# THE PAPERS OF

# THOMAS JEFFERSON

## RETIREMENT SERIES

# THE PAPERS OF
# Thomas Jefferson

## RETIREMENT SERIES

## Volume 7
## 28 November 1813 to 30 September 1814

J. JEFFERSON LOONEY, EDITOR

SUSAN HOLBROOK PERDUE AND ROBERT F. HAGGARD,
SENIOR ASSOCIATE EDITORS

JULIE L. LAUTENSCHLAGER, ELLEN C. HICKMAN, AND
CHRISTINE STERNBERG PATRICK, ASSISTANT EDITORS

LISA A. FRANCAVILLA, MANAGING EDITOR

ANDREA R. GRAY AND PAULA VITERBO, EDITORIAL ASSISTANTS

CATHERINE COINER CRITTENDEN AND SUSAN SPENGLER,
SENIOR DIGITAL TECHNICIANS

PRINCETON AND OXFORD
PRINCETON UNIVERSITY PRESS
2010

*Library of Congress Cataloging-in-Publication Data*

Jefferson, Thomas, 1743–1826
The papers of Thomas Jefferson. Retirement series / J. Jefferson Looney, editor . . .
[et al.] p. cm.
Includes bibliographical references and index.
Contents: v. 1. 4 March to 15 November 1809—[etc.]—
v. 7. 28 November 1813 to 30 September 1814
ISBN 978-0-691-14975-2 (cloth: v. 7: alk. paper)
1. Jefferson, Thomas, 1743–1826—Archives. 2. Jefferson, Thomas, 1743–1826—
Correspondence. 3. Presidents—United States—Archives.
4. Presidents—United States—Correspondence. 5. United States—
Politics and government—1809–1817—Sources. 6. United States—Politics
and government— 1817–1825—Sources.    I. Looney, J. Jefferson.
II. Title. III. Title: Retirement series.
E302.J442 2004b
973.4'6'092—dc22     2004048327

This book has been composed in Monticello

DEDICATED TO THE MEMORY OF

## ADOLPH S. OCHS

PUBLISHER OF THE NEW YORK TIMES

1896–1935

WHO BY THE EXAMPLE OF A RESPONSIBLE

PRESS ENLARGED AND FORTIFIED

THE JEFFERSONIAN CONCEPT

OF A FREE PRESS

THIS EDITION was made possible by a founding grant from The New York Times Company to Princeton University.

The Retirement Series is sponsored by the Thomas Jefferson Foundation, Inc., of Charlottesville, Virginia. It was created with a six-year founding grant from The Pew Charitable Trusts to the Foundation and to Princeton University, enabling the former to take over responsibility for the volumes associated with this period. Leading gifts from Richard Gilder, Mrs. Martin S. Davis, and Thomas A. Saunders III have assured the continuation of the Retirement Series. For these essential donations, and for other indispensable aid generously given by librarians, archivists, scholars, and collectors of manuscripts, the Editors record their sincere gratitude.

# FOREWORD

THE 526 DOCUMENTS printed in this volume cover the period from 28 November 1813 to 30 September 1814. The War of 1812 continued its negative impact on the American economy, which was further strained in Jefferson's neighborhood by a poor growing season. In a 23 February 1814 letter to William Short, Jefferson commented that the embargo, the blockade, and drought had caused him to suffer "more than any other individual." He kept abreast of current events through correspondents at home and abroad as well as newspapers that provided regular updates from American battlefronts and from Europe, including accounts of Napoleon's abdication in April 1814. Jefferson initially discounted reports of the destruction late in August 1814 of the public buildings in Washington D.C. When the reality could no longer be denied, he was quick to write his old friend, Samuel H. Smith, now federal commissioner of the revenue, enclosing a catalogue of his library and offering his massive book collection as a replacement for the Library of Congress. Ultimately, in January 1815 Congress bought Jefferson's 6,707 books for $23,950, an acquisition that has served as the nucleus for one of the world's great libraries.

During the months covered in this volume, Jefferson showed an interest in the documentation of history. In reviewing the extant sources on the 1765 Stamp Act crisis to aid William Wirt in preparing his biography of Patrick Henry, Jefferson observed that "It is truly unfortunate that those engaged in public affairs so rarely make notes of transactions passing within their knolege. hence history becomes fable instead of fact. the great outlines may be true, but the incidents and colouring are according to the faith or fancy of the writer." At the behest of Walter Jones, Jefferson recorded his largely positive impressions of George Washington's character. He also advised Joseph Delaplaine in his preparation of a series of biographies of famous Americans. Delaplaine was particularly anxious to locate suitable portraits of his subjects, and Jefferson went so far as to trace an image of Christopher Columbus for Delaplaine from the preface to a book in his possession, Theodor de Bry's *Americae Pars Quinta*. In response to his friend John Minor's request for a legal reading list, Jefferson transcribed and updated a document he had initially drawn up about 1773 for the namesake son of Bernard Moore. Jefferson's recommendations included Eugene Aram's 1759 defense at his murder trial, a speech printed elsewhere in this volume, which he considered to be a model of logic and style and one of the finest orations in the English language.

Jefferson sometimes claimed during this period that his advancing age was impairing his physical abilities. His activities demonstrate no evidence of weakness. Early in the spring of 1814 Jefferson became a trustee of the Albemarle Academy. He was soon actively involved in planning for the establishment of the school. Jefferson served on a committee to draft rules and regulations for the board of trustees and propose funding options for the institution. His 7 September 1814 letter to Peter Carr laid out an expansive vision for the school's future as an institution of higher learning. Although the Albemarle Academy never opened its doors under that name, it was the earliest direct ancestor of the University of Virginia. Jefferson further displayed his enthusiasm for the cause of education in correspondence and conversations exchanging ideas with such respected scholars as Thomas Cooper and José Corrêa da Serra. He also furnished Richmond educator Louis H. Girardin with his formula and explanation of John Napier's mathematical theorem and continued to help educate his grandson, Francis Eppes.

Jefferson's correspondents engaged him on a wide range of topics, from the arts and sciences to religion and politics. Oliver Evans defended himself against Jefferson's doubts about the validity of his patent. Miles King urged the retired president at great length to reflect on his personal religion, eliciting an eloquent and tolerant rejoinder. Edward Coles, an Albemarle County friend and neighbor, called on Jefferson as the author of the Declaration of Independence to use his prestige to promote the abolition of slavery. In his diplomatic response, Jefferson reiterated his view that slavery was evil, but he discouraged any measures beyond gradual emancipation and expatriation. Ultimately he declined further involvement and left the problem to the next generation: "this enterprise is for the young; for those who can follow it up, and bear it through to it's consummation. it shall have all my prayers, and these are the only weapons of an old man."

# ACKNOWLEDGMENTS

MANY INDIVIDUALS and institutions provided aid and encouragement during the preparation of this volume. Those who helped us to locate and acquire primary and secondary sources and answered our research questions include our colleagues at the Thomas Jefferson Foundation, especially Anna Berkes, Eric D. M. Johnson, Jack Robertson, Leah Stearns, and Endrina Tay of the Jefferson Library, and Carrie Taylor of the curatorial department. Also instrumental to our work were Margaret M. O'Bryant at the Albemarle Charlottesville Historical Society; Diann Benti, Jon Benoit, Jaclyn M. Penny, and Thomas Knoles at the American Antiquarian Society; Valerie-Anne Lutz van Ammers, Roy E. Goodman, Charles Greifenstein, Earle Spamer, and Keith Thomson at the American Philosophical Society; Bonnie Eisenman and David Farris at the Beth Ahabah Museum and Archives, Richmond; Stephen Z. Nonack at the Boston Athenæum; Russell Flinchum at The Century Association Archives Foundation; Kathleen Feeney at the Special Collection Research Center of the University of Chicago; Ila Furman at the Corcoran Gallery of Art; Laurent Ferri, Ana Guimaraes, and Eileen M. Heeran at the Kroch Library, Cornell University; Skip Hulett at the Georgiana Collection, Hargrett Rare Book & Manuscript Library at the University of Georgia; Denison Beach at the Houghton Library at Harvard University; Lewis Hobgood Averett at the Jones Memorial Library in Lynchburg; Edith Mulhern at the Library Company of Philadelphia; Barbara Bair, Jeff Flannery, and their colleagues at the Library of Congress's Manuscripts Division and Bonnie Coles at its Duplication Services Department; Marianne E. Julienne, Bill Luebke, and Brent Tarter at the Library of Virginia; Peter Drummey and Elaine Grublin at the Massachusetts Historical Society; Alessandra Merrill, Christine Nelson, and Eva Soos at the Morgan Library & Museum in New York; June Lucas and Martha Rowe at the Museum of Early Southern Decorative Arts; Deborah Mercer at the New Jersey State Library; Tammy Kiter at the New-York Historical Society; James D. Folts at the New York State Archives; Marilyn Schuster at Special Collections, Atkins Library, University of North Carolina-Charlotte; Nicholas P. Cole at the University of Oxford; Anna Bentson, Jack Gary, Travis C. McDonald, Gail Pond, and Octavia N. Starbuck at the Corporation for Jefferson's Poplar Forest; Anthony Grafton at Princeton University; Erin Clements Rushing at the Smithsonian Institution Libraries; Charles Lesser at the South Carolina Department of Archives and History; Darla

Brock at the Tennessee State Library and Archives; Leon C. Miller and his colleagues at Tulane University Library's Special Collections Department; at the University of Virginia, Edward Gaynor, Warner Granade, Margaret Hrabe, and Heather Riser, Albert and Shirley Small Special Collections Library, Cheryl Summers, Chemistry and Mathematics Library, Kent Olson, Law Library, and G. Edward White, School of Law; Margaret T. Kidd and Lee Shepard at the Virginia Historical Society; and Susan A. Riggs at the College of William and Mary's Special Collections Research Center. As always, we received advice, assistance, and encouragement from a large number of our fellow documentary editors, including Margaret Hogan from the Adams Papers; Martha King, John Little, and Linda Monaco from the Thomas Jefferson Papers in Princeton; Mary Hackett and Angela Kreider from the James Madison Papers; Daniel Preston from the James Monroe Papers; and C. M. Harris from the William Thornton Papers. Peter S. Baker gave us guidance on Anglo-Saxon; Genevieve Moene and Roland H. Simon transcribed and translated the French letters included in this volume; Coulter George helped us with passages in Greek; Jonathan T. Hine and Rosanna M. Giammanco Frongia provided aid with Italian; John F. Miller assisted us with Latin quotations; and David T. Gies counseled us on a passage in Spanish. Kevin B. Jones explained an astronomical document. The maps of Jefferson's Virginia and Albemarle County were created by Rick Britton. Stephen Perkins of Dataformat.com continued raising us to more sophisticated digital approaches. Our colleagues and friends at Princeton University Press have gone the extra mile to keep this series and this edition at the highest level. Departing assistant editor Deborah Beckel participated in the early stages of work. Finally, with this volume we say goodbye to Susan Holbrook Perdue, who completed eight years of dedicated service late in 2008 and moved on to direct an exciting new scholarly venture. Sue came to the Retirement Series when the project was less than a year old and made essential contributions to our development of a successful workflow and consistent editorial style, adoption of software, and creation of sophisticated indexing and tagging systems. Her cheerful collegiality and commitment to quality have had a huge impact, and she will be greatly missed.

# EDITORIAL METHOD AND APPARATUS

## 1. RENDERING THE TEXT

From its inception *The Papers of Thomas Jefferson* has insisted on high standards of accuracy in rendering text, but modifications in textual policy and editorial apparatus have been implemented as different approaches have become accepted in the field or as a more faithful rendering has become technically feasible. Prior discussions of textual policy appeared in Vols. 1:xxix–xxxiv, 22:vii–xi, 24:vii–viii, and 30:xiii–xiv of the First Series.

The textual method of the Retirement Series will adhere to the more literal approach adopted in Volume 30 of the parent edition. Original spelling, capitalization, and punctuation are retained as written. Such idiosyncrasies as Jefferson's failure to capitalize the beginnings of most of his sentences and abbreviations like "mr" are preserved, as are his preference for "it's" to "its" and his characteristic spellings of "knolege," "paiment," and "recieve." Modern usage is adopted in cases where intent is impossible to determine, an issue that arises most often in the context of capitalization. Some so-called slips of the pen are corrected, but the original reading is recorded in a subjoined textual note. Jefferson and others sometimes signaled a change in thought within a paragraph with extra horizontal space, and this is rendered by a three-em space. Blanks left for words and not subsequently filled by the authors are represented by a space approximating the length of the blank. Gaps, doubtful readings of illegible or damaged text, and wording supplied from other versions or by editorial conjecture are explained in the source note or in numbered textual notes. Foreign-language documents, the vast majority of which are in French during the retirement period, are transcribed in full as faithfully as possible and followed by a full translation.

Two modifications from past practice bring this series still closer to the original manuscripts. Underscored text is presented as such rather than being converted to italics. Superscripts are also preserved rather than being lowered to the baseline. In most cases of superscripting, the punctuation that is below or next to the superscripted letters is dropped, since it is virtually impossible to determine what is a period or dash as opposed to a flourish under, over, or adjacent to superscripted letters.

Limits to the more literal method are still recognized, however, and readability and consistency with past volumes are prime considerations. In keeping with the basic design implemented in the first volume of the Papers, salutations and signatures continue to display in large and small capitals rather than upper- and lowercase letters. Expansion marks over abbreviations are silently omitted. With very rare exceptions, deleted text and information on which words were added during the process of composition is not displayed within the document transcription. Based on the Editors' judgment of their significance, such emendations are either described in numbered textual notes or ignored. Datelines for letters are consistently printed at the head of the text, with a comment in the descriptive note when they have been moved. Address information, endorsements, and dockets are quoted or described in the source note rather than reproduced in the document proper.

## 2. TEXTUAL DEVICES

The following devices are employed throughout the work to clarify the presentation of the text.

| | |
|---|---|
| [ ... ] | Text missing and not conjecturable. The size of gaps longer than a word or two is estimated in annotation. |
| [ ] | Number or part of number missing or illegible. |
| [roman] | Conjectural reading for missing or illegible matter. A question mark follows when the reading is doubtful. |
| [*italic*] | Editorial comment inserted in the text. |
| <*italic*> | Matter deleted in the manuscript but restored in our text. |

## 3. DESCRIPTIVE SYMBOLS

The following symbols are employed throughout the work to describe the various kinds of manuscript originals. When a series of versions is included, the first to be recorded is the version used for the printed text.

| | |
|---|---|
| Dft | draft (usually a composition or rough draft; multiple drafts, when identifiable as such, are designated "2d Dft," etc.) |
| Dupl | duplicate |
| MS | manuscript (arbitrarily applied to most documents other than letters) |
| PoC | polygraph copy |

PrC  press copy
RC   recipient's copy
SC   stylograph copy

All manuscripts of the above types are assumed to be in the hand of the author of the document to which the descriptive symbol pertains. If not, that fact is stated. On the other hand, the following types of manuscripts are assumed not to be in the hand of the author, and exceptions will be noted:

FC  file copy (applied to all contemporary copies retained by the author or his agents)

Tr  transcript (applied to all contemporary and later copies except file copies; period of transcription, unless clear by implication, will be given when known)

### 4. *LOCATION SYMBOLS*

The locations of documents printed in this edition from originals in private hands and from printed sources are recorded in self-explanatory form in the descriptive note following each document. The locations of documents printed or referenced from originals held by public and private institutions in the United States are recorded by means of the symbols used in the *MARC Code List for Organizations* (2000) maintained by the Library of Congress. The symbols DLC and MHi by themselves stand for the collections of Jefferson Papers proper in these repositories. When texts are drawn from other collections held by these two institutions, the names of those collections are added. Location symbols for documents held by institutions outside the United States are given in a subjoined list. The lists of symbols are limited to the institutions represented by documents printed or referred to in this volume.

CoCCC   Colorado College, Colorado Springs
CSmH   Huntington Library, San Marino, California
     JF   Jefferson File
     JF-BA Jefferson File, Bixby Acquisition
     JF-SA Jefferson File, Smith Acquisition
CtY    Yale University, New Haven, Connecticut
DeGH   Hagley Museum and Library, Greenville, Delaware
DeWint-M Henry Frances DuPont Winterthur Museum, Joseph Downs Manuscript and Microfilm Collection, Winterthur, Delaware

| | |
|---|---|
| DFo | Folger Shakespeare Library, Washington, D.C. |
| DGW | George Washington University, Washington, D.C. |
| DLC | Library of Congress, Washington, D.C. |

> TJ Papers     Thomas Jefferson Papers (this is assumed if not stated, but also given as indicated to furnish the precise location of an undated, misdated, or otherwise problematic document, thus "DLC: TJ Papers, 213:38071–2" represents volume 213, folios 38071 and 38072 as the collection was arranged at the time the first microfilm edition was made in 1944–45. Access to the microfilm edition of the collection as it was rearranged under the Library's Presidential Papers Program is provided by the *Index to the Thomas Jefferson Papers* [1976])

| | |
|---|---|
| DNA | National Archives, Washington, D.C., with identifications of series (preceded by record group number) as follows: |

> | | |
> |---|---|
> | CD | Consular Dispatches |
> | CS | Census Schedules |
> | LAR | Letters of Application and Recommendation |
> | MLR | Miscellaneous Letters Received |
> | RCIAT | Records of the Cherokee Indian Agency in Tennessee |
> | RWP | Revolutionary War Pension and Bounty-Land Warrant Application Files |

| | |
|---|---|
| ICN | Newberry Library, Chicago, Illinois |
| ICPRCU | Polish Roman Catholic Union of America, Chicago, Illinois |
| ICU | University of Chicago, Illinois |
| LNT | Tulane University, New Orleans, Louisiana |
| MBAt | Boston Athenæum, Boston, Massachusetts |
| MdHi | Maryland Historical Society, Baltimore |
| MH | Harvard University, Cambridge, Massachusetts |
| MHi | Massachusetts Historical Society, Boston |
| MiU-C | Clements Library, University of Michigan, Ann Arbor |
| MoSHi | Missouri History Museum, Saint Louis |

> | | |
> |---|---|
> | TJC-BC | Thomas Jefferson Collection, text formerly in Bixby Collection |

| | |
|---|---|
| MWA | American Antiquarian Society, Worcester, Massachusetts |
| NcCU | University of North Carolina, Charlotte |
| NcD | Duke University, Durham, North Carolina |
| NcU | University of North Carolina, Chapel Hill |
| | NPT     Southern Historical Collection, Nicholas Philip Trist Papers |
| NhD | Dartmouth College, Hanover, New Hampshire |
| NHi | New-York Historical Society, New York City |
| NIC | Cornell University, Ithaca, New York |
| NjMoHP | Morristown National Historical Park, New Jersey |
| NjP | Princeton University, Princeton, New Jersey |
| NjVHi | Vineland Historical and Antiquarian Society, Vineland, New Jersey |
| NN | New York Public Library, New York City |
| NNC | Columbia University, New York City |
| NNGL | Gilder Lehrman Collection, New York City |
| NNPM | Pierpont Morgan Library, New York City |
| OCLloyd | Lloyd Library and Museum, Cincinnati, Ohio |
| PHi | Historical Society of Pennsylvania, Philadelphia |
| PLF | Franklin and Marshall College, Lancaster, Pennsylvania |
| PPAmP | American Philosophical Society, Philadelphia, Pennsylvania |
| | VMWCR     Visitors Minutes, University of Virginia and its predecessors, copy prepared after 7 October 1826 for William C. Rives |
| PPL | Library Company of Philadelphia, Pennsylvania |
| PPRF | Rosenbach Foundation, Philadelphia, Pennsylvania |
| PU-L | Biddle Law Library, University of Pennsylvania, Philadelphia |
| THi | Tennessee Historical Society, Nashville |
| TxH | Houston Public Library, Houston, Texas |
| TxNaSFA | Stephen F. Austin State University, Nacogdoches, Texas |
| Vi | Library of Virginia, Richmond |
| ViCMRL | Thomas Jefferson Library, Thomas Jefferson Foundation, Inc., Charlottesville, Virginia |
| ViFreJM | James Monroe Museum and Memorial Library, Fredericksburg, Virginia |
| ViHi | Virginia Historical Society, Richmond |

| | | |
|---|---|---|
| ViLJML | Jones Memorial Library, Lynchburg, Virginia | |
| ViU | University of Virginia, Charlottesville | |
| | GT | George Tucker transcripts of Thomas Jefferson letters |
| | TJP | Thomas Jefferson Papers |
| | TJP-CC | Thomas Jefferson Papers, text formerly in Carr-Cary Papers |
| | TJP-Co | Thomas Jefferson Papers, text formerly in Cocke Papers |
| | TJP-ER | Thomas Jefferson Papers, text formerly in Edgehill-Randolph Papers |
| | TJP-LBJM | Thomas Jefferson Papers, Thomas Jefferson's Legal Brief in *Jefferson v. Michie*, 1804–15, deposited by Mrs. Augustina David Carr Mills |
| | TJP-PC | Thomas Jefferson Papers, text formerly in Philip B. Campbell Deposit |
| | TJP-VMJB | Thomas Jefferson Papers, Visitors Minutes, University of Virginia and its predecessors, copy prepared after 7 October 1826 for James Breckenridge |
| | TJP-VMJCC | Thomas Jefferson Papers, Visitors Minutes, University of Virginia and its predecessors, copy prepared after 7 October 1826 for Joseph C. Cabell |
| | TJP-VMJHC | Thomas Jefferson Papers, Visitors Minutes, University of Virginia and its predecessors, copy prepared after 7 October 1826 for John H. Cocke |
| | VMJLC | Visitors Minutes, University of Virginia and its predecessors, copy evidently prepared for John Lewis Cochran |
| ViW | College of William and Mary, Williamsburg, Virginia | |

|  | TC-JP | Jefferson Papers, Tucker-Coleman Collection |
|---|---|---|
|  | TJP | Thomas Jefferson Papers |
| ViWC | | Colonial Williamsburg Foundation, Williamsburg, Virginia |
| WHi | | State Historical Society of Wisconsin, Madison |

The following symbols represent repositories located outside of the United States:

| FrN | Bibliothèque Municipale, Nantes, France |
|---|---|
| ItF | Biblioteca Nazionale Centrale, Florence, Italy |
| PlKMN | Muzeum Narodowe w Krakowie, Poland |
| StEdNL | National Library of Scotland, Edinburgh |

## 5. OTHER ABBREVIATIONS AND SYMBOLS

The following abbreviations and symbols are commonly employed in the annotation throughout the work.

Lb    Letterbook (used to indicate texts copied or assembled into bound volumes)

RG    Record Group (used in designating the location of documents in the Library of Virginia and the National Archives)

SJL    Jefferson's "Summary Journal of Letters" written and received for the period 11 Nov. 1783 to 25 June 1826 (in DLC: TJ Papers). This epistolary record, kept in Jefferson's hand, has been checked against the TJ Editorial Files. It is to be assumed that all outgoing letters are recorded in SJL unless there is a note to the contrary. When the date of receipt of an incoming letter is recorded in SJL, it is incorporated in the notes. Information and discrepancies revealed in SJL but not found in the letter itself are also noted. Missing letters recorded in SJL are accounted for in the notes to documents mentioning them, in related documents, or in an appendix

TJ    Thomas Jefferson

TJ Editorial Files    Photoduplicates and other editorial materials in the office of the Papers of Thomas Jefferson: Retirement Series, Jefferson Library, Thomas Jefferson Foundation, Charlottesville

d    Penny or denier

$f$    Florin

£    Pound sterling or livre, depending upon context (in doubtful cases, a clarifying note will be given)

s    Shilling or sou (also expressed as /)

₶ Livre Tournois

℗ Per (occasionally used for pro, pre)

## 6. SHORT TITLES

The following list includes short titles of works cited frequently in this edition. Since it is impossible to anticipate all the works to be cited in abbreviated form, the list is revised from volume to volume.

*Acts of Assembly* *Acts of the General Assembly of Virginia* (cited by session; title varies over time)

*ANB* John A. Garraty and Mark C. Carnes, eds., *American National Biography*, 1999, 24 vols.

*Annals* *Annals of the Congress of the United States: The Debates and Proceedings in the Congress of the United States . . . Compiled from Authentic Materials*, Washington, D.C., Gales & Seaton, 1834–56, 42 vols. (all editions are undependable and pagination varies from one printing to another. Citations given below are to the edition mounted on the American Memory website of the Library of Congress and give the date of the debate as well as page numbers)

APS American Philosophical Society

*ASP* *American State Papers: Documents, Legislative and Executive, of the Congress of the United States*, 1832–61, 38 vols.

Axelson, *Virginia Postmasters* Edith F. Axelson, *Virginia Postmasters and Post Offices, 1789–1832*, 1991

Bathe and Bathe, *Oliver Evans* Greville Bathe and Dorothy Bathe, *Oliver Evans: A Chronicle of Early American Engineering*, 1935, repr. 1972

*BDSCHR* Walter B. Edgar and others, eds., *Biographical Directory of the South Carolina House of Representatives*, 1974– , 5 vols.

Betts, *Farm Book* Edwin M. Betts, ed., *Thomas Jefferson's Farm Book*, 1953 (in two separately paginated sections; unless otherwise specified, references are to the second section)

Betts, *Garden Book* Edwin M. Betts, ed., *Thomas Jefferson's Garden Book, 1766–1824*, 1944

Biddle, *Lewis and Clark Expedition* Nicholas Biddle, *History of the Expedition under the command of Captains Lewis and Clark to the Sources of the Missouri, thence across the Rocky Mountains and down the River Columbia to the Pacific Ocean. Performed during the years 1804–5–6. By order of the Government of the*

*United States*, 2 vols., Philadelphia, 1814; Sowerby, no. 4168; Poor, *Jefferson's Library*, 7 (no. 370)

*Biog. Dir. Cong.* *Biographical Directory of the United States Congress, 1774–1989*, 1989

*Biographie universelle* *Biographie universelle, ancienne et moderne*, new ed., 1843–65, 45 vols.

*Black's Law Dictionary* Bryan A. Garner and others, eds., *Black's Law Dictionary*, 7th ed., 1999

Brant, *Madison* Irving Brant, *James Madison*, 1941–61, 6 vols.

Brigham, *American Newspapers* Clarence S. Brigham, *History and Bibliography of American Newspapers, 1690–1820*, 1947, 2 vols.

Bruce, *University* Philip Alexander Bruce, *History of the University of Virginia 1819–1919: The Lengthened Shadow of One Man*, 1920–22, 5 vols.

Bush, *Life Portraits* Alfred L. Bush, *The Life Portraits of Thomas Jefferson*, rev. ed., 1987

Butler, *Virginia Militia* Stuart Lee Butler, *A Guide to Virginia Militia Units in the War of 1812*, 1988

Cabell, *University of Virginia* Nathaniel F. Cabell, ed., *Early History of the University of Virginia as contained in the letters of Thomas Jefferson and Joseph C. Cabell*, 1856

Callahan, *U.S. Navy* Edward W. Callahan, *List of Officers of the Navy of the United States and of the Marine Corps from 1775 to 1900*, 1901, repr. 1969

Chambers, *Poplar Forest* S. Allen Chambers, *Poplar Forest & Thomas Jefferson*, 1993

Chandler, *Campaigns of Napoleon* David G. Chandler, *The Campaigns of Napoleon*, 1966

Clay, *Papers* James F. Hopkins and others, eds., *The Papers of Henry Clay*, 1959–1992, 11 vols.

Connelly, *Napoleonic France* Owen Connelly and others, eds., *Historical Dictionary of Napoleonic France, 1799–1815*, 1985

*DAB* Allen Johnson and Dumas Malone, eds., *Dictionary of American Biography*, 1928–36, 20 vols.

*DBF* *Dictionnaire de biographie française*, 1933– , 19 vols.

*Delaplaine's Repository* *Delaplaine's Repository of the Lives and Portraits of Distinguished Americans*, Philadelphia, 1816–18, 2 vols.; Poor, *Jefferson's Library*, 4 (no. 139)

Destutt de Tracy, *Commentary and Review of Montesquieu's Spirit of Laws* Antoine Louis Claude Destutt de Tracy, *A Commentary and Review of Montesquieu's Spirit of Laws. prepared for press from the Original Manuscript, in the hands of the publisher. To which are annexed, Observations on the Thirty-First Book, by the late M. Condorcet: and Two Letters of Helvetius, on the merits of the same work*, Philadelphia, 1811; Sowerby, no. 2327; Poor, *Jefferson's Library*, 10 (no. 623)

Dolley Madison, *Selected Letters*      David B. Mattern and Holly C. Shulman, eds., *The Selected Letters of Dolley Payne Madison*, 2003

*DSB*      Charles C. Gillispie, ed., *Dictionary of Scientific Biography*, 1970–80, 16 vols.

*DVB*      John T. Kneebone and others, eds., *Dictionary of Virginia Biography*, 1998– , 3 vols.

*EG*      Dickinson W. Adams and Ruth W. Lester, eds., *Jefferson's Extracts from the Gospels*, 1983, *The Papers of Thomas Jefferson, Second Series*

Fairclough, *Horace: Satires, Epistles and Ars Poetica*      H. Rushton Fairclough, trans., *Horace: Satires, Epistles and Ars Poetica*, Loeb Classical Library, 1926, repr. 2005

Fairclough, *Virgil*      H. Rushton Fairclough, trans., *Virgil*, ed. rev. by G. P. Goold, Loeb Classical Library, 1999–2000, 2 vols.

Ford      Paul Leicester Ford, ed., *The Writings of Thomas Jefferson*, Letterpress Edition, 1892–99, 10 vols.

Gaines, *Randolph*      William H. Gaines Jr., *Thomas Mann Randolph: Jefferson's Son-in-Law*, 1966

Haggard, "Henderson Heirs"      Robert F. Haggard, "Thomas Jefferson v. The Heirs of Bennett Henderson, 1795–1818: A Case Study in Caveat Emptor," *MACH*, 63 (2005): 1–29

HAW      Henry A. Washington, ed., *The Writings of Thomas Jefferson*, 1853–54, 9 vols.

Heidler and Heidler, *War of 1812*      David S. Heidler and Jeanne T. Heidler, eds., *Encyclopedia of the War of 1812*, 1997

Heitman, *Continental Army*      Francis B. Heitman, comp., *Historical Register of Officers of the Continental Army during the War of the Revolution, April, 1775, to December, 1783*, rev. ed., 1914

Heitman, *U.S. Army*      Francis B. Heitman, comp., *Historical Register and Dictionary of the United States Army*, 1903, 2 vols.

Hening      William Waller Hening, ed., *The Statutes at Large; being a Collection of all the Laws of Virginia*, Richmond, 1809–23, 13 vols.

Hoefer, *Nouv. biog. générale*      J. C. F. Hoefer, *Nouvelle biographie générale depuis les temps les plus reculés jusqu'a nos jours*, 1852–83, 46 vols.

*Hortus Third*     Liberty Hyde Bailey, Ethel Zoe Bailey, and the staff of the Liberty Hyde Bailey Hortorium, Cornell University, *Hortus Third: A Concise Dictionary of Plants Cultivated in the United States and Canada*, 1976

Jackson, *Papers*     Sam B. Smith, Harold D. Moser, Daniel Feller, and others, eds., *The Papers of Andrew Jackson*, 1980– , 7 vols.

*Jefferson Correspondence*, Bixby     Worthington C. Ford, ed., *Thomas Jefferson Correspondence Printed from the Originals in the Collections of William K. Bixby*, 1916

*JEP*     *Journal of the Executive Proceedings of the Senate of the United States*

*JHD*     *Journal of the House of Delegates of the Commonwealth of Virginia*

*JHR*     *Journal of the House of Representatives of the United States*

*JS*     *Journal of the Senate of the United States*

*JSV*     *Journal of the Senate of Virginia*

Kimball, *Jefferson, Architect*     Fiske Kimball, *Thomas Jefferson, Architect*, 1916

*L & B*     Andrew A. Lipscomb and Albert E. Bergh, eds., *The Writings of Thomas Jefferson*, Library Edition, 1903–04, 20 vols.

Latrobe, *Papers*     John C. Van Horne and others, eds., *The Correspondence and Miscellaneous Papers of Benjamin Henry Latrobe*, 1984–88, 3 vols.

Lay, *Architecture*     K. Edward Lay, *The Architecture of Jefferson Country: Charlottesville and Albemarle County, Virginia*, 2000

*LCB*     Douglas L. Wilson, ed., *Jefferson's Literary Commonplace Book*, 1989, *The Papers of Thomas Jefferson*, Second Series

Leavitt, *Poplar Forest*     Messrs. Leavitt, *Catalogue of a Private Library . . . Also, The Remaining Portion of the Library of the Late Thomas Jefferson . . . offered by his grandson, Francis Eppes, of Poplar Forest, Va.*, 1873

Leonard, *General Assembly*     Cynthia Miller Leonard, comp., *The General Assembly of Virginia, July 30, 1619–January 11, 1978: A Bicentennial Register of Members*, 1978

*List of Patents*     *A List of Patents granted by the United States from April 10, 1790, to December 31, 1836*, 1872

*Longworth's New York Directory*     *Longworth's American Almanac, New-York Register, and City Directory*, New York, 1796–1842 (title varies; cited by year of publication)

*MACH*     *Magazine of Albemarle County History*, 1940– (title varies: issued until 1951 as *Papers of the Albemarle County Historical Society*)

Madison, *Papers*    William T. Hutchinson, Robert A. Rutland, John C. A. Stagg, and others, eds., *The Papers of James Madison*, 1962– , 32 vols.

   *Congress. Ser.*, 17 vols.

   *Pres. Ser.*, 6 vols.

   *Retirement Ser.*, 1 vol.

   *Sec. of State Ser.*, 8 vols.

Malcomson, *Historical Dictionary*    Robert Malcomson, *Historical Dictionary of the War of 1812*, 2006

Malone, *Jefferson*    Dumas Malone, *Jefferson and his Time*, 1948–81, 6 vols.

Marshall, *Papers*    Herbert A. Johnson, Charles T. Cullen, Charles F. Hobson, and others, eds., *The Papers of John Marshall*, 1974–2006, 12 vols.

Mazzei, *Writings*    Margherita Marchione and others, eds., *Philip Mazzei: Selected Writings and Correspondence*, 1983, 3 vols.

*MB*    James A. Bear Jr. and Lucia C. Stanton, eds., *Jefferson's Memorandum Books: Accounts, with Legal Records and Miscellany, 1767–1826*, 1997, *The Papers of Thomas Jefferson*, Second Series

*Memorial to Congress on Evans' Patent*    *Memorial to Congress of sundry citizens of the United States, praying relief from the oppressive operation of Oliver Evans' Patent*, Baltimore, 1813

*Notes*, ed. Peden    Thomas Jefferson, *Notes on the State of Virginia*, ed. William Peden, 1955

*OCD*    Simon Hornblower and Antony Spawforth, eds., *The Oxford Classical Dictionary*, 2003

*ODNB*    H. C. G. Matthew and Brian Harrison, eds., *Oxford Dictionary of National Biography*, 2004, 60 vols.

*OED*    James A. H. Murray, J. A. Simpson, E. S. C. Weiner, and others, eds., *The Oxford English Dictionary*, 2d ed., 1989, 20 vols.

Papenfuse, *Maryland Public Officials*    Edward C. Papenfuse and others, eds., *An Historical List of Public Officials of Maryland*, 1990– , 1 vol.

Peale, *Papers*    Lillian B. Miller and others, eds., *The Selected Papers of Charles Willson Peale and His Family*, 1983– , 5 vols. in 6

*PMHB*    *Pennsylvania Magazine of History and Biography*, 1877–

Poor, *Jefferson's Library*    Nathaniel P. Poor, *Catalogue. President Jefferson's Library*, 1829

*Princetonians* James McLachlan and others, eds., *Princetonians: A Biographical Dictionary*, 1976–90, 5 vols.

*PTJ* Julian P. Boyd, Charles T. Cullen, John Catanzariti, Barbara B. Oberg, and others, eds., *The Papers of Thomas Jefferson*, 1950– , 34 vols.

*PW* Wilbur S. Howell, ed., *Jefferson's Parliamentary Writings*, 1988, *The Papers of Thomas Jefferson*, Second Series

Randall, *Life* Henry S. Randall, *The Life of Thomas Jefferson*, 1858, 3 vols.

Randolph, *Domestic Life* Sarah N. Randolph, *The Domestic Life of Thomas Jefferson, Compiled from Family Letters and Reminiscences by His Great-Granddaughter*, 1871

Shackelford, *Descendants* George Green Shackelford, ed., *Collected Papers to Commemorate Fifty Years of the Monticello Association of the Descendants of Thomas Jefferson*, 1965

Sowerby E. Millicent Sowerby, comp., *Catalogue of the Library of Thomas Jefferson*, 1952–59, 5 vols.

Sprague, *American Pulpit* William B. Sprague, *Annals of the American Pulpit*, 1857–69, 9 vols.

Stagg, *Madison's War* John C. A. Stagg, *Mr. Madison's War: Politics, Diplomacy, and Warfare in the Early American Republic, 1783–1830*, 1983

Stein, *Worlds* Susan R. Stein, *The Worlds of Thomas Jefferson at Monticello*, 1993

*Terr. Papers* Clarence E. Carter and John Porter Bloom, eds., *The Territorial Papers of the United States*, 1934–75, 28 vols.

*TJR* Thomas Jefferson Randolph, ed., *Memoir, Correspondence, and Miscellanies, from the Papers of Thomas Jefferson*, 1829, 4 vols.

True, "Agricultural Society" Rodney H. True, "Minute Book of the Agricultural Society of Albemarle," *Annual Report of the American Historical Association for the Year 1918* (1921), 1:261–349

*U.S. Reports* *Cases Argued and Decided in the Supreme Court of the United States*, 1790– (title varies; originally issued in distinct editions of separately numbered volumes with *U.S. Reports* volume numbers retroactively assigned; original volume numbers here given parenthetically)

*U.S. Statutes at Large* Richard Peters, ed., *The Public Statutes at Large of the United States . . . 1789 to March 3, 1845*, 1845–67, 8 vols.

*Va. Reports* *Reports of Cases Argued and Adjudged in the Court*

*of Appeals of Virginia*, 1798– (title varies; originally issued in distinct editions of separately numbered volumes with Va. Reports volume numbers retroactively assigned; original volume numbers here given parenthetically)

*VMHB*    *Virginia Magazine of History and Biography*, 1893–

Washington, *Papers*    W. W. Abbot, Dorothy Twohig, Philander D. Chase, Theodore J. Crackel, and others, eds., *The Papers of George Washington*, 1983– , 52 vols.

> *Colonial Ser.*, 10 vols.
>
> *Confederation Ser.*, 6 vols.
>
> *Pres. Ser.*, 14 vols.
>
> *Retirement Ser.*, 4 vols.
>
> *Rev. War Ser.*, 18 vols.

*William and Mary Provisional List*    *A Provisional List of Alumni, Grammar School Students, Members of the Faculty, and Members of the Board of Visitors of the College of William and Mary in Virginia. From 1693 to 1888*, 1941

*WMQ*    *William and Mary Quarterly*, 1892–

Woods, *Albemarle*    Edgar Woods, *Albemarle County in Virginia*, 1901, repr. 1991

# CONTENTS

### 1813

# CONTENTS

## · ❧ 1 8 1 4 ❧ ·

# CONTENTS

# CONTENTS

# CONTENTS

# CONTENTS

# CONTENTS

# CONTENTS

# CONTENTS

# CONTENTS

# CONTENTS

# CONTENTS

CONTENTS

# CONTENTS

# MAPS

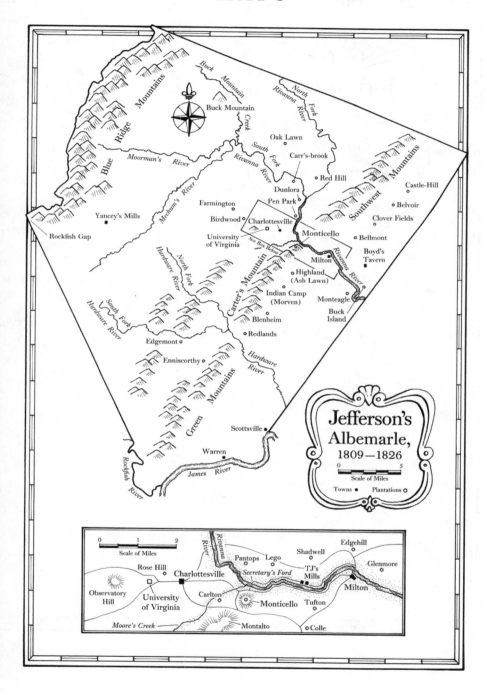

Jefferson's Albemarle, 1809—1826

0    5
Scale of Miles

Towns o    Plantations o

Buck Mountain Creek

Blue Ridge Mountains

North Fork Rivanna River

South Fork Rivanna River

Buck Mountain

Oak Lawn

Carr's-brook

Red Hill

Dunlora

Pen Park

Castle-Hill

Southwest Mountains

Belvoir

Clover Fields

Moorman's River

Yancey's Mills

Farmington

Birdwood

Charlottesville

University of Virginia

See Box Below

Monticello

Bellmont

Boyd's Tavern

Rockfish Gap

Mechum's River

Milton

Highland (Ash Lawn)

Indian Camp (Morven)

Monteagle

Buck Island

North Fork Hardware River

Carter's Mountain

Blenheim

Redlands

South Fork Hardware River

Edgemont

Enniscorthy

Hardware River

Rivanna River

Green Mountains

Scottsville

Warren

James River

Rockfish River

---

0    1    2
Scale of Miles

Rose Hill

Observatory Hill

University of Virginia

Charlottesville

Carlton

Rivanna River

Pantops

Lego

Secretary's Ford

Shadwell

TJ's Mills

Edgehill

Glenmore

Milton

Monticello

Tufton

Moore's Creek

Montalto

Colle

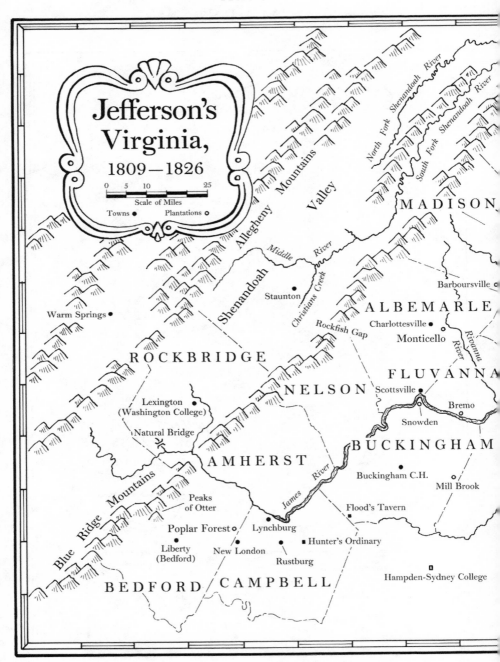

Jefferson's
Virginia,
1809—1826

0  5  10          25
Scale of Miles
Towns ●          Plantations ○

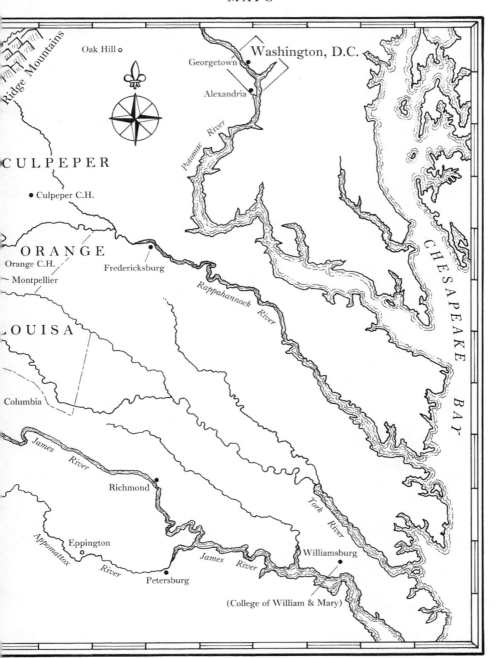

# ILLUSTRATIONS

*Following page 434*

## OLIVER EVANS BY BASS OTIS, ENGRAVED BY WILLIAM G. JACKMAN

Jefferson's cordial relationship with the inventor Oliver Evans (1755–1819) was interrupted by a contentious, public debate over the novelty of the milling machinery for which Evans is best known. The publication late in 1813 of Jefferson's letter to Isaac McPherson of 13 Aug. 1813, which cast doubts on the validity of Evans's patent, elicited an impassioned defense of his rights in Evans's letters of 7 and 29 Jan. 1814 to the ex-president. In 1816 Joseph Delaplaine commissioned the artist Bass Otis to paint two dozen portraits of famous Americans, including Evans and Jefferson, for use in *Delaplaine's Repository of the Lives and Portraits of Distinguished Americans.* Although an engraving of the Jefferson likeness was the only one of Otis's works ultimately included, Delaplaine exhibited all of them at his Philadelphia gallery the following year. Rubens Peale bought the artworks after Delaplaine's death in 1824, and he later sold the entire collection to the famed showman P. T. Barnum. The portrait of Evans was apparently consumed in one of the two fires that destroyed Barnum's New York City museum during the 1860s. The caption beneath William G. Jackman's nineteenth-century line engraving of the Otis original, which was published by D. Appleton & Company of New York, describes Evans as "The [James] Watt of America" (Roland H. Woodward and others, *Bass Otis: Painter, Portraitist and Engraver* [1976], 14–7; Eugene S. Ferguson, *Oliver Evans: Inventive Genius of the American Industrial Revolution* [1980], 8–9; *DAB,* 1:637).
*Courtesy of Smithsonian Institution Libraries, Washington, D.C.*

## CHRISTOPHER COLUMBUS AS ENGRAVED BY JEAN DE BRY

Theodor de Bry included an engraving of the explorer Christopher Columbus by his son, Jean de Bry, in his *Americae Pars Quinta* (Frankfurt am Main, 1595; Sowerby, no. 3977). This representation of the famed explorer seems to have been taken either from a copy of a portrait attributed to Sebastiano del Piombo (Sebastiano Luciani) (ca. 1485–1547), the original of which is owned by New York City's Metropolitan Museum of Art, or, less convincingly, from a shared artistic predecessor. Because both the signature and inscription identifying it as a painting of Columbus were apparently added long after its completion, both the artist and its subject are in doubt. Although a young Piombo might have painted Columbus (1451–1506) from life, few contend that he did so. Indeed, no life portrait of Columbus is known to exist. Furthermore, the visage depicted by "Piombo" and de Bry does not match up very well with contemporary written descriptions of Columbus, which most often portray him as long-faced, bright-eyed, and prematurely white-haired. Joseph Delaplaine ultimately chose to use a painting of Columbus by the Spanish artist Mariano Salvador Maella in the first volume of *Delaplaine's Repository of the Lives and Portraits of Distinguished Americans* (Philadelphia, 1816–18). It was engraved by Peter Maverick, who would on two occasions during the 1820s perform a similar service for the

# ILLUSTRATIONS

plan of Jefferson's University of Virginia (John Boyd Thacher, *Christopher Columbus: His Life, His Work, His Remains* [1904], 3:42–52; Paul M. Lester, "Looks Are Deceiving: the Portraits of Christopher Columbus," *Visual Anthropology 5* [1993]: 211–27; Jane Turner, ed., *Dictionary of Art* [1996], 20:77–8; *DAB*, 6:432; Stein, *Worlds*, 196–7).

*Courtesy of the Albert and Shirley Small Special Collections Library, University of Virginia.*

## ADDRESS COVERS

In 1809 Congress granted Jefferson the right to send and receive his letters and packages free of charge. His signature, or frank, on outgoing correspondence was the customary way of validating these gratis mailings. Autograph seekers have sometimes clipped away these signatures from surviving address covers. The postmarks and franks on incoming mail are either stamped or handwritten, with the former occurring predominantly in letters sent from larger municipalities, such as New York City and Charleston, South Carolina. The postage paid, if any, is generally inserted by hand. Jefferson's address is often given simply as "Monticello, Virginia," but the additional information that he lived in Albemarle County near Charlottesville or Milton is sometimes provided (*U.S. Statutes at Large*, 2:526, 552).

Jefferson to John E. Hall, 1 Jan. 1814, *Courtesy of Straus Autograph Collection, Manuscripts Division, Department of Rare Books and Special Collection, Princeton University Library.*

Abraham Howard Quincy to Jefferson, 10 May 1814, *Courtesy of the Special Collections Research Center, Swem Library, College of William and Mary.*

John L. E. W. Shecut to Jefferson, 17 Aug. 1814, *Courtesy of the Manuscripts Division, Library of Congress.*

## PETER CARR BY SAINT-MÉMIN

Peter Carr (1770–1815) was a favorite nephew of Jefferson, who supervised his education. Carr was a founding trustee of Albemarle Academy, and early in April 1814 he was elected president of its board. During the months that followed Jefferson joined him in overseeing the important early steps in the transformation of the nascent institution into Central College. Charles Balthazar Julien Févret de Saint-Mémin (1770–1852), artist, engraver, and museum director, immigrated in 1793 to the United States from France, by way of Switzerland. Within a few years he had established himself as one of America's preeminent miniature portraitists. His usual method was to take an exact profile of his subject with a physiognotrace, use a pantograph to reduce the image down to a little over two inches in diameter, and then make an engraving on a copper plate using a graver and roulette. In the years prior to 1810, Saint-Mémin took likenesses successively in New York City, Philadelphia, Baltimore, Washington, Richmond, and Charleston, South Carolina. His surviving artistic output, which totals nearly nine-hundred head-and-shoulder profiles, 90 percent of which were engraved, documents the wealthiest, best-connected, and most powerful Americans of the Early National period. The first three presidents are each represented, with Jefferson having sat late in November 1804. The engraving of Peter Carr dates from Saint-Mémin's 1807–08 sojourn in Richmond, during which he made more than one-hundred portraits. After Napoleon fell from power in 1814, Saint-Mémin returned to France and served for more than thirty years as a museum director in his native Dijon (*ANB*; *DAB*; Bush, *Life Portraits*, 51–3; Fillmore Norfleet, *Saint-Mémin in Virginia: Portraits and Biographies* [1942], 97, 149).

*Courtesy of the Corcoran Gallery of Art, Washington, D.C., Gift of William Wilson, 75.16.597.*

## JEFFERSON'S TAX RECEIPTS

On 23 Jan. 1814 Jefferson paid the $14 levied on his four-wheel phaeton and two-wheel gig by the 24 July 1813 federal "Act laying duties on carriages for the conveyance of persons." He made payment to and received signed receipts from the recently confirmed collector of the revenue for Virginia's nineteenth collection district, his son-in-law Thomas Mann Randolph. The vouchers were filled in and countersigned by the deputy collector, Jefferson's grandson Thomas Jefferson Randolph, who had been appointed to that post by his father under section 20 of the 22 July 1813 "Act for the assessment and collection of direct taxes and internal duties." The elder Randolph resigned as collector soon thereafter and was succeeded by his son late in March 1814 (*MB*, 2:1296 [24 Jan. 1814]; *U.S. Statutes at Large*, 3:23–4, 30, 40–1; *JEP*, 2:456, 461, 511, 515 [18, 21 Jan., 16, 26 Mar. 1814]).

*Courtesy of the Massachusetts Historical Society.*

## THE BURNING OF WASHINGTON, D.C.

On 14 Oct. 1814 George Thompson, a publisher of popular prints in West Smithfield, London, issued his wood engraving of "The Taking of the City of Washington in America." The caption beneath the print reads "THE CITY OF WASHINGTON THE CAPITAL OF THE UNITED STATES OF AMERICA WAS TAKEN BY THE BRITISH FORCES UNDER MAJOR GEN[L] ROSS On Aug[t] 24 1814 when we burnt and destroyed their Dock Yard with a Frigate and a Sloop of War Rope-walk Arsenal Senate House Presidents Palace War Office Treasury and the Great Bridge With the Flotilla the public property destroyed amounted to thirty Million of Dollars." The frigate in question was the USS *Columbia*, and the sloop was the second USS *Argus*. The "Great Bridge" across the Potomac River, a mile-long pile structure with draws at both ends, opened in May 1809. It was located at the site of the present-day 14th Street Bridge connecting Virginia to the District of Columbia (Malcomson, *Historical Dictionary*, 10, 110, 596; Washington *National Intelligencer*, 22 May 1809; DeBenneville Randolph Keim, *Keim's Illustrated Hand-Book. Washington and its Environs* [1874], 52; Joseph West Moore, *Picturesque Washington* [1887], 304).

*Courtesy of the Prints and Photographs Division, Library of Congress.*

## JEFFERSON OFFERS HIS LIBRARY TO CONGRESS

Jefferson's letter to Samuel H. Smith of 21 Sept. 1814 offered his library to the nation to replace the one lost when the British burned the United States Capitol a month earlier. Surprisingly, it seems to have been published first in the Georgetown *Federal Republican*, a newspaper founded by the Federalist congressman Alexander Contee Hanson. This version, which appeared on 18 Oct., is complete and accurate, aside from some regularized punctuation and spelling, four words italicized for emphasis, a bracketed editorial comment, and a few misread words. Immediately following Jefferson's letter the editors included one of a satirical nature supposedly written by a Johannes Vonderpuff to Jefferson on 1 Oct. 1814 from Missouri and proposing to sell his own library to Congress. Although almost certainly apocryphal, Vonderpuff's missive is sufficiently interesting to merit inclusion at its appropriate chronological place in a forthcoming volume (*DAB*, 4:231; Brigham, *American Newspapers*, 1:89–90).

*Courtesy of the American Antiquarian Society.*

RANGE OF OFFICES AT POPLAR FOREST

Although Jefferson reported to his son-in-law John Wayles Eppes in April 1813 that he had hired someone to build a range of "offices," or service rooms, at Poplar Forest, work did not begin in earnest for another year. Hugh Chisholm put up the walls of the wing, which stretched for one hundred feet from the main house to the eastern mound, in the spring and early in the summer of 1814. It was apparently roofed and finished during the following year. After its completion the range included a dairy or storage room, a kitchen, the cook's room, and a smokehouse. As at Monticello, it was built into the slope of the land (thus making it visible only from the back of the house) and boasted a covered walkway and a rooftop terrace that was often used by Jefferson and his guests for their evening stroll. The rooms were of various sizes, but through the regular spacing of the doorways the exterior was given a symmetrical appearance. Jefferson is not known to have contemplated the construction of a similar wing to the west of the main house. Demolished during the first half of the nineteenth century, the service rooms were rebuilt in 2008–09 by the Corporation for Jefferson's Poplar Forest (TJ to Eppes, 18 Apr. 1813; Chisholm to TJ, 22 May 1814; TJ to Jeremiah A. Goodman, 4 Oct. 1814; *MB*, 2:1300; Chambers, *Poplar Forest*, 80–4, 191).

*Courtesy of Thomas Jefferson's Poplar Forest, Les Schofer, photographer.*

# Volume 7

## 28 November 1813 to 30 September 1814

# JEFFERSON CHRONOLOGY

## 1743 · 1826

| | |
|---|---|
| 1743 | Born at Shadwell, 13 April (New Style). |
| 1760–1762 | Studies at the College of William and Mary. |
| 1762–1767 | Self-education and preparation for law. |
| 1769–1774 | Albemarle delegate to House of Burgesses. |
| 1772 | Marries Martha Wayles Skelton, 1 January. |
| 1775–1776 | In Continental Congress. |
| 1776 | Drafts Declaration of Independence. |
| 1776–1779 | In Virginia House of Delegates. |
| 1779 | Submits Bill for Establishing Religious Freedom. |
| 1779–1781 | Governor of Virginia. |
| 1782 | Martha Wayles Skelton Jefferson dies, 6 September. |
| 1783–1784 | In Continental Congress. |
| 1784–1789 | In France on commission to negotiate commercial treaties and then as minister plenipotentiary at Versailles. |
| 1790–1793 | Secretary of State of the United States. |
| 1797–1801 | Vice President of the United States. |
| 1801–1809 | President of the United States. |

## RETIREMENT

| | |
|---|---|
| 1809 | Attends James Madison's inauguration, 4 March. |
| | Arrives at Monticello, 15 March. |
| 1810 | Completes legal brief on New Orleans batture case, 31 July. |
| 1811 | Batture case dismissed, 5 December. |
| 1812 | Correspondence with John Adams resumed, 1 January. |
| | Batture pamphlet preface completed, 25 February; printed by 21 March. |
| 1814 | Named a trustee of Albemarle Academy, 25 March. |
| | Resigns presidency of American Philosophical Society, 23 November. |
| 1815 | Sells personal library to Congress. |
| 1816 | Writes introduction and revises translation of Destutt de Tracy, *A Treatise on Political Economy* [1818]. |
| | Named a visitor of Central College, 18 October. |
| 1818 | Attends Rockfish Gap conference to choose location of proposed University of Virginia, 1–4 August. |
| | Visits Warm Springs, 7–27 August. |
| 1819 | University of Virginia chartered, 25 January; named to Board of Visitors, 13 February; elected rector, 29 March. |
| | Debts greatly increased by bankruptcy of Wilson Cary Nicholas. |
| 1820 | Likens debate over slavery and Missouri statehood to "a fire bell in the night," 22 April. |
| 1821 | Writes memoirs, 6 January–29 July. |
| 1823 | Visits Poplar Forest for last time, 16–25 May. |
| 1824 | Lafayette visits Monticello, 4–15 November. |
| 1825 | University of Virginia opens, 7 March. |
| 1826 | Writes will, 16–17 March. |
| | Last recorded letter, 25 June. |
| | Dies at Monticello, 4 July. |

# THE PAPERS OF
# THOMAS JEFFERSON

·《══════》·

## To Destutt de Tracy

Nov. 28. 13.

I will not fatigue you, my dear Sir, with long and labored excuses for having been so tardy in writing to you; but shall briefly mention that the thousand hostile ships which cover the ocean render attempts to pass it now very unfrequent, and these concealing their intentions from all that they may not be known to the enemy are gone before heard of in such inland situations as mine. to this, truth must add the torpidity of age as one of the obstacles to punctual correspondence.

Your letters of Oct. 21. & Nov. 15. 1811. and Aug. 29. 1813. were duly recieved and with that of Nov. 15 came the MS. copy of your work on Oeconomy. the extraordinary merit of the former volume had led me to anticipate great satisfaction and edification from the perusal of this; and I can say with truth and sincerity that these expectations were compleatly fulfilled. new principles developed, former ones corrected, or rendered more perspicuous,[1] present us an interesting science, heretofore voluminous and embarrassed, now happily simplified and brought within a very moderate compass. after an attentive perusal which enabled me to bear testimony to it's worth, I took measures for getting it translated and printed in Philadelphia; the distance of which place prepared me to expect great and unavoidable delays. but notwithstanding my continual urgencies these have gone far beyond my calculations. in a letter of Sep. 26. from the editor in answer to one of mine, after urging in excuse the causes of the delay, he expresses his confidence that it would be ready by the[2] last of October; and that period being now past, I am in daily expectation of hearing from him. as I write the present letter without knowing by what conveyance it may go, I am not without a hope of recieving a copy of the work in time to accompany this. I shall then be anxious to learn that better health and more encouraging circumstances enable you to pursue your plan thro' the two remaining branches of Morals & Legislation, which executed in the same lucid, logical and condensed style, will present such a whole as the age we live in will not before have recieved. should the same motives operate for their first publication here, I am now offered such means, nearer to me, as promise a more encouraging promptitude in the execution. and certainly no effort should be spared on my part to ensure to the world such an acquisition. the MS. of the first work has been carefully recalled and deposited with me. that of the second, when done with shall be equally taken care of.

If unmerited praise could give pleasure to a candid mind I should have been highly exalted, in my own opinion, on the occasion of the first work. one of the best judges and best men of the age has ascribed it to myself; and has for some time been employed in translating it into French. it would be a gratification to which you are highly entitled, could I transcribe the sheets he has written me in praise, nay in rapture with the work; and were I to name the man, you would be sensible there is not another whose suffrage would be more encouraging. but the casualties which lie between us would render criminal the naming any one. in a letter which I am now writing him, I shall set him right as to myself, and[3] acknolege my humble station far below the qualifications necessary for that work: and shall discourage his perseverance in retranslating into French a work the original of which is so correct in it's diction that not a word can be altered but for the worse; and from a translation too where the author's meaning has sometimes been illy understood, sometimes mistaken, and often expressed in words not the best chosen. indeed when the work, thro' it's translation becomes more generally known here, the high estimation in which it is held by all who become acquainted with it, encorages me to hope I may get it printed in the original. I sent a copy of it to the late President of W$^m$ and Mary college of this state, who adopted it at once, as the elementary book of that institution. from these beginnings it will spread and become a political gospel for a nation open to reason, & in a situation to adopt and profit by it's results, without a fear of their leading to wrong.

I sincerely wish you all the health, comfort and leisure necessary to dispose and enable you to persevere in employing yourself so usefully for present & future times: and I pray you to be assured you have not a more grateful votary for your benefactions to mankind nor one of higher sentiments of esteem & affectionate respect

Th: Jefferson

PoC (DLC); at foot of first page: "M le Comte De-tutt Tracy." Enclosed in TJ to David Bailie Warden, 29 Dec. 1813, and TJ to John Graham, 6 Jan. 1814.

The FORMER VOLUME was Destutt de Tracy, *Commentary and Review of Montesquieu's Spirit of Laws*. The EDITOR of his most recent submission was William Duane. ONE OF THE BEST JUDGES AND BEST MEN OF THE AGE: Pierre Samuel Du Pont de Nemours. The LATE PRESI-DENT of the College of William and Mary was Bishop James Madison.

[1] Manuscript: "perspcuous."
[2] Preceding twenty-eight words interlined to correct a fault in the polygraph.
[3] TJ here canceled "take."

# From Joseph C. Cabell

DEAR SIR                                    Williamsburg. 29th novr 1813.

Your favor of 7th inst covering an abstract of the Bill respecting yourself & the Rivanna River Co, did not get to Warminster, till nearly a fortnight after I had left home for the lower country: and it was not untill the 26th inst that I received it at this place. This will account for the delay of my answer; as well as for my not calling at Monticello on my way down, agreeably to your obliging invitation.

I am happy to learn that the Bill of the last session as amended in the Senate, is satisfactory to the parties concerned, & that it will pass thro' both houses as a matter of course. To the verbal amendments suggested by yourself in red ink, I presume, there will be no objection from any quarter, as they only remove defects in the wording of the bill, & cause it to express more accurately the real intentions of the parties.

On the subject of the duration of the charter, I can only say that it was made as short as was supposed compatible with the success of the amendments made in the Senate. Mr Johnson advised me to attempt nothing further. I am extremely sorry that I cannot see your reasoning on the general question of the duration of charters, & the power of one generation to bind another. I should derive great satisfaction & advantage from such a communication; the more especially as it would throw light on the path of my official duties, in which I am desirous to move with all possible care & circumspection during the residue of the time that I have to act as the representative of the district. The ride from my house to monticello would have cheerfully been taken, for this object: had I not already have left home. I beg the favor of you to communicate this production to me, whenever in your opinion a suitable opportunity may occur.

Tho' I shall not be able personally to deliver Say's work to you, I hope you will not be disappointed in receiving it, by the period mentioned in your letter (7th Decr) as I shall take all possible care to cause it to be put into your hands by that time. I brought it[1] as far as

Richmond, where I left it;[2] & from which I intended to send it to Monticello at the close of the session. I feel ashamed of the length of time I have kept it from you. Soon after borrowing it, I determined on reading Smith's treatise first; which I did: & then in order to understand him more clearly, I read him a second time: afterwards I read Say twice, with the exception of a small part—During these perusals, I took frequent occasion to refer to small tracts on branches of the science—These readings, with my other studies & avocations, have filled up the long space of time that Say has been in my hands. I am much pleased with this author, & think he well deserves the praises you bestow on him. He is more concise, more methodical, more clear, &, in many passages, more correct than Smith. His work approximates perfection more nearly than Smith's—yet I consider it only as an approximation. On the theory of money my mind is not yet satisfied, and I doubt whether new views of that branch of the science are not to rise upon the Human mind. My studies on the subject of political economy, are, however, in an unfinished state: and things may appear to me obscure, because I do not understand them. This has been often the case in regard to Commentators on Smith, and the remark, I think, at least in some degree applicable to Ganihl, whose work I have partly read. I shall be happy to hear your opinion of this writer at a convenient opportunity.

I am d[r] Sir very respectfully & truly yours

JOSEPH C. CABELL.

RC (ViU: TJP-PC); at foot of text: "M[r] Jefferson"; endorsed by TJ as received 13 Dec. 1813 and so recorded in SJL.

Adam SMITH'S TREATISE was *An Inquiry into the Nature and Causes of the* *Wealth of Nations*, 2 vols. (London, 1776; Sowerby, no. 3546).

[1] Cabell here canceled "along in my carriage."

[2] Cabell here canceled "in my trunk at M[rs] Carrington's."

# To Pierre Samuel Du Pont de Nemours

MY VERY DEAR AND ESTIMABLE FRIEND.                    Nov. 29. 13.

In answering the several very kind letters I have recieved from you, I owe to yourself, and to the most able and estimable author of the Commentaries on Montesquieu to begin by assuring you that I am not the author of that work, and of my own consciousness that it is far beyond my qualifications. in truth I consider it as the most profound and logical work which has been presented to the present generation. on the subject of government particularly there is a purity and soundness of principle which renders it precious, to our country particularly, where I trust it will become the elementary work for the youth of our academies and Colleges. the paradoxes of Montesquieu have been too long uncorrected. I will not fail to send you a copy of the work if possible to get it thro' the perils of the sea.          I am next to return you thanks for the copy of the works of Turgot, now compleated by the reciept of the last volume. in him we know not which most to admire, the comprehensiveness of his mind, or the benevolence and purity of his heart. in his Distribution of Riches, and other general works, and in the great principles developed in his smaller works, we admire the gigantic stature of his mind. but when we see that mind thwarted, harrassed, maligned and forced to exert all it's powers in the details of provincial administration, we regret to see a Hercules laying his shoulder to the wheel of an ox-cart. the sound principles which he establishes in his particular as well as general works are a valuable legacy to ill-governed man, and will spread from their provincial limits to the great circle of mankind.          I am indebted to you also for your letter by mr Correa, and the benefit it procured me of his acquaintance. he was so kind as to pay me a visit at Monticello which enabled me to see for myself that he was still beyond all the eulogies with which yourself and other friends had preconised him. learned beyond any one I had before met with, good, modest, and of the simplest manners, the idea of losing him again filled me with regret: and how much did I lament that we could not place him at the head of that great institution which I have so long nourished the hope of seeing established in my country; and towards which you had so kindly contributed your luminous views. but, my friend, that institution is still in embryo as you left it: and from the complexion of our popular legislature, and the narrow and niggardly views of ignorance courting the suffrage of ignorance to obtain a seat in it, I see little prospect of such an establishment until the national government shall be authorised to take it up and form it on the comprehensive basis of all the useful sciences.          The inauspicious commencement of our war had damped at first the hopes of fulfilling your injunctions to add the Floridas and Canada to our confederacy. the former indeed might have been added but for our steady adherence to the sound principles of National integrity, which forbade us to take what was a neighbor's merely because it suited us; and especially from a neighbor under circumstances of peculiar affliction. but seeing now that his afflictions do not prevent him from making those provinces the focus of hostile and savage combinations for the massacre of our women and children by the tomahawk and scalping knife

[ 7 ]

of the Indian, these scruples must yield to the necessities of self defence: and I trust that the ensuing session of Congress will authorize
the incorporation of it with ourselves. their inhabitants universally
wish it and they are in truth the only legitimate proprietors of the soil
& government. Canada might have been ours in the preceding year
but for the treachery of our General who unfortunately commanded
on it's border. there could have been no serious resistance to the
progress of the force he commanded, in it's march thro' Upper
Canada. but he sold and delivered his army fortified and furnished as
it was, to an enemy of one fourth his number. this was followed by a
series of losses flowing from the same source of unqualified commanders. carelessness, cowardice, foolhardiness & sheer imbecility
lost us 4 other successive bodies of men, who under faithful and capable leaders would have saved us from the affliction and the English
from the crime of the thousands of men, women & children murdered
& scalped by the savages under the procurement & direction of
British officers, some on capitulation, some in the field, & some in
their houses and beds. the determined bravery of our men, whether
regulars or militia, evidenced in every circumstance where the
treachery or imbecility of their commanders permitted, still kept up
our confidence and sounder and abler men now placed at their head
have given us possession of the whole of Upper Canada & the lakes.
at the moment I am writing I am in hourly expectation of learning
that Gen$^l$ Wilkinson who about the 10$^{th}$ inst. was entering the Lake
of S$^t$ Francis in his descent upon Montreal, has taken possession of it,
the force of the enemy there being not such as to give us much apprehension. between that place and Quebec there is nothing to stop
us, but the advance of the season.        the atchievements of our little navy have claimed and obtained the admiration of all, in spite of
the Endeavors of the English by lying misrepresentations of the force
of the vessels on both sides to conceal the truth. the loss indeed of half
a dozen frigates and sloops of war is no sensible diminution of numbers to them; but the loss of the general opinion that they were invincible at sea, the lesson taught to the world that they can be beaten
by an equal force, has, by it's moral effect lost them half their physical force. I consider ourselves as now possessed of every thing from
Florida point to the walls of Quebec. this last place is not worth the
blood it would cost. it may be considered as impregnable to an enemy
not possessing the water. I hope therefore we shall not attempt it, but
leave it to be voluntarily evacuated by it's inhabitants, cut off from all
resources of subsistence by the loss of the upper country.

I will ask you no questions, my friend, about your return to the US.

at your time of life it is scarcely perhaps advisable. an exchange of the society, the urbanity, and the real comforts to which you have been formed by the habits of a long life, would be a great and real sacrifice. whether therefore I shall ever see you again, or not, let me live in your esteem, as you ever will in mine most affectionately and devotedly.

TH: JEFFERSON

P.S. Monticello Dec. 14. 13. we have been disappointed in the result of the expedition against Montreal. the 2ᵈ in command who had been detached ashore with a large portion of the army, failing to join the main body according to orders at the entrance of Lake Sᵗ Francis, the enterprize was of necessity abandoned at that point, and the inclemency of the winter being already set in, the army was forced to go into winter quarters near that place.—Since the date of my letter I have recieved yours of Sep. 18. & a printed copy of your plan of national education of which I possessed the MS. if I can get this translated and printed it will contribute¹ to advance the public mind to undertake the institution. the persuading those of the value² of science who possess none, is a slow operation.

RC (DeGH: Pierre Samuel Du Pont de Nemours Papers, Winterthur Manuscripts); at foot of first page: "M. Dupont de Nemours." PoC (DLC); endorsed by TJ. Enclosed in TJ to David Bailie Warden, 29 Dec. 1813, and TJ to John Graham, 6 Jan. 1814.

Anne Robert Jacques Turgot's piece on the DISTRIBUTION OF RICHES was *Réflexions sur la formation et la distribution des richesses* ([Paris], 1788; Sowerby, no. 2379), a work that Du Pont also included in the fifth volume of his edition of Turgot's *Oeuvres* (Sowerby, no. 2436). Preconized (PRECONISED): "announced; extolled; commended" (*OED*). The

GREAT INSTITUTION that TJ had long hoped to see established would eventually come to fruition as the University of Virginia (Jennings L. Wagoner Jr., *Jefferson and Education* [2004]; TJ to William Short, 9 Nov. 1813). TJ was convinced of the TREACHERY OF OUR GENERAL William Hull. THE LAKES: the Great Lakes. The 2ᴰ IN COMMAND during the abortive United States campaign against Montreal was Wade Hampton. Du Pont's letter to TJ was actually dated 8 Sept. 1813, not SEP. 18.

¹ Manuscript: "contibute."
² PoC: "benefit."

# To Tadeusz Kosciuszko

MY DEAR FRIEND AND GENERAL                    Nov. 30. 13.

I have to acknolege the reciept of yours of Dec. 1. 12. and it's duplicate of May 30. 13. and am pleased that our arrangement with mr Morton proves satisfactory.¹ I believed it would be so, and that a substantial & friendly house there might sometimes be a convenience, when, from the dangers of the sea, difficulty of finding good bills, or other casualties, mr Barnes's remittances might incur unavoidable delay. he is at this time making arrangements with mr Williams the correspondent of mr Morton for the usual remittance, having for some time past been unable to get a good bill.

You have heard without doubt of the inauspicious commencement of our war by land. our old officers of high command were all withdrawn by death or age. Scott closed the list of the dead a few weeks ago: and happy for us would it have been could we have followed your advice in appointing new generals; and could we have been directed in our choice to those only who were good. but this is a lottery in which are few prizes, and our first draught fell among the blanks. the first called into action, delivered his army and fort up to one fourth of his own numbers of the English. he might have taken possession of all upper Canada, almost without resistance. this was followed by cases of surprise, of cowardice, of fool hardiness and of sheer imbecility, by which bodies of men were sucessively lost as fast as they could be raised; and thus the first year of the war was lost. Gen$^l$ Wilkinson, whom you knew in the late war, has at length been called from the Southern department; Gen$^l$ Hampton also: and they are doing what their predecessors ought to have done the last year. we have taken all the posts and country on lakes Erie & Ontario; and Gen$^l$ Wilkinson on the 10$^{th}$ inst. was about entering the lake S$^t$ Francis in his descent to Montreal, and would in 3. or 4. days reach Montreal, where the British force is such as not to give uneasiness for the result. I trust he is now in possession of it, and there being neither a post nor a man between that & Quebec, we may consider ourselves as commanding the whole country to the walls of that city. the season however will probably oblige us to make Montreal our winter quarters. Kingston at the East end of Lake Ontario has been left unmolested, because being of some strength, and well garrisoned, it would have required a seige, and the advance of the season would have disappointed us as to all below. insulated as it is from succours and subsistence, it must capitulate at our leisure. this, my friend is the present state of things by land; and as I know not yet how or when this letter is to go, I may by a P.S. be able to add what shall have actually taken place at Montreal. it is a duty however to add here that in every instance our men, militia as well as regulars, have acted with an intrepidity which would have honored veteran legions, and have proved that had _their_ officers understood their duty as well as those of our little navy, they would have shewn themselves equally superior to an enemy who had dared to despise us. on the ocean we have taught a lesson of value to all mankind, that they can be beaten there with equal force. we have corrected the idea of their invincibility, which by it's moral effect annihilates half their physical force. I do not believe the naval history of the world has furnished a more splendid atchievement of skill and bravery than that of Perry on L. Erie. they threaten now to hang our prisoners, reclaimed by them altho' naturalised with us, and, if we retaliate, to burn our cities. we shall certainly retaliate, and, if they burn N. York, Norfolk, Charleston, we must burn London, Portsmouth, Plymouth: not with our ships, but by our money; not with our own hands, but by those of their own incendiaries. they have in their streets thousands of famished wretches who, for a loaf of bread to keep off death one day longer, and more eagerly for a million of dollars will spread to them the flames which they shall kindle in New York. it is not for those who live in glass houses to set the example of throwing stones. what is atrocious as an example becomes a duty to repress by retaliation. if we have taken, as I expect, the residue of their troops above Quebec, we have as many of their troops taken by honorable fighting, as they have of ours purchased or surprised.

I have less fear now for our war than for the peace which is to conclude it. your idea that our line of future demarcation should be from some point in Lake Champlain is a good one: because that would shut up all their scalp-markets. but that of their entire removal from the continent is a better one. while they hold a single spot on it it will be a station from which they will send forth their Henrys upon us to debauch traitors, nourish conspiracies, smuggle in their manufactures, and defeat our commercial laws. unfortunately our peace-commissioners left us while our affairs were still under the depression of Hull's treason, and it's consequences, and they would as soon learn their revival in the moon as in S$^t$ Petersburg. the English newspapers will still fill their ears, as those of all Europe with lies, and induce them to offer terms of peace under these erroneous impressions: and a peace which does not leave us the Canadas will be but a truce. as for the Floridas they are giving themselves to us. I hope therefore no peace will be made which does not yield us this indemnification for the thousand ships they took during peace, the thousands of our citizens impressed, their machinations for disseevering our Union, the insults they have heaped upon us, the inhuman war they have waged with the tomahawk & scalping knife of the savage, the suffocation of our prisoners in pestiferous jails and prison ships, and other atrocities against national and individual morality, which have degraded them from the rank of civilised nations. the longer the peace is delayed the more firm will become the establishment of our manufactures. the growth and extent of these can be concieved by none who does not see them. of coarse and midling fabrics we never again shall import. the manufacture of the fine cottons is carried also to great extent & perfection. a million of cotton spindles nearly being, I think, now employed in the US. this single advancement in oeconomy, begun by our embargo law, continued by that of non-importation, and confirmed by the present total cessation of commercial intercourse was worth, alone, all the war will cost us.

I have thus, my dear friend, given you the present state of things[2] with us, which I have done with the more minuteness because I know that no native among us takes a livelier interest in them than you do. the tree which you had so zealously assisted in planting, you cannot but delight in seeing watered and flourishing. happy for us would it have been if a valour fidelity and skill like yours[3] had directed those early efforts which were so unfortunately confided to unworthy hands. we should have been a twelvemonth ago where we now are, and now, where we shall be a twelvemonth hence. however from one man we can have but one life; and you gave us the most valuable and active part of yours, and we are now enjoying and improving it's effects. every sound American, every sincere votary of freedom loves and honors you, and it was it's enemies only, and the votaries of England who saw with cold indifference, and even secret displeasure your short-lived return to us. they love none who do not love kings, and the kings of England above all others. god bless you under every circumstance, whether still reserved for the good of your native country, or destined to leave us in the fulness of time with the consciousness of succesful efforts for the establishment of freedom in one country, and of all which man could have done for it's success in another. the lively sense I entertain of all you have done & deserved from both countries can be extinguished only with the lamp of life, during which I shall ever be affectionately & devotedly yours          TH: JEFFERSON

P.S. Monticello Dec. 14. We have been disappointed in the result of the expedition against Montreal, and again by the fault of a general who refused, with his large detachment ashore, to meet the main body according to orders at the entrance of Lake S[t] Francis. the expedition was of necessity suspended at that point, and the army obliged by the severity of the season to go into winter quarters near that place.

PoC (DLC); at foot of first page: "Gen[l] Kosciusko"; endorsed by TJ. Enclosed in TJ to David Bailie Warden, 29 Dec. 1813, and TJ to John Graham, 6 Jan. 1814.

The FIRST CALLED INTO ACTION was General William Hull. Twenty-three American soldiers captured on 13 Oct. 1812 at Queenston, Canada, had been sent to England to be tried for treason in consequence of Great Britain's refusal to recognize that they had been or could be NATURALISED by the United States. Under the British doctrine of indelible citizenship, natives who took up citizenship elsewhere could still be executed for taking up arms against king and country. Secretary of War John Armstrong responded on 15 May 1813 by ordering General Henry Dearborn to put twenty-three British prisoners into close confinement and hold them as hostages "for the safe keeping and restoration (on exchange)" of the abovementioned American servicemen. Lieutenant General George Prevost reacted by confining forty-six more prisoners of war and informing his American counterpart on 17 Oct. 1813 that if any British captives were put to death, the war would be prosecuted "with unmitigated severity against all cities, towns, and villages belonging to the United States." Undeterred by such

threats, General James Wilkinson replied to Prevost on 3 Dec. 1813 that he had placed forty-six additional British soldiers under arrest. The issue continued to generate controversy thereafter, but in the end none of those sent to England were tried, and the twenty-one survivors (two of the detainees having died in captivity) returned to America shortly after the conclusion of hostilities (*ASP, Foreign Relations*, 3:630–2, 635, 637; Ralph Robinson, "Retaliation for the Treatment of Prisoners in the War of 1812," *American Historical Review* 49 [1943]: 65–70). General Wade Hampton refused, according to TJ, TO MEET THE MAIN BODY of the American army advancing on Montreal (Stagg, *Madison's War*, 345–6).

[1] Manuscript: "saisfactory."
[2] Manuscript: "thing."
[3] Reworked from "if your valour fidelity and skill."

# To Lafayette

MY DEAR FRIEND                                    Nov. 30. 13.

The last letters I have recieved from you were of Apr. 22. May 20. July 4. of the preceding year. they gave me information of your health, always welcome to the feelings of antient and constant friendship. I hope this continues & will continue until you tire of that and life together.—the Sheperd dogs mentioned in yours of May 20. arrived safely, have been carefully multiplied, and are spreading in this and the neighboring states where the increase of our sheep is greatly attended to. of these we have already enough to clothe all our inhabitants, and the Merino race is wonderfully extended, & improved in size. our manufactures of fine cloths are equal to the best English, and those of cotton by their abundance and superior quality will compleatly exclude the English from the market. our progress in manufactures is far beyond the calculations of the most sanguine. every private house is getting spinning machines. I have four in operation in my own family for our own use, and carding machines are growing up in every neighborhood. insomuch that were peace restored tomorrow, we should not[1] return to the importation from England of either coarse or midling fabrics of any material, nor even of the finer woolen cloths. putting honor & right out of the question therefore, this revolution in our domestic economy was well worth a war.

You have heard how inauspiciously our war began by land. the treachery of Hull who, furnished with an army which might have taken Upper Canada with little resistance, sold it to an enemy of one fourth his strength was the cause of all our subsequent misfortunes. a second army was by surprise submitted to massacre by the Indians, under the eye and countenance of British officers to whom they had surrendered on capitulation. other losses followed these from cowardice, from foolhardiness and from sheer imbecillity in the commanders. in every instance the men, militia as well as regulars displayed an intrepidity which shewed it only wanted capable direction. these misfortunes however, instead of disheartening, only sunk deeper into our hearts the necessity of reexertion,[2] as in old times was the effect of the retreat across the Delaware. this has happily been crowned with success. every thing above the Eastern end of L. Ontario is already in our possession, and I might venture to say to the walls of Quebec: because on the 10th inst. Genl Wilkinson was entering the Lake St Francis on his passage down to Montreal where he would land within 3. or 4. days and not meet a resistance which gives us any apprehensions. between that place and Quebec there is neither post nor armed man. Kingston was wisely left to fall of itself. the St Laurence to the walls of Quebec being ours whenever the season will open it to us, this last place will never be worth the blood it would cost. cut off from subsistence by the loss of the upper country, it must be evacuated by it's inhabitants. our quarters for this winter will probably be in Montreal.

Of the glories of our little navy you will of course have heard. those on the ocean are no otherwise of value than as they have proved the British can be beaten there by an equal force. they correct the idea of their invincibility, and by this moral effect destroy one half their physical force on that element. but Perry's victory on L. Erie had the most important effects, and is truly the parent of all the subsequent successes. nor do I know that the naval history of the world furnishes an example of a more splendid action.

I join you sincerely, my friend in wishes for the emancipation of South America. that they will be liberated from foreign subjection I have little doubt. but the result of my enquiries does not authorise me to hope they are capable of maintaining a free government. their people are immersed in the darkest ignorance, and brutalised by bigotry & superstition. their priests make of them what they please: and tho' they may have some capable leaders yet nothing but intelligence in the people themselves can keep these faithful to their charge. their efforts I fear therefore will end in establishing military despotisms in the several provinces. among these there can be no confederacy. a republic of kings is impossible. but their future wars & quarrels among themselves will oblige them to bring the people into action, & into the exertion of their understandings. light will at length beam in on their minds and the standing example we shall hold up, serving as an excitement as well as a model for their direction may in the long run qualify them for self-government. this is the most I am able to hope for them; for I lay it down as one of the impossibilities of nature that ignorance should maintain itself free against cunning, where any government has been once admitted.

I thank you for making mr Correa known to me. I found him deserving every thing which his and my friends had said of him, and only lamented that our possession of him was to be so short-lived.          I will certainly send you another copy of the book you desire if it can possibly escape the perils of the sea.          I say nothing about your affairs here because being in the best hands I can say nothing important. I am happy you have been able to turn the just retribution of our country to some account in easing your mind from some of it's concerns. on our part it was a just attention to sacrifices you had made to make us what we are. I only lament it was not what it should have been. I write to M$^{de}$ de Tessé, M. de Tracy E$^t$c. and conclude with the assurance of my affectionate and unalterable friendship and respect.          TH: JEFFERSON

P.S. Monticello Dec. 14. I have kept my letter open that I might state with certainty the issue of the expedition against Montreal. our just expectations have been disappointed by another failure of a General commanding a large portion of the army ashore, and refusing to meet, the main body, according to orders at the entrance of Lake S$^t$ Francis. the expedition was of necessity abandoned at that point at which it was known to have arrived at the date of my letter: and the commencement of severe weather forced the army into winter quarters near that place. in the President's message at the meeting of Congress you will see a succinct & correct history of the transactions of the year.

RC (DLC: Kislak Collection). PoC (DLC); endorsed by TJ: "Fayette M. de la. Nov. 30. 13." Enclosed in TJ to David Bailie Warden, 29 Dec. 1813, and TJ to John Graham, 6 Jan. 1814.

On 23 Jan. 1813 a group of American prisoners of war captured at the recently concluded Battle of Frenchtown were subjected to a MASSACRE BY THE INDIANS, an event that excited outrage throughout the Northwest (Stagg, *Madison's War*, 225). General George Washington's retreat across the DELAWARE River early in December 1776 set the stage for his later triumphs at the battles of Trenton and Princeton (Edward G. Lengel, *General George Washington: A Military Life* [2005], 170–1). The BOOK TJ promised to procure for Lafayette was Destutt de Tracy, *Commentary and Re-* *view of Montesquieu's Spirit of Laws*. The GENERAL who refused to join the American forces advancing on Montreal was Wade Hampton (Stagg, *Madison's War*, 345–6). For President James Madison's 7 Dec. 1813 annual MESSAGE to Congress, see *JHR*, 9:162–6.

[1] Word interlined.
[2] Manuscript: "reextion."

# From Judith Lomax

(Port-Tobago.—Nov^ber 30^th /1813.

I send you my dear Sir, the promised Acacia Seed, together with a few of the Flowers, knowing you to be an admirer of the perfume.— The Filbert scions you will get, whenever an opportunity shall occur at the proper season for removing them.—My best wish's await M^rs Randolph, and M^rs C. Bankhead, I will send M^rs Randolph the flower seed I promised, so soon as I can make a collection worth offering.

I am Sir most respectfuly Y^rs           JUDITH LOMAX.—

RC (MHi); dateline at foot of text; endorsed by TJ as received 13 Dec. 1813 and so recorded in SJL.

At Monticello on 16 Feb. 1814, TJ planted "56 seeds of the ACACIA Nilotica" that he had received from Lomax. They descended from "the plant at Greenspring," the estate of colonial governor Sir William Berkeley, near Williamsburg (Betts, *Garden Book*, 83, 524).

# From John Clarke

DEAR SIR                                         near Richmond Dec^r 2^d 1813.

In addressing the first man of an enlightened nation, upon a political subject; I feel that diffidence which a consciousness of the great disparity between our respective intellects, naturally inspires.—The sun cannot borrow light from a twinkling star, nor can the brilliancy of your mind, receive additional lustre from the weak and obscure reflections of mine. But as the most able Generals sometimes receive salutary hints from the lowest subaltern, and even from the humble soldier; And as the most unenlightened citizen, may suggest ideas, which abler minds may improve into real benefits; I am tempted again to address you.

As we cannot subdue our enemy on the ocean, for want of a sufficient navy; And as the war on our part must therefore be carried on chiefly by land forces; it is a matter of the first importance, that we should adopt effectual measures for raising a strong and efficient Army. The efforts of our Marine force in the present war, have been crowned with the most brilliant success, and have filled the public mind with exultation; Whilst those of the Military, have, in several instances been so unsuccessful; as to fall far short of the public expectation. But as the success of Armies, as well as of Navies, depend upon the skill, as well as the courage, of the individuals who compose them; we should not expect that the success of our Military force, will equal that of the Marine; until the Army shall be composed of troops, voluntarily enlisted for regular service, and skilled in the arts of war. Until that object shall be accomplished; we must continue to employ the Militia, in our Armies. And notwithstanding they sometimes object, to passing beyond the limits of the United States; they must guard our frontiers. And although they are undisciplined, they must contend against a veteran enemy, until regular troops can be provided. It is true, that, during the period of life, in which our citizens are militia, they necessarily bear a greater portion of the burthens of war, than other members of the community; since they like others, meet the expenses of war, with the purse; And moreover, meet the enemy with the bayonet. But the militia of the present day, merely stand in the predicament in which others have stood, whom old age has exempted from militia duty; and the same in which, our male infants must stand, when they shall arrive at the proper age, to perform that duty. Our militia citizens are brave and patriotic, but they are unacquainted with military operations. A considerable portion of them, are married men, who follow the occupations of agriculture; And although they perform their respective tour's of military duty without complaint, and are anxiously disposed to support a vigorous prosecution of the war; yet the performance of that duty, is generally attended with much disadvantage and inconvenience to themselves. Moreover, the reluctance with which they leave their wives & children, and cease to cultivate the fields that yield them bread,—the consciousness, when in service, that their want of military skill, will render them unequal to the enemy in battle;—and their anxiety to return to the bosom of domestic enjoyment; Are considerations which operate on the minds of the married militia-men with such force, as to prevent them from receiving, even the rudiments of a military education; and disqualify them for the performance of their duty with the intrepidity and manly spirit of soldiers. But notwithstanding the militia is a mass too heterogeneous for an Army, if taken indiscriminately; yet the materials for gallant armies, are to be found amongst that class of our citizens. Let us then, seperate the metal from the dross; by enlisting from amongst the militia, the unmarried men, who feel the influence of military pride & valour, and are anxious to become the avengers of their country's wrongs. Men who possess those feelings, and are free from the cares & uninfluenced by the considerations above mentioned, are the materials, of which, our military columns should be composed. But in this country, the temptations are great, which agriculture, and the mechanic, arts; hold out to enterprise and industry; We should not therefore, expect that such men; should encounter the hardships & perils of war, for a smaller reward than their domestic labours would produce. And I may add, that it is owing more to the want of a liberal bounty, than perhaps to any other cause, that so few recruits are enlisted for regular service.

I now come to the object of this communication, which is; to suggest for your consideration, a method, not yet resorted to; for the enlistment of regular troops.—The project simply is; That the militia of the United States, shall be legally authorised or allowed, to furnish from time to time, such numbers of regular troops raised among themselves by their own voluntary contributions in money or other property, as may be sufficient for all the purposes of war; instead of performing military services themselves.

I may perhaps be mistaken in the effect of this project, but I am induced to believe it would succeed; not merely from my own reflections on the subject, but by the opinions of many militia officers of high rank, as well as of privates, of good judgment; to whom I have mentioned it.

If all the troops required for our armies were regulars, there would be no necessity for calling out the militia; but whilst there is not a sufficient number of regular troops, the militia are continually subject to be called into service: And the circumstances under which they perform military duty are such; that there is scarcely a man among them who, would not much rather contribute a small sum, for the enlistment of regulars, than perform that duty himself. It could not be deemed a hardship on the militia, that they should apply their own funds to the enlistment of regulars; because they would have the option, of doing so, or not; and if they should choose to enlist regulars, it would be for their own accomodation. Let us now consider, whether the pecuniary interest as well as the convenience of the militia, would not be promoted by their contributing money for the enlistment of regular troops, instead of performing military duty themselves.—Every militia-man who is possessed of health & strength, sufficient for the performance of military duty, has it in his power to earn (even by the most common occupations of husbandry) an hundred dollars per annum, But when he is called into service, one tour of duty for the usual term of six months, will deprive him of the profits of half a year's labour; which is equal to fifty dollars: and as he looses fifty dollars by the performance of a tour of duty; it may be presumed that he would rather pay that sum, and continue his attention to his own affairs at home; than, go into the army, even for the term of one tour. But for want of regular troops in the army, he may be made to perform many tour's; It would therefore be greatly to his interest, to contribute fifty dollars (which one tour of duty would cost him) for the enlistment of regular troops, who, by continuing in the army, would perhaps exonerate the militia-man from military service, during the whole war. I have endeavoured to shew, that the pecuniary interest, as well as the convenience, of the militia generally, would be promoted by their contributing fifty dollars each, for the enlistment of regular troops. But a contribution of only half that sum (to wit twenty five dollars) by each militia-man; would perhaps raise as many regulars, as the army now requires to make it so strong, as to render the service of the militia unnecessary. Although every militia-man, may by labour earn, an hundred dollars per annum; yet if a bounty of an hundred dollars should be offered for each citizen who would enlist to serve in the regular army during the war; I think it probable that the requisite number would soon be raised. Because the present war is not expected to be of long continuance; Because the occupation of a soldier, although, sometimes attended with hardship & danger; is not so laborious as the business of the Farm or the Work-shop: And because enterprising unmarried men, when the country is involved in war; are prompted to engage in it, by a natural impulse; and that impulse would be increased by a bounty of one hundred dollars. But suppose the bounty should be even greater than the annual amount of a man's labour while domesticated among the militia;—let it be an hundred and twenty five dollars:—It only requires five militia-men to contribute twenty five dollars each, and that bounty for a regular soldier is immediately made up. Twenty five dollars, is indeed a small sum to contribute to so important an object; especially when we consider, that every militia-man who is sufficiently able-bodied to perform military duty, may earn it, at any kind of business; in the course of two or three months,—in half the time that one tour of militia duty would require of him. As the burthen of war, falls more heavily on the militia, than any other class of citizens; every militia-man in the United States, should bear his portion of it; and when that shall be the case; the burthen will in reality be a light one.

If five militia-men by a contribution of Twenty five dollars each, can enlist a regular soldier for the war; every militia regiment of a thousand men, may in like manner enlist Two hundred; And the whole militia of the Union (by apportioning the proper number to each regiment,) might raise an army of regular troops, so strong; as, to render the military service of the Militia, unnecessary.

I merely suggest this outline of a project, in the hope; that, it may be so improved; as to add strength and vigour to the military force upon which we chiefly depend, in the present war.

The present belligerent state of the nations of Europe & America, and their respective relations to each other; furnish matter for deep & interesting speculation; but we cannot foretel the consequences that may result from such a state of things. It is pleasing however, to reflect; that, 'tho' robbed of commerce, and involved in war; yet happy is the condition of free, self-governed America, contrasted with that of miserable Europe, still smarting under the lash of Tyrants; still convulsed; and bleeding at every pore. But we should not depend for our happiness & prosperity, upon the Justice of foreign nations; We must rely upon the exertion of our own strength, and prudence. The ambition and pride, of kings and emperors; which inflames all Europe and sends forth its sparks to America; is sufficient to awaken us to a sense of our assailable & unprepared situation for war. It should stimulate our energies and call into action our resources; by means of which; we should be able to repel the most formidable efforts of our enemy. The anxious hope for peace, which we still cherish; is attributed, by our enemy, to our inability, and unwillingness to carry on the war. And whilst we trust to that hope, and rely on negotiation, as we now do upon the mediation of Russia; whilst public opinion wavers upon points that require the most prompt decision; we shall probably continue at war, without being prepared for it. As great Britain (with her european allies,) is now contending against the greatest military nation on earth; we should strike the blow, that would give us complete possession of her american provinces; And banish from the Florida's, her spanish allies; who make war upon us, through the instrumentality of the southern Indians;—those savages whose happiness, your philanthropy has long laboured to promote, by introducing among them, the blessings of peace and civilization. Should the present campaign, in Europe, terminate in favor of the allies; perhaps Britain; already elated with success in Spain; may be induced to send a considerable number of troops from thence to america.—That is an event that may happen, and one which we should be prepared to meet. The future

happiness of our country, and the stand which we shall hereafter occupy in the scale of nations; may perhaps depend upon the character,
which the present war will stamp upon us. Our love of peace, and
confidence in the Justice and moderation, with which our government has long endeavoured to prevent encroachments upon our
rights; have been considered, by the nations of europe, as a base submission to wrongs, which we had not sufficient energy to counteract:
But since we have buckled on[1] "the armour and taken the attitude
of war;" Since we have been compelled to lay aside the olive branch
and draw the sword; we ought ere it is sheathed; to engrave with its
point, the character of our nation. We ought to prove to piratical
Britain; that we are as brave and generous, as we have been moderate and Just; And convince imperial Europe, that republican America, though in peace like the lamb is, in war like the lion. By a
courageous & determined spirit, and by improvements in the science
of war; France has acquired a weight of character, which she could
not otherwise attain. She is now not only able to combat the most
powerful of her enemies, but to meet in battle, their whole united
force. And although we do not Justify the acts of her present ruler;
we may profit by the examples she has furnished, of bravery, activity
and perseverance.

But I fear, that any attempt to establish such a reputation as our nation deserves, will be ineffectual; whilst the salutary measures of the
national Executive, are trammelled & thwarted by the national Legislature. The honor and the interests of the nation are confided to its
agents; but they cannot be supported in war; without unanimity and
energy in our councils; aided by skill, and bravery, in our Army, and
navy. That the federalists or british partisans; should act in opposition to the administration of our government; is neither new nor
unexpected. But that men who, by professing a devotion to the principles of our government; were elected to represent a republican people, in the national legislature; should in time of war assist the enemy,
by counteracting the patriotic measures of the Executive branch of
the government; is a circumstance which could not have been expected by their constituents. It is a species of treachery that has the
effect of studied treason; and excites the warmest indignation of the
people. It is, perhaps, owing to the ambition and envy, of men of that
stamp; that we are now involved in war. Their hostility to the Executive; manifested to the british government; that beside the federal
party, there were republicans of high standing, in Congress;
who were equally inimical to the Administration;—that in the event
of a war; its measures would probably be cramped and paralyzed by

a republican, as well as a federal, opposition; And that war, could not therefore be carried on with great effect. And if such were the predictions of the british government; they have been most fully verified. For the President, since the commencement of the war; has scarcely appointed any citizen to an office of importance, either civil or military; or adopted any important measure relative to carrying on the war with vigour; or for making peace on honourable terms: but his appointments and his measures, have been invariably condemned by those pretended republicans, as well as the federalists; And all the means in their power exerted, to prevent any beneficial result from them.

yet not content with the opposition made while on the floor of Congress, nor with the opprobrious invectives uttered in private circles, against the Executive; We have recently seen, that the ambition & envy of a certain senator who _professes_ to be a republican; has lately prompted him to attack our patriotic President, through the medium of the public prints; Under the pretence of Justifying his own conduct. But he is mistaken in the estimate he has formed of the public discernment. The veil of sophistry with which he attempts to shroud his designs, is not impervious to the public eye. The american people behold him, as a public servant, who has abused their confidence; and as a statesman, who would sacrifice the interests of the nation, and the well-merited fame of our best patriots; at the shrine of his ambition. It is much to be regretted, that, the public voice, cannot now reduce this envious, ostentatious man, to the obscurity to which (at the last congressional election) it consigned a late celebrated demagogue of opposition, in the lower house, for a similar dereliction of political principles.

But the war, I trust; will be prosecuted with vigour, notwithstanding the opposition of monarchists, federalists, and pretended republicans. And if we can succeed in filling the ranks of our armies with regular troops; we may smile at the contemptible opposition made to it; by the tory governors of some of the eastern States; as we shall not then require the militia, to fight our battles.

I take this opportunity, to acknowledge the receipt of your favor of the 8th April, in reply to my letter of the 9th march last; And to tender you the assurance of my veneration and Cordial esteem.

JOHN CLARKE

RC (DLC: James Madison Papers); at head of text: "The hon'ble Thomas Jefferson, late President of the United States"; endorsed by TJ as a letter "relating to war" received 13 Dec. 1813 and recorded under that date of receipt in SJL. Enclosed in TJ to James Monroe, 27 Jan. 1814.

The 1813 campaigns of Great Britain and her continental allies against France, the GREATEST MILITARY NATION ON EARTH, achieved such success that by the end of the year French forces had been driven out of both central Europe and SPAIN (Chandler, *Campaigns of Napoleon*, 945). THE ARMOUR AND TAKEN THE ATTITUDE OF WAR references President James Madison's 5 Nov. 1811 annual message to Congress, in which he urged the legislature to put the nation "into an armour, and an attitude demanded by the crisis" (Madison, *Papers, Pres. Ser.*, 4:3). France's PRESENT RULER was Napoleon. William B. Giles, a United States senator from Virginia, repeatedly attacked President James Madison's policies THROUGH THE MEDIUM OF THE PUBLIC PRINTS. His letters "To the People of Virginia," dated between 20 Oct. and 25 Nov. 1813, were printed in newspapers across the country and also published separately (Washington *Daily National Intelligencer*, 16 Nov., 1, 13 Dec. 1813; *Address of the Honorable William B. Giles, to the People of Virginia* [n.d.]). The CELEBRATED DEMAGOGUE who lost his seat in the United States House of Representatives in the 1812 election was John Randolph of Roanoke (*DAB*).

[1] Manuscript: "on on."

# From John Adams

DEAR SIR                                        Quincy Dec[r] 3. 13

The Proverbs of the old greek Poets, are as Short and pithy as any of Solomon or Franklin. Hesiod has Several. His

Αθανατους μεν πρωτα θεους νομω, ως διακειται

Τιμα. Honour the Gods established by Law. I know not how We can escape Martyrdom, without a discreet Attention to this præcept. you have Suffered, and I have Suffered more than you,[1] for want of a Strict if not a due observance of this Rule.

There is another Oracle of this Hesiod, which requires a kind of dance upon a tight rope, and a Slack rope too, in Philosophy and Theology

Πίςις δ' ἄρα ὁμῶς καὶ ἀπίςιας ὤλεσαν ἀνδρας.

If believing too little or too much, is So fatal to Mankind what will become of Us all?

In Studying the Perfectability of human Nature and its progress towards perfection, in this World, on this Earth, (remember that) I have met many curious things, and interesting Characters.

About three hundred years ago, There appeared a number of Men of Letters, who appeared to endeavour to believe neither too little, nor too much. They laboured to imitate the Hebrew Archers who could Shoot to an hairs breadth. The Pope and his Church believed too much: Luther and his Church believed too little. This little band was headed by three great Scholars, Erasmus, Vives, and Budeus. This Triumvirate is Said to have been at the head of the Republick of Letters, in that Age. Had Condorcet been Master of his Subject, I fancy he would have taken more Notice in his History of the progress of Mind, of these Characters. Have you their Writings? I wish I had. I Shall confine myself at present to Vives. He wrote Commentaries on the City of God of St. Augustine, Some parts of which were censured by the Doctors of the Louvain as too bold and too free. I know not, whether the following passage of the learned Spaniard was among the Sentiments condemned, or not.

"I have been much afflicted," Says Vives, "when I have Seriously considered, how diligently, and with what exact care, the Actions of Alexander, Hannibal, Scipio Pompey, Cæsar and other Commanders: and the Lives of Socrates Plato Aristotle, and other Phylosophers, have been written and fixed in an everlasting Remembrance, So that there is not the least danger they can ever be lost: but then the Acts of the Apostles and Martyrs and Saints of our religion and of the Affairs of the rising and established Church, being involved in much darkness, are almost totally unknown, though they are of so much greater Advantage, than the Lives of the Phylosophers, or great Generals, both as to the improvement of our knowledge and Practice. For, what is written of these holy men, except a very few things is very much corrupted and defaced, with the mixture of many fables; while the Writer, indulging his own humour, doth not tell Us what the Saint did, but what the Historian would have had him done: and the fancy of the Writer dictates the Life and not the truth of things." And again, Vives Says

"There have been men, who have thought it a great piece of Piety, to invent Lies for the sake of religion."

The great Cardinal Barronius too, confesses "There is nothing, which Seems So much neglected to this day, as a true and certain Account of the Affairs of the Church, collected with an exact diligence. And that I may Speak of the more Ancient, it is very difficult to find any of them, who have published Commentaries on this Subject which have hit the truth in all points."

Canus, too another Spanish Prelate of great name Says "I Speak it with grief, and not by way of reproach, Laertius has written the lives of the Philosophers, with more care and industry, than the Christians have those of the Saints; Suetonius has represented the Lives of the Cæsars with much more truth and Sincerity, than the Catholicks have the Affairs, I will not Say of the Emperors, but even those of the Martyrs, holy Virgins and Confessors. For they have not concealed the Vices nor the very Suspicions of Vice, in good and commendable Philosophers or Princes, and in the worst of them, they discover the very colours or Appearances of Virtue. But the greatest part of our

Writers, either follow the Conduct of their Affections, or industriously fain many things; So that I, for my part am very often both weary and ashamed of them; because I know they have thereby brought nothing of Advantage to the Church of Christ, but very much inconvenience."

Vives and Canus are Moderns, but Arnobius the Converter of Lactantius was ancient. He Says "But neither could all that was done be written or arrive at the knowledge of all men. Many of our great Actions being done by obscure Men, and those who had no knowledge of Letters: and if Some of them are committed to Letters and Writings; yet even here, by the malice of the Devils, and of men like them, whose great design and Study it is to intercept and ruin this truth, by interpolating, or adding Some things to them, or by changing or taking out Words, Syllables, or Letters, they have put a Stop to the Faith of wise Men, and corrupted the truth of things."

Indeed, M$^r$ Jefferson, what could be invented to debase the ancient Christianism, which Greeks Romans, Hebrews, and Christian Factions, above all the Catholicks, have not fraudulently imposed upon the Publick? Miracles after Miracles have rolled down in Torrents, Wave Succeeding Wave, in the Catholic Church from the Council of Nice, and long before, to this day.

Aristotle, no doubt, thought his "Οὔτε πᾶσα πιςέυοντες, Οὔτε πᾶσιν ἀπιςοῦντες," very wise and very profound: but what is its Worth? What Man, Woman or Child, ever believed, every Thing, or nothing?

Oh! that Priestley could live again! and have leisure and means. An Enquirer after Truth, who had neither time nor means might request him to search and research for answers to a few Questions.

1. Have We more than two Witnesses of the Life of Jesus? Mathew and John?

2. Have We one Witness to the Existence of Mathews Gospel in the first Century?

3. Have We one Witness of the Existence of John's Gospell in the first Century?

4. Have We one Witness of the Existence of Marks Gospell in the first Century?

5 Have We one Witness of the Existence of Lukes Gospell in the first Century?

6. Have We any Witness of the existence of St. Thomas's Gospell, that is the Gospell of the Infancy in the first Century?

7. Have We any Evidence of the Existence of the Acts of the Apostles in the first Century?

8. Have We any Evidence of the Existence of the Supplement to the Acts of the Apostles, Peter and Paul, or Paul and Tecle, in the first Century?

Here I was interrupted, by a new book, Chataubriands Travels in Greece Palestine and Egypt[2] and by a Lung Fever, with which the amiable Companion [of][3] my Life has been violently And dangerously attacked.

December    13. I have fifty more questions to put to Priestley: but must adjourn them to a future opportunity.

I have read Chateaubriand, with as much delight, as I ever read Bunyan Pilgrims Progress, Robinson Crusoes Travels or Gullivers; or Whitefields; or Wesleys[4] Life; or the Life of St. Francis, St Anthony or St Ignatius Loyaula. A Work of infinite Learning, perfectly well written, a Magazine of Information: but an enthusiastic, biggotted, Superstitious Roman Catholic throughout. If I were to indulge in jealous criticism and Conjecture, I Should Suspect, that there had been an Œccumenical Counsel of Pope Cardinals and Bishops, and that this Traveller has been employed at their expence, to make this tour, to lay a foundation for the resurrection of the Catholic Hierarchy in Europe.

Have you read La Harpes Course de Litterature, in 15. Volumes? have you read St. Pierres Studies of Nature?

I am now reading the Controversy between Voltaire and Nonotte.

Our Friend Rush has given Us for his last Legacy, an Analysis of Some of the diseases of the Mind. Johnson Said We are all more or less mad; and who is or has been more mad than Johnson?

I know of no Philosopher, or Theologian, or Moralist ancient or modern more profound; more infallible than Whitefield, if the Anecdote that I have heard be true.

He began; "Father Abraham"! with his hands and Eyes gracefully directed to the Heavens as I have more than once Seen him; "Father Abraham," "who have you there with you"? "have you Catholicks?"[5] No. "Have you Protestants." No. "Have you Churchmen." No. "Have you Dissenters."[6] No. "Have you Presbyterians"? No. "Quakers"? No. "Anabaptists"?[7] No. "Who have you then? Are[8] you alone"? No.

"My Brethren,! you have the Answer to all these questions in the Words of my Text, He[9] who feareth God and worketh Righteousness, Shall be accepted of him."

Allegiance to the Creator and Governor of the Milky Way and the Nebulæ, and Benevolence to all his Creatures, is my Religion. Si quid novisti rectius istis, Candidus imperti. —

I am as ever                                                                  JOHN ADAMS

RC (DLC); at foot of text: "President Jefferson"; endorsed by TJ as received 24 Dec. 1813 and so recorded in SJL. FC (Lb in MHi: Adams Papers).

Ἀθανάτους μεν πρωτα θεους νομω, ως διακειται Τίμα ("Honor the immortal gods first, in the order appointed by custom") is from the first line of the *Carmen aureum*, which was not composed by Hesiod (Johan C. Thom, ed., *The Pythagorean Golden Verses: With Introduction and Commentary* [1995], ix, 15, 31–3, 57–8, 94–5). Πίςις δ' ἄρα ὁμῶς καὶ ἀπίςιας ὤλεσαν ἄνδρας: "for both trust and distrust have destroyed men" (Hesiod, *Works and Days*, 372, in *Hesiod*, trans. Glenn W. Most, Loeb Classical Library [2006], 1:116–7). Hebrew stone-throwers, not archers, were said to be able to hit AN HAIRS BREADTH in the Bible, Judges 20.16.

The two quotations by Juan Luis VIVES are from *De Tradendis Disciplinis*, book 5, chap. 2 (Foster Watson, ed., *Vives: On Education* [1913], 248–9). That ostensibly from Cesare Baronio (BARRONIUS) is in a preface added to a posthumous edition of his *Annales Ecclesiastici* (Antwerp, 1670–77), vol. 1. That by Melchor (Melchior) Cano (CANUS) is from *De Locis Theologicis*, book 11, chap. 6 (Salamanca, 1563). ARNOBIUS's quotation is from *The Seven Books of Arnobius Adversus Gentes*, book 1, chap. 56 (Alexander Roberts and James Donaldson, eds., *Ante-Nicene Christian Library* [1871], 19:46–7). In 325 A.D. the ecumenical COUNCIL OF NICE (Nicaea; present-day Iznik, Turkey) condemned Arianism and established the Nicene Creed.

Οὔτε πᾶσα πιςεύοντες, Οὔτε πᾶσιν ἀπιςοῦντες: "neither trusting nor distrusting all" (Aristotle, *Rhetoric*, 2.14, in *Aristotle with an English translation: The "Art" of Rhetoric*, trans. John Henry Freese, Loeb Classical Library [1926], 254–5). The Acts of PETER AND PAUL and of PAUL AND TECLE (Thecla) are apocryphal works of the New Testament (James K. Elliott, *The Apocryphal New Testament: A Collection of Apocryphal Christian Literature in an English Translation* [1993], 364–74, 428–9). The NEW BOOK was François René, vicomte de Chateaubriand, *Travels in Greece, Palestine, Egypt, and Barbary, during the years 1806 and 1807*, trans. Frederic Shoberl (Philadelphia, 1813). LUNG FEVER: "pneumonia" (*OED*). STUDIES OF NATURE: Jacques Bernardin Henri de Saint-Pierre, *Études de la Nature*, new ed., 5 vols. (Paris, 1804). The French Jesuit Claude Adrien Nonnotte (NONOTTE) engaged in an extended polemical debate with Voltaire over the latter's writings against religion.

WE ARE ALL MORE OR LESS MAD: Samuel Johnson wrote that "Disorders of intellect . . . happen much more often than superficial observers will easily believe. Perhaps, if we speak with rigorous exactness, no human mind is in its right state" (*The Prince of Abissinia. A Tale* [London, 1759], 2:116). The ANECDOTE about George Whitefield is substantially confirmed in Joseph B. Wakeley, *Anecdotes of the Rev. George Whitefield* (1872), 134–5. HE WHO FEARETH GOD AND WORKETH RIGHTEOUSNESS, SHALL BE ACCEPTED OF HIM is from the Bible, Acts 10.35. SI QUID NOVISTI RECTIUS ISTIS, CANDIDUS IMPERTI: "If you know something better than these precepts, pass it on, my good fellow," from Horace, *Epistles*, 1.6.67 (Fairclough, *Horace: Satires, Epistles and Ars Poetica*, 290–1).

[1] Remainder of sentence interlined.
[2] Preceding three words interlined.
[3] Omitted word editorially supplied. FC: "partner of."
[4] Manuscript: "Westleys."
[5] Omitted opening quotation mark editorially supplied.
[6] Omitted opening quotation mark editorially supplied.
[7] Omitted opening quotation mark editorially supplied.
[8] Superfluous opening quotation mark in front of this word editorially omitted.
[9] Superfluous opening quotation mark in front of this word editorially omitted.

# From David Ramsay

Dear Sir,                                    Charleston Dec^r 3^d 1813

The bearer Sir Egerton Leigh is the nephew of my father in law Henry Laurens. Though nominally an Alien he is a native of South Carolina from which he was taken by his father to England when in his infancy & before the revolution. You will find him a Gentleman & well informed on the subjects on which you delight to converse. He is a citizen of the world & his Philanthropy embraces the whole human family. His fortune rank & education entitle him to notice in every place but being an unknown Alien I have taken the liberty of informing you who he is & requesting your civilities to him. With my best wishes for your health & happiness I am with great respect sincerly yours                    David Ramsay.

RC (MHi); addressed: "Thomas Jefferson late President of the United States"; endorsed by TJ as received 5 Jan. 1814 and so recorded in SJL. Enclosed in Sir Egerton Leigh to TJ, 19 Dec. 1813.

David Ramsay (1749–1815), physician, public official, and historian, was born in Lancaster County, Pennsylvania. He received an A.B. degree from the College of New Jersey (later Princeton University) in 1765 and an M.B. degree from the College of Philadelphia (later the University of Pennsylvania) in 1773. After moving by 1774 to Charleston, South Carolina, Ramsay established a flourishing medical practice and entered politics. He served in the South Carolina House of Representatives, 1776–80 and 1782–90, sat in the Confederation Congress, 1782–83 and 1785–86, and was president of the South Carolina Senate, 1791–97. In 1787 he married Martha Laurens, the daughter of Continental Congress president Henry Laurens. In politics Ramsay proved to be a moderate Federalist. He backed the new United States Constitution at the 1788 state ratification convention and supported a stronger central government and John Adams's presidential aspirations, but he opposed the Jay Treaty. Ramsay achieved his greatest fame through his widely disseminated historical writings, which included a *History of the Revolution of South-Carolina*, 2 vols. (Trenton, N.J., 1785; Sowerby, no. 488; Poor, *Jefferson's Library*, 4 [no. 135]), *The History of the American Revolution*, 2 vols. (Philadelphia, 1789; Sowerby, no. 490), *The Life of George Washington* (New York, 1807; Sowerby, no. 511), *History of the United States*, 3 vols. (Philadelphia, 1816–17), and *Universal History Americanised*, 9 vols. (Philadelphia, 1819). At Ramsay's request, TJ arranged during his diplomatic service in France for the translation and publication of a French edition (Sowerby, no. 489) of the *History of the Revolution of South-Carolina*. Ramsay was fatally shot by a deranged former patient (*ANB*; *DAB*; *Princetonians, 1748–68*, pp. 517–21; N. Louise Bailey and others, eds., *Biographical Directory of the South Carolina Senate, 1776–1985* [1986], 2:1330–4; Robert L. Brunhouse, ed., "David Ramsay, 1749–1815: Selections From His Writings," APS, *Transactions*, n.s., 55, pt. 4 [1965]; Arthur H. Shaffer, *To Be an American: David Ramsay and the Making of the American Consciousness* [1991]; *PTJ*, 8:210–1; Sowerby, no. 3474; Charleston *City Gazette and Commercial Daily Advertiser*, 9 May 1815).

# From George Hay

SIR,                                         Richmond. Dec.ʳ. 6. 1813

You must have the goodness to excuse my failure, to answer your late letter on the Subject of Michie's motion in the general Court. I have been entirely occupied by various concerns, professional, <u>political</u>, & domestic.—I have now only to inform you that the intended motion was not made, nor did any person appear as far as I could learn, with a view to make it.—

I am with great respect yʳ mo: ob. St.                     GEO HAY—

RC (DLC); endorsed by TJ as received 17 Dec. 1813 and so recorded in SJL.

# To Alexander von Humboldt

MY DEAR FRIEND AND BARON                          Dec. 6. 13.

I have to acknolege your two letters of Dec. 20. & 26. 1811. by mr Correa, and am first to thank you for making me acquainted with that most excellent character. he was so kind as to visit me at Monticello, and I found him one of the most learned and amiable of men. it was a subject of deep regret to separate from so much worth in the moment of it's becoming known to us.          the livraison of your Astronomical observations, and the 6th and 7th on the subject of New Spain, with the corresponding Atlasses are duly recieved, as had been the preceding Cahiers. for these treasures of a learning so interesting to us, accept my sincere thanks. I think it most fortunate that your travels in those countries were so timed as to make them known to the world in the moment they were about to become actors on it's stage. that they will throw off their European dependance I have no doubt; but in what kind of government their revolution will end is not so certain. history, I believe furnishes no example of a priest-ridden people maintaining a free civil government. this marks the lowest grade of ignorance, of which their civil as well as religious leaders will always avail themselves for their own purposes. the vicinity of New Spain to the US. and their consequent intercourse may furnish schools for the higher, and example for the lower classes of their citizens. and Mexico, where we learn from you that men of science are not wanting, may revolutionise itself under better auspices than the Southern provinces. these last, I fear, must end in military despotisms. the different casts of their inhabitants, their mutual hatreds and jealousies, their profound ignorance & bigotry, will be plaid off by cunning leaders, and each be made the instrument of enslaving the others. but of all this you can best judge, for in truth we have little knolege of them, to be depended on, but through you.    but in whatever governments they end, they will be <u>American</u> governments, no longer to be involved in the never-ceasing broils of Europe. the European nations constitute a separate division of the globe; their localities make them part of a distinct system; they have a set of interests of their own in which it is our business never to engage ourselves. America has a hemisphere to itself: it must have it's separate system of interests, which must not be subordinated to those of Europe. the insulated state in which nature has placed the American[1] continent should so far avail it that no spark of war kindled in the other quarters of the globe should be wafted across the wide oceans which separate us from them. and it will be so. in 50. years more the US. alone will contain 50. millions of inhabitants; and 50. years are soon gone over. the peace of 1763. is within that period. I was then 20. years old, and of course remember well all the transactions of the war preceding it. and you will live to see the epoch now equally ahead of us, and the numbers which will then be spread over the other parts of the American hemisphere, catching long before that the principles of our portion of it, and concurring with us in the maintenance of the same system.—you see how readily we run into ages beyond the grave, and even those of us to whom that grave is already opening it's quiet bosom. I am anticipating events of which you will be the bearer to me in the Elysian fields 50. years hence.    You know, my friend, the benevolent plan we were pursuing here for the happiness of the Aboriginal inhabitants in our vicinities. we spared nothing to keep them at peace with one another, to teach them agriculture and the rudiments of the most necessary arts, and to encourage industry by establishing among them separate property. in this way they would have been enabled to[2] subsist and multiply on a moderate scale of landed possession; they would have mixed their blood with ours and been amalgamated and identified with us within no distant period of time. on the commencement of our present war, we pressed on them the observance of peace and neutrality. but the interested and unprincipled policy of England has defeated all our labors for the salvation of these unfortunate people. they have seduced the greater part of the tribes, within our neighborhood, to take up the hatchet against us, and the cruel massacres they have committed on the women and children of our frontiers taken by surprise, will oblige us now to pursue them to extermination, or drive them to new seats beyond our reach. already we have driven their patrons & seducers into

Montreal, and the opening season will force them[3] to their last refuge, the walls of Quebec, we have cut off all possibility of intercourse and of mutual aid, and may pursue at our leisure whatever plan we find necessary to secure ourselves against the future effects of their savage and ruthless warfare. the confirmed brutalisation, if not the extermination of this race in our America is therefore to form an additional chapter in the English history of the same colored man in Asia, and of the brethren of their own colour in Ireland and wherever else Anglo-mercantile cupidity can find a two-penny interest in deluging the earth with human blood.—but let us turn from the loathsome contemplation of the degrading effects of commercial avarice.

That their Arrowsmith should have stolen your map of Mexico, was in the pyratical spirit of his country. but I should be sincerely sorry if our Pike has made an ungenerous use of your candid communications here; and the more so as he died in the arms of victory gained over the enemies of his country. whatever he did was on a principle of enlarging knolege, and not for filthy shillings and pence of which he made none from that book. if what he has borrowed has any effect it will be to excite an appeal in his readers from his defective information to the copious volumes of it with which you have enriched the world. I am sorry he omitted even[4] to acknolege the source of his information. it has been an oversight, and not at all in the spirit of his generous nature. let me sollicit your forgiveness then of a deceased hero, of an honest and zealous patriot, who lived and died for his country.

You will find it inconcievable that Lewis's journey to the Pacific should not yet have appeared; nor is it in my power to tell you the reason. the measures taken by his surviving companion Clarke, for the publication, have not answered our wishes in point of dispatch. I think however, from what I have heard, that the mere journal will be out within a few weeks in 2. vols 8$^{vo}$. these I will take care to send you with the tobacco seed you desired, if it be possible for them to escape the thousand ships of our enemies spread over the ocean. the botanical & zoological discoveries of Lewis will probably experience greater delay, and become known to the world thro' other channels before that volume will be ready. the Atlas, I believe, waits on the leisure of the engraver.

Altho' I do not know whether you are now at Paris, or ranging the regions of Asia to acquire more knolege for the use of man, I cannot deny myself the gratification of an endeavor to recall myself to your recollection of assuring you of my constant attachment, and of renewing to you the just tribute of my affectionate esteem & high respect and consideration.                    TH: JEFFERSON

RC (NNPM: Heineman Collection). PoC (DLC); at foot of first page: "Baron de Humboldt." Enclosed in TJ to David Bailie Warden, 29 Dec. 1813, and TJ to John Graham, 6 Jan. 1814.

LIVRAISON: a part of a work published in installments (*OED*). The PEACE OF 1763 refers to the Treaty of Paris of that year, which ended the Seven Years' War.

Zebulon Montgomery PIKE was killed on 27 Apr. 1813 while leading a successful American assault on York (now Toronto), Canada (*ANB*; *New-York Weekly Museum*, 15 May 1813).

[1] Manuscript: "Amecan."
[2] TJ here canceled "main."
[3] Preceding nine words interlined.
[4] Word interlined.

# From Edward Ross

RESPECTED SIR.                    Mount Ida the 6th Decr. 1813.

In hopes that this letter may find you in good health, I take the liberty of addressing you a few lines upon a subject, which is at present of some importance to me and on which I wish, you may be pleased to favor me with your kind advice.—I have been very busy, ever since my return from your place of Residence, with the construction of a Saw Mill and it is now my intention to erect several other Mills and Machineries, such as a fulling Mill, flour & grist Mill &c—in especial however a <u>Slitting Mill</u> to manufacture Nails and other articles of a like nature which will cost a large Sum of Money and I therefore should be very happy, if you would be pleased to communicate to me your ideas on the subject as soon as convenient to you and whether you expect that such kind of machinery will answer well and will prove usefull to the Country, as well as profitable for the owner. Your long earned Experience will only and entirely guide me in my future operations, respecting this business, I therefore hope you will favor me with your best advice and should you know of any other Sort of Mill or Machinery, which by establishing might bring some Profit, I should be very happy, if you would let me know.

I pray you will please remember me kindly to M[rs] Randolph and all the rest of your amiable family and thanking you once more for the very friendly and hospitable Reception you have been good enough to give me, I remain with Sentiments of the highest Respect & Regard

Respected Sir Your most ob[d] hbl Servant

EDWARD ROSS.
<u>New Canton</u>
<u>Buckingham County</u>

RC (MHi); at foot of text: "Thomas Jefferson Esquire &c &c &c Monticello"; endorsed by TJ as received 17 Dec. 1813 and so recorded in SJL.

# From Joseph C. Cabell

DEAR SIR,                                            Richmond. Dec<sup>r</sup> 8<sup>th</sup> 1813.

I expected when I wrote you from Williamsburg, that my Servant would have come up with me from that place on the 5<sup>th</sup> inst; but one of my horses being unavoidably detained, I was compelled to leave him behind; & was consequently disappointed, for the moment, in sending him on with your books. I was only waiting for his arrival, when to-day, I fell in with Gen<sup>l</sup> Moore, who told me he should set out in the Charlottesville stage, in the morning, for the place of his residence, & politely consented to take charge of the packet, & to deliver it to Doct: Carr on his way thro' that place. I hope it will reach you in a few days. I return you my grateful acknowledgements for the use of the book for so great a length of time.

We have just formed the two houses, & are proceeding to business. I think Governor Barber will be reelected without opposition: notwithstanding the great discontents which have prevailed in many parts of the state.

I shall seek the earliest oppertunity of conferring with Doct Everett & m<sup>r</sup> Garth relative to the petition of the Rivanna River company. As yet we are scarcely placed in our respective lodgings. I expect to see them in the morning.

I am, d<sup>r</sup> Sir, with high esteem & respect
y<sup>r</sup> mo: ob<sup>t</sup>                                    JOSEPH C. CABELL.

RC (ViU: TJP-PC); endorsed by TJ. Recorded in SJL as received 13 Dec. 1813.

The TWO HOUSES of the Virginia General Assembly came to order on 6 Dec. 1813, with Charles Everette and Jesse Winston GARTH representing Albemarle County in the House of Delegates (Leonard, *General Assembly*, 273).

# To Madame de Tessé

Dec. 8. 13.

While at war, my dear madam and friend, with the Leviathan of the ocean, there is little hope of a letter's escaping his thousand ships; yet I cannot permit myself longer to withold the acknolegement of your letter of June 28. of the last year, with which came the Memoirs of the Margrave of Bareuth. I am much indebted to you for this singular morsel of history which has given us a curtain view of kings, queens & princes disrobed of their formalities. it is a peep into the stable of the Egyptian god Apis. it would not be easy to find grosser manners, coarser vices, or more meanness in the poorest huts of our peasantry. the princess shews herself the legitimate sister of Frederic, cynical, selfish, and without a heart.　　　notwithstanding your wars with England, I presume you get the publications of that country. the Memoirs of mrs Clarke and of her <u>Darling</u> prince, and the Book, emphatically so called, because it is the Biblia Sacra Deorum et Dearum sub-caelestium, the Prince regent, his Princess and the minor deities of his sphere,[1] form a worthy sequel to the memoirs of Bareuth; instead of the vulgarity and penury of the court of Berlin giving us the vulgarity & profusion of that of London, and the gross stupidity and profligacy of the latter, in lieu of the genius and misanthropism of the former. the whole might be published as a Supplement to M. de Buffon, under the title of the 'Natural history of kings & Princes,' or as a separate work & called 'Medecine for Monarchists.' the 'Intercepted letters' a later English publication of great wit and humor, has put them to their proper use by holding them up as butts for the ridicule and contempt of mankind. yet by such worthless beings is a great nation to be governed, & even made to deify their old king because he is only a fool and a maniac, and to forgive and forget his having lost to them a great & flourishing empire, added 900. Millions sterling to their debt, for which the fee simple of the whole island would not sell, if offered farm by farm at public auction, and increased their annual taxes from 8. to 70 millions sterling, more than the whole rent-roll of the island. what must be the dreary prospect from the son when such a father is deplored as a national loss. but let us drop these odious beings and pass to those of an higher order the plants of the field. I am afraid I have given you a great deal more trouble than I intended by my enquiries for the Maronnier or Castanea Sativa, of which I wished to possess my own country, without knowing how rare it's culture was even in yours. the two plants which your researches have placed in your own garden, it will be all but impossible to remove hither. the war renders their safe passage across the Atlantic extremely precarious, and, if landed any where but in the Chesapeak, the risk of the additional voyage along the coast to Virginia is still greater. under these circumstances it is better they should retain their present station, and compensate to you the trouble they have cost you.　　　I learn with great pleasure the success of[2] your new gardens at Aulnay. no occupation can be more delightful or useful. they will have the merit of inducing you to forget those of Chaville. with the botanical riches which you mention to have been derived to England from New Holland, we are as yet unacquainted. Lewis's journey across our continent to the Pacific has added a number of new plants to our former stock, some of them are curious, some ornamental, some useful, and some may by culture be made acceptable on our tables. I have growing, which I destine for you, a very handsome little shrub, of the size of a currant bush. it's beauty consists in a great produce of berries, of the size of currants, and literally as white as snow, which remain on the bush thro' the winter after it's leaves have fallen, and make it an object as singular as it is beautiful. we call it the Snow-berry bush, no botanical name being yet given to it, but I do not know why we might not call it Chionicoccos, or Kallicoccos. all Lewis's plants are growing in the garden of mr McMahon a gardener[3] of Philadelphia to whom I consigned them, and from whom I shall have great pleasure, when peace is restored, in ordering for you any of these, or of our other indigenous plants. the port of Philadelphia has great intercourse with Bordeaux and Nantes, and some little perhaps with Havre. I was mortified not long since by recieving a letter from a merchant in Bordeaux, apologising for having suffered a box of plants addressed by me to you, to get accidentally covered in his warehouse by other objects, and to remain three years undiscovered when every thing in it was found to be rotten. I have learnt occasionally that others rotted in the warehouses of the English pyrates. we are now settling that account with them. we have taken their Upper Canada, and shall add the Lower to it when the season will admit; and hope to remove them fully and finally from our continent. and what they will feel more, for they value their colonies only for the bales of cloth they take from them, we have established manufactures, not only sufficient to supercede our demand from them, but to rivalise them in foreign markets. but for the course of our war I will refer you to M. de la Fayette to whom I state it more particularly. our friend mr Short is well. he makes Philadelphia his winter quarters and New york, or the country, those of the summer. in his fortune he is perfectly independant and at ease, and does not trouble himself with the party politics of our country. will you permit me to place here for M. de Tessé the testimony of my high[4] esteem and respect, and accept for yourself an assurance of the warm recollections I retain of your many civilities & courtesies to me, and the homage of my constant and affectionate attachment and respect.

TH: JEFFERSON

RC (NNPM). PoC (DLC); at foot of first page: "M^de de Tessé." Enclosed in TJ to David Bailie Warden, 29 Dec. 1813, and TJ to John Graham, 6 Jan. 1814.

The LEVIATHAN OF THE OCEAN was Great Britain. When a new bull was selected as the manifestation of the EGYPTIAN GOD APIS, during the first forty days when only women were permitted to see him, they lifted their garments and exposed themselves to him (Diodorus Siculus, *Library of History*, 1.85, in *Diodorus of Sicily*, trans. Charles H. Oldfather and others, Loeb Classical Library [1933–67; repr. 1989], 1:290–1; for editions of this author owned by TJ, see Sowerby, nos. 37–8). The memoirs of Mary Anne CLARKE, the mistress of HER DARLING PRINCE, Frederick, duke of York, were contained in *Evidence and Proceedings upon the Charges preferred against the Duke of York, in 1809* (London, 1809; Sowerby, no. 409). For THE BOOK, see TJ to Samuel Pleasants, 11 Aug. 1813, and note. BIBLIA SACRA DEORUM ET DEARUM SUB-CAELESTIUM: "holy

book of the gods and goddesses under Heaven." PRINCE REGENT George was married to Caroline Amelia Elizabeth, PRINCESS of Wales, while the OLD KING was his father, George III. SJL does not record receipt in 1813 of a single LETTER FROM A MERCHANT IN BORDEAUX, and none has been found.

[1] Word interlined in place of "court and government."
[2] TJ here canceled "our."
[3] Preceding two words interlined.
[4] Word interlined.

# From Thomas Leiper

MY DEAR SIR                                    Philad^a Dec^r 9^th 1813—

Enclosed in my opinion is a very extraordinary letter which appeared in Poulson's Paper of the 6^th—The History of the letter from the information I have received The contents was wrote by you to Doctor Logan and by him handed to Poulson's Press—I trust it is a forgery—I have but one opinion and I am not singular in my opinion (for Twenty years) that every Battle obtained by the French was a Battle in favor of the Americans and I will add in favor of the Revelation of God which appears clear to me from the 7 Chapter[1] of Daniel and the 17 Chapter[2] of the Revelation of Saint John—How could this fisherman I would ask get his information that their would be Ten Kings or Kingdoms[3] formed out of the Western Empire which absolutly came to pass and that they should remain a certain period and should be cut off which at this day[4] comming to pass at the very time too the authors on the subject had pointed out— From your Answer to me on your receipt of Towers illustration of Prophecy it appeared to me the Book was in no great estimation with you—I sent the Book to M^r Madison he did not Vouchsafe to acknowledge the receipt[5] but at the same time I sent the Book to Judge Duvall and received for answer he had read the Book with great pleasure and satisfaction and would read it again and again Do read the Book for certain I am after you have read it you would not be at a Loss to know how the thing would wind up—Since I have read Towers I have seen Thomas Scott's Bible he was Rector of Aston Bucks he mentions he was Twenty years in finishing his notes—on[6] the 7 Chapter of Daniel he mentions[7] the Ten Kingdoms by name that were to be formed and to be destroyed and should Scott's Bible not be at hand give me leave to mention them 1st Senate of Rome 2[d] The Greeks of Ravina 3[d] The Lombards in Lombardy. 4th The Huns[8] in Hungary. 5th The Alemanes in Germany[9] 6th The Franks in France 7th The Burgundians in Burgundy[10] 8th The Goths in spain 9th The Britons 10th Saxon in Britain—Now Sir abstracted from the Above what is Bonaparte contending for the freedom of the Seas we have certainly the same thing in View by our War What has Great Britain in view by Bribing all the Crown'd Heads in Europe the Trade of the whole World and if she had it in her power I verily believe she would not suffer a Cock Boat of any other nation to swim the Ocean[11]— Bonaparte has drawn his Sword and has Declared it shall not return into the Scabbard untill the Ocean shall be a public high way for all nations and as I believe no permanent peace will take place 'till this thing is effected I hope and Trust he will keep his word as Providence has[12] put the means in his power—And as there are many of these Kingdoms are already down we have every reason to infere from the same Document the rest will follow and as Britain is one of them the sooner she goes the better it will be for the whole World With respect and esteem I am Your most obedient S[t]

THOMAS LEIPER

RC (DLC); addressed: "Thomas Jefferson Late President of the United States Monticello Virginia"; endorsed by TJ. Recorded in SJL as received 24 Dec. 1813. FC (Lb in Leiper Papers, Friends of Thomas Leiper House, on deposit PPL). Enclosure: extract from TJ to George Logan, 3 Oct. 1813, printed in Philadelphia *Poulson's American Daily Advertiser*, 6 Dec. 1813.

Thomas Leiper (1745–1825), merchant, was a native of Scotland who immigrated to Maryland in 1763. He relocated two years later to Philadelphia, where he became a leading tobacco merchant and the owner of quarries and snuff mills. During the Revolutionary War, Leiper supported the American cause both financially and through service as a sergeant in an elite volunteer unit, the First Troop Philadelphia City Cavalry. TJ rented a house in Philadelphia from him during his tenure as secretary of state, 1790–93, and sold him tobacco on a number of occasions thereafter. Leiper strongly opposed the imposition of excise taxes on snuff and other tobacco products

in petitions to Congress and to President George Washington in 1794. To transport stone from his quarries, he constructed a short, horse-drawn railroad in 1809–10 that is now thought to have been Pennsylvania's first. In addition, Leiper served regularly as president of the Philadelphia Common Council and as a director of the Bank of Pennsylvania, was a director of the Bank of the United States toward the end of his life, and helped found the Franklin Institute (*DAB*; *MB*; *PTJ*, esp. 17:267–9, 24:714, 25:529, 32:209–10; Gibson & Jefferson to TJ, [before 12 Apr. 1812]; James T. Callender, *A Short History of the Nature and Consequences of Excise Laws* [Philadelphia, 1795], 56–74, 78–9, 86–7; *Journal of the First Session of the Eleventh House of Representatives of the Commonwealth of Pennsylvania* [Lancaster, 1800], 246; Philadelphia *Gazette of the United States*, 15 Oct. 1802; *Philadelphia Repository and Weekly Register*, 22 Oct. 1803; *Albany Advertiser*, 18 Jan. 1817; Philadelphia *Franklin Gazette*, 20 Jan. 1820; Philadelphia *Aurora & Franklin Gazette*, 8 July 1825).

Leiper alluded to the WESTERN Roman Empire. He thought that TJ did not hold Joseph Lomas Towers's *Illustrations of Prophecy*, 2 vols. (London, 1796; repr. Philadelphia, 1808; Sowerby, no. 1548) in GREAT ESTIMATION because TJ contrasted it with "some other late writer (the name I forget) who has undertaken to prove contrary events from the same sources; and particularly that England is not to be put down" (TJ to Leiper, 21 Jan. 1809 [DLC]). ASTON BUCKS: Aston Sandford, Buckinghamshire, England.

[1] RC: "Chaper." FC: "chapter."
[2] RC: "Chaper." FC: "chapter."
[3] RC: "Kingdom." FC: "Kingdoms."
[4] FC: "Time."
[5] RC: "rceipt." FC: "receipt."
[6] RC: "finishing his notes—His notes on." FC: "finishing his notes—On."
[7] RC: "mention." FC: "mentions."
[8] RC: "Hunds." FC: "huns."
[9] RC: "Garmany." FC: "Germany."
[10] RC: "Burguny." FC: "Burgundy."
[11] FC ends here.
[12] RC: "his."

# From George Logan

DEAR SIR                                    Stenton Decb[r] 9th: 1813

Accept my thanks for your late friendly and interesting Letter. Your approbation of my visit to France in 1798 is highly satisfactory. Influenced by similar motives, I visited England in 1810. To a person so perfectly acquainted with the spirit of the constitution of the United States, as you are; it is not necessary for me to say any thing in justification of the acts of any private citizen, to promote the prosperity and happiness of his country.

During a residence of five months in England[1] I travelled one thousand miles thro' that country. I visited the principal commercial, and manufacturing cities; and became acquainted with the agricultural interest. I had a fair opportunity of ascertaining the sentiments of men in every situation of life, respecting the unhappy contest between the united States and Great Britain. I found a general anxiety to prevail; that harmony and peace should be restored, equally honorable and[2] beneficial to both countries.

An erronious opinion is entertained by some few men in the United States; of the decline and fall of the British empire. That country at no period of its history, was more free, powerful and respectable, than at this moment. The successful stand she has made, against the tyrant of Europe has occasioned the continental Powers to regard her with veneration. Knowing that the liberty of their country depends on the correct habits and information of the people. The princes, nobility, and patriotic citizens of every religious and political opinion; are uniting in distinct societies, for the purpose of educating, and[3] giving moral instruction to the destitute part of the community—This is the most honorable and beneficial measure, ever adopted by the citizens of that nation; and will secure its liberty and prosperity.

The sordid views of British merchants, under the falacious name of british interests, have less influence over the cabinet of S<sup>t</sup> James than formerly. The landed[4] agricultural interest is becoming more powerful—It is a great, but quiescent interest; on whose collective knowledge and integrity, the freedom and fate of that country depends. Such is the present favorable aspect of the British nation—The reverse is.

First. The immense issue and circulation of bank notes, beyond their intrinsic value.

Second. The extent of her manufacturing system, has in an alarming degree increased mendicity in her manufacturing towns; and has brutalized the manufacturing population; particularly since the introduction of machinery. Children from the tenderest infancy; as soon as their fingers are capable of twisting a thread, or feeding a carding machine; are by the misery or cupidity of their parents, immured in great manufacturing establishments; without the benefit of education, or moral instruction.[5] This is not the only evil: The working manufacturers, are united into jacobinical clubs against their employers; and in opposition to the laws of the land; frequently occasioning such tumults, as to render a military force necessary to suppress. An ignorant debauched population, is the most unstable support upon which a government can depend: The strength of a nation is in the moral character of its people. When that principle is debilitated; the country is fast approaching to ruin.

Third. The extent of her colonial establishments is contemplated with anxiety, by the best patriots in Great Britain; not only on account of the immense taxes, necessary to protect and support them; but as a great political evil; Those distant colonies affording lucrative offices, to be bestowed on the creatures of the minister; for the purpose of creating a parliamentary influence; repugnant to the spirit of the British constitution.

Notwithstanding these evils—The miserable contracted, and unjust policy towards Ireland; and the deprivations of the people of many of the comforts of life; owing to enormous taxes, to support an annual expenditure of more than one hundred millions sterling. Yet the energies of the Nation, appear to increase in proportion to the difficulties which she has to encounter; and her resources are still unquestionably great.

The orders in council of the British cabinet, as a measure of retaliation on France, for her Berlin and Milan decrees, is the strongest evidence of the want of foresight and political wisdom in her councils. Had the British government, instead of uniting with the tyrant of Europe, to annihilate the commerce of neutral nations; indignantly protested against the decrees of France, as a violation of the laws of nations: and declared herself, the friend and protector of neutral rights; she would by such an act of justice, and magnanimity; have united every neutral to her interest. In my conversations with members of the British government, I urged this measure, as founded on principles of the soundest policy. In my Letter to M$^r$ Perceval, I observe "The bickerings and semi state of warfare which has existed for several years between our nations; have been viewed with deep affliction, by the best men in both countries—Since my arrival in England; I have had an opportunity of conversing with many of your most eminent characters; as well as with respectable men of every situation in life. I have not met with one Person, who does not wish a reconciliation with the United States. My public and private situation in my own country, afforded me an opportunity of becoming fully acquainted with the sentiments of my fellow citizens—I know they anxiously desire to preserve peace with Great Britain. And as a manifestation of their sincerity, they have renewed their commerce with this country; and have removed every obstacle to an amicable negotiation Let Great Britain with the same laudable intent, remove her orders in council—Let her declare herself the advocate of neutral rights such as she claimed for herself; and conceded to others; before she adopted the execrable commercial warfare of the tyrant of Europe. A system of warfare, which will be depicted by the faithful pen of the historian, in the blackest colours—a warfare by decree and orders in council, dastardly attacking the humble cottage, the comforts, the subsistence of unoffending women and children; instead of meeting in an open and honorable conflict, the armed battalions of your enemy in the field—Let her return to that safe and honorable course of public law, which she has abandoned, and treat with the United States on terms of reciprocity; equally honorable and beneficial to both countries. A treaty of peace between the two nations, founded on such principles, will conciliate the citizens of the United States; and they will consider Great Britain as their real friend.

My dear sir—for heavens sake pause—and from the elevated and honorable situation on which your sovereign has placed you; contemplate agonizing nations, at the feet of a military despot: and say if it is not necessary, that Great Britain and the United States, at this momentous crisis of the world, should lay aside unfounded jealousies, and mutual bickerings; not only to protect their own existence, as independent nations, but to preserve the civil and political liberties of mankind.

[ 40 ]

I may appeal to your own superior information, and understanding; if you are acquainted with any truth, more thoroughly established than, that there exists in the affairs of nations, an indissoluble union, between the generous maxims of an honest and magnanimous policy; and the solid rewards of public prosperity and happiness." This nefarious, and profligate system[6] as connected with the license trade, must however be attributed to the minister; not to the nation. On the first enactment of the orders in council, the measure was opposed by many of the best informed men in and out of parliament. And when I was in London in 1810 I did not meet with one man, even amongst the friends of the minister, who could justify the act on principles of justice, or sound policy. In fact, such was the clamour of the nation against the minister on account of the orders in council, that himself contemplated having them revoked before the meeting of parliament—And that such was actually his intention, is confirmed by the last Letter of M$^r$ Foster to M$^r$ Monroe, previous to our unfortunate declaration of war: in which he observes "It was France, and afterwards America, that connected the question relative to the right of blockade, with that arising out of the orders in council. You well know, that if these two questions had not been united together, the orders in council would have been in 1810 revoked." Unfortunately for the peace of our country, not content with the revokation of the orders in council, as dictated by the law of Congress of May 1810,—M$^r$ Pinkney demands a repeal in his Letter to Lord Wellesley of Sep$^r$ 21: 1810 not only of the blockade from Elbe to Brest, but of those of Zealand, and of the Isles of Mauritious & Bourbon—And in his Letter of Jan$^y$ 14th 1811 to the same minister, he speaks also of other Blockades (including that of Zealand) which the United States expected to see recalled; besides the blockade of May.[7] In this Letter he suggests an idea, directly calculated, and perhaps designed to alarm the British ministry; as to the ulterior views of our government, on the subject of blockade in general; and to discourage them from a compliance with our demands. Concerning the blockade of May; he observes, "It is by no means clear, that it may not be fairly contended, that a maritime blockade is incomplete, with regard to States at peace; unless the place which it would affect, is invested by land, as well as by sea."

Apprehensive that some shuffling conduct of this kind, would be the result of an official communication with M$^r$ Pinkney, I urged in my Letter to Sir John Sinclair; and to other gentlemen in London with whom I conversed; that the king and council, should voluntarily, and immediately, remove or suspend the orders in council: not only as an act of justice to the United States—but as a measure of sound policy, with regard to the British nation; as tending to silence the jealous, and strengthen the well disposed real american citizens in the United States.

When I contemplate the unfounded jealousies, bickerings, and mutual acts of irritation; which for some years have taken place between the United States and Great Britain and which has finally terminated in a war equally injurious to both nations I consider both in the wrong—A genuine history of the errors and follies of the American and British cabinets towards each other; would form an important and instructive work. Governments would discover, that cupidity, cunning, and vindictive retaliation, have always been attended with the most pernicious effects. Let these statesmen who have conceived such notions of governing, go to the school of common sense; and abandoning the odious maxims of machiavelian politics; take as their guide Him, who preached the doctrine of peace and good will towards man. To be sensible of past misconduct, is the first step towards amendment; but this will be looked for in vain from men despising the admonitions of experience; and who appear ignorant that the strongest evidence of a magnanimous mind, is the candid acknowledgment of error.

The present is an awful period. The judgments of the Almighty are abroad on the earth, to recall its thoughtless inhabitants, to a sense of their duty. Whoever has marked the progress and seriously reflected on the consequences of the events which have convulsed every part of Europe must be blinded by more than common scepticism, to doubt this truth. The miseries under which the European world is groaning, have been but partially extended to the United States—Let us hope therefore that we shall be wise before it is too late; and that our councils may be guided by prudence, and their decrees founded in justice.

Let the present calamities of[8] the United States and the miserable prospect before us, induce the President to use his best efforts to restore peace to our country. Should he continue the unnecessary war in which we are engaged even to the conquest of Canada, from the British and Florida from Spain: at the expence of millions of money, and the loss of the lives of thousands of our fellow citizens—will such evils be balanced by the acquisition of new territories? the possession of which, will remain as baneful monuments of our ambition, and injustice, and will cherish and keep alive, those seeds of envy hatred and distrust, which sooner or later, will produce the same miseries with which the United States are now overwhelmed—

It may be generally observed, that the larger the extent of republics, the more they are subject to revolutions and misfortunes. Already the citizens of the United States, inhabiting the southern and northern portions of the republic regard each other with jealousy, and suspicion, What then of concord can be expected in our councils, from the hetorogenious population of Canada and Florida? On this account I am not afraid to say; it is almost equally unhappy for its government to succeed or miscarry in its enterprizes of conquest—The tranquillity of our republican government, depends upon preserving it within its present limits—We enjoy every advantage of extent of territory, climate and soil; to render us completely happy The true interest of the United States is to render her own interior condition such as may make her not only independent but respected by other nations. This is only difficult to Statesmen, who can conceive no other methods to effect it, than war and violence— methods that ought never to be pursued without the most absolute necessity.

In your friendly Letter, you observe "I repeat therefore that if you can suggest what may lead to[9] peace, I will willingly communicate it to the proper functionaries" Let the government of the United States adopt a candid just and magnanimous conduct, to allay[10] the storm, which its own imprudence in hastily declaring war has occasioned. Let the President immediately propose an armistice, as a prelude to negotiation. Let him nominate three citizens of honorable minds; unbiassed by personal or party feelings, as commissioners to restore peace and harmony between the two countries.[11] I am perfectly satisfied, from personal communications with many of the most respectable and best informed men in England, that if such a measure is adopted, peace, will be obtained, equally honorable and beneficial to both nations. The rashness of the United States,[12] has silenced our friends in Great Britain; but has not destroyed them[13]—they will again appear, to support our just claims, consistent with the honor and vital interest of that nation.

Whatever may be the corruption of the British parliament;—or the influence of the crown. The weight of public opinion is friendly to the United States; and that opinion when steadily firmly and temperately asserted, ultimately prevails over the projects of the most obstinate and conceited ministry.

I wish the President to act like an able statesman, whose views are not confined[14] within the narrow circle of those short sighted politicians, by whom he is surrounded—Let him employ his influence and power, to restore the blessings of peace to our distracted country—No other enterprize can be truely to him either honorable or successful.

Some of my observations may appear to you severe—but those are the best friends to their country, who have firmness of mind to point out errors; when there is a possibility of their being removed.

My Wife unites with me in best respects to yourself and family.[15]

Accept assurances of my friendship                    GEO LOGAN

RC (DLC); at foot of text: "Thomas Jefferson Esq"; endorsed by TJ as received 24 Dec. 1813 and so recorded in SJL. FC (PHi: Logan Papers); in Logan's hand; endorsed by Logan.

The TYRANT OF EUROPE was Napoleon, referred to later in the letter as a military despot. For Logan's letter of 3 Aug. 1810 to British prime minister Spencer PERCEVAL, see Deborah Norris Logan, *Memoir of Dr. George Logan of Stenton*, ed. Frances A. Logan [1899], 175–7. For the LAST LETTER written by British minister plenipotentiary Augustus John Foster to Secretary of State James Monroe prior to the American declaration of war, dated Washington, 14 June 1812, see *ASP, Foreign Relations*, 3:470. The LAW OF CONGRESS of 1 May 1810 was "An Act concerning the commercial intercourse between the United States and Great Britain and France, and their dependencies, and for other purposes" (*U.S. Statutes at Large*, 2:605–6). William Pinkney's letters to Lord Wellesley of 21 Sept. 1810 and 14 Jan. 1811 concerning the various British BLOCKADES are print-

ed in *ASP, Foreign Relations*, 3:368, 409–11. Logan's letter of 14 May 1810 to SIR JOHN SINCLAIR is printed in Logan, *Memoir of Dr. George Logan*, 178. Jesus WAS HIM, WHO PREACHED THE DOCTRINE OF PEACE AND GOOD WILL TOWARDS MAN.

[1] Preceding two words interlined.
[2] Preceding two words canceled in FC.
[3] FC here adds "by a general distribution of the Holy Scriptures."
[4] RC: "landid." FC: "landed."
[5] FC here adds "However monstrous this is."
[6] FC here adds "of the orders in council."
[7] Preceding five words underscored in FC.
[8] RC: "of of." FC: "of."
[9] FC here adds "a just."
[10] RC: "alay." FC: "allay."
[11] FC: "Governments."
[12] FC here adds "in declaring war."
[13] Dash supplied from FC.
[14] RC: "conconfined." FC: "confined."
[15] Sentence not in FC.

# Account with Reuben Perry

Reuben Perry in acc[t] with Th: Jefferson

|  | £ s d |  | D |
|---|---|---|---|
| Account for work on the house at Pop. For. | 63– 4–7 | = | 210.76 |
| d[o] for various jobs. | 11–11–0 |  | 38.50 |
| d[o] for barn at Monticello. |  |  | 329.68 |
|  | £ s d |  |  |
| error in Griffin's acc[t] of 1807. formerly settled, now corr[d] |  | 11–18–4 | 39.72 |
|  |  |  | 618.66 |

1813. By finding hands from Oct. 26. 12. to wit

    Jesse Perry 12. days (13/6 p[r] week) Hal & Mat 16. days

      (@ 10/ p[r] week)        £3–9–9 =     11.62

    May 8.   By acc[t] smith's work from

        J. A. Goodman 59/11         9.98

      By 13 bush–1 peck corn furn[d] at

        Monticello @ 20/         8.83

      By pd mrs Lewis for 124½ ℔ bacon

        @ 1/   £6–4–6        20.75

      By the price of Jame Hubbard    450.

      By Isham Chisolm's order      50.

      Balance due Reuben Perry     67.48

                           618.66

Dec. 10. 1813.

    Settled and the balance of sixty seven Dollars and 48. cents acknoleged due to Reuben Perry        TH: JEFFERSON

                                REUBEN PERRY

MS (ViW: TC-JP); in TJ's hand, signed by TJ and Perry; endorsed by TJ: "Perry Reuben Settlem[t] Dec. 10. 1813."

Jeremiah A. Goodman supplied TJ with documents respectively giving the number of days worked by Mat and Hal and by JESSE PERRY, and the value of the SMITH'S WORK performed by or for Goodman (MSS in ViW: TC-JP; in Goodman's hand; with TJ's summary of both documents on the verso of the lat-

ter). TJ settled his accounts with GOOD-MAN on 12 May 1813 and Mary Walker LEWIS on 5 Oct. 1813, and he paid Isham Chisolm's ORDER on 24 Jan. 1814. He finally cleared the BALANCE of his account with Perry early in November 1814 by drawing on Gibson & Jefferson for $75, noting on 4 Nov. that this "overpays our old balce. of 67.48 and it's interest" (MB, 2:1288, 1293, 1297, 1304; TJ to Perry, 3 Nov. 1814).

# From John C. Pryor

D SIR,                     Hermitage Prince Edward 10. Decr. 13

    I am desirous to obtain the office of Collector of the direct tax & am at a loss to know to what department to make application. relying on your superior acquaintance with public[1] business & your readiness to assist those who are ignorant must beg you to give me the proper information on the subject as it regards the department to which I must apply also the requisites of the law—credentials &C &C. You will be pleas'd direct to me. Prince Ed Hermitage. Your obt. & very hbl. serv[t]

                                JOHN C. PRYOR

RC (DLC); endorsed by TJ as received 17 Dec. 1813 and so recorded in SJL.

A 22 July 1813 "Act for the assessment and collection of direct taxes and internal duties" divided Virginia into twenty-six collection districts, of which the thirteenth comprised Amelia, Buckingham, Cumberland, and PRINCE EDWARD counties. The only stipulated CREDENTIALS were that each district collector be "a respectable freeholder and reside within the same." Samuel Jones was ultimately chosen as the collector for the thirteenth district (*U.S. Statutes at Large*, 3:23–4, 25; *JEP*, 2:455, 456, 461 [18, 21 Jan. 1814]).

[1] Reworked from "all."

# From John Barnes

DEAR SIR—                                        George Town, 12th Dec[r] 1813.

Inclosed, you recive M[r] Williams Letter to me, of the 9th recd the 15th Ult[o]—and such is the State of Affairs respecting a Remittance to be made Gen[l] K, that how, to govern my self I am at a loss to know—unless, M[r] Williams politeness will permit him (without—a positive Order—from the House of Morton & Russell of Borodeau)[1] to value himself upon them, per set of Exchange in my fav[r] and my remitting him[2] the Am[t], at Curr[t] exchange, which I much fear, he will not consent to. my only hope is—in M[r] Russells—Arrival or some other advices—may impower M[r] Williams to Act, with effect.—

I most sincerely Congratulate M[rs] Randolph—and the good family on Col[o] Randolphs safe return, After so fatiguing & hazardous a Campaign

I am Dear Sir, mst Respectfully
yr obed[t] serv[t]                                        JOHN BARNES,

16th Dec[r]—

PS. the within, has been detained—four days—expecting the good Col[o] to call on me before he left Town

his impatience to hasten to Monticello I do—most readily excuse
Yrs—                                                            J B—

RC (ViU: TJP-ER); adjacent to full signature: "Tho[s] Jefferson Esq[r] Montecillo"; endorsed by TJ as a letter of "Dec. 12. & 16. 1813" received 20 Dec. 1813, but recorded in SJL as received 24 Dec. 1813. Enclosure not found.

GEN[L] K: Tadeusz Kosciuszko. COL[O] Thomas Mann Randolph, who had recently participated in the FATIGUING & HAZARDOUS, but ultimately unsuccessful American attempt to capture Montreal, received a furlough and began his journey home from upstate New York by 20 Nov.

1813. Having passed through Albany, New York City, and Philadelphia, he reached Georgetown by 11 Dec. and arrived in Albemarle County shortly thereafter (Gaines, *Randolph*, 85–92; James Wilkinson to Randolph, 19 Nov. 1813 [MHi]; Edward B. Randolph to Randolph, 20 Nov. 1813 [MHi]; Randolph to James Madison, 11 Dec. 1813 [DLC: Madison Papers]).

[1] Omitted closing parenthesis editorially supplied.
[2] Word interlined.

# From Samuel M. Burnside

SIR,                                    Worcester Massa<sup>s</sup> Decem<sup>r</sup> 13th. 1813—

On the 24th of October 1812, the Legislature of Massachusetts formed a number of Gentlemen into a body Corporate and Politic, by the name of "The American Antiquarian Society."—The nature, views and objects of this Institution are stated and explained in a pamphlet, recently published by their order, a copy of which is transmitted to You, and will accompany this letter.—The Society, desirous to secure the good wishes, the patronage and Support of the friends of Science throughout our Country, have directed me to address you, Sir, as one of the fathers of American Literature, and to solicit Your aid in the advancement of the laudable objects of their establishment. American Antiquities, they trust, have never been Subjects of indifference to one, who has done more than any other individual to elevate the rank of our Country in the general Republic of letters.—I am Therefore instructed to ask, Sir, If you will honor the Society by permitting them to elect You a member, and by affording them Such assistance from time to time in their pursuits,[1] as may consist with the numerous other claims, which Your personal friends, and Your Country at large, may have upon Your attention.—With great consideration and

respect, I am, Sir, Your Obed<sup>t</sup> Servant

SAM<sup>L</sup> M. BURNSIDE. Sec<sup>y</sup>
A. A. S

RC (DLC); at foot of text: "Hon. Tho's Jefferson Esqr"; endorsed by TJ as received 24 Dec. 1813 and so recorded in SJL. Enclosure: *An Account of the American Antiquarian Society, incorporated, October 24th, 1812. published by order of the society* (Boston, Nov. 1813), p. 30 of which indicates that TJ had been elected a member even before the above letter asked him for permission to do so.

Samuel McGregore Burnside (1783–1850), attorney, was a native of Northumberland, New Hampshire, who received an A.B. degree from Dartmouth College in 1805. After two years as preceptor of a female academy in Andover, Massachusetts, he took up the study of law. Burnside was called to the Massachusetts bar in 1810 and admitted to practice at the state supreme court two years later. Having moved to Worcester in 1810, he helped found the American Antiquarian Society in that city in 1812. In the ensuing years Burnside held the offices of recording secretary, 1812–14, corresponding secretary, 1814–23, counsellor, 1823–50, and librarian, 1830–31. He also served on the Massachusetts General Court, 1826–27, was a trustee of the nearby Leicester Academy, and sat for many years on the local school committee. At the time of his death Burnside owned real estate worth about $52,000 (*General Catalogue of Dartmouth College and the Associated Schools, 1769–1925* [1925], 112; William Lincoln, *History of Worcester, Massachusetts* [1837], 238; *Boston Gazette*, 6 Apr. 1812; *Account of the American Antiquarian Society*, 15, 18; American Antiquarian Society, *Proceedings*, n.s., 1 [1880]: vi, vii, viii; DNA: RG

29, CS, Mass., Worcester, 1820, 1830, 1850; *Salem* [Mass.] *Gazette*, 5 May 1826; *Pittsfield* [Mass.] *Sun*, 15 Mar. 1827; MWA: Burnside Papers and finding aid; *Boston Daily Atlas*, 1 Aug. 1850).

On this day TJ received a report describing the annual meeting of the United States Military Philosophical Society held in New York City on 1 Nov. 1813. Contained therein were lists of the members present, officers chosen, resolutions passed, and candidates elected to membership, as well as a brief report on the society's finances by its president, Jonathan Williams (printed circular in MoSHi: TJC-BC; addressed: "Thomas Jefferson Esqr Monticello Charlotteville Virginia"; franked; postmarked Philadelphia, 1 Dec., and Charlottesville, 9 Dec.; endorsed by TJ as received 13 Dec. 1813).

[1] Preceding three words interlined.

# From Bela Fosgate, with Note from David Holt

RESPECTED SIR                    Herkimer 13th 12 mo 1813—

Altho I am an enemy to those wars which destroy the human race and desolate the earth yet I am friendly to the principle implanted with in us of self-preservation from which arises that of self defence. I am a friend[1] to Civil liberty and have long been pained in witnessing the violations of the rights and liberties of my fellow citizens. The estimation in which I hold thy charactir yeields an asurence that I may address thee in thy retirement with out being deemed an intruder. I have been grieved to find that the hostile ships of England those ingines of tyranny have been enabled to hover upon our Coast and remain in our water's unmolested and that the means hitherto used for their expulsion or destruction have proved abortive.—

My reflections upon the failure of sub-marine experiments have led me to imagine that the difficulty hitherto experienced in affixing tor-pedoes to the objects intended may be removed. I have supposed that the bodies to be operated upon posess with in themselves the power of attraction to such a degree that a loadstone may be connected with a torpedo. and answer the effect intended by being drawn (independent of or aside from the current) into contact with a ship of war that necssarily from the nature of her armamint caries with her the attractive power.—I am not suffiently versed in either philosophy or Chemistry to satisfy my own mind upon this subject and my situation in Society forbids my taking any active part in the struggles between nations altho I trust I Shall ever be found a true friend to my native and beloved Country.

If the ideas I have intertained respecting an improvment upon tor-pedoes be by thee considered visionary still my motives in making them known to thee are pure—I hope thou wilt so far indulge me as to inform me whether thou thinkest that the appendage I have suggested can be applied with a prospect of sucess—Should my notions be chemerical I do not wish to expose myself to the sneers of little minds and I have therefore ventured to address thee asured that with thee my motives will be duly appreciated—

with much esteem I am thy frie[nd]     BELA FOSGATE

SIR,

Permit me to inform you, that the writer of the foregoing letter is a very respectable member of the society of Friends,—a druggist, in this place, a warm friend to the republican administrations, and incapable of harboring a wish to trifle with you. Knowing your liability to be imposed upon by unknown enemies, I have deemed it incumbent on me to make this addition, for a part of which I have the permission of Mr. Fosgate. The knowledge of his having written at all is confined, I believe to himself and,

Your obedient servant,          DAVID HOLT, P. Master

RC (DLC); torn at seal; in Fosgate's hand, with subjoined note in Holt's hand; adjacent to Fosgate's signature: "To Thomas Jefferson Late President"; endorsed by TJ as a letter from Fosgate and Holt received 24 Dec. 1813 and so recorded in SJL.

Bela Fosgate (ca. 1775–1830), druggist, was born in Worcester, Massachusetts, and moved to Montgomery County, New York, by about 1800, when he reputedly developed an anodyne cordial medicine. After 1810 he relocated to Herkimer County, where he resided until at least 1819. In the latter year Fosgate ran unsuccessfully for the state assembly. He moved by 1822 to Auburn, New York, and died there (Cynthia L. Fosgate-Swan, "Family history of the Swan and Fosgate families" [undated typescript at TxH], 3–4; DNA: RG 29, CS, N.Y., Montgomery Co., 1810; Cherry-Valley [N.Y.] Gazette, 1 Apr. 1819; New-York Evening Post, 6 Jan. 1820; Utica, N.Y., Western Recorder, 26 Jan. 1830).

David Holt (1779–1853), printer, postmaster, and magistrate, was a native of New London, Connecticut. He learned the craft of printing from his brother Charles Holt, who also corresponded with TJ. During his long publishing ca-

reer Holt printed a number of newspapers, including the Farmer's Monitor, 1805–07, Bunker-Hill, 1809–10, and the Republican Farmer's Free Press in 1830, all in Herkimer, New York. He also served as Herkimer's postmaster, 1812–20, collector of direct taxes and internal revenue during the War of 1812, and county judge, 1817–23. Financial difficulties induced Holt to relocate by 1840 to Albany, where he continued to work as a printer. By 1850 he had moved to Madison, Wisconsin, where he died (Daniel S. Durrie, A Genealogical History of the Holt family in the United States [1864], 256–7; Lorraine Cook White, ed., The Barbour Collection of Connecticut Town Vital Records [1994–2002], 3:12; Nathaniel S. Benton, A History of Herkimer County [1856], 221, 222, 321–2, 484; Brigham, American Newspapers, 1:580; Washington National Intelligencer, 22 Feb. 1812; Otsego Herald, 4 Dec. 1813; JEP, 2:455, 465 [18, 31 Jan. 1814]; Palmyra [N.Y.] Register, 7 June 1820; Saratoga Sentinel, 21 Feb. 1821; DNA: RG 29, CS, N.Y., Albany, 1840, Wis., Madison, 1850; Albany Journal, 19 Jan. 1853).

[1] Manuscript: "fiend."

# To Isaac Cox Barnet

SIR                                    Monticello Dec. 14. 13.

My interior situation among the mountains and very far from any seaport, renders it extremely difficult for me to learn when vessels are going from any port of the United States to France, which might offer a tolerably safe conveyance for letters. this makes me a very tardy correspondent with that side of the water, and must be my apology for having so long delayed acknoleging the reciept of your letter accompanying a copy of the Memoires concerning M. Peron, for which I pray you to accept my thanks. I have read it with great pleasure and find him a very interesting character, and one with which I should have been unacquainted but for your kind attention. our booksellers in this country furnish us with nothing new from the European <u>continent</u>. with my thanks for this kindness be pleased to accept the assurance of my great respect & esteem.     TH: JEFFERSON

PoC (DLC); at foot of text: "M^r Isaac C. Barnet"; endorsed by TJ. Enclosed in TJ to David Bailie Warden, 29 Dec. 1813, and TJ to John Graham, 6 Jan. 1814.

For the MEMOIRES CONCERNING M. PERON, see note to Barnet to TJ, 21 Nov. 1812.

# To Valentín de Foronda

DEAR SIR                              Monticello Dec. 14. 13.

I have had the pleasure of recieving several letters from you, covering printed propositions and pamphlets on the state of your affairs, and all breathing the genuine sentiments of order, liberty & philanthropy with which I know you to be sincerely inspired. we learn little to be depended on here as to your civil proceedings, or of the division of sentiments among you: but in this absence of information I have made whatever you propose the polar star of my wishes. what is to be the issue of your present struggles we, here, cannot judge. but we sincerely wish it may be what is best for the happiness and reinvigoration of your country. that it's divorce from it's American colonies, which is now unavoidable, will be a great blessing, it is impossible not to pronounce on a review of what Spain was when she acquired them, and of her gradual descent from that proud eminence to the condition in which her present war found her. nature has formed that peninsul to be the second, and why not the first nation in Europe? give equal habits of energy to the bodies, and of science to the minds of her citizens, and where could her superior be found? the most advantageous relation in which she can stand with her American colonies is that of independant friendship, secured by the ties of consanguinity, sameness of language, religion, manners, and habits, and certain, from the influence of these, of a preference in her commerce. if, instead of the eternal irritations, thwartings, machinations against their new governments, the insults and aggressions which Gr. Britain has so unwisely practised towards us, to force us to hate her against our natural inclinations, Spain yields, like a genuine parent, to the forisfamiliation of her colonies now at maturity, if she extends to them her affections, her aid, her patronage in every court & country, it will weave a bond of union indissoluble by time.          We are in a state of semi-warfare with your adjoining colonies the Floridas. we do not consider this as affecting our peace with Spain or any other of her former possessions. we wish her and them well; and under her present difficulties at home, and her doubtful future relations with her colonies, both wisdom & interest will I presume induce her to leave them to settle themselves the quarrel they draw on themselves from their neighbors. the commanding officers in the Floridas have excited & armed the neighboring savages to war against us, and to murder & scalp many of our women and children as well as men, taken by surprise, poor creatures! they have paid for it with the loss of the flower of their strength, and have given us the right as we possess the power to exterminate, or to expatriate them beyond the Missisipi. this conduct of the Spanish officers will probably oblige us to take possession of the Floridas, and the rather as we believe the English will otherwise sieze them, and use them as stations to distract and annoy us. but should we possess ourselves of them, & Spain retain her other colonies in this hemisphere, I presume we shall consider them in our hands as subjects of negociation.

We are now at the close of our 2$^d$ campaign with England. during the first we suffered several checks from the want of capable and tried officers; all the higher ones of the revolution having died off during an interval of 30 years of peace. but this 2$^d$ campaign has been more succesful, having given us all the lakes & country of Upper Canada, except the single post of Kingston, at it's lower extremity. the two immediate causes of the war were the Orders of Council and impressment of our seamen. the 1$^{st}$ having been removed after we had declared war, the war is continued for the 2$^d$ and a 3$^d$ has been generated by their conduct during the war, in exciting the Indian hordes to murder & scalp the women & children on our frontier. this renders peace for ever impossible but on the establishment of such a meridian boundary to their possessions as that they never more can have such influence with the savages as to excite again the same barbarities. the thousand ships too they took from us in peace and the six thousand seamen impressed call for this indemnification. on the water we have proved to the world the error of their invincibility, and shewn that with equal force and well trained officers they can be beaten by other nations as brave as themselves. their lying officers and printers will give to Europe very different views of the state of their war with us. but you will see now, as in the revolutionary war, that they will lie and conquer themselves out of all their possessions on this continent.

I pray for the happiness of your nation, and that it may be blessed with sound views & succesful measures, under the difficulties in which it is involved: and especially that they may know the value of your counsels, and to yourself I tender the assurances of my high respect and esteem. TH: JEFFERSON

PoC (DLC); at foot of first page: "Don Valentin de Foronda. Coruña." Enclosed in TJ to John Graham, 6 Jan. 1814.

FORISFAMILIATION: the emancipation of a son from paternal authority through the gift of a piece of land (*Black's Law Dictionary*).

# To François André Michaux

SIR Monticello Dec. 14. 1813.

My interior situation among the mountains, and great distance from any seaport town, is extremely unfriendly to punctual correspondence with the other side of the Atlantic. vessels bound to that quarter are generally gone before I learn their destination by the public papers. I have recieved from you, at different times,[1] several livraisons of your excellent work on the forest trees of America. to wit the 1st and 2d sur les Pins et Sapins, et sur les Chenes, and the 9th and 10th on the Betula, Castanea, Fagus, Diospyros Etc. I have gone over them with great pleasure and recieved from them much information which had escaped my own notice, altho' the subjects lie under my eye. they contain a valuable addition to the knoledge of American trees, and claim for you the thanks of all who interest themselves in this most interesting branch of science. I pray you to accept my portion of that tribute, as being among those who set the highest value on your work.

I have not seen the work of M. Tessier, mentioned by you, on the subject of the Merinos. but that race of sheep is multiplying among us most extensively. the general attention paid to them will soon render their wool an article of export, altho' our own manufactures are fast increasing also, and will soon make us independant of England for manufactures of wool and cotton, as well as for many other articles. besides the domestic benefit to be derived from this economy, the political advantage of weakening permanently a bitter and permanent enemy are of real importance. with every wish for the succesful prosecution of the valuable labors you are engaged in, be pleased to accept the assurance of my great respect & esteem.

TH: JEFFERSON

RC (OCLloyd); addressed: "M. F. André Michaux à Paris." PoC (MoSHi: TJC-BC); endorsed by TJ. Enclosed in TJ to David Bailie Warden, 29 Dec. 1813, and TJ to John Graham, 6 Jan. 1814.

TJ had received LIVRAISONS ("parts") of Michaux's *Histoire des arbres forestiers de l'Amérique septentrionale* (Paris, 1810–12; Sowerby, no. 1083) on several occasions during the preceding three years. SUR LES PINS ET SAPINS, ET SUR LES CHENES: "on pine, fir, and oak trees."

[1] TJ here canceled "three."

# To Alexis Marie Rochon

Monticello. Dec. 14. 1813.

I have had the pleasure, my dear Sir, of recieving your letter of Aug. 7. 1812. and with it a copy of your voyages for the observations of the longitudes at sea, which I have read with great satisfaction, and pray you to accept my thanks for them. I recieved at the same time your pamphlet on the Micrometer of rock-chrystal, the advantages of which you had shewn to me in 1785 at D$^r$ Franklin's at Passy, on the telescope you gave him, which is now in my possession. the uses of this discovery at sea, as well as with land-armaments, are so many and great, that it is wonderful to me, that in a course of 30. years, it is not yet brought into general use. it is one of the remarkable proofs of the slowth with which improvements in the arts & sciences advance.

I am happy to learn that you are in the superintendance of the interests of manufactures. I shall rejoice to see them flourish every where, & every nation enabled to furnish itself with what it has hitherto taken from England, and withdrawing from her their quota of the aliment of her thousand armed ships, and of her piracies on the ocean, of which they are the instruments. we shall certainly hereafter call on her for very little. never has there been an instance of such rapidity in the establishments of manufactures; the capital of our former commerce being of necessity diverted to that object. we have already, or shall certainly have in the course of another year, a million of spindles engaged in spinning; which are sufficient for clothing our eight millions of people. but they will still continue to multiply. we are getting the spinning machines into all our farm houses, for the cloathing of our families. I work myself upwards of an hundred spindles merely for our own domestic use. we raise wool enough for all our purposes; so much the less being necessary with our abundance of cotton. the race of Merinos is very much multiplied and spread over all our states from hence Northwardly.          I give you these details because I know your partiality for the useful arts, and that you will see their importance in all their bearings, political and economical.          I am glad to learn that you are shewing us the way to supply ourselves with some of the most necessary tropical productions, and that the bette-rave, which we can all raise, promises to supplant the cane particularly, and to silence the demand for the inhuman species of labour employed in it's culture & manipulation. could you favor me with the details of the best process for the manufacture of sugar from the beet? I have the book of M. Parmentier; but that does not give us recipes of the process. very much gratified by this occasion of recalling myself to your recollection, I tender you the assurance of my great esteem and respect.          TH: JEFFERSON

PoC (ViW: TC-JP); at foot of first page: "M. l'Abbé Rochon"; endorsed by TJ. Enclosed in TJ to David Bailie Warden, 29 Dec. 1813, and TJ to John Graham, 6 Jan. 1814.

SLOWTH is a variant of "sloth," in this context meaning "sluggishness" (*OED*). BETTE-RAVE: "beet." Antoine Auguste

PARMENTIER was the author of *Aperçu des Résultats obtenus de la fabrication des Sirops et des Conserves de Raisins; dans le cours des années 1810 et 1811, pour servir de suite au Traité publié sur cette matière; avec une Notice historique et chronologique du Corps sucrant* (Paris, 1812; Sowerby, no. 1200).

# To André Thoüin

Monticello Dec. 14. 1813.

The perils of the ocean, my good and antient friend, are such that I almost despair of getting a letter to you. yet I cannot permit myself longer to withold the acknolegement of the reciept of your letters of Mar. 2. and Dec. 7. 11. and Mar. 15. 13. the boxes of seeds which you were so kind as to forward to me in 1810. 1811. came safely to hand,

and were committed to our best seedsmen, in order that they might be preserved and distributed so as to become general. the box announced in yours of March 15. 13. has, I presume, been captured on the high seas; as I have never heard of it's arrival in any port. I thank you for the pamphlet sent me with the letter by M. Correa, as well as for having made me acquainted with that most excellent character. he favored me with a visit at Monticello, which gave me opportunities of judging of his great science, worth and amability. when he left me he meant to leave our continent immediately for Portugal. but I learn that he changed his mind afterwards and winters in Philadelphia.      I learn with pleasure the success of several new cultures with you, and that you will by example teach us how to do without some of the tropical productions. the bette-rave, I am told, is likely really to furnish sugar at such a price as to rivalize that of the Cane. if you have any printed recipes of the process of manipulation, and could send me one, naming also the best species of beet, you would add a valuable item to the repeated services you have rendered us by a communication[1] of the useful plants. if ever we should get the sea open again, I shall take great pleasure in repaying some of your kindnesses by sending you a collection of the seeds & new plants which were brought to us by Lewis & Clark from the other side of our Continent. they have been well taken care of by M$^r$ M$^c$Mahon, seedsman and botanist at Philadelphia from which port they can be readily shipped. at present we are blockaded by our enemies; as we were indeed for many years while they called themselves our friends. I know not therefore how the present letter is to get to you: but should it be so fortunate, let it be the bearer to you of sincere assurances of my great friendship and respect.      TH: JEFFERSON

RC (StEdNL); addressed: "Mons$^r$ Thouin de l'Institut de France Museum d'Histoire Naturelle à Paris"; endorsed by Thoüin as received 14 May 1814 from David Bailie Warden; with Tr on verso of address leaf. PoC (DLC); endorsed by TJ. Tr (StEdNL); French translation; misdated 14 May 1814; on verso of address leaf of RC. Enclosed in TJ to David Bailie Warden, 29 Dec. 1813, and TJ to John Graham, 6 Jan. 1814.

José Corrêa da Serra delivered Thoüin's letter of 7 Dec. 1811 and its enclosed PAMPHLET to TJ on 31 July 1813. AMABILITY: "lovableness" (OED). BETTE-RAVE: "beet."

[1] Manuscript: "communiication."

# To Julian Ursin Niemcewicz

DEAR SIR                                    M[ontic]ello Dec. 15. 13.

Your letter of Sep. 4. 10. was 10. months on it's passage to me, having been recieved on the 7<sup>th</sup> of July 11. I addressed my answer to you without delay, acknoleging my obligations to the Royal society of the friends of science in Warsaw for their nomination of me as one of their members, expressing my sense of the honor of being associated with their body, and tendering any services which at this distance, I could render them. this having been sent by the way of Paris, was, I hope, duly recieved. writing now some letters to my friends there, I take the same occasion of recalling my self to your recollection, and of expressing the satisfaction I feel in reviewing the agreeable moments I have passed with you in Paris and Philadelphia.

we, like you, are now at war, but happily on our borders only, undisturbed at our altars & firesides. we recieved some checks in it's beginning, from the want of experienced and tried officers to command us, a peace of 30. years having deprived us of all those of high grades in the revolutionary war. our second campaign has been more succesful, having possessed ourselves of all the lakes and country of Upper Canada, except the single post of Kingston at it's lower extremity.        on the ocean, tho' we have but a very small force, in half a dozen actions, of vessel to vessel of equal force, we have captured them in every instance but one: and on Lake Erie, in an engagement of 8. or 10. vessels of a side, of the size navigating that water, we took their whole squadron, not a vessel or a man escaping. we have no doubt, if the war continues, of ousting them from the entire continent. this is very different from what their lying papers will tell you in Europe. but you have heard at least that in our revolutionary war the same papers were eternally announcing victories & changes of position, till they conquered themselves out [of a co]ntinent.        it would give me great pleasure to hear how you [are per]sonally affected by the wars around you, and to be assured that you do not participate of their calamities. when will this world be again at peace!

Your old friend, mr M<sup>c</sup>lure, paid us a visit some two or three years ago, and returned to Paris. his brother is living and still engaged in commerce, as I believe. Latrobe has been till lately engaged at Washington in the business of civil engineer, but is now gone to Pittsburg to take part in the enterprize of furnishing steam-boats for the Ohio and Missisipi. these boats, of the invention of mr Fulton, have obtained the most perfect success, and are now extending to all our rivers.

This notice of some of your friends here, I have thought might not be unacceptable, and among[1] them I pray you to count none as entertaining sentiments of higher esteem and respect for you than myself.                                                             TH: JEFFERSON

PoC (DLC); top edge torn; at foot of first page: "M. Julien Ursin Niemcewicz. Warsaw"; endorsed by TJ. Enclosed in TJ to David Bailie Warden, 29 Dec. 1813, and TJ to John Graham, 6 Jan. 1814.

No earlier ANSWER by TJ to Niemcewicz's letter of 4 Sept. 1810 has been found, nor is one recorded in SJL. Oliver Hazard Perry captured a WHOLE SQUADRON of British ships on Lake Erie on 10 Sept. 1813 (ANB). The distinguished American scientist William

Maclure (McLURE) (1763–1840) spent much of the period between November 1809 and May 1816 conducting geological investigations and collecting rock specimens from France, Italy, Russia, and Scandinavia. He visited Niemcewicz in Warsaw late in the summer of 1810. His BROTHER Alexander Maclure was a merchant in Norfolk (ANB; John S. Doskey, ed., The European Journals of William Maclure [1988], esp. 322; Thomas J. Wertenbaker, Norfolk [1931], 102).

[1] Word interlined in place of "with."

# From Horatio G. Spafford

HON<sup>D</sup> AND ESTEEMED FRIEND—                     Albany, 12 mo. 17, 1813.

I was duly favored with thy obliging favor of last autumn, & immediately sent the Gazetteer as directed. Did it arrive safe? & how dost thou like it?

But, this is only a minor cause of my writing at this time, though I confess myself anxious to learn thy opinion of my Work. I am tired of this unceasing jargon of politics, with which I am surrounded, this warring of principle against no principle, of natural right against old prejudices, & long to see it ended. Selfishness, & the basest twistings of deceit for the basest purposes, oppose the Government in every thing, & the merest trifler in Society knows more than the best of men, long tried in private & public service. Now it is said the Government is all in the wrong, & the partial advocate for any of its measures, is denouncd as worse than a devil, & more foolish than a fool. The Merchants, Lawyers, & p——s,[1] are almost all Monarchists, & they & their tools are plunging us into a preparation for a civil War. I see it plainly, & know too well their designs; & I would to God that thou & all the Southern people knew it as well. I deprecate the War, as much as any man; but though I disapprove of some measures, do not condemn all. The seizure & confinement of British Officers,[2] as hostages for our citizens, is now a chief topic of declamation, & for saying, just now, that, 'were I the President, I would take of these life for life,' I was treated most infamously by a set of these upstarts. They have proclaimed that the President <u>dare not do it</u>, nor would <u>I</u>, if in his place. But, God is my witness that I would, in defiance of all the frowns of hell, (or hades,) & I showed the ground of my reasons. This is truly a second war for independence. We took arms before, for the defence of national rights, & now we are fighting for independence of opinion; warring against the prejudices of those who <u>think</u> of the <u>garlics</u>, & other good things in <u>Egypt</u>. I have heard many say it was a great pity we were ever separated from Great Britain, & others that they prayed for a Monarchy. Commerce, that rapidly enriches the merchants, & the practise of Law, with a fat clergy, are all monarchical in their tendencies, which must be counteracted, or no republic can live. Why not as well take care of British advocates, although American Born, as of British Citizens? We shall finally have to do it, & the sooner it is done the better. I am ready to defend the Government quite as far as I think it ought to be defended, & that is as far as any one ought. The weakness of prejudice is opposed to reason; & prejudiced, bigotted advocates, but weaken the cause they would defend. In saying this much to thee, however, I may, I believe,[3] without impropriety add, that the General Government does not take counsel of the right kind of men, relative to its affairs in this State. And this is an opinion common amongst the best informed, moderate men, of all descriptions. The best men are all in the back-ground, & the only passport to public favor, is party violence, with little regard to merits of any other kind.

Turning from these disgusting scenes, I am glad to view thee safe & undisturbed by the storm—save so far as thy private portion of concern for our common country leads to an interest in the affairs of the State. May we not hope for peace soon? or what must we expect?

I shall be happy to be favored with another Letter, & remain, with very great esteem & regard, thy
friend,                                        H. G. SPAFFORD.

RC (MHi); at foot of text: "Hon. Thomas Jefferson"; endorsed by TJ as received 31 Dec. 1813 and so recorded in SJL.

TJ's letter to Spafford of LAST AUTUMN was actually dated 15 Aug. 1813. The Jews fondly recall the GARLICS, & OTHER GOOD THINGS IN EGYPT in the Bible, Numbers 11.5.

[1] Probably standing for "priests" and so construed by TJ in his 17 Mar. 1814 reply.
[2] Manuscript: "Offiers."
[3] Manuscript: "belieive."

# From Elizabeth Trist

MY MUCH HONORD FRIEND                                    Henry 17<sup>th</sup> Dec 1813

Your kind favor by last weeks mail, accompanied by one from my
daughter now Madame S<sup>t</sup> Julian de Tourneillon occasiond my heart
to glow with feelings that it has been long a stranger to, a reiteration
of your continued friendship and good wishes, and assurances of her
happiness in consiquence of the change in her condition were calculated to animate my mind to an enthusiastic degree of gratitude for
the goodness of Almighty God who has so far granted my petition
daily[1] offerd for the preservation of my friends, and happiness of my
dear Children, owing to the miscarriage of a letter I am unacquainted
with the particulars relating to her union with M<sup>r</sup> Tourniellon nor do
I know any thing of his general character, where he is from, or what
is his age but I have reason to conclude that he is rich, and that he is
liberal; and kind to all connected with her, the Boys are very much at-
tachd to him, Nicholas writes me that he is renderd very happy by his
Mothers marriage they have now a Father friend and protector, that
he is temperate mild and industrious rises at the dawn of day to superintend the Negroes who are clearing land and he has great expectation of making a good crop the next year, that If I was only with
them their happiness wou'd be compleat, I have also received a most
friendly and kind joint request that I wou'd spend the remainder of
my days with them and they will with pleasure answer the bills I may
choose to draw on them, for the expencese of my journey and Mary
observed that M<sup>r</sup> Tourneillon desired her to say that If I wish'd to
dispose of my half of the plantation that he will purchase it, that it
had long been her earnest wish to make me this offer as the only
means of making me independent of my friends, for my private expences, which she says she knows is necessary to my happiness begs
that I will not permit the interest of my Grandsons to deter me as It
is for them that he wishes to buy it,[2] at first my pride was a little
roused the Idea that I shou'd owe such obligation to a person that I
never Saw or heard of till now, Tis so unusual for generosity to shew
it self in this way, that the meanness of doubt took possession of my
mind as to his being what they thought him, but when I reflected
more calmly on the affair it struck my immagination in a new point of
view, that it was only a compliment to his wife by enabling her to render a being in whoes welfare she was deeply interested more comfortable and happy than she thought my situation admitted of, and
therefore concluded to accept the offer of the <u>purchase</u>, their kind invitation I was under the necessity of declining at present, there were

too many obsticles in the way of my getting there while the war lasted
though it wou'd be the delight of my Soul to see my children and witness their happiness yet it wou'd be a Severe operation to Sever me
from this family from whom I have experienced every kindness, the
children too, I shou'd be miserable to part from especially the two
youngest tho some times I feel a wish to emerge from this seclusion
and to see and hear a little of what is going forward in the world, tho
I believe no change wou'd increase my happiness, unless so situated
as to alternately pass the remnant of my days with connections so
dear to me, my health has certainly benefitted by my residence here
and tho the time <u>has</u> been when I Shou'd have look'd upon it with
horror I am satisfied that no situation under circumstances like mine
Cou'd have been found to suit me so well, and I shou'd leave it with
regret[3] M[r] and M[rs] Tourneillon were to set out for Orleans the last of
October to place the Boys at college, Nicholas past the last year there
and his Mother says his improvement has exceeded her most sanguine expectation, that he has grown five inches since She saw him
has a Northern complexion and robust health that I wou'd not suppose that he had been a Student for he was as wild as a Deer Browses
constitution is very delicate but I hope the change will benefit his
health in point of talents I am certain that he will not be inferior to
his Brother[4] Nicholas has been honord at the examination, his
Mother enclosed me the Presidents letter to her, and refers me to my
neice for translation but I find that she has forgotten her french in a
great measure for both Peachey and her self make a difficulty on acc[t]
of the handwriting and as I am interested I shou'd be glad to know
every word it contains and had it in contemplation to write to M[rs]
Randolph and request the favor of her to gratify me with a translation
but to impose any task upon her at this time woud be unkind therefore my D[r] good friend shall I ask that indulgence from you they can
make out that he has received a premium and crown in the translation and mathematical Classes which gives me unspeakable pleasure[5]
excuse my obtruding on your time by detailing occurrences that I am
sensible can not be very interesting to you—Your present has occasion'd us many laughs and will contribute to our amusement some
time to come its certainly a compleat satire on those characters who
rule the British Goverment Good God if I cou'd see them lash'd[6] to
the bone it wou'd delight me I presume that it is a production of Cole-
mans I have read his Parody on the Lady of the Lake and I think it is
in his Style, I look upon the Prince Regent as one of the most con-
temptable and vile characters in existence and I hope the House of

the Guelphs will terminate with him his Brothers are no better we have nothing to hope for from him his orders breathe nothing but destruction to our Towns or death to our citizens but I trust and hope the Torpedoes will be set in motion to good effect I tremble for the consiquences when ever I hear of any of our troops having fallen into their hands where will it end, if they put their threats into execution of puting those to Death who they call British subjects taken in arms against them those poor fellows who have been for many years living in our country naturalized citizens our attempt at retaliaton has exasperated them and will I fear occasion the death of hundreds I can not bear this cool Blooded warfare but we must not recede from the Presidents declaration tho it may terminate in the loss of many of our valuable countrymen I had great hopes that our Success in Canada wou'd be the means of emancipating those Officers from their Dungeons at Quebec before they cou'd be transported for sacrafice but I fear we have been too sanguine our last newspaper did not reach us but the report of our armey going into winter quarters[7] without effecting the Great object contemplatd is a great drawback on the success which has recently crownd our arms, we have reason for exultation in the heroic conduct of our brave Countrymen but our victories have been generally dearly bought I wonder if there is foundation for the report in circulation that Wilkinson and Hampton are at varience I shou'd be sorry if that is the case as it will procrastinate the fulfilment of our hopes and wishes The men that have gone to Norfolk from this part of the country have sufferd by death and sickness and are very dissatisfied with their treatment bad unsound provisions and little or no fuel, they are out of temper with the Governor and General Taylor who are Stigmatised with the name of Federalists, I shou'd not be surprised if at the next election a Tory Governor was elected and if the war was to continue that he wou'd make a Simmilar proclamation to Governor Chittenden, but I wou'd not say as much to every body I can not help feeling interested in the honor and Glory of france from a principle of gratitude and I hope Bonaparte will be spared as a scourge to the English as long as they continue their present System. I was very sorry to hear the fate of General Moreau for tho he had sufficient cause of displeasure against the Goverment of france I am grieved that he shou'd have fallen fighting against his Country you have no doubt heard of the Death of Daniel Clarke tho many I dare say will feel his loss I cant say that I regret it, with many good points about him he was too vindictive and wou'd have extirpated you if he cou'd, poor M^rs Randolph I feel most sensibly for her, but hope and pray that the clouds will all disperse that obscures her present happiness I think of Colonel Randolph continually and never knew till now how much I loved him I trust and hope that God will Strengthen his arm in the day of Battle and that he will return with Glory to his dear family please to present my affectionate love to them all and tell Patsy I lately received a letter from M$^{rs}$ Bache after a very long silence which has not added to my happiness she says that since she wrote to me that she has been greatly afflicted. the total suspension of commerse added to other causes had deprived them of the possibility of keeping their family together in Phila$^d$ and removed with her Girls to a Lodging in Frankford Benjamin was at school in Princeton and in August she sent her two youngest children to her Brothers and went to see him on her return she found her Daughter Emma very Ill which terminated her existance in two weeks after Suffering much her disorder was a dropsy on the Brain this circumstance added to other distressing causes induced her friends to approve of her spending the winter in Princeton with the remainder of her children I am afraid the Doc$^t$ has sunk never to rise again, I shall write soon to Patsy tho I had determined never to write again untill I rec$^d$ some proof that my letters wou'd be acceptable I shall I fear, never keep my resolution with her for I can not resist when I am very anxious about any event in which my friends are interested M$^r$ and M$^{rs}$ Gilmer unite with me in most respectful esteem and fervent regard for M$^{rs}$ Randolph and your self and believe me always your obliged and grateful friend

E, Trist

RC (MHi); endorsed by TJ as received 5 Jan. 1814 and so recorded in SJL. FC (NcU: NPT); in Elizabeth Trist's hand; ink stained; incomplete; differs substantially from RC, with only the most significant variations noted below. The enclosed letter to Mary Trist Jones Tournillon from Jules Davezac has not been found.

The BOYS were Nicholas Philip Trist and Hore Browse Trist. On 15 Oct. 1813 Nicholas P. Trist wrote his grandmother of the MARRIAGE of her daughter-in-law, MARY Trist Jones Tournillon (NcU: NPT). Trist's grandsons enrolled at Orleans COLLEGE in New Orleans (Shackelford, *Descendants*, 1:101). At this time she was staying with her NEICE Mary House Gilmer and the latter's husband,

Peachy R. Gilmer, at their home in Henry County, Virginia.

YOUR PRESENT was Thomas Moore's *Intercepted Letters; or, the Twopenny Post Bag. to which are added, Trifles Reprinted. By Thomas Brown, the Younger* (Philadelphia, 1813; Sowerby, no. 4519). George Colman's PARODY ON THE LADY OF THE LAKE was "The Lady of the Wreck; or, Castle Blarneygig: a poem" (Colman, *Poetical Vagaries* [London, 1812], 35–111). The GOVERNOR of Virginia was James Barbour.

Vermont governor Martin CHITTENDEN, a Federalist, issued a proclamation on 10 Nov. 1813 stating that "the Military strength and resources of this State, must be reserved for its own defence and protection, *exclusively*—excepting in cases provided for, by the Constitution of the United States; and then, under orders derived *only* from the Commander in Chief" (Middlebury, Vt., *Columbian Patriot*, 17 Nov. 1813).

Jean Victor MOREAU returned to Europe from his exile in the United States, joined the Allied armies in Saxony, and was mortally wounded at the Battle of Dresden in August 1813 (Connelly, *Napoleonic France*, 344). PATSY: Martha

Jefferson Randolph. The DOC[T] was probably William Bache, Catharine Wistar Bache's husband.

[1] Word interlined.
[2] Tr ends here.
[3] Tr resumes here.
[4] Tr ends here.
[5] Tr resumes here.
[6] RC: "lask'd." Tr: "lash'd."
[7] Tr ends here.

# From Paul Allen

Philadelphia Dec 18. 1813—

I trust that Your Excellency will do Me the justice to beleive that Your request with regard to the volumes of Lewis & Clarke would have been complied with long since & the books transmitted if the work had not been unexpectedly detained in the hands of the Printer They have now arrived at the conclusion of the work excepting the diary of the weather &c which comes in at the appendix. The delay has been occasioned by the press of other avocations which the Printers have been obliged to turn their more immediate attention to & particularly periodical works. My reason for troubling Your Excellency is an apprehension that You would deem Me neglectful of Your request of which [bele]ive Me Sir I am utterly incapable. With regard to the biographick [sketch] which You so condescendingly furnished Me with, I have to offer my sincerest thanks accompanied I must confess with some little chagrin that it was out of my power to requite the obligation. My mind was for sometime wavering on the propriety of annexing to Your biographick sketch a particular account of the melancholy death of Capt Lewis. That account has already been published by the late Alexander Wilson Esqr the celebrated ornithologist. But as this might notwithstanding in all human probability wound the sensibility of surviving relatives & freinds, I deemed it the most expedient to err on the side of humanity & rather to veil the severity of biographick fact than to have my motives misunderstood by the recital.—I should[1] have been much gratified by annexing a sketch of the life of Gov. Clarke but that has been long since abandoned as unattainable. The misfortune in such cases is that with regard to many of the Men who have adorned the character of their Country it is by One single act that they have rendered themselves illustrious. When that act is told the whole of the Life of the Individual so far as the Publick is interested becomes already known & precludes interesting biography. Thus this hazardous expedition is the only part of Capt Lewis life which were he now alive he would be willing probably to Submit to publick Notice—it was on one occasion only that his great talents were put to the proof & then they were found adequate to the emergen[cy.]

It is commonly beleived by Mankind that when one [...] Beings displays talents commensurate with the occasion [...] them forth, the whole of his previous life must exhibit some traces of that character. This is a great mistake which may be illustrated by an anecdote of my Countryman the late Gen. Greene. When he was a Militia General in Rhode Island he addressed a petition[2] to the Legislature of that State menti[o]ning that a bill of six shillings of Continental currency was accidentaly washed to peices in his Jacket pocket & praying compensation.[3]

Yet this was the same Nathaniel Greene who afterwards delivered the southern States from the tyranny of England!

Your Excellencys humble Servt &c                    P ALLEN

RC (DLC); torn at seal; at foot of text: "His Excellency T. Jefferson Esqr Monticello"; endorsed by TJ as received 31 Dec. 1813 and so recorded in SJL.

James Maxwell was the PRINTER of Biddle, *Lewis and Clark Expedition.* A letter from Alexander Wilson of 28 May 1811 giving a detailed account of the MELANCHOLY DEATH of Meriwether Lewis appeared in a Philadelphia journal, the *Port Folio,* n.s., 7 (1812): 34–47. Nathanael Greene successfully petitioned the Rhode Island legislature in the summer of 1775 for the reimbursement of £4.10, not SIX SHILLINGS (*August, 1775. At the General Assembly of the Governor and Company of the English Colony of Rhode-Island and Providence Plantations, in New-England, in America* [Providence, 1776], 93).

[1] Allen here canceled "likewise."
[2] Manuscript: "petitition."
[3] Allen here canceled "from the State."

# From John Adams

DEAR SIR                                  Quincy December 19. 1813

Ridendo dicere Verum, quid vetat. I must make you and myself merry or melancholly, by a little more Phylosophical Speculation about the formidable Subject of Aristocracy.

Not long after General Dearborn's return to Boston from the Army, a violent Alarm was excited and Spread in Boston and through the country, by a report at first only Secretly whispered in private circles that an Affair of Love was commencing between the

General and Madam Bowdoin the virtuous and amiable Relict of my Friend and your Ambassador James Bowdoin. The Surprise, the astonishment, were universal and the indignation very general. The exclamations were in every mouth. "Impossible"! "It cannot be"! "It is a false report." "It is too bad"! "It¹ is a Scandalous fiction"! "It is a malicious Calumny against M^rs Bowdoin"! "Would that Lady disgrace her Husband?" She was herself, a Bowdoin: "Would She degrade her own and her Husbands Name and Blood"?² "Would She disgrace the illustrious Name of Bowdoin which has been So long famous in France"? "Would She disgrace her Husband who has been an Ambassador? and her Father in Law, who was her Uncle, and had been Governor"?

This is no exaggeration. I have heard all these exclamations. Have you read Cecilia, or the Scottish Chiefs? Is there any thing in the Character of the Delville Family, or in any of the Scotch Thanes more outrageously Aristocratical, than these popular Sentiments, in this our Democratical Country?

I undertook like a genuine Knight Errant to be the Champion of the Lady: and Said Some things very Shocking to some Companies. To some very grave Ladies I said "Why; Madam, if M^rs Bowdoins object is Love and domestic comfort, The General is an healthy, robust and personable Man; which her former Husband was not. If her object is Ambition, She will advance her Degree and condition by this Alliance; for neither Governors nor Ambassadors nor Earls hold So high a Rank as a Secretary at War and Commander in Chief, of all the Armies of a great Nation. Her object cannot be Wealth: for She has enough; but if it was, Collectorships and other offices, must have given the General a Competency."³

Till very lately the French descent of the Bowdoins has been known to very few and never boasted by any body. But it has been published and proclaimed by M^r William Jenks, Secretary to the Board of Trustees of Bowdoin Colledge in his Eulogy on M^r Bowdoin. This Eulogy M^rs Bowdoin, I presume has Sent to you as well as to me. If not, I will Send you an extract.

The Race of Baudouins, it is true has long been notable in France. The Name I believe is to be found among the Crusaders, to Jerusalem, when, no doubt they were orthodox Catholicks: but afterwards, in the Crusades against the Albigenses, they were Suspected on both Sides. In all the Seiges and in all the battles, there were many Nobles and Cavaliers among the Sectaries. The Counts De Foix, De Comminges, De Besiers, De Bearn, and almost all the Lords who inhabited, towards the Pyrennes, were of the Sect, or at least favoured and protected it. The Count de Thoulouse, without declaring himself a Manichean, (So they called the Albigenses as well as the Waldenses) had for the Sect, and for their Preachers a respect, which bordered on extravagance, and laid the foundation of all the misfortunes, of his princely house. Baudouin, Brother of the Count De Thoulouse, was hanged on a Tree by the Hereticks, notwithstanding the Tenderness of the Family for them, and though he begged for time to confess and receive the Communion.

The Count De Thoulouse (Baudouin) acted a mysterious part. though he protested his orthodox faith, yet he obstinately protected the Hereticks. He made Promises, but could not determine to fullfill them. The Pope innocent the third, interrested himself in his favour, and arrested, for some time, the Proceedings of the Legates against him. But he knew Not how to take Advantage of these dispositions. Without Firmness, without Wisdom, without Prudence, he could not conquer the Secret Inclination he had for Heresy; nor foresee that he was commencing the misfortunes of his Family; nor that the Ambition of the neighbouring Potentate, would soon compleat its destruction. A Miracle it Seems was wrought for the destruction of this Family. Simon de Monfort with only Eight hundred Men, and one thousand Fantassins attacked the Army of the King of Arragon, and the Count de Thoulouse, which was of one hundred thousand men, and totally defeated them.

This I learn from Nonotte, the Scourge of Voltaire, whom Voltaire Scourges in his turn with a long Catalogue of "Sottises." This is however but a ray of the historical Glory of the name. Baudouin the eighth Count of Flanders was Emperor of Constantinople in 1204. Baudouin the 2$^d$ was the last latin Emperor of Constantinople in 1228. A Baudouin was King of Jerusalem in the 12$^{th}$ Century and Saladin or Noraddin his Enemy Said he had not left his equal. The name has been distinguished in Lettres as well as in War and Politicks. A Baudouin, was Solicited by Henry 3, then Duke of Anjou, to write in Justification of the Massacre of St. Bartholemy. But he was too honest a man. Another Baudouin, who died in 1650[4] translated all the Classicks and wrote many other Things.

All these litterary, civil, political, millitary, religious, noble, royal and imperial honours are now to be devolved[5] on the Bowdoin Family of Massachusetts. But the name is extinct in the male Line. To repaire this breach a law of the State has been procured, to alter the Name of a Sisters Son from Temple to Bowdoin, and to him the Family Estate is given. Sir John Temple too the Father of that Son has poured a Stream of English noble blood into the mighty river of Baw-doin. A Splendid Funeral Sermon of M^r Gardner has been printed "On the Death of Elizabeth Lady Temple." The name of Bowdoin is immortalized, by a flourishing University founded by the Family. you have immortalized the Name by making an Ambassador of it; and by making a Cousin, another Ambassador.

Do you call this natural or artificial Aristocracy? Aristocracy it is most certainly; for the Name of Bowdoin in this State has more in-fluence than the name of Russell or Howard has in England. So have the names of Livingston and Clinton in New York. We had a General Sterling, but that Title would not Satisfy.[6] He must be called Lord Sterling, and his Daughter "Lady Kitty Duer." Our Russell Family wear the Arms, and claim Relation to the Dukes of Bedford. Our Quincys are descended from Saer de Quincy, Marquis of Winchester, who extorted Magna Charta from King John, and whose Signature to that Instrument, "Sayer de Winton" you have Seen in the British Musæum and in Blacstones Copy. General Talmadge of Connecticutt is by Law a Member of the British House of Peers. And who knows but We may have Lord and Ladies Yrujo's from Spain and Lord and Ladies Mansfields from Great Britain? Aristocracy like Waterfowl, dives for ages and then rises with brighter Plumage. It is a Subtle Venom that diffuses itself unseen, over Oceans and Continents, and tryumphs over time. If I could prevent its deleterious influence I would put it all into "The Hole" of Calcutta: but as this is impossible as it is a Phœnix that rises again out of its own Ashes, I know no bet-ter Way than to chain it in a "Hole, by itself" and place a Watchfull Centinel on each Side of it.

An hundred other foreign Aristocracies have Sown and are Sow-ing their Seeds in this Country: and We have an Abundance of them Springing up in this Country not from Virtues and Talents So much as from Banks and Land Jobbing.      I am as ever      yours

JOHN ADAMS

RC (DLC); at foot of text: "President Jefferson"; endorsed by TJ as received 31 Dec. 1813 and so recorded in SJL. FC (Lb in MHi: Adams Papers).

RIDENDO DICERE VERUM, QUID VETAT: "what is to prevent one from telling the truth as he laughs," from Horace, *Satires*, 1.1.24–5 (Fairclough, *Horace: Satires, Epistles and Ars Poetica*, 6–7). Sarah Bowdoin Dearborn's

FATHER IN LAW, James Bowdoin (1726–90), was governor of Massachu-setts, 1785–87 (*ANB*). FANTASSINS: "foot soldiers" (*OED*). SOTTISES: "non-sense; foolishness." NORADDIN: Nured-din, sultan of Syria and Egypt.

To avoid extinction IN THE MALE LINE, two nephews of James Bowdoin (1752–1811) adopted his surname: James Bowdoin Temple became James Temple Bowdoin in June 1805 and

James Bowdoin Winthrop dropped his last name in June 1813 (*List of persons whose names have been changed in Massachusetts. 1780–1883* [1885], 15–6, 27–8; *Some Account of the Bowdoin Family* [1887], 9–15).

TJ appointed a Bowdoin COUSIN, George W. Erving, to several diplomatic posts during his presidency (*DAB*). William Alexander, claimant to the title of Lord Stirling (STERLING), served as a major general in the Continental army (*ANB*). More than one hundred British prisoners of war suffocated in the Black Hole of CALCUTTA in 1756 (Robert K. Webb, *Modern England* [1980], 70; memorial at Saint John's Church, Calcutta).

[1] Omitted opening quotation mark editorially supplied.
[2] Preceding eleven words not in FC.
[3] Omitted closing quotation mark editorially supplied.
[4] FC: "1680."
[5] FC: "devoted."
[6] FC: "answer."

# From John Devereux DeLacy

SIR                                    New York Dec[r] the 19th 1813

I take leave to enclose the report on the southern waters for your perusal and to subscribe myself most Respectfully

sir Your most Obed[t] Serv[t]                    JOHN DEV[x] DELACY

RC (DLC); dateline at foot of text; addressed: "Thomas Jefferson Esq[r] Monticello V[a]"; franked; postmarked New York, 19 Dec.; endorsed by TJ as received 31 Dec. 1813 and so recorded in SJL. Enclosure: Robert Fulton (working "from the surveys of John D. DeLacy"), *Report of the Practicability of Navigating with Steam Boats, on the Southern Waters of the United States, from the Chesapeak to the River St. Mary's, forming part of a line of Steam-Boat Communications, now establishing, from the northern extremity of Lake Champlain to East-Florida, a distance of fifteen hundred miles* (New York, 1813), in which Fulton stresses the "importance of cheap and rapid communication" to national prosperity (p. 3); argues that improved transportation will "encourage manufactures by a cheap conveyance of raw materials; promote and refine agriculture, increase population, and advance civilization throughout the whole range of our country—by giving to our citizens an easy intercourse, it will assimilate their customs, manners, and opinions, and bind them together as much by their habits as their interests" (pp. 3–4); suggests that American waters are uniquely suited to the use of steamboats; expresses a hope that Congress and the various state legislatures will take an interest in the issue; predicts that it will only cost about $40,000 to clear the shoals and cut all the portages between Norfolk and the Saint Marys River; describes the navigable waterways of North Carolina; provides a detailed summary of DeLacy's survey; and asks for friendly cooperation from affected states and landowners.

# From Sir Egerton Leigh

SIR                              Lexington–Virginia 19th Dec[r] 1813

The enclosed letter I received a few days back from D[r] Ramsay of Charleston S[o] Carolina. I am very sorry that I am prevented having the honor of personally delivering it to you by a severe Rheumatism or unfixed Gout which confines me to the house but hope in the Spring to be able to do myself the honor of paying my respects to you at Monticello

I have the honor to be Sir
Your Most Obedient Humble s^t

EGERTON LEIGH

RC (MoSHi: TJC-BC); dateline at foot of text; endorsed by TJ as received 5 Jan. 1814 and so recorded in SJL. Enclosure: David Ramsay to TJ, 3 Dec. 1813.

Sir Egerton Leigh (1762–1818), the son of a prominent South Carolina colonial official and Loyalist of the same name and grandnephew of Continental Congress president Henry Laurens, was educated at Westminster School in London, 1771–75, entered the British army at the age of fifteen, and saw service in and around New York City, 1780–81. He succeeded to the family baronetcy when his father died in the latter year. Leigh later married an English heiress and established households in London and Warwickshire. He also became an evangelical

preacher in the 1790s, helped to found a Baptist church in 1803, and served as pastor for its first eight years. Leigh apparently arrived in New York City in October 1812, was judged to be an enemy alien, and obtained his parole at Lexington sometime the following year. He was back in England when he died (*BDSCHR*, 2:396–9; George F. R. Barker and Alan H. Stenning, eds., *The Record of Old Westminsters* [1928], 2:567; Peter Wilson Coldham, *American Migrations, 1765–1799* [2000], 708–9; website of Rugby Baptist Church, Warwickshire, Eng., 13 Nov. 2009; Kenneth Scott, *British Aliens in the United States during the War of 1812* [1979], 150, 326; *Gentleman's Magazine, and Historical Chronicle* 100 [1830]: 179–80).

# From Patrick Gibson

SIR                                    Richmond 21^st Dec^r 1813

Your note for $2000– in bank falls due on the 28^th/31^st Ins^t to enable me to renew it I now send you inclosed a stamp for your signature which I will thank you to return to me in course of post, that is, so as to be here with the mail which arrives on Wednesday it had entirely escaped my recollection or I should have written to you sooner upon the subject—I have received three loads of your flour say 126 barrels 102 Sfine & 24 fine, the barrels are in very bad order, neither well made nor well hooped—There is at present no prospect of selling [at]¹ the nominal price, or rather that at which the last sale was made is 4½$ in fact no purchaser can now be met with, as it is impossible to get anything out now, the little trade we had with the West Indies being stopp'd by the Embargo—Respectfully I am

Your ob^t Serv^t                              PATRICK GIBSON

RC (ViU: TJP-ER); at head of text: "Thomas Jefferson Esq^re"; endorsed by TJ as received 24 Dec. 1813 and so recorded in SJL. Enclosure not found.

SFINE: superfine. On 17 Dec. 1813 Congress passed "An Act laying an EM-BARGO on all ships and vessels in the ports and harbours of the United States" (*U.S. Statutes at Large*, 3:88–93).

¹ Omitted word editorially supplied.

# From John Melish

DEAR SIR                                      Philadelphia 21 Dec^r <u>1813</u>

I beg leave to present you with a Copy of the military atlas, just published, which I hope will afford you a little amusement in your retirement, and be no unpleasing picture of the State of the arts in this City.—

With affectionate wishes for your welfare, and sentiments of veneration and respect—

I am Dear Sir Your obed. Ser^t                        JOHN MELISH

RC (DLC); at head of text: "Thomas Jefferson Esq"; endorsed by TJ as received 31 Dec. 1813 and so recorded in SJL. Enclosure: Melish, *A Military and Topographical Atlas of the United States; including the British Possessions & Florida . . . to which is added, A List of the Military Districts, A Register of the Army, and A List of the Navy of the United States* (Philadelphia, 1813; Poor, *Jefferson's Library*, 7 [no. 356]).

With this letter Melish also enclosed a prospectus for his "New General Atlas, And familiar Introduction to the Use of Maps," which he described as a revised and improved American edition of a work "originally published by Laurie and Whittle, very celebrated map engravers

in London." According to a newspaper advertisement, Melish's publication was to contain folio maps of the world as a whole, America, Europe, Asia, Africa, the United States, England, Scotland, Ireland, and an "Elementary Map"; as well as "a series of Statistical Tables, exhibiting at a general view, the Extent, Population, Government, Towns, Revenue, Religion, Produce, Trade, Manufactures, &c. of all the countries in the world." The atlas was to be engraved by John Vallance and H. S. Tanner, printed on high-quality paper, and bound with morocco backs, at a cost to subscribers of $5 if the maps were colored, with "a suitable deduction" if they were left uncolored (New York *Columbian*, 1 Sept. 1813).

# From William Champe Carter

DEAR SIR.                                      Culpeper Dec^r 22^d 1813

I have this moment received your letter of the 9^th ultimo, and have to express my regret at that of the 23 of September having never reached me. Had the wish of the parties for a meeting in order to run the lines between their respective estates been known at an earlier date, I should certainly have appointed for that purpose some day within the interval allowed in your letter as being convenient to yourself and C^olo Monroe.

The severity of the present season leads me to conclude that neither you nor he would choose to attend a survey sooner than the commencement of Spring, whether at that time I can be with you is uncertain, and indeed I consider my presence entirely unnecessary if the proposition, I have made to C^{olo} Monroe, to submit to your umpirage the adjustment of the divisional line,[1] be accepted, and as there can be on this subject no future collision between M^r Short and me, I flattered myself, that you would have no objection to decide the point in dispute. In case C^{olo} Monroe's view of the subject should prove correct, he agrees to receive from me, what I got for the land, with interest—I remain Dear Sir, with sentiments of esteem & respect

    yours truly                     WILLIAM CHAMPE CARTER

RC (ViW: TJP); endorsed by TJ as received 7 Jan. 1814 and so recorded in SJL. Enclosed in TJ to William Short, 9 Apr. 1816.

[1] Word interlined.

# To Jeremiah A. Goodman

DEAR SIR                    Monticello Dec. 22. 13.

Dick, Solomon and Philip are permitted to go and see their friends, and in returning will help to bring the hogs and beeves. I am in hopes you have procured the beds and given them to the women. in giving out their clothes I forgot the article of hats, which I give every other year; but as it will be more convenient to give about half one year and half another, we will give to the men only, this year, and to the women the next. be so good therefore as to get hats for all the men & lads who labour. we get them here at a dollar & 7/6. clover seed is now at 15.D. and may get higher. at this price we can only afford to sow mr Darnell's lower field which must be sowed at any price. I expect Gill's waggon will be with you about the latter end of the next week, and will bring, when she returns, the residue of the peas which Dick shall not bring. I shall be glad to learn by the return of the bearers what progress is made on the bear creek road and whether the tobacco is sold or got down.[1] were the weather to be very mild in Feb. or Mar. it is possible I might then pay you a visit. Accept my best wishes.

                                  TH: JEFFERSON

[*on address cover:*]

since writing the within Gill is taken very ill, which will delay his coming.                             TH:J.

RC (ICN); addressed: "M<sup>r</sup> Jeremiah A. Goodman Poplar Forest in Bedford by Dick, Solomon and Philip"; franked.

¹ Preceding nine words interlined.

## To Patrick Gibson

DEAR SIR                                    Monticello Dec. 24. 13.

While in Bedford I sent off two boat loads of flour, and a third was to follow, carrying in all between 140. & 150. barrels. we shall begin to send from hence immediately after the Christmas holidays. but we do not make half a crop here, nor more than half a one in Bedford. we shall soon see now whether the enemy mean to venture on riding in our bay through the winter. on that I suppose will much depend the price to be got. will not our merchants also venture as those of Baltimore do, to run thro them in dark and stormy nights?            I drew on you a few days ago for 25.D. in favor of D. Higginbotham, and must ask the favor of you to send me 75.D. by return of post to meet a paiment for corn of which I have been obliged to purchase to the amount of 8. or 900.D. which will fall due at different epochs from this to May 10. accept the assurance of my esteem & respect.

TH: JEFFERSON

PoC (DLC); at foot of text: "M<sup>r</sup> Gibson"; endorsed by TJ.

TJ borrowed $25 from David HIGGINBOTHAM on 21 Dec. 1813 and drew an order of Gibson & Jefferson for the same amount the following day "to replace the

above" (*MB*, 2:1295). On 4 Jan. 1814, one day after he had received the desired 75.D. from Gibson & Jefferson, TJ paid Richard Bruce $56.67 for twenty barrels of corn that Edmund Bacon had purchased on his behalf on 4 Oct. 1813 (*MB*, 2:1293, 1296).

## From Shotwell & Kinder

RESPECTED FRIEND                        New York 24th 12 mo 1813

Knowing the pleasure thou has in Improvements that promise Comfort to the Human Race; we have taken the liberty of sending thee a few yards of Cloth, sufficient for an over Coat which we beg thy acceptance of; it is the production of a great many Experiments, to render the Hair of Black Cattle from the Tanneries useful as Clothing, and various other Fabrics, and composed of one part common Wool and two parts Hair, we find that it can be worked with the same ease and facility as Wool alone, and believe it will prove equally durable; For Carpeting and some other uses we use no Wool—

We doubt not that at the present time, when our Country fears a want of similar Articles, it will be gratifying to thee to find that we have resources where they were the least looked for, and so extensive as to be of great importance to the American Family

We likewise hand thee a small pattern of one part Wool & three parts Hair, and are very Respectfully

Thy Assured Friends                    SHOTWELL & KINDER

RC (MoSHi: TJC-BC); beneath dateline and salutation: "Thomas Jefferson"; endorsed by TJ as received 4 Feb. 1814 and so recorded in SJL.

On 23 July 1813 William Shotwell (ca. 1760–1837) and Arthur Kinder (d. after May 1821), merchants in New York City, patented a process for making cloth from a mixture of cattle hair and wool. On 4 Nov. they took out two additional patents, one for spinning and the other for carding "the hair of neat or black cattle." The two men established the brokerage partnership of Shotwell & Kinder that same year and opened a factory to produce coarse cloth and carpeting in Rahway, New Jersey. With an initial capital of $400,000, the separately incorporated Patent Cloth Manufacturing Company was capable of producing 500 yards of their "Taurino" cloth daily. Shotwell's son and namesake joined the firm in 1815, two years prior to its dissolution by mutual consent. The elder Shotwell, a Quaker who had received several patents while visiting England during the first decade of the nineteenth century, was a longtime resident of New York City. He continued the busi-

ness as Shotwell & Son, brokers, into the mid-1820s (*List of Patents*, 127, 128; New York *Daily Advertiser*, 4 Mar. 1789; DNA: RG 29, CS, New York, 1790, 1810–30; London *Repertory of Arts, Manufactures, and Agriculture* 10 [1807]: 464; 14 [1809]: 217–21; *Longworth's New York Directory* [1813], 173, 281; [1821], 258; [1825], 382; *Baltimore Patriot & Evening Advertiser*, 28 Oct. 1813; New York *Commercial Advertiser*, 29 June 1815, 24 Apr., 30 June 1817; Washington *Daily National Intelligencer*, 13 Nov. 1815; *New-Bedford Mercury*, 25 Aug. 1837).

On this day Shotwell & Kinder sent a similar letter enclosing fabric samples to President James Madison (DLC: Madison Papers). A committee of the Society for the Promotion of Useful Arts in the State of New-York reported on 2 Mar. 1814 that Shotwell & Kinder's Taurino cloth was strong, moisture resistant, lighter than wool cloth, durable, and thus a viable substitute material for carpets and overcoats and for felting in paper manufacture (Society for the Promotion of Useful Arts in the State of New-York, *Transactions* 3 [1814]: 251–2).

# From John Adams

DEAR SIR                            Quincy Dec<sup>r</sup> 25<sup>th</sup> 1813

Answer my Letters at your Leisure. Give yourself no concern. I write as for a refuge and protection against Ennui.

The fundamental Principle of all Phylosophy and all Christianity is "Rejoice Always in all Things.[1] Be thankfull at all times for all good and all that We call evil." Will it not follow, that I ought to rejoice and be thankful that Priestley has lived? Aye! that Voltaire has lived?[+] That Gibbon has lived? That Hume has lived, though a conceited Scotchman? That Bolingbroke has lived, tho' a haughty arrogant Supercilious Dogmatist? that Burke and Johnson have lived, though Superstitious Slaves or Self deceiving Hypocrites both. Is it not laughable to hear Burke call Bolingbroke a Superficial Writer? To hear him ask "Who ever read him through?" Had I been present I would have answered him "I, I, myself, I have read him through, more than fifty years ago, and more than five times in my Life, and once within five years past. And in my opinion the epithat "Superficial" belongs to you and your Friend Johnson more than to him."[2] I might Say much more. But I believe Burke and Johnson to have been, as political[3] Christians, as Leo. 10$^{th}$.

I return to Priestley, though I have great Complaints against him for personal Injuries and Persecution, at the Same time that I forgive it all, and hope and pray that he may be pardoned for it all, above. D$^r$ Broklesby an intimate Friend and convivial Companion[4] of Johnson told me, that Johnson died in Agonies of Horror of Annihilation, and all the accounts We have of his death corroborate this account of Brocklesby. Dread of Annihilation? Dread of Nothing? A dread of Nothing I Should think would be no dread at all. Can there be any real Substantial rational fear of nothing? Were you on your deathbed, and in your last moments informed by demonstration or Revelation that you would cease to think and to feel, at your dissolution, Should you be terrified? you might be ashamed of yourself for having lived So long, to bear the proud Man's Contumely. you might be ashamed of your Maker, and compare him to a little Girl amusing herself her Brothers and Sisters by blowing Bubble[s] in Soap Sudds. you might compare him to Boys Sporting with Crakers and Rocketts: or to Men employed in making more artificial Fire Works; or to Men and Women at Farces[5] and operas, or Sadlers Wells Exploits; or to Politicians in their Intrigues; or to Heroes in their Butcheries; or to Popes in their Devilisms. But what Should you fear? Nothing. Emori nolo Sed me mortuum esse nihil estimo.

To return to Priestley. you could make a more luminous Book, than his upon "the Doctrines of Heathen Phylosophers compared with those of Revelation." Why has he not given Us a more Satisfac-

---

+ [*Note in margin:*] I Should have given my Reason for rejoicing in Voltaire &c. It is because I believe they have done more than Even Luther or Calvin, to lower the Tone of that proud Hierarchy that Shot itself up above the Clouds, and more to propagate religious Liberty than Calvin or Luther, or even lock.

tory Account of the Pythagorean Phylosophy and Theology? He barely names Ocellus, who lived long before Plato. His Treatise of Kings and Monarchy has been destroyed, I conjecture by Platonic Phylosophers, Platonic Jews or Christians, or by fraudulent Republicans or Despots. His Treatise of "The Universe"[6] has been preserved. He labours to prove the Eternity of the World. The Marquiss D'Argens translated it, in all its noble Simplicity. The Abby Batteux has Since given another translation. D'Argens not only explains the Text, but Sheds more light upon the antient Systems. His remarks are So many Treatisses, which devellope the concatenation of antient opinions. The most essential Ideas of the Theology, of the Physicks and of the Morality of the antients are clearly explained: and their different Doctrines, compared with one another, and with the modern discoveries. I wish I owned this Book and 100,000 more that I want every day, now when I am almost incapable of making any Use of them. No doubt he informs Us that Pythagoras was a great Traveller

Priestley barely mentions Timæus: but it does not appear that he had read him. Why has he not given Us an Account of him and his Book? He was before Plato and gave him the Idea of his Timæus, and much more of his Phylosophy. After his Master he maintained the existence of Matter: that Matter was capable of receiving all Sorts of forms: that a moving Power agitated[7] all the Parts of it: and that an Intelligence directed the moving Power; that this Intelligence produced a regular and harmonious World. This Intelligence had Seen a Plan, an <u>Idea</u> (Logos) in conformity to which, it wrought, and without which it would not have known what it was about, nor what it wanted to do. This Plan was the <u>Idea</u>, Image or Model, which had represented, to the Supream Intelligence, the World before it existed, which had directed it, in its Action upon the moving Power, and which it contemplated in forming the Elements the Bodies and the World. This Model was distinguished from The Intelligence which produced the World as the Architect is from his plans. He divided, The productive Cause of the World, into a Spirit, which directed the moving Force, and into an Image, which determined it in the choice of the directions which it gave to the moving Force, and the forms which it gave to matter.

I wonder that Priestley has overlooked this because it is the Same Phylosophy with Plato's and would have Shewn that the Pythagorean[8] as well as the Platonic Phylosophers probably concurred in the fabrication of the Christian Trinity. Priestley mentions the name of Archytas, but does not appear to have read him; tho he was a

Sucessor of Pythagoras, and a great Mathematician, a great Statesman and a great General. John Gram a learned and honourable Dane
has given a handsome Edition of his Works with a latin translation,
and an ample Account of his Life and Writings. Saleucus The Leg-
islator of Locris and Charondas of Sybaris were Disciples of Pythagoras, and both celebrated to immortality for the Wisdom of their
Laws, 500 years before Christ. Why are those Laws lost? I Say the
Spirit of Party has destroyed them. civil, political and ecclesiastical
Bigotry. Despotical, monarchical aristocratical and democratical
Fury, have all been employed in this Work of destruction of every
Thing that could give Us true light and a clear insight of Antiquity.
For every One of these Parties, when possessed of Power, or when
they have been Undermost and Struggling to get Uppermost, has
been equally prone to every Species of fraud and Violence, and
Usurpation.

Why has not Priestley mentioned These Legislators? The Pream-
ble to the Laws of Zaleucus, which is all that remains, is as orthodox
Christian Theology as Priestleys: and Christian Benevolence and forgiveness of Injuries almost as clearly expressed.

Priestley ought to have done impartial Justice to Phylosophy and
Phylosophers. Phylosophy which is the result of Reason, is the first,
the original Revelation of The Creator to his Creature, Man. When
this Revelation is clear and certain, by Intuition or necesary Induction, no Subsequent Revelation Supported by Prophecies or Miracles
can Supercede it. Phylosophy is not only the love of Wisdom, but the
Science of the Universe and its Cause. There is, there was and there
will be but one Master of Philosophy in the Universe. Portions of it,
in different degrees are revealed to Creatures. Phylosophy looks with
an impartial Eye on all terrestrial religions. I have examined all, as
well as my narrow Sphere, my Streightened means and my busy Life
would allow me; and the result is, that the Bible is the best book in
the World. It contains more of my little Phylosophy than all the Libraries I have Seen: and Such Parts of it as I cannot reconcile to my
little Phylosophy I postpone for future Investigation.

Priestley ought to have given Us a Sketch, of the Religion and
Morals of Zoroaster of Sanchoniathon of Confucius, and all the
Founders of Religions before Christ, whose Superiority, would from
Such a comparison have appeared the more transcendant.

Priestley ought to have told Us, that Pythagoras passed twenty
Years, in his Travels in India, in Egypt, in Chaldea, perhaps in
Sodom and Gomorrah, Tyre and Sydon. He ought to have told Us

that in India he conversed with the Brakmans and read the Shasta, 5000 years old, written in the Language of the Sacred Sanscrists with the elegance and Sentiments of Plato. Where is to be found Theology more orthodox or Phylosophy more profound than in the Introduction to the Shasta? "God is one, creator of all, Universal Sphere, without beginning, without End. God governs all the Creation by a general Providence, resulting from his eternal designs. — Search not the Essence and the nature of the Eternal, who is one; your research will be vain and presumptuous. It is enough that, day by day, and night by night, you adore his Power, his Wisdom and his Goodness, in his Works.[9] The Eternal willed, in the[10] fullness of time, to communicate of his Essence and of his Splendor, to Beings capable of perceiving it. They as yet existed not. The Eternal willed, and they were. He created Birma, Vitsnow, and Sib." These Doctrines, Sublime if ever there were any Sublime, Pythagoras learned in India and taught them to Zaleucus and his other disciples. He there learned also his Metempsychosis, but this never was popular, never made much progress in Greece or Italy, or any other Country besides India and Tartary, the Region of the Grand immortal Lama: And how does this differ, from the Possessions of Demons in Greece and Rome, from the Demon of Socrates[11] from the Worship of Cows and Crocodiles in Egypt and elsewhere. After migrating through[12] various Animals from Elephants to Serpents according to their behaviour, Souls that at last behaved well became Men and Women, and then if they were good, they went to Heaven. All ended in Heaven if they became virtuous. Who can wonder at the Widow of Malabar. Where is the Lady, who if her[13] faith were without doubt, that She Should go to Heaven with her Husband on the one, or migrate into a Toad or a Waspe on the other, would not lay down on the Pile and Set fire to the Fuel?

Modifications and disguises of the Metempsichosis had crept into Egypt and Greece and Rome and other Countries. Have you read Farmer on the Dæmons and Possessions of the New Testament?

According to the Shasta Moisazor, with his Companions rebelled against the Eternal, and were precipitated, down to Ondero, the region of Darkness. Do you know any thing of the Prophecy of Enoch? Can you give me a Comment on the 6th the 9th the 14th Verses of the Epistle of Jude?

If I am not weary of writing, I am Sure you must be of reading Such incoherent[14] rattle. I will not persecute you So Severely in future, if I can help it.     So farewell     JOHN ADAMS

RC (DLC); edge chipped, with loss from one word supplied from FC; at foot of text: "President Jefferson"; endorsed by TJ as received 14 Jan. 1814 and so recorded in SJL. FC (Lb in MHi: Adams Papers).

Edmund Burke famously asked "Who now reads Bolingbroke? WHO EVER READ HIM THROUGH?" in his *Reflections on the Revolution in France* (London, 1790), 133. SADLERS WELLS was one of London's oldest theaters (Dennis Arundell, *The Story of Sadler's Wells, 1683–1964* [1965]). EMORI NOLO . . . NIHIL ESTIMO: "Dying I shun: of being dead I nothing reck" (Cicero, *Tusculan Disputations*, 1.8.15, in *Cicero*, trans. John E. King, Loeb Classical Library [1927; repr. 1971], 20–1). Jean Baptiste de Boyer, marquis d'Argens, discussed THE ANTIENT SYSTEMS in *Ocellus Lucanus en grec et en françois avec Des Dissertations sur les Principales Questions de la Metaphisique, de la Phisique, & de la Morale des anciens* (Berlin, 1762; Poor, *Jefferson's Library*, 8 [no. 418]). SALEUCUS: Zaleucus. A shastra (SHASTA) is any sacred Hindu text (*OED*). Antoine Marin Le Mierre's play, THE WIDOW OF MALABAR (*La Veuve du Mal-*

*abar*), was first produced in Paris in 1770 (H. Gourdon de Genouillac, *Paris a travers les siècles* [1880], 3:340). The work by Hugh FARMER was *An Essay on the Demoniacs of the New Testament* (London, 1775). JUDE seems to quote from the apocryphal Book of Enoch in the Bible, Jude 14–5.

[1] Superfluous closing quotation mark editorially omitted.
[2] Omitted closing quotation mark editorially supplied.
[3] RC: "polilitical." FC: "political."
[4] Preceding three words interlined.
[5] FC: "Fares."
[6] Omitted closing quotation mark editorially supplied.
[7] RC: "agitatated." FC: "agitate."
[8] Word interlined in place of "Peripatetick."
[9] Superfluous closing quotation mark editorially omitted.
[10] Adams here canceled "plenitude of his Power."
[11] Preceding five words interlined.
[12] RC and FC: "throw."
[13] RC: "he." FC: "her."
[14] RC: "inchohent." FC: "inchoherent."

# To Mary Lewis

DEAR MADAM                                    Monticello Dec. 25. 13.

The news of the embargo reached me yesterday. this rendering the hope of getting money for our crop more than doubtful, makes it necessary to avoid new money engagements. I am therefore obliged to decline taking the cask of your good old brandy which you were so kind as to offer. the same circumstance affects deeply the question on which you consulted me, whether you ought to take 3/9 for your wheat. I am really not now able to give an opinion. I will take the liberty of[1] sending for some barrels of apples; and if a basket of them can now be sent by the bearer they will be acceptable[2] as accomodated to the season of mince pies. Accept the assurance of my friendship & respect                                    TH: JEFFERSON

PoC (MHi); at foot of text: "M^rs Lewis"; endorsed by TJ.

[1] TJ here canceled "apply."
[2] TJ here canceled "and enable us."

# To Charles Clay

Dear Sir                                    Monticello Dec. 28. 13.

Learning that mr Forber, one of those who have erected carding machines for us, was in the neighborhood, I asked the favor of him to call on me. he did so yesterday and agrees to go up to you in the 1st or 2d week of January. he tells me his price for a wool-carding machine is 500.D. & a Cotton carder 600.D. these prices being higher than I had supposed, and perhaps than I suggested to you, I have thought it advisable to state them to you, that should they be beyond the expence you meant to incur, you might save yourself the embarrasment of his visit by immediately countermanding it; as it is possible might be done by mail in time. Your's with all friendship

                                            Th: Jefferson

RC (ViU: TJP); at foot of text: "Mr Clay." PoC (DLC); endorsed by TJ.


# From Charles Willson Peale

Dear Sir                                Belfield December 28th 1813.

It is long indeed since[1] I have intended to answer your letter of April 17., at first I wished to finish my Corn-fields according to your directions, and after that I wanted to hear the observations of my Neighbours—and I must say that every one with whom I have conversed acknowledge the improvment of making hilly ground equally advantagous as level fields. your letter came to me at the proper Moment for me to make the experiment on some of my hills, though none of my land is very hilly—even my Garden which is on the side of a hill has received advantage by your lesson—about 3 years past I experienced the disadvantage of having furrows down hill, the land was considerably washed & the grain suffered by the floods of Rain. I was led to plow in that direction by the oppinion of Mr Job Roberts (author of the Penna farmer) who directed that Corn would be best planted North & South, by which he said the Sun would have greater access to the bottom of the Corn—The loss I sustained in the field above alluded to, brought me to think on what he had said, when I was satisfied that Corn planted East & west would have a better chance of the benefits of the Sun, as the Sun would shine between the rows both in the morning and evening, and the meridian Sun would not be intirely lost in our longest days.[2]

I am inclined to believe that my Corn has been improvd by this culture, for I have a greater quantity this year than on former years, if I was to make the estimate of the proportion of a$^{rs}$ planted each year, I could thus speak with greater certainty, but this one thing speaks to the purpose, I bought a wire-corn-sive of M$^r$ Nathan Sellers, and I think he has been careful to make such sives of the best size—on tryal of this Sieve I find my Corn will not pass through it, except the small grains taken from the ends of the Cobs—Perhaps the kind of Corn which I have choosen to plant may be generally of larger grain than the Gourd seed-corn—my Corn is the hard yellow corn— I have not yet tryed my Corn which I have grown[3] for Homony, which is white and flinty.

My attention has been engaged in making fences, and as far as yet that I have made tryal, it appears very plain that Hedges & ditches is not only the best kind of fence, but also, that they can be made nearly as cheap as the Post & rail fence, and by making a good ditch that they are defence against any kind of Cattle in the first year—It has been said that we loose some ground by the ditch, if that is a small loss, the obtaining a permanant fence makes up fully for that loss. Some Gentlemen have told me that I could not afford to make such fences, that in Europe where labour is so much cheaper, that they complain of the expence—It appears to strike me that the people in Europe do not manage the business properly, probably they depend on the Spade in making their ditches—My Method is to use my strongest plow, drawn by a p$^r$ of oxen with two horses to brake up the Soil, this is soon thrown up on the bank with shovels, and when the ditch is deepened, lastly we use a Single Horse plow, by this method, much labour is saved—but if the land is stoney, in such places we cannot have the full benefit of the plow. That many of my countrymen have not succeeded with their thorns is I believe owing to their neglect of weeding & dressing in the first 2 or 3 years after planting them—This is only the 3$^d$ year since I began, and some of my Thorns will be in 2 or 3 years more a complete fence with small ditches. It appears to me that the New Castle Thorn will make a better fence than the Virginia Thorn, as the spines are strong and large—and the Thorn is more bushy, That of Virginia grows fast, but spiring, to take benifit from its quicker groath we should cut it more freequently, I believe it[4] must be trimed twice in the year, early in the spring and again in midsummer. Thorn fences are indispensably necessary in the Vicinity of large Manufactories; to keep the people belonging to those factories from trespassing on our fields, in crossing our farms by every direction they are permited to go[5]—The Neighbourhood of Germantown promises to become the seat of much Manufactories—

The breeding of Sheep seems to engross much of the intentions of merchantile men as well as farmers, it appears to me as something of <u>mania</u>, at least the profit they speak of[6] must be exagerated—My Thorn fences must get their necessary groath before I shall attemp keeping any sheep—an increase of Manufatories no Doubt will call for much wool, and we are going so fast into making cloath as well as Cotton goods that should the war continue any length of time it will probably induce monied men to employ their funds in establish[g] manufatories—My two youngest Boys I have put in a Manufactory of machine making, the elder of them has considerable mechanic talents, He will in one year become master of all that is necessary to enable him to undertake that business, yet my view in puting Him[7] into such a manufactory was that he might qualify himself to undertake the management of the Cotton business, and knowing how to make the machines, will give an advantage of knowledge to keep his machines[8] in the best order.

My labour on the farm is not so active as you may imagine, occasionally I give my aid, but a great part of my time is imployed in making Machinery at my Mill, and it being a new work to me, has given me more labour than necessary, but accomplishing the several objects undertaken gives me content. I made a Thrashing Machine from a description given me by a mill-wright, It is the Scotch invention; a Drum with dashers to strike off the grain that is carried forward between fluted rollers, The sheaves carried to the Rollers in the manner of the carding machine i.e. a cloth mooving on two rollers—The whole of the moovment of this machine is perform'd by Straps—It was some time before I could determine the best proportion of moovements—at present I have make the Drum which has 6 dashers to give about 1000 strokes in a minute, the feeders give about $\frac{3}{4}$ Inch of length of the grain to each stroke. The Straw is considerably broken—I have seen another method, a Patent machine. It is also with a Drum, but with its surface studed with pins, the Grain passes between the Drum and an Iron bar, this bar is mooved by screws to give it a greater or less distance from the Drum—This Machine does not brake the Straw; it comes out flattened. I am told that it thrashes fast, for a long time I had my doubts whether I should not get this kind of Machine, but from what I have heard and seen of the Machine, I judge that the person who feeds it must be very careful in not feeding too fast, or the Machine would be liable to be stoped by choaking and thus injure the machinery—I cannot be a proper judge as I have not yet seen its opperation.[9]

I have a Machine for getting out clover seed, the invention of

Jonathan Roberts, who paid for a patent many years past, but would not let any person see this Machine, not even his children, after his death I bought his Machine, It is on the principle of a Coffee mill; the first he made was a conic cylinder whether he found it required more power than his Horse could give to work it, or whether the heads did not pass through it sufficiently quick, I have not been able to learn, but he substituted a perpendicular cylinder with the same kind of Gores as in the other, this Cylinder considerably smaller in the Diameter than his conic cylinder. This Machine seems to turn out the husk well broken—There was no sieves or fans, these I have added, and hope I shall get the seed pretty clean, which I find is not easily done, even with the use of the Common wheat Fan & screenes.[10]

I have attempted to make a Machine to take off the heads of Clover instead of moowing to get the seed—low Truck-wheels; the points are plates of Steel, they take off the heads with ease, but I found that the grass taken with them clogged the teeth, and prevents the heads from falling 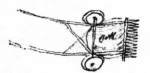 into the cloath back of them, I must devise some method to clear the teeth, which if I can accomplish, will make it a useful machine, if the heads can be taken off clear of the straw, the labour of thrashing will be saved[11]—For the farmers own use, perhaps simply thrashing of serving[12] the clover in the heads may very well answer the purpose— but if he wants seed for sale, it must be well cleaned—The dust attending the cleaning of Clover-seed is very offensive to the Lunges. I have heard that the men who work at Clover mills receive double wages in Lancaster.

In churning[13] of Butter by the mill, I find that a quick motion will make the best butter, but instantly the butter is come, it must be gathered very Slow. I see a piece in the news paper advising the boiling of the Cream, this method I tryed and found that it injured the butter, making it curdly, or in small lumps—and the butter took longer time before it came, the reverse of what the author said.[14]

I have sundry machines in the Mill to aid the farmers labour. Instead of feeding with whole corn, we grind it, which also gives us good small homoney, this I consider more wholesome than when fine to make <u>mush</u> of it.

Four stampers falling close togather in a Morter, beats us excellent Homony. a strong and hearty food, the liquor good for laying in Women &c.[15] Various stones for grinding our tools is a great conveniency, yet I have seen some loss by it, the Men are too apt to grind their sythes and axes too thin, and thus soon wear them out.

Grinding my plaster is no saving,[16] the few tons used on one farm, may as well be ground elsewhere[17] as to have the mill-stones cleaned & picked over again. but if a Machine I have, had a pair of large Bullets the weight of which in pushing them round the Kettle would brake the plaster fine, there would not be much trouble to put in, & take out the plaster when ground, I intend to make tryal as soon as I can purchase a p$^r$ 42[18] w Balls. I cannot perfectly reconsile to my Idea's the great benefit of the use of Plaster, and I follow the advice of others whose experiance they says is sufficient proof—I have had good crops of Hay, clover especially where I have used the plaster freely. If a good manure, it is certainly a cheap kind, compared to the cost of purchasing Stable manure.

Saving of labour may not be of any importance in some instances in Virginea, where there are many Negroes, whose time should be filled up in the evenings and in bad weather: such as the shelling of Corn, and this may also be done expediciously by treading out with Horses—but as I have nothing to write for your amusement, so likely to be acceptable as descriptions of Machines—and even in this I have but a small chance of giving any thing new to you.        Perhaps you have seen machines for shelling Corn—one was invented several years past & shewn at the Philosophical Society, it was a Cylinder of 20 Inches Diameter about 2 feet long—and studed with Iron points projecting about $\frac{1}{4}$ of an Inch, this Barrel had one half of it enclosed in a semi circular box with gratings at the bottom—to let the Corn through, I dont remember that there was any pins on the inner side of said Box, the distance of the Cylinder from the box just allowed the corn to enter, & the cob was thrown out on the opposite side, it was proposed that springs should admit the Cylinder to raise to take the largest Ears of Corn,—I have a Machine which I use by a strap from the Drum at the Mill, but which farmers in common drive by a treaddle.

It is 20 Inches Diameter & 2 feet long, a solid piece of White oak. studed with pieces of Iron drove in a small degree in spiral lines; the shape of these pins ▽ projecting $\frac{1}{4}$ Inch, each angle is about one Inch long—next is a small roller of $2\frac{1}{2}$ Inches Diam: with pins in spiral lines. The small roller is turned by a band from a Pully on the end of the large roller. on the frame below the small roller, is an Iron plate on the inside and Iron pieces[19] like those in the large roller drove in an oblike direction ⟶ a handle is put to the West end of the little roller to lift it when throwing the Corn between it & the large roller, by the spiral pins the Corn cobs is thrown out at the West end, as fast as the Ears of Corn is thrown in, so fast it is shelled; about 12 Bushels of Ears may with ease be shelled in an hour.[20]

For cutting of Straw I have a machine an English Invention, It has a Curved knife on a wheel, the axis of which has a crank to lift up and press down a board to compact the straw which is brought forward by cords round the axis of a ratchet wheel that has the forked rake fastened to the other ends of the Cords—It appears to me that this is an excellent Cutting box, better than most that has come within my knowledge—If I thought it had not come within your notice, I would have given you a Sketch with more particular description of it.[21]

I remember being present with you When Lord Dunmore shewed us a p[r] of Elks—I have a male that I have keept in an inclosure upwards of 3 years, his first horns was a single prong about one foot long, he drops His horns in the last week in April, or the first of May yearly, each year they are increased in size, and having heard of a p[r] of their Horns being full 6 feet long, I am induced to keep this Animal living to see to what length he will acquire horns, as to their having a branch increase for each year, it has no credit with me, & has no better foundation than the yearly increase of a rattle with the Rattle-Viper.

When your Son in Law M[r] Randolph was in Philadelphia lately, I was indisposed with a Diarrhaea, or I should have waited on him, and I was told that he intended to come to see me at my farm, It[22] would have been highly gratifying to me to see so distinguishd a farmer, on my place, especially the father of Thomas Jefferson.

Jan[y] 15th—14. While writing the foregoing, a thought came into my head that I could make a machine that might save labour and also wood, in cutting down Trees &c, and I posponed the finishing of this Scrawl in order to make a Model for tryal, and then to give you a sketch of it After digesting in my mind the several parts of the frame work in order to simplify[23] and meet all the different situations it might be placed in for use, I described the principle to 2 or 3 of my ingenous mechanical friends for their opinion of practibility and power of such a machine. and I had but little encouragement from them to proceed—My D[r] Sir by this you will find that I am not ashamed to shew any of my weaknesses; that I like to find out my irrors, and I hope that I am always willing to correct them. I write with the desire to give you a few moments of amusement, to give advantage I cannot expect. To proceed, suppose a Pendulum of 10 feet long, the Bob a 56 weight. a slight sketch will illustrate the principle, To the axis of the Pendulum is a fork 2 feet long, a piece of scant-ling with a pivot to moove in that fork by the swinging of the Pendulum, its joint to fixture of the frame at (a) which might also be a movable joint to give the Saw a greater or lesser motion, the piece of timber—connected to 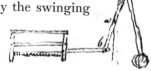 the Saw has a joint at (b). The Saw keept steady by a frame, which frame may be turned to place the Saw horisontally, in which case the Saw might[24] be drawn forward by a weight over a Pully. This Saw being in a frame may be of small size, of coarse will cut with less labour than one large and making a wider cut.

Speaking of my machine to a friend He thought my Pendulum would moove with great power as he had seen heavy logs that were bored to convey Water at his Mill, drove one into the other by means of a heavy Block suspended by a rope and mooved like a Pendulum to drive one log into the other.        I made a model of my Machine of the 4th part of the size I proposed for use, and on tryal of it I found that a machine of such construction would require immence strength about the axis of the Pendulum, its fork, and also in the frame to keep it sufficiently steady in use. And after all it is a question whether any power gained more than could be had by hand labour?

While writing this morning, my Son Rubens seeing the subject of this part of my letter, tells me that a Man living on the commons of Philaª has spent 2 or 3000$ in a plan of mooving Machinery by the power of a Pendulum of very great weight; that he first had two men to swing the Pendulum, and afterward added a fly-wheel with a crank to act on the Pendulum near the center of motion—had made a great quantity of wheels that were to be worked by his Pendulum power, and that many persons had conceived that this person had ac-complished a very important discovery. But after all, this Man can do nothing with all his labour and expence—

I have very often in like manner spent my time, labour & expence to no rail advantage, except that of amusing myself very innocently. It brings to my mind a sentiment I meet with last evening in reading the Memoirs of a young Lady, her words are, "happiness is a very common plant, a native of every soil; yet is some skill required in gathering it; for many poisonous weeds look like it, and deceive the unwary to their ruin." I wish you every happiness that can fall to the lot of man, and believe your Philosophy give you the powers to disreguard the blame sensure, or even applause of the multitude; an approving mind gives a sourse of perfect content.

I once more thank you for your desire to serve me and others by the example you desire me to make.

most affectionately yours                                    C W PEALE

RC (DLC); with marginal notations by TJ; endorsed by TJ as received 21 Jan. 1814 and so recorded in SJL. PoC (PPAmP: Peale Letterbook); bottom edge torn.

SPIRING: sprouting, shooting up into a stem or spire (*OED*). Peale's TWO YOUNGEST BOYS were Benjamin Franklin Peale (1795–1870) and Titian Ramsay Peale (1799–1885) (Peale, *Papers*, 5:xl). The SCOTCH INVENTION for threshing grain described by Peale was the handiwork of Andrew Meikle (*ODNB*). Virginia's last royal governor, John Murray, 4th Earl of Dunmore, had apparently exhibited a pair of ELKS to TJ and Peale in Williamsburg in May 1774 (Peale, *Papers*, vol. 2, pt. 1, p. 5n). TJ's grandson THOMAS JEFFERSON Randolph boarded with the Peale family, 1808–09 (*MB*). The quote HAPPINESS IS A VERY COMMON PLANT . . . AND DECEIVE THE UNWARY TO THEIR RUIN is from *Fragments in Prose and Verse, by Miss Elizabeth Smith, lately deceased. With some account of her Life and Character, by H. M. Bowdler* (Boston, 1810), 135.

[1] Manuscript: "simce."
[2] In RC to left of this paragraph TJ noted: "horiz^l ploughing."

[3] Reworked from "Sown."
[4] Manuscript: "is."
[5] In RC to left of this paragraph TJ noted: "hedges."
[6] Manuscript: "off."
[7] Reworked from "them."
[8] Manuscript: "machinees."
[9] In RC to left of this paragraph TJ noted: "threshing."
[10] In RC to left of this paragraph TJ noted: "clover seed."
[11] In RC to left of this paragraph TJ noted: "Gathering clov. seed."
[12] Thus in manuscript. Peale may have intended "or severing."
[13] Manuscript: "churming."
[14] In RC to left of this paragraph TJ noted: "butter."
[15] In RC to left of this paragraph TJ noted: "beating homony."
[16] Manuscript: "saying."
[17] Manuscript: "eslewere."
[18] Reworked from "40."
[19] Manuscript: "pices."
[20] In RC to left of this paragraph TJ noted: "Corn shelling."
[21] In RC to left of this paragraph TJ noted: "cutting straw."
[22] Manuscript: "I."
[23] Reworked from "simply."
[24] Word interlined in place of "must."

# From Patrick Gibson

SIR                                    Richmond 29th Dec[r] 1813

Your two favors of the 24th are received and agreeably to your desire I send you inclosed $75 in notes—no sale whatever for flour, the little wheat brought to market is purchased by the millers at 3/.— With great respect I am

Your ob[t] Serv[t]                                    PATRICK GIBSON

RC (ViU: TJP-ER); at head of text: "Thomas Jefferson Esq$^{re}$"; endorsed by TJ as a letter from Gibson & Jefferson received 3 Jan. 1814 and so recorded in SJL.

SJL records one letter from TJ to Gibson of 24 Dec. 1813, not TWO. The second document, not found, was most likely a brief note covering the return of the "stamp" that Gibson had sent for TJ's signature three days previously.

# To Philip Mazzei

Monticello Dec. 29. 1813.

The last letter I have recieved from you, my dear & antient friend, was of the 15$^{th}$ of Feb. 1811. that letter I answered two days after it's reciept, to wit, July 9. 1811. since which I have not heard from you. such an interval excites anxieties to learn that you continue in health. my health remains good; a diminution of strength being the principal indication of advancing years.

Since our last letters we have been forced by England into the war which has been so long raging. her Orders of council, which excluded us from the ocean, but on license and tribute to her, and took from us near 1000. vessels in a time of what she called peace, her impressment of between 6. and 7000. of our seamen, the Proclamation of her Prince regent that they never would repeal the Orders of council as to us, until France should have repealed her illegal decrees as to all the world, and the declaration of her minister to ours that no admissible precaution against the impressment of <u>our</u> seamen by her officers, other than their discretion, could be devised, obliged us at length to declare war. about the time of our declaration, she was forced, by the distresses of her manufactures and commerce, to issue a Palinodial Proclamation repealing her orders. this was unknown to us at the time of our Declaration. but the war, being commenced, is now continued for the 2$^d$ cause the impressment of our seamen. our 1$^{st}$ campaign of 1812 was unsuccesful through the treachery of the General who came first into contact with the enemy, and betrayed to them his army, fort and the country around it. this was the parent of all the subsequent misfortunes of the campaign, altho' immediately produced by the cowardice, carelessness or incompetence of other commanders; all new and untried men, all our officers of high grade in the revolutionary war, during 30. years of peace, having either died, or become superannuated. Scott died lately; and Starke the only surviving one I recollect, is past service. on the part of the enemy, all their successes, after the first which their money atchieved, were obtained by the immense body of Savages they engaged, and who under British direction, carried on the war in their usual way, massacring prisoners in cold blood & after capitulation, & tomahawking and scalping women and children on our frontiers.

In our 2$^d$ campaign,[1] altho' we have not done all to which our force was adequate, we have done much. we have taken possession of all Upper Canada, except the single post of Kingston, at it's lower extremity.          on the Ocean where our force consists only of a few frigates & smaller vessels, in 6. or 7. engagements of vessel to vessel of equal force, or very nearly so, we have captured their vessel in every instance but one. three of their frigates have been taken by us, & one only of ours by them. in a remarkable action on Lake Erie between about 8. or 10. vessels of a side, large and small from ships down to gunboats, the greater number of guns and men being on their side, we took their whole squadron, not a vessel or a man escaping. on this state of things our 3$^d$ campaign will open.          the President's message at the meeting of the present session of Congress will give you a more detailed account of our proceedings. knowing your affections for this country, & your anxieties for it's welfare, I have thought this summary view of our war and it's events would be acceptable. in the mean time the war has turned most of our commercial capital to manufactures. the rapidity of their growth is unexampled. we have already probably a million of spindles engaged in spinning cotton & wool, which will clothe sufficiently our 8. millions of people, & they are multiplying daily. we are getting the Spinning machines into all our farm houses. I have near 100. spindles in operation for clothing our own family. the Merino sheep are spreading over the continent and thrive well. we make as good broad cloth now in our larger manufactories as the best English; and come peace when it may, we shall return to them only for the finest & most exquisite manufactures. indeed I consider the most fatal consequence of this war to England to be the[2] transfer it has occasioned of her art in manufacturing into other countries. from this, and her impending bankruptcy, future history will have to trace her[3] decline and fall as a great power. exertions beyond her strength, and expences beyond her means, as in the case of private individuals, have given her a shortlived blaze, which must sink her the sooner to her original level.

Now as to the remains of your affairs here. I have the happiness to inform you that I have at length been able to make sale of your house and lot in Richmond for 6342 Dollars 21 cents, clear of the expences of sale, bearing an interest of 6. per cent from the 14$^{th}$ of July last. the close blockade of our ports by the enemy, a recent embargo by ourselves and the consequent suspension of our commerce and intercourse with all nations would have rendered the remittance of the price impracticable, had I supposed it your wish. but the higher interest it bears with us, and a belief that your views are not entirely withdrawn from this country would have alone prevented my displacing it until your special orders. in the mean time the same obstructions to our commerce render it a convenience to retain it for a while in my own hands. it shall be placed on landed security so as to be entirely safe, and if you desire it, the interest shall be remitted to you annually and regularly, being of 380. dollars a year. the principal sum being so considerable, a proportionable time must probably be allowed, say of one and two years, when it's remittance is called for. since the execution of the deed to the purchaser, in which Edmund Randolph joined me, he has died, having long been in a state which rendered it rather desirable for himself and his friends. our friend T. Lomax had paid this debt to nature a year or two before. I recollect no other death interesting to you which has happened since the date of my last letter. Derieux and his wife are living. they move often from place to place to seek relief from their distresses. I believe they have 10. or 12. children. he is now bar-keeper to a tavern in Richmond, and she keeping a little school in Petersburg. he sollicited me to mention him to you and that any crumbs from your property here would help him to subsist.

Let me hear from you as soon as you can, being anxious to know that you are well; and tendering to your family any services I can ever render them, with the assurances of my attachment and respect, accept for yourself those of my constant & affectionate friendship.

TH: JEFFERSON

RC (DLC: Mazzei Papers); holes in manuscript, with missing text supplied from PoC; at foot of text: "Philip Mazzei esquire." PoC (DLC); endorsed by TJ. Tr (DLC: Mazzei Papers); in Italian; in Mazzei's hand. Tr (NhD: Ticknor Autograph Collection); in Italian; in Mazzei's hand. Tr (ItF); in Italian. Enclosed in TJ to David Bailie Warden, 29 Dec. 1813, and TJ to John Graham, 6 Jan. 1814.

The American GENERAL WHO CAME FIRST INTO CONTACT WITH THE ENEMY was William Hull. Oliver Hazard Perry's REMARKABLE ACTION ON LAKE ERIE took place on 10 Sept. 1813 (*ANB*). The PURCHASER of Mazzei's house and lot in Richmond was Thomas Taylor.

[1] Manuscript: "campain."
[2] Manuscript: "the the."
[3] TJ here canceled "deposition."

# To David Bailie Warden

DEAR SIR                                        Monticello Dec. 29. 13.

I need much of your indulgence for the want of punctuality in acknoleging the reciept of your several favors. but my situation is so far
removed from the seaport towns, that no notice of vessels about to
sail ever reminds me of the duty of making these acknolegements;
and so they lie over from month to month, until my own conscience
is at length smitten by the delay. even at this moment I know not how
my letters are to go, shut up by an embargo law of our own, enforced
by the blockade of our enemy. I must wait however no longer, but
commit my letter to the department of state, and trust to their finding
some conveyance with their own dispatches.

I will begin with the acknolegement of your letters of Dec. 10. 11.
Nov. 1. 12. & Apr. 1. 13. the second of these, which was not recieved
till Sep. last, ($10\frac{1}{2}$ months after date) mentions your having written
me 4. letters preceding. of these, one only (that of Dec. 10. 11) ever
came to hand. with that I recieved the works of M. Tracy, Peuchet's[1]
Statistique, and the Atlas of Le Sage for mrs Randolph. the copy of
Toulongeon, mentioned in the letter of Nov. 1. 12.[2] to have been sent
by the Hornet, was not recieved. but the Voyage de Rochon, by D$^r$
Barraud, and the box of seeds from M. Thouin came safely. the seeds
were delivered to mr M$^c$Mahon of Philadelphia, as the most likely
person to preserve and distribute them. D$^r$ Stevens forwarded safely
the Codes de France, and mr Hasler the second copy of Toulongeon
you were so kind as to send, as mentioned in your letter of last April.
the box of seeds therein mentioned from M. Thouin committed to the
Bellona, I presume to have been captured, as I have never heard of it.
this is a faithful statement of the acknolegements I owe to you, and I
pray you to be assured I feel them most sensibly, and tender my
thanks with gratitude: and on the observation, in your last, that time
had not permitted you to have Toulongeon bound, permit me to pray
the omission of that circumstance on your favors, not only as unnec-
essarily increasing the burthen on you, but as they come lighter &
safer by the mail when unbound.

The President's message at the meeting of Congress, which you
will have recieved before you do this, has given[3] you a succinct and
correct history of our last campaign. we were very late in getting into
motion, for the main object, that of possessing ourselves of the
Canadas, as low as Montreal; and after we got into motion, a series of
such tempestuous weather as heaven never sent before retarded our
movements so as to leave barely the time possible for taking Mon-

treal. enough however remained. but when our main body had reached Lake S^t Francis, from whence in 3. or 4. days it would have been at Montreal, a disobedience of orders by a general with the body he had ashore, to meet at the point prescribed, suddenly arrested the enterprise, and closed our well grounded hopes of compleating this season the conquest of the country to that point. our army retired into Winter quarters near the place, deeply mortified with the disappointment in the object which was to have satisfied them for their unparalleled sufferings from the rigors of the climate and season. the enemy retains therefore, for the winter, Montreal & Kingston. all these evils have flowed from the original treachery of Hull, who is shortly to undergo the trial & punishment due to his crime. but all could have been speedily remedied, had not the resources of the Eastern states been witheld. the undertaking fell of course on those of the Middle & Southern states, most remote from the scene of action, and our exclusion from the water still increased the delays, and have finally prevented our obtaining for the present all we might have obtained. much however has been effected by our insulating the British from their savage allies, to whom alone, and not at all to themselves they are indebted for every success they have obtained. this unfortunate race, whom we had been taking so much pains to save and to civilize, have by their unexpected desertion and ferocious barbarities justified extermination, and now await our decision on their fate. the Creeks too on our Southern border, for whom we had done more than for any other tribe, have acted the same part (tho' not the whole of them) and have already paid their defection with the flower of their warriors. they will probably submit on the condition of removing to such new settlements beyond the Missisipi as we shall assign them.          our naval atchievements will shew what our men are when they have officers to command them who understand their business: and they have taught to the world the precious truth that the English can be beaten on their peculiar element with equal force. it is in vain that they endeavor, by exaggerating the force of our vessels, underrating that of their own, and otherwise lying in every form, to conceal the superiority we have displayed. it is equally vain for them to practise the same arts on the land. their lying victories in Canada are visibly driving them out of it; as, in the last war it was seen that they conquered themselves out of the continent. their accounts alone can find their way to the European nations, no channel being open to ours. but observation of their successive positions after every pretended victory will sufficiently shew on which side it really was.

[ 91 ]

Our embargo, if we can enforce it, will greatly increase their difficulties, both here and in Europe; and the prevailing spirit will, I think enforce it at the point of the bayonet. the game playing by a few base & cunning leaders in Massachusets, however degrading to the state, is a compleat dupery of the English. if the question of separation, with which they are tantalising the English were ever to be proposed to the people of that state not one tenth even of the federalists would countenance it. yet by decieving the enemy on this head they keep themselves unblockaded and their trade little disturbed.

We are all anxiety to learn the issue of the campaign in Europe. if the French arms are so far succesful as to enable the Emperor to close the Baltic, and compleatly exclude British manufactures from Europe, as they are from America, her starving manufacturers and bankrupt merchants must do the work of us all, and throw her thousand armed ships on her own resources, which would afford them but a short lived subsistence.

Our manufactures are spreading with a rapidity which could not have been expected. the whole capital of our merchants diverted from commerce turns of necessity into the channel of manufactures. the spinning machines are getting into every farmhouse, and I think we cannot be far short of a million of spindles at work, which will fully clothe our 8. millions of people. the root these have taken among the body of our people is so firm that there is no danger of it's not being permanent. it's houshold establishment will fix the habit where no future change of employment in the mercantile capital can ever affect it.

I inclose you many letters for my friends & correspondents in Europe, with whom, as with yourself, I was greatly in arrear. recommending them to your friendly attentions & particular care, I pray you to accept assurances of my sensibility of your kindnesses and of my affectionate esteem and respect.　　　　Th: Jefferson

RC (MdHi: Warden Papers); at foot of first page: "D. B. Warden esq."; endorsed by Warden. PoC (DLC); endorsed by TJ. Enclosures: (1) TJ to Destutt de Tracy, 28 Nov. 1813. (2) TJ to Pierre Samuel Du Pont de Nemours, 29 Nov. 1813. (3) TJ to Tadeusz Kosciuszko, 30 Nov. 1813. (4) TJ to Lafayette, 30 Nov. 1813. (5) TJ to Alexander von Humboldt, 6 Dec. 1813. (6) TJ to Madame de Tessé, 8 Dec. 1813. (7) TJ to Isaac Cox Barnet, 14 Dec. 1813. (8) TJ to François André Michaux, 14 Dec. 1813. (9) TJ to Alexis Marie Rochon, 14 Dec. 1813. (10) TJ to André Thoüin, 14 Dec. 1813. (11) TJ to Julian Ursin Niemcewicz, 15 Dec. 1813. (12) TJ to Philip Mazzei, 29 Dec. 1813. Enclosed in TJ to John Graham, 6 Jan. 1814.

The American general TJ regarded as guilty of DISOBEDIENCE OF ORDERS was Wade Hampton (Stagg, *Madison's War*, 345–6). General William Hull was placed on TRIAL in January 1814 for treason, cowardice, neglect of duty, and conduct unbecoming an officer. Although convicted of the second and third charges and sentenced to be shot, President James Madison remitted Hull's punishment (*ANB*; *Trial of Brig. Gen. William Hull* [Boston, 1814], esp. 26–8). General Andrew Jackson's victories at Tallushatchee on 2 Nov. and Talladega on 9 Nov. 1813 cost the Creek Indians the FLOWER OF THEIR WARRIORS (Stagg, *Madison's War*, 355–6).

[1] Manuscript: "Peuchel's."
[2] Manuscript: "Nov. 1. 13."
[3] Manuscript: "give."

# From David A. Leonard

DEAR SIR,                                    Bristol Dec[r] 30th 1813

Shall I, without[1] apology, intrude so far upon your attention, as to state to you the object of this letter? I, with several brothers as well as other friends, are now resolved on what, for two or three years passed, we have had in serious contemplation—that is, to remove into the Western Country. They look to me to make the necesary inquiries. But very few of us, if any, are personally acquainted with any part of that country. What we have heard of that country has strongly prepossessed us to remove thither. As the people who live in the several territories will be generally inclined to speak well of the country they have chosen for their home, we deemed it advisable to make a little enquiry of the author of 'Notes on Virginia,'[2] where the most inviting situation for 20. or 30 families, may be selected. Among our number may be found farmers, merchants, mechanicks labourers &c. Our general views are agriculture Manufactures, Culture of sheep (the merino) &c! We have been inclined toward the Missouri Ter[y] but cannot say we are without our fears whether that country be healthful for emigrants from N. England, & whether some part of the Illinois ter[y], Indiana Ter[y] or of the state of Ohio may be preferred. We should therefore feel ourselves under great obligation to you, Sir, for a word of instruction & advice, knowing that you have long contemplated the various local[3] circumstances of our Country & have the most correct judgement where those parts are that are now attended with the most liberal prospects & most inviting to settlers whose objects are like those of ours. We are wishing to fix upon a spot before the ensuing season as many of us have long been determined to remove from N. England. With us, to remove at so great a distance, is indeed a serious & important object; this, dear Sir, is our apology for thus presuming upon your kindness to give us some little general advice. Mr R. Easton of St. Louis[4] speaks very well of the Missouri Ter[y]—Mr Thos. Sloo entertains a very flattering opinion of the

[ 93 ]

Kaskaskia Country. Other gentlemen also speak well of other places. We feel prepared to repose great confidence in what you may please to inform us. Should you not find leisure to reply—Will you be so kind as to name to us the person or persons who could advise on this, to us, so interesting & important a subject.

Yours very respectfully     DAVID A LEONARD

RC (MoSHi: TJC-BC); between date-line and salutation: "Thomas Jefferson Esq"; endorsed by TJ as received 14 Jan. 1814 and so recorded in SJL.

David Augustus Leonard (1771–ca. 1819), clergyman, author, and merchant, was born in Bridgewater, Massachusetts, and graduated from Rhode Island College (later Brown University) in 1792. During the decade following his ordination as a Baptist evangelist in 1794, he served as a preacher in Massachusetts and New York City, published a number of sermons and orations, and opened a school. In 1805 Leonard moved to Bristol, Rhode Island, where he became a Unitarian and a merchant, edited the *Mount Hope Eagle*, 1807–08, supported the Republican party, and served for a dozen years as postmaster. In 1817 he relocated for health and financial reasons to Vincennes in the Indiana Territory, but he died insolvent two years later (D. Hamilton Hurd, comp., *History of Plymouth County, Massachusetts* [1884], 983; *Historical Catalogue of Brown University, 1764–1904* [1905], 79; Sprague, *American Pulpit*, 6:349–50; Thomas Baldwin,

*A Sermon delivered at Bridgewater, December 17, 1794, at the Ordination of the Rev. David Leonard to the Work of an Evangelist* [Boston, 1795]; *Longworth's New York Directory* [1800], 256; New York *Mercantile Advertiser*, 20 May 1800; Brigham, *American Newspapers*, 2:994; DNA: RG 29, CS, R.I., Bristol, 1810; Newport *Rhode-Island Republican*, 20 Mar. 1810; *Providence Gazette, and Moral, Political & Commercial Register*, 10 May 1817; *Providence Patriot*, 20 Nov. 1819; Providence *Rhode Island American, and General Advertiser*, 28 Jan. 1820).

Rufus EASTON, a former judge in the Missouri Territory, was elected its delegate to the United States Congress in 1814. Thomas SLOO served as a land-claims commissioner in the Illinois Territory's Kaskaskia District, 1812–13 (*Terr. Papers*, 14:79, 790, 16:340).

[1] Reworked from "with."
[2] Inconsistent closing double quotation mark editorially changed to single quotation mark.
[3] Word interlined.
[4] Preceding three words interlined.

# Account with William & Reuben Mitchell

[ca. 31 Dec. 1813]

M. Thomas Jefferson
In a/c with W. & R. Mitchell Dr

1813

| | | | | | | |
|---|---|---|---|---|---|---|
| May | To Flour over drawn equeal 6¾ bus. Wheat 7/6 | | | | | $8.43 |
| " | To Extra on 141 Barrels Flour | | | | 3/. | 70.50 |
| Dec<sup>r</sup> 31 | To Carriage | 44 | Bbls Flour to Richmond | | 2/. | 14.67 |
| " To ditto | | 40 | " | " | " | " | 13.33 |
| " To ditto | | 42 | " | " | " | " | 14.00 |

" To ditto        24[1]    "      "           "            "           8.00
" To Provisions furnished Boatmen                             33.29
" To 2$\frac{33}{60}$ Wheat over drawn                        1.70
" To Extra on 126[2] Barrels Flour            3/.             63.00
                              Due W. & R. Mitchell        $226.92[3]
Err[s] Excepted

                                        W. & R. Mitchell

MS (ViU: TJP-ER); in the hand of a representative of William & Reuben Mitchell and endorsed by him on verso as "A/c M. Jefferson to W. & R. Mitchell"; endorsed by TJ: "Mitchells Mess[rs] account of wheat & flour of 1813.

viz. bush        Bar.
827–57 = 126. SF
          25. F
         151."

TJ obtained the information given in his endorsement above from an undated "Statement of M[r] Jeffersons wheat a/c; crop of 1813," which additionally breaks down each shipment to Richmond into fine and superfine flour and notes that one hundred and fifty barrels of flour had been sent to Richmond and one barrel of superfine flour to Poplar Forest (MS in ViU: TJP-ER; in the hand of a representative of William & Reuben Mitchell and endorsed by him as "M[r] Jeffersons Wheat crop 1813").

On the verso of an undated list of wheat deliveries to William & Reuben Mitchell, TJ noted by way of summary that his "wheat of 1812. 780–45 b.," the equivalent, he claimed, of 141 BARRELS FLOUR, had been "deliv[d] spring of 1813" (MS in ViU: TJP-ER; in the hand of a representative of William & Reuben Mitchell, with notation by TJ; endorsed by TJ: "Mitchells").

[1] Below and to the right of this column, TJ recorded the total of the four preceeding lines as "150. Bar."
[2] Below this column in an unidentified hand is the sum "267," the total number of barrels in the two "To Extra" entries.
[3] In the margin to the right of this column an unidentified person broke most of this sum down into "83.29," the total transportation costs (carriage plus provisions), and "133.50," the amount due from the two "To Extra" entries.

# To John E. Hall

SIR                                    Monticello Jan. 1. 1814.

Your letter of Nov. 15. came during a long absence of mine from this place, which has occasioned this delay of the answer. the MS. notes in my pamphlet on the Batture, were only corrections of the press, I believe; for I have not a copy of it. these I inserted in most of the copies I sent out, but not in all of them; and I have no others to add. it was printed by mr Serjeant in N. York, who had the plate engraved, and charged me with it. this I presume would give me a property in it, which however I had never thought of exercising because the plate could be of no use to me. I presume also it can be of no further use with his establishment, and therefore very freely welcome you to whatever right I have in it, if it be worth looking after. I have never seen mr Livingston's answer and shall be glad of a copy of both his and my pieces when you shall have printed them, and will remit the price in bills of the Virginia bank which I presume are exchangeable in Baltimore. we have no other means of making small remittances to other states. Accept the assurance of my esteem and respect.                                                     TH: JEFFERSON

RC (NjP: Straus Autograph Collection); addressed: "M<sup>r</sup> John E. Hall Baltimore"; franked; postmarked Milton, 5 Jan. PoC (DLC); with missing dateline replaced by TJ's mistaken notation: "(not dated in the original, but believed to have been Dec. 31. 13)"; endorsed by TJ as a letter of 31 Dec. 1813 and so recorded in SJL.

For the publication of the legal PIECES by Edward Livingston and TJ in the *American Law Journal*, vol. 5 (1814), see notes to Hall to TJ, 15 Nov. 1813. TJ did not actually REMIT THE PRICE for this work until 6 Aug. 1817 (*MB*, 2:1337).

# To Thomas Leiper

DEAR SIR                                                   Monticello Jan. 1. 1814.

I had hoped, when I retired from the business of the world, that I should have been permitted to pass the evening of life in tranquility, undisturbed by the peltings and passions of which the public papers are the vehicles. I see however that I have been dragged into the newspapers by the infidelity of one with whom I was formerly intimate, but who has abandoned the American principles out of which that intimacy grew, and become the bigotted partisan of England and Mal-content of his own government. in a letter which he wrote me, he earnestly besought me to avail our country of the good understanding which subsisted between the Executive and myself, by recommending an offer of such terms to our enemy as might produce a peace towards which he was confident that enemy was disposed. in my answer I stated the aggressions, the insults and injuries which England had been heaping on us for years, our long forbearance in the hope she might be led by time and reflection to a sounder view of her own interests, and of their connection with justice to us: the repeated propositions for accomodation made by us, and rejected by her, and at length her Prince Regent's solemn Proclamation to the world that he would never repeal[1] the orders in council <u>as to us</u>, until France should have revoked her illegal decrees <u>as to all the world</u>; and her minister's declaration to ours that no admissible precaution against the impressment of our seamen could be proposed: that the unavoidable declaration of war which followed these was accompanied by advances for peace on terms which no American could dispense with, made thro' various channels, and unnoticed and unanswered thro' any: but that, if he could suggest any other conditions which we ought to accept, and which had not been repeatedly offered and rejected, I was ready to be the channel of their conveyance to the government: and, to shew him that neither that attachment to Bonaparte nor French influence, which they alledge eternally without believing it themselves, affected my mind, I threw in the two little sentences of the printed extract inclosed in your friendly favor of the 9th Ult. and exactly these two little sentences, from a letter of 2. or 3. pages he has thought proper to publish, naked, alone, and with my name, altho' other parts of the letter would have shewn that I wished such limits only to the successes of Bonaparte as should not prevent his compleatly closing Europe against British manufactures & commerce; and thereby reducing her to just terms of peace with us.

Thus am I situated. I recieve letters from all quarters, some from known friends, some from those who write like friends, on various subjects; what am I to do? am I to button myself up in Jesuitical reserve, rudely declining any answer, or answering in terms so unmeaning as only to prove my distrust? must I withdraw myself from all interchange of sentiment with the world? I cannot do this. it is at war with my habits and temper. I cannot act as if all men were unfaithful because some are so; nor believe that all will betray me, because some do. I had rather be the victim of occasional infidelities, than relinquish my general confidence in the honesty of man.

So far as to the breach of confidence which has brought me into the newspapers with a view to embroil me with my friends, by a supposed separation in opinion and principle from them. but it is impossible there can be any difference of opinion among us on the two propositions contained in these two little sentences, when explained as they were explained in the context from which they were insulated. that Bonaparte is an unprincipled tyrant, who is deluging the continent of Europe with blood, there is not a human being, not even the wife of his bosom, who does not see. nor can there I think be a doubt as to the line we ought to wish drawn between his successes & those of Alexander. surely none of us wish to see Bonaparte conquer Russia, and lay thus at his feet the whole continent of Europe. this done, England would be but a breakfast: and altho' I am free from the visionary fears which the votaries of England have affected to entertain, because I believe he cannot effect the conquest of Europe; yet put all Europe into his hands, and he might spare such a force, to be sent in British ships, as I would as lieve not have to encounter, when I see how much trouble a handful of British souldiers in Canada has given us. No. it cannot be our interest that all Europe should be reduced to a single monarchy. the true line of interest for us is that Bonaparte should be able to effect the compleat exclusion of England from the whole continent of Europe, in order, as the same letter said 'by their peaceable engine of constraint to make her renounce[2] her views of dominion over the ocean, of permitting no other nation to navigate it but with her license, & on tribute to her, and her aggressions on the persons of our citizens who may chuse to exercise their right of passing over that element.' and this would be effected by Bonaparte's succeeding so far as to close the Baltic against her. this success I wished him the last year, this I wish him this year; but were he again advanced to Moscow, I should again wish him such disasters as would prevent his reaching Petersburg. and were the consequences even to be the longer continuance of our war, I would rather meet them than see the whole force of Europe wielded by a single hand.

I have gone into this explanation, my friend, because I know you will not carry my letter to the newspapers, and because I am willing to entrust to your discretion the explaining me to our honest fellow-laborers, and the bringing them to pause and reflect, if any of them have not sufficiently reflected on the extent of the success we ought to wish to Bonaparte, with a view to our own interests only; & even were we not men to whom nothing human should be indifferent.— But is our particular interest to make us insensible to all sentiments of morality? is it then become criminal, the moral wish that the torrents of blood this man is shedding in Europe, the sufferings of so many human beings, good as ourselves, on whose necks he is trampling, the burnings of antient cities, devastations of great countries, the destruction of law and order, and demoralisation of the world should be arrested, even if it should place our peace a little farther distant?—No. you and I cannot differ in wishing that Russia, and Sweden, & Denmark, and Germany, & Spain, & Portugal, & Italy, and even England may retain their independance. and if we differ in our opinions about Towers and his 4. beasts and 10. kingdoms, we differ as friends, indulging mutual errors, and doing justice to mutual sincerity & honesty. in this spirit of sincere confidence and affection I pray god to bless you here and hereafter.      TH: JEFFERSON

P.S. altho' I do not believe the French minister will think worthy of notice this bald extract, unvouched by any testimony but that of a newspaper, yet, lest he should note it to the government, I have avoided all mention of it to them and all explanation of it in my own name which might amount to an avowal of the letter. because in this state the answer of the Executive is easy, that it is a mere newspaper paragraph, unauthorised, unavowed by any body, and which cannot be the legitimate subject of serious notice by any one.

RC (DLC); slightly damaged, with missing text supplied from PoC; at foot of first page: "M^r Lieper." PoC (DLC); endorsed by TJ. Enclosed in Leiper to TJ, 17 Apr. 1814.

TJ resented the INFIDELITY of George Logan and did not respond to his letters until after the War of 1812 ended, but he did not terminate their relationship (TJ to Logan, 15 Oct. 1815). LIEVE is a variant of "lief" (OED). The millennial publication of Joseph Lomas TOWERS discussed the contemporary significance of the four biblical BEASTS and 10. KINGDOMS of Daniel 7.3 and 7.7 and Revelation 4.6 and 17.12 (Towers, *Illustrations of Prophecy*, 2 vols. [London, 1796; repr. Philadelphia, 1808; Sowerby, no. 1548]). The FRENCH MINISTER was Louis Barbé Charles Sérurier.

[1] RC: "repeaal." PoC: "repeal."
[2] Preceding four words reworked from TJ's 3 Oct. 1813 letter to Logan, which stated "she can be made to renounce."

# To Archibald Thweatt

DEAR SIR                                    Monticello Jan. 1. 1814.

Your letter dated Oct. 26. but I presume for Nov. 26. came here during my absence in Bedford in December, and this is the first moment I have been able to reply to it. I am sorry it is not in my power to give you any information of the account of Farrel & Jones against mr Eppes. I do not know that I ever saw it, nor had I any information ever from him respecting it. I remember only to have heard mr Eppes complain that he was likely to lose whatever mr Cary had recieved of the produce of his estate while he was under age. I should have been highly gratified to have been able to give you information of it.            —I have never heard from mr Hay on the subject of the report in the suit of Skelton's exrs. I have ever looked upon it as a case wherein nothing could ever be got, and therefore always willing to let it go off the docket by consent. it will otherwise be in eternal lethargy in the court of Chancery.

I hope mrs Thweat is well, and that you enjoy the same state. present me affectionately to her, and accept the assurance of my great friendship and respect                                    TH: JEFFERSON

PoC (DLC); at foot of text: "Archibald Thweatt esq."; endorsed by TJ.

A missing letter from Thweatt to TJ of 26 Oct. 1813 is recorded in SJL as received 17 Dec. 1813 from Eppington. For the account of Farell (FARREL) & Jones with Francis Eppes (1747–1808), see note to TJ to Thweatt, 13 Jan. 1810. For the settlement of Bathurst SKELTON's estate, see note to TJ to David Copeland, 25 June 1809.

# To Walter Jones

Dear Sir                                            Monticello Jan. 2. 14.

Your favor of Nov. 25. reached this place Dec. 21. having been near a month on the way. how this could happen I know not. as we have two mails a week both from Fredericksburg and Richmond. it found me just returned from a long journey and absence during which so much business had accumulated, commanding the first attentions, that another week has been added to the delay.

I deplore with you the putrid state into which our newspapers have passed, and the malignity, the vulgarity, & mendacious spirit of those who write for them: and I inclose you a recent sample, the production of a New-England judge, as a proof of the abyss of degradation into which we are fallen. these ordures are rapidly depraving the public taste, and lessening it's relish for sound food. as vehicles of information, and a curb on our functionaries they have rendered themselves useless by forfieting all title to belief. that this has in a great degree been produced by the violence and malignity of party spirit I agree with you; and I have read with great pleasure the paper you inclosed me on that subject, which I now return. it is at the same time a perfect model of the style of discussion which candor and decency should observe, of the tone which renders difference of opinion even amiable, and a succinct, correct, and dispassionate history of the origin & progress of party among us. it might be incorporated, as it stands, and without changing a word, into the history of the present epoch, and would give to posterity a fairer view of the times than they will probably derive from other sources. in reading it with great satisfaction there was but a single passage where I wished a little more developement of a very sound and Catholic idea, a single intercalation to rest it solidly on true bottom. it is near the end of the 1$^{st}$ page, where you make a statement of genuine republican maxims, saying 'that the people ought to possess as much political power as can possibly consist with the order and security of society.' instead of this I would say 'that the people being the only safe depository of power, should exercise in person every function which their qualifications enable them to exercise consistently with the order and security of society; that we now find them equal to the election of those who shall be invested with their Executive and legislative powers, and to act themselves in the Judiciary, as judges in questions of fact'; that the range of their powers ought to be enlarged E$^{t}$c. this gives both the reason and exemplification of the maxim you express 'that they

ought to possess as much political power"[1] E[t]c.      I see nothing
to correct either in your facts or principles.

You say that in taking Gen[l] Washington on your shoulders, to bear
him harmless thro' the Federal coalition, you encounter a perilous
topic. I do not think so. you have given the genuine history of the
course of his mind thro the trying scenes in which it was engaged, and
of the seductions by which it was decieved, but not depraved.[2] I think
I knew General Washington intimately and thoroughly; and were I
called on to delineate his character it should be in terms like these.

His mind was great and powerful, without being of the very first
order; his penetration strong, tho' not so acute as that of a Newton,
Bacon or Locke; and as far as he saw, no judgment was ever sounder.
it was slow in operation, being little aided by invention or imagination, but sure in conclusion. hence the common remark of his officers,
of the advantage he derived from councils of war, where hearing all
suggestions, he selected whatever was best. and certainly no General
ever planned his battles more judiciously. but if deranged during the
course of the action, if any member of his plan was dislocated by sudden circumstances, he was slow in re-adjustment. the consequence
was that he often failed in the field, & rarely against an enemy in station, as at Boston & York. he was incapable of fear, meeting personal
dangers with the calmest unconcern. perhaps the strongest feature in
his character was prudence, never acting until every circumstance,
every consideration was maturely weighed; refraining if he saw a
doubt, but, when once decided, going through with his purpose
whatever obstacles opposed. his integrity was most pure, his justice
the most inflexible I have ever known, no motives of interest or consanguinity, of friendship or hatred, being able to bias his decision. he
was indeed, in every sense of the words, a wise, a good, & a great
man. his temper was naturally irritable and high toned; but reflection
& resolution had obtained a firm and habitual ascendancy over it. if
ever however it broke it's bonds he was most tremendous in his
wrath. in his expences he was honorable,[3] but exact; liberal in contributions to whatever promised utility; but frowning and unyielding
on all visionary projects, and all unworthy calls on his charity.
his heart was not warm in it's affections; but he exactly calculated
every man's value, and gave him a solid esteem proportioned to
it.       his person, you know, was fine, his stature exactly what
one would wish, his deportment easy, erect, and noble; the best
horseman of his age, and the most graceful figure that could be seen
on horseback. altho' in the circle of his friends, where he might be

unreserved with safety, he took a free share in conversation, his collo-
quial talents were not above mediocrity, possessing neither copious-
ness of ideas, nor fluency of words. in public when called on for a
sudden opinion, he was unready, short, and embarrassed. yet he
wrote readily, rather diffusely, in an easy & correct style. this he had
acquired by conversation with the world for his education was merely
reading, writing, and common arithmetic, to which he added surveying at a later day. his time was employed in action chiefly, reading
little, and that only in Agriculture and English history. his correspondence became necessarily extensive, and, with journalising his
agricultural proceedings, occupied most of his leisure hours within
doors. on the whole, his character was, in it's mass perfect, in nothing bad, in few points indifferent; and it may truly be said that never
did nature and fortune combine more perfectly to make a man great,
and to place him in the same constellation with whatever worthies
have merited from man an everlasting remembrance.[4] for his was the
singular destiny & merit of leading the armies of his country succes-
fully thro' an arduous war for the establishment of it's independance,
of conducting it's councils thro' the birth of a government, new in it's
forms and principles, until it had settled down into a quiet and or-
derly train, and of scrupulously obeying the laws, thro' the whole of
his career, civil and military, of which the history of the world furnishes no other example. how then can it be perilous for you to take
such a man on your shoulders? I am satisfied the great body of republicans thinks of him as I do. we were indeed dissatisfied with him
on his ratification of the British treaty. but this was short lived. we
knew his honesty, the wiles with which he was encompassed, and
that age had already begun to relax the firmness of his purposes: and
I am convinced he is more deeply seated in the love and gratitude of
the republicans, than in the Pharisaical homage of the Federal
monarchists. for he was no monarchist from preference of his judgment. the soundness of that gave him correct views of the rights of
man, and his severe justice devoted him to them. he has often declared to me that he considered our new constitution as an experiment on the practicability of republican government, and with what
dose of liberty man could be trusted for his own good: that he was determined the experiment should have a fair trial, and would lose the
last drop of his blood in support of it. and these declarations he repeated to me the oftener, and the more pointedly, because he knew
my suspicions of Col° Hamilton's views, and probably had heard
from him the same declarations[5] which I had, to wit, 'that the British
constitution with it's unequal representation, corruption and other

existing abuses, was the most perfect government which had ever been established on earth, and that a reformation of these abuses would make it an impracticable government.' I do believe that Gen¹ Washington had not a firm confidence in the durability of our government. he was naturally distrustful of men, and inclined to gloomy apprehensions; and I was ever persuaded that a belief that we must at length end in something like a British constitution had some weight in his adoption of the ceremonies⁶ of levees, birth-days, pompous meetings with Congress, and other forms of the same character, calculated to prepare us gradually for a change which he believed possible, and to let it come on with as little shock as might be to the public mind.

These are my opinions of General Washington, which I would vouch at the judgment seat of god, having been formed on an acquaintance of 30. years. I served with him in the Virginia legislature from 1769. to the revolutionary war, and again a short time in Congress until he left us to take command of the army. during the war and after it we corresponded occasionally, and in the 4. years of my continuance in the office of Secretary of state, our intercourse was daily, confidential and cordial. after I retired from that office great and malignant pains were taken by our Federal-monarchists⁷ and not entirely without effect, to make him view me as a theorist, holding French principles of government which would lead infallibly to licentiousness and anarchy. and to this he listened the more easily from my known disapprobation of the British treaty. I never saw him afterwards, or these malignant insinuations should have been dissipated before his just⁸ judgment as mists before the sun. I felt on his death, with my countrymen, that 'verily a great man hath fallen this day in Israel.'

More time and recollection would enable me to add many other traits of his character; but why add them to you, who knew him well? and I cannot justify to myself a longer detention of your paper. Vale, propriéque tuum, me esse tibi persuadeas.          TH: JEFFERSON

RC (ViHi); with later insertion glued on (see note 4 below); at foot of first page: "Doctʳ Walter Jones." PoC (DLC); with later insertion not glued on. Tr (DFo); posthumous copy; incomplete. Enclosures not found.

As commanding general of the Continental army, George Washington forced the British to evacuate Boston in March 1776 and to surrender Yorktown (YORK), Virginia, in October 1781 (ANB). For

TJ's dissatisfaction with the 1795 RATIFICATION OF THE BRITISH TREATY (Jay Treaty), considered by him to be an "infamous act, which is really nothing more than a treaty of alliance between England and the Anglomen of this country against the legislature and people of the United states," see PTJ, 28:400n, 466, 475–6, 540, 542. Elsewhere TJ repeated that in a conversation he had heard Alexander Hamilton state THAT THE BRITISH CONSTITUTION ... WAS THE

MOST PERFECT GOVERNMENT WHICH HAD EVER BEEN ESTABLISHED ON EARTH (TJ's Explanation of the Three Volumes Bound in Marbled Paper, 4 Feb. 1818; *PTJ*, 20:141). The biblical quote, VERILY A GREAT MAN HATH FALLEN THIS DAY IN ISRAEL, is in 2 Samuel 3.38. VALE, PROPRIÉQUE TUUM, ME ESSE TIBI PERSUADEAS: "Farewell, be assured I am entirely yours."

[1] Omitted closing quotation mark editorially supplied.
[2] Tr omits everything between salutation and dateline and this point.

[3] Word interlined in place of "liberal."
[4] The passage from this point through "no other example" was written separately on slips of paper, with one attached to the RC, presumably by Jones as TJ had instructed in his letter of 10 Jan. 1814, and the other filed with the PoC. As a guide for insertion, TJ included the word "remembrance" on the slips of paper as well as the original manuscript, later canceling the duplicated word on the PoC.
[5] Manuscript: "declartions."
[6] Preceding nine words not in Tr.
[7] Preceding four words interlined.
[8] Tr ends here.

# From Thomas Leiper

DEAR SIR                               Philad[a] Jan[ry] 2[d] 1813 [1814]

I wrote you on the 9th of last month to which I refere—In that letter was enclosed an extract of a letter wrote by you and the report of the day was it was adressed to Doctor Logan—

All your friends here were but of one opinion you never wrote it it was a forgery

But since their has appeared in the same paper on the 11th the same extract with a preface annexed which staggers our faith and we are obliged to believe the extract is yours[1] and sorry I am I ever saw it— Now I will take it for Granted that the extract is yours—now sir let me ask you what this virtuous Alexander has done for the benefit of Mankind—He has 28,000,000 of subjects $\frac{1}{10}$ of which are Nobles the Greatest Tyrants on earth[2] and they Tyrannise over the remainder who are slaves to them and one half of these slaves are but one degree removed from the Brute—now what has Alexander done to meliorate the condition of these Wretches <u>Nothing</u> then to annex Virtue to such a Sovereign in my opinion is a prostitution of the Word—Poulsons paper is formed for the Torries and the British only—He collects all the Trash published in the United States[3] against our own Goverment and the French and every thing in favor of England so from that circumstance he must publish many things that are not true and I expected your extract would have been numbered as one of them and this would have been the case had not the extract again been Published with the preface I hope the extract will never get to France for certain I am it will be of no service to M[r] Crawford—And I am of the opinion Logan had that in view when he sent it to the press Logan is an enemy to you and his country and it appears to me from this very thing he would sacrifice both to serve England—Notwithstanding[4] your extract which by the bye I do not like I shall never give you up for the good you have done—God Bless you and believe me to be[5] your friend sincerely and

your most Obedient Servant

THOMAS LEIPER

RC (DLC: TJ Papers, 197:35051–2); misdated; at foot of text: "Thomas Jefferson Late President of the United States"; endorsed by TJ as a letter of 2 Jan. 1814 received 14 Jan. 1814 and so recorded in SJL. FC (Lb in Leiper Papers, Friends of Thomas Leiper House, on deposit PPL); similarly misdated but followed in Lb by a letter dated 8 Feb. 1814.

The quotation from TJ's letter to George Logan reprinted on 11 Dec. in the Philadelphia *Poulson's American Daily*

*Advertiser* had a PREFACE ANNEXED identifying it as an "*Extract of a letter from* THOMAS JEFFERSON, *to a gentleman in Pennsylvania, dated* MONTICELLO, Oct. 3, 1813."

[1] RC: "your." FC: "yours."
[2] RC: "eath." FC: "Earth."
[3] RC: "State." FC: "States."
[4] RC: "Notwithstand." FC: "Notwithstanding."
[5] RC: "by." FC: "be."

# From David A. Leonard

DEAR SIR,

Bristol R. I. Jan^y 2. 1814

I am mortified to state to you that in my letter addressed to you a few days ago enquiring concerning the Westtern Country, I omitted to mention one important article in the object of our company in their removal thither that is; We wish for a situation on some navigable waters, where we may be able, if inclined, to build vessels that we may enjoy in the interiour of our country some of that kind of commerce that many of us have been accustomed to in N. England. The reason of our troubling you in your tranquil retreat from publick life, with our enquiry is sincerely from the great confidence we have in your extensive view into the future destinies of our blessed country. From what we have read & heard of you in this respect, we could not consider our enquiries finished without soliciting your opinion where we had better look for a place of settlement; & in particular what is your view in respect to the Missouri Territory. We have such a consideration of your disposition to assist the laudable objects of your fellow citizens, as prevents us from fearing our intrusion on your attention wholly inadmissible.[1] Dear Sir, A brief reply to our enquiry (should you deem it worthy your notice) would be the greatest kindness bestowed upon us.

Yours very respectfully

D. A LEONARD

RC (MoSHi: TJC-BC); endorsed by
TJ as received 14 Jan. 1814 and so
recorded in SJL.

[1] Manuscript: "inemissible."

# From Isaac McPherson

RESPECTED FRIEND,                                    Baltimore January 2nd 1814

Thy esteemed favour of the 3rd of September came safe to hand and I have the great satisfaction in saying that I have procured such testimony respecting the origin of the different parts of the machenery that O Evan's claims as his invention that I think every honest man must say when he peruses it that he has most grossly imposed upon the public and it may have its use. I have had 500 pamphlets printed containing the whole one of which I beg the favour of thee to accept it goes by the same mail as this—Major Martin has deceased was he living I think his testimony would be still more pointed but I think the whole so clear that either Congress or the Courts will do something to releave the public—

I have been most intimate with O E for many years & never had the smallest misunderstanding with him—I am not one cent dirictly or indirectly benefited or injured by the decition having nothing but the public good at heart, having spent some hundreds of dollars in collecting the testimony that I now, produce shoud the citisens at large be benifited I shall be satisfied I propose laying a pamphlet on the desk of each member of the Sanate and House of Represintatves I am thy friend

ISAAC McPHERSON

RC (DLC); between dateline and salutation: "Thomas Jefferson Esqr"; endorsed by TJ as received 7 Jan. 1814 and so recorded in SJL.

TJ's ESTEEMED FAVOUR was dated the 18th, not the 3RD OF SEPTEMBER. McPherson sent TJ one of the PAMPHLETS he had recently published anonymously, the *Memorial to Congress on Evans' Patent*, in which he and a group of fellow millers sought to prove that Oliver Evans should not benefit from his patent because he had neither created, nor newly applied, the inventions he claimed to have designed, including the elevator, conveyer, hopper-boy, drill, and kiln drier. Early in 1811 Evans had more than doubled his licensing fees for millers using his alleged improvements (Bathe and Bathe, *Oliver Evans*, 189–90; McPherson to TJ, 3, 28 Aug. 1813, and enclosure to latter; Evans to TJ, 7 Jan. 1814).

# To John Graham

DEAR SIR                                    Monticello Jan. 6. 14.

I trouble you with a package addressed to mr Warden containing many letters to my friends & correspondents in Europe which I must ask of your usual goodness to give a passage to under cover with the dispatches of your office. some of them being very confidential I would prefer their awaiting the safest passage, their <u>certain</u> conveyance being more important than their early one. accept my apology for repeating these troubles to you, with the assurance of my great esteem and respect.                    TH: JEFFERSON

P.S. the letter to Foronda I presume had better go to our Consul at Paris.

PoC (DLC); beneath signature: "John Graham esq."; endorsed by TJ. Enclosures: (1) TJ to Valentín de Foronda, 14 Dec. 1813. (2) TJ to David Bailie Warden, 29 Dec. 1813, and enclosures.

# From Oliver Evans

SIR                                    Washington City Jan^y 7th 1814

I have this day perused your learned discussion of my Claims to exclusive right to the use of Elevators Conveyors & Hopperboys &C, In a letter dated Monticello, August 13^th 1813. But I have not the Satisfaction of knowing who it was directed to, for in the publication of it the gentleman has concealed his name, making use of yours to press me down in the public estimation. If I knew whose letter you have answered I would inform him that it appears evident that he has missrepresented the case to your honour, by giving you the Idea that I have obtained a grant of exclusive right for useing Elevators Conveyors Hopperboys & drills, I beg leave to assure, you that I have no Such grant, nor do I Claim any Such right. My Patent is for my improvement in the process of the manufacture of flour and meal, by the application of certain principles to produce a new and very great and useful result, by means of an improved Elevator, an improved Hopperboy, &c which the law requires of me to describe a Set of Machinery that will carry my principles into operation, to secure to me the improvement without being confined to the Machinery discribed, but free to use any machinery that is known and free to the public. It is well that I knew better than to take a patent for Machines, for my invention or discovery was completed, and then machines sought after to put it in operation. I had a common right to chose and use the best I could find for my purpose, either Chain pump, Chain of Buckets, Archimides pump, Screw or[1] bellows or Hopperboy, if there had been Such a machine. If I had found them all perfect and Suitable for my purposes but applied to other uses, I had a right to take them, and combine them, to produce the great result that I had conceived, making an improvement of the utmost importance in the Art of manufacturing flour and meal, for which the patent law Said I was entitled to a patent. But so it was that neither of the Machines mentioned were to be found in a State, that would answer my purpose, and I had at great expense of Study time and labour, to improve invent,[2] arange, and combine them, Therefore the act for my relief directs a patent to be granted me, first to secure to me the exclusive right to my improvement in the art of manufacturing flour and meal, Secondly the exclusive right to my improved machines, for all other purposes to which they will apply in consequence of my improvement of them, leaving the Machines in their original State or as they were before known[3] and used, free to all as usual

I have reason to beleive that the gentleman who required your opinion in the case, knew well all that I have Stated, And it was his duty when approaching So elevated and dignifyed a character to have Stated the whole truth, more especially if he intended to draw forth an Opinion, to be published with intent to influence the public mind, in a case So important as private and public right, he Should also have Sent you a true report of the case tryed in the Circuit court for the district of Maryland, which I now Send accompanying this, also a copy of my Memorial now before Congress, that you may be informed of my persuits, and the persecutions and difficulties I have to encountre, which I beg you will be pleased to read. And as your letter printed in a pamphlet conected with a great number of affidavits memorials observations &c making 50 octavo pages, is now before congress, All of which I could better answer before a Court of Justice. I am constrained to beg of you to condescend to answer this my Statemint, as soon as your convenience and leisure will permit, with your consent, that I Shall publish both this letter and your answer, for I will be forced to say something in my defence I am

Hon^ble Sir with great Resp[ect] your Obedient Humble Ser

OLIVER EVANS

RC (DLC); torn at seal; dateline at foot of text; addressed: "The Hon^ble Thomas Jefferson Monticello Virginia"; franked; postmarked Washington, 9 Jan.; endorsed by TJ as received 14 Jan. 1814 and so recorded in SJL.

Oliver Evans (1755–1819), inventor, engineer, and author, was apprenticed to a wheelwright in his native Delaware. By 1774 he became engrossed in designing steam engines and steam-powered land carriages. Ridiculed for his ideas, Evans turned to other labor-saving projects. About 1778 he built a machine to produce textile cards, and in the 1780s he designed improvements for the manufacturing of flour and meal, for which he received state patents in the 1780s and a federal patent in 1790. Two years later Evans moved to Philadelphia, where he established mercantile and milling enterprises and began to prosper. He expended considerable energy and employed a network of family members and agents to defend his patent rights and licenses from infringement. Evans published a popular handbook, *The Young Mill-Wright & Miller's Guide* (Philadelphia, 1795, and later editions; Sowerby, no. 1180), and followed it a decade later with a work entitled *The Abortion of the Young Steam Engineer's Guide* (Philadelphia, 1805). After 1800 he focused increasingly on the construction of high-pressure steam engines for waterworks, mills, and steamboats. In 1804 Evans built an amphibious steam-powered dredge for cleaning docks. By 1806 he founded the Mars Works in Philadelphia, and about 1811 he helped his son George Evans establish the Pittsburgh Steam Engine Company. Prior to TJ's retirement he and the elder Evans communicated sporadically yet cordially regarding patent rights and inventions, as well as mill materials and licensing. In response to the opposition of TJ and others to his broad claims of patent rights, Evans disseminated a number of essays on patent law, including an angry, unsigned pamphlet, *A Trip made by a Small Man in a Wrestle with a Very Great Man. Answer to the Baltimore Millers' Memorial, and Thomas Jefferson's Letter* (n.p., 1814). Evans died in New York City, leaving an estate valued in excess of $30,000 (*ANB*; *DAB*; Bathe and Bathe, *Oliver Evans*; *List of Patents*, 4, 39–40, 62, 97; *PTJ*, 24:683–4; Isaac McPherson to TJ, 3, 28 Aug. 1813; TJ to McPherson, 13 Aug., 18 Sept. 1813; TJ to John Wharton, 10 July 1818; Philadelphia *Poulson's American Daily Advertiser*, 19 Apr. 1819).

TJ's letter of AUGUST 13TH 1813 was addressed to Isaac McPherson, who CONCEALED HIS NAME when he included this letter in a published memorial to Congress. The ACT for Evans's RELIEF is described at McPherson to TJ, 3 Aug. 1813. In the CASE TRYED IN THE CIRCUIT COURT of MARYLAND during its November 1812 term, *Oliver Evans v. Samuel Robinson*, all of Evans's patent rights were confirmed. The enclosed report on the case has not been identified. In Evans's view the verdict "demonstrated conclusively his right, as an inventor, to his patented improvements; depicted in severe and glowing colors the depravity and baseness of those who had combined to defraud him of the fruits of his ingenuity; and maintained his claims and pretensions beyond all controversy, and established his genius and merits on an exalted and triumphant eminence" (*Evans v. Robinson* and other items supplied by Evans and printed in Baltimore *Weekly Register*, Addenda, 3 [1813]: 1–16; *The Federal Cases: comprising Cases Argued and Determined in the Circuit and District Courts of the United States* [1894–97], 8:886–8 [case no. 4,571]). Other enclosure printed below.

[1] Preceding two words interlined.
[2] Word interlined.
[3] Manuscript: "know."

# Oliver Evans's Petition to the
# United States Congress

*To the honorable the Senators*
*and Representatives in Congress individually.*     [by 28 Dec. 1813]

THE subscriber, in behalf of himself and the patentees in the United States, begs leave to represent to the members of Congress:

That when any man discovers a piece of unlocated land, he is allowed by law to patent it, and on paying the public for their right to the soil, it is secured to him, and his heirs and assigns forever.—He can sell any part of it to others, to induce them to join with him in improving the same, by building mills, furnaces, forges, bridges, roads, canals, &c. for their own and the public benefit. But it is evident, that if the exclusive right to the land had been granted for only fourteen years, that he could neither afford to make such improvements, nor could he sell any part of his right to induce others to engage with him to do it; and the consequence would be that no prudent person would patent such lands, and no improvements would be made thereon, although it does not cost a man much to discover unlocated land, it being a fixed, existing thing, that can be easily found by any one who will go to it.

But to discover a new principle, or the means of applying a principle to make a new and useful improvement in science or art, oftentimes requires not only ingenuity, but great labor and exertion of both body and mind, in a long course of expensive experiments, for it is not an existing fixed thing, but has to be discovered, invented, and in a measure created by the inventor. The public can have no claim to it, or any thing that does not exist as proprietors of the soil. He that creates or produces a thing that never before existed, is by common consent, and the laws of nature, the only true proprietor, as no other person can possibly have any claim or right to it. Thus, inventors humbly conceive that they are entitled to be secured in their rights for more than fourteen years.—Inventors are so few in number, that they are never represented in legislation, and cannot defend their rights, but are subject to the rest of the community, who forget to legislate, to protect such property as inventors produce; therefore, the property of the inventor only, is left unprotected, and it is common to all, excepting only in such countries where the evil tendency of such policy has been discovered; there the inventor is protected in his rights for limited times; and even this partial justice has been productive of much good. But we have heard no good reason assigned why protection to them should be extended to fourteen years only, while all other classes are protected in the exclusive right to the fruits of their labor forever; they cannot, more than others, afford to surrender the fruits of their labors to the public, at the end of fourteen years; nor can they improve their inventions or discoveries, or sell any part of their right to others, to induce them to join with them to improve or extend their property for their own, or the public benefit.

A protection for fourteen years only, tends to suppress the inventive genius and labors of every prudent and wise man; for he knows that in so short a time, an improvement cannot be introduced against the prejudice and opposition it has to meet,* so as to yield any profit; therefore, discoveries must lay dormant or be produced at the expense, and to the injury and ruin of the inventor, which is so often the case, that the reader will acknowledge that he would not bear the name of a projector of new things for any consideration, as it would destroy his credit equal to a bankruptcy.

All inventors think themselves capable of carrying on regular business in the beaten track as well as others, and generally have in their latter days to lament that they have labored for the public, subjecting themselves to the frauds and jeers of knaves and wags, to deprivations and poverty, while they have expended labor, and exercised talents that would have soon raised them to independence if applied for their private interest. Believing that no further arguments need be used, and that he cannot make the case clearer, it remains with Congress to decide whether this state of things shall continue, and whether the public interest would not be greatly promoted by a further protection to the rights of inventors.

The writer, however, begs leave to declare that he believes that as early as 1786, he himself had conceived and discovered useful improvements, which, if they had been promptly and extensively put into operation, and the savings or gains by the use of them collected into the public treasury, it would have been sufficient to have discharged the public debt, defrayed the expense of government, and freed the people of the United States from taxes. But the most of them have been suppressed by the above stated policy, and are dormant at this day. But he knows that this assertion cannot be credited, for he has heretofore been deemed deranged for asserting much less. He hopes, therefore, that Congress will appoint a committee, to ascertain the improvements he has already got into use, as well as those which he has specified in the patent office, and are lying dormant, that they may judge how far the assertion may be true. If it prove true in but one hundredth part, there surely may be ninety-nine other inventors in the United States to supply the deficiency and make the case still worthy the attention of Congress to pass a supplement to the patent laws, granting patentees, their heirs and assigns, the privilege of renewing their patents for a second term of fourteen years, any time within the last seven years of their first term; for if such supplement should produce improvements operating in the United States, the profits of the use of which would be sufficient to discharge the public debt, and exempt the people of the United States from further taxation, it would be more than can be devised by any other means. The inventors will not fail on their parts to produce the improvements, and if others can devise the means of collecting the profits thereof into the treasury, the whole would soon be done; if not, the profits will remain somewhere in the United States; wealth is a good source from whence to draw supplies by loans or taxation.

If the protection now asked (for all patentees) had been granted to the subscriber when he petitioned the legislatures of Pennsylvania, Delaware, and Maryland, in the years 1786–7, and had he found assistance to put his discoveries in full operation, and have drawn one dollar out of every hundred dollars gained by their use, (as he now does from the use of his

---

*The greatest opposition is always to be met from those who are to be most benefited from the improvement; that is, from those who are to use it; they cannot be induced to leave their old track.

improvements for the manufacture of flour) he might have been able to have loaned government a large sum at this day; and those who used his improvements to have loaned or paid in taxes ninety-nine times as much from the same source. And it would be difficult to ascertain the injury that any person would have sustained from the wealth of either the inventor or the user of his improvements.

If it was right in the legislature of New-York to grant exclusive right to Messrs. Livingston and Fulton for thirty years, which did produce steam boats in operation in 1807, which had lain dormant twenty one years for want of such protection and aid, after having been invented and put in operation by others; it was an error in the legislature of Pennsylvania, in 1787, to reject my improvements, because they could not understand them, and wrong in the legislature of Maryland in limiting their grant to fourteen years, a term too short to enable me to produce them.

If it be an error in an individual to refuse to use a patented machine, which would save him one hundred dollars in any given time, for fear of paying one dollar, or even six dollars out of the hundred, to the inventor, still it may be best to accept of important improvements on the terms that they can be produced. What was wrong or right at one time may [not][1] be so now.

Great and expensive improvements, although they may be ever so important, cannot be produced without the protection that is asked; less will be thankfully received, but less will not, perhaps, answer the great purpose of stimulating genius to action, by remuneration equal to labors, expenses, and risks.

When we reflect that we ask neither money nor monopoly of any existing thing of Congress, that the grant cannot deprive any person of any thing, while it may enable us to produce many new and useful things of the utmost importance and benefit to the community, promising to do much good, without as we believe, a possibility of doing any harm—While we offer to produce things of high value to the public, on condition of their securing to us not more perhaps than one hundredth part of their value, equal to lending money, or its value, at one per cent. for one year, and then forgiving the debt—To serve our country in the way the God of nature has qualified us best to serve it—To enrich our country on the simple condition of its refraining from the use of our property without our consent for a limited time, doing us justice in but a small proportion as done to others—Allowing us to enrich ourselves by our own labors, while we shall enrich our neighbors and our country at the same time—Acknowledging ourselves entirely subject to the rest of the community, a class without protection, excepting for limited times, without the means of defending our rights—Anxious to do all the good that we conceive ourselves capable of, but sensible that we cannot do it at our own expense, without a prospect, tempted to abandon our natural pursuits, suppress our patriotism and bury our talents, that we may be free and independent, as others are. Under reflections like these, we cannot refrain from hoping that all we ask will be speedily granted. When we shall be able to form associations, obtain the necessary aid, give our minds full scope, with fair prospects, we will soon prove the good policy of extending to us, as to others, the full enjoyment of the fruits of our labors, although it be but for limited times. We will not be compelled to keep our discoveries and principles of art secret in our own defence; this sordid and execrable principle which we despise will be exploded for ever, as soon as our interest can be promoted by disclosing and publishing them.

I am, Sir, very respectfully, Your obedient humble servant,

OLIVER EVANS.

Printed circular (DLC: TJ Papers, 236:42310); undated.

On 28 Dec. 1813 Congressman Charles Jared Ingersoll presented this petition to the United States House of Representatives, which referred it to a select committee consisting of Ingersoll, Daniel Sheffey, Daniel Udree, Thomas Telfair, and John Lovett. Although the committee also considered at least three petitions opposing Evans's pretensions, on 17 Feb. 1814 it reported a bill that, without addressing Evans's broader concerns, did extend his patent on steam engines an additional seven years beyond its 1818 expiration date. The measure became law on 7 Feb. 1815 (*JHR*, 9:185, 302, 719; *U.S. Statutes at Large*, 6:147).

AS EARLY AS 1786 Evans had unsuccessfully petitioned the Pennsylvania legislature for the exclusive right to de-

velop USEFUL IMPROVEMENTS in steam-powered land travel, which he termed "steam waggons." The reaction to this proposal persuaded him that the lawmakers thought him DERANGED. Evans also petitioned the legislatures of other states, including MARYLAND, which ultimately granted him fourteen-year patents for both his steam wagons and milling improvements (Bathe and Bathe, *Oliver Evans*, 4, 6, 14–20). Robert LIVINGSTON, on behalf of himself and later his partner Robert FULTON, had obtained a monopoly on steam navigation in New York that had previously belonged to John Fitch, but they found it difficult at best to work within the framework of state and federal patent laws (Cynthia Owen Philip, *Robert Fulton: A Biography* [1985], 122, 210–2).

[1] Omitted word editorially supplied.

# From Robert M. Patterson

SIR,                    At the Hall of the Society,— january 7th., 1814.

I have the honor to inform you, that, at an election of the American Philosophical Society, held this day, you were unanimously reelected their President.

It gives me great pleasure, Sir, to announce to you this renewed proof of the high estimation with which you continue to be regarded by the Society.

Permit me, Sir, to take this opportunity of expressing to you my personal feelings of veneration and of gratitude.

R. M. PATTERSON,
Secretary A. P. S.

RC (MHi); dateline at foot of text; at head of text: "To Thomas Jefferson"; endorsed by TJ as received 14 Jan. 1814 and so recorded in SJL.

Robert Maskell Patterson (1787–1854), physician and educator, was a na-

tive Philadelphian and the son of TJ's longtime friend Robert Patterson. The younger Patterson received an undergraduate degree from the University of Pennsylvania in 1804 and a medical degree from that institution four years later. The American Philosophical Society elected him to membership in 1809. Later that year he traveled to Europe to continue his training, bearing letters of introduction from TJ to leading French scientists. Shortly after his return to America, in 1813 Patterson was appointed professor of natural philosophy in the medical department of the University of Pennsylvania. One year later he was given the chair of natural philosophy and mathematics in the university's arts faculty. He served his alma mater as vice provost, 1814–28, and trustee from 1836 until his death. From 1828–35 Patterson held the chair of natural philosophy at the University of Virginia. He returned to Philadelphia as director of the United States Mint, 1835–51. Patterson served the American Philosophical Society as a secretary, 1813–24, as a vice president, 1825–30 and 1836–44, and as president from 1849 until his death. He also helped manage the Franklin Institute, the Musical Fund Society of Philadelphia, and the Pennsylvania Institution for the Instruction of the Blind (Samuel Breck, *A Short Biography of Robert M. Patterson, M.D.* [1854]; PPAmP: Patterson Family Papers; Peale, *Papers*, 3:10n, 4:18n; APS, Minutes, 21 Apr. 1809, 1 Jan. 1813, 7 Jan. 1825 [MS in PPAmP]; Robert Patterson to TJ, 10 May 1809; TJ to Pierre Samuel Du Pont de Nemours, André Thoüin, and Bartelémy Faujas de Saint-Fond, 16 May 1809; TJ to Robert M. Patterson, 15 Feb. 1818; TJ to James Monroe, 22 July 1824; Joseph Carson, *A History of the Medical Department of the University of Pennsylvania* [1869], 117; Edward Potts Cheyney, *History of the University of Pennsylvania, 1740–1940* [1940], 435; *Catalogue of the Trustees, Officers, & Students of the University of Pennsylvania. Session 1851–52* [1852], 3–5; J. Thomas Scharf and Thompson Westcott, *History of Philadelphia, 1609–1884* [1884], 2:1943; Bruce, *University*, 2:162–4; *JEP*, 4:498, 501 [28 Dec. 1835, 5 Jan. 1836]; William L. Mactier, *A Sketch of the Musical Fund Society of Philadelphia* [1885], 51; APS, *Proceedings* 6 [1854]: 60–4).

# To Charles Clay

DEAR SIR                                      Monticello Jan. 8. 14.

I informed you on the 28th Ult. by letter that I had according to your request engaged mr Forber[1] to wait on you with a view to the erection of a carding machine for you. he proposes to set out the day after tomorrow, and will present himself to you with this letter. the success of the machine he has erected near me, persuades me he is fully competent to fulfill your wishes. Accept the assurance of my great esteem & respect.                          TH: JEFFERSON

RC (CoCCC); at foot of text: "Charles Clay esq." PoC (MHi); endorsed by TJ.

[1] TJ later corrected the PoC by interlining "Faber" above this word.

# From Patrick Gibson

SIR                                      Richmond 8th January 1814

Since the arrival of the Cartel at Annapolis bringing dispatches from England to our Government, there has been much speculation in our market, founded upon the supposition that peace would either directly or indirectly grow out of it—flour which last week would not command 4$ has this week been sold at 5½ Cash & 5¾$ 60ᵈ/.—these still continue to be the prices, altho little is now doing—letters from Alexandria mention the appointment and confirmation by the Senate of Rufus King as minister to London, I cannot learn that any information has been received from Washington to that effect—I have as yet made no sale of your flour, and shall be glad to receive your instructions as soon as convenient—I inclose you a Copy of your account current to the 31ˢᵗ Ultº leaving a balance in your favor of $1123.54—

With great respect I am Your obᵗ Servᵗ          PATRICK GIBSON

RC (MHi); at head of text: "Thomas Jefferson Esqʳᵉ"; endorsed by TJ as received 12 Jan. 1814 and so recorded in SJL. Enclosure not found.

The British CARTEL schooner *Bramble* reached Annapolis on 30 Dec. 1813. The dispatches it carried, which included Foreign Secretary Lord Castlereagh's call for direct peace negotiations between the warring parties, were immediately sent on to Washington (*Baltimore Patriot & Evening Advertiser*, 1 Jan. 1814; Stagg, *Madison's War*, 369–70). The rumor that the Federalist senator Rufus King had been appointed United States MINISTER TO LONDON was untrue.

# To Samuel M. Burnside

SIR                                        Monticello. Jan. 9. 1814.
    I have duly recieved your favor of the 13ᵗʰ of¹ December, informing me of the institution of the American Antiquarian Society and expressing it's disposition to honor me with an admission into it, and the request of my cooperation in the advancement of it's objects. no one can be more sensible of the honor and the favor of these dispositions, and I pray you to have the goodness to testify to them all the gratitude I feel on recieving assurances of them. there has been a time of life when I should have entered into their views with zeal, and with a hope of not being altogether unuseful. but, now more than Septagenary, retired from the active scenes and business of life, I am sensible how little I can contribute to the advancement of the objects of their establishment; and that I should be but an unprofitable member, carrying into the institution indeed my best wishes for it's success, and a readiness to serve it on any occasion which should occur. with these acknolegements, be so good as to accept, for the society as well as for yourself the assurances of my high respect & consideration.

THᴴ: JEFFERSON

RC (MWA: American Antiquarian Society Archives); addressed: "Mʳ Samuel M. Burnside Worcester. Massachusets"; franked; postmarked Milton, 12 Jan. PoC (DLC).

¹ Reworked from "inst."

## From Charles Clay

DEAR SIR,                                    Lynchburg Jan. 9. 1814
   about two Day Since I recieved yours informing me you had Seen & Spoken to the man who builds the carding Machines, the price for a wool carding one I always understood was about¹ $500. am therefore not disappointed in that, & of course wish the Man to come on, if you Suppose him to be Master of his business—with Respect to the Cotton one I can Make no decisive determination until he may come & view the situation, & quantity of Water I may have to Spare for such machinery, as might be proper to erect—the town is full of bustle, Conjectures are Various, & expectation on tiptoe from a Report in circulation, that a brittish Minister has come to the City of Washington, with an Olive branch in hand &c &c &c I salute you on the new year opening with Such flattering prospects & beg you to accept Assurances of my high Consideration & profound Respect.

                                             C. CLAY

RC (MHi); addressed (torn): "Tho. J[e]ff[erson Esquire] of Montichello Albemarle"; endorsed by TJ as received 12 Jan. 1814 and so recorded in SJL.

Newspapers put numerous premature rumors of peace into CIRCULATION, in- cluding one that "a flag of truce has arrived from England at Annapolis, with a despatch from the British minister to the Secretary of State" (Richmond *Enquirer*, 4 Jan. 1814).

¹ Word interlined.

## To Louis H. Girardin

                                             Jan. 9. 14.
   Th: Jefferson presents his compliments to M. Girardin and his regrets that his garden is so bare of kitchen herbs as to have but a single plant of sage, & that stripped of it's leaves: he has no translation of Quinctilian. Bonne's Atlas is sent by the bearer.

   P.S. T. Jefferson Randolph is in Richmond, but expected home daily.

RC (PPAmP: Thomas Jefferson Papers); dateline above postscript; addressed: "Mʳ Girardin." Not recorded in SJL. Enclosure: Abbé Grenet and

Rigobert Bonne, *Atlas Portatif à l'usage des Colleges, pour servir à l'intelligence des auteurs classiques* (Paris, 1779–82; Sowerby, no. 3837; Poor, *Jefferson's Library*, 7 [no. 307]).

# From Thomas Hornsby

Sir

January 9th 14

I received your favour November 11th a few days ago & am mutch surprised at the statement made by M Peyton. I send you incloased Mrs Henderson,s statement the rest of the family concuring as far as there knowledge extends in this business. James Henderson departed this life 9th day of last June the appeal to him therefore is useless I think it probable the news of his death had reached Mr Peyton or he would not have been so ready to have made this appeal I wrote to Mr Meriwather when I wrote to you last he answered me immideately, after weighting some time I wrote him again requesting him to reassume the agency for me and settle the business as soon as possible. my reason for this step was, not receiving an answer from you in that time and supposeing the information which my letter conveyed rendered farther communication on the subject unnecessary. after receiving Col Greenup,s first letter I addressed him twice the second time requesting[1] some positive answer: my letter was then answered but in a way that induced me to believe that nothing could be done between us. Col Greenup in his last requested to know what was the lowest price I would take for the property and said if the terms were such as he could[2] safely meet he would immediately[3] comply[4] with them this was a question which I could not answer as I did not know the value of the property. had left that part to Mr Meriwather. therefore did not answer him this was the only part of his letter which seemed to require an answer your request that I would[5] immediately withdraw the power of attorney from Mr Meriwather and appoint some other person would be attended with mutch illconvenience to me as my acquaintance[6] in Albermarle is very slight and I do not know of any other person to whom I should be willing to apply for such a favour: Mr Meriwaher,s assidulty & politeness has been such in attending to the business for me that I am mutch indebted to him on the score of favour,s I hope therefore that you will not think harde of confering whith him on the business. in Col Greenup,s last he requested to know what could be done respecting the mill race claimed by John Henderson to run through the dower land soald to you I communicated the question to Mrs Henderson.

she dose not know how the dificuty takes place but gave me the perusal of her papers. I finde a release given by John Henderson to Mrs
Henderson runing in this way that if any former right which she had
given to any other person should prevent him from runing a race
through the dower land that she was in no way responseble. John
Henderson it seems gave nothing for the liberty of the race but was
granted him by his mother provided it was not prevented by the former sale which she had made. if a coppy of this release can be of any
service to you it can be had: in M^r Peytons letter to James Henderson[7] he mentions a tract of land near the Big bone Lick mortgaged to
him for the security of the property he perchaised in Virginia. this
tract is likewise[8] equally the property of the other legatee,s. being
part of the estate of Col Bennett Henderson deceased it has been
since divided. and James Henderson has only an equal share with the
rest of the children each one having about 200 acres. the land very
hilly. & very mutch disputed by interfearing claims 100 dollars per
Shear I think would be a high price. it is what I have offered mine at
and have not been able to get it with the highest esteem & respect Sir

    I remain yours &ccc                Thomas Hornsby

RC (ViU: TJP); at foot of second page: "Thomas Jefferson esqr"; endorsed by TJ as received 23 Feb. 1814 and so recorded in SJL.

A letter from Craven Peyton to TJ of 5 Jan. 1814, not found, is recorded in SJL as received from Monteagle two days later.

On 18 Sept. 1802 and 25 Feb. 1805 James L. Henderson provided SECURITY that the underage Henderson heirs would make good on their agreements to sell their possessions in and around Milton to Peyton. On the former occasion he pledged to pay Peyton £5,000 if they backed out when they married or came of age, while on the latter he was joined by his mother, Elizabeth Henderson (ViU: TJP).

[1] Manuscript: "requsting."
[2] Hornsby here canceled "immediate-ly."
[3] Hornsby here canceled "meet them."
[4] Manuscript: "comply comply."
[5] Manuscript: "woul."
[6] Manuscript: "acquaintancce."
[7] Manuscript: "Henders."
[8] Manuscript: "likewis."

ENCLOSURE

## Statement by Elizabeth Henderson

                              December 25^th 1813
I do not recollect of any conversation ever takeing place between Mr. Peyton
James Henderson & myself respecting my daughters property in Verginia I
never consented for James[1] Henderson to Sell their property, and never
knew that it was soald, untill after James Henderson left this country for

Washita which was several years after the transaction seems to have taken place. when Craven Peyton was at my house any business transacted between himself and James Henderson was done in another house which they had to themselves. and I did not know that any sale of my daughters property was made by James Henderson to Craven Peyton

ELIZABETH HENDERSON

MS (ViU: TJP); in Thomas Hornsby's hand, signed by Henderson; endorsed by TJ: "Henderson mrs Elizabeth. Dec. 25. 13."

Elizabeth Lewis Henderson (1752–1829), a daughter of Charles Lewis, of Buck Island, was a cousin of TJ and also a sister-in-law of his sister Lucy Jefferson Lewis. She married Bennett Henderson in 1771. Eleven of the couple's twelve children survived infancy, and ten of them were under the age of nineteen when Bennett Henderson died in 1793. When her husband's Albemarle County estate was divided a few years thereafter, Henderson gave most of her portion to her children, retaining only a small parcel near the family millseat, some houses, lots, and other buildings in Milton, and a third of the profits from the Henderson's mill and warehouse. She moved to Shelby County, Kentucky, with her five minor children in 1801 (Merrow Egerton Sorley, *Lewis of Warner Hall: The History of a Family* [1935; repr. 1991], 371–2; Boynton Merrill Jr., *Jefferson's Nephews: A Frontier Tragedy* [1976], 59–66; Woods, *Albemarle*, 227–8, 388; *PTJ*, 28:474n; Haggard, "Henderson Heirs").

Henderson sold her Albemarle County interests to TJ's proxy, Craven Peyton, between September 1802 and July 1804. Her involvement in the extended litigation growing out of the sale of her children's property in Albemarle County to TJ through Peyton was extremely important and, from TJ's perspective, almost entirely detrimental. First, in 1803 Henderson strongly supported her son John Henderson's contention that she had already granted him the right to run a millrace through the property when she sold it to Peyton in 1802. Then in the above deposition she claimed that she had not been privy to the 1802 sale to Peyton of the Albemarle County possessions of her three youngest daughters—Frances, Lucy, and Nancy. Henderson's testimony helped extend the life of the case and, in the case of the three minor heirs, raised TJ's costs substantially (Haggard, "Henderson Heirs"; note to Peyton to TJ, 6 Aug. 1809; Craven and Jane Peyton's Conveyance of the Henderson Lands, [22 Aug. 1809]).

[1] Manuscript: "Jame."

# To John Pintard

SIR
Monticello Jan. 9. 14.

I have duly recieved your favor of Dec. 22. informing me that the New York Historical society had been pleased to elect me an honorary member of that institution. I am entirely sensible of the honor done me by this election; and I pray you to become the channel of my grateful acknolegements to the society. at this distance, and at my time of life, I cannot but be conscious how little it will be in my power to further their views: but I shall certainly, and with great pleasure, embrace any occasion which shall occur of rendering them any services in my power. with these assurances be so good as to accept for them and for yourself those of my high respect and consideration.

TH: JEFFERSON

RC (NHi: New-York Historical Society Archive); at foot of text: "John Pintard Rec. Sec$^y$ of the N. Y. Historical society." PoC (DLC).

John Pintard (1759–1844), merchant, insurance executive, and philanthropist, was a native of New York City who received an A.B. degree from the College of New Jersey (later Princeton University) in 1776. After several brief stints in the militia he spent three years with his uncle and guardian Louis (Lewis) Pintard trying to improve conditions for American prisoners of war held in New York City during the Revolutionary War. The receipt of a sizable inheritance in 1784 provided him with the financial wherewithal to become a merchant, but his interests extended far beyond buying and selling. Pintard worked as a United States government translator under John Jay and TJ, 1786–90. Although initially successful in business, his decision to countersign notes for William Duer in 1791 ruined him, and he eventually spent more than a year in debtors' prison, 1797–98. Only the passage of a national bankruptcy law in 1800 allowed Pintard to resume his normal activities. Despite support from Vice President Aaron Burr, he failed in an 1801 attempt to become United States consul at New Orleans. Pintard was a founder of the New-York Historical Society in 1804, and in the years prior to 1827 he was, at various times, its secretary, librarian, and treasurer. He was also a city alderman, a state legislator in 1791, a city inspector, 1804–09, sometime clerk of the corporation council, secretary of the New York chamber of commerce, 1817–27, and secretary of the Mutual Insurance Company, 1809–29. Pintard supported his friend DeWitt Clinton for president in 1812, was a founder and longtime officer of the American Bible Society, helped to organize New York's first savings bank in 1819, and was its president, 1828–41 (*DAB*; *Princetonians, 1776–1783*, pp.

89–99; "Walter Barrett" [Joseph Alfred Scoville], *The Old Merchants of New York City* [1863–69], 2:217–44; *PTJ*, 10:523, 17:352–3n, 23:447–9; Mary-Jo Kline and others, eds., *Political Correspondence and Public Papers of Aaron Burr* [1983], 2:609–11; Dorothy C. Barck, ed., *Letters from John Pintard to his daughter, Eliza Noel Pintard Davidson, 1816–1833*, 4 vols. [1940–41]; New York *Emancipator and Weekly Chronicle*, 26 June 1844).

Pintard's FAVOR OF DEC. 22, which he signed as recording secretary "in behalf of Samuel Miller. D.D. Correspond. Secretary," stated that "I have the honour to inform you, that at a Meeting of the New-York Historical Society, held on the *twelfth* day of *October, last* you were elected an HONORARY MEMBER of that Institution. By Order of the Society" (RC in MHi; printed form with words filled in by Pintard rendered in italics; at head of text: "New-York Historical Society"; at foot of text in Pintard's hand: "The Honourable Thomas Jefferson"; endorsed by TJ as a letter of 23 Dec. 1813 received 31 Dec. 1813 from Pintard writing for the "Historical Society of N. York" and so recorded in SJL).

The NEW YORK HISTORICAL SOCIETY was founded on 10 Dec. 1804 in order "to discover, procure, and preserve whatever may relate to the natural, civil, literary, and ecclesiastical history of the United States in general, and of this State in particular." It was to consist of resident and HONORARY members, with "the former to be persons residing in the State of New-York; the latter persons residing elsewhere." Resident members were expected to pay $10 upon admission and $2 a year thereafter. Honorary members were not required to contribute, and TJ apparently did not do so (*The Constitution and Bye-Laws of the New-York Historical Society* [New York, 1805], 3, 4; Robert W. G. Vail, *Knickerbocker Birthday: A Sesqui-Centennial History of the New-York Historical Society, 1804–1954* [1954]).

# From Joseph R. Darnall

VENERABLE SIR                    York District S° Cª Janʸ 10ᵗʰ 1814

On the 17ᵗʰ of last June I call'd on You, and Stayed until the next day. My business was of So disagreeable a nature that I did not make it known: and nothing but extreem & increasing necessity could force me to it at this time.

It is to humbly ask your assistance in releiving from indigence and distress Myself my Wife, and three small children.        So extraordinary a petition, requires that I should let you know the cause of my situation: It was the sudden decline of Trade in the Southern States: I was at that time engag'd in the Mercantile business, and altho' upon a small scale, with fair prospects of making a living. by that event I lost all.

Depriv'd of House & home, reduc'd to want, and being constitutionally as well as accidentally unable to follow a laborious occupation, having Studied the English & Latin Languages, Some of my Relations, and most respectable friends, advis'd me to the Study of Physic. Dr Thomas Henderson of Charlotte N° Carolina, a man highly esteem'd in his publick, private, and professional characters, offere'd to board and instruct me on reasonable terms: my Father-in-law, who liv'd about ten miles from the village offered to take my Wife and children to his house, so that I could see them once a week. I accordingly agree'd, and Studied 2 years during which time I read the common Systematic Authors on the practice of Physic & Surgery. With the assistance of a Father who is now no more, I paid off for the first year, but am still indebted $25 of the price of the last year; besides $15 for some Medicine & furniture I have since bought of another man.

My Situation is literally this, A Young Physician, with a small family, living in the settlement wherein I was rais'd, the practice engross'd by the old and emminent Physicians, of course I am unable to live here, and quite <u>Unable</u> to move to where I could live.

In this Situation I have been for several years, and the death of a kind Father has cut off the only assistance I have had in that time: You are the only person to whom the world has directed me to apply: If you think my case Merits your benificence, you will be so kind as to let me know by letter.

As my misfortune has not been the effect of prodigality, nor any imprudent conduct, I have the commiseration of the most intelligent and feeling part of my acquaintance, but that does not reach my case. The frowns of fortune, the Scorn of Wealthy fools, and my distress'd situation, has seriously injured me in body and mind, has left me no emulation but that of acquiring knowledge, and depriv'd me entirely of the only means of obtaining it. (viz.) Books & Society. You will please to write me an answer as Soon as convenient directed to Harrisburg. Lancaster District[1] South Carolina, it being the nearest post office

Accept Sir the Sincere petition and high Veneration of

JOSEPH R. DARNALL

P.S. When at Monticello last spring you enquired if there were any of the Magnolia's growing as high up as that part of S° C° in which I live. At that time I knew of none, but am since inform'd that there is one growing in the woods, in Lincoln County North Carolina 10 Miles from the Catawba River, 5 from Crowders Mountain, & 60 from the Blueridge. Mr Peter Smith on whose land it grows has sold Several Boxes of the twigs in Charleston S° C°. The tree is 105 feet high, and has been visited by one French, and one English Botanist. It is Said to be the only native Magnolia between that place & the Florida's          J R. D

RC (MHi); addressed: "Thomas Jefferson Esq^r Monticello Albemarle County Virginia" by "Mail"; stamped; postmarked Harrisburg, S.C., 10 Jan. 1814, and Charlottesville, 1 Feb.; endorsed by TJ as received 2 Feb. 1814 and so recorded in SJL.

Joseph Rush Darnall (b. ca. 1780), physician, was born probably in Mecklenburg County, North Carolina, near the border of York County, South Carolina. A census record of 1830 describes him as a doctor living in the latter county and owning three slaves. Darnall was no longer listed there in 1840 (Avlyn Dodd Conley, comp., *The Darnall, Darnell Family: in-cluding Darneal, Darneille, Darnielle, Darnold, Dernall, Durnall, Durnell, and names variously spelled, With Allied Familes* [1954–79], 2:264, 266–7, 276–7; Darnall to Mary Henderson, 25 Sept. 1812 (NcCU: Irwin Family Papers); DNA: RG 29, CS, N.C., Mecklenburg Co., 1810, S.C., York Co., 1820, 1830).

Darnall's FATHER-IN-LAW was Banks Meacham (Clarence E. Mitcham, comp., *Meacham, Mitcham, Mitchum Families of the South* [1974], 219).

[1] Superfluous period after "Lancaster" editorially omitted.

# To Walter Jones

TH: JEFFERSON TO D^R JONES                    Monticello Jan: 10. 14.

I have discovered that in copying my letter to you of the 2^d inst. I omitted a sentence, which contained a fact so important in the character of Gen^l Washington that my conscience will not permit me to let it go[1] uncorrected. the sentence is written on the inclosed scrip of paper, and is to follow the word 'remembrance' pa. 4. l.15. of the letter. I have so written it on this scrip, that if you will moisten the bits of wafer on the back, and stick it close under the 14^th line it will stand in it's place. affectionately farewell.

PoC (DLC); endorsed by TJ.

[1] Preceding three words interlined in place of "leave the letter."

For the enclosed SCRIP OF PAPER, see textual note 4 to TJ to Jones, 2 Jan. 1814.

## From William Johnson

SIR                                              Richmond 12^th Jan^y 1814
verey unexpectedly to me I have been detained here in the service of the State, my boat together with all those that were then in the Basin shared the same fate, we were impressed to go up the River in the neighbourhood of Goochland C House after Hay. The engagment which I made with you to do your work is now interrupted. But I trust It will be in my power to do ample Justice to you as well as the Cause of my Country, because I am providing boats to assist in the work and hope to reassume your employment in the course of about a fortnight I am Sir y^rs Gratefully                                         W^M JOHNSON

RC (MHi); endorsed by TJ as received 19 Jan. 1814 and so recorded in SJL.

The James River Canal BASIN was at Richmond.

## To Patrick Gibson

DEAR SIR                                         Monticello Jan. 13. 14.
Your's of the 8^th is just recieved, and I learn with pleasure that $5\frac{1}{2}$ & $5\frac{3}{4}$ D. can be had for flour. I have no hesitation in accepting these prices, preferring the latter at 60. days to the former in cash. if these prices therefore are still to be had, or even 5.D. be so good as to sell at once. I see nothing in the late news which may suddenly raise prices. the moment Johnson returns, I have 100. barrels ready for him to take off, and which may be comprehended in the sale, as it will be with you within a week from this time. the rest will follow as fast as he can carry it.
I must ask the favor of you to send me 300.D. by return of post in bills from 50. to 5.D. Accept the assurances of my esteem & respect.
                                                    TH: JEFFERSON

PoC (ViU: TJP); at foot of text: "M^r Gibson."

# To Jeremiah A. Goodman

DEAR SIR                                                 Monticello Jan. 13. 14.

Being desirous that Gill's waggon should go with Dick's, and having a job of hauling of corn from a distance and some other things to finish before Gill could go, I detained Dick to help dispatch it, and tomorrow both waggons will set out. the two beeves came in terrible order; the cow so poor that we are obliged to turn her out, and the steer in worse order than some of ours, so that we found it better to change him for one of our own in better order.

I pray you to spare nothing in fattening the remaining one. he may be sent on as soon after the 1ˢᵗ of March as he shall be fat enough. he should come by easy days journies of 12. or 15. miles, & highly fed on the way, or the journey will reduce him too low. he should set out with a good deal of fat to spare. I send by the waggon 17. hats for the men, to wit, Jame Hubbard, smith Will, Dick, Hall, armistead Jesse, Nace, Caesar, Austin, Gawen, Phill Hubard, Daniel, Reuben, Manuel Stephen, Evans, and Hercules. — considering the extravagant price to which salt has got (being from 4. to 6.D. a bushel here) we must suspend for a while the liberal allowance I had directed for the people and go on as we did before, making them do with what is absolutely necessary. if 6.D. at Lynchburg for my tobᵒ is not to be had, send it down as soon as you can, sparing no pains, and regarding no loss in making it of the 1ˢᵗ quality. two of my neighbors, Divers & Rogers, have been offered 8.D. for all they can make this year, and my land is of a quality to make as good as theirs. what you will now send down therefore I shall offer to the person who made the proposal to mr Divers and Rogers, and offer him my this year's crop for 8.D.

I send up a mare to be wintered. she may be worked in the waggon

Accept my best wishes                                       TH: JEFFERSON

RC (University Archives, Stamford, Conn., 1997). Recorded in SJL as a letter to "Goodman Jerem. A."

A letter from Goodman to TJ of 30 Dec. 1813, not found, is recorded in SJL as received 7 Jan. 1814 from Poplar Forest.

# To Thomas Cooper

DEAR SIR                                                 Monticello Jan. 16. 1814.

Your favor of Nov. 8. if it was rightly dated, did not come to hand till Dec. 13. and being absent on a long journey it has remained unanswered till now. the copy of your introductory lecture was recieved

& acknoleged in my letter of July 12. 1812. with which I sent you Tracy's 1st vol on Logic. your Justinian came safely also, and I have been constantly meaning to acknolege it, but I wished at the same time to say something more. I posessed Theophilus's, Vinnius's and Harris's editions; but read over[1] your notes, and the Addenda et corrigenda, and especially the parallels with the English law, with great satisfaction and edification. your edition will be very useful to our lawyers, some of whom will[2] need the translation as well as the Notes. but what I had wanted to say to you on the subject was that I much regret that, instead of this work, useful as it may be, you had not bestowed the same time and research rather on a translation and notes on Bracton, a work which has never been performed for us, and which I have always considered as one of the greatest desiderata in the Law.        the laws of England, in their progress from the earliest to the present times, may be likened to the road of a traveller, divided into distinct stages, or resting places, at each of which a review is taken of the road passed over so far. the 1st of these was Bracton's De legibus angliae: the 2'd Coke's Institutes, the 3d the Abridgment of the law by Matthew Bacon, and the 4th Blackstone's commentaries. doubtless there were others before Bracton which have not reached us. Alfred, in the preface to his laws, says they were compiled from those of Ina, Offa, and Aethelbert, into which, or rather preceding them, the clergy have interpolated the 20. 21st 22d 23d and 24th chapters[3] of Exodus, so as to place Alfred's preface to what was really his, awkwardly enough, in the body of the work an interpolation the more glaring as containing laws expressly contradicted by those of Alfred.[4] this pious fraud seems to have been first noted by Houard in his Coutumes Anglo-Normandes (I. 88.) and the pious judges of England[5] have had no inclination to question it. [of this disposition in[6] these judges I could give you a curious sample,[7] from a note in my commonplace book, made while I was a student; but it is too long to be now copied. perhaps I may give it to you with some future letter.] this Digest by Alfred of the laws of the Heptarchy, into a single code, common to the whole kingdom, by him first reduced into one, was probably the birth of what is called the Common law. he has been styled 'magnus juris anglicani Conditor,' and his code the 𝕯𝖔𝖒-𝖇𝖊𝖈, or doom book. that which was made afterwards under Edward the Confessor was but a restoration of Alfred's with some intervening alterations. and this was the code which the English so often, under the Norman princes, petitioned to have restored to them.        but, all records previous to the Magna charta, having been early lost, Bracton's is the first digest of the whole body of[8] law, which has come down to us entire. what materials for it existed in his time we know not, except the unauthoritative collections by Lambard & Wilkins, and the treatise of Glanville, tempore H. 2. Bracton's is the more[9] valuable, because being written a very few years after the Magna charta, which commences what is called the Statute law, it gives us the state of the Common law in it's ultimate form, and exactly at the point of division between the Common and Statute law. it is a most able work, complete in it's matter, and luminous in it's method. 2. the statutes which introduced changes began now to be preserved, applications of the law to new cases by the courts began soon after to be[10] reported in the Year books, these to be methodised and abridged by Fitzherbert, Brooke[11] Rolle[12] and[13] others, individuals continued the business of reporting, particular treatises were written by able men, and all these, by the time of L[d] Coke, had formed so large a mass of matter as to call for a new digest, to bring it within reasonable compass. this he undertook in his institutes, harmonising all the decisions and opinions which were reconcilable, and rejecting those not so. this work is executed with so much learning and judgment that I do not recollect that a single position in it has ever been judicially denied. and altho' the work loses much of it's value by it's chaotic form, it may still be considered as the fundamental code of the English law.

3. The same processes recommencing, of Statutory changes, new decisions, multiplied Reports, and special treatises, a new accumulation had formed, calling for new reduction, by the time of Matthew Bacon. his work therefore, altho' not pretending to the textual merit of Bracton's or Coke's, was very acceptable. his Alphabetical arrangement indeed, altho' better than Coke's jumble, was far inferior to Bracton's. but it was a sound digest of the materials existing on the several alphabetical heads under which he arranged them. his work was not admitted as authority in Westminster hall; yet it was the Manual of every judge and lawyer, and, what better proves it's[14] worth, has been it's daily growth in the general estimation.

4. a succeeding interval of changes and additions of matter produced Blackstone's Commentaries, the most lucid in arrangement, which had yet been written, correct in it's matter, classical in style, and rightfully taking it's place by the side of the Justinian institutes. but like them, it was only an elementary book. it did not present all the subjects of the law in all their details. it still left it necessary to recur to the original works of which it was the summary. the great mass of law books, from which it was extracted, was still to be consulted on minute investigations. it wanted therefore a species of merit

which entered deeply into the value of those of Bracton, Coke & Bacon. they had in effect swept the shelves of all the materials preceding them. to give Blackstone therefore a full measure of value, another work is still wanting, to wit, to incorporate with his principles a compend[15] of the particular cases subsequent to Bacon[16] of which they are the essence. this might be done by printing under his text a digest like Bacon's,[17] continued to Blackstone's time. it would enlarge his work[18] and increase it's value peculiarly to us, because just there we break off from the parent stem of the English[19] law, unconcerned in any of it's subsequent changes, or decisions.[20]

Of the 4. digests noted, the three last are possessed & understood by every one. but the first, the fountain of them all, remains in it's technical Latin, abounding in terms antiquated, obsolete, and unintelligible but to the most learned of the body of lawyers. to give it to us then in English,[21] with a Glossary of it's old terms, is a work for which I know no body but yourself possessing the necessary learning & industry. the latter part of it would be furnished to your hand from the glossaries of Wilkins, Lambard, Spelman, Somner in the X. Scriptores[22] the index of Coke & the law dictionaries. could not such an undertaking be conveniently associated with your new vocation of giving law lectures? I pray you to think of it.[†] a further operation indeed would still be desirable. to take up the doctrines of Bracton, separatim et seriatim, to give their history thro' the periods of L$^d$ Coke and Bacon, down to Blackstone; to shew when & how some of them have become extinct, the successive alterations made in others, and their progress to the state in which Blackstone found them. but this might be a separate work, left for your greater leisure, or for some future pen. [this has been done by Reeves in his History of the law][23]

I have long had under contemplation, & been collecting materials for the plan of an university in Virginia which should comprehend all the sciences useful to us, & none others. the general idea is suggested in the Notes on Virginia Qu. 14. this would probably absorb the functions of[24] W$^m$ & Mary college, and transfer them to a healthier and more central position. perhaps to the neighborhood of this place. the long & lingering decline of W$^m$ & Mary,[25] the death of it's last president, it's location and climate, force on us the wish for a new institution more convenient to our country generally, and better adapted to the present state of science.[26] I have been told there will be an effort in the present session of our legislature to effect such an establishment. I confess however that I have not great confidence

---

[†] Bracton has at length been translated in England.

that[27] this will be done. should it happen it would offer places worthy of you, and of which you are worthy. it might produce too a bidder for the apparatus and library of D[r] Priestly, to which they might add mine on their own terms. this consists of about 7. or 8[28] thousand volumes, the best chosen collection of it's size probably[29] in America, and containing a great mass of what is most rare and valuable, & especially of what relates to America.

You have given us, in your Emporium, Bollman's medley on political economy. it is the work of one who sees a little of every thing, & the whole of nothing; and were it not for your own notes on it, a sentence of which throws more just light on the subject than all his pages,[30] we should regret the place it occupies of more useful matter. the bringing our countrymen to a sound comparative estimate of the vast value of internal commerce, and the disproportionate importance of what is foreign, is the most salutary effort which can be made for the prosperity of these states, which are entirely misled from their true interests by the infection of English prejudices, & illicit attachment to English interests and connections. I look to you for this effort. it would furnish a valuable chapter for every Emporium; but I would rather see it also in the newspapers, which alone find access to every one.[31]

Every thing predicted by the enemies of banks, in the beginning, is now coming to pass. we are to be ruined now by the deluge of bank paper as we were formerly by the old Continental paper. it is cruel that such revolutions in private fortunes should be at the mercy of avaritious adventurers who, instead of employing their capital, if any they have, in manufactures, commerce & other useful pursuits, make it an instrument to burthen all the interchanges of property with their swindling profits, profits which are the price of no useful industry, of theirs. prudent men must be on their guard in this game of <u>Robin's alive</u> & take care that the spark does not extinguish in their hands. I am an enemy to all banks discounting bills or notes[32] for any thing but coin. but our whole country is so fascinated with this Jack lanthern wealth, that they will not stop short of it's total and fatal explosion.*

Have you seen the Memorial to Congress on the subject of Oliver Evans's patent rights? the memorialists have published in it a letter of mine containing some views on this difficult subject. but I have opened it no further than to raise the questions belonging to it. I wish we could have the benefit of your lights on these questions. the abuse

---

*this accordingly took place 4. years after.

of frivolous patents is likely to cause more inconvenience than is countervailed by those really useful. we know not to what uses we may apply implements which have been in our hands before the birth of our government, and even the discovery of America. the memorial is a thin pamphlet printed by Robinson in Baltimore, a copy of which has been laid on the desk of every member of Congress.[33]

You ask if it is a secret who wrote the Commentary on Montesquieu? it must be a secret during the Author's life. I may only say at present that it was written by a Frenchman, that the original MS. in French is now in my possession, that it was translated and edited by Gen[l] Duane, and that I should rejoice to see it printed in it's original tongue, if any one would undertake it. no book can suffer more by translation, because of the severe correctness of the original in the choice of it's terms. I have taken measures for securing to the author his justly earned fame, whenever his death or other circumstances may render it safe for him. like you, I do not agree with him in every thing, and have had some correspondence with him on particular points. but, on the whole, it is a most valuable work, one which I think will form an epoch in the science of government; and which I wish to see in the hands of every American student, as the elementary and fundamental institute of that important branch of human science.[†]

I have never seen the answer to Gov[r] Strong of the judges of Massachusets to which you allude, nor the Massachusets reports in which it is contained. but I am sure you join me in lamenting the general defection of lawyers and judges from the free principles of government. I am sure they do not derive this degenerate spirit from the father of our science, Lord Coke. but it may be the reason why they cease to read him, and the source of what are now called 'Blackstone lawyers.'

Go on in all your good works, without regard to the eye 'of suspicion and distrust with which you may be viewed[34] by some' and without being weary in well doing, and be assured that you are justly estimated by the impartial mass of our fellow citizens, and by none more than my self.                    TH: JEFFERSON

† the original has since been published in France, with the name of it's author, M. de Tutt Tracy.

PoC (DLC); brackets in original, with bracketed sections, authorial footnotes, and other emendations made after 1819, most likely to revise the letter when TJ shared a copy with Dabney C. Terrell in 1821; at head of text: "Th: Jefferson to D[r] Thomas Cooper"; at foot of first page: "Thomas Cooper esq." Tr (ViU: TJP); in the hand of Ellen Wayles Randolph (Coolidge); lacking TJ's footnotes and other revisions and probably based on the letter as it stood before its 1821 revision; incomplete. Tr (NjP: Thomas Jefferson Collection); including TJ's footnotes and other later revisions. Enclosed in TJ to Terrell, 26 Feb. 1821.

TJ acknowledged the receipt of Cooper's *Introductory Lecture* in his letter of 10 July 1812, not JULY 12. 1812. For the extract from TJ's legal COMMONPLACE BOOK, see TJ to Cooper, 10 Feb. 1814. MAGNUS JURIS ANGLICANI CONDITOR: "great author of English law." TEMPORE H. 2: "times of Henry II." WESTMINSTER HALL in London, the oldest portion of Westminster Palace, housed the law courts of King's Bench, Common Pleas, and Chancery. SEPARATIM ET SERIATIM: "separately and in succession." The LAST PRESIDENT of the College of William and Mary, Bishop James Madison, had died in 1812. In the GAME OF ROBIN'S ALIVE a lighted stick is passed from person to person. The one holding it when the flame goes out pays a penalty (William Wells Newell, *Games and Songs of American Children* [1883], 135–6). The MEMORIALISTS published TJ's letter to Isaac McPherson of 13 Aug. 1813 in their *Memorial to Congress on Evans' Patent*. Destutt de Tracy's *Commentary and Review of Montesquieu's Spirit of Laws* was first PUBLISHED IN FRANCE in 1819. The phrase regarding the SUSPICION AND DISTRUST WITH WHICH YOU MAY BE VIEWED BY SOME is loosely quoted by TJ from Cooper's letter of 8 Nov. 1813.

[1] TJ here canceled "again."
[2] Preceding four words interlined in place of "who for the most part." ViU Tr reproduces TJ's original wording, while NjP Tr retains the addition, with the verb following it mistranscribed as "read."
[3] Reworked from "the 21st and 22d chapters."
[4] Preceding fourteen words interlined in PoC, absent in ViU Tr, and present in NjP Tr.
[5] Preceding two words interlined in PoC, absent in ViU Tr, and present in NjP Tr, which also adds "in the zeal for church and State."

[6] TJ here canceled "our." ViU Tr retains this word and omits "these."
[7] NjP Tr: "example."
[8] NjP Tr here adds "common."
[9] NjP Tr: "most."
[10] Preceding sixteen words not in NjP Tr.
[11] PoC and ViU Tr: "Broke." NjP Tr: "Brooke."
[12] Word interlined in PoC and ViU Tr.
[13] TJ here canceled "perhaps by." These words are also canceled in ViU Tr.
[14] TJ here canceled "merit."
[15] Preceding two words interlined in PoC, replacing (after several intermediate cancellations) "a specification." ViU Tr retains the original wording, while NjP Tr reproduces the revised text.
[16] Preceding three words interlined in PoC, absent in ViU Tr, and present in NjP Tr.
[17] Reworked from "the digest of Bacon." ViU Tr retains the original wording, while NjP Tr reproduces the revised text.
[18] In PoC TJ here canceled "to the size of my Lord Coke's." Original wording retained in ViU Tr, but absent in NjP Tr. Sir Edward Coke's *Institutes of the Laws of England* ran to four folio parts (Sowerby, nos. 1781–4).
[19] Word interlined in PoC and absent in ViU Tr.
[20] Preceding two words not in ViU Tr.
[21] Marginal notation in ViU Tr, keyed to this place in the manuscript: "this has been lately done in Engld."
[22] Preceding five words interlined.
[23] In PoC TJ interlined above the bracketed note "* insert this as a Note at bottom." ViU Tr keeps bracketed note at end of paragraph and omits TJ's interlined instruction. NjP Tr renders the bracketed note as a footnote at the bottom of the page.
[24] Preceding three words interlined.
[25] TJ here canceled "& finally."
[26] TJ here canceled "all hopes of it's ever recovering it's usefulness."
[27] Reworked from "not sufficient confidence in their liberality to expect that."
[28] Preceding three words interlined in place of "ten."
[29] Word interlined.

30 Reworked from "than his whole page."

31 Paragraph not in NjP Tr.

32 Preceding three words interlined in place of "paper."

33 Preceding four paragraphs not in ViU Tr, which ends at the conclusion of the following paragraph.

34 Word interlined in place of "looked."

# To Oliver Evans

SIR
Monticello. Jan. 16. 1814.

In August last I recieved a letter from mr Isaac McPherson of Baltimore, on the controversies subsisting between yourself and some persons in that quarter interested in mills. these related to your patent rights for the elevators, conveyors, and hopper boys; and he requested any information I could give him on that subject. having been formerly a member of the patent board, as long as it existed, and bestowed in the execution of that trust much consideration on the questions belonging to it, I thought it an act of justice, and indeed of duty to communicate such facts and principles as had occurred to me on the subject. I therefore wrote the letter of Aug. 13. which is the occasion of your favor to me of the 7th instant just now recieved, but without the report of the case tried in the circuit court of Maryland, or your Memorial to congress, mentioned in the letter as accompanying it.    you request an answer to your letter, which my respect and esteem for you would of themselves have dictated: but I am not certain that I distinguish the particular points to which you wish a specific answer.    you agree in the letter that the chain of buckets, and Archimedes's screw are old inventions: that every one had, and still has, a right to use them, and the hopper boy if that also existed previously in the forms and constructions known before your patent: and that therefore you have neither a grant, nor claim, to the exclusive right of using elevators, conveyors, hopper boys, or drills, but only of the improved elevator, the improved hopper boy Etc. in this then we are entirely agreed, and your right to your own improvements in the construction of these machines is explicitly recognised in my letter.    I think however that your letter claims something more: altho' it is not so explicitly defined as to convey to my mind the precise idea which you perhaps meant to express. your letter says that your patent is for your improvement in the manufacture of flour by the application of certain principles, and of such machinery as will carry those principles into operation, whether of the improved elevator, improved hopper boy, or (without being confined to them) of any machinery[1] known and free to the public.       I can concieve how a machine may improve the manufacture of flour: but not how a <u>principle</u> abstracted from any machine, can do it. it must then be the machine, and the principle of that machine which is secured to you by your patent.       recurring now to the words of your definition, do they mean that, while all are free to use the old string of buckets, and Archimedes's screw for the purposes to which they had been formerly applied, you alone have the exclusive right to apply them to the manufacture of flour? that no one has a right to apply his old machines to all the purposes of which they are susceptible? that every one, for instance, who can apply the hoe, the spade, or the axe to any purpose to which they have not been before applied, may have a patent for the exclusive right to that application? and may exclude all others under penalties from so using their hoe, spade or axe? if this be the meaning, my opinion that the legislature never meant by the patent law to sweep away so extensively the rights of their constituents, to environ every thing they touch with snares, is expressed in the letter of Aug. 13. from which I have nothing to retract, nor ought to add but the observation that if a new application of our old machines be a ground of monopoly, the patent law will take from us much more good than it will give.       —Perhaps it may mean another thing: that while every one has a right to the distinct & separate use of the buckets, the screw, the hopper boy, in their old forms, the patent gives you the exclusive right to combine their uses on the same object. but if we have a right to use three things separately, I see nothing in reason, or in the patent law which forbids our using them all together. a man has a right to use a saw, an axe, and a plane separately; may he not combine their uses in fashioning the same piece of wood? he has a right to use a knife to cut his meat, a fork to hold it;[2] may a patentee take from him the right to combine their use on the same subject? such a law, instead of enlarging our conveniences as was intended, would most fearfully abridge them, and croud us by monopolies, out of the use of the things we have.

I have no particular interest however in these questions; nor any inclination to be made the advocate of either party; and I hope I shall be excused from it. I shall acquiesce chearfully in the decisions in your favor by those to whom the laws have confided them, without blaming the other party for being unwilling, when so new a branch of science has been recently engrafted on our jurisprudence, one with which it's professors have till now had no call to make themselves acquainted, one bearing little analogy to their professional educations or pursuits, that they should be unwilling I say, to admit that one or two decisions, before inferior & local tribunals, before the questions shall have been repeatedly & maturely examined in all their bearings, before the cases shall have presented themselves in all their forms and attitudes, before a sanction by the greater part of the judges on the most solemn investigations, and before the industry and intelligence of many defendants may have been excited to efforts for the vindication of the general rights of the citizen; that one or two precedents should for ever foreclose the whole of a new subject.

To the publication of this answer with your letter, as you request, I have no objection. I wish right to be done to all parties, and to yourself particularly & personally the just rewards of genius, and I tender you the assurances of my great esteem & respect.

Th: Jefferson

PoC (DLC); at foot of first page: "Oliver Evans esq."

While he served as United States secretary of state, TJ was leader ex officio of the three-member federal PATENT BOARD, known as the Board of Arts, which evaluated patent applications from 1790 until it was abolished when the patent act was revised three years later. During that time the board issued sixty-seven patents, among them one of 18 Dec.

1790 for Evans's improvements in the manufacturing of flour and meal (*U.S. Statutes at Large*, 1:109–12, 318–23 [10 Apr. 1790, 21 Feb. 1793]; Jeffrey H. Matsuura, *Jefferson vs. the Patent Trolls: A Populist Vision of Intellectual Property Rights* [2008], 79–111; *List of Patents*, 4).

[1] TJ here canceled "before."
[2] TJ here canceled "fast."

# To Joseph C. Cabell

DEAR SIR                                    Monticello Jan. 17. 14.

In your last letter to me you expressed a desire to look into the question Whether, by the laws of nature, one generation of men can, by any act of theirs, bind those which are to follow them? I say, by the laws of nature, there being between generation and generation, as between nation and nation, no other obligatory law: and you requested to see what I had said on the subject to mr Eppes. I inclose, for your own perusal, therefore, three letters which I wrote to him on the course of our finances, which embrace the question before stated. when I wrote the 1st I had no thought of following it by a 2d. I was led to that by his subsequent request, and after the 2d I was induced, in a 3d to take up the subject of banks, by the communication of a proposition, to be laid before Congress, for the establishment of a new bank. I mention this to explain the total absence of order in these letters as a whole. I have said above that they are sent for your own perusal, not meaning to debar any use of the matter, but only that my name may in no wise be connected with it. I am too desirous of tranquility to bring such a nest of hornets on me as the fraternities of banking companies: and this infatuation of banks is a torrent which it would be a folly for me to get into the way of. I see that it must take it's course, until actual ruin shall awaken us from it's delusions. until the gigantic banking propositions of this winter had made their appearance in the different legislatures, I had hoped that the evil might still be checked. but I see now that it is desperate, and that we must fold our arms, and go to the bottom with the ship. I had been in hopes that good old Virginia, not yet so far embanked as her northern sisters, would have set the example, this winter, of beginning the process of cure, by passing a law that after a certain time, suppose of 6. months, no bank bill of less than 10.D. should be permitted: that after some other reasonable term there should be none less than 20.D. and so on, until those only should be left in circulation whose size would be above the common transactions of any but merchants. this would ensure to us an ordinary circulation of metallic money, and would reduce the quantum of paper within the bounds of moderate mischief: and it is the only way in which the reduction can be made without a shock to private fortunes. a sudden stoppage of this trash, either by law or it's own worthlessness, would produce confusion and ruin. yet this will happen by it's own extinction, if left to itself. whereas by a salutary interposition of the legislature, it may be withdrawn insensibly and safely. such a mode of doing it too would give less alarm to the bank holders, the discreet part of whom must wish to see themselves secured by some circumscription. it might be asked what we should do for change? the banks must provide it, 1st to pay off their 5.D. bills, next their 10.D. d° and so on, and they ought to provide it to lessen the evils of their institution.—but I now give up all hope. after producing the same revolutions in private fortunes as the old continental paper did, it will die like that, adding a total incapacity to raise resources for the war.

Withdrawing myself within the shell of our own state, I have long contemplated a division of it into hundreds or wards as the most fundamental measure for securing good government, and for instilling the principles & exercise of self government into every fibre of every member of our commonwealth. but the details are too long for a letter, and must be the subject of conversation, whenever I shall have the pleasure of seeing you. it is for some of you young legislators to immortalise yourselves by laying this stone as the basis of our political edifice.

I must ask the favor of an early return of the inclosed papers, of which I have no copy. ever affectionately yours.

TH: JEFFERSON

RC (ViU: TJP); at foot of first page: "Joseph C. Cabell esq."; endorsed by Cabell as answered 23 Jan. PoC (DLC). Enclosures: TJ to John Wayles Eppes, 24 June, 11 Sept., 6 Nov. 1813. Enclosed in TJ to James Monroe, 3 Aug. 1814, and Monroe to TJ, 26 Apr. 1815.

By Cabell's LAST LETTER, TJ means his letter of 29 Nov. 1813, which was received at Monticello on the same day as the state senator's most recent communication, dated 8 Dec. 1813. For TJ's ideas about the necessity of dividing his home state into HUNDREDS OR WARDS, see his 1778 Bill for the More General Diffusion of Knowledge (*PTJ*, 2:526–35, esp. 527–8), TJ to John Tyler, 26 May 1810, and TJ to John Adams, 28 Oct. 1813.

# From Joseph Wheaton

EXCELLENT SIR                                    Richmond Jan$^y$ 17. 1814

I understand from M$^r$ William Johnson—that he is one of your overseers—and that he has been impressed into the Service of the united States by a M$^{rl}$ Nathan$^l$ Childers of Manchester Forage Master—Under Col W$^m$ Swan—Qu$^{tr}$ Mas$^{tr}$ Gen$^l$ Norfolk—this circumstance came to My knowledge by Settling Johnsons account— Childers had no authority to make any impressment whatever any inconvenience which you May have Suffered from this unauthorized Conduct—Nathaniel Childers is answerable for—. I am not Chargeable with any impropriety on this office—

I am Excellent Sir Sincerely & faithfully your obedient Humble Servant                                         JOSEPH WHEATON

A, D, Q, M, Gen$^l$

RC (DLC); adjacent to closing: "Thomas Jefferson Esq$^r$"; endorsed by TJ as received 23 Jan. 1814 and so recorded in SJL.

$^1$ Wheaton here canceled "Nicholas."

# From William Short

DEAR SIR                                          Philad$^a$ Jan 18—14

Your kind letter of the 9$^{th}$ of Nov: was recieved here at the time. You mentioned that you were setting off for Bedford & would be absent a month—I postponed therefore acknowleging its reciept so long that I determined to wait until I should again hear from you as to Carters affair after you had heard from him—so as to trouble you less often. But as I know my good countrymen of the Carter stamp I suppose it would be useless now to wait longer—& I therefore take up my pen to return you my very sincere thanks for your letter & particularly for the determination which you are so good as there to express, of not suffering this Carter business "to rest until it is finally & justly settled."—I am afraid it will give you a great deal of trouble & out of all proportion to the value of the object—but unsettled matters of this kind are so disagreeable to have on hand that I really have not the force to ask you to decline it, knowing as I do, that without your kind & friendly agency it would lye over until all the tombs of the Carters were filled—and I do not see how, even with your aid, Carter can be brought to the spot—Should he decline coming would there be no means of proceeding without him? and if it should be found that Monroe is well advised & entitled to the land, what would be my remedy against Carter? I should suppose a suit for damages—or perhaps he would give his obligation to refund—As to M$^r$ H: he has his remedy in his own hands—but I hope he will not avail himself of it to decline paying his bond in April.—Monroe would have saved us all a great deal of trouble if he would have urged his claim as he ought to have done, without leaving me to pay taxes on this land & finally sell it, if it really belong to him, which I hope will not be the case, when I consider that my survey must have been made so soon after his, & probably by the same surveyor—At any rate I am anxious for its final ascertainment. And I shall consider the termination as a desperate case, if it be necessary to have both Monroe & Carter present—but I hope there would be some means of proceeding without them—& that they might be brought to consent to the running of the line in the manner you mention by a surveyor.

M$^r$ Higginbotham has as yet said nothing of the rent which he assumed & which was due the 1$^{st}$ of this month. He will subject me both to disappointment & loss if he should not keep his engagement for April, because I intend to subscribe to the Government loan that is coming out. As the payment is made by installments in these loans, it adds much to the convenience, because a person can subscribe for a larger sum than he has on hand & count on future reciepts towards paying up future installments.

I regret as much as any person can, the lamentable change of system which has taken place as to our finances since you left the helm of government—but as I cannot prevent the present holders of the purse strings from spending so wantonly, & of course borrowing so ruinously, & as I am also to pay my proportion of the taxes consequent on these spendthrift extravagancies, it is my intention to save myself as much as I can by becoming a participator in the benefits of the lenders, as I must be in the burthens of the payers. Few people have an idea of the advantage of placing money in this way, & still fewer would believe that the power given to M$^r$ Gallatin for raising this money & the means he had of abusing that power to his own emolument (I am far from saying or believing that he did abuse it) was such as no British ministry ever had or could dream of having. And yet we all believe that we the people of these U.S. are the most cautious of trusting our power & have our servants the most under our control of all the others whom we consider as so many slaves & dupes to their Governors. The fact is that not one in an hundred of us sovereigns know in what manner this money was treated for—& yet the press is free & we are all wise & of course capable of judging—but the tone of public opinion is lost & buried in party spirit—Had this negotiation been in open day, & had M$^r$ G. obtained the loan at par, it would have been equally abused & complained of by the federal editors—And their abusing an operation is of itself sufficient to insure the full approbation of the opposite party—of course let the leaders of one party do what they may, (give the public bonds of 100 dollars for every fifty that they touch in cash, instead of for every 88—or 88$\frac{1}{4}$ dollars in cash as they did in the last two loans) they are sure of being abused by one set & this will insure their applause by the other—And where then is the subserviency of these servants of the people, or their responsibility to the people.—

Congress in the first instance gave the President the power of taking up 16. millions at any rate at which he could get it—he could only make the bonds bear 6. pc$^t$—but he could sell these bonds in the market for what they would bring—They advertized for a competition of lenders as the British Chancellor of the exchequer does—but there the parallel ends—for the whole loan not being subscribed, M$^r$ G.— came here & treated <u>à huis clos</u> for about 10. millions, in a tête à tête with M$^r$ Parish—& this agreement was in its nature final—neither the President or the Congress could have a vote after that—This loan was fixed at 88—It depended on M$^r$ G & M$^r$ P. of their own will jointly to fix it at any other rate—such a latitude, & to such an amount, never has been, for the play of <u>pots de vin</u> & all the other little expedients so well known to money dealers—I thought at the time how brave & undaunted M$^r$ G. must be when I recollected how much I had trembled when ordered to Amsterdam to borrow one tenth of that sum in the first instance.—I felt how much it put it in the power of suspicion & malevolence to abuse me—and at that date there was some bound to these hateful principles—There was one only remedy & that I was so fortunate as to be able to resort to, so as to put at defiance the possibility of suspicion—The bonus to be allowed the Bankers was the only part in which there could be deception, & I resolved therefore that it should be so low as to shew to all there could not be abuse—They resisted the reduction, which was so far below what had been allowed, & only[1] undertook to make the loan conditionally for it—saying they should be able to satisfy the President that it was less than it ought to be, & would rely on his justice & generosity to increase it—They appealed to him—stated the expences at which they were in procuring the loan & he thought it reasonable to allow the addition they asked—To this I had no objection because I did really believe it was just—but it showed to demonstration that I had not made such an allowance as could admit of the possibility of abuse. I then had the hope of being rewarded by the mission to Paris—& did suppose that by meriting the President's approbation I should stand before those who had not been at all employed abroad— The event did not, as you know, realize my hopes—& showed that other requisites are better under our form of Government, than experience or antecedent approbation of our conduct.

But this is an old story & a great aberration from the subject of the present letter. However, I find that in proportion as my ambitious propensities die away those of avarice increase—This is generally the case I believe & particularly as years increase—And the present government has so completely assumed the character of those young spendthrifts who have a large real estate, but no money for present exigencies & send their bonds into market with a mortgage on every thing, that every aviricous money holder is as much excited by present prospects as the Jews are when a young heir apparent comes on[2] the tapis. I count on 100. dollars at 6. p$^{ct}$ for every 88. or 90 dollars, perhaps for every 85—that I can command for the next six or eight months, during which the installments will probably be recievable. The appointment of such a man as Clay, who as a Kentuckian, surely cannot sign a treaty giving up the Canadas, or at least upper Canada, will make the loan several p.cent lower—the smallest gain that I have heard mentioned by the money lenders for them is 2. p.$^{ct}$—that is if he had not been appointed they expected to give 90 for the 100—but now not more than 88—So the world goes—& I really begin to feel great disgust with it.

Correa is here & has been for some time—He was enchanted with Monticello & delighted with its owner, & intends repeating his visit in the spring or summer—He is very partial to Virginia—but for the slave part he thinks it the first of the States—& says if ever there be an epic poem in the U.S. it will be born there.— I have recieved from the Abbe Rochon a micrometer of his invention—& also a telescope of Platina—If I should have an opportunity I should be very glad to show you the micrometer, as I think it would interest you—Let me if you please have the pleasure of hearing from you— Say to C^lo Randolph how much I regretted not finding him at home when here—I desired Co^l Coles to say the same to him—Believe me ever & truly, your friend & servant W SHORT

RC (MHi); endorsed by TJ as received 28 Jan. 1814 and so recorded in SJL.

The statute authorizing a new GOVERNMENT LOAN of up to $25 million was enacted on 24 Mar. 1814, while the laws for the LAST TWO LOANS were signed on 14 Mar. 1812 ($11 million) and 8 Feb. 1813 ($16 million), respectively (*U.S. Statutes at Large*, 2:694–5, 798–9, 3:111–2). À HUIS CLOS: "behind closed doors." POTS DE VIN: "bribes." Following TJ's departure from France in 1789, Short remained behind as chargé d'affaires and negotiated loans totaling roughly $12 million from bankers in AM-

STERDAM and Antwerp (*ANB*). On 14 Jan. 1814 James Madison nominated the KENTUCKIAN Henry Clay as one of the ministers plenipotentiary "to negotiate and sign a treaty of peace and a treaty of commerce with Great Britain." The Senate confirmed his appointment four days later (*JEP*, 2:451–2, 454). TJ already owned a MICROMETER ("lunette") of Alexis Marie Rochon (TJ to Robert Patterson, 27 Dec. 1812; Stein, *Worlds*, 352–3).

[1] Word interlined.
[2] Manuscript: "or."

# From Thomas Clark

SIR                              Philadelphia January 19^th 1814

I have taken the liberty to forward to you a copy of the second edition of the naval history of the U.S. I return you my sincere thanks for your kind communication. It was not in my power to avail myself of your two remarks on the Tripolitan war. M^r Carey was very desirous of having the work speedily published; & would not consent to the delay, which a recourse to official documents would have occasioned. There was nothing else in my possession[1] sufficiently authentic, on which to rest my narrative. This however shall certainly be attended to, should a third edition be called for by the public.

I have also enclosed proposals for the publication of a history of the United States, on which for several years past I have been employed.

Your patronage is earnestly solicited. Any Suggestions on the improvement of the work, or historical communication, will be thankfully received

In collecting materials all the printed documents & histories have been examined: & I Shall in succession consult the records of the several State Governments. I am desirous of knowing, whether in the government offices of Virginia there are not a number of valuable important records & papers for the historian. You would also very much oblige me by putting me in the way of obtaining an authentic & complete copy of the laws & transactions of the government of Virginia, from its settlement to the present time; likewise a file of some of your oldest & most respectable news-papers, or other local publications, that may contain any valuable or authentic historical matter. The policy of the British government; in the early part of our history, to prevent the establishment of printing presses, in the American colonies; renders the collection of materials a very arduous & difficult task.[2] & in your State particularly, where Sir William Berkeley used every[3] exertion to carry it into effect.

The first volume, intended as a specimen of the work, will immediately be put to press, It will contain an introductary account of the aborigines of America, & the history of the first period, ending with the commencement of the reign of James the first

I am Sir with great esteem your most humble & obedient servant

THOMAS CLARK

My address is N° 37 south second St.      Philadelphia

RC (DLC); addressed: "Thomas Jefferson Esq;"; endorsed by TJ as received 2 Feb. 1814 and so recorded in SJL. Enclosures: (1) Clark, *Naval History of the United States, from the Commencement of the Revolutionary War to the Present Time*, 2d ed., 2 vols. (Philadelphia, 1814; Sowerby, no. 531; Poor, *Jefferson's Library*, 4 [no. 142]). (2) Clark, "Proposals, for publishing by subscription, A History of the United States," stating that the work will be a general history of the United States, with sections about the various states and individuals important to the nation's development, chapters on civil, political, legal, military, ecclesiastical, local, scientific, literary, educational, and natural history, and information about the country's wealth, military resources, defenses, manners, customs, institutions, associations, and occupations "illustrative of the state and progress of society"; explaining that two octavo volumes of between five and six hundred pages are anticipated annually, at a cost of $3 per volume, "until the work be completed"; and advising that subscribers "will not be considered as obligated for the whole work, but, on notifying the publisher, may discontinue the taking of it" (printed broadside at MBAt).

The KIND COMMUNICATION was TJ's 19 June 1813 letter to Mathew Carey, Clark's publisher. In the preface to the second edition of his *Naval History*, Clark reported that "through want of proper documents, and the hurry of the work, it was not in my power to avail myself of two of the observations of Mr. Jefferson, late president of the United States, on the

Tripolitan war. They shall however not be neglected should the public call for another edition." Prior to the Revolutionary War, significant restrictions were placed on the ESTABLISHMENT OF PRINTING PRESSES in America. One early authority asserted that outside Massachusetts, "no presses were set up in the colonies till near the close of the seventeenth century"; and that as late as 1775 the fifty extant American printing establishments were all located in the various colonial capitals, where they might be reined in, if necessary, by the imperial regime (Isaiah Thomas, *The History of Printing in America* [Worcester, 1810; repr. 1970], 7–8). Longtime Virginia colonial governor SIR WILLIAM BERKELEY famously remarked

in 1671 that "I thanke God there are noe free schooles noe printing and I hope Wee shall not have these hundred yeares for learning has brought disobedience & heresye & sects into the world and printing hath divulged them, and libells against the best Government. God keepe us from both" (Warren M. Billings and Maria Kimberly, eds., *The Papers of Sir William Berkeley, 1605–1677* [2007], 397).

Clark sent the same enclosures to President James Madison on 24 Jan. 1814 (DLC: Madison Papers).

[1] Manuscript: "possion."
[2] Manuscript: "tasks."
[3] Manuscript: "evey."

# From Patrick Gibson

SIR                                      Richmond 19th January 1814

Immediately after my letter to you of the 8th Inst the price of flour became nominal, the few orders which had been received from Alexandria were complied with and no further purchases were made, so that, when on monday I received your favor of the 13th and endeavour'd according to your directions to effect a sale, I found that even 5$ could not be obtain'd—I have still hopes of getting that price, although I may be under the necessity of giving 60d/—I regret much I did not sell without waiting to hear from you, but like many others I thought it could not fall in the interim, but on the contrary expected it would rise—I send you $300. as you request in small notes

With great respect I am Your obt Servt          PATRICK GIBSON

RC (ViU: TJP-ER); at head of text: "Thomas Jefferson Esqre"; endorsed by TJ as received 23 Jan. 1814 and so recorded in SJL.

# To David A. Leonard

SIR                                      Monticello Jan. 20. 14.

I have duly recieved your two favors of Dec. 30. and Jan. 2. you could not have applied for counsel to one less personally acquainted with the Western country than myself; having never been 50. miles Westward of my own house. I have not however been uninquisitive as to the circumstances characteristic of the several parts of the

Western waters, of their comparative advantages, disadvantages, and preferences; and shall freely give you the result of my reflections. taking into view those considerations which weigh most in the choice of a residence, that is to say: 1. temperature of climate, 2. fertility of soil, 3. cheapness of land, 4. profitable objects of culture, 5. convenience to market. 6. navigation & 7. safety from external enemies, the Missisipi territory, and particularly the part of it in the neighborhood of the hither bank of the river, has appeared to me to have a preference over every other part of the Western country. the neighborhood of Washington, it's capital, has been represented by those acquainted with both, as corresponding in it's climate & healthiness with the middle and upper parts of N. Carolina, which is certainly as healthy a country as any to the North of it; altho' all[1] Northern people are prone to consider whatever is South of them as sickly and mortal. if this very general view can be of service in leading your enquiries, as to the points of preference, to persons better informed, it will have rendered you the only service it is in my power to offer: and with it accept my wishes that you may be fortunate in your choice, and prosperous in it's issue, with the assurance of my respect.        TH: JEFFERSON

PoC (MoSHi: TJC-BC); at foot of text: "M^r D. A. Leonard Bristol. R.I."; endorsed by TJ.

[1] Word interlined in place of "every."

# To Robert M. Patterson

SIR                                            Monticello Jan. 20. 14.

I have duly recieved your favor of the 7^th informing me that the American Philosophical society, at their meeting of that day, had been pleased unanimously to re-elect me as President of the society. I recieve with just sensibility this proof of their continued good will, and pray you to assure them of my gratitude for these favors, of my devotedness to their service, and the pleasure with which at all times I should in any way be made useful to them.        for yourself be pleased to accept the assurance of my great esteem and respect.

TH: JEFFERSON

RC (PPAmP: APS Archives); addressed: "R. M. Patterson Secretary of the A. Phil. Society Philadelphia"; franked; postmarked Milton, 26 Jan.; endorsed by an APS clerk as from "Jefferson 1814 on his re-election as President read. 4 Feb^y 1814." PoC (DLC).

# To Sir Egerton Leigh

SIR                                    Monticello Jan. 21. 14.

Your favor of Dec. 7. came to hand but a few days ago, and with it the letter of D[r] Ramsay. I learned with regret your detention on the road by sickness, and hope, if this finds you at the same place, it will be in a better state of health. presuming that the warm and hot springs of[1] Bath county are the objects of your journey, I cannot but wish to hear of your arrival there; as (living myself on one of the highroads to them) I have witnessed the most flattering instances of permanent cure of rheumatism and great relief to gout. there is a general idea that their waters are the most efficacious in the months of July, August & September. but these months have got into vogue by their being the sickly months of the tide waters and therefore the most apropos for leaving the lower country. I doubt myself whether either the temperature or impregnation of the waters are sensibly affected by the season. more precautions against taking cold will of course be necessary in colder weather: but precautions, more or less, are necessary in all seasons.          your letter giving me the hope that you may have occasion to pass this way, I pray you to be assured that I shall be happy to recieve you here, and to be favored with such an occasion of proving my respect for our friend D[r] Ramsay, as well as of doing justice to your own personal merit. I shall be absent from home about 3. or 4. weeks from the latter part of April, which I mention in the hope that this call upon my time may not be so unlucky as to deprive me of the gratification of your visit. Accept the assurance of my great respect & consideration.

TH: JEFFERSON

PoC (MoSHi: TJC-BC); at foot of text: "Sir Egerton Leigh"; endorsed by TJ.

Leigh's FAVOR was dated 19 Dec. 1813, not DEC. 7.

[1] TJ here canceled "Augusta."

# To John Melish

Monticello Jan. 21. 14.

Th: Jefferson presents his compliments to mr Melish and his thanks for the renewed mark of his attention in sending him a copy of his military Atlas, a very interesting work in the present state of things. he begs leave to become a subscriber for the New General

Atlas which mr Melish proposes to publish, of which he returns the Prospectus with his name to it. he salutes mr Melish with great esteem & respect.

PoC (DLC); dateline at foot of text; endorsed by TJ.

For the enclosed PROSPECTUS, see note to Melish to TJ, 21 Dec. 1813.

# From Joseph C. Cabell

DEAR SIR,                                              Richmond. 23ᵈ Jan: 1814.

The last mail from Charlottesville brought me your letter of 17ᵗʰ inst: accompanied by your three letters to mʳ Eppes on the subject of the ways & means of carrying on the war. Accept, I beseech you, my most sincere thanks for the communication of these papers which from the hasty perusal I have given them already promise me a fund of valuable & highly interesting matter. I shall observe your injunctions in regard to the use of them, and the time during which they may remain in my possession. They have come too late to produce any effect on the principal proceedings of our session in regard to Banks. The day the packet reached me, the senate voted for the Bill augmenting the Capital and extending the Charter of the Bank of Virginia. I was desirous to reduce the encreased capital from one million to half a million of dollars, but could not prevail. I have however brought myself under the lash of your censure by voting for this measure. I have thus voted from a wish thro' the instrumentality of the Bank to aid the state in the prosecution of the war. I have of late years, come into the opinion of a limited well regulated system of Banking in Virginia, not so much from any fondness I have for the system in the abstract, as that I regard it as a sort of defensive system, imposed on us by the circumstance of our being a member of a confederacy, the other members of which have surrounded us with banks. In the language of the mountain Hunters, "I am for firing against their fire." You have opened a vast horizon to my view. Indeed Sir, I most sincerely & heartily thank you for the high gratification you have given me in the perusal of these letters. A bill for the establishment of a small bank at Wheeling will probably come up to the Senate in a few days. On that occasion I shall[1] avail myself of some of your ideas. I cannot now go into this subject, but will be extremely happy to resume it in conversation at a future day. You would add greatly to the obligations already conferred on me, if you would inform me by letter what is your opinion in regard to the[2] Question,

"Whether the Legislature of a state has a right under the federal Constitution to restrict the residence of a member of the House of Representatives to the district by which he is chosen": and if your opinion should be in favor of the right, you would add greatly to the favor by stating the principal reasons on which your opinion is founded. This subject was agitated in the Assembly last winter: the Senate & the House of Delegates were opposed to each other on the question. I voted with the majority of the Senate ag$^t$ the right of the Legislature. A review of my opinion leaves me in some doubt as to its correctness. The subject is now before the House of Delegates—and probably it will be two weeks before the upper House will be called upon to vote on it. I should be much pleased to hear from you before the vote is taken, and should it be your desire that your Letter should not be used, I will consider it a duty to hold it from the view of others:

The bill respecting the Rivanna River Company is now progressing thro' the Lower House. It contains the verbal alterations you suggested. The Assembly will rise about the middle or 20$^{th}$ of February.

I am d$^r$ Sir, very truly & sincerely yours.

JOSEPH C. CABELL.

I shall be happy to learn your reasons for dividing the state into hundreds or wards. M$^r$ Coles mentioned this subject to me some years ago: but without stating the various considerations in favor of the measure.

I sent your books to you by Gen$^l$ moore, at the commencem$^t$ of the session: & hope they arrived safe & in a few days after [they lef]t$^3$ this.

RC (ViU: TJP-PC); mutilated at seal; addressed: "Thomas Jefferson esq. Monticello"; franked; postmarked Richmond, 26 Jan.; endorsed by TJ as received 28 Jan. 1814 and so recorded in SJL.

The Senate of Virginia approved a bill "For extending the CHARTER of the Bank of Virginia, and for other purposes" on 22 Jan. 1814, and it became law two days later (JSV [1813–14 sess.], 28; Acts of Assembly [1813–14 sess.], 67–71). The Senate rejected a bill from the House of Delegates for "Incorporating the Merchants' and Farmers' Bank of WHEELING" by a tie vote on 29 Jan., with Cabell among those who voted nay (JSV [1813–14 sess.], 31, 35).

On 6 Feb. 1813 the Virginia General Assembly, after an AGITATED debate and numerous amendments, approved "An Act for arranging the Counties of this Commonwealth into Districts to choose Representatives to Congress," section 2 of which stipulated that the electorate was to "vote for some discreet and proper person, qualified according to the constitution of the United States, as a member of the House of Representatives of the United States." A bill from the House of Delegates "Requiring members of Congress to reside in their respective districts" was committed to Cabell and four other senators on 24 Jan. 1814. He brought the proposed legislation back to the floor on 1 Feb., but the measure was killed by a vote tabling it until after the close of the session (*Acts of Assembly* [1812–13 sess.], 30–4, quote on p. 30; *JSV* [1812–13 sess.], 68, 73, 77, 79; [1813–14 sess.], 31, 42).

[1] Cabell here canceled "probably."
[2] Cabell here canceled "power."
[3] Missing text supplied from Cabell, *University of Virginia*, 18.

# To John Adams

DEAR SIR                                    Monticello Jan. 24. 14.

I have great need of the indulgence so kindly extended to me in your favor of Dec. 25. of permitting me to answer your friendly letters at my leisure. my frequent and long absences from home are a first cause of tardiness in my correspondence, and a $2^d$ the accumulation of business during my absence, some of which imperiously commands first attentions. I am now in arrear to you for your letters of Nov. 12. 14. 16. Dec. 3. 19. 25.

I have made some enquiry about Taylor's book, and I learn from a neighbor of his that it has been understood for some time that he was writing a political work. we had not heard here of it's publication, nor has it been announced in any of our papers. but this must be the book of 630. pages which you have recieved; and certainly neither the style nor the stuff of the author of Arator can ever be mistaken. in the latter work, as you observe, there are some good things, but so involved in quaint, in far-fetched, affected, mystical conciepts, and flimsy theories, that who can take the trouble of getting at them?

You ask me if I have ever seen the work of J. W. Goethens Schoristen? Never. nor did the question ever occur to me before Where got we the ten commandments? the book indeed gives them to us verbatim. but where did it get them? for itself tells us they were written by the finger of god on tables of stone, which were destroyed by Moses: it specifies those on the $2^d$ set of tables in different form and substance, but still without saying how the others were recovered. but the whole history of these books is so defective and doubtful that it seems vain to attempt minute enquiry into it: and such tricks have been plaid with their text, and with the texts of other books relating to them, that we have a right, from that cause, to entertain much doubt what parts of them are genuine. in the New testament there is internal evidence that parts of it have proceeded from an extraordinary man; and that other parts are of the fabric of very inferior minds. it is as easy to separate those parts, as to pick out diamonds from dunghills. the matter of the first was such as would be preserved in the memory of the hearers, and handed on by tradition for a long time; the latter such stuff as might be gathered up, for imbedding it, any where, and at any time.—I have nothing of Vives, or Budaeus, and little of Erasmus. if the familiar histories of the saints, the want of which they regret, would have given us the histories of those tricks which these writers acknolege to have been practised, and of the lies they agree have been invented for the sake of religion, I join them in their regrets. these would be the only parts of their histories worth reading. it is not only the sacred volumes they have thus interpolated, gutted, and falsified, but the works of others relating to them, and even the laws of the land. we have a curious instance of one of these pious frauds in the Laws of Alfred. he composed, you know, from the laws of the Heptarchy, a Digest for the government of the United kingdom, and in his preface to that work he tells us expressly the sources from which he drew it, to wit, the laws of Ina, of Offa & Aethelbert, (not naming the Pentateuch.) but his pious Interpolator, very awkwardly, <u>premises</u> to his work four chapters of Exodus (from the 20<sup>th</sup> to the 23<sup>d</sup>) as a part of the laws of the land; so that Alfred's <u>preface</u> is made to stand in the body of the work. our judges too have lent a ready hand to further these frauds, and have been willing to lay the yoke of their own opinions on the necks of others; to extend the coercions of municipal law to the dogmas of their religion, by declaring that these make a part of the law of the land. in the Year Book 34. H. 6. fo. 38. in Quare impedit, where the question was how far the Common law takes notice of the Ecclesiastical law, Prisot, Chief Justice, in the course of his argument says 'a tiels leis que ils de Seint eglise ont en <u>ancien scripture</u>, covient a nous a donner credence; car ces Common ley sur quels touts manners leis sont fondes: et auxy, Sir, nous sumus obliges de conustre lour ley de saint eglise E'c.' Finch begins the business of falsification by mistranslating and mistaking the words of Prisot thus 'to such laws of the church as have warrant in <u>holy scripture</u> our law giveth credence,' citing the above case & the words of Prisot in the margin. Finch's law. B. 1. c. 3. here then we find <u>ancien scripture</u>, antient writing, translated 'holy scripture.' this, Wingate in 1658. erects into a Maxim of law, in the very words of Finch, but citing Prisot, and not Finch. and Sheppard tit. Religion, in 1675 laying it down in the same words of Finch, quotes the Year Book, Finch and Wingate. then comes S<sup>r</sup> Matthew Hale, in the case of the King v. Taylor 1. Ventr. 293. 3. Keb. 607. and declares that 'Christianity is parcel of the laws of England.' citing nobody, and resting it, with his judgment against the witches, on his own authority, which indeed was sound and good in all cases into which no superstition or bigotry could enter. thus strengthened, the court in

1728 in the King v. Woolston, would not suffer it to be questioned whether to write against Christianity was punishable at Common law, saying it had been so settled by Hale in Taylor's case. 2. Stra. 834. Wood therefore, 409. without scruple, lays down as a principle that all blasphemy and profaneness are offences at the Common law, and cites Strange. Blackstone, in 1763. repeats in the words of S$^r$ Matthew Hale that 'Christianity is part of the laws of England,' citing Ventris and Strange ubi supra. and L$^d$ Mansfield in the case of the Chamberlain of London v. Evans, in 1767. qualifying somewhat the position, says that 'the essential principles of revealed religion are part of the Common law.' thus we find this string of authorities all hanging by one another on a single hook, a mistranslation by Finch of the words of Prisot, or on nothing. for all quote Prisot, or one another, or nobody. thus Finch misquotes Prisot; Wingate also, but using Finch's words; Sheppard quotes Prisot, Finch and Wingate; Hale cites nobody; the court in Woolston's case cite Hale; Wood cites Woolston's case; Blackstone that & Hale; and L$^d$ Mansfield volunteers his own ipse dixit. and who now can question but that the whole Bible and Testament are a part of the Common law? and that Connecticut, in her blue laws, laying it down as a principle that the laws of god should be the laws of their land, except where their own contradicted them, did any thing more than express, with a salvo, what the English judges had less cautiously declared without any restriction? and what I dare say our cunning Chief Justice would swear to, and find as many sophisms to twist it out of the general terms of our Declarations of rights, and even the stricter text of the Virginia 'act for the freedom of religion' as he did to twist Burr's neck out of the halter of treason. may we not say then with him who was all candor and benevolence 'Woe unto you, ye lawyers, for ye lade men with burdens grievous to bear.'

I think with you that Priestley, in his comparison of the doctrines of Philosophy and of revelation, did not do justice to the undertaking, but he felt himself pressed by the hand of death. Enfield has given us a more distinct account of the ethics of the antient philosophers; but the great work, of which Enfield's is an abridgment, Brucker's history of Philosophy, is the treasure which I would wish to possess, as a book of reference or of special research only, for who could read 6. vols 4$^{to}$ of 1000 pages each, closely printed, of modern Latin? your account of D'Argens' Ocellus makes me wish for him also. Ocellus furnishes a fruitful text for a sensible and learned commentator. the Abbé Batteux', which I have, is a meagre thing.

You surprise me with the account you give of the strength of family distinction still existing in your state. with us it is so[1] totally extinguished that not a spark of it is to be found but lurking in the hearts of some of our old tories. but all bigotries hang to one another; and this in the Eastern states, hangs, as I suspect, to that of the priesthood. here youth, beauty, mind and manners are more valued than a pedigree.

I do not remember the conversation between us which you mention in yours of Nov. 15. on your proposition to vest in Congress the exclusive power of establishing banks. my opposition to it must have been grounded, not on taking the power from the states, but on leaving any vestige of it in existence, even in the hands of Congress; because it would only have been a change of the organ of abuse. I have ever been the enemy of banks; not of those discounting for cash; but of those foisting their own paper into circulation, and thus banishing our cash. my zeal against those institutions was so warm and open at the establishment of the bank of the US.[2] that I was derided as a Maniac by the tribe of bank-mongers, who were seeking to filch from the public their swindling, and barren gains. but the errors of that day cannot be recalled. the evils they have engendered are now upon us, and the question is how we are to get[3] out of them? shall we build an altar to the old paper money of the revolution, which ruined individuals but saved the republic, and burn on that all the bank charters present and future, and their notes with them? for these are to ruin both republic and individuals. this cannot be done. the Mania is too strong. it has siesed by it's delusions & corruptions all the members of our governments, general, special, and individual. our circulating paper of the last year was estimated at 200. millions of dollars. the new banks now petitioned for, to the several legislatures, are for about 60. millions additional capital, & of course 180. millions of additional circulation, nearly doubling that of the last year; and raising the whole mass to near 400. millions, or 40. for 1. of the wholsome amount of circulation for a population of 8. millions circumstanced as we are: and you remember how rapidly our money went down after our 40. for 1. establishment in the revolution. I doubt if the present trash can hold as long. I think the 380. millions must blow all up in the course of the present year; or certainly it will be consummated by the reduplication to take place of course at the legislative meetings of the next winter. should not prudent men, who possess stock in any monied institution, either draw & hoard the cash, now while they can, or exchange it for canal stock, or such other as being bottomed on immoveable property, will remain unhurt by the crush? I have been endeavoring to persuade a friend in our legislature to try and save this state from the general ruin by timely interference. I propose to him 1. to prohibit instantly all foreign paper. 2. to give our own banks 6. months to call in all their 5. Dollar bills (the lowest we allow.) another 6. months to call in their 10.D. notes, and 6. months more to call in all below 50. Dollars. this would produce so gradual a diminution of medium as not to shock contracts already made; would leave finally bills of such size as would be called for only in transactions between merchant and merchant, and ensure a metallic circulation for those of the mass of citizens. but it will not be done. you might as well, with the sailors, whistle to the wind, as suggest precautions against having too much money. we must scud then before the gale, and try to hold fast, ourselves, by some plank of the wreck. god send us all a safe deliverance, and to yourself every other species and degree of happiness. TH: JEFFERSON

P.S. I return your letter of Nov. 15. as it requests: and supposing that the late publication of the life of our good & really great Rittenhouse may not have reached you I send a copy for your acceptance. even it's episodes and digressions may add to the amusement it will furnish you. but if the history of the world were written on the same scale, the whole world would not hold it. Rittenhouse, as an astronomer, would stand on a line with any of his time, and as a mechanician he certainly has not been equalled. in this view he was truly great. but, placed along side of Newton, every human character must appear diminutive, & none would have shrunk more feelingly from the painful parallel than the modest and amiable Rittenhouse, whose genius and merit are not the less for this exaggerated comparison of his over zealous biographer.

RC (MHi: Adams Papers); edge trimmed, with missing text supplied from PoC; addressed: "President Adams"; endorsed by Adams; docketed by Charles Francis Adams. PoC (DLC). Enclosure: Adams to TJ, 15 Nov. 1813.

TJ was IN ARREAR to Adams for a letter dated 15 Nov. 1813, not 16 Nov. J. W. GOETHENS SCHORISTEN: Johann Wolfgang von Goethe's *Schriften* ("writings"). For the YEAR BOOK 34. H. 6. FO. 38, see *Les Reports des Cases Contenus in les Ans vingt premier, & apres en temps du Roy Henry le VI* (London, 1679); the case in question does commence on page 38, but the quotation from Chief Justice John

Prisot appears two pages later. QUARE IMPEDIT: a writ or action enforcing a patron's right to fill a vacant benefice (*Black's Law Dictionary*).
A TIELS LEIS QUE ILS DE SEINT EGLISE . . . CONUSTRE LOUR LEY DE SAINT EGLISE: "We should give credence to the laws in the ancient writings of the holy Church; because they are the common law upon which all manners and laws are founded: and also, Sir, we are obliged to recognize the law of the holy Church." 3. KEB. 607: Joseph Keble, *Reports in the Court of Kings Bench at Westminster* (London, 1685; Sowerby, no. 2063), 3:607. In 1662 Mathew Hale presided over a famous trial in Bury Saint

Edmunds that resulted in the conviction and execution of two WITCHES (*ODNB*). UBI SUPRA: "as stated above" (*Black's Law Dictionary*).

TJ's refutation of the theory that the WHOLE BIBLE AND TESTAMENT ARE A PART OF THE COMMON LAW drew heavily on his Legal Commonplace Book (see TJ to Thomas Cooper, 10 Feb. 1814, and note). The CUNNING CHIEF JUSTICE, John Marshall, presided over the 1807 treason trial that acquitted Aaron Burr (*DAB*). Jesus is quoted as saying WOE UNTO YOU, YE LAWYERS, FOR YE LADE

MEN WITH BURDENS GRIEVOUS TO BEAR in the Bible (Luke 11.46). TJ's FRIEND in the Virginia legislature was Joseph C. Cabell.

TJ evidently sent separately A COPY of William Barton, *Memoirs of the Life of David Rittenhouse* (Philadelphia, 1813; Sowerby, no. 529; Poor, *Jefferson's Library*, 4 [no. 141]).

[1] Word interlined.
[2] Preceding nine words interlined.
[3] RC: "get get." PoC: "get."

# From Tadeusz Kosciuszko

MON CHER AMI                    Paris 24. Janvier–1814.
Je crois que la Guerre avec l'Angletaire à empeché la communication de l'Amerique avec la France, puis que je nai pas reçu de lettre de change pour l'Année passée, ni aucune de vos nouvelles. Cependant comme je suis pressé d'Argent—Ayez la bonté de m'en faire parvenir le plutot possible. ne pouriez vous pas charger quelque Americain ici ou même M^r Crawford votre Ministre c'est une petite Sômme pour lui mais trés grande pour moi—
Je vous embrasse Mille et Mille fois avec la plus grande Éstime et la
    Consideration la plus Distinguee                    T KOSCIUSZKO

EDITORS' TRANSLATION

MY DEAR FRIEND                    Paris 24. January–1814.
I believe that the war with England has hindered communications between America and France, as I have received neither a letter of exchange for last year nor any news from you. Yet, as I am short of money—please be so kind as to have some sent to me as soon as possible. Could you not entrust it to some American here or even to your minister Mr. Crawford? It is a small sum for him but a very large one for me—
I embrace you a thousand and a thousand times with the highest esteem and
    the most distinguished consideration                    T KOSCIUSZKO

RC (NNPM); dateline at foot of text; endorsed by TJ as received 2 Apr. 1814 and so recorded in SJL. Enclosed in TJ to John Barnes, 25 Apr. 1814, and Barnes to TJ, 18 May 1814. Translation by Dr. Genevieve Moene.

In a covering letter written from Berville on 24 Jan. 1814, Kosciuszko asked William H. CRAWFORD to forward "la lettre ci jointe à M^r Jefferson par le premier Navire a votre disposition" ("the enclosed letter to Mr. Jefferson by the first ship at your disposal") (RC in possession of The Century Association, New York City, 1948; addressed: "À Monsieur Monsieur Crawford Ministre Plenipotantiaire des Etats Unis de l'Amerique à Paris à son Hotel"; stamped; postmarked 27 Jan. 1814).

# From John Manners

DEAR SIR,                                          Flemington Jan. 24th 1814

Altho' I have not the honour of a personal Acquaintance with you, yet impelled by a desire of being informed on a subject of natural science, and knowing no person upon whose opinion I could place so much reliance, I have taken the liberty of writing to you—

Nor should I now obtrude[1] on your time, had I not known that you take pleasure in distributing useful knowledge—

The subject on which I wish to be informed is respecting the classification of animals—Whether with D[r] shaw and the British Zoologists you adopt the classification of Linnæus:—whether with the french naturalists you prefer that of M. Cuvier or of M. Blumenbach—whether you have not formed one peculiar[2] to yourself—or whether you, with the learned M Buffon reject all classification as injudicious and impracticable—

This opinion of the french naturalist certainly has its analogy— Diseases were formerly divided into classes orders genera species & varieties by D[r] Sydenham D[r] Cullen and other nosologists; and in fact nosology was adopted by the medical world—But these divisions have been shown to the satisfaction of most pathologists to be injudicious impracticable and even injurious by my illustrius and truly worthy friend and preceptor in medicine D[r] Rush; and disease proteiform as it is has been demonstrated to be an unit—But I think notwithstanding the ingenuity and erudition with which M. Buffon has defended his opinion, that the classification of animals stands on a more solid basis—But upon the propriety and manner of classification I must importune your opinion—

While a student of medicine I attended several courses of lectures on natural History in the Museum of M[r] Peale by D[r] Barton. He adopted the classification of M. Cuvier with some few modifications—

As the nomenclature of the Classes orders genera & even some of the species is highly objectionable—I have attempted to reform it, but have not dared to make it public—

Another subject upon which I wish to consult you is with respect to that curious genus of animals the <u>Ornothorhyncus</u>—I wish to know to what order, or even to what class you assign it: I say to what class; because it [dif]fers materially from the mammalia—[. . .] Home nor no other zootomist who has had an opportunity of desecting them ever find them to possess mammæ—They differ also in other important particulars—It seems to approximate more to the <u>Aves</u> in having the mandibles—Cloaca—and in having a spur on its leg (at least the O. paradoxus) I am ignorant where to give it a place; but am rather inclined to the opinion we shall have to constitute a new class for this anomalous genus—on this subject, however, it becomes me to be silent untill I hear your opinion

I am most respectfully Your ob[t] Servant  JOHN MANNERS

RC (DLC); mutilated at seal; addressed: "Thomas Jefferson Esq[r] Monticello Virginia"; stamped; postmarked Flemington, 24 Jan.; endorsed by TJ as received 4 Feb. 1814 and so recorded in SJL.

John Manners (1786–1853), physician, chemist, attorney, and public official, was a native of Hunterdon County, New Jersey. He established a medical practice in Philadelphia about 1811. The following year Manners graduated from the University of Pennsylvania's medical department, where he studied under Benjamin Rush. He married a daughter of Thomas Cooper and eventually became the latter's literary executor. Manners lectured on the institutes and practice of medicine at the Cabinet of Sciences of Philadelphia. He was also president of that institution and corresponding secretary for the Philadelphia Medical Society. Manners's published essays included descriptions of his chemical investigations and experiments. Returning to New Jersey, he established a medical practice in Hunterdon County. Manners was admitted to the New Jersey bar in 1820. From 1850 until his death he represented Hunterdon County in the state senate, winning a term as president of that body in 1852 (*The Biographical Encyclopædia of New Jersey of the Nineteenth Century* [1877], 453–4; James

Robinson, *The Philadelphia Directory, for 1811* [Philadelphia, 1811], 206; *Memoirs of the Columbian Chemical Society, of Philadelphia* [Philadelphia, 1813], vol. 1; *Kite's Philadelphia Directory for 1814* [Philadelphia, 1814]; *The Medical Repository of Original Essays and Intelligence relative to Physic, Surgery, Chemistry, and Natural History*, n.s., 2 [1815]: 15–9; Manners to TJ, 20 May 1817; TJ to Manners, 12 June 1817; William Riker Jr., *Rules of the Supreme Court of the State of New Jersey* [1901], 62; John Blane, *History of the District Medical Society for the County of Hunterdon* [1872], 47–8; *Journal of the Eighth Senate of the State of New Jersey*, 7–9 [76th sess., 13 Jan. 1852]; *New York Times*, 2 July 1853; *New Jersey Medical Reporter* 6 [1853]: 347–8).

PROTEIFORM: "assuming many forms, extremely variable" (*OED*). *Ornithorhyncus* (ORNOTHORHYNCHUS) *anatinus* is the scientific name for the platypus, of which Everard HOME published one of the first scientific descriptions in 1802 (Home, "A Description of the Anatomy of the *Ornithorhynchus paradoxus*," *Philosophical Transactions of the Royal Society* 92 [1802]: 67–84). A ZOOTOMIST studies the structure of animal bodies (*OED*). AVES: "birds."

[1] Manuscript: "obtruded."
[2] Manuscript: "one of peculiar."

# To Richard Randolph

DEAR SIR                                    Monticello Jan. 25. 14.

Will you be so good as to send me two gross of your beer jugs; the one gross to be quart jugs, and the other pottle dº. they are to be delivered to a mr William Johnson a waterman of Milton, who will apply for them about a week hence. mr Gibson will be so good as to pay for them on your presenting this letter. they should be packed in crates, or old hogsheads or such other cheap package as you use. Accept the assurance of my esteem & respect.          TH: JEFFERSON

PoC (MHi); at foot of text: "Mr Richard Randolph"; endorsed by TJ.

Richard Randolph (1782–1859), the eldest son of David Meade Randolph and Mary Randolph, of Tuckahoe, visited TJ at Monticello in September 1808. Five years later he established a stoneware factory a dozen miles east of Richmond on the James River in Henrico County. By 1816 Randolph's two-story "Potters Shop" was valued at $1,200. In 1822 he sent TJ six barrels of waterproof shale cement, a substance discovered by his father, and asked the ex-president for his opinion of it. Unfortunately, TJ found that "in every instance this cement dissolved on being put into water," and he was consequently unwilling to use it either at Monticello or for the construction of the University of Virginia (William G. Stanard, "Randolph Family," *WMQ*, 1st ser., 9 [1901]: 250; Randolph to TJ, 10 Jan. 1809 [ViW: TC-JP], 18 Mar., 30 May 1822; Richmond *Enquirer*, 22 Oct. 1813; Vi: Mutual Assurance Society, policy no. 1955 [29 Mar. 1816]; Washington *National Register*, 23 Aug. 1817; *MB*, 2:1384; TJ to Randolph, 13 May 1822; *Richmond Enquirer*, 18 Apr. 1828).

# To John Staples

SIR                                    Monticello Jan. 25. 14.

Understanding that you are the agent for disposing of mr Oliver Evans's patent screws for crushing the ear of corn, cob & all for grinding in a mill, I have to ask the favor of you to deliver one for me to mr William Johnson, a waterman of Milton, who will apply to you for it about a week hence. Mr Gibson will be so good as to pay you the price on presenting him this letter.

Accept the assurance of my esteem and respect

                                        TH: JEFFERSON

PoC (MHi); at foot of text: "Mr John Staples"; endorsed by TJ.

Evans had received his PATENT for an "Improvement called the screw mill for breaking and grinding different hard substances" on 14 Feb. 1804 (*List of Patents*, 39–40).

# From Mathew Carey

SIR                                          Philad[a] Jan. 26. 1814.

By this day's mail, I take the liberty of forwarding you a copy of the second Edition of the Naval History, for which I request a place in your Library, as a mark of the esteem & respect of

Your ob[t] h[ble] serv[t]                    MATHEW CAREY

RC (MHi); dateline at foot of text; at head of text: "His Excellency Thomas Jefferson, Esq[r]"; endorsed by TJ as received 4 Feb. 1814 and so recorded in SJL. Enclosure: Thomas Clark, *Naval* *History of the United States, from the Commencement of the Revolutionary War to the Present Time*, 2d ed., 2 vols. (Philadelphia, 1814; Sowerby, no. 531; Poor, *Jefferson's Library*, 4 [no. 142]).

# To Patrick Gibson

DEAR SIR                                      Monticello Jan. 26. 14.

I have duly recieved your favor of the 19th with the 300.D. inclosed. I was sorry to learn that my letter had not got to you in time to avail me of the momentary demand for flour. I wrote by the first mail after hearing there was such a demand. but these advices reach us too slowly, and therefore I had entertained a hope of your selling without waiting to consult me. I think it impossible but that stories will from time to time reach us as to the Gottenburg negociation which may give momentary spurs to adventurous merchants. I hope you will avail me of them according to your own discretion; for my purchases of corn for the subsistence of my people on the last years failure will go considerably beyond the balance in your hands these will be falling due from the 1st of March to the 10th of May. within that time I hope there may be sales. I have somewhere about 200. barrels now ready for Johnson who came up 2. or 3. days ago only & promises to take in a load to-day. I must ask the favor of you to send me by him a keg of powder of 25.℔. 6. gross of corks, or if very good I would be glad to take double that quantity, for I fear they will become difficult to get hereafter, also 9.[1] bundles of nail rod, assorted, to wit, 2. bundles of the size proper for 6[d] nails, 2 d[o] for 10[d] 2. d[o] for 16. pennies, 2 d[o] for 20. pennies, & 1. d[o] for spikes or half crown rod. I have written to Richard Randolph for 2. gross of beer-jugs & to mr Staples for one of Evans's corn-cob screws, and desired them to apply to you for paiment; and I shall within a day or two draw on you for between 30. & 40.D. in favor of D. Higginbotham. Accept the assurance of my great esteem and respect.          TH: JEFFERSON

PoC (facsimile in Profiles in History, Beverly Hills, Calif., catalogue 31 [ca. 2000], lot 102, p. 78); at foot of text: "M^r Gibson."

While declining Russian mediation, British foreign secretary Lord Castlereagh forwarded to his American counterpart on 4 Nov. 1813 the proposal that direct negotiations for ending the War of 1812 be initiated at either London or GOTTENBURG (Göteborg, Gothenburg), Sweden. In his reply of 5 Jan. 1814 Secretary of State James Monroe informed Castlereagh that "the President accedes to his proposition, and will take the measures depending on him for carrying it into effect at Gottenburg." Monroe notified the American peace commissioners on 27 June 1814 that they had the authority to transfer the talks to a more convenient site, such as Amsterdam, the Hague, or even a city in England. After receiving their thoughts on the subject, on 11 Aug. 1814 he communicated to them the president's approval of their decision to move the negotiations to Ghent, in present-day Belgium (*ASP, Foreign Relations*, 3:621–3, 704–5).

[1] Reworked from "7."

# To Joseph Wheaton

SIR                                   Monticello Jan. 26. 14.

I thank you for the information respecting the impressment of mr Johnson by Childers. Johnson is a tenant of mine, a very honest man, and usually employed by me in carrying my produce to market. this operation has been delayed by his detention, but whether to my injury or not, I do not yet know. it was certainly highly wrong in mr Childers to assume the public name and authority in committing an act of violence on the liberty and property of citizens, and one for which if they prosecute him, he will probably be made to pay very dear. it is a wearing out of the good will of the people before it is wanting and while it should still be spared & cherished. it should be left to the government to declare by law when they think the public necessities begin to require forced contributions. when they have decided this point, we shall all cheerfully acquiesce: but we ought not to be placed at the mercy of every individual who may usurp the powers of the government. Accept the assurance of my esteem & respect                                   TH: JEFFERSON

RC (CtY: Wheaton Papers); addressed: "M^r Joseph Wheaton Richmond"; franked; postmarked Milton, 29 Jan.; endorsed by Wheaton. PoC (CSmH: JF-BA); endorsed by TJ.

# To William Champe Carter

DEAR SIR                                    Monticello Jan. 27. 14.

Your favor of Dec. 22. came to hand on the 7th inst. I am duly sensible of the confidence you are so good as to repose in me in proposing that the question of boundary between Col° Monroe and mr Short should be left to my umpirage. but I could not trust myself with such a decision. for altho' I feel great and sincere friendship for all the parties, and a perfect desire that what is right may be done between them, I have been too much the sole agent for one of them, not to be in danger of entertaining impressions formed on a contemplation of the rights and interests of one only which might prevent a just view of those of others, without my being sensible of it. I hope therefore to be excused from it. and indeed the whole question turning on what is 'the run on the Eastern side of Dick's plantation, and where is it's source' the probability is that you could satisfy yourself and all others were you on the spot, either by your own recollections, or by calling on those to whom you may know the matter to have been intimate. I must therefore again sollicit your aid in settling this question, and leave to yourself entirely the choice of any time between this & the middle of April, till which time I shall be constantly at home & ready to attend you at a moment's warning. Col° Monroe however would need notice. the arrangement between you & him, that you shall refund the money you recieved and interest, if there has been a mistake, is exactly what is just; and as it amounts to an agreement that mr Short's line shall stand as marked, it seems to leave him & mr Higginbotham the purchaser, without further interest in the question, in which case we should give you no further trouble about it, & leave it to Col° Monroe & yourself to be settled between you at your leisure. a line from yourself & from Col° Monroe to this amount, would be the most acceptable termination of the difficulty with all parties, and just as between yourselves. should this or any other business bring you into this neighborhood I repeat the assurance of the pleasure it would give me to see you here, & add that of my great respect and esteem.

                                              TH: JEFFERSON

RC (Old South Association, on deposit MBAt); damaged, with missing text supplied from PoC; addressed: "William Champe Carter esq. near Culpeper C. H. recommended to the care of Cap[t] Shackleford"; franked; endorsed by Carter. PoC (DLC); endorsed by TJ.

TJ had served as William Short's SOLE AGENT in the negotiations leading up to the sale of Indian Camp to David Higginbotham in 1813. THE RUN ON THE EASTERN SIDE OF DICK'S PLANTATION, AND WHERE IS IT'S SOURCE quotes from Carter's 20 Sept. 1793 indenture of sale to

James Monroe of 1,000 acres adjoining Indian Camp (Albemarle Co. Deed Book, 11:163–5). DICK'S PLANTATION was a portion of the Indian Camp Quarter tract (note to TJ to Carter, 16 Jan. 1813).

# To John Clarke

SIR                                    Monticello Jan. 27. 14.

Your favor of Dec. 2. came to hand some time ago, and I percieve in it the proofs of a mind worthily occupied on the best interests of our common country. to carry on our war with success we want <u>able</u> officers, and a sufficient number of soldiers. the former, time and trial can alone give us; to procure the latter we need only the tender of sufficient inducements and the assiduous pressure of them on the proper subjects. the inducement of interest proposed by you is undoubtedly the principal one on which any reliance can be placed, and the assiduous pressure of it on the proper subjects would probably be better secured, by making it the interest and the duty of a given portion of the militia, rather than of a meer recruiting officer. whether however it is the best mode belongs to the decision of others; but satisfied that it is one of the good ones,[1] I forwarded your letter to a member of the government, who will make it a subject of consideration by those with whom the authority rests. whether the late discomfiture of Bonaparte will have the effect of shortening or lengthening our war is uncertain. it is cruel that we should have been forced to wish any success to such a destroyer of the human race. yet while it was our interest, & that of humanity that he should not subdue Russia, & thus lay all Europe at his feet, it was desirable to us that he should so far succeed as to close the Baltic to our enemy, and force him by the pressure of internal distress, into a disposition to return to the paths of justice towards us. if the French nation stand by Bonaparte, he may rally, rise again, and yet give Gr. Britain so much employment as to give time for a just settlement of our questions with her. we must patiently wait the solution of this doubt by time.

Accept the assurances of my esteem & respect.

TH: JEFFERSON

PoC (DLC); at foot of text: "Mʳ John Clarke."

On this day TJ sent Clarke's letter to Secretary of State James Monroe, A MEMBER OF THE GOVERNMENT. By Napoleon's LATE DISCOMFITURE, TJ presumably means his defeat at the Battle of the Nations (also known as the Battle of Leipzig) the preceding October and the expulsion of French forces from central Europe during the ensuing month (Chandler, *Campaigns of Napoleon,* 936–9).

[1] Reworked from "a good one."

# To James Monroe

I now return you the letter of mr Carter which was inclosed in yours of Nov. 3. and which was 6. weeks on it's passage to me. the reference to myself which you are both so kind as to propose I must beg leave to decline. I could not trust myself with such a decision. for altho' I should certainly endeavor to see nothing but the facts of the case, yet even as to these, my having been the sole agent, thro the whole of this business, for one of the parties only, and the particular interest which it was thus my duty to feel and to espouse, may but too possibly have left impressions, unpercieved by myself, which might prevent my seeing the subject in the original and unbiased view with which an umpire ought to enter into it. I have therefore requested mr Carter to attend at any time convenient to you and himself, between this and the 1st of April until which time I shall be constantly at home. a letter from him however of Dec. 2. informs me that you have agreed between you that if your claim proves correct, he is to pay you what he got for the land with interest. this amounts to an agreement that the line shall stand as marked for mr Short, and that whatever it shall take from you shall be paid for by him to you. this is certainly perfectly just, and it leaves mr Short and mr Higginbotham without further interest in the question, and the meeting & proceedings before proposed are in that case[1] become unnecessary. the question in this case remains between yourself and mr Carter only, to be settled at your leisure. if you will be so good as to signify this in a line to me, I shall be able to satisfy mr Short, and to remove mr Higgenbotham's scruples about the paiment of his bonds, the first of which is now at hand.

I inclose you a letter from mr John Clarke suggesting a mode of keeping the army filled up. whether it be the best or not, I am not to decide. but as it appears to be one of the good ones, I inclose it to you to be suggested where it may serve.

What effect will the disasters of Bonaparte have on the negociation of Gottenburg? not a good one I am afraid. the Salvo of maritime rights by the other party, leaves room to claim whatever the successes of her allies may embolden, or her own greediness stimulate her to grasp at. these successes will enable her to make the ensuing a warm campaign for us. Orleans, Pensacola, and the Chesapeak, one or the other, or all, are indicated by the number and construction of the boats they are preparing. their late proceedings too in the North seem to breathe the spirit of a bellum ad internecionem. it would be well if on some proper occasion the government should either justify or disavow M$^c$lure's proceedings at Newark. as it is possible our negotiators may not obtain what we would wish on the subject of maritime rights, would it not be well that they should stipulate for the benefit of those which shall be established by the other belligerents at the settlement of a general peace. remember me affectionately to the President. it is long since I have had occasion of writing to him, and I consider it a duty to suppress all idle calls on his attention. ever affection-ately yours.

Th: Jefferson

RC (DLC: Monroe Papers); at foot of first page: "Col$^o$ Monroe." PoC (DLC); endorsed by TJ. Enclosure: John Clarke to TJ, 2 Dec. 1813. Other enclosure not found.

William Champe Carter's letter to TJ was dated 22 Dec. 1813, not DEC. 2. In response to New York militia general George McClure's destruction of Niagara, Upper Canada, on 10–11 Dec. 1813, the British inaugurated a BELLUM AD INTERNECIONEM ("war of extermination") along the northern frontier that set the stage for the burning the following sum-mer of Washington, D.C. During the last half of December 1813 British forces destroyed the American towns of Black Rock, Buffalo, Lewiston, and Manchester. Although McClure claimed that his actions had been authorized by Secretary of War John Armstrong, the United States government quickly disavowed his PROCEEDINGS AT NEWARK (Niagara) (Malcomson, *Historical Dictionary*, 323–4, 374–6; *ASP, Military Affairs*, 1:84, 486, 487; *ASP, Foreign Relations*, 3:752).

¹ Preceding three words interlined.

# From William Cocke

Fort Strother Jan$^y$ 28$^{th}$ 1814

In my last I promis$^d$ to advise you of the Occurences that might take place in the Southern expedition against the hostile Creeks on the 22$^{nd}$ Instant we had two engagements near the E Muckfaw & another on the 24$^{th}$ at the hilabies or Enochepoo The brave Gen$^l$ Jackson has Added new laurels to his former victories; we have fought we have bled we have Conquereed Gen$^l$ Coffee has covered him Self with Glory his fame is made Rich with his Blood he is wounded Severely but not dangerously. Col$^o$ Carrol the intripid the brave Carrol by his great Example gave Courage to all who were near him, none Could excell that valuable¹ officer he is worthy of his Countrys first love & highest gratitude,

The enemy have been Confounded and defeated; in all their attacks but not with out the loss of Some of the best Blood that ever annimated human nature, Our loss in feild is 22 and double that number wounded among the Slain we have to lament Mag$^r$ Donnelson Aid to Gen$^l$ Coffee & the Brave Cap$^t$ Hill, The enemy Cannot have lost less than one hundred & eighty or perhaps two hundred killed they have not been able to Carry off[2] a Single Scalp—The Cherokees have distinguished them Selves & Some of the friendly Creeks have done well, Col⁰ Richard Brown, Capᵗ John thompson fought Bravely & the Son of the old path Killer Known by the name of the Bear Meat with ten of his Companions fought by My Side—in the last engagement & it is nothing more than Justice due them for Me to Say that they Rendered essensial, among them that were near me I have to lament the death of Mʳ Thomas Smith Son of Capᵗ Samuel Smith of Maury County a youth not more than Eighteen years of age he fought Bravely and[3] died gloriously Capᵗ William Hamilton of East Tennessee who joind the artillery Company is no more he fought like a heroe and expireed for his Country Capᵗ Lemˡ Childress assistant Quarter Master was wounded early in the action he Seemᵈ to be in Spireed with fresh ardor from the Blood that trickled down his Cheeks, Joshua Harskel deserves the highest applause for his gallant Conduct on this trying occation Much praise is Said to be due to Magʳ Boid Capᵗ Carr & Lieut Long Capᵗ Geo. W Mar and my Nephew Mʳ James Cocke was wounded on the evening of the 22ⁿᵈ Capᵗ Marr distinguished him Self and so did the brave men under his Command he set them an example worthy of him Self and they Retaliated tenfold for the blood that they lost the artillery Company Sustaind the heaviest Shock they had to Contend with the Strong force of the enemy Bird Evans of that Company was killed, & the Brave Lieuᵗ Armstrong wounded in the hip but not dangerously Also Jacob McGaffock Hyram Bradford & John Sigler of the Same Company Mʳ Syon perry Joseph & peter loony fought like heroes Magʳ thomas T Maury did him s[elf] great honour and was Slightly wounded Magʳ Joseph Pekins is truly brave and fought well, in[4] this Short Scetch and from the limited view I had of the action I feel my self incompetent to do Justice to many Brave and valuable men & officers but Merit has its best Reward in the pleasure that is felt in Concious rectitude I am you well know your old and Sure friend

Wᴹ COCKE

(I[5] know the following[6] note from my Genˡ will be Grattifying to you I their fore Send you a coppy)

RC (DLC); edge chipped; endorsed by TJ as received 16 Feb. 1814 and so recorded in SJL; with enclosure subjoined. Enclosure: Andrew Jackson to Cocke, Fort Strother, 28 Jan. 1814, commending him for his recent military service, which included "Entering the percuit exposing your person and their by Saving the life of Lieuᵗ Moss" as well as personally killing an Indian; expressing dismay at Tennessee's failure to supply his army with the troops and provisions it needs, particularly 1,500 men requisitioned for six months' service by the secretary of war and Major General Thomas Pinckney; alleging that those who have not supported his efforts lack patriotism; and asking that Cocke return to East Tennessee to see to it that Jackson receives the men and matériel necessary to bring his campaign to a speedy and successful conclusion (Tr in DLC: TJ Papers, 200:35647, entirely in Cocke's hand, undated; Dft in DLC: Jackson Papers, undated, but mistakenly endorsed in another hand as a letter of 29 Jan. 1814; printed, dated 28 Jan. 1814, in Washington *Daily National Intelligencer*, 12 May 1814; summarized in Sam B. Smith, Harold D. Moser, Daniel Feller, and others, eds., *The Papers of Andrew Jackson* [1980– ], 3:408).

Cocke's most recent letter to TJ, dated 15 May 1813, nowhere promises to keep him apprised of events in the SOUTHERN EXPEDITION against the Creek Indians. He is either mistaken or referring to a letter that never reached TJ. Jackson's January 1814 raid against the Red Stick Creek Indians resulted in indecisive engagements at Emuckfaw Creek and Enitachopco (ENOCHEPOO) Creek in what later became Tallapoosa County, Alabama (Heidler and Heidler, *War of 1812*, 135).

¹ Manuscript: "waluable."
² Manuscript: "of."
³ Manuscript: "and &."
⁴ Manuscript: "in in."
⁵ Omitted opening parenthesis editorially supplied.
⁶ Manuscript: "followin."

# From Elias Earle

SIR                                  Washaington City 28th Jany 1814

I have taken the liberty of Laying before Your Excllencey, the Statement of General Henry Dearborn, and the letter of Maj^r James Holland, touching the Conversation or contract respecting my Errecting Iron works &c in the cherokee nation—

the reason why I make this application to You is that I wish some arangement made with the present administration, who is totally unacquainted with the circumstances connected with it—I would therefore thank You for Such a statement as may be within Your recollection of the Subject—

a compliance of which will confer a perticular Obligation on Sir Your

most Obt & Very Humb^l Servt                    ELIAS EARLE

RC (DLC); between dateline and salutation: "His Excellencey Thomas Jefferson Esq^r"; endorsed by TJ as received 4 Feb. 1814 and so recorded in SJL. Enclosure: James Holland, a former North Carolina congressman, to Earle, Maury County, Tennessee, 28 Mar. 1812, stating that "In Yours of the 27th ulto, I am requested to Give You a statement of the Impositions of M^r Jefferson & H Dearborn, the then President and Secretary at War—touching Your Erecting Iron works &c in the Chirokee Country, which were so far as my memory Serves me as follows—You was to use Your influence to procure a purchase of a track [tract] <*of land*> for that purpose & if accomplished to Erect Iron works thereon & to manufacture Such Iron instruments of husbandry as the Goverment Anually supplies the Indians with, for which You was to be allowed a fair price—You was to have a fee simple in the land, or a long lease, & in the latter Case You was to be paid for all improvemints at the End of the lease, & if a fee simple You was to re-imburse the moneys Expended in the Ex-tinguishmint of the Indian title—I farther recollect that after You had by treaty Ob-tained a Grant from the Indians for the Above purpose & had returned to Wash-ington, nothing apeared to prevent the progress of the proceedings, but a doupt [doubt] of the tract being within the lim-its of the State of Tennessee, in which case measures were to be taken to obtain a title from the state or to Vary the place, to come within the Jurisdiction of the Unit-ed States" (Tr in DLC; in Earle's hand and endorsed by him). Other enclosure printed below.

Elias Earle (1762–1823), manufacturer and public official, moved in 1787 from his native Virginia to Greenville County, South Carolina. There he operated an iron foundry and amassed sizable land-holdings. A Republican, Earle represent-ed the Greenville District in the South Carolina House of Representatives, 1794–97, and in the state Senate, 1798–1804. He sat in the United States House of Rep-resentatives for five terms, 1805–07, 1811–15, and 1817–21. By 1811 he had moved to the Pendleton District and founded the town of Centreville. In the ensuing years Earle established a planta-tion, ironworks, gun factory, and other business ventures. He received a contract in 1815 to supply the federal government with ten thousand muskets, but his trans-fer of that obligation to another gunmak-er resulted in litigation resolved only a decade after Earle's death in Centreville (*BDSCHR*, 4:176–7; Joseph Earle Birnie, *The Earles and the Birnies* [1974], 59–72, 192–4; Ernest M. Lander Jr., "The Iron Industry in Ante-Bellum South Carolina," *Journal of Southern His-tory* 20 [1954]: 340–1; *U.S. Statutes at Large*, 6:510; Washington *Daily Nation-al Intelligencer*, 23 June 1823).

## Henry Dearborn's Statement Regarding Elias Earle's Ironworks

In the early part of the Year 1807 Col Elias Earle of South Carolina pro-posed to the Secretary of war the establishing of Iron works, with suitable Shops[1] in the Cherokee Nation—on the following conditions viz) that [a][2] suitable place should be looked out & selected, where suffcent quantities of Good ore Could be found in the Vicinity of Good[3] streams of water for such establishment, & that the Indians should be induced to make a cession of a tract of land Say Six miles square that should embrace the ore & the water priviledge—and that he should have so much of the land so ceeded, conveyed to him, as the President of the United States might deem proper, including the ore & water priviledge—on which he should be authorised to Errect Iron works, smiths shops &c—and on his part he would engage to erect such Iron works & shop as to enable him to furnish such quantities of Iron and imple-ments of[4] Husbandry, as should be Suffcent for the use of the Various Indian tribes in that part of the Country, including those on the western side of the Ohio and Mississippi—and to deliver anually to the order of goverment of the United States Such quantities of Iron & impliments as should be re-quired for the Indians—and on such reasonable tirms as should be mutually agreed on—and as Great delays & Disapointments had Very frequently oc-curred in procuring those articles for the Indians in that quarter of the coun-try, the Secretary of war refered the propositions to the President of the united States—and it was determined that Col° Meigs, the agent for the cherokees, Should be directed to endeavour to procure from the cherokees a cession of such a Tract as was proposed, as soon as Col° Earle Should have Explored the country and Selected a[5] suitable place for the proposed Establishment Col° Earle accordingly explored the Country & selected a suitable [place][6] for the proposed Establishment at the mouth of chickamaga creek,[7] where a sufficent quantity of Good ore & a[8] water priviledge combined—Col° Meigs was accordingly[9] directed to endeavour to obtain from the Indians a cession of[10] six miles Square, that should imbrace the ore & water priviledge—he accordingly held a treaty with the chiefs of the Cherokees[11]—and obtained the Cession & paid the Indians near three thousand dollars of the stipulated Concideration—Col° Earle attended the treaty & came on to Washington City with the result, at the next meeting of Congress—the president proposed the ratification to the Senate, but before It was acted upon, it was found by running[12] the Southerly line of the State of tennessee that the tract So ceeded[13] fell within that State—& the ratification was suspended with a hope on the part of the President, that the State of Tennessee would concent to give up its claim to the land—but he was disapointed and [no][14] further measures were taken, on the part of the goverment—Col° Earle returned home after bringing on the Treaty with a [full][15] Expectation that the treaty would be ratified and[16] Sent off Some hands & provisions for the purpose of erecting Some houses[17] for the workmen &c. his waggons & hands were Stoped on the way by a party of disafected cherokees and turned back— Col° Earle now claims[18] compensation for his time & Expenses in Exploring the country & selecting the place for the proposed Establishment, and for bringing on the treaty—or it would be more agreable[19] to him if the Goverment would make an adjustment[20] with the cherokees for an Exchange of the ceeded tract for one that should[21] be without the boundries of the State of Tennessee—but which Should embrace Similar advantages for such an Establishment as was proposed[22]—and to allow him to further[23] the establishment on[24] the same conditions as were Contemplated on the other tract—and Col° Earle thinks that such an Exchange would readily be[25] consented to by the Cherokees—and that a tract may be found within there Country, that will possess all the nessasary qualities for such an Establishment—and as the Indians have actually reced a great[26] part of the Stipulated Conciderations— they ought the more readily to agree to such an Exchange

Signed—H, DEARBORN

March 29th 1812—

Tr (DLC: TJ Papers, 195:34754–5); entirely in Earle's hand; at head of text and beneath signature: "Copy." Tr (DLC: Madison Papers); entirely in Earle's hand.

On 6 Apr. 1812 Earle had sent President James Madison copies of both Dearborn's statement and a covering note from Dearborn giving the secretary of war's opinion that Earle should either be compensated financially or allowed to select another tract in the Cherokee territory for his proposed ironworks (Madison, *Papers, Pres. Ser.*, 4:303–4).

[1] Madison Papers Tr: "with Smiths Shops."
[2] Omitted word supplied from Madison Papers Tr.
[3] TJ Papers Tr: "of a Good." Madison Papers Tr: "of Good."
[4] TJ Papers Tr: "of of." Madison Papers Tr: "of."

<sup>5</sup> TJ Papers Tr: "as." Madison Papers Tr: "a."

<sup>6</sup> Omitted word editorially supplied.

<sup>7</sup> In Madison Papers Tr, phrase from ampersand to this point reads "& found a place on chicamaga."

<sup>8</sup> Madison Papers Tr here adds "Suitable."

<sup>9</sup> Madison Papers Tr substitutes "then" for this word.

<sup>10</sup> Madison Papers Tr here adds "a Track."

<sup>11</sup> Madison Papers Tr: "chiefs of the Cherokee nation."

<sup>12</sup> Madison Papers Tr: "reviewing."

<sup>13</sup> Preceding five words not in Madison Papers Tr.

<sup>14</sup> Omitted word supplied from Madison Papers Tr.

<sup>15</sup> Omitted word supplied from Madison Papers Tr.

<sup>16</sup> Madison Papers Tr here adds "precipitatily."

<sup>17</sup> Madison Papers Tr substitutes "Commencing the Erection of some huts" for preceding three words.

<sup>18</sup> Madison Papers Tr here adds "some."

<sup>19</sup> TJ Papers Tr: "ageable." Madison Papers Tr: "agreable."

<sup>20</sup> Madison Papers Tr: "agreement."

<sup>21</sup> Madison Papers Tr: "shall."

<sup>22</sup> TJ Papers Tr: "proposed proposed." Madison Papers Tr: "proposed."

<sup>23</sup> Madison Papers Tr: "form."

<sup>24</sup> TJ Papers Tr: "on on." Madison Papers Tr: "on."

<sup>25</sup> TJ Papers Tr: "readily be readily be." Madison Papers Tr: "be readily."

<sup>26</sup> Madison Papers Tr: "received the greater."

# From Robert Mills

DEAR SIR            Philadelphia Jan<sup>y</sup> 28<sup>th</sup> 1814

Permit me to take the liberty of soliciting a favor at your hand, should you deem me worthy of the station for which I would ask the honor of your recommendation.

My worthy friend and preceptor M<sup>r</sup> Latrobe having resigned his office as Surveyor of the Public buildings of the U S<sup>ts</sup> at Washington, and retired to Pittsburg to reside, and that office being now vacant, I feel desirous to apply for this situation,—that when the state of our public affairs will warrant the completion of the public buildings at Washington, I may be prepared (in case of appointment) to suggest some plans for this purpose—

As I have the honor to be known in some degree to you Sir, and as you have been pleased to indulge me with your good opinion, I would presume to take the liberty to ask of you a letter of recommendation to M<sup>r</sup> Madison.

Having the good fortune to be the first American that has gone through a regular course of Architectural studies in his own country, I am anxious to acquire the honor which is offered, of contributing what talents I possess to the public service of my country—and endeavoring to prove to strangers, that the simplicity of native genius, is not innimical to correct taste in design, and that we may lay some claim to talent in Architecture as well as in painting.—

I would flatter myself Sir that the experience I have had, and the advantages I have derived from the instructions of a man so eminent in his profession as M^r Latrobe, (for which I am indebted to you Sir) that I shall be able to do justice to the station he so honorably filled—

In the hope that this my wish may meet your favorable approbation and support,

I salute you Sir with affection and respect      ROB^T MILLS

P.S.—I beg leave to inclose to you a copy of the Constitution and by-laws of the Columbian Society of artists which has the honor of your name at its head—

RC (DGW: W. Lloyd Wright Collection); at foot of text: "Thomas Jefferson Esq^r Monticello Virginia"; endorsed by TJ as received 4 Feb. 1814 and so recorded in SJL. Enclosure: *Charter and by-laws of the Columbian Society of Artists Instituted May, 1810* (Philadelphia, 1813). Enclosed in TJ to James Madison, 17 Feb. 1814.

Mills was INDEBTED to TJ for recommending him in 1803 to Benjamin Henry

Latrobe, with whom he studied architecture for much of the ensuing five years (Latrobe to TJ, 2 Oct. 1803 [DLC]; Latrobe, *Papers*, 1:330, 331n). TJ had been elected president of the COLUMBIAN SOCIETY OF ARTISTS at their annual meeting in Philadelphia on 5 Jan. 1814. Mills was chosen as secretary of the organization at the same time (Philadelphia *Poulson's American Daily Advertiser*, 8 Jan. 1814).

# To William Short

DEAR SIR                                    Monticello Jan. 28. 14.

I scarcely ever sat down to write a more painful letter than the present. when in Oct. 1812. I proposed to become the payer of a part of mr Higginbotham's purchase of you, at that time expected to be three paiments of 1800. or 2000.D. each, I gave you a particular statement of my resources, than which nothing could be more true. I have since that sowed regularly 800. bushels of wheat a year, and those who make least carry to market, after taking out their seed & table consumption, never less than a barrel of flour for every bushel sowed. we had for some time before that, recieved every year from 8. to 10.D. a barrel for our flour. I had a right then to state my income, from this article alone, at 7. or 8000. Dollars, a year, exclusive of tob° of rents, & other articles. but what has happened since was neither under my expectation nor view. in Jan. or Feb. following came upon us the blockade, before I was able to get my crop to market. the sale immediately failed, and after keeping it till I feared it would spoil on my hands, I sold at such a price as netted me 57. cents a bushel only for my wheat. this fell short in amount of the current engagements of the year, and left me in a crippled state for the ensuing one. this year a threefold calamity has befallen us. 1. such a drought as had not happened in 58. years before, which reduced our harvest to little more than double the seed, & destroyed the crop of bread-corn. 2. the blockade continued even thro' the winter. 3. our embargo, doubly barring the door of exportation. this overwhelming concurrence has rendered the fulfilment of engagements as impossible as an earthquake swallowing up the lands. the little wheat I made the last season if it could be sold, would not more than pay the bread bought for subsistence, taxes E$^t$c. but none is yet sold, nor does any early probability of sale appear. under these circumstances, my dear Sir, the total failure in my first paiment has become unavoidable, from disasters not within controul or foresight. I have sincerely regretted my taking on myself these paiments, because, on the merchants books the debt would of course have been expected to await the issue of crops, for which the merchant found compensation in the gains of the dealings which had produced it. but you have recieved no such compensation. yet I do not know that I can propose to you any thing but to place this first paiment on the footing of the public funds, that is to say, to pay the interest quarterly, or, what would be equivalent, instead of 4. quarterly remittances[1] of a quarters interest, which in my interior situation would be difficult, to make a remittance of the whole year's interest of 200.D. at such time within the body of the year as to be equivalent to the 4. quarterly remittances. this would include necessarily the postponement of the 1$^{st}$ bond till after the 2$^d$ & 3$^d$ shall have been paid off: because were exportation to be opened, I should not be able after the loss of two successive crops, to pay more than one bond a year, increased as they were from my first expectation of 600. to 1000 £. a year. that our exportation will be opened I have considerable expectation. England knows we are fighting now for nothing but such a regulation of impressments as she has twice agreed to altho' she flew off ultimately on both occasions. she cannot think this worth the additional expence of her war with us, and I presume had so made up her mind before proposing the negociation of Gottenburg. I do therefore think she means peace with us. as to maritime rights we had better stipulate to participate of those which shall be settled by the other belligerent powers at the general pacification, she suspending in the mean time her orders of council and paper blockades. altho Bonaparte is greatly crippled, if his nation stands by him, and he will confine himself to the defence of France (within the Rhine) and the conquest of the Peninsul, he may oblige his Northern enemies to keep their armies together at a distance from their homes, he may hover over the coast of England, oblige her to the continuance of overwhelming expences to subsidise the Northern armies, defend the Peninsul, and oppose the invasion of her own island. these considerations make me expect that England will be disposed to relinquish the small object of her war with us, in order to concentrate her force and lessen her expenditures.—mr Higginbotham is ready to make his 1st paiment, not depending for it, as I do, on the produce of his farms. I am happy to inform you that we shall be able to settle the question of boundary with Colo Monroe, so as to leave yourself & mr Higginbotham entirely unconcerned. Mr Carter & Colo Monroe have agreed to settle it between themselves, by mr Carter's refunding the principal and interest for so much as your line shall be found to have run in on Colo Monroe. I have this from mr Carter, and have written to Colo M. for a declaration of it from him, which will settle it.—I send you, as you desired, Dupont's work on National education.—is it not time to feel alarm for the fate of our bank institutions? they had 200. Millions of Dollars in circulation the last year, and those now petitioned for are said to amount to 60. Mills additional capital, and of course of 180. Mills additional circulation. near 400. Mills of paper afloat in a country of 8. Mills of people, whose wholesome circulation would be only of that number of Dollars, makes the medium of exchanges 40. or 50. times what it should be. should alarm at this or any other circumstance produce a run on the banks, no one supposes they have 400. Mills of cash in their vaults, or the 50th part of it. universal bankruptcy must follow, and a tax of 2. or 300. Millions be thus levied on us, and levied most unequally. I hope you are on your guard and that you may exchange, while you can, any bank stock you possess for canal stock or such other as is founded on realty, or for the stock of the US. which, if the war is short, will be perfectly safe, and if long, will give time for change. I am pressing a friend in our legislature to save this state from the wreck by immediately forbidding all foreign paper, by giving our banks so many months to call in their 5.D. bills, so many more for their 10.D. & so many more for all under 50.D. leaving these for mercantile transactions. they are too large to enter into those of farmers & other small people. but I do not expect it to be done. the bank mania has seised all classes, and it is difficult to persuade those of a certain measure of understanding that they can have too much money. ever & affectionately yours.

TH: JEFFERSON

RC (ViW: TJP); endorsed by Short as received 5 Feb. 1814. Enclosure: Pierre Samuel Du Pont de Nemours, *Sur l'éducation nationale dans les États-Unis d'Amérique* (Paris, 1812; Poor, *Jefferson's Library*, 5 [nos. 207, 209–10]).

TJ had offered to pay for A PART OF MR HIGGINBOTHAM'S PURCHASE of Indian Camp in his letter to Short of 17 Oct. 1812. William Champe Carter wrote TJ

on 22 Dec. 1813 of his willingness to refund to James Monroe the PRINCIPAL AND INTEREST on any land sold to David Higginbotham that rightly belonged to Monroe's Highland estate. TJ's FRIEND IN OUR LEGISLATURE was Virginia state senator Joseph C. Cabell.

¹ Word interlined in place of "paiments."

# From Horatio G. Spafford

ESTEEMED FRIEND—                    Albany, 1 Mo. 28, 1814.

I am so frequently asked, 'how does President Jefferson like the Gazetteer,' or 'what does he say of it,' that I hope thou wilt excuse my anxiety to learn. Possibly it may not have reached thee. I sent one in the Mail, a long time since. If that miscarried, I would send another.

I must not trouble thee with a long Letter, but permit to add assurances of my wishes for thy health & happiness. Should I outlive thee, I should deem it a great favor to have some trifling evidence of thy remembrance. But—I fear I am too importunate, & that, tiring thy patience, I forfeit thy esteem.

With great respect, thy friend,                    H. G. SPAFFORD.

RC (MHi); at foot of text: "Hon. Thomas Jefferson"; endorsed by TJ as received 11 Feb. 1814 and so recorded in SJL.

For Spafford's GAZETTEER, see Spafford to TJ, 27 Aug. 1813, and note.

# To John Barnes

DEAR SIR                    Monticello Jan. 29. 14.

Your letter of Dec. 12. was duly recieved and I now return you that of mr Williams which it covered. I wish you may have been able to procure a bill to go by some of the late flags which offered such safe conveyance.

It is time to ask if there is not great reason to feel alarm for our banking institutions. the notes they had in circulation the last summer were calculated to amount to 200. millions of Dollars. the banks now petitioned for are of 60. millions additional capital of course 180. millions of circulation; so that the ensuing summer we shall have near 400. Millions of paper afloat in a country of 8 millions of people, whose wholesome & competent circulation would be 8. millions of Dollars, or a 50th part of what it is to be. should any alarm[1] from this or any other circumstance produce a run on the banks, their bankruptcy is unquestionable, because no body imagines they have 400. Millions or the 50th part of it in their vaults. duty then to our friend Kosciuzko requires that we should save him while we can, by withdrawing his stock from the banks. this too is the fortunate moment, when the government is opening a loan on terms which will yield more profit than the bank stock. tho were the profit less, the superior safety would dictate the change. my opinion therefore is that we should subscribe for him to the government loan, to the whole amount of his bank stock, & sell out in the bank. I suppose that stock is above par, and it is expected the govmt will give 100.D. for every 88. or 90. which will increase his capital. I shall be glad of your opinion on this subject, as soon as possible that a final determination may be taken in time.

ever affectionately yours.                                    TH: JEFFERSON

PoC (DLC); at foot of text: "M[r] John          [1] TJ here canceled "arise."
Barnes"; endorsed by TJ. Enclosure not
found.

# From Oliver Evans

HONBLE SIR                              Washington City Jan[y] 29th 1814

I this day received yours of 16th inst I am sorry that I did not receive it sooner, I waited untill I lost hope and could no longer bear the injury that yours of 13th August to Isaac McPherson was evidently dooing me in Congress I therefore hastened to reply to it and the many misrepresentations of the memorial and affidavits taken expartee out of court accompanying it

I was sensible of my inability of contesting legal points with you in public print But conscious of having truth and Justice on my side I was certain that I could loose nothing while I might gain much When two bodies come in contact they are apt to assimilate in some degree the chance of gain then is entirely in my favour

I think it would be improper to publish your kind answer to me because you say you did not receive the report of the trials in the circuit court at Baltimore and if you have never seen it and have seen the affidavits Memorials and certificates published with your letter, I think it impossible that you could Judge fairly in the case from hearing one side only fraught with misrepresentations directly opposite to the testimony even of their own witness and Judicial decisions in court in the said trials

It appears to me very easie to answer all the questions you have stated if not already sufficently answered in the papers I have sent you, Copies of which I put in the post office with this fully enclosed that they may the more certainly reach you

you speak of exclusive rights for new improvements being monopolies I beleive that there exists no power in this country that can grant a monopoly according to the odious meaning of the word as described by lord Coke Congress can grant neither right Priviledge nor monopoly a patent right in this country can be good only for things that are new and useful that never existed in this country prior to the discovery of the patentee But if it be only an improvement on a knife hoe ax or spade that will cause it to apply usefully to a new purpose it is "a new and useful improvement on a <u>machine</u>" and a patent will be good for the improvement only and for the use should it be an improvement "<u>on any art</u>" The old machine will remain free there is no monopoly of any right that any person ever possessed therefore no injury done but a good or convenience added to the public stock as soon as the thing becomes public property

Congress can only protect natural right "<u>for limited times</u>" And they have promised their protection to inventors of "any new and useful art, machine manufacture,[1] &c or any improvement in any art machine manufacture[2] &c" by their "act to promote &c" in which they declare the inventor has the right to take such steps to obtain this protection for 14 years. did the error of the officer of state destroy this right or was the act for the relief of Oliver Evans totally unnessessary as well as the two provisos[*] And in the present disputed case the inventor has spent a life of the most arduous labour of mind and body perhaps ever known in this country to invent put in opperation to disseminate and teach others to use his improvements <u>in an art and in machines</u> Is their any power tantamount to the power that protects him, that can take away his right, and rob him of the prize he has so justly and fairly won Will any one say that he has not made a useful improvement, or Can they shew an instance in the world of so low a charge in proportion to the benefits? Can Congress withdraw their protection untill the term expires? or grant their protection to any other to use the said improvement by means of other machinery? Can two or more persons have exclusive right to

[*] This act was passed on the recommendation of Thomas Jefferson

the same thing at the same time? If any are dissatisfied with the patent law ought they not to submit to its opperations untill they can get one made to suit themselves? Or can one law Justify the patentee to receive the prices of his licences from the Just true and liberal, and protect the knave the hipocrite and illiberal in refuseing to pay anything and yet use his invention? Men who to save their country from sinking into slavery would not lend their money If they could persuade or deceive congress to repeal the act for the relief of Oliver Evans[3] would his right be at all impaired, or could he not take out his patent under the general law? These are questions worthy of consideration

Who could have thought that the name of Thomas Jefferson would ever have been used in defence of such men, While it is known that in 1803 he sugested to a committee of congress, the impropriety of legislating for the letter A alone while they could as easily legislate for the whole alphabet at once, for the patent term (he said) was too short, The state of the arts and scattered population was such that 28 years in this country was not as good as 14 years in England, that the patent term would expire before the patentee could make any profits, (These were nearly his words), The Committee reported accordingly, and the case has never been decided altho under consideration almost ever since

I have not yet been able to let in the idea that you are opposed to my rights My Case is now fairly at issue before the public, between those who wish to reward inventors on one side, And those who wish to seize prematurely on their rights on the other side, Should the later prevail and Congress refuse to grant the protection I ask I will never make another effort to offend my country men, by producing in operation a useful invention or improvment And I am sure none of my Children ever will, For they know the vexations calumnies and persecutions that I have suffered, the insults abuse poverty and deprivations, anxiety labour and loss of Credit that I have endured, While I have proved to them, that I was capable of Conducting business in such way as to have acquired as much as my persecutors has done, by the use of my inventions, and made a great estate with less anxiety and fatigue and in less time, than I have spent for the public good, and created no enemies It is poor encouragement indeed to inventors, to find that the wicked can excite the indignation of the good against them, if their invention should happen to be profitable

I declare that I have produced in operation but a Small proportion of the great and important improvements which I have invented, enough however to perpetuate my name, untill that of every enemy they have created me, and their crimes shall be totally forgotten, the rest must lay dormant untill god shall be pleased to offer them again through the medium of another, When that time shall come if hystory shall state the reason why they were not produced by Oliver Evans, who discovered them, will not the names of those who suppresed them be execrated—

Will you risque your immortal name at the head of the list, to be the only Surviveing one, for all the rest will be obliterated by time, faster perhaps than their bodies moulder, unless the crime they are now commiting should attract[4] the attention of the Heystorian, to perpetuate them

I hope you will excuse me consider what my feelings must be, not only my property, but my Character attacked, by men who would ruin me and deprive the public of all useful inventions, to save a paltry sum, they owe, and what others have freely paid

  sir with great Respect         OLIVER EVANS

RC (DLC); at foot of text: "The Hon&#7793;&#7793;&#7793; Thomas Jefferson"; endorsed by TJ as received 4 Feb. 1814 and so recorded in SJL. Enclosures: enclosures to Evans to TJ, 7 Jan. 1814.

TJ's letter to Isaac McPherson of 13 Aug. 1813 and related MEMORIALS AND CERTIFICATES were published in the *Memorial to Congress on Evans' Patent.* Sir Edward Coke defines and discusses MO-NOPOLIES, which he viewed as being "against the ancient and fundamental laws of this kingdome," in *The Third Part of the Institutes of the Laws of England* (London, 1644; Sowerby, no. 1784), chap. 85. Evans's sometimes inexact quotations, A NEW AND USEFUL IMPROVE-MENT ON A MACHINE, "on any art," and "any new and useful art . . ." are from the 21 Feb. 1793 "Act to promote the progress of useful Arts" (*U.S. Statutes at Large,* 1:318–23). The phrase FOR LIM-ITED TIMES is from the United States Constitution, article 1, section 8. For the TWO PROVISOS to the 1808 "Act for the relief of Oliver Evans," see TJ to McPherson, 13 Aug. 1813. The Commerce and Manufactures COMMITTEE OF the United States House of Representatives recommended on 22 Jan. 1805 that, "owing to the great extent of the United States, and the difficulties usually attending the introduction of improvements in new countries," Evans's patent on his milling machinery should be extended. At the same time, the committee proposed to draw up a bill increasing the duration of all patents from fourteen to twenty-one years. A bill containing the latter provision was introduced in the House of Representatives on 6 Feb. but rejected that same day (*Annals,* 8th Cong., 2d sess., 1002–3, 1180–1). TJ had indeed indicated that he thought the current PATENT TERM might be too short: "an inventor ought to be allowed a right to the benefit of his invention for some certain time. . . . how long the term should be is the difficult question. our legislators have copied the English estimate of the term; perhaps without sufficiently considering how much longer, in a country so much more sparsely settled, it takes for an invention to become known & used to an extent profitable to the inventor" (TJ to Evans, 2 May 1807 [DLC]).

[1] Word interlined.
[2] Word interlined.
[3] Manuscript: "Oliver Es."
[4] Manuscript: "should should atteract."

# To Joseph Graham

Monticello Jan. 29. 14.

Th: Jefferson presents his compliments to mr Graham and his thanks for the Discourse he has been so kind as to send him. he has observed with real pleasure the sentiments of pure patriotism which it breathes & inculcates, it's just applications of the precepts of the gospel which teach so emphatically the duties we owe to our country, and it's demonstrations of the incivism and heterodoxy of those who would derive from that authority sanctions for their insubordination to the government of their country. without the pleasure of knowing who is the author he begs leave to express here his respect for him.

PoC (DLC); endorsed by TJ.     INCIVISM: "want of good citizenship" (*OED*).

# To James Lyons

DEAR SIR     Monticello Jan. 29, 14.

Your favor of the 23ᵈ is just recieved. about 12. or 13. years ago having had to address your father in a matter respecting the estate of Bathurst Skelton, in answering my letter he took occasion to mention some claim against mr Wayles, as atty for Farrell & Jones: but what it was I do not remember. as the administration[1] of mr Wayles's estate had been entirely committed to mr Eppes for 20. years preceding that, and he was in possession of all the papers of the estate, I forwarded the letter to him, & informed mr Lyons that he alone could act in it. I think mr Eppes afterwards mentioned to me something in opposition to the claim, but what it was I do not recollect with precision. perhaps that mr Wayles's attorneyship for F. & J. having ceased with his life, and the accounts respecting it having been finally settled & closed in 1790. his executors could no further intermeddle with the affairs of F. & J. and that any application respecting them must be addressed to mr Hanson, their acting attorney.—mr Wayles's & mr Eppes's papers however are all in the hands of mr Archibald Thweat, the exr of mr Eppes, & authorised to close his administration of mr Wayles's affairs. he comes often to Richmond, and to him therefore I must refer you as solely enabled to act in the case which is the subject of your letter.

I avail myself with pleasure of this occasion of recognising our former acquaintance and of assuring you of my continued sentiments of esteem & respect.     TH: JEFFERSON

PoC (MoSHi: TJC-BC); at foot of text: "Doct<sup>r</sup> James Lyons"; endorsed by TJ as a letter to John Lyons and so recorded in SJL. Enclosed in TJ to Archibald Thweatt, 29 Jan. 1814.

James Lyons (ca. 1763–1830), physician, was a native of Hanover County and the son of Peter Lyons, a prominent Virginia jurist. The younger Lyons attended the College of William and Mary about 1776 and served under Lafayette at the Battle of Yorktown five years later. He received medical degrees in 1784 from the University of the State of Pennsylvania and the following year from the University of Edinburgh, where his dissertation was on cholera. While continuing his studies in London and Paris, Lyons transmitted correspondence to and from TJ and impressed the elder diplomat as "a sensible worthy young physician." In 1786 he returned to the county of his birth and established a successful medical practice, which he later moved to Richmond. Lyons also published a number of medical papers. He died at his home in Hanover County (*VMHB* 66 [1958]: 88; *William and Mary Provisional List*, 26; Wyndham B. Blanton, *Medicine in Virginia in the Eighteenth Century* [1931], 75, 82, 87; *PTJ*, 8:687, 9:58, 259, 10:107; Lyons account book, 1799–1806 [CSmH: Robert A. Brock Collection]; *Richmond Enquirer*, 1 Apr. 1806; *Philadelphia Medical and Physical Journal* 2, pt. 2 [1806]: 30–6, 41–2; *Richmond Commercial Compiler*, 27 Mar. 1830; *Richmond Enquirer*, 16, 23 Apr. 1830).

Lyons's FAVOR OF THE 23<sup>D</sup>, not found, is recorded in SJL as received 28 Jan. 1814 from Richmond. For the unsuccessful attempt by Peter Lyons in 1801 to collect his CLAIM AGAINST John Wayles for £20 plus interest from 1767, see *PTJ*, 35:726–7, 36:157–8.

<sup>1</sup> Manuscript: "administation."

# To Archibald Thweatt

DEAR SIR                                        Monticello Jan. 29. 14.

M<sup>r</sup> Peter Lyons in his life time (1801) sent me some claim on mr Wayles as atty for Farrell & Jones. I inclosed it to mr Eppes & referred<sup>1</sup> mr Lyons to him. I have just recieved a renewal of the claim from D<sup>r</sup> Lyons his son, which I send to you with a copy of my answer referring him to you.

I am obliged to remind you of the loan of my pamphlet on Livingston's case, of which I had only that copy. an answer to it having been published by him it is possible I may have occasion to turn to mine. ever affect<sup>ly</sup> to yourself and mrs Thweatt.

TH: JEFFERSON

PoC (DLC); at foot of text: "Archibald Thweatt esq."; endorsed by TJ. Enclosures: TJ to James Lyons, 29 Jan. 1814, and 23 Jan. 1814 letter from Lyons to TJ described there.

SJL records missing letters from Thweatt to TJ of 13 and 20 Feb. 1814 that were received 18 Feb. from Richmond and 4 Mar. 1814 from Eppington, respectively.

<sup>1</sup> Word interlined in place of "informed."

# To Joseph C. Cabell

DEAR SIR                                    Monticello Jan. 31. 14.

Your favor of the 23ᵈ is recieved. Say had come to hand safely. but I regretted having asked the return of him; for I did not find in him one new idea on the subject I had been contemplating; nothing more than a succinct, judicious digest of the tedious pages of Smith.

You ask my opinion on the question whether the states can add any qualifications to those which the Constitution has prescribed for their members of Congress? it is a question I had never before reflected on; yet had taken up an off-hand opinion, agreeing with your first, that they could not: that to add new qualifications to those of the Constitution, would be as much an alteration as to detract from them. and so I think the House of Representatives of Congress decided in some case; I believe that of a member from Baltimore. but your letter having induced me to look into the Constitution, and to consider the question a little, I am again in your predicament of doubting the correctness of my first opinion. had the constitution been silent, nobody can doubt but that the right to prescribe all the qualifications and disqualifications of those they would send to represent them would have belonged to the state. so also the constitution might have prescribed the whole, and excluded all others. it seems to have preferred the middle way. it has exercised the power in part, by declaring some disqualifications, to wit, those of not being 25. years of age, of not having been a citizen 7. years, and of not being an inhabitant of the state at the time of election. but it does not declare itself that the member shall not be a lunatic, a pauper, a convict of treason, of murder, of felony, or other infamous crime, or a non-resident of his district: nor does it prohibit to the state the power of declaring these or any other disqualifications which it's particular circumstances may call for: and these may be different in different states. of course then, by the 10ᵗʰ Amendment, the power is reserved to the state. if, wherever the constitution assumes a single power out of many which belong to the same subject, we should consider it as assuming the whole, it would vest the general government with a mass of powers never contemplated. on the contrary the assumption of particular powers seems an exclusion of all not assumed. this reasoning appears to me to be sound; but, on so recent a change of view, caution requires us not to be too confident, and that we admit this to be one of the doubtful questions on which honest men may differ with the purest motives; and the more readily as we find we have differed from ourselves on it.

I have always thought that where the line of demarkation between the powers of the general & state governments was doubtfully or indistinctly drawn, it would be prudent and praise-worthy in both parties never to approach it but under the most urgent necessity. is the necessity now urgent to declare that no non-resident of his district shall be eligible as a member of Congress? it seems to me that, in practice, the partialities of the people are a sufficient security against such an election; and that if in any instance they should ever chuse a non-resident, it must be in one of such eminent merit and qualifications as would make it a good, rather than an evil; and that in any event the examples will be so rare, as never to amount to a serious evil. if the case then be neither clear nor urgent, would it not be better to let it lie undisturbed? perhaps it's decision may never be called for. but if it be indispensable to establish this disqualification now, would it not look better to declare such others, at the same time, as may be proper?—I frankly confide to yourself these opinions, or rather no-opinions, of mine; but would not wish to have them go any further. I want to be quiet: and altho' some circumstances now and then excite me to notice them, I feel safe, and happier in leaving every thing to those whose turn it is to take care of them; and in general to let it be understood that I meddle little, or not at all with public affairs. there are two subjects indeed which I shall claim a right to further as long as I breathe, the public education and the subdivision of the counties into wards. I consider the continuance of republican government as absolutely hanging on these two hooks. of the first you will, I am sure, be an advocate as having already reflected on it, and of the last when you shall have reflected. ever affectionately yours

TH: JEFFERSON

RC (ViU: TJP); addressed: "Joseph C. Cabell esq. of the Senate of Virginia now at Richmond"; franked; postmarked Milton, 2 Feb.; endorsed by Cabell as answered 5 Feb. PoC (DLC).

Article 1, sections 2–3 of the United States Constitution list the qualifications for MEMBERS OF CONGRESS. In 1807 Joshua Barney contested the election of William McCreery, a MEMBER FROM BALTIMORE, arguing that McCreery had not met the residency requirements laid down by the Maryland legislature. The United States House of Representative's committee on elections examined the case and reported on 9 Nov. 1807 that no state had the right "to change, add, or diminish" the qualifications enumerated in the Constitution. In consequence, it deemed the Maryland law "restricting the residence of the members of Congress to any particular part of the district for which they may be chosen" to be unconstitutional and allowed McCreery to take his seat (ASP, Miscellaneous, 1:484). The United States Supreme Court, by a vote of 5–4, finally settled the issue in 1995 by explicitly prohibiting states from placing additional restrictions on those seeking election to Congress (U.S. Term Limits, Inc., v. Thornton [U.S. Reports, 514:779–926]).

# To Samuel Greenhow

Sir                                    Monticello Jan. 31. 14.

Your letter on the subject of the Bible society arrived here while I was on a journey to Bedford which occasioned a long absence from home. since my return it has lain with a mass of others accumulated during my absence, till I could answer them. I presume the views of the society are confined to our own country, for with the religion of other countries, my own forbids intermedling. I had not supposed there was a family in this state not possessing a bible and wishing without having the means to procure one. when, in earlier life I was intimate with every class, I think I never was in a house where that was the case. however, circumstances may have changed, and the society I presume have evidence of the fact. I therefore inclose you chearfully an order on Mess<sup>rs</sup> Gibson and Jefferson for 50.D. for the purposes of the society, sincerely agreeing with you that there never was a more pure & sublime system of morality delivered to man than is to be found in the four evangelists. Accept the assurance of my esteem & respect                                    TH: JEFFERSON

PoC (DLC); at foot of text: "M<sup>r</sup> Samuel Greenhow." Enclosure not found.

# To Elizabeth Trist

Dear Madam                          Monticello Feb. 1. 14.

Your letter of Dec. 17. was near three weeks on it's passage here. immediately on it's reciept I turned over to Ellen the letter you had inclosed me for translation, she being as much a mistress of the language as any of us and less occupied by correspondences and business. her translation is inclosed in a letter from herself, and I sincerely congratulate you on it's flattering purport. our Martha has had a poor time since the birth of her new daughter. harrassed with lingering fevers which have greatly debilitated her. she ought to have come out to day, but is not strong enough, and it is snowing. the grandchildren and great grandchildren are serenading us in every corner of the house with the whooping cough. most of them however have it favorably, some badly, but none dangerously. I have heard only of two deaths from it in the neighborhood. mr Randolph will probably leave us in the spring to try another campaign; tho' he does not seem decided. Jefferson has found a loadstone at Warren, which draws him there so often as to induce us to conclude the attraction of the two bodies mutual. mr Gilmer's brothers and their families here were all well a few days ago. the Doctor has removed from Milton to a place bought of one of the Keys near mr Minor's. this is our small news: and as for great, we may as well say nothing, as we have nothing comfortable, either behind or before us to say. we have had indeed some comfortable things from the ocean where they could do us no good, but on the land, where they would have been useful, neither courage nor conduct to cheer us. we must sympathise with our mutual friend who is doomed to see his wise measures all baffled in the execution. affectionate salutations and Adieu.

TH: JEFFERSON

RC (John Randolph Burke, Bryn Mawr, Pa., 1947; photostat in ViU: TJP); addressed: "M<sup>rs</sup> Elizabeth Trist at mr Gilmer's near Henry Court house"; franked; postmarked Milton, 4 Feb. PoC (MHi); endorsed by TJ.

Martha Jefferson Randolph's NEW DAUGHTER was Septimia A. Randolph (Meikleham). The LOADSTONE attracting Thomas Jefferson Randolph to Warren was his future wife, Jane Hollins Nicholas. OUR MUTUAL FRIEND: James Madison.

# To Jeremiah A. Goodman

DEAR SIR                                     Monticello Feb. 3. 14.

Your letter of the 27<sup>th</sup> Jan. came to hand last night, and this morning I have written to mr Gibson to inclose to you 30.D. by the mail to Lynchburg. he will recieve my letter on Monday next, the 7<sup>th</sup> and by the first mail leaving Richmond after that it will be at Lynchburg, which w[ill] [prob]a[b]l[y] [be] before you recieve this letter. let the clover be sown about the 1[. . .] of March, and if the earth has no crust on the top, the first rain will cover it sufficiently, without drawing a bush over it. clover sown at that time is pretty much out of danger of being injured by frost, and will get so strong before the heats set in as not to be hurt by them. I am glad to hear of your progress on the [r]oad, & hope when I come up it will be ready to be recieved by [. . .]t. not a dust of my flour is sold as yet. Acce[p]t my best [. . .]

TH: JEFFERSON

P.S. if my tobacco is not already engaged, send it off to Richmond, where the tobacco of this neighborhood sells for 9.D. and if that is well handled [I h]ave no fear of getting as much. in that case it is not to be inspected at Lynchburg. I should be glad the beef should start from Poplar forest the 1<sup>st</sup> of March if fat enough. Gill & his waggon must come with it, and he will return with a load of some things for the house at Poplar forest. with respect to salt for the people it has got to so exorbitant a price that I have been obliged to allowance my people here to a pint apeice a month for the grown people & half a pint for every child. and the same must be done at the fore[st.] I am told the assembly has laid a tax on all dogs over two at every planta[t]ion. I am not yet sure of the fact, but if it be true, every dog over that number at each plantation must be killed as soon as it is ascertained. you will know from the members when they return home or from the newspapers.

RC (ViCMRL, on deposit ViU: TJP); torn at folds and damaged at seal; addressed: "M$^r$ Jeremiah A. Goodman Poplar Forest near Lynchburg"; franked; postmarked Charlottesville, 9 Feb.

Goodman's LETTER OF THE 27$^{TH}$ JAN., not found, is recorded in SJL as received 2 Feb. from Poplar Forest. SJL also records a missing letter from Goodman to TJ of 5 Mar. 1814, received 9 Mar. from Poplar Forest, and missing letters from TJ to Goodman of 11 Mar. and 16 Apr. 1814. TJ's letter of THIS MORNING to Patrick GIBSON, not found, is recorded in SJL.

The Virginia General Assembly passed a tax on DOGS on 26 Jan. 1814, but Albemarle and Bedford were among the counties exempted from the legislation (*Acts of Assembly*, 1813–14 sess., 55–6).

# Notes on Account with David Higginbotham

[ca. 3 Feb. 1814]

| | | |
|---|---|---|
| Negroes | 1107. 80 | |
| * groceries | 312. 13 | ℔ |
| iron | 210. 14 to wit $\left\{ \begin{array}{l} 2200\frac{1}{2} \text{ iron} \\ 74\frac{1}{4} \text{ steel} \end{array} \right.$ |
| salt | 122. 14 = 13. sacks + $1\frac{1}{2}$ bush |
| spinn$^g$ cotton 230.℔ | 57. 50 | |
| Miscellanies | 164. 72 | |
| | 1974. 43 | |
| | ℔   oz. | |
| * white sugar | 271–4 | |
| brown sugar | 317. | |
| coffee | 66. 8 | |
| tea | 22. 2 | |
| spirits | $18\frac{1}{4}$ gall$^s$ | |

MS (MHi); in TJ's hand; undated; on verso of last page of TJ's Account with Higginbotham, 1 Aug. 1813.

On 3 Feb. 1814 TJ recorded in his memorandum books that "On settlement of my dealings with D. Higginbotham from Aug. 1. 1812. to July 31. 1813. the balance due him is 1903.50 for which I gave him my acknolegemt." He then copied the above "Analysis of the dealings in that period" with Higginbotham, to which he added a note indicating that

"The sawmill took upwards of 1000.℔." of iron (*MB*, 2:1297).

By NEGROES TJ meant fabric, blankets, and hats for distribution to his slaves.

# From Jason Chamberlain

DEAR SIR,     University of Vermont Burlington Vt. 4 of Feb. 1814.

Though I have not the honour of an acquaintance with you, I take the liberty to send you some Indian Pamphlets. From the excellent works which you have published, I learn that you have paid some attention to the Aborigines of this country. I thought you might have the curiosity to see a specimen of the Iroquois Language. There are many among the Iroquois who can read. They use the French Alphabet, and sounds of the Letters.

Among the thousands who follow you to your retirement with benedictions for your publick services, there is not one, whose good wishes are more

Sincere than those of your humble servant,

JASON CHAMBERLAIN.

RC (MHi); at foot of text: "Hon. Th. Jefferson"; endorsed by TJ as received 18 Feb. 1814 and so recorded in SJL. Enclosure: Eleazer Williams, *Good News to the Iroquois Nation: a Tract, on Man's Primitive Rectitude, his Fall, and his Recovery Through Jesus Christ* (Burlington, 1813; with copy at APS inscribed in an unidentified hand: "Specimen of the Iroquois Language 15 April 1814" and "Sent by Mᵣ Jefferson Presᵗ of APS From Jason Chamberlayne Burlington Vermᵗ").

Jason Chamberlain (1783–1820), Congregational minister, educator, and attorney, was a native of Holliston, Massachusetts, who graduated from the College of Rhode Island (later Brown University) in 1804. During service in 1806 as a supply minister at Thomaston, Maine, he officiated at the funeral of Henry Knox. Chamberlain was ordained in 1808 at the Congregational church in Guilford, Vermont, and remained there until 1811. In the latter year he became a professor of Greek

and Latin at the University of Vermont, a position he held until the university suspended classes in 1814 in order to accommodate United States soldiers during the War of 1812. Chamberlain saw military service himself in the autumn of 1814. He had become an attorney in 1813 and pursued this profession in Vermont until at least 1816. Chamberlain subsequently practiced law in the town of Jackson in the Missouri Territory, and later at Arkansas Post in the Arkansas Territory. He briefly served as clerk to the Arkansas Territory House of Representatives before he drowned trying to cross a creek in that territory (Pliny H. White, "History of the Congregational Church in Guilford, Vt.," *Congregational Quarterly* 8 [1866]: 286; *Historical Catalogue of Brown University, 1764–1904* [1905], 95; Cyrus Eaton, *History of Thomaston, Rockland, and South Thomaston, Maine* [1865], 1:266–7; Chamberlain to TJ, 30 Nov. 1814; *The Vermont Register and Almanac, for the Year of Our Lord 1816*

[Burlington, 1815], 69; *Terr. Papers*, 17:321–4; DNA: RG 59: LAR, 1809–17 and 1817–25; Dallas T. Herndon, ed., *Centennial History of Arkansas* [1922; repr. 1970], 1:412; *Arkansas Gazette*, 12 Feb., 12 Aug. 1820; Washington *Daily National Intelligencer*, 6 Sept. 1820).

With this letter or that of 10 May 1814, Chamberlain sent TJ another work by Williams, *Gaiatonsera Ionteweienstakwa Ongwe Onwe Gawennontakon: A Spelling-Book in the Language of the Seven Iroquois Nations* (Plattsburgh, N.Y., 1813; Poor, *Jefferson's Library*, 14 [no. 912]).

# From Samuel Greenhow

SIR.                                             Richmond 4ᵗʰ febʸ 1814

I have this day recᵈ your letter of the 31ˢᵗ Ultᵒ, covering a draft on Messʳˢ Gibson & Jefferson for $50—which has been paid. I have considered it proper to acknowledge the receipt of the money; and in doing so, can not avoid expressing to you, the Satisfaction I have derived from your attention to mine—your long silence left me under an impression, that I had been guilty of an impertinence in addressing a letter to you on the Subject of the Bible Society, which your reply has removed.—

I am also gratified, that my Application has been successful as to it's Object, because that Success assures me that you approve our Association, if the Bibles are wanted in our Country, by persons too poor to purchase them.—

Altho' perhaps twenty years younger than you, I also recollect when Bibles were generally found in each house; But, I respectfully suggest, that, they may be more scarce at this time, from a cause well calculated to reduce the number; Bibles were school books thirty years ago, at present, they are out of use in most schools—

Permit me farther to encroach on your time, by offering a few additional remarks.—

If the Bible contains a pure System of Morality—If it adds another sanction (Religious faith) to the practise of morality—If it bases moral Conduct on the amiable sentiment of diffusive charity; Should we wait for the expression of a wish, before we will give it? If our friend or neighbor would probably be benefited by our advice, we do not hesitate to give that advice, altho' we are aware that it may not be well received at first—If an intelligent Patriot believed that he could do some great good to his Country, he would not wait to be sollicited. Should we then wait for the expression of a wish to possess[1] the bible? Should we, holding a book which inculcates such morality, withhold it, until application is made—? Should we give only to those who are not able to purchase it? I think not—. For if the dona-tions were confined to such only, so fortunate are our people gener-ally as to pecuniary resources, that your donation would supply the demand in several Counties—

If the Bible is a Good—or may produce one, I would distribute it, as Heaven diffuses it's blessings, freely, and extensively as possible—I would give it to the believer and to the unbeliever—If possible, like the light of the sun or the rain of the Clouds, it should reach every house and every individual—If it shall not benefit the donee, it may benefit his heir or some member of his family—If it shall in any de-gree advance the morals of Society, it will arrest the progress of that Luxury, so rapidly increasing among us, and so baneful to the peace of Society and so destructive to free[2] elective governments—It has been abused and may still again be so—But, shall we refuse to do a good, because by improper use of it, an evil results—The Book can not be chargeable with the faults of Bigots and Enthusiasts.—

We mean not to interfere with the religion of others, But, we con-template only to distribute the book—By our Country, I presume you mean any of the United States or their Territories—The great defi-ciency of Bibles in Louisiana has been satisfactorily shewn—I am told that the Bishop of Orleans has expressed a wish that a french tes-tament may be distributed in Louisiana—An Edition of 5000 Copies is now (I believe)[3] in press—the translation in press, is that called the Geneva translation, which does not differ materially from that in use among Protestants here, and tho' not similar to the Latin Vul-gate, is approved (I am told) by the Church of Rome—To this Edi-tion our Society mean to subscribe—In this only, have we, as yet had a view, extending beyond this State—

    I am with great Respect
    y$^{rs}$ &c

SAMUEL GREENHOW

RC (DLC); endorsed by TJ as received 15 Feb. 1814 and so recorded in SJL.

The Bible Society of Virginia donated $150 to the Bible Society of Philadelphia to assist in the publication of a FRENCH TESTAMENT for dissemination in Loui-siana (Bible Society of Philadelphia, Re-port 6 [1814]: 9–10; *Nouveau Testament de Notre Seigneur Jesus-Christ* [Philadel-phia, 1814]).

[1] Word interlined in place of "own."
[2] Word interlined.
[3] Parenthetical phrase added in mar-gin.

# From Joseph C. Cabell

DEAR SIR,                                    Richmond. 5<sup>th</sup> Feb: 1814

Your favor of 31<sup>st</sup> ult has come to hand, and I am happy to learn from it that your books arrived in safety. The free communication of your opinion upon the subject of the alledged Right of the Gen<sup>l</sup> Assembly to annex additional qualifications to the members of the House of Representatives of Congress, places me under great obligations. Your letter did not get to hand before the subject was acted on in the Senate: yet it serves to satisfy my mind the more perfectly as to the course which I took on the occasion. I held the bill back as long as possible, in order to have time to get an answer from yourself, as well as to obtain some facts for which I had written to Washington. But the House growing every day thinner by the withdrawing of members, and the majority of the last year, being urgent that the decision of the House should[1] not be reversed by the accidental composition of the House at the moment of taking the question: I reported the Bill, and informed the body that I should vote as I had voted the last year, because I still doubted the constitutional power of the Gen<sup>l</sup> Assembly to pass the Bill: but that those doubts had in a considerable degree been removed, and perhaps might have been entirely dissipated if I could have continued my investigation a few days longer: At the same time I expressly reserved to myself the right of changing the vote I then gave should the subject again be brought to the view of the Senate. It was admitted on both sides that the subject was too important, & the period of the session too advanced to admit of its being then fairly & definitively disposed of, and it was agreed on both sides that the Bill should be postponed with a distinct understanding that it might be resumed with the consent of the House of Delegates at a future session, as if no such postponement had taken place. On this safe ground the subject now stands. It will probably give rise to considerable discussion next winter. Should it not be disagreeable to you, I should be infinitely indebted to you for any further views you may take of the subject at any time during the year. Your repose shall not be disturbed by an improper communication of your name, in connection with this or any other subject, on which you may favor me with information. My object is to be useful to my country in the station which I occupy: and in availing myself occasionally of your valuable aid, it would be highly improper to disturb the tranquility of your retirement.

I have had the pleasure of seeing Col: Randolph, from whom I learn that you are anxious to know the fate of the Rivanna Bill. I was about to write you on that subject, when he came to town. The Bill passed the two Houses a few days ago, in the shape agreed upon by yourself & M<sup>r</sup> Minor, including the two verbal alterations which were suggested by yourself, and not objected to by the Delegates from Albemarle. The reason of the bill's not being sooner acted upon is this. Doctor Everett expected that communications from the parties concerned might be addressed directly to himself and M<sup>r</sup> Garth, and to give time for that expectation to be fulfilled, I agreed that the bill might be detained in the House of Delegates as long as possible. At length he consented to take the letters addressed by you & M<sup>r</sup> Minor to myself, as his authority, and then the Bill passed into a law, as soon as the² forms of the two Houses would permit. I congratulate you on being now exonerated from the trouble & vexation which this subject has given you.

It was my wish to send by Col: Randolph the papers on the subject of finance, you were so kind as to lend me. But occupied as I am in the business of the Assembly, I cannot digest them as thoroughly as I could desire. I shall therefore take the liberty of keeping them in my possession, for about two weeks after the rising of the Assembly. I will send them to you by the 20<sup>th</sup> February—or at latest the 1<sup>st</sup> of March. If you should require them sooner, they shall be immediately forwarded. I availed myself of some of your facts, & reasoning in a discussion in the Senate, on the subject of a Small bank at Wheeling, which excit[ed] considerable interest, as it was contended on one side [&] admitted on the other that if this Bill should pass, it would be the commencement of the system of covering our state with small banks. The bill fell by an equal division of the Senate.

On the subjects of education & the division of the state into wards, I shall be much pleased to communicate with you at some future period of leisure.

With highest regard y<sup>r</sup> friend & humb: serv<sup>t</sup>

JOSEPH C. CABELL.

RC (ViU: TJP-PC); mutilated at seal; addressed: "Thomas Jefferson Esquire Monticello Care of Col: Randolph"; endorsed by TJ as received 8 Feb. 1814 and so recorded in SJL.

The FATE OF THE RIVANNA BILL is explained at TJ to Cabell, 7 Nov. 1813, and its enclosed Abstract of the Rivanna Company Bill, [ca. 7 Nov. 1813]. On 30 Dec. 1813 Dabney MINOR sent Cabell a short note explaining that "The directors of the Rivanna Company and m<sup>r</sup> Jefferson are agreed that the law as amended the last session in the Senate be passed into a law, will you D<sup>r</sup> Everett & m<sup>r</sup> Garth attend and have it made a law" (RC in ViU: TJP; addressed: "Joseph C. Cabell Richmond Care of Majr Ro Quarles"; endorsed by Cabell).

¹ Word interlined in place of "might."
² Cabell here canceled "authority."

# From Samuel Brown

Dear Sir,                                                    Natchez Feb$^y$ 8$^{th}$ 1814

On my return from New Orleans, a few days ago, I had the pleasure of receiving your letter of the 13$^{th}$ of November. It had remained in the Post office, at this place, during my absence, which was protracted, far beyond my calculations, by the illness & death of an intimate friend who had solicited me to witness his last moments—

The constant expectation of receiving an answer to your letter, which I had forwarded to Mr Henderson, prevented me, for some weeks, from replying to your very interesting letter of the 14$^{th}$ of July. An additional domestic misfortune, the loss of an infant daughter, which happened in Sep$^t$, affected me so sensibly that, for some time, I was almost incapable of attending to any kind of business. No calamity however could render me insensible of the honor you confer on me by your letters [whi]ch are always filled with instruction conveyed in the most agreeable form. I am indeed ashamed of the poor returns I make you—The last year of my life seems like a Dream & I ought scarcely to be accountable to God or man for what I have done or left undone in it.

Whilst I was in N. Orleans I obtained certain information that Mr James L. Henderson was dead but I could not learn when his death happened. Believing that his papers are in the hands of Mr Tho$^s$ Lewis the Judge of the Parish of Washita, I have addressed a letter to that Gentleman requesting him to examine your letter of April last & to search Mr Hendersons papers for the information you require & to communicate to you, without delay, the result of his investigations. Knowing Judge Lewis to be a Gentleman of a very obliging disposition & correct principles, I am confident he will execute this commission with pleasure & ability—As there is a Post now established between this place & Washita you may very soon expect a letter from Judge Lewis on the subject. I did not feel myself authorised to request the Judge to open your second letter to Henderson & have therefore returned it to you. If it shall appear that the Papers left by Mr H. can be useful to you I have no doubt copies of them can be easily obtained. I regret very much that Henderson did not answer your letter. I have no doubt he rec$^d$ it—& until I returned from N Orleans had hopes that he had transmitted his letter to you by some direct conveyance.

Our country is fast recovering from the shock occasioned by the War, which was, perhaps, as sensibly felt here, as in any part of the

Union. Within one month a most surprising revolution in our commerce has taken place. The demand for our Cotton to supply the manufacturers[1] of the U.S. trandscends all our calculations & the Barges which are four times as numerous as they were last year must be quadrupled before they will be sufficient to carry the produce already ordered up the River. The Wharves are crouded with these Barges of 60 90 & 100 tons & all the ships yards are more busily employed in rigging & repairing them than they have ever been since I have known N Orleans. It is said the merchants of Natchez have already rec[d] orders for cotton from the Atlantic states to the amount of 2 millions of dollars & the price has within a few days risen from 5 to 12 cents. The competition which is now established between domestic & foreign manufacturers will always ensure the Planter a good price for his cotton & the habits of economy & industry which our late necessities have formed will, it is [hope]d, long continue. With our present habits cotton can be afforded at 12 cents better than formerly at 25 when foreign luxuries of every kind were sought with the most rediculous avidity. I have felt real pleasure in seeing Servants in Gaudy Livery hawking Butter & Country Cotton through the streets of Natchez whilst the most wealthy Planters have worn[2] their own manufactures Our enemies will mark these changes with wonder & I am confident that they will contribute as much as our naval victories to recall an infatuated Gov[t] to a sense of justice. I began to think that the power of Napolean has attained its acme & that his tyranny will soon be effectually resisted. But will the continental powers admit, in their full extent, the maritime usurpations [of][3] Great Britain? I trust not. I never thought the Power of France so dangerous to us as the commercial monopoly of England.

I am much pleased with the simple Apparatus invented by D[r] Jennings & am persuaded it will be found useful in a variety of diseases particularly Gout & Rheumatism: and I even think it probable that by a judicious application of such an Atmosphe[re] the cold stage of an i[n]termittent might be prevented. It is certainly an ele[ga]nt substitute for what is called an Indian Sweat & is by far the most convenient Vapour bath that I have seen. Besides I am not sure that the Chemical properties of such an atmosphere are of no importance. To remove a Patient out of Bed when faint & exhausted by fever or when tortured with pain is often a dangerous & always an unpleasant undertaking. Indeed I have seen fatal accidents result from the attempt. I hope D[r] Jennings will conduct his Exp[ts] with zeal & regulate them by the Scientific Principles established by D[r] Currie in his inestimable work on the use of cold water in fevers for which he deserves a Statue of Gold. In Hospitals, Ships & other places where fuel is scarce the invention of D[r] Jennings will I think, soon be duely appreciated—I am greatly indebted to you for the trouble you have taken to explain it to me. I almost wish you had tried it in your Chronic Rheumatism But Sir W Temple says every man of sense ought to be his own Physician at 40. Your Diploma then is of an older date than mine & I submit to your riper judgment.

I am m[a]king great exertions to remove my little family to Kentu[c]ky in order that my Daughter may have the benefit of Mrs John Browns instruction. It is my wish to extend my journey to N York & Boston. Should I cross the Allegeheny I should travel a few hundred miles with great cheerfulness that I might have once more the pleasure of paying my respects to you. In the mean time let me assure you that it will always give me pleasure to serve you in any way in my power & that your letters are not more agreeable to any man in the world than to

Your Humble Sert                                         SAM[L.] BROWN

RC (DLC); torn at folds; endorsed by TJ as received 9 Mar. 1814 and so recorded in SJL. Enclosure: TJ to James L. Henderson, 12 Nov. 1813, recorded in SJL, but not found.

For TJ's letter of 21 APRIL LAST to James L. Henderson, see note to TJ to Brown, 24 Apr. 1813. James CURRIE wrote *Medical Reports, on the Effects of Water, Cold and Warm, as a remedy in* *Fever, and Febrile Diseases* (Liverpool, 1797). Brown's sister-in-law Margaretta Mason Brown (MRS JOHN BROWN) was a religious educator in Frankfort, Kentucky (William H. Averill, *A History of the First Presbyterian Church Frankfort Kentucky* [1901], 198, 220–2).

[1] Manuscript: "manufacturees."
[2] Manuscript: "won."
[3] Omitted word editorially supplied.


# From Patrick Gibson

SIR                                         Richmond 8th February 1814—

I send you by M[r] Johnson such parts of the nail rod mention'd in your letter of the 26th Ult[o] as I have been able to procure together with the Corks & powder as p[r] Mem[n] at foot—nothing has been doing in Flour since I wrote you last, the price is nominally 4$\frac{1}{2}$$—         With great respect I am

Your ob[t] Serv[t]                                         PATRICK GIBSON

| | | | | |
|---|---|---|---|---|
| Of Sam¹ G. Adams | 62 lbs hoop Iron | 9ᵈ | $ 7.75¹ = | .12½ |
| | 2 bundles 6ᵈ nail rod | 30/. | " 10.² = | .10 |
| | 2 " 10ᵈ " | " | " 10. | |
| | 1 " Spike " | " | " 5. | $ 32.75 |
| Jaˢ Brown Jʳ | a Keg Gun powder | | | " 21. |
| J & J Dick | 12 Gross Corks | 4/6 | | " 9. |
| | | Toll & drayᵉ | | " .37³ |
| | | | | $63.12⁴ |

RC (ViU: TJP-ER); in Gibson's hand, with two calculations in TJ's hand; at head of text: "Thomas Jefferson Esqʳᵉ"; endorsed by TJ as received 15 Feb. 1814 and so recorded (as a letter from Gibson & Jefferson) in SJL.

¹ Remainder of line added by TJ.
² Remainder of line added by TJ.
³ Reworked from ".25."
⁴ Reworked from "$63.—."

# From John Barnes

DEAR SIR                    George Town Colᵒ 9ᵗʰ Febuary 1814—

Your favʳ of the 29ʰ Ultᵒ receved last Evening—and duly Notice its Contents, with referance to the good Genˡ K—every exersion has been made by me to effect a remittanc—thro Mʳ Williams and others, but without effect,—the late Occurances in Europe as well here, has but increased the difficulty—

and to Attempt One at this Crisis—would be to hazard a still greater risque—what then I ask can possibly be done, in aid of the Genˡ but to wait—a more convenient season—let us hope! and trust ere long some favorable change of Circumstancs may Offer to effect so desirable a purpose—

With referance to your further request respecting my Opinion on the propriety of disposing of the Genˡ Pennᵃ Bank stock and placing the proceeds on Loan to Govermᵗ I must beg a day or two, for serious Consideration and reflection—on so Momentous¹—a question—          most Respectfully, Dear Sir

your mst Obedᵗ

JOHN BARNES,

RC (ViU: TJP-ER); at foot of text: "Thoˢ Jefferson Esqʳ Monticello"; endorsed by TJ as received 18 Feb. 1814 and so recorded in SJL.

GENˡ K: Tadeusz Kosciuszko.

¹ Manuscript: "Momentoues."

# To Mathew Carey

Monticello Feb. 10. 14.

Th: Jefferson presents his compliments to m<sup>r</sup> Carey and his thanks for the copy of the 2<sup>d</sup> edition of Clark's Naval history which has come safely to hand. he is happy to find that mr Clark is continuing the work, and ensuring to us the preservation of the facts as they occur. he has recovered more of those of the Revolutionary war than had been deemed practicable. Th:J. salutes mr Carey with esteem and respect.

PoC (DLC); dateline at foot of text; endorsed by TJ.

# To Thomas Clark

Sir                                                    Monticello Feb. 10. 14.

Your favor of Jan. 19. is recieved, and with it a copy of the 2<sup>d</sup> edition of your Naval history, for which be pleased to accept my thanks. I subscribe willingly for a copy of your History of the US. and shall readily render you any service I can towards the procuring information. Richmond is the present deposit of our public records, which however sustained great losses by wanton destruction by the enemy during the revolutionary war. my situation is distant from that place; but whenever you propose to come on thither I will furnish you with a letter to the Governor who will be able to procure you access to our public records. a collection of all our laws from the settlement of the colony to the present day is in a course of publication by mr Hening, who has already brought it to the year 1710. in 3. vols 8<sup>vo</sup>. another volume is soon expected. you will find it difficult to procure a file of newspapers of any extent. wishing you success in your undertaking, I tender you the assurance of my esteem & respect

TH: JEFFERSON

PoC (DLC); at foot of text: "M<sup>r</sup> Thomas Clark"; endorsed by TJ.

# To Thomas Cooper

Dear Sir                                               Monticello Feb. 10. 14.

In my letter of Jan. 16. I promised you a sample from my Commonplace book, of the pious disposition of the English judges to connive at the frauds of the clergy, a disposition which has even rendered them faithful allies in practice. when I was a student of the law, now half a century ago, after getting thro Coke Littleton, whose matter cannot be abridged, I was in the habit of abridging and common-placing what I read meriting it, and of sometimes mixing my own reflections on the subject. I now inclose you the extract from these entries which I promised. they were written at a time of life when I was bold in the pursuit of knolege, never fearing to follow truth and reason to whatever results they led, & bearding every authority which stood in their way. this must be the apology, if you find the conclusions bolder than historical facts and principles will warrant. Accept with them the assurances of my great esteem and respect.

Th: Jefferson

PoC (DLC); at foot of text: "Thomas Cooper esq."

TJ here enclosed a transcription of sections 873 and 879 of his legal COMMON-PLACE BOOK (MS in DLC: TJ Papers, ser. 5). The selections he sent to Cooper discussed and rejected the theory that Christianity had been incorporated into the English common law (PoC of Tr in DLC: TJ Papers, 200:35660–3, entirely in TJ's hand, undated, with minor differences from MS; Tr in MHi, posthumous copy based on PoC of Tr, undated, incomplete, lacking portions of section 873 and all of section 879).

# To Shotwell & Kinder

Messʳˢ Shortwell and Kindes      Monticello Feb. 10. 14.
Your favor of Dec. 24. came but by our last mail, and with it the piece of cloth made of wool and hair which you were so kind as to send me. I pray you to accept my thanks for this present, which, while it is an acceptable mark of good will, shews also how important a resource we have in an article hitherto mostly thrown away, towards supplying our stock of wool not yet quite equal to our wants. altho' our flocks of sheep are multiplying rapidly in this state, they are still so far short of what are necessary for clothing our laborers, that we are obliged to mix half cotton in their clothing. this has by no means the substance which you give with hair;[1] and if such cloth as your smaller sample, of $\frac{1}{4}$ only of wool, can be made reasonably cheap, I think much of it might find a sale in this state. the manufacture of cotton with us in a houshold way, has, for a century at least, been equal to the clothing the lower & midling classes of our fellow citizens. the introduction of the Spinning-machines has increased these manufactures of coarse and midling fabric to the full demand of all classes of our citizens.

I rejoice in this progress towards a real independance, and while I hope a permanent support to those generally to whose spirited enterprize we are likely to be indebted for it, I add sincere wishes for success to your particular exertions, and with a repetition[2] of my thanks, I tender the assurances of my respect.

TH: JEFFERSON

PoC (CSmH: JF-BA); endorsed by TJ. Printed in Philadelphia Society for Promoting Agriculture, *Memoirs* 3 (1814): 405–6.

[1] Remainder of paragraph not in *Memoirs*.

[2] Manuscript: "repetion."

# From John Barnes

MY DEAR SIR— George Town Col[a] 11th Febuary 1814.

You were pleased Sir—in your fav[r] of the 29[h] Ult[o] to ask my Opinion, on the propriety of your disposing of Gen[l] K[s] Penn[a] Bank Stock, and transpose the proceeds thereof on Loan to Goverm[t] by saying—

"it is time to ask, if there is not reason to feel Alarm, for our Overflowing Bank Institutions, that we have 400. Millions of paper afloat, a population of 8 Millions of people, whose compitant Circulation w[d] be, 8 Millions of Dollars, or, a 50th part of it, that in case of great Alarm,—a <u>Run</u> on the Banks, their Bankrupsey is unquestionable, Because, no Body imagine they have 400—Millions—or, a 50th part of it, in their Vaults."—

In Compliance with your Request, I submit my humble opinion— without reserve—w[th] the Frankness and sincerity of a disinterested individual—not only as to, its consequences, Respecting Bank Institutions but the Goverment—I admit Sir—your Calculations in the <u>Theory</u> to be Correct, and I admit also—the effects you describe may probably happen, to some individuals Banks, whose stability, and Credit, has not been proved—or Conducted by designing Men.— from Theory, let us advert to practice—when an individual, cannot pay, his Note, due at Bank, or meet his engagem[ts] made on <u>Change</u>— He commits an Act of Bankruptsey (in the Mercantile Usage of Business) and every Creditor <u>Runs</u> upon him, and demands—immediate paym[t]: the consequence is, The Unfortunate Man, is forced to Yield to the presure of his unfeeling C[rs] altho' perhaps, he possesses—(tho not, within his reach)—more then double the Amo of what he Owes—a total Stop, is put, to his prosecuting any further business untill the whole detail of his Affairs are adjusted—at great expence— loss of Credit—time &[c] &[c]

But, in the Case of Alarm, such as you have Noticed I do not

Apprehend—the like consequences—to follow—<u>A Run</u>—on an Established Bank—in full Credit, proceeding from no abuse or Mismanagem[t] but from the fears, and agitated state of Public Affairs & divided opinions—aided by the Views of designing Men—even, in such a state of Alarm—as you describe:—and in order to meet so unexpected—unmerited shock—the most effectual alternative—I presume—would be, to stop immediately the issuing of Specie—but in small change—with the Confidence of the Stock holrs & public. the fears, created by the Alarm—would soon subside—the exchange of paper—and even Specie from the Neighbouring Banks,—would hasten to their Assistance—to Reestablish the Institution in question—the very—existance of the Other Banks—and even Goverm[t] at such a Crisis—would—stretch out their friendly Aid to support em Upon that all[1] binding—Clause of Principle—<u>Self Preservation;</u> for a Precident of this only Alternative, expedient, We have the high Authority—of the Bank of England—

permit me Sir—here to contrast[2]—the good, with the bad effects of these Establishm[ts] for effects—will follow—their relative causes—has not, the Barren Wilderness been converted into fruitfull Valleys and Villages, and Towns into Cities—Cannals, Bridges—turnpike roads and public Buildings in almost every direction, the Value of Uncultivated Lands and Farms beyond Calculations by means of these Institutions? Altho perhaps—at first created thro self—individual Int. the first spring of Action—

the great evil we complain of—and justly too—is the abuse of them—nor do I see—any possible[3] means can be devised to remedy the growing Evil: effectualy—such then being the Actual state of the Case—

is it not, I ask, far better—to submit—and bear with an Evil, we cannot eradicate—in order to reap the superior Benefit—from that, overflowing Stream of (I am constrained[4] to admit of Superficial[5]) Wealth, in part, only for reality—the fact is—it is but of[6] little consequence of what Matereels Monies are composed of—even Specie—is but of Nominal Value. Established by Custom and Usage in Exchanges.—so it passes and repasses to the satisfaction of both the seller & the purchaser.—Upon the Whole—We can only judge from present existing Circumstances—and w[th] becoming patience & circumspection—await the final issue—of those—(very Usefull)—Complicated Engines of Speculation,

Nevertheless, should you be of Opinion that the Gen[ls] Penn[a] Bank Stock—would be more secure on Loan to U States I shall Use every endeav[r] to Effect it on the best tirms—this questionable subject is inexhaustable my Crude observations—the result of my feelings & opinion of mankind in general—the dreaded effects of the growing Evils—I fervently pray, may never be put to the tryal of the expedient.

with great Esteem & respect I am D[r] Sir

your most obed[t] servant—                                JOHN BARNES,

RC (ViU: TJP-ER); at foot of text: "Thomas Jefferson Esq[r] Monticello"; endorsed by TJ as received 18 Feb. 1814 and so recorded in SJL.

GEN[L] K[s]: Tadeusz Kosciuszko's. IT IS TIME TO ASK . . . IN THEIR VAULTS paraphrases a portion of TJ to Barnes, 29 Jan. 1814.

[1] Word interlined.
[2] Manuscript: "contras."
[3] Manuscript: "possibly."
[4] Manuscript: "constained."
[5] Manuscript: "Superfical."
[6] Manuscript: "of of."

# From Samuel R. Demaree

RESPECTED SIR,                          Shelby County, K. Feb. 13, 1814.

To me it is no small satisfaction to hear from men of general literature—especially such as live convenient to foci of Information, as the cities may be called. I too make a few observations on passing events; and am very willing that others, who are qualified, may employ them to enlarge the bounds of human knolege.

From a journal of the past year I discover peculiarities. On the first of Feb. '13 there was an excessive rain: on the 22d March[1] a gust of 20 or 30 minutes raised the waters beyond former example. April was rainy thro'out: not 4 clear days in it. It was very sickly in my naborhood. Cool May: frost 31st. Cutworm very destructive to corn till middl[e] of June. 3d week of this month very warm. Harvest unusually cool; frequent north wind till the 24th Exceedingly dry, in Kentucky generally. Dry again and warm the latter half of Aug. From the middle of Sept. till now, there have been few fair days: most cloudy with frequent light falls of rain or snow. 9th and 10th Oct. hard frost which injured nearly all the corn in the state—much of it ruined. Blight & fly had injured the wheat. The bad quality of grain and the prevalent moisture of the atmosphere probably occasiond the uncommon prevalence of sickness. The last expedition of volunteers to Canada also proved fatal to many of my country men. A fever, I suppose a typhus of malignant grade, is now rife in many parts: I thank God it has not visited my immediate naborhood.

The war has had I fear an injurious influence on the cause of Education: which was indeed too much neglected before. The sickness of our volunteers & the disasters about Ontario have very much lowered the war tone. Indeed there was too much exulting at the appeal to one of God's "sore judgments," and too much profane boasting of the mighty things which we would do. As a nation we had acknoleged the Soverin of the Universe, & having since generally paid idolatrous worship to Mammon, Bacchus & Venus, it is not to be wondered that the righteous Disposer of events should "enter into controversy" with us. Indeed the present state of the whole world indicates the speedy approach of "the harvest & the vintage"—a period of woful calamities: which however we may hope will usher in a day of universal peace and happiness—when "<u>war shall be learned no more</u>"

I have read[2] Telemaque in French. It is a fine work—which does honor to the hart & the hed of its author. I find the language much less difficult than I expected. I have just finished Godwin's "political Justice;" and am much surprized that a man who lived in society, where he had a chance to learn for himself, could be so <u>confident</u> of the practicability of his fine speculations. To me the arguments of T. R. Malthus appear resistless:—unless it can be proved "that man is not depraved"—a doctrine which the conduct of both its advocates and its oppugners most clearly proves—to be groundless. Scott in his "Family Bible" which has just come into my hands, elucidates many points which had long perplexed my mind. Can any man, when he looks at his departure out of this life, forbear to wish that he possessed the spirit & the hope which animated old Paul on many trying occasions?

With best wishes for your peace and just fame in life, and a joyful unfailing hope in death, I remain,

Very dear Sir

S. R. Demaree

RC (DLC); edge trimmed; addressed: "Hon. Thomas Jefferson Monticello Virginia"; franked; postmarked Frankfort, Ky., 20 Feb.; endorsed by TJ as received 4 Mar. 1814 and so recorded in SJL.

By one of God's sore judgements, Demaree means war (see Ezekiel 14.21). Other biblical allusions include the harvest & the vintage (Revelation 14.14–20) and war shall be learned no more (Isaiah 2.4). François de Salignac de la Motte Fénelon was the author of *Les Avantures de Telemaque*, a didactic novel first published in Paris in 1699. TJ owned copies in French, Spanish, and English (Sowerby, nos. 4305–7).

[1] Word interlined in place of "April."
[2] Word interlined.

# From James Madison

Dear Sir                                    Washington Feb^y 13. 1814

You will have noticed the propositions in the H. of Reps which tend to lift the veil which has So long covered the operations of the post off. Dep^t. They grew out of the disposition of Granger to appoint Leib to the vacant post office in Phil^a in opposition to the known aversion of the City & of the whole State; & to the recommendation of the Pen: delegation in Cong^s. Having actually made the appointment, contrary to my Sentiments also, which he asked & rec^d much excitement prevails ag^st him, and he is of course sparing no means, to ward the effects of it.

Among other misfeasances charged on him, is his continuance, or probably reappointment, of Tayloe, since his residence in this City, as post master of a little office near his Seat in Virg^a, no otherwise of importance than as it gives the post master the privilege of franking, which is said to amount to more than the income of the office, and which is exercised by the non-resident officer. The exhibition of this abuse to the public, is anxiously dreaded, by G. and as a chance to prevent it, a very extraordinary conversation has been held by him with a particular friend of mine with a view doubtless, that it might be communicated to me [& perhaps] to others of your friends.

Instead of denying or justifying the abuses he [stated] that whilst Doc^r Jones was a Candidate for Cong^s a [Baptist] Preacher, who electioneered for him, enjoyed a contract [for] carrying the mail; that Tayloe who became [an under-bidder for] the contract, was about to oust the Preacher; and that [the] only expedient to save & satisfy[1] the electioneering friend of the Doc^r [was] to buy off Tayloe, by giving Him the post office, which [was] brought about by Doc^r Jones <u>with your sanction</u>; that the present obnoxious[2] arrangement had that origin; and if the enquiry is pushed on him he must come out with the whole Story.

It would be superfluous to make remarks on the turpitude of character here developed. I have thought it proper to hint it to you, as a caution ag^st any snare that may be laid for you by artful letters, and that you may recollect any circumstances which have [been perverted] for So wicked a purpose.

I have nothing to add to the contents of the enclosed n[ewspaper.]

Affectionate [respects]                         [James Madison]
                                                [Prest U.S.]

RC (photocopy in TJ Editorial Files); photocopy blurred, with illegible words filled in from a 1958 typescript supplied by a former owner of the original, Roger W. Barrett, Chicago. Recorded in SJL as received 18 Feb. 1814. Enclosure not found.

As postmaster general, Gideon Granger had the authority to appoint postmasters without presidential oversight. During his tenure in office he used this privilege to appoint political allies. When the Philadelphia post office became vacant early in 1814, Granger selected Senator Michael LEIB, who was openly unfriendly to the Madison admin-istration. Madison responded by removing Granger and nominating in his place Return J. Meigs (ca. 1765–1825), who was confirmed as postmaster general on 17 Mar. 1814. Madison's 25 Feb. nomination of Meigs was his first notification to Congress that Granger had been dismissed. A 7 Mar. 1814 resolution that Madison be asked to "inform the Senate whether the office of Postmaster General be now vacant, and if vacant, in what manner the same became vacant" failed by one vote (Brant, *Madison*, 6:243–5; *JEP*, 2:499, 504, 511).

[1] Preceding two words interlined.
[2] Word interlined.

# From James Monroe

DEAR SIR                                   Washington Feby 14th 1814.
   my engagment in preparing instructions, for our ministers at got-tenburg, Russia, Sweden, & Paris, for Mr Clay & Mr Russell to take with them, prevented my answering sooner your favor of the 27th ulto.
   Mr Carter entirely misconceived[1] the import of my letter to him, relative to the mode in which the settlement of the interfering claims between Mr Short & me would affect Mr Short. I stated to Mr Carter, that, let it be settled as it might, he would have to pay the sum given for the land only with interest on it, according to my opinion. By this I meant that if I recoverd of Mr Short, he would only recover of Mr Carter that sum, and not the price at which he sold the land to Mr Higginbotham. If Mr Short recovers against me, I can have no claim against Mr Carter. the decision in Mr Shorts favor, could only be on the principle, that the boundary of my land, which was purchased first, had been correctly trac'd in my absence, in designating that sold to Mr Short afterwards. If Mr Short loses the small strip in dispute between us, his having purchased by a defind boundary, has a claim on Mr Carter for it. that will, I am inform'd, by those in practice, be settled on the principle above stated, except that as he may be consider'd as having had possession, till I gave notice of my claim, he cannot recover interest during that period.[2] For Mr Short I have a sincere friendship, but he will not expect from me in such a case, any sacrifi[ce] of interest, he being an old bachelor, rich & Œconomical—

I should have been happy that you would have taken the trouble to settle this affair between us, since it would have given content to all parties. I will however agree to leave it to some other person, on whom we will fix when I return to Albemarle.

The accounts rec<sup>d</sup> yesterday by a vessel just arrivd at Boston give reason to expect a peace in Europe we have papers as late as Decr 24., with letters of the same date from our commissy of prisoners in England, which communicate a speech of Boniparte to his legislative corps, from which that hope is drawn. we have also heard from M<sup>r</sup> G. & M<sup>r</sup> B., who were at Petersbg on the 15. of nov<sup>r</sup>, still waiting the answer of the British gov<sup>t</sup>, to the renewd proposition of the Emperor respecting his mediation. This communication is voluminous, & I have not yet read the whole of it. Boniparte states in his speech that he has accepted as the basis of negotiation, the preliminaries offerd by the allies, & the morning Chronicle, says, that it is reported, that these deprive him of all his conquests except Treves & Cologne. Your hint about the reservation of rights in case of a peace which may not secure every thing will be attended to. I am dear

Sir with great respect & esteem your friend & servant

JA<sup>s</sup> MONROE

RC (DLC: TJ Papers, 201:35833–4); edge chipped; endorsed by TJ as a letter of 14 "<*July*> Jan<sup>y</sup>" 1814 received 2 Mar. 1814 and so recorded in SJL. Tr (ViW: TJP); undated portion of second paragraph extracted in TJ to William Short, 26 Mar. 1814.

In his letter to Monroe of 24 Dec. 1813, Reuben G. Beasley, the American agent for PRISONERS IN ENGLAND, enclosed a copy of Napoleon's 19 Dec. 1813 speech to the French Corps Législatif announcing that he would be entering into peace negotiations with the Allied powers, as well as published responses to it

(DNA: RG 59, CD, London; Washington *Daily National Intelligencer*, 15 Feb. 1814). Albert Gallatin and James A. Bayard (M<sup>R</sup> g. & m<sup>R</sup> b.) had been in Saint Petersburg awaiting the British response to EMPEROR Alexander I's offer to mediate a peace treaty. As a condition of peace France was reported to be considering giving up all of its conquests except Trier (TREVES) and Mainz, former electorates of the Holy Roman Empire (London *Morning Chronicle*, 24 Dec. 1813).

<sup>1</sup> Tr: "misunderstood."
<sup>2</sup> Tr consists of paragraph to this point.

# From William Bentley

SIR,          Salem Mass USA. 16 Feb. 1814.

I saw your name, giving approbation to a Naval History, I have therefore taken the liberty to send you a Sermon delivered upon the death of a Naval Officer, mentioned in it. It has been printed nearly twenty years & not an article has been questioned. The Sermon may then be thought a testimony from the pulpit to the worth of our first Naval Heroes of the Revolution.

with every sentiment of personal respect, & with a share of the National gratitude for your unrivalled services, your devoted Servant,

WILLIAM BENTLEY.

The G. G. Father John, was the Worthy of Mather's Magnalia, who began the settlement at the confluence of the Concord & Merrimac rivers.

His G. Father Moses was in the settlements, where President Adams' Seat, now is, then Braintree.

His Father, was the third Minister in succession, & lived & died in Salem.

RC (DLC); adjacent to closing: "Hon Thomas Jefferson: former President of USA. Monticello. Virginia"; endorsed by TJ as received 4 Mar. 1814 and so recorded in SJL. Enclosure: Bentley, *A Funeral Discourse, delivered in the East Meeting-House, Salem, on the Sunday after the Death of Major General John Fiske* (Salem, 1797).

John Fiske was the second NAVAL OFFICER commissioned in the Massachusetts navy and participated in the capture of dozens of British vessels between 1776 and 1777 (*ANB*). Chelmsford (later Lowell), Massachusetts, is at the CONFLUENCE of the Concord and Merrimack rivers.

## To Elias Earle

SIR                                        Monticello Feb. 16. 14.

I have read and considered mr Holland's letter of Mar. 28. 1812. and Gen¹ Dearborn's statement of Mar. 29. 12. and find them in a general correspondence with my recollection of the transactions respecting the establishment of iron works proposed to have been made by yourself on the lands of the Cherokees. I must add a qualification however as to a single fact. I retain a strong impression that this proposition was on your own motion altogether, and not on the request or account of the government: that the exploring [of]¹ the country, looking out for a site for your works, and bargaining with the Indians were your own undertakings, for your own interest merely, & at your own expence; that the government thinking that, by such an establishment, the Indians would be more certainly and conveniently supplied with the utensils of iron necessary for them, willingly lent it's aid and agency with the Indians in the bargain you were to make with them, acting herein as a mutual friend between them and you, but especially as the patron and guardian of the Indian interests: and that in all this they took no part nor interest which could make them liable as parties for the expences of exploring the country or selecting the ground: that we learned (while the treaty I think was depending before the Senate) that a strong opposition to it had arisen among the Indians, and that a desire to understand the grounds of that opposition was one of the causes of suspension before the Senate. on this subject I am persuaded there are letters and documents in the War office. I should be glad that G[1] Dearborne's recollection could be drawn particularly to this point. he had the most to do in the communications with you on the subject, remembers better, I am sure, what part the government took in it, and if on reconsideration he recollects that we did any thing which made the government liable to the expences I shall acquiesce in the fact, in confidence that he is right, & that it is my own memory which is in default. with this imperfect information be pleased to accept the assurance of my esteem and respect                                      TH: JEFFERSON

PoC (DLC); at foot of text: "Col[o] Elias Earle"; endorsed by TJ. Tr (DLC: Madison Papers); entirely in TJ's hand; at head of text: "Copy." Enclosed in TJ to James Madison, 16 Feb. 1814.

James HOLLAND'S LETTER and Henry DEARBORN'S STATEMENT were enclosed in Earle to TJ, 28 Jan. 1814. TJ submitted Earle's treaty to the United States SENATE on 10 Mar. 1808. Although a majority of the Senate initially favored ratification, further consideration of the treaty was postponed to December 1808 and never resumed (*JEP*, 2:72, 78 [10, 14, 15 Mar. 1808]; ASP, *Indian Affairs*, 4:752–3; William G. McLoughlin, *Cherokee Renascence in the New Republic* [1986], 123–6, 133–4). Secretary of War John Armstrong awarded Earle $985 later in 1814 for "damage sustained by having his waggons stopped & detained on the road in the Cherokee nation by Cherokees in 1808." The following year the War Department renewed Earle's authorization to negotiate with the Cherokee or Chickasaw in order to obtain land for an ironworks. The new grant stipulated, however, that "after your having obtained their consent to erect the works no claim for losses or indemnity of any sort will be allowed you by this Government" (Return J. Meigs to Armstrong, 15 Apr. 1814 [DNA: RG 75, RCIAT]; James Monroe to Earle, 3 Feb. 1815, *Terr. Papers*, 6:498–9).

[1] Omitted word supplied from Tr.

# From Walter Jones

DEAR SIR,                                             Feb[y] 16th 1814.

I was much gratified by the receipt of yours of January the 10th, as it bestowed Some approbation on the matter & manner of my observations & the <u>temper</u>, in which they were written. it was my honest Intention to recall the mind to useful Truths, & to Show the possibility of writing <u>even</u> upon <u>Party</u>, without feeling that factious virulence & malignity, that appears to me, to be fast undermining the Safety & honour of our united republic.—Your Letter arrived, when I was much indisposed, and when an opportunity occurred of Sending the paper immediately to Richmond. I found I could not incorporate the very apposite addition you proposed, without writing the whole paper over again, for which I had niether time nor strength.—I thought it too of less Importance, as I had not meant, to make a full Enumiration of the Constituents of the republican Character, as will be Seen in the Expression "of these or of analogous maxims."—

I am extremely pleased with the admirable character you draw of Gen$^l$ Washington.—if you mean to prepare any Memoirs for Publication, as is generally Supposed by your friends, I hope this character will have a place in them.—If faction was Susceptible of the Emotion of Shame, or of a Consequent Blush, the perusal of this character, is Calculated to Call up both in your political adversaries.

I should be very glad to know your opinion of the Chances of Peace.—I have always thought that no nation upon Earth, that nearly approached us in populousness, was So weak & incapable of Carrying [on a?] war, as we are.—our people enjoy subsistence & freedom to Such a degree [as?] to make them extremely difficult & enormously expensive to be enlisted, [their?] republican equality render discipline uncommonly difficult, our vast destitution of military Science & <u>experienced</u> officers, and a Government of all others, most defective in that Sort of Energy that Can give Stability & Compactness to a military System, have long ago filled me with presages of a war, which Events have more than verified.—I think the Governing Party have never made allowance enough in their Calculations, for the counteracting & treacherous faction, which is Strong in N. England, & disseminated more or less through every other State—the violence of their domestic adversaries affords a Stimulu[s,] rather than a check, to their eagerness for foreign hostility.—their Forces daily crumbling away, thro Short enlistments, or the frauds in agents & Contractors of Supply, their Generals quarrelling, or Sick, or incompeten[t] or Captive, in Short impotence in every thing, but in legislative Declamations, and Executive Messages, while our implacable Enemy is at a Point of Power, Pride, and Triumph, which She has never before Seen.

The Legation sent on the Errand of peace, I apprehend, is too Numerous, and I wish they may not be of too discordant characters—the little middle faction, in the Senate, have placed M$^r$ Gallatin hors de Combat—M$^r$ Adams is an honest, Sensible man, but, I believe, very Self-willed & obstin[ate] M$^r$ Bayard is an <u>American</u>, but a very proud federalist, of M$^r$ Russe[ll] I know little, & heartily wish the Government may know enough, but I confess, as a <u>Peace-maker</u>, I distrust the ardent, aspiring, and fresh made States man & diplomatist, M^r Clay.—the premature prosperity of the western States, the bold Spirit of adventure or want that peopled them, have impressed upon the people a Character of Selfishness, Pride & impetuosity, that to me is Suspicious, as well as unamiable. their voracity for new lands, & the obstacles which <u>british</u> Canada presents, to their Extirpation of the Indian proprietors, would render a western man extremely pertinacious, in insisting on the Cession of Canada;[1] and however hopeless Success, might be, would persevere, tho the Desolation of the Who[le] atlantic Coast Should follow.—I think I have seen a temper in thos[e] people, which, if excited, would fall heavier on the old atlantic States, that nurtured them So fondly, than the whole mass of N. England Toryism

These are very gloomy thoughts, and may be as baseless, as they are gloomy But they have not been lightly taken up, and under Some pretty favourable opportunities for observation.—I should not have troubled you with them: but in a retirement like mine, it is a Relief to be unburthened of reflexions, where one can impart them with Confidence, and be Sure, they will be received with Candor.—

Yours, dear Sir, with affectionate & unabating Esteem

WALT: JONES

have the Goodness to present me, in the kindest manner, to Col^o Randolph & his Lady.—

RC (DLC); torn at seal, edge trimmed; addressed: "M^r Jefferson monticello Charlottesville"; franked; postmarked Farnham, Richmond Co., 19 Feb. 1814, and Charlottesville, 26 Feb.; endorsed by TJ as received 2 Mar. 1814 and so recorded in SJL.

Albert GALLATIN had been rendered HORS DE COMBAT by the United States Senate's initial rejection on 19 July of his 31 May 1813 nomination as a peace negotiator, which followed his departure for Europe. Federalist senator Jeremiah Mason took advantage of Gallatin's absence by calling on 24 Jan. 1814 for his removal from his treasury post. In order to salvage the confirmation of Gallatin as minister plenipotentiary and envoy extraordinary to join a negotiating team that included John Quincy ADAMS, James A. BAYARD, Jonathan RUSSELL and Henry CLAY, President James Madison replaced Gallatin as treasury secretary in February 1814 (*JEP*, 2:346, 348–9, 390, 470–1 [31 May, 2 June, 19 July 1813, 8, 9 Feb. 1814]; *JS*, 5:420–1; Raymond Walters Jr., *Albert Gallatin: Jeffersonian Financier and Diplomat* [1957], 269).

[1] Preceding two words interlined.

# To James Madison

DEAR SIR                                              Monticello Feb. 16. 14.

A letter from Col° Earle of S. C. induces me to apprehend that the government is called on to reimburse expences to which I am persuaded it is no wise liable either in justice or liberality. I inclose you a copy of my answer to him, as it may induce further enquiry, & particularly of Gen¹ Dearborn. the Tennisee Senators of that day can also give some information.          We have not yet seen the scheme of the new loan. but the continual creation of new banks cannot fail to facilitate it; for already there is so much of their trash afloat that the great holders of it shew vast anxiety to get rid of it. they percieve that now, as in the revolutionary war, we are engaged in the old game of Robin's alive. they are ravenous after lands, and stick at no price. in the neighborhood of Richmond, the seat of that sort of sensibility, they offer twice as much now as they would give a year ago. 200 Millions in actual circulation, and 200. Millions more likely to be legitimated by the legislative sessions of this winter, will give us about 40. times the wholesome circulation for 8. millions of people. when the new emissions get out, our legislatures will see, what they otherwise cannot believe, that it is possible to have too much money. it will ensure your loan for this year; but what will you do for the next? for I think it impossible but that the whole system must blow up before the year is out: and thus a tax of 3. or 400 millions will be levied on our citizens who had found it a work of so much time and labour to pay off a debt of 80. millions which had redeemed them from bondage. the new taxes are paid here with great cheerfulness, those on stills & carriages will be wonderfully productive. a general return to the cultivation of tob° is taking place, because <u>it will keep</u>. this proves that the public mind is made up to a continuance of the war. ever affectionately your's                          TH: JEFFERSON

RC (DLC: Madison Papers); addressed: "James Madison President of the US Washington"; franked; postmarked Milton, 17 Feb. PoC (DLC); endorsed by TJ. Enclosure: TJ to Elias Earle, 16 Feb. 1814.

# To James Madison

DEAR SIR                                              Monticello Feb. 17. 14.

In my letter of yesterday I forgot to put the inclosed one from mr Mills,[1] which I now send merely to inform you of his wishes, and to do on it what you find right. he is an excellent young man, modest, cautious & very manageable. his skill in architecture will be proved by his drawings & he has had a good deal of experience. he married a daughter of Col° Smith of Winchester formerly (perhaps now) a member of Congress.

Affectionately yours                                      TH: JEFFERSON

RC (University Archives, Stamford, Conn., 1997); addressed: "James Madison President of the US. Washington"; franked; postmarked Milton, 19 Feb.

1814. PoC (MHi); endorsed by TJ. Enclosure: Robert Mills to TJ, 28 Jan. 1814.

¹ Manuscript: "Mill."

## To Robert Mills

DEAR SIR                                      Monticello Feb. 17. 14.

Your letter of Jan. 28. came to hand a few days ago and I have with pleasure borne testimony to your merits in a letter to the President of this day's date. wishing you success on this and all other occasions, I tender you the assurance of my esteem and respect.

TH: JEFFERSON

PoC (DLC); at foot of text: "Mʳ Robert Mills"; endorsed by TJ.

## From Richard Randolph

DEAR SIR                                      Kaolin 18ᵗʰ Febʸ 14.

My best workman was in New york when I recieved your letter; he returned yesterday, and will make your jugs next week, when they shall be forwarded agreable to your directions.

I am respectfully your Humˡ servᵗ      RICHARD RANDOLPH

RC (MHi); at foot of text: "Thˢ Jefferson Esqʳ"; endorsed by TJ as received 22 Feb. 1814 and so recorded in SJL.

## From Arabella Graham

DEAR SIR                                      Pittsburgh Feb 20th 1814.

My husband James Graham haveing written to his Excellency J Madison some time cince requesting an apointmint in the Army and not haveing received a reply to that letter I have taking the liberty of Submitting the same request to your concideration trusting that You

will use your influence with Mr Madison for the purpose of procure-
ing my husband some imployment at which he would have an opportunity of exerting his tallents for the good of the Country as well as
for the suport of his familly

Should You think proper to do any thing for J Graham in that way
he would go on to the City with any recommendation that You may
advise

From the generosity of your heart which I have alwayes understood was feellingly alive to the distresses of your fellow Creatures I
flatter myself that You will Pardon the liberty which I am about to
take that of Requesting the loan of 4 hundred Dolls for the purpose
of Eastablishing a Morroco hat Store which would inable me to suport my 3 sisters who are all very Young and have no Father friend
or protecter in this world but Mr Graham and myself and we hav
nothing but what we maede by teaching which would scarcely afford
us a subsistance

In this distressing Cituation I aply to you for that council and assistance which I have no means of obtaining but through your means
should you favor me with that sum my husband will give you a Bond
for the payment of it at[1] the end of 4 years Dear Sir for the love of
Heaven grant me the means of suporting those destitute orphans who
are left under my care by a dying parent trusting that you will Pardon this liberty, I Remain Dear Sir Your Respectfully

ARABELLA GRAHAM

RC (DLC); between dateline and salutation: "to his Excellency Thomas Jefferson"; endorsed by TJ as received 18 Mar.
1814 and so recorded in SJL.

Arabella Graham and her husband
James Graham were TEACHING in Pittsburgh by April 1812, when they opened
adjoining schools on Second Street. He
provided "an English and classical education," while she taught "young ladies . . .
all things requisite to an English education, and a complete knowledge of needle-
work" (Sarah H. Killikelly, *The History of
Pittsburgh: Its Rise and Progress* [1906],
273–4).

[1] Manuscript: "a."

# From Gideon Granger

DEAR SIR,                                    Washington City: Feb: 22: 1814

a state of things exists here which in all probability will in a few
days force me to make a solemn appeal to the nation, in vindication
of my character as a man, my conduct as an officer of Government,
and the uniform tenor of my life in upholding those principles which

brought you into power; accompanied by an explanation of the causes of the several denunciations which have been put forth against me, with proofs in my own justification

That unhappy affair of Hunt, by which I lost my rank while I saved others, must be explained to the world.

In addition to this, I have been denounced as a Burrite; but you know that in 1800 I sent Erving from Boston to inform Virginia of the danger resulting from his intrigues; that in 1803–4 on your advice I procured Erastus Granger to inform De Witt Clinton of the plan to elevate Burr in N. York; and that in 1806 I communicated, by the first mail after I had gained knowledge of the fact, the supposed plans of Burr in his western expedition; upon which communication your Council was first called together to take measures in relation to that subject.

You will also bear in mind the activity I displayed on that occasion; that I bridled the whole country to the West, the South, and the S. West, by investing certain distinguished citizens, by us agreed on, with the full transferrable powers of my office, to dismiss those who were justly doubted, and provide on all occasions of public emergency; that you requested me to appoint a confidential agent to pass from here to N. Orleans, secretly clothed with all the powers which by law I could confer on him, to expedite the mails, to correct all errors, to remove the disaffected and substitute others in their places; and that I replied there was no man but my brother Pease to whom I would confide my honour: And, Sir, you know that he went the journey, and his conduct to you was so acceptable, that you made him Surveyor General of the Southern District without any request of mine.

Sir, I have also been denounced and charged with siding with federalism, for the part I took in silencing the Common-law, sedition prosecutions in Connecticut; at the same time you know, Sir, that at your request I wrote the members justifying your conduct in returning the money in the Marshall's hands to Callender, and in ordering Nolle Prosequis on all the prosecutions for sedition, on the principle that they were forbidden by the Constitution, and therefore were not lawful: That I had been useful in a case peculiarly interesting to your feelings, (which were not keener than mine are on the present occasion,) and that I silenced those prosecutions in conformity to your written request, in a manner which peculiarly exposed me to the censure of those republicans who had been my friends; while, by the respectful concessions of President Backus obtained by my management, I placed you on the vantage ground.

Though I possess the evidence which would incontrovertibly maintain most of these positions, yet I think to publish them at large could not be pleasing to you, and it would be distressing to me.

Under my present circumstances I have to propose, that in lieu of my giving a full developement of these things to the public by an elucidation of these subjects, that, if you please and deem it proper, you furnish me by letter with such materials as will not only forever silence calumny against me, but shew to my country that I have been useful on all these points, except the Hunt business where I cannot ask you to interfere

I pray you that it may be clear and explicit, not leaving a loophole whereby to hang a doubt, lest to solve that doubt I should be forced to a full explanation.

Sir, let me solicit your early reply.

Always your affectionate friend                    GID<sup>N</sup> GRANGER

RC (DLC); in a clerk's hand, signed by Granger; addressed by clerk: "Thomas Jefferson Esq<sup>r</sup> late President of the United States Monticello near Charlotteville—Albemarle Co. Virginia"; franked; postmarked Washington, 22 Feb.; endorsed by TJ as received 4 Mar. 1814 and so recorded in SJL.

When Federalist congressman Samuel HUNT allegedly slandered Dolley Madison in 1804, Granger came to her defense. However, he declined Hunt's challenge to

a duel (Brant, *Madison*, 4:243, 6:244). For Granger's role in exposing the IN-TRIGUES of Aaron Burr, his contribution to SILENCING THE COMMON-LAW, SEDITION PROSECUTIONS IN CONNECTICUT, TJ's issuance of a pardon and refund of a fine to James T. CALLENDER, and Granger's success in obtaining a softening by Rev. Azel BACKUS of his verbal attack on TJ, see Malone, *Jefferson*, 4:211, 5:240–1, 385–91; *PTJ*, 33:157–8, 309–10; TJ to Wilson Cary Nicholas, 13 June 1809, and note.

# To John Manners

SIR                                    Monticello Feb. 22. 14.

The opinion which in your letter of Jan. 24. you are pleased to ask of me on the comparative merits of the different methods of classification adopted by different writers on Natural history, is one which I could not have given satisfactorily even at the earlier period at which the subject was more familiar; still less after a life of continued occupation in civil concerns has so much withdrawn me from studies of that kind. I can therefore answer but in a very general way, and the text of this answer will be found in an observation in your letter, where speaking of nosological systems, you say that disease has been found to be an Unit. Nature has, in truth, produced Units only thro' all her works. Classes, orders, genera, species are not of her work. her creation is of individuals. no two animals are exactly alike; no two plants, nor even two leaves or blades of grass; no two crystallisations. and, if we may venture, from what is within the cognisance of such organs as ours, to conclude on that beyond their powers, we must believe that no two particles of matter[1] are of exact resemblance. this infinitude of Units, or individuals being far beyond the capacity of our memory, we are obliged, in aid of that, to distribute them into masses,[2] throwing into each of these all the individuals which have a certain degree of resemblance; to subdivide these again into smaller groupes, according to certain points of dissimilitude observable in them; and so on, until we have formed what we call a system of classes, orders, genera, and species. in doing this we fix arbitrarily on such characteristic resemblances & differences as seem to us most prominent & invariable in the several subjects, and most likely to take a strong hold in our memories. thus Ray formed one classification on such lines of division as struck him most favorably; Klein adopted another; Brisson a third, and other naturalists other designations, till Linnaeus appeared. fortunately for science, he concieved in the three kingdoms of nature, modes of classification which obtained the approbation of the learned of all nations. his system was accordingly adopted by all, and united all in a general language. it offered the three great desiderata 1. of aiding the memory to retain a knolege of the productions of nature. 2. of rallying all to the same names for the same objects, so that they could communicate understandingly on them. and 3. of enabling them, when a subject was first presented, to trace it by it's characters up to the conventional name by which it was agreed to be called. this classification was indeed liable to the imperfection of bringing into the same group individuals, which, tho resembling in the characteristics adopted by the author for his classification, yet have strong marks of dissimilitude in other respects. but to this objection every mode of classification must be liable, because the plan of creation is inscrutable to our limited faculties. Nature has not arranged her productions on a single & direct line. they branch at every step, and in every direction, and he who attempts to reduce them into departments is left to do it by the lines of his own fancy. the objection of bringing together what are disparata in nature lies against the classifications of Blumenbach & of Cuvier, as well as that of Linnaeus; and must for ever lie[3] against all. perhaps not in equal degree; on this I do not pronounce. but neither is this so important a consideration as that of uniting all nations under one language, in Natural history. this had been happily effected by Linnaeus, and can scarcely be hoped for a second time.

nothing indeed is so desparate as to make all mankind agree in giving up a language they possess for one which they have to learn. the attempt leads directly to the confusion of the tongues of Babel. disciples of Linnaeus, of Blumenbach, & of Cuvier, exclusively possessing their own nomenclatures, can no longer communicate intelligibly with one another. however much therefore we are indebted to both these naturalists, and to Cuvier especially, for the valuable additions they have made to the sciences of nature, I cannot say they have rendered her a service in this attempt to innovate in the settled nomenclature of her productions: on the contrary I think it will be a check on the progress of science, greater or less, in proportion as their schemes shall more or less prevail. they would have rendered greater service by holding fast to the system on which we had once all agreed, and by inserting into that such new genera, orders, or even classes as new discoveries should call for. their systems too, and especially that of Blumenbach, are liable to the objection of going too much into the province of anatomy. it may be said indeed that anatomy is a part of Natural history. in the broad sense of the word it certainly is. in that sense however it would comprehend all the natural sciences, every created thing being a subject of Natural history, in extenso. but in the subdivisions of general science, as has been observed in the particular one of Natural history, it has been necessary to draw arbitrary lines, in order to accomodate our limited views. according to these, as soon as the structure of any natural production is destroyed by art, it ceases to be a subject of Natural history, and enters into the domain ascribed to Chemistry, to Pharmacy, to anatomy E$^t$c. Linnaeus's method was liable to this objection so far as it required the aid of Anatomical dissection, as of the heart, for instance, to ascertain the place of any animal; or of a chemical process for that of a mineral substance. it would certainly be better to adopt as much as possible such exterior and visible characteristics as every traveller is competent to observe, to ascertain, and to relate. but with this objection, lying but in a small degree, Linnaeus's method was recieved, understood, and conventionally settled among the learned, and was even getting into common use. to disturb it then was unfortunate. the new systems attempted in Botany by Jussieu, in Mineralogy by Haüy, are subjects of the same regret; and so also the no-system of Buffon; the great advocate of individualism, in opposition to classification. he would carry us back to the days, and to the confusion of Aristotle and Pliny, give up the improvements of twenty centuries, and co-operate with the Neologists in rendering the science of one generation useless to the next, by perpetual changes of it's language. in Botany Wildenow and

Persoon have incorporated into Linnaeus the new discovered plants. I do not know whether any one has rendered us the same service as to his Natural history. it would be a very acceptable one. the materials furnished by Humboldt, and those from New Holland particularly require to be digested into the Catholic system. among these, the Ornithorhyncus, mentioned by you, is an amusing example of the anomalies by which Nature sports with our schemes of classification. altho' without Mammae, Naturalists are obliged to place it in the class of Mammiferae; and Blumenbach particularly, arranges it in his order of Palmipeds,[4] and toothless genus, with the Walrus and Manatee. in Linnaeus's system it might be inserted as a new genus, between the Anteater and Manis,[5] in the order of Bruta. it seems in truth to have stronger relations with that class than any other, in the construction of the heart, it's red and warm blood, hairy integuments, in being quadruped and viviparus, and, may we not say, in it's tout ensemble, which Buffon makes his sole principle of arrangement? the Mandible, as you observe, would draw it towards the Birds, were not this characteristic overbalanced by the weightier ones beforementioned. that of the cloaca is equivocal, because, altho a character of birds, yet some mammalia, as the beaver and sloth have the rectum and urinary passage terminating at a common opening. it's ribs also, by their number and structure are nearer those of the bird than of the Mammalia. it is possible that further opportunities of examination may discover the Mammae. those of the Opossum are asserted by the Cheval[r] d'Aboville, from his own observations on that animal made while here with the French army, to be not discoverable until pregnancy, and to disappear as soon as the young are weaned. the Duckbill has many additional particularities which liken it to other genera, and some entirely peculiar. it's description and history needs yet further information.

In what I have said on the Methods of classing I have not at all meant to insinuate that that of Linnaeus is intrinsically preferable to those of Blumenbach and Cuvier. I adhere to the Linnean because it is sufficient as a groundwork; admits of supplementary insertions, as new productions are discovered, and mainly because it has got into so general use that it will not be easy to displace it, and still less to find another which shall have the same singular fortune of obtaining the general consent. during the attempt we shall become unintelligible to one another, and science will be really retarded by efforts to advance it, made by it's most favorite sons. I am not myself apt to be alarmed at innovations recommended by reason. that dread belongs to those whose interests or prejudices shrink from the advance of truth and science. my reluctance is to give up an universal language of which we are in possession without an assurance of general consent to recieve another. and the higher the character of the authors recommending it, and the more excellent what they offer, the greater the danger of producing schism.

I should seem to need apology for these long remarks to you who are so much more recent in these studies: but I find it in your particular request and my own respect for it, and with that be pleased to accept the assurance of my esteem and consideration.

TH: JEFFERSON

PoC (DLC); at foot of first page: "Dr John Manners." Tr (ViU: GT); posthumous copy. Tr (ViHi: Hugh Blair Grigsby Papers); at foot of text: "To Dr John Manners Clinton N. J— (Copy) Mar 29th 1861."

DISPARATA: "segregated." Observations on the OPOSSUM by François Marie, chevalier (later comte) d'Aboville, appeared in François Jean, marquis de

Chastellux, *Travels in North America in the Years 1780, 1781 and 1782*, trans. and ed. Howard C. Rice Jr. (1963; see also Sowerby, nos. 4021, 4023), 2:465–8.

[1] ViHi Tr: "water."
[2] ViU Tr: "mass." ViHi Tr: "groups."
[3] ViU Tr: "be."
[4] Preceding ten words not in ViU Tr.
[5] Reworked from "Manatee."

# To John Barnes

DEAR SIR                                    Monticello Feb. 23. 14.

I have duly recieved and weighed your favors of the 9th and 11th. nobody would be farther from wishing a sudden crush to the banks than my self. that they are multiplied to a great abuse and evil is evident; and their reduction by degrees would be the safest for the public, and might save us if our legislatures were wise. but it is their folly which is hurrying us to the precipice, by the increase of these establishmts until they all fall together. it is this which convinces me they must fall and no one can say when it will happen. Manhattan is leading the way. that was one of our great banks; yet see how little cash they had in their vaults. why should we suppose any other better provided. I do not believe they are, and no one can say that this first alarm may not be immediately renewed with a 2d a 3d Etc till all go. under these circumstances we should be unfaithful stewards to leave the worthy Kosciusko in danger of wanting bread. it would be the less justifiable too because with greater security the government will offer greater advantages. I cannot therefore resist the sense of duty imposed on us, & must pray you to take immediate measures to sell out the General's stock in bank, and place it in the new government loan. perhaps the treasury would recieve the General's bank stock as cash in exchange for their new stock. I understand that a bonus of 10. or 12. per cent is expected which will add so much to the General's capital. every bank which cracks will give me great alarm until we are out of them. I shall be glad to learn your prospects in this business by a line when you begin to see your way thro' it. affectionately Yours

Th: Jefferson

RC (Wayne M. Hart, East Orange, N.J., 1950; photostat at ViU: TJP); addressed: "Mr John Barnes Georgetown Col."; franked; postmarked Milton, 24 Feb. PoC (DLC); endorsed by TJ.

Early in 1814 Boston's New England Bank withdrew more than $150,000 in specie from its New York counterparts in an attempt to prevent them from subscribing to a government loan. As a result the Bank of the MANHATTAN Company stopped discounting bills of exchange (*Boston Gazette*, 24 Jan. 1814; William Jay to John Jay, 10 Feb. 1814 [NNC: Jay Papers]; Stagg, *Madison's War*, 376–7).

## To Patrick Gibson

DEAR SIR                                    Monticello Feb. 23. 14.

I must ask the favor of you to send me an hundred Dollars by the return of post, in small bills. we have been told here that flour had risen with you to $5\frac{3}{4}$ D. but I know not how truly. I would not wish the sale of mine to be lost for a quarter dollar of difference. for altho' I think peace will grow out of the existing negociations, it will not be in time to dispose of the crop now on hand, and I see no other prospect offering the hope of a fair price. my corn purchases are now at hand. on the 1st of Mar. I shall have to draw on you for 280.D. and in April & May about the same sums will become due. Accept assurances of my great esteem and respect.          Th: Jefferson

PoC (photocopy in TJ Editorial Files); at foot of text: "Mr Gibson"; endorsed by TJ.

## To William Short

DEAR SIR                                    Monticello Feb. 23. 14.

I am first to thank you for the indulgences of yours of Feb. 6. I believe that by the combined effects of blockade embargo and drought, I have suffered more than any other individual. the two former would but have left me where I was, but the last threw me back by forcing me to buy a year's subsistence for my whole family. — on the reciept of your letter I saw mr Higgenbotham and stated to him the accomodation to you of paying his first bond immediately. he promised to endeavor to do it, and by the inclosed note from him yesterday I percieve it is done, and notice of it forwarded to you. he desires you to inclose his bond, and rent-note to me, to be given him in exchange for reciepts for the paiments made.

I sincerely rejoice that the career of Bonaparte is at length arrested, and that Europe is likely to be restored to it's antient divisions and governments: for bad as they were, they were better than the military despotisms of Bonaparte, those 'great designs of his, concieved and executed for the prosperity & happiness of the world.' the only thing to be lamented is that the tyrant of the ocean is not also dismounted. peace I suppose we shall have; but on the condition of navigating under her licenses; and altho I believe we have greatly overtraded ourselves, I should prefer a war ad internecionem to a peace on that condition. it will very possibly end in the total suppression of our navigation & commerce, and leave us to be a world by ourselves. my whole confidence as to the salvation of commerce is in Alexander, that he will not yield to the subjugation of the ocean. present me affectionately to M. Correa, whom I shall rejoice to see here, and the more were you to accompany him. I shall write to him soon, the engourdissement of the winter being over. affectionately yours

TH: JEFFERSON

RC (ViW: TJP); endorsed by Short as received 28 Feb. 1814. Enclosure not found.

Short's letter of FEB. 6., not found, is recorded in SJL as received 11 Feb. from Philadelphia. For the 19 Dec. 1813 speech in which Napoleon gave up his GREAT DESIGNS and announced that he would be negotiating peace, see note to James Monroe to TJ, 14 Feb. 1814. WAR AD INTERNECIONEM: "war of annihilation." ENGOURDISSEMENT: "dullness, drowsiness."

# From William DuVal

DEAR SIR,            Buckingham February 24th 1814

My Son John P DuVal obtained his Commission as first Lieutenant he says in Virtue of your Recommendation he is now a Captain in the 20th Regiment. He wishes for a Majority in one of the Three Rifle Regiments. My Son is in his Twenty Fifth Year. He has been in Service about two Years. He first Marched by Orders to Norfolk from thence to Niagara Last Spring he was Ordered to Recruit & has been tolerably successful. He lived in Kentucky at Bardstown about a Year. I believe if he was to receive the Appointment he, with his Brother William P. DuVals assistance, could raise a number of Men so as to complete the new[1] Regiment.

Kentucky, if he survives the War, is to be his place of Residence—

I do believe that my Son has seen as much Service as most of the Officers of his Grade. He has devoted[2] a part of his time to the Study of Military tacktics, & is well qualified to command a Battallion. He has never I believe applied for a Furlow, since he engaged in the Army. He and Lieut Col° Craughan are of the same Age were Fellow Students at the Coledge of William & Mary & intimate Friends. John P. DuVal possesses great coolness & Intripidity, He is sobor, Moral, and not addicted to any Vice—He writes me to request you to write to the Secretary at War in his behalf, he says he wishes to have an Opportunity to render his Country some essential Service, which with your Assistance will be an additional stimulous, with him, so to act as to deserve the Good opinion you have been[3] pleased to entertain of him

M[r] James Pleasants of Congress will render him what service he can, my Son writes me

I am with great Esteem & Respect Your mo. ob[t] Serv[t]

WILLIAM DUVAL

RC (MHi); endorsed by TJ as received 2 Mar. 1814 and so recorded in SJL.

John Pope DuVal (1790–1854), attorney and public official, was born in Richmond. He attended Washington Academy (later Washington and Lee University) in 1806–07 and the College of William and Mary at some point after that and before he was admitted to the bar in Richmond in 1811. DuVal served in the United States Army during the War of 1812, holding the rank of captain at his discharge in 1815. After the war he practiced law in Fauquier and Loudoun counties. About 1827 DuVal moved to Florida Territory, where in 1828 he was appointed commissioner of Tallahassee. In 1832 he relocated to Bardstown, Kentucky, from which place he raised volunteers as a brigadier general of the Texas forces during the Texas Revolution. DuVal returned to Florida in 1837, served as territorial secretary and sometime acting gov-

ernor, 1837–39, and oversaw the forced removal of the Apalachicola Indians. He also prepared a compilation of Florida laws. DuVal died in Tallahassee (Lyon Gardiner Tyler, ed., *Encyclopedia of Virginia Biography* [1915], 2:249; *Catalogue of the Officers and Alumni of Washington and Lee University, Lexington, Virginia, 1749–1888* [1888], 59; *William and Mary Provisional List*, 16; TJ to William Eustis, 25 Jan. 1812; Heitman, *U.S. Army*, 1:391; *Alexandria Herald*, 19 June 1820; *Terr. Papers*, esp. 23:1006, 25:391, 397–8, 649, 26:825–7; *JEP*, 5:31, 32 [19, 25 Sept. 1837]; DuVal, *Compilation of the Public Acts of the Legislative Council of the Territory of Florida, passed prior to 1840* [1839]; gravestone in Old City Cemetery, Tallahassee; Tallahassee *Floridian and Journal*, 9 Dec. 1854).

[1] Word interlined.
[2] Manuscript: "doveted."
[3] Manuscript: "be."

# From Lafayette

MY DEAR FRIEND                    La grange febur<sup>y</sup> 25<sup>h1</sup> 1814

This Letter will Be delivered By M<sup>r</sup> Jullien a Citizen distinguished By His Litterary and political knowledge as well as By His patriotic Sentiments. He Has Been for a Long time employ'd in the Commissariat and offices of the military department and Has particularly Applied His Studies to the Line of education. Being desirous to visit the U. S., altho' He is not on the lists of proscription, He will Be Highly gratified By this introduction to you, my dear friend. I know you will Be Satisfied with His information and principles. Most truly and affectionately

 Yours                                    LAFAYETTE

RC (MH); addressed: "Thomas Jefferson Esq Monticelo State of Virginia." Not recorded in SJL and probably never received by TJ.

[1] First digit reworked from "1."


# From Patrick Gibson

SIR                              Richmond 26<sup>th</sup> Feb<sup>y</sup> 1814

 Your note in bank for $2000. falling due on the 1<sup>st</sup>/4<sup>th</sup> of next month, I send you one inclosed for your signature, the prospect of peace altho' distant has had very considerable influence upon our Tobacco market, fine crops have been sold at from 9 to 10$ and for a few choice hhd<sup>s</sup> 12 and as high as 13.6 has been paid, low qualities have risen in a greater ratio under an expectation of an opening to Holland—I cannot perceive that it has had any sensible effect on the price of flour, our millers however hold it rather higher say $5\frac{1}{2}$$ still I can find no purchaser at 5$—         With great respect Your ob<sup>t</sup> Serv<sup>t</sup>                              PATRICK GIBSON

RC (ViU: TJP-ER); at head of text: "Thomas Jefferson Esq<sup>re</sup>"; endorsed by TJ as a letter from Gibson & Jefferson received 2 Mar. 1814 and so recorded in SJL. Enclosure not found.


# From John Barnes

DEAR SIR—                    George Town Col<sup>o</sup> 27<sup>th</sup> Feb<sup>y</sup> 1814—

 On receipt of your fav<sup>r</sup> 23<sup>d</sup> recd last Evening, I have by this days Mail wrote to my friend in Philad<sup>a</sup> (not to Alarm him in Case of any suspicion, as to the Cause) for his Advice & directions respecting the disposal of a few Shares (say ten)[1]—of Penn[a] Bank Stock, for a friend of mine—and sh[d] the Offer be Acceptable the Curr[t] & selling price terms &[tc] and withal, the probability of any Extra dividend—at 1[t] July—mean while, I shall inform my self of the terms & conditions of the new Loan—and whether or not—an exchange, of said Bank stock, for a loan Certificate w[d] be Accepted of[2]—all of which, I shall in due time, advise you—for your Govem[t]—Respecting the Manhattan Bank, the particulars not known[3] to me—but thro the Medium of the News papers, I still presume Originated—thro design.— however that may be, I also well know the effects may be severely felt by the Other Institutions—at least the fall in these Stocks will I Apprehend be the Consequence—It is most Assuredly high time—for the Several Goverm[ts] to put a final Stop to the increase of these most extravagant Institutions—but the rage is such that even in this Case (as in London) private Companies, Composed of respectable Names and Means, will I fear eventually be the Consequence—those already incorporated cannot be restrained Untill their Charter expires—are I presume—more by one half suff[t]—for a liberal Medium of Circulation.

Can the devize be thought of! towards releving the good Gen[l] K? If it were possible for him—to draw upon me at sight, for $1000—Thro the Aid of his Banker—even this expedient I fear is impracticable. the Merch[ts] on this side the Atlantic are all—indebted to France.—

most Respectfully—Dear Sir I am, Your Obed[t] serv[t]

JOHN BARNES,

RC (ViU: TJP-ER); at foot of text: "Thomas Jefferson Esq[r] Monticello"; endorsed by TJ as received 4 Mar. 1814 and so recorded in SJL.

GEN[L] K: Tadeusz Kosciuszko.

[1] Omitted closing parenthesis editorially supplied.
[2] Manuscript: "off."
[3] Manuscript: "know."

# From John Adams

DEAR SIR                                    Quincy Feb          1814

I was[1] nibbing my pen and brushing my Faculties, to write a polite Letter of Thanks to M[r] Counsellor Barton for his valuable Memoirs of D[r] Rittenhouse though I could not account for his Sending it to me; when I received your favour of Jan. 24th. I now most cordially indorse my Thanks over to you. The Book is in the modern American Style, an able imitation of Marshalls Washington, though far more entertaining and instructive; a Washington Mausolæum; an Egyptian Pyramid. I Shall never read it, any more than Taylors Aristocracy. M$^{rs}$ Adams reads it, with great delight, and reads to me, what She finds interresting, and that is indeed the whole Book. I have not time to hear it all.

Writtenhouse was a virtuous and amiable Man; an exquisite Mechanician; Master of the Astronomy known in his time; an expert Mathematician, a patient calculator of Numbers. But We have had a Winthrop an Andrew Oliver[2] a Willard a Webber, his equals and We have a Bowditch his Superior in all these particulars except the Mechanism.[3] But you know, Phyladelphia is the Heart, the Censorium, the Pineal Gland of U.S.—In Politicks, Writtenhouse was a good, Simple ignorant well meaning Franklinian Democrat, totally ignorant of the World, as an Anachorite, an honest Dupe of the French Revolution; a mere Instrument of Jonathan Dickinson[4] Sargent, D$^r$ Hutchinson, Genet and Mifflin, I give him all the Credit of his Planetarium. The Improvement of the Orrery to the Planetarium was an easy, natural thought and nothing was wanting but calculations[5] of orbits Distances,[6] and Periods of Revolutions all of which were made to his hands, long before he existed. Patience, Perseverance and Slight of hand is his undoubted Merit and Praise.

I had heard Taylor in Senate, till his Style was So familiar to me that I had not read[7] 3 pages before I Suspected the author. I wrote a Letter to him and he candidly acknowledged that the 650 Pages were sent me, with his consent. I wait with impatience for the Publication and Annunciation of the Work. Arator ought not[8] to have been adulterated with Politicks: but his precept "Gather up the Fragments that nothing be lost"[9] is of inestimable Value in Agriculture and Horticulture. Every Weed Cob, Husk Stalk ought to be Saved for manure.

Your research in the Laws of England, establishing Christianity as the Law of the Land and part of the common Law, are curious and very important. Questions without number will arise in this Country. Religious Controversies, and Ecclesiastical Contests are as common and will be as Sharp as any in civil Politicks foreign, or domestick? In what Sense and to what extent the Bible is Law, may give rise to as many doubts and quarrells as any of our civil political military or maritime Laws and will intermix with them all to irritate Factions[10] of every Sort. I dare not look beyond my Nose, into futurity. Our Money, our Commerce, our Religion, our National and State Constitutions, even our Arts and Sciences, are So many Seed Plotts of Division, Faction, Sedition and Rebellion. Every thing is transmuted into an Instrument of Electioneering. Election is the grand Brama, the immortal Lama, I had almost Said, the Jaggernaught, for Wives are almost ready to burn upon the Pile and Children to be thrown under the Wheel.

You will perceive, by these figures that I have been looking into Oriental History and Hindoo religion. I have read Voyages and travels and every thing I could collect, and the last is Priestleys "Comparison of the Institutions of Moses, with those of the Hindoos and other ancient Nations," a Work of great labour, and not less haste. I thank him for the labour, and forgive, though I lament the hurry. You would be fatigued to read, and I, just recruiting a little from a longer confinement and indisposition than I have had for 30 years, have not Strength to write many observations. But I have been disappointed in the principal Points of my Curiosity.

1. I am disappointed, by finding that no just Comparison can be made, because the original Shasta, and the original Vedams[11] are not obtained, or if obtained not yet translated into any European Language.[12]

2. In not finding Such Morsells of the Sacred Books as have been translated and published, which are more honourable to the original Hindoo[13] Religion than any thing he has quoted.

3 In not finding a full devellopement of the History of the Doctrine of the Metempsichosis which originated[14]

4. In the History of the Rebellion of innumerable Hosts of Angells in Heaven against the supream Being, who after Some thousands of years of War conquered them and hurled them down to the Region of total darkness, where they Suffered a part of the Punishment of their Crime, and then were mercifully released from Prison permitted to ascend to Earth and migrate into all Sorts of Animals, reptiles, Birds Beasts and Men according to their Rank and Character,[15] and even into Vegetables and Minerals, there to serve on probation. If they passed without reproach their Several gradations they were permitted to become Cows and Men. If as Men they behaved well, i.e to the Satisfaction of the Priests, they were restored to their original rank and Bliss in Heaven.

5 In not finding the Trinity of Pythagoras and Plato, their contempt of Matter, flesh and blood, their almost Adoration of Fire and Water, their Metempsicosis, and even the prohibition of Beans So evidently derived from India.

6. In not finding the Prophecy of Enoch deduced from India in which the fallen Angels make Such a figure.

But you are weary. Priestly has proved the superiority of the Hebrews to the Hindoos, as they appear in the Gentoo Laws and Institutes[16] of Menu: but the comparison remains to be made with the Shasta.

In his remarks on M^r Dupuis. p. 342. Priestley Says, "The History of the fallen Angels is another Circumstance, on which M^r Dupuis lays much Stress. 'According to the Christians,' he says, Vol. 1. p. 336, 'there was from the beginning, a division among the Angels; Some remaining faithful to the light, and others taking the part of Darkness' &c.[17] But this Supposed history is not found in the Scriptures. It has only been inferred, from a wrong interpretation of one passage in the 2^d Epistle of Peter, and a corresponding one in that of Jude, as has been Shewn by judicious Writers. That there is such a Person as The Devil is no part of my Faith, nor that of many other Christians; nor am I sure that it was the belief of any of the christian Writers. Neither do I believe the doctrine of demoniacal possessions, whether it was believed by the Sacred Writers or not; and yet my unbelief[18] in these Articles does not affect my faith in the great facts of which the Evangelists were eye and ear Witnesses. They might not be competent Judges, in the one case, tho perfectly So, with respect to the other."

I will[19] ask Priestley, when I See him, Do you believe those Passages in Peter and Jude to be interpolations? If so; by whom made? and when? and where? and for what End? Was it to Support, or found the doctrine of The Fall of Man, Original Sin, the universal Corruption depravation and guilt of human nature and mankind; and the Subsequent Incarnation of God to make Attonement and Redemption! —Or do you think that Peter and Jude believed the Book of Enoch to have been written, by the 7^th from Adam, and one of the Sacred cannonical Books of the Hebrew Prophets? Peter, 2. Ep. c. 2. v. 4, Says "For if God Spared not the Angels that Sinned, but cast them down to <u>Hell</u> and delivered them into chains of <u>Darkness</u>, to be reserved unto Judgment." Jude v. 6^th Says "And the Angels which kept not their first Estate, but left their own habitations, he hath reserved in everlasting Chains under darkness, unto the Judgment of the great day."[20] v. 14^th "And Enoch also, the 7^th from Adam, prophesied of these Saying, behold the Lord cometh with ten thousands of his Saints, to execute Judgment upon all &c" Priestley Says "a wrong Interpretation" has been given to these Texts. I wish he had favoured Us with his right interpretation of them.

In another place. p. 326. Priestleys Says "There is no Circumstance of which M^r Dupuis avails himself So much, or repeats So often, both with respect to the Jewish and Christian religions, as the history of the Fall of Man, in the beginning of the Book of Genesis. I believe with him, and have maintained in my Writings, that this history is either an Allegory, or founded on uncertain Tradition: that it is an hypothesis to account for the origin of evil, adopted by Moses, which by no means Accounts for the Facts."

March 3^d So far, was written almost a month ago: but Sickness has prevented Progress. I had much more to Say about this Work. I Shall never be a Disciple of Priestley. He is as absurd inconsistent, credulous and incomprehensible as Athanasius. Read his Letter to The Jews in this Volume. Could a rational Creature write it? Aye! Such rational Creatures as Rochefaucault and Condorsett and John Taylor in Politicks, and Towers's, Jurieus and French Prophets in Theology.

Priestleys Account of the Philosophy and Religion of India appears to me to be much Such a Work, as a Man of busy research would produce, who Should undertake to describe Christianity from the Sixth to the twelfth Century, when a deluge of Wonders overflowed the World; when Miracles were performed and proclaimed from every Convent and Monastry, Hospital, Church Yard, Mountain Valley Cave and Cupola

There is a Work, which I wish I possessed. It has never crossed the Atlantic. It is entitled Acta Sanctorum, in forty Seven Volumes in Folio. It contains the Lives of the Saints. It was compiled in the beginning of the 16^th Century by Bollandus, Henschenius and Papebrock. What would I give to possess in one immense Mass, one Stupendous draught all the Legends, true doubtful and false. These Bollandists dared to discuss Some of the Facts and to hint that Some of them were doubtful. E.G. Papebrock doubted The Antiquity of the Carmellites from Elias; and whether the Face of J. C. was painted on the Handkerchief of St Veronique; and whether the Prepuce of the Saviour of the World, which was Shewn in the Church at Antwerp, could be proved to be genuine? For these bold Scepticisms he was libelled in Pamphlets and denounced to the Pope and the Inquisition in Spain. The Inquisition condemned him: but the Pope not daring to acquit or condemn[21] him, prohibited[22] all Writings, Pro and Con. But as the Physicians cure one disease by exciting another, as a Fever by a Salivation, this Bull was produced by a new Claim. The Brothers of the Order of Charity asserted a Descent from Abraham 900 Years anterior to the Carmelites.

A Phylosopher who Should write a description of Christianism from the Bollandistic Saints of the Sixth or the tenth Century would probably produce a Work tolerably parallel[23] to Priestleys upon the Hindoos,
                                                                                                     JOHN ADAMS

RC (DLC: TJ Papers, 200:35682–4); partially dated; at foot of text: "President Jefferson"; endorsed by TJ as a letter of Feb.–3 Mar. 1814 received 18 Mar. 1814, and so recorded in SJL. FC (Lb in MHi: Adams Papers).

ARISTOCRACY was the title of the first section of John Taylor of Caroline's work, *An Inquiry into the Principles and Policy of the Government of the United States* (Fredericksburg, 1814; TJ's copy documented in his MS Retirement Library Catalogue, DLC: TJ Papers, ser. 7, p. 88 [no. 656]). CENSORIUM: "sensorium." Adams WROTE A LETTER to Taylor on 12 Dec. 1813, and in his response of 24 Dec. 1813 (both in MHi: Adams Papers), Taylor CANDIDLY ACKNOWLEDGED authorship of *Arator; being a series of Agricultural Essays, Practical & Political* (Georgetown, 1813; Sowerby, no. 814). GATHER UP THE FRAGMENTS THAT NOTHING BE LOST is from the Bible, John 6.12. Vedas (VEDAMS) are the four ancient sacred texts of Hinduism (*OED*). The TRINITY of Pythagoras consisted of unity, wisdom, and the soul, while Plato's substituted goodness for unity (E. Cobham Brewer, *Dictionary of Phrase and Fable* [1900], 1246). According to Diogenes Laertius, Pythagoras abstained from a variety of foods, including BEANS (Diogenes Laertius, *Lives of Eminent Philosophers*, trans. Robert D. Hicks, Loeb Classical Library [1925; repr. 1979], 2:337). The GENTOO LAWS were a compilation used by the British in administering Hindu populations in India, translated by Nathaniel Brassey Halhed (*ODNB*) and published as *A Code of Gentoo Laws, or, Ordinations of the Pundits, from a Persian*

*Translation, made from the Original, written in the Shanscrit Language* (London, 1776). The Laws of Manu (MENU) are a Sanskrit legal code (*OED*). Joseph Priestley included an address TO THE JEWS in his work, *A Comparison of the Institutions of Moses with those of the Hindoos and Other Ancient Nations* (Northumberland, Pa., 1799), 393–428. J. C.: Jesus Christ.

[1] FC here adds "sitting."
[2] Preceding three words interlined.
[3] Preceding three words interlined.
[4] Word not in FC.
[5] RC: "caculations." FC: "calculations."
[6] RC: "Distrances." FC: "Distances."
[7] Word not in FC.
[8] Word not in FC.
[9] Omitted closing quotation mark editorially supplied.
[10] FC: "Faction."
[11] FC: "Vendams."
[12] Preceding five words not in FC.
[13] RC: "Hindo." FC: "Hindoo."
[14] Sentence not in FC. RC: "orignated."
[15] RC: "Charater." FC: "Character."
[16] FC: "Institutions."
[17] Preceding two sets of double quotation marks, surrounding material in which Priestley is quoting Charles François Dupuis, editorially altered to single quotation marks for clarity.
[18] FC: "belief."
[19] Word interlined in place of "would."
[20] Omitted closing quotation mark editorially supplied.
[21] FC: "condemn or acquit."
[22] RC: "prohited." FC: "prohibited."
[23] RC: "parrallel." FC: "parallel."

# From Patrick Gibson

SIR Richmond 2ⁿᵈ March 1814—

I wrote to you by last mail inclosing a note for your signature to renew the one in bank due the 4th Inst and am apprehensive it may not be received in time to meet it, having again too long delayed forwarding it, I shall however pay the one due on Friday and offer the new one when received—You will have observed by my letter that the information you had received relative to flour was incorrect I have continued to offer what I have on hand at 5$ without meeting with a purchaser, the offering price is $4\frac{1}{2}$ to $4\frac{3}{4}$$—I inclose you as requested one hundred dollars in small notes—

With great respect I am
Your obt Servt PATRICK GIBSON

RC (ViU: TJP-ER); between dateline and salutation: "Thomas Jefferson Esqre"; endorsed by TJ as received 4 Mar. 1814 and so recorded in SJL.

# From John Graham

DEAR SIR Washington 2d March 1814—

I have the pleasure to inform you, that I forwarded by Mr Clay the Packet for Mr Warden, which you sent to me, and as Mr Clay will have occasion to dispatch a Courier to Mr Crawford at Paris, very soon after his arrival at Gottemburg, there is every reason to beleive that it will reach its destination in safety and without delay—

It will be some time, I fear, before I meet with so good a conveyance for the Letter to Mr Foronda; but I will not fail to do the best I can with it. I have understood that a Despatch vessel will probably be sent to Europe very soon—Should you wish to write by her, it will give me great pleasure to forward any Letters which you may think proper to direct to my Care.

With Sentiments of the Highest Respect—
I have the Honor to be, Sir your Mo: Obt Sert

JOHN GRAHAM

RC (DLC); at foot of text: "Thomas Jefferson Esqr"; endorsed by TJ as received 11 Mar. 1814 and so recorded in SJL.

# From William Short

DEAR SIR                                                  Philad<sup>a</sup> March 3—14

I had the pleasure of writing to you on the 26<sup>th</sup> ul<sup>to</sup>—& have since recieved your favor of the 23<sup>d</sup>—for which I beg leave here to return my thanks.—Conformably with what I then announced I now send the work of Dupont which you were so good as to lend me. I despair of seeing any general system of education established during my day. I should however be much gratified if I could live to see a fair experiment of what would be the effect on our people, of such a system. The good, I think, would be great indeed—It would certainly be the best means of extirpating the very great evil of "Blackstone Lawyers & Sangrado Doctors" who are increasing in the country as fast as another dreadful evil, the Banks; & for which I see no preventative, & no cure but after very great suffering—To the old Bankphobia has succeeded an incurable Bankmania. I foresaw this evil from the time of my arrival in this Country & made my arrangements accordingly—I have ceased for many years being a share holder—Those who continue, may by the fluctuation of things gain a good deal in speculating, but ultimately must lose I should suppose.

Your opinion as to the probability of peace gives me real pleasure—I have kept it to myself, because I know how it would fly. When asked for my own opinion, as I frequently am, I give it without hesitation stating always that I consider it of little worth, as indeed is the case—but if your opinion were known it would be decisive with many, who insist on thinking that your influence on M<sup>r</sup> M. is without a balance.—I have no doubt that M<sup>r</sup> M. must from the nature of things wish for peace—but it seems to me there must be great obstacles in the way—There is no reason certainly why England should yield any point now, that was refused when the war begun, & at the same time I do not see how M<sup>r</sup> M. can, after having subjected us to all the horrors of war, all the demoralization & distress which it has brought on, all the danger to liberty, which, he has so often & so well told us, laid embosomed in an increasing debt, onerous loans & consequent taxes, how he can, I say, let us down precisely where he took us up, in a statu quo ante. If the boon of peace arrive, I suppose it must be by some of those mezzi termine which it is the talent of able negotiators to discover. I do not think M<sup>r</sup> Clay is a very skilful choice for such a search. The last sentiment of the public will of Kentucky which he carries with him is a resolve not to yield the Canadas. Should he be daring enough[1] to go against this in putting his signature to a treaty, it would not surprize me to hear he was tarred &

feathered on his return there. As he is, no doubt sufficiently aware of this, & as indeed the Kentucky democracy is the only basis on which he stands & which could have possibly put him into an Ambassadorial chair, he will not, I should think, let that slip from under him. However, there are enough to sign without him, & if we the people should not have the benefit of his signature, we shall not the less have to pay for his services. For my part I shall be happy to see peace once more in the land. Experience has sufficiently confirmed what reason foresaw that the happy form of our Government is not calculated for military enterprize & glory—It has always seemed to me absurd to be endangering our domestic liberty in pursuit of other objects, even if we could attain them. It is the fable revived of the Dog losing the substance in catching at the shadow. I cannot help regretting that the experiment was not made of allowing Commerce to take care of itself. Dr Priestley has somewhere suggested this in a way that might have been beneficial to our Legislators. So far as any objection is derivable from the idea of national honor, the moment was a favorable one. For when such nations as France & England have resolved to abolish all public law & put force in the place of right & usage, I do not see that there can be any more disgrace in weak Governments allowing individuals (their Citizens whom they are unable to protect) to shift for themselves on the Ocean, & make their own way, than in the Governments of France & England descending, (from a view to political expediency) to purchase exemption & safety for their subjects, from the Dey of Algiers, for instance. I once gave a hint of this sort to Monroe after he became sec. of State—But he probably could not listen then with that ear,—& I have no doubt he acted much more prudently & properly for himself.—We are told now his chance for the Presidency is the best—It certainly would have been no chance at all if he had adopted these ideas. The Western States would never have pardoned his thus abandoning the Sailors rights. And now that a war has been undertaken on the subject, I will not pretend to decide that it could be relinquished with honor, for the purpose of trying a different remedy. Still I regret that it was not tried at its proper time. Every year in this way would have been giving us more bone & made us more able to act efficiently when we should have found it necessary.

I rejoice with you that the devastating career of Bonaparte has been stopped & his conquests rescued from him—Had the great & good Moreau lived, relief would have been extended also to France—& I do not doubt the new Dynasty would have become an abortion. As it is, the issue is doubtful—Correa says the affair is now taken into

Chancery & will of course be long—He is much pleased by your kind recollection of him, & will be still more so to hear from you, as you promise. It would make me very happy indeed to be able to accompany him & pay you my respects in person—As I remain stationary during the winter I shall be obliged in the spring to go to N. York, where I have interests that require my presence. I flatter myself every year with the hope of again seeing Monticello—but I find myself so controlled by my New York affairs that I am often disappointed. It shall certainly not be my fault if I do not realize the hope of again seeing you & renewing the assurances of those sentiments which have grown up with me, which time has fortified, & with which I am, dear sir, most truly & affectionately

Your friend & servant W: SHORT

RC (MHi); endorsed by TJ as received 11 Mar. 1814 and so recorded in SJL. Enclosure: Pierre Samuel Du Pont de Nemours, *Sur l'éducation nationale dans les États-Unis d'Amérique* (Paris, 1812; Poor, *Jefferson's Library*, 5 [nos. 207, 209–10]).

Short's letter to TJ of the 26TH ULTO, not found, is recorded in SJL as received from Philadelphia on 4 Mar. 1814. The fictional SANGRADO was a quack physician whose patients often died in his care (Alain René Le Sage, *Histoire de Gil Blas de Santillane*, 4 vols. [Paris, 1715–35; repr. London, 1769; Sowerby, no.

4346]). MR M.: James Madison. Mezzo termini (MEZZI TERMINE): "halfway measures, compromises" (*OED*). A DOG loses a piece of meat by reaching for its reflection in *Aesop's Fables*. For Joseph Priestley's proposal that United States commerce TAKE CARE OF ITSELF, see note to Short to TJ, 10 Apr. 1809. When James MONROE became secretary of state, Short cited Priestley in suggesting that American maritime interests be left to fend for themselves (Short to Monroe, 22 May 1811 [ViFreJM]).

[1] Manuscript: "enought."

# From Martin Dawson & Company

DEAR SIR Milton 4th March 1814

We hold your agreements with Mr Craven Peyton for Corn with Order on you for the Proceeds two hundred and eighty dollars payable the first of this month, a Dft on Richmond or the money at Charlotsville on Monday next for the same will oblige

Yo. Ob. Hu. Sevts MARTIN DAWSON & CO

RC (ViU: TJP-ER); in Dawson's hand; addressed: "Thomas Jefferson esqre Monticello"; endorsed by TJ as received 4 Mar. 1814 and so recorded in SJL.

# From Elizabeth Trist

My D<sup>R</sup> FRIEND                        Bird wood March 5<sup>th</sup> 1814

I received your kind favor of the 1<sup>st</sup> of last month[1] with my usual feelings of gratitude for the many kind and friendly attentions I have experienced from you,[2] my having obtruded M<sup>r</sup> Davèzac letter upon you for translation was inexcuseable for you mention'd in your last, from poplar Forest the little leisure you had for writing while at Monticello but that consideration never came into my head till it was too late but I know your goodness will excuse it. for tho we take the greatest liberties with our best friends generally speaking we are not justifiable in imposing too much on their good nature. Ellen[3] has done ample justice in the elegant translation and has afforded me great pleasure. I was grieved to hear that M<sup>rs</sup> Randolph was not restored to health and that Colonel R— had not relinquish'd the Idea of another Campaign[4] tho such Men are wanted in our Armey I think he might be readily excused for he has great and important duties to perform as well as that of fighting the enemies of his Country one campaign was a great undertaking for a man with so large a family I am sorry that more success did not attend our Arms but at the same time I dont think the enemy had great cause of triumph for the check given to Proctor and his savage Allies and many other exploits of our Country men prove that they are not cowards our republican System dont admit of Standing Armies in time of Peace and they must have time to learn the Art, I am not apprehensive of being conquor'd or even driven to accept terms that are not just and honorable notwithstanding these malcontents[5] in the New England States and elsewhere I hope there is sperit and virtue sufficient to save our Country[6] I heard from a friend in Orleans that they were in commotion[7] in that City a number of french men who claim'd the priviledge of voting refused to stand a draft to drive the enemy from their Shores[8] The poor Governor has been Courting these people for ten years and the moment he interferes with their Comforts they abandon and abuse him[9] their plea is that they are french Subjects but that is a poor excuse[10] for the english are the enemies of france as well as America[11] I am glad to hear that the Creoles are not of the Party. another draft of Melitia are call'd for from this County and are to march next week to Norfolk I expect our Dear Peachey will have to go, tho' he is placed in rather an awkward Situation to avoid the frequent musterings which interfered with his Professional duties he got Colonel Hairston to place him on the Staff as Surgeons mate tho he had no skill in that art he cou'd tell if a man was fit for duty that had nothing the matter

with him but he cou'd not take upon him to perform the necessary duties of that Office when they might be in a situation to need assistance in that line, the duty as well as inclination wou'd lead him to perform his tour of melitia duty[12] he dont much like going into the ranks with such associates marching to the tune of the white Cockade play'd on an old half Strung fiddle a few days will detirmine the matter as the Colonel has written to General Leftwhich to know if it is necessary to take the Staff Officers if he must go it is better that he shou'd go now than later in the Season I hope there will be a truce at any rate while they are negociating for a General Peace Alas poor Napolien his proud heart must feel this Stroke of adverse fortune M[r] and M[rs] Gilmer unite with me in devoutly wishing you all that can render you happy, long life good health and every other good that you can desire and believe me your ever obliged and faithful friend
E, TRIST

RC (MHi); addressed: "Thomas Jefferson Esq[r] Monticello Albemarle" via "mail"; franked; postmarked Rocky Mount, Va., 9 Mar. 1814; endorsed by TJ as received 23 Mar. 1814 and so recorded in SJL. Dft (NcU: NPT; filed at reel 17, frames 42–4 of 1991 microfilm ed.); undated, unsigned, and unaddressed; differs substantially from RC, with only the most significant variations noted below.

The POOR GOVERNOR of Louisiana was William C. C. Claiborne.

[1] Dft: "of this month."
[2] Instead of remainder of this sentence and all of next, Dft reads "After sending off my letters I was struck with the impropriety of my request knowing the little leisure you must have, but it has been my misfortune thro life to be hurried on by the first impulses and I have been by so doing led to commit errors that have been attended with mortifications which I might have escaped with common prudence, and I lament that age dont operate to my amendment."
[3] Dft here adds "I am sure."
[4] Instead of next section of letter, Dft reads "our want of success must be attributed to the want of Unanimity in our County-men the report that the Eastern States are about to raise an Army of thirty thousand men to oppose the measures of our Goverment fills my mind with horror the consiquences are so dreadful God only knows where it will end they abuse'd you for not going to war, these very people that are now so clamorous against it."
[5] RC: "male contents."
[6] Dft resumes here.
[7] Dft: "in a dreadful state."
[8] In place of preceding twenty-three words, Dft reads "The french to put Blanque and Roufeignice and others in the Legeslature claim'd the previledge of voting but have refused to stand a draft to drive the enemy from their Shores, and they look forward to an unpleasant Issue—The Balize having been abandond leaves the enemy in possession of the mouth of the River a schooner was taken some miles up the River and the inhabitants were in dread of their paying them a flying visit."
[9] Dft here adds "it seems it is not the creoles of the Country but french men that have married in the Country."
[10] Dft here adds "for their cowardice."
[11] Instead of remainder of letter, Dft reads "I am not surprised that Tyrrany has had such sway in the world for half the human Race are only to be kept in subjection by the scourge I am so out of temper with those malecontents that I think I cou'd see them put to Death or banish'd the Country with pleasure there is nothing desireable in the Office that M[r] Madison is elected to fill for there is not sufficient emolument to console for the

chagrine and trouble attending such a situation without effecting the great object; we have reason to exult in the bravery of our men and the recent success that has attended our arms but it has cost us dear and if there is truth in the report that Hampton and Wilkinson are at varience I fear a procrastination to our hopes and wishes M^r Randolph occupies my thought continually God grant that he may be spared to his family and friends but I wou'd rather here that he was kill'd than taken prisoner for they surely wou'd on your acct make a sacrifise of him—I hope Bonaparte will be spared as long as Britain continues her arrogant system of Tyranny I can not help feeling interested in the honor and Glory of the french nation both from principles of gratitude as will as dislike to the english I was sorry to hear of Moreaus death the more grievious for having taken up arms against his Country tho he had been ill treated I cou'd have wishd him superior to that kind of resentment."

[12] Trist here canceled "but."

# From William Wardlaw

DEAR SIR                                      Richmond 5 Mar. 1814

I am very anxious to procure the Session Acts for the year 1748. After the most careful enquery they can not be found in any of the publick offices here. M^r Henning who has been publishing the Statutes at large says he can not procure them. The Object with me is to see the law dividing the Counties of Henrico & Chesterfield to asscertain whether the southern, the Northeren shores or the[1] middle of the river is the line. This has become a question of some importance on ac^t of Mill sites on both sides of the river at the fall near this place.

If you have the law will you do me the favour to quote to me that part of it which relates to this subject. If a juditial question should hereafter arise on the subject I might have to ask the favour of the law itself

I am with much esteem Your friend &c                W WARDLAW

RC (DLC); endorsed by TJ as received 16 Mar. 1814 and so recorded in SJL; with TJ's notation on verso: "1748. c. 85."

An 11 May 1749 LAW DIVIDING Chesterfield from Henrico County put the former on the south side of the James River and the latter on the north without addressing the question of jurisdiction over the river itself (Waverly K. Winfree, *The Laws of Virginia, being a Supplement to Hening's The Statutes at Large, 1700–1750* [1971], 446–7, 463).

[1] Manuscript: "or the or the."

# From Charles Burrall

SIR,                           Baltimore March 6, 1814.

In consequence of the removal of M$^r$ Granger, there will be many efforts made to remove the subordinate officers in our Dep$^t$ especially where their offices are worth having, and already have individuals began to practice their insiduous arts to obtain mine—From, your personal knowledge of me, and from an opinion entertained by myself, that your sentiments have been favorable to me I have presumed Sir, to address you on this subject.—I have held my office upwards of fourteen years, and altho' I have had various dispositions to consult, yet I believe no city postmaster has performed his duties more free from complaint, or given more general satisfaction than myself.—I am confident that if I were to solicit the <u>real letter interest</u> of this city, that I could obtain at least nine tenths of it, but after having served such a length of time faithfully & impartially, before I would solicit the support of the citizens individually, I would submit to removal from office, if the new Postmaster General should be disposed to treat me with so much injustice.—I can plead no party services in my behalf, nor can any be laid to my charge, I have never voted myself, or attempted to influence any mans vote since I have lived in this city, nor have I contributed a dollar to the support of any news-paper, or caused a paragraph to be inserted in any of them relative to men or measures.—

In the summer of 1812 I had a trying time here, and although I would not go thro' the same scene again for any office within the gift of the President that I am capable of filling, yet I have the consolation of knowing that I then served M$^r$ Madison with as much fidelity as I flatter myself, in your estimation, I heretofore served you—I believe I may say without vanity that I at that time contributed as much as any other individual to prevent his coming into collision with the riotously disposed of this City.—I send you a copy of my deposition (which I caused to be laid before the President at the time) that you may see what was my conduct on that occasion.—Should you be disposed to serve me, and feel yourself perfectly at liberty to do it, by addressing a few lines to the President in my behalf, you will confer a particular favor on me.

I am Sir with sentiments of the highest respect your Obedient Servant                          CHA$^s$ BURRALL

RC (DLC: James Madison Papers); addressed: "The Honb$^{le}$ Thomas Jefferson Monticello Virginia"; endorsed by TJ as received 11 Mar. 1814 and so recorded in SJL. Enclosed in TJ to Madison, 16 Mar. 1814.

Charles Burrall (ca. 1763–1836) served as a clerk at the general post office in Philadelphia in 1791, as assistant postmaster general, 1792–1800, and as postmaster of Baltimore, 1800–16. During the years 1797–99 he and TJ stayed at the same Philadelphia boardinghouse, and thereafter Burrall wrote TJ a handful of letters in his professional capacity. After leaving the postal service, he was president of the Baltimore and Reister's-Town Road Company. Burrall remained in Baltimore until at least 1824. By 1830 he was living in Goshen, New York, where he died (*PTJ*, 33:426–7; *Gazette of the United States, and Philadelphia Daily Advertiser*, 31 Mar. 1800; *Federal Gazette & Baltimore Daily Advertiser*, 20 May 1800; TJ to Madison, 16 Mar. 1814; Washington *Daily National Intelligencer*, 7 May 1816, 9 June 1836; *Executive Communication to the General Assembly of Maryland, at December Session, 1818, on the Subject of Turnpike Roads* [Annapolis, 1819], 26–31; *Baltimore Patriot & Mercantile Advertiser*, 8 Oct. 1821; *Matchett's Baltimore Directory, for 1824* [Baltimore, 1824], 46; DNA: RG 29, CS, N.Y., Orange Co., 1830; *New-York Spectator*, 12 May 1836).

Burrall had a TRYING TIME as postmaster in August 1812 when mobs attempted to seize copies of the antiwar *Federal Republican* at the Baltimore post office when they arrived there from Georgetown for distribution (Donald R. Hickey, *The War of 1812: A Forgotten Conflict* [1989], 67). For the DEPOSITION, see Burrall to TJ, [7 Mar. 1814]. Burrall had his testimony LAID BEFORE President Madison in January 1813 with Postmaster General Gideon Granger's assistance (Madison, *Papers, Pres. Ser.*, 5:575n).

# From Joseph C. Cabell

DEAR SIR,                                    Carey's brooke. 6 March. 1814.

I have got thus far on my way home, and entrust to the neighbouring post office, your letters on Finance, which I hope will safely reach you. I must beg your pardon for having detained them longer than the period of my engagement. My private business in the lower country took up much more time than I had anticipated, and I was compelled to keep your letters thus long in order thoroughly to digest them. I have read them many times over, and most sincerely thank you for the perusal. The principal topics will form subjects of reflection for me, during the residue of the year. I have suffered M^r W. Rives, M^r Tucker, M^r Thomas Ritchie & M^r Cocke, to peruse them, on a promise from each not to communicate your name. I have also taken the liberty to transcribe a good many passages for my private use. You will, I hope, pardon these liberties. I write in great haste, in the midst of company. I hope to have the pleasure to see you between this & June.

I am d^r Sir, most respectfully & truly yours.

JOS: C: CABELL.

RC (ViU: TJP-PC); endorsed by TJ as received 12 Mar. 1814 but recorded in SJL as received 12 Apr. 1814. Enclosures: TJ to John Wayles Eppes, 24 June, 11 Sept., 6 Nov. 1813.

# From Martin Dawson & Company

DEAR SIR                                    Milton 6<sup>th</sup> March 1814

We are favourd with your letter to the writer covering your Df<sup>t</sup> on Gibson & Jefferson for two hundred and eighty dollars, in his fav<sup>r</sup> for Mr Craven Peytons Order on you for that sum ℔ said Order receipted and under cover—for which you have our thanks—as respects your bond to Edmund Bacon in our hands, it is the property of John Bacon—when he may call for the money we Know not untill he calls, we shall have no use for the money

    With Esteem Yo. Ob. Hu. Sevts      MARTIN DAWSON & C<sup>o</sup>

RC (MHi); in Dawson's hand; addressed: "Thomas Jefferson Esq<sup>re</sup> Monticello"; endorsed by TJ.

TJ's LETTER TO THE WRITER is not recorded in SJL and has not been found.

It presumably covered the draft on GIBSON & JEFFERSON in favor of Dawson that TJ recorded on this date (*MB*, 2:1298). For the BOND, see TJ's Promissory Note to Edmund Bacon, 7 Apr. 1813.

# From Charles Burrall

SIR                                         [7 Mar. 1814]

Since writing my letter of yesterday an insiduous piece has appeared against me in the Whig, which I enclose—It contains many unfounded suggestions to my prejudice, altho it tacitly admits that I have done my duty with correctness & impartiality—I have loaned to government more money than I could make by my office in Six years, and of six people employed in my office there is but one, a poor Letter carrier, of the Fedral party in politics. My deposition refered to in my letter of yesterday, will be found in a pamphlet that I send you by this days[1] mail—It commences on Page 153 & ends on Page 159. This pamphlet contains much information relative to our disturbances that you may not have seen—

    I am Sir respectfully your &c      CHA<sup>S</sup> BURRALL

RC (DLC: James Madison Papers); undated; endorsed by TJ as a letter of 7 Mar. 1814 received four days later and so recorded in SJL, which indicates that it came from Baltimore. Enclosed in TJ to James Madison, 16 Mar. 1814.

Burrall's DEPOSITION of 18 Dec. 1812 describes his efforts in the summer of that year to protect the Baltimore post office

from Republican mobs intent on seizing copies of the *Federal Republican*. It was printed on pp. 153–9 of at least two pamphlets, *Testimony taken before the Committee of Grievances and Courts of Justice, Relative to the Late Riots and Mobs in the City of Baltimore* (Annapolis, 1813) and *Report of the Committee of Grievances and Courts of Justice of the House of Delegates of Maryland, on the Subject of the Recent*

[ 231 ]

*Mobs and Riots in the City of Baltimore, together with the Depositions Taken Before the Committee* (Annapolis, 1813). A manuscript version dated 18 Dec. 1812 is in DLC: Madison Papers and described in Madison, *Papers, Pres. Ser.,* 5:575n. Other enclosure not found.

[1] Word interlined.

## From Thomas Clark

SIR                                              Philadelphia March 7 1814

I received your letter of the 10 February. I return you my sincere thanks for your patronage of my arduous undertaking; & for your kind offer of assistance. I intend soon to visit Richmond: a letter of introduction from you to the Governor of Virginia would be very acceptable.

There appears, in the public, a disposition to encourage my proposed history of the U.S. I have taken the liberty to enclose some proposals & circulars, which I entreat you, if not too much trouble, to direct to those gentlemen of your state, who may be disposed to patronise the work, or who may render me any assistance in the collection of materials.

I am Sir with respect & esteem

Your obedient servant.                          THOMAS CLARK

RC (DLC); at foot of text: "Thomas Jefferson Esq;"; endorsed by TJ as received 11 Mar. 1814 and so recorded in SJL. Enclosure: enclosure no. 2 to Clark to TJ, 19 Jan. 1814.

## From George Frederick Augustus Hauto

SIR                              Germantown March 7th 1814 near Philad[a]

I must plead, the high Idea, I entertain of you, as a Philosopher, and as a Patron to every Invention, which promises to be usefull to our Contry, as an excuse for the liberty I take of adressing you, and of submitting to your examination the enclosed Engraving & Description of the Hydrostatic Engine—patented to M[r] Long & myself;—begging your protection for the Engine, if you should find it deserving of it.

The Engine, we errected in this Village, for M[r] Bayly—has been in operation for more than five months—and has been examined by Judge Cooper Professor at Dickinson College, Gen[l] Swift, of the Engineer Corps—M[r] Large Steam Engineer and many other Gentlemen, acquainted with the Subject—

I shall be happy to send you a Model of the Engine, if you wish it, and give you any Information on the Subject—beg to be favor'd with your opinion on the Engine and have the honor to be with the greatest respect—

Sir Your most obd$^t$ humb Serv$^t$         GEO FRED$^K$ AUG$^S$ HAUTO

RC (DLC); between dateline and salutation: "Thom$^s$ Jefferson Esq$^{re}$ Monticello"; endorsed by TJ as received 18 Mar. 1814 and so recorded in SJL.

George Frederick Augustus Hauto (ca. 1781–1825), merchant and inventor, emigrated by 1802 from his native Germany to the United States, and three years later he was residing in Philadelphia, where he was a merchant. He and Stephen H. Long were in Germantown when they patented their hydrostatic and steam engines on 3 Sept. 1813. About 1816 Hauto opened an office in Philadelphia, and two years later he joined with that city's wire manufacturers Josiah White and Erskine Hazard in developing coal mines and improving navigation on the Lehigh River. White and Hazard bought out Hauto in 1820, after he failed to raise promised funds. Hauto left an estate valued at $7,418.81 and consisting mostly of coal and canal stock (Hauto's naturalization record, Philadelphia County Court of Common Pleas, 7 Dec. 1805, 23 Jan. 1808 [Philadelphia City Archives]; James Robinson, *The Philadelphia Directory, for 1808* [Philadelphia, 1808]; *List of Patents*, 128; Robinson, *The Philadelphia Directory, for 1816* [Philadelphia, 1816]; DeGH: Lehigh Coal Mine Company Records;

*Acts of the General Assembly of the Commonwealth of Pennsylvania, 1817–18* sess., 197–205 [20 Mar. 1818]; Alfred Mathews and Austin N. Hungerford, *History of the Counties of Lehigh and Carbon, in the Commonwealth of Pennsylvania* [1884], 595, 661–2; "Eleanor Morton" [Elizabeth G. Stern], *Josiah White: Prince of Pioneers* [1946]; Hauto's will and estate inventory [Philadelphia Register of Wills] Philadelphia *Aurora and Franklin Gazette*, 7 Feb. 1825; Reading, Pa., *Readinger Adler*, 15 Feb. 1825).

The ENCLOSED ENGRAVING & DE-SCRIPTION OF THE HYDROSTATIC EN-GINE (*Hydrostatic Engine* [undated broadside in DLC: TJ Papers, 200:35689]) described the water-powered engine invented by Hauto and LONG, included a diagram of the machine keyed to the text ("Engraved by H. Anderson, from an original drawing by W. Lehman"), and mentioned an engine that had been constructed at the brewery of a Mr. BAYLY in Germantown "for the purpose of grinding malt." Thomas COOPER reprinted the broadside with cautiously supportive commentary of his own later this year (*Emporium of Arts and Sciences* 3 [June 1814]: 166–70; Poor, *Jefferson's Library*, 14 [no. 920]).

# From John Barnes

DEAR SIR—                 George Town, 8$^{th}$ March 1814—

I have the pleasure: handing you, my friend M$^r$ Taylors letter of the 3$^d$ by which, to regulate your proposed transfer—the present Curr$^t$ price at 141. ℔Ct is equal to $564. per Share, on 20 shares produces $11,280—by my Calculation.—

it is however to be observed, in Case of a present Sale, the purchaser would be intitled to The 1$^t$ July dividend, say $400—on the Other hand—immediately After, the 1$^t$ July the same stock would probably fall to 38 ℔Ct—increasing Monthly—at all events, it would not be advisable to sell out, before you receive that dividend—the terms of the New Loan (if passed) are not yet Known—it is however presumed (as Usual) the paym$^{ts}$ will be made by installm$^{ts}$ perhaps, the two first say $\frac{1}{8}$h for the 3$^d$ 4$^h$ & 5$^h$ a $\frac{1}{4}$ each, on all such paym$^t$ your Int. commences—but sh$^d$ you wish to pay down the whole Subscribed for—they will receive it,—no Extra Int. but on the Acco$^t$ of the Installm$^t$ will be Allowed—from these several particulars—you may form—the result of your wishes and determination.

previous to, and immediately After the 1$^t$ July, it will be Necessary—for you to furnish me with your Order, to receive the Devid$^d$ due 1$^t$ Jan$^y$ last and 1$^t$ July—I shall have to regret, the closing Gen$^l$ K— Acco$^t$ with Penn$^a$ Bank—Allowed to be equal, to any, in the Union—as to its stability—productive of 10 ℔Ct and of increasing Value—as well a surplus dividend—every 2 or 3 years: in preferance—to a loan Certificate of Stationary Value and at less Interest,—

with great Respect I am Dear Sir—Your most Obed$^t$ serv$^t$

JOHN BARNES, COL$^A$

be pleased to return me M$^r$ Taylors letr for my goverm$^t$—

RC (ViU: TJP-ER); at foot of text: "Thomas Jefferson Esq$^r$ Monticello Virg$^a$"; endorsed by TJ as received 18 Mar. 1814 and so recorded in SJL. Enclosure not found.

GEN$^L$ K–: Tadeusz Kosciuszko.

# To Gideon Granger

DEAR SIR                                    Monticello Mar. 9. 14.

Your letter of Feb. 22. came to hand on the 4$^{th}$ instant. nothing is so painful to me as appeals to my memory on the subject of past transactions. from 1775. to 1809. my life was an unremitting course of public transactions, so numerous, so multifarious, and so diversified by places and persons, that, like the figures of a magic lanthern, their succession was with a rapidity which scarcely gave time for fixed impressions. add to this the decay of memory consequent on advancing years, and it will not be deemed wonderful that I should be a stranger as it were even to my own transactions. of some indeed I retain recollections of the particular, as well as general circumstances; of others a strong impression of the general fact, with an oblivion of particulars; but of a great mass, not a trace either general or particular remains in my mind. I have duly pondered the facts stated in your letter, & for the refreshment of my memory I have gone over the letters which passed between us while I was in the administration of the government, have examined my private notes, and such other papers as could assist me in the recovery of the facts, and shall now state them seriatim from your letter, and give the best account of them I am able to derive from the joint sources of memory and papers.

'I have been denounced as a Burrite: but you know that in 1800 I sent Erving from Boston to inform Virginia of the danger resulting from his intrigues.'    I well remember mr Erving's visit to this state about that time, and his suggestions of designs meditated in the quarter you mention: but as my duties on the occasion were to be merely passive, he of course, as I presume, addressed his communications more particularly to those who were free to use them. I do not recollect his mentioning you; but I find that in your letter to me of Apr. 26. 04.[1] you state your agency on that occasion, so that I have no reason to doubt the fact.

'that in 1803.–4. on my advice, you procured Erastus Granger to inform DeWitt Clinton of the plan to elevate Burr in N. York.'    here I do not recollect the particulars; but I have a general recollection that Col° Burr's conduct had already at that date rendered his designs suspicious; that being for that reason laid aside by his constituents as Vice President, and aiming to become the Governor of New York, it was thought advisable that the persons of influence in that state should be put on their guard; and mr Clinton being eminent, no one was more likely to recieve intimations from us, nor any one more likely to be confided in for their communication than yourself. I have no doubt therefore of the fact, and the less because in your letter to me of Oct. 9. 06. you remind me of it.

About the same period, that is, in the winter of 1803.–4. another train of facts took place which altho' not specifically stated in your letter, I think it but justice to yourself that I should state. I mean the intrigues which were in agitation, and at the bottom of which we believed Col° Burr to be; to form a coalition of the five Eastern states, with New York & New Jersey, under the new appellation of the seven Eastern states; either to overawe the Union by the combination of their power and their will, or by threats of separating themselves from it. your intimacy with some of those in the secret gave you opportunities of searching into their proceedings, of which you made me daily and confidential reports. this intimacy to which I had such useful recourse, at the time, rendered you an object of suspicion with many as being yourself a partisan of Col° Burr, and engaged in the very combination which you were faithfully employed in defeating. I never failed to justify you to all those who brought their suspicions to me, and to assure them of my knolege of your fidelity. many were the individuals, then members of the legislature, who recieved these assurances from me, and whose apprehensions were thereby quieted. this first project of Col° Burr having vanished in smoke he directed to the Western country those views which are the subject of your next article.

'that in 1806 I communicated by the first mail after I had gained[2] knolege of the fact, the supposed plans of Burr in his Western expedition; upon which communication your council was first called together to take measures in relation to that subject.'—not exactly on that single communication. on the 15th and 18th of Sep. I had recieved letters from Col° George Morgan, and from a mr Nicholson of N. York suggesting in a general way the maneuvres of Col° Burr. similar information came to the Secretary of state from a mr Williams of N. York. the indications however were so vague that I only desired their increased attention to the subject, and further communications of what they should discover. your letter of Oct. 16. conveying the communications of Gen¹ Eaton to yourself and to mr Ely gave a specific view of the objects of this new conspiracy, and corroborating our previous information, I called the Cabinet together, on the 22d of Oct. when specific measures were adopted for meeting the dangers threatened in the various points in which they might occur. I say your letter of Oct.[3] 16. gave this information, because it's date with the circumstance of it's being no longer on my files induce me to infer it was that particular letter, which having been transferred to the bundle of the documents of that conspiracy, delivered to the Attorney General, is no longer in my possession.

Your mission of mr Pease on the route to New Orleans, at the time of that conspiracy, with powers to see that the mails were expedited, & to dismiss at once every agent of the Post office whose fidelity could be justly doubted, and to substitute others on the spot was a necessary measure, taken with my approbation; and he executed the trusts to my satisfaction. I do not know however that my subsequent appointment of him to the office of Surveyor General was influenced, as you suppose, by those services. my motives in that appointment were my personal knolege of his mathematical qualifications, and satisfactory informations of the other parts of his character.

With respect to the dismission of the prosecutions for sedition in Connecticut, it is well known to have been a tenet of the republican portion of our fellow citizens, that the Sedition law was contrary to the Constitution and therefore void. on this ground I considered it as a nullity wherever I met it in the course of my duties; and on this ground I directed Nolle Prosequis in all the prosecutions which had been instituted under it. and as far as the public sentiment can be inferred from the occurrences of the day, we may say that this opinion had the sanction of the nation. the prosecutions therefore which were afterwards[4] instituted in Connecticut, of which two were against printers, two against preachers, and one against a judge, were too inconsistent with this principle to be permitted to go on. we were bound to administer to others the same measure of law, not which they had meted to us, but we to ourselves, and to extend to all equally the protection of the same constitutional principles. these prosecutions too were chiefly for charges against my self, and I had from the beginning laid it down as a rule to notice nothing of the kind. I believed that the long course of services in which I had acted on the public stage, and under the eye of my fellow citizens, furnished[5] better evidence to them of my character and principles than the angry invectives of adverse partisans in whose eyes the very acts most approved by the majority were subjects of the greatest demerit and censure. these prosecutions against them therefore were to be dismissed as a matter of duty. but I wished it to be done with all possible respect to the worthy citizens who had advised them, and in such way as to spare their feelings which had been justly irritated by the intemperance of their adversaries. as you were of that state and intimate with these characters, the business was confided to you, and you executed it to my perfect satisfaction.

These I think are all the particular facts on which you have asked my testimony; and I add with pleasure, and under a sense of duty the declaration that the increase of rapidity in the movement of the mails which had been vainly attempted before, were readily undertaken by you on your entrance into office, and zealously and effectually carried into execution: and that the affairs of the office were conducted by you with ability and diligence, so long as I had opportunities of observing them.

With respect to the first article mentioned in your letter, in which I am neither concerned nor consulted, I will yet as a friend volunteer my advice. I never knew any thing of it, nor would ever listen to such gossiping trash. be assured, my dear Sir, that the dragging such a subject before the public will excite universal reprobation, and they will drown in their indignation all the solid justifications which they would otherwise have recieved and weighed with candor. consult your own experience, reflect on the similar cases which have happened within your own knolege, and see if ever there was a single one in which such a mode of recrimination procured favor to him who used it. you may give pain where perhaps you wish it; but be assured it will react on yourself with double tho' delayed effect; and that it will be one of those incidents of your life on which you will never reflect with satisfaction. be advised then; erase it even from your memory, and stand erect before the world on the high ground of your own merits, without stooping to what is unworthy either of your or their notice. remember that we often repent of what we have said, but never of that which we have not. you may have time enough hereafter to mend your hold, if ever it can be mended by such matter as that. take time then, and do not commit your happiness and public estimation by too much precipitancy. I am entirely uninformed of the state of things which you say exists, and which will oblige you to make a solemn appeal to the nation, in vindication of your character. but whatever that be, I feel it a duty to bear testimony to the truth; and I have suggested with frankness other considerations occurring to myself, because I wish you well, & I add sincere assurances of my great respect and esteem.                                                      TH: JEFFERSON

RC (DLC: Granger Papers). PoC (DLC); at foot of first page: "Gideon Granger esq."

Granger's letters to TJ of APR. 26. 04. and OCT. 9. 06. are in DLC: TJ Papers. Letters to TJ of 29 Aug. 1806 from COL° GEORGE MORGAN, of 6 Sept. 1806 from John NICHOLSON, and of 16 Oct. 1806 from Granger, do not appear to be extant. The 5 Sept. 1806 letter to SECRETARY OF STATE James Madison from Nathan WILLIAMS is in DLC: Madison Papers. This letter, with its apparent failure to provide Granger with the full VINDICATION that he sought, ended his correspondence with TJ. Granger ultimately decided not to take his case to the public. He moved to the state of New York, where he was an attorney and state senator (*ANB*; Brant, *Madison*, 6:243–5).

[1] Reworked from "02."
[2] In enhancing a faint PoC, TJ here substituted "got."
[3] Reworked from "Aug."
[4] Word interlined.
[5] Word interlined in place of "was."

# To James Madison

DEAR SIR                                          Monticello Mar. 10. 14.

Your favor of Feb. 7. was duly recieved. that which it gave me reason to expect from mr G. did not come till the 4th inst. he mentioned in it that a state of things existed which probably would oblige him to make a solemn appeal to the public, and he asked my testimony to certain specific facts which he stated. these related solely to charges against him as a Burrite, and to his agency in dismissing the prosecutions in Connecticut under the Sedition law. the facts alledged as disproving his Burrism were 1. that he thro' mr Erving in 1800. put Virginia on her guard against the designs of Burr. 2. that in 1803–4. at my request he communicated to DeWitt Clinton Burr's aspiring to the government of New York. 3. that in 1806. he gave us the first effectual notice of Burr's Western projects, by which we were enabled to take specific measures to meet them. 4. his mission of mr Pease on the route to N. Orleans to expedite the mails, and remove suspected agents of the Post office. these appeals to my very defective memory are very painful. I have looked over my papers, and answered his enquiries as exactly as I could, under a sense not only of the general duty of bearing testimony to truth, but of justice to him personally, for his conduct towards me was ever friendly and faithful, and I on several occasions used his services to the advantage of the public.

He said nothing on the subject of Tayloe's post office. but I remember the substance, altho' not the minutiae of that case. he informed me that mr Tayloe held a post office near Mount Airy, and exercised it by his steward as a deputy, himself residing at Washington, merely for the purpose of carrying on his plantation correspondence free of postage. I advised his immediate appointment of another, as well on the ground of the abusive use of the office, as to suppress the example of non-residents holding local offices, which would otherwise lead immediately to the most pernicious practices of sinecure.          of the Baptist preacher, and mr Tayloe's underbidding him I recollect nothing. I remember that mr Granger, soon after he came into office, informed me of a devise practised by the federalists in the Eastern states to favor the circulation of their papers and defeat that of the republicans, which was, whenever a republican rider was employed, to underbid to a price below what the business could be done for, submitting to that loss for one year, and the next to demand the full price, the republican being thus removed from the competition, by the disposal of his horses E<sup>t</sup>c. I desired him whenever a bidder should offer below the real worth, & there should be reason to suspect this fraud, to reject him, and I would take on myself the responsibility. If I was consulted on the competition of Tayloe and the baptist preacher, and gave an opinion on it, it must have been stated as a case of this class. as to the compromise alledged of giving up the one case for the other, no such idea was ever presented to me, nor would mr G. have ventured to present it, and I am certain that not a word ever passed between Doct<sup>r</sup> Jones & myself on the subject. the true remedy for putting those appointments into a wholesome state would be a law vesting them in the President, but without the intervention of the Senate. that intervention would make the matter worse. every Senator would expect to dispose of all the post-offices in his vicinage, or perhaps in his state. at present the President has some controul over those appointments by his authority over the Postmaster himself. and I should think it well to require him to lay all his appointments previously before the President for his approbation or rejection. an expression in mr G's letter gave me ground to advise him to confine his vindication to it's important points whatever they might be, and not to let his passions lead him into matter which would degrade himself alone in the public opinion, and I have urged it in such terms as I trust will have effect.          Our agriculture presents little interesting. wheat looks badly, much having been killed by the late severe weather. corn is scarce, but it's price kept down to 3.D.[1] by the substitute of wheat as food both for laborers and horses, costing only 3/6 to 4/. they begin to distill the old flour, getting 10. gall$^s$ of whiskey from the barrel, which produces 5. to 6.D. the barrel & consequently more than we can get at Richmond for the new. tobacco is high, from it's scarcity, there having been not more than $\frac{1}{3}$ of an ordinary crop planted the last year. this year there will probably be $\frac{2}{3}$ ever affectionately yours          TH: JEFFERSON

RC (DLC: Madison Papers, Rives Collection); addressed: "The President of the United States Washington"; franked; postmarked Milton, 16 Mar. PoC (DLC); endorsed by TJ.

Madison's FAVOR OF FEB. 7. was actually dated 13 Feb. 1814. The letter IT GAVE ME REASON TO EXPECT was Gideon Granger to TJ, 22 Feb. 1814.

[1] Preceding two words interlined.

# Recommendation of William McClure by Thomas Jefferson and Thomas Mann Randolph

The bearer W$^m$ M$^c$lure removed from N.C. to this neighborhood under an engagement to instruct us in the use of the Spinning Jenny. several of these machines have been made by him & by our own workmen, and our Spinners are taught to use them so completely as to ensure our being able to clothe our own people by the labor of a few of the least useful of them. his principal profession is that of weaving, of which we have no other experience than his having taught some of our people to weave single & double cloth, being all our wants have hitherto called for. he has lived here between 2. & 3. years and I have found him to be an honest, disinterested man, good humored, accomodating and sober. I have thought it a duty, at his request, to state these truths

Mar. 12. 14

Th:J.

TMR.

PoC (MoSHi: TJC-BC); entirely in TJ's hand; endorsed by TJ: "M^clure W^m"; with wax seal on verso. Not recorded in SJL.

# From Patrick Gibson

Sir                                                    Richmond 13^th March 1814

I wrote to you on the 2^nd inclosing $100 in small notes, and have since received your favor of the 3^d together with the blank sign'd— although, my not having received it in time to renew your note due in bank has caused me no inconvenience, it might have been otherwise, and to guard against my negligence in future, as well as accidents by the mail &c, I think it adviseable to adopt the plan you propose, and for that purpose inclose you two notes for your signature—Flour instead of getting better is becoming daily more unsaleable, it is dull even at $4\frac{1}{2}$\$ from the prevalence of the opinion, even among those most sanguine in their expectations as to peace that it will come too late to save the present crop. I have just received instructions to sell at that price—With great respect I am

Your ob^t Serv^t                                    Patrick Gibson

RC (ViU: TJP-ER); between dateline and salutation: "Thomas Jefferson Esq^re"; endorsed by TJ as received 18 Mar. 1814 and so recorded in SJL. Enclosures not found.

TJ's favor of the 3^d is recorded in SJL, but neither it nor the blank sign'd note enclosed in it have been found.

# From John E. Hall

Sir                                                    Baltimore 15^th March 1814

I should have answered your letter sooner, but that I have been kept in almost daily expectation of receiving the Law Journal from my printer at Philadelphia. It has at length arrived, & I take the earliest opportunity of sending you a copy. I trust you will approve of the corrections, which it was thought proper to make in your "Defence." I thought myself justified in the act, by your MS. acknowledgment of the existence of such inadvertencies, in the copy which you transmitted to my friend, Judge Cooper.

I am Sir

respectfully yr obt Servt                                    J. E. HALL

RC (DLC); endorsed by TJ as received 18 Mar. 1814 and so recorded in SJL.

For the reprinted version of TJ's DEFENCE in the batture controversy enclosed here, see note to Hall to TJ, 15 Nov. 1813. TJ TRANSMITTED a copy of his original 1812 pamphlet on the subject to Thomas COOPER in a letter dated 10 July 1812.

# To William Bentley

SIR                                                Monticello Mar. 16. 14.

I thank you for the sermon on the death of Gen$^l$ Fiske, which I have read with pleasure. he appears to have been truly a model of merit. and the more deserving of praise inasmuch as his good works being performed in the still walks of private life, were not to be blazoned on the great theater of the world. what a contrast does a character of so much benevolence hold up to view with that of the Attilas and Bonapartes, the flagella dei, sent to scourge kings & nations for their crimes & follies!

Accept the assurance of my great esteem & respect.

TH: JEFFERSON

RC (NNGL, on deposit NHi); at foot of text: "the rev$^d$ mr Bentley." PoC (DLC); endorsed by TJ.

FLAGELLA DEI: "scourges of God" (*OED*).

# To Henry M. Brackenridge

Monticello Mar. 16. 14.

Th: Jefferson presents his thanks to mr Brackenridge for the copy of his much esteemed 'Views of Louisiana' which he has been so kind as to send him. in doing this he does but render his portion of the general gratitude due for this valuable contribution towards the knolege of a great country which nature has destined to become the most interesting portion of the Western world. he salutes mr Brackenridge with great respect and esteem.

RC (ViU: TJP); torn at crease, with missing text supplied from PoC; dateline at foot of text; addressed, with a series of redirections in different hands: "M^r Henry M. Brackenridge Baton Rouge Louisiana <*recommended to the care of M^r* [...]>"; franked; postmarked twice. PoC (DLC); endorsed by TJ.

## To Charles Burrall

DEAR SIR                              Monticello Mar. 16. 14.

Your favor of the 7^th was recieved by our last mail and I have, by it's return written to the President, bearing testimony with pleasure to the merit of your conduct and character through every stage of my acquaintance with them. no one whose conduct has been so rational and dutiful as yours ever had, or has now any cause to fear. those only who use the influence of their office to thwart & defeat the measures of the government under whom they act, are proper subjects of it's animadversion, on the common principle that a house divided against itself must fall. you were faithful, as you ought to have been to the administration under which you were appointed, & you were so to that which succeeded it. be assured you have nothing to fear under so reasonable and just a character as the President. I am happy in having been furnished with an occasion of proving my readiness to be useful to you, and of manifesting my esteem for merit and respect for honest opinions when acted on correctly; and I pray you to accept the assurance of my friendly attachment.                    TH: JEFFERSON

PoC (DLC); at foot of text: "M^r Charles Burrall. P.M. Baltimore"; endorsed by TJ.

The principle that A HOUSE DIVIDED AGAINST ITSELF MUST FALL comes from the Bible, Matthew 12.25.

## To Jason Chamberlain

SIR                                   Monticello Mar. 16. 14.

I thank you for the Indian pamphlets you have been so kind as to send to me. they add to the remains of a considerable collection of their vocabularies which I had availed myself of every opportunity of procuring, but the greater part of which was lost by an accident. if ever we are to know any thing of their early relations with the other nations of the world, I am persuaded it is to be sought in the filiation of their languages. the copy for the Philosophical society shall be duly forwarded. I recieve with just sensibility the kind expressions of your letter towards myself personally, and beg you to be assured of my great respect & esteem.                    TH: JEFFERSON

PoC (DLC); at foot of text: "M^r Chamberlain"; endorsed by TJ as a letter to Jason "Chamberlayne" and so recorded in SJL.

A trunk containing TJ's CONSIDERABLE COLLECTION of Indian vocabularies was stolen and most of its contents destroyed during its shipment to Monticello at the end of his presidency (Samuel J. Harrison to Gibson & Jefferson, 16 July 1809; TJ to Benjamin Smith Barton, 21 Sept. 1809).

# To James Madison

DEAR SIR                                    Monticello Mar. 16. 14.

I inclose you two letters from mr Burrall, postmaster of Baltimore. you will percieve by them that the removal of mr Granger has spread some dismay in the ranks. I lodged in the same house with him (Francis's) during the sessions of Congress of 97. 98. 99. we breakfasted, dined E^tc at the same table. he classed himself with the federalists, but I did not know why, for he scarcely ever uttered a word on the subject, altho' it was in the reign of addresses, of M^cpherson's blues & of terror. he would sometimes make a single observation in support of the administration. he is an honest and a good man, and, as far as I have observed him, has been correct, faithful and obliging in the conduct of his office. altho' I am sure it is unnecessary, yet I could not when requested refuse this testimony to the truth. ever & affectionately yours                              TH: JEFFERSON

RC (DLC: Madison Papers); addressed: "The President of the United States Washington"; franked; postmarked Milton, 17 Mar.; with penciled notation in Madison's hand: "For perusal, & to be returned." PoC (DLC); endorsed by TJ. Enclosures: Charles Burrall to TJ, 6, [7] Mar. 1814.

M^cPHERSON'S BLUES was a volunteer militia unit composed entirely of Federalists, raised in Philadelphia by William McPherson (James Russell Young, ed., *Memorial History of the City of Philadelphia* [1898], 2:155).

# To Henry Muhlenberg

DEAR SIR                                    Monticello Mar. 16. 14.

I thank you for your catalogue of North American plants. it is indeed very copious, and at the same time compendious in it's form. I hardly know what you have left for your 'Descriptio uberior.' the discoveries of Gov^r Lewis may perhaps furnish matter of value, if ever they can be brought forward. the mere journal of the voyage may be soon expected; but in what forwardness are the volumes of the botany, natural history, geography and meteorology of the journey, I am uninformed. your pamphlet came during a long absence from home, and was mislaid or this acknolegement should have been sooner made. with my wishes for the continuance and success of your useful labors I embrace with pleasure this first occasion of assuring you that I have had long and much gratification in observing the distinguished part you have borne in making known to the literary world the treasures of our own country and I tender to you the sentiments of my high respect and esteem

TH: JEFFERSON

PoC (CSmH: JF-BA); at foot of text: "The rev^d Henry Muhlenburg"; endorsed by TJ.

Henry (Gotthilf Heinrich Ernst) Muhlenberg (1753–1815), Lutheran clergyman, botanist, and educator, was the son of Henry Melchior Muhlenberg, a German immigrant and eminent Lutheran Church leader in America. A native Pennsylvanian, the younger Muhlenberg was educated at Halle, Saxony (1763–70), including study at its university. Soon after returning home in 1770, he was ordained a Lutheran minister and served several congregations in the Philadelphia area. In 1780 Muhlenberg moved to Lancaster, Pennsylvania, where he spent the rest of his life as pastor at Holy Trinity Church. He served as secretary of the Ministerium of Pennsylvania for six terms and president for eleven terms. Muhlenberg pursued the systematic study of botany, examining and documenting the flora surrounding Lancaster, collecting the earliest important American herbarium, and investigating the economic and medicinal uses of plants. About 1783 he began collaborating with other American and European botanists, and in 1785 he was elected to the American Philosophical Society. Muhlenberg was the first principal of Franklin College (later Franklin and Marshall College), 1787–1815. His published works include an

English-German dictionary and works on native and exotic plants of North America (*ANB*; *DAB*; Paul A. W. Wallace, *The Muhlenbergs of Pennsylvania* [1950]; Sprague, *American Pulpit*, 9:59–66; Herbert H. Beck, "Henry E. Muhlenberg," *Castanea* 3 [1938]: 41–53; APS, Minutes, 22 Jan. 1785 [MS in PPAmP]; James A. Mears, "Some Sources of the Herbarium of Henry Muhlenberg (1753–1815)," APS, *Proceedings* 122 [1978]: 155–74; Joseph Henry Dubbs, *History of Franklin and Marshall College* [1903]; Philadelphia *Poulson's American Daily Advertiser*, 26, 30 May 1815).

Muhlenberg's CATALOGUE OF NORTH AMERICAN PLANTS, entitled *Catalogus Plantarum Americæ Septentrionalis huc usque cognitarum Indigenarum et Cicurum: or, A Catalogue of the hitherto known Native and Naturalized Plants of North America, arranged according to the sexual system of Linnæus* (Lancaster, 1813; Sowerby, no. 1088), was followed by the posthumously published DESCRIPTIO UBERIOR ("richer description"), entitled *Descriptio Uberior Graminum et Plantarum Calamariarum Americæ Septentrionalis Indigenarum et Cicurum* (Philadelphia, 1817). For the publication of Meriwether Lewis's JOURNAL, see editorial note at TJ to Paul Allen, 18 Aug. 1813.

# From Samuel P. Parsons

RESPECTED FRIEND                    Richmond 3rd Mo 16th 1814

With this letter I put in the care of P. Gibson, a Drill plough (for planting corn peas &Ct) to be forwarded to thee, by the first oppertunity; It may seem strange that an entire stranger shoud presume to intrude on a person with whom he has no personal[1] knowledge; particularly one who has been so far elivated above the ordinary community; But when it is recollected that we are both children of a free & enlitened republic, our rights, & privilages are the same; & our interest shoud be equally so, as respects the good of the whole, I can but flatter myself, I shall stand entirely excused for this address, & shall state the motives, which induces me to send the plough; In the Regester of a few weeks past, I read a letter from thee on the subject of Olliver Evans machine for Manufactoring[2] flour &Ct, in which letter thee stated thee had a plough invented by a Majr Martin for Drilling Corn (I have never seen the plough invented by Martin;) For several years past I have been pursuing a Mechanical business embracing most of the useful utencils used in Husbandry (particularly wheat fans & ploughs[3] with considerable improvement) having suggested the Idear of expediting the general mode[4] of Drilling corn, last spring, I set a bout making myself a plough to plant my crop of corn, which came fully up to my expectation, but never found that an improvement was practicable, & accordingly, made one for one of my neighbours; this last seemed to fix the principal & the utility, upon a purmenant basis & no doubt remain of its meeting with encuragement, when corn is Drilld: from actual expereance, I find that with this plough a boy & horse can plant 10 Acres of ground in the day of 8 feet rows; It is useless for me to explain the principle; to one who is so well acquainted with mechanical principles: generally.[5] suffice to say, it is the greatest saving labour machine in husbandry that I have seen It not only lays off & Drops the corn, but covers it up at the same time; leaving every hill at eequal distance from each other,

Thee will please try it (shoud thee[6] be in the practice of Drilling) & upon such tryals find it of sufficient importance to adopt it, thee will know doubt keep it, & remit me 18 Dollars the price through P. Gibson; if thee is not in want of such a Machine, thee will return it (free of any cost) thro the same chanel, that thee receives it,

It will render me a singular faver (shoud it not be too much trouble) to give me thy Idears on the propriety of obtaining a patent as I have it in contemplation;[7] Its simplicity may induce most farmers to

[ 246 ]

use it in preferance to any other, if I meet with sufficient incurrage-
ment I intend having the axel & roller (in which the cups are that
drops the grain) made of Cast Iron which will make the ploughs of
more duribility & less subject to get out of order, I have ploughs for
fallowing that I shoud like to send thee on tryal, shoud thee feal disposed to add to thy (no dout) already large supley,       With
great respect I am thy
    ass<sup>d</sup> friend

SAML. P. PARSONS

RC (ViW: TC-JP); at head of text: "Thomas Jefferson"; endorsed by TJ as received 12 Apr. 1814 and so recorded in SJL.

Samuel Pleasants Parsons (1783–1842), manufacturer and public official, was born in Charles City County. From about 1804–09 he worked in partnerships with his father and others, selling wire, wheat fans, lumber, and tools. By 1813 Parsons operated his own wagon manufactory, and he continued to make and sell farm implements for several years. He served twice as superintendent of the state penitentiary in Richmond, from about 1816–22 and 1824–32. Parsons was a member of the Agricultural Society of Virginia, an advocate of slave emancipation, and a supporter of the African colonization movement, both as a private citizen and in his capacity as prison superintendent. In 1838 he incorporated the Cottage ironworks in Hanover County (Lyon Gardiner Tyler, *Encyclopedia of Virginia Biography* [1915], 4:311; William Wade Hinshaw and others, *Encyclopedia of American Quaker Genealogy* [1936– ], 6:201–2, 262; Richmond *Virginia Argus*, 2 June

1804, 15 Mar. 1808, 3 Mar. 1809, 25 Nov. 1813, 29 Apr. 1815; Richmond *Enquirer*, 22 Dec. 1808; *The Virginia Farmers' Almanac, for the year of our Lord 1817* [Fredericksburg, 1816]; Parsons letters in Vi: RG 3, Governor's Office, Letters Received; *JSV*, 1830–31 sess., 134 [8 Mar. 1831]; *Memoirs of the "Society of Virginia for Promoting Agriculture"* [Richmond, 1818], xii; Mount Pleasant, Ohio, *Genius of Universal Emancipation* 1 [1821]: 31; *Philadelphia Recorder* [1825]: 339; *Acts of Assembly* [1838 sess.], 193–4; Henrico Co. Will Book, 11:35–8; *Richmond Enquirer*, 17 Feb. 1842; gravestone inscription in Hollywood Cemetery, Richmond).

TJ's 13 Aug. 1813 letter to Isaac McPherson concerning the patent claims of Oliver EVANS was printed in Hezekiah Niles's Baltimore *Weekly Register* 5 (1813–14): addenda, 2–6.

<sup>1</sup> Manuscript: "pesonal."
<sup>2</sup> Manuscript: "Manufactoing."
<sup>3</sup> Manuscript: "ploghs."
<sup>4</sup> Manuscript: "mote."
<sup>5</sup> Word interlined.
<sup>6</sup> Manuscript: "the."
<sup>7</sup> Manuscript: "comtemplation."

# To Charles J. Ingersoll

Monticello Mar. 17. 14.

Th: Jefferson returns thanks to mr Ingersoll for the copy of his
speech on the Loan bill which he has been so kind as to send him. he
has read it with great satisfaction, and felicitates his country on having in it's councils so able an advocate of sound principles, and whose

age may promise them a long course of his valuable services. he hopes & doubts not mr Ingersoll will recieve the highest of all rewards to an honest and patriotic mind, the love and gratitude of his fellow citizens. he salutes him with great esteem and respect.

RC (R. Sturgis Ingersoll, Philadelphia, 1946); dateline at foot of text; addressed: "The honble M^r Ingersoll of the Pensylvania delegation in Congress Washington"; postmarked Milton, 23 Mar.; endorsed by Ingersoll. PoC (DLC).

Ingersoll's SPEECH ON THE LOAN BILL, probably enclosed in Ingersoll to TJ, 3 Mar. 1814 (not found, but recorded in SJL as received 11 Mar. 1814 from Washington), supported the War of 1812, summarizing its causes and arguing that, despite the trials of war, the United States was unified and financially sound (Ingersoll, *Mr. Ingersoll's Speech on the Loan Bill, Tuesday, 15 February, 1814* [1814]).

# To Horatio G. Spafford

DEAR SIR                                              Monticello Mar. 17. 14.

I am an unpunctual correspondent at best. while my affairs permit me to be within doors, I am too apt to take up a book, and to forget the calls of the writing table. besides this I pass a considerable portion of my time at a possession so distant, and uncertain as to it's mails that my letters always await my return here. this must apologise for my being so late in acknoleging your two favors of Dec. 17.[1] and Jan. 28. as also that of the gazetteer which came safely to hand. I have read it with pleasure, and derived from it much information which I did not possess before. I wish we had as full a statement as to all our states. we should know ourselves better our circumstances and resources, and the advantageous ground we stand on as a whole. we are certainly much in debted to you for this[2] fund of valuable information.—I join in your reprobation of our merchants, priests and lawyers for their adherence to England & monarchy in preference to their own country and it's constitution. but merchants have no country. the mere spot they stand on does not constitute so strong an attachment as that from which they draw their gains. in every country and in every age, the priest has been hostile to liberty. he is always in alliance with the Despot abetting his abuses in return for protection to his own. it is easier to acquire wealth and power by this combination than by deserving them: and to effect this they have perverted the purest religion ever preached to man, into mystery & jargon unintelligible to all mankind & therefore the safer engine for their purposes. with the lawyers it is a new thing. they have in the mother country been generally the firmest supporters of the free principles of their constitution. but there too they have changed. I ascribe much of this to the substitution of Blackstone for my Lord Coke, as an elementary work. in truth Blackstone and Hume have made tories of all England, and are making tories of those young Americans whose native feelings of independance do not place them above the wily sophistries of a Hume or a Blackstone. these two books, but especially the former have done more towards the suppression of the liberties of man, than all the million of men in arms of Bonaparte and the millions of human lives with the sacrifice of which he will stand loaded before the judgment seat of his maker. I fear nothing for our liberty from the assaults of force; but I have seen and felt much, and fear more from English books, English prejudices, English manners, and the apes, the dupes, and designs among our professional crafts. when I look around me for security against these seductions, I find it in the wide spread of our Agricultural citizens, in their unsophisticated minds, their independance and their power if called on to crush the Humists of our cities, and to maintain the principles which severed us from England. I see our safety in the extent of our confederacy, and in the probability[3] that in the proportion of that the sound parts will always be sufficient to crush local poisons. in this hope I rest, and tender you the assurance of my esteem and respect.

Th: Jefferson

RC (NjMoHP: Lloyd W. Smith Collection); addressed: "M[r] Horatio G. Spafford, Albany"; franked; postmarked Milton, 23 Mar.; endorsed by Spafford: "3. 30, '14," with "31" on the line beneath the "30"; additional calculations by Spafford on address leaf, subtracting "born 1745" from "1815" to yield "70 years of age" (see Spafford to TJ, 24 Feb.

1815). PoC (DLC); endorsed by TJ. Tr (ViU: GT); posthumous copy.

[1] Reworked from "31," the day TJ received that letter.
[2] Word interlined in place of "such a."
[3] RC and PoC: "probality." Tr: "probability."

# To William Wardlaw

Dear Sir                    Monticello Mar. 17. 14.

Your letter of the 5th came to hand yesterday (the 16th) only, or it should have been sooner answered. if I own the Sessions acts of 1748. they are bound up in a volume of Sessions acts which I lent to mr Hening, and which can be resorted to in his hands; but I do not believe I ever had them; and as far as my recollection serves me, no copy of them was ever to be found in my time. and the reason for this, as presumed, was that the Revisal of 1748. coming out at that time and containing every public act of that session, the Sessions acts disappeared immediately. you will find the <u>title</u> of the act you want in the Revisal of 1748. c. 85. but this is matter of memory and conjecture only, in which I may be mistaken. you will oblige me by asking of mr Hening whether the laws of that session are bound up in the volume of Sessions acts which he has of mine, and by dropping me a line. the volume I refer to is lettered on the back 'Laws of Virginia Vol. V. Monticello library.'　　　Accept the assurance of my great esteem and respect.　　　　　　　　　　　　　　　　Th: Jefferson

PoC (DLC); at foot of text: "D$^r$ William Wardlaw"; endorsed by TJ.

# To Louis H. Girardin

Dear Sir　　　　　　　　　　　　　　　Monticello Mar. 18. 14.

According to your request of the other day, I send you my formula and explanation of L$^d$ Napier's theorem for the solution of right angled Spherical triangles. with you I think it strange that the French mathematicians have not used, or noticed, this method more than they have done. Montucla, in his account of Lord Napier's inventions, expresses a like surprise at this fact, and does justice to the ingenuity, the elegance, and convenience of the theorem, which, by a single rule, easily preserved in the memory, supplies the whole Table of Cases, given in the books of Spherical trigonometry. yet he does not state the rule; but refers for it to Wolf's Cours de Mathmatiques. I have not the larger work of Wolf's and in the French translation of his abridgment (by some member of the congregation of S$^t$ Maur) the branch of Spherical trigonometry is entirely omitted. Potter, one of the English authors of Courses of mathematics, has given the Catholic proposition, as it is called, but in terms unintelligible, and leading to error, until, by repeated trials, we have ascertained the meaning of some of his equivocal expressions. in Robert Simson's[1] Euclid we have the theorem, with it's demonstrations, but, less aptly for the memory, divided into two rules; and these are extended, as the original was, only to the cases of right angled triangles. Hutton, in his Course of Mathematics, declines giving the rules as 'too artificial to be applied by young computists.' but I do not think this. it is true that, when we use them, their demonstration is not always present to the mind: but neither is this the case generally in using mathematical theorems, or in the various steps of an Algebraical process. we act on them however mechanically, & with confidence as truths of which we

[ 250 ]

have heretofore been satisfied by demonstration, altho we do not at the moment retrace the processes which establish them. Hutton however in his Mathematical Dictionary, under the terms 'Circular parts' & 'Extremes' has given us the rules, and in all their extensions to oblique spherical, & to plane triangles. I have endeavored to reduce them to a form best adapted to my own frail memory, by couching them in the fewest words possible, & such as cannot, I think, mislead, or be misunderstood. my formula, with the explanation which may be necessary for your[2] pupils, is as follows.[3]

L[d] Napier noted first the parts, or elements of a triangle, to wit, the sides & angles: and, expunging from these the right angle, as if it were a non-existence, he considered the other five parts, to wit, the 3. sides and 2. oblique angles, as arranged in a circle, and therefore called them the Circular parts; but chose, (for simplifying the result) instead of the hypothenuse & 2. oblique angles, themselves, to substitute their complements. so that his 5. circular parts are the 2. legs themselves, and the Complements of the hypothenuse & of the 2. oblique angles. if the 3. of these, given and required. were all adjacent, he called it the case of Conjunct parts, the middle element the Middle part, and the 2 others the Extremes conjunct with the middle, or Extremes Conjunct; but, if one of the parts employed was separated from the others by the intervention of the parts unemployed, he called it the case of Disjunct parts, the insulated or opposite part, the Middle part, and the 2. others the Extremes disjunct from the middle, or Extremes Disjunct. he then laid down his Catholic rule, to wit;

'the Rectangle of the Radius & Sine of the Middle part is equal to the Rectangle of the <u>Tangents</u> of the 2. Extremes Conjunct, and to that of the <u>Cosines</u> of the 2. Extremes Disjunct.'

And to aid our recollection in which case the Tangents, and in which the Cosines are to be used, preserving the original designations of the inventor, we may observe that the <u>tangent</u> belongs to the <u>Conjunct</u> case, terms of sufficient affinity to be associated in the memory; and the Sine-<u>Complement</u> remains of course for the <u>Disjunct</u> case: and further, if you please, that the initials of Radius and Sine, which are to be used together, are Alphabetical consecutives.

L[d] Napier's rule may also be used for the solution of Oblique Spherical triangles. for this purpose a perpendicular must be let fall from an angle of the given triangle internally on the base, forming it into 2. right angled triangles, one of which may contain 2. of the data. or, if this cannot be done, then letting it fall externally on the prolongation of the base, so as to form a right angled triangle comprehending the oblique one, wherein 2. of the data will be common to both. to secure 2. of the data from mutilation this perpendicular must always be let fall from the end of a given side, and opposite to a given angle.

But there will remain yet 2. cases wherein L$^d$ Napier's rule cannot be used, to wit, where all the sides, or all the angles, alone, are given. to meet these 2. cases, L$^d$ Buchan & D$^r$ Minto devised an analogous rule. they considered the sides themselves, and the Supplements of the angles as Circular parts in these cases; and, dropping a perpendicular from any angle from which it would fall internally on the opposite side, they assumed that angle, or that side, as the Middle part, and the other angles, or other sides, as the Opposite or[4] Extreme parts, disjunct in both cases.          then 'the rectangle under the tangents of $\frac{1}{2}$ the sum, and $\frac{1}{2}$ the difference of the Segments of the Middle part is equal to the rectangle under the tangents of $\frac{1}{2}$ the sums & $\frac{1}{2}$ the difference of the Opposite parts.'

And, since every plane triangle may be considered as described on the surface of a sphere of an infinite radius, these 2. rules may be applied to plane right angled triangles, and, through them, to the Oblique. but as L$^d$ Napier's rule gives a direct solution only in the case of 2. sides and an uncomprised angle, 1. 2. or 3. operations, with this combination of parts, may be necessary to get at that required.

You likewise requested,[5] for the use of your school, an explanation of a method of platting the courses of a survey which I mentioned to you as of my own practice. this is so obvious and simple, that as it occurred to myself, so I presume it has to others, altho' I have not seen it stated in any of the books. for drawing parallel lines, I use the triangular rule, the hypothenusal side of which being applied to the side of a common strait rule, the triangle slides on that, as thus always parallel to itself. instead of drawing meridians on his paper let the pupil draw a parallel of latitude, or East and West line, and note in that a point for his 1$^{st}$ station. then applying to it his protractor, lay off the 1$^{st}$ course and distance in the usual way to ascertain his 2$^d$ station.

—for the 2$^d$ course, lay the triangular rule to the E. and W. line, or 1$^{st}$ parallel, holding the strait- or guide-rule[6] firmly against it's hypothenusal side. then slide up the triangle (for a Northernly course) to the point of his 2$^d$ station, and pressing it firmly there, lay the protractor to that, and mark off the 2$^d$ course and distance as before, for the 3$^d$ station.

—then lay the triangle to the 1$^{st}$ parallel again, and sliding it as before to the point of the 3$^d$ station, there apply to it the protractor for the 3$^d$ course & distance, which gives the 4$^{th}$ station: and so on.     Where a course is Southwardly, lay the protractor as before to the Northern edge of the triangle but prick it's reversed course, which reversed again in drawing, gives the true course. when the station has got so far from the 1st parallel as to be out of the reach of the parallel rule sliding on it's hypothenuse[7] another parallel must be drawn[8] by laying the edge, or longer leg of the triangle to the 1st parallel as before, applying the guide-rule to the end, or short leg (instead of the hypothenuse) as in the margin, & sliding the triangle up to the point for the new parallel.—I have found this in practice the quickest and most correct method of platting which I have ever tried, and the neatest also, because it disfigures the paper with the fewest unnecessary lines.

If these Mathematical trifles can give any facilities to your pupils, they may in their hands become matters of use, as in mine they have been of amusement only. ever and respectfully yours

Th: Jefferson

PoC (DLC); at foot of first page: "Mr Girardin." Tr (ViU: GT); posthumous copy.

The edition of Christian von Wolff's *Cours de Mathématique* owned by TJ was translated by Antoine Joseph Pernety and Jean François de Brézillac, both members of the CONGREGATION OF St MAUR (Paris, 1747; Sowerby, no. 3682). TJ also cited John POTTER, *A System of Practical Mathematics* (London, 1759; Sowerby, no. 3667); Robert SIMSON's *The Elements of Euclid* (Glasgow, 1756; Sowerby, no. 3702); and Charles HUTTON, *A Course of Mathematics* (New York, 1812; Sowerby, no. 3683) and *A Mathematical and Philosophical Dictionary* (London, 1795; Sowerby, no. 3684).

David Steuart Erskine, 11th Earl of BUCHAN, and Walter MINTO discussed their analogous rule in *An Account of the Life, Writings, and Inventions of John Napier, of Merchiston* (Perth, 1787), 99.

[1] Tr: "Simons's."
[2] Tr: "our."
[3] Letter from this point to end of paragraph concluding with "to get at that required" is either based on or the basis for TJ's Notes on Napier's Theorem, [ca. 18 Mar. 1814].
[4] Preceding two words interlined.
[5] Tr: "request."
[6] Reworked from "strait rule."
[7] Preceding four words interlined.
[8] Remainder of sentence interlined.

# Notes on Napier's Theorem

[ca. 18 Mar. 1814]

Ld Nepier's Catholic rule for solving Spherical rt angled triangles.
He noted first the parts, or elements of a triangle, to wit, the sides and angles, and, expunging from these the right angle, as if it were a non existence, he considered the other 5. parts, to wit, the 3. sides, & 2. oblique angles, as arranged in a circle, and therefore called them the Circular parts; but chose (for simplifying the result) instead of

the hypothenuse, & 2. oblique angles themselves, to substitute their complements: so that his 5. circular parts are the 2. legs themselves, & the Complements of the hypothenuse, & of the 2. oblique angles. if the 3. of these, given & required, were all adjacent, he called it the case of Conjunct parts, the middle element the <u>Middle part</u>, & the 2. others the Extremes conjunct with the middle, or Extremes Conjunct: but if one of the parts employed was separated from the others by the intervention of the parts unemployed, he called it the case of Disjunct parts, the insulated, or opposite part, the Middle part, and the 2. others the Extremes Disjunct from the middle, or Extremes Disjunct. he then laid down his Catholic rule, to wit, 'the rectangle of the Radius, & Sine of the Middle part, is equal to the rectangle of the Tangents of the 2. $\begin{bmatrix}\text{adjacent parts}\\\text{Extremes Conjunct}\end{bmatrix}$ and to that of the Cosines of the 2. $\begin{bmatrix}\text{opposite parts}\\\text{Extremes Disjunct.'}\end{bmatrix}$ or R. $\times$ Si. Mid. part $= \Box$ Tang. of the 2 $\begin{bmatrix}\text{adjacent parts}\\\text{Extr. Conj.}\end{bmatrix} = \Box$ of Cos. of 2. $\begin{bmatrix}\text{opposite parts}\\\text{Extr. Disjunct.}\end{bmatrix}$

In applying the Catholic rule, instead of using literally the Sine of a Complement, seek at once the Cosine; for the Tangent of a Complement, seek the Cotangent, and for the Cos. of a complement, use the Sine of the same side or angle.

And to fix this rule artificially in the memory, it is observable that the 1$^{st}$ letter of <u>A</u>djacent parts is the 2$^d$ of the word T<u>a</u>ngents to be used with them; & that the 1$^{st}$ letter of <u>O</u>pposite parts is the 2$^d$ of C<u>o</u>sines, to be used with them: and further, that the initials of <u>R</u>ad. and <u>S</u>ine, which are to be used together, are consecutive in the alphabetical order.

L$^d$ Napier's rule may also be used for the solution of Oblique spherical triangles. for this purpose a perpendicular must be let fall from an angle of the given triangle, internally, on the base, forming it into two right angled triangles, one of which may contain 2. of the data. or, if this cannot be done, then letting it fall externally on the prolongation of the base, so as to form a right angled triangle, comprehending the oblique one, wherein 2. of the data will be common to both. to secure 2. of the data from mutilation this perpendicular must always be let fall from the end of a given side, & opposite to a given[1] ∠. and if the sides, or angles adjacent to the base be of the same character, i.e. both of 90° or of less, or more, it will fall on the base internally: if otherwise, externally.

The sides and angles are of the same, or different characters under the following circumstances. 1. in a r$^t$ angled triangle the angles adjacent to the hypoth. are of the same character each as it's opposite leg. 2. in a r$^t$ angled $\triangle$ if the hypoth. is of less than 90° the legs & angles will be of the same character; if of more, different. 3. in a r$^t$ angled $\triangle$ if a leg or angle be of less than 90° the other & the hypoth. are of the same character; if more, different. 4. in every spherical $\triangle$, the longest side & greatest angle are opposite: & the shortest side and least angle.

But there will remain yet 2 cases wherein L$^d$ Napier's rule cannot be used, to wit, where all the sides, or all the angles alone are given. to meet these 2 cases, L$^d$ Buchan & D$^r$ Minto devised an analogous rule. they considered the sides themselves, & the supplements of the angles as Circular parts in these cases, & dropping a perpendicular from any $\angle$ from which it would fall internally on the opposite side, they assumed that $\angle$ or that side as the middle part, & the other $\angle^s$ or other sides as the opposite, or Extreme parts, disjunct in both cases. then the rectangle under the Tangents of $\frac{1}{2}$ the Sum, & $\frac{1}{2}$ the Difference of the segments of the middle part, = the $\square$ under the Tangents of $\frac{1}{2}$ the sums, & $\frac{1}{2}$ the difference of the Opposite parts.

Corollary. since every plane $\triangle$ may be considered as described on the surface of a sphere of an infinite radius, these 2. rules may be applied to plane r$^t$ angled $\triangle^s$ & thro' them to the Oblique: but as L$^d$ Napier's rule gives a direct solution only in the case of 2. sides & an uncomprised $\angle$. 1. 2. or 3. operations, with this combination of parts, may be necessary to get at that required.

In using the analogous rule, when unknown segments of an $\angle$ or base are to be subtracted the one from the other, the greatest segment is that adjacent to the longest side, or to the least angle at the base.

MS (NjVHi); entirely in TJ's hand; undated, with conjectural date based on identical or similar language in TJ to Louis H. Girardin, 18 Mar. 1814; all brackets beneath dateline in original.

John Napier of Merchiston (1550–1617), mathematician, was a minor Scottish nobleman with a deep interest in millennialism. He wrote important arithmetical and algebraic treatises, developed concrete aids to calculations, and won lasting fame as the inventor of logarithms (*DSB*; *ODNB*). Napier developed his analogies for the solution of right-angled spherical triangles in book 2, chapter 4 of his *Mirifici Logarithmorum Canonis descriptio* (Edinburgh, 1614), 30–9, published in English as *A Description of the Admirable Table of Logarithmes* (London, 1616; trans. Edward Wright), 43–57.

[1] Manuscript: "gven."

# To James Barbour

DEAR SIR                                        Monticello Mar. 20. 14.

M[r] Thomas Clark of Philadelphia, author of the Naval history of the US. published not long since, has extended his views to a general history of the US. in order to furnish himself with materials he proposes to visit the several seats of the government of the separate states, in the hope of being permitted to collect in their depositories of records such materials as may contribute to his object. as Richmond is one of those depositories I have taken the liberty of recommending him to your patronage and good offices in procuring for him access to such public papers as you may think may be laid open to him. and indeed I presume there are none relating to public[1] history which may not; for in a time of peace we can have little occasion for secrecy. the aid and attentions you may favor him with will be acknoleged as additional claims to those sentiments of high respect and esteem of which I have the honor of repeating to you sincere assurances.                                        TH: JEFFERSON

PoC (DLC); at foot of text: "His Excellency Governor Barbour"; endorsed by TJ. Enclosed in TJ to Thomas Clark, 20 Mar. 1814.

[1] TJ here canceled "off."


# To Thomas Clark

SIR                                        Monticello Mar. 20. 14.

Your favor of the 7th is duly recieved, and I now, according to your request, inclose you a letter to Govern[r] Barbour from whom I am persuaded you will recieve every aid and facility in his power towards the furthering your object. at the same time I fear that the destruction of our records by the British during the war, not only at all the County courthouses they could visit, but at the seat of government also, has left little which may be useful to you.          I would gladly use the papers you have sent me for subscriptions to your work, but that I go so little from home as to have no opportunities of circulating them. our neighborhood too (for I live among the mountains) consists almost wholly of farmers, who seldom buy books, and never perhaps till they see them, & can judge for themselves. if I can get a friend in Richmond to recieve & dispose of them, it will be the best means which are in my power of rendering you the services which I would wish to do. Accept the assurance of my great esteem and respect. Th: JEFFERSON

PoC (DLC); at foot of text: "Mʳ Thomas Clark"; endorsed by TJ. Enclosure: TJ to James Barbour, 20 Mar. 1814.

# From Thomas Cooper

DEAR SIR                                    Carlisle March 20 1814

I am much obliged by your two Letters, and instructed by the legal suggestions they contain. I never knew the origin of Christianity becoming parcel of the Laws of England before. I see the Judges of New York state are determined to engraft the Christian code with their State Code; but I hope some event will take place to bring this imposition into discussion. There is in America a strange mixture of theoretical tolerance, and practical bigotry. A generation or two must die off, before things are set right.

I have Bracton, but not Fleta. I am fully aware of the utility of such a book as you propose, but let it be ever so well written, who would buy it?

This is a consideration, necessary 1ˢᵗ to the public utility of a book: and 2ˡʸ what is to me of no small consequence, to its private utility. Whatever book I write, must have two qualities, it must benefit my reputation, and benefit my pocket. For, I _must_ subsist my family by literary exertion: my income as a chemical professor here, does not afford me half maintenance.

I issued proposals, or rather for about two years, I have continued to issue proposals for what I deem a very useful work; namely a compilation of all such British reports (at full length) as bear upon the Law of our own country, with notes and references to home decisions: Leaving out, by the cases, corporation cases, franchise cases, pauper cases, bankrupt cases, cases of practice &c which must depend upon the wording of our Laws at home: I could by this means condense the body of reporters into little more than a third of the space. But I can find no Law bookseller to undertake it. Of my introductory lecture there has not been ante enough to pay the printer and paper maker, two thirds of their demands. so that however glad I should be to contribute to the Stock of public information, I must combine it if

I can, with private emolument. But, many an enterprize of great pith
and moment

 with this regard its current turns away
 losing the name of action.

In the last number of the present volume of the Emporium (now
printed) I have adopted your suggestion, and given a summary of the
Law of patents with proposals for a new system. If any amelioration
occurs, pray let me have the benefit of your opinion, and I will reconsider the subject in my next number. Also, it w^d contribute to the improvement of the work and to all my views connected with it, if you
would have the goodness to point out to me when you have leisure to
look over it, any thing in the conduct of the work, that appears ex-
ceptionable, or that would contribute to its utility, or to extend its
sale. I hope by the time I have done with it, to make it the Repository
for information on the manufacturing subjec[ts?] treated in it. I have
this at heart; but I fear the sale will not continue to support the work,
till I have exhausted my collections and my plans.

 M^r Ogilvie, who I find was for some time your neighbour, spent a
week here. I was greatly pleased with his talent and his manners; but
the political complexion of this place did not suit him, nor he the people. There is, both here and in Baltimore, a general, unspecific ki[nd
of?] rumour operating against him, about the bad tendency of his
principles; what is meant, I could never ascertain; but I suspect he
must have been, in the warmth of youthful research, too unguarded
in his religious expressions.[1] Northward of Virginia at least, this is a
crime of deep dye: and though the writ be obsolete, the spirit of burning heretics, religious or political, is not. It is here as else where, the
strongest among those who know the least, and feel the least, and
care the least about religion of any sect or kind. Prudential motives
have kept locked up a manuscript of mine, for these fourteen years,
and will induce me one day or other to commit it to the fire. I really
have not yet made up my mind, whether it be not in the order, and
conformable to the will of providence, that for some centuries at least
to come, men shoul[d] be deceived by frauds and lies: and whether
these be not necessary to keep them in good order, and whether a
sudden blaze of truth would not do as much harm to the mass of
mankind, as sudden emancipation to the negroes. I fear too, that experience will too well justify the comparison of the public to an Ass,
kicking at any one who attempts to ease him of his Burthens. If there
were not an habitual pleasure attached to the act of doing good, independant of all regard[2] for the persons to whom you do it, very little

would be done. I should say with the worldly-wise,[3] si populus vult decipi, decipiatur.

I see the allied powers are entering France. I am glad of it. You do not like Buonaparte; nor I. But I am satisfied, a much stronger case might be [m]ade out in his defence for these last twenty years, than theirs. I sincerely [h]ope, they may be cut up, and quarrel among themselves.

I am grossly mistaken, if Russia does not again mean to become the head of an armed neutrality: which God grant. Adieu. Believe me with great respect and sincerity, your obliged friend.

THOMAS COOPER

RC (DLC); edge trimmed and chipped; endorsed by TJ as received 9 Apr. 1814 and so recorded in SJL.

MANY AN ENTERPRIZE . . . NAME OF ACTION is paraphrased slightly from William Shakespeare, *Hamlet,* act 3, scene 1, and substitutes "away" for "awry." Cooper's SUMMARY, "On Patents. By The Editor," appeared in the *Emporium of Arts and Sciences* 2 (Apr. 1814): 431–55. SI POPULUS VULT DECIPI, DECIPIATUR: "if the people wish to be deceived, let them be deceived."

[1] Word interlined in place of "opinions."
[2] Manuscript: "rgard."
[3] Manuscript: "wordly-wise."

# To Nicolas G. Dufief

SIR                                  Monticello Mar. 20. 14.

I possess the Abbé Auger's translations of Demosthenes, Aeschines, Isocrates, and the Minor orators in 9.v. 8$^{vo}$ but he published also a translation of Lysias in a single vol. which I have not. can you help me to it? it is some time since I have squared accounts with you. be so good as to send me a note of what I am in your debt and it shall be remitted immediately. I must still request you to keep in mind my former unsatisfied commissions. the book on brewing from Indian corn, particularly, if yet published will be acceptable. I salute you with esteem and respect.          TH: JEFFERSON

PoC (DLC); at foot of text: "M. Dufief"; endorsed by TJ.

# To Samuel Pleasants

SIR                                    Monticello Mar. 20. 14.

To compleat my collection of the latter Sessions acts I need those of the sessions which commenced in

Dec. 1809.

Dec. 1812.[1]

Dec. 1813. will you be so good as to furnish me with them by the stage, adding to the packet one of Hopkins's razor straps, without a drawer or any thing but the strap.

I subscribed for a doz. copies of miss Lomax's poems. be so good as to send me a single copy, and to keep the rest for sale for her benefit, drawing at the same time the price of the 12. for her use from mr Gibson with that of the other articles above requested. Accept assurances of my esteem and respect                        TH: JEFFERSON

PoC (MHi); at foot of text: "Mr Pleasants"; endorsed by TJ.

[1] TJ placed a check mark in the left margin next to preceding two words, presumably after receiving Pleasants's 26 Mar. 1814 reply.

# From Isaac A. Coles

DR SIR,                                Enniscorthy. 21st mar 1814

I have at length been able to steal a few days from my duty in Staunton to spend with my frnds here, & since my arrival have been examining the Deer & find there are three Does and a Buck that can very conveniently be spared. I have ordered a pen to be made in which they shall be fed, & in which it will hereafter be easy to secure them whenever it may be convenient for you to send for them—If the waggon cld bring me a few small Chub. I shld consider it a great favor—with

sincere & respectful Attachmt—yrs                        I. A. COLES

RC (DLC); addressed: "Thomas Jefferson Monticello"; endorsed by TJ as received 22 Mar. 1814 and so recorded in SJL.

On 1 June 1814 TJ had A BUCK and a doe from Enniscorthy put into "the Paddock inclosing the brick yard" (Betts, *Garden Book*, 525).

# To John Barnes

Dear Sir            Monticello Mar. 22. 14.

Your favor of the 8<sup>th</sup> is recieved and I now return you mr Taylor's letter, but so unacquainted am I with every thing relating to stock that I am not able to calculate the effect of converting G<sup>l</sup> K's bank shares into public stock, altho you have furnished me materials. I must therefore trouble you again to make out for me 2. statements, the 1<sup>st</sup> stating the market value of his principal in the Pensylvania bank, and the average annual nett[1] sum recieved on it including every thing & deducting costs; and 2<sup>dly</sup> what that principal sum converted into the new loan with the addition of the bonus, will amount to, and what nett sum he will recieve on that annually? from these two statements I shall be enabled to judge what to do.     I trouble you with a little[2] commission for me with Gen<sup>l</sup> Armstrong; and as it may be necessary to shew him my letter explaining it, I have written it separately from this. you will percieve that in it I ask you to refund to him a sum of 40. francs, about 8. or 10.D. paid for me in Paris in 1810, with any little additions attending it[3] which I will replace to you in a remittance I have to make shortly to your place. be so good as to return me the French letter inclosed in that after shewing it to the General. ever & affectionately yours

Th: Jefferson

PoC (DLC); at foot of text: "M<sup>r</sup> John Barnes"; endorsed by TJ. Enclosure not found.

[1] Word interlined.
[2] Word interlined.
[3] Remainder of sentence interlined.

G<sup>l</sup> K: Tadeusz Kosciuszko.

# To John Barnes

Dear Sir            Monticello Mar. 22. 14.

In August last I recieved from mr Rembrandt Peale 2. or 3. pieces of Agate which had been purchased for me, by some person in France, who says I desired him to purchase them while I was resident in France. I have totally forgotten it, & his name subscribed in his letter to me (now inclos<sup>d</sup>)[1] being in illegible characters, I am unable to make out who it was who[2] after so long an interval was so kind as to think of me, altho' I had so long ago left the country. but he called on Gen<sup>l</sup> Armstrong, left the articles with him, and he writes me that the General was so kind as to reimburse him their cost, which was 40.

francs. this last circumstance is that alone which occasions my troubling you at present. it is to ask the favor of you to call on the General and refund to him whatever the amount is in our money, and to return him in my name a thousand cordial thanks for this kindness. the delay needs explanation. the articles were sent by the Gen¹ in a box of books to the Pensylva Academy of fine arts in which they remained unnoticed, when mr R. Peale discovered & forwarded them to me. Gen¹ Armstrong's absence at the time on the frontiers occasioned my postponing the subject till his return, since which it had escaped my memory. with my respects to him be pleased to accept the assurance of my constant esteem.     TH: JEFFERSON

PoC (CSmH: JF); at foot of text: "M<sup>r</sup> John Barnes"; endorsed by TJ. Enclosure: Claude Antoine Prieur Duvernois to TJ, 5 Sept. 1810.

[1] Parenthetical phrase added in margins.

[2] In margin TJ here added "Prieur?"

# From Charles Burrall

DEAR SIR,       Baltimore March 22<sup>d</sup> 1814.

I have the honor to acknowledge the receipt of your letter of the 16<sup>th</sup> Ins<sup>t</sup> and to assure you that although the favorable sentiments you have expressed of my character and conduct, would at all times have been highly gratifying to my feelings, yet that they are peculiarly so at this period, when I have been so unjustly assailed; and indeed Sir, that I want language to express to you, the gratitude I feel for the friendship you have manifested towards me, by bearing testimony to the President of my claim to the patronage and support of the present administration.

With best wishes for your health and happiness, I beg you Sir, to believe that it will ever be one of the first objects of my desire, to preserve your good opinion, by discharging with zeal and fidelity any duties with which I may be entrusted.

I am Dear Sir, with sentiments[1] of the highest respect and esteem, Your Obd<sup>t</sup> Servant     CHA<sup>S</sup> BURRALL

RC (DLC); at foot of text: "The Hon-b<sup>le</sup> Thomas Jefferson"; endorsed by TJ as received 26 Mar. 1814 and so recorded in SJL.

[1] Manuscript: "sentments."

# From David Gelston

DEAR SIR,                                    New York March 22ᵈ 1814.

I do my self the pleasure, to enclose to you a few pumpkin seeds, which were taken from one raised in my garden the last summer, that weighed 226ˡᵇˢ—from two seeds, the weight of seven raised, was upwards of 1000ˡᵇˢ—

It is said, for feeding cows, nothing equals them—if they should prove to be of any advantage to you, or, afford you either amusement or satisfaction, I shall be gratified,

with great regard, I am—Dear Sir, your obedient servant,

DAVID GELSTON

RC (MHi); at foot of text: "Thomas Jefferson esquire"; endorsed by TJ as received 2 Apr. 1814 and so recorded in SJL.

# To Patrick Gibson

DEAR SIR                                    Monticello Mar. 22. 14.

Your's of Mar. 2. with the 100.D. inclosed had been duly recieved and that of the 13ᵗʰ is now at hand. I inclose you the [two notes?] for renewal for the 6ᵗʰ of May & 8ᵗʰ of July, ready signed. I some time ago pressed my manager in Bedford to send off immediately the little tobᵒ I have there (about 5. M̶) and am in hopes it is with you by this time. they had strong charges to spare no pains in the handling, and being made on new lands of 1ˢᵗ quality I hope it will bring a just price. there being no reason to hold that up, I wish you to sell it immediately on the best terms you can. this is necesary to provide for my corn[1] contracts, & an additional draught of between 3. and 400.D. which I shall have to make in April or May. my flour I should be willing to hold up for the price before noted to you, until May or June, if my corn draughts will admit. for one of these I must now ask the favor of you to remit me by post 275.D. of which about 75.D. may be in 10. & 5.D. bills. the following month of May[2] will call for an equal sum, & June about 100.D. I hope the sales of tobacco and flour between them will keep you in funds. Accept the assurance of my great esteem and respect                    TH: JEFFERSON

PoC (NHi: Thomas Jefferson Papers); two words faint; at foot of text: "Mʳ Gibson"; endorsed by TJ. Enclosures not found.

[1] Word interlined.
[2] Reworked from "the next month."

# From Horatio G. Spafford

ESTEEMED FRIEND—                                 Albany, 3 Mo. 22, 1814.

Highly as I appreciate the favor of thy friendly regards, I can but feel mortified at the length of time that has elapsed Since my last, & often admire at the cause. Sometimes I fear that the latitude allowed to my remarks, has given displeasure; then that, possibly, I asked too much, & I know that it is painful to deny some gratification. If, in any case, I have offended, pray have the goodness to excuse it. I often regret the warmth of my feelings, or rather the want of prudence. But—I never was formed for any policy of design; & at best can never be more than a zealous drudge. It appears, too, that I had formed too high an estimate of my own merits & talents, & I acquiesce in the wisdom of official neglect.

I hope my Gazetteer has duly reached thee, & that it affords thee some information of this section of the Union, which must be a pleasure. I hope, too, that it meets, in some degree, thy approbation. Most devoutly do I wish thee a long continuance of life, health, & happiness in time & eternity. With much esteem & respect, thy friend,

                                         HORATIO GATES SPAFFORD.

RC (MHi); at foot of text: "T. Jefferson, Esq."; endorsed by TJ as received 2 Apr. 1814 and so recorded in SJL.

# The Founding of the University of Virginia: Albemarle Academy, 1803–1816

MINUTES OF THE ALBEMARLE ACADEMY BOARD OF TRUSTEES,

25 MAR. 1814

## EDITORIAL NOTE

On 12 Jan. 1803 the Virginia General Assembly passed "An Act to establish an academy in the county of Albemarle, and for other purposes." Although it never educated a single student, the Albemarle Academy is important because it served as midwife to one of Jefferson's proudest achievements, the founding of the University of Virginia a few miles west of Monticello. The legislature named fourteen trustees, including Jefferson's friends George Divers and Wilson Cary Nicholas, his nephews Dabney Carr and Peter Carr, and his son-in-law Thomas Mann Randolph, and authorized the board thus created to collect subscriptions; hold a lottery or lotteries to raise up to $3,000; purchase land, goods, and chattels; name additional trustees and select officers; and draw up bylaws. However, during the ensuing eleven years nothing was apparently done to bring the school to life.

On 25 Mar. 1814 five of the trustees met in Charlottesville and agreed, with the later concurrence of a sixth, to add thirteen members to the board. The impetus behind the revival of the Albemarle Academy at this particular time has never been satisfactorily explained. Nor has Jefferson's nomination as one of the new trustees been convincingly accounted for. The historian Dumas Malone and others have cast grave doubts on the oft-repeated story that the ex-president was accosted while riding through town and asked, on the spur of the moment, to join in the deliberations. Indeed, no evidence confirms that Jefferson even attended the March 1814 meeting. He did appear on 5 Apr. at the next gathering, where he was appointed, along with the board's newly elected president Peter Carr and three others, to draft the board's rules and regulations and propose ways to raise funds for the institution's establishment and maintenance. On 3 May Jefferson was placed, in his absence, on a committee with Carr and Thomas Mann Randolph to draft a petition to the General Assembly requesting that a portion of the money arising from the sale of the county's Anglican glebe lands be given to the academy. The resulting petition and associated draft legislation went much farther than that, however. Not only did the trustees request an annual appropriation from the state Literary Fund, they asked the legislature to transform the school into a renamed "Central College."

Although Jefferson is recorded as attending only two of the six known meetings of the Albemarle Academy Board of Trustees, the evidence that he was the primary force behind the decision to push for collegiate status is compelling. In 1810 he had postulated that the best way to educate college students was through the creation of an "academical village." Just two months prior to his appointment as trustee, Jefferson wrote his friend Thomas Cooper on 16 Jan. 1814 that he had "long had under contemplation, & been collecting materials for the plan of an university in Virginia . . . this would probably absorb the functions of W$^m$ & Mary college, and transfer them to a healthier and more central position. perhaps to the neighborhood of this place." Late in August 1814 he informed Cooper, in reference to his earlier letter, that "we are about to make an effort for the introduction of this institution." Having been asked by the board to spell out his views, Jefferson sent President Carr on 7 Sept. a detailed description of the courses and professorships necessary for an institution of higher learning. Also about this time, he made preliminary drawings of an academic institution and its component parts. Whether Jefferson joined the board with the idea of transforming Albemarle Academy into Central College or had an epiphany shortly after signing on, by the summer of 1814, at the latest, he was fully behind the attempt to make a reality of the dream that he had expressed to Cooper in January.

The Albemarle Academy board had its last documented meeting on 19 Aug. 1814, but it seems very likely that the members did come together thereafter (perhaps on or around 18 Nov., the date selected for the next gathering) to discuss Jefferson's letter to Carr and approve the petition and proposed legislation being sent to the General Assembly. At some point late in the year Carr forwarded all three documents plus Jefferson's letter to Cooper of 7 Oct. 1814 to David Watson, a delegate from neighboring Louisa County and later a member of the University of Virginia's Board of Visitors, for presentation to the state legislature. As it turned out, Watson failed to do so, because the packet reached him in Richmond late in the legislative session, which had opened on the unusually early date of 10 Oct. Jefferson wrote state senator Joseph C. Cabell early in January 1815 complaining about the delay and enclosing additional copies, but to no avail.

The trustees' petition was finally read in the House of Delegates on 7 Dec. 1815, during its next session. Having been examined by the Committee of Propositions and Grievances and deemed reasonable, the Central College bill was formally introduced on 19 Dec. in the lower house. Albemarle County delegates Thomas W. Maury and Charles Yancey joined Senator Cabell in shepherding it through the legislative process over the next two months. When it passed into law on 14 Feb. 1816, the Albemarle Academy phase ended (*Acts of Assembly*, 1802–03 sess., 23–4; 1815–16 sess., 191–3; Bruce, *University*, 1:121; Malone, *Jefferson*, 6:241–5; Jennings L. Wagoner Jr., *Jefferson and Education* [2004], 78–83, 87, 90, 92; Leonard, *General Assembly*, 277; *JHD*, 1815–16 sess., 23, 38, 56 [7, 14, 19, 20 Dec. 1815]; TJ to the Trustees of the Lottery for East Tennessee College, 6 May 1810; TJ to Cooper, 16 Jan., 25 Aug., 7 Oct. 1814; Minutes of the Albemarle Academy Board of Trustees, 5, 15 Apr., 3 May, 17 June, 19 Aug. 1814; TJ to Carr, 7 Sept. 1814; TJ's Estimate, Elevation, and Plan of Albemarle Academy, Pavilion and Dormitories, [ca. 18 Nov. 1814]; TJ's Draft Bill to Create Central College and Amend the 1796 Public Schools Act, [ca. 18 Nov. 1814]; TJ to Cabell, 5 Jan. 1815; Yancey to TJ, 26 Sept. 1815; Cabell to TJ, 16 Jan. 1816; TJ to Benjamin Henry Latrobe, 3 Aug. 1817).

# Minutes of the Albemarle Academy Board of Trustees

We John Harris John Nicholas, John Kelly, Peter Carr, and John Carr, five of the persons appointed Trustees by the Act of the General Assembly entitled "An act to establish an Accademy in the County of Albemarle and for other purposes," having met at the house of Triplet T Estes, in the town of Charlottesville, for the purpose of taking into consideration the said recited Act, and there not appearing the majority, as required by the s$^d$ Act have agreed, in order to fill such vacancies as have occured by deaths, removals and resignations, to nominate the following Citizens, to wit: Thomas Jefferson, Jonathan B. Carr, Robert B Streshly, James Leitch, Edmund Anderson, Thomas Wells, Nicholas M Lewis, Frank Carr, John Winn, Alexander Garrett, Dabney Minor, Sam$^l$ Carr and Tho$^s$ Jameson, to fill such vacancies, and whenever one other (making a majority) of the Trustees in the said Act named, shall concur therein, they shall be considered as appointed for the purposes of carrying the Said recited Act into execution. And we hereby recommend a general meeting at the house of Triplet T Estes in the town of Charlottesville on the fifth day of the next month.

signed

March 25. 1814.

JOHN HARRIS

JNO: NICHOLAS

JNO: KELLY

PETER CARR

JOHN CARR

I Edward Garland concur in the above nomination

ED. GARLAND

Tr (ViU: TJP-VMJCC). Tr (ViU: TJP-VMJHC). Tr (ViU: TJP-VMJB). Tr (ViU: VMJLC). Tr (PPAmP: VMWCR).

John Nicholas (ca. 1758–1836) was a captain in the Continental army who succeeded his father and namesake as Albemarle County clerk, serving from 1792 to 1815. In the latter year he moved to Buckingham County, although he retained substantial property holdings in Albemarle. A committed Federalist, Nicholas is best known for his role in the Langhorne incident of 1797, in which he accused TJ's nephew Peter Carr of forging a letter to George Washington that unsuccessfully attempted to elicit an undiplomatic response from the president. Nicholas was an active trustee of the Albemarle Academy in 1814. Although TJ privately condemned him in 1811 as a "miserable scribbler," they corresponded amicably in 1819 about Nicholas's efforts to obtain a state pension (*PTJ*, 16:139–45; Manning J. Dauer,

"The Two John Nicholases: Their Relationship to Washington and Jefferson," *American Historical Review* 45 [1940]: 338–53; V. Dennis Golladay, "Jefferson's 'Malignant Neighbor,' John Nicholas, Jr.," *VMHB* 86 [1978]: 306–19; Heitman, *Continental Army*, 413; Woods, *Albemarle*, 289–90, 294, 368; Washington, *Papers, Retirement Ser.*, 1:373–5, 475–7; TJ to James Monroe, 8 Jan. 1811; Nicholas to TJ, [received 9 Nov.], 25 Nov. 1819; TJ to Nicholas, 10, 28 Nov. 1819; *Lynchburg Virginian*, 12 May 1836).

John Carr was admitted to the bar in 1783 and subsequently served as deputy clerk of Albemarle County. He was clerk of the Albemarle County District Court, 1805–19, and first clerk of the Circuit Court of Albemarle, 1809–19 (*PTJ*, 28:477, 31:84; Edson I. Carr, *The Carr Family Records* [1894], 73, 111; Woods, *Albemarle*, 159, 380; *MB*; Frederick Johnston, *Memorials of Old Virginia Clerks* [1888], 24, 32).

Edward Garland (d. 1817) rose from lieutenant in the 1st Virginia Regiment to captain in the 14th Virginia Regiment of the Continental army, 1775–77, and served as an adjutant in the militia during the War of 1812. He acted as a sheriff in the 1790s, became a county magistrate in 1801, and represented Albemarle County in the Virginia House of Delegates, 1800–04. He left an estate with personal property valued at $7,334.25, including seventeen slaves (Woods, *Albemarle*, 199, 364, 372; Heitman, *Continental Army*, 243; DNA: RG 15, RWP; *MB*, 2:931, 993, 1006; Leonard, *General Assembly*, 219, 223, 227, 231; Charles Yancey to TJ, 22 Aug. 1814; Albemarle Co. Will Book, 6:206–7, 318–20).

# From Thomas Jefferson Randolph

MY DEAR GRANDFATHER        Carys-brook March 25 1814

M$^r$ Cary is unfortunately from home; I have ordered Phil to wait and have left a message for him with his wife. I am afraid there is little prospect of getting him:[1]

your sincerely affectionate grandson       TH: J. RANDOLPH

RC (ViU: TJP-ER); endorsed by TJ as received 26 Mar. 1814.

[1] Randolph here canceled "Will you sign my bond," preceded by extra space.

# From Patrick Gibson

SIR        Richmond 26$^{th}$ March 1814

I have received your favor of the 22$^{nd}$ with the two notes inclosed, and now send you as you request Two hundred and seventy five dollars in bank notes—With great respect I am

Sir Your ob$^t$ Serv$^t$       PATRICK GIBSON

RC (ViU: TJP-ER); between dateline and salutation: "Thomas Jefferson Esquire"; endorsed by TJ as a letter from Gibson. Recorded in SJL as a letter from Gibson & Jefferson received 31 Mar. 1814.

# To George Frederick Augustus Hauto

SIR        Monticello Mar. 26. 14.

Your letter of the 7$^{th}$ has been duly recieved with the plate therein inclosed describing your hydraulic engine on which you are pleased to ask my opinion. it's combinations are full of ingenuity, and especially that for converting a rectilineal into a rotatory motion without the great loss of force occasioned by the ordinary means of a crank.

but long experience and multiplied disappointments have taught me to be cautious in pronouncing on the effect of a new mechanical invention, from it's theory only. there are so many circumstances which theory does not embrace, and which still affect the execution that nothing but the actual trial of the machine itself at large can assure us of it's effect. I confess too that in the present case I do not see the benefit derived from the interposition of the rack work between the stroke of the water, and the spur wheel intended to be the first mover of whatever machinery is applied to it: why the water should be made to give a direct motion first, to be converted afterwards by machinery into a rotatory one, rather than let the same quantity of water from the same height strike at once a bucket in the periphery of the fly wheel, and give thus the same rotatory motion, without the intervention and consequent friction of any machinery. however I must say that I have but little studied this machine. I am out of the habit of these studies, and disposed at present to lighter attentions only. but you have the machine itself in action at German town. you have in Philadelphia mathematicians and mechanics of the first order in the US. their examination and report of the effects they see must silence all the doubts & questions arising from a mere view of a paper drawing. wishing you therefore every success which your time & ingenuity may be found to have justly merited I add the assurances of my respect. Th: Jefferson

PoC (DLC); at foot of text: "Mr Geo. Fred. Augs Hauto"; endorsed by TJ.

# To James Madison

Dear Sir                                  Monticello Mar. 26. 14.

The inclosed from Dr Brown is this moment come to hand, and supposing it may possibly be of some importance I send it off immediately to the post office on the bare possibility it may get there in time for the mail of this morning. if it fails it will have to wait there 4. days longer. ever affectly yours              Th: Jefferson

PoC (MHi); at foot of text: "The Pres. US."; endorsed by TJ.

The INCLOSED letter, Samuel Brown to TJ, 22 Feb. 1814, not found, is recorded in SJL as received 26 Mar. 1814 from Natchez.

# From James J. Pleasants
## (for Samuel Pleasants)

SIR                      Richmond March 26th 1814
Agreeably to your request I have sent by the stage, such of the articles ordered in your letter of 20th inst as could be procured. The sessions acts of 1809, are not to be had in this place
     Respectfully yrs.               SAMUEL PLEASANTS
                               By J. J. PLEASANTS

Thos Jefferson Esqr
Bot of S. Pleasants

| | |
|---|---|
| 1[1] Sessions acts 1812 | $ 1.00 |
| 12 Copies Miss Lomax's poems @ 50 cts | 6.00 |
| 1 Copy "The[2] Book" | 1.12½ |
| 1 Hopkins Razor Strop | 2.50 |
| | $10.62½ |

ps. Sessions acts of 1813 not yet done. so soon as they are a Copy shall be sent

RC (MHi); in James J. Pleasants's hand; endorsed by TJ as a letter from Samuel Pleasants received 2 Apr. 1814 and so recorded in SJL.

James Jay Pleasants (1797–1849) was a native of Hanover County. He worked in the Richmond printing- and bookshop of his uncle Samuel Pleasants before moving to Alabama, where he served as secretary of state, 1821–24. Pleasants was later a member of the New Orleans cotton firm of Martin, Pleasants & Company. He died in Huntsville, Alabama (Thomas McAdory Owen, *History of Alabama and Dictionary of Alabama Biography* [1921],

4:1372; Norma Carter Miller and George Lane Miller, *Pleasants and Allied Families: an historical genealogy of the descendants of John Pleasants (1644/5–1698) of Henrico County, Virginia* [1980], 227, 229, 231; *Richmond Enquirer*, 13 Nov. 1821, 24 Sept. 1824; Huntsville *Democrat*, 22, 29 Aug. 1849).

A letter of 20 July 1814 from Samuel Pleasants to TJ, not found, is recorded in SJL as received 22 July 1814 from Richmond.

[1] Reworked from "2."
[2] Omitted opening quotation mark editorially supplied.

# To William Short

Dear Sir                              Monticello Mar. 26. 14.

In my letter of Feb. 23. I desired you to send me mr Higgin-botham's rent-note, as well as his bond. but the bond happened to be on the way at the time, and expecting that on the reciept of my letter you would send on the rent note also, I kept up the bond to deliver both together. two days ago however I recieved the inclosed note from mr Higgenbotham, by which it appears the rent is paid. I send him his bond now therefore, with a promise of the rent-note as soon as you can forward it in compliance with this.

I was sorry to recieve from Col⁰ Monroe a letter in answer to mine, in which is the following paragraph. 'Mʳ Carter entirely misunder-stood the import of my letter to him, relative to the mode in which the settlement of the interfering claims between mr Short and me would affect mr Short. I stated to mr Carter that, let it be settled as it might, he would have to pay the sum given for the land only, with interest on it, according to my opinion. by this I meant that if I recovered of mr Short, he would only recover of mr Carter that sum, and not the price at which he sold the land to mr Higinbotham. if mr Short recovers of me, I can have no claim against mr Carter. the decision in mr Short's favor could only be on the principle that the boundary of my land, which was purchased first, had been correctly traced in my absence, in designating that sold to mr Short after-wards. if mr Short loses the small strip in dispute between us, he having purchased by a defined boundary has a claim on mr Carter for it. that will, I am informed, by those in practice, be settled on the principle above stated; except that as he may be considered as hav-ing had possession till I gave notice of my claim, he cannot recover interest during that period.' he then promises to procure a meeting of mr Carter and himself, to chuse arbitrators here and end the matter; to which I will certainly give every aid and urgency in my power. he is certainly mistaken in supposing you to be in possession until he notified his claim. the rule of law is unquestionable that where two coterminous tenants claim both a particular space of ground, the law always considers him in the actual possession in whom the property shall be ultimately found to be: hence the act of limitation never runs between two such tenants. and the fact is that he has been as much in the actual possession as you, neither having cultivated or inclosed it. ever and affectionately yours

Th: Jefferson

RC (ViW: TJP); endorsed by Short as received 2 Apr. 1814.

The INCLOSED NOTE from David Higginbotham is not recorded in SJL and has not been found.

SJL records a missing 15 Apr. 1814 letter from Higginbotham, received from Milton the same day. A 2 Apr. 1814 letter from Short to TJ, not found, is recorded in SJL as received 15 Apr. from Philadelphia and described by Short in his epistolary record as: "Jeffn. inclose Higginbotham assumpsit of rent" (DLC: Short Papers; abstract in Short's hand from a portion of his epistolary record containing entries of July 1813 to June 1814, written on a half sheet folded to form narrow pages).

# From Benjamin Galloway

SIR,        Hagers Town Washington County M—d March 30. —14—

I was at M$^r$ Secretary Munroe's house in the city of washington a few weeks since, when I mentioned to him my wish to pay you a visit at Monticello in the months of May or June next: M$^r$ M observed, that Congress would probably adjourn about the middle of April; and that if no business of importance more than he foresaw, should demand his immediate attention, he intended with M$^{rs}$ Munroe to visit their cottage in the neighbourhood of Monticello in a few weeks after the termination of the session; and signified a desire, that I would postpone my contemplated visit to you, untill he might have it in his power to entertain me at the Cottage. In consequence, I promised so to regulate my movements towards Monticello, as to be enabled to spend a day at the Cottage with my good friends in return for the polite attention and hospitality which I have received from them at the City—

Should it not be altogether convenient to receive me at, or about the time above mentioned I beg, Sir, you will so say to me; as it will be equally convenient to me at some other, but not far distant day, to have an opportunity of gratifying a wish which I have long entertained partly to be a beholder of the beauties with which The Heavenly Mountain is represented to abound, but, more especially, to have an opportunity of assuring you Sir, that I am, as a citizen US, with unfeigned gratitude for the many, and important services, which you have rendered to my country

Yrs Respectfully                        BENJAMIN GALLOWAY.

RC (MHi); endorsed by TJ as received 15 Apr. 1814 and so recorded in SJL.

The COTTAGE was James Monroe's Highland estate, near Monticello.

# From Horatio G. Spafford

ESTEEMED FRIEND—                              Albany, 3 Mo. 30, 1814.

Thy very interesting Letter of the 17th instant came duly to hand, & will form a kind of guide to my future life. Those sentiments were my own, except that in relation to the Lawyers, I was not informed of a possible cause, having read very little Law or Lawyers' books. I hope I have an implied permission to show the Letter to some friends, for I have done so already.

Ere this can reach thee, thou wilt have received a late Letter from me, of little other interest than to inform of my curiosity to learn thy opinion of the Gazetteer. In some former Letters, I have acquainted thee that I had never sought for political or official honors, & thou knowest the moderation of my religious, moral & political creeds. Lately, I have written to the new P. M. General to inform him how much I wish to be the Post Master in this City. The present incumbent has held the office many years, (since Pickering was Post-Master General,) has made a large fortune by it, & is independently rich. I have stated these things, as also that $D^r$ Mancius is a worthy man, & keeps a good office, He has a partner, & associate. $D^r$ M. is a Federalist; his partner is any thing, for the times, to save his office. If such a [league?] can perpetuate for 25 or 30 years, why not patent the offices at once? Threats are even thrown out now by the Federalists, that the President dare not remove Dr. Mancius. Rotation in office, is a part of my Republicanism. Would it be too much to ask of thee to aid my wishes in this matter? If thou couldest do so, I should be greatly obliged. If I have not done as much as some others to excite the friendship of a party & its influence, I have not neglected the public interests—I have a large expensive family to support, & my whole fortune is absorbed in my copy-rights. Besides, the distresses among my connexions, principally frontier inhabitants, occasioned by the war, press heavily on me. My Parents, far advanced in years, & my Father a cripple, have been more than a year past driven from their home, dependent on their Sons for support. Two of my own Cousins, active, useful farmers, of Genesee in this state, fell lately in battle at Buffalo—& two of my Brothers are detained in Canada. I had a little property in England, which is detained by the War, & indeed I expect to lose it entirely by the War. How many men find this their opportunity! but I suffer extremely & am overlooked or unattended to. Would I go to England, I have a support there, if not even a fortune; & to my entreaties for permission to draw it thence, I have

[ 273 ]

not even an answer to my Letters, nor any acknowledgement during 6 or 8 months! I pray thee to forgive my importunity, & to interest thyself in my application. Mine is a hard case, & I am very reluctant to ask any thing of the government.

And now—though thou art tired of my Letter, I pass to the main object of it. For a long time I have been engaged in investigations of mechanics—or rather the philosophy of motion, & the powers of moving bodies. Philosophers & Mechanics have failed to perceive one grand consequence of the Laws of motion & moving bodies, which I discovered, to my own satisfaction, about 14 years ago: it will be 14 years in May next. During this long period, I have been busily employed at intervals, on these investigations; & I am very happy to have it in my power to inform thee that I have lately succeeded to complete demonstration. My discovery will prove of vast utility to the poor & midling classes of people; & nothing of the present age will outlive it in fame. I long to see thee, & to show thee what no man hath ever seen but myself—& to receive the coveted boon of thy entire approbation. My discovery rests as yet with myself—& at the moment of receiving thy late Letter, I was meditating a journey to Washington on business, & thence to Monticello, to present first to thee, the greatest discovery of the age in which we live. Slender finances retard my operations, & this only will prevent my purpose, at no distant day, should we both live.        Don't startle at these suggestions;—they are all the sober reflections & facts of a sober & practical mind, not given to speculation, & whose projects have never been deemed visionary by others, nor have they ever deceived me. In my mind's eye, thou art the man, of all others in the world, to whom I would first disclose, a great discovery, hidden hitherto, for purposes which Divine Providence alone can assign. Flattery is far from my present purpose—& so devoutly am I engaged in this wish, that I am this moment in tears, humbly craving the blessing of Heaven upon it. To a man who loves peace as I do, our Patent laws do not afford an inducement to make public so important a discovery & invention—& I want to be governed by thy advice in this matter. Sooner than incur all the evils attendant upon a profitable patent, in this country, I would carry my discovery to a foreign government, & present it to the nation, for a reward which I am Sure would be liberal. On these terms, I would present it to America, recommended by the Man who drew its Declaration of Independence, & in whose mind rest the seeds of all that has kept us Republican to the present day. Secured by his patronage, (& to him alone would I disclose my great secret,) I could with confidence approach the National Councils, & offer to the Nation, for a National indemnity, or a competent reward, a source of incalculable wealth & national honor.

Aware that it is presumption in me to ask so much attention, I offer an apology that will, I hope, be accepted—the greatness & perfect justice of my objects in so doing. To do this, I have long hesitated; & I sincerely regret to give thee so much trouble. Let me still live in thy kind remembrance, & I should be much obliged by knowing that thou wilt attend to these numerous requests: If so, I shall hope to see thee before midsummer, & perhaps within 4 or 5 weeks.

Presuming that thy wishes would be duly respected by the President, & the Post-Master General, I have taken a liberty in soliciting that attention, which, I hope thy goodness will excuse—With very sincere esteem & respect, thy grateful friend,

HORATIO GATES SPAFFORD.

Postscript. Albany, 4 Mo. 7, 1814. I have determined to go for Washington in a few days—probably within ten days or two weeks at most. A part, (& indeed that part is a very considerable one,) of my object, is an intention to submit to thee in person, the mechanical demonstration of my discovery & invention. I shall be governed by thy advice in endeavoring to secure my right, or in rendering it useful to myself & the public. There is such a species of successful piracy operating against useful rights, that I dare not trust to the patent Laws. Pray have the goodness to forward to Washington a Letter, informing if I shall find thee at Monticello, & at what time? My Wife accompanies me as far as Philadelphia, & perhaps to Washington.

I have informed my friends of my intention to see & first submit to thee my mechanical inventions, who all approve of the design, but without knowing what it is. They are all ignorant of it, except that I have long been employed upon it, & without knowing how, or with what success.

With the most sincere esteem & respect,     H. G. SPAFFORD.

RC (MHi); one word illegible; postscript on separate sheet and filed separately at 7 Apr. 1814; at foot of postscript: "Thomas Jefferson, LL.D."; endorsed by TJ on verso of postscript as a letter of 30 Mar. 1814 received 22 Apr. and so recorded in SJL.

The NEW P. M. GENERAL was Return J. Meigs. George W. MANCIUS served as postmaster of Albany, 1792–1814 (Robert J. Stets, *Postmasters & Postoffices of the United States 1782–1811* [1994], 51, 173; Joel Munsell, *Annals of Albany* [1855], 6:105; Joseph Fry, *The Albany Directory, for the year 1814* [1814], 42; Fry, *The Annual Register, and Albany Directory, for the year 1815* [1815], 61).

# From Benjamin Taylor

SIR,                                                    New York, March [30]. 1814.

I take the liberty of annexing a representation of what is considered by myself and others a valuable improvement in Submarine-Explosion as a cheap and just defence against a maritime enemy: an art to which all seamen are hostile and which the people here, generally speaking, regard as diabolical; but which I contemplate as the future & only[1] defence of nations against a naval despotism.

The Exploders described in the annexed half sheet, cannot cost $50. each; but were they to cost much less than $50. it is not in the power of any individual to carry them into execution, as this would require not only the whole of his time, but a stock of at least 500 Exploders. An Establishment (a laboratory, boats, workmen, &c.) is indispensible, & this would demand a capital of $10.000.

On the 18 Jan. last I communicated this improvement with the method of constructing Exploders[2] to M^r Irving, on[e] of our representatives in Congress, that he might lay it before that body, & at the same time shew them, that their act to encourage sub-marine explosion was, in fact, a mockery, and would encourage no-body. On the 5^th Ult° he writes me, "That the naval committee & secretary of the Navy were annoyed with Torpedo projects.—That the only thing that could & would be done, was already done by a law to pay for any property destroyed by their means.—That the Sec. of the Navy declared he could not spare time to read my long letter."

On receipt of this answer from M^r Irving, fearing this improvement might become lost, (I am 53 years of age & in a declining state of health)[3] I sent it, with the same view I now send it to you, most respectable Sir, to "The Mayor of Baltimore," the "First Magistrate of the Port of Norfolk," & to "Commodore Decatur, at New London"; but am, as yet, without notice from any of them.

With great respect I remain, Sir, Your mo. ob^t Serv^t

BENJAMIN TAYLOR.

N° 84 Washington St.

RC (DLC: TJ Papers, 201:35719); edge trimmed, chipped, and torn, with missing day supplied from endorsement; addressed: "The Hon^ble Thomas Jefferson, Monticello, Virginia"; franked; postmarked New York, 1 Apr.; endorsed by TJ as a letter of 30 Mar. 1814 received 15 Apr. 1814 and so recorded in SJL.

Benjamin Taylor (b. ca. 1761), cartographer, was appointed a city surveyor of New York in 1794 and held the position until at least 1815. He operated a circulating library, 1809–11 (*Minutes of the Common Council of the City of New York, 1784–1831* [1917–30], 2:111; *The New-York Directory, and Register for the year 1795* [New York, 1795], 210; *Longworth's New York Directory* [1809], 349; [1811], 287; [1814/15], 274).

[1] Preceding two words interlined.
[2] Preceding six words interlined.
[3] Parenthetical phrase interlined.

# Benjamin Taylor's Annotated Drawings of Underwater Mines

The drawings below represent an improvement in Submarine Explosion for crippling Enemies Ships of War.

Nº 1. Represents a Swimming Exploder to act without the aid of a Time-piece.

**A.** is its float, about 2 feet diameter.

**B.** is the Exploder itself suspended in the water by its float, **A.**

**C.** is a table, its upper side convex, with a concave bed in its centre, to carry a 6 or 8 lb. ball, with a staple cast in it, as seen at a. which is the ball rolled off its bed.

**D.** is a wire, communicating with a Gun-lock in the chamber of the Exploder.—1. 2. 3. are light hoops, to keep the suspending lines and the exploding line clear & apart.

Now, these mechanical arrangements being well understood, it must appear, that when the wire (**D**) is pulled upwards the Gun-lock will be struck; and this is effected by the descent of the ball (**a**) which is kanted off its bed whether the Exploder runs foul of the Ship, or the Ship runs foul of the Exploder.

---

These Exploders are the result of three years of study, & experiments made at a very considerable expence.

---

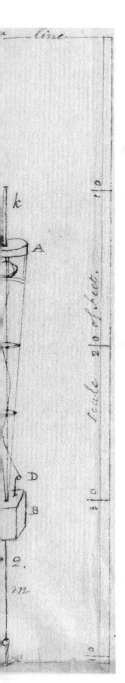

N° 2. Represents a Blockading Exploder.

The letters **A. B. C. D.** and the figures 1. 2. correspond with the same in N° 1. m. is its mooring-line, and k. is its kanting-pole, the top of which is 10 feet below the surface of the water; consequently vessells drawing less than 10 feet may pass over it in safety, while vessells drawing more than 10 feet will strike the kanting-pole, the discharging ball will be rolled off its bed, and an explosion will instantly follow.

The charge of Gunpowder in the Exploder should be always calculated to cripple and not wantonly to destroy the ship: In the former case it would be regarded as an instrument of humanity; but in the latter it would be looked upon, & justly, as an infernal machine. It is conjectured that $\frac{2}{3}^{ds}$ the weight of a 42 lb. shot, or 28 pounds of Gunpowder, will be found sufficient, when properly exploded, to make any ship of war a very leaky vessel; and no good reason can be given, why the charge should be carried any higher than is necessary to put her "hors de combat."

The "Torpedo," when launched & its clock set will explode in a certain <u>time</u>; but it is not known in what <u>place</u>; and it has on this account been hitherto an unprofitable instrument. These Exploders, on the contrary, are always in the right <u>place</u>—the right depth—for doing execution, & their cost is but the tenth part of a "Torpedo."

MS (DLC: TJ Papers, 201:35720); entirely in Taylor's hand; undated.

# From William Cook

SIR          Monticello (Geo) 31ˢᵗ March 1814.

SIR          Monticello (Geo) 31ˢᵗ March 1814.

I have been induced through motives of humanity to investigate the claim of an old revolutionary soldier, who alledges that by the misfortune of losing his papers he has been deprived of a pension formerly allowed him by Government: for a number of years, He is by the name of Benjamin Fry, and informs me that he served in the 14ᵗʰ Virginia Regiment: commanded at that time by Col. Charles Lewis, and that after receiving the wound for which he was considered as entitled to a pension, you drew the pension for him and was the chief instrument in causing him to be provided for in that way, That you drew for him in the year 1778.[1] at which time he lived in Albemarle County, afterwards he removed into Amherst and John Gilmer drew for him the five years immediately subsequent; that if not forgotten he is known to you, his father having lived with yours, perhaps in the capacity of an Overseer or mechanic, I have been thus particular in order to refresh your memory of him—he is now an old man, has a large and needy family, and it will be indeed an Act of humanity and benevolence to assist the old gentleman in obtaining what he has been so unfortunately deprived of, and what he is So justly intitled to, I shall be very thankful if you will write me on this subject giving me all the information in your power, and particular any thing which may serve as a clue to obtain a reestablishment of the lost papers, In writing to a person of your standing Sir upon an Ordinary subject some apology from me would be proper, being wholly unknown to you. But when I am pleading the cause of humanity I know you will lend a willing ear, and give such aid as may be in your power, I am very respectfully

Yʳ Obt servant          WILLIAM COOK

RC (MHi); between dateline and salutation: "The Hon. Thomas Jefferson"; endorsed by TJ as received 27 Apr. 1814 and so recorded in SJL.

William Cook, attorney, served as postmaster of Monticello, Georgia, from about the end of 1809 until at least 1819. He served in the Georgia legislature, 1819–21, and was still living in Monticello when he unsuccessfully applied to become a district attorney in the Florida Territory in 1822 (Robert J. Stets, *Postmasters & Postoffices of the United States 1782–1811* [1994], 111; *Table of Post-offices in the United States, with the Names of the Post-Masters, the Counties and States in which they are situated* [Washington, 1819], 41; Georgia Department of Archives and History, *Georgia's Official Register, 1925*, comp. Ruth Blair [1925], 283; Cook to George R. Gilmer, 7 Dec. 1822 [DNA: RG 59, LAR, 1817–25]; Stephen F. Miller, *The Bench and Bar of Georgia: Memoirs and Sketches* [1858], 2:250; Tad Evans, *Georgia Newspaper Clippings, Jasper County Extracts* [1999–   ], vol. 1).

Benjamin Fry received a PENSION from Virginia beginning in 1778 after losing the use of his arm due to a wound he received at the Battle of Brandywine. By 1813 he was receiving $60 a year from the federal government. As an invalid pensioner Fry was receiving $96 a year in 1818 (*JHD*, 1778 sess., 15 [19 May 1778]; *Letter from the Secretary of War communicating a Transcript of the Pension List of the United States* [Washington, 1813], 44; *Message from the President of the United States, transmitting a Report of the Secretary of War, in Compliance with a Resolution of the Senate, "To cause to be laid before them, a list of all the Pensioners of the United States"* [Washington, 1818], 160).

¹ Reworked from "1779."

# To Benjamin Smith Barton

DEAR SIR                                    Monticello Apr. 3. 14.

At the request of mr Jason Chamberlayne of Burlington in Vermont, a professor of the college there, I inclose for the American Philosophical society a pamphlet presenting a specimen of the language of the Iroquois, among whom he informs me there are many who can read. this however is beginning at the wrong end for the improvement of their faculties and conditions.

the care of domestic animals,

agriculture

the useful houshold arts,

the acquisition of property,

the use of money

arithmatic to estimate it

writing to note it

then reading printed books, & first those of a popular character, and last of all those of religion as distinguished from morality; seems to mark the order of progression which has best succeeded in developing their faculties, enlarging their understandings, and advancing their physical happiness.

I am gratified by every opportunity of renewing to you the assurances of my great esteem and respect.                    TH: JEFFERSON

PoC (DLC); at foot of text: "Doctʳ Benjamin S. Barton one of the V. Presidents of the A. P. Society"; endorsed by TJ. Enclosure: Eleazer Williams, *Good News to the Iroquois Nation: A Tract, on Man's Primitive Rectitude, his Fall, and his Recovery through Jesus Christ* (Burlington, Vt., 1813; with copy at APS inscribed in an unidentified hand: "Specimen of the Iroquois Language 15 April 1814" and "Sent by Mʳ Jefferson Presᵗ of APS From Jason Chamberlayne Burlington Vermᵗ").

At its 15 Apr. 1814 meeting the AMERICAN PHILOSOPHICAL SOCIETY recorded receiving "a specimen, of the Iroquois Language transmitted by Thoˢ Jefferson through hands of D Barton V. P." and "Presented by J. Chamberlayne of Burlington Vermont" (APS, Minutes [MS in PPAmP]).

# To Nicolas G. Dufief

DEAR SIR                                              Monticello Apr. 3. 14.

I wrote to you on the 20th of March, since which I have seen in the Aurora of Mar. 23. an advertisement of Newton's Principia for sale by mr M[c]lure and a reference to your bookstore. if the above work be either in English or French, I will thank you to send me a copy of it. Accept my friendly salutations                    TH: JEFFERSON

PoC (DLC); at foot of text: "M. Dufief"; endorsed by TJ.

# To David Gelston

Monticello Apr. 3. 14.

Th: Jefferson presents his compliments to mr Gelston and his thanks for the pumpkin seed he has been so kind as to send him. he will with pleasure give them a trial; the pumpkin being a plant of which he endeavors every year to raise so many as to maintain all the stock on his farms from the time they come till frost, which is from 2. to 3. months. besides feeding his workhorses, cattle & sheep on them entirely they furnish the principal fattening for the pork slaughtered. a more productive kind will therefore be of value. he is happy in the occasion furnished by this kind remembrance of mr Gelston, of assuring him of the continuance of his great and friendly esteem & respect.

RC (Grace Floyd Delafield Robinson, Greenport, N.Y., 1947); dateline at foot of text; addressed: "David Gelston esq. New York"; franked; endorsed by Gelston. PoC (MHi); endorsed by TJ.

# Minutes of the Albemarle Academy Board of Trustees

Agreeable to the recommendation of the twenty fifth of March last past, on this fifth day of April 1814. appeared at the house of Triplet T Estes, in Charlottesville, Thomas Jefferson, Jonathan B Carr, Robert B Streshly, James Leitch, Edmund Anderson, Tho[s] Wells, Nicholas M Lewis, Frank Carr, John Winn, Alexander Garrett, Peter Carr, Edward Garland, John Kelly, Jno: Nicholas, Rice Garland, Samuel Carr, Thomas Jameson, and John Carr, and the nomination made on the twenty fifth of March last having been duly approved of by Edward Garland, making a majority of the remaining trustees under the Act aforesaid, and thereupon the board of Trustees proceeded to an election of a President and Secretary.

> Peter Carr was elected President and
> John Carr          Secretary.

On motion to designate the place where the proposed establishment shall be made, the decision thereon is postponed until the 15<sup>th</sup> day of the present month.

A committee consisting of the following members to wit: Thomas Jefferson, Peter Carr, Frank Carr, John Nicholas, and Alexander Garrett, were chosen to draft rules and regulations for the government of the board of Trustees.

The same committee are instructed to report to the next meeting, a plan for raising funds for the erection and support of the institution.

And thereupon the board is adjourned, till the 15<sup>th</sup> Inst at the house of Triplet T. Estes.

> Signed
> P. Carr.

Tr (ViU: TJP-VMJCC). Tr (ViU: TJP-VMJHC). Tr (ViU: TJP-VMJB). Tr (ViU: VMJLC). Tr (PPAmP: VMWCR).

# From John Barnes

Dear Sir             George Town Co<sup>a</sup> 5<sup>th</sup> April 1814

The proposition and statem<sup>ts</sup> required is founded on the presumed sale of $8000. Penn<sup>a</sup> Bank Stock, producing 10 pC<sup>t</sup> paid half yearly—(of increasing Value) and Curr<sup>t</sup> price say, 40 pC<sup>t</sup> above par—and if so disposed of[1]—And the Net proceeds invested in the New Loan Certificates—supposed to be Created—at 88 for every 100 dolls, bearing 6 per Cent paid quarterly—If this is Correctly the proposition and statement required—the probable result, would be Nearly—I Apprehend—as follows—Viz—

| | |
|---|---|
| The $8000 Bank Stock made sale of | |
| at 40 per Cent above par would produce | $11,200— |
| and whilst in Bank produce, 10 pC<sup>t</sup> in | $ 800— |
| The above $11,200—converted into the New loan Certificates on the above scale of 88 for $100— would produce $12,700, shares 8$\frac{27}{100}$ of d° a | 760 |
| in fav<sup>r</sup> of Bank Stock | $ 40 |
| The one Stock rising in Value the Other Stationary— | |

Note also. the extra Expenses on sale & transfering—the proceeds would not be less—I presume than a $\frac{1}{4}$ of 1 pC$^t$ & Other exp$^s$—very near a \$50—

so that the 1$^t$ years Net Int woud not exceed very little—more than \$700—in lieu of \$800—

it is therefore self Evident (—barring unforeseen Accidents—and unexpected—risque—or Danger in Bank of Penn$^a$) said Stock is Confessedly the most profitable—Stock—

a hoarsness and Cold still hangs on me—has prevented my waiting on Gen$^l$ Armstrong. hope in a few days, to be able to present to that Gent$^n$ your seperate letter and inclosure for his perusal[2] and recollection—

most Respectfully I am Dear Sir—your Obed$^t$ serv$^t$

JOHN BARNES,

PS. since the preceding—to days paper Announce$^{g}$[3] the terms—or rather Conditions perscribed—of which I cannot at present form any correct opinion Shall however—endeav$^r$ to Obtain—the best Acc$^t$—I presume—they cannot but—be equal if not superior to the last loan—Otherwise it will not, I, sh$^d$ suppose fill so readily—and I have no doubt of its being Compleatly filled before the Money—is required for the public use—

RC (ViU: TJP-ER); addressed: "Thomas Jefferson Esquire Monticello Virginia"; franked and postmarked; endorsed by TJ as received 15 Apr. 1814 and so recorded in SJL.

YOUR SEPERATE LETTER AND INCLOSURE: TJ to Barnes, 22 Mar. 1814 (second letter), and enclosure. The TERMS of the new government loan were given in the Washington *Daily National Intelligencer*, 7 Apr. 1814.

[1] Manuscript: "off."
[2] Manuscript: "persual."
[3] Reworked from "Announced."

# From Nicolas G. Dufief

MONSIEUR,                                  A Philadelphia Ce 6 Avril 1814

Il vient de m'arriver une affaire désagréable dont vous pouvez, par votre déclaration, me tirer le plus complètement du monde. Voici ce dont il S'agit. Un nommé Bécourt publia, l'été dernier, un livre intitulé la Création. On l'a poursuivi pour cet ouvrage & je me trouve très-innocemment compris dans la poursuite pour vous en avoir vendu un exemplaire. Comme cela est absolument faux, vous m'obligerez infiniment de me mettre, le plutôt possible, à même de faire tomber l'accusation que mes ennemis personnels ont fait intenter contre moi & dont ils tirent le plus grand parti pour me nuire. Ce qui a pu, cependant, donner naissance à un prétexte qu'ils ont Saisi avec avidité, c'est que Bécourt me fit voir une lettre où vous lui mandiez que la première fois que vous me feriez une remise, vous y comprendriez two dollars pour lui. En qualité de votre correspondant & pour obliger cet homme Je crus póuvoir prendre Sur moi de payer votre petite dette Sans y être autorisé

Je n'ai point la traduction de Lysias par Auger—Je tâcherai de vous la procurer—Je vais écrire à New York pour Savoir Si l'American Brewer & Malster assistant a enfin paru. Je conserve Soigneusement tous les ordres dont vous m'avez honoré, afin de les remplir dans l'occasion.

J'ai l'honneur d'être avec tous les Sentimens que je vous dois à tant de titres, Monsieur, votre très-respectueux & très-devoué Serviteur                                                                 N. G. Dufief

P.S. Je vous envoye notre compte courant, puisque vous l'avez demandé

EDITORS' TRANSLATION

Sir,                                                                 Philadelphia 6 April 1814
Something unpleasant has just happened to me and, by your testimony, you can exonerate me completely before the world. The situation is as follows. Last summer a man named Bécourt published a book entitled La Création du Monde. He was prosecuted for this work, and although I am totally innocent I find myself included in the proceedings for having sold a copy of it to you. As this is absolutely false, you would infinitely oblige me by enabling me, as soon as possible, to dismiss the accusation that my personal enemies have brought against me and from which they are taking full advantage to harm me. The pretext that they have seized on so eagerly to justify this action is the fact that Bécourt showed me a letter in which you informed him that the first time you sent money to me, you would enclose two dollars for him. As your correspondent, and in order to oblige that man, I believed that I could take it on myself to pay your small debt without authorization

I do not have the translation of Lysias by Auger—I will try to procure it for you—I will write to New York to find out whether the American Brewer & Malster assistant has finally come out. I carefully save all the orders with which you honor me, so as to be able to fill them when I get the chance.

I have the honor to be with all the sentiments that I owe you for so many reasons, Sir, your very respectful and very devoted servant

N. G. Dufief

P.S. I am sending you our current account, according to your request

RC (DLC); endorsed by TJ as received 15 Apr. 1814 and so recorded in SJL. Translation by Dr. Genevieve Moene.

## Account with Nicolas G. Dufief

Th Jefferson Esqr in a/c with N G Dufief

| 1812 | | | | | | |
|---|---|---|---|---|---|---|
| Nov | 4 th | Simp Fluxion | 6.18 | May 25 1813[1] | | |
| | " | Mellish Map | 1.00 | By Cash | | 40.00 |
| 1813[2] | | | | | | |
| Jany | 4 | Tacitus | 8.00 | | | |
| Feb[y] | 15 | Titus Livius | 12.50 | | | |
| June | 28 | Cash Paid | 2.00 | | | |
| July | 10 | Directory | 1.25 | | | |
| | 14 | Dictionary | 11.50 | | | |
| Aug | 31 | Heathan Phi[y] | 1.00 | | | |
| Nov[r] | 18 | Traité de Mo[r] | 1.50 | Balanc due N G Dufief | | 4.93 |
| | | | $44.93 | | | 44.93 |

Due N G Dufief April 6th 14               $4.93

MS (DLC: TJ Papers, 201:35730); in a clerk's hand; undated; with top horizontal rule and double vertical rule in red ink and additional entries at foot of text in TJ's hand recording the purchase on 14 Apr. 1814 of Isaac "Newton's Philosophy" (*Philosophiæ Naturalis Principia Mathematica*) for $18 (see note to Dufief to TJ, 14 Apr. 1814) and, without listing a date or price, "another copy" of

Dufief's *A New Universal and Pronouncing Dictionary of the French and English Languages*, 3 vols. (Philadelphia, 1810; Sowerby, no. 4822; Poor, *Jefferson's Library*, 14 [no. 881]).

[1] Manuscript corrected from "1814" based on TJ to Patrick Gibson, 20 May 1813, and TJ to Dufief, 21 May 1813.

[2] Reworked from "1812."

# From Peter Carr

D[R] SIR,                       [received 7 Apr. 1814]

The young gentleman, who will hand you this, is a son of my particular friend D[r] John D Orr, of Jefferson County. He is at present, a student with M[r] Girardin, and is very anxious to see Monticello and it's inhabitants. Permit me to ask y[r] attention to him

Affectionately y[rs]             P[R] CARR

RC (ViU: TJP-CC); undated; endorsed by TJ as received 7 Apr. 1814 and so recorded in SJL.

Thomas Lee Orr (d. 1848), attorney, was the son of John D. Orr, a physician, and Lucinda Lee Orr. By 1820 he was practicing law in Washington, D.C. He died in Fairfax County, leaving a will that

freed his four slaves (Cassius Francis Lee Jr. and Joseph Packard Jr., *A Record of the Descendants of Col. Richard Lee, of Virginia* [1872], 5; Frederick Co. Will Book, 10:62–7; Washington *Daily National Intelligencer*, 29 June 1820, 11 Apr. 1848; Fairfax Co. Will Book, V:228, X:338–40).

# From José Corrêa da Serra

Sir                                 Philadelphia 10 April. 1814

M$^r$ Short tells me that you intend to give me an invitation to visit you at Monticello; for which i give you my sincere thanks, because no moments of Life can i consider more precious than those i would pass in your company. In the summer or in the fall i will attempt to profit of your Kindness. In the mean time as i am determined to visit Kentucky and the Ohio, an excursion which i presume will take about three months, i intend to begin it about the first of May, and enter Kentucky by Virginia, to return afterwards by Pittsburg. In this manner i shall be able by stopping a day at Charlottesville to pay once more my respects to you, and of presenting to you my <u>compagnon de voyage</u> M$^r$ Walsh, whose name you know by its first productions, which were rather of another hemisphere, but there has been a gradual and great change in his ecliptic; as will naturally happen to every man, who is <u>avant tout</u> a good and sincere American. Such men easily find the high road, only by observing the deviations of party spirit, which are to well meaning persons equivalent to a demonstration <u>ad absurdum</u>

I dare entreat your favour for an object about which i feel the greatest curiosity. There grows in Louisiana a tree called by the French <u>Bois d'arc</u>, and by the Americans Bow wood. I am sure a word from you to Gov$^r$ Claiborne can obtain for me a young branch of it or two, pressed in brown paper with their Leaves, and both the male and female flowers, also some of the fruit, either dry, or in a mixture $\frac{1}{3}$ wiskey, $\frac{2}{3}$ water, also in the proper season some ripe seeds. All this i will consider as a very great favour. I ta[ke] the Liberty of reminding you of the Louisiana springs being very early.

My three months residence in New England have afforded me occasion of studying both the sickness and the curative, you will best judge when i meet you; if my view of the matter is correct. I expect i will be so happy as to find Col. Randolph at Monticello, but wherever he may be, my most sincere respect and good wishes are for him.

I am Sir with the highest consideration
Your most faithful obedient serv$^t$

JOSEPH CORRÈA DE SERRA

RC (DLC); dateline at foot of text; edge chipped; endorsed by TJ as received 22 Apr. 1814 and so recorded in SJL.

Corrêa da Serra's COMPAGNON DE VOYAGE ("traveling companion") was Robert Walsh, whose FIRST PRODUCTIONS included several works on Europe and on American foreign affairs (M. Frederick Lochemes, *Robert Walsh: His*

*Story* [1941], 229–30). AVANT TOUT: "above all." AD ABSURDUM: "to absurdity." The Osage orange tree is also known as the BOIS D'ARC or BOW WOOD because of its use by Native Americans in making bows (*OED*).

# From George Divers

DEAR SIR                                              Farmington Ap[r] 11th 1814

You will be pleas'd to accept of a Bushel of the Mazzei pea which I send by your servant, which are all I have to spare. plant them about the middle of next month. I am sorry they are so much mix'd with the Cow pea, as you want them to put you in stock it will be well to have the latter pick'd from them—my Health has improv'd very much since the weather has become moderately warm,[1] The first asparagus we had was 5 or 6 days ago, since that we have had several dishes and we have it in plenty for dinner today, I wish you were with us to partake of it, I will come to see you when I am able but wish you would make us a visit in the mean time—

Your friend                                              GEO: DIVERS

RC (MHi); addressed: "Thomas Jefferson esq Monticello"; endorsed by TJ as received 11 Apr. 1814.

[1] Manuscript: "worm."

# From Benjamin Smith Barton

DEAR SIR,                                    Philadelphia, April 12th, 1814.

This will be handed to you by Judge Woodward, whose great merits, in various respects, are not unknown to you. The Judge is about to visit you,[1] concerning a work on the "classification of human knowledge," in which he has long been engaged. I have had frequent conversations with M[r] Woodward, who has developed to me, at length, the outlines of his plan, in which, so far as I am capable of apprehending, and properly estimating, a subject so mixed and multifarious, and difficult, I perceive a great deal deserving of the highest praise. Judge Woodward is fully sensible, that no other person, in the United-States, is so eminently qualified by his learning and general Knowledge, as well as by his liberality of sentiment, to form a proper estimate of the new plan, as you are. he will depend much upon your opinion and advice.

---

Since I began this letter, I have received your's, dated April 3[d]. The enclosed pamphlet shall be safely lodged with the Philosophical Society.

I agree with you, Sir, that we have not, in general, begun at the right end "for the improvement of the faculties and conditions" of the Indians. Even the Missionaries, though often sensible, and always, I hope, well disposed to do what is right, have shown themselves children, as it were, in their intercourse with the Indians. With respect to these poor people, there seems to have been a singularly unhappy destiny. Yet, in the midst of the wars in which we are engaged, and are likely to be engaged with them, I flatter myself, that <u>Your</u> efforts, and the efforts of a few other good and influential men, will place a remnant of the vast Indian population of the United-States, where it ought to be placed, by the side of their brethren of another colour.

I am, Dear Sir, with very great respect, your affectionate friend, &c., BENJAMIN SMITH BARTON.

RC (DLC); dateline beneath signature; endorsed by TJ as received 29 Apr. 1814 and so recorded in SJL.

[1] Barton here canceled: "for the purpose of [...] your position."

# From Bradford & Inskeep

SIR                                   Phila[a] April 12th 1814

At the request of M[r] Paul Allen we have packed & sent to the care of Gibson & Jefferson as directed thirteen copies, one of which we beg you will accept, they were forwarded by mail Stage & we think will go safe—

We are your Ob[t] Ser[ts]          BRADFORD & INSKEEP

RC (MHi); in an unidentified hand; subjoined to MS of enclosure; endorsed by TJ as a letter of 7 Apr. 1814 (the date of the enclosed account) received 22 Apr. and so recorded in SJL.

Bradford & Inskeep was a publishing partnership established by 1808 in Philadelphia by Samuel Fisher Bradford (1776–1837) and John Inskeep (1786–1820). Before it failed in 1815, the firm published a variety of works, including the *Port Folio*, a literary magazine; Alexander Wilson's *American Ornithology; or, the Natural History of the Birds of the United States*, 9 vols. (Philadelphia, 1808–14; Sowerby, no. 1022); and Bid-dle, *Lewis and Clark Expedition*. Bradford belonged to a prominent Philadelphia family of printers. He was in business in 1798–99 with his father, Thomas Bradford, before establishing his own firm. After his partnership with Inskeep ended, Bradford continued printing until at least 1833. Inskeep, Bradford's brother-in-law and the namesake son of a two-time mayor of Philadelphia, later entered the ministry and died in New Orleans (Henry Darrach, *Bradford Family 1660–1906* [1906], 2, 7, 12; Henry Edward Wallace Jr., "Sketch of John Inskeep, Mayor, and President of the Insurance Company of North America, Philadelphia," *PMHB* 28 [1904]: 131,

133, 135; baptismal record of Inskeep at Christ Church, Philadelphia, 21 Sept. 1792; Brigham, *American Newspapers*, 2:924, 955–6; H. Glenn Brown and Maude O. Brown, *A Directory of the Book-Arts and Book Trade in Philadelphia to 1820, Including Painters and Engravers* [1950], 23, 65; *MB*, 2:1218, 1302; TJ to Samuel F. Bradford, 13 Dec. 1807, and Bradford to TJ, 18 Dec. 1807 [MHi]; Philadelphia *Poulson's American Daily Advertiser*, 2 Feb. 1808, 6, 9 Feb. 1815, 27 Sept. 1820; *Desilver's Philadelphia Directory and Stranger's Guide, for 1833* [Philadelphia, 1833], 21; Philadelphia *United States Gazette*, 19 Apr. 1837).

E N C L O S U R E

## Account with Bradford & Inskeep

Philad<sup>a</sup> April 7. 1814

Thomas Jefferson Esq<sup>r</sup>
            To Bradford & Inskeep dr

| | | | | | | | |
|---|---|---|---|---|---|---|---|
| For | 10 | Lewis & Clarkes travels[1] bds @ | 6.00— | 60.00 |
| | 2 | ditto | do | " | cf g<sup>t</sup> | 10.00— | 20.00 |
| | | | | | | | 80.00 |
| | | | | 15 p<sup>r</sup> Ct off | | | 12.00 |
| | | | | | | | 68.00 |
| | | | | Box &c | | | 75 |
| | | | | | | | $68.75 |

MS (MHi); in an unidentified hand different from that of subjoined covering letter.

BDS: "boards." CF G<sup>T</sup>: "calf gilt."

[1] Manuscript: "traves."

# To Patrick Gibson

DEAR SIR                              Monticello Apr. 12. 14.

Our newspapers having come lately more irregularly than usual I have as yet seen nothing later than the President's recommendation to repeal the embargo. what act of England has produced this change of policy, we do not yet know; but I presume an armistice, or something equivalent has been proposed, and the rather, as we are told that vessels pass freely in & out of our bay. under these circumstances it is advisable to hold up my flour for a better price than had been before expected; and indeed if exportation be free of both embargo & blockade, I see no reason why the prices should not be quite high. I leave therefore the disposal of my flour, as to price, to your discretion altogether, to be governed by circumstances & prospects; and the rather as I must draw on you within 2. or 3. weeks in favor of Robert S. Sthreshly for 230. Dollars for corn bought of him.

I must ask the favor of you to send me a quarter cask of powder either by Johnson's boat if down; if not, then by mr Randolph's. accept my friendly salutations. Th: Jefferson

PoC (NHi: Thomas Jefferson Papers); at foot of text: "M^r Gibson"; endorsed by TJ.

James Madison recommended on 31 Mar. 1814 that Congress REPEAL THE EMBARGO Act of 17 Dec. 1813, and the statute was duly repealed on 14 Apr. 1814

(Washington *Daily National Intelligencer*, 1 Apr. 1814; *U.S. Statutes at Large*, 3:123). On 2 May 1814 TJ drew on Gibson & Jefferson for $230 to be paid to John M. Perry, assignee of Robert B. STHRESHLY, for corn purchased the previous October (*MB*, 2:1299; Sthreshly to Edmund Bacon, 13 Oct. 1813).

# From Luis de Onís

Monsieur          Philadelphie ce 13. Avril 1814.

L'interet que Votre Excellence a toujours temoigné pour le bonheur et prosperité de la Nation Espagnole, m'encourage à lui offrir un exemplaire de la Constitution de sa Monarchie. J'espere que Votre Excellence voudra bien l'accepter comme un hommage de ma consideration pour les talents, qui distinguent si eminemment sa personne; et je me flâte que Votre Excellence verra avec plaisir tracés dans cette constitution une partie de loîx sages que Votre Excellence a sugerer à cette Republique pour consacrer la liberté et l'independance dont elle jouit avec tant de gloire.

J'ai l'honneur d'etre avec la plus haute consideration

De Votre Excellence Le trés humble et trés obeiss^t Servit^r

Le Chevalier de Onis

EDITORS' TRANSLATION

Sir          Philadelphia 13. April 1814.

The interest that Your Excellency has always taken in the happiness and prosperity of the Spanish nation encourages me to offer you a copy of its monarchy's constitution. I hope that Your Excellency will accept it as an expression of my respect for the talents that so eminently distinguish your person; and I flatter myself that Your Excellency will be pleased to see written in this constitution some of the wise laws that Your Excellency suggested to this republic in order to perpetuate the liberty and independence that it enjoys with such glory.

I have the honor to be with the highest respect

Your Excellency's very humble and very obedient servant

Le Chevalier de Onis

RC (DLC); at foot of text: "A Son Exc^ce Thomas Jefferson. & & &"; endorsed by TJ as received 22 Apr. 1814 and so recorded in SJL. Translation by Dr. Genevieve Moene. Enclosure: *Constitution of the Spanish Monarchy. Promulgated at Cadiz on the 19th of March, 1812* (Philadelphia, 1814; Sowerby, no. 2424).

# From William Wardlaw

DEAR SIR          Richmond 13^th1 April 1814

I have at length seen M^r Henning and have mentioned to him your request to me of last month. M^r H. informs me that he has the Vol of the laws of Virginia that you mention, but that in the sessions acts of 1748 several pages are missing among which is the act that I am so anxious to find

I find in the 4^th Vol of "The Statutes at large," which is about to appear, that the titles of the private acts in many cases are only given. This will not meet the intention of the Legislature or be of service to men versed in the laws of the State

I am with much esteem Your friend &c        W WARDLAW

RC (DLC); endorsed by TJ as a letter of 12 Apr. received 19 Apr. 1814.      The 4^TH VOL of Hening was not in fact published until 1820.

1 Reworked from "12^th."

# From Nicolas G. Dufief

MONSIEUR,         A Philadelphie ce 14 d'Avril. 1814

Je vous envoye par le courrier de demain le 1^er volume de l'ouvrage de Newton que vous me demandez par votre lettre du 3 du Courant: J'en avais un exemplaire <u>cartonné</u> mais croyant que vous le préféreriez relié Je m'en Suis procuré un par échange. Vous recevrez tout l'ouvrage dans le tems fixé dans une de vos précédentes

Je Suis fâché d'apprendre d'un libraire de New York que "The American Brewer & Malster's assistant" ne Soit point Sous presse. En attendant, Si quelque autre ouvrage pouvait également remplir vos vues, je m'empresserais de vous en donner avis. J'ai noté tous les ouvrages que Je n'ai pu vous procurer lorsque vous me les avez demandés

J'ai l'honneur d'être avec le plus profond respect votre très-dévoué Serviteur        N. G. DUFIEF

EDITORS' TRANSLATION

SIR,                                              Philadelphia 14 April. 1814
I am sending you by tomorrow's post the first volume of the work by New-ton that you requested in your letter of the third of this month: I had this in boards but thinking that you would prefer a bound copy I procured one by exchange. You will receive the whole work within the time frame fixed in one of your previous letters
I am sorry to learn from a New York bookseller that "The American Brewer & Malster's assistant" has not gone to press. In the meantime, if some other work could equally meet your needs, I will lose no time in informing you of it. I have noted all the works that I was unable to obtain for you when you asked me for them
I have the honor to be with the most profound respect your very devoted servant                                        N. G. DUFIEF

RC (DLC); endorsed by TJ as received 22 Apr. 1814 and so recorded in SJL. Translation by Dr. Genevieve Moene.

With this letter Dufief may have en-closed a brief account indicating that on this date he had given Philip H. Nick-lin $3 in cash and a copy of "Newton's Philosophy" in boards valued at $15 in exchange for a bound copy of the same publication (MS in DLC: TJ Papers, 201:35729; written on a scrap in a clerk's

hand; undated; edge trimmed; with nota-tion by TJ on verso: "1813 Sep. 6. Priest-ley's to J. Adams," "Dufief's dict.," and "Directory 1.2[5]"). The work by Isaac NEWTON was probably *The Mathematical Principles of Natural Philosophy*, trans. Andrew Motte, new ed. by William Davis, 3 vols. (London, 1803; Sowerby, no. 3721; for a Latin ed. of the *Philosophiæ Naturalis Principia Mathe-matica*, see Sowerby, no. 3720).

# Minutes of the Albemarle Academy Board of Trustees

At a meeting of the Trustees of the Albemarle Accademy held at the house of Triplet T Estes in Charlottesville the 15th day of April 1814—agreeable to adjournment, present Peter Carr President, Thomas Jameson, Frank Carr, Jno: B Carr, Robt B Streshly, James Leitch, John Kelly, Jno: Nicholas, Edward Garland, Nicholas M Lewis, Jno: Winn, Edmund Anderson, and Jno: Carr. The number of members present constituting a bare majority, and it being desir-able that a full board should be had to take into consideration the im-portant subjects submitted to the committee appointed at the last session. It is therefore ordered that the board be adjourned until Tuesday the third day of May next.

Signed
P. CARR.

Tr (ViU: TJP-VMJCC). Tr (ViU: TJP-VMJHC). Tr (ViU: TJP-VMJB). Tr (ViU: VMJLC). Tr (PPAmP: VMWCR).

# From John Barnes

DEAR SIR— George Town, 16th April 1814.—

since my letter of the 4th Ins[t] inclosing a sketch on the difference between continuing G K'[s] $8,000. Penn[a] Bank stock, with its being made sale of a 40 ℔C[t] and converted into the New Loan, a 88 for $100—bearing 8 ℔C[t]—I was induced to apply Thro a friend to a M[r] Parker a Clerk in the Treasury departm[t] a Gent[n] well qualified—with Calculations on finance—<u>Copy</u> of his statem[t] with a Counter one of mine—with my several Minutes—on the probable result Accruing— from all such well regulated Established Institutions (barring unforeseen accidents.)—I am still compelled, to adhear to the latter—for the several reasons—therein assigned—

still however—you will be pleased—on your close examination—to determine for your self

from 800 a $900. ℔ ann[m1] instead of $762—without any extra exp[s] or trouble—in making Sale of the one, and placing it in the other—with the loss of Int. on both, from 2 a 3 M[os] for although you pay the whole Am[t] at Subscribing—you are not allowed an Ins[t2] but on the sum Stated ℔ Instalm[t] would not be less—I presume than $\frac{1}{8}$ of the $762—℔ ann[m3] say '95 to $100—

my hoarsness & cold—tho much abated—have not quite left me— but I promise my self soon, to have the Honor of presenting your letter &[c] to the Sect[y] of war—for the good purpose, mentiond in your fav[r] of the 22[d] Ult[o]—

I am, always most Respectfully—Dear Sir, your Obed[t] serv[t]

JOHN BARNES,

PS. was the Gen[ls] Capital in any Other less Valuable and less productive Bank—I should readily agree with M[r] Parkers statem[t] but the Bank of Penn[a] Possessing the Revenue of the State—discounting twice a week—to a vast Amo[t] and when profits (to an indiff[t] Spectator)[4]—are but lightly perceived—but when duly estimated—its productive Interest and growing Capital—possessed of any part thereof, I should rest perfectly satisfied with its Continuance,—<u>to increase and Multiply</u>—

RC (ViU: TJP-ER); postscript on separate page; beneath signature: "Thomas Jefferson Esquire Monticello"; endorsed by TJ as received 22 Apr. 1814 and so recorded in SJL. Enclosures not found.

Barnes's LETTER was dated 5 Apr. 1814, not THE 4ᵀᴴ. G K'S: General Tadeusz Kosciuszko's. The SECTʸ OF WAR was John Armstrong.

[1] Manuscript: "annⁿ."

[2] Thus in manuscript. Barnes appears to mean "Interest."
[3] Manuscript: "annⁿ."
[4] Omitted closing parenthesis editorially supplied.

# From Joseph Delaplaine

SIR,                                                    Philadelphia April 16ʰ 1814

I once more take the freedom of encroaching on your kindness with a request that you would allow me the privilege of having engravings made from two original pictures which I am informed by Doctor Barton are in your possession: One of them the portrait of Columbus, the other that of Americus Vespusius. Intending to render the work I have already had the honor to announce to you, a complete American Biographical work, it has occurred to me that the first discoverers ought to be allowed a nitche in it as well as the founders and perfecters of our republic; and my idea has been approved by several persons of distinction in this quarter. To me your approbation will be much more gratifying and to the work itself of infinite importance, since whatever its intrinsic merit may be, its success will greatly depend upon the first impression the expectation of it will make upon the people. Should the plan I mention, the proposals for which I take the liberty of enclosing (a rough proof just from the hands of the printer) have the good fortune to obtain your approbation, no more efficacious testimony of it can be given to the public than your condesending to supply the pictures. In which case you will add to the great weight of obligations I have to acknowledge, by giving your compliance to me as soon as possible, as the address to the public on the subject is to be with-held 'till I have the honor of receiving your reply.

And may I, sir, without being charged with presumption, intreat you to trust the pictures to my custody, in order to their being put into the hands of Mʳ Edwin whose great professional talents will do the utmost justice to those august subjects. I pledge my honor that the pictures shall be restored to you in perfect safety, as soon as the engraver[1] is done with them.

Mʳ Madison some little time ago sent to me his picture painted by Stuart—governor Tompkins has done the same & so have other gentlemen, as my plan appears to be highly & universally approved of.

I enclose for your kind inspection the portrait of Dʳ Rush to enable you to see the style of the engravings for the work; for the first volume of which, with others, I purpose to have your portrait engraved, but at present I am at a loss to know how I shall get either of your portraits painted by Stuart, as you inform me in your favour of the 30 of May last that the two portraits he painted of you are in his possession. I have since heard by Mʳ Wood the portrait painter that he believes he saw one of these portraits in Mʳ Madison's house. Please to inform me if this is correct to enable me to take the proper steps to procure it.

Hoping to be honored with a letter

I remain with the highest respect & regard your obedᵗ humbˡ servᵗ

JOSEPH DELAPLAINE
Bookseller
Philadelphia

RC (DLC); at foot of text: "His Excellency Thomas Jefferson"; endorsed by TJ as received 30 Apr. 1814 and so recorded in SJL.

The enclosed ROUGH PROOF of the proposal for *Delaplaine's Repository* has not been found. Multiple versions of Delaplaine's prospectus were published, as broadsides, pamphlets, and newspaper advertisements (Gordon M. Marshall, "The Golden Age of Illustrated Biographies: Three Case Studies," in Wendy Wick Reaves, ed., *American Portrait Prints: Proceedings of the Tenth Annual American Print Conference* [1984], 39). An undated broadside version (NHi) entitled *Proposals For Publishing a Great National Work, In Perpetual Commemoration of Those Illustrious Men who have most distinguished themselves, By Their Virtues, Talents, and Public Services: to be entitled Delaplaine's Repository, of the Portraits and Lives of the Heroes, Philosophers, and Statesmen of America* noted that the work would include likenesses from portraits by "the most celebrated artists," to be "engraved by Messrs. Edwin, Leney, Fairman, Lawson, and Tiebout," accompanied by short biographies of each subject; asserted its importance as a reference work; promised that the engravings would be vetted by individuals acquainted with the originals, with only the most accurate to be published; pledged to keep the publication free from partisan bias; indicated that the work would be printed on quarto paper, that twelve portraits and biographies would constitute a volume to be published in two installments during one year, that each volume would include an "elegant title page and vignette, designed and engraved by Mr. Fairman," that the volume would conclude with a list of subscribers and an index, that William Brown would execute the typography, and that subscribers would pay eight dollars per volume and nonsubscribers nine; and specified that because of varying opinions respecting the most genuine likeness of George Washington, engravings would be included derived both from the Gilbert Stuart portrait and the Jean Antoine Houdon bust, the latter of which Bushrod Washington had endorsed as an "accurate likeness of his uncle." Thomas Sully's portrait of Benjamin RUSH (reproduced above in Vol. 4, opp. p. 371) was engraved and included in *Delaplaine's Repository*, 1:26.

¹ Reworked from "engraving."

# To William Shirman

S<small>IR</small> Monticello Apr. 16. 14.

I have about 80. or 100. perch of stone work to be laid at Poplar Forest in Bedford, 10. miles from Lynchburg; and also from one to two hundred perch to lay at this place; in all of which I should be willing to employ you. the work in Bedford might be done by the perch; but for that here I would rather pay you a reasonable monthly hire, because difficulties & delays in hauling materials sometimes unavoidably occur, which I would rather should be at my own loss, than to have complaints. there is moreover in this neighborhood generally & in the two towns of Charlottesville & Milton, about 3 miles each from me, abundant employment for a workman in your line, and I have every year some thing considerable to do; so that, if you should like the situation, you might be sure of work enough; there being no stone mason in the neighborhood now. while about my work, you could satisfy yourself as to the prospect; and mr Chisolm, the bearer of this letter, a bricklayer of this neighborhood can give you full information of the subject. he is now on his way to Poplar Forest to do some plaistering and brickwork for me. it is while he will be there that I should want you to do the stone work at that place. I shall be there the first or second[1] week in May, and should be glad if you could come then and let us agree on this subject. in the meantime if you will immediately on the reciept of this write me a line of information whether I may count on seeing you, and contrive it to Nelson court on Monday the 25th instant, my Grandson Thomas J. Randolph will be there, and will bring it to me, if delivered to him. he will be readily found at court[2] as attending on the business of the Collectorship of the district. should any accident prevent his being there, if put into the post office there, I may by possibility get it before I set out for Bedford. I am Sir    your humble serv[t]

T<small>H</small>: J<small>EFFERSON</small>

PoC (MHi); at foot of text: "M[r] Sherwin"; endorsed by TJ.

[1] Preceding two words interlined.
[2] Preceding two words added in margin in place of "there."

# From Thomas Leiper

D<small>EAR</small> S<small>IR</small> Philad[a] April 17th 1814.—

I wrote you on the 9th of Dec[r] and the 2d of January since I have received yours of the 1st of January which I have read again and again but none other has nor never shall because I believe it would not advance your standing with a number of your friends of which number you may put me down as one—I observe you are affraid that Bonaparte will Conquer Europe and by that means will conquer England—England has been at War with us for upwards of Twenty years and will conquer us if she can and as she has been at the Bottom of all the Wars in Europe these Centenaries past from that circumstance the sooner she is conquered the better—You and I read the same history let us look at the origin of the present War of France and the Allies The people of France agreed to establish a republican goverment which you and I agree they had a right to do they sent their Embassador to England their request was a reasonable One for England to let them alone and establish their Goverment in their own way I do not correctly remember their answer but it amounted in substance to this—You are a set of scoundrels for attempting any thing like a republican Goverment you shall leave England in Fourteen days and they did oblige him to go within the time—In the mean time the Duke of Brunswick was put in Battle array Look at his friendly Proclaimation and again look at the Compacts formed at Coblentz & Pelnuntz where they did agree to divid France and Blot it out of the Map of Europe Again a Treaty was made at Amies by the whole powers of Europe who broke it the British—Prelemenories were established lately but Bonaparte has been given to understand since They cannot be complied with till they consult their Allies that is Castleraegh and Company from this very circumstance their will be no peace for Castlereagh has got with him the whole funds of England in his possession and money you know has a very powerfull effect on the great men as they are called in Europe—Now Sir my mind is made up that the Executive of England is the Cause of all the bloodshed and not Bonaparte for these Twenty years and my opinions proceed from the foregoing facts—You are affraid that Alexander will be dispossessed of his Title of Emperior the sooner the better from the history I have read of Russia they cannot have a worse[1] Goverment—Let us take a Look of the Virtuous Kings all in a Bunch Russia Austria & Prussia what did they do they Cut up Polland and each took a slice and the Virtuous King of Great Britian looked on and suffered this thing to take place Indeed she makes no[2] calculations but in the way of Trade for if she finds that object can be advanced by any exchange she will agree to it for she never had and believe never will have any other object in view—What was the principle cause of the brecking the Treaty of Amies it was Trade—England found that Bonaparte was going to every part of France inquiring to every species of manufactures &ca and giving every eade[3] in his power to premote them—England found it would not do especially as the Marquiss of Lands doun told them in the House of Lords that the Taxes in France per head was only One Pounds ten shillings and in England they were six Pounds and that it was impossible for them to manufacture with them on the same Terms and I have no doubt at this period they are some 20 per Cent higher in England—Thus far had I wrote when the enclosed Made its appeerence in Ralf's paper should it by the bye be yours which I hope it is not I must beg leave to differ from you in opinion General Armstrong on his return from the Lines said had the embargo been strickly observed the British could not have supported their Fleets and Armies and would have been obliged to return from whence they came I am with the Utmost esteem and respect　　　Your most Obedeint Ser[t]　　　　　　　　　　　　THOMAS LEIPER

PS Enclosed is your letter to me of the 1st of January 1814 which was my intention to have returned at this date but it has been with this letter under lock & Key ever since

RC (DLC); addressed: "Thomas Jefferson Late President of the United States Monticello Virginia"; with apparently unrelated calculations by TJ on address cover; endorsed by TJ (brackets in original) as a letter of "Apr. 17. [1814] for 1815" received 12 May 1815 and recorded in SJL under this date of receipt as a letter of 17 Apr. 1815. Enclosures: (1) TJ to Leiper, 1 Jan. 1814. (2) newspaper article alleging that in a letter to an unnamed "gentleman residing in the neighborhood" of Philadelphia, "the *Recluse of Montecello*" had expressed "his utter disapprobation of the restrictive system of the administration—He is represented to say, that an embargo during war is a political solecism; and intimates that nothing but the energetic interference of the good sense of the people of the United States can arrest the mad and suicidal career of Mr. Madison's administration—We have not seen this letter; but are satisfied that one of this sort really exists—When will political phenomena cease? It will be recollected that Mr. Jefferson in a letter to Dr. Logan, gave up the 'super-eminent' Napoleon Bonaparte: It appears now that he has also given up the *sub eminent* James Madison" (*Relf's Philadelphia Gazette*, 11 Apr. 1814). No such letter by TJ criticizing the Madison administration has been found, and he emphatically denied its existence in his 12 June 1815 reply to Leiper.

In his 25 July 1792 manifesto the DUKE OF BRUNSWICK justified his forthcoming invasion of France as an effort to save that country from anarchy and threatened to destroy Paris if the royal family were harmed (William Doyle, *The Oxford History of the French Revolution* [1989], 188; Philadelphia *National Gazette*, 19 Sept. 1792). The German city of Koblenz (COBLENTZ) was a center for émigré activity during the early years of the French Revolution. In the 1791 Declaration of Pillnitz (PELNUNTZ), Holy Roman Emperor Leopold II and Frederick William

II, the king of Prussia, threatened to use force to restore the powers and prerogatives of the French monarchy (William Doyle, *The Oxford History of the French Revolution* [1989], 147, 156–7, 171, 302). The 1802 Treaty of Amiens (AMIES) established a peace between France and Great Britain that lasted about a year (Connelly, *Napoleonic France*, 16).

[1] Manuscript: "wrorse."
[2] Word interlined.
[3] Thus in manuscript, presumably meaning "aid."

# To John H. Cocke

DEAR SIR                                                      Monticello Apr. 19. 14.

M[r] Patterson, and my grandson T. J. Randolph inform me you have a dark bay horse which you are disposed to sell at the price of 50.£ and which, from their description would suit me. they speak of him as a steady carriage horse, and a tolerable riding horse. if their information as to your purposes of selling him be right, I shall be glad to recieve him by the bearer, with the privilege of returning him within a week, if he should not answer my purpose, particularly as to the carriage which is the principal object. I should have sent for him some time ago, but have been awaiting the sale of my crop of flour in Richmond, that I might at the same time send you an order on my correspondents there, Gibson & Jefferson, for the money. but they are holding it up for the effect of the repeal of the embargo; and as the horse would be useful to me on a journey I am about making to Bedford, I have concluded to ask an indulgence for the price until my flour is sold, when you shall recieve an order for the money. this may be a delay of a few weeks; but I shall have it all sold in May,[1] be the price what it may. accept the assurance of my great esteem and respect.

TH: JEFFERSON

RC (ViU: TJP-Co); addressed: "General Cocke Bremo"; endorsed by Cocke, with his additional signed notation at foot of text: "The above paid a few months after the above mentioned time with interest." PoC (DLC); endorsed by TJ.

The DARK BAY HORSE was Bremo. In recording his agreement to the purchase price of £50 on the following day, TJ described the animal as a "dark bay, star in forehead, by Knowesly, 8. y. old this present spring." On 23 Oct. 1814 he paid Cocke $167 in settlement of this debt (*MB*, 2:1299, 1304).

[1] Manuscript: "sold in all May."

# From John H. Cocke

DEAR SIR, Bremo April 19. 1814

I send herewith the Horse mentioned to you by M<sup>r</sup> Patterson & your grandson M<sup>r</sup> T. J. Randolph He answers the description they have given of his qualities as a Carriage & riding Horse. I have driven him chiefly in double Harness—he has been seldom in a gig but when tried performed very well & I am sure from his docile character may be trusted without risk. You are at liberty to take him on your journey to Bedford and return him when you get back if you find that he does not suit you—

He has been occasionally subject to a spasmodic affection something like the Thumps—which I once thought alarming—but am now induced to beleive that it is nothing more than Hickup, as it always succeeds a hearty meal or draught of water.

As to payment for the Horse, the arrangement you mention is perfectly satisfactory—I only regret that you permitted any considerations on this score to prevent your sending for him as soon as you wanted him. Yours with much Esteem & respect

JN<sup>o</sup> H. COCKE

RC (CSmH: JF); at foot of text: "M<sup>r</sup> Jefferson"; endorsed by TJ as received 20 Apr. 1814 and so recorded in SJL.

The THUMPS are a condition in horses characterized by a beating of the chest due to spasmodic contractions of the diaphragm, analogous to the human HICK-UP (*OED*).

# To José Corrêa da Serra

DEAR SIR Monticello Apr. 19. 14.

M<sup>r</sup> Randolph first, and latterly mr Short have flattered me with the hope that you would pay us a visit with the returning season. I should sooner have pressed this but that my vernal visit to Bedford was approaching, and I wished to fix it's precise epoch, before I should write to you. I shall set out now within a few days, and be absent probably all the month of May; and shall be very happy to see you here on my return, or as soon after as may be. it will give me the greatest pleasure, and our whole family joins in the invitation, if, consulting your own convenience and comfort, you would make as long a stay with us as these should permit. you know our course of life. to place our friends at their ease we shew them that we are so ourselves; by pursuing the necessary vocations of the day, and enjoying their company at the usual hours of society. you will find the summer of Monticello much cooler than that of Philadelphia, equally so with that of the neighborhood of that place, and more healthy. the amusements it offers are such as you know, which, to you, would be principally books and botany. mr Randolph's resignation of his military commission will enable him to be an associate in your botanical rambles. come then, my dear Sir, and be one of our family as long as you can bear a separation from the science of the world. since Bonaparte's discomfiture I wish much to see you, to converse with you on the probable effect that will have on the state of the world, of it's science, it's liberty, it's peace & prosperity, and particularly on the situation of our literary friends in Europe. percieving the order of nature to be that individual happiness shall be inseparable from the practice of virtue, I am willing to hope it may have ordained that the fall of the wicked shall be the rise of the good.

I can readily fulfil M. Cuvier's request for the skin & skeleton of the Mink. I have procured a fine skin, and can at any time get the entire subject. the difficulty will be to find a vessel which would recieve so large a subject, and preserve the spirits in which it would be immersed. but this shall be an article of consultation when you are with us. the cranium of the buffalo cannot be procured but from the other side of the Missisipi. there I can readily obtain it. but it must go thence by the way of New Orleans, which cannot well be till peace.          I have done for mr Warden what you and himself wished as to his commission. it's effect with the government I have not learned. I also suggested to the government your observation on the difference of structure in vessels which the difference of specific gravity between salt & fresh water might render useful. Accept my thanks for Fossombroni's book, which tho topographical, presents circumstances of curiosity. I salute you with sincere affection and respect.

TH: JEFFERSON

PoC (DLC); at foot of first page: "M. Correa de Serra"; endorsed by TJ.

On 20 Feb. 1814 TJ paid his slave Philip fifty cents for a MINK skin (*MB*, 2:1298).

# From Joseph Delaplaine

SIR,                                            Philadelphia April 19th 1814

I took the liberty a few days ago of writing to you on the subject of two pictures which Doctor Barton informed me are in your possession, and at the same time requested the favour of you to forward them to me for the purpose of having engravings taken from them for my national biographical work; I mean the portraits of Columbus & Americus Vespusius. In my letter I enclosed one of the portraits (that of D^r Rush) to enable you to see a specimen of the engravings, for a work, which, if I receive the countenance of the American people, I intend shall far surpass any thing of the kind that has been executed in England.

I have already received letters from nearly all the eminent men of America who have unanimously agreed that I shall be furnished with their portraits, and at the same time expressed their approbation of the plan.

I omitted in my letter to request the favour of you to take the trouble of informing me whether you have any other portraits in your possession which you may conceive suitable subjects for my work beside those of Columbus & Vespusius.

Your portrait I shall have the pleasure of putting into the hands of the engraver as soon as I ascertain whether the information is correct that One of the portraits of you painted by Stuart is in M^r Madison's house. Be pleased to inform me whether this is the fact or not.

I take the liberty of enclosing a corrected proposal of the work.

With the highest respect & regard I remain, your obed hum^l serv^t

JOSEPH DELAPLAINE

RC (DLC); at foot of text: "His Excellency Thomas Jefferson"; endorsed by TJ as received 30 Apr. 1814 and so recorded in SJL.

For the enclosed PROPOSAL OF THE WORK, see note to Delaplaine to TJ, 16 Apr. 1814.

# To Nicolas G. Dufief

DEAR SIR                                    Monticello Apr. 19. 14.

Your favor of the 6^th inst. is just recieved, and I shall with equal willingness and truth state the degree of agency you had respecting the copy of M. de Becourt's book which came to my hands. that gentleman informed me by letter that he was about to publish a volume in French 'sur la Creation du monde, ou Systeme d'organisation primitive,' which, it's title promised to be either a geological, or astronomical work. I subscribed; and, when published, he sent me a copy; and as you were my correspondent in the book-line in Philadelphia, I took the liberty of desiring him to call on you for the price, which he afterwards informed me you were so kind as to pay him for me, being, I believe, 2. Dollars. but the sole copy which came to me was from himself directly, and, as far as I know, was never seen by you.

I am really mortified to be told that, <u>in the United States of America</u>, a fact like this can become a subject of enquiry, and of criminal enquiry too, as an offence against religion: that a question about the sale of a book can be carried before the civil magistrate. is this then our freedom of religion? and are we to have a Censor whose imprimatur shall say what books may be sold, and what we may buy? and who is thus to dogmatise religious opinions for our citizens? whose foot is to be the measure to which ours are all to be cut or stretched? is a Priest to be our Inquisitor, or shall a layman, simple as ourselves, set up his reason as the rule for what we are to read, & what we must believe? it is an insult to our citizens to question whether they are rational beings or not; and blasphemy against religion to suppose it cannot stand the test of truth and reason. if M. de Becourt's book be false in it's facts, disprove them; if false in it's reasoning, refute it. but, for god's sake, let us freely hear both sides, if we chuse. I know little of it's contents, having barely glanced over here and there a passage, and over the table of contents. from this the Newtonian philosophy seemed the chief object of attack, the issue of which might be trusted to the strength of the two combatants; Newton certainly not needing the auxiliary arm of the government, and still less the holy author of our religion as to what in it concerns him.[1] I thought the work would be very innocent, and one which might be confided to the reason of any man; not likely to be much read, if let alone, but if persecuted, it will be generally read. every man in the US. will think it a duty to buy a copy, in vindication of his right to buy, and to read what he pleases.          I have been just reading the new constitution of Spain. one of it's fundamental[2] bases is expressed in these words. 'the <u>Roman Catholic</u> religion, the only true one, is, & always shall be that of the Spanish nation. the government protects it by wise & just laws, and prohibits the exercise of any other whatever.' now I wish this presented to those who question what you may sell, or we may buy, with a request to strike out the words 'Roman catholic' and to insert the denomination of their own religion.[3] this would ascertain the code of dogmas which each wishes should domineer over the opinions of all others, & be taken like the Spanish religion, under the 'protection of wise and just laws.' it would shew to what they wish to reduce the liberty for which one generation has sacrificed life and happiness. it would present our boasted freedom of religion as a thing of theory only, & not of practice, as what would be a poor exchange for the theoretic thraldom, but practical freedom of

Europe. but it is impossible that the laws of Pensylvania, which set us the first example of the wholsome & happy effects of religious freedom, can permit these inquisitorial functions to be proposed to their courts. under them you are surely safe.

At the date of yours of the 6<sup>th</sup> you had not recieved mine of the 3<sup>d</sup> inst. asking a copy of an edition of Newton's principia which I had seen advertised. when the cost of that shall be known, it shall be added to the balance of 4. D 93 c and incorporated with a larger remittance I have to make to Philadelphia. Accept the assurance of my great esteem & respect                    TH: JEFFERSON

PoC (DLC); at foot of first page: "M. Dufief." Tr (ViU: GT); at head of text: "ex<sup>d</sup>"; posthumous copy.

[1] Preceding seven words interlined.
[2] Word interlined.
[3] Word interlined.

# To Benjamin Galloway

DEAR SIR                              Monticello Apr. 19. 14.

Your favor of Mar. 30. is but just recieved, and I am much gratified by the prospect it holds up of my seeing you at Monticello; I hope, if you do not make it your head quarters, you will at least divide your time between Col° Monroe and myself. as you are kind enough to mention that the exact time of your journey will not be material, it gives me room to observe that I am within a fortnight of setting out for a distant possession of mine, which I visit three or four times a year and stay at a month or more at a time. it will be the last of May before I can get back. this will still admit your journey before the entrance of the hot season. adhering ever to the principles which distinguish our political brethren, I am made happy by every mark of their approbation, and sensibly therefore, in this view, feel the gratification of your visit as well as of the kind expressions in your letter, as testimonies of an esteem I highly value: and in the hope excited by your letter I tender you the assurances of my great esteem and respect.                    TH: JEFFERSON

PoC (DLC); at foot of text: "Benjamin Galloway esq."; endorsed by TJ.

# To Samuel P. Parsons

Sir Monticello Apr. 19. 14.

Your letter of Mar. 16. was recieved on the 12<sup>th</sup> inst. only, & the corn-drill arrived at the same time by a boat. possessing already one of Martin's drills, this will be returned in the same way it came. for this reason as well as because you ask my opinion, I shall go into explanations. your's came without the pieces which go into the 3. mortises having chains appended to them: but I presume the foremost was the helve, either with or without a small hoe for opening the furrow, and the 2. hinder ones carrying mould boards to cover the seed. these Martin's has also, so that for opening & covering the furrow they are equal. but his has other valuable advantages over yours, in it's present state.

1. your's has it's buckets cut into the solid of the axle, adapted solely to the size of grains of corn, & the distances for dropping them. his has shifting bands of tape or leather, with sets of metal buckets to each, adapted to seed of every size from the turnip to the pea: and one size larger would do for corn.

2. his has a single wheel only, as light as a cotton spinning wheel, about 2.f. distant from the beam, turning an axis not bigger than the wrist, with a broken joint in that axis enabling the wheel to mount over stones & moderate stumps without interrupting the motion of the buckets. it depends on it's 3. legs for steady motion on the ground, & these with a clevis regulate the depth of the furrows.

3. his whole machine does not weigh as much as the beam of yours. a man may draw his. I used it however with a little Jenny or mule.

4. his costs 8. Dollars, yours 18.D.

His may be[1] easily improved so as to sow several rows, at given distances, at the same time. but so might your's, by lengthening the axis & digging different circles of buckets round it. it would be easy too to vary your buckets with the size of the seed, by digging, in the axis, square mortises instead of buckets, and filling these with plugs of wood, in different sets, each plug having a bucket dug into it, proportioned to the size of the seed. the distance of dropping too might be varied by making the mortises of each circle close to each other, & filling occasionally those not wanted with blank plugs. still it would have no advantage over Martin's, and would be heavier & dearer: and possessing as I before observed one of these, yours would be of no utility to me. the expence of bringing and returning it shall be mine. Accept the tender of my best wishes & respects.

Th: Jefferson

PoC (ViW: TC-JP); at foot of first page: "M[r] Sam[l] P. Parsons"; endorsed by TJ.

[1] TJ here canceled "made."

# From Patrick Gibson

SIR                                              Richmond 20th April 1814—

I have received your favor of the 12th Ins[t] and am happy to find that I have acted conformably to your wishes in holding up your flour, the repeal of the restrictive system brought into market a few purchasers at 5$, which I refused under an impression that it would in a short time be followed by an Armistice—this opinion altho generally prevalent has not tended to raise the price, for the present I hold what I have on hand at $5\frac{1}{2}$$ & should be glad to meet with a purchaser—I have sold your 4 hhd[s] Tobacco to M[r] Vibert at $8.90—and should have obtained a higher price had not 2 of the Hhd[s] been rather soft—The Cask of powder shall be sent by the first of the two boats you mention, which comes down—

With great respect I am
Your ob[t] Serv[t]                                    PATRICK GIBSON

RC (ViU: TJP-ER); at head of text: "Thomas Jefferson Esq[re]"; endorsed by TJ as received 27 Apr. 1814 and so recorded in SJL.

# From John Rhea

SIR                                              Washington 20th April 1814

Inclosed is a copy of a circular letter please to accept it from most respectfully
Your ob[t] serv[t]                                    JOHN RHEA
                                                       of Tennessee

RC (MHi); at foot of text: "Thomas Jefferson Esq[r] Late President of the U States"; endorsed by TJ as received 30 Apr. 1814 and so recorded in SJL. Enclosure not found.

# From David Gelston

DEAR SIR,                                          New York 21st April 1814—

Perceiving by your note of the 3[d] instant, that, the seeds I sent to you may be more useful than I had contemplated, and having plenty on hand, which are of the same species, but were taken from a pumpkin of a smaller growth, I do my self the pleasure, to enclose a further supply,

I will just mention, that I have observed the greatest growth in a potatoe patch of strong new ground, and it appeared to me the moisture of the ground under the potatoe vines contributed greatly to the growth of the plant, a single seed in the situation here described, produced more than in any other way, without apparently injuring the crop of potatoes.—

very sincerely & truly your's                    DAVID GELSTON

RC (MHi): at foot of text: "Mr Jefferson"; endorsed by TJ as received 30 Apr. 1814 and so recorded in SJL.

# From Augustus B. Woodward

SIR,                                          Washington, April 21. 1814.

I have been diverted by public business from waiting on you so early as I expected.

I contemplate setting out for Monticello to-morrow, or the day after.

I am charged with two packages for you from Dr Barton, of Philadelphia; which I shall have the honor of presenting you, on my arrival.

Accept, Sir, my veneration, and respect.

                                          A. B. WOODWARD.

RC (DLC); at foot of text: "The Honorable Thomas Jefferson"; endorsed by TJ as received 30 Apr. 1814 and so recorded in SJL.

# From Augustus B. Woodward

                                          Alexandria, April 22. 1814.

I left Washington this afternoon in prosecution of my journey to Monticello, and shall proceed on, in the stage, to Fredericsburgh, to-morrow morning. Presuming that the mail will travel faster than the state of the roads and weather will allow me to do I forward this line, from this place; not contemplating to write again on the road, unless detained by some unexpected contingency.

Col. Monroe requested me to mention to you that he expected to be in Albemarle in three weeks. Dr Tucker, Dr Leib, Mr Law,[1] Mr Ringgold, charged me with their respects to you. The President expects to visit Orange next week.

I flatter myself I shall find you at home, and some-what disengaged. I entertain the hope of meeting Col. Randolph at Monticello. If any of your other scientific friends, or neighbors, should be at leisure to bestow an hour, for a few days, say from twelve to one p.m., each day, or every other day, on the subject which I propose exhibiting to your attention, it would be gratifying. Every suggestion, from whatever quarter, will be carefully noted, and if what is in[2] contemplation should hereafter meet the favor and adoption of the scientific world it will not be uninteresting to recollect its progress and developement. To yourself, Sir, as the father of your country, and cherishing peculiarly the wish of seeing it equal, and, if possible superior, to Europe in scientific attainment, I deem it a duty to make the first exposition of the enterprize in contemplation. I rely greatly on the accuracy of your judgment, not only in relation to the correctness of the division, and demarcation, of the sciences, but also in the selection of the most appropriate terms in the nomenclature; and shall, with equal pride and pleasure, distinguish the improvements which I anticipate as the result of my expected interview with you.

accept, Sir, my sincere esteem, and respect.

A. B. WOODWARD.

RC (DLC); addressed: "The Hon. Thomas Jefferson. Monticello. Virginia"; endorsed by TJ as received 30 Apr. 1814 and so recorded in SJL.

During a visit to TJ that lasted from either 29 Apr. or 1 May until at least 22 May 1814, Woodward and TJ conversed ON THE SUBJECT of the classification of knowledge, and Woodward copied TJ's library organization scheme (Woodward, *A System of Universal Science* [Philadelphia, 1816; Poor, *Jefferson's Library*, 14 (no. 930)], 192, 213–24).

[1] Preceding two words interlined.
[2] Woodward here canceled "agitation."

# From Hugh Holmes

DEAR SIR                                                 M[r] Divers Alb[e] April 23rd 14

The unusual protraction of the Orange Court and forbidding weather to travelers has denied to me the pleasure of Visiting Monticello and obliged me to take the nearest rout to my next court—I have however snatched a moment on the wing to mention another assurance from our manufacturer of your cloth that he w[ld] finish it before the first of May—if he breaks this promise, it will be I think without any plausable excuse, for his workman whom he expected from the North since last November had arrived about a fortnight before I left home and was only waiting for some brushes which it was said w^d arrive the first week in this month—

In haste
y^r friend

H^H HOLMES

RC (MHi); at foot of text: "The Hon- ble Tho^s Jefferson Esq^r"; endorsed by TJ as received 25 Apr. 1814 and so recorded in SJL.

The cloth MANUFACTURER was Cyrus B. Baldwin.

## Joseph Jones Monroe to James Monroe

DEAR BROTHER. Albemarle April 23^d 1814.

Altho I did not receive your letter till after the election, my conduct on that occasion, was regulated, as nearly as circumstances woud admit, by the course it pointed out. I have long been convincd, that moderation, & forbearance, is the best course one can pursue, to- wards his enemies, & that heat & impetuosity, will, in all public dis- cussions, give them a vast ascendency over you.

M^r Carr having, at the preceding court, in a very rude, & unbecom- ing manner alluded to my conduct, I justified it, upon the principle of his being oppos'd to the admn, & asserted that I had my information, from M^r Nelson, which I had been previously authorizd to do. He then without any obliquity, was proceeding to invalidate my testi- mony, & I woud not suffer him to go on. Thus trammel'd he at length under many modifications, disclos'd what he had said to M^r Nelson, & threw himself on his vote at the last presidential election. I know- ing that his drift, & that of his abettors, was to gull the people, coud not permit him to elude the charge in this way, & repeated the sub- stance of M^r Nelson's communication to me, & assurd the people that he woud at any time verify it. On the day of the election, the polling commenc'd at an unusually early hour, & I arrivd just in time to hear him deny the charge of his being inimical to the admn, & I forthwith read M^r Nelsons certificate which had been furnish'd me by D^r Everett; after which I made a few remarks, purporting, that I knew a large majority of the people, was friendly to the admn, & if the gen- tleman had satisfied them that he was so, I had nothing to urge ag^t him, but if he concur'd in political opinion, with his friend & connex- ion, a distinguish'd member of the Senate of the U:S from Marylan'd, who had thwarted the executive in two important cases, which had recently occurd, & who I believ'd woud ere long systematically oppose, all the measures proceeding from that quarter, I did not think him a proper representative. If I had not acted in this manner I am fully assurd, that I shoud have been stigmatiz'd as a framer of falsehood, & a base calumniator.

I am the better, satisfied with having taken the above step, since I am persuaded that it effectually settled the point as to him, & has brought out into the fair & open field of public view, the arch juggler, who was by every secret sinister, & tortuous art, & machination, endeavoring to subvert the admn. As far as I can fathom their depths their plan was to get into the next legislature, as many of their creatures as possible, who woud act as leaven upon that body, & prepare it, for ulterior & more important operations. The dismission of Granger, (combin'd with other subordinate considerations) has bro<sup>t</sup> them out earlier than they had contemplated. Of this I am well assurd. You will have seen an account of a letter said to have been written by M<sup>r</sup> Jefferson to a gentleman near Philadelphia, publish'd in the Phil: Gaz: in which he inveighs ag<sup>t</sup> M<sup>r</sup> Madison, & says that nothing but the energy & good sense of the people can rescue the nation, from the effects of the mad career of that gentleman. Every word of this is true as will ere long be made to appear[1] for he has express'd himself to the post master at Milton & others, in terms unfavorable of certain recent acts of the admn,[2] & is fomenting discontents, by all the means in his power. It was ascertaind at what time this letter, woud make its appearance, in the prints here, & Wilson Nicholas was to take his stand in Richmond to give it every possible eclat, if on sounding the public mind there, he found it ripe for the meditated change; if not, to denounce it as a federal fabrication, & thus for a time the matter woud rest M<sup>r</sup> Nicholas was at his post.[3] In the interim, you & M<sup>r</sup> Madison, woud receive assurances of his most friendly & affectionate regard &c. It woud, shoud you hear of his declarations at Milton, be ask'd of you as it was on a former occasion; "Do you not know him better, than to suppose that he woud confide in such drivellers"? I believe that the destinies of the nation, are not in the hands of these people, & that they are only formidable when they act in the dark. I therefore rejoice that the curtain is drawn up, on them, & that they will be exhibited to public view in their true colors, & exact dimensions. This being done I have little doubt of the weight of the admn crushing them.

The cause assign'd by M<sup>r</sup> Jefferson for this dereliction, is, the recommendation of the late embargo law by the president. He said that restrictive measures had been tried in their fullest extent & found nugatory & unavailing. Ag$^t$ the repeal thereof, he also protests, & declaims ag$^t$ the imbecility & fickleness of the president. But this is only grimace. He knows that he does not now[4] direct the helm of our national affairs, is discontented, & thirsts for power. He sees in the admn, a disposition to compromise our differences with G. Britain, & that goads him to the soul. He has Sempronius like, been too open for the war, to take that ground, besides, it woud arrange him with the federalists. By & bye, however, he will descant upon the feebleness with which it has been conducted, & shoud a peace be form'd, he will rail ag$^t$ it as one dishonorable to the nation. The letter which he wrote to D$^r$ Logan denouncing the tyrant of the European Continent was ad captandum vulgus: & his present apostacy is with the same view. I have given you these crude & desultory reflections, because, I am thoroughly convinc'd of their truth: & if not fully known to you already, I conceive it, to be my duty from the many & important favors you have done me, independent of other ties, to communicate them to you. Hereafter on such topics I will be silent. That my opinions of this old gentleman, on whose acc$^t$ I have been twice on the eve of a duel, & have not hesitated to express have been radically changd I frankly admit it[5] whenever questiond on that subject, nor at my time of life, do I think, you ought to interdict any future development that I may think proper to make, since this change has been operated by circumstances with which You are not concern'd. But rest assur'd, that I will never wantonly, by any act of mine, give you pain or inquietude, far less cause to you deep affliction. I am most sincerely yr friend & brother.

JO: JO. MONROE

RC (ViU: George Carr Papers).

Peter Carr was a CONNEXION of Samuel Smith, United States senator from Maryland, through his marriage to Smith's sister. Smith and his fellow senatorial Tertium Quids THWARTED President James Madison in his attempt to make Albert Gallatin his secretary of state in 1809 and then forced Gallatin to give up his treasury post in 1813 when he joined the peace commission in Russia.

For the supposed letter from TJ TO A GENTLEMAN NEAR PHILADELPHIA, see note to Thomas Leiper to TJ, 17 Apr. 1814. The POST MASTER AT MILTON was Charles Vest. For the wide publicity given to a short extract DENOUNCING

Napoleon taken from TJ to George Logan, 3 Oct. 1813, see Thomas Leiper to TJ, 9 Dec. 1813. The fictional character SEMPRONIUS favored war with Julius Caesar in act 2 of Joseph Addison, *Cato: A Tragedy* (London, 1713), 18. AD CAPTANDUM VULGUS: "designed to please the crowd" (*OED*).

Apparently Joseph Jones Monroe later threatened to issue a pamphlet attacking TJ, but the publication never came to fruition (James Monroe to Charles Everett, 1 June [ViU: Monroe Papers], 17 June 1814 [ViW: Jay Johns Collection], both printed in *Tyler's Historical Quarterly* 4 [1923]: 407–8; Harry Ammon, *James Monroe: The Quest For National Identity* [1971], 352).

[1] Preceding eight words interlined.
[2] Preceding twelve words interlined.
[3] Preceding six words interlined.

[4] Preceding two words interlined.
[5] Preceding eight words interlined.

# From Horatio G. Spafford

RESPECTED FRIEND—                                    Albany, 4 Mo. 24, 1814.

Detained by some business, beyond the time that I assigned in my last, I think proper to inform thee, & that I still am preparing to go to Washington, & to see thee, as I informed thee before. In the mean time, I presume to trouble thee with a solicitation in behalf of some interest I wish to make at Washington. The present Post-Master of this city, is a most worthy man, my intimate friend. From him I have just learnt that I have been named at Washington, as his Successor. Doct. Mancius has long held the office, & though he does not wish to decline a reappointment, I believe he expects not to be continued. There are 2 other Candidates—Allen, & Dox, both young & active, capable men, & warm & zealous political partizans, friends of the administration. Dox is a batchelor, in trade, & rich enough; Allen is getting rich very fast, by a kind of broker's business, & as a trader. With these, I am willing to compete, but not on the same ground. Let the public decide, & I will be satisfied. But—they have probably made interest by long lists of names, & party friendships—I have only said that I wish the office. But I have also said that if names are necessary, I will engage to get as much of popular weight & weight of character as they can, if necessary. May I ask thy friendly regards? & be excused for the trouble I give thee? Really, I cannot see why I may not enjoy some official favor, as well as others. I have <u>done</u> as much, & <u>can</u> do as much, as these, for my country—& I pray thee to aid me with an expression of thy good wishes in this matter.

I learn that the Vice-President wishes my appointment, & that is all I have learnt about it. I have written to the President, & to the Post-Master General, soliciting the appointment; but have no Knowledge how they stand disposed. Will thy goodness excuse my solicitude, & my importunities, & extend a hand to Washington for my aid! That hand would not be extended in vain, nor its favors ill bestowed: Nor would the Administration cherish for nought.

Conscious that I trouble thee too often, I will be brief this time. Should my life & health be spared, I shall probably leave here for the South within 10 or 15 days. My Mechanical combinations are in readiness, & I go to offer thee, first of all, a discovery that rests yet solely with myself, & which I deem of vast importance. My Wife desires to join me in a very respectful assurance of high esteem, with devout wishes for thy health & happiness. Thy grateful friend,

HORATIO GATES SPAFFORD.

RC (MHi); at foot of text: "Thomas Jefferson"; endorsed by TJ as received 7 May 1814 and so recorded in SJL.

Peter P. DOX succeeded George W. Mancius as postmaster at Albany (Joseph Fry, *The Annual Register, and Albany Directory, for the year 1815* [1815], 40).

The VICE-PRESIDENT was Elbridge Gerry. No letters have been found from Spafford to PRESIDENT James Madison or to POST-MASTER GENERAL Return J. Meigs seeking appointment as Albany postmaster.

# To John Barnes

MY DEAR SIR                                   Monticello Apr. 25. 14.

Your letter of the 16th is just recieved, and I have maturely considered it, as well as the papers you were so kind as to inclose in it. it is with real pain that I feel myself irresistably forced to a conclusion which I percieve to be different from what would be yours. mr Parker's estimate of the proceeds of Gen¹ Kosciuzko's 8000.D. in 13. years, makes a difference of 2046.D. in favor of employing it in the new loan of the US. while yours makes one of 1234 D. in favor of it's remaining in the bank of Pensylvania. both go of necessity on conjectural ground as to what will be the course of these establishments during the next 13. years; he counting on a stationary interest in the bank of 9.p.c. and a value of 40.p.c. above par; and you on a progressive rise both of interest and value, the former to 11.p.c. & the latter to 55.p.cent. both suppose either a stationary or progressive course without giving sufficient weight, I think, to the progressive multiplication of banks and banking capital; a progression far more rapid than that of our population. the new banks must of necessity circumscribe the business of the old, lessen of course their profits, and the value of their capital. while the increase of our population is not more than of 3. or 4.p.c. a year, every winter's sessions of the different legislatures adds 50.p.c. to the existing number of banks, and amount of banking capital. and it is impossible to foresee where this progression, or it's effects on the present banks will stop. one effect however we cannot be decieved in, that their discounts must be curtailed, and all their surplus paper flow back upon them, and drain their vaults. considering them as having reached their maximum, & that their future values will be retrograde, I think it important to sieze the present moment of advantage, and to advance Gen[l] K.'s capital from 8000.D. to 12,700.D. at which it will be fixed in the hands of the government; & altho' it will yield a lower rate of interest, yet this being on a greater capital, it's amount will be equal; 6.p.c. for instance on 12,700.D. yielding something more [than][1] 9.p.c. on 8000.D. the amount of interest too being the same, every one would prefer to own the larger, rather than the smaller principal. while G[l] Kosciuzko will be recieving from this[2] stock between 7. & 800.D. interest in either way, it is better he should own a deposit of 12.700 D than of 8000.D. the difference of value will be palpable enough when pay-day comes. suppose at the end of 13. years, when he will recieve 12,700 D. instead of 8000.D.            there is another consideration too of which we must not lose sight, because no man on earth feels it more powerfully than Gen[l] Kosciuzko; that, our profit remaining the same in both cases, it is a duty to aid our country, of preference, with the use of our principal, during the pressure of a war for the most sacred of rights.

But there is a more serious view of this subject to be offered yet. taking a mean between the wildest and the soundest estimates of the quantum of circulating medium necessary for a country under all the circumstances of ours, we might carry it to an amount of 30. millions of Dollars, while the soundest principles really fix it at not more than 8. millions, or a dollar a head on the population. before the legislative sessions of the last winter the existing capital employed in banking thro' the whole US. was about 70. millions of Dollars, which authorised an issue of 200. millions. the legislatures of the last winter have made up the capital 100. millions, and the circulation authorised 300. millions; which is ten times more than the highest, and 40. times more than the soundest estimate of our competent circulation; and in fact advancing fast to the point of 40. for 1. at which the paper money of the revolution began generally to be refused. bank paper then must depreciate, has depreciated, and will be refused, and it would be against the evidence of our senses to suppose the banks have cash enough in their vaults to meet their issues of paper, if any circumstance of alarm should produce a run on them. the single consideration that this is the fact, whenever any accident shall draw the public attention to it, will produce that run; and this, once begun, on 2. or 3. banks, the alarm will become general. and it will be too late then to begin to save ourselves.

I will not say that this <u>will</u> take place on the bloated circulation of

<u>this</u> year; yet I think it possible and probable. but if it should not this year, the next winter adds 150. Millions more: for the bankmania raging among our legislatures is such that it will not be stopped but by a general bankruptcy. in this crush the holder of stock incurs it's total loss, because if worth any thing at all, it must go to pay the debts of the bank. their credits are a fallacious resource; for the same crush which prostrates them, bankrupts most of those who are in their debt. that this event is to take place, and that it is not distant, I as firmly believe, as that the hand of death is suspended over us all. in this belief, how could I suffer a beloved friend to remain exposed to a loss which would trench so deeply into the resources for his daily subsistence: and especially when a deposit is opened & offered to us, yielding an equal profit, and a security as stable as the earth we stand on. for such I deem the abilities and the faith of the US. I could not answer it to my friend, or to my conscience. after such a calamity to him I could never have another sound night's sleep.          we must then, my dear friend, place our General in safety. we must transfer his stock into the hands of the US. on the newly proposed loan. all the details in the execution of this change I leave to you; and will at a moment's warning execute any power or do any other act which you shall inform me to be necessary. the two certificates, one of them for 18. shares & the other for 2 shares are in my possession, and shall be forwarded to you if requisite. it will be well so to time the sales as to interrupt as little as possible the course of the current interest; and if in this way there should be some little loss, the object justifies it. for this would be the only consequence of the error of my opinion, if it be erroneous. whereas that of the contrary opinion would be a total loss. I pray you then to proceed in this matter, as being ultimately decided, and not to let slip the opportunities of subscribing.

I inclose you a letter from the General expressing his distress for want of remittance. return it to me if you please, and tell me what you think I can say to him. as to the channel of mr Crawford, I have no expectation we can use it. perhaps on a consultation with the Secretary of the Treasury, he could help us to a channel; and perhaps in the new loan the government may have the means of paying in Europe the interest of lenders residing there.          the necessity of my departure for Bedford the first week in May requires that you should be so good as to inform me quickly of whatever may be necessary for me to do to enable you to proceed in the business of transfer. ever & affectionately yours          TH: JEFFERSON

PoC (ICPRCU); at foot of first page: "Mͬ Barnes"; endorsed by TJ. Enclosure: Tadeusz Kosciuszko to TJ, 24 Jan. 1814.

George W. Campbell was the newly ap-

pointed SECRETARY OF THE TREASURY (*JEP*, 2:470, 471 [8, 9 Feb. 1814]).

[1] Omitted word editorially supplied.
[2] TJ here canceled "fund."

# From Charles Caldwell

SIR,                                         Philad͙ April 25ᵗʰ 1814

Although personally unknown to you, at least, I fear, unrecollected, I address you frankly as a man of letters, in relation to and in behalf of the literature of our country. Amidst other numerous and to me more important engagements, I have allowed myself to be prevailed on lately to take charge of the editorial department of the Port Folio, a monthly Journal with the reputation of which you are not, probably, altogether[1] unacquainted. For many years past, this work has been devoted almost[2] exclusively to American literature. Its numbers have rarely contained[3] more than a very few pages of foreign or extracted matter. It has been kept, moreover, perfectly free from party politics, polemical theology, and every other topic calculated to enkindle the passions and to inveterate prejudices, rather than to improve the intellect or ameliorate the heart. Nor is it my intention to suffer, in these respects, any change to occur in it while under my direction. But for information touching the general character and bearing of the Journal, permit me to solicit your attention to the editorial address, a copy of which accompanies this letter.

You will perceive that American biography is intended hereafter to constitute[4] a prominent department[5] in the pages of the Port Folio. It is not possible, however, that materials for filling up this in a manner creditable either to the work, the country, or the personages whose names may be introduced, can be in the possession of any individual. In relation to this point the joint contribution of numbers, and those widely scattered throughout the country, will be essential.

To you it would be worse than superfluous to speak of the importance of American biography. Fortunately the period has arrived when our fellow citizens at large have become sensible of its utility. They are delighted, moreover, with the variety of character and incident which it contains. It seems, in fact, essential to the popularity and, therefore, to the usefulness of a periodical work.

Virginia abounds and has long abounded in characters whose virtues and talents, learning and achievements are worthy to be recorded, as well in honour of the individuals[6] themselves, as for the good of[7] others. The names and merits of our revolution[ary] worthies, in particular, should never be forgotten. Yet forgotten they will be, and that at no very distant period, unless handed down by some more permanent vehicle than mere traditionary story:

I have no doubt, sir, but by this time you fathom my meaning, should I even decline being more explicit. I have read and am delighted with your biographical notice of the late Governor Lewis, prefixed to the account of his expedition to the Pacific Ocean.[8] Something of the kind from your pen, in relation to Patrick Henry, the Lees, the Randolphs or any of the other distinguished Virginians, with whom you have acted and been intimate, would be recieved as a favour of the highest order. I say from <u>your own pen</u>, in preference to any other. Should this, however be more than I am entitled to expect, or than your more important engagements will allow; perhaps you can inform me to what sources I may apply with a prospect of success—Possibly it might be practicable, by means of your personal influence with some of your literary friends, to induce them to embark in the undertaking. If under any and all of these shapes I ask too much, let my apology be the object I have in view—to rescue from oblivion American characters, to awaken in the minds of our youth those elevated and ennobling sentiments for which well written biography is so eminently calculated, and to subserve the cause of letters in our country.

The character of Patrick Henry would be peculiarly acceptable to me—so indeed would any one from your pen or through your influence.

Communications for the Port Folio are usually addressed to Bradford and Inskeep, Booksellers, Philadelphia. Any note you may have the goodness to forward in answer to this will bear my own address— viz D<sup>r</sup> Charles Caldwell, Philadelphia.

Should you have in possession any original articles other than biographical, suitable for a monthly miscellany, I need not express to you with what pleasure I would receive them.

I have the honour to be, with the highest consideration,

Your obedient and Very Humble servant     CH: CALDWELL

RC (DLC); chipped; at foot of text: "Thomas Jefferson Esq<sup>r</sup>"; endorsed by TJ as received 7 May 1814 and so recorded in SJL, which describes it as a letter from Dr. John Caldwell.

Charles Caldwell (1772–1853), physi-cian, author, editor, and medical educator, was a native North Carolinian. After serving as a schoolmaster in that state, in 1792 he moved to Philadelphia, where he studied under Benjamin Rush and received a medical degree in 1796 from the University of Pennsylvania. In the latter year he was elected to the American Philosophical Society. After establishing a practice in Philadelphia, Caldwell joined the Academy of Medicine, the Philadelphia Medical Society, and the city board of health. He delivered medical lectures at the Philadelphia Almshouse, 1805–11, and served as a professor of geology and the philosophy of natural history at the University of Pennsylvania, 1816–19. Initiating a long career as a translator and author of medical works by 1795, Caldwell also wrote widely on biographical, literary, political, and scientific topics. He contributed to the *Port Folio* by 1809 and edited the journal from 1814 until 1816. Caldwell moved in 1819 to Lexington, Kentucky, to accept a faculty position in the new medical department at Transylvania University. In 1837 he became the first professor of the Louisville Medical Institute (later the University of Louisville), remaining in this position until 1849. Caldwell played a leading role at both of these trans-Appalachian medical schools. In 1825 he visited TJ at Monticello (*ANB*; *DAB*; Harriot W. Warner, ed., *Autobiography of Charles Caldwell, M.D.* [1855; repr. 1968 with introduction by Lloyd G. Stevenson], esp. p. 346; Albert H. Smyth, *The Philadel-*

*phia Magazines and Their Contributors: 1741–1850* [1892], 142–5; APS, Minutes, 21 Oct. 1796 [MS in PPAmP]; William Wirt to TJ, 11 June 1825; Lunsford P. Yandell, "A Memoir of Dr. Charles Caldwell," *Western Journal of Medicine and Surgery* 12 [1853]: 101–16).

INVETERATE: "to root or implant deeply" (*OED*). In an EDITORIAL ADDRESS dated 11 Apr. 1814 and appearing in the following month's issue, the new editor of the *Port Folio* expressed his intention to continue promoting American literature and solicited contributions, particularly examples of American biography (*Port Folio* 3 [1814]: 383–98; Poor, *Jefferson's Library*, 14 [no. 921]). For TJ's biography of Meriwether LEWIS see TJ to Paul Allen, 18 Aug. 1813, printed at that date as the first in a group of documents on TJ's Biography of Meriwether Lewis.

[1] Manuscript: "alogether."
[2] Word interlined.
[3] Word interlined.
[4] Manuscript: "contitute."
[5] Word interlined in place of "article."
[6] Manuscript: "indiduals."
[7] Caldwell here canceled "posterity."
[8] Word interlined.

# From John Waldo

SIR, Geo Town. S C. April 25th 1814

For your obliging and highly esteemed favour of August 16th please[1] to accept my warmest thanks. My apology for not presenting them at a much earlier period, is this; My business of teaching leaves but a little of my time unoccupied, & the preservation of my health requires a great proportion of that little to be devoted to relaxation & exercise. Had I contemplated writing only the few lines to which I am even now, confined, I should certainly have sent you my immediate acknowledgment. But the subject on which you have honoured me with your very ingenious and learned remarks, is truly interesting to me & in a great measure novel. It therefore excited my curiosity, and induced me to think of bestowing some attention upon it; & of making you the poor return of some additional remarks of my own. I have however the mortification of finding myself after this long interval, no nearer obtaining the object of my wish than I was at first. When I received the letter I was suffering from more than usually bad health, which for months put it out of my power to do more than to attend to the duties of my school. Since, I have recov[ere]d my usual, but infirm health, I have been engaged, the few leisure moments I could catch, in abridging my grammar, and in preparing my spelling books for the press. As the warm[2] weather returns, my health becomes more feeble; and some additional private business also requires my attention for some time. I have therefore, altho' the above works are off my hands, not a moment that has not its regular business. That my situation thus limits my pursuits, and almost wholly denies me the satisfaction of attending to literary subjects, except the first elements, to which the business of teaching confines me, and which lose their relish by their daily recurrence, would be to me the subject of severe regret, were I not satisfied that the duties Providence has imposed upon me, tho' humble and laborious, are most important to society, and that it is the part of wisdom, as well as of our duty to acquiesce with cheerfulness, in that disposition of ourselves & of our time, which we find not left to our own choice to alter.

I had an opportunity of shewing your letter to many of yours, as well as my own friends, who think with me, that it is ably written, and that you ought to consent to its publication. Tho' I was satisfied that you could have no objection to its being presented to the public, I did not think it correct to do it without your express approbation. I will therefore thank you to write me on the subject.

Your ob[t] Serv[t]                                JOHN WALDO

RC (DLC); one word illegible; endorsed by TJ as received 17 May 1814 and so recorded in SJL.

The works that Waldo was PREPARING for publication included *An Abridgment of Waldo's Rudiments of English*

*Grammar* (Philadelphia, 1814) and *The Dictionary Spelling Book* (Georgetown, S.C., 1816).

[1] Manuscript: "plase."
[2] Manuscript: "worm."

# To José Corrêa da Serra

DEAR SIR                                Monticello Apr. 26.[1] 14.

Your favor of the 10th by the delays of our winter post, is but just recieved and mine of the 19th I presume reaches you about this time. they have passed each other by the way. I am sorry that your visit to us will be delayed until your return from Kentucky; mais tout ce qui est differé n'est pas perdu; and it will then and always be welcome.

you promise also to call on us en passant. should I have set out on my journey to Bedford, you will find mr & mrs Randolph here who will recieve you with the pleasure your society gives us all; as they will also your companion mr Walsh. his visit I should lose personally with real regret, entertaining equal esteem for his worth and talents. it is still however possible that I may be detained some days longer than I expect; as my departure hangs on certain circumstances not within my controul. should you therefore have left Philadelphia on the 1st of May as you propose, and make no stay at Washington, I do not entirely despair of participating of your company here, altho' you may not have recieved this letter apprising you of the possibility.

The first Western mail shall carry a letter to Gov$^r$ Claiborne, or perhaps to a friend in Natchez more conversant in Botanical researches, to engage an execution of your request as to the Bowwood.　　　　not entirely without a hope of seeing yourself & mr Walsh here, but in every case wishing you a pleasant journey & safe return, I salute you with affection & respect.　　Th: Jefferson

PoC (DLC: TJ Papers, 201:35743); at foot of text: "M. Correa de Serra"; endorsed by TJ.

mais tout ce qui est differé n'est pas perdu: "but not all that is postponed is lost." The friend in natchez was Samuel Brown, to whom TJ wrote on 28 Apr. 1814.

[1] Reworked from "25."

# From David Isaacs

Ap$^l$ 26$^{th}$ 1814

I rec$^d$ the 5 $ Note by the Boy but my Boys nor Fish have not come yet and i do not expect them till to Night or tomorrow morning, when i will with Pleasure sent M$^r$ Jefferson 6 of the best Shad the boys Brings and also the Change　　　　am Respectfully yours

David Isaacs

RC (MHi); dateline beneath signature; addressed: "Tho$^s$ Jfferson Esquire Monticelloe"; endorsed by TJ.

David Isaacs (ca. 1761–1837), merchant, was a German native who initially settled in Richmond, where he and his brother Isaiah Isaacs joined Jacob Cohen in the mercantile firm of Cohen & Isaacs and helped found the Beth Shalome synagogue. Early in the 1790s both of the Isaacs brothers moved to Charlottesville, where David Isaacs worked for many years as a merchant. TJ called on him for a wide range of food, books, and supplies from about 1799 until his own death in 1826. Isaacs contributed $50 in 1825 to the nascent University of Virginia. During the last decade of his life he was involved in legal proceedings related to his common-law marriage to a free woman of color and to the settlement of his brother's estate, and in 1832 his daughter Julia Ann Isaacs married Eston

Hemings, TJ's freed slave and probably his son by Sally Hemings (Joshua D. Rothman, *Notorious in the Neighborhood: Sex and Families across the Color Line in Virginia, 1787–1861* [2003], 54–91; *MB,* esp. 2:1007; Isaacs to TJ, 5 Sept. 1816, 1 Feb. 1818; ViU: Proctor's Papers; Albemarle Co. Will Book, 12:366–70, 396–7; gravestone in Hebrew Cemetery, Richmond).

# To Horatio G. Spafford

DEAR SIR                                                   Monticello Apr. 26. 14.

Your letter of the 7th inst. is just recieved and finds me within a few days of my departure for a distant possession which I visit 3. or 4. times a year & am absent a month at a time. the suspension of these visits during winter renders indispensable as early a one as practicable in spring, and I expect to be absent all May. I hasten therefore to mention this, lest we should both be disappointed by my absence at the time of the visit with which your letter flatters me. this would be a subject of regret, and, as from the letter I understand that your journey is not restrained to a particular moment, I hope this may enable you so to time it as to find me at home.          I very much doubt the effect of the application you propose at Washington. the principle of rotation is not that of our constitution; nor has it ever been acted on by our government. I believe there has never been an instance of removing an officer who has well done his duty, merely on the consideration that he has been long enough in office, and ought to give way to some other.

I am sensible of the kindness of your confidence in me, when you propose to communicate to me a discovery in mechanics of the importance you intimate, and which you have not trusted to any other. that the secret should be kept by me, I am not afraid to say. but I have so long laid aside all mechanical studies, and indeed all subjects which requiring a severe application of the mind my age indisposes me to, that I have lost my familiarity with them, and feel a consciousness that to a mind long occupied on a particular problem in mechanics, it would not be likely that any thing I could offer, would be new or not before contemplated. tho' therefore I should be ready to render any aid or service in my power, I feel it a duty to apprise you of this disqualification, while I express my wishes for it's complete success & the assurance of my great esteem & respect.

TH: JEFFERSON

RC (NjMoHP: Lloyd W. Smith Collection); edge torn, with missing text supplied from PoC; addressed: "Mr Horatio G. Spafford at Albany"; franked; postmarked Charlottesville, 27 Apr.; endorsed by Spafford as received 4 May 1814. PoC (DLC); endorsed by TJ.

Spafford's LETTER OF THE 7TH INST. was actually a letter of 30 Mar. with a postscript dated 7 Apr. 1814.

# From John Barnes

DEAR SIR                                          George Town 27ʰ April 1814—

I had this morning the pleasure of Presenting—your letter of the 22ᵈ Ultº with the inclosed (herewith returned you) to Genˡ Armstrong—and—withal tendered to him—your many thanks, for his politeness—in receiving paying, & forwarding the Articles therein mentioned—it had escaped his recollection, inquiring After your health &ᵃ beged I would tender to you his most respectfull good wishes for its continuance—          I tendered[1] the Genˡ ten dollars—but, he would not receive more than Eight—rating five francs to the dollar—

waiting your Answer to mine of the[2] 16 Insᵗ

I am Dear Sir, your very Obedᵗ                              JOHN BARNES.

PS. The good President left Washington this Morning abᵗ 9. ºCk. for Montpelier. I was a ¼ of an hour too late—in paying my respects, and in wishing him a pleasant & safe Journey. After the fatigue of an Anxious and most interesting long session

We are not to expect any More Cossack dinners—Their Orator—Mʳ Harper having proved to be but, a false prophet!—

RC (ViU: TJP-ER); postscript on verso of address leaf; addressed: "Thomas Jefferson, Esquire, Monticello—Virginia"; franked and postmarked; endorsed by TJ as received 7 May 1814 and so recorded in SJL. Enclosure: Claude Antoine Prieur Duvernois to TJ, 5 Sept. 1810.

Federalist Robert Goodloe HARPER proclaimed in a speech at a 5 June 1813 dinner celebrating the recent French defeats in Russia that the "triumphal car of other conquerors has passed over the necks of prostrate nations. As the tri-

umphal car of Alexander advances, prostrate nations rise up and hail him as their deliverer" (*Correspondence respecting Russia, between Robert Goodloe Harper, Esq. and Robert Walsh, Jun. together with the Speech of Mr. Harper, commemorative of the Russian Victories. Delivered at Georgetown, Columbia, June 5th, 1813. and An Essay on the Future State of Europe* [Philadelphia, 1813], quotation on p. 27).

[1] Manuscript: "tended."
[2] Manuscript: "of the of the."

# From Nicolas G. Dufief

MONSIEUR,                                    A Philadelphie ce 27 Avril 1814

J'ai reçu, avec bien de la reconnaissance, la déclaration que vous vous êtes donné la peine de m'envoyer. Elle est amplement Suffisante pour lever tous les doutes qu'on aurait pu avoir au Sujet de l'affaire désagréable que des ennemis m'ont Suscité. Mais comme il pourrait peut-être arriver qu'il me[1] fût utile de produire une pareille pièce en Justice, Je vous prie de m'en envoyer une autre où vous déclariez Simplement le Seul fait que je ne vous ai ni vendu, ni envoyé l'ouvrage intitulé: la création par R. De Bécourt.[2] Je Suis assuré d'avance que vous approuverez mes motifs. J'aimerais mieux perdre ma cause que de la gagner en manquant aux règles de la Bienséance, & en causant le moindre déplaisir aux personnes qui comme vous ont des bontés pour moi.

Je vous adresse par le courrier de demain le 3ème & dernier volume de Newton

J'ai l'honneur d'être avec tous les Sentimens qui vous Sont dus
Votre très-dévoué Serviteur                              N. G. DUFIEF

P.S connaissant votre extrême obligeance, Il est de mon devoir de vous prémunir contre les pièges que pourrait tendre à votre génêrosité Bécourt de l'Immoralité & de l'ingratitude duquel J'ai été la victime

EDITORS' TRANSLATION

SIR,                                          Philadelphia 27 April 1814

I have received, with much gratitude, the testimony that you took the trouble of sending me. It is more than enough to remove any doubts one could have had regarding the unpleasant affair that some of my enemies stirred up against me. But as it may prove useful for me to produce such a document in court, I ask you to forward me another copy in which you would simply state the single fact that I have neither sold nor sent you the work entitled: *La Création du Monde*, by R. de Bécourt. I am certain that you will approve of my motives. I would rather lose my case than win it by failing to observe the proprieties, and by causing the slightest displeasure to people who like you have been kind to me.

I am sending Newton's third and final volume to you by tomorrow's post
I have the honor to be with all the sentiments which are your due
Your very devoted servant                              N. G. DUFIEF

P.S. Knowing your great kindness, it is my duty to warn you about the traps that Bécourt, of whose immorality and ingratitude I have been the victim, might set to take advantage of your generosity

RC (DLC); endorsed by TJ as received 7 May and so recorded in SJL. Translation by Dr. Genevieve Moene.

[1] Word interlined.
[2] Manuscript: "Bécout."

# To Samuel Brown

DEAR SIR                                                 Monticello Apr. 28. 14.

Your favor of Feb. 8. was recieved on the 9th of March. I thank you for the trouble you have taken respecting Henderson, whose testimony would have been valuable to me: but I doubt if he would have given it, having latterly had reason to suspect that himself was the cheat by whom I lose 2000. Dollars. I sincerely sympathise[1] with you in the affliction mentioned in your letter. experience of every loss which can rend the human heart has taught me that time and occupation are the only medicines for grief. one of the misfortunes of living too long is the loss of all one's early friends and affections. when I review the ground over which I have passed since my youth, I see it strewed like a field of battle with the bodies of deceased friends. I stand like a solitary tree in a field, it's trunk indeed erect, but it's limbs fallen off, and it's neighboring plants eradicated from around it. I do not know whether we should rejoice in such inventions as D[r] Jenning's, which promises, or rather threatens, to make us live beyond our time. his vapor bath is rising into notice. like all new things it is to do every thing. I have no doubt however that when sobered down by sound observation, it will be found to do much. I inclose something on that subject, cut out of a newspaper, on the presumption it may not have reached you.          We are all, as you describe your neighbors, getting into home spun; and so universally is houshold manufacture established that I am certain it will never again be abandoned. I have three spinning Jennies employed for clothing ourselves; and the consumption of the US. will offer a great market for your cotton independant of piracies by sea & prohibitions on the land. our merchants agree that their future dealings will be confined to groceries & fancy goods.          I rejoice with you in the downfall of Bonaparte. this scourge of the world has occasioned the deaths of at least ten millions of human beings, and for what? that he may be called a conqueror, a Robin Hood of the big breed, and end at last in bringing on his own nation the devastation he has spread over others. how fortunate for mankind if the tyrannies of England could have been arrested and retorted in like manner, that both the land and sea robbers could have been suppressed at the same time. but I see no term to her piracies but in that bankruptcy in which mad expences, so much beyond her resources, must end.

I have carefully committed to the earth the seeds you were so kind as to send me the last summer. the Capsicum I am anxious to see up; but it does not yet shew itself. nor do the garavances appear. I do not yet however despair of them. I have just recieved from an European friend, M. Correa de Serra, a request to engage some friend on the Missisipi to send me a young branch or two of the Bow-wood, or bois d'arc of Louisiana, pressed in brown paper with their leaves, and both the male & female flowers. also some of the fruit, either dry, or in a mixture of $\frac{1}{3}$ whiskey & $\frac{2}{3}$ water. the dry no doubt can come most conveniently by mail. also in the proper season some ripe seeds. can I get the favor of you to execute the commission? M$^r$ Correa is now at Philadelphia, setting out on a visit to Kentuckey. he is perhaps the most learned man in the world. not merely in books, but in men & things. and a more amiable & interesting one I have never seen. altho' a stranger to no science, he is fondest of Botany. should you have gone to Kentucky as your last letter seemed to contemplate, take him to your bosom, and recommend all the attentions to him by which our brethren of Kentucky can honor themselves. you spoke in your letter of a visit to the Atlantic states, & of the possibility even of our seeing you at Monticello. 'calculo albo diem notarem' as the Antients did their days of good fortune. here, and every where I wish you all the health and felicities of life. TH: JEFFERSON

RC (ViU: TJP); torn at creases, with missing text supplied from PoC; addressed: "Doct$^r$ Samuel Brown Natchez"; franked; postmarked Charlottesville, 29 Apr. PoC (DLC); endorsed by TJ.

The enclosed NEWSPAPER cutting may have been an article and series of testimonials from the Richmond *Enquirer*, 19 Mar. 1814, indicating that Samuel K.

Jennings had recently relocated to that city and published a pamphlet about his portable bath (see note to Jennings to TJ, 30 Oct. 1813). CALCULO ALBO DIEM NOTAREM: "I would signify the day with a white pebble," a reference to the practice by which the ANTIENTS marked their personal calendars with white or black pebbles respectively for good or bad days.

[1] Word interlined in place of "condole."

# To Luis de Onís

Monticello Apr. 28. 14.

I thank you, Sir, for the copy of the new constitution of Spain which you have been so kind as to send me; and I sincerely congratulate yourself & the Spanish nation on this great stride towards

political happiness. the invasion of Spain has been the most unprecedented & unprincipled of the transactions of modern times. the
crimes of it's enemies, the licentiousness of it's associates in defence,
the exertions and sufferings of it's inhabitants under slaughter &
famine, and it's consequent depopulation, will mark indelibly the
baneful ascendancy of the tyrants of the sea and continent, & charac-
terise with blood & wretchedness the age in which they have lived.
yet these sufferings of Spain will be remunerated, her population restored & increased, under the auspices and protection of this new
constitution; and the miseries of the present generation will be the
price, and even the cheap price[1] of the prosperity of endless generations to come.          there are parts of this constitution however in
which you would expect of course that we should not concur. one of
these is the intolerance of all but the Catholic religion; and no security provided against the reestablishment of an inquisition, the exclusive judge of Catholic opinions, and authorised to proscribe & punish
those it shall deem a-catholic. 2$^{dly}$ the aristocracy, quater sublimata,
of her legislators: for the ultimate electors of these will themselves
have been three times sifted from the mass of the people, and may
chuse from the nation at large persons never named by any of the
electoral bodies.          but there is one provision which will immortalise it's inventors. it is that which, after a certain epoch, disfran-
chises every citizen who cannot read and write. this is new; and is
the fruitful germ of the improvement of every thing good, and the
correction of every thing imperfect in the present constitution. this
will give you an enlightened people, and an energetic public opinion
which will controul and enchain the aristocratic spirit of the government. on the whole I hail your country as now likely to resume
and surpass it's antient splendor among nations.          this might
perhaps have been better secured by a just confidence in the self-
sufficient strength of the Peninsul itself; every thing without it's limits being it's weakness not it's force. if the mother country has not the
magnanimity to part with the colonies in friendship, thereby making
them, what they would certainly be, their natural and firmest allies,
these will emancipate themselves, after exhausting her strength and
resources in ineffectual efforts to hold them in subjection. they will be
rendered enemies of the mother country, as England has rendered us
by an unremitting course of insulting injuries and silly provocations.
I do not say this from the impulse of national interests. for I do not
know that the US. would find an interest in the independance of
neighbor nations, whose produce and commerce would rivalize ours.

it could only be that kind of interest which every human being has in the happiness and prosperity of every other. but putting right and reason out of the question, I have no doubt that on calculations of interest alone, it is that of Spain to anticipate voluntarily, and as a matter of grace and friendship, the independance of her colonies, which otherwise necessity will enforce.

I avail myself of this occasion of entering into some explanations which my daughter mrs Randolph is anxious should be conveyed to Madame de Onis. about the time (in 1809.) when you honored me with a letter, inclosing one from my friend mr Yznardi, Madame de Onis was so kind as to address a note to mrs Randolph covering a letter from mrs Hackley. this seemed to have been entrusted to a Member of Congress for conveyance, as it came inclosed from one, who perhaps mislaid or forgot it, till some months had elapsed. it found her under a long and afflicting spell of sickness, & among the first acts of her convalescence was the writing an answer expressing her thanks to M$^e$ de Onis and the assurances of her great respect. this answer she was afterwards made to apprehend, by information from mrs Hackley, had never got to hand; and that she might have suffered in the estimation of M$^e$ de Onis as guilty of an omission of duty of which she is incapable. it is at her request that I take the liberty of placing this transaction here, and of praying thro' this channel to pass to Madame de Onis the renewed assurances of her great respect and consideration; and joining with them my own, I beg leave to tender to yourself the same, with sincere wishes for your health and happiness. Th: Jefferson

PoC (DLC); at foot of first page: "Le Chevalier de Onis." Tr (TJ Editorial Files); 1957 typescript by an Onís descendant; at head of text: "To His Excellency Don Luis De Onis." Tr (ViU: GT); at head of text "ex$^d$"; posthumous copy.

QUATER SUBLIMATA: "four times raised." Members of the Spanish Cortes were to be THREE TIMES removed from the MASS OF THE PEOPLE, in that they would be chosen following elections at the parish, district, and provincial levels, only the first of which would be by a popular vote. 1830 was the EPOCH after which illiterate citizens would be disfranchised (*Constitution of the Spanish Monarchy. Promulgated at Cadiz on the 19th of March, 1812* [Philadelphia, 1814; Sowerby, no. 2424], 7, 9).

[1] Preceding five words not in 1957 Tr.

# From Charles Caldwell

SIR, Philad$^a$ April 30$^{th}$ 1814.

As it is not known to me whether or not you have had an opportunity of becoming acquainted with the character of the Port Folio, your acceptance of a copy of it is respectfully solicited. Being a perfect tyro in the direction of a public journal, I possess, as yet, on that subject, neither pride to be wounded, nor prejudices to be overcome. Any opinion, therefore, you may have the goodness to express touching the merit of the number I inclose, or the manner in which the work may be improved, will be thankfully received. The decision of enlightened and liberal criticism I hold myself bound to listen to and regard: for, as far as I am personally concerned, my object is reputation and self-improvement rather than emolument.

While I again solicit[1] from you, proximately or indirectly, such aid as it may suit your views and your convenience to afford, suffer me to repeat the sentiments of high consideration, with which I have the honour to be

Your Obedient and Very Humble servant        Ch: Caldwell

P.S. The Port Folio is published on the first day of each month, and shall be regularly forwarded to you hereafter, as soon as prepared.

C. C

RC (DLC); between signature and postscript: "Thomas Jefferson Esq<sup>r</sup>"; endorsed by TJ as received 7 May 1814 and so recorded in SJL, which describes it as a letter from Dr. John Caldwell. Enclosure: an unidentified issue of the *Port Folio* (Poor, *Jefferson's Library*, 14 [no. 921]).

[1] Word interlined in place of "request."

# From Francis Corbin

The Reeds. April 30<sup>th</sup> 1814
Dear Sir                near White Chimnies Post office Caroline County.
I have just heard of M<sup>rs</sup> Paradise's death.

M<sup>r</sup> Wales, M<sup>r</sup> Waller, and my Father were Col: Ludwell's Trustees for his Daughters and their descendants. you, Col: Skipwith, M<sup>r</sup> Benjamin Waller & myself are the sole surviving Executors of those Trustees. A Trusteeship, I think, the Lawyers say, never dies. Are we not bound then to look to the Estate left by M<sup>rs</sup> Paradise, who has several Grandchildren in Italy? The decision of the Court of Appeals, relative to Aliens, I presume, does not affect the Rights & Interests of these Children. Is it not our duty then to take possession of the Estate, & hold it till we can fulfil our Trust?

Be good enough, Sir, to give me your opinion on this subject that I may co-operate with you, Col: Skipwith and M<sup>r</sup> Benj: Waller in doing what may be proper. I am unwilling to run risques if I can avoid them, tho' the size of my family, the state of my health, and the scantiness of my Fortune afford me no leisure to attend to other business than my own.

With great Respect,

I have the Honor to be, Dear Sir, Your Mo: ob^t Serv^t

FRANCIS CORBIN

RC (DLC); dateline beneath signature; at foot of text: "Thomas Jefferson Esq^r Monticello"; endorsed by TJ as received 17 May 1814 and so recorded in SJL.

Francis Corbin (ca. 1759–1821), planter and public official, was probably a native of King and Queen County. In 1773 he was sent to be educated in England, where he was admitted to the Inner Temple of the Inns of Court for legal training in 1777. He returned to Virginia after the Revolutionary War. Corbin represented Middlesex County in the Virginia House of Delegates, 1784–94, and at the state ratification convention of 1788, where he supported the new United States Constitution. He ran unsuccessfully for the United States House of Representatives in 1789, 1790, and 1793. Corbin lost a bid to serve in the United States Senate in 1792 and subsequently withdrew from public life to manage The Reeds, his large Caroline County estate. In 1817 he was named a director of the Richmond branch of the Second Bank of the United States, a position he held at his death (*DVB*; *PTJ*, esp. 30:286–7; numerous letters in DLC: Madison Papers; *VMHB* 30 [1922]: 315–8; Leonard, *General Assembly*; Merrill Jensen, John P. Kaminski, and others, eds., *The Documentary History of the Ratification of the Constitution* [1976– ], vols. 8–10; William P. Palmer and others, eds., *Calendar of Virginia State Papers* [1875–93], 5:448; Norfolk *American Beacon and Commercial Diary*, 5 Feb. 1817; *Richmond Enquirer*, 1 June 1821; Washington *Daily National Intelligencer*, 9 June 1821).

TJ's father-in-law John Wayles (WALES), Benjamin WALLER and Richard Corbin were named as trustees to Lucy Ludwell Paradise and the other daughters of Philip LUDWELL in 1767 (Archibald Bolling Shepperson, *John Paradise and Lucy Ludwell of London and Williamsburg* [1942], 34). The Virginia COURT OF APPEALS upheld the confiscation of land from the heirs of Lord Fairfax in 1810 but the United States Supreme Court overturned the decision in 1813 and confirmed that judgment three years later (*Va. Reports*, 15 [1 Munford]: 218–38; *U.S. Reports*, 11 [7 Cranch]: 603–32; Marshall, *Papers*, 8:108–26).

# From Joseph Delaplaine

SIR,                                        Philadelphia April 30. 1814.

Since I took the liberty of writing to you respecting the portraits of Columbus & Americus Vespusius, I am enabled to send you a perfect proposal of my Biographical work, in the first volume of which your portrait & a Biographical sketch of your life will be given.

I shall be happy if you will authorize me to put [your]¹ name with others on my list as a subscriber.

With the highest respect & esteem

I am your obed^t hum^l serv^t                JOSEPH DELAPLAINE

RC (DLC); at foot of text: "The Hon^ble Thomas Jefferson late Pres^t of the U. States"; endorsed by TJ as received 7 May 1814 and so recorded in SJL.

For the PROPOSAL OF MY BIOGRAPHICAL WORK see note to Delaplaine to TJ, 16 Apr. 1814.

[1] Omitted word editorially supplied.

# From William Shirman

SIR                                           Bent Creek, Ap^l 30^th 1814

I had the pleasure of Recving your letter the 16^th Ins^t & the Contents truely observ^d had I Recv^d it in time, Should been happy to have Complide as to Writing you[1] an answer By M^r Th^s Randolph from Nelson Court, you will please to excuse me for not meeting you at your place in Bedford as I was at that time So Ingage^d put it out of my power.

It is my firm resurlution to acomidate you in perfoming your Business to your Satisfaction Provided you Can wate untill I Comply with my Present Ingagements here

If It will Sute you I Can Commence business for you by the 15^th of July next

If it is agreeable to you to wate untill then I will thank you for a few lines as Soon as posible If you wish me to Come to your house, before the 15^th of July, I will take a pleasure in doing So, Wherein wee Can Come on pointed Turms—

I am Your Humble Sev^t                         W^M SHIRMAN

RC (MHi); endorsed by TJ as received 26 June 1814 and so recorded in SJL.

[1] Manuscript: "you you."

# From Abraham Small

SIR                                    Philadelphia April 30^th [1814]

Perhaps it would best become me to apologise, for the liberty I take in requesting your acceptance of the Book which accompanies this—My heart tells me it is but a poor expression of my veneration for you

If you should have leisure to look through it, I hope it will indicate the bias of the Compilers mind, & those principles to which your life has been devoted

The little time it has been before the public, seems to promise another Edition—Could I through your instrumentality improve the

Indian department of it?—nothing of that nature has I believe escaped your notice—my endeavors here, have been either ill-directed or in vain—however this may be, I hope you will forgive the expression of what you can never be divested

the fervent & heartfelt affection—of your most h^ble Ser^t

ABR^M SMALL

RC (MiU-C); corner torn; at foot of text: "The Hon^ble Thomas Jefferson"; endorsed by TJ as a letter of 30 Apr. 1814 received 13 May 1814 and so recorded in SJL. Enclosure: Small, *The American Speaker; a Selection of Popular, Parliamentary and Forensic Eloquence; particularly calculated for the Seminaries in the United States*, 2d ed. (Philadelphia, 1814; Poor, *Jefferson's Library*, 13 [no. 819]).

Abraham Small (1765–1829), printer, was a native of Taunton, England. He was in Philadelphia by 1796, when he formed a three-year-long partnership with John Thompson for the purpose of printing America's first hot-pressed

Bible. From about 1800 until 1813 Small partnered with William Young Birch, after which he worked independently as a printer and stationer until at least 1825 (H. Glenn Brown and Maude O. Brown, *A Directory of the Book-Arts and Book Trade in Philadelphia to 1820, Including Painters and Engravers* [1950], 20, 110, 118; *MB*, 2:979, 984, 996; Thomas Wilson, ed., *The Philadelphia Directory and Stranger's Guide for 1825* [Philadelphia, 1825], 128; Edward L. Clark, *A Record of the Inscriptions on the Tablets and Grave-Stones in the Burial-Grounds of Christ Church, Philadelphia* [1864], 579; Philadelphia *United States Gazette*, 16 Sept. 1829).

# To Louis H. Girardin

May 1. 14.

Th: Jefferson returns his thanks to M^r Girardin for the Sabots, which will be of real value to him. he sends him all the Tomata seed he has. he had rode out when mr Girardin's note came, or it should have been then sent. it should be planted immediately.

RC (PPAmP: Thomas Jefferson Papers); dateline at foot of text; addressed: "M^r Girardin." Not recorded in SJL.

MR GIRARDIN'S NOTE is not recorded in SJL and has not been found. SJL also records a missing letter from Girardin to TJ of 9 Apr., received the same day.

# From David Isaacs

SIR                                                                          May 1 1814

The Boy just arrived and i hasten to forward you Six of the best they Brot the trip has been a long one, and the Fish cost 1/6 a peice on Shore I cant Sell them for less than 3/—to Save myself—I hope they will meet your approbation

Your &^c

D ISAACS

RC (MHi); dateline beneath signature; at foot of text: "Thos Jefferson Esqr"; endorsed by TJ as a letter of May 1814.

TJ recorded paying Isaacs $3 on this date for SIX shad (*MB*, 2:1299).

# From John Barnes

MY DEAR SIR—                                        George Town 2d May 1814—
   Your much Esteem'ed, very Particular and interresting favr of the 25h Ulto recd by Yesterdays Mail—has been Attentively perused—Yr reasoning and determination fully conclusive—the Confidential deposit, of an Absent friend—wholly dependent on your Judgement, for the safety[1] of his property do not admit (at these eventfull times) even the shadow of a Risque—less then Goverment security. I shall therefore hasten to Execute your final Commands, respecting the sale of Genl Ks 20. shares of Penna Bank stock. and transpose their Net proceeds—in Subscribing—to the New loan <u>U States.</u> for which purpose, it will (—I presume)—be Necessary for you, to Authorize me, by power of Atty—to sell—in your behalf—as Agent, and sole Atty— for the said Genl T. K:—meanwhile—I shall use my, best endeavrs to effect the sale, so, as to meet—and secure the whole subscription—for which purpose I have by this days Mail—wrote Mr Taylor to prepare himself, by stating to me the present Currt price, and certainty of Sale, terms &c for my govermt—the first subscription per Advertizt takes place the 25h Inst—

|  |  | $\frac{1}{4}$ say |
|---|---|---|
| The Amot I contemplate to subscribe— |  |  |
| (if agreele)[2] | $10,000. | 2,500. |
| I have now in hand—of the Genls | 1694.50. |  |
| with the proceeds of dividend due | } say 390 " |  |
| 1t Jany last (not recd—waiting yr order,)[3] |  |  |
| together with your Years Int due last Mo | 360 " | 2,444.50 |
| deficient on 1t Subn only |  | 55.50 |
| for 2d Subn 25h June | 2,500 " |  |
| " 3d do 25h July | 2,500 " |  |
| " 4h do 25th Aug. | 2,500 " | 7,500 " |
|  |  | $7,555.50 |

The presumed Net proceeds of <u>$8000</u> " ⎫
penna Bank Stock Clear of all            ⎬
exps say a 40 ℌCt—may be  $11.200.  ⎭  will leave,
the good Genl an Ample surplus for a Remittance
the present—and with the growing Int. for the coming Year—

with these particulars—if nearly Correct, you will be pleased to signify—your Assent.—or—Correction—,
the next most essensial—and Anxious Concern will be to furnish the
good Gen$^l$ with a suitable Remittance and sh$^d$ be happy to be furnished—with a letter of introduction to the Sect$^y$ of the Treasury, to
whom I am a perfect stranger—or, to M$^r$ Monroe—either of whom I,
should suppose could fav$^r$ me, with their Aid in conveying—a Remittance ( —if to be effected)—either by Bill of ex: or, on M$^r$ Crawford—
either—on his Acco$^t$ w$^h$ the Treasury or his own family Acc$^t$—
　with perfect Esteem & Respect,
　I am Dear Sir—Your most Obed$^t$ serv$^t$　　　JOHN BARNES,

Note. $10,000, if a 88 for $100 will produce $11,363$\frac{50}{100}$ on Loan a
　　6 ℔C$^t$ is $681–$\frac{81}{100}$ ℔ Anm?
Q$^{re}$ as the Gen$^{ls}$ 20 shares are in 2 Certificates viz 1 of 18 & 1. of 2,
　　whether or not they require—seperate powers—said Certifi-
　　cates—must I presume be endorsed—the Gen$^l$ Letter not yet
　　translated shall be forwarded to you, ℔ next opportunity—

RC (ViU: TJP-ER); at foot of text:
"To Thomas Jefferson Esq$^r$ Monticello";
endorsed by TJ as received 7 May 1814
and so recorded in SJL.

GEN$^L$ K$^S$: Tadeusz Kosciuszko's. THE
GEN$^L$ LETTER: Kosciuszko to TJ, 24 Jan.
1814.

[1] Manuscript: "safty."
[2] Omitted closing parenthesis editorially supplied.
[3] Omitted closing parenthesis editorially supplied.

# From John Barnes

DEAR SIR　　　　　　　　　Monday 2 °Ck PM—2$^d$ May 1814,
　since the close of my letter & deposit in the post Office—I waited
on the Cash$^r$ of Bank of Columbia—for information respecting Subscribing[1] to the loan—he informed me—this being the last day for receiving Offer, & terms—he was then preparing his—in order to wait
on the Sect$^y$ of the Treasury.—he had two distinct offers to make—
viz a 85$\frac{1}{2}$ & 88; and lest a further delay might protract the business I
did not hesitate to have your Name (as Sole Agents & Att$^y$ for Gen$^l$
Kosciusko)—for $10,000—a 88 for 100—which may possibly be
reduced to 85$\frac{1}{2}$—
　and hope to be prepared in time for its final Consumation—
　I am D$^r$ Sir most Respectfully your Obed$^t$　　　JOHN BARNES,

RC (ViU: TJP-ER); at foot of text: "Thomas Jefferson Esq$^r$ Monticello— Virg$^a$"; endorsed by TJ as a letter received 7 May 1814 from Georgetown and so recorded in SJL.

The CASH$^R$ of the Bank of Columbia in Georgetown was William Whann.

[1] Manuscript: "Subscibing."

# Minutes of the Albemarle Academy Board of Trustees

At a meeting of the board of Trustees of the Albemarle Accademy held at the house of Triplet T. Estes in Charlottesville the third day of May 1814, agreeable to adjournment.

Present Peter Carr President, John Harris, Dabney Minor, Thomas Wells, Sam$^l$ Carr, Jno: Kelly, Jno: Winn, Rice Garland, Jno: Nicholas, Robt B. Streshly Jno B Carr, Frank Carr, Thomas Jameson, James Leitch, and Edmund Anderson.

Wilson Nicholas by letter dated the second day of May 1814. declines acting as one of the Trustees of the Accademy, whereupon Nimrod Bramham, was chosen to fill the vacancy occasioned by the resignation of the said Wilson C. Nicholas, and it is ordered that the Secretary inform the said Bramham of his election.

The committee appointed by an order of the board made the fifth day of April 1814, to draft rules and regulations for the Government of the board: and who were also directed to report on the ways and means of raising funds for the establishment and support of the institution, made a report in these words, to wit: The committee appointed at the last meeting of the board of Trustees of the Albemarle Accademy to frame rules and regulations for the government of the same, submits the following.

Resolved that the meetings of this board of Trustees shall always be held at the place of there last meeting unless when otherwise prescribed.

That to constitute a quorum for the transaction of business the presence of a majority. 12. of the legal number of members shall be necessary.

That there shall be four stated meetings in every year, to wit: on the third Friday in March, June, August, and November and at the hour of 10. A.M.

That the president of the board shall be authorised to call a special meeting at any time on the written recommendation of any seven members, using his best endeavours that notice either verbal or written be given to every member before the day appointed for the meeting.

That a President, Secretary, and Treasurer, be chosen at the first stated meeting of the board in every year.

That the functions of the President be to preside at the meetings of the board, and to sign there proceedings, of the Secretary to take minutes of there proceedings, preserve there papers, for which purpose he is authorised and required to procure a paper[1] book, and attest copies of them[2] and orders of the board: and of the treasurer to receive and disburs all monies accruing to the board for the purposes of the institution under the direction of the board of Trustees.

That in the absence or non existence of a President a vice president may be appointed to act on the special occasion.

That all nominations of persons to supply vacancies in the body of Trustees shall be openly made previous to there being ballotted for.

That all appointments shall be by ballot on the vote of a majority of those present, removable at will by the vote of two thirds of the legal number of the board.

That the President, Secretary, and Treasurer, and all other officers and functionaries of the board being members thereof shall have a right to vote on every question without exception

That all proceedings of the board, when assembled, shall be according to parliamentary usages, except in cases otherwise specially declared.

That executive measures may be ordered whenever proposed, but that all general rules and laws shall lie over for consideration until the meeting next ensuing that at which they are proposed and if not then acted on or adjourned, shall be considered as discontinued.

Resolved that the object of the creation of this board is to provide such means as may be in there power for the establishment within the county of Albemarle, of a seminary for the instruction of youth already well grounded in the knowledge of reading and writing and Common Arithmetic previous to the commencement by the pupil of the Study of the Mathematical Sciences, in Such useful Sciences as Shall be within the competence of the means they may provide, begining first with those branches of Science deemed the most useful, and extending afterwards to others next in the order of usefulness, in proportion to the increase of the means they may acquire.

That the course of the Studies to be pursued, of the instruction to be given, the ordinary visitation and dicipline of the institution shall be confided to a standing committee of visiters to consist of three members of the board, to be elected at its first stated meeting in every year subject however to the controul of the board in all there proceedings whenever it shall think proper to interfere.

That the regulations of the ordinary expenses and domestic[3] economy of the institution be confided to a standing executive committee to consist of three members of the board to be elected at there first stated meeting in every year, subject to the controul of the board in all there proceedings whenever it shall think proper to interfere.

That whenever the board shall think proper to receive any proceeding of any standing committee, they shall appoint a special committee of enquiry of five persons, not being members of the committee whose proceedings are to be received whose duty it shall be to enquire into and report facts, and there opinions on them.

It was likewise made the duty of your committee to enquire into and report the ways and means of carrying the institution into effect. On this subject they beg leave to propose.

first, A Lottery to raise 3000 D. as authorised by law.

Second, A subscription either of a sum in gross or an annual sum for a given number of years at the convenience of the Subscriber.

Third, the monies for which the Glebes of the parishes of St. anne and Fredericksville[4] were sold.

Scheme of the Lottery

It is proposed that the price of the tickets be five dollars. It will require then, that four thousand be sold to raise the sum on which the discount of 15 p Cent the usual discount in Lotteries will give three thousand dollars, the sum proposed to be raised.

A sale of tickets to the above amount will place at our disposal twenty thousand Dollars to be distributed into prizes. Your committee would recommend that it be thrown into the following prizes, to wit: into one prize of 5000 D. one of 2000 D. and three of 1000 D. Thus 10000 D. will be disposed of. The remaining 10.000 might be distributed in the following manner[5] to wit: into one prize of 500 D. into five of Sixty Dollars, into four of 50 D. into fifty of twenty Dollars, into one hundred of 15$ into 150 of ten dollars and into one thousand of five Dollars. This will give 1315. prizes and will leave 2685 tickets to be met by blanks.

The drawing shall commence certainly at the end of 18 months from the date of the sale of the first tickets, at Charlottesville, or at any time within that period which the board of trustees shall deem proper. The first drawn ticket on the third days drawing shall be entitled to a prize of 3000 D. the first drawn ticket on the fifth days drawing shall be entitled to a prize of 1000 D. and the first drawn ticket on the eleventh days drawing shall be entitled to a prize of 500 D. If a prize be drawn opposite to the tickets which shall be entitled to the above three stationary prizes of 500 D. or less the amount so drawn shall go to the making up of the stationary prize the residue of which or the whole in case there should be no prize drawn opposite to the tickets entitled to them, shall be made up of the prizes in the wheel at the time of there being drawn of a less denomination than 50 D. begining with the 5$ prizes, and if they are insufficient proceeding upwards to the tens and[6] twenties. If a prize of more than 500 D. be drawn opposite to the ticket entitled to the stationary prize the said stationary prize shall be the property of the next drawn ticket on the same day. If when the drawing shall commence at the end of 18 months the whole 4000 Tickets shall not have been disposed of, your committee would recommend that the board reserve to itself the right of proceeding in the drawing and of proportioning the prizes to the number of Tickets which shall be sold. In this way altho we may fail in raising the sum authorised by law, the discount on the sum which we may be able to command, may be a considerable aid to the means which we may derive from other sourses, and enable us to Commence the opperation of the Accademy. Your committee would suggest finally that a committee of five members of the board be immediately chosen by ballot to carry the preceding plan as speedily as possible into effect, who shall be empowered to regulate at there discretion the times of drawing and the number of tickets to be drawn on each day.

A subscription either of a sum in gross or an annual sum for any given number of years at the will of the subscriber.

It is recommended by your committee, that a committee of three members be appointed who shall be authorised and required to open subscription papers prepared with lines necessary to designate the amount and character of the sum subscribed.

The views of the board might perhaps be promoted if the treasurer were directed to vest the moneys that may be derived from all these sourses when he shall have received sufficient for that purpose in stock of the bank of Virginia subject to the order of the board of Trustees.

Monies arrising from the Sale of the Glebe Lands.

By an Act of the General Assembly passed the 13th day of Febuary 1811. the court of Albemarle county is authorised to appoint a commissioner whose duty it is to vest the money arrising from the sale of the Glebe Lands of St Anne and Fredericksville[7] parishes in stock of the bank of Virginia, and to appropriate the interest of the money so vested to the establishment & use of a public School or schools in the county according to the provisions of the act passed the 22$^d$ December 1796. entitled, an act to establish public Schools. It is unnecessary to recite the provisions of that Act, both togeather place the money arrising from the sale of the Glebe lands entirely beyond the reach of the board, except through an application to the General Assembly. In the mean time the circulation of papers to obtain the consent of the freeholders of the County to the appropriation[8] of the money to the purposes of the contemplated Accademy, under the controul of the board of trustees, would essentially aid the success of any application to the general assembly, which may be deemed expedient. Your committee would therefore recommend that it shall be the duty of the last mentioned committee to forward the views of the board in that respect, by giving the papers already put into circulation, a circulation as extensive as possible, and by using any other means which may seem to the members of it proper and useful. It would be well too that a committee of three members of the board be appointed to draft a petition to the next general assembly praying the passage of an Act placing the monies, already by an order of the court of the County in the hands of Mr Winn as commissioner under the Law of the 13$^{th}$ Febuary 1811 and vested in Bank stock as made his duty by that act under the controul of the board of trustees for the purpose of carrying the proposed Accademy into effect.

All which is respectfully Submitted.

Which being submited to the Consideration of the board was unanimously adopted.

The board then proceeded to the choice[9] of a committee to carry into effect, that article of the report which relates to the management of the Lottery, when John Winn, Jno: Kelly, James Leitch, Frank Carr, and Alexander Garrett were chosen.

The board then further proceeded to choose a Treasurer and President of the board of[10] Lottery managers, to which office Jno Kelly was chosen.

Dabney Minor, Thomas Wells and Edmund Anderson were then chosen a committee to open subscription papers agreeable to the article of the Report of the committee on that subject, and for the purpose of forwarding subscriptions to petitions to the next Assembly praying an appropriation of the monies arrising from the sale of the Glebe lands to the use of the contemplated accademy.

Thomas Jefferson, Thomas M Randolph and Peter Carr, were

elected a committee to draft a petition to the next assembly asking an appropriation of the money arrising from the Sales of the glebe,[11] for the benefit of the Accademy.

Adjourned until the third friday in June next.

Signed

PETER CARR President
JNO: CARR Secretary.[12]

Tr (ViU: TJP-VMJCC). Tr (ViU: TJP-VMJHC). Tr (ViU: TJP-VMJB). Tr (ViU: VMJLC). Tr (PPAmP: VMWCR).

[1] VMJB Tr: "proper."
[2] VMJCC Tr: "thm." Other Trs: "them."
[3] Word not in VMJHC Tr.
[4] VMJCC, VMJHC, and VMWCR Trs: "Frederickville." VMJB and VMJLC Trs: "Fredericksville."
[5] Word not in VMJCC Tr.
[6] VMJCC Tr: "an." Other Trs: "and."
[7] VMJCC, VMJHC, and VMWCR Trs: "Frederickville." VMJB and VMJLC Trs: "Fredericksville."
[8] VMJHC Tr: "application."
[9] VMJCC Tr: "choise." Other Trs: "choice."
[10] VMJCC and VMWCR Trs: "the board of the board of." Other Trs: "the board of."
[11] Other Trs: "Glebe Lands," with varying capitalization and "Lands" interlined in all but VMJLC Tr.
[12] Other four Trs have "teste" above this line.

# To Joseph Delaplaine

SIR                                          Monticello May 3. 14.

Your favors of Apr. 16. and 19. on the subject of the portraits of Columbus and Americus Vespucius were recieved on the 30th. while I resided at Paris, knowing that these portraits, & those of some other of the early American worthies were in the gallery of Medicis at Florence, I took measures for engaging a good artist to take and send me copies of them. I considered it as even of some public concern that our country should not be without the portraits of it's first discoverers. these copies have already run the risks of transportations from Florence to Paris, to Philadelphia, to Washington, & lastly to this place, where they are at length safely deposited. you request me 'to forward them to you at Philadelphia for the purpose of having engravings taken from them for a work you propose to publish, and you pledge your honor that they shall be restored to me in perfect safety.' I have no doubt of the sincerity of your intentions in this pledge; and that it would be complied with as far as it would be in your power. but the injuries and accidents of their transportation to Philadelphia and back again are not within your controul. besides the rubbing thro' a land carriage of 600. miles, a carriage may overset in a river or creek, or be crushed with every thing in it. the frequency of such accidents to the stages renders all insurance against them impossible. and were they to escape the perils of this journey, I should be liable to the same calls, and they to the same or greater hasards, from all those in other parts of the Continent who should propose to publish any work in which they might wish to employ engravings of the same characters. from public therefore as well as private considerations, I think that these portraits ought not to be hazarded from their present deposit. like public records, I make them free to be copied, but, being as originals in this country, they should not be exposed to the accidents & injuries of travelling post. while I regret therefore the necessity of declining to comply with your request, I freely and with pleasure offer to recieve as a guest any artist whom you shall think proper to engage, and will make them welcome to take copies at their leisure for your use. I wish them to be multiplied for safe preservation, and consider them as worthy a place in every collection. indeed I do not know how it happened that mr Peale did not think of copying them while they were in Philadelphia; and I think it not impossible that either the father or the son might now undertake the journey for the use of their Museum. on the ground of our personal esteem for them, they would be at home in my family.

When I recieved these portraits at Paris, mr Daniel Parker of Massachusets happened to be there, and determined to procure for himself copies from the same originals at Florence; and I think he did obtain them, and that I have heard of their being in the hands of some one in Boston. if so, it might perhaps be easier to get some artist there to take and send you copies. but be this as it may, you are perfectly welcome to the benefit of mine in the way I have mentioned.

The two original portraits of myself taken by mr Stewart, after which you enquire, are both in his possession at Boston. one of them only is my property. the President has a copy from that which Stewart considered as the best of the two; but I believe it is at his seat in this state.

I thank you for the print of D$^r$ Rush. he was one of my early & intimate friends, and among the best of men. the engraving is excellent as is every thing from the hand of mr Edwin. Accept the assurance of my respect, and good wishes for the success of your work.

TH: JEFFERSON

RC (LNT: George H. and Katherine M. Davis Collection); addressed: "M$^r$ Joseph Delaplaine Philadelphia"; franked; postmarked Milton, 4 May; endorsed by Delaplaine, including a misrecording of his 17 Aug. 1814 reply:

"Wrote 18 Aug 1814." PoC (DLC). Tr (ViU: GT); at head of text: "ex^d"; posthumous copy.

In 1788 Philip Mazzei engaged the ARTIST Giuseppe Calendi on TJ's behalf to copy portraits of Christopher Colum- bus, Amerigo Vespucci, Hernán Cortés, and Ferdinand Magellan (*PTJ*, 15:xxxv– xxxvi; Stein, *Worlds*, 73, 132–3). The version of Gilbert Stuart's portrait of TJ owned by PRESIDENT James Madison is now at Colonial Williamsburg (Bush, *Life Portraits*, 59).

# From Thomas Law

DEAR SIR.                                        Washington May 3^rd 1814

I submit to you a production intended to be perused by the female sex which has so much influence on man from the cradle to the grave—

There is a case in the quarterly review of Octo^r 1811 page 286— which shews the distressing effects of oppression & contempt shewn to a boy of sensibility, & of the benefits resulting by a change to encouragement & benevolence, which strongly corroborates my sentiments—

"The phenomena of mind are influenced by a peculiar conformation of the brain, & also by its chemical composition, directly by the blood & indirectly by air, exercise & food"—this the physiologists acknowledge, but in my opinion, man is actuated very much by education which exercises the brain—Thus as printing disseminates moral sensations arising from novel circumstances, the human race is more & more spiritualised or operated upon by divine moral laws as violations of right are more execrated—

[Forgive?] me for th[us?] claiming your attention to a subject which many persons deem unimportant, but which I am convinced is deem'd by You worthy of attention

I remain

With sincere Esteem Yr m^t Ob^t St                        T LAW—

RC (DLC); top edge damaged; endorsed by TJ as received 20 May 1814 and so recorded in SJL. Enclosure: Law, *Second Thoughts on Instinctive Impulses* (Philadelphia, 1813; Sowerby, no. 3250).

The October 1811 issue of the QUARTERLY REVIEW repeated an anecdote by educator Andrew Bell in which a student who had been the victim of relentless bul- lying improved dramatically when he was treated kindly (*Quarterly Review* 6 [1811]: 285–6, quoting from Bell, *An Analysis of the Experiment in Education, made at Egmore, near Madras*, 3d ed. [London, 1807], 74–5). Law's quote on the PHENOMENA OF MIND comes from a discussion of the work of Philippe Pinel (*Edinburgh Review*, 7th ed., 2 [1814]: 166).

# From Joseph H. Nicholson

MY DEAR SIR Baltimore May 3. 1814

M[r] James H. MCulloch, the son of our Collector, is going westward on some scientific Pursuits, and as he wishes to take Monticello in his way, I beg leave to introduce him to you—I flatter myself when you know him, you will not find him unworthy of your acquaintance—One of his Objects is to look into the Mineralogy and aboriginal History of our Country, and as these are Subjects which you have not suffered to escape you, permit me to ask for him such aids, in the furtherance of his Views, as you may think useful to him—

After a separation of such a length of Time, with very little Hope of again meeting you, I cannot address you without the warmest Emotions. May I therefore tell you of the deep Interest which I always take in every thing that concerns you, and respectfully offer you the best wishes of a Heart sincerely devoted to you?

JOSEPH H. NICHOLSON

RC (MHi); endorsed by TJ as a letter from "Nicholson Joseph A." received 18 May 1814 and so recorded in SJL, with the added notation: "by mr M[c]Culloch."

Joseph Hopper Nicholson (1770–1817), legislator and judge, was a native of Maryland's Eastern Shore. After studying law, he served in the Maryland House of Delegates, 1796–98, and in the United States House of Representatives, 1799–1806. Nicholson strongly supported TJ during the 1800 presidential election and became a Republican leader closely allied with fellow congressmen John Randolph of Roanoke and Nathaniel Macon. From 1806 until his death Nicholson served as chief justice of Maryland's sixth judicial district, in which capacity he also served on the Court of Appeals, the state's highest tribunal. In 1810 he became president of the Commercial and Farmers' Bank of Baltimore. During the War of 1812 Nicholson raised and commanded a company of artillery and was present at the successful September 1814 defense of Baltimore. Shortly thereafter he assisted his brother-in-law Francis Scott Key in publishing "The Defense of Fort McHenry," a poem that became better known as "The Star Spangled Banner." TJ and Nicholson

corresponded occasionally on governmental matters early in the 1800s (DAB; PTJ, esp. 32:512–3; Scott S. Sheads, "Joseph Hopper Nicholson: Citizen-Soldier of Maryland," Maryland Historical Magazine 98 [2003]: 133–51; Baltimore Niles' Weekly Register, 8 Mar. 1817).

James H. McCulloh (ca. 1792–1869), physician, banker, and author, attended the College of New Jersey (later Princeton University) and earned a medical degree from the University of Pennsylvania in 1814, with a final essay on the castor-oil plant. That same year he was appointed a garrison surgeon in the United States Army in his native Maryland, serving until 1816. McCulloh assisted Louis H. Girardin in 1822 in organizing the Academy of Science and Literature in Baltimore. He served as deputy collector for the port of Baltimore under his father, James H. McCulloch (1756–1836), from roughly 1827 until about 1835. McCulloh served as president of the Bank of Baltimore, 1841–53. He wrote books on the origins of Native Americans and on Christianity (General Catalogue of the American Whig-Cliosophic Society of Princeton University [ca. 1952], 63; Catalogue of the Alumni of the Medical Department of the University of

*Pennsylvania, 1765–1877* [1877], 113; Heitman, *U.S. Army,* 1:661; TJ to McCulloh, 7 Nov. 1817; McCulloh to TJ, 14 Nov. 1817; John R. Quinan, *Medical Annals of Baltimore From 1608 to 1880* [1884], 32; R. J. Matchett, *Matchett's Baltimore Directory for 1827* [1827], 177; *Matchett's Baltimore Director, Corrected up to September, 1835. For 1835–6* [1835], 170; J. Thomas Smith, "The National Bank of Baltimore," *Bankers' Magazine* 52 [1896]: 620–32; McCulloh, *An Impartial Exposition of the Evi-*dences and Doctrines of the Christian Religion* [1836]; McCulloh, *On the Credibility of the Scriptures* [1867]; DNA: RG 29, CS, Md., Baltimore City, 1850, 1860; *Baltimore Sun,* 25, 28 Dec. 1869).

McCulloh's work on the ABORIGINAL HISTORY of the United States resulted in a book entitled *Researches on America; being an attempt to settle some points relative to the Aborigines of America, &c.* (Baltimore, 1816; Poor, *Jefferson's Library,* 5 [no. 173]).

# From John F. Watson

Philad 3 May 1814

Permit me Sir, thus, to lay before you the Prospectus for those eminent publications the Edinb^gh & Quarterly Reviews & to solicit your patronage to either or both of them, from the last N^os or from the beginning—

It is possible you may receive them from some other Bookseller already, if so, forgive this trespass upon your time & notice—

Yrs respectfy                                                    JOHN F WATSON

RC (DLC); dateline beneath signature; addressed: "The Hon^ble Thomas Jefferson Esq^re Monticello V^a"; franked; postmarked Philadelphia, 3 May; endorsed by TJ as received 13 May 1814 and so recorded in SJL. Enclosure not identified.

John Fanning Watson (1779–1860), businessman and antiquarian, was born in New Jersey and received commercial training in Philadelphia and in his native state. He served as a clerk in the United States War Department from about 1800 until 1804, when he became the New Orleans mercantile agent for a Pennsylvania business firm and subsequently a provisions agent for Louisiana army posts. Watson moved to Philadelphia and there commenced a book and stationery business in 1809, and he expanded to publishing by 1811. During his tenure as cashier of the Bank of Germantown, 1814–48, he authored religious works and devoted himself to the collection and preservation of historical materials, buildings, and artifacts. These activities facilitated the 1824 founding of both the Historical Society of Pennsylvania and the Society for the Commemoration of the Landing of William Penn. After exhaustive research, including the use of oral history, questionnaires, and archaeological evidence, Watson issued his somewhat idealized *Annals of Philadelphia* (1830 and later eds). He followed this with comparable works chronicling the city and state of New York. From about 1848 until his retirement in 1859, Watson was treasurer and secretary of the Philadelphia, Germantown and Norristown Railroad. He died in Germantown (*DAB*; Deborah Dependahl Waters, "Philadelphia's Boswell: John Fanning Watson," *PMHB* 98 [1974]: 3–52; Benjamin Dorr, *A Memoir of John Fanning Watson* [1861]; DeWint-M: Watson Family Papers; *Philadelphia Inquirer,* 25 Dec. 1860).

# From Samuel Brown

Dear Sir.                              Natchez May 4<sup>th</sup> 1814

The last mail from Catahoula brought me The enclosed Letter from Judge Lewis which seems to close all prospect of obtaining the information you wished from the papers of M^r Henderson. From the statement of the time of his Death, I am disposed to beleive, that your communication of may last never reached him but has probably been returned to the General Post office, from that of Catahoula where it was deposited about the beginning of June by my friend D^r Smith.

Although we submitted to the Embargo without much murmuring it never was a very popular measure here as is sufficiently evinced by the joy manifested by the people on receiving the news of its repeal. In time of war money is what we most want and I would rather sell my superfluous provisions to my enemy to enable me to buy arms & amunition to blow his brains out than attempt the less heroic measure of starving him to Death—In time of war taxes must be paid and <u>unanimity</u> at[1] home is essential to national power & I fear this has not been promoted by the restrictive system—A few speculators have engrossed the greatest part of our last years crop of cotton at about six or seven cents per lb and many of our farmers are not able to pay the current expences of their plantations. What benefit the community at large may have derived from the measure I do not pretend to determine—as my means of information are extremely limited.

What will be the event of the great struggle in Europe? Will the usurper be able to transmit his throne and titles to his Son or will the Bourbons be restored?—

A fatal disease the Typhoid Pleurisy has spread itself over a great part of the western Country. From the beneficial effects of hot bathing I am persuaded that D^r Jennings' apparatus would have saved a multitude of lives had it been in general use. There are few families among the middling & poorer classes of people where a hot bath can be obtained without expos[ing] the patient to many inconveniences & the attendants to much trou[ble.] I long to see a good history of this Epidemic. It exhibited some features of a very peculiar kind. Every evil has its benefit—It will check the rage for <u>Bleeding</u> which had become perniciously fashionable in the Philadelphia school of medicine—and with the indiscriminate and unlimited use of mercury has done more mischief than a dozen of Epidemics—

With sentiments of perfect respect & the most sincere wishes for your happiness

I am Yo mo obt

SAM BROWN

RC (DLC); edge trimmed; at foot of text: "M^r Jefferson"; endorsed by TJ as received 26 June 1814 and so recorded in SJL. Enclosure: Thomas C. Lewis to Brown, Ouachita Parish, 7 Mar. 1814, stating that "I am confident Maj^r Henderson never Rec^d the letter You mention from M^r Jefferson to him relative to the Title of a certain tract of Land, or I should certainly have heard him speak of it. neither is there any such letter among his Papers; Nor any Note or Memo^m touching the subject, upon diligent search, which I have made with Pleasure, tho sorry not to have found any information required, P^r Your Request: Ja^s L. Henderson departed this life at the House of M^r Ja^s Barlow's of this Parish on the 9^th of June last past"; the letter also welcomes the possibility of peace, argues that the war has fostered industry and prosperity in the South, and complains of the difficulty in obtaining news with the nearest post office eighty miles away (RC in DLC: TJ Papers, 201:35706–7; addressed: "Doct^r Samuel Brown Natchez fav^d by M^r Cudy"; stamped; postmarked Catahoula Court House, 23 Apr. 1814).

For TJ's letter to James L. Henderson of 21 Apr. 1813 (not MAY LAST), see note to TJ to Brown, 24 Apr. 1813.

A letter from Brown to TJ of 15 Aug. 1814, not found, is recorded in SJL as received 2 Sept. 1814 from Natchez.

¹ Manuscript: "a."

# From Patrick Gibson

SIR                                        Richmond 4^th May 1814

I received by the last mail your favor of the 28^th Ult° and Send you hereinclosed $150 in notes—there is no¹ change in flour since I last wrote you, nor can we expect a rise until an armistice take place—

With great respect I am
Your ob^t Serv^t

PATRICK GIBSON

RC (ViU: TJP-ER); between dateline and salutation: "Thomas Jefferson Esq^re"; endorsed by TJ as received 7 May 1814 and so recorded in SJL.

TJ's missing FAVOR of 28 Apr. 1814 is recorded in SJL.

¹ Word interlined.

# To John Staples

SIR                                        Monticello May. 4. 14.

I send you the model of the mouldboard of a plough of a form of my own, and ask the favor of you to cast me two dozen in iron. I presume you will preserve the mould, as I shall probably call annually for a supply. I will thank you to have them ready as soon [a]s you can, and I will direct them to be called for. they had better be tied together in manageable bundles by bits of nailrod passing thro' their holes. mr Gibson will be so good as to pay your bill for them. accept the assurance of my respect. Th: Jefferson

PoC (MHi); one word faint; at foot of text: "Mʳ John Staples"; endorsed by TJ.

## From Joseph Wheaton

Excellent Sir                                    Richmond May 4ᵗʰ 1814

I had once the honor of rendering to the United States Some Service in the Creek nation of Indians—(Missippie Territory) in the establishing the mail rout to New Orleans—and in Some measure under your directions—. The only motive I had then, was to evince to you my zeal for the public interest, I Should have fully obtained that object—of intigrity and a proper treatment of the Indian charector with my industry—had not the vile Mʳ Granger induced you to believe What was false was true, and what was true was false—His official weight of charecter prevailed—and I have been persecuted to the ruin of my property by that base man—of which you have lately had Strong presumtive evidence.

The high Sense which I have ever entertained of you induces me to call to your recollection the past—the enclosed papers will Shew you Some evidence that I am, under the Excellent Mʳ Madison pursuing the public interest with Some zeal and attention—with the homage of my heart I remain Sir

Your most obed. Servant                          Joseph Wheaton
                                                 A, D. Q, M, Genˡ only

RC (MoSHi: TJC-BC); at foot of text: "Thoˢ Jefferson Esqʳ"; endorsed by TJ as received 6 May 1814 but recorded in SJL as received the following day. Enclosures not found.

Wheaton sent TJ evidence regarding his dispute with Gideon Granger in his letter to TJ of 20 July 1809.

## From John T. Mason

Dear Sir                                         Montpelier 5ᵗʰ May 1814

My old friend Doc. Wallace has just paid us a kind visit. The picture that he has presented to Mʳˢ Mason & my self of the happiness you enjoy in your retirement from public life, is to us both, very pleasing & interesting. But when he described your efforts to make our

Country more independent by promoting domestic manufactures we were gratified to find that what we were pursuing with industry and persevereance had been by you deemed an object worthy of your attention. When we retired from Geo. Town to Sᵗ Marys County in 1805 we found ourselves in a Country where the materials for manufactures were unattainable. But when in May 1808 we crossed the Mountains and reached this place, the first thing we did was formally to declare War against Europe, by refusing to buy her merchandize, except such articles as ladies cannot well do without, and as cannot be made in private families. We have ever since adhered and still do adhere to this determination. Since that time we have not bought a Carpet, Blanket, Sheet or any other species of house linnen coarse or fine, we make our own stockings, cloths coarse and fine and indeed almost every thing else. To shew you the Style in which we conduct our Warfare, but more particularly to evince her respectful and affectionate remembrance of yourself, Mʳˢ Mason has prevailed on Doc. Wallace to be the bearer to you of a Counterpain a table cloth and a napkin made by herself of which she begs your acceptance. I sincerely wish that those who direct and manage the political concerns of our Country had been as much in earnest as we were, and had persevered with as much firmness as we have done, in this mode of Warfare.

Mʳˢ Mason, in wishes for a continuance of your health and happiness, unites with dear Sir your sincere friend and

Humˡ Servᵗ                                JOHN T. MASON

RC (DLC); endorsed by TJ as a letter from "Mason John Thompson" received 25 June 1814 and so recorded in SJL, which indicates that TJ received it at Warren.

John Thomson Mason (1765–1824), attorney and public official, was a native of Virginia. He practiced law in Georgetown and campaigned for TJ in the elections of 1796 and 1800. Mason ran unsuccessfully for the Maryland House of Delegates in 1800. TJ appointed him United States attorney for the District of Columbia in 1801, and he served in this capacity until 1804, but Mason rebuffed TJ's attempts to make him the nation's attorney general in both 1802 and 1805. He served briefly as attorney general of Maryland in 1806, as a state senator by appointment, 1807–08, and as a state delegate, 1813–14. Mason moved in 1805 to Saint Mary's County, Maryland, and then to Montpelier, his estate in Washington County, Maryland, where he lived from 1808 until his death (*PTJ*, 32:128–9, 225–6, 33:380; *JEP*, 1:402, 405 [6, 26 Jan. 1802]; Mason to TJ, 17 Mar. 1802 [DNA: RG 59, LAR, 1801–09], 20 July 1805 [DLC]; TJ to Mason, 12 Aug. 1804 [DNA: RG 59, LAR, 1801–09]; Papenfuse, *Maryland Public Officials*, 23, 42, 264; Easton, Md., *Eastern Shore General Advertiser*, 24 Nov. 1807; Baltimore *North American, and Mercantile Daily Advertiser*, 15 Nov. 1808; Washington *Daily National Intelligencer*, 18 Dec. 1824).

# To William Richardson

SIR                [M]on[ticello] Apr. [May] 6. 14.

My grandaughter Ellen Randolph purchased for me at your store about six weeks[1] ago 15. yds of scarlet rattinett. we want 2. yds more to compleat the lining of the carriage it was intended for. I will be obliged to you if you will do up that much compactly in the size and form of a moderate letter and put it into the post office, to come by our first mail as it is the last article we want to finish a carriage, for which I am waiting to set out on a journey. if you have no more of the stuff, you would oblige me by procuring it elsewhere to prevent disappointment and delay. mr Gibson will be so good as to pay the price on your presenting him this letter. Accept my respects

TH: JEFFERSON

PoC (MHi); misdated, but endorsed as a letter of 6 May 1814 and so recorded in SJL; one word faint; at foot of text: "M^r Richardson."

William Richardson was a merchant in Richmond (*The Richmond Directory, Register and Almanac, for the Year 1819* [Richmond, 1819], 65).

ELLEN W. Randolph (Coolidge) visited Richmond from roughly the end of Feb-ruary until late in April 1814 (Ellen W. Randolph [Coolidge] to Martha Jefferson Randolph [ca. 2 Mar.], 30 Mar., 24 Apr. 1814 [ViU: Ellen Wayles Randolph Coolidge Correspondence]). Rattinet (RATTINETT) is a plain-woven fabric with a rough surface used for upholstering (*OED*).

[1] Preceding two words interlined in place of "a fortnight."

# From David Bailie Warden

DEAR SIR,                Paris, 6 may 1814.

yesterday I had the pleasure of receiving your letter, of the 29th of December last, with those inclosed, which I have delivered to their address, with the exception of two, one for Gen. Kosciusko: the other, for mr. mazzei: these I shall forward by the first[1] conveyance: the former lives in the Country near <u>Fontainbleau</u>. Madame De Tessé is no more: she died some months ago. gen. La Fayette is now at Paris, with his son and daughter. His Son in law has been a prisoner in Russia, since the affair of moscow, and is daily expected here. The General has lately become heir to a very considerable property by the death of Relations.—

I cannot conceive what became of the seeds by the <u>Bellona</u> the Supercargo—mr. Breuil of Philadelphia promised to take great care of them: they were delivered to his agent, at nantes, and their receipt acknowledged: this vessel certainly[2] arrived at Philadelphia.—The first

[ 349 ]

Copy of <u>Toulongeon</u>, was left with other volumes, at cherburg; the Captain of the <u>Hornet</u> refusing to take the case which contained them, on board. In autumn last, I forwarded to you, through our minister, a copy of my essay on <u>Consular Establishments</u>, which I presume you have not received—I now send another by a friend—mr. Corran, who promises to leave it at the office of the Department of State. The change of Government here, with which You will be acquainted before this reaches you, has occasioned an enquiry concerning parliamentary practise; and your <u>manual</u>, on this subject, has been sought by several Officers of the Government. no copy can be found here.—I hope soon to receive one from Philadelphia.—

I feel much obliged to you for the information which you have been pleased to give me concerning our public Affairs. The English are deeply mortified at our Naval success, and profiting of the wonderful influence which they have lately acquired, they Seem determined to Send a considerable force to Canada, consisting of Several Regiments of Lord Wellingtons' army, and several thousand Seamen destined for the Lakes, with the <u>pieces</u> and prepared materials of frigates, which are to be constructed, as if by enchantment, in their ports.—During the present coalition we can hope for nothing more than neutrality from the northern powers: their interests must soon induce them to oppose the English doctrine concerning naturalisation and the impressment of Seamen.—I am now occupied with this Subject; and if political circumstances do not prevent, I shall probably publish the result of my researches. I inclose two Brochures—one on the french Constitution: the other <u>Notice</u> des <u>travaux de la</u> classe <u>des beaux Arts</u>—[3]

I also inclose a copy of the <u>prospectus</u> of <u>Michaux'</u> work—He is much gratified by your letter—

Please Sir to present my respects to mr & mrs Randolph: and to Accept of my thanks and gratitude for the Attention which you are pleased to shew me

your very obedient Servant        DAVID BAILIE WARDEN

RC (DLC); at foot of text: "Thos Jefferson Esquire, monticello"; endorsed by TJ as received 15 Sept. 1814 and so recorded in SJL. 1st Dupl (DLC); dated 5 May 1814; at head of text: "Copy—The original sent by Mr Corran." 2d Dupl (DLC); dated 5 May 1814; adjacent to dateline: "Duplicate"; conjoined with RC of Warden to TJ, 1 Aug. 1814; endorsed by TJ as received 12 Oct. 1814. FC (MdHi: Warden Letterbook); in Warden's hand; dated 5 May 1814; endorsed by Warden as sent "By Corran." Enclosure: unidentified issue of *Notice des travaux de la Classe des Beaux-Arts de l'Institut Royal de France*. Other enclosures not found.

TJ had not received the previous copy of Warden's ESSAY, *On the Origin, Na-*

ture, *Progress and Influence of Consular Establishments* (Paris, 1813; Poor, *Jefferson's Library*, 12 [no. 712]), sent through William H. Crawford, the American minister plenipotentiary to France. The CHANGE OF GOVERNMENT was the abdication of Napoleon and restoration of the Bourbon monarchy (Connelly, *Napoleonic France*, 3–5).

¹ Dupls and FC here add "safe."
² Word not in Dupls or FC.
³ 1st Dupl and FC end here. 2d Dupl concludes here with "I am sir, with great respect, your very obliged Servant."

# From James Monroe

DEAR SIR                                    washington may 7. 1814.

The bearer Mʳ McCullock of Baltimore was introduc'd to me by a particular friend there, with a request that I would make him known to you. He is the son of the collector of that port, & represented to have made considerable progress in the knowledge of natural history, for which science he is said to have much taste and a strong passion. He has studied medicine¹ in Philª, & passed the examination with credit. He intends making a visit to the western country, with a view to his more favorite study.

I hope soon to have the pleasure of seeing you in Albemarle. Some affairs keep me here for the present, but they do not menace a very long detention.

with great respect & esteem yr friend & servt.

JAS MONROE

RC (MHi); endorsed by TJ as received 18 May 1814 and so recorded in SJL, which gives the added notation: "by mr McCulloch."

¹ Manuscript: "studed medicne."

# To Craven Peyton

DEAR SIR                                    Monticello May 7. 14.

Your letter of the 4ᵗʰ came to hand yesterday. I do assure you that I never have entertained a moment's doubt of the truth of the transaction between Jaˢ Henderson, mrs Henderson & yourself as to the sale of the lands of the 3 youngest daughters, and of her full knolege & consent to it as you have ever stated it. I believe her denial of it to be a sheer falsehood. it was impossible such a transaction should have passed at her house without her knolege; you could have no motive to conceal it from her, but on the contrary every reason to be assured of her approbation; and it is less probable that James Henderson would keep it from her than that she may now wish to decieve Hornsby by a false denial. I have always however apprehended that James Henderson might evade giving us the benefit of his testimony, as there is not one grain of honesty in the whole family. and I pray you to rest assured of my entire belief and satisfaction as to the zeal and integrity with which you acted for me in the whole of the transactions with that family, and my perfect conviction of the truth with which you communicated them to me.     I inclose you John Henderson's deed of quitclaim for the lands of the 3. younger daughters, and his rec$^t$ for £100. in consideration which you will be so good as to return at your convenience, and I tender you the assurance of my esteem & friendship.                              TH: JEFFERSON

RC (John Peyton, Staunton, 1958); at foot of text: "M$^r$ Craven Peyton." PoC (MHi); lower left corner of page torn away; endorsed by TJ. FC (ViU: TJP, TB [Thurlow-Berkeley] no. 909); on a small scrap; abstract in TJ's hand reading as follows: "May 7. 14. at the request of Craven Peyton I inclosed to him John Henderson's deed for the lands of Francis, Lucy & Nancy Hend. adjac$^t$ to Milton with a quitclaim. also J. Hend's rec$^t$ for 100£ the considn. which he is to return to me." Enclosure: receipt from John Henderson to Peyton, Milton, 17 Nov. 1807, for £100 paid by Peyton in exchange for the right to the lands of Frances, Lucy, and Nancy Henderson (MS in ViU: TJP; in an unidentified hand, signed by John Henderson and witnessed by Fleming Turner; endorsed in an unidentified hand: "Recep$^t$ Henderson to Peyton £100"). Other enclosure printed below.

Peyton's letter to TJ OF THE 4$^{TH}$, not found, is recorded in SJL as received 6 May from Monteagle.

ENCLOSURE

## John Henderson's Deed of Milton Property to Craven Peyton

Know all Men by these presents that I John Henderson of the County of Albemarle And State of Virginia have this day bargained soald And delivared Unto Craven Peyton of s$^d$ State And County all the right tittle And interest which the three youngest children of Bennett Henderson Decs$^d$ are intitled in And adjacent to the town of Milton in the County of albemarle., the Names, of the children Are, Frances. L. Lucy. L. And Nancy Henderson, And I do hereby for evar warrant & defend a good And lawfull right & title in s$^d$ proparty to s$^d$ peyton for And in consideration of the Som of One Hundred pound$^s$ to me in hand p$^d$ by the s$^d$ peyton, And do furthar hereby bind my self my heirs &. in the Som of One Thousand pound$^s$ Nevar to interfere in Any way whatsoevar directly Or indirectly[1] with Any part of the proparty, herein soald. Or Any part of the proparty which the s$^d$ peyton has baught of the othar legatees of the s$^d$ Bennett Henderson Decs$^d$, And do furthar oblige my self, to forward to the s$^d$ peyton compleat titles to the above mentioned proparty immediately on the three above mentioned legates becomes of law-full age. given Undar my hand & Seale this Seventeenth day of novembar Eighteen hundred & Seven

JOHN HENDERSON

(Sealed)

guardian
For the three Legatees

Signed Sealed And
delivared in the presence of
FLEMING TURNER
M DAWSON
JAMES BULLOCK

MS (ViU: TJP); in an unidentified hand, signed by Henderson, Turner, Martin Dawson, and Bullock; on verso in unidentified hand: "Deed Henderson to Peyton"; endorsed by TJ: "John Henderson for Frances, Lucy & Nancy to Craven Peyton. 1807. Nov. 17. £100. all their rights in & adjacent to Milton and a quit. claim on his part."

John Henderson (b. 1771), was the eldest son of Bennett Henderson and Elizabeth Lewis Henderson, of Albemarle County. Following his father's death in 1793, Henderson was appointed the legal guardian of his ten surviving siblings. Henderson's oversight of the family milling operation and his role in managing the division of his father's estate brought him into legal conflict with TJ by 1795. They differed first over Henderson's attempt to raise the height of the family milldam and, later, over his claim to have retained the right to construct a canal to carry water to his mill that would run through property that TJ had purchased through Peyton. Although the latter case was decided in his favor, insolvency prevented Henderson from reaping the fruits of this victory. Because of his partnership with David Michie, however, the threat of litigation over the millrace continued until at least 1817 (Woods, *Albemarle*, 228; Haggard, "Henderson Heirs"; Peyton to TJ, 6 Aug. 1809; Michie to TJ, 18 June 1812).

[1] Manuscript: "indiretly."

# To John Barnes

DEAR SIR                                    Monticello May 8. 14.

I recieved yesterday your favors of Apr. 27. and May 2. & 2. and I now inclose you Gen[l] Kosciuszko's 2. certificates for 18. and 2. shares in the bank of Pensylvania, with my endorsement, duplicate powers of Attorney to dispose of them, and letters to the Secretaries of State and the Treasury requesting their aid in the remittances of interest. these I have left open for your perusal, after which be so good as to seal them before delivery. Judge Woodward being with me at present and to return soon to Washington or Philadelphia, he can be applied to there to attest the powers of Attorney before a Notary. sincerely praying for the best success in your use of all these documents I tender you the assurance of my affectionate respect.

TH: JEFFERSON

PoC (DLC); at foot of text: "M^r Barnes"; endorsed by TJ. Enclosures: (1) TJ to George W. Campbell, 8 May 1814. (2) TJ to James Monroe, 8 May 1814. Other enclosures not found.

# To George W. Campbell

DEAR SIR                                                    Monticello May 8. 14.

Gen^l Kosciuszko whose revolutionary services and general devotion to the cause of liberty have rendered him dear to this country, made a deposit of all his funds in the monied institutions of this country, placing them under my general superintendance, which is exercised through mr Barnes who will have the honor of handing you this letter, and whom I take this occasion to make known to you for his great worth. I have instructed him to dispose of the General's bank-stock and to invest it in the new loan of the US. but the immediate object of this letter is to observe that during the war we have found it impracticable to remit to the General his annual interest, in consequence of which his letters inform me of his great distress in Paris, which must I know be great indeed. I have supposed it possible that he might perhaps be availed of some of the money transactions of your department so as to recieve his remittances thro' them. any facility you may be so kind as to offer to mr Barnes for this purpose, besides being recieved as a personal favor to myself, will extend a much needed relief to one of our great revolutionary worthies.

I avail myself of this first occasion of congratulating you on your accession to the honorable and important station you now occupy. it is always a gratification to me to see the public offices confided to those whom I know to come into them with singleness of view to the public good. Accept the assurance of my great respect & esteem.

TH: JEFFERSON

RC (ICPRCU); addressed: "The honble George W. Campbell Secretary of the Treasury Washington handed by mr Barnes"; endorsed by Campbell as answered 9 Sept. 1815. PoC (DLC); endorsed by TJ. Enclosed in TJ to John Barnes, 8 May 1814.

George Washington Campbell (1769–1848), attorney and public official, was a native of Scotland whose family immigrated to the United States in 1772, settling in Mecklenburg County, North Carolina. He entered the College of New Jersey (later Princeton University) in 1793 and graduated the following year. Campbell was admitted to the bar in North Carolina and then in Tennessee in 1798. After establishing a highly successful practice in Knoxville, he served in the United States House of Representatives, 1803–09. As a leading Jeffersonian Republican in an intensely partisan atmosphere, Campbell helped manage the impeachment trials of two Federalist judges, chaired the Ways and Means Committee,

1807–09, and wounded Federalist congressman Barent Gardenier in a duel in 1808. Campbell served on the Tennessee Supreme Court of Errors and Appeals, 1809–11, and he moved to Nashville in 1810 to oversee his landholdings. He represented Tennessee from 1811 to 1814 in the United States Senate, where he supported the war with Great Britain and chaired the Foreign Relations and Military Affairs committees. Campbell succeeded Albert Gallatin as secretary of the treasury, serving from February to September 1814, but he struggled with that difficult wartime position. Late the following year he resumed his seat in the Senate. In 1818 President James Monroe appointed Campbell envoy extraordinary and minister plenipotentiary to Russia, where he proved to be an able diplomat. After his return to Tennessee in 1821, he resumed his law practice and expanded his landed wealth. In 1832 President Andrew Jackson appointed Campbell to the French Spoliation Claims Commission, where for three years he led the American officials evaluating claims against France under the terms of the Rives Treaty. He died in Nashville, leaving a large estate (*ANB*; *DAB*; *Princetonians*, 1791–94, pp. 341–51; Weymouth T. Jordan, *George Washington Campbell of Tennessee, Western Statesman* [1955]; *JEP*, 2:470–1, 3:183, 4:276–7 [8, 9 Feb. 1814, 16 Apr. 1818, 14 July 1832]; Nashville *Republican Banner*, 18 Feb. 1848; Nashville *Daily Union*, 19 Feb. 1848).

## To James Monroe

MY DEAR SIR                                   Monticello May 8. 14.

I know that your esteem for our mutual friend Kosciuszko will interest you in relieving the sufferings under which he now is in Paris. all his funds are in our monied institutions, and we are now transferring them into the hands of the government on the new loan. but the cause of his distress is our inability to find the means of remitting his annual interest, the sole source of his subsistence. the entire destruction of all the relations of commerce, has swept away the resource of private bills. the object of this letter is to beseech you to avail mr Barnes of any means which your department may offer of remitting to the General his annual funds. mr Barnes will have the honor of asking your advice on this subject.

I shall set out for Bedford in about 8. or 10. days. I shall regret it very much should it deprive me of the pleasure of seeing you here. my absence will be of 3. or 4. weeks.          Affectionately yours

TH: JEFFERSON

RC (NNGL, on deposit NHi); addressed: "The honble James Monroe Secretary of State Washington handed by mr Barnes." PoC (DLC); endorsed by TJ. Enclosed in TJ to John Barnes, 8 May 1814.

# To Bernard Peyton

Sunday May 8. 14.

Th: Jefferson asks the favor of Cap[t] Peyton's company to dinner tomorrow on peas.

RC (DLC); written on a small scrap; dateline at foot of text. Not recorded in SJL.


# To William Cook

SIR                                                    Monticello May 9. 14.

Your favor of Mar. 31. came to hand about a week ago, and I have taken that time to look over such old papers as are of about the date of the transactions respecting mr Fry, and I am sorry that none of these contain his name or throw any light on his case. nor can my memory supply the defect. I well remember that a person of the name of Fry was in the service of my father at the time of his death in 1757. and that he then left us. but of what became of him afterwards or what family he had I have no recollection. I think he was a one-handed man, & from what I retain of his physiognomy he must have been 40 years of age. I was out of the county from the death of my father till 1763. either at school; college, or as a student, which accounts for my losing sight of the family. the circumstances mentioned by mr Fry render his statement probable; for Col[o] Charles Lewis of this county did command a Virginia regiment raised partly in the county (Albemarle) and John Gilmer was a resident here. that I aided him as to his pension is probable, because I was in the habit of doing this for all who applied to me, but I rarely made any notice of these merely neighborly offices. the want of this, the distance of time, now 50. years, and the mass of transactions which have passed thro' my mind within that period will account for the evanition from my memory of all traces respecting mr Fry personally. I should have been happy if a better recollection had enabled me to be of some service to him in his old age. but I should think his case might be traced at the War-office thro' the aid of some of your representatives in Congress. be pleased to accept for yourself the assurance of my great respect

TH: JEFFERSON

PoC (MHi); on verso of reused address cover to TJ; at foot of text: "M[r] William Cook"; endorsed by TJ.

On 27 Apr. 1778, ABOUT THE DATE that Benjamin Fry remembered TJ assisting him with his pension, TJ "Gave Ben Fry a wounded soldier 42/" (MB, 1:462). EVANITION: "disappearance" (OED).

# From Jason Chamberlain

SIR,                                        Burlington, May 10, 1814.

I have the honour to acknowledge the receipt of your[1] note. I shall think myself happy to have done the least, to oblige a man to whom every virtuous <u>American</u> will readily acknowledge himself under so many obligations.

I take the liberty to send you one of my Orations. It was written in haste, and in obedience to the wishes of our Corporation. It became my duty to defend the study of the Languages, which I sincerely think is useful. I would not, however, introduce them to the exclusion of one of the sciences, and I would also recommend the study of the modern Languages, and particularly the French, to the one, who is desirous of a finished education.

We have every reason to believe that our Lake, (Champlain,) was formerly much larger than at present. Our large flats have every appearance of having been overflowed. Lake shells are found in great abundance, in the rocks, more than two miles from the Lake. They may be taken entire, by breaking the stones of which they compose a part. The aspect of the land, and the quality of the soil, indicate that the waters have receded some distance from their former banks. I believe that some of the barriers, in the St. Lawrence, have, in times past, broken away, and that all the Lakes are much smaller than they were in former ages. I suggest this idea, because I know that you have not been inattentive to the natural history of our country, while your Administration forms so splendid a period in our civil history.

With veneration for your publick character, and private worth,
I am your most obedient,                    JASON CHAMBERLAIN.

RC (MHi); at foot of text: "The Hon. Tho. Jefferson, Esq."; endorsed by TJ as received 26 June 1814 and so recorded in SJL. Enclosure: Chamberlain, *An Inaugural Oration delivered at Burlington, August 1, 1811. by Jason Chamberlain, A. M.,* *professor of the learned languages in the University of Vermont. published by order of the Corporation, and at the request of the students* (Burlington, Vt., 1811).

[1] Manuscript: "you."

# To Hugh Chisholm

DEAR SIR                                    Monticello May 10. 14.

I have been detained by the carriage maker at Charlottesville far beyond my expectation. the carriage however comes home to day and will take about a week to paint dry and finish here. this now depending on ourselves alone, I may count with certainty, and shall not suffer an hour to be lost, nor wait one hour after it is done. I suppose I shall be with you certainly by the 20<sup>th</sup>. I have thought it best to drop you this line, that you may not be on uncertainty. accept my best wishes.                                                    TH: JEFFERSON

RC (MHi); addressed: "M<sup>r</sup> Hugh Chisolm at Poplar Forest near Lynchburg"; franked; postmarked Charlottesville, 11 May; endorsed by TJ. PoC (MHi); endorsed by TJ.

On 21 May TJ gave CARRIAGE MAKER Elijah Rosson an order on Gibson & Jefferson for $30.50, "the balance after deducting 72.D. for 120l.f. of ash delivered him," for work on a landau. Although TJ intended to be at Poplar Forest BY THE 20<sup>TH</sup>, he did not arrive until 24 May 1814 (*MB*, 2:1300).

# From George Creager

SIR                                   May 10 1814 Washington City
I Saw a Racommandation under sined by your Name Last spring it was Handed to me by one James M<sup>c</sup>Keny the Recommadation was in ditleing him as a Vary Honest men and of such a carractor that indused me to belive that it was the Case and on the stranght I took him and his Son in as Bordars and was Compliatly taken in he at first paid of Every week for three weeks and then stoped payment and in the month of July I took sick when he took the atvendage of me and— Left me and I had sometime before Give his Son two dollars for being inclined to assist me in times in my Buisness to by him a pair of shoos and as the old Gendlemen left me he put his old shoos in the place of his sons and took the pair which I bought for the son and wend of and the first I heard of him he wrote a letter to M<sup>r</sup> John napp in this place and in the letter he mentioned of the mony he owed to me and said I should not be afread of loosing what he owed me that as soon as he Could Collact mony that was owing to him he would sent it by Post but[1] Never did as yet I would thank you if you would Speck to him on the subgact as on the Good Recommandation of yours I Give him Cradit other wise I would helt him to pay Every week or Stoped Bording him and after he left me I got furter aquendet of his prinsibles whear I was much surprised of as I think your Recommandation was Gon to far acording to his Cunduct I wish to hear from you and Remain with Respect your frend          [GEOR]GE CREAGER

his acount is for Bording and washing & for money lent for him only as for his son I made no garge after he took to assist me in my Buisness as I and father had agreed that he should help me for his Bording and the garge was only of the old mens to the amount of thirty two Dollars which he ows Justly to me now—

GEORGE CREAGER

RC (DLC); torn at seal; addressed: "M$^r$ Thomas Jafforson Esqe Albemare County Verginia"; franked; postmarked Washington, 12 May; endorsed by TJ as received 20 May 1814 and so recorded in SJL.

George Creager (ca. 1753–1815) served as sheriff of Frederick County, Maryland, from 1803–06, and sought an additional term unsuccessfully in 1809. Afterwards he moved to Washington, D.C., where he died (J. Thomas Scharf, *History of Western Maryland* [1882; repr. 2003], 1:480–1, 487, 493; Fredericktown (now Frederick), Md., *Republican Advocate*, 10 Dec. 1802; *National Intelligencer and*

*Washington Advertiser*, 1 Feb. 1805; Fredericktown *Hornet; or, Republican Advocate*, 4 Oct. 1809; *Creager v. Brengle*, reported in Thomas Harris and Reverdy Johnson, *Reports of Cases Argued & Determined in the Court of Appeals of Maryland* [1821–27], 5:234–45 [case decided in June 1821]; Washington *Daily National Intelligencer*, 20 July, 10 Oct. 1815; *Frederick-Town Herald*, 26 Aug. 1815).

The RACOMMANDATION of James McKinney (M$^c$KENY) was probably TJ to Richard M. Johnson, 26 Jan. 1813.

¹ Manuscript: "put."

# From James Madison

DEAR SIR                                      Montpelier May 10. 1814

Having particular occasion and the state of business at Washington not forbidding, I am on a short visit at my farm. M$^{rs}$ M. as well as myself would gladly extend it to Monticello; but with a certainty that our return to Washington must be very soon. I am obliged moreover to hold myself in readiness to hasten it, at any moment of notice. We must postpone therefore the pleasure of paying our respects then, till the autumn when I hope we shall be less restricted in time.

We have rec$^d$ no information from our Envoys to the Baltic for a very long time. From those last appointed there has not been time to hear after their arrival at Gothenburg. Neither have we any acc$^{ts}$ from England, other than the newspaper paragraphs which you have seen. The B. Gov$^t$ cannot do less than send negociators to meet ours; but whether in the spirit of ours is the important question. The turn of recent events in Europe, if truly represented, must strengthen the motives to get rid of the war with us; and their hopes by a continuance of it, to break down our Gov$^t$ must be more & more damped, by occurrences here as they become known there. The election in N. York alone crushes the project of the Junto faction so long fostered by and flattering the expectations of the B. Cabinet. Still it is possible that new fallacies may suffice for a willingness to be deceived. Our difficulties in procuring money without heavy taxes, and the supposed odium of these, will probably be made the most of by our internal enemies, to reconsider the experiment of prolonged hostilities.

The idea of an armistice so much bandied in the newspapers rests on no very precise foundation. It is not doubted that it is wished for in Canada, and might co-incide with the opinions of the Naval Commander; but it is presumable that the latter has no commensurate power, and it is taken for granted that the power in Canada, is limited to operations of land forces.

I found my wheat fields uncommonly flourishing with the exception of parts under the depredation of the Hessian fly. The appearance changes for the worse so rapidly, that the crop must be greatly reduced, and may be in a manner destroyed. I know not the extent of the Evil beyond this neighbourhood. I hope yours is exempt from it.

Accept assurances of affect<sup>e</sup> respect  JAMES MADISON

RC (DLC: Madison Papers); at foot of text: "M<sup>r</sup> Jefferson"; endorsed by TJ as received 17 May 1814 and so recorded in SJL.

Republicans won the majority in both the New York state legislative and federal congressional contests in the April 1814 ELECTION (Heidler and Heidler, *War of 1812*, 383).

# To Craven Peyton

DEAR SIR  Monticello May 10. 14.
M<sup>r</sup> Rosson is finishing a carriage for me and has not a pair of handles left. but he has the fellow to one which he lately put to your carriage. if you can accept of the one now sent and which he says is much superior to the one you have, and can let me have that, I shall then be able to get my carriage finished for which I am waiting to set out to Bedford. I shall be thankful to you for the accomodation, and I send the new handle by my workman who is able to put it on for you.

I [ho]pe you recieved in time the letter I lodged for you [...]day at the post office. Accept the assurance of [my esteem?] & respect.
  TH: JEFFERSON

PoC (MHi); corner torn; at foot of text: "[...]yton"; endorsed by TJ as a letter to Craven Peyton and so recorded in SJL.

# From Abraham Howard Quincy

SIR, New York May 10<sup>th</sup> 1814

My new System travels with Snail like motion, but sure, it has friends, but wants more, it is in satisfactory operation in this City in the New & Elegant city Hall & with many persons in private families, I have almost the whole Literary world against the principle of compressing flued fire by multiplied passages in Stone, but from what cause I am unable to deturmine, as I have never yet been favored with a rational Objection, altho courted & challenged repeatedly, my greatest greif arrises from the circumstance that I am not fairly opposed, but have a concealed Enemy to contend with, whose only instruments of Anoyance are little insinuations accompanied with great characters, fact however is fast undermining the Throne & hopes of Superficial greatness, I was in hopes M<sup>r</sup> Dashcoff the Russian Minister would have Seen you at Washington & given you his opinion of my general design, particularly as m<sup>r</sup> Fulton could not have made you a Satisfactory report, as his Visit, on the Occation requested by you, was in the moments of hurry, he called on me with his Lady last Spring & I accompanied them to a Gentlemans House in which the principle had been in Successful Operation the Season then past, he asked no questions of importance, Solicited no account of its Operations or effects, & under the influence of prejudice, which I had evidence existed prior to this Visit, he had not the power to communicate to you existing & interesting facts, From the discouraging Scenes through which I pass, opposed rather than investigated, I am convinced that like the Sturdy oak, my discovery is doomed to advance by degrees proportioned to its duration.

Do we desire to avoid the thousand bodily infirmaties & torments produced by irregular action in the fluids of the Same, that liquid life & death which nourishes & distroys alternately, this System effects the object; by equalising the atmosphere of our appartments & expelling the deadly damps of unfavorable Seasons & climates. does not artificial heat produce changes in air? Do we desire to control the powerful element of fire rather than be controled by its ravaging authority—Compression effects it.

Do we desire to Save nine parts out of ten of the expence & inconvenence attending the use of fuel in the common way & to remove all the usual hassards incident to Infancy & Infirmity, by this System we fully accomplish the Same.

Do we desire superior elegance, unusual cleanliness, or to gratify the most systematic or Romantic Schemes in conducting this all important element to usefulness By the use of this System & this Stone our desires are gratified to the full.

now, Sir, these are not the Vissions of a Sickly brain but experemental facts, & not the less so, because not believed in by great men, it will be recollected that the great question, that now supports the living & dying christian, once hung in Suspence, & that, in an enlightened age, on this grave query "have any of the Rulers believed on him" I am Very Sorry it has not been in my power to gratify your desire by giving you the means of information which many gentlemen have had relative to this Subject, I hope however Soon to devise means of Sending you Such a Specimen of the principle, & So applied, as Shall give correct ideas of its utility, which the unceartainty of water[1] Carriage has heretofore prevented, General Dearborn has partially inspected other Systems as intended in mettals for cooking in Ships & Camps, he will Soon be supplied with one for his quarters[2] here & give his opinion, I propose that one man shall supply one Hundred & Eighty men with good clean wholesome cooking all weathers in the open camp in two hours with one fire, in place of that unceartainty & waste that now attends the Operations, this System I Showed to General Dearborn last fall, it is a double Swinging Stove with the furnice beneath & with boilers hanging by the Sides with projections runing from each into all Sides of the furnice & the smoak or flame rising from the fire between the inner & outer Surfaces, rising by one Side, runing over the top, decending by the other Side; then rising up the back & runs off,[3] thus forming a large holow Square with Shelves, & to open like a closset for the purpose of baking & roasting, five Sides out of Six of the Same Square is covered with flame, the Side boilers mentioned, are rather Steam kettles, in to each of which Ten Camp kettles are intended to be put, when this System is used on Ship board it is intended to hang by chain & Swivel; & to be no more Subject to the motion of the Ship than the hanging Compass, or the swinging hammock, when hung under deck its funel will rise So as to have motion in a thing resembling a reversed tunnel passing through[4] the deck, to prevent the fluid escaping with its best power through the pores of the mettals before have[g] gone through the System, we put a thin Sheet Iron case over the S[d] double Stove or Caboose, through which also the boilers pass, I may be too troublesome to you Sir, but am confident when you shall percieve I am aiming at blessing Scociety by means any way practical I shall have your patronage,

with great respect I am at your command,

ABR[M] HOWARD QUINCY

I would remark that my System in Stone when extensively patronised will come Very low in price, as I have an inexhaustable Quarry on Connecticut river or within 80 rods of its banks at a Town in New Hamshire Called Orford, which Doct[r] Mitchel pronounces the best quality he has yet Seen.

RC (ViW: TC-JP); addressed: "Tho[s] Jefferson Esqr late President of the United States Montecelo Virginia"; stamp replaced by frank; postmarked New York, 12 May; endorsed by TJ as received 20 May 1814 and so recorded in SJL.

HAVE ANY OF THE RULERS BELIEVED ON HIM comes from the Bible, John 7.48.

[1] Preceding two words interlined.
[2] Manuscript: "quaters."
[3] Manuscript: "of."
[4] Manuscript: "throug."

# From John Barnes

DEAR SIR—                                   George Town 13th May 1814.—
M[r] Taylors unfavorable Acc[t] ℔ last Evening Mail, says— "Bank stock, in general is falling Considerably."[1]—that he sold— yesterday Penn[a] Bank stock a 135 ℔ Ct. Owing to the Rumour of Peace—as well the demand for Cash—Subscribers to the New Loan—        that the Certificates with a regular power of Atty— will be requiset to make the Sale—        that Bills on France cannot be depend[d] upon—at this most Critical Moment—
the $10,000—Subscribed for viz. $2,500—must be paid 25th Instant.—and sh[d] Necessity require it I will attempt—(After making good the 1[t] Instalm[t]) a Journey to Philad[a] however inconvenient in Order to Effect a permanent and Conclusive Adjustm[t] that no default may intervene[2]—dispatch—on these particular Occasions—is—Necessary.—        most respectly and truly.
I am Dear Sir—Yrs &[c]                                   JOHN BARNES,

RC (ViU: TJP-ER); at foot of text: "Thomas Jefferson Esq[r] Monticello"; endorsed by TJ as received 20 May 1814 and so recorded in SJL.

[1] Omitted closing quotation mark editorially supplied.
[2] Manuscript: "interene."

# From Tadeusz Kosciuszko

MON CHER AMI                                   Paris 15. Mai 1814.
Je Crois que nous souffrons tout deux cette Année Vous par l'Angleterre et moi par vous, Car je nai pas touché les interets de ma petite Somme placée chez vous[1] pour l'année passée de 1813. et dont

cependant jaurais un grand besoin. Je conçois que la Guerre a pu empecher les communications avec la France; Mais tachez de m'envoyer par l'Angleterre ou par la Hollande.

Je vous embrasse mille fois avec toute mon Amitié et mon Estime Sincere T Kosciuszko

EDITORS' TRANSLATION

MY DEAR FRIEND                    Paris 15. May 1814.
I believe we are both suffering this year, you because of England, and me because of you, for I have not received the interest for last year, 1813, on the small sum placed with you, and which I still greatly need. I understand that the war may have hindered communications with France; but try to send it to me through England or Holland.

I embrace you a thousand times with all my friendship and sincere[1] esteem T Kosciuszko

RC (MHi); dateline at foot of text; endorsed by TJ as received 15 Sept. 1814 and so recorded in SJL. Dupl (facsimile, lacking verso with endorsement, in Sotheby Parke Bernet auction catalogue, New York City, 14 Nov. 1978, item 460); catalogue indicates that TJ's en-dorsement noted receipt on 12 Oct. 1814, but recorded in SJL as received two days later. Translation by Dr. Genevieve Moene. Enclosed in Levett Harris to TJ, 22 June 1814.

[1] Preceding three words not in Dupl.

# To Henry Dearborn

MY DEAR FRIEND AND GENERAL          Monticello May 17. 14.
I present to you mr Rives, the bearer of this, an eleve of mine in law and politics. he is able, learned, honest, & orthodox in his principles. being just about to enter on the stage of public life he wishes first to see something more of our country at large. he will be one of the distinguished men of our state, & of the United States. in taking him by the hand while in Boston you will render service to distinguished[1] merit, plant the seeds of gratitude in a grateful soil, and lay under particular obligations

Your's sincerely & affectionately          TH: JEFFERSON

RC (DLC: William C. Rives Papers); addressed: "His Excellency Major General Dearborne Boston by mr Rives." PoC (DLC); endorsed by TJ.

The BEARER, William C. Rives, was TJ's student, or ELEVE (OED).

[1] Word interlined.

# To John Langdon

MY DEAR AND ANTIENT FRIEND Monticello May 17. 14.

I present to you mr Rives, an eleve of mine in law and politics: honest, able, learned, & true in the holy republican gospel. bestow on him your native kindness, not only for the gratification of your own benevolent dispositions, but to shew him the degree of estimation in which you hold your

affectionate friend TH: JEFFERSON

RC (DLC: William C. Rives Papers); addressed: "The honorable John Langdon Portsmouth by mr Rives." PoC (DLC); endorsed by TJ.


# To James Madison

DEAR SIR Monticello May 17. 14.

The inclosed paper came to me for I know not what purpose; as it came, just as you see it, without a scrip of a pen: perhaps that I might join in the sollicitation. Augustus Chouteau, the first signer, I always considered as the most respectable man of the territory, and the more valuable as he is a native. of the other signers I know nothing; and I know how easy it is to get signers to such a paper, and that no man possesses that art more perfectly than the one recommended. he must have changed character much if he is worthy of it. I remember we formed a very different opinion of him; and I think he was removed for faction and extortion or champerty from some office he held; either that of Attorney for the US. or of land Commissioner, or something of that sort. perhaps you will recollect it better than I do. it is probable you have recieved such a paper; but lest you should not, I send you this. We learnt your arrival at home about a week ago. I was then, as I am now, on the point of setting out to Bedford, delayed from day to day for a carriage daily promised. my present prospect is to set out in two days. this will prevent my intruding a visit on you during your present stay at Montpelier, and the rather as I am sensible that all visits must be inconveniently intrusive on the objects which bring you home. I sincerely congratulate you on the success of the loan, and wish that resource may continue good. I have not expected it could be pushed very far, from the unfortunate circumstance of our circulating medium being delivered over to enrich private adventurers at the public expence, when in our own hands it might have been made a competent supplement to our other war resources. mrs Randolph joins me in friendly respects to mrs Madison. mr Randolph is at Varina. ever affectionately yours

Th: Jefferson

I have this moment been called on for Wynne's life of Jenkins, & find it not in the library. the last I remember of it was the carrying it to Washington for your use while engaged on the subject of neutral rights. I suspect therefore it may still be in the Office of state. can you recollect, or will you be so good as to enquire after it. I have re-opened my letter to state this.

RC (DLC: Madison Papers); beneath signature: "The President of the US."; postscript on verso; endorsed by Madison. PoC (DLC); lacking postscript; endorsed by TJ, with additional notation: "Specht Gen$^l$." Enclosure: petition by "Members of the General assembly of the Territory of Missouri" to Madison and the United States Senate, 5 Dec. 1813, certifying "that from a Knowledge of the uprightness, talents and ability of Rufus Easton Esquire of the Town of S$^t$ Louis, formed on a personal acquaintance, we believe him a character eminently qualified for the office of a Judge for this Territory," and recommending his appointment (MS in DNA: RG 59, LAR, 1809–17, in a clerk's hand, signed by Auguste Chouteau and fourteen other legislators, with two additional signatures on separate sheets; Tr in same, with all seventeen signatories; certified in Saint Louis, 10 Dec. 1813, by Marie Pierre Le Duc, notary public, with his notarial seal; Tr in same, with original fifteen signatories; printed in *Terr. Papers*, 14:716–7).

In 1805 Easton had been charged with fraud. Although he was acquitted, neither TJ nor Madison reappointed him to the OFFICE of judge of the territorial superior court (Lawrence O. Christensen and others, eds., *Dictionary of Missouri Biography* [1999], 271–2). William WYNNE'S work was *The Life of Sir Leoline Jenkins*, 2 vols. (London, 1724; Sowerby, no. 374).

# To William Short

MY DEAR FRIEND                    Monticello May 17. 14.

The bearer mr Rives, the son of one of our wealthiest citizens and of the neighboring county of Amherst, is an eleve of mine in law & politics. before he commences practice he wishes to visit the country North of us. an honester, abler, or better informed man could not be presented to you. make him sensible of my high estimation of him by the kind offices which you as my friend may render him in Philadelphia, and charge all to the account of

Your's affectionately                    Th: Jefferson

RC (ViW: TJP); at foot of text: "William Short esq."; endorsed by Short as "rec$^d$ by M$^r$ Reevs, at the end of May." Recorded in SJL as a letter to be delivered "by mr Rives."

# To John F. Watson

I have long been a subscriber to the edition of the Edinburgh review first published by mr Sargeant, and latterly by Eastburn Kirk and co. and already possess from N° 30. to 42. inclusive; except that N^os 31. & 37 never came to hand. these two and N° 29. I should be glad to recieve, with all subsequently published thro the channel of mess^rs Fitzwhylson & Potter of Richmond, with whom I originally subscribed, and to whom it is more convenient to make paiment by a standing order on my correspondent at Richmond. I willingly also subscribe for the republication of the first 28. N^os to be furnished me thro the same channel for the convenience of paiment. this work is certainly unrivalled in merit, and if continued by the same talents, information and principles which distinguish it in every department of science which it reviews, it will become a real Encyclopaedia, justly taking it's station in our libraries with the most valuable depositories of human knolege. of the Quarterly Review I have not seen many numbers. as the Antagonist of the other it appeared to me a pigmy against a giant. the precept 'Audi alteram partem,'[1] on which it is republished here, should be sacred with the judge who is to decide between the contending claims of individual & individual, it is well enough for the young who have yet opinions to make up on questions of principle in ethics or politics. but to those who have gone thro' this process with industry, reflection, and singleness of heart, who have formed their conclusions and acted on them thro' life, to be reading over and over again what they have already read, considered and condemned, is an idle waste of time. it is not in the history of modern England or among the advocates of the principles or practices of her government, that the friend of freedom, or of political morality, is to seek instruction. there has indeed been a period, during which both were to be found, not in her government, but in the band of worthies who so boldly and ably reclaimed the rights of the people, and wrested from their government theoretic acknolegements of them. this period began with the Stuarts, and continued but one reign after them. since that the vital principle of the English constitution is <u>Corruption</u>, it's practices the natural result of that principle, and their consequences a pampered aristocracy, annihilation of the substantial middle class, a degraded populace, oppressive taxes, general pauperism, & national bankruptcy. those who long for these blessings here will find their generating principles well developed and advocated by the Antagonists of the Edinburgh Review. still those who doubt should read them; every man's reason being his sole rightful umpire. this principle, with that of acquiescence in the will of the Majority will preserve us free & prosperous as long as they are sacredly observed.     Accept the assurance of my respect.

TH: JEFFERSON

RC (PHi: Dreer Collection); addressed: "Mr John F. Watson Bookseller Philadelphia"; franked; postmarked Charlottesville, 18 May; endorsed by Watson as received 23 May and answered 2 June 1814, with added notation: "Books—11.25." PoC (DLC). Tr (MHi); posthumous copy.

AUDI ALTERAM PARTEM: "hear the other side."

Sometime before this date, South Carolina Episcopal bishop Theodore Dehon and a friend visited TJ at Monticello. Dehon's biographer and probable companion, Christopher E. Gadsden, later described the visit as follows: "On his journey to attend the Convention at Philadelphia, (May, 1814,) the road brought him within a half-day's ride of Monticello. His companion having expressed an earnest wish to see both that seat and its illustrious proprietor, he kindly and promptly surrendered his own inclination. Unprovided with a letter, we were nevertheless hospitably invited to pass the night. The extensive and varied scenery from this mountain—the arrangements of the grounds, and of the interior of the mansion, and its scientific decorations, presented many interesting novelties; but our attention was chiefly engaged by the presence and the conversation of the great man. Mr. Jefferson's large person seemed the appropriate tenement of his capacious and largely stored mind. He moved with great ease and more rapidity, than one unaccustomed to it could have done, over his well-waxed, tessellated mahogany-floor. He spoke, almost constantly, on various topics seasonably introduced, very sensibly, and seemed never to hesitate for a thought or a word. The impression was unavoidable, that he was a master mind. The regret was equally unavoidable, that it had been so indifferent, if not averse, to moral studies, important beyond all comparison—studies which had deeply interested Newton, Locke and Bacon. Having breakfasted with Mr. Jefferson, we proceeded to the seat of President Madison, with whom Bishop Dehon was acquainted" (Christopher E. Gadsden, *An Essay on the Life of the Right Reverend Theodore Dehon, D. D.* [1833], 239).

[1] Opening double quotation mark editorially altered for consistency.

## To John Adams

MY DEAR SIR                    Monticello May 18. 14.

This will be handed you by mr Rives a young gentleman of this state and my neighborhood. he is an eleve of mine in law, of uncommon abilities, learning and worth. when you and I shall be at rest with our friends of 1776. he will be in the zenith of his fame and usefulness. before entering on his public career he wishes to visit our sister states and would not concieve he had seen any thing of Massachusets were he not to see the venerable patriot of Braintree. I therefore request your indulgence of his wishes to be presented to you, a favor to which his high esteem for your character will give double value. but his wishes would be but partly gratified were he not presented to mrs Adams also. may I then ask this additional favor of you, which I shall value the more as it will give him the opportunity which I hope of bringing back to me a favorable report of both your healths. Accept as heretofore the assurances of my affectionate esteem & respect                                          TH: JEFFERSON

RC (DLC: William C. Rives Papers); addressed: "John Adams late President of the United States Braintree by mr Rives." PoC (DLC).

# From John Barnes

DEAR SIR—                                    George Town—18th May 1814
My two last to you, were of the 2[d] and 13th—I am Anxiously waiting your power of Atty—Accompanied with the two Certificates—for the 20 Shares of Penn[a] Bank Stock—
without which, I am unable to proceed a Step further, then to provide for the $2500—the first paym[t] to be made, 25th Ins[t]. for this purpose I was Compell'd—to ask the fav[r] of a friend—to indorse (for my Note of $1480)[1]—the last resort—the only inconvenence on this Occasion is—my friend—can—with equal propriety—Ask the like fav[r] of me— (which Otherwise—I could with propriety refuse—at this eventfull Crisis). as the 25th June Approaches—I shall be Anxious to provide for it, lest some, unforeseen Accd[t] might—intervene—hope you had not left Monticello—for Bedford—ere mine of the 2[d] Ins[t] had reached Milton—if unfortunately—you had set out—for Bedford.— the business might be so protracted as to hazard my effecting a Sale in time to make good—your 2[d] paym[t]—25th June—
I trust however, my fears will, in Course of a post or two—prove ground less—
and relieve
Dear Sir—your very Obed[t]                              JOHN BARNES,
inclosed I return you Gen[l] Kosicuszko—letter,

RC (ViU: TJP-ER); at foot of text: "Thomas Jefferson Esq[r] Monticello"; endorsed by TJ as received 26 June 1814 and so recorded in SJL. Enclosure: Tadeusz Kosciuszko to TJ, 24 Jan. 1814.

[1] Omitted closing parenthesis editorially supplied.

# To Daniel D. Tompkins

SIR                                                    Monticello May 18. 14.

Altho' I have not had the honor of a personal acquaintance with you, yet our respective public duties have heretofore produced an intercourse of letters which rendering us not entire strangers furnish the grounds of addressing this letter to you. it will be handed by mr Rives, a young gentleman of this state, an eleve of mine in the law, of great abilities, learning and worth, and one who will undoubtedly in the fulness of time become one of the prominent characters of our Union. before entering on the stage of public life, he wishes to see more of our country at large, and proposes to take New York in his course. I take the liberty of presenting him to your attentions, which cannot be bestowed on a more worthy subject; which I do the more willingly, as it furnishes me the occasion of assuring you of the high estimation in which I hold your character and public services and of repeating former assurances of my great esteem & respect

TH: JEFFERSON

RC (DLC: William C. Rives Papers); at foot of text: "H. E. Governor Tompkins." PoC (DLC); endorsed by TJ. Recorded in SJL as a letter to be delivered "by mr Rives."

Daniel D. Tompkins (1774–1825), attorney and public official, was a native of Westchester County, New York. He graduated from Columbia College (later Columbia University) in 1795 and was admitted to the New York bar two years later. Tompkins soon embarked on a political career as a Jeffersonian Republican. He served in New York State constitutional conventions in 1801 and 1821, sat in the lower house of the state legislature in 1803, and was appointed to the New

York Supreme Court the following year. Tompkins was governor of New York, 1807–17, strongly supporting the Embargo of 1807 and the War of 1812, and vice president under James Monroe, 1817–25. At his request the New York legislature passed a law in 1817 that abolished slavery in the state effective ten years later. Tompkins's final years were strained by political and financial complications resulting from his wartime management of state finances. He died on Staten Island (*ANB*; *DAB*; Hugh Hastings, ed., *Public Papers of Daniel D. Tompkins*, 3 vols. [1898–1902]; TJ to Tompkins, 10 Dec. 1807 [DLC]; *New-York Evening Post*, 13 June 1825).

# To Francis Corbin

DEAR SIR                                                Monticello May 20. 14.

Your favor of Apr. 30. is just recieved and conveys the first information of the death of mrs Paradise. it finds me on the eve of a journey of length, on which I shall be a month absent, and the preparations for which permit me only to give you my first thoughts on the subject of your letter.

I happen to possess an outline of the marriage settlement between mr and mrs Paradise, reciting so much of Col° Ludwell's will as relates to our purpose. this, with some little aid from my memory, furnishes a scanty supply of the facts of the case.    By the will, dated Feb. 28. 1767. he devises his lands to Richard Corbin E<sup>t</sup>c in trust for the use of his three daughters, <u>and their heirs</u>, specifying by description the particular lot each was to have, and providing, if either died before age or marriage, that her part should be equally divided between the survivors <u>and their heirs</u>: and he appoints persons in England their guardians. he died Mar. 25. 1767. one of the daughters, Frances, died Sep. 7. 1768. whereon her portion passed to the other two sisters. Lucy was afterwards married to John Paradise, and by previous deed of May 10. 1767. her estate was settled on the husband & wife for life, then on their children for such estates, not exceeding estates tail, as they should appoint, with other limitations not concerning the trustees.

On these facts I observe, 1. that the devise of the legal estate to the trustees was a jointenancy, which on their deaths survived successively, so as to vest wholly in the last survivor and his heirs. mr Wayles died first; and whether mr Waller or your father next, I do not know; but I believe mr Waller; & if so, your father became solely invested with the trust, which has descended on his heirs.

2. But the legal estate could not vest in the trustees without their acceptance, consent being as necessary to recieve, as to convey an estate. now did the trustees ever accept the trust expressly, or do any act amounting to an acceptance? I very much suspect they never did; for there was no act for them to perform, unless they had been called on to convey, and the act of conveyance would have been a full and final discharge of the trust. I believe they acted as Col° Ludwell's friends in the direction of his estate during his absence in England where he died; but that I suppose was by a power of attorney; for I know it was before the date of his will creating the trust: and their delivering over the estate to Paradise after the death of Col° Ludwell was but a closure of their transactions as attornies. if they never accepted the trust, then the legal estate never moved out of Col° Ludwell, but descended on his heirs, & became consolidated with the Use.

3. If they accepted the trust, it was still but a very nugatory one, the Use being given to the daughters in feesimple, and the possession also. there was nothing for the trustees to do but to convey the legal estate as the daughters should require. a simple conveyance of mrs Paradise's moiety, for the purposes of the marriage settlement

would have closed, and would now close the duties of the trustees; for, the estate having always been in possession of the Cestuys que usent, and the trustees having touched nothing, can be responsible for nothing.

If these hasty opinions, or any of them, be incorrect, and the trustees or their representatives, or any of them, be answerable for any thing, I think they should instantly file a bill in chancery stating the whole case truly, & praying that they may be permitted to make a conveyance of the legal estate to those entitled to the use, that they may stand discharged of the trust, and that those claiming or possessing the estate may be left to settle their rights among themselves, or by due course of law, at their will.        I think further it would be very unsafe for the representatives of the trustees to touch an article of the estate; as it would make them trustees in their own wrong, embarras the object of their application to the Chancellor, and make them liable to future suits by every person interested in the estate.

These, as before observed, are but the results of a sudden view of the case. should further reflection induce me to believe them incorrect, it shall be the subject of another communication; altho' at present the case appears to me tolerably simple and plain.

The agency I had in mr Paradise's affairs while I was in Europe, 1st by the mutual confidence of himself and his creditors, who left to me to settle absolutely the provisions for their debts, and for his intermediate support, which I did; then on the joint appeal by himself and his son in law the Count Barziza to make arrangements for them, makes me feel it incumbent, as the common friend of all parties, to convey intelligence to Count Barziza of the death of mrs Paradise, that he may look to the rights of his children. their citizenship is liable to question, and their claims may otherwise be rendered litigious by mrs Paradise's will, if she made one. of this I am uninformed, and of the dispositions she has made. to this interference is opposed my age, my aversion to trouble, particularly to the labors of the writing table, and the difficulties of transmitting a letter to Venice in the present disturbed state of the ocean and continent of Europe. I shall consider further of it, and perhaps be influenced by the dispositions of mrs Paradise's will, if I can get information of them.

If the representatives of mr Wayles stand any ways implicated in the affairs of the trust, I shall be happy to act in perfect union with yourself and according to your wishes; and I pray you to be assured of my continued and friendly sentiments of esteem and respect.

Th: Jefferson

PoC (DLC); at foot of first page: "Francis Corbin esq."; endorsed by TJ.

For the OUTLINE OF THE MARRIAGE SETTLEMENT between John Paradise and Lucy Ludwell Paradise, see TJ to Philip I. Barziza, 24 Dec. 1815. JOINTE-NANCY (joint tenancy): possession in which each joint tenant has a right of survivorship to the other's share. CESTUYS QUE USENT: the person for whose benefit a piece of property is held by another (*Black's Law Dictionary*).

# To Abraham Small

SIR                                            Monticello May 20. 1814.

I thank you for the copy of the American Speaker which you have been so kind as to send me. it is a judicious selection of what has been excellently spoken on both sides of the Atlantic; and according to your request I willingly add some suggestions should another edition be called for. to the speeches of L$^d$ Chatham might be added his reply to Horace Walpole on the Seamen's bill in the H. of Commons in 1740; one of the severest which history has recorded. indeed the subsequent speeches on order, to which that reply gave rise, being few short and pithy well merit insertion in such a collection as this. they are in the 12$^{th}$ vol. of Chandler's Debates of the H. of Commons. but the finest thing in my opinion which the English language has produced is the Defence of Eugene Arum, spoken by himself at the bar of the York Assizes in 1759.[1] on a charge of murder, and to be found in the Annual Register of that date, or a little after. it had been upwards of 50. years since I had read it, when the reciept of your letter induced me to look up a MS. copy I had preserved, and on re-perusal at this age & distance of time, it loses nothing of it's high station, in my mind, for classical style, close logic, and strong representation. I send you this copy which was taken for me by a school-boy, replete with errors of punctuation, of orthography, and sometimes substitutions of one word for another. it would be better to recur to the Annual Register itself for correctness, where also, I think, are stated the circumstances and issue of the case. to these I would add the short, the nervous, the unanswerable speech of Carnot, in 1803. on the proposition to declare Bonaparte Consul for life. this creed of republicanism should be well translated, and placed in the hands & heart[2] of every friend to the rights of self government. I consider these speeches of Arum, & Carnot, and that of Logan, inserted in your collection, as worthily standing in a line with those of Scipio and Hannibal in Livy, and of Cato and Caesar in Sallust. on examining the

Indian speeches in my possession, I find none which are not already in your collection, except that my copy of the Cornplanter's has much in it which yours has not. but, observing that the omissions relate to special subjects only, I presume they are made purposely, and indeed properly.

I must add more particular thanks for the kind expressions of your letter towards myself. these testimonies of approbation from my fellow citizens, offered too when the lapse of time may have cooled and matured their opinions, are an ample reward for such services as I have been able to render them, and are peculiarly gratifying in a state of retirement & reflection. I pray you to accept the assurance of my respect.                                         TH: JEFFERSON

P. S. since writing the above I have undertaken to transcribe the schoolboy copy of Arum's speech, and to correct some of it's errors: but some, I am persuaded, still remain. the book therefore should be recurred to.

PoC (DLC); at foot of first page: "Mr Abraham Small." Tr (MHi); posthumous copy; at head of text: "ext."

The next edition of Small's *American Speaker* did not include the 6 Mar. 1741 speech in Parliament by William Pitt, later 1st earl of CHATHAM, opposing provisions of the SEAMEN'S BILL that gave British justices of the peace rights to issue search warrants and impress men into the navy. It did, however, contain the 1759 defence of EUGENE Aram printed below and the 1 May 1804 speech of Lazare CARNOT that opposed making Napoleon consul for life (Small, *The American Speaker; A Selection of Popular, Parlia-* *mentary and Forensic Eloquence; particularly calculated for the Seminaries in the United States*, 3d ed. [Philadelphia, 1816], 114–20, 355–61). Small's text of CORNPLANTER'S speech (printed as "Speech of the Chiefs of the Seneca nation to the President of the United States—1790") omitted large sections of the speech that appear in the manuscript version owned by TJ (*American Speaker*, 2d ed. [Philadelphia, 1814; Poor, *Jefferson's Library*, 13 (no. 819)], 376–9; Tr in DLC: TJ Papers, 58:9949–58; undated; in John Wayles Eppes's hand).

[1] Reworked from "1769."
[2] Preceding two words not in Tr.

ENCLOSURE

## Eugene Aram's Defense at his Trial for Murder

[3 Aug. 1759]
The defence of Eugene Arum on his trial at the York Assizes.
First, my Lord, the whole tenor of my conduct in life contradicts every particular of this indictment. yet I had never said this, did not my present circumstances extort it from me, and seem to make it necessary. permit me here, my Lord, to call upon malignity itself, so long and cruelly busied in this prosecution, to charge upon me any immorality, of which prejudice was not the author. no, my lord, I concerted no schemes of fraud, projected no violence, injured no man's person or property. my days were honestly laborious, my

nights intensely studious. and I humbly concieve my notice of this, especially at this time, will not be thought impertinent or unseasonable; but at least deserving some attention. because, my lord, that any person, after a temperate use of life, a series of thinking & acting regularly and without one deviation[1] from sobriety, should plunge into the very depth of profligacy precipitately and at once, is altogether improbable & unprecedented, and absolutely inconsistent with the course of things.[2] villainy is always progressive, and declines from right step by step, till every idea[3] of probity is lost, and every sense of moral obligation[4] totally perishes.

Again, my lord, a suspicion of this kind, which nothing but malevolence could entertain and ignorance propagate, is violently opposed by my very situation at that time with respect to health; for, but a little space before, I had been confined to my bed, and suffered under a very long and severe disorder, and was not able, for half a year together, so much as to walk. the distemper left me indeed; yet slowly & in part; but so emaciated,[5] so enfeebled, that I was reduced to crutches; and was so far from being well about that[6] time I am charged with this fact, that I never to this day have[7] perfectly recovered. could then a person in this condition take any thing into his head so unlikely, so extravagant? I, past the vigor of my age, feeble & valetudinary, with no inducement to engage, no ability to accomplish, no weapon wherewith to perpetrate such a fact, without interest, without power, without motive, without means.

Besides, it must needs occur to every one that an action of this atrocious nature is never heard of, but, when it's springs are laid open, it appears that it was to support some indolence, or supply some luxury, to satisfy some avarice, or oblige some malice; prevent[8] some real, or some imaginary want. yet I lay not under the influence of any one of these. surely, my lord, I may, consistent with both truth and modesty affirm thus much; & none who have any veracity, & know me, will ever question this.

In the second place, the disappearance of Clark is suggested as an argument of his being dead. but the uncertainty of such an inference from that, and the fallibility[9] of all[10] conclusions from such circumstances,[11] are too obvious, & too notorious to require instances. yet, superseding many, permit me to produce a very recent one, and that afforded by this castle. in June 1757 William Thompson, for all the vigilance of this place, in open day light, and double ironed, made his escape. notwithstanding an immediate enquiry set on foot, the strictest search, and all advertisement, was never seen nor heard of since. if then Thompson got off unseen, thro' all these difficulties, how very easy was it for Clark, when none of them opposed him? but what would be thought of a prosecution commenced against any one seen last with Thompson?

Permit me, my lord, to observe a little upon the bones which have been discovered. it is said, which perhaps is saying very far, that these are the skeleton of a man. it is possible indeed they may: but is there any certain known criterion which incontestably distinguishes the sex in human bones? let it be considered, my lord, whether the ascertaining of this point ought not to precede any attempt to identify them. the place of their depositum too claims much more attention than is commonly bestowed on it: for of all places in the world none could have mentioned any one wherein there was greater certainty of finding human bones, than a hermitage; except he should point out a church yard; hermitages in times past being not only places of religious retirement, but of burial too; and it has scarcely[12] ever been heard of but that every cell now known contains, or contained, these relicks of humanity, some mutilated, and some entire. I do not inform, but give me leave to remind your lordship, that here sat solitary sanctity, and here the hermit or the Anchoress, hoped that repose for their bones when dead, they here enjoyed when living.

All this while, my lord, I am sensible this is known to your lordship, & many in this court, better than to me.[13] but it seems necessary to my case that others, who have not at all perhaps adverted to things of this nature, and may have concern in my trial, should be made acquainted with it. suffer me then, my lord, to produce a few of many evidences that those cells were used as repositories of the dead, and to enumerate a few in which human bodies have been found, as it happened in this in question; lest to some that accident might seem extraordinary, & consequ[e]ntly occasion prejudice. 1. the bones, as was supposed, of the Saxon saint Dubritius were discovered buried in his cell, at Guy's cliff near Warwick, as appears from the authority of S^r William Dugdale.      2. the bones that were[14] thought to be those of the Anchoress Rosia were but lately discovered in a cell at Royston, entire, fair & undecayed; tho' they must have lain interred for several centuries, as is proved by Doctor Stukely.[15]      3. But our own country, nay almost this neighborhood, supplies another instance. for in January 1747. was found by mr Stovin, accompanied by a reverend gentleman, the bones, in part, of some recluse in the cell at Lindholm near Hatfield. they were believed to be those of William of Lindholm, a hermit, who had long made this cave his habitation.      4. in February 1744. part of Woburn abbey being pulled down, a large portion of a corpse appeared, even with the flesh on, and which bore cutting with a knife; tho' it is certain this had laid above 200.[16] years, and how much longer is doubtful: for this abbey was founded in 1145. and dissolved in 1538. or 9. what would have been said, what believed, if this had been an accident to the bones in question?

Further, my lord, it is not yet out of living memory that a little distance from Knaresborough, in a field part of the manor of the worthy and patriot baronet who does that borough the honor to represent it in parliament, were found, in digging for gravel, not one human skeleton only, but five or six, deposited side by side, with each an urn placed at it's head, as your lordship knows was usual in antient interments. about the same time, and in another field almost close to this borough was discovered, also in searching for gravel, another human skeleton. but the piety of the same worthy gentleman ordered both pits to be filled up again, commendably unwilling to disturb the dead. is the invention of these bones forgotten then, or industriously concealed, that the discovery of those in question may appear the more singular and extraordinary? whereas in fact there is nothing extraordinary in it. my lord, almost every place conceals such remains. in fields, in hills, in highway sides, in commons, lie frequent and unsuspected bones. and our present allotment of rest for the departed is but of some centuries. another particular seems to claim not a little of your lordship's notice, and that of the gentlemen of the jury; which is that perhaps no example occurs of more than one skeleton being found in one cell; and in the cell in question was found but one;[17] agreeable in this to the peculiarity of every[18] known cell in Britain. not the invention of one skeleton then, but of two, would have appeared suspicious & uncommon.

But then, my lord, to attempt to identify these, when even to identify living men has proved so difficult, as in the case of Perkin Warbeck, & Lambert Symnal[19] at home, and Don Sebastian abroad, will be looked upon perhaps as an attempt to determine what is indeterminable. and I hope too it will not pass unconsidered here, where gentlemen believe with caution, think with reason, and decide with humanity, what interest the endeavor to do this is calculated to serve in assigning proper personality to these bones, whose particular appropriation can only appear to eternal omniscience.

Permit me, my lord, also[20] to remonstrate that as human bones appear to have been the inseparable adjunct of every cell, even any person naming such a place at random as containing them in this case, shews him rather unfortunately prescient, than conscious;[21] and that these attendants on every hermitage accidentally concurred with this conjecture; a mere casual coincidence of words & things.[22]

But, it seems, another skeleton has been discovered by some laborer which was full as confidently averred to be Clark's as this. my lord, must some of the living, if it promotes some interest, be made answerable for all the bones that earth has concealed, or chance exposed? and might not a place where bones lay be mentioned by a person by chance, as well as found by a laborer by chance? or is it more criminal accidentally to name[23] where bones lie, than accidentally to find[24] where they lie?

Here too is a human skull produced, which is fractured. but was this the cause,[25] or was it the consequence of death? was it owing to violence, or the effect of natural decay? if it was violence, was that violence before or after death? my lord, in May 1732 the remains of William, Lord archbishop of this province, were taken up by permission in this cathedral, and the bones of the skull were found broken. yet certainly he died by no violence offered to him alive that could occasion that fracture there.      let it be considered; my lord, that upon the dissolution of religious houses, and the commencement of the reformation, the ravages of those times both affected the living and the dead. in search after imaginary treasures coffins were broken up, graves & vaults dug open, monuments ransacked, and shrines demolished. your lordship knows that these violations proceeded so far as to occasion parliamentary authority to restrain them; and it did, about the beginning of the reign of Q. Elizabeth. I intreat your lordship, suffer not the violence, the depredations, and the iniquities of those times to be imputed to this.

Moreover, what gentleman here is ignorant that Knaresborough had a castle, which tho now run to ruin, was once considerable both for it's strength and garrison? all know it was vigorously besieged by the arms of the parliament. at which siege, in sallies, conflicts, flights, pursuits, many fell in all the places round it, and where they fell were buried; for every place, my lord, is burial earth in war; and many, questionless, of these rest yet unknown whose bones futurity shall discover.

I hope, with all imaginable submission, that what has been said will not be thought impertinent to this indictment, and that it will be far from the wisdom, the learning, and the integrity of this place, to impute to the living what zeal in it's fury may have done, what nature may have taken off, and piety interred; or what war alone may have destroyed, alone deposited.

As to the circumstances that have been racked,[26] I have nothing to observe; but that all circumstances whatsoever are precarious, and have been but too frequently[27] [fou]nd lamentably fallible. even the strongest have failed. they may rise to the utmost degree of probability; yet are they but probability still. why need I name to your lordship the two Harrisons recorded in Doctor Howel who both suffered upon circumstances, because of the sudden disappearance of their lodger, who was in credit, had contracted debts, borrowed money, and went off unseen, and returned again a great many years after their execution? why name the intricate affairs of Jacques de Moulin, under King Charles the second, related by a gentleman who was Counsel of the crown? and why the unhappy Coleman, who suffered innocently, tho' convicted upon positive evidence, and whose children perished for want because the world uncharitably believed the father guilty? why mention the perjury of Smith, incautiously admitted King's evidence, who, to screen himself, equally accused Faircloth and Loveday of the murder of Dun?[28] the first of whom in 1749. was executed at Winchester; and Loveday was about to suffer at Reading had not Smith been proved perjured, to the satisfaction of the court, by the Surgeon of the Gosport hospital?

Now, my lord, having endeavored to shew that the whole of this process is altogether repugnant to every part of my life; that it is inconsistent with my condition of health about that time; that no rational inference can be drawn that a person is dead, who suddenly disappears; that hermitages were the constant repositories of the bones of the recluse; that the proofs of this are well authenticated; that the revolutions in religion, or the fortune of war, has mangled, or buried the[29] dead; the conclusion remains, perhaps no less reasonably than impatiently wished for. I, last, after a year's confinement equal to either fortune, put myself upon the candor, the justice, and the humanity of your lordship, and upon yours, my countrymen, gentlemen of the jury.

PoC of Tr (DLC: TJ Papers, 201:35779–81); entirely in TJ's hand; undated; torn; one word faint. Printed in the *Annual Register, or a view of the History, Politicks, and Literature, of the year 1759* (London, 1760), 356–60, and in Abraham Small, *The American Speaker; A Selection of Popular, Parliamentary and Forensic Eloquence; particularly calculated for the Seminaries in the United States*, 3d ed. (Philadelphia, 1816), 114–20. Small's version generally follows TJ's transcription.

Eugene Aram (ca. 1704–59) was a British schoolmaster accused of murdering an associate named Daniel Clark. In 1745 Clark disappeared from his home in Knaresborough, Yorkshire, after borrowing large sums of money. Aram fled soon after, when suspicion of collusion fell on him. In 1758 a skeleton believed to be Clark's was found, and the cause of death was determined to be a blow to the head. After Aram was found and arrested, he composed this defense speech during the year he spent in York Castle prison. He was convicted of murder and executed. Aram was also a self-taught philologist who advanced the theory that the European family of languages descended from a common Celtic-based tongue (*ODNB*; Nancy Jane Tyson, *Eugene Aram: Literary History and Typology of the Scholar-Criminal* [1983]; *Annual Register*, 351–65).

DEPOSITUM: a place where things are stored (*OED*).

[1] *Annual Register*: "one single deviation."
[2] *Annual Register* here includes "Mankind is never corrupted at once."
[3] *Annual Register*: "regard."
[4] *Annual Register*: "every sense of all moral obligations."

<sup>5</sup> *Annual Register*: "macerated."
<sup>6</sup> *Annual Register* and *American Speaker*: "the."
<sup>7</sup> Word not in *Annual Register*.
<sup>8</sup> *Annual Register*: "to prevent."
<sup>9</sup> *Annual Register*: "infallibility."
<sup>10</sup> Manuscript: "of all of all."
<sup>11</sup> *Annual Register*: "conclusions of such sort, from such a circumstance."
<sup>12</sup> *Annual Register*: "scarce or."
<sup>13</sup> *Annual Register*: "better than I."
<sup>14</sup> Preceding two words not in *Annual Register*.
<sup>15</sup> *American Speaker*: "Shikely."
<sup>16</sup> *Annual Register*: "100."
<sup>17</sup> *Annual Register* italicizes this word and, earlier in the sentence, "one" and "one cell."

<sup>18</sup> *Annual Register*: "every other."
<sup>19</sup> *Annual Register*: "Symnel."
<sup>20</sup> *Annual Register*: "also very humbly."
<sup>21</sup> *Annual Register*: "rather unfortunate than conscious prescient."
<sup>22</sup> *Annual Register* italicizes this word and, earlier in the sentence, "words."
<sup>23</sup> *Annual Register* italicizes this word.
<sup>24</sup> *Annual Register* italicizes this word.
<sup>25</sup> *Annual Register* italicizes this word.
<sup>26</sup> *Annual Register*: "raked together." TJ placed a question mark above this word in manuscript.
<sup>27</sup> Manuscript: "frequenly."
<sup>28</sup> *Annual Register*: "Dunn."
<sup>29</sup> Manuscript: "the the."

# To Joseph H. Nicholson

DEAR SIR                           Monticello May 21. 14.

I thank you for making me acquainted with mr M<sup>c</sup>Culloch. he staid with me but part of a day. but that was sufficient to let me see that he was capable, well informed and modest. he left us on the 18<sup>th</sup> for the Natural bridge, from whence he intended to return, and to postpone for a while his Western expedition.

I recieve the kind expressions of your letter with sensibility & gratification, and reciprocate them cordially. your zealous & steady cooperation in atchieving & maintaining the republican ascendancy, and rescuing our constitution from the hands of those who were rapidly monarchising it, ought never to be forgotten; and I assure you with pleasure that there has never been a moment in which I have not honored and esteemed you for this as well as for your great personal merit. these sentiments have prevailed uninterruptedly in my mind, their impression is still the same, and assurances of the same attachment, esteem and respect are now given with truth and sincerity.

TH: JEFFERSON

RC (PPAmP: Thomas Jefferson Papers); addressed: "The honble Joseph Nicholson Baltimore"; franked; postmarked Milton, 25 May; with subsequent notation on address cover: "Given by M<sup>rs</sup> Nicholson to F F C—. 1823." PoC (MHi); endorsed by TJ.

# From Hugh Chisholm

SIR                                          Paplor forrist May 22<sup>th</sup> 1814

I have done the plaistring and have begon To Lay the Stone wall myself as you have maid a much Longer stay in albermarle than I Expected—I have been afraid that some accident must have Happened
from your delay—if it should be the case I pray you would write ame-
diately the size of the Bilding and the openings and whether I shall
Bild the pillers with Circulor Brick or with Squar Bricks the people
are all well at Both Places—Exept my Best wishes

HUGH CHISHOLM

RC (MHi); at foot of text: "M<sup>r</sup> Thomas
Jefferson"; endorsed by TJ as received 26
June 1814 and so recorded in SJL.

Chisholm laid the STONE WALL during
construction of a wing of offices at Poplar
Forest (Chambers, *Poplar Forest*, 81).

# From John Barnes

DEAR SIR—                                    George Town 24<sup>th</sup> May 1814—

Your very Acceptable fav<sup>r</sup> of the 8<sup>th</sup> with its several inclosures,
came safe to hand 21 Ins<sup>t</sup> viz The two Certificates of the 20 shares
of P. B. Stock with power of Att<sup>y</sup> and duplicate thereof, as well
yr letters to the Sect<sup>y</sup> of State & Treasury,—sealed & presented
yesterday—with Assurances that soon as the Momentous Crisis of
Affairs—in Paris—had subsided & arranged they would with great
pleasure, Aid me—in conveying your Remittance &<sup>c</sup> to the good
Gen<sup>l</sup> K—but at present nothing could be done,—with any Certainty
of Success,

that I was preparing for Philad<sup>a</sup> in Order to Effect a Sale of the
Gen<sup>ls</sup> Stock, &<sup>c</sup> and Asked the liberty—to wait on them on my return—when perhaps some more favorable turn of Affairs in Europe
might Offer to effect, the desired purpose—

The first instalm<sup>t</sup>—say $2,500, I deposited in the Bank of Col<sup>a</sup> yes-
terday—w<sup>th</sup> the Cashier—And to guard against any Unforeseen Occurances should the price of the B. S: or the want of purchasers
fail—my expectations, or your wishes—the struggle with me,[1] would
be,—whether or not I ought to sacrifice the Gen<sup>l</sup> Stock at its then Reduced price—or wait—with <u>trembling fear</u>, to fall upon some expe-
dient—with yr Assistance—to provide for the 2<sup>d</sup> Instalm<sup>t</sup> the 25<sup>h</sup>
June that effected, the 1<sup>t</sup> July at hand. y<sup>r</sup> ½ y<sup>rs</sup> dividend say $400—
would come in Aid—of the falling price of the stock—after the said

date—would at least be in fav$^r$—of the Gen$^l$—but of this while in Philad$^a$ I shall be inabled to judge more Correctly—

still permit me to suppose no efficient sale is effected—Unfortunately my funds in Bank—are already exhausted. my late Note for $1480. running upon me—of course sh$^d$ another be required to be issued and meet with a Refusal—I should in deed! be much mortified—If you could but Aid me w$^{th}$ a Moiety say $1250—I would Attempt to borrow the like sum even for a M$^o$ or two—would favor me with a Chance of selling to a better advantage. to sacrifice the Stock at too considerable a loss. I cannot think of it—with any degree of patience—it has I presume escaped your recollection—to favor me with your Order on the Cashier M$^r$ Smith for the last 6 M$^{os}$ dividend due 1$^t$ Jan$^y$—on Monday[2] next the 30$^h$ Ins$^t$ I purpose leaving this for Philad$^a$ any Commands you may think proper to Honor me with—addressed in Care of M$^r$ George Taylor Jun$^r$ I shall receive—at least to the Middle—or 18$^{th}$[3] June—will be particularly Attendd too—

By Dear Sir—
your very Obt servant,

JOHN BARNES,

RC (ViU: TJP-ER); addressed: "Thomas Jefferson Esq$^r$ Monticello—Virginia"; franked; postmarked 25 May; endorsed by TJ as received 26 June 1814 and so recorded in SJL.

P. B.: Bank of Pennsylvania. GEN$^L$ K: Tadeusz Kosciuszko. The cashiers of the

Bank of Pennsylvania and the BANK OF COL$^A$ (Columbia) were Jonathan SMITH and William Whann, respectively.

[1] Reworked from "us."
[2] Manuscript: "Mondy."
[3] Reworked from what appears to be "20$^{th}$."

# From James Mease

DEAR SIR                                      Philadelphia May 24$^{th}$ 1814—

The "Philadelphia Soc: for promoting Agriculture," are about publishing a third vol: of Memoirs, and in it will be contained a paper by Judge Wynkoop of Buck's County on making Cyder from the Hughe's Crab—and another on a Crab apple that originated on the farm of Col: Roan of Virginia and which is preferred by many to Hughe's Crab for Cyder.—

Being anxious to Collect all the facts respecting our native fruits, and especially our Cyder apples, I take the liberty to apply to You for Some account of the Crab, called The Gloucester white, Taliafero, a Robinson apple, which M$^r$ Coxe of Burlington, a zealous orchardist,[1]

lately informed me, he had heard in Washington you had praised very much for the excellent Cyder it produced.

I have tried to procure the history of the Hughe's Crab, but without effect

I Sincerely hope you enjoy good health, and that your life and energies may be long preserved.—

Accept My perfect respect. JAMES MEASE

RC (DLC); at foot of text: "The Honble Thos Jefferson"; endorsed by TJ as received 26 June 1814 and so recorded in SJL.

James Mease (1771–1846), physician and author, was a native of Philadelphia. He received an A.B. from the University of the State of Pennsylvania in 1787, and five years later he was awarded an M.D. by the University of Pennsylvania. Mease served as a hospital surgeon during the War of 1812. Though he did not establish a private practice, he was an acknowledged expert on rabies and offered courses privately on medicine, pharmacy, and veterinary medicine. Mease was heavily involved in Philadelphia's intellectual community and published on a wide range of topics, including agriculture, geology, medicine, and prisons. He was elected to the American Philosophical Society in 1802, serving as a curator about 1824–30 and a councillor, 1832–39. Mease was also a member and sometime secretary of the Philadelphia Society for Promoting Agriculture and a founder of both the Athenaeum of Philadelphia and the Pennsylvania Horticultural Society. He corresponded sporadically with TJ for many years on agricultural, historical, and scientific topics. Mease died in Philadelphia (ANB; DAB; PTJ, esp. 23:620; APS, Minutes, 16 Jul. 1802, 2 Jan. 1824, 6 Jan. 1832 [MS in PPAmP]; Philadelphia North American, 15 May 1846).

In its MEMOIRS (3 [1814]: 43–9, 392–5), the Philadelphia Society for Promoting Agriculture printed an article by Henry WYNKOOP on making cider from the Hewes (HUGHE'S) or Virginia crab apple and Timothy Pickering's account of the apples cultivated by John Roane (ROAN).

[1] Manuscript: "orchadist."

# To George Creager

SIR, May 28 1814.

I recieved your letter of May 10. just as I was setting out on a journey, from the end of which I write this. I am sorry you have been taken in as you mention by McKinney, and by a recommendation having my name undersigned. be assured that I never signed such a paper, nor ever saw it, we have been decieved in mr McKinney as you have been, and I have lost upwards of 1000. Dollars by him, and certainly therefore should never have assisted in taking in any other person. he is removed to some of the Southern counties of this state bordering on North Carolina, but where I do not know. but out of the line of communication with us. I should have been better pleased to have been able to give you a better account of him, and of the prospect of your recovering your money from him; but this I think small as he is not worth a copper, altho' I believe he has got into some kind of business. Accept my wishes that you may be able to succeed with him better than I expect                    TH: JEFFERSON

PoC (DLC); at foot of text: "M<sup>r</sup> George Crager"; endorsed by TJ as written from Poplar Forest.

# From John Vaughan

D SIR                                             Philad. 28 May 1814

My particular friend M<sup>r</sup> Nicholas Biddle, with his Lady, daughter of the late M<sup>rs</sup> Craig, are travelling to some of the springs in Your State, to reestablish health & tranquility of mind, which had been much affected by their late Domestic afflictions—Should they have the opportunity—I should feel gratified at being the means of bringing you personally acquainted—M<sup>r</sup> Biddle's tour to Europe has led him to appreciate more correctly, the Otium cum Dignitate which Monticello affords, & M<sup>rs</sup> B with a taste formed by that of her accomplished mother will not be less pleased with your elegant retirement— With regret that I cannot Indulge myself by a similar gratification I remain D sir

Your friend & ser<sup>t</sup>                              JN VAUGHAN

RC (DLC: Nicholas Biddle Papers); addressed: "Thomas Jefferson Monticello." Not recorded in SJL and probably never received by TJ.

Jane Margaret Craig Biddle (1793–1856) was the daughter of John and Margaret Murphy Craig. She was raised and educated in Philadelphia and at Andalusia, her family's estate in Bucks County, Pennsylvania. She married Nicholas Biddle in 1811, and their family eventually took up residence at Andalusia (Nicholas B. Wainwright, "Andalusia, Countryseat of the Craig Family and of Nicholas Biddle and His Descendants," *PMHB* 101 [1977]: 18–27; *ANB*, 2:734–6; Washington *Daily National Intelligencer*, 15 Aug. 1856; gravestone inscription in Saint Peter's Episcopal Church cemetery, Philadelphia).

The Biddle family's LATE DOMESTIC AFFLICTIONS included the death on 28 Jan. 1814 of Margaret Murphy Craig (*Port Folio* 3 [1814]: 284–9).

# From Henry M. Brackenridge

SIR,                                Baton Rouge 30<sup>th</sup> May 1814

I take the liberty of expressing the sense of gratitude which I feel, at the flattering notice you have been pleased to take, of the volume

[ 383 ]

lately published by me, on the subject of Louisiana. I am truely sensible, that, it is exceedingly emperfect; and further oppertunities, of information, have disclosed many errors. This, induces me, to think of a second edition, should the first, meet with a ready sale.[1] I regard the work, merely as a contribition towards something of a higher kind, which, I hope, may be undertaken by some one, possessed of the necessary qualifications: should this be the case, instead of attempting a second edition, I will be content, to become a correspondent, and a contribitor, in this way, as far as my information will enable me.

I might make appologies for the defects which occur in the volume, but I know that according to correct principles these are inadmissible, for no man ought to appear before the publick with his work until completely satisfied that it has received all the finish which it may be in his power to bestow; Indeed, I have done wrong in publishing so soon, but I was actuated [by][2] a belief that a regular work on such a subject could not be expected from one whose pursuits were of a different nature, and in some degree incompatible with the undertaking. My essays were hastily written, and in irregular desultory manner, often in the bar room of a country tavern, or in a boat as I passed along, and not composed in privacy and retirement. They were printed at the distance of two thousand miles from me, the manuscript forwarded by mail generally as it was written.

Louisiana, is at this moment far from being prosperous. The pressure of war has been more severely felt here than in any other state of the Union. The scenes of calamity and distress are very numerous in the city; in the country they are less striking, for notwithstanding,[3] the diminution in value of propety of all kinds, and the numerous sacrafises for the payment of debts, the obsolite means of subsistence are still possessed. It is not the case in the city. The merchants and the banks have but small real capital, and commerce ceasing their credit no longer buoys them up. There have been many failures, and the banks three in number no longer pay their[4] notes; nothing but a mutual sense of danger, and a dread of the possible extent of the mischief prevented their total failure. Bank notes have therefore lost their former currency[5] and many are unwilling to take them unless at a considerable discount. Persons who have thousands in notes can with difficulty purchace previsions in market. New Orleans has undergone a surprising depopulation within the last eighteen months.

I contemplate passing through Virginia this coming Autumn or the Spring following, and hope to have it my power to [pay]⁶ my respects in person at Monticello.

I am, Sir, with great respect

Your most obed<sup>t</sup> Hmble Servant.        H: M: BRACKENRIDGE

RC (DLC); addressed: "Thomas Jefferson, Esq<sup>r</sup> late President of the United States Monticello, Virginia"; franked; postmarked Baton Rouge, 19 June; endorsed by TJ as received 8 July 1814 and so recorded in SJL.

Three years later Brackenridge did publish a SECOND EDITION of his *Views of Louisiana; containing Geographical, Statistical and Historical Notices of that*

*Vast and Important Portion of America* (Baltimore, 1817), with a dedication to José Corrêa da Serra.

¹ Manuscript: "a ready a sale."
² Omitted word editorially supplied.
³ Manuscript: "nothithstanding."
⁴ Brackenridge here canceled "bills in [sp?]."
⁵ Manuscript: "curreny."
⁶ Omitted word editorially supplied.

# From Thomas Cooper

DEAR SIR                                        May 31. 1814 Carlisle

I say nothing about the affairs of Europe, for they are so clouded that no reasonable conjecture can be afforded by present facts. I am most willing to believe that the progress of knowledge cannot be stopt, and the dark ages renewed, even should the Bourbons again ascend the throne, but there is nothing to be expressed but hope and good wishes. Yet from the beginning of history, it appears that excepting the short period of the blood thirsty, restless and unprincipled republics of Greece, the world has been governed hitherto by royal Dynasties, which must inevitably degenerate in a few successions into Ideocy, like those of Britain, France Spain, Portugal, Prussia, Sweden of the present day. I begin to fear that as it was in the beginning, it is now and ever will be world without end. All knowledge and all virtue consists in discovering and counteracting the natural tendencies and propensities of the System whereof we form a part.

I have been reading very carefully, with great interest and instruction the work of Cabanis. It ranks in my estimation (considering the respective periods at which they were published) on a par with Hartley. Cabanis has boldly drawn the unavoidable conclusion, which Hartley was obliged to compromise about, and talk nonsense to the multitude; but which is unavoidable to every man who considers metaphysical questions in a physiological point of view; and who studies fact instead of logomachy. I should greatly like to translate

Cabanis, but I fear the public would not bear it. Too much light is apt to blind us. Then again who w$^d$ read it, except some few young Physicians, who w$^d$ lose all their practice if they were known to approve of it; for readers who w$^d$ not expend the time necessary to study and digest such a work, would be the most likely to seize hold of obnoxious passages.

some thirty years ago I published a first volume of tracts, which went nearly the whole length of Cabanis; but if I sh$^d$ republish them with what I have since written, I must expunge much of what I sacrificed to popular prejudice.

Oliver Evans has written me a long letter of abusive complaint for not speaking <u>decidedly</u> in his favour in the Emporium. I thought I said what I did say, as impartially as possible. But I have now copied from the Dictionaire des Arts et des sciences, from Belidor, from Prony, and from Townsend's travels into Spain, a selection of Elevators, Norias &c so similar to his own, that he who runs may read. I c$^d$ not find the edition of Desaguliers which contained the Noria you allude to, but I found one very like it in Belidor. His patent is an imposture; but as I do not like to go to the expence of getting my drawings engraved for the benefit of the Millars, they must remain as they are, & he must go on and levy his tax on a class of men who deserve to pay, because they will not be at the expence of an united effort to get rid of the burthen. The application of the Baltimore Millars to Congress was nugatory: the matter now rests with the Courts of Law; and you know as I know, how very ignorant those gentry are out of their own vocation. Adieu. I remain with sentiments of sincere respect Dear Sir

Your friend

THOMAS COOPER

RC (DLC); endorsed by TJ as received 16 June 1814 but recorded in SJL as received ten days later.

The phrase AS IT WAS IN THE BEGINNING, IT IS NOW AND EVER WILL BE WORLD WITHOUT END is drawn from a common Christian doxology. The WORK OF CABANIS was *Rapports du Physique et du Moral de l'Homme*, 2 vols. (Paris, 1802; Sowerby, no. 1246). That of David HARTLEY was *Observations on Man, his Frame, his Duty, and his Expectations*, 2 vols. (London, 1749). The quote TOO MUCH LIGHT IS APT TO BLIND US comes from Blaise Pascal, *Thoughts on Religion, and other curious Subjects*, 4th ed. (London, 1749; Sowerby, no. 1516), 211.

Cooper published a single VOLUME entitled *Tracts Ethical, Theological and Political* (Warrington, Eng., 1789). He discussed Oliver Evans's patent claims in the EMPORIUM 2 (1814): 445–55. NORIAS are chain-pumps. HE WHO RUNS MAY READ is in the Bible, Habakkuk 2.2. In January 1814 Congress rejected the petition of a group of BALTIMORE millers protesting Evans's patent (Bathe and Bathe, *Oliver Evans*, 205–6, 324).

# Account with William Steptoe

| 1813 | | Thos Jefferson Esqr to Will: Steptoe | Dr |
|---|---|---|---|
| Jany | 17th To | Visit to negroe woman Aggy | £0: 8:0 |
| | " | Blistering Plaister & Prescriptn Verbl | 7:6 |
| Feby | 2d " | Visit to Do Cantharides 3/ Ven. Sectn & | |
| | | Prescrpt | 18:0 |
| | 6th " | Visit to Ditto—Ven. Sect 2/6—Box Pills¹ | 13:6 |
| | 7th " | Visit in the night & attendance | 1: 1:0 |
| | 10th " | Visit—Cantharides 3/—Elixr Paregoric—1/— | 12:0 |
| | 15th " | Visit—16th Do Pills—4/ | 1: 0:0 |
| | 18th " | Do in the night 15/—Tinct. Cast. Russia | 16:6 |
| | 22d " | Do to Do 8/— 25th Do & Prescript. Verb | 1: 0:6 |
| March | 5th " | Do—to Do 8/— ℥ 1 Spt Nit. dulc. 2/6 | 10:6 |
| | " | Gum Arabic & Prescript. Verb | 6:3 |
| | 8th " | Visit in the rain at night | 18:0 |
| Augt | 18th " | Visit to Maria at Mr Darnels | 8 |
| | " | Antihemorrhagic powder to Do 6/— | |
| | | Pills laxativ 3/ | 9: |
| Sept. | 24th " | Making incision in Ambrose's leg & | |
| | | extracting bone | 13:6 |
| | 27th " | Enlarging wound to Do Dressing & Prescript. | 15 |
| | 30th " | Visit to Maria 8/ Prescript. Verb—4/6 | 12:6 |
| Oct. | 2nd " | Cutting off negroe boys finger | 10:6 |
| | 5th " | Examining & dressing Do | 9 |
| | 22nd " | Visit & extracting bone out of Ambrose's leg | 12:0 |
| | 27th " | Visit to Sally & extracting Tumor | |
| | | on her Arm | 1: 10:0 |
| Novr | 1st " | Visit to Do Dressing wound & Directions | 18:6 |
| | | | £15: 9:9 |
| 1814² | | To amount of my bill this year | 5: 1:3 |
| | | | £20: 11:0 |
| Cr | | By order on Mr Clay £3:8:4. By shop acct—£5:7:10 | 9: 16:2 |
| | | By—8 bushells of wheat | 2: 8:0 |
| | | By Cash £1:10:0 (see the other bill) | 1: 10:0 |

[*on verso:*]

£20:11: 0

13:14: 2

£ 6:16:10  Due W S. June 1st 1814—

MS (ViU: TJP-ER); in Steptoe's hand; addressed "Tho<sup>s</sup> Jefferson Esq<sup>r</sup>"; with additional notation in Steptoe's hand: "£15:9:9"; endorsed by TJ: "Steptoe D<sup>r</sup> W<sup>m</sup>."

William Steptoe (1785–ca. 1863), physician, was a son of TJ's longtime friend James Steptoe. After defending his thesis on "Animal sympathy," he received a medical degree from the University of Pennsylvania in 1807. Returning to his native Bedford County, Steptoe provided medical services at TJ's plantations in that area and occasionally dined with TJ at Poplar Forest. He lived between Poplar Forest and the town of New London, where he maintained a shop and office. In 1817 Steptoe helped organize a local Bible society. By 1830 he owned about twenty-six slaves (James Steptoe family Bible record, photocopy at ViLJML; Philadel-phia *Aurora General Advertiser*, 15 Feb. 1805; Philadelphia *Medical Museum* 4 [1808]: lviii–lix; Will J. Maxwell, comp., *General Alumni Catalogue of the University of Pennsylvania* [1917], 568; *MB*, 2:1314; TJ's Instructions for Poplar Forest Management, Dec. 1811; *Lynchburg Press*, 4 Aug. 1814; TJ to Steptoe, 13 Sept. 1815, 8 Dec. 1820; Steptoe to TJ, 24 July 1819; Richmond *Christian Monitor* 2 [1817]: 319–20; DNA: RG 29, CS, Bedford Co., 1830; Bedford Co. Will Book, 19:250–1; *Daily Lynchburg Virginian*, 16 Jan. 1863).

℥ 1 SP<sup>T</sup> NIT. DULC.: one fluid ounce sweet spirit of nitre.

[1] Steptoe here canceled "antihyst<sup>c</sup>" (antihysteric pills were prescribed to combat hysteria [*OED*]).

[2] Manuscript from this point written in a different ink.

# From John F. Watson

SIR,                                     Philad<sup>a</sup> 2<sup>nd</sup> June 1814.

I acknowledge myself much obliged by your polite attention to the letter, I had the honour to send you respect<sup>g</sup> the Edinburgh & Quarterly Rev<sup>ws</sup>. The Edinburgh, has indeed a decided preference, even among those who are its political opponents. This is sufficiently manifested, by my Sub<sup>on</sup> List. Lawyers & Federalists are the principal Sub<sup>ers</sup>. As a profound mataphisical work it is certainly unequalled. I could however, point to several very able articles in the Quarterly Reviews.

In consequence of your letter I have sent on to N York & have now rec<sup>d</sup> for you the 29, 31 & 37<sup>th</sup>[1] N<sup>os</sup> which you needed to complete your sets. These, with the early Vol<sup>s</sup> (to wit: the 1, 2 & 3<sup>d</sup>) you may expect to be delivered in packages to <u>your address</u>, to your Agents Mesrs Fitzwhylson & Potter at Richmond<sup>x</sup>—The subsequent Vol<sup>s</sup> to 14.[3] inclusive will be sent on to you in intervals of 2 M<sup>os</sup> until the whole is completed. It occurs to me however to suggest, whether it might not be more acceptable to you to receive the future Vol<sup>s</sup> by mail? It would much facilitate their receipt with you. I perceive for instance, that you have not yet rec<sup>d</sup> the 43<sup>d</sup> N<sup>o</sup> altho' the 44<sup>th</sup> is now in press & will be

x in 2 weeks hence[2]

out in 8 or 10 days—I speak however exclusively in relation to the early Vol<sup>s</sup> as I should not wish to supply <u>future</u> N<sup>os</sup>, for this would be an interference with Mesrs Fitzwhylson & P—You could however (I should suppose) receive them from N York by having them charged there to their Account—

As respects the early Vol<sup>s</sup> & deficient N<sup>os</sup> which you request of me, a remittance ℔ mail once in a year will be satisfactory to me. Any fraction of a dollar which may occur, will be freely given in, by me— for instance: 11D<sup>r</sup> only is enough for the present bill.

I make free to annex the titles of a few books, which are scarce & which might possibly interest you—

I am Sir most respectfully Yrs          JOHN F WATSON

List of Books for Sale by J F Watson Philad<sup>a</sup>

2<sup>nd</sup> Voyage dans l'interieur de l'Afrique, par le cap de
Bonne Espérance dans les années 83, 84 et 85 par F La
Vaillant Paris Ed<sup>n</sup> 3 Vol<sup>s</sup> with many plates—sheep gilt.          8.00
Lettres d'un voyageur Anglois—sur la France, la suisee et
l'allemagne—traduit de l'anglois de M Moore—3 Vol<sup>s</sup>          8.00
C.S. Sonninis travels in upper & lower Egypt, with
many plates—Lond<sup>n</sup> 4<sup>to</sup> calf gilt          12 —
Boothroyds history of the Ancient borough & renowned
sieges of the ancient Castle of Pontefract with much
curious biography of Contemporaries—calf gilt with plates          6.00
Secret history of the Court & reign of Charles II by a
member of his Privy Council—2 Vol<sup>s</sup> calf gilt 8<sup>vo</sup>          5 25
Nobles memoirs of the House of Cromwell & family
history with much collateral matter—in 2 Vol<sup>s</sup> &
many plates          sheep gilt 8<sup>vo</sup>          5.00
Rouseau's original correspondence with Latour &
Du Peyrou in 2 Vol 8<sup>vo</sup>          4.00
Gesners Works—Lond<sup>n</sup> in 3 Vol<sup>s</sup> many elegant plates          7.50
D'Israeli's Literary miscellanies & dissertation on anecdotes          2.25
Remarks on Selkirks highlands of Scotland <u>and a view of</u>
<u>the causes & consequences of Emigration</u> clf glt          2.50
Beaumonts travels through the Lepontine Alps from
Lyons to Turin with 27 superb Views—hot prest
<u>Folio</u> calf gilt folio size          22 —

RC (DLC); with verso of address cover containing postscript and a brief account consisting of two entries for purchases by TJ, one for $7.50 dated 23 May 1814: "the 1, 2 & 3<sup>d</sup> Vol<sup>s</sup> of the Edinb<sup>g</sup> Reviews on sub<sup>on</sup> continuation, sent forward this day in a package to his address, to care of mesrs Fitzwhylson & P.—sent via Sam<sup>l</sup>

Pleasants"; and another for $3.75 dated 2 June 1814: "for the 29, 31 & 37 N<u>os</u> of the Edinburgh Reviews, sent this day in the above manner"; and giving an overall total of $11.25; addressed: "Thomas Jefferson Esq<sup>re</sup> Monticello Virg<sup>a</sup>"; franked; postmarked Philadelphia, 2 June; endorsed by TJ as received 26 June 1814 and so recorded in SJL.

[1] Check marks, most likely by TJ, are placed above this and the preceding two numbers.
[2] Note written perpendicularly in margin of first page.
[3] Reworked from "15."

# From Luis de Onís

MONSIEUR                Philadelphie ce 3. Juin 1814.

Je suis trés charmé Monsieur d'aprendre par la lettre du 28. Avril, dont vous m'avez honnoré, que la Constitution de la Monarchie Espagnole, que je me suis pris la liberté de vous offrir, a été de votre aprovation. L'aprovation d'une personne si distinguée par son talent que par ses connoissances profondes dans le droit publique, et sur tout par la part qu'il a eu dans la redaction de la Constitution si admirée des Etats Unis, ne saurait qu'être trés flateuse à tous egards à la Nation Espagnole, et à moi en particulier: recevez Monsieur je vous prie mes remerciments de la peine que vous vous étes pris de la parcourrir, et de me communiquer vos observations lumineuses sur les points sur les quels vous apreendez que nous difererrons; mais permettez moi aussi, que j'essaye de vous transmettre mes reflexions au sujet des deux points, que vous m'avez cité dans votre lettre: Peut-être je serai assez heureux de dissiper les doutes que vous avez, et de vous mêttre d'accord avec les representants Espagnols, qui ont consacrés ses interessants travaux pour faire le bonheur de la Nation à la vue de l'Ennemy, et au milieu même des grenades et bombes dont la ville de Cadix etoit foudroyée.

Un des points que vous remarquez c'est l'intolerance d'autre Réligion que la Catholique: le peu de securité que l'inquissition ne soit retablie tribunal qui juge exclusivement des opinions, et qui est autorisé de punir ceux qui se separent des dogmes Catholiques.

Pour aprecier Monsieur la sagesse des Representants du Peuple dans le Cortes, et l'energie dont ils se sont revetus pour rediger cet article, il faut vous representer, que le Clergé d'Espagne, lors de notre glorieuse insurrection etoit le corps le plus puissant de l'Etat: que le Peuple etoit rempli des prejugés religieux contre les quels on ne pouvait pas heurter de front; sans s'exposser à tomber plus que jamais dans les tenebres du fanatisme: que les Representants ont tout pesé, ont tout consideré; et que sa sagesse et prevoyance a sçu tirer partie de toutes ces circonstances pour amener le peuple, non seulement a abolir l'inquisition, source de tous les maux qui ont afligé la Nation depuis tant de siecles, mais à declarer qu'elle etoit incompatible avec la Constitution, et avec la liberté de la Monarchie; Quelle garantie plus forte peut-on avoir Monsieur contre le retablissement de l'Inquisition que la declaration dont je viens de faire mention, et l'etablissement de la liberté de la presse, comme point constitution-nelle? On devroit croire qu'il n'etoit pas possible d'en faire davantage. Cependant les representants Espagnols sont allès plus loin: Ils ont etablis comme basse constitutionelle l'education et instruction publique, boulevard impenetrable au fanatisme, et le seul rempart contre le despotisme et la tirannie. Vous m'avouerez j'espere Monsieur que c'est precissement dans la redaction de cet article que les representants du Peuple Espagnol se sont excedé à eux mêmes: Ils desiroient detruire l'hidre du fanatisme, assurer la tranquillité des consciences à tous les Individus qui se fixeroient sur le sol Espagnol, et empecher qu'ils fussent inquietés pour ses opinions religieuses: La redaction de l'article $2^{de}$ titre $2^{de}$ de la constitution, et l'abolition de l'Inquisition garantissent l'un et l'autre. Il est vrai qu'il n'est pas per-mis aucune autre culte publique que le catholique, mais il n'est pas defendu à aucune personne de quelque religion que ce soit de s'etablir dans les états Espagnols, d'avoir ses opinions à lui, de don-ner son culte privé à ses Dieux, et de leur faire ses prieres. La Con-stitution et l'abolition de l'Inquisition lui donne toute la garantie necessaire à cet egard. Je vais plus loin Monsieur. Je pense que l'ar-ticle, decretant qu'aprés huit ans la constitution sera revissée et amendée, si on trouveroit qu'il etoit necessaire, est une porte que les peres de la Patrie ont voulu laisser ouverte, pour faire inserer à l'ex-piration de ce terme la liberté absolue des Cultes, qui fait la base du bonheur dont aujourd'huy jouit votre Republique. Je me flâte Mon-sieur que l'explication que je me suis pris la liberté de donner sur cet article à l'homme le plus marquant de l'Amerique, sera suffissante pour dissiper les craintes que son Coeur bienfaissant avoit conçu sur l'imperfection de l'article en question, et je me flâte d'après cela que nous serons d'accord sur ce point, et même que nous reconnoitrons que c'est precissement le point qui fait le plus d'honneur aux repre-sentants de la Nation Espagnole.

Quant au second point dont vous me faites l'honneur de me parler, c'est à dire, sur ce que vous craignez que notre representation na-tionale soit un peu aristocratique, attendu que les elections doivent passer par trois differents scrutins ou ballotages, et que les derniers Electeurs sont autorissés à nommer pour representants des Individus, qui peut-être ne se seront pas trouvés dans la liste des Electeurs, je vous rappellerais Monsieur ce que vous savez mieux que moi, que c'est un axiome incontrovertible en droit publique, que la liberté est d'autant plus assurée, que les elections sont plus epurées, et les ballotages se multiplient. Il n'y a point de doute que l'election tumultueuse est plus sujette à se resentir de l'esprit de partie, à être seduite par l'influence des riches, et qu'il est plus dificile de gagner ou d'influer trois diferentes chambres qui doivent faire les elections, que de gagner ou d'acquerir de l'influence dans une seule. Dailleurs en Espagne la noblesse titrée est peu nombreuse, trés considerable la noblesse proprement ditte, et la Constitution n'en connoit aucune pour la representation nationale, en sorte que le pretre, le grande d'Espagne, le Gentilhomme, et le roturier sont tous des Citoyens egaux devant la loi, et ils n'ont aucune preéminence quelqu'onque pour etre elus deputés aux Cortes. c'est ainsi que nous avons vu qu'il y en a eu depuis l'établissement de notre liberté des Deputés de toutes les Clases dans les Cortes, et que toujours a été la plus nombreuse celle du Peuple, mais du peuple qu'il a quelque moyen de subsister afin de les mettre à couvert de la seduction, et de s'assurer que dans toutes les deliberations de cet auguste Congrés, tous les Deputés ont un interet reel à apuyer ce qu'il est utile à la generalité des habitants, puisqu'ils y trouvent en cela leur propre avantage. Vous conviendrez j'espere avec moi Monsieur qu'une election de cette nature loin d'etre aristocratique, a toutes les provabillités d'etre plus populaire, qu'on l'a adopté avec une parfaite connoissance des defauts des elections tumultuaires, et avec l'idée d'empecher que des gens ignorants, immorales, ou qui n'ont rien à perdre puissent s'introduire dans les deliberations sacrées qui doivent faire le bonheur de la Nation. Je me flâte Monsieur que nous serons d'accord encore sur ce point, si vous arretez votre consideration sur la solidité de tout ce que je viens de vous exposer.

Il ne me reste donc que de vous dire mon opinion sur celle que vous avez enoncé, de ce qu'il seroit avantageux à l'Espagne d'abandonner toutes ses Colonies, de leur donner la liberté, et de les rendre independants. Je suis parfaitement d'accord avec vous sur ce point: L'Espagne et tous les Individus qui compossent cette grande Nation, la plus marquante dans l'histoire par son courage, sa generosité, loyauté, et par ses sentiments philantropiques, connoit fort bien que les Provinces d'Amerique ne peuvent rien ajouter à sa puissance: elle a été avant la découverte de l'Amerique, elle est, et elle sera toujours une puissance de prémier ordre, digne de l'admiration de tous les êtres sensibles: Les tresors du Mexique et du Perou si comboités par les Puissances étrangeres, ne servent qu'à afeblir l'Espagne, et à diminuer sa population et sa force: une preuve bien claire du peu que l'Espagne a besoin des Ameriques, nous l'avons dans le projet presenté dernierement aux Cortes, pour eteindre completement sa dette en dix ans, sans compter avec un seul liard de l'Amerique, et tout en diminuant considerablement les contributions qui existoient du tems de Charles 4. L'Espagne connoit et sait aprecier la solidité de ces verités, et elle n'hesiteroit pas a abandonner les Ameriques et à leur accorder son independence, si elle pourroit compter de trouver la même bonne foi, qu'elle mêt dans ses transactions parmi les puissances du globe, et si elle ne craignoit pas qu'en les abandonnant elle ne les laisserait en proie aux dissentions, guerres civiles, meurtres, assassinats, et tous les horreurs auxquels l'ambition des puissances etrangéres ne laisseroit de les amener, soit pour les asservir, soit pour empecher qu'elles prosperent. vous ne pouvez pas nier Monsieur que le plan de la reduction a été employé avec succés dans diferentes de ses provinces par les puissances étrangeres, pendant la glorieuse insurrection de l'Espagne, dans le tems meme que cette Puissance etoit avec elles dans la plus parfaite paix, et qu'elle faissois des glorieux efforts pour rafermir sa liberté, et pour la donner à toute l'Europe. Vous n'ignorez pas Monsieur que du sein de votre Republique (sans doute sans l'aveu, et contre les ordres du Gouvernement) on a fourni des armes, des vivres, des soldats, des officiers pour allumer la guerre civile dans plusieures des possessions Espagnoles, et les masacres de Tejas, des Caracas, des Florides, du Mexique, et de Buenes Ayres sont encore fameuts, pour que l'Espagne sache, que l'humanité exige, qu'elle donne toute la protection qu'ils meritent aux descendants de ses ancetres, trop jeunes encore, et qui ont trop peu d'experience pour ce gouverner par eux memes. La constitution formée par la Republique de Caracas, et toute sa conduite depuis sa revolution est une demonstration frapante, que ces Provinces abandonnées à elles mêmes ne sauroient se gouverner; qu'elles ont besoin des conseils et de la direction de la Mére Patrie, et que ceux qui leurs conseillent l'independence, ne vissent qu'à causer sa ruine; tout comme celui qui conseilleroit à un enfant de cinq ans de se soustraire de la domination paternelle, et qu'il se gouverna par lui même. Mon opinion donc, (et je differe en ceci de l'opinion de M$^r$ de Foronda mon predecesseur) est d'après tous ces fondements que l'Espagne ne doit pour le present abandonner ses provinces de l'Amerique, malgré qu'elles ne lui soient pas d'aucune avantage reelle; qu'elle doit les defendre au risque de son existence, comme un Pere defende ses enfants contre tous ceux qui veulent leur faire du mal; qu'elle doit les amener graduellement à ce but, en les faissant, comme elle l'a fait dejà par la Constitution partie integrante de la Monarchie, egales en droits et prerrogatives, en leur accordant enfin le droit de dicter ses loix et de se gouverner par ses propres representants, ce qui acomplit tout ce qu'elles pourroient obtenir si elles se separoient de la Mere patrie.

J'espere Monsieur que vous m'excusserez la franchise avec la quelle j'ai osé vous donner mon opinion: Je parle à un Philosophe renommé par sa philantropie, et son talent superieure; je cherche à m'illustrer, et je vous serois extremement redevable, si vous pouvez mes donner des idées, comme homme publique et comme Philosophe, qui puissent rectifier mon opinion: Celle ci est en deux mots, que je pense comme vous, en ce que les Ameriques ne sont pas necessaires à l'Espagne pour sa gloire et sa prosperité, mais qu'il est de la gloire et de l'humanité de l'Espagne, vu qu'elle ne peut pas compter sur la bonne foie des Nations etrangeres, et qu'elle prevoit qu'elles feront tout son possible pour rendre malheureuses les provinces de l'Amerique de les proteger à toute outrance, comme un bon Pere protege et defende un enfant seduit par des mauvais Conseils, qui a une conduite irreguliere.

Madame de Onis est extremement sensible aux politesses de Madame Rendorph votre fille: elle me charge de lui temoigner toute sa reconnoissance, ainsi que son regret de n'avoir pas eu l'avantage de faire sa connoissance personnelle: elle espere qu'elle ne tardera pas à avoir ce plaisir, et en attendant elle me prie de l'assurer de son respect. J'oserai vous prier aussi d'offrir les miens à Madame de Hackley, et d'étre bien persuadé des voeux que je fais pour votre prosperité.

Agréez Monsieur les assurances de la plus haute consideration avec laquelle j'ai l'honneur d'être

Monsieur votre trés humble et trés obéiss^t Serv^r

LE CHEVALIER DE ONIS

EDITORS' TRANSLATION

SIR                                        Philadelphia 3. June 1814.

I am delighted, Sir, to learn from the letter with which you honored me on 28 April that the constitution of the Spanish monarchy, which I took the liberty of presenting to you, met with your approval. The approbation of a person as distinguished as you are for your talent, your deep knowledge of public law, and most of all for the part you took in writing the much admired Constitution of the United States, can only be flattering from every point of view to the Spanish nation and to me in particular. Please accept, Sir, my thanks for the trouble you took in reading it and communicating to me your enlightened observations on the areas in which you think we will differ, but allow me also to try to convey my reflections on the two points you raised in your letter. Perhaps I will be so fortunate as to dispel any doubts you may have and persuade you to agree with the Spanish representatives, who were hoping through their interesting labor to make the nation happy in full view of the enemy and even while grenades and bombs were striking the city of Cádiz.

One issue you raise is the intolerance for religions other than Catholicism: the lack of security that the Inquisition, a tribunal that judges opinions exclusively and is authorized to punish those who reject Catholic dogma, will not be reestablished.

In order to appreciate, Sir, the wisdom of the representatives of the people in the Cortes and the energy needed for them to write this article, I must explain to you that during our glorious insurrection the Spanish clergy was the most powerful body in the state, that the people were full of religious prejudices that one could not confront head-on without exposing oneself to the risk of falling more than ever into the darkness of fanaticism, that the representatives considered and weighed everything, and that in their wisdom and foresight they knew how to take advantage of all of these circumstances in order to lead the people not only to abolish the Inquisition, the source of all the evils that have afflicted the nation for so many centuries, but to declare that it was incompatible with the constitution and the liberty of the monarchy. What stronger guarantee can one have, Sir, against the reestablishment of the Inquisition than the declaration I just mentioned and the establishment of the freedom of the press as a constitutional right? One would think that it was impossible to do more than this. However, the Spanish representatives went even further. They established public education, the impenetrable bulwark against fanaticism and the only rampart against despotism and tyranny, on a constitutional basis. I hope, Sir, that you will admit that it is precisely in the composition of this article that the representatives of the Spanish people have surpassed themselves. They wanted to destroy the hydra of fanaticism, insure tranquility of conscience to all persons who settle on Spanish territory, and prevent them from being persecuted for their religious opinions. The drafting of article 2 of the second section of the constitution and the abolition of the Inquisition guarantee these things. While it is true that no religion other than Catholicism is allowed, people of other religions are not forbidden from settling in the Spanish states, from having their own opinions, or from worshiping and praying privately to their own gods. The constitution and the abolition of the Inquisition provide all the necessary guarantees on this issue. I will go even further, Sir. I believe that the article stipulating that the constitution will be revised and amended after eight years, if it is found necessary to do so, is a door that the nation's fathers wanted to leave open in order to insert at the end of this term absolute religious freedom, which is the foundation of the happiness enjoyed by your republic today. I flatter myself, Sir, that as the most remarkable man in America, you will find my explanation of this article sufficient to dissipate the fears that your kind heart may have had about the imperfection of the article in question, and this leads me to hope that we will agree on this point and even recognize that it is precisely this which most honors the representatives of the Spanish nation.

As to your second point, which is your fear that our national representation is a little aristocratic, remember that the elections must go through three different polls or ballots and that the final electors are authorized to name as representatives individuals who would perhaps not have been placed on the electors' list. I will remind you, Sir, of something you know better than I, that the following is an uncontested axiom of public law: the more refined and numerous the elections, the more secure freedom is. Tumultuous elections are no doubt more likely to be influenced by party mentality and be seduced by the influence of the rich. It is more difficult to win over or influence three different electoral bodies, than to win over or acquire influence over only one. In any case, in Spain titled noblemen are not numerous, although the nobility as a whole is properly speaking very considerable, and the constitution does not recognize nobility with regard to national representation. Therefore the priest, the Spanish elite, the gentleman, and the common people are all equal citizens in the eyes of the law, and they enjoy no advantage of any kind in the election of representatives to the Cortes. Thus we have seen that since the establishment of our liberty, representatives of every class have served in the Cortes. The people have always been the most heavily represented, but only the sort of people who are self-supporting, so as to avoid their being bought off and to insure that in all the deliberations of this august congress the deputies have a real interest in supporting that which is advantageous to themselves and thus also useful to the bulk of the inhabitants. I hope, Sir, you will agree with me that an election of this nature, far from being aristocratic, has every chance of being more representative of the people, and that it was adopted with a perfect knowledge of the flawed nature of tumultuous elections and concerned with keeping away ignorant, immoral people, who have nothing to lose, and preventing them from insinuating themselves into the sacred deliberations necessary to insure the nation's happiness. I flatter myself, Sir, that we will also be in agreement on this point, if you stop to consider the solidity of the arguments I have just presented to you.

My only remaining task is to respond to your opinion that Spain could advantageously abandon all of its colonies, give them their freedom, and make them independent. I agree with you completely. Spain and all the individuals that compose this great nation, the most noted in history for its courage, generosity, loyalty, and philanthropic sentiments, know quite well that the American provinces can add nothing to its power. Spain was a power of the first order before the discovery of America, it still is, and it always will be, worthy of the admiration of all thinking people. The treasures of Mexico and Peru, which are so coveted by foreign powers, only serve to weaken Spain and diminish its population and strength. Spain gave a very clear proof that it has little need for America in the plan recently presented to the Cortes, in which it is proposed to extinguish its debt in ten years without using a single cent from America and while diminishing considerably the sums levied under Charles IV. Spain knows and appreciates the importance of these truths and would not hesitate to abandon the Americas and grant them their independence if it could rely on other global powers to manifest the same good faith it shows in its transactions with them, and if it did not fear that by abandoning its colonies, it would expose them to discord, civil wars, murders, assassinations, and all the horrors that the ambition of foreign powers will bring them, either by enslaving them or by preventing them from prospering. You cannot deny, Sir, that the scheme of subjugation has been used successfully by foreign powers in various provinces during the blessed Spanish insurrection and at the very same time that this power was in a state of the most perfect peace with them and was making glorious efforts to strengthen its liberty and extend it to all of Europe. You are not ignorant of the fact that from the bosom of your own republic (probably without consent and against government orders) arms, food, soldiers, and officers were provided to start civil wars in several Spanish possessions. The massacres of Texas, Caracas, the Floridas, Mexico, and Buenos Aires are still infamous. Spain therefore recognizes its humanitarian obligation to give the descendants of its ancestors all the protection they deserve, because they are still too young and inexperienced to govern themselves. The constitution created by the Caracas Republic and its behavior since its revolution gives striking proof that these provinces, if left to themselves, would not know how to govern themselves, that they need the advice and leadership of the mother country, and that those who advise independence only aim to bring about their ruin, as much as if someone advised a five-year-old child to escape paternal domination and govern himself. From these basic facts I therefore conclude (and in this I differ from Mr. Foronda, my predecessor), that for the moment Spain must not abandon its American provinces, even though they are of no real advantage to it, that it must defend them even at the risk of its own existence, just as a father defends his children against all those who want to harm them, that it must gradually bring them to maturity by making them equal in responsibilities and privileges, as it has already done in making the constitution an integral part of the monarchy. Eventually granting them the right to make their own laws and govern themselves through their own representatives, the colonies will achieve everything they could obtain if they separated from the mother country.

I hope, Sir, that you will excuse the frankness with which I have dared to give you my opinion; I speak to a philosopher renowned for his philanthropy and superior talent; I am trying to enlighten myself, and I would be extremely obliged if, as a public man and philosopher, you would help me to rectify my opinion. In brief, while I agree with you that Spain does not need the Americas for its glory and prosperity, its glory and humanity do demand that, since Spain cannot count on the good faith of foreign nations and predicts that they will do everything in their power to make the American provinces miserable, it do its utmost to protect them, like a good father protects and defends a poorly advised child, who is behaving badly.

Madame de Onís is extremely thankful for the kindnesses of your daughter Mrs. Randolph. She asks me to send her word of her utmost gratitude as well as her regret at not having had the good fortune of yet making her acquaintance. She hopes to have this pleasure in the near future, and in the meantime, she asks me to send her respectful regards. I will also dare to ask you to offer mine to Mrs. Hackley and to accept all my wishes for your prosperity.

Please accept, Sir, the assurances of the highest regards with which I have the honor to be,

Sir, your very humble and very obedient servant

LE CHEVALIER DE ONIS

RC (DLC); at foot of text: "M^r Jefferson"; endorsed by TJ as received 16 June but recorded in SJL as received ten days later. Translation by Dr. Genevieve Moene.

The REPRESENTANTS ESPAGNOLS composed their 1812 constitution in Cádiz, to which they had been driven by French forces during the Peninsular War (Michael Broers, *Europe Under Napoleon, 1799–1815* [1996], 208–15). The REPUBLIQUE DE CARACAS declared its independence from Spain in July 1811 and drafted a constitution in December of that same year, but it fell to Spanish forces in 1812 (John Lynch, *The Spanish American Revolutions, 1808–1826* [1973], 195–8).

# From John Wilson

SIR,                                        Washington City June 3^d 1814

Please to accept the enclosed, you were so good to examine the M.S., you will peruse it, I hope, with more satisfaction now it is in print. I thank you for having said the reformation would be desirable if it could prevail, because, I think, on reviewing the subject in a fairer form, you will be convinced, that admitting the custom is to change ey into ies or y preceded by a consonant, yet you will more cordially unite with me, as you would to reform an unreasonable law or custom of any kind. You know, sir, it is only by exercising our reason that prejudice can be dispelled & reformation effected.

Yours very respectfully                                   J^no WILSON

RC (CSmH: JF-BA); at foot of text: "Th. Jefferson, Esq^r"; endorsed by TJ as received 26 June 1814 and so recorded in SJL. Enclosure: Wilson, *A Volume for all Libraries . . . Being a System of Philological Entertainments, Comprising Altogether an Extensive Ground Work for Immense Improvements in the English Language* (Washington, 1814; Sowerby, no. 4888).

# From William Barton

SIR,                                        Lanc^r (Penn^a) June 6^th 1814.

In consequence of your polite and liberal attention to my "Memoirs" of the Life of the late D^r Rittenhouse, I take the liberty of inclosing, herewith, the Prospectus of a pretty arduous Work in which I am now engaged. I shall be much gratified, if it should meet Your approbation; and it shall be my endeavour to render it worthy of the

Patronage of the American Public. — The publication of a work some-what similar to the one proposed by me, has been recently announced by a bookseller in Philad[a] a M[r] Delaplaine, formerly of New York. But the plan on[1] which he means to conduct his, is such, as, I believe, will not interfere with mine. M[r] Delaplaine's undertaking (for his work is anonymous, as to its author or compiler,) seems to be intended to contain <u>Sketches</u> of the Lives of eminent persons, — drawn up for the purpose of accompanying engraved portraits of the subjects of them; — in the manner, I presume, of <u>Birch's Lives</u>, which are short biographical notices of sundry distinguished characters, designed to illustrate <u>Houbraken's Heads</u> of those persons. I hope to render mine a more extensive and a more scientific work. Besides, by making mine a much <u>cheaper</u> book, I flatter myself it will be more useful; as it will, thereby, be accessible to the generality of readers. —

I have been prompted to this undertaking, by the persuasion of several gentlemen of abilities & literary taste; and some of them have given me assurances of assistance & support. My brother, the Doctor, appears much pleased with my having engaged in it. His extensive & valuable Library will be at my service, and I shall derive much interesting information from himself. I trust that many other gentlemen will favour me with occasional communications, suitable for my purpose; and should you, Sir, be pleased to contribute any thing in this way, from your ample magazines of literature & science, the highest obligation will be thus conferred, and it shall be most thankfully acknowledged. —

I have the Honour to be, With the highest Respect, Sir, Your most obed[t] h[ble] serv[t]                                        W. BARTON

RC (DLC); at foot of text: "The Honourable Th. Jefferson, Esq."; endorsed by TJ as received 26 June 1814 and so recorded in SJL. Enclosure: *Select American Biography: or, An Account of the Lives of Persons, Connected By Nativity, or Otherwise, with the History of North America . . . constituting Memorials of Many Eminent Men, whose Characters are Worthy of being Perpetuated in the Annals of America* (Lancaster, 1814), amplifying the claim that biography is one of the most useful and interesting branches of history; asserting that many American statesmen, magistrates, soldiers, clergy, moralists, philosophers, men of letters, lawyers, physicians, artists, mechanics, explorers, agricultural improvers, and merchants have earned renown; proposing to publish a biographical work focused on the lives of these worthies, including those already documented and others "of whom no public record has yet appeared"; soliciting pertinent "facts, literary notices or anecdotes, letters, or memoirs of other kinds" from men of science and information; advising that the projected three volumes will contain more than six-hundred pages apiece, each issued in three numbers, with a new number to be released every four months until the work is completed, and with the possibility of extension into a new series should the first three volumes be well received; and stating that the terms of subscription are $4.50 per volume, and that "no greater number of copies will be printed, than shall be subscribed for."

Thomas BIRCH's biographical work was *The Heads of Illustrious Persons of* *Great Britain, Engraven By Mr. Houbraken, and Mr. Vertue. With Their Lives and Characters*, 2 vols. (London, 1743–51).

¹ Manuscript: "on on."

# To Martha Jefferson Randolph

MY DEAR MARTHA                                     Poplar Forest June 6. 14.

I have for some time been sensible I should be detained here longer than¹ I had expected, but could not till now judge how long. Chisolm will finish his work in about 10. days, and it is very essential that I should see the walls covered with their plates, that they may be in a state of preservation. this will keep me 3. or 4. days longer, so that I expect to be here still about a fortnight longer. there have not been more than 2. or 3. days without rain since I came here, and the last night the most tremendous storm of rain, wind & lightening I have ever witnessed. for about an hour the heavens were in an unceasing blaze of light, during which you might at any moment have seen to thread a needle. they had been deluged with rain before I came; and the continuance of it threatens injury to our wheat, which is indifferent at best. I have not seen a pea since I left Albemarle, and have no vegetable but spinach and scrubby lettuce. Francis and Wayles Baker are with me. my journey was performed without an accident. the horses & postilions performed well. James will be an excellent driver, and Israel will do better with more strength and practice. you will always be perfectly safe with their driving. if Wormly & Ned should get through the ha! ha! and cleaning all the grounds within the upper roundabout, they should next widen the Carlton road, digging it level and extending it upwards from the corner of the graveyard up, as the path runs into the upper Roundabout, so as to make the approach to the house from that quarter on the North side instead of the South. present me affectionately to all the family, and be assured of my warmest love                                     TH: JEFFERSON

RC (NNPM); at foot of text: "Mrs M. Randolph"; endorsed by Martha Jefferson Randolph. PoC (MHi); endorsed by TJ.

A ha-ha (HA! HA!) is a sunken fence in a garden or park that does not interfere with the view from within and is invisible until closely approached (*OED*). In September 1812 TJ recorded construction of the CARLTON "path on the high mountain, thro' the woods & exceedingly steep. Wormley & Ned did about 50. yds a day, 4 f. wide. which is 25. yds apiece" (Betts, *Farm Book,* 1st section, 70). Carlton was the farm adjoining Monticello where TJ's

granddaughter Ann C. Bankhead and her
husband Charles L. Bankhead lived (*MB*,
2:1269–70n).

[1] Manuscript: "that."

# From Robert Mills

My dear Sir                                    Richmond June 7th 1814
    As I believe it will prove gratifying to you to be made acquainted
with the progress of the Fine arts in our country and with the state of
the institution which has the honor of calling you its president, I beg
leave to enclose for your examination, a Catalogue of the paintings &c
now exhibiting in Philadelphia—As I left that City immediately after
the opening of the Exhibition I had no opportunity of examining[1] the
particular merits of the peices, so as to point out to your attention any,
peculiarly interesting—it seem'd the opinion of such as were col-
leagued with me in the arrangement of [the] exhibition, that much
more <u>merit</u> was [...]ed to the pictures &c this year exhibited than at
any previous exhibition—It is a pleasing consideration to reflect upon
the progress of talents in our country—and it is flattering to observe
how rapidly we are gaining that purety of taste, which if combined
with knowledge will advance us to the honor of becoming rivals of
European artists.—
In the hope of your enjoying your usual health and in prospect of the
pleasure of hearing from you at Ph[a] I salute you dear Sir with affectionate respect                                    Rob[t] Mills

RC (DLC); torn at seal; endorsed by
TJ as received 26 June 1814 and so
recorded in SJL. Enclosure: *Fourth Annual Exhibition of the Columbian Society*

*of Artists and the Pennsylvania Academy.*
*May 1814* (Philadelphia, 1814).

[1] Manuscript: "examing."

# To Patrick Gibson

Dear Sir                                    Poplar Forest June 9. 14.
    I have been here a fortnight, and am likely to continue a fortnight
longer, and therefore not in a situation to hear any thing about the
price or prospect for flour. but I see nothing which promises such a
change for the better as makes it advisable to keep what we have on
hand, on the contrary a competition with the new crop will soon
lessen our chance of selling the old. I would therefore wish you to sell

the whole of mine in the course of this month, unless you should see strong reasons to the contrary; and the rather as I shall of necessity have to make draughts on that fund.

Mess<sup>rs</sup> Mitchells, of the Blackwater mills have presented me an account of 83.29 D for the transportation of 150. Bar flour paid by them, and of half a dollar a barrel extra, on 141. Bar. flour of the crop of 1812. and 126. Bar. of the crop of 1813. on the presumption that all passed as Superfine. being uninformed myself what proportion of each of those crops passed as **SF**. I must ask your information, as the mill marks will have enabled you to distinguish the Albemarle from the Bedford flour, a distinction which I must pray you always to note, as the conditions of sale render an after reckoning necessary for the **SF**. be so good as to direct your answer to me at Monticello, after the reciept of which I shall draw on you in favor of the mr Mitchells for their balance whatever it may be. Yours with friendship & respect.

TH: JEFFERSON

PoC (NHi: Thomas Jefferson Papers); at foot of text: "M<sup>r</sup> Gibson"; endorsed by TJ.

# From William Short

DEAR SIR                                           Philadelphia June 9—14

M<sup>r</sup> Rives has presented to me the letter by which you were so kind as to make us acquainted—He has been here now some days & I have been very much pleased with him. His being your friend would have insured him at any rate my attention—but I really return you my thanks for having procured me so agreeable an acquaintance. I have taken pleasure in introducing M<sup>r</sup> Rives to such of my friends here as I thought would be most agreeable to him—It is however an unfavorable season for a stranger to visit Philadelphia, as many of the inhabitants are absent, in the country—I have procured M<sup>r</sup> Rives the means of seeing the loom you wished him to examine, which was more than I had done myself—but it always so happens that what we can see at any time, we are apt to postpone at all times—This at least was always the case with me to a great degree—but now more than ever—for I percieve a general <u>insouciance</u> growing on me—I endeavour to persuade myself that this mode of acting, with me is the result of sound philosophy—but it is probable that I flatter myself, & that in fact I am indebted for it, to disposition & circumstances—I see nothing within my attainment worth taking any trouble about, & content myself therefore with avoiding evil rather than pursuing any positive good.—In this way I have gone on so far without even having a house to live in myself or recieve a friend—merely to avoid the trouble of housekeeping. I purchased a house here on my return to America for the purpose—but on closer examination gave up the plan—& I believe I have done better, in my present disposition, of mind, to content myself with the life of a boarding house—my friends urge me much to change my "free & unhoused condition"—but though I have no apprehension from the example of Othello, yet I do not feel that exclusive attraction to one particular object, which with me would be a sine qua non to a contract of this kind—I have no doubt however that I should have done wiser to have adopted this measure in earlier life—Probably the having been once on the very border of this state & finding the effect which time produced on that disposition would make me more cautious as to the entering into it without the possibility of return. I do not the less however believe that in this country more than any other the married state is a desirable one—Our friend Correa says that it is a country where there is beaucoup de bonheur & peu de plaisir—& this seems to me a good definition of the state of mariage, perfectly conformable to the maxim of la Rochefoucauld.

Apropos of Correa; He has left us for his western excursion via Pittsburgh—he will go through Ohio, Kentucky &c. & enter Virginia by the Southwestern frontier & pay you a visit en passant. This is a long & painful journey for a man at his time of life, & what is worse, with a disorder that disables from riding on horseback—It is being roué indeed to go on wheels over such a distance of such roads. The prospect of Monticello at the end of his route, he says, will support him in it.

I do not know whether the manner in which the Allies have conducted themselves at Paris will reconcile Correa to their having passed the Rhine. He wished the end of Bonaparte as much as any body—but he was not reconciled to the counter revolution by the Allies—In his plan they were not to have crossed the Rhine, & when he left us he had not yet pardoned them for it—It is difficult however to concieve that this great & momentous business could have been effected in an easier & better manner than was done after the allies entered Paris—It is the best thing that could have happened for France & all Europe.—Indeed for many years back, from the time that Bonaparte proved that his only object was to erect a permanent despotism on the anarchy he had destroyed, I was convinced that the restoration of the Bourbons was the most desirable event for France—I used every argument in my power to inspire the great & the good Moreau with this sentiment—He came to this country very differently impressed with respect to the Bourbons, notwithstanding he was banished under the pretext of being their partisan—His mind whilst here had undergone a total change on this subject—Our friend Correa refuses to subscribe to this opinion however, & he was certainly intimate with Moreau—but I think his own feelings have led him into error on this point—For Moreau who was made up of honor & candor was incapable of duplicity—I saw the progress of this revolution in his sentiments—it was slow & perceptible, & proceeded from his acquaintance & intimacy with a fellow exile & companion in misfortune, more than from any other circumstance—This was de Neuville (who brought you a letter from M$^{de}$ d'houdetot) one of the best, most noble, honest & disinterested hearts that I ever met with— He was the active & intrepid agent of Louis 18—& exiled to this Country after running ten thousand risks—here his acquaintance with Moreau begun—they had a common enemy—they were both strangers in a foreign land—both good Frenchmen—an unreserved intimacy soon grew between them—Moreau knew that de Neuville was incapable of deception or dissimulation—de Neuville was personally acquainted with the character & disposition of L. 18—& thus by degrees removed the prejudices with which Moreau had grown up in his public life against the whole of that race—that done, the great difficulty was overcome—In the last conversation which I had with Moreau, I found that no apprehension remained in his mind but that which arose from the influence of the priests, which he feared would exist under the Bourbons—but on the whole he had no doubt that their restoration by the will of the French people would be the most desirable event that could take place for France. I sincerely hope & believe that the consequences will be such as Moreau contemplated.—And now that the general interests are provided for, all my anxiety is to hear of my private friends & learn what has been their fate in this new, & I hope, last revolution—Poor lafayette & his Merinos were on the very route by which the armies passed & I much fear the Cossacks will have been wolves in his fold—The country seat of M$^{de}$ de la Rochefoucauld was also on the route; the allied armies were three times in advancing & retiring at La Ferté sous Jouarre—Her house is the most visible object in the neighborhood, & will without doubt have attracted their notice. She herself was not there at that season, & she had no Merinos—but the furniture was valuable.—

In the midst of my rejoicing for this return of peace to France I cannot help feeling a drawback on account of our unfortunate situation—I have little hope of peace for ourselves—It could now only come from our enemy copying the magnamity & disinterested policy of the virtuous Alexander—I should as soon expect, with Horace, to see the wild deer suspended in the branches of the lofty forest—We have, I fear, nothing but disaster before us, a long & disgraceful war followed by an humiliating & disgraceful peace—As we have as yet sent only five ministers in pursuit of this peace, & as our rulers seem to have confidence in numbers, I think when Congress meet they would do well to send the whole committee of foreign relations—If they could have disposed of this committee at the time of declaring war with the virtuous patriotic & brave Peter B. Porter at their head we might perhaps have preserved peace, & been able now with all Europe to sit down to a table of concord instead of the war feast which they called us to—

If I were not ashamed I would again trouble you as to the boundary business—But you have had so much trouble already—& I am so sure you will have it settled if you can that I will not importune you at this moment—Monroe must have so many other important subjects in his head that this must be to him invisible—I will for the present bid you adieu, then, with renewed assurances of the invariable sentiments with which I am,

dear sir, Your friend & servant                                 W SHORT

RC (MHi); endorsed by TJ as received 26 June 1814 and so recorded in SJL.

By FREE & UNHOUSED CONDITION Short means his own unmarried state, referencing William Shakespeare, *Othello*, act 1, scene 2. BEAUCOUP DE BONHEUR & PEU DE PLAISIR: "much contentment and little pleasure." The MAXIM may be the observation that "Il y a de bons Mariages, mais il n'y en a point de délicieux" ("There are good marriages, but

no delightful ones"), from *Reflexions et Maximes Morales de M. le Duc de La Rochefoucault*, new ed. [Amsterdam, 1772], 368. For the LETTER FROM M$^{DE}$ D'HOUDETOT, see TJ to James Madison, 31 Dec. 1811. The allusion to WILD DEER SUSPENDED IN THE BRANCHES OF THE LOFTY FOREST paraphrases a passage from Horace, *Odes*, 1.2.9–12 (*Horace: Odes and Epodes*, trans. Niall Rudd, Loeb Classical Library [2004], 24).

# To William Thornton

DEAR DOCTOR                    Poplar Forest near Lynchburg. June 9. 14.

Your kindness has emboldened me, whenever I want information of what relates to the arts, to apply to you, and especially when for an object deposited in your office. the inclosed description of Janes's improvement of the loom has excited my attention. that the force of the stroke of the batton should also move the shuttle and treadles is certainly practicable by proper machinery; but we who live in the country where we have only common workmen have other questions to ask, and I address them as usual to your friendship. does the stroke of the batton in Janes's[1] loom competently work the shuttle and the treadles? is it of such simplicity as that it can be made by our country workmen, and kept in order by the common ingenuity in our families? can the machinery be affixed to a common loom, or does it require a new loom of special construction? if applicable to a common loom, can the apparatus be made in Washington, & within the volume which the stages would undertake to bring? what the price of the apparatus separately, or of loom & apparatus together[2] if both must be had together, and what the volume of both together? this letter is written at a place 2. or 3. days distant from Monticello, to which I pay 3. or 4. long visits a year, but I will ask your answer to be addressed as usual to Monticello. After trying several spinning machines, I have settled down with the antient Jenny, because it's simplicity is such that we can make and repair it ourselves. mr Randolph & myself have four of these at work in our family, 3 of them of 24. spindles each and one of 40. but there is an improvement of D[r] Allison's enabling them to spin from the roll, without previous roving, which, when I have leisure I shall try to make, having obtained the Doctor's permission. he has given me some directions additional to those in Cooper's Emporium, which render the executing of the machine quite easy.

at the return of peace I think Gr. Britain will find that the country demand for her coarse goods is for ever lost to her: at least if I may judge from the houshold establishments of this state.

with respectful compliments to the ladies of your family accept the assurance of my great esteem & respect          TH: JEFFERSON

RC (DLC: Thornton Papers); addressed: "Doct[r] William Thornton Washington, Columbia"; franked; postmarked. PoC (DLC); endorsed by TJ.

The INCLOSED DESCRIPTION OF JANES'S IMPROVEMENT OF THE LOOM was probably a brief article published in the Washington *Daily National Intelligencer* on 11 May 1814 under the heading "The Useful Arts," which notes that an improved loom has been on display "in an apartment of the capital" for two or three weeks; describes the invention as smaller than a common loom but constructed so that when a person uses one arm to operate the batten or slay "in the common manner, motion is given to a spring shuttle, works the treadles, and, at proper times, lets out the warp and winds up the cloth, keeping the whole well tightened and in proper order"; asserts that the shuttle can be thrown two-hundred times per minute, that an average day's work yields thirty yards of common cloth, and that "two inches of ordinary size have been woven in one minute"; indicates that the writer has witnessed its operations himself; names the inventor as Walter Janes, of Connecticut; and concludes that the loom is suitable for the manufacture of any fabric, "from the finest silk to the coarsest bagging; and from its cheapness and superiority for family use will prove a benefit to the community, as we hope of wealth to the inventor and proprietors."

¹ TJ here canceled "mach."
² Word interlined.

# From Dudley Leavitt

SIR.                                Centre-Harbor, N.H. June 10ᵗʰ 1814.

I have taken the liberty to send You the enclosed Table, which, after You have inspected to Your satisfaction, I would thank You to lay before the Am. Philos. Society, of which I am informed You, Sir, are, or have been the President.—May You long live to diffuse that light, both Philosophical and Political, which has, under Providence, been the means of leading the zealous and enterprising Sons of America, from a State of ignorance and oppression to the Temple of Freedom and Science.—If You, Sir, and the Society, may think the Table in any degree useful, (being a genuine American Production,) You are at liberty to publish it among Your Memoirs.—This Table, of which I am the Inventor, will give the true time of the Moon's Quarters with as much or <u>more</u> accuracy than Ferguson's will the New and Full Moon, which is frequently of great use to find, and sufficiently accurate for <u>common</u> Almanacks.—The reason which induced me to invent the Table was, having ever made Astronomy my favorite study, and amused myself in making various calculations, I found that <u>Ferguson's</u> Tables, altho' they gave the <u>Change</u> and <u>Full</u> tolerably correct, would not give the Quarters by 5 h. + or − !—After employing considerable time in investigating the cause, I discovered it, as hereafter explained. I should esteem it a great favor to receive a line from your Excellency on any Scientific Subject, if such condescension might not be repugnant to your more important Concerns,

With Sentiments of the profoundest respect
I am, Sir, Your most obedient friend and humble Servant,
DUDLEY LEAVITT.

RC (PPAmP: Thomas Jefferson Papers); on sheet folded to form four pages, with enclosure on pp. 2–3 and address on p. 4; addressed: "Hon. Th. Jefferson, Esqʳ Monticello, Va.—Late President of U.S. of America"; franked; postmarked Center Harbor, 12 June; endorsed by TJ as received 26 June 1814 and so recorded in SJL. Enclosed in TJ to Robert Patterson, 29 June 1814.

Dudley Leavitt (1772–1851), educator, author, and maker of almanacs, was a native of New Hampshire. Beginning with *The New England Calendar: or, Almanack, for the year of our Lord 1797*

(Concord, N.H., 1796), he issued farmer's almanacs under a variety of titles, settling eventually on *Leavitt's Farmer's Almanack and Miscellaneous Year Book*. The annual publication became remarkably popular and continued to be issued well after Leavitt's death, aided by calculations he had prepared in advance. He settled his family by 1806 on a farm in Meredith, New Hampshire, where he kept a school, served occasionally as a local official, compiled the *New Hampshire Register* annually from 1811 to 1817, and authored or edited widely circulated textbooks on arithmetic, astronomy, geography, grammar, literature, music,

pedagogy, and science (*DAB*; Bruce D. Heald, *New Hampshire Learnin' Days: Dudley Leavitt, "Master" [1772–1851]* [1987]: 25–53; Emily Leavitt Noyes, *Leavitt: Descendants of John, the Immigrant Through His Son, Moses* [1941], 65–9; Amherst, N.H., *Farmers' Cabinet*, 24 Sept. 1851).

James FERGUSON's work was entitled *Astronomical Tables and Precepts, For calculating the true Times of New and Full Moons, And shewing the method of projecting Eclipses, from the Creation of the World to A.D. 7800. To which is prefixed, A Short Theory of the Solar and Lunar Motions* (London, 1763).

ENCLOSURE

## Dudley Leavitt's Table for Determining the Moon's Quarters

Table.—Second Equation from the Mean to the True Time of the Moon's Quarters.—Argument— ☽'s Equated Anomaly.—

| | 0 Signs. | | 1 Sign. | | 2 Signs. | | 3 Signs. | | 4 Signs. | | 5 Signs. | | |
|---|---|---|---|---|---|---|---|---|---|---|---|---|---|
| | Add. | | | | | | | | | | | | |
| Deg. | H. | M. | H. | M. | H: | M. | H. | M. | H. | M. | H. | M. | Deg. |
| 0 | 0 | 0 | 7 | 35 | 13 | 11 | 15 | 6 | 12 | 7 | 7 | 34 | 30 |
| 1 | 0 | 18 | 7 | 50 | 13 | 17 | 15 | 2 | 11 | 56 | 7 | 20 | 29 |
| 2 | 0 | 30 | 8 | 5 | 13 | 20 | 15 | 1 | 11 | 48 | 7 | 15 | 28 |
| 3 | 0 | 48 | 8 | 15 | 13 | 26 | 15 | 0 | 11 | 40 | 7 | 5 | 27 |
| 4 | 1 | 5 | 8 | 30 | 13 | 32 | 14 | 57 | 11 | 35 | 6 | 45 | 26 |
| 5 | 1 | 23 | 8 | 45 | 13 | 40 | 14 | 53 | 11 | 25 | 6 | 28 | 25 |
| 6 | 1 | 38 | 8 | 58 | 13 | 50 | 14 | 50 | 11 | 15 | 5 | 48[1] | 24 |
| 7 | 1 | 54 | 9 | 10 | 13 | 55 | 14 | 45 | 11 | 10 | 5 | 54 | 23 |
| 8 | 2 | 9 | 9 | 20 | 14 | 2 | 14 | 40 | 11 | 0 | 5 | 36 | 22 |
| 9 | 2 | 25 | 9 | 35 | 14 | 10 | 14 | 35 | 10 | 50 | 5 | 25 | 21 |
| 10 | 2 | 40 | 9 | 45 | 14 | 13 | 14 | 30 | 10 | 45 | 5 | 4 | 20 |
| 11 | 2 | 57 | 10 | 2 | 14 | 15 | 14 | 28 | 10 | 35 | 4 | 51 | 19 |
| 12 | 3 | 7 | 10 | 12 | 14 | 20 | 14 | 24 | 10 | 25 | 4 | 32 | 18 |
| 13 | 3 | 21 | 10 | 22 | 14 | 25 | 14 | 15 | 10 | 15 | 4 | 17 | 17 |
| 14 | 3 | 36 | 10 | 33 | 14 | 30 | 14 | 10 | 10 | 10 | 3 | 53 | 16 |
| 15 | 3 | 54 | 10 | 45 | 14 | 35 | 14 | 5 | 9 | 55 | 3 | 43 | 15 |
| 16 | 4 | 8 | 11 | 0 | 14 | 38 | 13 | 58 | 9 | 52 | 3 | 31 | 14 |
| 17 | 4 | 24 | 11 | 10 | 14 | 40 | 13 | 55 | 9 | 45 | 3 | 20 | 13 |
| 18 | 4 | 35 | 11 | 21 | 14 | 42 | 13 | 45 | 9 | 35 | 3 | 5 | 12 |
| 19 | 4 | 52 | 11 | 31 | 14 | 44 | 13 | 35 | 9 | 25 | 2 | 55 | 11 |
| 20 | 5 | 10 | 11 | 40 | 14 | 46 | 13 | 30 | 9 | 20 | 2 | 45 | 10 |

| 21 | 5 | 24 | 11 | 50 | 14 | 48 | 13 | 22 | 9 | 9 | 2 | 25 | 9 |
|---|---|---|---|---|---|---|---|---|---|---|---|---|---|
| 22 | 5 | 35[2] | 12 | 0 | 14 | 52 | 13 | 17 | 8 | 54 | 2 | 15 | 8 |
| 23 | 6 | 50 | 12 | 10 | 14 | 54 | 13 | 10 | 8 | 44 | 1 | 54 | 7 |
| 24 | 6 | 9 | 12 | 20 | 14 | 55 | 13 | 0 | 8 | 34 | 1 | 43 | 6 |
| 25 | 6 | 12[3] | 12 | 25 | 14 | 56 | 12 | 55 | 8 | 24 | 1 | 24 | 5 |
| 26 | 6 | 40 | 12 | 32 | 14 | 57 | 12 | 43 | 8 | 14 | 1 | 15 | 4 |
| 27 | 6 | 50 | 12 | 42 | 14 | 58 | 12 | 30 | 8 | 4 | 1 | 0 | 3 |
| 28 | 7 | 10 | 12 | 56[4] | 15 | 2 | 12 | 25 | 7 | 54 | 0 | 45 | 2 |
| 29 | 7 | 20 | 12 | 56[5] | 15 | 4 | 12 | 15 | 7 | 44 | 0 | 31 | 1 |
| 30 | 7 | 35 | 13 | 11 | 15 | 6 | 12 | 7 | 7 | 34 | 0 | 0 | 0 |
| Deg. | 11 Signs. | | 10 Signs. | | 9 Signs. | | 8 Signs. | | 7 Signs. | | 6 Signs. | | Deg. |
| Subtract.[6] | | | | | | | | | | | | | |

Explanation of the Table.—

Principle.—The reason why Ferguson's Tables will not give the true approximate time of the ☽'s Quarters, is, because the Excentricity of the lunar orbit at the Syzygies, is always greater than at the Quadratures.— This hint will be sufficient to explain the Principle, and for further improving the Table.—

Practice.—In finding the ☽'s Quarters, proceed as in finding the Change and Full, according to Ferguson, only the 2$^d$ Equation must be taken from this Table instead of Ferguson's 2$^d$ Equation,—

N.B.—This method gives the mean or Equal time, Per Clock.

| | |
|---|---|
| MS (PPAmP: Thomas Jefferson Papers); undated; written on pp. 2–3 of sheet containing RC of covering letter on p. 1 and address leaf on p. 4. Enclosed in TJ to Robert Patterson, 29 June 1814. | [1] Thus in manuscript.<br>[2] Thus in manuscript.<br>[3] Thus in manuscript.<br>[4] Thus in manuscript.<br>[5] Thus in manuscript.<br>[6] Page ends here. |

# To Elizabeth Trist

DEAR MADAM                    Poplar Forest June 10. 14.

My visits to this place, considered as a halfway-house, rekindle the desire of bringing myself to your recollection, and afford me at the same time more leisure to do so. I left all your friends at Monticello well, and the happier that mr Randolph had resigned his military commission. at Farmington not so much health: mrs Divers generally indisposed; and mr Divers has been all the winter, and still is kept at home by complicated complaints. we are all too more or less laboring under political fever, and variously affected by the ups and downs of Europe. our warmest zealots see nothing bad but in England, nor salutary but in Bonaparte. others see both good & evil, whichever tyranny prevails. if the recent news be true that Bonaparte has the two emperors and two kings in his possession, and consequently the whole continent of Europe at his nod, this may humble England to give us peace & justice. but that peace will be ground enough with Bonaparte for excluding us from the continent of Europe: besides, once master of the Continent, the conquest of England is inevitable, and with English fleets and French armies, our distance becomes an equivocal security.          if, on the other hand, the allies dethrone Bonaparte, we may have commerce with them in their bottoms; but England, in the insolence of triumph and hatred to us, full-armed, and without other employment or support for her pyratical power, may think us beneath her peace, and view us rather as desirable subjects for the exercise of her military faculties, and for the indulgence of her ambition, her avarice & her vindictive spirit. whichever scale then preponderates gives us both good and evil. if that of Bonaparte, we have peace with England, and exclusion from the rest of the world: if that of the allies, we have war with England, and commerce with them. which commerce however will be so far an amelioration of our present condition. such then is the present crisis, that we know not what to hope or fear; and, only standing to our helm, must abide, with folded arms, the issue of the storm. if George and his Prince regent however afflict us with these anxieties, let us enjoy the comfort and revenge of deriding and despising their individual rottenness. with this view I send, for a place on your book-shelf, from which you can take occasional doses, the famous 'Book,' written by Percival. it will confirm the moral truth that, independantly of another world, the wicked have their torment here also. turning from this ghastly subject to the sweeter consolations of friendship be assured that mine remains ever affectionately with you.          TH: JEFFERSON

RC (facsimile in NcU: Jefferson Photostats); addressed: "M<sup>rs</sup> Elizabeth Trist at mr Gilmer's near Henry Court house"; franked; endorsed by Nicholas P. Trist. PoC (MHi); endorsed by TJ.

In February 1814 Napoleon won a series of victories that slowed but did not stop the Allied advance on Paris and his own abdication in April (Chandler, *Cam-* *paigns of Napoleon*, 975–6; Connelly, *Napoleonic France*, 181, 192–3). The TWO EMPERORS AND TWO KINGS in the false rumor repeated by TJ presumably included Czar Alexander I of Russia, Emperor Francis I of Austria, and King Frederick William III of Prussia. For the FAMOUS 'BOOK' sent with this letter, see TJ to Samuel Pleasants, 11 Aug. 1813.

# To Charles Caldwell

SIR                              Poplar Forest near Lynchburg June 12. 14.
     Your letters of Apr. 25. & 30. came to me by the same mail as I was leaving Monticello on a journey to a distant place, from which this

acknolegement of them is now written. I had before known something of the Portfolio by character, but had never seen a N° of it till that you have been so kind as to send me. it is certainly a favorable specimen of the candor and abilities by which it is likely to be conducted in your hands. I shall gladly become a subscriber, with your permission, and especially if you have any agent who can recieve the annual subscription within this state, the remittance of small sums to a distant state, in a medium recievable there, being a considerable obstacle to such engagements. the objects of this publication are useful & worthy of encouragement, and no part of them more so than that of preserving the biography of our distinguished characters. there is a gentleman of this state, of the first order of talents, engaged in preparing something of this kind. but whether his particular vocations will permit him to pursue it, when it may appear, or whether during his life, I am not able to say. his views are confined to this state alone.

I recieve with due acknolegements your invitation to myself to lend a hand to this useful undertaking, and should not perhaps have declined it at a period of life when the energies of the mind might have been a safe pledge for performance. but I sensibly feel the effect of years on the active powers of the mind as well as of the body. perhaps too a surfiet of the labors of the writing table, during a long course of public employment, may have increased my repugnance to them, strengthened the desire of retirement from them, and of consigning the close of life to the rest & tranquility suitable to it's state of decay.

when too I review the characters which were of principal effect in the stand which was made, in the public councils of this state, against British usurpation, I am sensible of being little able to contribute to their biography. these were Patrick Henry, Richard Henry Lee, George Mason, Richard Bland, George Wythe, Edmund Pendleton, Peyton Randolph, John Page, Mann Page, of the dead, and others doubtless who do not now occur. nearly the whole of these, being country gentlemen, residing in different parts of the state distant from one another, & from my own residence also, I knew little of their private lives, connections or situations. among those who were their cotemporaries and now living, I see one person only who could render you worthy aid in this way. D$^r$ Walter Jones, late a member of Congress, was intimate with R. H. Lee, lived not distant from Mason, Pendleton, one of the Pages, was the particular friend of both, and was personally acquainted with all the others named. his information is extensive, he has industry, ability, leisure, and a good pen. he is well known to some of the elder physicians of Philadelphia, & should not want encouragement from myself to engage in this business, so far as my exhortations might have any effect. should he be induced to cooperate with you, you will have more than an equivalent for any services which I might at any time have been able to render: and with my wishes that he may, I pray you to accept assurances of my high esteem and respect.                                                        TH: JEFFERSON

PoC (DLC); at foot of first page: "Doct<sup>r</sup> Charles Caldwell"; endorsed by TJ.

The GENTLEMAN OF THIS STATE was probably William Wirt.

# From Patrick Gibson

SIR                                         Richmond 13<sup>th</sup> June 1814—
I have not written you since the 4<sup>th</sup> ult° when I forwarded you $150.—flour has been gradually declining and cannot without difficulty be sold at $4—I fear we have allowed the only favorable moment to escape, and regret extremely that I did not accept of the offer of 5$—60<sup>d</sup>/. of which I inform'd you in mine of the 20<sup>th</sup> April— should no change occur, so as to enable us to ship in the course of this or next month, of which at present I see very little probability, the present crop will be but little better than the last; and even $4. low as it is, will no longer be obtainable,—I shall continue to hold yours at your limit until I hear from you
With great respect I am Your ob<sup>t</sup> Serv<sup>t</sup>            PATRICK GIBSON

RC (ViU: TJP-ER); between dateline and salutation: "Thomas Jefferson Esq<sup>re</sup>"; endorsed by TJ as received 26 June 1814 and so recorded in SJL.

# To Thomas Law

DEAR SIR                         Poplar Forest near Lynchburg. June 13. 14.
The copy of your Second thoughts on Instinctive impulses with the letter accompanying it, was recieved just as I was setting out on a journey to this place, two or three days distant from Monticello. I brought it with me, and read it with great satisfaction; and with the more, as it contained exactly my own creed on the foundation of morality in man. it is really curious that, on a question so fundamental, such a variety of opinions should have prevailed among men; and those too of the most exemplary virtue and first order of understanding. it shews how necessary was the care of the Creator in making the moral prin-

ciple so much a part of our constitution as that no errors of reasoning or of speculation might lead us astray from it's observance in practice. of all the theories on this question, the most whimsical seems to have been that of Woollaston, who considers <u>truth</u> as the foundation of morality. the thief who steals your guinea does wrong only inasmuch as he acts a lie, in using your guinea as if it were his own. truth is certainly a branch of morality, and a very important one to society. but, presented as it's foundation, it is as if a tree, taken up by the roots, had it's stem reversed in the air, and one of it's branches planted in the ground.        Some have made the <u>love of god</u> the foundation of morality. this too is but a branch of our moral duties, which are generally divided into duties to god, and duties to man. if we did a good act merely from the love of god, and a belief that it is pleasing to him, whence arises the morality of the Atheist? it is idle to say as some do, that no such being exists. we have the same evidence of the fact as of most of those we act on, to wit, their own affirmations, and their reasonings in support of them. I have observed indeed generally that, while in protestant countries the defections[1] from the Platonic Christianity of the priests is to Deism, in Catholic countries they are to Atheism. Diderot, Dalembert, D'Holbach Condorcet, are known to have been among the most virtuous of men. their virtue then must have had some other foundation than the love of god.

The το καλον of others is founded in a different faculty, that of taste, which is not even a branch of morality. we have indeed an innate sense of what we call beautiful: but that is exercised chiefly on subjects addressed to the fancy, whether thro' the eye, in visible forms, as landscape, animal figure, dress, drapery, architecture, the composition of colours E$^t$c. or to the imagination directly, as imagery, style, or measure in prose or poetry, or whatever else constitutes the domain of criticism or taste, a faculty entirely distinct from the moral one.        Self-interest, or rather Self love, or <u>Egoism</u>, has been more plausibly substituted as the basis of morality. but I consider our relations with others as constituting the boundaries of morality. with ourselves we stand on the ground of identity, not of relation; which last, requiring two subjects, excludes self-love confined to a single one. to ourselves, in strict language, we can owe no duties, obligation requiring also two parties. self-love therefore is no part of morality. indeed it is exactly it's counterpart. it is the sole antagonist of virtue, leading us constantly by our propensities to self-gratification in violation of our moral duties to others. accordingly it is against this enemy that are erected the batteries of moralists and religionists, as the only obstacle to the practice of morality. take from man his selfish propensities, and he can have nothing to seduce him from the practice of virtue. or subdue those propensities by education, instruction, or restraint, and virtue remains without a competitor. Egoism, in a broader sense, has been thus presented as the source of moral action. it has been said that we feed the hungry, clothe the naked, bind up the wounds of the man beaten by thieves, pour oil and wine into them, set him on our own beast, and bring him to the inn, because we recieve ourselves pleasure from these acts. so Helvetius, one of the best men on earth, and the most ingenious advocate of this principle, after defining 'interest' to mean, not merely that which is pecuniary, but whatever may procure us pleasure or withdraw us from pain, [de l'Esprit. 2. 1.] says [ib. 2. 2.] 'the humane man is he to whom the sight of misfortune is insupportable and who, to rescue himself from this spectacle, is forced to succour the unfortunate object.' this indeed is true. but it is one step short of the ultimate question. these good acts give us pleasure: but[2] how happens it that they give us pleasure? because nature hath implanted in our breasts a love of others, a sense of duty to them, a moral instinct in short, which prompts us irresistibly to feel and to succour their distresses; and protests against the language of Helvetius [ib. 2. 5.] 'what other motive than self interest could determine a man to generous actions? it is as impossible for him to love what is good for the sake of good, as to love evil for the sake of evil.' the creator would indeed have been a bungling artist,[3] had he intended man for a social animal, without planting in him social dispositions. it is true they are not planted in every man; because there is no rule without exceptions: but it is false reasoning which converts exceptions into the general rule. some men are born without the organs of sight, or of hearing, or without hands. yet it would be wrong to say that man is born without these faculties: and sight, hearing and hands may with truth enter into the general definition of Man. the want or imperfection[4] of the moral sense in some men, like the want or imperfection of the senses of sight and hearing in others, is no proof that it is a general characteristic of the species. when it is wanting we endeavor to supply the defect by education, by appeals to reason and calculation, by presenting to the being so unhappily conformed other motives to do good, and to eschew evil; such as the love, or the hatred or rejection of those among whom he lives and whose society is necessary to his happiness, and even existence; demonstrations by sound calculation that honesty promotes interest in the long run; the rewards & penalties established by the laws; and ultimately the prospects of a future state of retribution for the evil as well as the good done while here. these are the correctives which are supplied by education, and which exercise the functions of the moralist, the preacher & legislator: and they lead into a course of correct action all those whose depravity is not too[5] profound to be eradicated. some have argued against the existence of a moral sense, by saying that if nature had given us such a sense, impelling us to virtuous actions, and warning us against those which are vicious, then nature must also have designated, by some particular ear-marks, the two sets of actions which are, in themselves, the one virtuous, and the other vicious: whereas we find in fact, that the same actions are deemed virtuous in one country, and vicious in another. the answer is that nature has constituted <u>utility</u> to man the standard & test of virtue. men living in different countries, under different circumstances, different habits, and regimens, may have different utilities. the same act therefore may be useful, and consequently virtuous, in one country, which is injurious and vicious in another differently circumstanced. I sincerely then believe with you in the general existence of a moral instinct. I think it the brightest gem with which the human character is studded; and the want of it as more degrading than the most hideous of the bodily deformities. I am happy in reviewing the roll of associates in this principle which you present in your 2ᵈ letter, some of which I had not before met with. to these might be added Lᵈ Kaims, one of the ablest of our advocates, who goes so far as to say, in his Principles of Natural religion, that a man owes no duty to which he is not urged by some impulsive feeling. this is correct if referred to the standard of general feeling in the given case, and not to the feeling of a single individual. perhaps I may misquote him, it being fifty years since I read his book.

The leisure and solitude of my situation here has led me to the indiscretion of taxing you with a long letter on a subject whereon nothing new can be offered you. I will indulge myself no further than to repeat the assurances of my continued esteem & respect.

TH: JEFFERSON

RC (ViU: TJP); brackets in original. PoC (DLC); at foot of first page: "Thomas Law esq."

The work by William Wollaston (WOOLLASTON) was *The Religion of Nature Delineated*, 7th ed. (Glasgow, 1746; Sowerby, no. 1252). THE το καλον:

"the good." The Good Samaritan aided the MAN BEATEN BY THIEVES in the Bible, Luke 10.33–4. TJ provided paraphrased translations of selections from the first volume of Claude Adrien HELVETIUS, *Œuvres Complettes de M. Hélvetius. Nouvelle Édition, corrigée & augmentée sur les Manuscrits de l'Auteur, avec sa Vie & son Portrait* (London, 1781; Sowerby, no. 1242). Law divided his book by LETTER rather than chapter. Henry Home, Lord Kames (KAIMS), wrote *Essays on the Principles of Morality and Natural Religion*, 1st ed. (Edinburgh, 1751; Sowerby, no. 1254).

[1] Reworked from "deflections."
[2] TJ here canceled "is that grati."
[3] Preceding two words canceled by an unidentified hand in RC but undeleted in PoC.
[4] Preceding two words interlined.
[5] Reworked from "so."

# From Jean Baptiste Say

MONSIEUR                                    Paris 15 Juin 1814.

J'ai eu le bonheur de recevoir il y a dix ans la lettre que vous me fites l'honneur de m'adresser le 1$^{er}$ fevrier 1804, en m'accusant reception d'un exemplaire de la premiere édition de mon Traité d'Economie politique. Les vues que cette lettre renferme Sur la population et Sur la question de Savoir Si les Etats-unis doivent desirer que les manufactures Se multiplient chez eux avant que leur agriculture Se Soit étendue davantage, ces vues, dis-je, me Semblent d'un haut interet, et dans le tems, j'en tirai parti pour mon instruction Sans avoir les moyens de vous en remercier.

Depuis ce moment un excellent commentaire français Sur l'Esprit des lois de Montesquieu, parfaitement traduit dans votre pays, et imprimé en amérique, ayant parlé avantageusement de mon Ouvrage, m'a donné une nouvelle preuve que je pouvais esperer d'obtenir quelque estime dans votre hemisphère.

Je me Suis envelopé dix ans dans l'obscurité pour laisser passer les tristes momens d'une tirannie Sauvage qui a fait retrograder la France de plusieurs Siecles; mais comme ma fortune n'etait pas suffisante pour faire Subsister Sans un travail lucratif, une famille assez nombreuse, j'ai etabli à 50 lieues de Paris une manufacture pour filer du coton, manufacture qui a prosperé jusqu'au moment où des droits excessifs imposés par le gouvernement et un appauvrissement général dans lequel est tombé la nation et qui Supprimait presque toute consommation, m'ont forcé de quitter mon entreprise.

Les momens de loisir que me laissait une vie occupée, mais au fond d'une campagne, m'ont permis de recommencer, de refaire entièrement mon Traité d'Economie politique, et les derniers événemens politiques ont enfin fait tomber les obstacles qui S'opposaient à l'impression de cet ouvrage. Il vient de paraître et je l'ai mis Sous la Sauvegarde de l'empereur de Russie pour qu'on n'en arretât pas la circulation; car la liberté de la presse n'est que dans nos proclamations publiques. Dans la réalité elle n'existe pas, et il n'est permis d'e-crire que pour prouver que le gouvernement a raison, quoiqu'il fasse.

Telle est l'histoire Succincte du livre dont je prends la liberté de vous adresser un exemplaire comme un hommage que je rends à vos vertus et à vos lumieres. Veuillez le recevoir, Monsieur, avec votre indulgence accoutumée. Si vous prenez la peine de le parcourir, je me flatte que vous trouverez qu'une meilleure methode, m'a permis d'asseoir l'Economie politique Sur des fondemens tellement Sûrs, qu'elle est desormais entrée dans le domaine des connaissances positives. Je ne pense pas qu'elle puisse offrir maintenant une Seule difficulté insoluble; et les conséquences qu'on en peut tirer pour le perfectionnement de l'art Social et pour le bonheur des hommes, me paraissent immenses.

Mon fils, jeune homme de Vingt ans, envoyé aux Etats unis, comme Subrecargue, par une respectable maison de commerce de Nantes, a dû dans le courant du mois d'avril dernier faire le voyage par terre de Charlestown à New-York. M$^r$ Warden, votre consul général en france, a eu la bonté de lui remettre une lettre d'introduction pour vous, Monsieur et s'il n'a pas été contrarié dans Ses projets, il aura été vous rendre Son hommage. Il est possible que le cours d'affaires où ce fils est engagé, l'entraine à former un etablissement de Commerce aux Etats-unis; et je vous avouerai que je Songe Serieusement à m'y fixer moi-même avec ma femme et quatre autres enfans plus jeunes. La Seule consideration qui m'arreterait Serait l'incertitude de pouvoir vivre en consacrant ma fortune qui n'est pas fort grande, à l'achat d'une terre que je ferais valoir.

Dans cette position, éprouvant en outre le besoin de respirer l'air d'un pays libre, et n'ayant pas l'esperance que la France Soit bien administrée, je regarderais comme une faveur Signalée de votre part, que vous voulussiez bien me donner, ou me faire donner, une reponse aux questions Suivantes, pour éclairer ma conduite.

Pourrait-on trouver, dans les cantons tels que ceux qui environnent Charlotteville en Virginie, une terre defrichée, ou du moins en partie, où il y eût deja des batimens Soit pour le logement Soit pour l'exploitation?

Combien faudrait-il qu'elle contînt d'âcres pour que l'acquereur qui la ferait valoir, pût y vivre avec Sa famille composée de Sept à huit maîtres?

Dans le canton designé et avec des batimens Suffisans pour pouvoir Se loger et faire valoir la terre dès en arrivant, combien coûterait l'acre de terre?

Ces questions resolues me permettraient d'asseoir un jugement et de prendre un parti.

Je designe le Canton de Charlotteville parce qu'il n'est ni assez près des ports pour que les terres y Soient fort chères, ni assez reculé pour qu'on y Soit exposé aux premieres rigueurs d'un etablissement nouveau. Sa latitude etant mitoyenne, n'expose ni aux froids cuisans des Etats du nord, ni aux chaleurs etouffantes de ceux du Sud. Je n'ai aucun autre motif de preference, ni aucune objection contre tout autre canton où Se rencontreraient les mêmes avantages. Toutes choses d'ailleurs égales, les cantons les plus habités, me conviendraient le mieux; car ce ne Sont pas les hommes que je fuis, mais les hommes de la vieille Europe qui Sont corrompus et vains. Au Surplus à l'age de 47 ans où je Suis parvenu, je Sais bien qu'en cherchant des hommes, je ne dois pas esperer de trouver des anges.

C'est Sur ce projet que j'ose reclamer, Monsieur, de votre bienveuillan[ce,] de votre philantropie, des conseils qui puissent me guider; et Si votre Santé ou vos occupations ne vous permettaient pas de me donner les renseignemens que je demande, j'ose esperer que vous Seriez assez bon, pour me les faire adresser par quelqu'un qui eût votre confiance. Les plus detaillés Seront les plus acceptables; mais quels qu'ils Soient, et quels qu'en Soient les resultats, croyez, Monsieur, que j'en aurai une tres vive gratitude.

Permettez-moi, Monsieur, de vous offrir en finissant l'hommage de la plus haute Vénération et de mon respectueux devouement.

J. B. SAY
Rue des fossés Saint-Jacques N° 13
a Paris

EDITORS' TRANSLATION

SIR                                                                   Paris 15 June 1814.

Ten years ago I was happy to receive the letter you did me the honor of sending on 1 February 1804, which advised me that you had gotten a copy of the first edition of my *Traité d'Economie Politique*. The opinions contained in that letter about population and the question of whether it is desirable to multiply factories in the United States before agriculture is extended more widely, these opinions, I say, seem to me to be of the greatest interest, and at that time I took advantage of them for my instruction without having the means of thanking you for them.

Since then, an excellent French *Commentary and Review of Montesquieu's Spirit of Laws*, perfectly translated in your country and printed in America, mentioned my work in a flattering manner and gave me a new proof that I might hope to obtain some recognition in your hemisphere.

For ten years I enveloped myself in obscurity in order to allow the sad period of savage tyranny that has set France back several centuries to pass; but as my assets were insufficient to support a rather large family without paid employment, I established, fifty leagues from Paris, a cotton-spinning factory that prospered until the excessive taxes imposed by the government and the general impoverishment that befell the nation and ended almost all consumption forced me to give up my enterprise.

The moments of leisure left to me by a life that is busy, albeit in a remote, rural setting, allowed me to recommence and entirely rework my *Traité d'Economie Politique*, and the most recent political events finally eliminated the obstacles that prevented the printing of this book. It has just come out, and to keep its circulation from being stopped I have put it under the protection of the emperor of Russia, because freedom of the press exists only in our public proclamations. In reality, it is not to be found, and writing is only allowed when it proves that the government is right, whatever it may do.

Such is the succinct story of the book, a copy of which I am taking the liberty of sending as an homage to your virtues and enlightenment. Please receive it, Sir, with your usual indulgence. If you take the trouble to skim it, I flatter myself that you will find that a better method has enabled me to establish political economy on foundations so sure that from now on it has entered the realm of positive knowledge. I now think that it does not leave a single insoluble difficulty, and that immense inferences may be drawn from it for the improvement of the social arts and the happiness of mankind.

My son, a young man of twenty who has been sent to the United States as supercargo by a respectable commercial company in Nantes, had to travel by land from Charleston to New York during this past April. Mr. Warden, your consul general in France, was so kind as to give him a letter of introduction addressed to you, Sir, and if nothing has interfered with his plans, he will have paid you his respects. The affairs in which my son is engaged may call for him to create a commercial establishment in the United States, and I must admit that I am thinking seriously of settling there myself with my wife and four youngest children. The only consideration that would prevent me would be my uncertainty that I could support myself by dedicating my fortune, which is not large, to the purchase and cultivation of a tract of land.

In this position and suffering, furthermore, from the need to breathe the air of a free country, while harboring no hope that France will become well administered, I would consider it a great favor on your part if you would give me or have somebody else provide me with answers to the following questions, in order to help me decide my course of action.

Could one find, in areas such as those around Charlottesville, Virginia, a piece of cleared or at least partially cleared land, where there are buildings either for living or for the cultivation of the land?

How many acres of land must the buyer cultivate in order to support a family with seven or eight members?

In the designated region, what would be the cost per acre for a piece of land with enough buildings to live in and ready to farm upon arrival?

Answers to these questions will allow me to form an opinion and make a decision.

I mention the Charlottesville region because it is neither too close to the ports, where land is very expensive, nor so remote as to expose one to the hardship of developing a new establishment. Its latitude is intermediate and

[ 419 ]

does not expose one to either the extreme cold of the northern states or the stifling heat of the southern ones. I have no other reasons for my preference, nor any objections against any other region that would offer similar advantages. All things being equal, the most inhabited areas would suit me best, because I am running away not from men, but from the corrupt and vain men of old Europe. Furthermore, at the age of forty-seven, I know quite well that in looking for men, I must not hope to find angels.

It is about this project, Sir, that I dare request your kindness, your philanthropy, and any advice that might guide me; and if your health or occupations do not allow you to give me the requested information, I venture to hope that you would be so kind as to have somebody you trust send it to me. The more detailed it is, the better; but whatever it may be, and whatever the results may be, please believe, Sir, that I will be most grateful.

Allow me, Sir, in closing, to offer you my regards, my highest veneration and my respectful devotion.

J. B. SAY
Rue des Fossés Saint Jacques Number 13
in Paris

RC (DLC); dateline at foot of text; edge trimmed; at head of text: "Monsieur Thomas Jefferson aux Etats-Unis"; endorsed by TJ as received 9 Dec. 1814 and so recorded in SJL; further notation by TJ beneath endorsement: "ans^d Mar. 2. 15." Translation by Dr. Genevieve Moene. Enclosure: Say, Traité d'Économie Politique, 2d ed., 2 vols. (Paris, 1814; Poor, Jefferson's Library, 11 [no. 697]; TJ's copy at ViU inscribed by the author: "offert par l'auteur à Monsieur Thomas Jefferson comme un témoignage de Son attachement et de Son respect" ["presented by the author to Mr. Thomas Jefferson as a testimony of his affection and respect"]).

Jean Baptiste Say (1767–1832), French political economist, author, and lecturer, was educated in his native Lyon and through commercial apprenticeships in Paris and England. He joined republican intellectual circles by 1789, when he issued a pamphlet in Paris on the freedom of the press and was introduced to Adam Smith's work. A member of the liberal group of economists known as the Idéologues, Say was a founder, contributor, and editor of La Décade philosophique, 1794–1800. A prolific author on practical political economy and the development of commerce and industry, his best-known work, Traité d'Économie Politique, 2 vols.

(Paris, 1803; Sowerby, no. 3547), was lauded by TJ and went through five editions in Say's lifetime, but it also led to a rupture with Napoleon. Say's experience as a cotton-mill owner, 1804–12, and proprietor of a distillery deepened his economic analyses. He was granted chairs at the Conservatoire des Arts et Métiers in 1819 and at the Collège de France in 1831 (Biographie universelle; Hoefer, Nouv. biog. générale; Jean Pierre Potier and André Tiran, eds., Jean-Baptiste Say: Nouveaux Regards Sur Son Œuvre [2003], esp. 631–52, 699–714, 737–60; Evelyn L. Forget, The Social Economics of Jean-Baptiste Say: Markets and Virtue [1999]; TJ's preface to Destutt de Tracy, A Treatise on Political Economy [Georgetown, 1817 (1818)]; Gilbert Chinard, Jefferson et les Idéologues, d'après sa correspondance inédite avec Destutt de Tracy, Cabanis, J.-B. Say et Auguste Comte [1925], 13–8; TJ to Say, 2 Mar. 1815, 14 May 1817).

TJ's LETTRE of 1 Feb. 1804 (DLC) discussed the relative merits of agricultural and manufacturing pursuits for laborers. The American translation of Destutt de Tracy's EXCELLENT COMMENTAIRE FRANÇAIS, which TJ revised, praised Say as "undoubtedly the author of the best work on political economy, that has yet appeared" (Commentary and Review of Montesquieu's Spirit of Laws,

187–8). Say dedicated the enclosed second edition of his *Traité* to Alexander I, the EMPEREUR DE RUSSIE, stating that "Un livre comme celui-ci, où l'on cherche de bonne foi à découvrir les sources de la prospérité publique, ne peut être présenté qu'à un bon Prince" ("A book like this one, in which one searches in good faith to discover the sources of public prosperity, can only be presented to a good Prince") (1:viiii). The LETTRE D'INTRODUCTION from David Bailie Warden to TJ for Say's son, Horace Emile Say, was not recorded in SJL, has not been found, and was probably never received by TJ.

# From John Barnes

MY DEAR SIR—                     George Town Co^a 16^h June 1814.

That you may form a pretty Correct idea of the prospect I had in View in effecting a Sale of the 20 shares Penn^a Bank stock I inclose for y^r Perusal[1] M^r Taylors last letter recd 26^th Ult^o a few days prior to my departure for Philad^a where I arrived the 1^st Instant,

fortunately there were no Penn^a B. S. at market, I proposed to M^r Taylor to offer the 2 Shares Certificate a 140 ℔ C^t merely to feel the pulse of the buyer,[2]—if any—and though not expecting—an offer for 3 Shares (not Accept^d) a 138—was at least rising the Market from 135 & 136—2 a 3 ℔ Ct—Another most fortunate offer from an Execut^r for some Orphan Children—purchased 12 shares at same rate, but would not exceed that advance—the Remaining Six—Continued on hand without any Chance of Rising but the Contrary—the former offer for 3. was Accepted, and the remaining 3 went to two diff^r purchasers at same price—and finally closed the whole—much to my satisfaction I then opened an Acc^t with the Bank and closed it.—taken the Cash^r draft for Balance on the Cash^r for the Bank of Columbia in Order to make good my paym^ts to the Loan of $10,000 as well for the purchase of a Bill of Exchange—to Remit the good Gen^l—the mode of purchase & Conveyance most eligible—M^r Nourse has Recommended—is, for you to address the firm of Mess^s          Barings Bankers in London—who has great Concern with the Bankers at Paris—(in which 1^st & 2^d)—I can put under Cover—each of which M^r Nourse has promised to convey to them thro the Treasury Departm^t to Mess^s Barings—with whom he Corresponds so that any further Application to either the Sect^y of State, or Treasury will be Unnecessary.

I arrived late last Even^g the excessive & continual Rains—for 15 days passed has so gutted & flooded the Roads that they are almost impassable—many Carriages stuck fast, and others Broken down— but tho many difficulties[3] Occured—the Carriages which fell to my lot escaped—tho somewhat detained—instead of arriving as Usual at 3 or 4 in the afternoon I was perfectly satisfied, on my Arrival—without any material Accid$^t$ between 9 & 10—for further particulars of no immediate moment, I ask leave—to defer for the present—not being Honored with any of your favors since I left George Town—your order for the 6 M$^{os}$ dividend due 1$^{st}$ Jan$^y$—will be Acceptable—

with perfect Esteem—and most Respectful Complm$^{ts}$ to the good families—

I am Dear Sir—Your Very Obed$^t$ servant     JOHN BARNES,

RC (ViU: TJP-ER); addressed: "Thomas Jefferson Esq$^r$ Monticello—Virginia"; franked; postmarked; endorsed by TJ as received 26 June 1814 and so recorded in SJL. Enclosure not found.

The GOOD GEN$^L$: Tadeusz Kosciuszko.

[1] Manuscript: "Persual."
[2] Manuscript: "buryer."
[3] Manuscript: "difficultes."

# From William H. Crawford

DEAR SIR.                                        Paris 16$^{th}$ June 1814.

I have the honor of transmitting to you a very voluminous letter from your friend Mr. Dupont de Nemours. From the tenor of the note[1] accompanying this letter, it appears that he wishes it to be translated into English, & printed in the united States.

You have no doubt been informed, thro' the channels of the newspapers, of the great events which have occurred here, and which have entirely changed the political state of Europe. Of the causes of these events, you know as much as we do, who were on the spot. The absolute suppression of the liberty of the press, and the extreme vigilance of the police, under the late Emperor, prevented the disclosure of every circumstance which was offensive to the government. We were wholly unacquainted with the relative forces of the belligerents. We knew as little of the temper and disposition of the French nation. The state of the negociations at Chatillon—the demands which were made—the pretensions which were urged, on the one part, and the other, were wholly unknown, at the moment the Allies entered Paris.

The same extinction of the liberty of the press, and a considerable part of the vigilance of the police[2] which characterized the late reign, still continue to exist. Neither the Allies, or the present government, seem disposed to give publicity to the official correspondence, which was carried on at Chatillon.[3] The British minister had promised the

Parliament, to produce this correspondence, but the abdication of the Emperor has induced him to retract this promise. The Paris journals, and the venal writers of the day, assert, that the peace is more favorable than would have been granted to Buonaparte. France is therefore indebted to the King for this advantageous treaty. If this assertion is true, nothing is more easy than to prove it. The publication of the official papers presented at Chatillon, by the ministers of the Allies and of France, would put this question at rest. The omission, justifies the conclusion, that the peace which was offered Napoleone, was more advantageous than that which has been imposed upon Louis, the 18th. From the time that I saw Lord Castlereagh was to be sent to the continent I believed that no peace would be made with the late Emperor. To draw on the Emperor of Austria step by step, to consent to dethrone his grand son, was a task of great delicacy, and no doubt put in requisition all the art and address of the British Secretary. The obstinacy and arrogance of Napoleone strongly seconded his efforts. The man who has $10\frac{1}{2}$ Millions sterling in his pocket, cannot well fail to be very eloquent, and entirely Conclusive in his arguments. This was Lord Castlereaghs situation. Terms of peace, were no doubt offered, which the Emperor of Austria thought reasonable & just, but which his son in law, held to be very unreasonable. These terms, were from time to time modified, and the stupid old Emperor was led imperceptibly to agree, that if these terms were not accepted, that the other sovereigns might adopt such measures as they should deem expedient. Lest he should repent, and cha[nge] his mind, they kept him at a great distance from Paris, and placed Lord Castlereagh aided by Prince Metternich to watch him, and soothe him into an acquiescence in the measures which were to preclude his grand son from the first throne in the world. The Allies assert in their declaration, issued immediately after the rupture of the negociation at Chatillon, that they were ready to treat with Buonaparte up to the 15th of march. Lord Wellington in his[4] proclamation dated the 1st of February at S[t] Jean De Luz puts up the family of the Bourbons, and hoists the white flag which he declares shall precede him. There can be no doubt that Lord Wellington acted according to his instructions. There can be no doubt also, that this act of his Lordship's was kept from the knowledge of the Emperor of Austria, until the declaration of the Emperor Alexander was made, in which he states that no treaty would be made with Napoleone or any of his family. Count D'Artois on the 27th of Jan[y], issued such a proclamation as Lord Wellington's[5] at Vesoul, and the

Emperor of Austria suppressed it, & compelled the Count to leave France, which he did not re-enter until after the Allies were in possession of Paris.

At the present day, it is asserted, that the principal officers of the Emperor had conspired against him for more than twelve months before his downfal. This is incredible. It presupposes, that these officers reposed that personal confidence in each other, which can be found only among men of principle. I believe that many of his officers, in the civil, and military line, wished his downfal, and contributed to it, as far as they could, individually, without incurring the danger of detection. It is however a matter of no great importance how the change has been effected. The change itself must be eventually serviceable to the world. The reduction of France within its ancient limits will ultimately be for the interest of the United States. The time, and manner in which this reduction has been effected, cannot fail to be immediately injurious to us. The subsidies which England has advanced to the Allies, & the access of artful and designing men of that nation, to the councils of these sovereigns, have enabled them to poison their minds against the United States. The manner in which the Bourbons have been restored—the leading part which the British general has acted in that restoration, must have made some impression upon the mind of the present King. At the moment of his restoration certainly nothing like sympathy for the United States was manifested in any European cabinet. The Stipendiaries of England, if sensible to this impression, could not with any decency manifest it. I know the American government expected the good offices of the Emperor Alexander. Our ministers in the approaching negociation at Ghent entertained the same expectations. Admitting the disposition to exist, we have no right to expect any favorable result from its exertion. England has twice refused his mediation in circumstances more favorable to his views than at present. He will not therefore renew the offer unless he intends to resent the refusal. In the present state of maritime Europe, no effectual opposition can be made to the English navy. Time is necessary to restore order in the fiscal departments of all Europe. A few years will be sufficient for this. The struggle which the great continental powers have made against the gigantic power of the late Emperor, have convinced them of their capacity to accomplish any thing which they shall undertake. The struggle itself has imparted to these nations a degree of energy which never heretofore existed. The Continuance of the American war will make them feel practically, the effects of the maritime usurpations of England. When felt, the remedy will be applied. We must therefore exert our energies, and prosecute the war, until our enemy becomes rational, or until her injustice, and arrogance shall confederate against her, all the maritime states of Europe. Three years I think will effect this.

If the negociations at Ghent fail to procure peace, they can hardly fail to produce a considerable degree of unanimity at home. In this event we have nothing to apprehend. We can never negociate under more inauspicious circumstances.

You will have seen the French constitution before you receive this letter. It is a strange medly. In religion it is greatly in advance of England. The temper and disposition of the nation is very bad. Every thing is unsettled. The demands and expectations of the old, & new nobility, are entirely irreconcilable, & must give the King much trouble. The propensity which he has manifested to restore all the ostentatious pomp of the Roman Catholic religion, & to make his reign a reign of devotion, incites the ridicule of the great body of the people, and the disgust and discontent of the Protestants. If I am not entirely mistaken Europe was never more unsettled. The peace will be nothing but an armed truce. If the Allies had left the great body of Belgium annexed to France, the peace might have had some duration. As it is, the people of Belgium & of France have been equally disappointed, and are equally dissatisfied.

I am sensible that I have trespassed too long upon your patience, but when I assure you, that my error is the result of the high respect which I bear towards your person, & for the distinguished services you have rendered your country, I confidently rely upon your indulgence for my pardon. With sentiments of the highest esteem I am sir your most ob$^t$ & very humb$^l$ serv$^t$      W$^M$ H CRAWFORD

RC (DLC); torn; adjacent to signature: "Tho$^s$ Jefferson. late President of the US. A."; endorsed by TJ as received 14 Oct. 1814 and so recorded in SJL.

William Harris Crawford (1772–1834), attorney and public official, was a native of Amherst County whose family moved to South Carolina and then to Georgia by 1783. He established a law practice in 1799 in Lexington, Georgia. Crawford was elected to the Georgia state legislature in 1803 and served until he was elected to fill a vacant United States Senate seat in 1807. He was a politically independent Jeffersonian Republican, initially opposing TJ's embargo policy but later fighting its repeal. Crawford also gained recognition leading the unsuccessful effort to recharter the First Bank of the United States. His election as president pro tempore of the Senate in March 1811 obliged him to preside continuously after Vice President George Clinton died the following month. Crawford served as the United States minister plenipotentiary to France, 1813–15, as secretary of war for more than a year after his return to the United States, and as secretary of the treasury, 1816–25. Despite strong support for his own presidential prospects in 1816, he supported James Monroe in the name of party unity. Crawford was a leading hopeful to succeed Monroe as president when he experienced a severe attack of paralysis in 1823 that substantially weakened his candidacy and subsequent political career. TJ communicated sporadically with Crawford, with whom he visited in 1823, and he seems to have favored his candidacy in 1824. Refusing President John Quincy Adams's offer to keep him at the Treasury, Crawford returned to Georgia in 1825 and recovered his health enough to serve as a superior court judge until his death (*ANB*; *DAB*; Chase C. Mooney, *William H. Crawford, 1772–1834* [1974]; TJ to Crawford, 20 Mar. 1808 [DLC], 21 Sept. 1824, 15 Feb. 1825; TJ to James Madison, 13 Oct. 1814; Virginia J. Randolph [Trist] to Nicholas P. Trist, 21 Oct. 1823 [DLC: Nicholas P. Trist Papers]; Washington *Daily National Intelligencer*, 26 Sept. 1834).

Pierre Samuel Du Pont de Nemours's VOLUMINOUS LETTER to TJ was a revision of the treatise on political economy that he had sent to TJ four years earlier (Du Pont de Nemours to TJ, [ca. 28 July 1810]; TJ to Du Pont de Nemours, 28 Feb. 1815). The Congress of CHATILLON was a gathering of the Allied leaders, February–March 1814. They offered to leave Napoleon on the throne of France if he would accept the boundaries of 1792. After his refusal the Allies signed the Treaties of Chaumont, in which they agreed that they would maintain a coalition against France for twenty years and that none of them would conclude a separate peace with that nation. The EMPEROR OF AUSTRIA was Francis I. His daughter, Marie Louise von Habsburg, married Napoleon and bore Francis's GRAND SON Napoleon François Joseph Charles, to whom Napoleon gave the title of King of Rome (Connelly, *Napoleonic France*, 109, 194–5, 324–5). STIPENDIARIES: "mercenaries" (*OED*).

[1] Word interlined in place of "letter."
[2] Preceding three words interlined.
[3] Manuscript: "Chattillon."
[4] Crawford here canceled "declaration."
[5] Preceding three words interlined.

# Minutes of the Albemarle Academy Board of Trustees

At a meeting of the board of Trustees of the Albemarle Accademy at charlottesville the 17th day of June 1814.

In the absence of the Secretary, Frank Carr was nominated and appointed Secretary.

On motion made and Seconded, the scheme of a Lottery heretofore reported to the board was amended by the adoption of the following substitute.

Lottery for the establishment of an Accademy in the County of Albemarle.

Scheme.

| 1 Prize of | 3000 D. | is | $3000. |
|---|---|---|---|
| 1 Ditto of | 2000. | " | 2000 |
| 4 Ditto of | 1000. | " | 4000. |
| 4 Ditto of | 500. | " | 2000. |
| 10 Ditto of | 100. | " | 1000. |

| 50 Ditto of | 20. | " | 1000. |
| 100 Ditto of | 10 | " | 1000. |
| 1000 Ditto of | 6. | | 6000. |
| 1170 Prizes | | | $20.000 |
| 2830 Blanks | | | |
| 4000 at five Dollars | | | $20.000 |

The first drawn Ticket on the third days drawing will be entitled to[1] $1000.

The first drawn on the twentieth will be entitled to $1000.

The first drawn on the 30th will be entitled to $2000.

The last drawn ticket on the last days drawing will be entitled to $3000.

The first five Hundred blanks drawn will be entitled to Six Dollars each.

The prizes will be payable 90 days after the drawing is compleated subject to a deduction of 15 pr Cent.

Prizes not claimed within 6 months after the drawing is finished are forfeited for the use of the Accademy.

And the same committee appointed at the last meeting to carry the former Scheme into effect are authorised and required to act on that which is adopted as its substitute.

Resolved that a committee of five to wit, John Winn, James Leitch, Jno Nicholas, Frank Carr, and Alexander Garrett be appointed to view the different situations in the County of Albemarle for the purpose of Locating the Albemarle Accademy, and to enquire into the relative expense of building on the best and most economical plan, and of purchasing a situation already improved, and they report there reasons at large, in favour of the situation to which they give the preference.

Ordered that the board adjourn until the meeting in course.

Tr (ViU: TJP-VMJCC). Tr (ViU: TJP-VMJHC). Tr (ViU: TJP-VMJB). Tr (ViU: VMJLC). Tr (PPAmP: VMWCR).

[1] VMWCR Tr here adds "a prize of."

# From David Bailie Warden

SIR,                                                          Paris, 18 June, 1814.

I am induced by feelings of gratitude to send for your perusal the inclosed communication relating to my removal from office—and am, with great respect, your most obedt Sert

DAVID BAILIE WARDEN

RC (DLC); dateline at foot of text; addressed: "Thomas Jefferson Esquire monticello"; endorsed by TJ as received 14 Oct. 1814 and so recorded in SJL. Enclosures: (1) Isaac Cox Barnet to Warden, Paris, 25 Aug. 1813, stating that William H. Crawford has delivered to him a 30 July 1813 letter to Crawford from William Daines, that in response Crawford has requested "a list of the Americans detained as Prisoners of War," and expressing Barnet's hope that Daines will be "<u>liberated to serve in a privateer of the United States</u>. If he will go of preference into the french Service, he must apply to others." (2) Warden to Crawford, Paris, 6 June 1814, asserting that in May the secretary of the American legation at Paris delivered to him Crawford's undated letter stating that he had been "directed by the President to remove me from the office of Consul, and to fill the vacancy by a temporary appointment, that therefore I was removed from the Consulate, and required to deliver possession of the Seals and records of the office to Henry Jackson Esquire"; noting that he delivered the relevant official papers but stating that he has retained the seals of office out of a belief that "their delivery might be deferred without injuring the interests of my country or derogating from the respect which I owe to your Excellency"; arguing that his nomination by the president and unanimous approval by the Senate "cannot be destroyed except by a revocation emanating from the same authority"; reporting his intention to await official notification of his removal, under the impression that "a Minister is superior in dignity to a consul, but the former according to the american constitution and laws, has no Control over the functions of the latter which are quite distinct and independent"; claiming that the charges alleged against him are "grounded on circumstances susceptible of misrepresentation" and that the death of Joel Barlow, the American minister plenipotentiary to France, did not negate Warden's powers as consul; declaring that the French government has acknowledged him as "Consul général" and insisting on the propriety of this title; observing that, as the legal consignee of Commodore

John Rodgers, Warden was "solemnly bound to prevent a person from taking possession of the proceeds, who being a bankrupt, did not merit this confidence," indicating that the American merchants supported him in this action, and reporting that all documents related to the Rodgers case have been submitted to the minister of commerce at Paris and that it was on Crawford's orders that Warden wrote to that minister "requesting him to commit the whole management of the case to M. Lee, and thus prevent all interference on the part of M.M. Martin and Russell to whom I had transferred my powers. I refer to the defence of my conduct in this affair dated the 31st of August 1813"; contending that Crawford's letter of 20 Aug. 1813 was intended to censure Warden; claiming that he has not forwarded or responded to "a long letter full of abuse" addressed to Warden by William Lee; stating that his 26 May 1814 letter to Crawford concerning the exhibition of consular signs in Paris originated from a sense of duty and complaining that Crawford has authorized interference by Barnet in consular matters; alleging that Crawford's accusations are calculated to ruin him; refusing to cease his functions until "my commission be regularly withdrawn"; and informing Crawford that "By the abdication of Napoleon late Emperor of france, your powers have naturally ceased, and therefore, you can have no ministerial authority untill you receive new instructions from the United States," and certainly not the power to replace "a Consul regularly acknowledged by the new government whose signature and acts are duly legalised at the office of foreign affairs." (3) Warden to James Monroe, Paris, 10 June 1814, forwarding copies of the preceding enclosures; identifying his 26 May 1814 letter to Crawford as the proximate cause of his removal; emphasizing Crawford's refusal to prove that he has the authority to remove Warden and underscoring Crawford's questionable status following the change of government; maintaining that the first enclosure confirms Crawford's approval of Barnet's meddling; claiming that Barnet violated United States law by delivering American passports to British prisoners in France; and stating that he will retain the seals of office until he hears from Monroe, but that he will refrain from legalizing documents or executing consular acts. (4) Warden to Monroe, Paris, 12 June 1814, stating that James A. Bayard, an American peace commissioner, has informed him that he saw the instructions for Warden's removal from office that Crawford has refused to reveal; that he will accordingly "cease from Consular functions," but that he will await further orders from the United States government (Trs in DLC: TJ Papers: 199:35417, 201:35795–7, with no. 3 on verso of no. 1 and no. 4 subjoined to no. 2, in an unidentified hand, with all except no. 4 signed by Warden; Trs of nos. 2 and 4 in DLC: Madison Papers, in an unidentified hand, signed by Warden).

# From Joseph Delaplaine

SIR, Philadᵃ June 19ʰ 1814

I have been favoured with your very obliging and satisfactory letter respecting the portraits of Columbus & Americus Vespusius; and shall avail myself of your kind offer whenever an opportunity offers.

I have taken the liberty to mention your name in the prospectus enclosed, & hope it will meet your approbation.—

Mʳ Madison, & the different heads of departments have given me their names as patrons to this work, which occupies my exclusive means & attention. Many other distinguished men of our country approbate the plan & have patronized the undertaking, and I cherish a hope that your patronage will not be wanting; not so much from the pecuniary consideration of it, as from its respectability. An individual subscription, in a pecuniary point of view cannot at any time be of any consequence.

Hoping to be honored with a letter, I remain with perfect regard your obedᵗ humˡ sᵗ JOSEPH DELAPLAINE

P. S. Your portrait will appear in the first volume but I should prefer Stuart's portrait of you to that of Mʳ Peale: How I am to manage this I cannot tell, if Mʳ Stuart will refuse to lend me the portrait I mean the original one.

RC (DLC); addressed: "Thomas Jefferson Esquire Monticello Virginia"; postmarked Philadelphia, 19 June; endorsed by TJ as received 26 June 1814 and so recorded in SJL.

A newspaper version of the enclosed PROSPECTUS for *Delaplaine's Repository* highlighted TJ's role in providing access to portraits of "Columbus and Americus Vespusius" and reported that the "prompt compliance of Mr. Jefferson in giving every facility to meet the views of the publisher, will enable him to render additional value to this publication" (Wilmington *Delaware Gazette*, 30 June 1814). In most other respects the prospectus closely followed the earlier version described in note to Delaplaine to TJ, 16 Apr. 1814.

# To Christopher Clark

DEAR SIR                                    Poplar Forest June 21. 14.

The road which now leads thro' the middle of my land from Abner Callaway's to Johnson's, a distance of 3 miles–32 po., and the branch of it leading from the Double branches of Bear creek up into the other 162 po.–15 links in all 3 mi.–192 po. will occasion me upwards of 7. miles of fencing, when we shall have cleared up to it on both sides, as the quality of the land on both sides the whole way[1] will call for. by turning it from the Double branches down the creek about $1\frac{1}{8}$ mile & then off to Johnson's, it will go just within my line the whole way, except about $\frac{3}{8}$ of a mile after it quits the creek that it will pass on mr Radford's side of our line, but still near it, his agreement to which was provided for when I conveyed him the lands. this will be 3 poles 19. links further for the people coming from the mountains, and the hill from the creek up into the present[2] road more gradual. for those who come from New London & that quarter by Abner Callaway's, it will be about 47. poles, say 250. yds further than the present road. I have been engaged the last winter in making the new road, keeping it on firm ground the whole way, and expected now to have asked your aid in obtaining the change from the Court. but I find that my people were not able to compleat it the last winter; for indeed it is a heavy job, and of course we must take another winter for it. the object of this letter therefore at present is to engage your assistance the next spring when it will be compleated and the objection will be removed which might have arisen from the burthen of making it. I avail myself with pleasure of this occasion of assuring you of my great esteem and respect                    TH: JEFFERSON

PoC (MHi); at foot of text: "Christopher Clarke esq."; endorsed by TJ.

Land to William Radford and Joel Yancey, 7 Dec. 1811.

For TJ's AGREEMENT with William Radford, see Conveyance of Bear Branch

[1] Preceding three words interlined.
[2] Word added in margin.

# To Archibald Robertson

DEAR SIR                                    Poplar Forest June 21. 14.

My flour of the last year being still unsold, I have said nothing to you yet on the subject of a payment out of it. but I have desired mr Gibson not to keep it on hand after the last of this month, but to take whatever he can then get for it. what that will be I know not: tho' probably but little, and the drought of the last summer reduced the quantity one half. the same cause having destroyed our corn in Albemarle almost totally, I had to buy bread there for nearly the year's subsistence. so that on the whole it has been the most calamitous year I have experienced since the year 1755. and will afflictingly abridge my means of making paiments this year. what I can do towards my account with you shall be done. a single year of midling produce & price would relieve me from the necessity of further delays; and I cannot but hope that either peace or neutral commerce will enable us to make something of the growing crop. to double my chance, I am aiming at a considerable crop of tobacco. I pray you to accept the assurance of my great esteem and respect          TH: JEFFERSON

PoC (ViU: TJP); at foot of text: "M<sup>r</sup> Archibald Robinson"; endorsed by TJ as a letter to Archibald Robertson and so recorded in SJL.

# From John Barnes

MY DEAR SIR                              George Town 22<sup>d</sup> June, 1814.

Anxious to expedite a Remittance to Gen<sup>l</sup> Kosciusko—I have engaged[1] a sett of ex—(expected soon to be at par) a $7\frac{1}{2}$ ₱ Cent under—Am<sup>t</sup> £400 ster<sup>g</sup> as you will perceive by the inclosed statem<sup>t</sup> &c<sup>a</sup>

as I have great expectations being able to convey my Letter &c—thro the hands of M<sup>r</sup> Nourse—who is expected in Town the insuing week,—I judged it proper for me to Accompany the Gen<sup>l</sup> a/c therewith duplicate also herewith for your goverm<sup>t</sup> as well a Copy of my letter to the Gen<sup>l</sup>—you will perceive the two last items—on the Credit side—as they will—eventualy be filled up & compleated—at your Leisure

I flatter my self these Arangem<sup>ts</sup> will meet your Approval.—and yet hope your expected Letters and even Ans<sup>r</sup> to this in time to go—by same conveyance

I am D<sup>r</sup> Sir
your most Obed<sup>t</sup>                              JOHN BARNES

RC (ViU: TJP-ER); at foot of text: "Thomas Jefferson Esqr Monticello"; endorsed by TJ as received 26 June 1814 and so recorded in SJL. Enclosure: Barnes to Tadeusz Kosciuszko, Georgetown, 22 June 1814, informing him that he had received Kosciuszko's letter of 20 May 1813 acknowledging "the safe conveyance of 5,500 franc's transmitted thro our mutual friend M<sup>r</sup> Morton 16 May 1812"; explaining that the delay in sending the remittance had caused him great distress but was unavoidable due to the "extensive Blockade of the Enemy—whereby all intercourse was at an End"; inclosing through "Messrs Baring Brothers & Comp<sup>y</sup> London—Messrs Bowie & Kurtz, sett of Ex: for £400 sterling a $7\frac{1}{2}$

℔Cᵗ under par, equal to 1644–44. dollars, passed to your Debit—in Accoᵗ Currᵗ herewith also inclosed—for the Sale of your late Pennᵃ Bank stock—and transposing the same in the U States New Loan To which I subscribed by Order of Mr Jefferson $10,000—The particulars of which—when Compleated—I shall do my self the Honor of transmitting you particulars—&ca"; taking note of the

"Astonishing and almost incomprehensible Epoch, of Human Affairs" that had recently transpired; and wishing Kosciuszko a "quiet retirement" (Tr in ViU: TJP-ER; entirely in Barnes's hand; at head of text: "Copy"; at foot of text: "To Genˡ Thadˢ Kosciuszko Paris"). Other enclosure printed below.

¹ Manuscript: "enaged."

ENCLOSURE

## Tadeusz Kosciuszko's Account with John Barnes

Genˡ Thadˢ Kosciusko, at Paris. In a/c wᵗʰ John Barnes Geo Town Coᵃ

| 1812 | | | | |
|---|---|---|---|---|
| May 16ᵗʰ | By Balᵉ due Genˡ K—per Accᵗ rendered | | $ | 173.50 |
| Oct 17— | By 6 Mᵒ divᵈ Pennᵃ Bᵏ due 1ᵗ July | 400. | | |
| 1813. | Negoⁿ | 10. | 390—" | |
| Janʸ 29. | By 6 Mᵒ divᵈ Pennᵃ Bk. due 1ᵗ Insᵗ | 400 | | |
| | Negⁿ | 10. | 390—" | |
| May 31ᵗ | By Mʳ Jeffersons 12 Mᵒ Int due 1ᵗ Apˡ | 360. | | |
| | Negⁿ | 9. | 351 " | |
| Augᵗ 7ʰ | By 6 Mᵒˢ divᵈ Pennᵃ Bk. due 1ᵗ July | 400. | | |
| | Negⁿ | 10. | 390 "— | |
| 1814. | | | | |
| June | By 6 Mᵒˢ divᵈ Pennᵃ Bk. due 1ᵗ Janʸ | 400. | | |
| | Negⁿ | 10. | 390—" | |
| June | By Mʳ Jeffersons 12 Mᵒˢ Int. due 1ᵗ Aprˡ | 360. | | |
| | Negⁿ | 9. | 351.— | 2262.— |
| | per Contra— | | | 2435.50. |
| June 22ᵈ | To Messʳˢ Bowie¹ & Kurtz's sett of Exchange In favʳ of John Barnes on Wᵐ Murdock London a 60 days sight endorsed payable to Baring, Brothers & Cᵒ London for the Use & a/c of Genˡ Kosciusko at Paris— | | | |
| | ex a 7½ ℔ Ct under par. for £400 Sterᵍ | | 1644.44 | |
| | Negⁿ 2 ℔ Cent | | 32 56 | |
| | | | 1677.00. | |
| | sundry postages &ᵃ to & from Baltᵉ &c | | 2.62. | 1679.62 |
| | Balᶜᵉ due Genˡ K. Carᵈ to New Accᵗˢ dollars. Errors & omissⁿˢ Excepted. George Town Coᵃ 22ᵈ June 1814 | | | $755.88 |

JOHN BARNES,

Tr (ViU: TJP-ER); entirely in Barnes's hand; at head of text: "Copy."

¹ Manuscript: "Borie."

# To Patrick Gibson

DEAR SIR                                    Poplar Forest June 22. 14.

I wrote to you from hence on the 9th instant, requesting that my flour might not be kept on hand after this month, as the competition of the new crop would influence the sale of it. the prospect either of a peace in which we shall be included, or at least a continental peace which will open all the continent of Europe to our produce in neutral vessels may I hope give a spur to prices, tho' still I would not wait after this month. having plantation debts here to the amount of about 240.D. I must ask the favor of you to inclose that sum to mr Archibald Robinson of Lynchburg to be paid to the order of Jeremiah A. Goodman. I leave this for Monticello the day after tomorrow. Accept the assurance of my esteem & respect

TH: JEFFERSON

PoC (NHi: Thomas Jefferson Papers); at foot of text: "Mr Gibson"; endorsed by TJ.

# From Levett Harris

SIR,                                        London 22 June 1814.

The inclosed letter was handed me a few days since by our mutual friend Prince Adam Czartoryski, who accompanied the Emperor Alexander hither from Paris.

The Prince, in recommending this letter to my attention, particularly requested me to bring him to your remembrance; & to renew to you those sentiments of admiration & attachment which originated with his early acquaintance with you at Paris, & which have had all their effect Since, by his review of your exalted character & eminent public services.

Prince Adam continues Still the admired friend of Alexander, & may possibly again become a principal member of his Majesty's Government.

I have been here about two months—I left St Petersburg with Messs Gallatin and Bayard with an intention of returning with these gentlemen to America—but having since received an instruction from my Government to take charge of the Legation to Russia, in the absence of Mr Adams, named a Commissioner to Ghent to treat there of peace with this Country, I Shall lose no time in retracing my Steps.

The Emperor leaves here to day on his return to the seat of his Empire. I seldom am honored with a private conversation with His Majesty (which has Occurred twice Since he has been here) that his Majesty does not make Special enquiries after you. His Sentiments of us, I can assure you, are always the same; & let me add they could have lost none of their effect by his visit to this Country—These Sentiments with which You Sir, have mainly Contributed to inspire the Emperor, I trust will be[1] improved into the happiest consequences to our Country.

I hope after Mr Adams's mission to Ghent is terminated that I Shall be releived by his resuming his function at St Petersburg; & that I Shall thereby be enabled to pursue the design I have So long had in view of revisiting my native land. Among the first gratifications to be imparted by this return to America, will be that derived by the duty I Shall immediately fulfil of paying my homage to you at Monticello, & there personally assure You of the deep sense I have of the confidence I have enjoyed under Your Government & my gratitude for the interest You have been pleased to take in my welfare.

Receive I pray You Sir, the renewed sentiments of the highest consideration & respect with which I am ever

Your most obedient humble servant          LEVETT HARRIS.

RC (DLC); dateline adjacent to signature; at foot of text: "The honorable Thomas Jefferson Monticello"; endorsed by TJ as received 15 Sept. 1814 and so recorded in SJL. Enclosure: Tadeusz Kosciuszko to TJ, 15 May 1814.

[1] Harris here canceled "Still."

# To Archibald Robertson

DEAR SIR                                Poplar Forest June 22. 14.

Having some plantation debts to discharge here amounting to about 240.D. I have this day written to mr Gibson to remit that sum and believing it would come safer under your address than if inclosed to mr Goodman directly, I have taken the liberty of desiring mr Gibson to inclose it to you, & have to ask the favor of you to recieve, and pay it when recieved[1] to the order of Jeremiah A. Goodman. be pleased to send me by the bearer 2. loaves of sugar, and accept the assurances of my esteem & respect.          TH: JEFFERSON

PoC (ViU: TJP); at foot of text: "Mr Archibald Robinson"; endorsed by TJ as a letter to Archibald Robertson and so recorded in SJL.

[1] Preceding two words interlined.

Oliver Evans by Bass Otis, Engraved by William G. Jackman

Within the engraving:

QVI RATE VELIVOLA OCCIDVOS PENETRAVIT AD IDOS
PRIMVS ET AMERICAM NOBILITAVIT HVMVM

CHRISTOPHORVS COLVMBVS LIGVR INDIARV PRIM INVET A°1493

ASTRORVM CONSVLT ET IPSO NOBILIS AVSV
CHRISTOPHOR° TALI FRONTE COLVMB° ERAT

## THEODORVS DE BRY LECTO-
ri salutem.

IN superiore libro historiæ Americanæ ( beneuole lector) in qua res noui orbis nuper inuenti mirandæ atq;
insignes non tantum scripto recitatur sed & iconibus
exprimuntur & repræsentantur, dictum est eas terras
Christophori Columbi Genuensis industria mirabiliter ac præter spem eorum omnium quos ea de re com-
pellarat, repertas fuisse. Quoniam autem ille Columbus vir erat cordatus
magnique ingenij & animi, Rex & Regina Castiliæ antequam ab illis
discederet, eius effigiem ab eximio aliquo pictore ad viuum exprimi ius-
serunt, vt si ab illa expeditione non rediret aliquod eius monumentum
apud se haberent. Huius autem effigiej exemplar nuper post absolutum

a 2        quartum

Christopher Columbus as Engraved by Jean de Bry

John L. E. W. Shecut to Jefferson,
17 Aug. 1814

Abraham Howard Quincy to Jefferson,
10 May 1814

Address Covers

Jefferson to John E. Hall, 1 Jan. 1814

Peter Carr by Saint-Mémin

No. 13

This is to certify, that *Thomas Jefferson* of the or of in the county of *Albemarle* in the 19th collection district of *Virginia* paid the duty of *Ten* dollars,

or,

for and upon a *four* wheel carriage for the conveyance of persons,

called a *Phaeton* owned by *him* or

This certificate to be of no avail any longer than the aforesaid carriage shall be owned by the said *Thomas Jefferson* unless said certificate shall be produced to the collector by whom it was granted, and an entry be made thereon, specifying the name of the then owner of said carriage, and the time when he or she became possessed thereof.

Given in conformity with an act of the Congress of the United States, passed on the 24th day of July, 1813.

*ThMRandolph* Collector of the Revenue
for the 19th Collection District of *Virginia*

Countersigned this 23 day of *January* 1814
*Thomas Randolph* Deputy Collector.

No. 14

This is to certify, that *Thomas Jefferson* of the or of in the county of *Albemarle* in the 19th collection district of *Virginia* paid the duty of *four* dollars,

or,

for and upon a *two* wheel carriage for the conveyance of persons,

called a *Gig* owned by *him* or

This certificate to be of no avail any longer than the aforesaid carriage shall be owned by the said *Thomas Jefferson* unless said certificate shall be produced to the collector by whom it was granted, and an entry be made thereon, specifying the name of the then owner of said carriage, and the time when he or she became possessed thereof.

Given in conformity with an act of the Congress of the United States, passed on the 24th day of July, 1813.

*ThMRandolph* Collector of the Revenue
for the 19th Collection District of *Virginia*

Countersigned this 23 day of *January* 1814
*Thos Randolph* Deputy Collector.

Jefferson's Tax Receipts

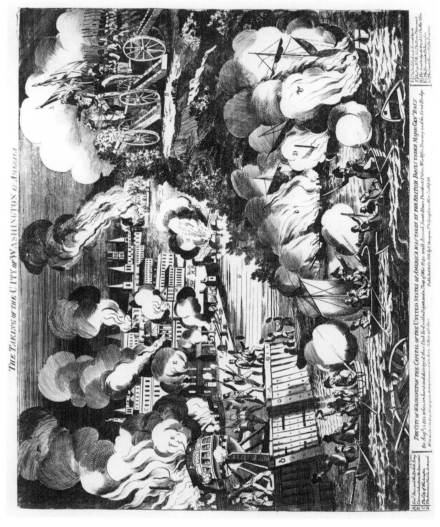

The Burning of Washington, D.C.

Jefferson Offers his Library to Congress

Range of Offices at Poplar Forest

# From Archibald Robertson

DEAR SIR                                          Lynchburg 22nd June 1814
   Your favors of yesterday & todays date have recd, altho: we are
much in want of money at present, your situation would prevent our
calling on you, yet hope you will as soon as in your power aford us
some aid—
You are at liberty at all times to make any remitances through us to
Mr Goodman, which shall be attended to with pleasure—
   Respectfully your ob St                        A. ROBERTSON

RC (ViU: TJP); endorsed by TJ as received 22 June 1814 and so recorded in SJL.


# From Israel B. Kursheedt

HONOR'D SIR!                                  Richmond June 24th 1814
In consequence of the stationers having refused to offer to the public
a work lately published in Boston from a fear to offend—. and with a
view to remunerate the author for the expences he has been at—a few
copies have been Sent to the care of Mr David Isaacs of Charlottsle for
him to dispose of <u>only</u> to the <u>liberal</u> & <u>enlightend</u>
   with the highest respect I am your obt          I B KURSHEEDT

RC (MWA: Thomas Jefferson Papers); dateline beneath signature; at foot of text: "Thos Jefferson Esqr"; endorsed by TJ as received 28 June 1814 and so recorded in SJL. Enclosures: (1) George Bethune English, *The Grounds of Christianity Examined, by Comparing the New Testament with the Old* (Boston, 1813; Sowerby, no. 1708). (2) Samuel Cary, *Review of a Book Entitled "The Grounds of Christianity Examined, by Comparing the New Testament with the Old, By George Bethune English, A. M."* (Boston, 1813; Sowerby, no. 1709). (3) English, *A Letter to The Reverend Mr. Cary, containing Remarks Upon His Review of the Grounds of Christianity Examined, by Comparing the New Testament with the Old* (Boston, 1813; Sowerby, no. 1710). Enclosed in David Isaacs to TJ, 28 June 1814.

Israel Baer Kursheedt (1766–1852), Jewish lay leader, was a German native who received Talmudic training at Frankfurt under Rabbi Nathan Adler. In 1796 he immigrated to the United States, settling in New York City and becoming active in religious and educational endeavors at Shearith Israel Synagogue. Kursheedt became recognized as an American authority on Judaism. In 1812 he moved to Richmond, where he helped reorganize the Beth Shalome Synagogue and served as a cantor for twelve years. His business ventures did not prosper, and in 1824 Kursheedt returned to New York and was a founder of a separatist congregation, B'nai Jeshurun. He helped organize a Hebrew Mutual Benefit Society in 1826 and served as its president, and in 1834 he founded the Hebrath Terumath Hakodesh, an organization to relieve poor Jews in Palestine. Kursheedt died in New York City (Kenneth Libo and Abigail Kursheedt Hoffman, *The Seixas-Kursheedts and the Rise of Early American Jewry* [2001], 26–49; Myron Berman, *Richmond's Jewry, 1769–1976: Shabbat in Shockoe* [1979], 47–9; Morris U. Schappes, *A Documentary History of* the Jews in the United States 1654–1875 [1971], 200, 211, 212, 596; Israel Goldstein, *A Century of Judaism in New York: B'nai Jeshurun, 1825–1925, New York's Oldest Ashkenazic Congregation* [1930], esp. 90–2; New York *Evening Post*, 5 May 1852).

Kursheedt was acquainted with the AUTHOR, George Bethune English (Herbert T. Ezekiel and Gaston Lichtenstein, *The History of the Jews of Richmond from 1769 to 1917* [1917], 132). In the enclosed publications, English argued that the gift of religious freedom in the United States

should induce all devout individuals to examine the tenets of their faith and test them against reason and scripture. English's inability to reconcile the divine revelations of the Old and New Testaments led him to question the foundations of Christianity. He then defended his position against attacks by Samuel Cary and William Ellery Channing, both of whom were Unitarian ministers. In his copy of the second enclosure (DLC), TJ penciled a note suggesting that Cary's position on miracles was circular (Sowerby, no. 1709).

# From William Lambert

SIR,                                    Lancaster County, Virg[a] June 24.[th] 1814.

The reformation of the Julian calendar by pope Gregory **XIII**, in the year 1582, is so near the truth, that it will not want correction until 3600 years after the change of stile took place. It has been found by a series of observations noticed in Vince's astronomy, that the tropical year is 365 days, 5 hours, 48 minutes, 48 seconds; if this be multiplied by 3600 years, the product will be 1,314,872 days, without the fraction of a second. In this period of 3600 years there will be 873 leap years and 2727 common years, which would make one day or 24 hours more than the product above mentioned; it will be necessary therefore, that the 3600th or some intermediate year, reckoned as Bissextile, should be made a common year; or in other words, that there must be 872 leap years and 2728 common years; for if we multiply 872 by 366 days, and 2728 by 365, the sum of the products will be 1,314,872 days, agreeing exactly with 3600 tropical years, according to the most accurate observations hitherto made. I wish to turn your attention and that of the American Philosophical Society to this subject, for altho' the time is so far distant as not to affect many generations to come, yet I should be glad that the correction should be proposed in the United States of America, rather than in Europe, or any other part of the world.

I am, Sir, with great respect, Your most obed[t] servant,

WILLIAM LAMBERT.

RC (PPAmP: APS Archives, Manuscript Communications); addressed: "Hon[ble] Thomas Jefferson, late President of the United States, and President of the American Philosophical Society. Monticello"; stamped; postmarked Kilmarnock, 24 June; endorsed by TJ as received 8 July 1814 and so recorded in

SJL; endorsed in an unidentified hand at APS: "Comm[n] on Gregorian Callender read Aug[t] 20. 1814 report. 7 Oct[r] Enclosed." Tr (DLC); entirely in TJ's hand; abstract subjoined to PoC of TJ to Robert Patterson, 23 July 1814, and reading as follows: "The paper quoting Vince's Astronomy for the tropical year being 365 d–5 h–48'–48" observes that this will produce an error of exactly 1. day in 3600. years; because 365 D–5 H–48'–48" × 3600 = 1,314,872 days within which are 873. leap years & 2727. common years, which would make 1. day more than the above number, to a single second. he proposes therefore that the 3600th year should be a common year because 872 × 366 + 2728 × 365 = 1,314,872 days."

Enclosed in TJ to Patterson, 23 July 1814.

This letter was read at a meeting of the American Philosophical Society on 19 Aug. 1814 and referred to a committee consisting of John Gummere, Robert Patterson, and Jonathan Williams. On 7 Oct. 1814 the society accepted the committee's recommendation that Lambert's communication "be filed among the papers of the Society" (APS, Minutes [MS in PPAmP]).

Lambert took the OBSERVATIONS from Samuel VINCE's book entitled *A Complete System of Astronomy* (Cambridge, Eng., 1797), 52–7. BISSEXTILE: a leap-year, or the extra day that the Julian calendar adds to it (*OED*).

# From John Barnes

DEAR SIR— George Town Co[a] 27th June 1814—

I have great satisfaction in advising you, that yesterday, I had the pleasure meeting M[r] Monroe (at the Presidents)—to whom I presented my sealed packet addressed to Baring Brothers & C[o] London Covering, Bowie & Kurtz first of Exchange on W[m] Murdock for £400 ster[g] for Acco[t] & Use of Gen[l] Koscuisk—in Paris—as well, my Letter & a/— to said Gen[l]—Copies thereof[1] I addressed to you 22[d] Instant

These dispatches with M[r] Monroes—goes Off, this day, for France—the most safe & certain Conveyance we could possibly wish for—

Nothing New but what you see in the late papers—in Phila[d]—&[a] &[a] the Cry of Peace—Peace—we shall, and must have—a Peace— says the Malignant,[2] restless, and daring Madness—of the hired[3] papers—of the F——[4] & interested Merch[ts] British Agents—Speculators—& others—

Peace! the most desirable—Event, & Anxiously the first wish of every good Man,—But unless,—it is, to be obtained on Honorable terms—I Hope—and trust—the Eventfull struggle—will prove the rising Hero's, equal to their Patriotic—sires—and Cover themselves alike, with never fading Laurels—of Honor and Glory,—

Accept Dear Sir

The best wishes—of Your Obed[t] servant JOHN BARNES,

[ 437 ]

RC (ViU: TJP-ER); at foot of text: "Thomas Jefferson Esq<sup>r</sup> Monticello"; endorsed by TJ as received 1 July 1814 and so recorded in SJL.

<sup>1</sup> Manuscript: "said Gen<sup>l</sup> Copies—thereof."

<sup>2</sup> Manuscript: "Maligant."
<sup>3</sup> Manuscript: "hirered."
<sup>4</sup> Presumably an abbreviation for "Federalists."

# From William Thornton

DEAR SIR                                 City of Washington 27<sup>th</sup> June 1814.

I only received your favour of the 9<sup>th</sup> Inst: a few Days ago, & I have been trying to get a copy made of the Drawing & Specification &c of m<sup>r</sup> Janes's Patent, but fearing it might take more time to do it correctly than your call for it would admit, I thought it best to run the risk of sending the Papers, and take the responsibility on myself, for I know that nothing but a miscarriage of the same can endanger their safe return.—It always gives me pleasure to endeavour to fulfil your commands, but I am sorry that I am not able to answer the questions you have put to me:—for not knowing that the Improvements m<sup>r</sup> Janes made in his former Loom, when he took out his last patent were important<sup>1</sup> I did not require another model, which I now lament, as the Invention appears to claim attention. I was repeatedly invited by M<sup>r</sup> Clopper, who resides between here & Harper's Ferry, to go to the Capitol & see the Loom in operation. I wished to see it, but was so much engaged while the Congress were here that I really had not time—As soon as they departed I had more leisure & went to Alexandria to see it, but it was gone—m<sup>r</sup> Clopper I understood had either purchased a share in it, or was the Agent for sales of Patent rights. If you, on examination of the Principles, think it would be worth your possession, I will make the necessary inquiries of the Patentee who resides at Ashford; Windham County; Con<sup>t</sup> or of his agent m<sup>r</sup> Clopper—

This morning, a Gentleman from Boston informed me he was the Bearer of the model of<sup>2</sup> a water Loom to be deposited in my office—invented by m<sup>r</sup> Pope of Boston, which he does not yet wish to patent, as he is engaged in making some Improvements on it, that he thinks will render it much more perfect.—Pope was engaged in the Invention of the Card-making machine in 1787—I saw him, at that time in Boston—He made a very beautiful orrery, and when such ingenious men as he, begin to apply their Talents to the common concerns of life we may expect great Improvements.—The number of ingenious

Looms in my office at this time, would, if amply described, fill a volume—The Arts have made an astonishing progress in this Country within a few years, & the number of patents applied for since the commencem$^t$ of the present year amount to ab$^t$ 140—yet some of the members of Congress think the whole Establishment ought to be burnt.—It would be a good deal like burning the Alexandrian Library—I am pleased that you have employed part of your time in the manufacturing of Cloth—I hope it will not only tend to your benefit but as an excellent Example, to the benefits that the Country must ultimately derive from such Establishments.

I have had a Person, for several months, employed in making a musical Instrument that I invented ab$^t$ 12 or 14 y$^{rs}$ ago—It will be the size of a large chamber organ—played by an endless band, on 68 Strings which by Keys in the manner of the piano Forte, will give all the tones of the violin—violincello—bass—double bass &c—It answers my utmost wish—and produces notes which equal the above Instruments, I have neither Catgut nor horse hair, but have imitated both, by compositions that are far superior, & these arose from necessity—I shall give you a better account when the Instrument is finished—(the mail is going & I have not time to read this).$^3$—

I am dear Sir yours very sincerely    WILLIAM THORNTON—

RC (MHi); at foot of text: "Hon: Thomas Jefferson"; endorsed by TJ as received 1 July 1814 and so recorded in SJL. Enclosures not found.

Joseph POPE, a clock- and watchmaker in Boston, built an ORRERY that Harvard University purchased in 1789 with the proceeds of a lottery (Justin Winsor, ed.,

*The Memorial History of Boston including Suffolk County, Massachusetts. 1630–1880* [1886], vol. 4, pt. 2, 500–2). He did not patent his water loom.

$^1$ Preceding two words interlined.
$^2$ Preceding three words interlined.
$^3$ Omitted closing parenthesis editorially supplied.

# To Baring Brothers & Company

Monticello in Virginia.
MESS$^{RS}$ BARINGS BROTHERS & CO.    June 28. 14.

Gen$^l$ Kosciuzko of Paris having a deposit in the banks & funds of the US. and depending considerably for his ordinary expences on the regular remittance of the interest and dividends, has been subjected to great inconveniences by the difficulties proceeding from the circumstances of the general war, and especially for the last year or two. we have embraced the first moment of the peace of Europe to relieve him by a bill of exchange for 400.£ sterling drawn by mess$^{rs}$ Boice &

Kurtz on W<sup>m</sup> Murdoch of London, at 60. days sight, in favor of John Barnes, endorsed to your house, for the use of Gen<sup>l</sup> Kosciuzko at Paris. we have made this endorsement from a knolege of the extensive foreign connections of your house, and a belief in the favorable dispositions you entertain towards the worthy Kosciuzko. I take the liberty of adding my personal sollicitations that you will have the goodness to facilitate as early a remittance of the money to the General as circumstances will admit, and will be thankful for a line of notice of it addressed either to mr John Barnes at George town, district of Columbia, or to myself. I avail myself with pleasure of this occasion of tendering you the assurance of my high esteem & consideration.

Th: Jefferson

RC (FrN); salutation clipped, with missing text supplied from PoC. PoC (DLC); endorsed by TJ. Enclosed in TJ to John Barnes, 28 June 1814.

Baring Brothers & Company, long a powerful British merchant-banking firm, received its initial capital from the textile enterprises of John Baring and Elizabeth Vowler Baring. In 1762 their sons formed the interlocking firms of John and Charles Baring & Company in Exeter, and John and Francis Baring & Company in London. Sir Francis Baring (1740–1810) developed the London establishment into a leader in international finance. His firm became known as Sir Francis Baring & Company in 1801 and changed its name to Baring Brothers & Company six years later. The company helped finance British war efforts in America and Europe. The efforts of Francis Baring's son Alexander Baring (1773–1848) strengthened a longstand-

ing alliance with the prestigious Amsterdam banking house of Hope & Company and culminated in the two firms joining to finance the American purchase of the Louisiana Territory from France. Baring Brothers & Company continued to supply capital thereafter for United States foreign trade and governmental activities. Imprudent investments severely weakened the company and led to its reorganization in 1890 as Baring Brothers & Company, Limited. After a further century as a prominent financial institution, the firm collapsed suddenly in 1995 (*ODNB*; John Orbell, *Baring Brothers & Co., Limited. A History to 1939* [1985]; Philip Ziegler, *The Sixth Great Power: A history of one of the greatest of all banking families, the House of Barings, 1762–1929* [1988]; Stephen Fay, *The Collapse of Barings* [1996; American ed. 1997]; Rufus King to TJ, 5 Sept. 1825).

BOICE & KURTZ: Bowie & Kurtz.

## To John Barnes

Dear Sir                                        Monticello June 28. 14.

After an absence of five weeks, I returned home the day before yesterday, and found here your favors of May 18. & 24. & June 16. and 22. I am much rejoiced that you have been able to compleat the sale of Gen<sup>l</sup> Kosciuzko's Pensylva bank stock, and to transfer it to the new loan of the US. there I know it will be safer than in any deposit on earth and will place him beyond those risks which might close his days in want. altho' the sale has not been quite as advantageous as was counted on in the estimates made by yourself & mr Parker & inclosed in your letter of April 16. yet the superior safety of the present deposit compensates the little difference in the proceeds of sale.

the 20. shares, being a capital of 8000.D. sold at 138.D. enlarges the capital to 11,040 D. our subscription to the US. loan being for 10,000 D. only, I suppose there will be a surplus to be still invested in the same US. stock by purchase. or do I see the particulars of this commutation in their true light? for I am so little conversant in these operations as not to be sure that I exactly understand the result of this one.

I inclose you the order for the interest due from the bank of Pensv[a] as you desired. my own payment, due in April, has not been forwarded because you had not as yet found the means of investing it in a remittance to the Gen[l]. the delay gave me a chance of a rise in the price of flour, mine of the last year having been in the hands of Mess[rs] Gibson & Jefferson since last Christmas, & still on hand unsold, as 4.D. cannot yet be obtained for it in Richmond. but if you will be so good as to name the day on which it will be wanting to make good your subscriptions, that amount shall be sold at any price and the money placed in your hands punctually before the day. we have daily hope that the prospect of peace will give some spur to prices. with the order above ment[d] and mr Taylor's letter, I inclose you the one you desired to the Barings, and one for the General which I pray you to have sent by the same conveyance, & to be assured of my constant friendship. TH: JEFFERSON

PoC (DLC); at foot of text: "M[r] Barnes"; endorsed by TJ. Enclosures: (1) TJ to Baring Brothers & Company, 28 June 1814. (2) TJ to Tadeusz Kosciuszko, 28 June 1814. Other enclosures not found.

# From David Isaacs

SIR                                            June 28th 1814

I sent 3 Books which ware handed to me yesteday with a letter, by a freind from Richmond who says that an acquaintance of mine in Richmond Sent them to me and desere for me to forward them to you which i take the Earliest opportunity to do so, he also has sent a good many more Setts[1] of them, and desires to sell them to those who Choose to buy them, the Price of the sett is 3\$25,[2] it is to be hoped if you should be Please after reading them—you will recoment Some costomers to me for them your Freind

Respectfully                                               DAVID ISAACS

RC (MHi); dateline beneath signature; addressed: "Tho⁵ Jefferson Monticelloe"; endorsed by TJ as received 28 June 1814 and so recorded in SJL. Enclosure: Israel B. Kursheedt to TJ, 24 June 1814, and enclosures.

On 7 May 1814 Isaacs sold TJ a side of veal weighing 48 pounds for $4. An extant account records this purchase along with an undated entry for unspecified

BOOKS, probably those mentioned above. TJ settled this account with a payment of $7.50 on 11 July 1814 (account with Isaacs [MS in MHi], written on a small scrap in a clerk's hand, undated, with additions in TJ's hand, endorsed by Isaacs and TJ; *MB*, 2:1301).

¹ Word interlined.
² That is, "$3.25."

# To Tadeusz Kosciuszko

MY DEAR FRIEND AND GENERAL                    Monticello June 28. 14.

Your letter of Jan. 24. has been recieved and has realised the fears we had for some time entertained that you would be suffering from the failure of the annual remittance from hence. mr Barnes had been constant in his endeavors to find some channel of remittance: but from the embargo & blockade and consequent cessation of nearly all intercourse with Europe, it had been absolutely impracticable. the medium of mr Morton, with which you had been so well contented, was particularly pressed on his correspondent here, and had failed, as well as other public and private channels which he tried. he has availed himself of the first moment we heard of the peace between France & England to procure a remittance thro' the latter country; and now forwards¹ a bill of exchange for £400. sterl. = 1644. D 44 c drawn by Boice & Kurtz on Wᵐ Murdoch of London at 60. Days sight. this bill he has endorsed to Messʳˢ Barings, brothers & co. of London; to whom I have written urgently to remit the proceeds to you as speedily as may be.

The abuse of the institution of banks in this country by their infinite multiplication, and the immense mass of paper they have thrown into circulation beyond the competent amount, has brought on a great depreciation of their paper, and imminent danger that all will blow up and end in universal bankruptcy. and as the particular moment, like that of the day of judgment, cannot be foreseen, but, when it comes, involves irrecoverable loss, I thought I owed it to your friendship & confidence to attend to the danger in time, and secure you against a total loss of your capital. it happened fortunately too, that the US. opened a loan at the same time, the permanent security of which is beyond that of any other deposit, I believe, in the world; and altho' the annual interest they give is less than the bank profits, yet as we found we could get an advance of 38.[2] per cent on the original amount of your bank stock, so as to increase your capital of 8000.D. in the Pensylvania bank to upwards of 11,000 D. in the funds of the US. the smaller rate of interest on a capital so much enlarged, will be something more than equivalent to the larger profit on a smaller capital, in bank stock. I accordingly directed mr Barnes to subscribe 10,000.D. for you in the loan of the US. and to sell out your bank stock. this he has effected, and after the operation shall be compleated, and the balance remaining on hand, after paying the subscription of 10,000.D. shall be known, the surplus also shall be invested in the same loan by a purchase of it's stock. you will experience no difference in your present income; but should you chuse to recieve the capital at the epoch of paiment, it will be of about 11,000 D. instead of 8000. and on the whole I am in hopes you will approve the transfer, as well for it's ultimate profit as it's permanent security.

Great events, my dear friend, have happened at Paris. I hope and believe they will be for the benefit of the world in general, and I especially wish they may be so to your country, & to yourself personally. how they will operate on us is doubtful, but we have minds prepared to meet any thing rather than dishonor. but the transactions in Europe generally are too little known here to justify any further observations or conjectures. under all circumstances I am faithfully your affectionate friend.                                    Th: Jefferson

RC (PlKMN); edge trimmed, with missing text supplied from PoC; addressed: "General Kosciuzko at Paris recommended to the care of H.E. mr Crawford Min. Plen. of the US. of America at Paris." PoC (MHi); endorsed by TJ. Enclosed in TJ to John Barnes, 28 June 1814.

boice & kurtz: Bowie & Kurtz.

[1] Word interlined in place of "incloses."

[2] TJ recopied this number below the line on RC for clarity.

# To Robert Mills

Monticello June 20. [28] 14.

Th: Jefferson presents his compliments to mr Mills and his acknolegements for the copy sent him of the annual exhibition of the

Columbian society of artists. he congratulates him on the success which seems likely to attend the instituti[on] and is particularly thankful to mr Mills for these repeat[ed] proofs of his personal attentions. he salutes him with grea[t] esteem and respect.

PoC (DLC: TJ Papers, 201:35810); misdated; edge trimmed; dateline at foot of text; endorsed by TJ as a letter of 28 June 1814 and so recorded in SJL.

# To Joseph Delaplaine

Monticello June 29. 14.

Th: Jefferson presents his respects to Mʳ Delaplaine & willingly becomes a subscriber to the publication stated in the Prospectus sent him. he presumes there will be some agent within this state who can recieve the subscription money, the difficulty of making remittances of small & fractional sums to a distance & in a paper recievable there being a principal obstruction to these subscriptions. since the date of his letter he has found in his library[1] a very fine print of Vespucius done in Florence from the same original from which his portrait is taken. it is the frontispiece of an Eulogium on Vespucius, 6.I. by $4\frac{1}{4}$ I. should mr Delaplaine find it more convenient to copy this, whenever his engraver proceeds to that part of his work, Th:J. will cut it out of the book and forward it to him, to be returned when done with.

RC (LNT: George H. and Katherine M. Davis Collection); dateline at foot of text; addressed: "Mʳ Joseph Delaplaine Philadelphia"; franked; postmarked Milton, 30 June; endorsement by Delaplaine includes a misrecording of his 17 Aug. 1814 reply: "Wrote 18 Augᵗ 1814." PoC (DLC); endorsed by TJ.

[1] Preceding three words interlined.

# To James Mease

Dᴇᴀʀ Sɪʀ                                   Monticello June 29. 14.

On my return home after an absence of five weeks, I find here your letter of May 24. of the history of the Hughes's crab apple I can furnish nothing more than that I remember it well upwards of 60. years ago, & that it was then a common apple on James river. of the other apple after which you enquire I happen to know the origin. it is not a crab, but a seedling which grew alone in a large old field near Williamsburg where the seed had probably been dropped by some bird. Majʳ Taliaferro of that neighborhood remarking it once to be very full of apples got permission of the owner of the ground to gather them. from these he made a cask of cyder which, in the estimation of every one who tasted it, was the finest they had ever seen. he grafted an orchard from it, as did also his son in law our late Chancellor Wythe. the cyder they constantly made from this was preferred by every person to the Crab or any other cyder ever known in this state, and it still retains it's character in the different places to which it has been transferred. I am familiar with it, and have no hesitation in pronouncing it much superior to the Hughes's crab. it has more body, is less acid, and comes nearer to the silky Champaigne than any other. Maj$^r$ Taliaferro called it the Robertson apple from the name of the person owning the parent[1] tree, but subsequently it has more justly & generally been distinguished by the name of the Taliaferro apple, after him to whom we are indebted for the discovery of it's valuable properties. it is the most juicy apple I have ever known, & is very refreshing as an eating apple.

Accept the assurance of my great esteem & respect.

TH: JEFFERSON

RC (NNGL, on deposit NHi); at foot of text: "D$^r$ James Maese." PoC (DLC); with unrelated words "Convention Guards" in TJ's hand on verso; mistakenly endorsed by TJ as a letter of 30 June and so recorded in SJL.

Mease included this entire letter in his "Account of the Virginia Cyder Apple, called Gloucester White," read at the Philadelphia Society for Promoting Agriculture in July 1814 and printed in its *Memoirs* 4 (1818): 49–51. His preface to the letter stated that "Having heard from William Coxe, Esq. a very favourable account of a cyder apple in Virginia, which went by the name of Gloucester White, Robertson, or Taliaferro apple, and being told by him that Mr. Jefferson could give some information concerning its origin, I wrote to him for it; and deeming also the history of the Hugh's crab (a cyder apple of more general note), well worthy of in-

quiry, I requested him to favour me with such facts as he possessed respecting it. The following was his reply." Mease followed TJ's letter with (1) a paragraph by Coxe commenting that the Taliaferro was an "immense bearer, a very fine cider apple, and by many, thought the finest table apple of the season, in Virginia," and indicating that "Mr. Jefferson described it as much superior to the Hugh's crab for cyder, as that is to any other fruit"; and (2) a brief covering letter from Coxe to Mease, Burlington, New Jersey, 21 May 1814, in which he stated that he supposed the Taliaferro to be "of Virginia origin, that is, first cultivated there, but cannot vouch for the fact." The Hewes Crab and the Taliaferro (also called the Robinson) apples are described in Peter J. Hatch, *The Fruits and Fruit Trees of Monticello* (1998), 74–6.

[1] Word interlined in place of "mother."

# To Robert Patterson

DEAR SIR                                    Monticello June 29. 14.
The inclosed paper came to my hand for communication to the
Philosophical society as you will percieve by it's contents. this I beg
leave to do thro' you, and to avail myself of this as of every occasion
of assuring you of my friendship & respect.      TH: JEFFERSON

RC (PPAmP: Thomas Jefferson Papers); addressed: "Doct^r Robert Patterson Philadelphia"; franked; postmarked
Milton, 30 June. PoC (MHi); with TJ's
correction of polygraph errors along right
margin; endorsed by TJ. Enclosure:
Dudley Leavitt to TJ, 10 June 1814, and
enclosure.

# To John Wilson

Monticello June 29. 14.
Th: Jefferson presents his compliments to mr Wilson & his thanks
for the copy of his Philological entertainments which he has been so
kind as to send him. with wishes for the success of his efforts to reconcile the orthography & pronunciation of our language he salutes
him with great respect.

PoC (MoSHi: TJC-BC); dateline beneath body of letter; at foot of text: "M^r John
Wilson Washington"; endorsed by TJ.

# To William Barton

DEAR SIR                                    Monticello June 30. 14.
Your favor of the 6^th inst. is just now recieved, informing me of
your purpose to undertake the biography of some of the prominent
characters of our country. no work can be more useful, agreeable or
desirable. I fear however that the collection of materials, spread over
so extensive a region, may be attended with considerable difficulty.
still partial notices will be valuable, as they will be so much saved
from the wreck of time, and may perhaps be added to hereafter. a
gentleman of abilities is engaged in such a work for this state; altho'
I doubt whether his professional occupations will permit him to pursue it; and in any event he is determined I believe not to publish it
during his own life, which may be a long one. I shall gladly become a
subscriber to your work, and would willingly furnish toward it any
facts within my knolege: but the circumstance of having been absent

from the state so great a portion of my life has permitted me to learn little of the private history of my cotemporaries, or to witness much of their public services; and at present a necessary attention to my affairs, with the inert habits of age keep me chiefly at home, and withdrawn from either intercourse or acquaintance with those by whom some materials might perhaps be furnished. with my wishes for the success of your undertaking, accept the assurances of my great esteem & respect.                                    TH: JEFFERSON

PoC (DLC); at foot of text: "William Barton esq."; endorsed by TJ.

The GENTLEMAN OF ABILITIES was probably William Wirt.

## To Jason Chamberlain

SIR                                              Monticello July 1. 14.
I thank you for the copy of the Iroquois Spelling book, as also for your inaugural oration on the subject of Classical learning: and I entirely concur in your estimate of the great value of the latter. to the models left us by the Greeks & Romans are we principally indebted for the chaste and rational style of modern composition, instead of the inflated & vague manner of the Eastern & Northern nations, into which our Northern ancestors might have been seduced by the examples they possessed.        Were we to consider Classical learning merely as a luxury in literature, I should feel myself more indebted to my father for having procured it to me, than for any other luxury I derive from his bounty.        We might too, in our academies and colleges, avail ourselves of the study of the Greek & Roman languages, to economise both the time and expence employed in these institutions. in most of them we have Professorships of Antient history, Ethics, Rhetoric & Belles lettres. but the teacher of Latin and Greek, with very little additional trouble, might supply the functions of all these; since the very books which are resorted to for instruction in these languages, are those also which form the basis of the other studies.
in Antient history Herodotus, Thucydides, Xenophon, Diodorus Siculus, Cornelius Nepos, Livy, Sallust, Caesar, Tacitus form such a body as the Student would easily fill up in the after-portions of his[1] life. in Ethics Epictetus, the Socratic writers, Antoninus, Cicero, Seneca, would require such occasional observations only from the teacher, as might systematise their matter; and what finer specimens could he produce & comment on in Rhetoric than Cicero, Demosthenes, Aeschynes & the other Grecian orators; and in Belles lettres

than Homer, Anacreon, Theocritus, Virgil, Horace, Terence & the Greek tragedians, all of them school books? I really think that the grammar schools might thus be made to supply these distinct professorships to the equal advantage, in time & expence, of the institution and it's students; both of which, in our country, are considerations of moment. I do not however pretend to have matured these speculations, nor to have examined minutely how they would work in practice. they have occurred when occasionally reflecting on the subject, and being recalled to my mind by the matter of your inaugural oration, I hazard them for consideration. be pleased to accept with them the assurances of my esteem and respect.

TH: JEFFERSON

RC (NjP: Thomas Jefferson Collection); addressed: "Jason Chamberlain, Esq. Burlington Vermont," with corrections of address in other hands successively forwarding it to Philadelphia and Washington; franked; postmarked, Milton, 6 July, and Philadelphia, 23 July; endorsed by Chamberlain. PoC (DLC); endorsed by TJ.

[1] Word interlined.

## To Joseph Darmsdatt

DEAR SIR                                Monticello [J]uly 1. 14.

I must ask the favor of you to send me 12. barr[els] of herrings and one of Shad: one half of the herrings to be sent to Lynchburg to the care of mr Robertson mercha[nt] of that place, and the other half with the barrel of sha[d] to be sent here by any of the Milton boats. my flour not being as yet sold, I cannot fix the paiment exactl[y,] but it shall be as soon as in my power. accept the assurances of my esteem & respect.                                TH: JEFFERSON

PoC (MHi); dateline faint; edge trimmed; at foot of text: "Mr Darmsdadt"; endorsed by TJ.

## To William Shirman

SIR                                Monticello July 1. 14.

Your letter of Apr. 30. arrived here after my departure for Bedford, from which place I returned but three days ago. not meeting you there I was obliged to have that job done by the Bricklayer who went to do the brick work. we are now engaged in our harvest which will employ us in cutting & getting out the grain till the middle of next month, before which time therefore I could not find you attendance. but at that date I shall be very glad to recieve you, and shall have work enough to employ you through the season, which will give you time enough to become acquainted with the neighborhood, & to see whether it would not be an advantageous position for you. I am myself persuaded you will find it so. in expectation therefore of seeing you about the middle of August I tender you my best wishes & respects.                    TH: JEFFERSON

PoC (MHi); at foot of text: "M$^r$ W$^m$     The BRICKLAYER was Hugh Chisholm.
Shirman"; endorsed by TJ.


# To John Waldo

SIR                              Monticello July 1. 14.
   A long absence from home has prevented an earlier acknolegement of your favor of Apr. 25. and I learn from it with regret the circumstance of your habitual ill health. I did not mean by my answer to trouble you with any particular attention to it's subject. it conveyed thoughts which had occurred to me sometimes in the course of a busy life, which had never allowed me time to examine them: and being called up by the occasion of your letter, I hazarded them for consideration, conscious that, the subject being so much more familiar to you, they would recieve from you their just estimate. of committing them to the public I had not the smallest idea. neither their merit nor my inclinations looked towards that tribunal. my present object is tranquility, & retirement from public notice, relieving sometimes, by literary speculations, the ordinary cares of a farming life; but never hazarding my quiet by provoking public controversy. I feel much indebted therefore to your justice & discretion in considering what I wrote as not meant for the public eye, but a mere indulgence of a course of thought produced by the occasion of your letter, and of the book you had been so kind as to send me. permit me to repeat to you the assurances of my esteem and respect.           TH: JEFFERSON

RC (CtY: Franklin Collection); addressed: "M$^r$ John Waldo George-town S. Carolina"; franked; postmarked Milton, 3 July. PoC (DLC); endorsed by TJ.

# To Louis H. Girardin

DEAR SIR                                        Monticello July 2. 14.

Before I went to Bedford I asked the favor of you to let me know the amount of my debt to you for the books you were so kind as to let me have, which was referred however until my return. on my return I found you had left the neighborhood; but the hope that some remnant of business might give us the pleasure of seeing you soon, occasioned me to wait a while. but finding that gratification delayed, I trouble you with the same request, and on recieving information of the amount, I will inclose you an order for it on Richmond. to this I will add the year's subscription for the Compiler, of which I learn from that paper that you are become the editor. I sincerely wish it may be profitable, as I am sure that in your hands it will have the merit of correctness of fact and moderation & decency of discussion united with sound principles. I fear more for your health than for success in your new situation. Accept my sincere prayers for both.

TH: JEFFERSON

RC (PPAmP: Thomas Jefferson Papers); addressed: "Mr L. H. Girardin Richmond"; franked; postmarked Milton, 16 July. Not recorded in SJL.

After serving as an EDITOR, Girardin joined William C. Shields from 1815–16 as a publisher of the *Daily Compiler and Richmond Commercial Register* (Brigham, *American Newspapers*, 2:1137).

# To William Duane

DEAR SIR                                        Monticello July 3. 14.

The intercourse with France being now open, I expect every hour a letter from M. de Tutt Tracy, on the subject of his book. what shall I be able to say to him? is it translated? is it in print? & when may it be expected? on the late change of government, he will probably print the original there, and as it will be instantly translated ours may be anticipated.

We are looking to new arrivals for interesting news. the allies having reestablished their brother king on his throne, & the honey-moon now over, the lion, the tyger, the panther & bear are now to divide their spoil with magnanimity. some snarling already appears. maritime rights are to be settled. Ferdinand & his Cortes have a bone to contend for; the old and new Noblesse of France have some little questions of property to settle. I think we may see in all this the seeds of new contentions, and that the present is but a cessation of arms, until the new objects & new coalitions may be formed. in this state of things, none of the powers will be precipitate in disarming; nor great Britain in detaching much of her force to this country. perhaps she may find new motives for peace with us, and by suspending her views on the fisheries, relieve the heart-ache of the Yankees, who will now be able to decide on which side of the water is their safest dependance. all these things make the present a moment of great interest, and induce me to view them but as the 1st chapter of a new history of which I shall not see much. Accept assurances of great esteem & respect.

TH: JEFFERSON

PoC (DLC); at foot of text: "Gen^l Duane"; endorsed by TJ.

The BROTHER KING was Louis XVIII of France, and THE LION, THE TYGER, THE PANTHER & BEAR represented Great Britain, Austria, Prussia, and Russia.

Napoleon had forced FERDINAND VII to abdicate in 1808, but he regained the Spanish throne in 1814 after Napoleon's downfall. Ferdinand renounced the Spanish consititution of 1812 and persecuted the liberal faction in his country (Connelly, *Napoleonic France*, 175–6).

# To John Adams

DEAR SIR                                          Monticello July 5. 14.
    Since mine of Jan. 24. your's of Mar. 14. was recieved. it was not acknoleged in the short one of May 18. by mr Rives, the only object of that having been to enable one of our most promising young men to have the advantage of making his bow to you. I learned with great regret the serious illness mentioned in your letter: and I hope mr Rives will be able to tell me you are entirely restored. but our machines have now been running for 70. or 80. years, and we must expect that, worn as they are, here a pivot, there a wheel, now a pinion, next a spring, will be giving way: and however we may tinker them up for awhile, all will at length surcease motion. our watches, with works of brass and steel, wear out within that period. shall you and I last to see the course of[1] the seven-fold wonders of the times will take? the Attila of the age dethroned, the ruthless destroyer of 10. millions of the human race, whose thirst for blood appeared unquenchable, the great oppressor of the rights & liberties of the world, shut up within the circuit of a little island of the Mediterranean, and dwindled to the condition of an humble and degraded pensioner on the bounty of those he has most injured. how miserably, how meanly, has he closed his

inflated career! what a sample of the Bathos will his history present! he should have perished on the swords of his enemies, under the walls of Paris

| 'Leon piagato a morte | Cosi fra l'ire estrema |
|---|---|
| Sente mancar la vita, | rugge, minaccia, e freme, |
| Guarda la sua ferita, | Che fa tremar morendo |
| Ne s'avilisce ancor. | Tal volta il cacciator.' |

Metast Adriano.

But Bonaparte was a lion in the field only. in civil life a cold-blooded, calculating, unprincipled Usurper, without a virtue, no statesman, knowing nothing of commerce, political economy, or civil government, & supplying ignorance by bold presumption. I had supposed him a great man until his entrance into the Assembly des cinq cens, 18. Brumaire (an. 8.) from that date however I set him down as a great scoundrel only. to the wonders of his rise and fall, we may add that of a Czar of Muscovy dictating, in Paris, laws and limits to all the successors of the Caesars, and holding even the balance in which the fortunes of this new world are suspended. I own that, while I rejoice, for the good of mankind, in the deliverance of Europe from the havoc which would have never ceased while Bonaparte should have lived in power, I see with anxiety the tyrant of the ocean remaining in vigor, and even participating in the merit of crushing his brother tyrant. while the world is thus turned upside down, on which side of it are we? all the strong reasons indeed place us on the side of peace; the interests of the continent, their friendly dispositions, & even the interests of England. her passions alone are opposed to it. peace would seem now to be an easy work, the causes of the war being removed. her orders of council will no doubt be taken care of by the allied powers, and, war ceasing, her impressment of our seamen ceases of course. but I fear there is foundation for the design intimated in the public papers, of demanding a cession of our right in the fisheries. what will Massachusets say to this? I mean her majority, which must be considered as speaking, thro' the organs it has appointed itself, as the Index of it's will. she chose to sacrifice the liberty of our seafaring citizens, in which we were all interested, and with them her obligations to the Co-states; rather than war with England. will she now sacrifice the fisheries to the same partialities? this question is interesting to her alone: for to the middle, the Southern & Western states they are of no direct concern; of no more than the culture of tobacco, rice & cotton to Massachusets. I am really at a loss to conjecture what our refractory sister will say on this occasion. I know what, as a citizen[2] of the Union, I would say to her, 'take this question ad referendum. it concerns you alone. if you would rather give up the fisheries than war with England, we give them up. if you had rather fight for them, we will defend your interests to the last drop of our blood, chusing rather to set a good example than follow a bad one.' and I hope she will determine to fight for them.—with this however you and I shall have nothing to do; ours being truly the case wherein 'non tali auxilio, nec defensoribus istis Tempus eget.' quitting this subject therefore I will turn over another leaf.

I am just returned from one of my long absences, having been at my other home for five weeks past. having more leisure there than here for reading, I amused myself with reading seriously Plato's republic. I am wrong however in calling it amusement, for it was the heaviest task-work I ever went through. I had occasionally before taken up some of his other works, but scarcely ever had patience to go through a whole dialogue. while wading thro' the whimsies, the puerilities, & unintelligible jargon of this work, I laid it down often to ask myself how it could have been that the world should have so long consented to give reputation to such nonsense as this? how the soi-disant Christian world indeed should have done it, is a piece of historical curiosity. but how could the Roman good sense do it? and particularly how could Cicero bestow such eulogies on Plato? altho' Cicero did not wield the dense logic of Demosthenes, yet he was able, learned, laborious, practised in the business of the world, & honest. he could not be the dupe of mere style, of which he was himself the first master in the world. with the moderns, I think, it is rather a matter of fashion and authority. education is chiefly in the hands of persons who, from their profession, have an interest in the reputation and the dreams of Plato. they give the tone while at school, and few, in their after-years, have occasion to revise their college opinions. but fashion and authority apart, and bringing Plato to the test of reason, take from him his sophisms, futilities, & incomprehensibilities, and what remains? in truth he is one of the race of genuine Sophists, who has escaped the oblivion of his brethren, first by the elegance of his diction, but chiefly by the adoption & incorporation of his whimsies into the body of artificial Christianity. his foggy mind, is for ever presenting the semblances of objects which, half seen thro' a mist, can be defined neither in form or dimension. yet this which should have consigned him to early oblivion really procured him immortality of fame & reverence. the Christian priesthood, finding the doctrines of Christ levelled to every understanding, and too plain to need[3] explanation, saw, in the mysticisms of Plato, materials with which they might build up an artificial system which might, from it's indistinctness, admit everlasting controversy, give employment for their order, and introduce it to profit, power & pre-eminence. the doctrines which flowed from the lips of Jesus himself are within the comprehension of a child; but thousands of volumes have not yet explained the Platonisms engrafted on them: and for this obvious reason that nonsense can never be explained. their purposes however are answered. Plato is canonised: and it is now deemed as impious to question his merits as those of an Apostle of Jesus. he is peculiarly appealed to as an advocate of the immortality of the soul; and yet I will venture to say that were there no better arguments than his in proof of it, not a man in the world would believe it. it is fortunate for us that Platonic republicanism has not obtained the same favor as Platonic Christianity; or we should now have been all living, men, women and children, pell mell together, like the beasts of the field or forest. yet 'Plato is a great Philosopher,' said La Fontaine. but says Fontenelle 'do you find his ideas very clear'?—'oh no! he is of an obscurity impenetrable.'—'do you not find him full of contradictions?'—'certainly, replied La Fontaine, he is but a Sophist.' yet immediately after, he exclaims again, 'oh Plato was a great philosopher.'—Socrates had reason indeed to complain of the misrepresentations of Plato; for in truth his dialogues are libels on Socrates.—but why am I dosing you with these Ante-diluvian topics? because I am glad to have some one to whom they are familiar, and who will not recieve them as if dropped from the moon. our post-revolutionary youth are born under happier stars than you and I were. they acquire all learning in their mothers' womb, and bring it into the world ready-made. the information of books is no longer necessary; and all knolege which is not innate, is in contempt, or neglect at least. every folly must run it's round; and so, I suppose, must that of self-learning, & self sufficiency; of rejecting the knolege acquired in past ages, and starting on the new ground of intuition. when sobered by experience I hope our successors will turn their attention to the advantages of education. I mean of education on the broad scale, and not that of the petty <u>academies</u>, as they call themselves, which are starting up in every neighborhood, and where one or two men, possessing Latin, & sometimes Greek, a knolege of the globes, and the first six books of Euclid, imagine & communicate this as the sum of science. they commit their pupils to the theatre of the world with just taste enough of learning to be alienated from industrious pursuits, and not enough to do service in the ranks of science. we have some exceptions indeed. I presented one to you lately, and we have some others. but the terms I use are general truths. I hope the necessity will at length be seen of establishing institutions, here as in Europe, where every branch of science, useful at this day, may be taught in it's highest degrees. have you ever turned your thoughts to the plan of such an institution? I mean to a specification of the particular sciences of real use in human affairs, and how they might be so grouped as to require so many professors only as might bring them within the views of a just but enlightened economy? I should be happy in a communication of your ideas on this problem, either loose or digested. but to avoid my being run away with by another subject, and adding to the length and ennui of the present letter, I will here present to mrs Adams & yourself the assurance of my constant & sincere friendship and respect.

TH: JEFFERSON

RC (MHi: Adams Papers); edge trimmed, with missing text supplied from PoC; addressed: "John Adams late President of the US. Quincy. Massachusets"; franked; postmarked Milton, 7 July; endorsed by Adams; docketed by Charles Francis Adams. PoC (DLC).

YOUR'S OF MAR. 14.: Adams to TJ, Feb.–3 Mar. 1814. The ATTILA OF THE AGE was Napoleon. LEON PIAGATO A MORTE . . . TAL VOLTA IL CACCIATOR: "The dying lion fiercely looks at his wounds, and roars and threatens in his last breath, so as to make his pursuer tremble," quoting from act 2, scene 2 of Pietro Metastasio, *Adriano in Siria* (London, 1765; Italian, with English translation on facing pages), 24, 25. TJ owned a copy of Metastasio's *Poesie*, 12 vols. (Paris, 1755–83; Sowerby, no. 4560). CINQ CENS (cents): "five hundred." On 18. BRUMAIRE in year 8 (9 Nov. 1799) Napoleon began the coup d'état that ultimately made him sole ruler of France.

Speculations that Great Britain might demand the cession of the rights of the United States to FISHERIES in Canadian waters were based on reports from British publications. Although these rights, which had been guaranteed by Article 3 of the 1783 Treaty of Paris, were discussed during peace negotiations, the commissioners included nothing on that subject in the final Treaty of Ghent ending the War of 1812 (Richmond *Enquirer*, 23 Apr., 4 June 1814; Hunter Miller, ed., *Treaties and other International Acts Of The United States Of America* [1931–48], 2:98; Malcomson, *Historical Dictionary*, 211–4).

NON TALI AUXILIO, NEC DEFENSORIBUS ISTIS TEMPUS EGET: "the hour calls not for such aid or such defenders," in Virgil, *Aeneid*, 2.521 (Fairclough, *Virgil*, 1:350–1). The dialogue between Jean de La Fontaine and Bernard le Bovier de Fontenelle discussing whether PLATO IS A GREAT PHILOSOPHER is recounted by Claude Adrien Helvétius in *Œuvres Complettes de M. Helvétius. Nouvelle Édition, corrigée & augmentée sur les Manuscrits de l'Auteur, avec sa Vie & son Portrait* (London, 1781; Sowerby, no. 1242), 72.

[1] Preceding three words interlined.
[2] Reworked from "as an American citizen."
[3] TJ here canceled "understanding."

# From John Barnes

Dear Sir                  George Town Co<sup>a</sup> 7<sup>th</sup> July 1814.

Your fav<sup>r</sup> 28<sup>h</sup> Ult<sup>o</sup> now before me—Acknowledge my several letters, up to 22<sup>d</sup>—my last was of 27<sup>h</sup> June Announc<sup>g</sup> my dispatch, to Baring Brothers & C<sup>o</sup> Covering £400. Sterling—together with my letter to the good Gen<sup>l</sup> Kosciusko—delivered in Care of M<sup>r</sup> Monro—already—on its passage to Europe—of course your letters to those Gent<sup>s</sup> will be reserved to go by the next favorable Opertunity with my Seconds—or Duplicates—to enable you to judge of my late proceedings (all circumstances taken into view) I persuade my self—will be found satisfactory—

some few Arrangem<sup>ts</sup> were necessary, previous to my departure for Philad<sup>a</sup> viz to discount my Note for $1480—to inable me to make my first paym<sup>t</sup> of $2500. on Subscrib<sup>s</sup> to the New Loan for $10,000—as well to guard against unforeseen Accidents—in my Absense, in my Sale & Returns, &c<sup>a</sup> &<sup>a</sup>—An Absense of ten Years from Philad<sup>a</sup> unused to fatigue in traveling—late and Early with irregular living—ill suited to my increasing infirmities a 84—but, I had already taken upon me the Responsibility of the Trust, reposed in me, And <u>Nothing Short</u>—of a total inability, could prevent me from Attempting the task Assign'd No friend—or Neighbour Offered to Accompany me, I judged it prudent, to take my Col<sup>d</sup> servant Charles to Attend me, in Case of Accident, this Necessaryly increased my Exp<sup>s</sup>—upon the whole; I weathered the threatend[1] storm, without any Material Accident—save, the excessive rains— Bad roads, and Nightly traveling—the favorable Occurances in the Sales of the Gen<sup>ls</sup> Bank Stock, you are Already Apprized of. it is only Necessary for me to add, that in the Course of these transact<sup>ns</sup> my present a/c—with the Gen<sup>l</sup> will close, with my late remittance Appearant Bal<sup>c</sup> $756$\frac{88}{100}$ of w<sup>ch</sup> I transmitted a statem<sup>t</sup>—will be carried to his Credit in New Acco<sup>t</sup>—of Sale & proceeds of his Bank Stock—and said Acco<sup>t</sup> Debited To paym<sup>ts</sup> made,—and to be made, on the Loan—After deduct<sup>g</sup>

1 ℔Ct—will I presume—leave him a Net Bal<sup>c</sup> of      $802–
which together with his former Bal<sup>c</sup> of         755. 88.
           a total Balance (nearly Correct, of   $1557– 88.

And thereby inable you, to make him a further Remittance on Receipt of your late one of $1644.44.—The growing Int. on the New Loan will not I presume—for some M<sup>os</sup> to come, be in Operation— My Calculations on the $10,000 Subscribed say 88 for $100 stock, will produce 113$\frac{56}{88}$ Shares of $100 each Ann<sup>y</sup> $11.300$\frac{63}{100}$ stock a 6

℔$C^t$ is $678$$\frac{9}{100}$ Annualy or $169$$\frac{53}{100}$ $q^{rly}$ together with your $360 Annu$^y$ Constitutes—the whole of the Gen$^{ls}$ funds here. it may be proper for me, to Observe—that my Usual remittance—was $1000 ℔ Ann$^{m2}$ his Acc$^t$ still encreasing—my last in 1812—was for $1100— the pres$^t$ for 2 y$^{rs}$ $1644—before the close of the year—will leave him a Clear Bal$^c$ as stated—of $1557—in Reserve for your Next Re- mittance—the growing Int on the Loan for 12 M$^{os}$ to come will not exceed $640 Net, which together with your $360—will nearly Com- pleat the $1000—as Usual—to leave your Bank bare—in making an Additional purchase of $1000—at this present time—might in Case of unforeseen misfortune—a total miscarriage—of the late Remit- tance &$^c$ &c$^a$ might be Attended with disagreable Consequences—

for although the Gen$^{ls}$ Capital Stock, by these late transfers is in- creased—from $8,000 to $11,300—his pres$^t$ Am$^t$ of Int. thereon is Reduced from $800—to $676—a deficiency of $128—

By these statm$^{ts}$ & Calculations—you will judge of their Correct- ness—and propriety—and if in your Judgem$^t$ they are found in any wise deficient—or incorrect—you will have the goodness—to point out (if any) my Unintenteal Errors & omiss$^{ns}$—

with great Esteem & Respects I am Dear Sir Yr mst Obed$^t$

JOHN BARNES,

PS. for my narretive of traveling incidents & occurances during my short stay in Philad$^a$ I beg leave to defer for a Seperate letter—at my better leisure

RC (ViU: TJP-ER); adjacent to signa- ture: "Thomas Jefferson Esq$^r$ Monticel- lo"; endorsed by TJ as received 15 July 1814 and so recorded in SJL.

[1] Preceding two words interlined.
[2] Manuscript: "Ann$^n$."

# From Patrick Gibson

SIR        Richmond 7$^{th}$ July 1814

I am favor'd with your two letters, of the 22$^d$ ult$^o$ from Poplar For- est, and of the 1$^{st}$ Ins$^t$ from Monticello upon receipt of the former I endeavour'd to make sale of your flour at 4$ but could not succeed— I am not certain that I could obtain even $3$\frac{1}{2}$ but think it probable, in the event of my not receiving instructions from you to the contrary I shall dispose of it for what it will bring—I remitted M$^r$ A Robertson $240 as you directed and now inclose your $175. as requested in your last—      with great respect I am

Your ob$^t$ Serv$^t$        PATRICK GIBSON

RC (MHi); between dateline and salutation: "Thomas Jefferson Esq^re"; endorsed by TJ as received 8 July 1814 and so recorded in SJL.

TJ's missing letter of the 1^ST INS^T to Gibson & Jefferson is recorded in SJL.

# To Louis H. Girardin

DEAR SIR          Monticello July 7. 14.

I send you by the bearer the parallel ruler you desired and return the catalogue you were so kind as to leave with me. I find on it the following books which I shall be glad to purchase whenever you decide on the disposing of your library. to wit. Tertullianus 1.v. 16° Charron. Virey. Thornton's family Herbal. Modern Gr. & Ital. dictionary. Conciones ex Histor. Lat. excerptae & Clarke's exercises. there are some others I may wish to examine & consider of hereafter. with respect to the following you can inform me verbally when I shall have the pleasure of seeing you next, to wit

Bezout. is stated at 5. vol^s does it want a vol. because there should be 6.

Hutcheson's Mor. Phil. stated as 1. vol. is it compleat? it is usually in 2. vol^s

Simpson's Mathem. problems. is this what is called his Select exercises for young proficients in Mathematics?

Accept the assurance of my great esteem and respect.

TH: JEFFERSON

RC (PPAmP: Thomas Jefferson Papers); at foot of text: "M^r Girardin."

Girardin probably requested the PARALLEL RULER and enclosed the CATALOGUE in a letter to TJ of 7 July 1814, not found, but recorded in SJL as received from Glenmore on the day it was written. The works in question include Quintus Septimus Florens TERTULLIANUS, *Apologeticus et ad Scapulam Liber* (Cambridge, 1686; Sowerby, no. 1587); Pierre CHARRON, *De La Sagesse* (Bordeaux, 1601; for English eds. acquired by TJ see Sowerby, nos. 1616–7; for French eds. see Poor, *Jefferson's Library*, 9 [nos. 462–3]); Julien Joseph VIREY, *Histoire Naturelle Du Genre Humain*, 2 vols. (Paris, 1801; Sowerby, no. 1051); Robert John THORNTON's *A New Family Herbal: or Popular Account of the Natures and Properties of the various Plants used in*

*Medicine, Diet, and the Arts* (London, 1810); Joachim Périon and Henri Estienne, eds., CONCIONES *et Orationes ex Historicis Latinis Excerptæ . . . in usum Scholarum Hollandiæ & West-Frisiæ* (Oxford, 1667; Sowerby, no. 4670); John CLARKE's *A New Grammar of the Latin Tongue, Comprising All in the Art necessary for Grammar-Schools* (London, 1754; Sowerby, no. 4785); Étienne BEZOUT, *Cours De Mathématiques, A L'Usage Des Gardes Du Pavillion Et De La Marine* (Paris, 1781; Sowerby, no. 3680); Francis HUTCHESON's *A Short Introduction To Moral Philosophy In Three Books; containing the Elements of Ethicks and the Law of Nature* (Glasgow, 1747; Poor, *Jefferson's Library*, 9 [no. 460]); and Thomas SIMPSON's *Select Exercises for Young Proficients in the Mathematicks* (London, 1752; Poor, *Jefferson's Library*, 8 [no. 398]).

# From Thomas Lehré

DEAR SIR,                                        Charleston July 7th 1814

By this days mail, I have Sent you three news papers of this City, by which you will See from the Toasts drank on the 4th Inst, we still Continue to hold in grateful remembrance, the very great Services you have rendered your Country.

Our Political Horizon; at present seems to wear a gloomy aspect, however, as long as we remain true to ourselves, and will support our Government & Country; with firmness, we have, in my humble opinion, nothing to fear,—our Republic will yet triumph over all it's enemies. Repeated enquiries are made of me by your old Friends, from different parts of this State, they Seem extremely desirious to know if you enjoy good health, & have a prospect of a long life; it will afford us great pleasure if you would drop me a line on the Subject, & if it would not be intruding too much on your time, to give at the Same time your opinion on our foreign relations

I remain with the highest consideration D[r] Sir Your Obed[t] Serv[t]

THOMAS LEHRÉ

RC (DLC); endorsed by TJ as received 18 July 1814 and so recorded in SJL.

The Charleston *City Gazette and Commercial Daily Advertiser* of 8 July 1814 printed the Seventy-Six Association's 4

July 1814 TOASTS, which included one to "*Thomas Jefferson*—He has lived to see the love and admiration of his Countrymen increase after the splendor of station has vanished, and the influence of power ceased."

# To Patrick Gibson, with Note on Corn Contracts

DEAR SIR                                        Monticello July 8. 14.

Altho' I have not heard yet of the actual sale of my flour, yet in the hope it has taken place, and urged by some of my corn contracts, I have been obliged to draw on you this day in favor of W[m] Steevens or order for 105.D. which will probably be presented to you with this advice. Accept the assurance of my esteem & respect.

TH: JEFFERSON

July. 9. the draught for 105. was taken in & one given for 70.D. payable to Jos. Bishop[1] there are still 20.D. due.

PoC (Mr. W. B. Jefferson, San Francisco, 1946); beneath signature: "M[r] Gibson"; endorsed by TJ as a letter to Gibson & Jefferson and so recorded in SJL.

TJ's memorandum books contain a deleted record for 8 July 1814 of having drawn on Gibson & Jefferson for the transaction described above, to pay for "35. barr." CORN. The following day TJ repeated the information in his subjoined note, indicating that he had revised the original agreement and that the $20 still due to Stevens was for "30. bar. corn"

(*MB*, 2:1301). The absence of an additional message to Gibson may suggest that Bishop was to present the letter above to the firm in person, with the note TJ added to the PoC possibly describing his revision to the missing RC.

[1] Manuscript: "given for 70.D. payable to Jos. Bishop given."

# From James W. Wallace

DEAR SIR                                    Fauquier July 8th
   The Gentleman who was to have deliver'd Mrs Mason's bundle at Charlottsville, has declined his Journey—Mrs Wallace in my absence sent a boy to Monticello with it, the boy was taken sick & returned, leaving the bundle at Major Claytons Culpeper CHouse—I have sent the Saw of a fish, which I hope will be acceptable.
   My best wishes to the Monticello family Mrs & Mr Bankhead
   God bless You sir                        JAMES W. WALLACE

RC (DLC: TJ Papers, 201:35825); partially dated; endorsed by TJ as received 25 July 1814 and so recorded in SJL.

# From Hugh Holmes

DEAR SIR                                    Winchr July 10th 1814
   Yesterday your Cloth was received from the Factory and is this day forwarded to the care of Judge Stuart of Staunton—some who have examined it, think that the finishing is equal to any american Manufacture and but little inferior to that of the English—I confess that I am disappointed, it does not feel soft enough to my touch; which may probably arise from being too often shorn—it was first dyed a blue; but not succeeding in his expectation the Manufacturer changed it to a black—the workmen say that broad Cloths such as yours will require 2 ℔ of Merino wool (washed) to the yard—if so the 10 yds now sent have consumed the 39 lb of unwashed wool
   I have not reced the bill of charges but from some hints dropped I presume it will cost more than our estimate—he sells such Cloth as yours at $10—when I Shall have the pleasure of seeing you at Monticello in September we can arrange the expences—
   Your friend & sevt                        HH HOLMES

RC (MHi); at foot of text: "The honble Tho⁸ Jefferson Esqʳ"; endorsed by TJ as received 16 July 1814 and so recorded in SJL.

The MANUFACTURER was Cyrus B. Baldwin.

# To Jeremiah A. Goodman

DEAR SIR:                                   MONTICELLO, July 11, '14

I duly received your letter by Mr. Chisholm. The difficulty of the saw mills in sawing longer stocks than their saw-frame has never been regarded here. We take out the head block which holds the slab end of the stock; let the stock shoot back beyond that as far as it will go, and leave the slab end to be sawed by hand, for a stock of 24 f in a mill of 21 f. there would remain 3 f. of every plank to be cut by hand.—There is some trouble in taking out the head-block: but this would be well paid in allowing for the whole stock as if sawed to the whole length. It requires too a double set of dogs, if this should be a difficulty let Will make the extra dogs for me to be lent to the mill, unless they should be willing to keep them in part payment for the plank. If the stocks would be too heavy after they were sawed for your teams to bring home, split them into halves, or otherwise to suit the strength of your team, leaving as many planks together as you can haul. We must get Mr. Adkinson to have the slab ends sawed out. This matter is so important to the preservation of the work we have done that I hope you will get over all difficulties and have it accomplished.[1] We have a poor crop of wheat here, occasioned by the rust. I am sorry to learn yours are the same. Our oats are fine. Send Will's wagon off so as to be here in a fortnight from this time. Accept my best wishes.                           TH: JEFFERSON.

Printed in the *Gordonsville Gazette*, 18 Dec. 1873; at head of text, in part: "The following original letter from MR JEFFERSON was handed us by Mr. Chas. G. Goodman of Louisa, who has some fifty of his letters in his possession, all pertaining to business matters."

Goodman's LETTER of 2 July 1814, not found, is recorded in SJL as received from Poplar Forest on 5 July 1814.

[1] *Gordonsville Gazette*: "accompllshed."

# From Thomas C. Flournoy

S IR .                                                 Georgetown, Ky. 12<sup>th</sup> July, 1814.

I take the liberty of sending you the draught of a speech, which I had the honour of delivering in Frankfort on the 4<sup>th</sup> instant. It is not because I am very much taken with my performance, but purely out of regard for the man I send it to. I have nothing better to offer, for your amusement.

I should be much pleased to know your opinion, as to the consequences that will result to the U. States, from the changes that are taking place in Europe; and particularly in France.

THOMAS C. FLOURNOY.

RC (DLC); on verso of enclosure, with address written perpendicularly beneath it; addressed: "Thomas Jefferson esq. Monticello, Va." by "Mail"; franked; postmarked Georgetown, 14 July; endorsed by TJ as received 29 July 1814 and so recorded in SJL.

ENCLOSURE

## Thomas C. Flournoy's Fourth of July Speech

[4 July 1814]

Speech.

Citizens of Frankfort.

We have met here to day, for the purpose of celebrating the 4<sup>th</sup> of July. This is a duty which Kentuckians perform, with the greatest pleasure. They know that the noblest emotions of the human heart may languish and decay, through mere inattention, and thoughtlessness: And they are determined to omit nothing, that may establish, and perpetuate in their minds, the sacred love of liberty. This I imagine, is the chief, if not the only good, that can arise from meetings of this kind, they cherish in our memory, the holy love of <u>free-dom</u>, the fairest gift of Heaven to man. After the lapse of thirty eight years; after the hundreds and thousands, of 4<sup>th</sup> of July speeches, delivered in the United States, since the year 1776, it might justly be considered as presumption, to attempt to throw new light, upon this <u>exhausted subject</u>. All that any man can do, at this late period, is to remark upon facts that have occurred, since the declaration of independence: And all that I can promise you at this time, is a feeble effort to prove two things, 1<sup>st</sup> That England <u>ought not</u>; and 2<sup>nd</sup> <u>cannot</u> succeed, in the present war against the U. States.

When I say that England ought not to succeed, I mean to convey an idea, that justice is on our side. In order to prove this, it will be necessary to look back for a moment, on the relations that subsisted between the U. States, England, & France, immediately before the declaration of war. In this view, the first thing that strikes our attention, is the blockade of France, published by England in May 1806. This blockade extended from the harbour of Brest, at the mouth of the British channel, on the Atlantic side, even to the Elbe.

This aggression on the part of England, this throwing the gauntlet, so highly injurious to the rights of neutral nations, has been defended on no other ground than this; that it was a fair, and legitimate blockade, and intended to be carried into full operation in all its parts—weak, & pitiful subterfuge: It is not contended, that any conduct of France had justified this measure; but only that England had taken it into her head, that she could effect the blockade of this very extensive coast, and that she had the <u>right</u> to do it, because she <u>could</u> do it. This blockade was calculated entirely to prohibit the ingress, and egress, of all French ships, through the whole coast to which it extended, and also to preclude effectually, the entrance of merchant-ships, from every neutral state, or nation in the world.

This gave rise to the Berlin, and Milan decrees, in the beginning of 1807, which go to invest England with a blockade. I look upon it as an act of justice, which the French nation owed to itself, to have adopted the Berlin & Milan decrees, or similar retaliatory measures. It was only saying to England, if you will not allow the U. States, and other neutral nations to trade with us, we will endeavour to hinder you from reaping the benefits of their commerce. The Berlin & Milan decrees furnished a <u>pretence</u> for England to issue her orders in council, of November 1807. These orders in council, prevented neutral ships, from trading with France, or her dependencies, unless they would consent to touch at some English port, and pay transit duties, on all the articles contained in said neutral ships: And as France in her Berlin & Milan decrees, had denied admittance to any neutral ships, that had passed through English ports; the U. States found herself necessitated, either to relinquish commerce altogether, or to adopt such measures of retaliation, as might seem calculated to restore to herself the privileges of trade. She preferred the latter; and with that view, the act of May the 1st 1810, was passed, called the nonintercourse. This law contained a provision, by which the President was authorized, to suspend its operation, as to Great Britain, upon the repeal of the orders in council: and as to France, upon an extinguishment of the Berlin & Milan decrees. The offer was made to both France, and England in the spirit of conciliation, and sincerity. France accepted the proposition. Accordingly, on the 5th of August following, the Duke de Cadore, the French minister, notified the U. States, that the Berlin & Milan decrees were revoked, and that they would cease to operate, on the 1st of November of the same year.

England had all along declared her willingness, to rescind the orders in council, whenever France should revoke her Berlin and Milan decrees: And now that France had done so, it was confidently expected by the U. States, that England would comply with her promise. But this she has refused to do, and by refusing she has given to the U. States, and to the world, the clearest, the most incontrovertible evidence of English deception, & insincerity, that ever one nation afforded to another, upon earth.

The excuses conjured up by the British, for this violation of honour, on the part of England, are too gross, and too contemptible, to be seriously refuted. They say that England had a right to wait, & see, whether the decrees of Bonaparte, were indeed repealed, in truth, & in <u>practice</u>. If she had a right to wait one day for that, she had a right to wait till the day of judgment. England had promised repeatedly, that whenever the Berlin & Milan decrees were revoked, that the repeal of the orders in council, should follow immediately. Now what better proof of the revocation of these decrees, could England require, than the official notification of the French minister, that they were revoked. This notification was given to England, on the 5th of August 1810; and yet, contrary to every principle of national truth, and national honour, the British orders in council, were not repealed, until eighteen months, or two years afterwards. But why spend time upon this part of my subject? It were as absurd, as to enter into all the depths, & mazes of rhetoric, to show that a certain man had committed a few trivial faults, when it could be proved that he had murdered his father. Admit the charge, of insincerity & deception, to be as true as demonstration, and it is equally so; Yet even this were a virtue compared to the enormity of England's crimes.

We will now consider the right of <u>impressment</u>, claimed & exercised by England. This memorable controversy, about the right of search and of impressment, has undergone so many changes, that at present, it will require some nicety to explain, or even to understand it.

At one time, it would seem, that England claimed the right of impressing <u>neutral seamen</u>, from on board of <u>neutral ships</u>. Her impressment of our seamen, will justify this presumption.

At another time, the Prince regent comes forward, and tells us, in his official declaration, that "The impressment of British seamen, found on board of neutral merchant-ships, is no violation of a neutral flag." This he asserts in direct contradiction to the law of nations: For Vattel lays it down expressly, that one belligerent nation, has no right under heaven, forcibly to enter a neutral ship, but for the purpose alone of ascertaining, whether it contain any troops, or military stores, to be used in the service of the other belligerent; and if any be found, to seize upon them. If then the citizens of a belligerent nation, can only enter the ships of a neutral state, for the purpose above mentioned; it results of course, that they have no right to enter, them for the purpose of taking out their own seamen, who may have deserted. The seas are defined to be the common highway of nations: And ships do certainly carry with them the rights of sovereignty, appertaining to the state to which they belong. How then can it be contended, that British officers had a right to enter our <u>ships</u>, and take out British seamen, when it is acknowledged on all hands, that no nation has a right to enter the <u>territory</u> of a neutral state, to exercise any authority whatever; much less that of seizing men, and carrying them away by force.

And lastly, some of the British writers, acknowledge they have not the right of entering neutral ships, in order to impress British seamen: but they contend for the right of entering neutral, in search of articles contraband of war, and that when they are once there, they may then impress British seamen—Gross absurdity: You must not enter your neighbours house, with the express design to kill him; no but you may walk in to shake hands with him; and when you are in the house, it will then be lawful to commit any unlawful act you please; even the murder of your friend.

In every step which the U. States has taken towards the declaration of war, the justice of her cause is conspicuous. War was declared, after the maturest deliberation, and a clear conviction, that any longer forbearance would be disgraceful to the U. States. If there had been no other ground of difference between us & England than the impressment of our seamen, that alone was ample cause of war. This evil of impressment bears lighter on Kentucky, than on any other state in the union. Not one of us perhaps who are here to day has a blood relation, that he knows to be impressed in the British service: But shall we on this account, forget the relation we bear to these unfortunate men, as citizens of the same free government with ourselves? Men equally entitled to all the rights that belong to freemen—to Americans.

It has been the practice of the British, for a number of years past, to seize upon American seamen, wherever they could find them, and to force them, ignominiously to force them on board their ships of war, there to remain, not for a voyage of six or eight months only, but for life. And for the purpose too of fighting the battles of a despot, George the third, in opposition to their own beloved countrymen. It is a melancholy truth that upwards of six thousand, free-born Americans, are at this very time, confined in the British service, manacled, & scourged, in the support of a venal ministry whom we & they despise, with all the bitterness of our souls. It is a fact which the British themselves do not deny. It is one which they admit in express terms. Captain Dacres says, in his official letter to Admiral Sawyer, that he would not have surrendered the Guerriere, to Captain Hull only he had a great many Americans on board, who did not fight bravely. After this plain statement of facts; after the ackno[w]ledgment of the British themselves, that they do inslave our citizens, no man who is a Kentuckian indeed, & in truth, will preten[d] to take the part of England in the slightest degree, in opposition to his own country. It is evident that a man who sides with England under these circumstances, must be the most contemptible sheep in nature. He must be either a fool or a tory. For if he disbelieve the fact of the impressment, after it has been acknowledged, he must be the biggest of all fools. And if he believe the impressment, & yet oppose the war his country is engaged in, he is a despicable tory, and deserves to be treated as a slave. But I am happy in believing, that there are none such. I have already said more upon this division of my subject, than I at first designed to say. It is a subject upon which I could not at once, check the impulse of my feelings: And I have gone on to say more than was necessary, either to prove the justness of our cause, or to show, that England ought not to succeed in the present war against the U. States.

We will now proceed to examine the second division of our text, which is, that England cannot succeed in the present war against the U. States. In remarking upon this head, I promise to consume as little time as possible. Fortunately it is not [n]ecessary here to enter into a lengthy detail of diplomatic shuffling, & maneuvering, between the U. States, & England, or between any [ot]her states, or nations in the world. All we have to do is to attend to a few plain, simple facts. Theories may sometimes be true, but [facts?] can never be otherwise. In the first place then, we may recollect the war, that has already taken place between the U. States, and England; and the particular circumstances of that war. At the commencement of the American revolution, the population of the U. States, amounted to about three million; while that of Great Britain, was more than three times as numerous. At that period England was at peace with all the world, and comparatively free from debt: at this time she is at war with nearly all Europe, & with the U. States in the bargain, and her national debt amounts to the enormous sum of seven hundred million of pounds sterling—a sum that never was coined, & perhaps never will be. If we look farther into the relative condition of the U. States, &

England, we find the contrast equally disparaging to the latter. Forty years ago, England was not able to enforce the payment of oppressive taxes in the U. States. Since that time she has[1] been constantly losing strength, while we have been gaining it. How vain then, & how ridiculous, must be all British efforts now, to enforce a system of impressment, still more odious. I naturally conclude, that a man cannot now perform a certain job, which he was too weak to do, when he was ten times as strong as he is at present. From the view which we have taken of this subject, and from every other view which can be taken, it is most evident that England cannot succeed in the present war against the U. States.

In forming this conclusion, we reason only from probability, and the nature of things. Without pretending to prophesy, I am bold to affirm, that the U. States, in point of physical force, has nothing to fear from all the powers of Great Britain put together. The dethronement of Bonaparte or any other event that could take place in Europe, has nothing to do with our independence. We are fighting for our inalienable rights: And I trust, they will never be given up, while we have a man left to defend them. United we may safely set the world at defiance. But from faction, and discord, we shall have the sad choice of a variety of evils. What power so great that may not be weakened by division? For Heaven's sake, let us never differ among ourselves. I had rather fight all the world beside, than fight the smallest state in the union. One or two observations more, & I shall have done.

I have witnessed with extreme regret, the spirit of opposition, that has been shown to persons, who are denominated federalists. I do not pretend to know the exact points of difference between the two parties—federalists & republicans. But I have always considered the dispute, as a most unfortunate affair. M^r Jefferson had a view, no doubt, to the suppression of this fuss about nothing, when he says "We are all republicans, we are all federalists." For my part I never cared one cent, what ideas any man entertained upon the subject of administration, or expediency in politics. If I believed him to be a sincere friend, to the genuine interests of the U. States, & to the federal constitution, I was satisfied with him, by whatever name you may please to call him. If on the other hand, his conduct shows him to be the enemy of his country, and of the constitution, not even the blessed name of republican itself, could shelter him from my detestation & contempt.

I know men in Kentucky who are called federalists, whose exertions in defence of liberty, or the constitution, would not [be] surpassed by those of any other person in the U. States: And whose intelligence is equal to their patriotism. I do hope sin[ce]rely, that all distinctions, as to republicans, and federalists, will cease in the U. States: And that we may henceforward [k]now each other only as whigs or tories—friends or enemies to the constitution. And I do hope, with all the devotion [o]f a christian, that whenever the U. States shall cease to be a free & independent nation; whenever our liberties are gone, that I for one may cease to exist upon earth.

THOMAS C. FLOURNOY.

MS (DLC: TJ Papers, 201:35827–8); entirely in Flournoy's hand; undated; edge chipped; with RC of covering letter on verso of final page.

The ACT OF MAY THE 1ST 1810 was Macon's Bill No. 2. Flournoy paraphrased a declaration of the British PRINCE REGENT dated at Westminster, 9 Jan.

1813 (*European Magazine, and London Review* 63 [Jan./June 1813], 55). Captain James R. DACRES wrote to Vice ADMIRAL Herbert Sawyer from Boston on 7 Sept. 1812 describing the capture of HMS *Guerriere* by the American frigate *Constitution*. During Dacres's subsequent court-martial, he stated that he had weakened his defenses by "permitting the *Americans* belonging to the ship to quit their quarters on the enemy hoisting the colors of that nation, which, though it deprived me of the men, I thought it was my duty" (Providence *Rhode-Island American, And General Advertiser*, 15 Dec. 1812; *Otsego Republican Press*, 12 Feb. 1813). TJ stated in his first inaugural address that WE ARE ALL REPUBLICANS, WE ARE ALL FEDERALISTS (*PTJ*, 33:149).

[1] Manuscript: "have."

# From Thomas Law

DEAR SIR—                                    Philadelphia July 12. 1814.

I was highly gratified by your favor of the 13th Ult[o] from Poplar Grove. Laudari a laudato is a real satisfaction—your observations comprise in a small compass all that has been written on the important subject: the remark that selfishness is the impulse of the individual & that moral feelings are excited by another or more, simplifies all that I have endeavored to prove—few have read my Pamphlet & of the few, I fear that one or two bigots under prejudices have deem'd it to contain irreligious doctrines—I met the other day with a novel of Holcrofts "Bryan Perdue" in which there is an excellent short Sermon on Truth, in which the preacher says "matters of fact alone meaning thereby those things which are common & subject to the examination of the senses, are the only things that can be called truths, as known to man—Concerning higher truths, which doubtless are, but which it is impossible that he should know what they are, if he saith that he hath knowledge thereof, he doth utterly shame himself, for he speaketh that which is wickedly false. Yea this falsehood, has in it the root & wickedness of hell, for it hath at all times & among all nations, engendered the worst passions,[1] hatred revenge,[2] yea, & it spreadeth fire sword & universal destruction. &c[a]" You recommend Lord Kaimes, I have taken a very pointed extract from him in my first Essay, to illustrate my position—Bonapartes fate I predicted in my lines "But soon the pigmys hurl'd &c[a]"[3] in my note explanatory of a verse in the Chapter on politicks or rather on the Constitution of the U.S—Robespierre & Bonaparte are the Scylla & Charybdis for Jacobinic & Despotic power to avoid—both of them governed by fear—affection gratitude & all the feelings which attach the multitude to a ruler were despised or not heeded—Thank Heaven all this slaughter & devastation has not been in vain. The Spaniards & the

French have benefited; the Potentates of Europe have received awful lessons, & different nations have become better acquainted with each other—My own Country alas, is the only one which will not benefit— Russia has obtained too much territory, my countrymen will become jealous—The intercourse with Asia will be opened by Cabul Cashmere &c[a]—from the Caspias Sea—at Lahore the Seiks are all Deists & have made many proselytes amongst the Hindoos—the perturbed spirits of Europe now unoccupied will carry new lights Easterly & set fire to combustible materials, sixty million can only be kept in subjection by 20,000 during ignorance. During the last short peace with France, the British spent more than 12 M$^n$ st$^g$ abroad—cheapness of living, the loco motive spirit, & the gratification of curiosity caused so much emigration—I perceive that already 10,000 passports have been given—the taxes press so heavy on all classes, & such a field is opened abroad for men of genius & industry, that not only income is spent abroad but much of the capital transferred—

This Gov$^t$ has been embarrassed for want of a good financial System, I have one which would have saved millions & which would have kept the 6 ℔C$^{ts}$ about par, but I did not perceive a disposition to receive it as I wished—it is my <u>opus maximum</u>—if I did not feel an aversion to intrude, I would avail myself of your former polite invitation [...] it to your perusal at Monticello—[...] Octo$^r$ Finance call'd by M$^r$ C. Ingersoll the [m]odern Elusinian mistery would appear an A.B.C study when the principles were seen—My memorial on the records of Congress two Years ago for a national bank to discount at 5 ℔C$^t$ unfolds some of the advantages of low interest—

I am going to the Yellow Springs. with much esteem regard & respect

I remain           T LAW—

RC (DLC); torn at seal; addressed: "To Thomas Jefferson Esq$^r$ Monticello Virginia"; franked; postmarked Philadelphia, 13 July; endorsed by TJ as received 25 July 1814 and so recorded in SJL.

LAUDARI A LAUDATO: "to be praised by a man who has himself been praised" (Cicero, *Epistolae ad familiares*, 5.12, in his *Letters to Friends*, ed. and trans. David R. Shackleton Bailey, Loeb Classical Library [2001], 164). Law quoted from the SHORT SERMON in Thomas Holcroft's *Memoirs of Bryan Perdue: A Novel* (London, 1805; repr. 1979), 1:85–6.

Law's *Thoughts on Instinctive Impulses* (Philadelphia, 1810; Sowerby, no. 3250), 12, 18, 34–5, quoted Henry Home, Lord Kames (KAIMES). Law predicted BONAPARTES FATE in his *Second Thoughts on Instinctive Impulses* (Philadelphia, 1813), 101: "But soon his dream dissolv'd, the pigmy's hurl'd / To shame and hate, a warning to the world."

By MY OWN COUNTRY Law meant his native Great Britain. In a 15 Feb. 1814 speech to the United States House of Representatives, Congressman Charles J. INGERSOLL observed that "finance is still a political secret. It is the modern

Eleusinian mystery of politics" (*Annals*, 13th Cong., 2d sess., 1427–8). For Law's MEMORIAL ON THE RECORDS OF CONGRESS, see Law to TJ, 1 Oct. 1813, and note.

[1] *Memoirs of Bryan Perdue* here adds "of the soul."

[2] *Memoirs of Bryan Perdue* here adds "the ignorance that confusion createth."

[3] Omitted closing quotation mark editorially supplied.

# From John Barnes

DEAR SIR                                        George Town Coᵃ [ca. 13] July 1814.

My friend Mʳ S. had Notice from Mʳ Taylor my being in Town— and inquired where I lodged—he gave him the Nᵒ 96. 3ᵈ Sᵗ Sᵒ opposit Sᵗ Pauls Church—I purposᵈ waiting Upon him—on Compleating my business—but he exceeded me in politeness, by calling on me the Next day—expressed the pleasure he felt, at seeing me look so well &cᵃ &cᵃ—and withal begg'ed I would call on him at Mʳˢ Bensons in Chesnut Street—without flattering him—I could with great propriety and did—return him the like Complimᵗ for be Assured his Countenance and person Appeared to me more Corpulant and ruddy—his Health and Viversity seemed perfectly at ease, with his growing wealth, for that also—is rapidly increasing—a stranger might reasonbly have guessed his age to be nearly forty—tho in reality he is—I verely believe verging on Sixty—the fashionable Curly Wig, both in front and rear—has a most powerfull effect I Assure you—on the Advanced Beau—Bachelor—Mʳ T. had previously informed me Mʳ S. had a year or two since—made a purchase[1] of a House Cost him $10,000—and furnished it, in Eligant Stile, that he Also solicited LᵉMaire to superintend it—which you may readily suppose he politely declined—it struck me Instantly—the restless Arch Urchen—had been playing off his Accustomed Gambols, upon our unsuspecting friend, and that, the Cruel rebut, of the unknown fair—rather than the refusal of LᵉMaire—had changed the Scene of action—and of necessity forced him—to a silent retreat—is altogether Conjecture—not Material here to Account for,

but as effects will take their Natural course—from whatever Cause—they Originate—the guiltless House and spotless furniture— were both consigned to suffer Under the unrelenting Hammer of the Auctioneer—

still however Unfortunate and perplexing these distressing Occurences might prey upon the tender feelings—of a Young impetuous Lover—Our friend has had the Fortitude of the Stoic—the whirlwind of Fortune—has proved him Superior to the powers of the Obdurate fair,—amidst the Bustle and Croud of Speculators—in Stock and ground Lotts—he has found Consolatery—if not <u>content</u>—of the latter—in some few ground Lotts—M$^r$ T. informd me his purchase[1] a few Yrs since cost him $14,000—for which he was lately offered, but refused $28,000—by such turns of the wheel, he seems perfectly at Ease, in his running a/c as to profit & Loss—still I fear—he will be found Wanting in the Balance As to the real Comforts of Social—happiness—what then I ask save Honor, remains— but to Unite, Arm, and Meet the Ruthless foe, and however long painfull and destressing—the eventfull Struggle! I, trust, and doubt not, will terminate—with shame and disgrace on the Avengers head—whose tyranny extents over the four quarters of the Globe—

for my interview & observation on my friend M$^r$ S. I beg leave to refer you in a seperate address—here Annexed—

And am most Respectfully My Dear Sir—your most Obed$^t$

JOHN BARNES,

RC (ViU: TJP-ER); partially dated; at foot of text: "Thomas Jefferson Esq$^r$ Monticello." Endorsed by TJ on final page of accompanying letter as a single letter from Barnes dated 13 July 1814, received 15 July 1814, and so recorded in SJL.

MY FRIEND M$^R$ S.: William Short. The RESTLESS ARCH URCHEN was Cupid.

[1] Manuscript: "puchase."

# From John Barnes

MY DEAR SIR,                    George Town Co$^a$ 13$^{th}$ July 1814.

Previous to my leaving Town, I had formed the Resolution to desist from the Use of either Wine Spirits—or even Porter—of which I am most fond off, or, to Accept of any invitation to dine at, either of my former Acquaintances—while in Philad$^a$ where friendly Congratulations were indeed very gratefull to my feelings—some of them looked nearly as Usual—others tottering under the weight of their infirmities—the Young out grown—my Recollection—while some— Alas! lye mouldring—in the silent Grave—cast a damp on our former Associations not easily assuaged—

This <u>friendly City</u>—the Pride and Boast—of America—so much increased and improved in Superb Buildings—both Public & private— in Churches for the improvement of our Morals—Edifices for the Arts & sciences—for Industry—Amusement as well of Correction—a

sucession of New streets vieing with each other—in Magnificence—
together with the display—truly Eligant the Numberless Varigated
stores—presents to the Astonished stranger—a grandeur—almost
beyond describing—with all these flattering prospective Views, of
this inviting City—the Contras drawn from my Observations, ought
not,—must not, be concealed—Alas! when I contemplated—on the
Review—of the Majestic Delaware (the Spring of Enterprize) in all
her former greatness—bearing the Rich products of every distant
Clime—her Stately ships—stripped of their Costly Apparel—hiding
their drooping heads in Sackcloth—in Solemn silence, by the deserted wharfs—I could not—I confess, repell the sigh of Sorrow's
and with it, the recollection—of the Sturdy Sailor—and busy labourers—with their Noisy drays—whose Jocund Ribaldry—was wont to
contest—the Superiority of their <u>Dear</u> Country—in Stile and Manners—their jokes & songs alike beguiling each labourous task—is not
the least of Rural injoyments—

still—still, it is the effects of Commerce—(the Idol of the adven-
tious Merchant) that brings with it the intoxicating draught, of Luxury—extravagance and folly—Unnerves the sober Habits, of frugality
and Industry—but these, are not the only evils they produce—

G.B—Jealous of our Liberty prosperity & growing population a
spirit of envy and rancorus Enmity—waiting only—the eventfull
Moment, to wreck their fury—on our forbearing[1] patience—Aided
by their Merciless Savages,—we are indeed!—(as M$^r$ Adams Observed[2]) fallen—on Evil times—
in Conversing with him at his lodgings, I took the liberty of observing—how he could confine himself to the dirty City at this Blooming
Season—when the best Company—were collecting at the waters—
He was in want of a Steady coachman (I rather supposed—aside)
that the Coachman was in Want of a steady employer—for M$^r$ T. had
informed me, he could not keep—one for any length of time—

I do indeed!—most sincerely pity him—with all his wealth and superior Accomplishm$^t$ I flatter myself I am his superior—in Content
and Homely Happiness—still waveing his trivial foiables—which are
wholly to himself—he has many great & Amiable good Qualities
most Excelant Company—<u>lively</u>—<u>Witty</u> & <u>friendly</u>, He most Assuredly deprive himself of many Comforts.—Abstracted from family
Connections—he would otherwise partake of. Noticing every triffling
foiable of his servants which other Gent$^n$ pass over—unnoticed—yet
even in these Cases—it is but Momentary with him—
I very much Esteem the Gentleman but I cannot avoid Censuring—

nor forbear Criticising—on the Humour & deversities of so singular—a Character—and I pray you my D[r] Sir excuse me making the
remarks—which Accident alone has excited in me to portray[3]—to
you—without the slighest Shadow of disrespect to the object—they
are drawn from—and whom I much Esteem as a friend—to be passed
over with a smile at the adventures they produce,

    with great sincerity—I am always Sir Your Obed[t] serv[t]

JOHN BARNES,

RC (ViU: TJP-ER); at head of text: "Narrative Promised"; at foot of text: "Thomas Jefferson Esq[r] Monticello"; endorsed by TJ with preceding partially dated letter as a single 13 July 1814 letter from Barnes, received 15 July 1814, and so recorded in SJL.

G.B: Great Britain. M[R] T.: George Taylor. The GENTLEMAN was William Short.

[1] Manuscript: "forbering."
[2] Manuscript: "Oberved."
[3] Manuscript: "protray."

# From Patrick Gibson

SIR                     Richmond 13th July 1814

    I have endeavour'd to procure the nail rod mention'd in your favor
of the 2nd but am sorry to inform you, that there is not a bundle to be
obtaind in the City

    With great respect Your ob[t] Serv[t]         PATRICK GIBSON

PS:—I inclose your Acco[t] Cur[t] to the 1st Ins[t] balance due me $752.29

RC (ViU: TJP-ER); between dateline and salutation: "Thomas Jefferson Esq[re]"; endorsed by TJ as received 15 July 1814 and so recorded in SJL. Enclosure not found.

TJ's missing FAVOR OF THE 2ND to Gibson & Jefferson is recorded in SJL.

# From Destutt de Tracy

a paris ce [14] juillet 1814.

c'est toujours un grand bonheur pour moi, Monsieur, quand je reçois
une de vos lettres. celle dont vous m'avez honoré le 28. 9[bre] 1813 et
qui m'est arrivée le 5. May dernier m'a fait un bien Sensible plaisir en
m'aprenant que vous aviez reçu mon quatrieme volume qui traite de
l'economie politique, que vous l'aviez acceuilli avec la meme indulgence que le commentaire Sur Montesquieu, et que vous aviez eu
l'extreme bonté de vous occuper de le faire traduire. j'ai un bien vif

regret que cette traduction n'ait pas encor pu me parvenir, car je Suis
aussi fier que reconnoissant quand je vois mes idées exprimées dans
votre langue et par vos Soins. il me Semble alors qu'elles tiennent
quelque chose de vos pensées.

c'est Sans doute cette illusion qui a Seduit celui de mes compatri-
otes dont vous me parlez. je le connois et je respecte Ses lumieres autant que je cheris Ses vertus. mais il S'est laissé emporter par Son
imagination, qualité dont il est aussi trés abondamment pourvu, et
par Sa vivacité que l'age ne Sauroit diminuer; et moi, je l'avoue, je
n'ai pas eu le courage de le detromper, et je crains bien que ce ne Soit
autant par vanité que par discrétion, tant je Suis glorieux qu'on ait pu
me prendre pour vous.

mais ma vraye passion, Monsieur j'ose vous en assurer, c'est le
desir d'etre utile. vous comblez tous mes vœux en m'apprenant que le
commentaire Sur l'esprit des loix peut Servir aux habiles Professeurs
du college de votre etat. j'espere que pour ce qui regarde l'economie
ils employeront encor plus facilement mon quatrieme volume parce
qu'il est, ce me Semble, plus methodique. je n'ose vous parler des
trois premiers qui composent le traité de l'entendement. je Sais que
dans votre raisonable nation on met tout de Suitte Sa Sagesse en
action; et par consequent je pense que l'on doit faire peu de cas d'une
théorie Speculative qui n'offre pas l'avantage d'une application
immédiate. cependant comme enfin dans les ecoles il faut bien parler
de logique, et comme jusqu'a present il me paroit qu'on en a parlé
assez mal, faute d'etre remonté jusqu'a la maniere dont Se forment
les idées dans nos têtes et dont elles Se peignent dans nos langues, je
crois que Si ces premiers volumes etoient traduits on pourroit en
tirer parti.

je Sens neanmoins[1] que ce Sont les derniers qui Seroient plus
usuels. Si je puis terminer ceux qui doivent traiter de la Morale et
de la Legislation, je ne manquerai Surement pas de les mettre tout de
Suitte Sous votre protection, je ne Saurois assez vous remercier de
l'extreme bonté que vous avez eue d'y Songer d'avance. c'est pour moi
le plus puissant des encouragements.

Sous tous les rapports, Monsieur, vous etes mon ange tutélaire. je
vous ai des obligations infinies a l'autre extremité du monde, Sans
meme que vous vous en doutiez. mon malheureux fils etoit en russie
prisonnier, malade, abandonné. j'ai invoqué votre nom. je me Suis
reclamé de vous auprés de M^r quiny adams et Galatin. tout de Suitte
il a été protegé, acceuilli; Son retour a été accéléré; et j'ai deja eu le
plaisir avec lui de temoigner toute notre reconnoissance a M^r Galatin

dans le court Sejour qu'il vient de faire ici. jugez vous meme, Monsieur, de tout ce que vous doit un pere tendre, et veuillez bien croire que tout ce que j'ai eprouvé de malheurs ne me rend que plus Sensible a des consolations Si touchantes, et que mon cœur est egalement penetré pour vous d'attachement, de reconnoissance, d'admiration et de respect.                                         DESTUTT DE TRACY

EDITORS' TRANSLATION

Paris [14] July 1814.

It is always a great happiness for me, Sir, to receive one of your letters. The one with which you honored me on 28 November 1813, and which reached me on 5 May, gave me much pleasure, because it let me know that you had received my fourth volume, which deals with <u>political economy</u>, that you had treated it with the same indulgence you had shown the *Commentary and Review of Montesquieu's Spirit of Laws*, and that you had been so extremely kind as to have it translated. I deeply regret that this translation has not yet reached me, as I am as proud as I am grateful to see my ideas expressed in your language, thanks to your efforts. It gives me the impression that my work contains some of your own thoughts.

This illusion is undoubtedly what misled the fellow citizen of mine whom you mentioned. I know him and respect his intellect as much as I cherish his virtues. He has, however, let his imagination, a quality with which he is very amply supplied, and his vivacity, which age has been unable to diminish, get the better of him; and I confess that I have not had the courage to put him right. I fear that this is due as much to vanity as discretion, as I glory in having been mistaken for you.

But I dare avow, Sir, that my true passion is the desire to be useful. You fulfill all my wishes by letting me know that the *Commentary and Review of Montesquieu's Spirit of Laws* might be of use to the skillful professors of your state college. I hope that regarding <u>economy</u> they will find my fourth volume even easier to use, because it is, I think, more methodical. I dare not mention to you the first three, which make up the <u>treatise on understanding</u>. I know that in your reasonable nation wisdom is promptly put into action; and consequently I think that one must not make much of a speculative theory that lacks the advantage of immediate application. One must talk about logic in the schools, however, and until now it seems to me that justice has not been done to this topic, because no one has traced to its origin the manner in which ideas are formed inside our heads and the ways in which they are expressed in our languages. I therefore believe that if these first volumes were translated, they might be useful.

Nevertheless, I feel that the last ones would attract the most habitual use. If I am able to finish the volumes dealing with morality and legislation, I will not fail to put them immediately under your protection, and I cannot thank you enough for the great kindness you have shown me by thinking of this in advance. It is for me the most powerful encouragement.

In every respect, Sir, you are my guardian angel. I am infinitely obliged to you from the other side of the globe, without your even suspecting it. My unhappy son was a prisoner, sick, and abandoned in Russia. I invoked your name. I mentioned my acquaintance with you to Mr. Quincy Adams and to Gallatin. He was immediately protected and sheltered; his return was accelerated; and he and I have already had the pleasure of expressing our gratitude to Mr. Gallatin during the short time he just spent here. Judge for yourself, Sir, all that a tender father owes you, and please believe that all the misery I have suffered only makes me more sensitive to such touching consolations and that my heart is full of attachment, gratitude, admiration and respect for you.                                                   DESTUTT DE TRACY

RC (DLC: TJ Papers, 201:35831); brackets in original, with bracketed text apparently added by TJ after the receipt of Destutt de Tracy's letter of 4 Feb. 1816, which supplies the full date; endorsed by TJ as a letter of July 1814 received 12 Oct. 1814 and so recorded in SJL. Translation by Dr. Genevieve Moene. Enclosed in David Bailie Warden to TJ, 1 Aug. 1814.

Pierre Samuel Du Pont de Nemours had labored under the ILLUSION that TJ wrote Destutt de Tracy's *Commentary and Review of Montesquieu's Spirit of Laws*. Victor Destutt de Tracy was the MALHEUREUX FILS whose French military service in 1812 in Russia culminated in imprisonment at Saint Petersburg (Hoefer, *Nouv. biog. générale*, 45:566–7).

[1] Manuscript: "neammoins."

# From Tadeusz Kosciuszko

MON CHER AMI                                              Paris 14. Juliet 1814.
Le tems se passe en attente et la nécessité augmente en proportion de mon petit revenu, de Grace cherchez moi un autre moyen de m'envoyer de l'argent; Je suis deja aux emprunts ce qui me fache beaucoup. et je ne voudrais pas manquer à ma parole donnée pour le monde entier. Que fait M^r Barnes de qui je n'ai réçu aucune nouvelle ni l'année passée ni celle ci; Obligez Le je vous prie à m'envoyer plusieures Lettres d'echanges par differents voys, afin qu'avec une parvenue je puisse toucher l'argent ou la négocier. Je nai pas Le tems de repondre à Votre Lettre datée d'octobre 1813. mais agreez je vous prie L'assurance de mon Amitié et de ma Consideration La plus distinguée                                              T KOSCIUSZKO

EDITORS' TRANSLATION

MY DEAR FRIEND                                           Paris 14. July 1814.
Time passes in waiting and necessity increases in proportion to my small income; for goodness sake try to find another way of sending me money. I am already borrowing, which makes me very unhappy, and I would not for all the world like to break my word. What is Mr. Barnes doing? I have received no news from him either last year or this one. Compel him, I beg you, to send me several bills of exchange by different routes, so that on successfully

receiving one I can cash or negotiate it. I do not have time to reply to your letter dated October 1813 but please accept the assurance of my friendship and my most respectful regards                                    T Kosciuszko

RC (MHi); dateline at foot of text; endorsed by TJ as received 14 Oct. 1814 and so recorded in SJL. Translation by Dr. Genevieve Moene.

TJ's only known letter to Kosciuszko of the preceding year is dated 30 Nov. 1813, not OCTOBRE.

# From John Adams

DEAR SIR                                                    Quincy July 16. 1814
I rec$^d$ this morning your favour of the 5$^{th}$ and as I can never let a Sheet of your's rest I Sit down immediately[1] to acknowledge it.

Whenever M$^r$ Rives, of whom I have heard nothing, Shall arrive he shall receive all the cordial Civilities in my power.

I am sometimes afraid that my "Machine" will not "Surcease motion" Soon enough;[2] for I dread nothing So much as "dying at top" and expiring like Dean Swift "a driveller and a Show" or like Sam. Adams, a Grief and distress to his Family, a weeping helpless Object of Compassion for years.

I am bold to Say that neither you nor I, will live to See the Course which "the Wonders of the Times" will take.[3] Many Years, and perhaps Centuries must pass, before the current will acquire a Settled direction. If the Christian Religion as I understand it, or as you understand it, Should maintain its Ground as I believe it will; yet Platonick Pythagoric, Hindoo, and cabballistical Christianity[4] which is Catholic Christianity, and which has prevailed for 1500 Years, has rec$^d$ a mortal wound of which the Monster must finally die; yet So Strong is his constitution that he may endure for Centuries before he expires. Government has never been much Studied by Mankind. But their attention has been drawn to it, in the latter part of the last Century and the beginning[5] of this, more than at any former Period: and the vast Variety of experiments that have been made of Constitutions, in America in France, in Holland, in Geneva in Switzerland, and even in Spain and South America, can never be forgotten. They will be Studied, and their immediate and remote Effects, and final Catastrophys noted. The result in time will be Improvements. And I have no doubt that[6] the horrors We have experienced for the last forty Years, will ultimately terminate in the Advancement of civil and religious Liberty, and Ameliorations, in the condition of Mankind. For I am a Beleiver, in the probable improvability and Improvement, the

Ameliorability[7] and Amelioration in human Affaires: though I never could understand the Doctrine of the Perfectability of the human Mind. This has always appeared to me, like the Phylosophy or Theology of the Gentoos, viz that a Brachman, by certain Studies for a certain time pursued, and by certain ceremonies a certain number of times repeated, becomes Omniscient and Almighty.

Our hopes however of Sudden tranquility ought not to be too Sanguine. Fanaticism and Superstition will Still be Selfish, Subtle, intriguing, and at times furious. Despotism will Still Struggle for domination; Monarchy will Still Study to rival nobility in popularity; Aristocracy will continue to envy all above it, and despize and oppress all below it; Democracy will envy all, contend with all, endeavour to pull down all; and when by chance it happens to get the Upper hand for a Short time, it will be revengefull bloody and cruel. These and other Elements of Fanaticism and Anarchy will yet for a long time continue a Fermentation, which will excite alarms and require Vigilance.

Napoleon is a Military Fanatic like Achilles, Alexander, Cæsar, Mahomet[8] Zingis Kouli, Charles 12$^{th}$ &c. The Maxim and Principle of all of them was the Same "Jura negat Sibi Cata, nihil non arrogat Armis."

But is it Strict, to call him An Usurper? Was not his Elevation to the Empire of France as legitimate and authentic a national Act as that of William 3$^{d}$ or the House of Hanover to the throne of the 3 Kingdoms. or as the Election of Washington to the command of our Army or to the Chair of the States.

Human Nature, in no form of it, ever could bear Prosperity. That peculiar tribe of Men, called Conquerors, more remarkably than any other have been Swelled with Vanity by any Series of Victories. Napoleon won So many mighty Battles in Such quick Succession and for So long a time, that it was no Wonder his brain became compleatly intoxicated and his enterprises, rash, extravagant and mad.

Though France is humbled, Britain is not. Though Bona is banished a greater Tyrant and wider Usurper Still domineers. John Bull is quite as unfeeling, as unprincipled, more powerful, has Shed more blood, than Bona. John by his money his Intrigues and Arms, by exciting Coalition after coalition against him made him what he was, and at last, what he is. How Shall the Tyrant of Tyrants, be brought low? Aye! there's the rub. I Still think Bona great, at least as any of the[9] Conquerors. "The Wonders of his rise and fall," may be Seen in the Life of King Theodore, or Pascall Paoli or Rienzi, or Dyonisius or Mazzionetti, or Jack Cade or Wat Tyler. The only difference is that between miniature and full length pictures.[10] The Schoolmaster at Corinth, was a greater Man, than the Tyrant of Syracuse; upon the Principle, that he who conquers himself is greater than he who takes a City. Tho the ferocious Roar of the wounded Lion, may terrify the Hunter with the possibility of another dangerous leap; Bona was Shot dead at once, by France. He could no longer roar or Struggle growl or paw he could only gasp the[11] Grin of death.[12] I wish that France may not Still regret him. But these are Speculations in the Clouds. I agree, with you that the Milk of human kindness in the Bourbons is Safer for Mankind than the fierce Ambition of Napoleon.

The Autocrator, appears in an imposing Light. Fifty Years ago English Writers, held up terrible Consequences from "thawing out the monstrous northern Snake." If Cossacks and Tartars, and Goths and Vandalls and Hunns and Ripuarians,[13] Should get a taste of European Sweets, what may happen? Could Wellingtons or Bonapartes, resist them? The greatest trait of Sagacity, that Alexander has yet exhibited to the World is his Courtship of the United States. But whether this is a mature well digested Policy or only a transient gleam of thought, Still remains to be explained and proved by time.

The "refractory Sister"[14] will not give up the Fisheries. Not a Man here dares to hint at So base a thought.

I am very glad you have Seriously read Plato: and Still more rejoiced to find that your reflections upon him, So perfectly harmonize with mine. Some thirty Years ago I took upon me the Severe task of going through all his Works. With the help of two Latin Translations, and one English and one French Translation[15] and comparing Some of the most remarkable passages with the Greek, I laboured through the tedious toil. My disappointment was very great, my Astonishment was greater and my disgust was Shocking. Two Things only did I learn from him. 1. that Franklins Ideas of exempting Husbandmen and Mariners &c from the depredations of War, were borrowed from him. 2. that Sneezing is a cure for the Hickups. Accordingly I have cured myself and all my Friends of that provoking disorder, for thirty years with a Pinch of Snuff.

Some Parts of Some of his Dialogues are entertaining, like the Writings of Rousseau: but his Laws and his Republick from which I expected most, disappointed me most. I could Scarcely exclude the Suspicion that he intended the latter as a bitter Satyre upon all Republican Government,[16] as Xenophon undoubtedly designed by his Essay on Democracy, to ridicule that Species of Republick. In a late letter to the learned and ingenious Mr Taylor of Hazelwood, I Suggested to him the Project of writing a Novel, in which The Hero

Should be Sent upon his travels through Plato's Republick, and all his Adventures, with his Observations on the principles and opinions, the Arts and Sciences, the manners Customs and habits of the Citizens Should be recorded. Nothing can be conceived more destructive of human happiness; more infallibly contrived to transform Men and Women into Brutes, Yahoos, or Dæmons than a Community of Wives and Property. Yet, in what, are the Writings of Rousseau and Helvetius wiser than those of Plato? "The Man who first fenced a Tobacco yard, and Said this is mine ought instantly to have been put to death" Says Rousseau. "The Man who first pronounced the barbarous Word 'Dieu,' ought to have been immediately destroyed,"[17] Says Diderot.

In Short Philosophers antient and modern appear to me as mad as Hindoos, Mahomitans and Christians. No doubt they would all think me mad, and for any thing I know this globe may be, the bedlam, Le Bicatre of the Universe.

After all; as long as Property exists, it will accumulate in Individuals and Families, As long as Marriage exists,[18] Knowledge, Property and Influence will accumulate in Families. Your and our equal Partition of intestate Estates, instead of preventing will in time augment the Evil, if it is one.

The French Revolutionists Saw this, and were So far consistent, When they burned Pedigrees and genealogical Trees, they annihilated,[19] as far as they could, Marriages, knowing that Marriage, among a thousand other things was an infallible Source of Aristocracy. I repeat it,[20] So sure as the Idea and the existence of <u>Property</u> is admitted and established in society, Accumulations of it will be made, the Snow ball will grow as it rolls.

Cicero was educated in the Groves of Academus where the Name and Memory of Plato, were idolized to such a degree, that if he had wholly renounced the Prejudices of his Education his Reputation would have been lessened, if not injured and ruined. In his two Volumes of Discourses on government We may presume, that he fully examined Plato's Laws and Republick as well as Aristotles Writings on Government. But these have been carefully destroyed; not improbably, with the general Consent of Philosophers, Politicians and Priests. The Loss is as much to be regretted as that of any Production of Antiquity.

Nothing Seizes the attention, of the Stareing Animal, So Surely, as Paradox, Riddle, Mystery, Invention, discovery, Mystery, Wonder, Temerity.

Plato and his Disciples, from the fourth Century Christians, to

Rousseau and Tom. Paine, have been fully Sensible of this Weakness in Mankind, and have too Successfully grounded upon it their Pretensions to Fame. I might indeed, have mentioned, Bolingbroke, Hume, Gibbon Voltaire Turgot[21] Helvetius Diderot, Condorcet, Buffon De La Lande[22] and fifty others; all a little cracked! Be to their faults a little blind; to their Virtues ever kind.

Education! Oh Education! The greatest Grief of my heart, and the greatest affliction of my Life! To my mortification I must confess, that I have never closely thought, or very deliberately reflected upon the Subject, which never occurs to me now, without producing a deep Sigh, an heavy groan and Sometimes Tears. My cruel Destiny Seperated me from my Children, allmost continually from their Birth to their Manhood. I was compelled to leave them to the ordinary routine of reading writing and Latin School, Accademy and Colledge. John alone was much with me, and he, but occasionally. If I venture to give you any[23] thoughts at all, they must be very crude. I have turned over Locke, Milton, Condilac Rousseau and even Miss[24] Edgeworth as a bird flies through the Air. The Præceptor, I have thought a good Book. Grammar, Rhetorick, Logic, Ethicks[25] mathematicks, cannot be neglected; Classicks, in Spight of our Friend Rush, I must think indispensable. Natural History, Mechanicks, and experimental Philosophy, Chymistry &c at[26] least their Rudiments, can not be forgotten. Geography Astronomy,[27] and even History and Chronology, tho' I am myself afflicted with a kind of Pyrrhonism in the two latter, I presume cannot be omitted. Theology I would leave to Ray, Derham, Nieuenteyt and Payley, rather than to Luther[28] Zinzindorph, Sweedenborg Westley, or Whitefield, or Thomas Aquinas or Wollebius. Metaphysics I would leave in the Clouds with the Materialists and Spiritualists, with Leibnits, Berkley Priestley and Edwards, and I might add Hume and Reed. Or if permitted to be read, it should be with Romances and Novels. What Shall I Say of Musick, drawing, fencing, dancing and Gymnastic Exercises? What of Languages Oriental or Occidental? Of French Italian German or Russian! of Sanscrit or Chinese?

The Task you have prescribed to me of Grouping these Sciences, or Arts, under Professors, within the Views of an inlightened Economy, is far beyond my forces. Loose indeed and indigested must be all the hints, I can note. Might Gramar, Rhetoric, Logick and Ethicks be under One Professor? Might Mathematicks, Mechanicks, Natural Phylosophy, be under another? Geography and Astronomy[29] under a third. Laws and Goverment, History and Chronology under a fourth. Classicks might require a fifth.

Condelacs course of Study has excellent Parts. Among many Systems of Mathematicks English, French and American, there is none preferable to Besouts Course La Harps Course of Litterature is very valuable.

But I am ashamed to add any thing more to the broken innuendos except assurances of the continued Friendship of

JOHN ADAMS

RC (DLC); at foot of text: "President Jefferson"; endorsed by TJ as received 3 Aug. 1814 and so recorded in SJL. FC (Lb in MHi: Adams Papers).

Samuel Johnson described Jonathan SWIFT expiring like A DRIVELLER AND A SHOW in *The Vanity of Human Wishes: The Tenth Satire of Juvenal, imitated by Samuel Johnson* (London, 1749), 25. Condorcet championed the DOCTRINE OF THE PERFECTABILITY OF THE HUMAN MIND. GENTOOS: non-Muslim inhabitants of Hindustan (*OED*). BRACHMAN: Brahman. KOULI: Nader Shah, one-time leader of a band of Turkish bandits who became King of Persia. JURA NEGAT SIBI CATA, NIHIL NON ARROGAT ARMIS: "let him claim that the laws are not for him, let him ever make appeal to the sword," from Horace, *Ars Poetica*, 122 (Fairclough, *Horace: Satires, Epistles and Ars Poetica*, 460–1). KING THEODORE: Theodor von Neuhof, a German adventurer, collaborated with exiles and briefly involved the Corsican throne as Theodore I. Dionysius II, the ruler or tyrant of Syracuse, was deposed twice. During his second banishment he allegedly became a SCHOOLMASTER AT CORINTH (*OCD*, 477; Justin, *Epitome of the Philippic History of Pompeius Trogus*, trans. J. C. Yardley, ed. R. Develin [1994], 171). MILK OF HUMAN KINDNESS is from William Shakespeare, *Macbeth*, act 1, scene 5.

In a 7 June 1814 letter Adams queried John TAYLOR of Caroline: "Will M$^r$ Taylor profess himself, a downright Leveller? Will he vote for a community of Property? Or an equal division of Property? And a Community of Wives and Women?" Adams added that if he were a "young Man, I should like to write a Romance; and Send a Hero upon his Travels, through Such a levelling Community of

Wives and Wealth. It would be very edifying to record his Observations, on the Opinions, Principles, Customs, Institutions, and manners of this Democratical Republick, and Such a virtuous and happy Age" (MHi: Washburn Autograph Collection). THE MAN WHO FIRST FENCED . . . PUT TO DEATH paraphrases the opening lines of the second part of Jean Jacques Rousseau's *Discours Sur L'Origine et les Fondements De L'Inégalité Parmi Les Hommes*, first published in Amsterdam in 1755.

DIEU: "God." Le Bicêtre (LE BICATRE) was an institution near Paris that served as a hospital, orphanage, asylum, and prison. BE TO THEIR FAULTS A LITTLE BLIND; TO THEIR VIRTUES EVER KIND is from Matthew Prior's poem, *An English Padlock* (London, 1705), 2. PRÆCEPTOR: Robert Dodsley compiled *The Preceptor: Containing A General Course of Education. Wherein The First Principles of Polite Learning Are laid down In a Way most suitable for trying the Genius, and advancing the Instruction of Youth*, 2 vols. (London, 1748; Sowerby, no. 1116). Benjamin RUSH had proposed that educators replace the teaching of Greek and Latin with modern languages and scientific topics (Lyman H. Butterfield, *Letters of Benjamin Rush* [1951], 1:516–8, 604–8).

[1] RC: "immdiately." FC: "immediately."
[2] Adams is quoting from TJ's 5 July 1814 letter.
[3] Adams is quoting from TJ's 5 July 1814 letter.
[4] Preceding five words interlined.
[5] RC: "begining." FC: "beginning."
[6] RC: "thatt." FC: "that."
[7] RC: "Ameliorabity." FC: "Ameliorability."
[8] Word interlined.

⁹ FC: "his."

¹⁰ Preceding nineteen words interlined.

¹¹ FC: "his."

¹² Preceding eleven words interlined.

¹³ FC: "Ripurians."

¹⁴ Omitted closing quotation mark editorially supplied. Adams is quoting from TJ's 5 July 1814 letter.

¹⁵ Reworked from "and English and French Translations."

¹⁶ FC: "Governments."

¹⁷ For consistency, closing single quotation mark editorially altered, and quotation marks around "Dieu" changed from double to single.

¹⁸ RC: "exits." FC: "exists."

¹⁹ RC: "annilated." FC: "annihilated."

²⁰ Preceding three words interlined.

²¹ Word interlined.

²² Word interlined.

²³ FC: "my."

²⁴ Reworked from "Mʳˢ."

²⁵ Word interlined.

²⁶ RC: "att." FC: "at."

²⁷ RC: "Astomy." FC: "Astronomy."

²⁸ Preceding two words interlined.

²⁹ RC: "Astromy." FC: "Astronomy."

# To John Wayles Eppes

DEAR SIR                                   Monticello. July 16. 14.

Mʳ Estin Randolph has shewed me a letter from you, proposing to sell him Pantops, in order to lay out the money in lands in your neighborhood for Francis. I had hoped that we had concurred in our purposes on that subject, altho' we did not in the immediate execution of them. my view & wish was when Francis should come of age, or the Pantops lease expire, or whenever else you pleased, to assign, in exchange for that, equivalent lands in Bedford, adjacent to what I might hereafter give him additionally, so as to make up an establishment of value consolidated in one body, rather than divided, and so distantly, into two. with this view I had built a most excellent house, and, since our correspondence on the subject, have been doing much towards it's completion. the inside work is mostly done, and I have this summer built a wing of offices 110. feet long, in the manner of those at Monticello, with a flat roof in the level of the floor of the house. the whole, as it now stands, could not be valued at less than 10,000.D. and I am going on. I am also making such improvements of the grounds as require time to perfect themselves: and instead of clearing on the lands proposed for him once in 5 years only as formerly mentioned, I clear on them every year; and by the time he comes of age, there will probably be 300. acres of open land. so that he would be comfortably and handsomely fixed at once, and in a part of the country which I really consider as the most desirable in this state, for soil, climate and convenience to market. Lynchburg is a most thriving place, already second in it's business to none but Richmond, and Richmond itself is convenient also by water carriage. these circumstances give an extraordinary rise in value to lands there.

a tract adjoining the Poplar Forest, but of very inferior value as to quality, was sold, when I was there last, for 21. D 90 C     I was much pleased too that Francis was placed at school at Lynchburg, as, besides giving me opportunities of seeing him, it will habitualize him to the neighborhood, and give him those early attachments of friendship and acquaintance which carry their impression and value through life. in opposition to these considerations I see no great advantage which can result to him from the disjunction of his property by the purchase you contemplate. no doubt indeed it would be a great comfort to you, & satisfaction to him also to be placed near you. but the limits of life render that temporary, and it would in a great measure be supplied by the superlative excellence of the roads between you. these are so fine and level, that with a little exertion it is but the journey of a day. I have suggested these things for your consideration, from a view to his happiness & advantage, which no one, I am sure, can wish for more than yourself; and I have developed my own intentions because they might become motives of action with you; altho' in his case, as in that of the other members of my family, I follow the accustomary course of not making them of irrevocable obligation, but reserve the rights which parents do for their own lives usually, and usefully for their children themselves. having the whole under your view, you will be enabled to decide ultimately & rightfully what will be most for the benefit of him who is the object of our mutual affection and sollicitude.     Mr Halcomb has permitted Francis to come and stay with me during my visits to Poplar Forest, on the condition of my carrying him on in his lessons, which I have been able to do with some advantages he would not have had in the school. I think my visits and stay at that place are sufficient to enable me to learn him French, of which there is no teacher there. I have accordingly procured the necessary books for that purpose, and shall carry them with me on my next visit. with my respects to mrs Eppes, accept the assurance of my affectionate esteem and attachment

Th: Jefferson

PoC (CSmH: JF); endorsed by TJ: "Eppes John W. July 16. 14."

An illustration of the WING OF OFFICES at Poplar Forest appears elsewhere in this volume.

# From John Crookes

SIR,        Office of the Mercantile Advertiser, New York, July 20. 1814.

I inclose you a Versification of the Speech of Logan, which I have just published. The knowledge that it had your approbation would be more gratifying to me than to have the applauses of "the million."

I am, Sir,        Yours very respectfully,        JOHN CROOKES.

RC (MHi); dateline adjacent to signature; addressed: "Hon. Mr. Jefferson, Montpelier, Virgᵃ"; franked; postmarked New York, 20 July; endorsed by TJ as received 31 July 1814 and so recorded in SJL.

John Crookes (ca. 1769–1818), newspaper publisher, editor, and author, of New York City, began his career at the New York *Register of the Times* and the New York *Diary* in 1797. From 1798 until his retirement in 1816, he was the printer of the New York *Mercantile Advertiser*, serving also as publisher beginning in 1806. Crookes also wrote biographical and poetic pieces that were published in various newspapers and journals (Crookes to TJ, 25 Mar. 1807 [DLC]; *MB*, 2:1249; Brigham, *American Newspapers*, 1:627, 661, 683; *New-York Columbian* and New York *Mercantile Advertiser* [reporting age at death as forty-nine years] and New York *Commercial Advertiser* [reporting death in forty-seventh year], all 29 June 1818).

Crookes had translated into rhyming couplets the SPEECH of 1774 in which the Mingo Indian James LOGAN mourned the murder of his family by white settlers (New York *Shamrock*, 30 July 1814). TJ had praised the eloquence of the original in his *Notes on the State of Virginia* (*Notes*, ed. Peden, 62–3).

# To Joseph Miller

DEAR SIR        Monticello July 21. 14.

I feel myself bound in candor to communicate to you the step which the dangers impending over[1] us, and the great change of circumstances since you left Charlottesville, have required me to take. the permission you requested to visit Norfolk was for a fortnight only which however I asked for a month, on my own responsibility; and in such terms as produced from the Marshal a permission without any particular limitation of time. your stay thro' the winter, while military operations in that vicinity were suspended by the season, gave me no concern, nor perhaps should I have felt any now but for the hourly expectation of invasion by a great hostile army, of which Norfolk may probably be the first object. altho' I still confide in the sentiments of attachment to this country which you often expressed here, yet you are sensible that the opportunities of your becoming intimately known to me have not been such as to justify unlimited confidence under the new dangers threatening our country, nor an indefinite continuance of my responsibility, however it might be warranted as I presume it would be, were your character more fully known to me. under these circumstances my duties as a citizen have obliged me, in a letter of this day to the Marshal, to withdraw the responsibility I had taken on myself with him, which possibly may occasion a revocation of your furlough, or it's suspension at least during the season of active operations in the neighborhood of Norfolk. should this take place, it will probably be but temporary; and this storm having once blown over you may rely on my readiness to be useful to you in obtaining any new indulgence, or rendering any other service your situation may require. I have asked of the Marshal should he revoke his license, still to indulge you with time, for necessary arrangements, which may perhaps be lengthened by your early reciept of this previous notice from myself. Accept my best wishes for your health and success in your pursuits                    TH: JEFFERSON

PoC (DLC); at foot of text: "Cap^t       ¹ TJ here canceled "our country."
Joseph Miller"; endorsed by TJ.

# To Andrew Moore

DEAR SIR                                      Monticello July 21. 14.
    I am first to thank you for the indulgence which, in October last, at my request, you were so kind as to extend to Cap^t Miller, stationed as an Alien at Charlottesville. he requested a fortnight only to go to Norfolk, to settle his affairs, and look after the property there which he claimed: but as I thought it would take him longer, I extended his request to a month. you were so kind as to fix no particular limit to his absence, and he seems disposed to avail himself of it indefinitely; having, as I am informed, engaged in a partnership business with a mr Hay in Norfolk who had in charge from the Escheator the property there claimed by mr Miller. had he stayed thro' the winter only, while military operations were suspended, in that vicinity, I should have felt no uneasiness for the responsibility I had undertaken for him. but we have reason now to expect a great hostile army hourly, and that Norfolk will be it's first enterprise. in such a case, personal confidence should not controul the cautious provisions of the law; and certainly I should not be willing to assume such a responsibility. I still have a favorable opinion of Cap^t Miller, altho' some who know him more particularly have less confidence in his candor. but without regard to this, having taken a furlough of nine months where one only was requested, he has had more than the full benefit of the object asked by

himself. I think it a duty therefore to recall the case to your recollection as scenes are approaching which command caution. should you think it prudent to require a return to his station, at least till the campaign is over, or till your further permission, which he can always ask, the indulgence of a few days after notice (if the enemy do not arrive in the mean while) to arrange with his partner the business he has engaged in, may perhaps be of value to him.—not knowing whether you may be in Richmond or Lexington, I send a copy of this letter to each place, lest time may be lost when every day & hour may bring forth the crisis apprehended. Accept the assurance of my friendly esteem and great respect          TH: JEFFERSON

PoC (DLC); at foot of text: "<$Col^o$> Gen$^l$ Andrew Moore"; endorsed by TJ.

## To Robert Patterson

Monticello July 23. 14.

Th: Jefferson incloses to D$^r$ Patterson a paper from M$^r$ Lambert proposing a correction of the Julian calendar additional to that of Gregory, which paper was intended for the use of the society; and he salutes D$^r$ Patterson with sincere friendship & respect.

PoC (DLC); dateline at foot of text, followed by abstract of enclosure described above at William Lambert to TJ, 24 June 1814.

## To William Thornton

DEAR SIR                                             Monticello July 23. 14.

I return you Janes's description of his loom with many thanks for the communication of it. the improvement for moving the treadles without using the feet is highly valuable, inasmuch as our weavers are for the most part women. it appears too to be sufficiently simple for country use. the winding up the cloth is also useful, & not complicated. I do not well understand the mechanism for shooting the shuttle, nor consider it important, because it may be as well to employ both hands as one. if I knew the price, and where and how I could get one of these looms, I might be tempted to try them. perhaps mr Clopper could give the[1] information. I think with you that the burning the Machine office would really be like burning the temple of Ephesus. it would be better to employ the surplus of it's funds in having engravings made of the select machines, & sold out to the public for reimbursement of the expence of engraving. I have endeavored to be supplied with your annual report of the titles of the patents of inventions, but have never been able to get but those printed in 1811. and 1813. I am steadily pursuing the business of homespun & will never give it up.　　I am glad to hear of your invention of a new musical instrument, altho' I shall never have the benefit of hearing it. it will give happiness to succeeding generations for whom a great portion of our labors and cares are employed: and with every wish that your immediate utility may be promoted by it, I tender you the assurance of my great esteem and respect.

TH: JEFFERSON

PoC (MHi); at foot of text: "Doct^r Thornton"; endorsed by TJ. Enclosure not found.

The great TEMPLE of Artemis was located at EPHESUS (*OCD*, 184, 528).

[1] Manuscript: "the the."

# From James Monroe

DEAR SIR　　　　　　　　　　Washington July 25. 1814.

I think you showd me last summer a note of the courses and distances, taken by M^r R. Lewis, of my land, lying between the old road, passing by my house, & the top of the mountain, being, the first purchase, which I made of M^r Carter. M^r Lewis made this survey at the time & in consequence of Mr Shorts purchase. I will thank you to have the goodness to send me a copy of that survey, as it may save me the trouble & expence of another.

The present appearing to be a favorable time for the sale of land in our state, I advertised my tract in Loudoun some months past, in the hope of profiting of the high price given for such land in that county. In this I have not yet succeeded. As I lately passed thro' Richmond, it was intimated to me, that I might obtain a very advantageous price for my tract in Albemarle, in consequence of which I authorised M^r T. Taylor to sell it, provided that suggestion could be realised. It is my intention to sell one of these estates, and to apply the money arising from the sale, to the payment of my debts, and improv'ment of the other. By this arrangment I shall try the market for both & dispose of that which can be sold to greatest advantage, intending however not to sell that in Albemarle, unless the price shall be such, as to indemnify me for the sacrifice I shall make in relinquishing a residence of 26. years standing, as mine in Albemarle has been, and near old friends to whom I am greatly attached.

Our financial affairs seem likely to take the course which it was easy to anticipate under all the difficulties of our situation. of monied men there are few in the country, and we cannot expect to obtain loans equal to the demand, from our monied institutions, many of which are not disposed to make them. I do not know, nor do I think, that an absolute failure in that respect, would do us any injury, as it would lead to some substitute, more œconomical, as well as consistent with the state of our country, and the genius of our gov't & people. Your ideas had much weight on my mind, but so wedded were our financiers to the plan in operation that it was impossible to make any impression on them, then, in favor of any other. will you have the goodness to confide to me a copy of your thoughts on this subjct with which I was favor'd last year? The moment for promoting the arrangment contemplated by them is now more favorable, & I shall be happy to avail myself of it.

with great respect I am very sincerely
your friend & servant                                    JAS MONROE

RC (DLC); endorsed by TJ as received 31 July 1814 and so recorded in SJL.

Years previously Monroe had offered to sell his Oak Hill estate, nearly two thousand acres in LOUDOUN County, located ten miles from Leesburg and thirty-five from Alexandria, along with its livestock and about twenty-five slaves (Leesburg *Washingtonian*, 6 Feb. 1810).

# To William Richardson

July 25. 14.

hav'g rec'd no answer to my l're of the 2'd inst. I wrote again to W'm Richardson, Richmond, for ½ doz. yds scarlet Rattinet, to be forwarded by mail stage mr Gibson to pay for it.

FC (MHi); abstract in TJ's hand; on verso of reused address cover to TJ; endorsed by TJ.

TJ's letter to Richardson of THE 2'D INST., not found, is recorded in SJL, as are missing letters from Richardson to TJ of 9 May and 29 July 1814, respectively recorded as received from Richmond on 13 May and 1 Aug. 1814.

# From David Bailie Warden

SIR,                                                      Paris, 25 July [1814]

I have already taken the liberty of transmitting to you, by mr Todd, a copy of my defence in reply to the accusation presented by mr Crawford as the ground of my removal from office, or suspension of my Consular powers. Since the date of that Communication, I have been informed that the real motive for this decision of the Government was grounded on information, that I corresponded with the french Government and went to Court[1] after the arrival of mr. Crawford. I beg leave to justify my conduct on this head by a plain statement of facts.

At my first interview with mr. Crawford, after his arrival at Paris, I communicated to him my resolution from which I never swerved, to consult him on every doubtful, or difficult subject, to execute no other business than that which he chose to leave to my direction; and to do every thing in my power to merit his approbation. I asked his advice, and instructions concerning every case, or circumstance not formally explained in the Consular laws, or instructions. I offered my Services as Interpreter, and on every occasion when he might call for them. In the affair of the prizes of Commodore Rodgers and every other, I submitted entirely to his ministerial decision—my correspondence, and particularly that of which I herewith send a copy, will shew how I endeavored even to anticipate his wishes. I was so far from desiring to correspond with the minister of foreign affairs that I refused to acknowledge the receipt of Several letters, after having twice requested mr. Labernardierre, Counsellor of State, who acted as minister, not to address them to me, observing, that mr. Crawford, though not acknowledged as minister, was the only person who could authorize this correspondence. on the 20th of September, I prayed mr. Jackson, Secretary of Legation to communicate to me the ministers' decision on this subject, which he promised to do, but I recieved no reply. again I requested mr. Labernardiere, through mr. Cazeaux, formerly Vice-Consul, at Portsmouth, to address his letters to mr. Crawford, and his answer was still the Same, as made to mr. Jackson, when I introduced him to the foreign department, "that untill mr. Crawford was acknowledged, the minister could not do otherwise than correspond with mr. Warden as the only accredited agent of the United States, at Paris." If mr. Crawford, on his arrival at Paris, or afterwards, had expressed, in the most indirect manner, his wishes on this Subject, I should have immediately ceased all relations with the minister of foreign affairs. I sent him a copy of every letter as soon as received, and nothing was more easy than to give me instructions thereon. It was by his positive authorisation, that I delivered passports, and I submitted every thing to his decision, though I was not always fortunate enough to receive a reply.

The second accusation, that I continued to go to Court is equally groundless. I was so far from wishing to interfere in Court-affairs, that after the arrival of mr Crawford, tickets were sent to me as usual for messrs Carrol, Consul for Barcelona, van Rensselaer, [Sears?], [Wilkes?], Smith, for the theatre of the Court, which I regularly transmitted to mr. Crawford.

It is true, that I dined with the Empress Josephine and was at her evening parties after mr. Crawfords' arrival but she was not considered as having any connection with the Court. Besides, I had the same honor before mr. Barlows' death, and the privilege of presenting to her any American Ladies, or Gentlemen, whom I might consider as worthy of this honor. mr. and mrs Sears of Boston, whom I introduced to her, as also the above-named Gentlemen are acquainted with this fact. This attention of the Empress was not altogether owing to my consular situation, but also to other circumstances, which I need not here explain. It is also true, that I dined with the Duke of Bassano, and with the Prince Cambaceres, in company with mr. Crawford, but it never entered my thoughts that this circumstance could give offence.

on the 13th of august, the grand Chamberlain by the orders of the empress Queen and Regent, invited me to the theatre of the palace of the Thuelleries, and the grand master of ceremonies to the Diplomatic circle. on the 10th of Sept, I was again invited to the Diplomatic circle; and on the 19th of that month, to the theatre of the Court—I declined all these invitations.

on the 11th of Sept. I was again invited, by the grand Master of ceremonies to attend the Diplomatic circle; and on the Same day, I received an invitation from the Duchess of montibello, first Lady of honor to the Empress Queen and Regent to dine at St Cloud: it was necessary to give an answer to this invitation; and I wrote the note to mr Crawford, and received the reply of which I inclose a copy. I should not have made this written enquiry, if I had been able in conversation to discover his wishes on this subject: I knew not what his answer meant; but I knew well, that all my relations with this Government have been strictly honorable—after the abdication of Napoleon, I was immediately acknowledged by the New Government; and the suspension of my powers has left me the consolation of a good conscience, the regret of my friends, and I venture to say, the esteem of all ministers, Secretaries, and chiefs, with whom I had any further relations—                    DAVID BAILIE WARDEN

Dupl (DLC: TJ Papers, 201:35842–3); partially dated; two words illegible; at head of text: "Copy"; endorsed by TJ as a letter of 25 July 1814 received 12 Oct.   1814 and so recorded in SJL. Enclosures: (1) Warden to William H. Crawford, 11 Sept. 1813, advising him that Warden had received an invitation "from the

Grand Master of Ceremonies to attend the Diplomatic Circle tomorrow," as well as an invitation to "dine tomorrow with the Duchess of Montebello," and asking "whether I Should or not accept these invitations. My duty, in all Such Circumstances, is to be directed by You, and my utmost desire to merit Your approbation & that of my Government" (FC in Lb in MdHi: Warden Papers). (2) Crawford to Warden, 11 Sept. 1813, stating that "It is impossible for me to have any Wish upon the Subjects which it embraces. You Know Your relation to this Government, and You also Know that it Cannot be a concern of mine, where You go, or with whom you dine"; and adding that he has received a letter from William Lee informing him that "the affair of the Maria has been adjusted, by his Yielding a point, which in my judgment, he ought not to have Yielded. This fact proves also the correctness of my Opinion, that the interference Of the Minister of Commerce, Could have been removed, without a reference to the Duke of Bassano. The affair is now Settled. I wish to hear no more of it, and trust that nothing of the Kind will occur in future" (Tr in Lb in MdHi: Warden Papers). Enclosed in TJ to James Madison, 13 Oct. 1814, and Madison to TJ, 23 Oct. 1814 (second letter).

THE EMPRESS QUEEN AND REGENT was Marie Louise von Habsburg, second wife of Napoleon.

[1] Preceding four words interlined.

# From Patrick Gibson

SIR                                    Richmond 27th July 1814

I have received your favor of the 23[d] Ins[t] and am sorry to inform you that owing to the present distressd state of the banks, no addition to your note can be obtained, indeed so far from their increasing their discounts, they have been reduced to the disagreeable necessity of curtailing the one 10 the other 15 p[r]C[t] for every 60 [d]/.—this has been the case with the Farmer's bank for 4 months past, and must be continued by both, until a change takes place in our affairs. they have been driven to this, by the continual demands upon them from the North, which are rapidly draining them of their specie, and will inevitably if times continue deprive them of every dollar—I have never witnessed such a scarcety of money, indeed the pressure is already very severe & becomes daily more so. to this is to be attributed my not being able to obtain even 3¼$ for your flour, at which I have offer'd it I send you inclosed $200 and shall attend to your dft in favor of Joseph B Proctor $63.91—With great respect I am Your ob[t] Serv[t]

PATRICK GIBSON

RC (MHi); between dateline and salutation: "Thomas Jefferson Esq[re]"; endorsed by TJ as received 31 July 1814 and so recorded in SJL.

TJ's FAVOR OF THE 23[D] INS[T], recorded in SJL but not found, presumably directed Gibson to pay Joseph B. PROCTOR. The payment was for unspecified quantities of cotton and whiskey (MB, 2:1301).

Joseph B. Proctor later gave TJ a receipt, dated 23 Aug. 1814, for TJ's purchase for $3 of "12[tb] of cotton @ 1/6"

(MS in DLC; mutilated; endorsed by TJ). Proctor, a resident of Albemarle County from whom TJ also bought cotton, oats, and tar on 2 May 1814, died later that year (*MB*, 2:1299; Albemarle Co. Order Book [1813–15], 411 [5 Dec. 1814]).

# From James Mease

DEAR SIR                                          Philad[a] July 27th 1814.

I am much obliged by your history of the Robinson Apple; I read it at the last Stated meeting of the Agric. Soc: on the 12th ins[t] and regret that your absence prevented my receiving it at a more early date, as I wished to insert it in the third vol: of the memoirs of the Soc: now publishing. I fear the number of papers is complete, for it, but should it be possible, I will insert it. The knowledge of the apple should be spread extensively: M[r] Cox of Burlington procured Some grafts, and has now the apples on his farm.—

I have the pleasure to send you a printed specification of the patent of Janes for his newly invented loom which is now in operation in this City. I visited the manufactory established by the person who has bought the right of this State, and of those to the south; and was much gratified:—He Says a loom will Cost about $50.—We may Say with respect to the loom what the French Soc: of Agric. said of your plough,—America Received the loom from Europe, and returned it perfected.—

Accept my Sincere esteem—                         JAMES MEASE

RC (DLC); at foot of text: "Tho. Jefferson Monticello"; endorsed by TJ as received 3 Aug. 1814 and so recorded in SJL. Enclosed in TJ to Thomas Ritchie, 15 Aug. 1814, and Ritchie to TJ, 9 Oct. 1814. Extract, consisting of second paragraph except for the sentence giving the cost, printed in Richmond *Enquirer*, 20 Aug. 1814. Enclosure not found.

TJ gave his HISTORY OF THE ROBINSON APPLE in his 29 June 1814 letter to Mease.

# From William Wirt

DEAR SIR.                                          Richmond. July 27. 1814.

The summer vacation of our courts, gives me an opportunity of taking up the materials which I have been for several years collecting for a life of Patrick Henry, and seeing what I could make of them. Will you have the goodness to excuse the following questions suggested, in a great degree, by a comparison of the communication you were so kind as to make, with others, from different quarters.

You mention a display made by M$^r$ Henry in 1762, a year later or sooner, in resisting the project of a loan office devised to cover a delinquency of the treasurer Robinson. I have not the journal of the House of Burgesses of '61 or 62, nor can they be found at the public offices here. But I am apprehensive that there may possibly be some inaccuracy in your recollection of the date of that incident or of M$^r$ Henry's participation in the debate. My doubts are founded on these circumstances. 1. That it appears from the concurrent statements of his countymen[1] (W$^m$ O. Winston, Charles Dabney, George Dabney, Thomas Trevilian, Colo Samuel Meredith & Judge Edmund Winston) that M$^r$ Henry's talent for speaking was not so much as suspected until the winter of 1763, when the trial of the celebrated cause called The Parson's cause took place. Judge Tyler, who seems to have been very intimately acquainted with M$^r$ Henry's life, by a separate statement, confirms this circumstance. 2. These gentlemen concur in stating that M$^r$ Henry never was a member of the assembly 'till '65: which he himself confirms by an indorsement on a copy of his resolutions left sealed among his papers and directed to be opened by his executors: he does not indeed say that he never had been a member before; but he calls himself a new member who had just taken his seat, & unacquainted with the forms of the house. 3. I am in possession of the journals from '63 to '67, inclusive: and in '67 (the year after the Speaker Robinson's death and the explosion of his[2] delinquency) I find the project of a loan brought forward, when M$^r$ Henry was a member; but the object was to borrow & not to lend; and it passed the house, but was rejected by the council. This is obviously a different measure from that to which you allude. But the measure you do speak of could not have occurred between '63 & 67—and if prior to '63, M$^r$ Henry was either not a member, or all my other statements are wrong, in assigning '63 as the epoch of his first display of eloquence, and '65 as the year in which he became a member of the house of Burgesses. If you have the journals of '61 and '62 and will take the trouble to turn to them, you will do me a favor to save me from the hazard of error on this head.

The Parson's cause (as it was called) arose, you will recollect on the act of '58, commuting the 16000 lbs tobacco stipend, for cash at 16/8 per C.W$^t$. The record of the court (Hanover) which is in my possession, shews that it was tried in nov. '63 on a demurrer, in dec$^r$ following on a writ of enquiry. It is the case of the rev$^d$ Ja$^s$ Maury &

his vestry ag$^t$ the collector of the county. It is agreed that this is the case in which M$^r$ Henry first distinguished himself at the bar. Judge Winston says that shortly after the trial some strictures were published at Williamsburg by a M$^r$ Greene—in which he spoke of M$^r$ Henry with great contempt as an obscure attorney. I mention these circumstances in the hope that it may revive something in your memory that may contribute to give interest to my story: and of this I have the stronger hope, because I observe that you were at this time a student and of an age likely to be struck with so singular and animated a contest as that was.

On the same account I beg leave to ask you if you have any recollection of M$^r$ Henry's having made a very distinguished figure in a contested election before the committee of privileges & elections[3] in 1764? Judge Winston & the late Judge Tyler state it to have been in the case of his brother John Syme. But neither the Journals of '63 or '64 both which are in my possession shew any such contest to have taken place. In '64 there was a contest before that commee between Nat. W. Dandridge, petitioner and James Littlepage the sitting member from Hanover, in w$^c$ it appears that the parties were heard by their counsel before the commee. From the county & the parties, I have thought it probable that this was the case to w$^c$ the two gentlemen have alluded in their statements. The report of the commee in this case was made on the 26 nov. 1764. The petition[4] was resolved to be frivolous and vexatious & Littlepage confirmed in his seat. If you recollect any circumstance which can clear this incident of doubt, or may give it more interest than a naked statement would do, I would thank you to communicate it.

I send you a copy of the resolutions from the journal of '65, as also of M$^r$ Henry's statement; by comparing which you will see that the 5$^{th}$ resolution reported by him is not on the journal; confirming your statement of the rescission of the last resolution—and by comparing both with Judge Marshall's note N$^o$ IV. at the end of his second volume of the life of Washington copied by him from prior documents, you will see what inaccuracy is already creeping into the American history.—I do not perceive that the 5$^{th}$ resolution on M$^r$ Henry's statement, is of a nature so much stronger than the four found on the journal as to explain the solicitude to rescind it: the two additional ones which M$^r$ Marshall says were agreed to by the committee but rejected in the house (and w$^c$ are not found either on the journal or M$^r$ H's copy) are of that nature—is it not possible that the bloody debate may have taken place on those two—but if rejected by the house as

M$^r$ M. states, there could be no necessity to rescind them. The resolutions themselves now sent may refresh your memory so far as to enable you to clear this difficulty for me. would you have any objection to being quoted as to the fact of rescinding the last resolution.—

It would increase the interest of the narrative very much, if I could give any thing like an outline of M$^r$ Henry's speech on his resolutions. The topics w$^c$ would naturally arise from the subject, are easily enough imagined:—but his views had something peculiar in them—and having never seen him, much less heard him, I sh$^d$ be much gratified by such a sketch as I have mentioned, if it were possible to procure it.

The resolutions were introduced in a committee of the whole house: was it before the committee, or in the house that he made his celebrated exclamation of "Cæsar had his Brutus, Charles the 1$^{st}$ his Cromwell—and George the third may profit by their example—" It is said that when he had proceeded so far in this, as to name George the 3$^{rd}$ the speaker from the chair cried out "treason!" which was echoed from various parts of the house—when Henry proceeded firmly,—"may profit by their example—if this be treason make the most of it—" from this narrative the committee must have arisen, the speaker being in his chair, & the house have been formed—& yet the period of introducing his resolutions in the committee seems the most natural for such an appeal. I take it for granted from the universal concurrence about it that the incident really occurred. Have you any recollection of the time place & manner of it—and if so, will you be so good as to state it—It is said by one who professes to have heard M$^r$ H's speech on this occasion, that M$^r$ H. was so ignorant of the forms of the house as to march out into the middle of the floor & wheel about to face the speaker instead of speaking in his place—have you a recollection of this fact.

M$^r$ Henry was much censured by M$^r$ Ed. Randolph, in the convention of 1788, on account of the attainder of a man by the name of Phillips, while Henry was Gov$^r$. I have read M$^r$ Henry's message to the speaker of the House of Burgesses on this subject & perceive that you were at the head of the committee that brought in the Bill of attainder. I cannot perceive that M$^r$ R. had any just ground for his censure in that case. Can you recal the facts?—

I perceive that M$^r$ Henry after serving three years as Gov$^r$ wrote a letter to the speaker, declining the office farther, on a doubt whether under the constitution he was eligible, for a longer term: Was a contrary opinion held by any one?

I beg you to excuse all this trouble—and to believe me, devotedly, Your friend & servant                    W^M WIRT

Can you give me any particular information as to a project said to have been once entertained of making M^r Henry a dictator?—

RC (DLC); postscript written perpendicularly along left margin of first page; endorsed by TJ as received 9 Aug. 1814 and so recorded in SJL. Tr (MdHi: Wirt Papers).

The COMMUNICATION YOU WERE SO KIND AS TO MAKE was TJ's Notes on Patrick Henry, [before 12 Apr. 1812], Document II in a group of documents on TJ's Recollections of Patrick Henry, printed above under that date. The ACT OF '58 was a one-year measure passed by the Virginia General Assembly in September 1758 that authorized the payment of debts in specified cash equivalents rather than previously contracted weights of tobacco, which had increased in value due to a bad crop (Hening, 7:240–1).

In June 1788 at the Virginia ratification convention, Edmund Randolph and Patrick Henry disagreed on the justice and necessity of the BILL OF ATTAINDER obtained ten years earlier against Josiah Philips, a Virginia Loyalist regarded as a brutal criminal by state authorities. After consultation with Governor Henry, TJ had drafted this measure, which was introduced in the House of Delegates on 28 May 1778 and approved by the Senate two days later (*PTJ*, 2:189–93; Merrill Jensen, John P. Kaminski, and others, eds., *The Documentary History of the Ratification of the Constitution* [1976–    ], 9:972, 1004, 1038, 1050–72, 1086–7).

In his 28 May 1779 LETTER TO THE

SPEAKER, DECLINING further election as he neared the end of his third consecutive term as governor, Henry stated that "The term for which I had the honour to be elected governor by the late assembly, being just about to expire, and the constitution, *as I think*, making me ineligible to that office, I take the liberty to communicate to the assembly through you, sir, my intention to retire in four or five days." The Virginia Constitution of 1776 stipulated that the governor "shall not continue in that office longer than three Years successively nor be eligible until the expiration of four Years after he shall have been out of that office." Wirt later suggested that Henry may have based his DOUBT on the "impression . . . that his appointment for the first year, not having been made by delegates who had themselves been elected under the constitution, ought not to be counted as one of the constitutional years of service" (Wirt, *Sketches of the Life and Character of Patrick Henry* [Philadelphia, 1817; Poor, *Jefferson's Library*, 4 (no. 131)], 225; William J. Van Schreeven, Robert L. Scribner, and Brent Tarter, eds., *Revolutionary Virginia, the Road to Independence: A Documentary Record* [1973–83], vol. 7, pt. 2, pp. 651–2).

[1] Tr: "countrymen."
[2] Tr: "the."
[3] Preceding two words not in Tr.
[4] Tr: "petitioner."

ENCLOSURE

# Patrick Henry's Stamp Act Resolves, with Notes by William Wirt

Patrick Henry's Resolutions copied from the Journal of the House of Burgesses in 1765. May 30.
[1]Resolved That the first adventurers and settlers of this his Majesty's Colony and Dominion of Virginia brought with them and transmitted to their

posterity, and all other his Majesty's subjects since inhabiting in this his Majesty's said colony, all the Liberties, Privileges, Franchises and Immunities, that have at any time been held, enjoyed and possessed by the people of Great Britain.

[2]Resolved That by two Royal Charters, granted by King James the First the colonists afores[d] are declared entitled to all Liberties, Privileges and Immunities of Denizens and natural Subjects to all intents & purposes, as if they had been abiding & born within the realm of England.

[3]Resolved That the taxation of the people by themselves, or by persons chosen by themselves to represent them, who can only know what taxes the people are able to bear, or the easiest method of raising them, and must themselves be affected by every tax laid on the people, is the only security against a burthensome taxation, and the distinguishing characteristic of British freedom, without which the ancient constitution cannot exist.

[4]Resolved That his Majesty's liege people of this his most ancient and loyal colony have without interruption enjoyed the inestimable right of being governed by such laws, respecting their internal polity and taxation, as are derived from their own consent, with the approbation of their Sovereign or his substitute; and that the same hath never been forfeited or yielded up but hath been constantly recognized by the Kings & People of Great Britain.

Here the Journal stops:—these are the resolutions as amended in the House—For the Journal says that they were passed, with amendments.—M[r] H's seems to be the copy as reported by the committee of the whole house.

MS (DLC: TJ Papers, 201:35848); entirely in Wirt's hand. Printed in *Journal of the House of Burgesses* (Williamsburg, 1765), 149–50; preceded by "Mr. Attorney, from the Committee of the whole House, reported, according to Order, that the Committee had considered of the Steps necessary to be taken in Consequence of the Resolutions of the House of Commons of *Great Britain* relative to the charging certain Stamp Duties in the Colonies and Plantations in *America*, and that they had come to several Resolutions thereon; which he read in his Place, and then delivered in at the Table, where they were again twice read, and agreed to by the House, with some Amendments, and are as follow."

Texts of resolves drafted by Henry but not finally approved by the HOUSE OF BURGESSES are given in note to TJ to Wirt, 14 Aug. 1814.

# From Joseph Delaplaine

SIR,                                     Philadelphia July 28th 1814

I acknowledge, most sincerely, the receipt of your kind and obliging favour of the 29th of the last month.—

It was my intention from the commencement of my undertaking to have placed your portrait in the first half volume of the Repository, and I regret, greatly regret, that any circumstances should induce me to depart from it.

On this subject I have reflected much. I perceive from your letter of the 3$^d$ of May that the two <u>original</u> portraits of you are in the hands of M$^r$ Stuart at Boston. I know of no means by which I can procure one of these long enough to have an engraving taken from it, unless, indeed, you will be so kind as to write to M$^r$ Stuart on the subject. One of the portraits being your property, I can see no obstruction to my obtaining it, which will be very gratifying. I cannot reconcile to myself to have an engraving taken from the Copy of one of these portraits by M$^r$ Stuart, which you tell me is the property of the President. The moment, sir, it was discovered that the engraving was made from the <u>Copy,</u> when it was known that two <u>originals</u> existed, that moment the character of my work would be blasted, and my reputation as the publisher of this great National work destroyed. I leave you to judge sir, of the delicate situation in which I am placed.

In consulting my friends, under these circumstances, they advise me to defer the engraving until I can obtain one of the original pictures by your direction. They say, "still M$^r$ Jefferson can be given in the first volume of the work." This then is the arrangement    Washington,

Washington,
Franklin
General Green
Hamilton    } first half volume
Ames
Rush

The second half volume will appear with your portrait, Hancock and other worthies making six[1] other portraits. So that the Twelve portraits & lives will be bound up together which form the First volume of the work.

Have the goodness to make the necessary arrangements to enable me <u>in time</u> to have an engraving taken, & if it is found necessary I will go to Boston & bring the picture with me.

I am now prepared to put the portrait of Americus Vespusius in the hands of the engraver, & therefore request the favour of you sir to transmit it to me in the manner you propose. The print will be better for my purpose to have an engraving from, than to engrave from a drawing of the picture. I sincerely wish there was also an equally good print of Columbus.—M$^r$ Wood a very distinguished likeness painter, proposes to go to Washington, when[2] Congress sits, if he does, he purposes having the honor of waiting on you to paint Columbus for me.—

Hoping to be honored with a letter,

I remain with great respect & regard, Your very obed. hum$^l$ serv$^t$

JOSEPH DELAPLAINE

[ 498 ]

P.S. The print of Vespusius shall be taken special care of & returned to you when done with.

RC (DLC); addressed: "Thomas Jefferson Esq^r Monticello Virginia"; franked; postmarked Philadelphia, 29 July; endorsed by TJ as received 3 Aug. 1814 and so recorded in SJL.

The names and sequence of the subjects eventually included in *Delaplaine's Repository* differed significantly from the tentative listing given above.

[1] Reworked from "five."
[2] Manuscript: "wh."

# From John Barnes

DEAR SIR—                                          George Town 29 July 1814.

My last to you on Business, was of 7^th Ins^t in Answer to yours of the 28^th Ult^o since when I deposited with M^r Plasentson—(in M^r Monroes Office) for next conveyance—my second of exchange—as well, your letter to Baring Brothers & C^o to Gen^l K— and to M^r Crawford, and made good my 3^d paym^t of $2,500—to the Loan—your order and Remittance recd—for the Gen^ls last dividend due 1^st Jan^y and wait only—your Ann^l April Int: to close the Gen^ls former Acco^t Curr^t and to Carry the Balance to his New a/c up to 25. Aug^st

We are still, Anxiously, waiting the Result of the Commiss^rs at Ghent, of whose favourable issue—I must, confess I never had but faint hopes of, and less so, since the Un-toward—unexpected—and prompt—effect so suddenly effected—and at a time too—so very unfavorable to our Affairs—has so Materially—inhansed their Arogance & superiority their pride, and Revenge—as to put—to silence—both Reason & Justice—that I cannot—with my most Anxious wishes—and endeavours to persuade myself to the Contrary—feel disposed—to expect any Stable—adjustment, will be Acceded to—and however Dear the Love of Peace—is, to these United States—they must not—be suffered to stain this Land of perfect Freedom—without the most determined struggle for her existance—but once United—not all, their Ships—their Legions—incendiaries and Savages combined, could not wrest it—from US—they may indeed! and will—Murder—Plunder Burn, and Destroy—with Ruthless Vengance—and thereby Retard the aspiring growth of this happy Country—to Subjugate, to their Merciless fury, it is Utterly impossible and the British Ministers themselves are convinced of it, but they also Know—that without War—they must soon Submit—to become a Bankrupt Nation—     If in 1776—the US. had Neither Money nor Ships—Cannon—Arms—Ammunition[1] nor

Cloathing—&c^a &c^a and but 3 Millions of Inhabitants—and <u>Now</u> that they are 9 Millions, and food Suff^t for as Many more <u>what</u>, is there to fear—Unless as Gov^r Morris—said We are, our own, worse Enemies,—

It is only necessiary—to bear & meet our dificulties however great[2] with becoming fortitude—and the issue—<u>must</u>—finally be successfull.—

Most Respectfully—
I am Dear Sir Your Obedient                                   JOHN BARNES,

RC (ViU: TJP-ER); at foot of text: "Thomas Jefferson Esq^r Monticello—Virg^a"; endorsed by TJ as received 3 Aug. 1814 and so recorded in SJL.

GEN^L K—: Tadeusz Kosciuszko. Gouverneur MORRIS gave his opinion on the role of government in an 8 Jan. 1802

speech to the United States Senate: "Why are we here? To save the people from their most dangerous enemy; to save them from themselves" (*Annals*, 7th Cong., 1st sess., 41).

[1] Manuscript: "Ammuition."
[2] Preceding two words interlined.

# From Elizabeth Trist

Bird wood Henry 29^th July —14

Nothing is more grateful to my heart than assurances of friendship and remembrance from those I love and esteem. your favor therefore with the Book you may be assured was most joyfully received to hear that M^r Randolph had resign'd his Military Commissi[on] and that the family were all well gave a Zest to the pleasure, God grant that every blessing may be extended to them, that your health and spirits may be long preserved to give pleasure and comfor[t] to your family and friends—often do I triumph in your escape from the Helm before the storms became violent poor M^r Madison with all his precaution to steer clear of censure has got his full portion and I make no doubt he will be heartily tired of his situation before the time arrives when he can disburthen him self from the cares of state and eat his Hog meat and Homony, in his native Dwelling I never thought the Presidents an enviable situation and I do expect from the want of unanimity in our country that it will become worse and worse—I trembled at one time at the impending ruin of France and for the fate of Bonaparte I never contemplated his being let down so easily, he ought to rejoice at the change for he has a much greater chance of happiness himself his family and connections all liberaly provided for, I shou'd have been delighted at the restoration of the Bourbons, as they have settled matters, if I did not apprehend greater evils wou'd attend our

own Country, we have little mercy to expect from great Britan She
will now have it in her power to distress us more than ever, her well
disciplined Armies will now be turn'd upon us her arrogance will increase with her late success and I have not the most distant hope that
she will give us peace on terms such as we ought accept I shou'd not
care about the Fisheries the Yankies are most interested in that trade
and they deserve to suffer but the impressing our Seamen is what I
can never be reconciled to, the rights of those brave men I hope will
be contended for till there is not a being left to fight for them, Oh
God! if we were only United I shou'd not fear them but I trust and
hope there are true-Blooded Americans enough to prevent our being
subdued—we have sustaind a heavy loss in the crew of the Essex but
their bravery will reflect honor on their Country and immortalize
their renown to the latest ages, I weep for the loss of my Countrymen,
at the same time exult in their Glorious exits we now and then hear
of Brilliant feats being perform'd by the land forces, the late news of
the capture of Erie is pleasing I expect every week to hear of Chauncy
engaging the British fleet on the Lakes but I dont suffer my self to be
too Sanguine of our success in capturing them, but this I am certain
of that our Brave Tars will do their duty, as to Canada I think we may
as well give up the Idea of possessing that Country but if we can get
command of the Lakes it will be a great point gain'd

I have been questioning Francis Gilmer as to the improvements at
Monticello he tells me except an observatory everry thing remaind as
when I left it. what exclaim'd I, are not the Porticoes compleated no,
alas I fear that monument of taste will not long Survive the present
possessor for if he does not finish them they will stand a poor chance
of ever being compleated tho I have not the most distant prospect[1] of
ever visiting Albemarle again I feel interested in all that relates to you
M^r Divers has done nothing towards compleating his establishment
I am afraid you are both become weary of the world, I suppose it is
natural as we advance in life to lose our energy of character, for I feel
that mine has departed tho I some times think if I had the means I
shou'd undertake to superintend building a comfortable House for
I really am sickend with log cabins and want of conveniences but
notwithstanding I feel more contented and happy than I have been
for many years tho I am daily admonish'd that my race is almost run
tho I am never Ill the feebleness of age has come upon me It may
be increased by the continuel wet weather yesterday and last night
the flood gates of Heaven were open'd upon us and the first this
morning was that all was destroy'd on the low ground the mill carried way and some of our poor Neighbours will be ruin'd and what is

more distressing I heard that all the mills in the Neighbourhood have shared the same fate of ours, we have heretofore been very fortunate and must find consolation as old Jemmy did in the loss of his Turkys that others have sufferd equally with ourselves—

Please to present me tenderly and affectionately to M$^{rs}$ Randolph and all her dear connections M$^r$ and M$^{rs}$ Gilmer join me in sincere wishes for your health and long happiness          E— TRIST

pray excuse my long epistles I fear I weary my friends by their want of conciseness I did not intend to obtrude so much on your time or patience and to have written to M$^{rs}$ Randolph but I found that my paper was all consumed

RC (MHi); edge trimmed; endorsed by TJ as received 13 Aug. 1814 and so recorded in SJL.

The USS ESSEX, under the command of Captain David Porter, was captured on 28 Mar. 1814 by the British after a bloody battle off the coast of Valparaiso, Chile. The first action in Major General Jacob Brown's Niagara campaign was the capture of Fort ERIE on 3 July 1814 (Heidler and Heidler, *War of 1812*, 170–1, 174–5).

[1] Manuscript: "prospet."

# From Frank Carr

MY DEAR SIR,                                   July 31$^{st}$ 1814

I am called on as surgeon to this regiment, to attend the late requisition of militia from this brigade, to the lower country. The detatchment left Charlottesville today; and I shall follow them as soon as I can make the necessary arrangements. This will put it out of my power to attend your boy, & will compell me, very reluctantly, to request those of my friends who have thought me worthy of their confidence, to make a temporary transfer of it to some other person. The distance of D$^r$ John Gilmer from Monticello[1] would probably render an application to him too inconvenient: of those physicians more convenient who reside in Charlottesville, permit me to recommend D$^r$ Ragland to you—

Very respectfully y$^{rs}$ &c                    FRANK CARR

RC (DLC); addressed: "M$^r$ Jefferson Monticello"; endorsed by TJ as received 31 July 1814 and so recorded in SJL.

John C. Ragland (ca. 1787–1823), physician, graduated from the College of William and Mary in 1808 and received a medical degree from the University of Pennsylvania in 1813. Ragland frequently provided medical services at Monticello between 1817 and his death (*William and Mary Provisional List*, 33; *Eclectic Repertory and Analytical Review* 3 [1813]: 540; *MB*; Woods, *Albemarle*, 243; James Monroe to Charles Everette, 5 Jan. 1824, printed in *Tyler's Quarterly Historical and Genealogical Magazine* 5 [1923]: 22; *Richmond Enquirer*, 6 Jan. 1824).

An undated letter from Ragland to TJ, not found, is recorded in SJL as received 22 July 1817.

[1] Word interlined in place of "this place."

# From Edward Coles

DEAR SIR                                    Washington July 31st 1814

I never took up my pen with more hesitation or felt more embarrassment than I now do in addressing you on the subject of this letter. The fear of appearing presumptuous distresses me, and would deter me from venturing thus to call your attention to a subject of such magnitude, and so beset with difficulties, as that of a general emancipation of the Slaves of Virginia, had I not the highest opinion of your goodness and liberality, in not only excusing me for the liberty I take, but in justly appreciating my motives in doing so.

I will not enter on the <u>right</u> which man has to enslave his Brother man, nor upon the moral and political effects of Slavery on individuals or on Society; because these things are better understood by you than by me. My object is to entreat and beseech you to exert your knowledge and influence, in devising, and getting into operation, some plan for the gradual emancipation of Slavery. This difficult task could be less exceptionably, and more successfully performed by the revered Fathers of all our political and social blessings, than by any succeeding statesmen; and would seem to come with peculiar propriety and force from those whose valor wisdom and virtue have done so much in meliorating the condition of mankind. And it is a duty, as I conceive, that devolves particularly on you, from your known philosophical and enlarged view of subjects, and from the principles you have professed and practiced through a long and useful life, pre-eminently distinguished, as well by being foremost in establishing on the broadest basis the rights of man, and the liberty and independence of your Country, as in being throughout honored with the most important trusts by your fellow-citizens, whose confidence and love you have carried with you into the shades of old age and retirement. In the calm of this retirement you might, most beneficially to society, and with much addition to your own fame, avail yourself of that love and confidence to put into complete practice those hallowed principles contained in that renowned Declaration, of which you were the immortal author, and on which we bottomed[1] our right to resist oppression, and establish our freedom and independence.

I hope that the fear of failing, at this time, will have no influence in preventing you from employing your pen to eradicate this most degrading feature of British Coloniel policy, which is still permitted to exist, notwithstanding its repugnance as well to the principles of our revolution as to our free Institutions. For however highly prized and influential your opinions may now be, they will be still much more so when you shall have been snatched[2] from us by the course of nature. If therefore your attempt should now fail to rectify this unfortunate evil—an evil most injurious both to the oppressed and to the oppressor—at some future day when your memory will be consecrated by a grateful posterity, what influence, irresistible influence will the opinions and writings of Thomas Jefferson have on all questions connected with the rights of man, and of that policy which will be the creed of your disciples. Permit me then, my dear Sir, again to intreat you to exert your great powers of mind and influence, and to employ[3] some of your present leisure, in devising a mode to liberate one half of our Fellowbeings from an ignominious bondage to the other; either by making an immediate attempt to put in train a plan to commence this goodly work, or to leave human Nature the invaluable Testament—which you are so capable of doing—how best to establish its rights: So that the weight of your opinion may be on the side of emancipation when that question shall be agitated, and that it will be sooner or later is most certain—That it may be soon is my most ardent prayer—that it will be rests with you.

I will only add, as an excuse for the liberty I take in addressing you on this subject, which is so particularly interesting to me; that from the time I was capable of reflecting on the nature of political society, and of the rights appertaining to Man, I have not only been principled against Slavery, but have had feelings so repugnant to it, as to decide me not to hold them; which decision has forced me to leave my native state, and with it all my relations and friends. This I hope will be deemed by you some excuse for the liberty of this intrusion, of which I gladly avail myself to assure you of the very great respect and esteem with which I am, my dear Sir, your very sincere and devoted friend

EDWARD COLES

RC (MHi); at foot of text: "Th: Jefferson"; endorsed by TJ as received 3 Aug. 1814 and so recorded in SJL. FC (NjP: Coles Papers); entirely in Coles's hand; at head of text: "Copy to Th: Jefferson"; with penciled notation by Coles at foot of text: "The original reply of M[r] Jefferson to this is in my possession, but has been published two or three times, & is in one of the Scrap books I sent you. E C." Tr (NjP: Coles Papers); entirely in Coles's hand.

[1] Reworked in Tr to "founded."
[2] Tr: "taken."
[3] RC: "emply." FC and Tr: "employ."

# To Baron Karl von Moll

SIR                         Monticello July 31. 1814. in Virginia.

Within a few days only I have recieved the letter which you did me the honor to write on the 22$^{\text{d}}$ of July 1812. a delay which I presume must be ascribed to the interruption of the intercourse of the world by the wars which have lately desolated it by sea and land. still involved ourselves with a nation possessing almost exclusively the ocean which separates us, I fear the one I have now the honor of addressing you may experience equal delay.          I recieve with much gratification the Diploma of the Agronomic society of Bavaria, conferring on me the distinction of being honorary member of their society. for this mark of their goodwill I pray you to be the channel of communicating to them my respectful thanks. age and distance will add their obstacles to the services I shall ardently wish to render the society. yet sincerely devoted to this art, the basis of the subsistence, the comforts, and the happiness of man; & sensible of the general interest which all nations have in communicating freely to each other discoveries of new and useful processes and implements in it, I shall with zeal at all times meet the wishes of the society, & especially rejoice in every opportunity which their commands may present of being useful to them. with the homage of my respects to them, be pleased to accept for yourself the assurances of my particular & high consideration.                         TH: JEFFERSON

PoC (DLC); at foot of text: "The Baron de Moll, privy counsellor of his Majesty the King of Bavaria, Secretary of the Academy of Sciences for the class of mathematical & physical sciences, and of the Agronomic society of Bavaria    at Munic."

# From David Bailie Warden

1. August, 1814.

I have forwarded a trunk, to the care of mr. Shaler, at gand, and addressed to Mr. Short, Philadelphia, containing volumes and brochures for yourself and this gentleman, from mr. Rochon—

I saw General Kosciusko yesterday who bids me present you his respects, and to inform you, that he has transmitted a letter to you through Mr. Parker.—He was preparing to set out for his place near Fontainbleau—He forwarded the letter to Mr. nimsewitz—General La Fayette proposes to write to you.—

I have forwarded a letter and documents to you, by mr. Shaler, under cover to General Mason, concerning the suspension of my Consular functions.—I had proposed to visit Washington, but I have not been able to procure a passport from London, without which, Mr. Gallatin informs me, I cannot be received on board the <u>John Adams</u>—This circumstance, and the strong conviction that I have zealously and actively discharged the duties of my office, have determined me to wait at Paris for further orders—I trust that you will find my justification satisfactory, and that I have done no voluntary act to render me unworthy of your further protection: though indeed I feel ashamed to trouble you again on the same subject—

mr. La Harpe, the preceptor of the Emperor of Russia has spoken to mr. Gallatin in my behalf; so has Mr. Say—the Baron De Humboldt has written to the President in the warmest manner for my reestablishment—so have other distinguished personages—

I inclose a letter from mr. De Tracey—To whom I have presented a copy of the Commentary on montesquieu.—

D. B. WARDEN—

RC (DLC: TJ Papers, 201:35760–1); subjoined to 2d Dupl of Warden to TJ, 6 May 1814; addressed: "His Excellency, Thomas Jefferson Esquire Monticello"; franked; postmarked Washington, 9 Oct.; endorsed by TJ as received 12 Oct. 1814 and so recorded in SJL. Enclosure: Destutt de Tracy to TJ, 14 July 1814.

GAND: Ghent. Alexander von Humboldt wrote PRESIDENT James Madison on Warden's behalf on 26 Aug. 1813 (Madison, *Papers, Pres. Ser.*, 6:559–60).

Alexis Marie ROCHON wrote TJ a letter in support of Warden on 2 Aug. 1814, of which only the following extract has been found: "Il vient de perdre sa place et c'est pour moi, et pour notre ami, m. Le Ray de Chaumont un vrai sujet d'affliction: c'est un excellent homme et toutes les personnes de mes amis et de mes amis connoissances eprouvent un vrai regret de la perte qu'il a fait d'une place qu'il remplissoit avec zele et assiduité" ("He has just lost his post and it is for me and our friend M. Le Ray de Chaumont a very afflicting subject: he is an excellent man and all my friends and acquaintances truly regret his loss of a position that he filled with such zeal and assiduity") (Tr in MdHi: Warden Letterbooks; entirely in Warden's hand; partially dated "2 aout" ["2 Aug."]; followed by a letter dated 4 Aug. 1814; in left margin: "Rochon to mr. Jefferson"; not recorded in SJL and probably never received by TJ).

# From William Thornton

DEAR SIR City of Washington 2<sup>d</sup> Aug<sup>st</sup> 1814.—

DEAR SIR City of Washington 2<sup>d</sup> Aug<sup>st</sup> 1814.—

I had this Day the honor of your Letter of the 23<sup>d</sup> Ult<sup>o</sup> inclosing Janes's Papers, which came in safety.—At the same time I received the inclosed Letter from Janes, and wrote immediately to M<sup>r</sup> George Greer of Baltimore to know his Terms.—I enclose a Copy of my

Letter to him, & shall transmit his answer as soon as received. I should have written to M<sup>r</sup> Clopper, but do not know where he is at present.—I should not have failed to have sent you a Copy of each of the annual lists of Patents, but they were only accidentally received even in my Office, & it was considered next to a favour to grant me a single copy.—I offered to revise the whole, & bring them into a smaller compass, if the Congress would have them reprinted, but they refused; wishing really, without making the proper & necessary expenditures, to draw from the Office a revenue.—My labours encrease so much, that the office brings in about 7000 Doll<sup>s</sup> now, & when I undertook it the receipts amounted to only ab<sup>t</sup> 1400—& tho' I rec<sup>d</sup> after the receipts doubled 2000 Doll<sup>s</sup> the Congress have not appropriated more than 1400 for several years back; so that I am worse situated than I was twenty years ago—having then 1600 Doll<sup>s</sup> which were equal to 2500 Doll<sup>s</sup> now—I am dear Sir with the highest respect & consideration Y<sup>r</sup> &c             WILLIAM THORNTON—

RC (MHi); at foot of text: "Honor<sup>ble</sup> Thomas Jefferson"; endorsed by TJ as received 10 Aug. 1814 and so recorded in SJL. RC (MHi); address cover only; on verso of TJ to Peter Cottom, 17 Aug. 1814; addressed: "Honorable Thomas Jefferson Monticello"; franked; postmarked Washington, 4 Aug.

ENCLOSURES

I

## Walter Janes to William Thornton

SIR                                    Ashford 12<sup>th</sup> [July] 1814

I recieved your Letter dated July 1<sup>st</sup> yesterday, enclosing a line from M<sup>r</sup> Jefferson, proposing certain questions relative to my Patent Loom, to which you request of me specific answers—and first he enquires to know if "the treadles and shuttle are compleatly worked by the stroke of the Batten"[1]—I answer they are—"Is it of such simplicity as that it can be made by our Country workmen, and kept in order by t[he co]mmon ingenuity in our families"? With a very little practice in either case, it is.—"Can the Machinery[2] be fixed to a common Loom &c—"? It cannot—It will require a New Frame and Machinery throughout—But its construction is simple, and its operation[3] easy to become acquainted with.—

You also enquire "what I would charge M<sup>r</sup> Jefferson for the privilege of using the Improvement &c."[4]—For such privilege, I must refer him to M<sup>r</sup> George Greer of Baltimore, or Robert Miller of Philadelphia, they having lately purchased My right for the southern and Western States—

They have some of the Looms in operation in Phil<sup>a</sup> and in Baltimore, and probably will soon have some agoing at Washington Yours &c—

WALTER JANES

RC (DLC: TJ Papers, 203:36102); partially dated; mutilated, with missing text supplied from TJ to Thornton, 9 June 1814; addressed: "William Thornton Esq[e] Washington Columbia."

Walter Janes (1779–1827), musician and inventor, moved between 1807 and 1810 from Dedham, Massachusetts, to Ashford, Windham County, Connecticut. He taught and conducted music and published two tune books that included many of his own compositions: *The Massachusetts Harmony* (Boston, 1803) and *The Harmonic Minstrelsey* (Dedham, 1807). Janes was a prominent Mason and author of *A Masonic Poem, Delivered at Mansfield, (Conn.) Before Trinity Chapter of* *Royal Arch Masons* (Brookfield, Mass., 1819). Between 1810 and 1826 he received six patents, for improved looms and wagon springs and for machines for weaving, shelling corn, and bending wheel tires (Frederic Janes, *The Janes Family: A Genealogy and Brief History of the Descendants of William Janes* [1868], 140, 195–7; *List of Patents*, 79, 85, 124, 205, 315, 316; *Masonic Mirror: And Mechanics' Intelligencer* 3 [1827]: 383).

[1] Omitted closing quotation mark editorially supplied.
[2] Manuscript: "Machinry."
[3] Janes here canceled "considered."
[4] Omitted closing quotation mark editorially supplied.

# II

## William Thornton to George Greer

SIR City of Washington 2[d] Aug[t] 1814

The late President of the U.S. M[r] Jefferson being desirous of knowing how & where he could obtain one of the Looms of M[r] Janes's Improvem[t] I wrote to M[r] J: & received this day his answer, referring me to you or to M[r] Robert Miller of Philadel[a]—you having purchased his right for the Southern & Western States—M[r] Jefferson would wish such parts as could be taken in the Stage or in a Cart to Monticello—but such only as would require attention in the construction, because his own carpenters are very good workmen, & he is well acquainted with the construction & operation of common Looms; therefore if you would be so obliging as to favor him with the essential parts and could pack them in a Box which could be safely sent to him by the Stages you would not only render him, but yourself a very essential service; for if he bring the improvement into use, it will extend over the Country, much to your benefit as the proprietor; & be assured he is no common patron of the Arts. He not only labours to serve the whole Community, but particularly those who are engaged in advancing the Arts; & by the industry of his own family sets an Example to the Country. As early an Answer as you can favor me with, I particularly request, containing an Account of the several parts, with their prices, & what it will cost to have them all executed in the best manner—Also what you will charge him for the right to set up as many Looms for his own use as he pleases, also the right of individual looms, if he should confine himself to two or three.—This you know as well as I, that whatever liberality you shew it will not be in any manner abused; but greatly rewarded—by its consequences—

I am Sir very respectfully &[c] W: T.

Tr (MHi); between dateline and salutation: "(Copy)"; at foot of text: "M[r] George Greer."

George Greer (ca. 1778–1827), merchant in Baltimore, traded with Port-au-Prince and imported madeira and coffee.

He was severely wounded at Fort McHenry in September 1814 during service as a private in the Baltimore Independent Artillerists. Greer received a United States pension in 1823 and unsuccessfully sought a federal appointment the following year (William M. Marine, *The British Invasion of Maryland, 1812–1815* [1913], 173, 303; *Pension Roll of 1835* [1835; indexed ed., 1992], 3:22; *Baltimore Price Current*, 22 July 1815, 16 Jan. 1819; Charleston, S.C., *City Gazette*, 12 June 1816; *Baltimore Patriot & Mercantile Advertiser*, 11 Aug. 1824, 18 Aug. 1826; Robert Oliver and others to James Monroe, 1 Mar. 1824 [DNA: RG 59, LAR, 1817–25]; gravestone in Old Saint Paul's Cemetery, Baltimore).

# To Robert Gillespie

SIR                                                    Monticello Aug. 3. 14.

Your favor of June 10. has come to hand after a long passage. no one however is less qualified than myself to judge of the merits of your invention of the Log still. for altho' not unacquainted with the general theory of distillation, yet I never had occasion to examine the structure even of the common still. but I do not understand how you can have been <u>refused</u> a patent whether the invention were new or not. the law (unless it has been altered since my attention to it) has made the issuing a patent a matter of right to whoever pays the sum of 30.D. and gives in the specification E$^t$c of their invention; and leaves it to be settled by a court and jury whether the invention be new. and this is to be done by the patentee's bringing an action against any[1] individual who uses the invention without having purchased the right to do so. if it be found not to have been new the patentee fails in his action; if otherwise he recovers the damages prescribed by law. this I believe to be the state of the law at present, and that a patent cannot be refused to you. supposing that the drawing you favored me with may be useful to yourself and that it ought not to get into other hands, I return it with the assurances of my respect & esteem.                                                    TH: JEFFERSON

PoC (DLC); at foot of text: "M$^r$ Robert Gillespie"; endorsed by TJ. Enclosure not found.

Robert Gillespie, inventor, spent time in New York, Virginia, Kentucky, and Tennessee. In 1810 he patented a perpetual still and evaporator, which he described in his *A New Plan For Distilling With Greater Facility Than Has Ever Been Heretofore Practised In Any Country* (Baltimore, 1810). Five years later he received a patent for a steam still. Gillespie became embroiled in a bitter and public patent dispute with James Wheatley, of Fauquier County, recipient of an 1813 patent for an improvement in the still and condensing tub. The men continued to quarrel even after agreeing to divide their rights by region according to a contract recorded in the Culpeper County Court (*List of Patents*, 81, 129, 149; Washington *Daily National Intelligencer*, 12, 18 May, 13 July 1815; Gillespie to James Monroe, 11 Mar. 1816 [DNA: RG 59, MLR]; Gillespie, *Observations on*

*Mashing* [Knoxville, 1817; broadside at NcU]; Harrison Hall, *The Distiller* [Philadelphia, 1818], 62–7).

Gillespie's letter of JUNE. 10, not found, is recorded in SJL as received from Nashville on 6 July 1814. The patent law of 1793, which TJ helped to draft, required a 30.D. fee from inventors submitting patent requests. In 1800 the law was amended to set the penalty in-curred by an individual who used an invention WITHOUT HAVING PURCHASED THE RIGHT TO DO SO at triple the actual damages sustained by the patentee, his or her executors, administrators, or assigns (*PTJ*, 22:359–62, 25:398–9; *U.S. Statutes at Large*, 1:318–23, 2:37–8).

[1] Word interlined in place of "some."

# To James Monroe

DEAR SIR                                        Monticello Aug. 3. 14.

Yours of July 25. was recieved on the 31st. I learn by it with[1] extreme concern that you have in contemplation the sale of the lands here. I had ever fondly hoped for your return to our society when you should have run out your career of public usefulness. perhaps however my age should relieve me from the pain of such long prospects. the survey of mr Short's land which you saw in my hand belonging properly to mr Higgenbotham, I have taken an exact copy of it, which I inclose to be kept for your own use. I very much wish we could get the disputed line settled: but this can never be done without the attendance of mr Carter. I hope therefore you will engage him to come at some fixed time which may suit yourself in the course of this autumn. you know the anxious dispositions of mr Short to be clear of all litigations, and to keep his affairs clear and distinct. say something to me in your first letter which I may write to him.

I send you the letters you desired and a short one to mr Cabell to whom I communicated them, because it expresses my entire despair on the subject, and at the same time the limitations under which I made the communication, to him, as now to yourself. if I had thought the President had time to read such voluminous speculations, I should have submitted them to him; but knowing his labors, I spared him on a principle of duty, & further because, altho' they might go further into details than his time had permitted him, yet they offered no principle or fact which was not familiar to him. should you think the communication of them to mr Campbell would be acceptable to him, you will be so good as to do it in my name: but there let it stop for the reasons explained in my letter to mr Cabell. keeping no copy of them, I shall be glad of their return after perusal. be assured of my affectionate esteem & respect.                        TH: JEFFERSON

RC (DLC: Monroe Papers); at foot of text: "Col⁰ Monroe." PoC (DLC); endorsed by TJ. Enclosures: (1) Robert Lewis's 18 Apr. 1795 survey of William Short's Indian Camp property (extant texts described at *PTJ*, 28:333–4n; a more detailed survey, undated but compiled during Short's ownership, shows the property in question and its surroundings [CSmH: JF-SA]). (2) TJ to John Wayles Eppes, 24 June, 11 Sept., 6 Nov. 1813. (3) TJ to Joseph C. Cabell, 17 Jan. 1814.

[1] Manuscript: "with with."

# From Augustus B. Woodward

Philadelphia, August 3. 1814.

M^r Woodward has the honor to transmit a small Philadelphia publication, which contains among other singular cases the case and speech of Eugene Aram; and to present his respects.—

RC (DLC); endorsed by TJ as received 12 Aug. 1814 and so recorded in SJL. Enclosure: *The Criminal Recorder: or, An Awful Beacon to the Rising Generation of Both Sexes, Erected by the Arm of Justice to Persuade Them from the Dreadful Miseries of Guilt*, 3d American ed. (Philadelphia, 1812; Sowerby, no. 2096; Poor, *Jefferson's Library*, 10 [no. 597]).

# From William Barton

SIR,                                    Lancaster, Aug. 4. 1814.

I was duly favoured with yours of the 30^th of June, and acknowledge myself much indebted to You for your polite attention to my proposed biographical work. I am aware of the difficulties to be encountered in conducting an undertaking of that Kind: they are such, however, as must be experienced by any man who shall engage in such a work; and although some of the obstacles, which stand in the way of a complete American Biography, are insurmountable, many others may be overcome by industry & perseverance. I shall not be easily deterred from prosecuting my plan; but I shall be in no haste to accomplish it.—The times are very inauspicious to literary pursuits. Our Country seems likely to become the theatre of a desolating War; the extent and duration of which, no man can foresee. In its consequences, I fear, it will prove destructive of some of our best interests. By grasping at imaginary advantages, we may perhaps forfeit, forever, the most important & substantial benefits a country can possess. Circumstanced as the United States now are, I am persuaded that the speedy establishment of a liberal Peace is the only means by which we can ensure a state of national prosperity and private happiness. I ask pardon for having obtruded these sentiments upon you:—feeling as I do on the occasion—with the most anxious solicitude for the welfare & honour of my native country,—I have been involuntarily led into an expression of opinions, which I know are not merely mine, but those of vast multitudes of the best men in the community;—I mean, intelligent & virtuous men of all Parties.—

Having been very lately in Philadelphia, my Bookseller informed me he had forwarded to you the six copies of my "Memoirs"—Will you permit me to request, that the amo$^t$ of your Subscription ($18–) may be remitted to me.—

I have the Honour to be,

With great Respect, Sir, Y$^r$ Mo. obed$^t$ Serv$^t$      W. Barton

RC (DLC); at foot of text: "Hon. T. Jefferson"; endorsed by TJ. Recorded in SJL as received 10 Aug. 1814.

# From George Hargraves

Sir                                Bedford, Aug$^t$ 4. 1814

The enclosed description and drawing of a Torpedo is an original paper which has lately fallen into my possession. Not being a judge of such matters, I shou'd probably have thrown it by as useless paper had I not known the Inventor to be a man of science, and more capable, in my opinion, of judging correctly of the efficacy of such things than any other person I know of—I am induced to send it to you not only because he mentions your name, but because after examining it, shou'd you think it deserving notice, you will have it in your power to forward it to some man of genius capable of making the experiment. Every exertion I think ought to be made at this time to check the predatory warfare carried on by the Enemy on our Sea board, and cou'd any plan be adopted to prevent maritime warfare altogether it wou'd doubtless be productive of great good to the World—From that part wherein your name is mentioned, you will readily conjecture who the Inventor is—: Doctor Ramsay, in his History of the revolutionary War, mentions him among the ingenious men of that time—I have no objection to your communicating the plan to any one you think proper, but for particular reasons, I beg of you to conceal his name, and to withhold from publick view that part which may lead to a discovery—

Shou'd a trial be made I shou'd be highly gratified to know the

[ 512 ]

result. I am now at the Bedford Springs drinking the Waters for my health—my place of residence is Warrenton, Georgia—

I am Sir, very respectfully, your most humble Serv<sup>t</sup>

GEO: HARGRAVES

RC (DLC); endorsed by TJ as a letter received from "Bedford?" on 17 Aug. 1814 and so recorded in SJL. RC (DLC); address cover only, with PoC of TJ to Nicolas G. Dufief, 21 Aug. 1814, on verso; addressed: "The Honorable Thomas Jefferson Monticello Virginia"; franked; postmarked Bedford, 5 Aug. Enclosure not found.

George Hargraves (ca. 1772–1849) served as a notary public and justice of the peace for Warren County, Georgia. He formed a business partnership with John Maury Fontaine and became a director of the Bank of the State of Georgia and of the branch Bank of the United States at Augusta (*Journal of the House of Representatives of the State of Georgia* [1799 sess.], 44, 49, [1805 sess.], 45; *Acts of the General Assembly of the State of Georgia* [1815 sess.], 27; *Niles' Weekly Register*, 18 May 1816; *The Planters' and Merchants' Almanac For The Year Of Our Lord 1817 . . . Calculated for the States of Carolina & Georgia* [Charleston, 1817];

Winston Francis Fontaine, *From Riches To Rags To Respectability: The History of a Fontaine Family and Kinfolks* [1987], 99; DNA: RG 29, CS, Ga., Warren Co., 1830, Muscogee Co., 1840; Greenville, S.C., *Mountaineer*, 5 Oct. 1849).

The INVENTOR mentioned by DOCTOR RAMSAY was David Bushnell, whose pioneering submarine, the *Turtle*, unsuccessfully attacked British warships in 1776. He also developed naval mines. Bushnell relocated to Georgia after the American Revolution and lived under the pseudonym "David Bush." Hargraves served as an executor of his estate in 1826 (David Ramsay, *The History of the American Revolution* [Trenton, 1811; Sowerby, no. 490], 2:404; *ANB*; Frederick Wagner, *Submarine Fighter of the American Revolution: The Story of David Bushnell* [1963], 120; Alex Roland, *Underwater Warfare in the Age of Sail* [1978], 62–88, 193–8; *PTJ*, 12:303–5; *Augusta Chronicle and Georgia Advertiser*, 25 Mar. 1826).

# To John H. Cocke

DEAR SIR                                        Monticello Aug. 5. 14.

I had expected long ere this that the sale of my flour in the hands of Mess<sup>rs</sup> Gibson & Jefferson in Richmond would have enabled me to send you an order on them for the price of the horse you were so kind as to furnish me with: and the rather as I had desired mr Gibson, as I informed you, to sell it for whatever he could get, & this I have been constantly repeating & expecting. but by our last mail he assures me he has not been able to sell a barrel, altho he has offered it at $3\frac{1}{4}$.D. and in fact that none can be sold at any price.        the great collection of force at Norfolk gives hope of a sensible demand as their consumption will be considerable, and can be supplied only from James river. the prospects of peace too, which every symptom favors, the moment they make impression on the merchants, will put them into motion. I can only hope then that a speedy change in the present state of things, may enable mr Gibson to comply with my instructions, and myself to send you the order promised. in the mean time I am constrained to ask your indulgence. with my regret for this unexpected failure be pleased to accept the assurance of my great esteem and respect. Th: Jefferson

RC (ViU: TJP); addressed: "Gen¹ John H. Cocke Bremo near New Canton"; franked; postmarked Milton, 7 Aug.; endorsed by Cocke. PoC (DLC); endorsed by TJ.

# From James Ogilvie

[ca. 5 Aug. 1814]

This speculation on Neology appears to me equally valuable & new: It perfectly concurs with the opinion I was led to form, when I had occasion to examine this subject several years ago: Language & especially the modern languages of civilised nations are necessarily in a state of incessant mutation & flux: As new discoveries are made new terms must be provided to designate[1] these discoveries: As errors are detected & exploded, the terms by which they were expressed are exploded also: It sometimes happens that the nomenclature of a whole science must undergo a radical change—Commerce too, in modern times so immensely extended by making common to every country the natural & artificial productions of every other, is constantly introducing new words.—

RC (MHi); undated; at head of text: "To Mᵣ Jefferson"; endorsed by TJ: "Ogilvie James      Aug. 5. 14."

[1] Word interlined in place of "express."

# To Reuben Perry

Dear Sir                                        Monticello Aug. 5. 14.

I promised you that on the completion of the bill of scantling I gave you, and the reciept of your account, I would give you an order on Richmond, for the amount of that & of the old balance. this I did on the confidence that my last year's crop of flour, in the hands of Gibson & Jefferson in Richmond, (400. Barrels) would be sold for something. but mr Gibson in his last letter informs me that he has offered it for $3\frac{1}{4}$.D. in vain, & that he does not believe it can at this time be disposed of at any price. I had further confided that, even if the sale was deferred, I could obtain a small and short accomodation from the bank of Richmond, which I would have done rather than keep you out of your money. but he further informs me that the bank has suspended discounts, & is calling in their debts. I have not learnt whether mr Adkinson has compleated the bill; but whether he has or not, I am sincerely mortified to be obliged to inform you that I shall not be able to make good my word, for the causes before stated. the great collection of force at Norfolk, which can only be supplied with bread from James river ought to produce soon a sensible demand; and the increasing prospects of peace, which acquire more and more strength, may set the exporters in motion, and enable us to turn our produce into money. until this happens, it seems vain to name days of paiment; but you may be assured that not a day shall be passed over after either the sale of my flour or return of the usual course of business at the bank of Richmond shall enable me to give you a draught as promised. Accept my best wishes.                    TH: JEFFERSON

PoC (ViW: TC-JP); at foot of text: "M$^r$ Reuben Perry"; endorsed by TJ.

# To John Watts

DEAR SIR                                        Monticello Aug. 5. 14.
I had expected with great certainty ere this to have been able to pay off my 2$^d$ bond to Griffin in your hands, having, as I informed you, desired mr Gibson to make sale of my flour in his hands (400. Bar.) for whatever he could get; and this I have constantly urged. by our last mail however he informs me that he has offered it at $3\frac{1}{4}$ Dollars & cannot get that, nor at this time can it be sold for any thing. however afraid of banks, I would have applied to that of Virginia in Richmond, which had very readily offered me an accomodation once before. but so far from making new discounts, they are calling in their debts. these difficulties, so unexpected, have placed me under the mortification of being unable to discharge that bond, as I had counted with confidence. nor do they open any precise prospect as to the moment when they may be expected to cease. the great collection of force at Norfolk offers some hope of a demand for flour, as their consumption is sufficient to produce a sensible demand, & they cannot get supplies but from James river. the opening prospects of peace too, between England & us, which every symptom indicates,

and which, the moment it obtains confidence, will put the merchants into motion, give hopes that this state of things will shortly be changed. notwithstanding the random shot of the English & Canada newspapers, there is not the least authentic ground to believe they have sent, or intend to send more than the 15. to 1800. men arrived at Quebec. if they had not meant peace, with their large disposible force, a much greater one would have been here ere the season had so far past over. during the present state of things therefore, and the hope of an early change, I am forced to request your indulgence, altho' I cannot specify a particular term to it, under the assurance that the very first moment it is brought within my power, the bond shall be discharged. with my regrets for this failure, be pleased to accept the assurance of my great esteem & respect      TH: JEFFERSON

P.S. at the date of writing this letter, the state of our information was as is therein mentioned. but before it goes to the Post office we recieve the Nat[l] Intelligencer of Aug. 2. quoting London papers which state that an embarcation of 8000 men had taken place at Bordeaux, destined for America, that more were to follow, and further the departure of Commissioners to Ghent for the negociation of peace. the embarcation of 8000. men does not seem inconsistent with views of peace, because not more than they would chuse to place there in a state of peace.

PoC (MHi); at foot of recto: "Col° William Watts" and "turn over"; postscript on verso; endorsed by TJ; identity of addressee corrected based on MB, 2:1309.

John Watts (ca. 1756–1830), Bedford County landowner, was a captain of dragoons during the Revolutionary War. In January 1799 he was commissioned a lieutenant colonel of dragoons in the United States Army, serving until his honorable discharge in June 1800. Ellen W. Randolph (Coolidge) later described Watts as TJ's "only decided enemy" in the vicinity of Poplar Forest (TxNaSFA: Watts Family Papers; Washington, Papers, Retirement Ser., 3:101–2, 229, 240, 335; Heitman, Continental Army, 576; Heitman, U.S. Army, 1:1010; Ellen W. Randolph [Coolidge] to Virginia J. Randolph [Trist], 4 Aug. 1819 [ViU: Ellen Wayles Randolph Coolidge Correspondence]; Lynchburg Virginian, 17 June 1830; Washington Daily National Intelligencer, 22 June 1830; Bedford Co. Will Book, 7:376–8).

# To Patrick Gibson

DEAR SIR                                    Monticello Aug. 7. 14.
    Your letter of July 27. was duly recieved, and the 200 D. inclosed in it. I find that in making my draughts, I had had too much confi-

dence that a sale of my flour could be effected on some terms, and that the deficiency produced by sacrifice in price, might be obtained from the bank until the crop, growing and severed might be got to market. I was not aware of their stopping discounts, & calling in their debts; an operation however which I verily believe is salutary & necessary for their security. for that a great crush must happen from the abuse of these institutions in the North seems certain. I think therefore what they are doing is wise, notwithstanding it's effect on my own situation. immediately on the reciept of your letter I set to work to accomodate in point of time, the money engagements I was under, and believe I can postpone all of them except one of 370.D. to be remitted to mr Barnes of Geo. T. on an account of so particular a character that I should stand on no sacrifice to make it good; and the remittan[ce]s to Philadelphia, which I mentioned to you, amounting to about 140.D. these are for several individuals, who giving credit to a person so distant and out of their reach, are entitled to have them considered peculiarly as debts of honor. I am not without hope that some demand for flour for the force collecting at Norfolk will arise; and that the prospect of peace, which the late embarcation of troops at Bordeaux does not disturb, will soon set the market in motion. yet these will not be in time to meet these two calls which press. I could not ask further advances from you; because the new operations of the banks may require cautions which I would not press upon certainly, from a sense of much kindness in our preceding relations. but having, for many years, had no other medium but your house for the transaction of my affairs, I have no other from whom I could make the enquiry whether, in such a place as Richmond, any private resource exists, of short accomodation, on any terms, & on any security I could give; which so far as regards property may be as ample as desired.          altho' this, would be new to me, yet for the particular calls stated, I would do it, confident that as it is the first, so it would be the last instance of being so far off my guard, as to expose myself to such a necessity. I look forward with great anxiety to the return of peace, and of a regular course in the transactions of life, where fair and rational calculations may not be defeated of their consequences by arbitrary causes.          there will be two small bills presented to you for articles ordered some months ago, and which, not seeing them in your account, I presume are still out. the one will be by mr Staples for some castings, the other by mr Rich^d Randolph for some of his earthen ware. of the remittances for Philadelphia, 68.75 D are for Bradford & Inskeep booksellers there, who in a letter of

Apr. 7. informed me they had sent by the mail stage, to your care, some copies of Lewis & Clarke's voyage. have they ever come to hand. Accept assurances of my perfect esteem & respect.

TH: JEFFERSON

PoC (NHi: Thomas Jefferson Papers); one word faint; at foot of first page: "M$^r$ Gibson"; endorsed by TJ.

# To Lancelot Minor

DEAR SIR                                         Monticello Aug. 7. 14.

I am now so frequently and long in Bedford, & find such accumulations of letters on my return, that I am long answering them, and especially those which press least. yours of Jan. 20. had been recieved in February, that of June waited here till my last return from Bedford. both contained copies of your accounts. in the former you mention that the risks of the mail prevented your sending the vouchers by that conveyance. but, my dear Sir, no vouchers are necessary as to yourself, and as against those who might demand a second paiment, they are more convenient in their deposit with you. I therefore now return you one of the accounts forwarded, with an acknolegement at the foot of it which supersedes the removal of the vouchers from their present deposit.          mr Buck lately presented an account against mr Marks. mrs Marks having been for some time absent on a visit to our brother, I could not recur to her for information; but told mr Buck that if you considered the account as right it should be placed among the debts of the estate, and paid as soon as we had funds. I must say the same as to D$^r$ Meredith's and mr Turner's accounts, and indeed as to what is due to Col$^o$ Callis's estate, to the settlement of which on the principles proposed by me and accepted by him, I agree and make final. we have some prospect of selling one of the negroes, which sale, or that of the land which we earnestly desire, would enable mrs Marks to pay up every thing now remaining due. indeed the estate should have been again aided from my own funds, but that my crop of the last year remains still unsold, having offered it in Richm$^d$ for $3\frac{1}{4}$ D. a barrel without success. should the sale of the negro take place, there shall be no further delay. one of them, the woman Isabel, died some time ago, so that only one remains able to work, except him we are endeavoring to sell.          I duly recieved the volume of mr M$^c$Calla's sermons. their style is remarkably good, and never I think did any compositions bear stronger internal proofs of the pure virtue and piety of their author. we are all here anxious for peace. and altho' the late embarcation of 8000 men for America discourages some, it does not me. these are no more than such an additional force as England would chuse to place in her American possessions in a time of peace. I know that war would be congenial with her hatred of us: but her own interests, and the wishes of all mankind for peace will probably prevail. the two causes of war, blockade & impressment being at an end with the war, if neither party has new views, peace must follow, and I am very much persuaded it will. Accept the assurance of my great esteem & respect.

Th: Jefferson

RC (WHi); addressed: "Lancelot Minor esquire near Yanceyville Louisa"; franked; postmarked Milton, 10 Aug.; endorsed by Minor. Enclosure not found.

Missing letters from Minor of JAN. 20, 9 JUNE, and 8 Sept. 1814 are recorded in SJL as received from Louisa on 2 Feb., 26 June, and 16 Sept. 1814, respectively. A letter from TJ to Minor of 25 Oct. 1814, not found, is also recorded in SJL. OUR BROTHER: Randolph Jefferson.

The SERMONS, *The Works of the Rev. Daniel M'Calla, D.D.*, 2 vols. (Charleston, S.C., 1810; Sowerby, no. 1713), included two vindications of TJ, both dated Aug. 1800 and signed "Amyntas." The first, addressed to newspaper publishers Peter Freneau and Seth Paine, responds to criticisms of TJ's character, politics, and religion; describes his role in promoting religious freedom; and concludes that "religious opinions have never been made among us, the test of qualification for civil offices. Whether in appointing governors, envoys, heads of departments, or even Presidents, we have never considered their religion, but their talents, and other qualifications necessary to discharge their respective offices to the public advantage. It is, therefore, most partial, and injurious, to demand of Mr. Jefferson, a qualification for public service, which we have never demanded of any other public officer" (2:428–9). The second claims that the uproar over TJ's religious views was politically motivated and observes that his adversaries have "been wrought up, by the passion of party, the impatience of opposition, and the envy of superior merit, and reputation! while he, with the tranquility becoming a philosopher, and the patience worthy of a Christian, has borne it all! Such immobility of temper, amidst the outrage of injury, is neither compatible with profligacy of principle, nor the meanness of an ambitious mind. Whatever it be, Mr. Jefferson is in possession of some strong, coercive principle, which maintains his equanimity entire, where few men would be capable of less than retaliation" (2:433–4).

# Promissory Note to Hugh Nelson

I promise to pay to the honble Hugh Nelson or order on or before the 1ˢᵗ day of January next one hundred and five Dollars for value recieved. witness my hand this 7ᵗʰ day of August 1814.

Th: Je[ffers]on

MS (MoSHi: TJC-BC); canceled by mutilation of signature; endorsed by TJ: "Nelson Hugh"; with TJ's later notation adjacent to signature: "paid the 105.
June 21. paid      2.38 as int for 4½ months."

TJ owed Nelson for a purchase of cattle. He recorded payment of $105.87 on 11 May 1815 and of $2.38 on 20 June 1815, with Edmund Bacon delivering both sums to Nelson (*MB*, 2:1301, 1308, 1311).

# To Samuel M. Burnside

SIR                                    Monticello Aug. 8. 14.

I have recently recieved your favor of July 12. informing me that the American Antiquarian society had done me the honor of electing me a member of their body. duly sensible of this honor, and thankful for such a mark of their favor, I pray you to be the channel of communicating to them these sentiments. from the circumstances of age and distance, I fear I shall be able to carry into their service little more than sincere dispositions to be useful to them whenever it shall be in my power.

I avail myself of this occasion of placing a paper, which has long been in my possession, in a deposit where, if it has any value, it may at sometime be called into use. it is a compilation of historical facts relating, some of them to other states, but the most to Massachusets, and especially to the Indian affairs of that quarter, during the first century of our settlement. this being the department of our history in which materials are most defective, it may perhaps offer something not elsewhere preserved. it seems to have been the work of a careful hand, and manifests an exactitude which commands confidence. it was given to me about 50. years ago by William Burnet Brown who removed to Virginia, from Massachusets I believe. he told me he had found it among the archives of his family. I understood he was a descendant of your Governor[1] Burnet, son of the bishop of that name. the writer speaks of himself in one place only (pa. 11. column 1.) and I should have conjectured him to have been Governor Burnet himself but that in pa. 7. col. 3. the Gov[r] is spoken of in the 3[d] person. all this however is much more within the scope of your conjecture, & I pray you to accept the paper for the use of the society, & to be assured of the sentiments of my high respect and consideration.

TH: JEFFERSON

RC (MWA: American Antiquarian Society Archives); at foot of text: "Samuel M. Burnside Sec[y] of the Amer. Antiq. So-ciety at Worcester"; endorsed by Burnside. PoC (DLC); endorsed by TJ. Enclosure: chronological description of

English discoveries and settlements in North America, French discoveries and settlements in North America, and the "State of the Indian Tribes in North America," with entries from 1620 through 1691 (MS in MWA: Indians of North America, Miscellaneous Papers; in an unidentified hand; undated, but compiled after 1703 and probably before 1727; containing twenty-five pages of text organized in three columns and additional blank sheets randomly interleaved; docketed on page 1: "Presented to the American Antiquarian Society by the Hon. Thomas Jefferson, late President of the United States. Aug^t 1814"; with similar information appearing on a separate cover sheet, but there mistakenly recording date of receipt as "1815"; cover sheet also notes that "This MS. was presented to M^r Jefferson by a Gentleman, M^r Bur-net, from New England, about the year 1763").

Burnside's FAVOR OF JULY 12. consisted of or enclosed a certificate, signed and dated by Burnside as recording secretary, informing TJ that at its recent meeting the American Antiquarian Society had elected him to membership, asking that he communicate his acceptance of that status, and including a postscript: "N. B. Each member pays annually to the Treasurer Two Dollars," with handwritten ad-dition by Burnside: "if he belong to Massachusetts" (MS in MHi, printed form with dateline, signature, and final five words of postscript filled in by Burnside; either this document or a missing covering letter from Burnside is recorded in SJL as received 25 July 1814). A later membership diploma gave TJ's date of election as 1 June 1814 (note to TJ to Rejoice Newton, 8 Dec. 1821).

The enclosed COMPILATION OF HISTORICAL FACTS is based in part on records of the New York Commissioners for Indian Affairs that are no longer extant, and in some instances provides unique evidence of treaty proceedings between English, Iroquois, and Mohican negotiators (Daniel K. Richter, "Rediscovered Links in the Covenant Chain: Previously Unpublished Transcripts of New York Indian Treaty Minutes, 1677–1691," American Antiquarian Society, *Proceedings*, n.s., 92 [1982]: 45–85). On PA. 11. COLUMN 1, the enclosure's author begins his notes on 26 Dec. 1677 by describing "The Transactions of the Commissioners at Albany Which I have by me." On PA. 7. COL. 3, under the date 1664, the author notes that "Gov^r Burnets Manuscript Extracted from french author says . . ."

¹ TJ here canceled "Brown, son."

# To John Crookes

Monticello Aug. 8. 14.

Th: Jefferson returns his thanks to mr Crookes for the copy he has favored him with of the versification of the speech of Logan, the Mingo chief. acceptable as it is in every form, he thinks mr Crookes has strictly preserved the strong & dignified sentiments of his original. he salutes mr Crookes with respect and consideration.

PoC (MHi); dateline at foot of text; endorsed by TJ.

# To Thomas C. Flournoy

Monticello Aug. 8. 14.

Th Jefferson presents his compliments and his thanks to mr Flournoy for the copy he has been so kind as to send him of his oration on the 4th of July. it has stated with great truth & justice the causes of the war in which we are engaged, and which he trusts will be deemed in history sufficient thro' all time. if the sentiments expressed by mr Flournoy, and which are the peculiar honor of Kentucky, could have animated some other states more at hand for offensive exertions, the war would ere this have been at an end. this consummation will probably be effected without delay by the interests of England and the desire of all mankind to see once more a general peace, and free and friendly commerce reestablished among all nations. he salutes mr Flournoy with esteem and respect.

RC (NjMoHP: Lloyd W. Smith Collection); dateline at foot of text; addressed: "Mr Thomas C. Flournoy Georgetown Kentucky"; franked; postmarked Milton, 12 Aug. PoC (DLC); endorsed by TJ.

# To Joseph Delaplaine

SIR                                                         Monticello Aug. 9. 14.

Your favor of July 28. is just recieved, and I now inclose you the print of Vespucius, which I have cut out of the book, & which is taken from the same original in the gallery of Florence from which my painting was taken.          With respect to the portrait in the hands of mr Stewart, I have thought it best to write to him, and to inclose the letter to you for perusal. if you think the object worth the trouble of having it brought to Philadelphia, then be so good as to seal the letter and put it into the post office immediately, that mr Stewart may be prepared by it for recieving your application. you will of course have the portrait so packed as to recieve no injury by a land transportation; and I should suppose if you could get this done by a friend there, and the package put into the care of some passenger coming on in the stage from Boston to Philadelphia, it would come safely and speedily enough in that way. when done with, I will ask the favor of it's being forwarded to Richmond under the like care of a stage passenger, addressed to mr Gibson my correspondent there, who will pay all charges and forward it to me.

Between the 4th & 5th parts of the great work of De Bry, is a print of Columbus, and an account of it which should give it some authority. it is very small, and not very much resembling my copy of his portrait from the Florentine gallery. De Bry's book is very rare and very expensive. yet probably it may be in some of the libraries of Philadelphia, perhaps the Loganian. if not, mr Wood, if he comes on to copy my Columbus, may copy this print also from my Debry. both may be worth inserting in your work. DeBry says his was given to him by the painter who drew the portrait of Columbus. Accept the tender of my esteem & respect                                    TH: JEFFERSON

RC (LNT: George H. and Katherine M. Davis Collection); at foot of text: "Mr Delaplaine"; endorsed by Delaplaine, with his notation that he "Wrote 18 Aug: 1814." PoC (DLC); endorsed by TJ. Enclosures: (1) frontispiece to Stanislao Canovai, *Elogio d'Amerigo Vespucci* (Flo-rence, 1788; Sowerby, no. 4163). (2) TJ to Gilbert Stuart, 9 Aug. 1814.

Delaplaine published a version of the PRINT OF VESPUCIUS in *Delaplaine's Repository*, 1:18.

# From George Greer

RESPECTED SIR                                    Baltimore August 9th 1814

I on the 5th Instant received a Letter from William Thornton Esqr City of Washington, Wishing me to forward for you such parts of Janes's Domestic & factory Loom, & Such parts only as would require attention in the Construction. from which I inferr that the frame is not included

Mr Francis C Clopper of montgomery County in this State is proprietor of the patent right for the state of Virginia, and has, I have understood sent a loom through Several of the Counties to Show the many advantages it posesses over the Common Loom, And dispose of his right. Whether he will be in your neighbourhood I am not Enabled to Say, however, as few if Any of those looms have yet been Constructed to the Southward of this place, And a little practice as well as attention is necessary to properly Connect the different parts, And do Justice to the inventor; I would with much pleasure have One made complete for you, by a mechanic who has for Some months been engaged in building Said Looms, for a Mr Sullivan & myself in this city, And after puting in a piece, I would with Care have the Loom taken down & safely packed, as well as the gears or headdle[s] Temples & Shuttle, Each of which has been improved by the ingenious inventor

In Connecticut where Mr Janes resides[1] the price of a loom is forty Dollars, here we can not get them made for less than fifty, measurably oweing to the increased price of metereals. We have in maryland, for the right of using Each Loom twenty Dollars, & suppos[e] the charge in your State would not Exceed that Sum.

Those looms that have been put in operation here fully Answer Our Expectations & with proper management we have no doubt of their becoming to Our Country, Invalueable

Should the improvement be patronised by you it would I am Satisfied be the means of making its usefulness, much sooner and more generally Known, which induces me again to repeat that I will with much pleasure attend to your Order Should you think proper to Command me

Very Respectfully I remain

Your Obe<sup>dt</sup> Serv<sup>t</sup>                                        GEORGE GREER

RC (MHi); edge trimmed; endorsed by TJ as received 12 Aug. 1814 and so recorded in SJL. RC (MHi); address cover only; with PoC of TJ to Bradford & Inskeep, 17 Aug. 1814, on verso; addressed: "Thomas Jefferson Esqr Monticello Virginia"; franked; postmarked Baltimore, 9 Aug. Enclosed in TJ to Thomas Ritchie, 15 Aug. 1814, and Ritchie to TJ, 9 Oct. 1814.

A loom's heddles (HEADDLES) guide the warp threads. Its TEMPLES keep the cloth stretched to its correct width (*OED*).

[1] Manuscript: "resideds."

# To Thomas Lehré

DEAR SIR                                        Montic[el]lo Aug. 9. 14.

Your favor of July 7. is recieved, with the papers inclosed. the testimonies they furnish of a favorable remembrance, by my fellow citizens, of my endeavors to serve them, are highly gratifying. you are so kind as to ask particularly after the habitual state of my health. it is generally as good as at my age (of 71.) ought to be expected, and not such as to threaten too long a protraction of life. I am much enfeebled in body, and this condition is sensibly advancing.

I learn with pleasure the stedfast dispositions of your quarter of the Union in support of the just war in which we are engaged. had those at our other extremity been animated by the same sentiments, the war might have been over in fact, altho' not in form, by this time. I think however it will now cease; and that British antipathies will yield to British interest and the desire of all nations to see once more a return of peace & free & friendly intercourse thro the world. I am much gratified that before it's conclusion the reputation of our arms by land is rising from it's depression. Gen<sup>ls</sup> Brown & Scott, in the first action at Chippeway gave our enemies a sample of what they are to expect from us, when a little more experienced in war: but still more in a 2ᵈ action of which we have just recieved the account; and which according to first general statements has been as sanguinary as we have ever known, in proportion to the numbers engaged; one of their Generals (Riall) taken, and two of ours badly wounded. this action, altho' a severe one, is a subject of congratulation. it is a great thing to find out Browns & Scotts, instead of a Hull and Boerstler. Accept the assurance of my great esteem & respect.

TH: JEFFERSON

PoC (DLC); one word faint; at foot of text: "Colᵒ Lehré"; endorsed by TJ.

Major General Jacob BROWN and Brigadier General Winfield SCOTT led the United States forces to victory at the battle of Chippewa (CHIPPEWAY) on 5 July 1814. Phineas RIALL, the British major general in command, retreated from Chippewa and reengaged the Americans on 25 July at the battle of Lundy's Lane. Brown, Scott, and Riall were wounded and Riall was captured. With this bloody standoff the American advance into Canada ended (Malcomson, *Historical Dictionary*, 95–7, 298–300, 472–3).

## From Thomas Ritchie

SIR—                                    Richmond, August 9. 1814.

In ransacking some Papers, which I had laid by, I lit upon the enclosed Paper, which you were so kind as to transmit to me, some time last year. I am sorry I have detained it so long.

However I flatter myself that this <u>Sin of Omission</u> is not so great as to cut me off from the Grace of similar favours.

Most Respectfully,

yours,                                  THOMAS RITCHIE

RC (MHi); dateline at foot of text; endorsed by TJ as received 16 Aug. 1814 and so recorded in SJL. Enclosure: Obituary Notice for Joel Barlow by Konrad E. Oelsner and Pierre Samuel Du Pont de Nemours, [before 10 Feb. 1813], printed above as an enclosure to Du Pont de Nemours to TJ, 10 Feb. 1813.

## To Gilbert Stuart

DEAR SIR                              Monticello Aug. 9. 14.

You wished to retain the portrait which you were so kind as to make of me while in Washington, until you should have time to have a print copied from it. this, I believe has been done, at least I think I have seen one which appeared to have been taken from that portrait.

M<sup>r</sup> Delaplaine of Philadelphia is now engaged in a work relating to the general history of America, and, wishing it to be accompanied with prints, has asked permission to have one taken from the same original, adapted to the size of his volume. I have therefore authorised him to ask for the portrait in your possession, to copy his print from it, & return it to me. this I have done on the supposition that I had not been mistaken in believing it had already answered in your hands the purpose you had meditated.

With a high veneration for your talents, & sincere good wishes that they might have abundant employment for the establishment of your own happiness and fame, I learned with pleasure the extensive work in which you were engaged in Boston. yet nature having spread with pretty equal hand her gifts of worth and wisdom over the different parts of the Union, it would have been more consonant with her plan, & our wishes, that your talents should have been applied to their commemoration with the same equal hand. your former central position was more favorable to this, and certainly you could never there have been without more than you could do. I do not think, with some, that man is so far the property of society as that it may command the use of his faculties without regard to his own will or happiness: but it is at least to be wished that the inclination should generally be coupled with the power of aiding the reasonable objects of those with whom we live; and I am not without a hope that you will resume the function of leaving to the world your own excellent originals rather than copies from inferior hands of characters of local value only. pardon these observations. they flow not merely from considerations of public concern, but equally from great personal regard, and the desire that the employment of your talents should be worthy of their dignity. I add with great sincerity assurances of my high respect and consideration. 

TH: JEFFERSON

PoC (PPRF); at foot of first page: "Gilbert Stewart esq."; endorsed by TJ. Enclosed in TJ to Joseph Delaplaine, 9 Aug. 1814.

Gilbert Stuart (1755–1828), artist, was born in Rhode Island. His childhood friend Benjamin Waterhouse noted that he exhibited talent for drawing and painting at an early age. When Stuart met the Scottish portrait painter Cosmo Alexander in 1769, he began formal training and eventually traveled with that artist in the colonies and finally to Edinburgh. After Alexander's sudden death in 1772, the young Stuart returned to Rhode Island and continued working as a portrait artist. In 1775 he relocated to London, where he became a student and assistant to Benjamin West. Stuart eventually established himself as a leading portraitist and remained in London until he left for Ireland in 1787 to escape his creditors. In 1793 Stuart moved back to the United States, settling first in New York City and moving successively to Philadelphia in 1794, to Washington in 1803, and to Boston in 1805, where he remained. Renowned for his skill in capturing lifelike images, he painted each of the first six presidents, in addition to numerous other prominent Americans of his time. Stuart realized that portraits of George Washington, in particular, would be marketable to the American public, and he made numerous replicas of his best-known, Athenaeum portrait of the first president. Although immensely popular and successful, Stuart was a poor financial manager and died in debt (*ANB*; *DAB*; *ODNB*; Lawrence Park, John Hill Morgan, and Royal Cortissoz, *Gilbert Stuart: An Illustrated Descriptive List of His Works*, 4 vols. [1926]; Dorinda Evans, *The Genius of Gilbert Stuart* [1999]; *Providence Patriot & Columbian Phenix*, 16 July 1828).

For the PORTRAIT YOU WERE SO KIND AS TO MAKE OF ME WHILE IN WASHINGTON, see TJ to Delaplaine, 30 May 1813, and note.

# From William Duane

RESPECTED & DEAR SIR,    Phil[a] 11 Aug. 1814

The translation has been completed several months but business of every kind has been thrown into new channels, and of the Six presses which were formerly employed for my benefit only one which prints the Aurora is now employed—There was not work to pay wages, and the Mss. remains on hand. Unless a change of Some kind takes place I see no prospect of doing any thing for I am too low in purse to be able to contribute any thing to my wishes and the cause of truth.

The state of things in Europe has baffled all human anticipations— where it will end is as difficult to foresee. Unless as they[1] affect our own country I feel no deep interest in them—the French have fallen from the loftiest pinacle of renown to the lowest abyss of contemptibility; and one is equally at a loss whether to despise them or to abhor the author of all the wars of Europe most. Spain is to be sure a kind of foil to elevate France, by exhibiting the force and brutality of superstition[2] on the unfortunate species. But they are all very appropriately assimilated to bears, and lions, and panthers and tygers—

I think seriously however of the effect on our own affairs, and the more seriously when I reflect on the state of the government and the apathy into which the people have fallen: a state perhaps the like of which never was before seen in a nation an apathy which like the state of the human stomach in certain cases, will admit of no wholesome aliment; and receives no nourishment but thro' a poisonous medium.

The country appears to me in a state very much resembling that of Holland in the time of the illustrious DeWitts, I believe about 1670 or thereabout; and menaced by the same enemy and by the same kind of agency. Hume describes it briefly but truly and I am afraid the moral condition of the country is not much better than was that of the

Dutch who could be prevailed on to murder their benefacters, to sub-serve the rapacious avarice and jealousy of England and to elevate a family who were to be their tyrants as the price of the subserviency of the tyrant to England

The Dutch would not believe—I mean the Dutch republicans the DeWitts, would not believe the British meant to play them foul; they believed in British friendship; they believed the professions and promises of British Ministers—in defiance of the daily acts of con-tumely and outrage committed on their people

I see the same credulity in our government—I see the power of England in the sneers of her agents as they walk our streets—I see the predominancy of that influence in the midst of war, and—forgive me—I see our own government temporising with this abominable government, and inviting their contempt—and their insolence by treating them in a manner which they must consider: with exulta-tion—as they must judge by themselves—and always, have been truckling and mean in adversity, as they have been insolent and over-bearing in Prosperity.

Our Government will never accomplish any thing by reasoning or appealing to justice, whose policy is established on the injury of all other nations and whose habitual passions as a nation are hatred, envy, jealousy, and hardness of heart towards every other people.

How will the bear and the lion settle the question of neutral rights—as the French say, I fear it is en l'air—it is something like the balloons thirty years ago, no longer an object worth contending for—the Deliverer of Europe will probably commute for Poland, all pre-tensions to the freedom of the Seas My respect for Kings and statesmen is not encreased by the experience of twenty years past. The possession of power appears to operate like a Tourniqet on the moral faculties, as soon as men possess power, the moral artery ap-pears to be screwed up—and the statesman becomes as frigid as a frog—Alexander the Deliverer has had his Sop. I believe he will sit down "infamous and contented"; but Poland is an immense bastion, flanking Silesia, Bohemia, Lusatia, Moravia, Austria, and Hun-gary—the[3] road by Krems over which Suwaroff marched for Italy & Switzerland is within a few miles of Vienna.

Saxony proper is portioned to aggrandize Prussia, this reduces Prussia to vassalage to Russia, and enables Russia to keep Austria counterpoised—the Austrian Empress is I believe a Saxon! There is to be a grand farce at Vienna, the parade of Plenipotentiaries, who are to act as the arch jugglers Talleyrand & Castleragh, seduce by cunning or purchase by gold—those grand <u>arsons</u> who set fire to nations and retire by the light of the conflagration they kindle to collect the spoils of desolation amidst the ruins. But where am I running

England cannot at this moment sit down quietly in peace, without greater danger than she can incur by continuing the war. This may appear a paradox—Her condition cannot at any time be suddenly changed—it is now <u>wholly military</u>—her circulation and social subsistence circulates through military channels—her means and experience are now more commensurate to war than at any former period—she may reduce as many of her land and naval forces as can with safety be admitted into Society—but she will be obliged to send abroad or to abandon a larger portion, which would perhaps enter the armies of her rivals, or carry themselves to america, to augment american population or man american vessels in commerce or war England has experienced the want of Generals, it has taken her 20 Years to produce one, and she will endeavor to keep up the breed; she has discovered that what Vegetius said long ago is true—"neither length of years, nor knowlege of state affairs, do back the art of war, but <u>continual exercise.</u>"

What does this lead to, you will ask? It leads to considerations that disturb my sleep, and induce me to look at the little flock of innocents around me; I recollect what I have seen of English policy, I recollect the traditionary history of three generations of my ancestors—I have seen in three quarters of the earth beside my country the policy of England—the national character of its policy—I am ready to meet it, but I cannot be therefore insensible to what must be inevitable—if the Government does not act as becomes the exigency—if they slumber like the DeWitts over a Volcano; if they temporise with disaffection, and exhibit in all their measures the same melancholy evidences of discord which characterises the extremities of the nation—we are undone

England has purchased every goverment in Europe—by her gold she has arrayed them all in arms—and in the midst of what was reputed the best organized tyranny that ever was framed she organized a conspiracy for its overthrow—and succeeded. Are we to expect this haughty power will in the insolence of her unexampled success, treat us with delicacy or justice—O fatal expectation!—fatal because it is even supposed to be possible!

But what is wrong or what would be right? Pardon me as usual for the freedom and unreserve with which I speak to you—I pretend to nothing more than common sense. And if I speak with confidence and firmness, it is to be attributed only to the earnestness & sincerity of my convictions What is wrong? Why the war from the first movement towards Tippacanoe to the last movement in to Canada by Niagara has been a series of futile and wasteful measures, productive if successful of no positive and comprehensive or durable good, but productive of disaster and destruction as they have been conceived and conducted. It was a fatal mistake not to declare war at the period of the Chesapeake, but the most fatal of all mistakes was the repeal of the Embargo. But I cannot conceive how any man who has considered the world for a life of forty Years only could expect anything but war after that repeal, or could think of accomplishing any solid object of peace but by a vigorous exercise of the whole energies of the nation. The embargo repeal indeed deceived the enemy fortunately as much as it deceived ourselves, for M$^r$ Quincey only echoed what Henry and other English emissaries said in Boston, that <u>we could not be kicked into a war</u>

The measures taken and the manner in which the war has been conducted, is the true cause of the apathy that prevails in Society. The friends of the Government, that is the Whigs of 1798 are the most disgusted and disappointed. They recollect the proscriptions and tyranny that prevailed during the last years of General Washington and all M$^r$ Adams' presidency, and they tremble at the idea of their recurrence; and they see that to be inevitable unless there be a different System, and unless the Executive pursues means to rouse the country to a sense of its danger.

I sent you a little memoir in 1812, I send you a copy of it again— you will see that what I there suggested, was not only practicable, but that some part of it has since been proposed but not executed; I mean the passage of the Cadaraqui, and the occupation of a position cutting off the communication with Lower Canada

The expeditions from Detroit against Malden—against Queenstown, against Fort George, against York in Upper Canada, could never at any time accomplish a purpose decisive of the war. It was the duty of this Government not to have made discursi[ve] expeditions; the Militia should have maintained a defensive war and protected their frontier; the regular force should have been all concentrated; and they were not only fully adequate to conquer all upper Canada by one battle; but to overwhelm lower Canada with the force possessed in the month of July last or in the month of March of the present year. The gallantry of Miller, Croghan, Johnson, and Holmes[4] of Perry and Elliot, do not compensate the loss of the expeditions under Harrison and the shameful transactions of his command

The victory at York was dearly purchased by the life of Pike—but what did it or what could it accomplish even if he survived

The design against Montreal was one of the most infatuated that the mind of man ever conceived, whether the season, the position, the mode of access, the force and means possessed for the service, or the condition of the enemy be considered; it was passing into a well without a ladder to reascend, and the enemy above to cut off all supplies or access to you. The shocking imbecility of Hampton at Chateauguay was alike disgraceful to him and the Goverment which under the shelter of his wealth suffered him to Escape in contempt of all discipline—indeed his first appointment was a reproach to the government, since every man who knew him must know, that neither education nor God had qualified him for a military command—and it must be an implisit belief in the possibility of miracles which could alone Sanction it

How can the people believe that the Government was in Earnest when such men as Morgan Lewis was made first a Quarter master General, one function of which he was not fit to Execute, and then a Major General when found unfit to be a Q$^r$ M$^r$

I could go more into particulars but I have already written too much. The measures as now conducted will lead only to the same calamitous issues as last year—The force now under Gen. Izard if carried against Prescott on the Cadaraqui might decide the campaign by the surrender of all upper Canada and render all our seamen now on Ontario & Erie, disposable on Champlain; our force now dispersed might be concentrated; and our line of defence would be reduced to the line between the Cadaraqui and Sorrel, instead of from Mackinaw to Champlain. The Indians would be quelled for want of subsistence and English agents; and our forces could be in training for the opening of the Spring, when I expect to see a British army landed on our coasts

In reflecting on the events which are to be expected, I have conceived a project, the policy of which I will submit to you in a concise way; I have no doubts or fears about its sucess or efficacy myself, but there are so many prejudices on the subject that I am well aware of the delicacy with which it ought to be touched; tho' once carried into operation, it would be in my mind one of the most powerful and effective means of public defence that could be devised by the wisdom of man—I shall give it on a separate sheet—

The enemy are now establishing a depot on the extreme of Long Island—I do not expect that they will attempt any thing on a large Scale this fall—unless they should attempt a <u>Coup De Main</u>—but I expect they will in the Spring be prepared with a force to shake our country to the centre.

Our government could lose nothing by acting upon this principle—they may sacrifice every thing by acting upon any other

With great esteem and respect Your friend & Sv$^t$

W$^M$ DUANE

RC (DLC); edge chipped; endorsed by TJ on final page of enclosure printed below as received 17 Aug. 1814 and so recorded in SJL.

The TRANSLATION was of Destutt de Tracy's manuscript of the fourth volume of his *Élémens d'Idéologie*. The MURDER of Dutch statesman Johan de Witt and his brother Cornelius by an Orangist mob in 1672 is described in David Hume, *The History of England* (London, 1762), 6:224–7 (for another edition, see Sowerby, no. 370). EN L'AIR: "in the air." INFAMOUS AND CONTENTED quotes from a 14 Feb. 1770 letter of the pseudonymous "Junius" (*The Letters of Junius*, ed. John Cannon [1978], 180).

NEITHER LENGTH OF YEARS, NOR KNOWLEGE OF STATE AFFAIRS, DO BACK THE ART OF WAR, BUT CONTINUAL EX-ERCISE paraphrases Flavius Vegetius Renatus, *Epitome of Military Science*, trans. N. P. Milner (1996), bk. 2, ch. 23. Josiah Quincy (QUINCEY) observed in the United States House of Representatives on 19 Jan. 1809 that "no insult, however gross, offered to us by either France or Great Britain, could force this majority into the declaration of war. To use a strong, but common expression, it could not be kicked into such a declaration by either nation" (*Annals*, 10th Cong., 2d sess., 1112). The enclosed LITTLE MEMOIR has not been found.

$^1$ Manuscript: "the."
$^2$ Manuscript: "supersticen."
$^3$ Manuscript: "the the."
$^4$ Manuscript: "Croghan and Johnson, Holmes," with "Johnson" interlined.

ENCLOSURE

## William Duane's Notes on the Expediency of Using Black Troops

Would it be expedient to use black troops?

The probability of an extensive and perhaps durable war, renders it important to anticipate every means by which the public safety may be endangered or secured. There are many who fear a rising of the colored people, this suggests an enquiry,—on three several points

1. What would be the effect of the employment in war of the white population alone?

2. What would be the effect on the colored population?

3. What would be the policy of the enemy?

1. Obliged to act on the defensive, the U.S. army must at all time consist of not less than 50000 effective men regulars

Militia 100,000 for short periods

If only one tenth of this number be diminished every year by the casualties of camps and war, then the annual diminution each year would be 15000 men; say only 10000, as our people are more hardy and better adapted to endure fatigue than Europeans.

If there be any foundation for the apprehension of revolt, then the danger is encreased by the employment of whites alone; while the colored men, are exempted from any participation in the dangers or privations of war; and their relative strength will be augmented to excess equal to the number taken from the whites

It must be here observed that the hypothesis presumes the revolt probable; I however do not believe it probable, without a foreign excitement.

2. The relative effect on the numbers of the colored population is touched in a particular sense in the preceding observations. In another point of view it is very important. The American born blacks, even in the Southern states where slavery is yet suffered, feel a sentiment of patriotism and attachment to the US. Those who doubt it know very little of human nature, and the force of habit on the human mind. There is nothing in the African traditions that can awaken either the affections of the heart, or that enthusiasm which is the effect of lost or promised happiness or glory. Slavery is congenial to the habits of thinking and to the condition of the actual Africans and their immediate descendants, their past condition was no better than the present; and the present condition of the descendant ten thousand cases to one, is better than in Africa or any other country where they are numerous. If climate be the consideration, the descendants know it only by description, and the climates of the Southern States identify everything that can be desirable in Africa. Their ideas of liberty, like all other ideas, are derived from association; and apt as they are frequently to desire to imitate the whites, very few of them ever rise to much above their condition as feel the sentiment of equality of rights in the dissimilarity of colors. I have known Africans of highly cultivated minds, I never found but one who was not content to be an external imitator of the manners and habits of white men

To gratify their passion for imitation to a certain extent, would I believe secure their affections, and assure the exercise of all their faculties. The Asiatics are by no means more intelligent than the Africans and their descendants, in what relates to their social relations to the whites. The Asiatics equal the hardiest and proudest and bravest of human species; their valor, contempt of danger, and of pain and death, are not to be surpassed; yet they are susceptible of the most rigid discipline; so would the descendants of the Africans serve and be serviceable in the United States. To employ them as soldiers would be to save so many of the whites and if loss be to be calculated, to assure a proportional suffering, and thereby a proportionate Security

To employ the blacks would be to carry against the British a force to them on many accounts most terrific, and to us a bond not only of security against the external enemy, but the best force by which the refractory of their own color could be kept in subjection. I need not point out the effect on the minds of the ignorant of any color, when one part is Elevated into a better condition, or more honored than his fellows. I do not admire the trait, I only speak of what is, and what I fear ever will be the human character.

3 There can be no doubt, from what has been already seen in the waters of the Chesapeake, that the enemy will endeavor to use the black population against us. It is the policy of the British in every part of the globe. They have corrupted and arrayed the Whites of N. Eng. against the Whites South of them—they have arrayed the white Protestant against the White Catholic in Ireland—they arrayed the blacks of St Domingo against the whites—they

array Mahomedans against Hindus in India and govern <u>seventy millions</u> of an ingenious people, by about forty brigades of troops enlisted out of the mass of the people whom they rule; they reign with a white population of about 20000 military and civil scattered over a country of 2000 square miles, in perfect security and as safe as in the midst of England.

Their policy would not overlook our apprehensions, or the resource which a revolt would present to them. Counteract them:—defeat them by turning the resources upon which they calculate against them. They have already erected a standard and issued an invitation in the South. My proposition would be to embody a single brigade to establish the first economy and discipline of the corps, and the mildness of the East India companys sepoy system is exactly such as is adapted to the purpose; they might then be augmented, one battalion of 500 men, to every white Reg$^t$ of one thousand; confining them to Infantry of the line, sappers and advance corps

I feel a perfect persuasion of the efficacy and security of such corps—and that to overlook or neglect to use them for military service will not only be a fatal blindness, but perhaps the only mode by which the colored population can become dangerous or injurious.

I could enter into more detail, but the object is so important and novel to the mind, that it is presented in this concise form to give it a fair opportunity for examination

MS (DLC: TJ Papers, 201:35868–9); entirely in Duane's hand; undated.

On 2 Apr. 1814 British Vice-Admiral Sir Alexander Cochrane ISSUED AN INVI- TATION to slaves in the United States to join the British military or accept freedom and passage to British colonial possessions (Salem *Essex Register*, 4 June 1814).

# From John Nicholas

Aug$^t$ 12th 1814—

John Nicholas also presents his Comp$^{lts}$ to M$^r$ Jefferson, & informs him that he saw his Sister, M$^{rs}$ Marks, a few days ago, who requested him to desire[1] M$^r$ J— to postpone sending for her untill he heard from her; M$^{rs}$ R. Jefferson being then very sick & M$^{rs}$ Marks not wishing to leave her untill her entire recovery—

RC (MoSHi: TJC-BC); dateline at foot of text; endorsed by TJ: "Nicholas John." SJL records receipt on 12 Aug. 1814 of either this letter or a missing document of the same date that probably ac- companied it, for which see Peter Carr to TJ, 14 Aug. 1814, and note.

[1] Word interlined in place of "inform."

# To Craven Peyton

DEAR SIR                                        Monticello Aug. 13. 14.

The deed of Sep. 10. 1805. from Charles L. Lewis to yourself is sufficient in it's form to convey to you all the estate he then held in the lands.[1] the circumstance of it's not having been recorded within the 8. months prescribed by law, subjects it to a question which I understand from the gentlemen of the law, has not been settled by our courts. but this can arise only in the case of a creditor or subsequent purchaser without notice of the conveyance to you. my own opinion has been that the deed became good after it's actual admission to record, & that purchasers between the 8. months and the admission to record could alone avail themselves of the failure to record in time. an act of the last session has expressly provided this as to future conveyances but has left the past under the former doubt. Accept the assurances of my esteem & respect.                    TH: JEFFERSON

RC (ViU: TJP); addressed: "Craven Peyton esq. Monteagle." PoC (MHi); lower left corner of page torn away; endorsed by TJ.

The 1792 Virginia "Act for regulating Conveyances" allowed 8. MONTHS to record a conveyance after it was sealed and delivered. As amended, the act specified that "any conveyance which shall hereafter be recorded after the expiration of the time now allowed by law for recording the same, shall take effect and be valid in law as to creditors and subsequent purchasers, from the time of such recording, and from that time only" (*Acts of Assembly* [1792–93 sess.], 48–50; [1813–14 sess.], 35–7).

Missing letters from Peyton to TJ of 24 July and 13 Aug. 1814 are recorded in SJL as received from Monteagle on 25 July and 13 Aug. 1814, respectively.

[1] At this point in RC an unidentified hand keyed the penciled note: "✳ These lands constituted the estate of Monteagle."

# From Peter Carr

DEAR SIR.                                        Carr's-brook. Aug. 14th 14

The committee of which J. Nicholas speaks in his note, was appointed for the purpose, of viewing the different situations in, and about Charlottes-ville, and reporting their opinion, to the next meeting of the board; this, by our constitution will take place on friday next. I was not of that committee. As well as I recollect, John Winn, Jas Leitch, J. Nicholas, Dr Carr & Alexr Garrett, were the persons who formed it. If they were all present, we should be quite safe—I rather believe, we shall as it is but still I would rather not risque it. I suppose the meeting tomorrow, has been called by the chair-man, in order to consult, compare &c, before the stated meeting of the board. When that time comes, we must endeavour so to arrange matters, as to postpone the important question of location, 'till we can be pretty certain of a favorable issue.

I will endeavour to see you at Monticello, before friday. Not being of the committee, I shall not attend at Charlottesville tomorrow. I return you the paper asked for by J. Nicholas, in order that you may give it the direction you think best. With great and sincere esteem Y$^{rs}$ most

Affectionately. P$^R$ CARR

RC (ViU: TJP-CC); endorsed by TJ as received 14 Aug. 1814 and so recorded in SJL.

The NOTE from John Nicholas and the enclosed PAPER he asked for have not been found. The former probably accom-

panied Nicholas to TJ, 12 Aug. 1814. Missing letters from ALEX$^R$ GARRETT to TJ of 20, 21 Aug., and 20 Sept. 1814, not found, are recorded in SJL as received from Charlottesville on 20, 22 Aug., and 21 Sept. 1814, respectively.

# From Lafayette

MY DEAR FRIEND La Grange August 14$^h$ 1814

Your Letters to me Nov. 30 and to our Beloved Mde de tessé decemb. 8$^h$ are the Last I Have Received—She Has Not lived to enjoy this token of your Rememberance—m. de tessé who Had Been declining Rapidly was the first of the two for whom we Had to mourn—she assisted Him to the Last Hour—She Regretted Him with the feelings of lively affection and old Habits—Her delicate frame Could not Bear Such a Sorrow—ten days after Her Husband's death She was no more—Her illness was Slight—Her departure gentle—You know what a woman Has Been lost to Society, what a friend to me—poor m. de mun, the eldest, yet the Survivor of the three, feels His fate with the warmth of a passionate youth, and Bears it with the fortitude of an old man who depends upon Speedy Relief—the few days He must Submit to are Spent in the Society of His children, chiefly at a Country Seat, two Leagues from La Grange—You Remember our Happy Hours, and Animated Conversations at chaville—How far from us those times, and those of the venerable Hôtel de la Rochefoucauld! and we who still number among the living do we not chiefly Belong to what is no more?

the news papers and Ministerial Correspondance will Have Apprised you of the Successive Events which Have overthrown Bonaparte, introduced the Bourbons, and once more thrown the dice for the liberties of france And of Course of Europe—the Strong powers and Singular Genius of Napoleon Had Been disharmonised by the folly of His Ambition, the immorality of His mind, and this[1] Grain of madness, not incompatible with Great talents, But which is developped By the Love and Succes of despotism—He trifled with and utterly Lost immense Armies, Sent abroad all the military stores of france, Left the Country defenseless and Exhausted, and avowed a determination to Have the Last man the last shilling of Europe—yet Such were His Generalship, the Superiority of our troops, and the Spirit of the people, that after He awoke He maneuvred with Skill, that under an inferiority of numbers the french arms Supported their fame, and that the inhabitants, determined not to defend Him, Could not Refrain, on the passage of the foreigners, from Rousing Against them—But an unlucky stroke of His, By which He expected to Become Master of the Emperor of Austria, and draw the others to the Rhine, oppened for the allies the Road to paris—He Could not Have Recovered Himself But By making the Capital a Seat of murder, fire, and desolation, nor did He appear to object to it—But the Senate, the national guards, and at Headquarters His Lieutenants were of an other mind—Emperor Alexander and the king of prussia Behaved Handsomely—the Heads of Government Had fled—a Capitulation Retarded By a Subsisting fear of Bonaparte took place—talleyrand who Had for Some month Held a Secret Correspondance with the Hostile princes and with the Emigrant Bourbons, Being also the only grand dignitary to be found in paris, took the lead of Course,—you Have Seen the decrees of the Senate, the proclamations, and the Roïal ordinnance Called Constitutional Charter.

My wishes and just Hopes Had Been different—I was with my family in paris nor Could I with propriety Have inhabited La grange under the invasion of the allies—I wanted a national insurrection against domestic despotism the Succes of which would lead to a treaty with or a Spirited attack upon the foreigners—in Both Cases we were masters of our own Government—I applied to military chiefs first in Rank, to Senators, and principal Citizens in the national guards who all were well disposed But thought imperial tyranny too well organised to Render it possible to shake it up—Even on the Last day, while the Bonapartian Government were flying off,[2] king Joseph among them, the national grenadiers, my Son and one Son in law in the Ranks, Being under arms, and twenty Senators Having assembled at m^r Lambrecht's House, the Habits of twelve years did prevail upon the offered opportunity—paris was occupied By foreign troops—two monarchs, Happily very Honest and impressed

with liberal ideas, entered our Capital—I Had no inclination to oppose measures tending to Expel the able and professional destroyer of
Liberty in Europe, and giving to france a chance to Recover Constitutional freedom—there was no way to Remove foreign influence and
interior intrigue But in joining the desperate, destructive Rage of
Bonaparte. My friends in the Senate and else where Supported the
change, Endeavouring to make it as national and liberal as possible,
and we all agreed to Range under the Restored Constitutional throne
of the Bourbons.

in the mean while talleyrand who Had not Scrupuled to treat with
the Hostile powers and Emigrant pretenders, who now felt no Reluctance to act with the invaders of paris, was, enabled to form a
provisory Government—there He mistook His and the public interest—to the liberal Sentiments of Alexander and His prussian friends
He, and His Collaborators were indebted for Every Encouragement
to form a national Constitution. it Became a Court intrigue—the forwardness of the Bourbons was invited—the Senate who Had too
Long Been the tools of Bonaparte, were Led into Selfish provisions
for themselves which Spoiled their Constitutional decree and gave
the king the means to Evade it—Hardly was the imperial Sun Set,
that the Royal globe Began to attract the Hopes, and impress the
fears—the Engagements ended into a Charter not accepted But given
By the king which the two first Bodies of the Nation thought proper
to Receive in that form. the torrent of the Restoration overwhelmed
those Barriers which weak and unpopular Hands Had with diffidence Endeavoured to Erect—nor Could it Be Stopped without
Recurring to Bonapartian discontents, unpatriotic in their Source,
Ruinous in their effects—it Became the part of good Citizens to
direct this turn of the Revolution towards the original principles
upon which it Had Been Begun—How far we may Succeed is yet
uncertain—the Aristocratical party is the Same as you Have known
it—Constitutionals and Republicans are united into one Brother-
hood—the Strength of Bonapartism wholly depends upon the Conduct of this new Government—Egregious Blunders Have Been
Committed—it Suffices to point out the Relinquishment of 42 fortified towns and thirteen thousand pieces of Cannon, by Count d'artois and talleyrand, in a morning, Before any thing was organised
and Compensations Could be talked of—yet among inexcusable
faults[3] and deplorable weaknesses two Evident facts must Be
aknowledged. there Has been a more proper Sense, and positive Care
of public liberty under this Restoration than at the time of charles the
Second, and there are now more Symptoms and chances of freedom

than Could Have Been expected under the masterly despotism and iron Hand of Bonaparte.

While I was writing we Have just now Lost a great Battle—a Bill Against the Liberty of the press Has passed the chambre des deputés—we Hoped for a majority—out of 217 members, eighty only voted Right—our friends will make a stand in the House of peers— But the question must be Against my Hopes, Considered as Lost— you Have observed that the Court Have thought it their interest to preserve for two years a Rump chamber of deputies whose election Had not been direct, whose time is out, and to Couple it with an House of peers Composed of old[4] Senators Some of whom Have been left out, most of the others Having long Habits of Servage, the new ones men of ancient birth and chiefly of Recent Emigration, all named for life, not Having the Sorry independance of Heredity, and preserving the Hope to attain it—to point out the illegality of a charter where the Sovereignty of the people is flatly denied, and the improprieties, insufficiencies, nay the impossibilities of that Royal and ministerial fabrick would be in a letter directed to you and permit me to Say writen by me, quite Superfluous—the Ancien Regime ideas are upper most—the pretensions of Aristocratic are a Compost of non Sense and madness—the ministry is an Heterogeneous Mixture—patriotic Opposition is Embarrass'd with the intrigues and miens of Bonapartists who plainly Regret their living upon the pillage of Europe and the Oppression of france—Ruin, Vengeance, and Redoubled folly would mark the Return of their patron—the mass of the people is fatigued, disgusted,—nothing So unpopular now as Revolutionary Language—out of seven princes of the House of Bourbon, duke d'orleans is the only one, on account of His education, whose opinions are Constitutional—So far as I may judge Having Seen Him But once—of the others the king Seems to be the most moderate— duke de Berry's more popular demeanour is all military—Bonaparte or the Bourbons Have Been, and still are the Alternative in the Country where the idea of a Republican Executive Has Become Synonimous with the Excesses Committed under that name. in the mean while you See the king of Spain, a vile fool, Restoring inquisition after Having expelled the Cortès, the pope Reestablishing the old System, the king of Sardinia destroying Every useful innovation in piemont, and Austria Submitting Her Ancient possessions to the illiberal System of Her Cabinet—yet the advantages derived from the first impulse, the philantropic intent of the Revolution, notwithstanding all what Has Since Happened, are widely extended, and deeply Rooted—most of them Have Resisted the powerful Hand of

[ 539 ]

Bonaparte—they are more than a match for the feeble, uncertain devices of their present adversaries—Should this french government feel their true interest and adopt a Liberal Constitutional Line, all Would be Easy in france and Beneficial to Europe—in the Contrary Case we are exposed to desagreable intervals of time and oscillations of Events—But I am Convinced that those Rights of mankind which, in 1789, Have Been defined under the encouragement of your approbation, and ought to Have Been the Blessing of the end of the last Century, shall Before the end of the present one be the undisputed Creed and insured property not only of this, but of Every European Nation.

My own Situation does not much differ from what it was under the imperial System—Had I Been Supported in my wishes of a double opposition to domestic tyranny and foreign invasion, this Crisis would Have proved Glorious to france, useful to the Cause of political freedom—Had the Courtiers of foreign and Emigrant influence Been endowed with a Capacity Superior to the Combinations of palace or exchange Business, Had their minds Been So Comprehensive as to Encompass their own interests as Revolutionary men, I, and with me a great number of patriots would Have aided in Securing a true and Stout Constitutional System—nay the Bourbons themselves ought to Have seeked in it a more national title to their throne, and a shield against the Extravagancies of their own party—I Have waïted upon the king, Some days after His Arrival—He was pleased to Receive me with a remarkable politeness. from His Brother I am also to aknowledge a very good Reception. I Have not Hitherto Gone farther in my Communications with them—and altho' I am not, in any manner, upon the footing of disgrace or disgust, and number personal friends Among the members of that government, and So I did to a degree under the late one, I Have no Call or inducement to Abandon my Retirements of La grange—to my friend I may allow myself to add that I enjoy the Confidence of Several in a more active life, and the good will of the public, Among whom I Could place in the first Rank, more particularly Since the Restoration, the parties and the men who, at the time of my proscription, Had Been the most prejudiced and Exesperated Against me. a disposition to which Comparative Restrospection on their Leaders Has not a Little contributed.

Altho' I Have not much mixed with our illustrious visitors it Has Been my Happy Lot to Be Some what Employ'd in the Service of the u.S.—I found means Better than My own assertions to Convey proper ideas to lord Castelreagh and Gentlemen on that Side—with the duke of Wellington I Had a Conversation on the Subject—I Saw

Lord Landsdown and other opposition members and am going to paris on a visit to Lord Holland whom an indisposition Has prevented on His passage to Come to La Grange—I Have Confered with Some of the Continental diplomats, particularly with the very Sensible and influencing brother of our friend Humboldt—Emperor Alexander I Have Seen But once with a Small party, during one Evening, at mde de staël's House—I Had three days before Requested A Confidential person who for fear of the british interest insisted upon my Secreting His name, to put under the Emperor's Eyes[5] the inclosed Letter—it Became the Subject of a Long particular Conversation where I endeavoured to dispel and explain inimical Representations, and to impress the great and good monarch with a disposition to make a new, and personal effort to accomodate matters on proper and Honorable terms—He promised He would do, and I know He Has done it. these particulars I give to you, my dear friend, as I know you are at a great distance from washington and in private Retirements. But Having done the Little I Could do in Concert with and under the direction of the worthy and Enlightened minister of the u.S. mr Crawford, and the Commissioners particularly mr Gallatin Having been informed of those transactions, I Refer myself to their dispatches for the information of the president and Secretary of state—nor shall I trouble them with Accounts of the Business of france, england, and ghent which will Come through much better channels. I fervently Hope there may be a peace—should it be other wise I Hope both parties in the United States will join to lay the fault upon, and Consequently to Rise Hand in Hand Against the Invader—an union very necessary in the present Crisis, which if I thought I might Contribute to produce, I would, instead of this letter, Smuggle myself in the Cartel ship of the Commissioners.

the expressions of your esteem for Emperor Alexander, as I Saw them in your Letter to mde de Staël, are well founded indeed— I Regret, and He was pleased to Express the Same Sentiment, to Have Seen Him So Late—But my objections to foreign influence, my Retired Situation, the intrigues of the people about the Helm and the people about Him were So many obstacles to an Early Communication.

it Has Been a Great Relief to me to Hear you Had Approved the Sale of the pointe Coupee Lands—if I am put in possession of the town tract for which Sir John Coghill is willing to purchase Such claims as might make up the deficiency, my share would be much benefited by the acquisition of this wealthy partner—in the mean while, thanks to the munificence of Congress and the kindness of my friends, I now am perfectly clear of debts and pecuniary Embarassments—I feel a grateful Satisfaction in giving you the pleasure to Hear it.

My children and grand children to the number of Sixteen are well and Beg, Such as Can talk, to be Respectfully Remembered to you— be pleased to present my affectionate Respects to mrs Randolph— Receive the tender wishes and most Lively affection of

Your old Constant friend                                    LAFAYETTE

RC (DLC); endorsed by TJ as received 9 Dec. 1814 and so recorded in SJL. Tr (NIC: Dean Collection); incomplete.

The restored French king Louis XVIII put the CONSTITUTIONAL CHARTER of 1814 into effect. It established a government on the British model, with chambers of appointed peers and elected deputies. However, the charter's bill of rights was later modified to suppress free-

dom of religion, speech, and the press (Connelly, *Napoleonic France*, 107). For TJ's collaboration with Lafayette in defining the RIGHTS OF MANKIND in 1789, see *PTJ*, 15:230–3.

[1] Tr: "his."
[2] RC and Tr: "of."
[3] Tr ends here.
[4] Word interlined.
[5] Tr resumes here.

ENCLOSURE

## From Lafayette to an Unidentified Correspondent

MONSIEUR                                        Paris 22. Mai 1814.
J'ai eu la bonne idée de me prévaloir des droits que me donnent mes Sentiments pour vous, votre amour du bien public, et votre affection pour la gloire de l'Empereur Alexandre; ce Secret sera d'autant mieux gardé que je connais votre répugnance à vous mêler d'affaires etrangères à votre païs.

Voici une note que j'ai demandée à M^r Crawford digne Ministre des Etats Unis. Il s'est adressé à M^r le C^te de Neselrode pour être présenté à l'Empereur et n'a pas eu de réponse. J'ai voulu qu'il pût au moins faire, comme Simple Citoyen, le peu qui dépend de nous.

Sa note etablit l'etat de la question jugée d'ailleurs par le refus qu'ont fait les anglais de la médiation de leur Auguste allié tandis que les Etats Unis S'etaient emprêssés de lui envoyer des Négociateurs choisis dans les deux partis nationaux

On y voit 1° Que les Américains Sont restés en Arriere de ce que Catherine Seconde et les autres puissances avaient cru nécessaire à l'Indépendance de tous les peuples.

2° Que le Sistême des blocus imaginaires n'etait pas soutenable et que les Anglais ont rapporté, depuis la déclaration de guerre, leurs Vexatoires ordres du Conseil

3° Que la presse des matelots sur des bâtimens neutres, au gré du premier officier Anglais etait d'autant plus intolérable que tandis que tout matelot étranger Se trouve naturalisé, malgré lui, en angleterre, par deux ans de Navigation, il faut, pour etre naturalisé en Amérique, cinq années de résidence à terre; les Americains ont même offert de nouvelles précautions pour prévenir les Contraventions à Cette Loi.

Mais ce qu'on y voit de plus important pour le moment actuel, c'est que la paix Européenne met fin à l'exercice de ces deux prétentions Britanniques, les blocus extensifs et la presse des matelots en pleine mer

Les Américains ont pris plus de terrain qu'ils n'en ont perdu; ils rentreront volontier[s] dans les limites respectives; Il serait non seulement ridicule mais coupable de leur demander plus; car ce ne pourrait etre qu'avec le projet d'entretenir l'humeur guerriere des Sauvages et de Contrarier les mesures adoptées pour leur Civilisation.

Il parait que d'anciens souvenirs d'une lutte favorable à la liberté du nouveau monde, des blessures d'amour propre dans les combats maritimes de la guerre présente, quelques intérêts de monopole ou de Captures qui ne Sont pas les vrais intérêts de l'angleterre y ont fomenté une disposition contraire à cette paix Si facile, puisque toutes les causes de litige Se trouvent anéanties par le fait

L'Empereur Alexandre peut et par conséquent doit completter en cette occasion Sa noble fonction de pacificateur. Celui qui ramenant la gloire à Sa vraie source et la puissance à son légitime usage ne s'est placé à la tête du genre humain que pour en rechercher les droits et le bonheur, ne mettra pas hors de sa bienfaisante influence un peuple le plus libre et le plus heureux de la terre, dont les intérêts sont Communs avec ceux de la Russie, et dont le voeu unanime a été de s'abandonner à Sa médiation.

Agréez, Monsieur, l'assurance de ma haute Considération et de mon Sincère attachement.

Signé LAFAYETTE

EDITORS' TRANSLATION

SIR                                               Paris 22. May 1814.
I had the clever idea of taking advantage of the rights that my feelings for you, your love of the public good, and your affection for the glory of the Emperor Alexander give me; this secret will be all the better kept as I am aware of your aversion to meddling in the affairs of countries outside of your own.

Here is a note that I requested from Mr. Crawford, worthy minister of the United States. It was addressed to the Count von Nesselrode for presentation to the emperor but received no reply. I wanted him, as a simple citizen, to at least do the little that we can do.

His note establishes the state of the question, judged, moreover, on the basis of the British refusal of the mediation of their august ally, while the United States lost no time in sending him negotiators chosen from among the two national parties

One can see, first of all, that the Americans have stopped short of what Catherine II and other powers had believed to be necessary for the independence of all peoples.

Second, that the system of imaginary blockades could not be sustained and that, since the declaration of war, the English have reimposed their vexatious Orders in Council

Third, that the impressment of sailors on neutral ships, at the whim of the first English officer they encounter, was all the more intolerable because, while any foreign sailor is naturalized in England, in spite of himself, after two years at sea, he must live for five years on land to be naturalized in America; the Americans have even offered new precautions to prevent violations of this law.

But, more importantly, it is now clear that the European peace puts an end to these two British pretensions of extensive blockades and the impressment of sailors at sea

The Americans have taken more territory than they have lost; they will gladly retire within their original borders; it would be not only ridiculous but unfair to ask more of them, since doing so would only serve to encourage the bellicosity of the savages and thwart the measures taken to civilize them.

It appears that old memories of the successful struggle to secure the liberty of the New World, hurt feelings arising from the naval battles of the present war, and monopolistic interests or those relating to the capture of American ships, which are not the true interests of England, have fomented a disposition contrary to the easy reestablishment of peace, as all the causes of the dispute are, in fact, eliminated

Emperor Alexander can and therefore must on this occasion undertake the noble function of peacemaker. He who has returned glory to its true source and power to its legitimate use, who has placed himself at the head of mankind only in order to seek its rights and happiness, such a man will not exclude from his beneficial influence the most free and happy people on earth, whose interests are the same as Russia's and whose unanimous wish has been to surrender itself to his mediation.

Please be assured, Sir, of my highest consideration and my sincere attachment.

Signed LAFAYETTE

Tr (DLC); edge chipped; at head of text, with ellipsis in original: "Copie d'une Lettre à M. . . . pour etre mise sous les yeux de l'Empereur de Russie, et qui a Servi d'introduction à ma Conversation avec lui Sur les affaires d'Amérique" ("Copy of a letter to Mr. . . . to be brought to the attention of the emperor of Russia, and which served as an introduction to my conversation with him about American affairs"). Translation by Dr. Genevieve Moene. Enclosure not found.

# To William Wirt

DEAR SIR          Monticello Aug. 14. 14.

I have been laying under contribution my memory, my private papers, the printed records, gazettes & pamphlets in my possession to answer the enquiries of your letter of July 27. and I will give you the result as correctly as I can. I kept no copy of the paper I sent you on a former occasion, on the same subject, nor do I retain an exact recollection of it's contents. but if in that I stated the question on the loan office to have been in 1762. I did it with too slight attention to the date, altho' not to the fact. I have examined the journals of the House of Burgesses of 1760.1.2. in my possession, and find no trace of the proceeding in them. by those of 1764. I find that the famous Address to the king, and Memorials to the Houses of Lords & Commons, on the proposal of the stamp act, were of that date; and I know that mr Henry was not a member of the legislature when they were passed. I know also, because I was present, that Robinson (who died in May 1766.) was in the chair on the question of the loan office. mr Henry then must have come in between these two epochs, and consequently in 1765. of this year I have no journals to refresh my memory. the first session was in May, and his first remarkable exhibition there was on the motion for the establishment of an office for lending money on mortgages of real property. I find in Royle's Virginia gazette of the 17th of that month, this proposition for the loan office brought forward, it's advantages detailed, and the plan explained; and it seems to have been done by a borrowing member, from the feeling with which the motives are expressed; and to have been preparatory to the intended motion. this was probably made immediately after that date, and certainly before the 30th which was the date of mr Henry's famous resolutions. I had been intimate with mr Henry from the winter of 1759.60. and felt an interest in what concerned him, & I can never forget a particular exclamation of his in the debate which electrified his hearers. it had been urged that from certain unhappy circumstances of the colony, men of substantial property had contracted debts which, if exacted suddenly, must ruin them & their families, but with a little indulgence of time might be paid with ease. 'what, Sir, exclaimed mr Henry, in animadverting on this, is it proposed then to reclaim the Spendthrift from his dissipation and extravagance, by filling his pockets with money?' these expressions are indelibly impressed on my memory. he laid open with so much energy the spirit of favoritism on which the proposition was founded, & the abuses to which it would lead, that it was crushed in it's birth. abortive motions are not always entered on the journals, or rather they are rarely entered. it is the modern introduction of Yeas and Nays which has given the means of placing a rejected motion on the journals: and it is likely that the Speaker, who, as treasurer, was to be the loan officer, and had the direction of the journals, would chuse to omit an entry of the motion in this case. this accounts sufficiently for the absence of any trace of the motion on the journals. there was no suspicion then (as far at least as I knew) that Robinson had used the public money in private loans to his friends, and that the secret object of this scheme was to transfer those debtors to the public, and thus clear his accounts. I have diligently examined the names of the members on the journals of 1764. to see if any were still living to whose memory we might recur on this subject, but I find not a single one now remaining in life.

Of the parsons' cause I remember nothing remarkable. I was at school with mr Maury during the years 1758. & 1759. and often heard him inveigh against the iniquity of the act of 1758. called the two-penny act. in 1763 when that cause was decided in Hanover, I was a law-student in Williamsburg, and remember only that it was a subject of much conversation, and of great paper-controversy, in which Camm, & Col° Bland were the principal champions.

The disputed election in which mr Henry made himself remarkable must have been that of Dandridge & Littlepage in 1764. of which however I recollect no particulars, altho' I was still a student in Williamsburg, & paid attention to what was passing in the legislature.

I proceed now to the Resolutions of 1765. the copies you inclose me and that inserted by judge Marshal in his history, and copied verbatim by Burke, are really embarrassing by their differences. 1. that that of the 4. resolutions taken from the records of the House is the genuine copy of what they passed, as amended by themselves, cannot be doubted. 2. that the copy which mr Henry left sealed up is a true copy of these 4. resolutions, as reported by the committee, there is no reason to doubt. 3. that judge Marshal's version of 3. of these resolutions (for he has omitted one altogether) is from an unauthentic source, is sufficiently proved by their great variation from the record in diction, altho equivalent in sentiment. but what are we to say of mr Henry's 5th and of Marshal's two last, which we may call the 6th and 7th resolutions? the 5th has clearly nothing to justify the debate and proceedings which one of them produced. but the 6th is of that character, and perfectly tallies with the idea impressed on my mind of that which was expunged. Judge Marshal tells us that two were disagreed to by the house, which may be true. I do not indeed recollect it, but I have no recollection to the contrary. my hypothesis then is this, that the two disagreed to were the 5th and 7th. the 5th because merely tautologous of the 3d & 4th and the 7th because leading to individual persecution, for which no mind was then prepared: and that the 6th was the one passed by the House, by a majority of a single vote, & expunged from the Journals the next day.     I was standing at the door of communication[1] between the house and lobby during the debate and vote, & well remember that after the numbers on the division were told, and declared from the chair, Peyton Randolph (then

Atty Gen¹) came out at the door where I was standing, and exclaimed 'by god, I would have given 100. Guineas for a single vote.' for one vote would have divided the house, and Robinson was in the chair who he knew would have negatived the resolution.     mr Henry left town that evening, or the next morning; and Col° Peter Randolph, then a member of the Council, came to the H. of Burgesses about ten aclock of the forenoon, and sat at the clerk's table till the house-bell rang, thumbing over the volumes of Journals to find a precedent of expunging a vote of the house, which he said had taken place while he was a member, or clerk of the house, I do not recollect which. I stood by him at the end of the table a considerable part of the time, looking on as he turned over the leaves; but I do not recollect whether he found the erasure. in the mean time some of the timid members, who had voted for the strongest resolution, had become alarmed, and as soon as the house met a motion was made and carried to expunge it from the journals. and here I will observe that Burke's statement of mr Henry's consenting to withdraw two resolutions, by way of compromise with his opponents is entirely erroneous. I suppose the original journal was among those destroyed by the British, or it's obliterated face might be appealed to. it is a pity this investigation was not made a few years sooner, when some of the members of the day were still living. I think enquiry should be made of judge Marshal for the source from which he derived his copy of the Resolutions. this might throw light on the 6ᵗʰ and 7ᵗʰ which I verily believe and especially the 6ᵗʰ to be genuine in substance.     On the whole I suppose the 4. resolutions which are on the record were past and retained by the House; that the 6ᵗʰ is that which was passed by a single vote and expunged, and the 5ᵗʰ & 7ᵗʰ the two which judge Marshal says were disagreed to.     that mr Henry's copy then should not have stated all this is the remaining difficulty. this copy he probably sealed up long after the transaction; for it was long afterwards that these resolutions, instead of the Address & Memorials of the preceding year, were looked back to as the commencement of legislative opposition. his own judgment may, at a later date, have approved of the rejection of the 6ᵗʰ and 7ᵗʰ altho' not of the 5ᵗʰ and he may have left & sealed up a copy, in his own handwriting, as approved by his ultimate judgment. this, to be sure, is conjecture, and may rightfully be rejected by any one to whom a more plausible solution may occur: and there I must leave it.

the address of 1764. was drawn by Peyton Randolph. who drew the Memorial to the Lords I do not recollect: but mr Wythe wrote that to the Commons. it was done with so much freedom that, as he has told me himself, his colleagues of the Committee shrunk from it as wearing the aspect of treason, and smoothed it's features to it's present form. he was indeed one of the very few, (for I can barely[2] speak of them in the plural number) of either character, who, from the commencement of the contest, hung our connection with Britain on it's true hook, that of a common king. his unassuming character however, made him appear as a follower, while his sound judgment kept him in a line with the freest spirit.         by these resolutions mr Henry took the lead out of the hands of those who had heretofore guided the proceedings of the House, that is to say, of Pendleton, Wythe, Bland, Randolph, Nicholas. these were honest and able men, had begun the opposition on the same grounds, but with a moderation more adapted to their age and experience. subsequent events favored the bolder spirits of Henry, the Lees, Pages, Mason E[t]c. with whom I went in all points. sensible however of the importance of unanimity among our constituents, altho' we often wished to have gone faster, we slackened our pace, that our less ardent colleagues might keep up with us: and they, on their part, differing nothing from us in principle, quickened their gait somewhat beyond that which their prudence might of itself have advised, and thus consolidated the phalanx which breasted the power of Britain. by this harmony of the bold with the cautious, we advanced with our constituents in undivided mass, and with fewer examples of separation than perhaps existed in any other part of the Union.

I do not remember the topics of mr Henry's argument: but those of his opposers were that the same sentiments had been expressed in the Address and Memorials of the preceding[3] session, to which an answer was expected and not yet recieved. I well remember the cry of treason, the pause of mr Henry at the name of George the III[d] and the presence of mind with which he closed his sentence, and baffled the charge vociferated.[4]         I do not think he took the position in the middle of the floor which you mention. on the contrary I think I recollect him standing in the very place which he continued afterwards habitually to occupy in the house.

The censure of mr E. Randolph on mr Henry in the case of Philips, was without foundation. I remember the case, and took my part in it. Philips was a mere robber, who availing himself of the troubles of the times, collected a banditti, retired to the Dismal swamp, and from thence sallied forth, plundering and maltreating the neighboring inhabitants, and covering himself, without authority, under the name of a British subject. mr Henry, then Governor, communicated the case to me. we both thought the best proceeding would be by bill of attainder, unless he delivered himself up for trial within a given time. Philips was afterwards taken; and mr Randolph being Attorney Gen$^l$ and apprehending he would plead that he was a British subject, taken in arms, in support of his lawful sovereign, and as a prisoner of war entitled to the protection of the law of nations, he thought the safest proceeding would be to indict him at Common law as a felon & robber. against this I believe Philips urged the same plea; but was overruled and found guilty.

I recollect nothing of a doubt on the re-eligibility of mr Henry to the government, when his term expired in 1779. nor can I concieve on what ground such a doubt could have been entertained; unless perhaps that his first election in June 1776. having been before we were nationally declared independant, some might suppose it should not be reckoned as one of the three constitutional elections.[5]

Of the projects for appointing a Dictator there are said to have been two. I know nothing of either but by hear-say. the 1$^{st}$ was in Williamsburg in Dec. 1776. the assembly had, the month before, appointed mr Wythe, mr Pendleton, George Mason, Thomas L. Lee and myself to revise the whole body of laws, & adapt them to our new form of government. I left the House early in December to prepare to join the Committee at Fredericksburg, the place of our first[6] meeting. what passed therefore in the House in December, I know not, and have not the journals of that session to look into. [it is even possible that it was the absence of the members of this commee which encoraged the movers of a Dictatorship to hazard that enterprize.][7]       the 2$^d$ proposition was in June 81. at the Staunton session of the legislature. no trace of this last motion is entered on the journals of that date,[8] which I have examined. this is a further proof that the silence of journals is no evidence against the fact of an abortive motion. among the names of the members found on the journal of the Staunton session, are John Taylor of Caroline, Gen$^l$ Andrew Moore, and Gen$^l$ Edward Steevens of Culpeper now living. it would be well to ask information from each of them, that their errors of memory, or of feeling may be corrected by collation.[9]

You ask if I would have any objection to be quoted as to the fact of rescinding the last of mr Henry's resolutions. none at all as to that fact, or it's having been passed by a majority of one vote only; the scene being as present to my mind as that in which I am now writing. but I do not affirm, altho' I believe it was the 6$^{th}$ resolution.

It is truly unfortunate that those engaged in public affairs so rarely make notes of transactions passing within their knolege. hence history becomes fable instead of fact. the great outlines may be true, but the incidents and colouring are according to the faith or fancy of the writer. had judge Marshal taken half your pains in sifting & scrutinising facts, he would not have given to the world, as true history, a false copy of a record under his eye. Burke again has copied him, and being a second writer on the spot, doubles the credit of the copy. when writers are so indifferent as to the correctness of facts the verification of which lies at their elbow, by what measure shall we estimate their relation of things distant, or of those given to us thro' the obliquities of their own vision? our records it is true, in the case under contemplation, were destroyed by the malice and Vandalism of the British military, perhaps of their government under whose orders they committed so much useless mischief. but printed copies remained as your examination has proved. those which were apocryphal then ought not to have been hazarded without examination. should you be able to ascertain the genuineness of the 6th and 7th resolutions, I would ask a line of information, to rectify or to confirm my own impressions respecting them. ever affectionately yours.          TH: JEFFERSON

RC (ViU: TJP); at foot of first page: "Mr Wirt." PoC (DLC). Tr (PPAmP: Thomas Jefferson Papers); extract entirely in TJ's hand; on verso of reused address cover to TJ; enclosed in TJ to Louis H. Girardin, 13 Dec. 1814.

The PAPER I SENT YOU ON A FORMER OCCASION was TJ's Notes on Patrick Henry, [before 12 Apr. 1812], Document II in a group of documents on TJ's Recollections of Patrick Henry printed under that date. John Daly Burk COPIED VERBATIM Henry's 1765 Stamp Act resolves as given in John Marshall's *The Life of George Washington* (Philadelphia, 1804–07; Sowerby, no. 496), vol. 2, backmatter, pp. 25–7 (Burk, *The History of Virginia, from its First Settlement to the Present Day* [Petersburg, 1804–05; Sowerby, no. 464; Poor, *Jefferson's Library*, 4 (no. 127)], 3:305–7).

Marshall OMITTED the third resolve recorded in the *Journal of the House of Burgesses* and printed above as a part of the enclosure to Wirt to TJ, 27 July 1814. Marshall indicated that the House had approved four resolves, the last of which is a version of MR HENRY's 5TH. Henry's retained text of this resolution gave it as

"Resolved Therefore that the General Assembly of this Colony have the only and sole exclusive Right & Power to lay Taxes & Impositions upon the Inhabitants of this Colony and that every Attempt to vest such Power in any Person or Persons whatsoever other than the General Assembly aforesaid has a manifest Tendency to destroy British [as] well as American Freedom" (Tr in ViWC: chipped; with notes in Henry's hand; printed in Wirt, *Sketches of the Life and Character of Patrick Henry* [Philadelphia, 1817; Poor, *Jefferson's Library*, 4 (no. 131)], 56–8).

Marshall evidently drew on contemporary newspaper accounts for the 6TH AND 7TH RESOLUTIONS, which affirmed "That his Majesty's Liege People, Inhabitants of this Colony, are not bound to yield Obedience to any Law or Ordinance whatsoever, designed to impose any Taxation upon them, other than the Laws or Ordinances of the General Assembly as aforesaid. That any Person who shall, by Speaking, or Writing, assert or maintain, That any Person or Persons, other than the General Assembly of this Colony, with such Consent as aforesaid, have any Right or Authority to lay or impose any Tax whatever on the Inhabitants thereof, shall be Deemed, an ENEMY TO THIS HIS MAJESTY'S COLONY" (Annapolis *Maryland Gazette*, 4 July 1765).

The ORIGINAL JOURNAL for 30 May 1765 disappeared almost immediately after its creation, well before it could have been DESTROYED BY THE BRITISH (Wirt, *Sketches*, 62). The contemporary account of an unidentified French visitor to Williamsburg suggests that Henry's speech was not interrupted by a CRY OF TREASON, but rather that the Speaker leveled such a charge at Henry when he paused after saying "that in former times tarquin and Julus had their Brutus, Charles had his Cromwell, and he Did not Doubt but some good american would stand up, in favour of his Country"; with Henry then pleading the heat of passion and asking pardon ("Journal of a French Traveller in the Colonies, 1765," *Ameri-can Historical Review* 26 [1921]: 726–9, 745; Edmund S. Morgan and Helen M. Morgan, *The Stamp Act Crisis: Prologue to Revolution*, rev. ed. [1963], 121–32).

[1] Manuscript: "communition."
[2] Word interlined in place of "hardly."
[3] TJ here canceled "year."
[4] Sentence quoted in Wirt, *Sketches*, 65.
[5] Tr begins here.
[6] Word interlined.
[7] Bracketed sentence, not in RC or PoC, supplied from Tr.
[8] Remainder of this and whole of next sentence not in Tr, which substitutes "because a rejected motion was never entered on the journals. that practice was introduced first by authorising the entry of the Yeas & Nays."
[9] Tr ends here.

# To Major Clayton

SIR                                          Monticello Aug. 15. 14.

By a letter of July 8. from D[r] Wallace, lately recieved, I am informed that a servant of his coming on to this place with a packet[1] addressed to me, was taken sick at Culpeper court house & returned home, and that you had been so kind as to recieve the packet. on this ground I send the bearer for it, and ask the favor of it's being delivered to him, tendering at the same time my thanks for your care of it, and the assurances of my respect.                    TH: JEFFERSON

PoC (MHi); at foot of text: "Maj[r] Clayton"; on verso of reused address cover to TJ; endorsed by TJ.

[1] Reworked from "bun."

# To Patrick Gibson

DEAR SIR                                     Monticello Aug. 15. 14.

M[r] Johnson going down with his boat gives me an opportunity of getting a bale of cotton brought up, which I will ask the favor of you to procure for me, say of 3. or 400. weight.          your favor of Aug. 4. is recieved, and lightens my anxieties. I now return the note for the bank, signed, but left blank to be filled by yourself according to circumstances.          1500.D. additional is about the sum which would answer my calls. the remittances to Philadelphia, & perhaps that to mr Barnes & some trifles here are the only ones for which I will avail myself of your permission to draw in the mean time. on those to Philadelphia I will write to you more specially by post. Accept the assurance of my great esteem and respect.

Th: Jefferson

P.S. on reflection I withold the note for the bank thinking it will go more safely in my letter by post.

PoC (NHi: Thomas Jefferson Papers); above postscript: "Mr Gibson"; endorsed by TJ.

On 13 Aug. 1814 TJ recorded that he had drawn on Gibson & Jefferson in favor of William JOHNSON "for 7.D. for bringing up fish &c. and the additional price of bringing up mould boards should he get them." TJ was awaiting the delivery of plow moldboards from John Staples (*MB*, 2:1301–2; TJ to Staples, 4 May 1814). Gibson's FAVOR OF AUG. 4., not found, is recorded in SJL as received 9 Aug. 1814 from Richmond.

# To Thomas Ritchie

DEAR SIR                                    Monticello Aug. 15. 14.

It is probable that a mr Clopper of Maryland is now in Richmond exhibiting a loom of the most beautiful invention imaginable. nobody was more pleased than myself with it's construction, when shewn here, and I was willing to have procured one of them altho' at a price which I deemed exorbitant. while it was here I recieved a letter from Dr Maese of Philadelphia, informing me that one of these looms cost there about 50.D. which letter I shewed to mr Clopper, & observed to him that perhaps he might find one or two other individuals in this county who might be willing to give 100.D. the price he asked; but I was sure he would find 100. if he reduced it to 50.D. he adhered however to his price, altho' I think with an intimation that he expected in time to lower it. since this I have recd a letter from the purchaser of the patent right for Maryland informing me that in Connecticut these looms are sold for 40.D. and in Baltimore for 50.D. his price for the right to construct and use a single loom is 20.D. while for the same right Clopper asks 50.D. from us. nobody wishes more to encorage useful arts and inventions than myself. but I think the present a very unwarrantable attempt to make our citizens pay the double of what is asked from those of other states, and that not to reward the author of the invention, but the forestaller of the Virginia market. but the taking from a few wealthy individuals 100. instead of 50.D. is not the git of the evil. it is the exclusion of the great body of our citizens from the benefit of the machine, by asking a price beyond their faculties: it is the placing the weavers of other states on a footing so much better than ours, that by underworking us, they may draw our own demands to the Northern manufactories, and put down the competition of ours. I certainly do not mean to bring myself into controversy with mr Clopper or any one else. yet I think our citizens should be put on their guard. perhaps this kind of information is properly within the[1] functions of the public papers. if you think so, and think proper to give it I inclose you the two letters which vouch the facts. I would rather however they should not be used, unless such a contradiction should arise as may require it in justification of the facts. I have heard it supposed that mr Harris of Richm^d will be the most likely person to be taken in by a want of information. perhaps it may be friendly to put him personally on his guard. be so good as to return me the letters when done with, and accept assurances of my constant esteem and respect.                                      TH: JEFFERSON

PoC (DLC); at foot of first page: "M^r Ritchie"; endorsed by TJ as a letter of 14 Aug. 1814 and so recorded in SJL. Enclosures: (1) James Mease to TJ, 27 July 1814. (2) George Greer to TJ, 9 Aug. 1814.

A newspaper article on "Mr Janes's Loom" called for a reduced price and quoted from the beginning of this letter as follows: "Mr. Jefferson, of whose skill in the arts we cannot say too much, terms it 'a loom of the most beautiful invention imaginable'—and says, 'Nobody was more pleased than myself with its construction'" (Richmond *Enquirer*, 20 Aug. 1814).

By GIT TJ may have been alluding to "gît," an archaic form of "gist" that was still current in law books (*OED*).

[1] Manuscript: "th."

# From John Barnes

DEAR SIR—                                Geo[rge] Town Co^a 16^th Aug^st 1814.

In making my Arangem^ts for the 1^st paymt to the loan 25^th May for $2500. I was Necessitated,[1] to procure a disc^t for $1480—and now find—my self deficient nearly—$1000—(exclusive of your expected $360—) to be provided for, against 25^h Instant, when the 4^th and last paym^t is to be made for $2500—soon as you can make it convenient—to remit me—will be very Acceptable—the times are become— so very pressing, that the Banks—thro. Necessity—are Obliged—to curtail their disc^t and former endorsing—friends (unless an Accomodating One) will not even lend you his Name—much less his purse—

whose strings are drawn titer and titer, as the times presses on him—
is readily to be Accounted for—the Natural effects of War, and its
distressing Consequences—

We begin to Assume a Confidence of Defence—against any Attempts that may be made upon the Capitol—and worthy possesors—
though I could never suppose, the Madness of the Enemy—ever had
it, in their serious Contemplation—but to excite the fears and jealousies—of the weake and diseffected—still, it is proper, to be prepared—for the worse, that might happen, and thereby quiet the
Minds of the people—in general,—to prevent a Repetition of the
Ravages daily made on individuals—Considering the deversity of
their defenseless situations, it is impossible for Goverm$^t$ to Afford
them that effectual aid, they severally stand in Need Off—to remove
their Slaves—Stock &c$^a$ &c—to the interior part of the Country—and
to avail themselves of a more favorable Season for their returns—is,
the only sure mode, of preserving the sad Remains of their property—and many of the late sufferers—are endeavouring to affect so
desirable a purpose

> with great respect,
> I am Dear Sir, Your mst Obed$^t$

JOHN BARNES,

RC (ViU: TJP-ER); torn; at foot of
text: "Thomas Jefferson Esq$^r$ Monticello"; endorsed by TJ as received 19 Aug.
1814 and so recorded in SJL.

[1] Manuscript: "Necessiated."

# To Nicolas G. Dufief

DEAR SIR                                    Monticello Aug. 16. 14.

The difficulty of remitting small & fractional sums to Philadelphia
obliges me generally to wait till my debts there[1] amount to something
of a round sum, and then to ask the favor of some one of those to
whom money is due to recieve the whole remittance and pay it out to
the others. this favor I am obliged now to ask of you.

|                                                    | D    c  |
|----------------------------------------------------|---------|
| I owe to J. F. Watson bookseller                   | 11.25   |
| Bradford & Inskeep, d$^o$                          | 68.75   |
| W$^m$ Barton, Lancaster, (for Rittenh's life)      | 18.     |
| Gen$^l$ Duane, 3. years of the Aurora              | 15      |
|                                                    | 113     |

besides what I am indebted to yourself. I have therefore desired mr
Gibson of Richmond to remit to you 150.D. out of which I will re-

quest you to pay the above sums to the several persons, whom I shall desire, by letters to them, to call on you, that you may have as little trouble as possible. the balance which will remain be pleased to place to my credit with you. I will ask the favor of you to send me another copy of your Dictionary by mail, but separatim as heretofore; as also Brown's history of the Shakers. pardon this trouble and accept the assurance of my esteem & respect.                    TH: JEFFERSON

RC (NjP: Andre deCoppet Collection); addressed: "M$^r$ Nich$^s$ G. Dufief Philadelphia"; franked; postmarked Milton, 17 Aug. PoC (DLC); on verso of reused address cover to TJ; endorsed by TJ.

SEPARATIM: "apart, separately." TJ acquired the first edition of Thomas BROWN's *An Account of the People called Shakers: their Faith, Doctrines, and Practice* (Troy, N.Y., 1812; Sowerby, no. 1707).

[1] Word interlined.

# To Patrick Gibson

DEAR SIR                                        Monticello Aug. 16. 14.
   In my letter of yesterday by mr Johnson, I mentioned that I would write to you more specially on the subject of the remittance to Philadelphia; I find that my different accounts there for books and newspapers amount nearly to 150.D. which sum I will therefore ask the favor of you to remit to mr Nicholas G. Dufief bookseller Philadelphia, on my account. I write to him now as to the disposal of it. I inclose the note for the bank as mentioned in my letter of yesterday. the box of books spoken of in a former letter came to hand yesterday. Accept assurances of esteem & respect.
                                                 TH: JEFFERSON

PoC (Joseph Bransten, San Francisco, 1950); at foot of text: "M$^r$ Gibson"; endorsed by TJ. Enclosure not found.

The BOX OF BOOKS contained thirteen copies of Biddle, *Lewis and Clark Expedition*, sent by Bradford & Inskeep early in April 1814.

# To William Barton

DEAR SIR                                        Monticello Aug. 17. 14.
   Your favor of the 4$^{th}$ is recieved. the difficulty of making small and fractional remittances to Philadelphia having no paper of common currency, obliges me to let little debts lie there, till I may remit a round sum covering the whole. I have just now made such a remittance to mr

Dufief bookseller there, and desired him to pay 18. Dollars of it to yourself or order; which therefore be so good as to authorize some one to call on him for, and accept the assurance of my esteem & respect.

TH: JEFFERSON

PoC (DLC); at foot of text: "W<sup>m</sup> Barton esq."; on verso of reused address cover to TJ; endorsed by TJ.

# To Bradford & Inskeep

MESS<sup>RS</sup> BRADFORD AND INSKEEP            Monticello Aug. 17. 14.

Your favor of Apr. 7. was recieved Apr. 22. the books never got to hand, or were heard of by me till the day before yesterday. I deferred remitting the amount in the hope of acknoleging their reciept at the same time. having to make a remittance to mr Dufief, bookseller in Philadelphia, I have included in it 68. D 75 C for you, for which I must ask the favor of you to call on him within a few days after your reciept of this, by which time it will have got to hand from mess<sup>rs</sup> Gibson and Jefferson of Richmond my correspondents. accept my thanks for the extra copy sent me and assurances of my respect

TH: JEFFERSON

PoC (MHi); on verso of reused address cover of George Greer to TJ, 9 Aug. 1814; endorsed by TJ.

Bradford & Inskeep's FAVOR OF APR. 7 was actually a letter of 12 Apr. 1814 enclosing an account dated 7 Apr. 1814.

# From William Caruthers

D<sup>R</sup> SIR                                Lexington 17<sup>th</sup> Aug<sup>t</sup> 1814

Some Years ago You requested me to find a purchaser for a Small Tract of land you hold in this county including the natural Bridge— in which I did not Suceed at that time—I have lately Taken a notion of purchaseing it, if You are Still Disposed to Sell and do Not Set too high a price on it. if the War continus I have Some Idia of manufacturing Shot at the Bridge

If You are Disposed to Sell, Will You please to Say by letter On What Terms—(the price[1]) and if it Will Suit You to Give Some Accomodiation in time for payment it Will Suit me Best as it Will Require a Good Deal of active cappital to Start the Business proposed—

I am Sir with the highest Respect[2]

Your Ob<sup>t</sup> Hmb<sup>l</sup> Ser<sup>t</sup>

W<sup>M</sup> CARUTHERS

RC (MHi); between dateline and salutation: "Tho⁵ Jefferson Esq"; endorsed by TJ as received 22 Aug. 1814 and so recorded in SJL.

On 7 Sept. 1809 TJ REQUESTED that Caruthers find a purchaser for his Natural Bridge TRACT in Rockbridge County, but he retracted that proposal in a letter dated 9 Oct. 1810.

¹ Manuscript: "pric."
² Manuscript: "Respet."

# From Thomas Cooper

DEAR SIR                    Northumberland August 17ᵗʰ 1814

I am here on business for a few days with more leisure than I usually have, and sitting down to write a few lines to you, my pen begins at once on politics, and the rather perhaps because it is a subject the more irritating as it is the more unpleasant. I brood over the events of Europe, with melancholy forebodings of what may be the case here, and with no violent predilection in favour of this best of all possible worlds. It seems to me as though "Chaos were come again." I shall doubt hereafter about all wise "saws" and moral and political axioms. I shall no longer unhesitatingly agree that <u>Magna est Veritas et prevalebit</u>: I shall no longer declare it as my opinion that in political struggles "no effort is ever lost." Heretofore I have enlisted under Leibnitz and Candide, but <u>Le disastre de Lisbon</u>, and the French Revolution, have shaken my Optimism. Doubtless I am bound to acknowledge that the Manichees were sad heretics; but their mistakes [m]ight happen to minds no stronger than mine.

Malthus's book goes far to shew that political improvement even if unobstructed by power, has its limits: that human perfectibility, is not thoroughly defensible either in posse or in esse: and that when amelioration passes a certain line, it loses gradually its character, and assumes the opposite, like the properties of attraction and repulsion in Boscovich's curve.

Indeed I am persuaded from what I see, that in a nation, where in the mass of the People are (as Reformers wᵈ wish them to be) perfectly free from political oppression—in a state of tolerable equality, as to the distribution of property and political influence—having at command all the comforts of life, in consequence of a high price for labour—and maintaining but few of the unproductive classes—there neither is or can be, the same quantity of energy exerted, bodily or mental, or the same quantity of knowledge prevail—or the same security in the means of defence of home, or offence abroad, as in a Country like England where the reverse of all this is to be found.

I do not like the english constitution in theory, I detest the british government in practice: I cannot approve of the State of a Country, where out of 10 or 11 million of people between 2 and 3 are supported as paupers at the expence of five & twenty million of dollars a year: and where the public policy is, to convert the mass of population into mere animal machines. But with all these evils, and out of these evils, so much solid good arises—so many benefits to the British which the Americans want, that I am compelled to hesitate and to consider before I absolutely decide. They have in that country incalculable means of defence, and of offence too—from superior knowledge as an article incessantly in demand there and not here, they are a superior[1] people; they live more, for the range of Ideas is much wider, and their succession quicker, where all energies mental and bodily are kept in perpetual, unrelenting requisition: there is certainly more misery in England than here, but I doubt whether there may not also be as much happiness.

In this country time is wasted among all ranks of people, particularly among the lower ranks to whom it is most valuable, because there is a general feeling & persuasion that they can afford to waste it: <u>occasional</u> energy may be and is exerted, sometimes surprisingly; but of <u>habitual</u> persevering energy, there is little, for the all powerful stimulus of poverty is wanting. You cannot excite the people to turn out even to defend their country, for they are so happy and idle at home, that danger and exertion are dreaded untill the moment arrives when they <u>must</u> be met. How can you fill your armies with men, who by an idle kind of Labour at home, under gone when the fit takes them during 4 or 5 days in the week, can earn all that nature requires and whiskey enough for intoxication into the bargain?

For want of Manufactures we have no science: it is not only not in request becau[se] it is not needed, but it is despised: this is une nation bouticaire. shew a farmer or a storekeeper, or a merchant if you please, a piece of Calico printed with three or four colours: he will stare at it much like an Indian, without having any Ideas excited; save perhaps, how it may be bought cheap and sold dear. But introduce the manufacture itself of printed Calicoes generally among this Community, and observe the inevitable consequences—you introduce concomitantly all the knowledge necessary to the Steam engine; all the accurate and scientific part of hydrostatics and hydraulics; you introduce accuracy and precision too in all [th]e branches of your iron manufacture; you introduce all the mechanical knowledge necessary to the complicated machinery of the spinning manufactory; you introduce the working of copper plates and copper cylinders, and the art of engraving on copper steel and wood; you introduce all the complicated chemical knowledge necessary [...] the bleaching, the dyeing, the printing, the discharging of white and coloured goods; and all the mercantile knowledge necessary to obtain from foreign parts the dungs and salts required in these operations; a mass of knowledge unthought of before is now put in requisition, and your tradesmen are called upon to become Men of Science: they are so in the old Country to an eminent degree. Is not this better than the faculty of making long speeches de omni scibile et de quolibet ente without attention to the substance of them? Where one sterling line, is spread out through a dozen newspaper columns, and the reader who wishes for real [i]nformation searches anxiously for two grains of wheat among three bushels of chaff? It is not true that (with as much natural capacity at least as any people) we are the most enlightened nation on the face of the earth, as some very ignorant and silly orators were pleased to call us: we are a people to whom political wrangling, and political speech making are as food of the first necessity, and sufficient to satisfy all other mental cravings.

It may be said if you introduce manufactures, you introduce capitalists who live by the life blood of the starving poor whom they employ—where pride and Luxury dispense their insolent commands to [cr]ouching[2] misery—where the man is converted into a machine, his constitution worn down, his intellect weakend, his character depraved, and his morals destroyed—where he is systematically kept in abject poverty, and to all real intents and purposes enslaved! Granted to a great extent. But manufactures are carried in England to an extent that renders the nation itself too sensibly alive to their loss; & they are carried on up[on] a system congenial with the spirit that pervades the political government of the Country. They need not be so here, or any where else. In fact, it appears to me that no nation is safe, where there are not some such classes of Society who can be made to work and fight for the rich and idle: a description of people, who neither in this or in any other country will work or fight for themselves. There has been m[uch?] silly outcry (by the way) about conscription, a most fair and equal system which we shall have to resort to, or I am much mistaken.

It is not true in practise, however plausible it may be in theory, that a people enjoying to the utmost, equal rights and comfortable subsistence, diffused throug[h] the whole mass of population, are stimulated to defend so desireable a situati[on] in life, in proportion as

[ 559 ]

they are more comfortable. I think the reverse is true. I wish I c<sup>d</sup> be persuaded that I am wrong, for I have every inclination to think otherwise and I never hear or think of Malthus with<sup>t</sup> unpleasant associations connected with his name; which on my part is silly prejudice. But enough of Politics de bene esse.

M<sup>r</sup> Ogilvie I hear is now Earl of Findlater. I have not heard of him or from him of late. M— Correa told me he meant to spend part of the month of Sept<sup>r</sup> at y<sup>r</sup> house. I wish my avocations w<sup>d</sup> permit me to pay you a visit. Corre[a] is full of all kind of information, and very entertaining as well as instructive. Pray tell him that in consequence of a short conversation between him and me in Phila<sup>a</sup> in which he expressed a decided opinion that none of the motions of plants originated from stimulus ab intra, I have considered the subject, and written two papers on vegetable life in the Portfolio for July & August, which I beg he will read when he has time. Also that in the next Portfolio, I shall have a dissertation on the punic origin of the Irish Language, adding some remarks of my own to Vallancey's proofs. His friend Walsh, is of opinion on the federalists that John Quincy Adams will make a very excellent President. Walsh is so ingenious, that I should not wonder at his discovering qualities far concealed from common eyes.

Adieu: pray accept my sincere respects and kind wishes.

THOMAS COOPER
Carlisle

RC (DLC); edges chipped; endorsed by TJ as received 2 Sept. 1814 and so recorded in SJL.

CHAOS WERE COME AGAIN draws on William Shakespeare, *Othello*, act 3, scene 3. In the same year as the catastrophic 1755 LISBON earthquake, Voltaire wrote a *Poème sur le désastre de Lisbonne*, which argued against the existence of a just and compassionate deity. MANICHEES: followers of Manichaeism; religious or philosophical dualists (*OED*). IN POSSE OR IN ESSE: "potentially or actually in being" (*Black's Law Dictionary*). Ruggiero Giuseppe Boscovich illustrated his law of forces with a CURVE showing oscillations of attraction and repulsion between two elements of matter in space (Zeljko Marković, "Boscovich's *Theoria*," in Lancelot Law Whyte, *Roger Joseph Boscovich, S.J., F.R.S., 1711–1787:*

*Studies of his Life and Work on the 250th Anniversary of His Birth* [1961], 127–52, esp. 137–8). UNE NATION BOUTICAIRE: "a nation of shopkeepers." DE OMNI SCIBILE ET DE QUOLIBET ENTE: "to dispute with any person in any science."

In December 1796 the United States House of Representatives debated and ultimately rejected including in its response to President George Washington's annual message to Congress the assertion that America was the MOST ENLIGHTENED NATION in the world (*Annals*, 4th Cong., 2d sess., 1612, 1614). DE BENE ESSE: "in anticipation of a future need" (*Black's Law Dictionary*). AB INTRA: "from within."

Cooper's two-part article ON VEGETABLE LIFE appeared in the *Port Folio*, 3d ser., 4 (July–Aug. 1814): 59–74, 176–91. He claimed to advance no personal opinion on the subject of plant sensation and voluntary motion, and stated that "it

seems to me of no great practical consequence which way the question is determined; it is a discussion curious but not
very useful, and certainly not worth any
anxiety as to the event of the controversy."
Cooper indicated, however, that he was
"somewhat prejudiced in favour of that
opinion which confers upon the vegetable
system, the property of sensation, and the
concomitant susceptibilities of pleasure
and of pain. As to voluntarity, unless as
implying sensation, I have no bias in its

favour; but as there can be no power of
voluntary motion unless what arises from
a sensation *ab intra*, I shall use the facts
that bear upon both" (p. 63). Cooper's
DISSERTATION ON THE PUNIC ORIGIN
OF THE IRISH LANGUAGE came out in the
same journal, 4 (Oct.–Nov. 1814): 409–
18, 480–5.

¹ Manuscript: "supeior."
² Word obscured by tape.

# To Peter Cottom

SIR                                        Monticello Aug. 17. 14.
  Being a subscriber for the Port folio, and observing by a notification on it that you are agent in Richmond for it, I ask the favor of you
to inform me what is it's annual price, which is unknown to me, and
I will send you [an?] order to recieve the 1ˢᵗ year's subscription in
Richmond. [...] begun with that of May last. Accept the assurance of
my respect                                        TH: JEFFERSON

PoC (MHi); torn; on verso of address
cover of William Thornton to TJ, 2 Aug.
1814; at foot of text: "Mʳ Peter Cottom
Richmond"; endorsed by TJ.

  Peter Cottom (d. 1849), bookseller, entered into partnership in Alexandria with
John Stewart in 1798 to form Cottom &
Stewart. In 1813 this association dissolved, Cottom relocated to Richmond,
and there he established himself as a
bookseller and stationer. He opened a
shop in 1815 in Lynchburg, which TJ patronized at least once. From 1813 until at
least 1819 Cottom published almanacs,
and he also operated a circulating library
in Richmond. He was a longtime Mason,
in which capacity he attended the funeral
of George Washington, and an honorary

member of the Richmond Light Infantry
Blues (Franklin L. Brockett, *The Lodge
of Washington: A History of the Alexan-
dria Washington Lodge . . . 1783–1876*
[1899], 153–4; *Alexandria Advertiser*, 26
Jan. 1798; *Alexandria Gazette, Commer-
cial and Political*, 20 Apr. 1813; Rich-
mond *Enquirer*, 13 July 1813, 18 Mar.
1815, 9 July 1830; *MB*, 2:1344; *Cottom's
Virginia Almanac, For The Year Of Our
Lord 1814* [Richmond, 1813]; *Cottom's
New Virginia & North-Carolina Al-
manack, For The Year Of Our Lord 1820*
[Richmond, 1819]; *Richmond Whig and
Public Advertiser*, 12 June 1849).
  Cottom's missing response of 27 Aug.
1814 is recorded in SJL as received 29
Aug. 1814 from Richmond.

# From Joseph Delaplaine

DEAR SIR,                           Philadelphia August 17th 1814

I have been favoured with your obliging letter of the 9th instant, accompanied by another to Mr Gabriel Stuart, and at the same time received your engraved portrait of Americus Vespusius in perfect safety. For these marks of your kindness be pleased to accept my sincere thanks

The print of Vespucius is much admired by our artists, and is to be engraved in the line by one of our best engravers.

Have the goodness to inform me what date the eulogium, from which the print is taken, bears. This will be mentioned with my engraving, & at the same time I shall also state that it was furnished by yourself, an attention which I conceive to be justly due to you.[1]

Your letter to Mr Stuart* I read with peculiar pleasure and believe[2] it to be, in every respect, well calculated to answer my purpose, and cannot fail to be perfectly satisfactory to himself. Agreeably to your request I lost no time in forwarding it to him.

At your suggestion I enquired at the Loganian & other libraries for the work of De Bry, but in vain. In speaking to my worthy friend Dr Barton on the subject, he informed me that he believed the work was not in America except in your possession. He spoke of its great value, and I at the same time mentioned that it contained an engraved portrait of Columbus, and that De Bry says it was given to him by the painter who drew the portrait of Columbus. That I derived this information from you & it added further, that an account of the print accompanied it which should give it some authority.

After this Dr Barton went to his library & produced the History of America in Spanish, entitled "Historia Del Nuevo-Mundo Escribíala D. Juan Baut. Munoz Tomo 1.

En Madrid Por La viuda De Ibarra M.D.C.C.X.C.I.I.I."[3] a work with which you are doubtless acquainted. It is in one vol. when that was finished the author died. It contains an engraved portrait of Columbus beautifully executed[4] in the line. Dr Barton spoke in high terms of the print & presumed it bore the stamp of unquestionable authority, as the work was undertaken at the instance of the King of Spain, and as an account of the print and painting, which he conceived favourable, was given by the Author of the book, which I now transcribe for you lest the work should not be in your possession. Several gentlemen enjoying a literary name with us attempted

---

*He spells his name <u>Stu</u>, I am informed, and not <u>Stew</u>

its translation, each differing from the other, and neither satisfying me. My object is, of course, to ascertain, positively, whether the painting from which the engraving is taken, bears the marks of genuine authenticity. I fear it does not, because from what I can gather from the account, the picture was in some degree effaced by time when it was presented to Antonio del Rincon,* who, at the suggestions of Columbus['s] son Fernando supplied the defects and made such corrections and alterations,† as he conceived would exhibit the best resemblance of his father, and in this state it went to the engravers' hands.

I shall trouble you no further, but come immediately to the original account of the picture.

"Este primer tomo lleva al principio el retrato del descubridor, dibujado y gravado con esmero. Entre muchos quadros y estampas que se venden falsamente por tales retratos, solo uno he visto que pueda serlo, y es el que se conserva en la casa del excelentisimo señor duque de Berwick y Liria, descendiente de nuestro héroe: figura del natural pintada al parecer en el siglo pasado por un mediano copiante, pero en que aparecen indicios de la mano de Antonio del Rincon, pintor célebre de los reyes católicos. Las señas dadas por Fernando Colón del rostro de su padre han servido para elegir la efigie mas semejante, y para enmendar los defectos que se advierten en algunas facciones, ó mal entendidas por el artífice, ó desfiguradas por las injurias del tiempo."

At the bottom of the print is engraved Mariano Maella lo dibuxó. Pilkington gives no account of him. The name of the engraver is Fernando Selma.

I beg of you sir, to have the goodness to examine this subject & compare the supposed genuineness of this portrait with that in De Bry's work, which, I strongly suspect, from De Bry's account of it, is of more satisfactory origin. If this should be the case, can I take the liberty of requesting the favour of you to take it from the work & forward it to me. I am certain that no injury can arise to that nor the one

*According to Pilkington in his Dictionary of Painters, he was born in 1446 and died in 1500, of Guadalaxara, is named among the first reformers of Spanish art. He travelled to Rome, and made himself master of the elements which began to distinguish that school. At his return his success was equal to hi[s] endeavours; he was made painter to the court, chamberlain & Knight of S[t] Jago, by Ferdinand the catholic. Of his works the greater part perished, and what remains is retouched. He left a son, Fendando, of some, though inferior name.

†or they were made by some other painter. Or perhaps the translation ought to be, that this picture was painted after the manner of del Rincon originally, & afterwards altered by another.

of Americus Vespusius, and when M$^r$ Fairman & M$^r$ Kearny, who are to engrave them in the line, have done with them, they shall be promptly sent to you to be replaced in the works from which they came.

The portrait of Columbus of which I have been speaking, has a youthful appearance, a smooth & beautiful face, & I fear does not exhibit those characteristic marks of age & expression which I presume Columbus himself possessed, nor, probably, of that given in De Bry's work.

I am compelled to be particular, because my work ought to bear a [g]enerally approved[5] stamp of authenticity.

Hoping to receive as early a reply as you can make it convenient, I remain with the highest respect & esteem,

Dear sir, your obed$^t$ hum$^b$ serv$^t$     JOSEPH DELAPLAINE

P.S. If I should be favoured with the portrait of Columbus contained in De Bry's work & it should be preferred,[6] I shall mention, of course, in the copy, that it was derived from your kindness.

RC (DLC); edge trimmed; at foot of text: "Thomas Jefferson Esq$^r$"; endorsed by TJ as received 26 Aug. 1814 and so recorded in SJL.

By ONE OF OUR BEST ENGRAVERS, Delaplaine meant Gideon Fairman. TJ provided a translation of the ORIGINAL ACCOUNT OF THE PICTURE in his 28 Aug. 1814 response to Delaplaine. LO DIBUXÓ: "drew it."

[1] TJ wrote perpendicularly in the left-hand margin of the page containing this paragraph: "Elógio d'Amerigo Vespucci che ha riportato il premio dalla nobile ac-cademia Etrusca di Cortona nel dì 15. d'ottobre dell' anno 1788 del P. Stanislao Canovai della scuole pie publico professore di fisica-matematica, in Firenze 1788. nella stamp. di Pietro Allegrini." For his use of this text, see TJ to Delaplaine, 28 Aug. 1814.

[2] Manuscript: "belive."

[3] Omitted closing quotation mark editorially supplied.

[4] Word interlined in place of "engraved."

[5] Preceding two words added in margin.

[6] Preceding five words interlined.

# To William Duane

DEAR SIR     Monticello Aug. 17. 14.

Since my letter to you of the 3$^d$ I have had occasion to make a remittance to mr Dufief bookseller of Philadelphia out of which I have desired him to pay my arrears for the Aurora, being of two years I believe besides the current year. if you will be so good as to call on him for it within a few days after your reciept of this, the remittance will by that time have got to his hands from Gibson & Jefferson my correspondents of Richmond. if you had any reciever at this last place, the paiment should be very regularly made every year. Accept the assurance of my esteem and respect.      TH: JEFFERSON

PoC (DLC); at foot of text: "Gen¹ Duane"; on verso of reused address cover to TJ. TJ's missing letter OF THE 3ᴰ is recorded in SJL.

# From John L. E. W. Shecut

MUCH ESTEEMED SIR  Charleston South Carolina. August 17th 1814.

I take leave once again to trespass upon your goodness, but, not until I was fully satisfied you wou'd pardon this intrusion. I am greatly straitened for the want of advice, & as I have ever held your opinion as of the utmost value, have selected you, to aid me, in preference to all others. I have been for the last nineteen years, taking notes, on the Theory and Practise of Medecine Having at that period, discovered many inconsistencies in both. I did believe that there was a primary cause of disease, which if once discovered, wou'd lead to a more successful & Philosophical practice, than had yet been adopted. I had learnt by experience, that the Theory of Nosologists were much the Same, but in practice there was a direct opposition, The doctrine of phlogiston, and the Antiphlogistic treatment appear'd to be the leading features in the practice of Physicians, but the success attending this doctrine was not such as answered the high expectations of its advocates. As yet, I knew nothing of the Theory of Doct Brown, I had been practising twelve years in the Interior, where the most of my Notes were originated—On my reading this most elegant production, I was truly charmed with the Style and more than gratified with the Philosophy of his reasoning. His doctrine of excitement and excitability, is a monument of human wisdom, which cannot be destroyed, but with Time. But even Here, as with Dʳ Cullen & our illustrious Countryman Professor Rush, there was still a clashing as to the Theory and Practice of Medecine. I felt myself still authorised to pursue my original Plan, much however upon the Principles of Doctor Brown. I have therefore progressed in my work which I have termed, Medical and Philosophical Aphorisms, or the Universal Doctrine of Medicine.—I have treated Disease as a Unit. And the primary Causes, as of two kinds the first, as Stimulant, the latter as debilitating.—The application of one of those kind of powers of each of which there are endless variety, produces <u>Sthenic</u> disease, of the latter <u>Asthenic</u>. By which it is obvious that there are two, and only two General States of disease, peculiar to Man, throughout all the World. The Practise necessary to be adopted in either case, is at once obvious, and is directly opposed to that of the other.—I consider the Electric fluid, as a "fifth element—a kind of Soul of Nature" Oxygenizing, and giving vitality and circulation to the blood, that the vast train of diseases heretofore termed Nervous, indeed owe their origin to the excess or deficiency of this fluid—I have therefore considered those diseases, as <u>Electroses</u> which arise from an excess of this fluid in the System, & those as <u>Neuroses</u> from a defect. And upon this principle I account for the reason, why one Practitioner, has cured, Palsy, Rheumatism, Epilepsy &c by means of Electricity, while others have aggravated the Symptoms. all of which happen from the misapplication of the fluid, in these and many other diseases, which are properly <u>Electroses</u> and in which this fluid is then prejudicial. In short I have made so many new remarks, founded on Practice, and actual observation, as to have procured for me, from my esteemed Preceptor D<sup>r</sup> David Ramsay, the most flattering remarks He has done me the Honor to assure me, that it was indeed, a New and valuable doctrine of Medicine, and which woud ultimately procure for me an imperishable monument in the bosoms of the friends of Science. It was true, that he had Seen in various other writers on Medicine, many of the remarks which were blended in my work, but woud at the Same time do me the justice to Say, He had not seen them any where, So happily blended nor So strikingly exemplified, that in fact, I had left no room or very little for controversy, particularly on the Subject of Medical Electricity. I acknowledge to be highly flattered with such compliments from Doctor Ramsay, the Rush of Carolina. But while he So highly appreciated the merits of the work, with me he had to lament the want of encouragement in this State particularly to works of Science, He touch'd upon the Flora Caroliniensis, and I was done.

With a desire therefore, to prevent if possible the failure of the publication of my New doctrine, I have selected your Excellency as I before mentioned, and will now unbosom myself as to a Father and a Friend.—I have been more than unfortunate thro Life, The Love of my Country and of Science, has made me poor indeed. add to which I have Seven Children now living, the eldest of whom are females, all incapable[1] of doing for the rest, So that it is upon my success in

life they all depend at present. I cannot think of publishing in S°
Carolina, for the reasons already stated. And I am an entire stranger
elsewhere, nor have I funds to carry me any where else.—It was suggested to me, to attempt its publication in Europe, or the Northern
States. I can get to neither situated as I am, and being determined to
avoid the contracting any debt, I consequently will not ask a loan of
Money of any friend whatever. I have therefore come to the determination of soliciting your advice which I have assured myself you will
cheerfully give me. Whether, I coud not procure an appointment
under Government with a moderate tho competent Salary, as Secretary to Some of the legation, either going to Europe, or in any of the
Northern States?—I have though[t] of such a thing and if your Excellency conceives any thing like an impropriety therein, I hope He
will have the Candour to advise me thereof. I submit the whole to the
consideration of your Excellency, and look up to you for the plan
which I shoud pursue, assured that your Superior judgment will
point to the most appropriate.* In the mean time I take leav[e] to add
that the <u>Capsicum minutissimum</u> flourishes luxuriantly in the open
gardens of Charleston & I expect to distribute them widely and extensively, they have obtained the name here of Jefferson Pepper, as
having been obtained from your Excellency. The Literary & Philosophical Society are greatly increasing & have commenced a Museum
in the City.—

  With Sentiments dictated by a heart truly grateful permit me to
subscribe myself, your Excellencys most obliged and obed$^t$ Serv$^t$

J L E W Shecut

*I imagine that with such a station, I coud find both the means and leisure, to have
printed as also to superintend the correction of the work in question. which has indeed
given rise to the thought.

RC (DLC); edge chipped; with author's endnote on verso of address leaf;
addressed: "His Excellency Thomas
Jefferson Esq$^r$ Monticello State of Virginia P$^r$ Mail"; stamp canceled and replaced by frank; postmarked Charleston,
18 Aug.; endorsed by TJ as received 31
Aug. 1814 and so recorded in SJL.

  The British physician John BROWN
taught that human health depended on
balancing EXCITEMENT, a property of
the nervous system, and stimulation. In
Brown's system, known as Brunonian-
ism, an excess of EXCITABILITY caused

STHENIC disease (*OED*). Brown based
his work in part on the teachings of his
mentor William CULLEN but contemporaries saw it as a rival theory (*ODNB*;
Sowerby, no. 897).

  On the nature of the ELECTRIC FLUID,
Shecut paraphrased Patrick Brydone, *A
Tour through Sicily and Malta* [London,
1773], 1:216–7, which described electricity as "the great vivifying principle of nature, by which she carries on most of her
operations.—It is a fifth element, perfectly distinct, and of a superior nature to the
other four, which only compose the corpo-
real parts of matter: But this subtile and

active fluid is a kind of soul that pervades and quickens every particle of it." In his letter to Shecut of 29 June 1813, TJ enclosed seeds of the CAPSICUM *annuum* var. *glabriusculum*, commonly called bird pepper (*Hortus Third*, 219).

[1] Manuscript: "incaple."

# To William Thornton

DEAR SIR                                                 Monticello Aug. 17. 14.

Your favor of Aug. 2. was duly recieved, and I thank you much for the information it has procured me. I have recieved a letter from mr Greer informing me that the price of Janes's loom in Connecticut is 40.D. and in Baltimore 50.D. where they sell the patent right for a single loom at 20.D. D$^r$ Maese in a letter to me from Philadelphia says the price of a loom there is 50.D. here mr Clopper asks 100.D. for a loom & 50.D. for the patent right to make & use a single one. he exhibited his loom in Charlottesville where I saw it, and think I have never seen a superior improvement. I advised him to abate his price, observing that I would give him 100.D. for a loom, & perhaps one or two others in the county[1] would do it, while there were 100. who would take them at 50.D. he is now exhibiting in Richmond at these prices: but he will be the dupe of his own avarice. he has not the means of furnishing a single loom, & were we to buy the right to make one for ourselves, we have no model. mr Greer offers to furnish me with one for 50.D. and I would willingly send a cart for it; but then I should have no right to use it, because we have been sold to mr Clopper. a few rich persons with us may buy at 100.D. of 40,000 looms in this state I verily believe that 10,000 would be exchanged for Janes's at 50.D. but at Clopper's prices I do not believe 100. will be bought. affectionately yours                          TH: JEFFERSON

RC (DLC: Thornton Papers); addressed: "Doct$^r$ William Thornton Washington"; franked; postmarked Milton, 24 Aug. PoC (MHi); endorsed by TJ.

[1] Preceding three words interlined.

# To John F. Watson

SIR                                                      Monticello Aug. 17. 14

Your favor of June 2. has been recieved, as also N$^{os}$ 29. 31. & 37. and vols 1. 2. 3. of the Edinburgh review. the 4$^{th}$ and subsequent volumes had better come on by mail, singly as they are published. I have directed a remittance to be made by my correspondents in Richmond, Gibson & Jefferson, to mr Dufief bookseller in Philadelphia, out of which I have desired him to pay you 11.25 D for which be so good as to call on him within a few days after you recieve this, and accept the assurances of my respect.        Th: Jefferson

PoC (DLC); on verso of reused address cover to TJ; at foot of text: "Mr John F. Watson"; endorsed by TJ.

## To Augustus B. Woodward

Monticello Aug. 17. 14.

Th: Jefferson presents his compliments to Judge Woodward and his thanks for the volume containing the defence of Eugene Arum. there is in it an Exordium of some length which he had never seen before. he presents him[1] also the thanks of the younger members of his family for the volumes he was so kind as to send them, and salutes him with esteem and respect.

PoC (DLC); dateline at foot of text; on reused address cover to TJ; endorsed by TJ.

[1] Manuscript: "hims."

## To John T. Mason

Dear Sir        Monticello Aug. 18. 14.

Your letter of May 5. was handed me by Dr Wallace on the 25th of June, & I have added to the delay of answering it by waiting the arrival of the specimens of mrs Mason's skill in manufactures which your letter mentd. these (after various accidents of delay immaterial to explain) arrived yesterday, and excite the admiration of us all. they prove that mrs Mason is really a more dangerous adversary to our British foes, than all our Generals. these attack the hostile armies only, she the source of their subsistence. what these do counts nothing because they take one day & lose another: what she does counts double, because what she takes from the enemy is added to us. I hope too she will have more followers than our Generals, but few rivals I fear. these specimens exceed any thing I saw during the revolutionary war, altho' our ladies of that day turned their whole efforts to these objects, & with great praise & success. the endeavors which Dr Wallace informed you we were making in the same line, are very humble indeed. we have not as yet got beyond the cloathing of our laborers. we hope indeed soon to begin finer fabrics, and for higher uses, but these will probably be confined to cotton & wool. our Spinning Jennies working from 24. to 40. spindles each, produce an impatience of the single thread of the flax-wheel. 2. oz. of cotton, for each spindle[1] is a moderate days work; and these, the simplest of machines, are made by our country joiners & kept in order by our overseers. very different from the clock-work of Arkwright's machines whose tooth & pinion work requires a clockmaker to make & keep in repair. I have lately also seen the improvement of the loom by Janes, the most beautiful machine I have ever seen; wherein the hand which pulls the batten moves the shuttle, the treadles, the temples, the web and cloth beams, all at the same time: so that a person with one hand, & without feet, or using only one hand, may weave as well as with all their members. I am endeavoring to procure this improvement also. these cares are certainly more pleasant than those of the state; and were happiness the only legitimate object the public councils would be deserted. that corvée once performed however the independant happiness of domestic life may rightfully be sought & enjoyed. mrs Randolph joins me in thanks and friendly respects to mrs Mason, and I add assurances of constant esteem & affection to yourself.

TH: JEFFERSON

PoC (DLC); at foot of first page: "John Thompson Mason esq."; endorsed by TJ.

[1] Preceding three words interlined.

# Minutes of the Albemarle Academy Board of Trustees

At a stated meeting of the Trustees of the Albemarle Academy, held at the house of Triplett T. Estes, in Charlottesville, the 19th day of August, 1814:

Present—Peter Carr, President, Thomas Jefferson, Dabney Minor, John Winn, Thomas Wells, Rice Garland, Alexander Garrett, Jonathan B. Carr, Robert B. Streshley, Nicholas M. Lewis, James Leitch, Edward Garland, John Nicholas, John Kelly, Samuel Carr and John Carr.

The committee to whom was referred the subject of location, made a report in these words, to wit:

"The committee to whom was referred the resolution of the Board of Trustees of the Albemarle Academy of the 17th of June, 1814, relative to the location of said Academy, have had the same under consideration, and thereupon agreed to the following report:

Your committee have viewed the different sites on which it would be advisable to locate the Academy in the town of Charlottesville and its vicinity, and in their opinion it would be most advisable to locate the same in the vicinity of the town, distant not more than one-half mile, provided such location, building, &c. would not cost the institution more than a situation in town already improved suitable to the purpose. To form some idea of the probable cost of improving a site in the vicinity of the town, your committee beg leave to submit the annexed plan, and recommend its adoption by the Board as one best suited to the purpose, provided the work can be completed according to the terms of the estimate.

Your committee have in vain attempted to ascertain the cost of a site unimproved in the vicinity of town, not being able to propose any particular terms of purchase, there being no funds at present at command of the Board of Trustees; they therefore beg of the Board to indulge the committee in a report on this part of the said resolution until a fund shall have been raised necessary to the purchase of such site. When this shall be accomplished, your committee will then be enabled to propose the terms of purchase with certainty, and the proprietors of the sites enabled to make proposals of sale accordingly.

All of which is respectfully submitted.

> JOHN WINN,
> JAMES LEITCH,
> JOHN NICHOLAS,
> ALEX. GARRETT.

19th August, 1814."

Which report is ordered to be recorded.

It is ordered and directed, that the President of the Board cause notice to be given in the public prints, according to law, that a petition will be presented to the next General Assembly praying an appropriation of the money arising from the sale of the glebes to the benefit of the Academy.

The meeting is now adjourned till the third Friday in November next.

> P. CARR.

Printed in Cabell, *University of Virginia*, 382–3.

The ANNEXED PLAN has not been found.

# To John Barnes

Dear Sir                                    Monticello Aug. 20. 14.

Immediately on reciept of your favor of July 29. I wrote to mr Gibson desiring him to make sale of my flour for whatever he could get for it in cash. it had been laying on hand since christmas in hopes of a rise of price. he accordingly made sale of it for 2. D 61 c a barrel which netted me for my wheat 48 cents a bushel. he informed me at the same time he could not sell at all for ready money, & had sold at 60. days but that I might draw on him in the mean time. on the reciept of your letter therefore of the 16^th which came to hand last night, I have written to him to remit to you without delay 380 D. and our Richm^d1 mail not going out till tomorrow, nor reaching him till the 22^d or 23^d I fear he will barely have time to find a bill and get it to your hands by the 25^th. the sum named is to cover the 360.D. for G^l Kosciuzko, the 8.D. you were so kind as to pay for me to G^l Armstrong, & the balance to lie in your hands to meet the transportation of a patent[2] loom from Baltimore to Georgetown where my cart will meet it, should I order one as I have some thought of doing, altho not yet decided. I am anxious that mr Gibson's remittance should get to hand by the day, & I shall think little of my sacrifice to cover yourself & the General from inconvenience. I salute you with affectionate respect                          Th: Jefferson

PoC (DLC); at foot of text: "M^r Barnes."

[1] Word interlined.
[2] Word interlined.

# To Patrick Gibson

Dear Sir                                    Monticello Aug. 20. 14.

In my letter of the 15^th by Johnson I mentioned that excepting for some small matters of current expence here I should not[1] avail myself of your permission to draw, but for my remittances to Philadelphia and to mr Barnes, until the proceeds of the note for my flour, or that for the bank were in hand. and I had hoped that the remittance for mr Barnes might have lain over a month or two. but a line from him by yesterday's mail informs me it is called for by the 25^th inst. I must therefore avail myself of your kindness so far as to ask that remittance of 380.D. to be made to him immediately, as there is barely time for it to reach him by the day. Accept assurances of my great esteem & respect.                                    Th: Jefferson

PoC (NHi: Thomas Jefferson Papers); at foot of text: "M^r Gibson"; endorsed by TJ.          [1] Word interlined.

# From Miles King

DEAR SIR,                    Mathews County V^a Aug: 20^th 1814

It is not without a considerable struggle in my mind arising from the conflict between a concieved duty, and many weighty and powerful objections, that I have ventured at some length to address you on the all important subject of vital religion. And it is highly probable, that both the theme, and writers name, may surprize you, and cause some astonishment; Yet I cannot help indulging the hope, that neither will be thought by you on mature reflection, too insignificant to be attended to, especially the former, as it should be the constant companion and solace of every great and polished mind.          The religion of the gospel of our Lord Jesus Christ!! is the welcome guest of every truly wise man that liveth under its salutary dispensation, or it must become so, If he would be happy and comfortable in the serious and solemn contemplation of death! judgement! & Eternity!—for it must be allowed by every one that before such awful and stupendous Scenes as those, all other subjects in a measure vanish; The splendour of the world and all its wisdom flee-eth away! The philosophy of Greece & the power of Rome in comparison of these, becomes a bursted bubble! a mere empty void.          I am still farther encouraged to hope, that this unexpected letter, and its principal design, will be regarded by you Sir in a favourable light, from the slight personal acquaintance, I have had with you during your Presidency over these united states; and as it may not be altogether irrelative to the main purpose of this epistle, I will briefly state that I was introduced to your notice, early in the congressional session of 1806, by M^r Tho^s Newton a member from the Borough of Norfolk, at which place I then resided.          your politeness, urbanity, and general condescension, won me so entirely, that I have not yet forgotten the circumstance & probably never shall in this life. This particular I should not have mentioned to you Sir, if Sincerity and frankness had not urged it as a strong reason for the hope above Expressed. Believe me Sir it is not my aim to flatter but rather to convince; that conviction may serve as a motive for humility in you, that I now write, and it is my intention, so far as I can to strip the mind of its artificial and deceitful covering—its borrowd ornaments from Art or Science, and Expose to your veiw its latent deformity, so that pride may be abashed & confounded, unbelief put to flight, skepticism exterminated, and reason, the handmaid of religion become subordinate to sublimer revelation.      But in attempting this I am not unconscious of my insufficiency for so great a task, and therefore rely upon Divine aid to inspire my mind whilst employed in my great masters-Service, in the development of truth, to offer such Ideas for your consideration as by his help shall make forcible entry into your heart, and leave indelible impressions on your mind. A proper subject presents itself to me in the person of an old Lady that now lies at the point of Death, at the threshold of Eternity or on the margin of another world, in an adjoining room—she is I believe turned of ninety—her maiden name was Plater, and I am informed was sister to the Gov<sup>r</sup> of Maryland of that name during our colonial vassalage—She has ever lived in affluent circumstances—Been bless'd with a good constitution, and a liberal Education—she yet enjoys all her mental powers—and hesitates not to Join with Solomon in pronouncing all sublunary Joys abstract from Christ!! but Vanity! she is wasting fast and seems to long for a better rest—a permanent dwelling beyond the reach of Death or fell diseasd Sins foul offspring—Oh! Sir I would have you to contemplate this last scene of human suffering and wreck of worldly granduer, which you must also ere long Exhibit in your own person, and now whilst you have opportunity. let me urge you to seize upon some moments of retirement, which are ever favourable to meditation—or should you awake, at the silent and impressive hour of midnight, when tired nature is hushd in calm repose around you, Ask thyself these important questions! Who, and Whence am I? For what purpose was I born? It could not be merely to fill up so short a space as comprises human life, to be tossed upon the Boisterous waves of this unfriendly world, or agitated by the storms of life, for threescore years, and then Sink into endless oblivion, that I came forth! reason & revelation both forbid such a conclusion. what then remains for me to fix upon, If after Death I become not annihilate? what but immortality? here I am constrained to rest, all else[1] is wild conjecture: where am I faste or rapidly hastening upon the Gospel scheme? to Heaven or to Hell? and what other scheme is offerred to my understanding, that will bear so critical an investigation, relative to my ulterior fate as the Gospel of Jesus Christ!!? On what other solid foundation can I Erect[2] my hope of happiness? But when O my Soul shall I experience the awful realities of another world? does not the time draw nigh? when I shall leave this present world for ever?

and am I fully prepared by an inflexible faith in Jesus Christ!! as the Son of God! and Saviour of the world, to stand at my Great Judges bar and hear my ever lasting doom pronounced, to happiness or woe—? And now permit me to ask dear Sir, are you not an old man well stricken in years, and laden with the highest honours that a grateful country can bestow? But what will these avail you in a dying hour? "or what can it profit any man if he gain all the world[3] & yet should loose his soul." your high standing in the great community is undeniable & there are but few, if any persons that more sincerely wish you a long enjoyment of a nations love than I do, long may you enjoy every Earthly Bliss, and the evening of your days be gilded with the mild and cheering rays of an approving conscience; the common harbinger of eternal and unfading Bliss. But to secure so great a blessing it is not sufficient that we have the applause of mortals, or ourselves alone, for we must have the approbation of Our God! his spirit witnessing with ours, that we are his children: This we cannot have unless we are converted & changed by the operation of his spirit!!! at our earnest request from a state of Nature to one of Grace! in short sir we must be born again or die for ever!—Oh that I had but a fourth part of your erudition & extensive knowledge, methinks I could easily persuade you by divine assistance of this indispensable fact: But I do not despair altho' I labour under the disadvantage of a Shallow understanding and but a superficial education, by the help of God! to make Some lasting impression on your highly cultivated and ingenuous mind.          And Sir if my prolixity be not tiresome to you, or does not obtrude upon your useful employment of Times fleeting moments, too far; I would again call your attention to the contemplation of some prominent features in my own life, not to gratify vanity—but to elucidate truth, and corroborate the doctrines of the Gospel of our Lord Jesus Christ!! in respect to the new birth & the progressive operations of the Holy Spirit!!! so that you might become enamoured of the same to the salvation of your precious and immortal soul! in doing this Sir I will endeavour as briefly as the confined limits of a letter will allow, to follow the plan furnished by the great apostle of the gentiles S$^t$ Paul when arraigned before King Agrippa and Gov$^r$ Festus, (that is to give a true history of my own conversion) & altho the Occasion be different, and Some slight shade of diff: as to the title of our auditors, yet will I presume to express a hope and fervently pray to my Heavenly Father for his dear sons sake, that you my highly respected & venerable Sir, may become not only almost, but altogether a <u>Christian</u>! and consequently attain that everlasting felicity, which I fear Festus, nor Agrippa ever did.

I will say no more of my parentage, being but an obscure individual, than My being the second son of John King of Virg<sup>a</sup> long deceased, and Nephew of Miles King lately dec<sup>d</sup> whom If I mistake not I have heard say, you were once at his house in Hampton on your return from an embassy to France—I was born in Prince George county V<sup>a</sup> and Brought up to the Sea, early in life I obtained command of a Vessel and traded to Europe for many years; I was commissioned & served a year or two as a L<sup>t</sup> in the Navy of the U.S. during the administration of M<sup>r</sup> Adams, and after the peace establishment took place, about the time of your inauguration to the presidency: I purchased a vessel & again traded to Europe, was generally successful and thought, but little or nothing of religion—was much disposed to a luxurious life of debauch and intrigue, accustomed to move in higher circles, than usually falls to the lot of ship masters— In short I lived a life of pleasure and gaiety, with now and then a hair Breadth escape from death, either by shipwreck or other casualty— untill it pleased God! to take from me my second wife, an amiable and affectionate woman; This affliction caused me for a short time, during the first paroxism of violent grief. to pause in my carreer and reflect on the uncertainty of human life—how fleeting its Joys & how certain death would oertake every child of man! It was not long after this chasm in my domestic happiness, that I visited the city of Washington, to get rid of Melancholy, and as I before observed, had the Satisfaction of being introduced to you—which circumstance, I can assure you Sir, trivial as it may appear to you, did not fail to augment my vanity considerably: you may perhaps smile at this; but I question if candour was to search the archives of your own memory, if it might<sup>4</sup> not be discovered, that in early life, perhaps when in your diplomatick carreer, on being introduced at court &c &c you felt sensations similar to those I have glanced at—Vanity Sir, was ever one of my besetting Sins, and a Knowledge but very lately acquired thro' grace, of this part of my own character; together with an accompanying fear lest I should be overcome by the tempter on this evil score again, in writing such a letter as this, with familiarity and entire freedom to one of the most distinguished characters of my country—I had almost said of the Age, has operated so powerfully on my mind, as to prevent me from writing for Some months past. How it came first into my mind to write to you at all, I will relate so well as my memory serves.      Some time early this spring I awaked about midnight, perhaps Just after I might have been dreaming something about you—And in consequence, my thoughts were much employ<sup>d</sup> about your spiritual estate—for I had often heard you indignantly called, deist, infidel, illuminati &c &c a thought sprung up within me, that it would not be considered by you an unpardonable crime, for me to write you a letter on this subject! that is to make an enquiry of yourself as to your real and candid sentiments respecting the religion of the Gospel of Christ!! what your hopes and fears? whither you have or ever had either? or if there is any consideration on Earth, that would induce you if required, deliberately, to sign a formal renounciation of any hope of Eternal happiness, that might Occur to you from the infinite Merit of Jesus Christ!! or in other words, whither you would for any consideration, forego all your interest in his sufferings, Death, Resurrection, assencion &c? But sir on viewing the great disparity between our situation, standing, acquirements &c I felt so little and insignificant in my own Eyes, that I endeavoured to get rid of the thought of writing and to treat it as a temptation from the Devil to ensnare me, but after having slept and again waking, the mind was reoccupied with the same Subject, and it was clearly represented to me in thought, that if I would write, it might do much good—infinitely more than I then had any Idea of, and I might moreover state, that the draught of a letter, the very words and sentences, were unfolded to my mind—But I treated all these things with indifference, merely mentioning them in my own family.          a month or more passed away without one similar thought, that I recollect—when to my utter Surprize and astonishment, I spent just such another night Sir, in contemplating your life. Services, learning, honors and probably speedy Exit from this to an Eternal state, & the phraseology of another letter differing but a little from the first was again presented—both these were certainly couched in more elegant language than I am accustomed to, or indeed than I am capable of using, But both seemed to Exhibit simplicity & perspicuity: and after resolving and reflecting on these strange thoughts I was seemingly destitute of a plausible excuse, for writing on such a topick to a character of such eminen[ce.] But it was soon Suggested to me by my invisible director, that in your most exalted situation you had condescended to notice me and ask me to dine with you, which I had done, and wherefore should I then doubt your attentive perusal of a letter from me, especially on so important a business as the Salvation of your own immortal Soul! furthermore it seemed as tho' I was urged to make use of our former (tho so slight) acquaintance as the basis of a new one, that might last for ever, unless you should frustrate it either thro' apathy or high mindedness.          As plain as the case now stood, I merely mentioned it in a light way to my companion, who perhaps observed that it was singular, that I should be thus Exercised, about so st[range] a circumstance as writing a Spiritual letter to M$^r$ Jefferson—this likewise passed off a month or two untill yesterday, when after breakfast I retired into my room set apart for study and devotion and whil[e] pausing to consider what author I should take up, a thought darted into notice as if a man had spoken to me thus; write the letter to M$^r$ Jefferson and discharge the obligation you owe him for former attention and acquit your conscience, in the Sight of God! I felt a purturbation of mind & went to prayer, became tranquil after having committed the whole affair to God! and asked his Blessing. I set down immediately to commu[nicate] such thoughts as might Occur—thus Sir you have a brief view of my reasons and motive for writing: your goodness must excuse the want of connection and all other deficiencies, and be assured, that however it might gratify my feelings to have an answer from you in reply to this letter; Yet it will not at all mortify me if you should treat it with contempt, except in as much as it might militate against you in another world.           another of my scruples about writing arose from a consideration of these eventful times, this alarming crisis of the publick welfare, wherein our Nations very Existence as a republic, seems to be involved or threatened; And at such a time as this, I calculated that your advice & Counsel would be much sought for, by our present worthy and enlightened President & that under these publick exigencies of the state, you would not perhaps take leisure enough to attend (not indeed to the merits of this letter, for I am truly conscious as before Expressed of many defects, which I do not exactly know how to remedy—) to the important theme, to wit vital religion—contained herein. But again I thought if I could be so happy as to enlist, by any suggestions whatever, the enlightened Chiefs of my nation in the cause of God! of holiness & of truth, I feel well assured, that it will tend more to the restoration of public tranquility—National & individual peace & happiness—than if we had all the legions of Europe at our Beck without religion—and do not my dear Sir mistake me herein or suppose me capable of insinuating that Armies are of no avail in procuring peace, for I am too well assured of the consistent method in which our Heavenly Father Governs the universe and does all things agreeably to his Divine perfections, not to allow that certain causes will produce in general certain effects—But I would be understood as saying—that if peace were obtained th[ro a] by any[5] secondary means, such as augmentation of fleets & armies &c it could not be either truly hon[orable] or Durable. for this plain reason, that unless a proper understanding or sense of true religion prevails & pervades the nations—there can be no other Bond found, sufficiently strong to ensure peace if the ambition, mistaken policy or supposed interest of nations dictate a Breach—for it is written "there is no peace to the wicked," this applies to Nations or individuals—I am also clearly of opinion that our impiety hath provoked this war upon us, and that nothing short of National reformation can do the Nation real good. Hence it is incumbent on every real patriot, to set a speedy example to his fellows; of true [piety?] & holiness & no examples are so powerful as those furnished by the higher orders of the community—It is not sufficient that our rulers & private worthies—Legislators & Judiciaries, merely tolerate religion: they must themselves become religious—thier Light must shine to the Glory of God! & the illuminating of others—more over I am of opinion that the present order of human affairs, is ere long to undergo a radical change and a more glorious arrangement to succeed, as promised in the Millenial Reign of our Lord Jesus Christ! on Earth, which I expect is to be a spiritual Reign, during which "the Earth shall be covered with righteousness as the waters cover the face of the great Deep"—and "the[6] Kingdoms of this world shall become the Kingdoms of our God! & his Christ"!! spiritually no doubt, for they are now his by creation & sovereign right—but then all the world shall worship him & Jew and Gentile, be fed by one shepherd and become the inmates of one fold! Furthermore I am convinced that God is over all his works Blessed for ever more—that he now does & for ever will rule the destiny of Nations, so long as they are permitted to Exist: that war, famine, and Pestilence are the three instruments of his wrath, wherewith[7] he generally Scourges nations for their impiety and afflicts them for transgression—that he builds up & pulls down Kingdoms, not capriciously as mortals do & then undo thier pigmy perishing works—but in righteousness, and according to thier conduct "as it is written, Proverbs 14 Ch: Righteousness exalteth a nation; but Sin is a reproach to any people." again we learn from the 18 ch: of the Prophet Jeremiah, (which I request you to read) "At what instant I shall speak concerning a Kingdom, to pluck up and to pull down, and to destroy it; If that nation against whom I have pronounced turn from thier evil: I will repent of the evil that I thought to do unto them. And at what instant I shall speak concerning a Kingdom and concerning a nation to Build and to plant it: If it do evil in my sight, that it obey not my voice, then will I repent of the good, wherewith I said I would benefit them."        On examining our nations history and meditating on these sacred and important truths—I was led to conclude, that God! in his infinite wisdom, goodness, and mercy! had done great things for us as a people in Emancipating us from A yoke of Tyranny and foreign domination and giving us a name and rank among the other nations of the Earth; but instead of these things, and a course of unparalleled prosperity exciting in us the liveliest thanksgiving and praise—It appears to me that we have like the Jews of old, repaid, this Bounteous efflux of Divine love, with the Blackest ingratitude & have continued to sin with a high hand—It would seem as if Our chiefs, I mean the rulers of the realm & those high in authority—thought that enough was done, by merely tolerating religion, as I have before hinted—But I again repeat it Sir this is not sufficient—However good in its place, for the National Legislature to recommend publick humiliation at particular times—yet we must go farther than this rulers, chiefs & People must not only be found performing occasional acts of devotion—but all must become habitually Devoted to God! to insure either a lasting peace or prosperity—Excuse me Sir for Observing in this place, nor deem it flatery (for that I hate)—when I say that the Embargo laid in 1808 was under all circumstances, the wisest political measure, that could have been at that time concerted to avert both the wrath of God! and the nations sufferrings—and had our New England Brethren been possessed of even half the religion they profess to How differently might we now be circumstanced—and permit me to add, that the failure of that excellent measure, may in no inconsiderable degree be attributed to your personal destitution of true religion—But this I do not pretend to assert as positively true, not Knowing your heart—But yet I am clear in saying that personal Examples of holiness—are wanting in our Presidents & others and by thier loose conduct in these particulars, the people in the gross become like them—And the Love of money that Bane of human happiness, hath in our peoples hearts Eclipsed the Love of God! especialy amongst the mercantile part of our Citizens—this class in particular appear to have then & do yet count gain for Godliness. Oh Sir I could say many truths upon this subject—but I would rather adhere to my purpose to persuade you to look into these things and unite with me in supplicating a rich throne of grace! and by timely humiliation and spiritually drawing nigh to God! avert his just Judgements, that hang lowering oer our afflicted country—as well as those that may be registered in the records of Heaven against us individually.　　　I will now resume the Narrative, from which I have made so lengthy a digression, and proceed to state, that some short time after I saw you in washington—I revisited Europe, and returned after a prosperous voyage to my native state, soon after the general Embargo was laid; here I had an opportunity of seeing something of the cupidity of <u>Southern merchants</u>, by the persuasive arguments used with me in order that I might violate it for the sake of gain—But I now return God! thanks once more, that a common Sense of Honesty—out weighed with me every other lure. Having some leisure now upon my hands in consequence of the Embargo, and being a lover of pleasure I took an Excursion into this part of the country, here for the first time I saw my present amiable companion, who was a widow, about my own age, possessed of a considerable fortune in her own right, which she generously gave to me not long after our union; this acquisition of wealth, added wings to my pleasure, I lived high, entertained most polite strangers, kept a neat Equipage, introduced weekly routs, card parties &c &c amongst my affluent neighbours & then had much of the company of old M^r P. Tabb of Gloucester—whom I mention because I believe he is personally Known to you, and also because he is a rich old devotee to the pleasures of Sense—But whom I as highly respect for many valuable traits in his character, as I can respect a worldly minded man—In short Sir I gratified every wish of my heart; and had no thought of the nature of true religion, altho from custom, I sometimes went to church, here too often to see & be seen, Sometimes tho seldom to the Baptist and methodist meetings—these I visited to my shame I now speak it, more to cavil at thier doctrines or thro' any aparent Blunder of thier preachers, find some excuse to my conscience for my own prodigality, I had almost said profligateness.　　　my wife having belonged to the methodist church during her first husbands life, But for non attendance after marying me, her name had been dropp'd—[8] amidst all our gaiety would often hint to me her wish to attend thier meetings—But Sir such was my aversion to what these people termed vital religion—that I would sooner order the carriage and go a trip of 20 miles off to her Brothers, than go but three to the meeting house. As it would be tedious perhaps to relate more of my Experience at this time—suffice it to say, that it pleased Almighty God! in corroboration of his Blessed Gospel to make use of the weak things of this world to confound the mighty. 1 Cor: 1 ch—for I was a mighty opposer of divine truth in my own Eyes—but he in mercy made use of a weak unlettered woman in the Neighbourhood, of the methodist society whilst setting at my own table and I trying to deride her religion & shake her faith, to open my spiritual Eyes, which had been by me hitherto closed, voluntarily against the truths of the Gospel—But now for the first time in my life I was taught to feel & perceive, that God! was a Spirit!!! and must be worshipped in spirit and in truth—

I was Sir like one awaking out of a deep sleep and began now to feel somewhat like Belshazzer—when he saw the hand, writing upon the wall—I felt in an instant that I was an accountable being, a probationer here & that I should soon have to leave this present scene, and be Judged in Righteousness for all my mispent life—from these first convictions, which were but light in comparison of what I afterwards underwent: I resolved to attend the methodist meetings—having no faith in the Church ministers—and at every meeting, I was more and more convinced I had lived in Sin & Error, that I was an alien—far gone from original righteousness—so that I resolved as I would secretly sigh, that I would Amend my life & make it more conformable to the holy Scriptures—and Sir, I vainly thought I had the power as of myself to do so—this mistake ruins many, who thinking virtue to be an inate quality a principle of the Soul, put off thier conversion, on the supposition, that they can become holy and truly religious at any moment—even if it be but a few hours before death! deluded infatuated mortals! you have no strength as of yourselves to renew yourselves unto righteousness hence it was that I found altho I would make firm resolutions against every species of vice I was notwithstanding, as certain to be overtaken, & overthrown by my enemy in almost every instance, especially in those Bosom & besetting sins, that delighted the Soul—my resolutions were as easily Broken as the wyths that bound unshaven Samson—I was frequently told by the preachers, that I must ask the assistance of Gods! grace & favour to help me to believe in the Lord Jesus Christ!! as Gods! son and the only Saviour of the world—that he would enable me to Keep my engagements & virtuous resolutions, for that I had no righteousness belonging to me by nature—neither had any person since Adams apostacy—but that God! would count to any one for righteousness, thier faith in Jesus Christ!! and this great boon is of his free Grace! at length after I had attended meetings for 5 or 6 months, regularly, and become sensible that I had no power over Sin, but that it Tyranized over me—and kept me in Bondage, so that I could say with a Poet—"Here I repent and sin again—now I revive and now am slain!

Slain with the same unhappy dart: Which Oh too [often][9] wounds my heart." I felt Sir I expect similar pangs to those described so well by Horace in these lines—"my reason this, my passion that persuades, I see the right and I approve it too; Condemn the wrong; and yet the wrong pursue." or to come yet nigher, I felt like the convicted man discribed in the 7th Ch: of St Pauls epistle to the Romans—"for the good that I would, I do not—But the evil which I would not that I do." and when like him in writhing agony of soul I exclaimed Oh wretched man that I am who shall deliver me from this Body of Death? (my sins) I found the same deliverer which he describes, even Jesus Christ!! I felt and witnessed all that Cowper so elegantly pourtrays under the allegory of a wounded deer—"I was a stricken Deer, that left the herd, (of worldlings) long since: with many an arrow deep infix't my panting side was charged, when I withdrew to seek a tranquil death in distant shades; there I was found by one who had himself been hurt by the (Jewish) archers; In his side he bore, and in his hands and feet the cruel scars, with gentle force soliciting the Darts, he drew them forth & healed & bade me live.—in like manner my gracious Lord! deliverd me & will do all who sincerely call upon him—He Broke the power of cancell'd sin, and fully set my spirit free; his blood can make the foulest clean; His blood availed for me—" for on the last Sabbath of the year 1811 he converted my soul in publick worship, soon after having rec$^d$ the sacrament—Oh Sir I felt that thro deep contrition I passed spiritually from Death unto Life—I felt regenerated & Born again of Gods! Holy Spirit!!! adopted as an hier of Heavenly Joys, this faith in Jesus Christ!! and for his merit only—and this adoption I feel Sir, is conditional, that it ultimately depends on myself in a great measure—for to obtain this inheritance I must live a new life of holiness and persevere untill Death shall close the present scene, then shall Our happy Souls rest for a Season in the Paradise of God! untill the great day of Judgement when Our Bodies shall arise from the dust in a new order of Being—be united to the soul & both be happy or miserable for ever—yes Sir it is indeed true, that after a painful gloom of sorrow & remorse for a mispent life, when I humbled myself in the dust as it were before the Lord! & besought his pardon, for the Lord Jesus'!! sake, my almighty Father changed his countenance towards me, (if I may so express myself) and liberty like Day Broke into my soul! This liberty thro mercy I have continued to enjoy with encreasing rapture unto this present moment; for which believe me my dear Sir I feel as if I could never sufficiently praise my God[!] Not long after my conversion, I was siezed with violent & sudden illness, something of the nature as the Physician said, of that malady that terminated the useful life of the great Washington—myself and all around thou[ght] that I must die, for respiration was very difficult, owing to the extreme inflamation of the throat, in that moment I felt all the consolations of faith, that flow from the promises of the Gospel of Christ!! It was [then] that every doubt of my acceptance vanished & I felt my witness Brightened—I saw by faith the Lord Jesus[!] who had apparently Just been crucified for me, (with all[10] others) he was Just arisen from the Dead & his precious Blood that seemed trickling from his pierced side, by a supernatural Divine power, was imparted & besprinkled my immortal Soul, to its entire cleansing! and I have never doubted of his sufferings—Death, resurrection and Ascension to Glory! from that hour to this; and humbly pray that you might obtain a like satisfaction. During my convalescence from this painful attack, I was truly astonished, to find an entire new thought spring up within me, that seemed to urge me to employ those hours that I was compelled to pass witho[ut] doors to the praise and Glory! of that Great God! & Saviour!! who had done so much for me—by writing a history of my Experience, in corroboration of Gospel promises, and throwing it into the form of a Sermon, adapted to the pulpit—I hesitated for some time, not thinking it possible for me to execute anything of this kind, that could either redound to the Glory of God! or the good of mankind; and I knew so little of the scriptures, that I even could not conjecture where to find a text; But after some agitation of mind & my unwillingness to do what I then & now concieve to have been the dictates of Gods! holy spirit!!! this invisible monitor, which seemed to be directing all my thoughts, (for I know not what else to ascribe it to) led me to the 5th ch: & [2 ver.] of the Gospel according to St matthew—and from this text, It is wonderful even now to me, with what facility I wrote of 23 or 4 pages of such sized letter paper as this, without having to stop for consideration, for tis true [that] I lost many strong and beautiful Ideas, thro' inability to pen them down so fast as they flowed—But I [must] acknowledge that this Sermon, if it deserve such a title, could not be compared with any advantage to the productions of Learned men, nor does it exhibit, the instructive model of Grecian Logick or Rhetorick being much after the manner of this letter, written without any preconcieved plan of arranging its [matter] but is simply the ebulitions of the Soul! Kept by divine power—within the precincts of Gospel truth: And it is worthy of remark, that notwithstanding the freedom of thought—the rapid succession of Ideas whilst writing—I had no sooner finished, than uncommon Barreness took place—in so much that I scarcely seemed to feel possessed of common understanding: And I verily thought, however novel the Situation or sublime the Theme, it appeared to me that I had in this discourse express'd the substance of everything I Knew upon religious Subjects & that it would be impossible for me to write another, no matter what was the text [without?] Borrowing expressions already used in this—But Sir, guess my surprize when two days afterwards, I was [thrown] into the same Kind of agitation as at first, and urged to write again, but was more embarrassed to find a text on which I could Expatiate, than at first if it be possible—But as I had heard the preachers of the Gospel quote [the] writings of St John, saying we should try the diff: spirits that assail us to discriminate between the Good & Evil[!] I determined in my mind, if this strange propensity for Sermonizing was of God! this should be the Criterion—to wit If I could write as lengthy a discourse as the former, upon any text in the whole volume of scripture, without borrowing from The first and this done without study or delay in writing—I would conclude it was the spirit!!! of God! teaching me to do this thing which I conjectured might, in the appointment of his wisdom, benefit Some one when I should be no more seen on Earth! not thinking they were ever to see the light in my life time, altho the phraseology indicated my delivering them in person. I was led to the 20 ver: of Same chap: for a text or Basis—from this I wrote full as much as from the former, with equal ease, more perspicuity, and arrangement of matter & without borrowing a Single Expression, that I can recollect! hence I concluded it was the will of God! that I should write, but for what particular purpose I had no clear Idea unless it might be what I have before hinted: In about ten days after I wrote five, and by this time had so far recovered my health as to attend to my secular bussiness, which at this time was multifarious[11]—But I felt an astonishing desire to[12] Bring all my bussiness to a close, that is to be circumscribed within certain limits—my feelings I expect were like those persons, whom I have often heard of as men of extensive bussiness, when of a sudden, they feel a presentiment of Death! Here it may be proper to relate, that after weighing the matter well and upon mature deliberation, having read the Gospel of Christ!! previously—I cast in my lot with those too generally dispised worshippers called methodists. Believing, in my Judgement then & now that thier Doctrine & discipline is nearest to the primitive Apostolic church of Christ!! and thinking this Junction would be promotive of my present & future welfare, by conducing to the establishment of my faith in the religion of the Gospel! in as much as the Society of pious people must unquestionably be an Auxiliary to the exercises of faith: I could say a great deal upon the advantage of christian fellowship—But feel that I must now forbear, and merely observe that I have not as yet discovered as too many suggested—that it has led to the least degree of bigotry—for I find within me Universal philanthopy exists in its fullest sense—I love the whole of mankind & whilst I pity and love the sinner, do hate & loath his sins; I feel drawn out in a particular manner toward the truly religious of every county. or sect. that embrace the Gospel of Christ!! I pity the ignorant who Knows it not—but am firmly persuaded it will be made Known in a very few years to every nation on Earth! antecedent to the ushering in of the Glorious Millenium so beautifully described by the Prophet Isaiah 11 & 12<sup>th</sup> Chap:—This Idea of the universal spread of the Gospel and its happy effects upon the Human Race, I think Sir your good Sense and candour must allow, is strongly indicated in the recent rise, and astonishingly rapid growth & progress of the Bible Societies—which I believe never existed untill within about 10 or 11 years ago, a Bible Society was first Organized in England & has since been patronized by most of the European nations, and seems to be particularly nourished & fostered by England and these United States—Indeed I am informed that Bibles are already, or are about to be sent to the Isles of the Ocean, and also to the vast hordes of native tribes that roam up and down this great continent of America. So that divine light & truth will ere long I humbly hope, Oer spread the Earth, to the Glory of God! and the unspeakable felicity of the great human family, uniting all nations in the bonds of Love & golden zone of coalescing charities Thus establishing the Object, that Christianity was intended to produce! For "Christianity, (says a chaste writer) bears all the marks of a divine original—It came down from Heaven and its gracious purpose is to carry us up thither—It was foretold by prophecies which grew clearer and Brighter as they approached the period of thier accomplishment—It was confirmed by miracles! which continued till the religion they illustrate was established. It was ratified by the Blood of its Author. Its doctrines are pure, sublime, consistent. Its precepts Just and holy. Its worship spiritual. Its service reasonable and rendered practicable, by the offers of divine aid to human weakness. It is sanctioned by the promise of Eternal happiness to the faithful, and the threat of Everlasting misery to the disobedient. It had no collusion with power, for power sought to crush it. It could not be in any league with the world, for it set out by declaring itself the Enemy of the world. It reprobates the maxims of the world, shews the vanity of its glories—the Danger of its riches—the Emptiness of its fading pleasures." In less than four months after I experienced a change of heart; I felt it my duty to preach what I had written, together with the whole Gospel of Christ!! and altho I then felt and yet feel poorly qualified for so arduous an undertaking—yet after much agitation, embarrassment, and long hesitation, I ventured to hold forth in publick—for I could not

rest day or night untill I consented to have an appointment made—
and when I did take up this heavy Cross, it was with much weakness
and trembling—and rest assured Sir, it was a severe trial to my weak
faith! especially if you consider that many of my first Auditors, were
my old companions at cards, wine, & conviviality—and appeared to
have met in consequence of the novelty, and to ridicule what I might
say; esteeming me now no better than a deluded fanatick; a mere maniac, because I had abandoned their sinful society—the allurements
of Sense, and the farther prodigality of that precious time only lent to
prepare me for Eternity! and because I had now told them of my rational determination to try & save my own Soul and as many as would
listen to truth!—I have continued to preach in my Local sphere &
God! has Owned and Blessed my labours, in town & Country! and I
fervently hope it may ever be a cheif delight of my Soul, to Labour in
the Lords Vineyard, and that I may be the humble & happy instrument in his hands of turning many of the children of disobedience to
the wisdom of the Just: and lead my hearers of every rank from the
power of Sin & satan unto God!—        As a methodist preacher
I now write to you my dear Sir, not so much for the purpose of
persuading you to become a member of our church, tho we be
methodists, as to intreat your espousal of the christian System of Salvation—and to be so far a methodist as to be methodical in religious
worship—in Devotion, & every Known duty whether it relates to the
life that now is—or that which is soon to come—for without method
none will be saved under our dispensation. My prayer to God! now is
that you may be disposed, by his grace to seek untill you shall find
Christ Jesus!! by faith revealed in you the hope of Glory! ere you go
hence and be no more seen on Earth! for the place that Knows you
now will Soon Know you no more for Ever! and do my friend and illustrious fellow-citizen, timely consider, even now lay it close to your
heart, that God! hath commanded all men every where to repent, because he hath appointed a day in which[13] he will Judge this world in
Righteousness, by that man—(God-man) whom he hath ordained—
Jesus Christ!! wherof he hath given an assurance to all men in that he
hath raised him up from the dead!—I would here by the help of your
immagination, draw aside the curtain of time, and for a few moments,
unfold Eternity to you. Behold now, coming forth from the Dark
chambers of Death—to Judgement (& this administered by Jesus
Christ!!) Such Characters as Voltair, D'Alembert, Didoret, Zwack,
Nigge, Nicholai, Condorcet &c &c what a horrid figure will these illuminati cut, in the presence of Christ!! Thier Eternal Judge—what
wil[l][14] all thier learning or Philosophy avail them—Say, will it not

rather aggravate thier Guilt! that God! should have so enlightened thier minds & that they in return, like the fabled adder, endeavour to turn and sting him—for it is said in Scripture, "in as much as you have done it unto one of the least of these little ones, you have done it unto me"[15] saith the Lord!! I presume there can be no doubt in the Breast of any candid man, but the writings of these & many other such characters have poisoned the minds & proved fatally ruinous to many, for whom Christ!! died—It is clear they were not supporters of the Christian Religion—but its enemies—there is no neuter ground in religion, as it is written "he that is not for me is against me—and whosoever does not gather with me Scattereth abroad"! Does this quotation not rub you pretty close Sir—? I hope it does not! But I would ask you to consider, that the End of all things is at hand, henc[e][16] the necessity that we should be sober & watch unto prayer—for what will it profit a man, again I ask, if he should gain all the world and should loose his own Soul?? I would make anot[her][17] appeal to your candour, and ask If the precepts of the Gospel of Christ!! does not demand the attention of every upright man or those who desire to be so—If the[18] Gospel has not a direct tendency to promote virtu[e][19] & destroy vice? and if as Neckar Justly Observes, it is not more consistent with reason and huma[nity][20]—rather to prevent crimes if possible, than to be compelled to punish them?—upon the score of [d]uty[21] then as a good Citizen, I may expect you Sir, to lend your influence, which must be very [c]onsiderable[22] for many reasons—especially on account of your Services—your high attainments & ven[e]rable[23] age! Oh let me solicit you once more, as you value happiness—Give Christianity your firm support & do not rest merely here, and be satisfied with bare historic faith! or what is called head religion! never rest untill you feel it in the heart! influencing all Your words and actions & regulating the thoughts of your heart! for it is written, "not every one that saith Lord! Lord! shall enter into the Kingdom of Heaven, but he that doeth the will of my father: which is in Heaven!"[24]—I would more over observe, that the religion of Jesus!! is most mercifully adapted to us fallen creatures—so much so that the most simple and illiterate, with the Learned and great, may participate in all its Blessings, without distinction—all that choose may understand and embrace it to thier eternal salvation—"For what says the Righteousness of faith? It speaketh on this wise; say not in thier heart, who shall ascend up into Heaven? that is to bring Christ!! down from above: Or who shall descend into the deep? that is to bring up Christ!! again from the dead! But wh[at][25] saith it? The word is nigh thee O man, even In thy mouth and in thy heart; [that

is?][26] the word of faith which we preach: That if thou shalt confess with thy mouth the Lord Je[sus][27] and Shalt believe in thine heart, that God! hath raised him from the Dead! thou shalt be Saved. For with the <u>heart</u>, man believeth unto righteousness, and with the mouth confession is made unto Salvation." Rom: 10 Ch. So that God! has left all men where ever this Gospel is or has been preached, without excuse. But I am truly Sorry to find in the course of my short Experience So many and they too of enlightened minds, that know[28] nothing of Experimental religion, nothing of that genuine faith that sweetly works by love and purifies the heart and life! Many are seemingly contented with a mere assenting to the Scriptures—or embracing a few Orthodox opinions whilst thier lives are squandered away in vanity—dissipation or folly! Such people remind me of children, that are satisfied with shadows only—and are as well contented with thier toy Guns, or the stick hobby's as if they were realities. But I hasten to conclude by observing that I have heard that you were or had been reading with deep attention the prophecy of Isaiah! if this is true deem me not impertinent for applying the Question of Philip the Evangelist to the Ethiopian Eunuch on a similar occasion and Say! "understandest thou what thou readest therein"?—should you condescend to reply to this letter, it would get to hand by directing to me at mathews C^t House. In the mean time I shall continue to offer up my prayers to God! thro Jesus Christ!! for your peace, prosperity and Eternal happiness, and if I should never see you in this world I hope to meet you in a much better—in the Kingdom of Everlasting Glory to dwell for ever more. As I am but a poor Scribe once more I ask you to excuse all defects, and Believe me to be with every Sentiment of Esteem and Respect          Dear Sir
   Your friend and Servant in the Gospel!          MILES KING

---

RC (DLC); bracketed words obscured by tape except as indicated below; addressed: "Thomas Jefferson Esq^re Late President of the United States Monticello Virginia p^r mail"; stamped; postmarked North End, Va., 28 Aug., and Charlottesville, 8 Sept.; endorsed by TJ as received 9 Sept. 1814 and so recorded in SJL.

Miles King (d. 1834) served in the United States Navy as a lieutenant from July 1799 until May 1801. He also served as a shipmaster based in Norfolk. King was instrumental in the early establishment of the Methodist Protestant Church in Virginia, forming a society about 1829 in Mathews County, becoming its minister, and attending church conferences (Callahan, *U.S. Navy*, 315; John Paris, *History of the Methodist Protestant Church* [1849], 272–3, 299; Edward J. Drinkhouse, *History of Methodist Reform Synoptical of General Methodism 1703 to 1898* [1899], 2:239, 245, 253, 256, 298; *American Beacon and Norfolk and Portsmouth Daily Advertiser*, 27 Sept. 1834).

George PLATER died early in 1792, three months after his election as governor of Maryland (*ANB*). The biblical quotation OR WHAT CAN IT PROFIT ANY

MAN . . . LOOSE HIS SOUL is in Mark 8.36. ST PAUL faced trial before King AGRIPPA II and the Roman procurator of Judea, FESTUS, in Acts 25–6. MILES KING, the recently deceased namesake uncle of the author, served on a committee of the Virginia House of Delegates that congratulated TJ on his service as United States minister plenipotentiary to France (*Boston Daily Advertiser*, 30 June 1814; *PTJ*, 16:11). THERE IS NO PEACE TO THE WICKED: Isaiah 57.21. THE EARTH SHALL BE COVERED . . . paraphrases Isaiah 11.9. BELSHAZZER saw a HAND, WRITING UPON THE WALL in Daniel 5.1–5. King quotes from "Hymn IV" by the POET John Austin (*Devotions in the Ancient Way of Offices* [Paris, 1668], 51).

King misidentifies lines from HORACE that in fact come from Ovid's *Metamorphoses*, 7.19–21 (Frank Justus Miller, *Ovid in Six Volumes* [3d. ed., rev. by George P. Goold, 1977, Loeb Classical Library], 3:342–3). OH WRETCHED MAN . . . BODY OF DEATH: Romans 7.24. William COWPER includes the ALLEGORY OF A WOUNDED DEER in book 3 of *The Task, A Poem, in Six Books* (London, 1785), 96–7. In Charles Wesley's hymn, "For the Anniversary Day of One's Conversion," Christ can break THE POWER OF CANCELL'D SIN and HIS BLOOD CAN MAKE THE FOULEST CLEAN; HIS BLOOD AVAILED FOR ME (John Wesley and Charles Wesley, *Hymns and Sacred Poems* [London, 1740], 121). The CHASTE WRITER being quoted is Hannah More, who wrote on the nature of Christianity in *Practical Piety; or, the Influence of the Religion of the Heart on the Conduct of the Life* (London, 1811; repr. Albany, 1811), 1:9.

Xavier von ZWACK and Adolph Franz Friedrich Knigge (NIGGE) were members of the freethinking Bavarian Illuminati, and Cristoph Friedrich Nicolai (NICHOLAI) edited a periodical that opposed authoritarian religion. King quotes three times from the biblical book of Matthew: IN AS MUCH . . . UNTO ME (25.40); HE THAT IS NOT FOR ME . . . (12.30); and not every one that saith Lord! Lord! . . . (7.21). The quotation from Jacques Necker (NECKAR) is in his *Of the Importance of Religious Opinions*, trans. Mary Wollstonecraft (London, 1788; for the French original see Sowerby, no. 1520), 69. PHILIP THE EVANGELIST questioned the ETHIOPIAN EUNUCH in Acts 8.30.

On 29 June 1816 King composed a similar and only somewhat shorter letter to President James Madison (DLC: Madison Papers).

[1] Manuscript: "esle."
[2] Reworked from "ground."
[3] Manuscript: "wold."
[4] Manuscript: "migt."
[5] Thus in manuscript.
[6] Omitted opening quotation mark editorially supplied.
[7] Manuscript: "wherlwith."
[8] King here canceled "however."
[9] Omitted word editorially supplied.
[10] Word interlined.
[11] Manuscript: "mutifarious."
[12] Manuscript: "to to."
[13] Manuscript: "in the which."
[14] Edge trimmed.
[15] Omitted closing quotation mark editorially supplied.
[16] Edge trimmed.
[17] Word obscured by crease.
[18] Manuscript: "the the."
[19] Word obscured by crease.
[20] Word obscured by crease.
[21] Word obscured by crease.
[22] Word obscured by crease.
[23] Word obscured by crease.
[24] Omitted closing quotation mark editorially supplied.
[25] Torn at seal.
[26] Torn at seal.
[27] Torn at seal.
[28] Manuscript: "now."

# To William Short

Dear Sir                                    Monticello Aug. 20. 14.

Since my short letter by mr Rives I have to acknolege the reciept of your two favors of June 9. & July 30. a few days before the last came to hand I had written to Col° Monroe & prayed him to name a day in the autumn (when the fall of the leaves shall have rendered a survey in the woods practicable) and to procure an engagement from Champe Carter to attend and let us have a surveyor and arbitrators on the spot to settle the questioned boundary. I delayed answering your last letter in the hope that he might, in the instant of recieving my letter write to me off-hand. having failed to do this the time of his answering is too indefinite to postpone further the giving you the present state & prospect of the business which you desire.

The state of the case is this. John Carter, eldest son of the family sold to Monroe, bounding him 'on the South by a run on the Eastern side of Dick's plantation, & running thence to the source of the sd run.'[1] but no line was actually marked or examined by either party. it is said that John Carter had no right to sell but that Champe from family considerations concluded to acquiesce. I do not know that this fact is true, having it only from neighborhood report. Champe afterwards sold to you, and attended us in surveying & marking the line. ascending the run far above Dick's plantation, it forked each run being equally large & extending nearly to the top of the mountain, but the Southern branch something the nearest. we knew nothing of the line specified in Monroe's deed, but mr Carter professing to know it & to lead the surveyor, started from the fork and run a straight line between the two branches to the top of the mountain, thus dividing the interval which the two branches rendered doubtful; but not a word of any doubt was then expressed; I presumed he knew what was right, and was doing it. Col° Monroe, sometime after his return from Europe ment[d] to me in conversation that the line as run between you & him by mr Carter was, as he had been informed questionable, but he could not then explain to me how: nor did I ever learn how till after the sale to Higgenbotham. indeed from the continued silence on the subject I believed the claim dropped till I recieved a line from Higgenbotham informing me mr Hay had notified him of it, and Col° M. soon afterwards called on me, shewed his deed, and explained to me for the first time the nature of his claim. we agreed that mr Carter should be desired to attend, that we would take two neighbors as arbitrators, go on the land and settle the question on view. the topics of your right are these. I. if Champe Carter's confirmation of John's sale

[ 591 ]

were necessary to supply the defect of title, then the demarcation of the line which he made in person was a declaration of the precise extent to which he did confirm. II. the run which was made the boundary to it's source, branching by the way, and each branch being equally entitled to be considered as the run whose source was to decide, neither could claim exclusively to be called Dick's run; the compromise made by mr Carter by running the line between them was a fair one, and after an acquiescence of 21. years, and that length of actual & adverse possession in you, ought to be considered as satisfactory to the parties; and especially when no effective step had been taken to maintain a contrary claim till after the land had been long notified as for sale & a sale actually made. the delay of the settlement has entirely rested with the other party. Price, who knows the two branches, thinks there may be about 25. acres between them, one half of which only is within the actual line.

Next as to the prospect. on closing this letter I shall write to John Carter, who lives in Amherst, for information as to his right, and his idea of the boundary, & if his information is of consequence I shall either get his deposition taken by consent of parties, or require his personal attendance as a witness. I must press upon Col° Monroe the fixing a day when he can attend, and some one to act for him, if he does not attend. Champe Carter I suppose will readily agree to be bound if he does not attend. I should have been very confident of finishing this at Monroe's next visit, for he is anxious to finish it but that the call of Congress the 19th of Sep. will render his attendance difficult. if so, I will endeavor to prevail on him to appoint some one here to act for him; for his personal presence[2] cannot be of much importance.

I think the downfall of Bonaparte a great blessing for Europe, which never could have had peace while he was in power. every national society there also will be restored to their antient limits, and to the kind of government, good or bad, which they chuse. I believe the restoration of the Bourbons is the only point on which France could be rallied, and that their re-establishment[3] is better for that country than civil wars whether they should be a peaceable nation under a fool or a warring one under a military despot of genius. to us alone this brings misfortune. it rids of all other enemies a tyrannical nation, fully armed, and deeply embittered by the wrongs they have done us. they may greatly distress individuals in their circumstances; but the soil and the men will remain unconquerable by them, and drinking deeper daily a more deadly, unquenchable and everlasting hatred to them. how much less money would it cost to them,[4] and pain to us, to nourish mutual affections & mutual interests & happiness. but the destructive passions seem to have been implanted in man, as one of the obstacles to his too great multiplication. while we are thus gnawed however by national hatreds we retire with delight into the bosom of our individual friendships in the full feeling of which I salute you affectionately.                                                   TH: JEFFERSON

RC (ViW: TJP); endorsed by Short as received 21 Sept. in New Brunswick. PoC (MHi); endorsed by TJ.

Short's missing letter of JULY 30 is recorded in SJL as received 5 Aug. 1814 from Philadelphia.

[1] Omitted closing quotation mark editorially supplied.
[2] In RC TJ here canceled "must." In enhancing the PoC, he did not reproduce the same deletion.
[3] Reworked from "establishment."
[4] Reworked from "less would it cost them."

# To James W. Wallace

DEAR SIR                                              Monticello Aug. 20. 14.
I am very thankful to yourself and particularly so to mrs Wallace for the trouble you have been so kind as to take with mr Mason's present of homespun. I sent to Culpeper C.H. a few days ago and recieved it safely, as I did also the fish-saw for which my Hall is indebted to you as for many previous curiosities. mrs Mason's work puts us all to shame, for as yet we have not attempted beyond the coarse cloathing of our people. we hope however shortly to try something higher: but not in flax; there is no thinking of the single thread of that wheel after using Jennies from 24. to 40. threads.—we have been in hopes of seeing you here, and the more so as our most promising is absent on a tour of militia duty. we are in hourly expectation of great news from the lakes, but whether good or bad will perhaps depend on the state of Chauncey's fever, who I fear has been forced by public impatience before either his body or mind are sufficiently reinforced for such an encounter. Accept my friendly & respectful salutations.                                                   TH: JEFFERSON

PoC (DLC); at foot of text: "Dr Wallace"; endorsed by TJ.

The MOST PROMISING physician was Frank Carr (see Carr to TJ, 31 July

1814). Commodore Isaac Chauncey had a FEVER for eighteen days starting late in July 1814 (New-York Spectator, 14 Sept. 1814).

# To William Wardlaw

DEAR DOCTOR                                    Monticello Aug. 20. 14.

I observe getting into use for the making of punch an acid called Lemon acid, which I am told you can furnish. it is in small earthen jars or phials of an ounce or somewhat more. Johnson's boat from Milton having gone down three days ago, I am in hopes it may be in Richmond at the moment of your recieving this. I will pray you therefore to send me by him a dozen of those small vials or jars of lemon acid. mr Gibson is so good as to pay these small calls for me, and will pay the bill for the above. Accept my friendly and respectful salutations.                                    TH: JEFFERSON

PoC (DLC); at foot of text: "D^r Wardlaw"; endorsed by TJ.

An advertisement for "Pure Lemon Acid" asserted that it could be used for MAKING "Punch, Lemonade, Sauces, Jellies, and every other purpose in cookery" (Washington *Daily National Intelligencer*, 27 July 1814).

# To John C. Carter

SIR                                            Monticello Aug. 21. 14.

Something upwards of 20. years ago you sold a piece of land adjoining Colle, part of your father's estate here, to Col° Monroe. the deed says it is bounded 'on the South by a run on the Eastern side of Dick's plantation, and running thence to the source of the sd run and thence in a straight line to the top of the S. W. mountains.' above Dick's plantation & far up the mountain the run forks into two branches nearly equal in size & in length. were these branches known at the time? was there any contemplation in your mind or any explanation verbal or written, which of the two was intended as the line? or do you recollect any thing which will throw light on the subject? this matter is now in question between Col° Monroe & mr Short, to whom your brother Champe Carter sold the adjacent land. on that sale mr Champe Carter himself directed the surveyor in marking the line, and when he came to the fork, he took the ridge between the two & run straight to the top of the mountain.

It has been said, but I know not on what grounds; having never seen your father's will, that your sale of that land was not valid until confirmed by your brother Champe. will you be so good as to set me right in that fact, by informing me of the nature of your title and whether mr Champe Carter's confirmation was necessary? having made the purchase for mr Short and always in his absence acted for him as to the lands, I feel my self bound to do so on the present occasion, and will therefore esteem it as a favor done to myself if you will endeavor to refresh your recollection on this subject, and give me the fullest information in your power Accept the assurance of my esteem & respect. TH: JEFFERSON

PoC (DLC); at foot of text: "John Carter esquire"; endorsed by TJ.

John Champe Carter (ca. 1759–1826) was commissioned an ensign in the 7th Virginia Regiment of the Continental army in 1776 and resigned the following year. Later in 1777 he became a captain in the 1st Continental Artillery. He was captured in 1780 at Charleston, South Carolina, and not released until the end of the war, when he was given the rank of brevet major. Carter was later awarded three-hundred acres of bounty land. His Nelson County estate included thirty-nine slaves in 1820 (Heitman, *Continental Army*, 147; Washington, *Papers, Rev. War Ser.*, 17:342–3; DNA: RG 15, RWP; George Selden Wallace, *The Carters of Blenheim: A Genealogy of Edward and Sarah Champe Carter of "Blenheim" Albemarle County, Virginia* [1955], 18; Woods, *Albemarle*, 164; DNA: RG 29, CS, Nelson Co., 1820; Lynchburg *Virginian*, 20 Apr. 1826).

For the FATHER'S WILL, that of Edward Carter, see note to TJ to William Champe Carter, 23 Sept. 1813.

## To Nicolas G. Dufief

Monticello Aug. 21. 14.

Th: Jefferson presents his salutations to mr Dufief and asks the favor of him to procure and send him a copy of Evanson's Dissonance of the four Evangelists.

PoC (DLC); dateline at foot of text; on verso of reused address cover of George Hargraves to TJ, 4 Aug. 1814; endorsed by TJ.

TJ sought Edward EVANSON's *The Dissonance of the four Generally Received Evangelists, and the Evidence of their Respective Authenticity Examined* (Ipswich, Eng., 1792; revised ed. Gloucester, Eng., 1805).

## From Samuel M. Burnside

SIR, Worcester, August 22. 1814.

I have received your favor of the 8th inst. enclosed in a very valuable Manuscript, relating to the first Settlement of New England by our venerable Ancestors.—On behalf of the A. A. Society, permit me, Sir, to tender You their thanks for this communication.—The Gentleman, from whom you received it, Mr. Wm. Burnet Brown, did remove, as You suppose, from this Commonwealth and was a native of

Salem.—He was of a very respectable family, but not descended, I believe, from Gov. Burnet, who left no children, as I am told.—His mother, however, was an adopted daughter of Gov. Burnet.—

I beg leave to assure You, Sir, that independently of any aid, which you may afford in advancing the useful and interesting objects of the Institution, of which You consent to become a member, your acceptance is very grateful.—The mere name, the friendly wishes, and weight of personal character of him, who has sustained a rank so elevated in the literary and political world, cannot fail to be highly useful to any Society.—

With much respect, I am, Sir, Your Obed$^t$ Serv$^t$

S M BURNSIDE

P.S.—It is usual with me to reply to all letters enclosing communications or presents for the Society, in order to remove all anxiety from the benevolent donors respecting the [receipt?] of their letters.

SMB.

RC (DLC); torn at seal; addressed: "Hon. Thomas Jefferson. L.L.D. Monticello.—Virginia"; franked; postmarked Worcester, 23 Aug.; endorsed by TJ as received 2 Sept. 1814 and so recorded in SJL.

William BURNET was the royal governor of New York and New Jersey, 1720–28, and of Massachusetts and New Hampshire, 1728–29. He had three children with his second wife. William Burnet Brown was the son of Governor Burnet's daughter Mary (*ANB*; William Nelson, *William Burnet Governor of New-York and New Jersey 1720–1728: A Sketch Of His Administration In New-York* [1892], 175).

# To Thomas Hornsby

SIR                                                    Monticello Aug. 22. 14.

Your letter of Jan. 9. was duly recieved. in that you are so kind as to inform me, on the subject of mrs Henderson's permission to John Henderson to pass a canal thro' the Dower lands near Milton, that there was among her papers an original release of John Henderson to her of all responsibility for any former right which she had given to any other person, & which might be a bar to that permission. this paper is so important to repel the fraudulent claim of Michie, that in order to obtain an authentication of it, I have taken out a commission from the court of Albemarle and inclosed it to Governor Greenup to have mrs Henderson's deposition taken: and besides the establishment of this paper I wish her deposition to go to the fact you mention that her permission to John, both the verbal & written ones, were for no valuable consideration but merely voluntary, and generally to the transactions stated in the Extract inclosed from the deposition of her son James L. Henderson who was present with her when they passed. Gov$^r$ Greenup will be so good as to appoint persons to take the deposition who can wait on mrs Henderson for the purpose, and Michie is notified that this will be done at her house on Tuesday the 11$^{th}$ of Oct. next. seeking nothing but truth and justice, I hope I am not unreasonable in requesting mrs Henderson to bear testimony to whatever she knows on the subject, and that you will be so good as to give any facility towards it in your power. Accept the tender of my esteem and respect.                     TH: JEFFERSON

RC (Mrs. Ethel A. Worsham, Jacksonville Beach, Fla., 1950); addressed: "M$^r$ Thomas Hornsby near Frankfort Kentucky"; franked; with notation in Christopher Greenup's hand: "NB: The extract of M$^r$ James L. Hendersons Deposition will be forwarded to M$^{rs}$ Hendersons on the 11$^{th}$ Oct$^o$ next 1814    Christ$^o$ Greenup." PoC (ViU: TJP); endorsed by TJ. Enclosure not found.

A letter of this date from TJ to GREENUP, in which the above letter was probably enclosed, is recorded in SJL but has not been found. Missing letters from Greenup to TJ of 29 Apr., 1 Oct., and 9 Nov. 1814 are recorded in SJL as received from Frankfort on 13 May, 14 Oct., and 1 Dec. 1814, respectively.

# To David Michie

SIR                                   Monticello Aug. 22. 1814

In the suit in Chancery which I have instituted against you in the county court of Albemarle for the purpose of perpetuating the testimony of certain witnesses in the bill named, & under the authority of commissions issued from the sd court, I intend to take the depositions of the following persons at the times & places following, to wit, the depositions of

Craven Peyton and Richard Price at ten aclock of Thursday the 8$^{th}$ of the ensuing month of September, at the tavern of John Watson in Milton:

Dabney Carr at 12. aclock of Tuesday the$^1$ 13$^{th}$ of the same month of September at his dwelling house in Winchester:

Elizabeth Henderson at 12. aclock of Tuesday the 11$^{th}$ of October next at her dwelling house in the neighborhood of Frankfort in Kentucky

James Lewis at 12. aclock of Tuesday the 25$^{th}$ of the same month of October at his dwelling house in Franklin county in Tenissee

of all which be pleased to recieve this as notice for your attendance

TH: JEFFERSON

RC (THi); at foot of text: "To M^r David Michie Albemarle." Not recorded in SJL.

[1] TJ here canceled "11^th of October next."

# From Jean Baptiste Say

MONSIEUR                                              Paris 22 août 1814.

J'ai eu l'honneur de vous ecrire le 15 juin dernier en vous adressant un exemplaire de mon nouveau Traité d'Economie politique, que les circonstances générales où nous nous Sommes trouvés, m'ont permis de publier. Je Souhaite vivement que cet ouvrage vous Soit parvenu, car votre approbation est une de celles dont je fais le plus de cas; je la regarde comme un veritable titre de gloire. La lettre et le livre étaient recommandés aux Soins de M^r Todd, alors à Paris, actuellement à Gand.

Je prenais la liberté dans cette lettre de vous parler de mon fils, jeune homme de Vingt ans envoyé en Amérique par une respectable maison de commerce de ce pays-ci. M^r Warden avait eu la bonté de lui donner une lettre d'introduction auprès de Vous, Monsieur; j'ignore encore s'il a eu l'honneur de vous presenter Ses devoirs.

M^r Warden a depuis ce moment eu le malheur d'encourir la défaveur de l'Ambassadeur des Etats-unis; ce qui l'a arreté dans une carriere où il m'a Semblé qu'il Se conduisait avec honneur, et ce qui a fort affligé Ses amis. Il Se flatte qu'on rendra justice à ses intentions et qu'il pourra reprendre Ses fonctions de Consul. Il etait fort bien vu de toutes les personnes qui tiennent à notre gouvernement.

Quant à moi, Si je reste en France, ce Sera par la difficulté de changer de place avec une famille nombreuse et une fortune médiocre. J'aimerais à habiter un pays libre, et je ne peux guère me flatter que celui-ci le devienne. Ce n'est pas que le gouvernement actuel Soit assez fort et assez habile pour etre oppresseur; mais le peuple est trop peu instruit pour échaper à l'oppression. On s'imagine en France que defendre Ses droits, c'est attaquer l'autorité; que contenir le gouvernement dans de justes bornes, c'est être indiscipliné; et c'est ainsi que la crainte des desordres nous plonge dans la Servitude. Aussi, Si je pouvais avec 60 mille francs disponibles, devenir cultivateur dans votre pays et y faire Subsister confortablement ma famille je crois que je m'y deciderais. C'est ce qui m'avait déterminé, Monsieur, à vous demander quelques informations Sur le prix actuel des terres, dans les pays habités et avec un commencement de defrichement et de bâtimens[1] tel qu'on pût y Subsister dès la première année mais je crains d'avoir été indiscret en vous entretenant de mes interets privés.

Je me borne donc à vous prier, Monsieur, de reclamer la seconde édition de mon Economie politique Si contre mes intentions elle ne vous avait pas été remise, et d'agréer favorablement l'expression de mon Sincère dévouement et de mon profond respect

J. B. SAY

Rue des fossés Saint Jacques N° 13

P.S. Si je pouvais obtenir d'etre agregé à la plus estimée de vos Societés Savantes, je regarderais cela comme un très grand honneur.[2]

EDITORS' TRANSLATION

SIR
Paris 22 August 1814.

I had the honor of writing you last 15 June and of sending you a copy of my new *Traité d'Economie Politique*, which I was allowed to publish, given the general circumstances in which we found ourselves. I very much wish this work to reach you, for I value your approbation more than that of any other; and I would consider receiving your approval to be a very great honor. The letter and book were entrusted to the care of Mr. Todd, who was then in Paris, and is now at Ghent.

In that letter I took the liberty of mentioning my son, a young man of twenty who has been sent to America by one of our respectable commercial houses. Mr. Warden was so kind as to give him a letter of introduction to present when he sees you, Sir; I still do not know whether he has had the honor of paying you his respects.

Since then, Mr. Warden has been so unfortunate as to incur the disfavor of the United States ambassador, which ended a career in which he seemed to be conducting himself very honorably, and which has saddened his friends very much. He flatters himself that his intentions will be fairly judged, and that he will be able to resume his role as consul. All the people who support our government had a very high opinion of him.

As for me, if I stay in France, it will be because of the difficulty of moving with a large family and a modest fortune. I would like to live in a free country, and I cannot delude myself that this country will become one. Even though the current government lacks the strength or skill to be oppressive, the people are too poorly educated to escape oppression. In France it is thought that to defend one's rights is to attack authority; that to contain the government within just limits is to be undisciplined; and this is how a fear of disorder plunges us into servitude. Thus, if with sixty thousand francs in hand I could become a farmer in your country and support my family comfortably, I believe I would make up my mind to do it. This is what prompted me, Sir, to ask you for some information about the current price of partially cleared land with a few buildings in populated regions, with which one could make a living starting the first year. But I fear that I have been indiscreet in writing to you about my private interests.

Therefore, I will limit myself to asking you, Sir, to request a copy of the second edition of my *Traité d'Economie Politique* if, contrary to my wishes, it has not yet reached you, and to accept my sincere devotion and profound respect

J. B. SAY

Rue des Fossés Saint Jacques Number 13

P.S. I would consider it a very great honor if I were admitted into the most esteemed of your scholarly societies.

RC (DLC); dateline beneath postscript; addressed: "A Monsieur Th. Jefferson a Monticello Etats-unis d'Amérique"; franked; postmarked New York, 4 May; notation on address leaf: "forwarded New York 3ᵈ May 1815 Your most ob Servᵗ H. C. De Rham"; endorsed by TJ as received 11 May 1815 and so recorded in SJL. Translation by Dr. Genevieve Moene.

¹ Preceding three words interlined.
² Manuscript: "honneurs."

# From Charles Yancey

Dᴿ Sɪʀ                                                 camp Fairfield 22ⁿᵈ Augᵗ 1814

I perform a duty gratefull to my feelings in communicating to you our Military Movements or operations since our arrival at this place. we were organized into two Regᵗˢ on ____ insᵗ and altho' more officers were called out, under the requisition from the State, than what are necessary under the requisition Adopted by the U.S. which gave disquietude to the supernumeraries, yet like good Citizens, they have honorably acquiesced under the Arrangement, & thereby given high evidence of public virtue. I have the honor to inform you that I command the 1ˢᵗ Regᵗ & Coln Belew of Buckingham the 2ⁿᵈ. with the officers & men under my Command, I am perfectly satisfied, They will do their duty; & acquit themselves with honor If met by the foe. Colˡ Edward¹ Garland who was a Soldier of 76, come down as my adjutant on his arrival here, he found that Station required, more activity, labor, & exertion, than a man of his advanced age could perform. has quietly Returned to his family, & his place is filled by Capᵗ B. Stanard. an officer of merit. who comes well Recommended to me, these instances of devotion to our country must be pleasing to its friends & I am Sure to no One more than yourself. we expect Shortly to remove to the Holly Spring where it is Said, the Water is better than it is here altho' our men considering our w[eat]her have had but few on the Sick list. I sha[ll] be happy as I am fully pursuaded² that you feel a deep Interest in every thing which relates to our Common Country, whose liberties You were So instrumental in establishing, that in the recess of More important avocations you wou'd drop me a line, & be assured that I shall feel high Gratification, from time to time to give You Such Inteligence as may be entitled to your notice I have the honor to be respectfully Your Mo Obd$^t$ S$^t$     C' Yancey

RC (DLC); torn at seal; endorsed by TJ as received 26 Aug. 1814 and so recorded in SJL.

Camp FAIRFIELD was near Richmond. Lieutenant Colonels Thomas Ballowe (BELEW) and Charles Yancey command-

ed the 1st and 2nd Virginia Regiments, respectively (Butler, *Virginia Militia*, 22, 254–5).

[1] Manuscript: "Eward."
[2] Manuscript: "pursuded."

# To Dabney Carr

DEAR SIR                                   Monticello Aug. 24. 14.

M$^r$ Michie having flown from his agreement to take depositions by consent, in the questions between him and myself, I filed a bill against him to take them de bene esse, and to perpetuate them, which the court has decreed. among others I have taken out a commission for obtaining your deposition. this I now inclose and pray you to fill it with the names of justices who can attend at the time & place notified to the def. you know so much of the case as to be able to direct your own testimony to the proper point, to wit, his fraudulent concealment of his claim on the examination at which you were present. the deposition when taken and inclosed to the clerk had perhaps better come under cover to me for greater safety.

Your friends here are all well. your brothers suffered severely by the late flood, having lost most of their crops. Sam is indemnified by the amelioration of his land. Peter's is bettered in some parts & injured in others. Peter Minor lost his entire crops, but with a vast improvem$^t$ to his grounds. these losses have not been confined to river sides. every creek & branch committed ravages of which they were thought incapable.

You recieve public news as early as we do. the late reinforcement in the Chesapeake, & the course it has taken puts us in fear for Washington. I have little doubt we shall have peace in the course of the year, but with a vast increase of hatred to the nation which to such aggravated causes of war has added so flagitious a course of pursuing it, by multiplying such private distresses as can have no effect on the event of the war, other than to prolong it, and envenom it's course. ever affectionately yours                    TH: JEFFERSON

PoC (ViU: TJP-CC); at foot of text: "Dabney Carr esq."; endorsed by TJ; unrelated notation by TJ on verso: "1813. Nov. 20. began on this ream." Enclosure not found.

DE BENE ESSE: "in anticipation of a future need" (*Black's Law Dictionary*).

# From Patrick Gibson

SIR                                                    Richmond 24th August 1814

Since writing to you on the 4th Inst I have received your several letters of the 7th 15th 16th & 20th—finding it impracticable either through the medium of our banks or of individuals to remit to the North, and not deeming it prudent to risk bank notes—I wrote to Mr Dufief and Mr Barnes to draw upon me at sight for the sums you mention'd—

I sent yesterday a bale of Cotton by Mr Johnson, who also took up some castings—not a bundle of nail rod can be procured in the City, nor has Mr Randolph any more of his earthenware ready—         With great respect

Your obt Servt                                        PATRICK GIBSON

Mr R has promised to send some of his earthenware up tomorrow

RC (ViU: TJP-ER); between dateline and salutation: "Mr Thomas Jefferson"; endorsed by TJ as received 26 Aug. 1814 and so recorded in SJL.

# From William Wardlaw

DEAR SIR                                              Richmond 24th Augt 1814

Your favour of the 20th was not recd from the post office till to day. on enquiry I found the boat that you mentioned had left the Basin. I have not the lemon acid but have purchased a doz which I will send to the stage office this evening packed in a very small box directed to the care the post master Milton the price I paid for it was $3.25.

I am with much esteem Your friend &c                  W WARDLAW

RC (DLC); endorsed by TJ as received 26 Aug. 1814 and so recorded in SJL.

# To Edward Coles

Dear Sir                                        Monticello Aug. 25. 14.

Your favor of July 31. was duly recieved, and was read with peculiar pleasure. the sentiments breathed thro' the whole do honor to
both the head and heart of the writer. mine on the subject of the slavery of negroes have long since been in possession of the public, and
time has only served to give them stronger root. the love of justice
& the love of country plead equally the cause of these people, and it
is a mortal[1] reproach to us that they should have pleaded it so long
in vain, and should have produced not a single effort, nay I fear not
much serious willingness to relieve them & ourselves from our present condition of moral and political reprobation. from those of the
former generation who were in the fulness of age when I came into
public life, which was while our controversy with England was on
paper only, I soon[2] saw that nothing was to be hoped. nursed and educated in the daily habit of seeing the degraded condition, both bodily & mental, of those unfortunate beings, not[3] reflecting that that
degradation was very much the work of themselves & their fathers,
few minds had yet doubted but that they were as legitimate subjects
of property as their horses or cattle. the quiet & monotonous course
of colonial life had been disturbed by no alarm, & little reflection on
the value of liberty. and when alarm was taken at an enterprise on
their own, it was not easy to carry them the whole length of the principles which they invoked for themselves. in the first or second session of the legislature after I became a member, I drew to this subject
the attention of Col° Bland, one of the oldest, ablest, and most respected members, and he undertook to move for certain moderate extensions of the protection of the laws to these people. I seconded his
motion, and, as a younger member, was[4] more spared in the debate:
but he was denounced as an enemy to his country, & was treated with
the grossest[5] indecorum. from an early stage of our revolution other
and more distant duties were assigned to me, so that from that time
till my return from Europe in 1789. and I may say till I returned to
reside at home in 1809. I had little opportunity of knowing the
progress of public sentiment here on this subject. I had always hoped
that the younger generation, recieving their early impressions after
the flame of liberty had been kindled in every breast, and had become
as it were the vital spirit of every American, that the generous tem-
perament of youth, analogous to the motion of their blood, and above
the suggestions of avarice, would have sympathised with oppression
wherever found, and proved their love of liberty beyond their own

share of it. but my intercourse with them, since my return, has not been sufficient to ascertain that they had made towards this point the progress I had hoped. your solitary but welcome voice is the first which has brought this sound to my ear; and I have considered the general silence which prevails on this subject as indicating an apathy unfavorable to every hope. yet the hour of emancipation is advancing in the march of time. it will come; and whether brought on by the generous energy of our own minds, or by the bloody process of S$^t$ Domingo, excited and conducted by the power of our present enemy, if once stationed permanently within our country, & offering asylum & arms to the oppressed, is a leaf of our history not yet turned over.[6]

As to the method by which this difficult work is to be effected, if permitted to be done by ourselves, I have seen no proposition so expedient on the whole, as that of emancipation of those born after a given[7] day, and of their education and expatriation at a proper age. this would give time for a gradual extinction of that species of labor and substitution of another, and lessen the severity of the shock which an operation so fundamental cannot fail to produce. the idea of emancipating the whole at once, the old as well as the young, and retaining them here, is of those only who have not the guide of either knolege or experience of the subject. for, men, probably of any colour, but of this color we know, brought up from their infancy without necessity for thought or forecast, are by their habits rendered as incapable as children of taking care of themselves, and are extinguished promptly wherever industry is necessary for raising the young. in the mean time they are pests in society by their idleness, and the depredations to which this leads them. their amalgamation with the other colour produces a degradation to which no lover of his country, no lover of excellence in the human character can innocently consent.

I am sensible of the partialities with which you have looked towards me as the person who should undertake this salutary but arduous work. but this, my dear Sir, is like bidding old Priam to buckle the armour of Hector 'trementibus aevo humeris et inutile ferrum cingi.' no. I have overlived the generation with which mutual labors and perils begat mutual confidence and influence. this enterprise is for the young; for those who can follow it up, and bear it through to it's consummation. it shall have all my prayers, and these are the only weapons of an old man.          but in the mean time are you right in abandoning this property, and your country with it? I think not. my opinion has ever been that, until more can be done for them, we should endeavor, with those whom fortune has thrown on our hands, to feed & clothe them well, protect them from ill usage, require such reasonable labor only as is performed voluntarily by freemen, and be led by no repugnancies to abdicate them, and our duties to them. the laws do not permit us to turn them loose, if that were for their good: and to commute them for other property is to commit them to those whose usage of them we cannot controul. I hope then, my dear Sir, you will reconcile yourself to your country and it's unfortunate condition; that you will not lessen it's stock of sound disposition by withdrawing your portion from the mass. that, on the contrary you will come forward in the public councils, become the Missionary of this doctrine truly Christian, insinuate & inculcate it softly but steadily thro' the medium of writing & conversation, associate others in your labors, and when the phalanx is formed, bring on & press the proposition perseveringly until it's accomplishment. it is an encoraging observation that no good measure was ever proposed which, if duly pursued, failed to prevail in the end. we have proof of this in the history of the endeavors in the British parliament to suppress that very trade which brought this evil on us. and you will be[8] supported by the religious precept 'be not wearied in well doing.' that your success may be as speedy and compleat, as it will be of honorable & immortal consolation to yourself I shall as fervently & sincerely pray as I assure you of my great friendship and respect.    TH: JEFFERSON

P.S. will you give to the inclosed letter the proper address of place to find your brother?

RC (NjP: Coles Papers); addressed: "Edward Coles esquire at the President's house Washington"; franked; postmarked Milton, 1 Sept. PoC (DLC); lacking postscript. Tr (Thomas F. Jackson, Westfield, N.J., 1946); lacking postscript. Printed in Alexandria *Phenix Gazette*, 10 Feb. 1825, from an unidentified issue of the Vandalia *Illinois Intelligencer*. Enclosure: TJ to Isaac A. Coles, 27 Aug. 1814.

The effort by TJ and Richard BLAND to promote CERTAIN MODERATE EXTENSIONS OF THE PROTECTION OF THE LAWS to slaves is not documented in the journals of the Virginia House of Burgesses, which did not routinely record failed motions. In his 1821 autobiography TJ indicated that "I made one effort in that body for the permission of the emancipation of slaves, which was rejected: and indeed, during the regal government, nothing liberal could expect success" (Ford, 1:5; *PTJ*, 2:22–4). TREMENTIBUS AEVO HUMERIS ET INUTILE FERRUM CINGI: "armor, long unused, on shoulders trembling with age," a paraphrase of Virgil, *Aeneid*, 2.509–11 (Fairclough, *Virgil*, 1:350–1). BE NOT WEARIED IN WELL DOING quotes from the Bible, Galatians 6.9 and 2 Thessalonians 3.13.

[1] *Phenix Gazette*: "moral."
[2] Word added in margin.
[3] *Phenix Gazette*: "but."
[4] *Phenix Gazette* here adds "no."
[5] *Phenix Gazette*: "greatest."
[6] Sentence not in *Phenix Gazette*.
[7] Tr: "certain."
[8] Preceding three words interlined in place of "we are."

# To Thomas Cooper

DEAR SIR                                    Monticello Aug. 25. 14.

In my letter of Jan. 16. I mentioned to you that it had long been in contemplation to get an University established in this state, in which all the branches of science useful to us, and at this day, should be taught in their highest degree; and that this institution should be incorporated with the college and funds of W^m & Mary. but what are the sciences useful to us, and at this day thought useful to any body? a glance over Bacon's arbor scientiae will shew the foundation for this question, & how many of his ramifications of science are now lopt off as nugatory. to be prepared for this new establishment, I have taken some pains to ascertain those branches which men of sense, as well as of science, deem worthy of cultivation. to the statements which I have obtained from other sources I should highly value an addition of one from yourself. you know our country, it's pursuits, it's faculties, it's relations with others, it's means of establishing and maintaining an institution of general science, and the spirit of economy with which it requires that these should be administered. will you then so far contribute to our views as to consider this subject, to make a statement of the branches of science which you think worthy of being taught, as I have before said, at this day, and in this country? but to accomodate them to our economy, it will be necessary further to distribute them into groups, each group comprehending as many branches as one industrious Professor may competently teach, and, as much as may be, a duly associated family, or class, of kindred sciences. the object of this is to bring the whole circle of useful science under the direction of the smallest number of professors possible, and that our means may be so frugally employed as to effect the greatest possible good. we are about to make an effort for the introduction of this institution.

On the subject of patent rights, on which something has passed between us before,[1] you may have noted that the patent board, while it existed, had proposed to reduce their decisions to a system of rules as fast as the cases presented should furnish materials. they had done but little when the business was turned over to the courts of justice, on whom the same duty has now devolved. a rule has occurred to me, which I think would reach many of our cases, and go far towards securing the citizen against the vexation of frivolous patents. it is to consider the invention of any new mechanical power, or of any new combination of the mechanical powers already known, as entitled to an exclusive grant; but that the purchaser of the right to use the invention should be free to apply it to every purpose of which it is susceptible. for instance, the combination of machinery for threshing wheat, should be applicable to the threshing of ryes, oats, beans E$^t$c the spinning machine to every thing, of which it may be found capable; the chain of buckets, of which we have been possessed thousands of years, we should be free to use for raising water, ore, grains, meals, or any thing else we can make it raise. these rights appear sufficiently distinct, and the distinction sound enough, to be adopted by the judges, to whom it could not be better suggested than thro' the medium of the Emporium, should any future paper of that furnish place for the hint.

Since the change of government in France, I am in hopes the author of the Review of Montesquieu[2] will consent to be named, and perhaps may publish there his original work: not that their press is free; but that the present government will be restrained by public opinion, whereas the late military despotism respected that of the army only. I salute you with friendship & respect.

TH: JEFFERSON

PoC (DLC); at foot of first page: "Thomas Cooper."

Destutt de Tracy wrote the REVIEW OF MONTESQUIEU.

ARBOR SCIENTIAE: "tree of knowledge." TJ based his own universal breakdown of knowledge on that advanced by Sir Francis Bacon (Sowerby, 1:x).

[1] Remainder of paragraph printed anonymously with Cooper's note of approbation in *Emporium of Arts & Sciences*, n.s., 3 (1814): 459.

[2] Manuscript: "Montesquiu."

# To Caspar Wistar

DEAR SIR                                  Monticello Aug. 25. 14.

It seems an age since I have had particular occasion to recall myself to your memory; and to that circumstance must be ascribed my long silence; and not to any abatement of my great esteem for you. perhaps the desire to say so may have entered somewhat into the motives for giving you the trouble I am now about to propose. we are desirous of establishing in my neighborhood an academy, on a moderate scale at first, but susceptible of being extended with time to every branch of science considered useful at this day, and for our country. to aid in the digest of our plan, I have wished to procure those of the institutions which have already obtained celebrity with us. among these I consider the University of Philadelphia as the first. the favor I have to ask of you is to give me a list of the professorships & of the branches of science ascribed to each Professor. I know that your medical department is branched into many professorships. we mean nothing of that kind; because a school of medecine, to make practical men, can only be where there is a large hospital. in this department we shall aim only at such a general view of anatomy, and the Theory of medecine as every man of education would wish to possess.

I am in hopes the late revolution in France will be favorable to science: inasmuch as no systematic plan will be ventured on for it's restraint. there was reason to fear this was meditated by the late military despotism. now perhaps we may consider the National institute as safe, and that it may venture to restore it's original construction.        I have not heard of Correa since he left Philadelphia. he promised to take this place in his return and to pass some time with us. I think it probable the botany of Kentucky may detain him longer than he expected. Accept assurances of great and sincere esteem and respect.                                        TH: JEFFERSON

PoC (DLC); at foot of text: "Doct^r Wistar"; endorsed by TJ.

The PHILADELPHIA institution of higher education was actually the University of Pennsylvania.

# From John H. Cocke

DEAR SIR,                                             Bremo Aug: 27. 1814

I rec^d your letter dated the 5 Aug: two posts past, and owe you an apology for not acknowledging it sooner.—The last eight days every moment of my time has been employ'd in placing my affairs in the best posture I can for my absence in the public service—The call upon me was entirely unexpected and found me unprepared.—

I am sorry that you deem'd it necessary to trouble yourself upon the subject of payment for the Horse—the understanding between us & the course of events prevented my expecting the money at this time— and be assured Sir, that I wish you to consult your convenience entirely about it in future.—Accept the assurance of my highest
    Esteem & respect—                                    JN^O H. COCKE

RC (CSmH: JF); endorsed by TJ as received 30 Aug. 1814 but recorded in SJL as received the following day. RC (MHi); address cover only; on verso of PoC of TJ to Richard Randolph, 27 Sept. 1814; addressed: "M^r Jefferson Monticello"; stamped; postmarked Columbia, Va., 28 Aug.

Cocke was a brigadier general in the

Virginia militia. He was preparing for AB-
SENCE IN THE PUBLIC SERVICE after the
organization of his brigade at Camp
Fairfield in August 1814 (Stuart L. Butler, "Gen. John Hartwell Cocke in the
War of 1812," *MACH* 65 [2007]: 19–43,
esp. 28–9).

# To Isaac A. Coles

DEAR SIR                                  Monticello Aug. 27. 14.

I thank you for the pamphlet you have been so kind as to send me.
altho' ignorant of the pretences for the opposition you had experienced in your regiment, your friends here, to whom you were best
known, never doubted that your conduct had been proper & honorable under every circumstance. they are gratified by the knolege of
the facts detailed in this[1] pamphlet, as proving specially what they
had concluded on the general knolege of your character and conduct
thro' life. it is with real sorrow I see such a spirit of insubordination
even in the officers of our army. they have been loud in their complaints of the existence of this spirit among their men; but how can it
be otherwise with such an example from their officers? if the privates
of the 12th regiment were to declare against duty under the signers of
the Memorial[2] to the Secretary at war, what could these gentlemen
say in reprobation of it? would they retire from their duties because
not acceptable to their men? or would they meet a challenge from one
of them? yet as the private is to his captain, such is the captain to his
colonel. as citizens all are equal; it is commission alone which gives a
superiority of rank, & against that superiority the officer may offend
as well as the private, & does offend by the same acts. this example
leads to an election of officers by the privates, & to a continuance in
command during the caprice of the latter.

Your friends here are well. your brother Tucker is on a tour of
militia[3] duty. we are all on the alert as to the fate of Washington. our
last information places the enemy at Benedict, an awkward situation
enough for an attack on Washington. it commits them to a land attack,
and an Englishman, like a fish, is diselemented when out of water. if
their numbers be such only as circumstances indicate, they ought not
to be a breakfast for those who may gather round them.            ever
affectionately yours                                  TH: JEFFERSON

PoC (MHi); at foot of text: "Col° Isaac
A. Coles"; endorsed by TJ. Enclosed in
TJ to Edward Coles, 25 Aug. 1814.
THE PAMPHLET, an appeal by Coles *To
the Public* (Washington, 1814), includes
seventeen documents related to Coles's

defense from charges brought against him by James C. Bronaugh, an army surgeon serving under him in the 12th Infantry Regiment. It begins with a preface by Coles noting that "As it respects the unworthy and dishonourable conduct which has been imputed to me, this rests for the present on nothing better than the infuriated denunciations of Bronaugh, and will be found to have no foundation but the dark and malignant passions to which he has given himself up." The 21 Aug. 1813 MEMORIAL TO THE SECRETARY AT WAR, the third text in the publication, is signed at Fort George by eighteen officers of the 12th, including Bronaugh, and requests that the secretary of war remove the recently promoted Coles from leadership of the unit and restore Colonel James P. Preston to command. The pamphlet concludes with a letter from Coles to the secretary of war, Washington, 7 July 1814, asking to be arrested and placed on trial, because "He feels that his reputation has greatly suffered in the estimation of many, and until he can again be placed on the ground on which he is conscious that he is entitled to stand, it would be truly painful to him to join his companions in arms. On the justice of his country therefore he throws himself, to which none should appeal in vain, and asks that the proper tribunal may be ordered immediately to pass upon him."

TJ also received Bronaugh's printed defense, dated 5 July 1814 (TJ's copy in DLC; endorsed by him as a letter from Bronaugh received 3 Aug. 1814), which includes an extract from Bronaugh's letter to Secretary of War John Armstrong, Fort George, 23 Aug. 1813, offering his own version of Coles's actions and giving Bronaugh's rationale for resigning his post; stating that Coles is "personally my enemy, and that from the proof already given of the meanness of his disposition, he would leave nothing undone to injure me. I solemnly believe that Col. Coles is a dastardly coward, and cannot reconcile it to my feelings to serve under a man of that character; I am not alone in this belief, many officers of high standing think so also, and do not hesitate to declare it

publicly"; two letters from Bronaugh to Coles, Grenadier Island, 25 Oct. 1813, in the second of which he demands "that satisfaction, which, as a gentleman, I am entitled to receive at your hands"; a statement of support for Bronaugh by Captain Roger Jones; Bronaugh's 25 Oct. public posting of Coles as "a base liar, infamous scoundrel, and coward," which he pledges to prove "in a court of judicature"; an extract from the army's general orders, Grenadier Island, 27 Oct. 1813, placing Bronaugh under arrest for challenging his superior officer to a duel; and concluding with General James Wilkinson's order of the same date, following a court-martial that sentenced Bronaugh to be cashiered from the service but then recommended clemency, that "In consequence of the recommendation of the court, the high professional merits of Dr. Bronaugh, and the calamitous situation of the sick, the punishment is remitted, and the Doctor will resume his sword."

Coles was eventually exonerated of all charges against him. On 26 July 1815 he published a statement (printed text in DLC; addressed: "Thomas Jefferson Monticello"; endorsed by TJ: "Coles Isaac A.") presenting correspondence related to his court-martial, including the court's conclusion early in that year that the charges were "unsupported by even a shadow of testimony" and that Coles's conduct had been "altogether correct and honorable"; a statement from Daniel Parker, the adjutant and inspector general, ordering that "The President of the United States having approved the foregoing sentence of the Court Martial, Colonel Coles is honorably restored to his command. He will resume his sword, and report himself for duty"; and a final exchange between Bronaugh and Coles between 19 and 21 July 1815, which Coles, having been honorably discharged from the service on 15 June, began by offering Bronaugh "the meeting, which, as your commandant, I denied you. I await your answer"; Bronaugh replied on 20 July that "In your note of last evening you state, that as a citizen, you seek me here to offer the meeting, which, as my commandant, you denied me. When I made the demand upon you at Grenadier Island, in Oct. 1813, through my friend, Colonel Jones, you refused me satisfaction, under the pretence that you were not bound to hold yourself responsible for any act that might emanate in your official capacity. This refusal made necessary a course less grateful to my own feelings, but more wounding to your's; it compelled me to post you, publicly, as a coward, &c. I cannot, therefore, become the challenger, and if we meet at all, it must be on your demand. This will be handed to you by my friend, Major Tillotson. I can receive no communication from you, except through the medium of gentlemen"; and Coles concluded this exchange by stating that "I have ever doubted your readiness to give the meeting, which, when my hands were fettered, you pretended so eagerly to desire. This impression your letter of yesterday has confirmed. I shall not, therefore, indulge your caprice, by changing the form of my note; but if you still persist in declining the offer it contained, shall post you, without delay, in your real character, to the world. I remain at Rhinebeck until to-morrow."

¹ TJ here canceled "statement."
² Manuscript: "Memoal."
³ Manuscript: "milia."

# To Joseph Delaplaine

Sir                                             Monticello Aug. 28. 14.

Your letter of the 17th is recieved. I have not the book of Muñoz containing the print of Columbus. that work came out after I left Europe, and we have not the same facility of acquiring new continental publications here as there. I have no doubt that entire credit is to be given to the account of the print rendered by him in the extract from his work, which you have sent me: and as you say that several have attempted translations of it, each differing from the other, & none satisfactory to yourself, I will add to your stock my understanding of it, that by a collation of the several translations the author's meaning may be the better elicited.

Translation. 'This first volume presents at the beginning the portrait of the Discoverer, designed and engraved with care. among many paintings and prints which are falsely sold as his likenesses, I have seen one only which can be such, & it is that which is preserved in the house of the most excellent Duke of Berwick & Liria, a descendant of our hero; a figure of the natural size, painted, as should seem, in the last century, by an indifferent copyist, in which nevertheless appear some catches from the hand of Antonio del Rincon, a celebrated painter of the Catholic kings. the description given by Fernando Colon of the countenance of his father has served to render the likeness more resembling, and to correct the faults which are observed in some of the features, either imperfectly siesed by the artist, or disfigured by the injuries of time.'

Paraphrase, explanatory of the above. Columbus was employed by Ferdinand and Isabella, on his voyage of discovery in 1492. Debry tells us that 'before his departure, his portrait was taken, by order of the King & Queen,' & most probably by Rincon their first painter. Rincon died in 1500. & Columbus in 1506. Fernando, his son, an ecclesiastic, wrote the life of his father in 1530. and describes in that his father's countenance. an indifferent hand in the 17th century copied Rincon's painting, which copy is preserved in the house of the duke of Berwick. in 1793, when a print of Columbus was wanting for the history of Muñoz, the artist, from this copy, injured as it was by time, but still exhibiting some catches of Rincon's style, and from the verbal description of the countenance of Columbus in the history by his son, has been enabled to correct the faults of the copy, whether those of the copyist, or proceeding from the injuries of time, and thus to furnish the best likeness.

The Spanish text admits this construction, and well known dates & historical facts verify it.

I have taken from the 2d vol. of De Bry a rough model of the leaf on which is the print he has given of Columbus, and his preface. it gives the exact size and outline of the print, which, with a part of the preface, is on the 1st page of the leaf, and the rest on the 2d. I have extracted from it what related to the print, which you will percieve could not be cut out without a great mutilation of the book. this would not be regarded as to it's cost, which was 12. guineas for the 3. vols in Amsterdam, but that it seems to be the only copy of the work in the US. and I know from experience the difficulty, if not impossibility of getting another. I had orders lodged with several eminent booksellers, in the principal book-marts of Europe, to wit, London, Paris, Amsterdam, Frankfort, Madrid, several years before this copy was obtained at the accidental sale of an old library in Amsterdam, on the death of it's proprietor.

We have then three likenesses of Columbus from which a choice is to be made 1. the print in Muñoz' work, from a copy of Rincon's original, taken in the 17th century by an indifferent hand, with conjectural alterations suggested by the verbal description of the younger Columbus of the countenance of his father.

2. the Miniature of De Bry, from a copy taken in the 16th century from the portrait made by order of the K. & Queen, probably that of Rincon.

3. the copy in my possession, of the size of the life, taken for me from the original which is in the gallery of Florence. I say, from an

original, because it is well known that in collections of any note, & that of Florence is the first in the world, no copy is ever admitted; and an original existing in Genoa would readily be obtained for a royal collection in Florence. Vasari, in his lives of the painters, names this portrait in his catalogue of the paintings in that gallery, but does not say by whom it was made. it has the aspect of a man of 35. still smooth-faced, & in the vigor of life, which would place it's date about 1477. 15 years earlier than that of Rincon—accordingly in the miniature of De Bry, the face appears more furrowed by time. on the whole I should have no hesitation at giving this the preference over the conjectural one of Muñoz, and the miniature of De Bry.

The book from which I cut the print of Vespucius which I sent you has the following title and date. 'Elogio d'Amerigo Vespucci che ha riportato il premio dalla nobile accademia Etrusca di Cortona nel dì 15. d'Ottobre dell' anno 1788. del P. Stanislao Canovai delle scuole pie publico professore di fisica-Matematica, in Firenze 1788. nella stamp. di Pietro Allegrini.' this print is unquestionably from the same original in the gallery of Florence from which my copy was also taken. the portrait is named in the catalogue of Vasari, and mentioned also by Bandini in his life of Americus Vespucius, but neither gives it's history—both tell us there was a portrait of Vespucius taken by Domenico, and a fine head of him by Da Vinci, which however are lost, so that it would seem that this of Florence is the only one existing.

With this offering of what occurs to me on the subject of these prints accept the assurance of my respect. Th: Jefferson

RC (LNT: George H. and Katherine M. Davis Collection); endorsed by Delaplaine, in part: "Answered 3ᵈ October 1814 Sent him a portrait of Mʳ Madison." PoC (DLC); at foot of first page: "Mʳ Delaplaine."

Ferdinand Columbus (FERNANDO COLON) was the son of Christopher Columbus. The LIFE OF HIS FATHER is The Life of the Admiral Christopher Columbus by his son Ferdinand, trans.

Benjamin Keen, 2d ed. (1992). ELOGIO D'AMERIGO VESPUCCI . . . DI PIETRO ALLEGRINI: "Eulogy of Amerigo Vespucci, which won the prize of the noble Etruscan Academy of Cortona on 15 October 1788 with a dissertation in support of this renowned navigator by Father Stanislao Canovai of the Pie Scuole [the University of Florence], professor of physics and mathematics. Florence, 1788. Pietro Allegrini Printing Press."

# I

## Extract from Theodor de Bry's Preface to *Americae Pars Quinta,* with a Drawing Depicting Christopher Columbus

### PRÆFATIO

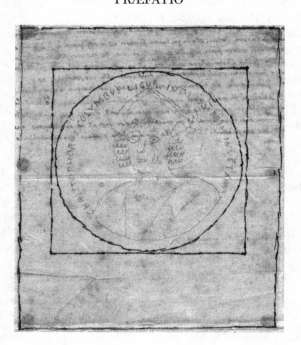

n superiore libro historiae Americanae (benevole lector) in qua res novi orbis nuper inventi mirandae atq; insignes non tantum scripto recitantur sed et iconibus exprimuntur et repraesentantur, dictum est eas terras Christophori Columbi Genuensis industria mirabiliter ac praeter spem eorum omnium quos ea de re compellarat, repertas fuisse. Quoniam autem ille Columbus vir erat cordatus magnique ingenii et animi, Rex et Regina Castiliae antequam ab illis discederet, ejus effigiem ab eximio aliquo pictore ad vivum exprimi jusserunt, ut si ab illa expeditione non rediret aliquod ejus monumentum apud se haberent. hujus autem effigiei exemplar nuper post absolutum quartum librum superiorem, à quodam amico meo qui illud ab ipso pictore acceperat magno cum gaudio nactus sum, cujus te quoque participem facere volui, atque in hunc finem eam effigiem à filio meo exigua forma quam fieri potuit perfectissimé in aes incidi curavi, quam et tibi hoc libro offero atque exhibeo. et revera digna est viri virtus cujus imago bonorum oculis obversetur. fuit enim ille vir probus, comis, magnanimus, ac moribus honestis, pacis justitiaeque amantissimus. quòd si Hispani ejus aemuli consilium ipsius secuti fuissent, tot tantaque mala in novo illo orbe non accidissent, neque ipsi tanta rabie non solùm in sua mancipia et in miseros Indos sed et in semetipsos mutuis caedibus saeviissent. E^tc [the residue of the preface has no relation to the print.]

EDITORS' TRANSLATION

## PREFACE

n the previous book of American history (kind reader) in which the wondrous, extraordinary facts of the recently discovered New World are not only recounted in writing but also reproduced and depicted with images, it was said that those lands had been found through the industry of Christopher Columbus of Genoa, amazingly and against the expectations of all those to whom he had appealed concerning that project. Since, however, Columbus was a prudent man and endowed with a great intellect and spirit, the king and queen of Castile ordered a lifelike portrait of him to be executed by an outstanding painter before he took his leave of them, so that, if he did not return from that expedition, they would have some memorial of him at their court. Shortly after completing the fourth book, moreover, I very happily obtained a copy of this portrait from a certain friend of mine who had received it from the painter himself, a copy which I wanted to share with you as well. To that end, I had this portrait etched in bronze in miniature by my son as perfectly as possible, and in this book I offer and display it also to you. Worthy indeed is the virtue of a man whose image is shown to the eyes of the good. For he was an upright man, kind, magnanimous, with a respectable character, and very devoted to peace and justice. If the Spaniards emulating him had followed his advice, so many and such great evils would not have happened in that New World, nor would they have brutalized with such great fury not only their own slaves and the wretched Indians, but also themselves by mutual slaughter. E^tc [the residue of the preface has no relation to the print.]

MS (LNT: George H. and Katherine M. Davis Collection); entirely in TJ's hand; undated; with following enclosure subjoined; brackets in original. Translation by Dr. John F. Miller. The Editors express their appreciation to the Louisiana Research Collection, Tulane University Libraries, for permission to use the image from this text reproduced above.

TJ copied the above from Theodor de Bry, *Americae Pars Quinta*, the fifth part (Sowerby, no. 3977) of *The Great or American Voyages, Parts I to XI, in Latin* (Frankfort and Oppenheim, 1590–1619). The first page is reproduced elsewhere in this volume.

# II

## Notes on the Likeness of Christopher Columbus

Note by Th:J.

The 1st vol. of Debry was printed in 1590. & the 2d to which the preface is here given, was printed in 1595. it was between these two dates then that the copy [exemplar] of the portrait which had been taken by order of the king & Queen, and of which his son made the miniature here exhibited, was given by his friend who recieved it from the painter himself [i.e. the copyist.] and the copy must have been taken between 1492. and 1590. i.e. in the 16th century. it was probably then a different copy from that in possession of the D. of Berwick, supposed to have been taken in the 17th century, altho' it might be from the same original.

MS (LNT: George H. and Katherine M. Davis Collection); entirely in TJ's hand; undated; subjoined to preceding enclosure; brackets in original.

# To Louis H. Girardin

Th:J. to mr Girardin.                                    Monticello Aug. 28. 14.

I send you the 1st vol. of Tucker's Blackstone & the 1st & 2d of Botta. I think I have nothing on the Revolutionary finances which answers your view except the Article 'Etats Unis' of the Encyclopedie, which article I have seperately bound with some pamphlets on the Finances of France & England, and now send you. De Meunier had prepared a poor article on that head, and sent it to me for correction before it was printed. I found it necessary to write the Article entire. he retained his own, but added mine. you will readily distinguish the ideas of a stranger from those of one who had had a part in the transactions. I wrote it when every thing was fresh in my mind, and when I was fully master of the subject. if this does not answer your view, you had better come & examine for yourself, when you can recieve also the sequel of my letters. we shall be happy to see you at all times.

Of the stories flying abroad of the burning of Washington, I believe nothing. they may be true, but are not the more likely for being reported. when Washington is in danger, we shall see mrs Madison and mrs Monroe, like the doves from the ark, first messengers of the news. I salute you with esteem and respect.

P.S. since writing this I recieve information undoubted that Washington is burnt.

RC (PPAmP: Thomas Jefferson Papers); dateline above postscript; addressed: "M^r Girardin Glenmore."

TJ here sent St. George TUCKER's *Blackstone's Commentaries*, 5 vols. (Philadelphia, 1803; Sowerby, no. 1807), vol. 1, and Carlo Botta's *Storia della guerra dell' Independenza degli Stati Uniti d'America*, 4 vols. (Paris, 1809; Sowerby, no. 509), vols. 1–2. TJ made significant contributions to Jean Nicolas Démeunier's ARTICLE on the United States for the section *Économie Politique et Diplomatique* in the *Encyclopédie Méthodique*. TJ had had the article BOUND with two other pamphlets under the general heading "Political tracts on the finances of France, Engl^d and the U.S. 89. 90. 4^to," and he enclosed that volume here (*PTJ*, 10:3–11; Sowerby, no. 2948–50). The DOVES are released from Noah's ARK in the Bible, Genesis 8.8–12.

A letter from TJ to Girardin, 3 Aug. 1814, not found, is recorded in SJL, as is a missing letter from Girardin to TJ of 28 Aug. 1814, recorded as received from Glenmore that day.

# From John Barnes

MY DEAR SIR,  George [T]own Monday 29^h Aug^t 1814

Your fav^r 20^th recd last Evening—I am really concerned to learn the sacrifice made to advance the $380—thro M^r Gibson—who without remitting me—either in Bank Notes—or, depositing that Amo^t in the Bank of Richmond and place^g it to my Credit, in the Bank of Col^a either of which, he might, and Ought to have done, he Requested of me—to draw—on him—Or—give him instructions to forward the Amo^t in Bank Notes,—

I have Answered him by this days Mail—and Begged leave to decline[1]—interfering with your Orders—to him, (at this particular Crisis of Public Affairs)[2] and that I will not be responsible for any—but my own Acts: and however desirable[3] the sum, would've been in Aid of the $2,500, payable the 25^h fortunately—in the last extremity, I had the Credit with both the Bank I have, Concerns w^th (though not the Cash) to effect the payment Notwithstanding—the confused state of the City, and this Town—whose situation—owing to the perverse[4] and most Unfortunate Occurances however distressing—will yet I hope & trust, be preserved from further distruction & disgrace— our remaining troops—and Others expected are pressing forward, and every preparation that our feeble situation will admit of—is in Activity to oppose the Enemys further depredations—against our desolated City &c^a—our good President—is Out—inimating and incouraging the troops & Citizens—not to dispair—and be the Event whatever it may even a total defeat—however distressing—will at least preserve—the Remnant of our lofted Honor—by the most unaccountable retreat from Bladensburg thro the City & Geo Town—

toward Tennlytown—instead of forming (which our troops in general expected and wished for) on the high grounds nearly opposit the Navy Yard. this fatal Error—<u>must</u>, however unavailing—be Accounted for—what has—or will be done, at Alexandria the confused Acco<sup>ts</sup> are so Various—nothing can be depended upon—but should the Enemy be amused but for a few days.—I trust they may judge it proper—after availing themselves of the resources they stand in need off, Flour—Tobacco &c<sup>a</sup> they may probably—drop down the Potomac—and proceed to Attack some more favorable point of Annoyance—My public papers I removed a week since—for my Private effects (excepting a few necessaries—) remain<sup>d</sup> with me <u>Alone</u> M<sup>rs</sup> Ratcliffe and servants removed—I was at Ease on that Score—Contented to Risque—what it was not in my Power to preserve—leaving the unavoidable Result—to time and Chance—and still in hopes the issue—may be more favorable than our fears induce us—to expect

Beleive me Dear Sir, most truly and Respectfully Your Obed<sup>t</sup> servant                                          JOHN BARNES,

PS. M<sup>rs</sup> R. & serv<sup>ts</sup> returned—to wait the fatal Alarm

RC (ViU: TJP-ER); torn; at foot of text: "Thomas Jefferson Esq<sup>r</sup> Monticello"; endorsed by TJ as received 2 Sept. 1814 and so recorded in SJL.

<sup>1</sup> Manuscript: "declinee."
<sup>2</sup> Omitted closing parenthesis editorially supplied.
<sup>3</sup> Manuscript: "desiable."
<sup>4</sup> Manuscript: "preverse."

# From Daniel F. Carr

D<sup>R</sup> SIR                                          Charlottesville 29<sup>h</sup> Au<sup>t</sup> 14

Necessity compels me to call on you, for money at this time I am here on my way to Richmond with out any, and there is none to be had in town. If you can furnish me with any it will be particularly acceptable. You can send it by the boy and I will leave a Rec<sup>t</sup> for the same with any person you'll name

Y<sup>rs</sup> Resptl.                                          DAN<sup>L</sup> F. CARR

RC (ViU: TJP-CC); dateline beneath signature; addressed: "Thomas Jefferson Eq<sup>r</sup> Monticello"; endorsed by TJ as received 29 Aug. 1814 and so recorded in SJL; with TJ's incorrectly dated notation at foot of text: "Dec. [Aug.] 29. 14. gave ord. on Gibson & Jeff. for 50.D. on acc<sup>t</sup>."

Daniel Ferrell Carr (1786–1847), the son of Garland Carr and brother of Frank Carr, succeeded his father at Bentivar, the family estate in Albemarle County. Carr later owned a house in Charlottesville designed and constructed about 1830 by one of TJ's master builders. Carr was an early member of the Agricultural Society of Albemarle, served as a director, secretary, and treasurer of the Rivanna Company, and was a subscriber for Central College (*VMHB* 3 [1895]: 208–10; True, "Agricultural Society," 26; Betts, *Farm Book*, 515; Woods, *Albemarle*, 161, 403; Lay, *Architecture*, 105, 106; ViU: Rivanna Navigation Company, Directors' Minutes, 1828–51; Cabell, *University of Virginia*, 404; Albemarle Co. Will Book, 18:123–4).

TJ noted in his financial records under 1 and 7 Aug. 1814 that after a $50 payment on the earlier date, he owed Carr MONEY totaling $192, plus interest, for sixty-four barrels of corn. TJ satisfied this obligation with the $50 payment noted above and a further payment of $109.56 on 8 Jan. 1815. Later, on 15 Jan. 1817 TJ indicated that he had "Delivered 555.D. to E. Bacon to pay D. F. Carr for 111. barrels of corn" (*MB*, 2:1301, 1302, 1306, 1330; TJ to Carr, 29 Aug. 1814).

# To Daniel F. Carr

SIR                                                Monticello Aug. 29. 14.

Having no cash in hand, I do the best in my power by sending you an order on Richmond for 50. Dollars which will be paid on sight. I am in hopes it may enable you to procure in Charlottesville enough for the road if that is wanting.

I wish you health and success.             TH: JEFFERSON

PoC (ViU: TJP-CC); at foot of text: "Mʳ Danˡ F. Carr"; endorsed by TJ. Enclosure not found.

# To Samuel Carr

DEAR SIR                                       Monticello Aug. 29. 14.

Roland Goodman who has lived with me as a carpenter since January last, informs me he is a member of your company, now called into service, and desires me to inform you of the state of his health. in May last he broke a blood vessel, in the lungs as was supposed, and voided a vast quantity of blood from it by the mouth, insomuch that he was long in imminent danger of dying, & was under the care of Dʳ Carr. after about a month (I believe) he got so that he could work a little, but had several relapses afterwards, was taken with a cough, and is (as I verily believe, altho I have avoided saying so to him) in a consumption. his hectic cough, paleness, emaciated body, & reduced strength will make it visible to you. he works on light things, but cannot do half work in that way, nor any thing at all requiring strength—and I doubt if he could ride to Richmond. I am satisfied if he is exposed to get wet & should catch cold it will fix the disease of his lungs & end in his certain death. I should be the last man to propose excusing a single person from service at this moment if he were able to perform it. every member of my own family has gone with my entire approbation. but this man is really unable and will only add one to your sicklist from the start, & to that of the dead in a very short time. health & victory attend you.     TH: JEFFERSON

PoC (ViU: TJP-CC); on verso of reused address cover to TJ; at foot of text: "Capt Sam¹ Carr"; endorsed by TJ.

On 23 Aug. 1813 TJ recorded his agreement that Rolin GOODMAN would "serve me as a Carpenter for a year, for which I give him 250.D. and 20. Barrels of corn for which he is to allow me 3.D. a barrel: in other words I give him 190.D. and 20. barr. corn. He finds himself all other provisions." Goodman remained in TJ's service until 1817 (*MB*, esp. 2:1292, 1339; Conveyance of Slave to Jeremiah A. Goodman, 30 Nov. 1815).

# To William Caruthers

SIR                                    Monticello Aug. 29. [1814]
Your favor of the 17ᵗʰ is duly recieved. there was a short time, about that of my leaving Washington, when to square my accounts there, I would have been willing to have parted with the Natural bridge and some other unproductive property; and that merely for the value of the soil as land, without attention to it's value either as a site for machinery, or as a curiosity, certainly the greatest in America elements of value which might fairly have entered into the consideration of price. but the difficulty of that moment having been surmounted, and the object of selling it otherwise answered, all thought of parting with it was abandoned, and so continues, and I should not think I fulfilled a duty to the public in permitting such an object to be obstructed by any constructions upon it. Accept the assurance of my great respect & esteem.     TH: JEFFERSON

PoC (DLC: TJ Papers, 202:35924); partially dated, but endorsed by TJ with full date of composition and similarly recorded in SJL; on verso of reused address cover to TJ; at foot of text: "Mʳ Caruthers."

# To George Hargraves

SIR                                    Monticello Aug. 29. 14.
Your favor of Aug. 4. came safe to hand, covering the description of a torpedo. I should readily have forwarded it to the government had it been within their plan to try the experiments which these machines require. but I understand that so many of these flowed in upon

them as to oblige them to decline attention to them; and to leave it to individuals to put them in practice, offering a great reward for every vessel destroyed, the value of the vessel I believe. I therefore return the paper to you. I doubt moreover whether the description is such as that a machine could be made from it. from a circumstance mentioned in your letter I presume the paper is of mr Bushnell who sent me, while in Europe, a description of his Turtle, which I had inserted in the Philosophical transactions, and is one of the most ingenious devices which has been yet proposed in this way.

Accept the assurance of my respect      TH: JEFFERSON

PoC (DLC); on verso of reused address cover of missing letter from Alexander Garrett to TJ, 21 Aug. 1814; at foot of text: "M$^r$ George Hargrave"; endorsed by TJ. Enclosure not found.

TJ sent David Bushnell's DESCRIP-TION OF HIS TURTLE to the American Philosophical Society, which reported it "worthy of publication" on 22 June 1798 (APS, Minutes [MS in PPAmP]) and published it in APS, *Transactions* 4 (1799): 303–12.

# From James W. Wallace

D$^R$ SIR                                    Fauq$^r$ Aug. 29. 14

I am pleased that the fish-Saw merits a place in your Hall. I hope soon to send you a pair of Swans, which, if not acceptable to you, I hope you will with my best wishes send to M$^{rs}$ Bankhead. I am anxious to get to Charlottsville but such is at present the state of private as well as public concerns that I can't say exactly when I shall see you, for I expect an immediate call for all the Militia en masse.

Being sent from the field of Battle, and hearing on the road every thing but the truth, and supposing you will be filled with false reports, I will give you such a statement as my situation on the Battle ground allows me.

About 10 oclock on Wednesday y$^e$ 24 Inst. the Army on Capitol Hill moved on towards Bladensburgh. I followed the Army expecting to see, what I have always anxiously[1] wished, an engagement by land, having seen one at sea. hearing the Enemy was in sight, I pushed on, when I arrived near Bladensburgh, our army stationed there, was drawn up in line of Battle on a commanding Eminence on the left, composed of, as I understood 2,500 Baltimore troops,[2] and 3,000 which had been stationed at Bladensburgh for some days, the Baltimore troops had arrived the night before the Action. Near the Centre of the line were two heavy cannons, on the left of the line the Cavalry, 150 regular and 94 militia. below the line, 400 yds was a breast work on which was placed four six pounders, short guns—and about 120 rifle men. the breast work, about 350 yds from Bladensburgh.

On the right hand hill, were placed two lines, the one 150 yards above the other—on the top of the hill were two pieces of Artillery (one brass) six pounders. between these two hills runs the main road leading to Bladensburgh. in, and near this road, were placed our cannons, in different situations.

The Enemy approached the Town, marching up the Eastern branch and formed on the side of a very large hill back of the Town. Soon as the first battalion formed, it ran up the hill & through the Town to commence the action. I feared the worst, I hoped the best. I am incapable of expressing my feelings, fearing what I did Soon[3] see, might come to pass. Now a Six pounder from the breast work spoke, a huzza ran through the lower line on the right hand hill. the other cannons on the breast work soon commenced a brisk fire and were answered by rockets from the Town. whilst this scene was going on, the Enemies Cavalry (about 40) charged the cannon on the back of the breast work. the riflemen flew, the artillery men soon followed. the cannon from the centre roared; the cavalry (ours)[4] at this moment were in quick motion going from the Enemy. the breast work is in an orchard, which prevented my seeing what passed. but sir, this settles the account of the breast work. the Enemies cannon (small) was now firing, when a heavy platoon firing commenced and ran from right to left of the line, in full blaze, smoke and roar, now the fire was general, and awfully tremendous, both from the musketry and cannon. a sight when taken all together, except a fine woman, was the most magnificant I have ever seen. all the sights I have ever seen are ignes fatua to this. the troops to the right of the line broke, as they were again coming up, others broke which carried them off again. they now continually broke, untill the Baltimore Uniform companies stood alone, who not being able to stand longer,[5] also ran off, having driven off, the left hand hill troops, composing the main body, they fell on the troops on the right hand hill (when I say right and left hand hill, I mean as the road leads to Bladensburg from the City) where a spirited fire commenced with the lower line (there being two lines 150 yds apart) soon a huzza rang through the line—a cry they run; and an advance on the Enemy, this I suppose arose from the lively play of the Artillery; but poor fellows they soon had to run like the rest helter Skelter, pell-mell—the second line now took up the fire, but soon followed suit, and away they went. the Artillery now was silent. there sir ended the contest for the metropolis of the U.S.A. a contest, which began & ended in, (I think) thirty minutes. all I have written I saw. fool that I am, to expose myself unarmed to such showers of Bullits to gratify curiosity. for there were not 200 men left on the field & they running when capt Jackson of the Prince George militia & myself came off in Showers of bullits. the Enemy fired so high, that I would not have given a worm eaten Quinque open for choice whether to be shot at or not, untill the last moments when the bullits flew from the ground (as the dust showed) to many feet over my head. I am made of strange materials, I really suffer more by sympathy for others, than I suffer for myself, I suffered more seeing Col Randolph walk on the top of your house, in half a second, than I suffered in the thick of the bullets, indeed I neither feared or cared. I am now clearly of opinion that I could make a Soldier[6] the Reports from the city are Numerous and contradictory. I expect it may be depended on that they have left the City, reports say[7] for Baltimore, for Harpers ferry, for Marlborou, the latter is I believe[8] true—the same report says Winders Army is near Baltimore—tis believed, the President is in the City. he is said to look very calmly over the ruins. the better to be depended reports say Armstrong is missing. if he gets to the City again popular fury will endanger him indeed If the President don't dismiss him, he will incur additional censure—Armstrong is suspected generally.

the Navy yard was burnt by order of our Government—

Tis said we lost 70—Killed. this I do not believe[9]—the Enemy 300—tis impossible.

Camp, & other statements of our numbers

| | |
|---|---|
| Winders Army | 2,700 |
| Bladdensburg Army | 3,000 |
| Baltimore troops | 2,500 |
| Flotilla men | 0,700 |
| Annapolis Regiment | 0,800. |

Amongst these were 150 regular cavalry & 280 Infantry, the Infantry not in battle. Sad arrangements, sad doings indeed, treachery I think, cowardice I saw, the Maryland Militia won't fight. there was not one Virginia Soldier in the Battle, unless the fairfax cavalry, which I do not think were there—the fleet is off alexandria carrying away the flour and Tobacco. troops are voluntarily going on, in, small numbers, but the Governor as yet has called out no more—I fear sir, I tire you, and my Eyes being much injured by a Rocket I conclude with best wishes to Mrs & Mr[10] Bankhead and the Montichello family—God bless you sir                   JAMES W. WALLACE

NB 30ᵗʰ

> 7 oclock A.M. a gentleman has just arrived who confirms, that the President is in the City & Enemy on their way to Marlboro—that the fleet is off Alexandria loading with Tobacco and Flour                                    J W WALLACE

RC (DLC); addressed: "Thomas Jefferson Monticello"; endorsed by TJ as received 9 Sept. 1814 and so recorded in SJL.

The Battle of Bladensburg was fought in very hot weather on 24 Aug. 1814 in the vicinity of the Anacostia River, an EASTERN BRANCH of the Potomac River that passes Lowndes Hill BACK OF THE TOWN. The inglorious American defeat there led to the evacuation of Washington and the burning of its public buildings by British forces later that day (a contemporary image of this event is reproduced elsewhere in this volume). As one result of this catastrophe, John ARMSTRONG resigned as secretary of war on 4 Sept., and President James Madison appointed

James Monroe as his successor on 26 Sept. 1814 (Malcomson, *Historical Dictionary*, 11–2, 41–2; *ANB*; *JEP*, 2:530 [26, 27 Sept. 1814]). A FAIRFAX County militia company did participate in the Battle of Bladensburg (Butler, *Virginia Militia*, 80–1).

[1] Manuscript: "anxously."
[2] Manuscript: "trops."
[3] Word interlined.
[4] Word interlined.
[5] Word interlined.
[6] Preceding five words interlined in place of "I am truly a firm man."
[7] Reworked from "one report says."
[8] Manuscript: "belive."
[9] Manuscript: "belive."
[10] Preceding two words interlined.

# To Charles Yancey

SIR                                         Monticello Aug. 29. 14.

I thank you for your letter of the 22ᵈ and the information it contained. your proposal of continuing to favor me with the occurrences, now become doubly interesting, cannot but be acceptable; while I fear it would not be in my power to offer any thing interesting in exchange for your favors. here we believe ourselves free from danger, and all our young men therefore are thronging to the standard of their country. the silver greys who remain, will of course have to keep their eye on any danger which might arise within their houshold, of which however there is not the least apprehension.[1] My son in law & grandson are already set out for the field, and my grand-son in law, mr Bankhead, is now setting out, and will be the bearer of this. if I were able either to walk or ride I would join them. mr Bankhead goes as a volunteer, without any commission. if you can befriend him with any birth better than that of the ranks it would be thankfully acknoleged. you know him personally I believe, and therefore I need add nothing more than the assurances of my great esteem & respect and wishes for your health and success        TH: JEFFERSON

PoC (DLC); at foot of text: "Col°
Yancey"; endorsed by TJ.

TJ's SON IN LAW was Thomas Mann
Randolph and his GRANDSON was
Thomas Jefferson Randolph.

[1] TJ here deleted "Accept the as."

# To Charles Yancey

SIR                                      Monticello Aug. 29. 14.
An express of the name of Roddie, to whom Cap[t] Samuel Carr furnished a horse, promised to leave him at your house. in the mean time
Cap[t] Carr being suddenly called on with his troop, I have furnished
him with a horse, and he has given me the inclosed order to recieve
his, for which the bearer now waits on you with the assurances of my
respects.
                                         TH: JEFFERSON

PoC (DLC); on verso of reused address cover to TJ; at foot of text: "M[r] Yancey";
endorsed by TJ. Enclosure not found.

# To John Minor, including an earlier
# letter to Bernard Moore

DEAR SIR                                 Monticello Aug. 30. 14.
I have at length found the paper of which you requested a copy. it
was written near 50. years ago for the use of a young friend whose
course of reading was confided to me; and it formed a basis for the
studies of others subsequently placed under my direction, but curtailed for each in proportion to his previous acquirements and future
views. I shall give it to you without change, except as to the books
recommended to be read; later publications enabling me in some of
the departments of science to substitute better, for the less perfect
publications which we then possessed. in this the modern student has
great advantage. I proceed to the copy.

'TH: JEFFERSON TO BERNARD MOORE.                    [ca. 1773?]
Before you enter on the study of the law a sufficient ground-work
must be laid. for this purpose an acquaintance with the Latin and
French languages is absolutely necessary. the former you have; the
latter must now be acquired. Mathematics and Natural philosophy
are so useful in the most familiar occurrences of life, and are so peculiarly engaging & delightful as would induce every person to wish an
acquaintance with them. besides this, the faculties of the mind, like

the members of the body, are strengthened & improved by exercise. Mathematical reasonings & deductions are therefore a fine preparation for investigating the abstruse speculations of the law. in these and the analogous branches of science the following elementary books are recommended.

Mathematics. Bezout, Cours de Mathematiques. the best for a student ever published.

Montucla or Bossu's histoire des Mathematiques.

Astronomy. Ferguson, and Le Monnier, or de la Lande.

[Geography. Pinkerton.][1]

Nat. Philosophy. Joyce's Scientific dialogues. Martin's Philosophia Britannica.

Mussenbroek's Cours de Physique.

This foundation being laid, you may enter regularly on the study of the Law, taking with it such of it's kindred sciences as will contribute to eminence in it's attainment. the principal of these are Physics, Ethics, Religion, Natural law, Belles lettres, Criticism, Rhetoric and Oratory. the carrying on several studies at a time is attended with advantage. variety relieves the mind, as well as the eye, palled with too long attention to a single object. but, with both, transitions from one object to another may be so frequent and transitory[2] as to leave no impression. the mean is therefore to be steered, and a competent space of time allotted to each branch of study. again, a great inequality is observable in the vigor of the mind at different periods of the day. it's powers at these periods should therefore be attended to in marshalling the business of the day. for these reasons I should recommend the following distribution of your time.

Till **VIII**. aclock in the morning employ yourself in Physical studies, Ethics, Religion, natural and sectarian, and Natural law, reading the following books.

Agriculture. Dickson's husbandry of the antients. Tull's horse-hoeing husbandry.

    L<sup>d</sup> Kaim's Gentleman farmer. Young's Rural economy.

    Hale's body of husbandry. De-Serres Theatre d'Agriculture.

Chemistry. Lavoisier. Conversations in Chemistry.

Anatomy. John and James Bell's Anatomy.

Zoology. Abregé du Systeme de Linnée par Gilibert.

    Manuel d'histoire Naturel par Blumenbach.

    Buffon, including Montbeillard & La Cepede.

    Wilson's American Ornithology.

Botany. Barton's elements of Botany. Turton's Linnaeus. Persoon Synopsis plantarum.

Ethics. & Nat$^l$ Religion. Locke's Essay. Locke's Conduct of the mind
    in the search after truth.
        Stewart's Philosophy of the human mind. Enfield's history
          of Philosophy.
        Condorcet, Progrès de l'esprit humain.
        Cicero de officiis. Tusculana. de senectute. somnium Scipi-
          onis. Senecae Philosophica.
        Hutchinson's Introduction to moral Philosophy. L$^d$ Kaim's
          Natural religion.
        Traité elementaire de Morale et Bonheur. La Sagesse de
          Charron.
Religion, sectarian. Bible. New Testament. Commentaries on them
    by Middleton in his works, and by Priestley in his Corrup-
    tions of Christianity, & Early opinions of Christ.
        Volney's Ruins. the Sermons of Sterne, Massillon &
          Bourdaloue.
Natural law. Vattel Droit des Gens. Reyneval, Institutions du droit
    de la$^3$ Nature et des Gens.

From **VIII.** to **XII.** read Law. the general course of this reading
may be formed on the following grounds. L$^d$ Coke has given us the
first view of the whole body of law worthy now of being studied: for
so much of the admirable work of Bracton is now obsolete that the
student should turn to it occasionally only, when tracing the history
of particular portions of the law. Coke's Institutes are a perfect
Digest of the law as it stood in his day. after this, new laws were
added by the legislature, and new developements of the old laws by
the Judges, until they had become so voluminous as to require a new
Digest. this was ably executed by Matthew Bacon, altho' unfortunately under an Alphabetical, instead of Analytical arrangement of
matter. the same process of new laws & new decisions on the old
laws going on, called at length for the same operation again, and
produced the inimitable Commentaries of Blackstone.      In the
department of the Chancery, a similar progress has taken place. L$^d$
Kaims has given us the first digest of the principles of that branch of
our jurisprudence, more valuable for the arrangement of matter, than
for it's exact conformity with the English decisions. the Reporters
from the early times of that branch to that of the same Matthew
Bacon are well digested, but alphabetically also in the Abridgment
of the Cases in Equity, the 2$^d$ volume of which is said to have been
done by him. this was followed by a number of able reporters, of
which Fonblanque has given us a summary digest by commentaries
on the text of the earlier work ascribed to Ballow, entitled 'a Treatise

of equity.' the course of reading recommended then in these two branches of Law is the following.

Common law. Coke's institutes.

> select cases from the subsequent reporters to the time of Matthew Bacon.
> Bacon's abridgment.
> select cases from the subsequent reporters to the present day.
> select tracts on Law, among which those of Baron Gilbert are all of the first merit.
> the Virginia laws. Reports on them.

Chancery. L^d Kaim's Principles of Equity. 3^d edition.

> select cases from the Chancery reporters to the time of Matthew Bacon.
> The Abridgment of Cases in Equity.
> select cases from the subsequent reporters to the present day.
> Fonblanque's Treatise of Equity.
> Blackstone's Commentaries (Tucker's edition) as the last perfect Digest of both branches of law.

In reading the Reporters, enter in a Common-place book every case of value, condensed into the narrowest compass possible which will admit of presenting distinctly the principles of the case. this operation is doubly useful, inasmuch as it obliges the student to seek out the pith of the case, and habituates him to a condensation of thought, and to an acquisition of the most valuable of all talents, that of never using two words where one will do. it fixes the case too more indelibly in the mind.

From **XII.** to **I.** read Politics.

Politics general. Locke on government. Sidney on Government.

> Priestley's First principles of Government. Review of Montesquieu's Spirit of laws. Anon.
> De Lolme sur la constitution d'Angleterre. DeBurgh's Political disquisitions.
> Hatsell's Precedents of the H. of Commons. select Parliam^y debates of England & Ireland.
> Chipman's Sketches of the principles of government. The Federalist.

Political Economy. Say's Economie Politique. Malthus on the principles of population.

> Tracy's work on Political Economy. <u>now</u> about to be printed. (1814.)

In the **Afternoon.** read History.

History. Antient. the Greek and Latin originals.

> select histories from the Universal history. Gibbon's decline of the Rom. empire.

> Histoire Ancienne de Millot.

Modern. Histoire moderne de Millot. Russel's History of Modern Europe.

> Robertson's Charles V.

English. the original historians. to wit. the Hist. of E. II. by E. F.—Habington's E. IV. More's R. III. L^d Bacon's H. VII. L^d Herbert's H. VIII. Goodwin's H. VIII. E. VI. Mary. Cambden's Eliz. & James. Ludlow. M^cCaulay. Fox. Belsham.

> Baxter's History of England. (Hume republicanised & abridged.) Robertson's Hist. of Scotland.

American. Robertson's History of America.

> Gordon's History of the independance of the US. Ramsay's Hist. of the Amer. revolution.

> Burke's Hist. of Virginia. Continuation of d° by Jones & Girardin. nearly ready for the press.

From **Dark** to **Bed-time.** Belles letters. Criticism. Rhetoric. Oratory. to wit.

Belles letters. read the best of the Poets, epic, didactic, dramatic, pastoral, lyric E^tc but among these Shakespear must be singled out by one who wishes to learn the full powers of the English language. of him we must advise, as Horace did of the Grecian models, 'vos exemplaria Graeca Nocturnâ versate manu, versate diurnâ.'

Criticism. L^d Kaim's Elements of criticism. Tooke's Diversions of Purley.

> of Bibliographical criticism the Edinbg Review furnishes the finest models extant.

Rhetoric. Blair's lectures on Rhetoric.

> Sheridan on Elocution. Mason on Poetic and Prosaic numbers.

Oratory. this portion of time (borrowing some of the afternoon when the days are long and the nights short) is to be applied also to acquiring the art of writing & speaking correctly by the following exercises. Criticize the style of any books whatever, committing your criticisms to writing.—translate into the different styles, to wit, the elevated, the midling, and the familiar. Orators and Poets will furnish subjects of the first, historians of the second, & epistolary and Comic writers of the third.—undertake, at first, short compositions, as themes, letters E$^t$c paying great attention to the correctness and elegance of your language.—read the Orations of Demosthenes & Cicero. analyse these orations, and examine the correctness of the disposition, language, figures, states of the cases, arguments E$^t$c.—read good samples also of English eloquence. some of these may be found in Small's American speaker, and some in Carey's Criminal Recorder, in which last the defence of Eugene Arum is distinguishable as a model of logic, condensation of matter, & classical purity of style.—exercise yourself afterwards in preparing orations on feigned cases. in this observe rigorously the disposition of Blair into Introduction, Narration E$^t$c. adapt your language & figures to the several parts of the oration, and suit your arguments to the audience before whom it is supposed to be spoken. this is your last and most important exercise. no trouble should therefore be spared. if you have any person in your neighborhood engaged in the same study, take each of you different sides of the same cause, and prepare pleadings according to the custom of the bar, where the pl. opens, the def. answers, and the pl. replies.—it would farther be of great service to pronounce your orations (having before you only short notes to assist the memory) in the presence of some person who may be considered as your judge.

Note, under each of the preceding heads, the books are to be read in the order in which they are named. these by no means constitute the whole of what might be usefully read in each of these branches of science. the mass of excellent works going more into detail is great indeed. but those here noted will enable the student to select for himself such others of detail as may suit his particular views and dispositions. they will give him a respectable, an useful, & satisfactory degree of knolege in these branches, and will themselves form a valuable and sufficient library for a lawyer, who is at the same time a lover of science.'

So far the paper; which I send you, not for it's merit, for it betrays sufficiently it's juvenile date; but because you have asked it. your own experience in the more modern practice of the law will enable you to give it more conformity with the present course; and I know you will recieve it kindly with all it's imperfections, as an evidence of my great respect for your wishes, and of the sentiments of esteem and friendship of which I tender you sincere assurances.

Th: Jefferson

RC (PU-L: Special Collections); with undated letter to Moore, written decades earlier but containing subsequent revisions, included in its body; at foot of first page: "General Minor." PoC (DLC).

No earlier version of the letter to BERNARD MOORE has been found. The original letter was likely written for the namesake son of TJ's friend Bernard Moore. The elder Moore (d. ca. 1775) lived at Chelsea plantation in King William County, married the daughter of Governor Alexander Spotswood, and sat regularly in the House of Burgesses. TJ served as a trustee for Moore in a 1771 property sale to benefit his creditors. After the death of Dabney Carr (1743–73), TJ's brother-in-law and a fellow attorney, TJ extended the younger Moore credit toward the purchase of books from Carr's estate. Moore represented King William County in the House of Delegates for four sessions, 1782 and 1786–88. The highly conjectural date assigned above to TJ's original letter to Moore is based on the assumption that it was written shortly before or after Moore's purchase of Carr's books (*Virginia Gazette* [Dixon & Hunter], 15 Apr. 1775; Morris L. Cohen, "Thomas Jefferson Recommends a Course of Law Study," *University of Pennsylvania Law Review* 119 [1971]: 823–32; Louise Pecquet du Bellet, *Some Prominent Virginia Families* [1907; repr. 1976], 2:703–7; Leonard, *General Assembly*; *PTJ*, 1:59–60, 64–5, 6:431, 11:623, 15:627, 639; *MB*, 1:62, 82, 206, 290).

HIST. OF E. II. BY E. F.: Elizabeth Cary, Viscountess Falkland, *The History of The Life, Reign, and Death of Edward II. King of England, and Lord of Ireland. With The Rise and Fall of his great Favourites, Gaveston and the Spencers* (London,

1680; Sowerby, no. 347; for authorship, see *ODNB*). HABINGTON'S E. IV.: William Habington, *The Historie of Edvvard the Fourth, King of England* (London, 1640; Sowerby, no. 349). MORE'S R. III.: Sir Thomas More, *The history of king Richard the thirde (unfinished) writen . . . about the yeare of our Lorde. 1513*, in *The workes of Sir Thomas More Knyght . . . wrytten by him in the Englysh tonge* (London, 1557; Sowerby, no. 350). BACON'S H. VII.: Francis Bacon, *The Historie of the Reigne of King Henry The Seventh . . . Whereunto is now added a very usefull and necessary Table* (London, 1641; Sowerby, no. 352). L^D HERBERT'S H. VIII.: Edward Herbert, *The Life and Reign of King Henry the Eighth* (London, 1683; Sowerby, no. 353). GOODWIN'S H. VIII. E. VI MARY: Francis Godwin, *Annales of England. Containing the Reignes of Henry the Eighth. Edward the Sixt. Queene Mary. Written in Latin . . . Thus Englished, corrected and inlarged with the Author's consent, by Morgan Godwyn* (London, 1630; Sowerby, no. 354). CAMBDEN'S ELIZ. & JAMES: William Camden published the first important biography of Elizabeth I, 1615–25, and he kept notes for a similar chronicle of James I that was published posthumously in 1691 (*ODNB*). TJ does not seem to have owned either work. VOS EXEMPLARIA GRAECA NOCTURNÂ VERSATE MANU, VERSATE DIURNÂ: "For yourselves, handle Greek models by night, handle them by day" (Horace, *Ars Poetica*, 268–9, in Fairclough, *Horace: Satires, Epistles and Ars Poetica*, 472–3).

[1] Preceding two words interlined in PoC and lacking in RC.
[2] Preceding two words interlined.
[3] Manuscript: "las."

# From Jeremiah Yancey
## (for Charles Yancey)

SIR                    Hopefull Mills Albemarle 30<sup>th</sup> Aug: 14.

The express of the name of Rody was here this morning, and said that he, promised cap<sup>t</sup> Samuel Carr, to leave his horse at this place, provided that he could get another here, he made all the exertions that was in his power, but could not succeed[1] consequently he rode cap<sup>t</sup> carrs horse, on to charlottesville, where he said he intended to leave him, I am with due respect yours &c.

JEREMIAH YANCEY JR
agent for
C YANCEY

RC (DLC); entirely in Jeremiah Yancey's hand; addressed: "Tho: Jefferson Esq<sup>r</sup> Monticello"; endorsed by TJ as a letter from Charles Yancey received 30 Aug. 1814 and so recorded in SJL.

[1] Manuscript: "secede," reworked from an illegible word.

# From Thomas Jefferson Randolph

MY DEAR GRANDFATHER             Richmond Aug 31<sup>th</sup> 1814

You are no doubt anxious to hear what we are doing and what are our expectations as it respects defence, and the arrival of the enemy. Our governor as pompous, perhaps, as patriotic, has taken the field, and is encamped at fairfaild, two miles from town, with M<sup>r</sup> Lee Mercer, H. Nelson, aid, and about 2500, men under the immediate command of Gen. Cocke. There are 2,000 at Camp Holly 10 miles below this under Gen. Porterfield and about 5 or 600 in town, local militia and volunteer corps; making an aggregate of about 5,000. Volunteers, are hourly arriving. They are to be organised, both horse and foot under command of my father as a legion to meet the enemy, where he lands, and fight him incessantly until he reaches the town, at the same time impeding his march by breaking up bridges and felling trees in the road. There is no confusion here, because the enemy is not at their doors, and not[1] from a confidence in the march, or activity in their preparation. they rest satisfied, as the enemy did not destroy private property at Washington, that they will not here, The federalists allways the least active in their preparation are as usual more violent and abusive upon every miscarriage. I have made yet, no disposition of myself I find all my young friends and acquaintances here and will be able to fix myself agreably, God forbid, that I should have been last to come forward in defence of my country, for which I shall always be proud to sacrifice my life

Your most devoted and affectionate grand son

TH: J. RANDOLPH

RC (MHi); endorsed by TJ as received 2 Sept. 1814 and so recorded in SJL. RC (MHi); address cover only; with PoC of TJ to Thomas Ritchie, 27 Sept. 1814, on verso; addressed: "Thomas Jefferson, Esquire Monticello Albemarle"; franked; postmarked Richmond, 31 Aug.

Virginia GOVERNOR James Barbour was accompanied by inspector general Charles Fenton MERCER and aides Benjamin W. Leigh (Lee), Hugh NELSON, and Philip N. Nicholas (Richmond *Enquirer*, 3 Sept. 1814; Butler, *Virginia Militia*, 21–2, 304).

[1] Word interlined.

# From Nicolas G. Dufief

MONSIEUR,                                   A Philad^e ce 1^er Septembre. 1814

Il m'a été impossible, Jusqu'à présent, de vous procurer l'ouvrage d'Evans. Je continuerai mes recherches. Vous avez du recevoir le 1^er & 2^d vol. de mon dictionnaire & l'histoire des <u>Shakers</u>

Plusieurs Personnes Sont venus me trouver, d'après vos lettres, pour me prier de leur compter les petites Sommes qui leur sont dues J'ai promis de les leur envoyer dès que M^r Gibson (a qui J'ai ecrit en reponse à une de Ses lettres dans laquelle il me demandait de quelle maniere il devoit envoyer l'argent) m'aura fait passer un <u>draft</u> Sur Philad^a ou des billets de Banque de cette ville ou de New York qu'il peut facilement Se procurer à Richmond, la Somme n'étant pas considérable

Agreez, Je vous prie, les assurances du profond respect avec lequel j'ai l'honneur d'étre

Votre très-humble Serviteur                          N. G. DUFIEF

EDITORS' TRANSLATION

SIR,                                           Philadelphia 1 September. 1814

I have been unable so far to obtain for you the work by Evanson. I will continue to look for it. You must have already received the first and second volumes of my dictionary and the history of the <u>Shakers</u>

Several people came to see me, after receiving your letters, to ask for the small sums due them. I have promised to pay them as soon as Mr. Gibson (to whom I wrote in response to a letter in which he asked me how he should send the money) provides me with a <u>draft</u> on Philadelphia or bank notes from this city or New York, which he can easily obtain in Richmond, the amount not being very large

Please accept the assurances of the profound respect with which I have the honor to be

Your very humble servant          N. G. Dufief

RC (DLC); endorsed by TJ as received 9 Sept. 1814 and so recorded in SJL. Translation by Dr. Genevieve Moene.

# From Edward Caffarena

Sir,        Genoa 5th 7ber 1814. American Consular Office

I avail myself of the favorable occasion per Mr Baker now here with family, to have the honor to address you, and to pray you, Sir to receive a few select seeds of choiced flowers and plants produced on this soil, I hope they may prove fruitful in yours, if So, it will afford me the highest gratification to remit you Annual samples.

Praying you Sir to excuse this liberty I have the honor to be with the utmost respect

Sir

Your Most Obedient and humble Servant.

         Edward Caffarena

Dupl (MHi); dateline beneath signature; at head of text: "Monticello Virginia To the Honorable Thomas Jefferson"; adjacent to salutation: "Duplicate"; endorsed by TJ as received 6 June 1816 and so recorded in SJL.

Edward Caffarena was appointed American vice-consul at Genoa in 1805 by Peter Kuhn, the American consul there. After Kuhn was banished from the city in 1807, Caffarena represented American interests until a replacement as consul was appointed in 1818 (Caffarena to James Madison, 7 Nov. 1807, 27 Jan. 1808, and Caffarena to James Monroe, 24 July 1816, 12 July 1817 [DNA: RG 59, CD, Genoa]; Caffarena to Madison, 27 July 1816, 12 July 1817, Dec. 1820 [DLC: Madison Papers]; *JEP*, 1:476, 3:138 [11 Dec. 1804, 18 Apr. 1818]).

# To Craven Peyton

Dear Sir        Monticello Sep. 6. 14.

I gave notice some time ago to mr Michie that I would take your deposition and that of mr Price at mr Watson's in Milton the day after tomorrow at ten aclock. I must ask the favor of your attendance there, and if you will be punctual to the hour you shall not be detained. Accept my friendly respects.        Th: Jefferson

Thursday the 8<sup>th</sup> of Sep. at 10. aclock in the morning was the hour appointed.

P.S. after writing the above I sat down to sketch the facts which were within your knoleg[e] and which I wished to perpetuate by your testimony. I am afraid it is not legible to you, but I send it that you may recall them to your memory before we meet, when you will be so good as to return me the paper, as it will guide me in taking your deposition. if you have not seen the deeds of Henderson & Michie therein ment<sup>d</sup> I will have them with me and shew them to you.

RC (Mrs. Charles W. Biggs, Lewisburg, W. Va., 1950); edge trimmed; adjacent to signature: "Craven Peyton esq." PoC (MHi); upper and lower left corners torn away; for second postscript TJ substituted a brief summary: "[...] [him] a sketch of the facts within his knolege to which I [...] him"; on reused address cover to TJ; endorsement by TJ torn.

The enclosed SKETCH was probably the Dft of the Deposition by Craven Peyton in *Jefferson v. Michie*, 20 Sept. 1814.

# To Thomas Jefferson Randolph

MY DEAR JEFFERSON                                          [Sep. 6. 14]

I thank you for your letter of Aug. 31. it was our first authentic information of what was passing at Richmond, and we are so flooded with lies that all is as blank paper to me which does not come thro' a known channel. you see therefore, how acceptable your Letters will be to me. I can give you nothing in exchange but the state of health of the family, which at present is all in perfect health. Anne left us yesterday, believing her affairs did not go on so well in her absence. we shall try to get her back again. we have not heard a tittle of mr Bankhead since he went away. our county is a desert. we meet no body now in the roads but grey heads of 60. or 70. who shew their age by their creeping along. mr Ogilvie left us this morning. he and mr [...] set out for the upper country indefinitely. it is uncertain whether we shall see him again. he proposes to embark from New York. I can tell you nothing of your affairs but that your fall sowing is going on, as may be seen from hence. ever feelingly & affectionately

yours                                                    TH: JEFFERSON

RC (facsimile in an unidentified dealer's catalogue, a blurred photocopy of which was supplied by Martin Doblmeier, Alexandria, 1997); undated, with supplied date parenthetically added to text in an unidentified hand; one word illegible; at foot of text: "Th: J. Randolph"; endorsed in an unidentified hand. Recorded in SJL as a letter of 6 Sept. 1814.

In SJL TJ recorded the receipt of two missing letters from Charles L. BANKHEAD, one of 28 Apr. 1814 received two days later from "Wilderness" and the other of 29 June inconsistently described as received 28 June 1814 from Carlton.

# To Peter Carr

DEAR SIR  Monticello Sep. 7. 14.

On the subject of the Academy or College proposed to be established in our neighborhood, I promised the trustees that I would prepare for them a plan, adapted in the first instance to our slender funds, but susceptible of being enlarged either by their own growth or by accession from other quarters. I have long entertained the hope that this our native state would take up the subject of education, and make an establishment, either with or without incorporation into that of William & Mary, where every branch of science, deemed useful at this day, and in our country, should be taught in it's highest degree. with this view I have lost no occasion of making myself acquainted with the organisation of the best seminaries in other countries, and with the opinions of the most enlightened individuals on the subject of the sciences worthy of a place in such an institution. in order to prepare what I had promised our trustees, I have lately revised these several plans with attention and I am struck with the diversity of arrangement observable in them, no two being alike. yet I have no doubt that these several arrangements have been the result of mature reflection, by wise and learned men, who, contemplating local[1] circumstances, have adapted them to the condition of the section of society for which they have been framed. I am strengthened in this conclusion by an examination of each separately, and a conviction that no one of them, if adopted without change, would be suited to the circumstances and pursuits of our country. the example they have set then is authority for us to select from their different institutions the materials which are good _for us_, and with them to erect a structure whose arrangement shall correspond with our own social condition, and shall admit of enlargement in proportion to the encoragements it may merit and recieve. as I may not be able to attend the meetings of the trustees, I will make you the Depository of my ideas on the subject, which may be corrected as you proceed by the better views of others, and adapted from time to time to the prospects which open on us, and which cannot now be specifically foreseen and provided for.

In the first place we must ascertain with precision the object of our institution, by taking a survey of the general field of science, and marking out the portion we mean to occupy at first, and the ultimate extension of our views beyond that, should we be enabled to render it in the end as comprehensive as we would wish.

It is highly interesting to our country, and it is the duty of it's func- I. Elementary tionaries to provide, that every citizen in it should recieve an educa- Schools. tion proportioned to the condition and pursuits of his life. the mass of our citizens may be divided into two classes, the laboring, & the learned. the laboring will need the first grade of education to qualify them for their pursuits and duties: the learned will need it as a foundation for further acquirements. a plan was formerly proposed to the legislature of this state for laying off every county into Hundreds or Wards of 5. or 6. miles square, within each of which should be a school for the education of the children of the ward, wherein they should recieve three years instruction gratis, in reading, writing, arithmetic as far as fractions, the roots and ratios, and Geography. the legislature, at one time, tried an ineffectual expedient for introducing this plan, which having failed it is hoped they will some day resume it in a more promising form.

At the discharge of the pupils from this elementary school, the two II. General classes separate: those destined for labor will engage in the business Schools. of agriculture, or enter into apprenticeships to such handicraft art as may be their choice: their companions destined to the pursuits of science will proceed to the College, which will consist of 1$^{st}$ General schools and 2$^{d}$ Professional schools. the General schools will constitute the second grade of education. The learned class may still be subdivided into two sections. 1. those who are destined for learned professions as a means of livelihood; and 2. the Wealthy who possessing independant fortunes may aspire to share in conducting the affairs of the nation, or to live with usefulness & respect in the private ranks of life. both of these sections will require instruction in all the higher branches of science, the wealthy to qualify them for either public or private life, the Professional section will need those branches especially which are the basis of their future profession, and a general knolege of the others as auxiliary to that, and necessary to their standing and associating with the scientific class. all the branches then of useful science ought to be taught in the General schools to a competent extent,[2] in the first instance. these sciences may be arranged into 3. departments, not rigorously scientific indeed but sufficiently so for our purpose. these are I. Language. II. Mathematics. III. Philosophy.

1. Language.    I. In the 1st department I would arrange as distinct sciences, 1. Languages and history, antient and modern. 2. Grammar. 3. Belles lettres. 4. Rhetoric and Oratory. 5. a school for the deaf, dumb and blind. history is here associated with languages not as a kindred[3] subject, but on a principle of economy, because both may be attained by the same course of reading, if books are selected with that view.

2. Mathematics.    II. in the department of Mathematics I should place distinctly 1. Mathematics pure. 2. Physico-mathematics. 3. Physics. 4. Chemistry. 5. Natural history, to wit, Mineralogy. 6. botany. and 7. Zoology. 8. anatomy. 9. the Theory of Medecine.

3. Philosophy.    III. in the Philosophical department I should distinguish 1. Ideology. 2. Ethics. 3. the Law of Nature & Nations. 4. Government. 5. Political economy.

but some of these terms being used by different writers in different degrees of extension, it is necessary to define exactly what I mean to comprehend within each of them.

I. 3. within the term of Belles lettres I include poetry & composition generally, and Criticism.

II. 1. I consider pure mathematics as the science of 1. Numbers. and 2. Measure in the abstract. that of numbers comprehending[4] Arithmetic, Algebra, & Fluxions; that of Measure, under the general appellation[5] of Geometry, comprehending Trigonometry plane and Spherical. Conic sections and Transcendental curves.

II. 2. Physico-Mathematics treat of Physical subjects by the aid of Mathematical calculation. these are Mechanics, Statics, hydrostatics, hydraulics, hydro-dynamics, navigation, astronomy, geography, optics, pneumatics, Acoustics.

II. 3. Physics, or Natural philosophy (not entering the limits of chemistry) treat of natural substances, their properties, mutual relations and action. they particularly examine the subjects of motion, attraction, magnetism, electricity, galvanism—light[6] meteorology with an Etc not easily enumerated.        these definitions and specifications render immaterial the question whether I use the generic terms in the exact degree of comprehension in which others use them. to be understood is all that is necessary to the present object.

---

III. Professional Schools.    At the close of this course the Students separate, the wealthy retiring with a sufficient stock of knolege to improve themselves to any degree to which their views may lead them, and the Professional section to the Professional[7] Schools constituting the IIId Grade of education, and teaching the particular sciences which the individuals of this section mean to pursue with more minuteness and detail than was within the scope of the General schools for the 2ᵈ grade of instruction. in these Professional⁸ schools each science is to be taught in the highest degree it has yet attained. they are to be in the

Iˢᵗ Department, the Fine arts, to wit, civil Architecture, Gardening Painting, Sculpture & the theory of Music.        in the

IIᵈ Department, Architecture military and naval, Projectiles, Rural economy (comprehending agriculture, horticulture, and veterinary) Technical philosophy, the Practice of Medecine, Materia medica Pharmacy,⁹ and Surgery.     in the

IIIᵈ Department, Theology & Ecclesiastical history, Law municipal and foreign.

To these Professional¹⁰ schools will come those who separated at the close of their 1ˢᵗ Elementary course, to wit,

the Lawyer to the school of Law.

the Ecclesiastic to that of Theology & Ecclesiastical history.

the Physician to those of the Practice of medecine, Materia Medica, Pharmacy and Surgery

the military man to that of military & naval architecture & Projectiles:

the Agricultor¹¹ to that of Rural economy:

the Gentleman, the Architect, Pleasure-gardener, Painter & Musician to the school of Fine arts:

and to that of Technical philosophy will come the mariner¹² carpenter, ship-wright, plough-wright, wheel wright, mill wright, pump-maker, clock-maker, machinist, optician, metallurgist, founder, cutler, druggist, brewer, vintner, distiller, dyer, painter, bleacher, soap-maker, tanner, powder maker, salt maker, glass maker, to learn as much as shall be necessary, to pursue their art understandingly, of the sciences of geometry, mechanics, statics, hydrostatics, hydraulics, hydrodynamics, navigation, astronomy, geography, optics, pneumatics, acoustics, physics, chemistry, natural history, botany mineralogy & pharmacy.

The school of Technical philosophy will differ essentially in it's functions from the other Professional¹³ schools. the others are instituted to ramify and dilate the particular sciences taught in the schools of the 2ᵈ grade on a general scale only: the Technical school is to abridge those which were taught there too much in extenso for the limited wants of the artificer or practical man. these artificers must be grouped together, according to the particular branch of science in which they need elementary and practical instruction, and a special lecture or lectures must be prepared for each groupe. and these lectures should be given in the evening, so as not to interrupt the labors of the day. this school particularly should be maintained wholly at the public expence, on the same principle with that of the ward schools. Through the whole of the Collegiate course, at the hours of recreation on certain days, all the Students should be taught the Manual exercise, Military evolutions and manoeuvres, should be under a standing organisation as a military corps, and with proper officers to train and command them.

---

A Tabular statement of this distribution of the sciences will place the system of instruction more distinctly in view.

I<sup>st</sup> or Elementary grade, in the Ward schools.

    reading, writing, arithmetic, geography.

II<sup>d</sup> or General[14] grade.

  1. Language & History, antient and modern.

  2. Mathematics. viz

      Mathematics pure.

      Physico-mathematics.

      Physics.

      Chemistry.

      Anatomy.

      Theory of Medecine.

      Zoology.

      Botany.

      Mineralogy.

  3. Philosophy. viz.

      Ideology

      Ethics.

      Law of nature & nations.

      Government.

      Political economy.

III<sup>d</sup> or Professional grade.

      Theology and Ecclesiastical history.

      Law, municipal & foreign.

      Practice of Medicine.

      Materia Medica and Pharmacy.

      Surgery.

      Architecture military & naval, and Projectiles.

      Technical Philosophy.

      Rural economy.

      Fine arts.

On this survey of the field of science, I recur to the question, what portion of it do we mark out for the occupation of our Institution?

with the 1ˢᵗ grade of education we shall have nothing to do. the sciences of the 2ᵈ grade are our first object, and to adapt them to our slender beginnings, we must separate them into groupes, comprehending many sciences each, and greatly more in the first instance than ought to be imposed on, or can be competently conducted by, a single professor permanently. they must be subdivided from time to time, as our means increase, until each professor shall have no more under his care than he can attend to with advantage to his pupils, & ease to himself. in the further advance of our resources the Professional[15] schools must be introduced, and Professorships established for them also. for the present we may groupe the sciences into Professorships as follows, subject however to be changed according to the qualifications of the persons we may be able to engage.

| Iˢᵗ professorship | IIᵈ professorship | IIIᵈ professorship. | IVᵗʰ professorship. |
|---|---|---|---|
| Lang. & Hist. Antᵗ & Mod. | Mathematics pure. | Chemistry | Philosophy, Ethical & Civil.[16] |
| Belles Lettres. | Physico-Mathematics | Zoology | |
| Rhetoric & Oratory. | Physics. | Botany | |
| | Anatomy Medecine. theory. | Mineralogy. | |

The organisation of the branch of the Institution which respects it's government, police, and economy depending on principles which have no affinity with those of it's course of instruction, may be the subject of separate & subsequent consideration.

with this tribute of duty to the board of trustees, accept the assurance of my great esteem & consideration          Tʜ: Jᴇꜰꜰᴇʀsᴏɴ

FC (DLC); entirely in TJ's hand; with wide margins characteristic of TJ's drafts and texts on which he invited the comments of others; at foot of first page: "Peter Carr, President of the board of trustees." PoC (ViU: TJP); lacking marginal headings. Enclosed in TJ to Thomas Cooper, 10 Sept. 1814, TJ to Joseph C. Cabell, 5 Jan. 1815, and Cabell to TJ, 26 Feb. 1816. Printed in Richmond *Enquirer*, 17 Feb. 1816, and *Sundry Documents on the subject of a System of Public Education, for the State of Virginia*, Published by the President and Directors of the Literary Fund, in obedience to a Resolution of the General Assembly (Richmond, 1817), 12–8.

As a member of the committee to revise Virginia's laws, in 1778 TJ drafted "A Bill for the More General Diffusion of Knowledge," in which he proposed that each county be divided into ʜᴜɴᴅʀᴇᴅs that would each host an elementary school (*PTJ*, 2:526–35, esp. 527). The ɪɴᴇꜰꜰᴇᴄᴛᴜᴀʟ ᴇxᴘᴇᴅɪᴇɴᴛ was "An Act to establish Public Schools" (*Acts of Assembly* [1796 sess.], 3–4).

[1] Word interlined in place of "the."
[2] Reworked from "in a College to a general extent."
[3] TJ here canceled "science."
[4] Word interlined in place of "consisting of."
[5] Word interlined in place of "term."
[6] Word interlined.
[7] Preceding two words interlined in place of "Special."
[8] Word interlined in place of "Special."
[9] Word interlined.
[10] Word interlined in place of "Special."
[11] Reworked from "Agriculturer."
[12] Word interlined.
[13] Word interlined in place of "Special."
[14] Word interlined in place of "Collegiate."
[15] Word interlined in place of "Special."
[16] Preceding three words not in *Enquirer* or *Sundry Documents*.

# From John Wayles Eppes

DEAR SIR,                                          Sep. 7. 1814.

Having occasion to send to Milton I have directed the servant to call and enquire after your health and that of the family—

We are all in a bustle here since the destruction of the public buildings at Washington. The feeble resistance made and the total want of any thing like an efficient force even of militia notwithstanding the Government had timely notice, is a subject of triumph to the foes of the administration, & has confounded and silenced its best friends—I fear it will greatly injure us in Europe—increase the insolence of our foe and protract the period of peace—Is it not probable that the strength and resources of other parts of the Union will be rated very low after the imbecility shewn at the seat of Government under the immediate superintendance of the Executive[1] of the United States?—

accept for the health of yourself and family my friendly wishes.
Yours sincerely.                          JNO: W: EPPES

RC (DLC); endorsed by TJ as received          [1] Manuscript: "Excecutive."
8 Sept. 1814 from Millbrook.

# From James W. Wallace

DEAR SIR                                   Dumfries 7th Sept 14

The day before yesterday the Enemies ships after loading with flour Tobacco & merchandize, with the ships surrenderd to them at alexa came down the Potomac—12 miles below alexandria at the white house on the Virginia side, Com Porter with the militia was stationd—the whole number marines and militia 3,000. Porters cannons were 3–18 Pounders—2–12 Pounders, four six[s] & 4 four pounders—two frigates anchored 150 yds from the fort, and in 40 minutes drove off the marines &c having dismantled the greater part of the Cannons—the Enemy continued firing furiously for two hours, after they could not see a man, supposing they might injure them in the woods—leaving the white house com— Perry at the Indian head 4 miles below on the Maryland Shore commenced his fire, which continued longer than Porters, but was also very soon silenced— the Enemies fire kept up at the trees & hills—they are now,[1] sailing down the river, not having noticd this place—the troops stationd at the mouth (75 infantry—32 cavalry) of the creek (4 miles below Dumf's,) are coming up. the fire at the white house was not mischievous I beleive to either side—we lost 10 killed—15 Wounded I expect the troops on this side of the Potomac will march to Richmond, tis supposed their next[2] attack will be there—I attentively viewed the fleet, I could only see the fore top Gallant mast of one frigate missing, & no other mark of injury, but heard their hammers—Men and things seem much confused wherever I go—the people seem to have lost confidence in all men, party spirit, rather abates, but something worse, threatens

my respects to the montechello famely & Mrs B
God bless You sir

JAMES W. WALLACE

RC (DLC); endorsed by TJ as received 12 Sept. 1814 and so recorded in SJL. RC (DLC); address cover only; with PoC of TJ to John Barnes, 30 Sept. 1814, on verso; addressed: "Thomas Jefferson Monticello"; franked; postmarked Dumfries, 7 Sept., and Charlottesville, 11 Sept.

WHITE HOUSE, Virginia, is located a few miles below Mount Vernon in Fairfax County (John K. Mahon, *The War of 1812* [1972], 303). MRS B: Ann C. Bankhead, TJ's granddaughter.

[1] Word interlined.
[2] Word interlined.

# From John Minor

Fredericksburg Sep. 8th [1814]

Accept, Dear Sir, my thanks for your kind Letter, I shall give it to my Son as the most valuable Present I can make him;

You, no doubt, have heard of the disgraceful disasters that have overwhelmed our Country, I need not, therefore, wring your Heart by the Painful repetition of the sad Tale—The Enemy have gone down the River with their—(I was about to call it their plunder)— but think it more correct to call it the Donations of Alexandria, I saw them yesterday opposite to Boyds Hole, about 20 in number; I blushed for my Country, but could not, at the same time, suppress, (perhaps) the uncharitable[1] wish that they had the Town of Alexandria[2] on board, Houses and all: That I might never see the monument of my country's compleated disgrace—The wish, I fear is too general to be just—it may be that there were <u>five</u> just person going among them—this may <u>be</u>, but there were not many more—it is reported that the Mayor, Col° Simm remonstrated with Com. Rodgers on his hoisting the American Flagg in the Town, (when he took possession of it, by order of the President,) the Reply was short, that <u>he</u> had raised it and that <u>he</u> the Mayor might pulle it down—if he Dared.

The passage of the Fleet gives us some relief here for the <u>Executive</u> in their <u>wisdom</u> have called all[3] the natural defence of this part of the Country to defend Richmond, leaving us with about 200 Men

May God bless you my dear Sir                    J MINOR

RC (MHi); partially dated; addressed: "Thos Jefferson Esquire Monticello"; stamp canceled and frank substituted; endorsed by TJ as a letter of 8 Sept. 1814 received the next day and so recorded in SJL.

BOYDS HOLE was in King George County (Joseph Martin and William H. Brockenbrough, *A New and Comprehensive Gazetteer of Virginia, and the District of Columbia . . .* [1835], 202). The citi-zens of ALEXANDRIA, led by MAYOR Charles Simms, surrendered their defenseless town on 29 Aug., agreeing to give up their commercial flour, tobacco, and other merchandise if their homes and personal possessions were not molested (Heidler and Heidler, *War of 1812*, 538).

[1] Manuscript: "uncharible."
[2] Manuscript: "Alexandia."
[3] Word interlined.

# From Thomas B. Wait & Sons

SIR,                                   Philadelphia, 8th Sept 1814.—

In January of the present year we issued proposals (a copy of which is inclosed) for publishing the State Papers & Public Documents of the Un. States that affect our Foreign Relations; commencing with your accession to the Presidency—and at the same time announced our intention of issuing proposals for publishing the Docts of a prior date; as soon as the present undertaking should be completed.

One of the most learned men and accurate politicians of our state consented to superintend the publication, and to aid us in making the collection perfect, many of the distinguished political characters of our own and the neighbouring states, cheerfully gave us access to such papers as were in their possession.—But notwithstanding the assistance that was generously afforded us from every quarter, many papers were not to be found,—and we were at length satisfied that New England did not afford them.—

While prosecuting a journey to Washington, in the hope of there completing the collection, our progress was arrested by tidings of the destruction of that city;—and we have since learnt, that it entered into the project of the enemy to destroy books and papers as well as warlike materials, and that the mass of documents upon which our reliance was placed for perfecting the work, had been consumed by fire.—

The facilities toward effecting our object that this city affords, are indeed very inconsiderable, and we can learn of no collection that gives any promise of assistance.—

In our dilemma, the idea occurred, that you sir, would more probably have in your possession a complete series of Amer. State Papers, than any man in the country; and the remarks of many of our friends strengthened us in the hope that the desired papers—might be found in your hands.

The principal deficiency of our collection occurs in the series prior to your administration.—The collection of the subsequent period is more complete altho' yet imperfect.—

Will you Sir, have the kindness to inform us whether you possess a collection of the State Papers & Public Docts of the U. States,— and—if such papers are in your possession, whether you would consent that we may have access to them for the purpose of making copies of those that we are unable to procure elswhere?—

With the greatest respect, Sir, Your very h^le servts.

THOMAS B. WAIT & SONS.

P.S.—Should you favour us with a speedy answer—its direction to the city of Philadelphia would oblige us.—

RC (DLC); in an unidentified hand; adjacent to signature: "Th: Jefferson, Esq."; endorsed by TJ as received 15 Sept. 1814 and so recorded in SJL. Enclosure: Thomas B. Wait & Sons, printed prospectus for *State Papers and Publick Documents of the United States*, Boston, Jan. 1814, making the case for a publication collecting American state papers, with the need amplified by the war with Great Britian and tangled relations with other European states; asserting that the documents printed by Congress to date have had inadequate print runs and reached only "the favoured correspondents of members of congress"; promising that the proposed work will be "equally useful to persons of both parties," that it will "have no party character," that it will "print all the publick documents relating to our intercourse with foreign nations, commencing with the accession of Mr. Jefferson to the Presidency," that "Nothing will be omitted, and no political remarks will be made," and that it will be "merely a book of useful reference on the plan of 'Debrett's State Papers'"; explaining that the work commences with TJ's administration because "the more recent events are much the most interesting," but that proposals for the publication of earlier documents will be made immediately after completion of the current work; and announcing that the work will probably consist of three or four 500-page volumes and conclude with a "copious index," that it will be printed "on a good paper, and with fair type," and that it will cost $2.50 per volume for subscribers and $3 for the general public, with payment due on delivery of each volume.

Thomas Baker Wait (1762–1830), newspaper editor, printer, and publisher, was a native of Massachusetts who spent his early years in Boston, where he worked in the printing and stationery business. With his partner, the printer Benjamin Titcomb, in 1785 Wait launched Maine's first newspaper, the weekly *Falmouth Gazette*. After one year of publication, Wait became sole proprietor and changed the name to the *Cumberland Gazette*. He changed the title again in 1792, to the Portland *Eastern Herald*, and sold out entirely in 1796. From 1795–96 Wait also published the Hallowell *Tocsin*. In 1798 President John Adams appointed him surveyor and revenue inspector for the port of Thomaston. He continued to work as a printer, pub-

lishing an edition of William Blackstone's *Commentaries on The Laws of England* (Portland, 1807). Wait was once again in Boston in 1810, when he was issued a patent as coinventor of a circular printing press. He continued printing and publishing into the 1820s (Philip Marsh, "Maine's First Newspaper Editor: Thomas Wait," *New England Quarterly* 28 [1955]: 519–34; Brigham, *American Newspapers*, 1:201, 204, 206, 209; Lawrence C. Wroth, *The Colonial Printer*, 2d ed. [1938; repr. 1964], 15, 27–9, 59, 60; *JEP*, 1:272, 273 [1, 3 May 1798]; Wait to George Thacher, 5 Jan. 1810 [MHi: Wait-Thacher Letters]; *List of Patents*, 78; Portland *Eastern Argus*, 2 Mar. 1830).

Thomas B. Wait & Sons was established as a Boston printing and publishing house in 1813. The firm published two editions of *State Papers and Publick Documents*, with the volume covering 1801–06 appearing first, in 1814. The remaining volumes of the first edition were issued in 1815, with a second edition following in 1817. The copartnership consisted of Thomas B., William S., and Silas L. Wait. It was dissolved in 1818. The following year Thomas B. Wait published the third edition of the *State Papers*, including "confidential documents" (*Boston Daily Advertiser*, 27 Dec. 1813; Boston *Columbian Centinel*, 22 Aug. 1818; Marsh, "Maine's First Newspaper Editor," 532).

# From Nicolas G. Dufief

Monsieur,                                          Philadelphie ce 9. Sept. 1814

J'ai eu l'honneur de vous envoyer par le courrier de ce matin le 3ème & dernier volume du dictionnaire universel—Je n'ai pas réussi Jusqu'à présent à trouver l'ouvrage d'Evanson—Aussitôt après avoir reçu les 150$^{dlls}$ de Mr Gibson, Je me Suis empressé d'aller regler avec Mr Bradford, chez qui l'on m'a donné le reçu inclus. Les autres personnes Seront payées dès qu'elles Se présenteront

Je Suis avec le respect profond qui vous est du

Votre très-dévoué Serviteur                                    N. G. Dufief

EDITORS' TRANSLATION

SIR,                                                    Philadelphia 9. Sept. 1814

By this morning's post I had the honor of sending you the third and final volume of the *New Universal and Pronouncing Dictionary of the French and English Languages*—I have not yet succeeded in finding Evanson's book—As soon as I received the 150 dollars from Mr. Gibson, I immediately went to settle your account with Mr. Bradford, at whose house I was given the enclosed receipt. The other people will be paid as soon as they present themselves

I am with the profound respect which is your due
Your very devoted servant

N. G. DUFIEF

RC (DLC); endorsed by TJ as received 15 Sept. 1814 and so recorded in SJL. Translation by Dr. Genevieve Moene. Enclosure not found.

# To Francis Eppes

Monticello Sep. 9. 14.

My first wish, my dear Francis, is ever to hear that you are in good health, because that is the first of blessings. the second is to become an honest and useful man to those among whom we live. you are now in the high road of instruction for this object, and I have great confidence you will pursue it with steadiness and attain the end which will make all your friends happy. I shall carry with me to Poplar Forest the proper books for instructing you in French. whether you can pass your time with me while there, and be employed in learning French must depend on the will of your father and of your tutor. I expect to go there within about three weeks, and to make a longer stay than usual. if that should be employed wholly on French, and you can afterwards pass your Christmas at Monticello where your aunt and cousins can assist me in helping you on, you will afterwards be able to proceed of yourself—in this you will be obliged to separate from your cousin who is too young for an undertaking to be pursued afterwards alone. in the hope of seeing you soon, and conveying to you the wishes of your aunt and cousins to be remembered to you, be assured of my affectionate love.

TH: JEFFERSON

PoC (CSmH: JF); on verso of reused address cover to TJ; at foot of text: "Francis Eppes"; endorsed by TJ.

Eppes's TUTOR was Thomas A. Holcombe. His AUNT was Martha Jefferson Randolph, and his COUSIN was John Wayles Baker.

# To John Wayles Eppes

Dear Sir                                            Monticello Sep. 9. 14.

I am sorry to learn by Francis's letter that you are not yet recovered from your rheumatism, and much wonder you do not go and pass a summer at the Warm springs. from the examples I have seen I should entertain no doubt of a radical cure.          the transactions at Washington and Alexandria are indeed beyond expectation. the circumjacent country is mostly disaffected, but I should have thought the motions of the enemy long enough known, and their object probable enough to have called the well affected counties of Virginia & Maryland into place. nobody who knows the President can doubt but that he has honestly done every thing he could to the best of his judgment. and there is no sounder judgment than his. I cannot account for what has happened but by giving credit to the rumors which circulate against Armstrong. who is presumptuous, obstinate & injudicious. I should[1] hope the law could lay[2] hold of Sims E$^t$c. if it could lay hold of any thing after the experiment on Burr. but Congress itself can punish Alexandria, by repealing the law which made it a town, by discontinuing it as a port of entry or clearance, and perhaps by suppressing it's banks. but I expect all will go off with impunity. if our government ever fails, it will be from this weakness. no government can be maintained without the principle of fear as well as of duty. good men will obey the last, but bad ones the former only.—our county is a desert. none are to be met in the roads but grey heads. about 800. men are gone from it, & chiefly volunteers. but I fear they cannot be armed. I think the truth must now be obvious that our people are too happy at home to enter into regular service, and that we cannot be defended but by making every citizen a souldier, as the Greeks & Romans who had no standing armies, & that in doing this all must be marshalled, classed by their ages, & every service ascribed to it's competent class. ever affectionately yours'

                                                        Th: Jefferson

RC (Mrs. Francis Eppes Shine, Los Angeles, 1946); endorsed by Eppes. PoC (DLC); at foot of text: "John W. Eppes"; endorsed by TJ.

The LETTER from Francis Eppes may have been that of 15 July 1814, not found, recorded in SJL as received 29 July 1814 from Lynchburg.

[1] Word interlined.
[2] Manuscript: "law."

# From Thomas Jefferson Randolph

MY DEAR GRANDFATHER                          Timberlake, Sep 9ᵗʰ 1814

By accident I have obtained in this wretched country paper enough to write a letter upon,           we arrived at camp (on the sixth) about two miles from West point, in want of every thing necessary for the support of the army both man and horse; we get some beef but never, enough, and that such as we find in the old fields, not good, without salt and often without bread, the supply of which is allways precarious; our horses go often twenty four hours without food We have nothing in abundance, but ticks and musketoes not as many of the latter as we expected to find,           If we remain here many days longer, we must[1] depend entirely upon supplies brought from Richmond as the country between this and that place was found too poor to support us on our march

We very often see large establishments apparently the abode of, wealthy persons upon approaching them we find them occupied by squalid indigent, wretches who cannot give a meal of any kind to two persons

Our sick list is rapidly encreasing; The water drank by part of the corps is such as our horses in Albemarle would not drink,

Your kind offer[2] of a draught upon Gibson would be very acceptable

Your affectionate Grandson                          TH J. RANDOLPH

RC (MHi); endorsed by TJ as received           [1] Word interlined.
26 Sept. 1814 and so recorded in SJL.           [2] Word interlined in place of "promise."


# To Thomas Cooper

DEAR SIR                          Monticello Sep. 10. 14.

I regret much that I was so late in consulting you on the subject of the academy we wish to establish here. the progress of that business has obliged me to prepare and address to the President of the board of trustees, a plan for it's organisation. I send you a copy of it with a broad margin, that, if your answer to mine of Aug. 25. be not on the way, you may be so good as to write your suggestions either in the margin or on a separate paper. we shall still be able to avail ourselves of them by way of amendments.

Your letter of Aug. 17 is received.[1] mr Ogilvie left us four days ago, on a tour of health, which is to terminate at N. York from whence he will take his passage to Britain to recieve livery and seisin of his new dignities and fortunes. I am in the daily hope of seeing M. Correa, and the more anxious as I must in two or three weeks commence a journey of long absence from home.

A comparison of the conditions of Great Britain & the US. which is the subject of your letter of Aug. 17. would be an interesting theme indeed. to discuss it minutely and demonstratively would be far beyond the limits of a letter. I will give you therefore, in brief only, the result of my reflections on the subject.        I agree with you in your facts, and in many of your reflections. my conclusion is without doubt, as I am sure yours will be, when the appeal to your sound judgment is seriously made.        The population of England is composed of three descriptions of persons, (for those of minor note are too inconsiderable to affect a general estimate) these are 1. the Aristocracy, comprehending the Nobility, the wealthy commoners, the high grades of priesthood, and the officers of government. 2. the laboring class. 3. the eleemosinary class, or paupers, who are about one fifth of the whole. the Aristocracy, which has the laws and government in their hands, have so managed them as to reduce the 3$^d$ description below the means of supporting life, even by labor; and to force the 2$^d$ whether employed in agriculture or the arts, to the maximum of labor which the construction of the human body can endure, & to the minimum of food, & of the meanest kind, which will preserve it in life, and in strength sufficient to perform it's functions. to obtain food enough, and clothing, not only their whole strength must be unremittingly exerted, but the utmost dexterity also which they can acquire; and those of great dexterity only can keep their ground; while those of less must sink into the class of paupers. nor is it manual dexterity alone, but the acutest resources of the mind also which are impressed into this struggle for life; and such as have means a little above the rest, as the master workmen for instance, must strengthen themselves by acquiring as much of the philosophy of their trade as will enable them to compete with their rivals, & keep themselves above ground. hence the industry & manual dexterity of their journeymen & day-laborers, and the science of their master-workmen keep them in the foremost ranks of competition with those of other nations, and the less dexterous individuals, falling into the eleemosinary ranks furnish materials for armies & navies to defend their country, exercise piracy on the ocean, and carry conflagration, plunder and devastation on the shores of all those who endeavor to withstand their aggressions. a society thus constituted possesses certainly the means of defence. but what does it defend? the pauperism of the lowest class, the abject oppression of the laboring, and the luxury, the riot, the domination, & the vicious happiness of the Aristocracy. in their hands, the paupers are used as tools to maintain their own wretchedness, and to keep down the laboring portion by shooting them whenever the desperation produced by the cravings of their stomachs drives them into riots. such is the happiness of scientific England: now let us see the American side of the medal.

And, first, we have no Paupers. the old and crippled among us, who possess nothing and have no families to take care of them, being too few to merit notice as a separate section of society, or to affect a general estimate. the great mass of our population is of laborers; our rich, who can live without labor, either manual or professional, being few, and of moderate wealth. most of the laboring class possess property, cultivate their own lands, have families, and from the demand for their labor² are enabled to exact from the rich and the competent such prices as enable them to be fed abundantly, clothed above meer decency, to labor moderately and raise their families. they are not driven to the ultimate resources of dexterity and skill, because their wares will sell, altho' not quite so nice as those of England. the wealthy, on the other hand, and those at their ease, know nothing of what the Europeans call Luxury. they have only somewhat more of the comforts & decencies of life than those who furnish them. can any condition of society be more desirable than this?          Nor in the class of laborers do I mean to withold from the comparison that portion whose color has condemned them, in certain parts of our Union, to a subjection to the will of others. even these are better fed in these states, warmer clothed, & labor less than the journeymen or day laborers of England. they have the comfort too of numerous families, in the midst of whom they live, without want, or the fear of it; a solace which few of the laborers of England possess. they are subject, it is true, to bodily coercion: but are not the hundreds of thousands of British soldiers & seamen subject to the same, without seeing, at the end of their career, & when age & acciden[t] shall have rendered them unequal to labor, the certainty, which the other has, that he will never want? and has not the British seaman, as much as the African been reduced to this bondage by force, in flagrant violation of his own consent, and of his natural right in his own person? and with the laborers of England generally, does not the moral coercion of want subject their will as despotically to that of thei[r] employer, as the physical constraint does the soldier, the seaman or the slave? but do not mistake me. I am not advocating slavery. I am not justifying the wrongs we have committed on a foreign people, by the example of another nation committing equal wrongs on their own subjects. on the contrary there is nothing I would not sacrifice to a practicable plan of abolishing every vestige of this moral and political depravity. but I am at present comparing the condition & degree of suffering to which oppression has reduced the man of one color, with the condition and degree of suffering to which oppression has reduced the man of another color; equally condemning both. now let us compute by numbers the sum of happiness of the two countries. in England, happiness is the lot of the Aristocracy only; and what proportion they bear to the laborers & paupers you know better than I do. were I to guess that they are 4. in every hundred, then the happiness of the nation would be to it's misery as 1. to 25.　　　in the US. it is as 8. millions to Zero, or as all to none.　　But it is said they possess the means of defence, and that we do not. how so? are we not men?—yes; but our men are so happy at home that they will not hire themselves to be shot at for a shilling a day. hence we can have no standing armies for defence, because we have no paupers to furnish the materials. the Greeks and Romans had no standing armies, yet they defended themselves. the Greeks by their laws, and the Romans by the spirit of their people, took care to put into the hands of their rulers no such engine of oppression, as a standing army. their system was to make every man a soldier, & oblige him to repair to the standard of his country, whenever that was reared. this made them invincible; and the same remedy will make us so. in the beginning of our government we were willing to introduce the least coercion possible on the will of the citizen. hence a system of military duty was established too indulgent to his indolence. this is the first opportunity we have had of trying it. and it has compleatly failed: an issue foreseen by many, and for which remedies have been proposed. that of classing the militia according to age, and allotting each age to the particular kind of service to which it was competent, was proposed to Congress in 1805. and subsequently; and, on the last trial, was lost, I believe, by a single vote only. had it prevailed, what has now happened would not have happened. instead of burning our Capitol, we should have possessed theirs in Montreal and Quebec. we must now adopt it, & all will be safe. we had in the US. in 1805. in round numbers, of free able bodied men, 120,000. of the ages of 18. to 21. inclusive.

|  |  |
|---|---|
| 200,000. of | 22. to 26. |
| 200,000 | 27. to 35. |
| 200,000 | 35. to 45. |
| in all 720,000 of | 18. to 45. |

with this force properly classed, organised, trained, armed and subject to tours of a year of military duty, we have no more to fear for the defence of our country than those who have the resources of despotism and pauperism.

But, you will say, we have been devastated in the meantime. true. some of our public buildings have been burnt, and some scores of individuals on the tide waters have lost their moveable property and their houses. I pity them; and execrate the barbarians who delight in unavailing mischief. but these individuals have their lands and their hands left. they are not paupers. they have still better means of subsistence than $\frac{24}{25}$ of the people of England. again, the English have burnt our Capitol and President's house by means of their force. we can burn their S$^t$ James's and S$^t$ Paul's, by means of our money, offered to their own incendiaries, of whom there are thousands in London who would do it rather than starve. — but it is against the laws of civilised warfare to employ secret incendiaries. — is it not equally so to destroy the works of art by armed incendiaries? Bonaparte, possessed at times of almost every capital of Europe, with all his despotism & power, injured no monument of art. if a nation, breaking thro' all the restraints of civilised character, uses it's means of destruction (power, for example) without distinction of objects, may we not use our means (_our_ money and _their_ pauperism) to retaliate their barbarous ravages? are we obliged to use, for resistance, exactly the weapons chosen by them for aggression? when they destroyed Copenhagen by superior force, against all the laws of god and man, would it have been unjustifiable for the Danes to have destroyed their ships by torpedoes? clearly not. and they and we should now be justifiable in the conflagration of S$^t$ James's and S$^t$ Paul's. and if we do not carry it into execution, it is because we think it more moral and more honorable to set a good example, than follow a bad one.

So much for the happiness of the people of England, and the morality of their government, in comparison with the happiness & the morality of America. — let us pass to another subject.

The Crisis then of the abuses of banking is arrived. the banks have pronounced their own sentence of death. between 2. and 300. millions of Dollars of their promisory notes are in the hands of the people, for solid produce & property sold, and they formally declare they will not pay them. this is an act of bankruptcy of course, and will be so pronounced by any court before which it shall be brought. but cui bono? the law can only uncover their insolvency, by opening to it's suitors their empty vaults. thus by the dupery of our citizens, and tame acquiescence of our legislators, the nation is plundered of 2. or 300. millions of Dollars, treble the amount of debt contracted in the revolutionary war, and which, instead of redeeming our liberty, has been expended on sumptuous houses, carriages & dinners. a fearful tax! if equalised on all: but overwhelming and convulsive by it's partial fall. the crush will be tremendous; very different from that brought on by our paper money. that rose & fell so gradually that it kept all on their guard, and affected severely only early or long-winded contracts. here the contract of yesterday crushes in an instant the one or the other party. the banks stopping payment suddenly, all their mercantile and city debtors do the same, and all in short except those in the country, who, possessing property, will be good in the end. but this resource will not enable them to pay a cent in the Dollar. from the establishment of the United states bank to this day I have preached against this system, but have been sensible no cure could be hoped but in the catastrophe now happening. the remedy was to let the banks drop gradatim, at the expiration of their charters, and for the state governments to relinquish the power of establishing others. this would not, as it should not, have given the power of establishing them to Congress. but Congress could then have issued treasury notes payable within a fixed period, and funded on a specific tax, the proceeds of which, as they came in, should be exchangable for the notes of that particular emission only. this depended, it is true, on the will of the state legislatures, and would have brought on us the phalanx of paper-interest. but that interest is now defunct. their gossimer castles are dissolved, and they can no longer impede and over-awe[3] the salutary measures of the government. their paper was recieved on a belief that it was cash on demand. themselves have declared it was nothing: and such scenes are now to take place as will open the eyes of credulity, and of insanity itself, to the dangers of a paper medium abandoned to the discretion of avarice and of swindlers. it is impossible not to deplore our past follies, and their present consequences: but let them at least be warnings against like follies in future. the banks have discontinued themselves. we are now without any medium; and necessity, as well as patriotism and confidence, will make us all eager to recieve treasury notes, if bottomed on specific taxes. Congress may now borrow of the public and without interest, all the money they may want, to the amount of a competent circulation, by merely issuing their own promisory notes, of proper denominations for the larger purposes of circulation, but not for the small. leave that door open for the entrance of metallic money. and, to give readier credit to their bills, without obliging themselves to give cash for them on demand, let their Collectors be instructed to do so, when they have cash, thus, in some measure, performing the functions of a bank, as to their own notes. Providence seems indeed, by a special dispensation to have put down for us, without a struggle, that very paper enemy which the interests of our citizens long since required ourselves to put down, at whatever risk. the work is done. the moment is pregnant with futurity; and if not siesed at once by Congress, I know not on what shoal our bark is next to be stranded. the state legislatures should be immediately urged to relinquish the right of establishing banks of discount. most of them will comply, on patriotic principles, under the convictions of the moment; and the non-complying may be crouded into concurrence by legitimate devices.—Vale, et me, ut amaris, ama.                    Th: Jefferson

PoC (DLC); edge chipped and trimmed; at foot of first page: "Thomas Cooper esq." Enclosure: TJ to Peter Carr, 7 Sept. 1814.

In his 1805 annual message TJ PROPOSED TO CONGRESS "the expediency of so modifying our militia system as, by a separation of the more active part from that which is less so, we may draw from it, when necessary, an efficient corps, fit for real and active service, and to be called to it in regular rotation." The resulting bill for classing the militia failed in the Senate on a vote of 8 to 19. Similar measures subsequently failed, including one defeated 55 to 58 in the House of Representatives in 1812 (*JS*, 4:6, 47 [3 Dec. 1805, 25 Feb. 1806]; *JHR*, 8:161 [5 Feb. 1812]). GRADATIM: "step by step; gradually" (*OED*). VALE, ET ME, UT AMARIS, AMA: "farewell, and love me as you are loved."

[1] Manuscript: "recived."
[2] Preceding six words interlined.
[3] Preceding two words interlined.

# From John C. Carter

Sir                              Nelson County 12 Sept 1814

I receiv<sup>d</sup> your letter of the 21<sup>st</sup> Aug<sup>t</sup> respecting the land which I sold to Col Monroe, It is true that the benefit of the sale was for myself & the sale also made by me. but the right was in my Brother Champe, who transferd it to Co<sup>l</sup> Monroe. I am sorry that it is not in my power to through any light on the subject. as not being present at the Survey, nor never having any particular knowledge of the, boundarys.

With Esteem Y<sup>r</sup> Most Ob S<sup>t</sup>                    John C. Carter

RC (DLC); endorsed by TJ as received 21 Sept. 1814 and so recorded in SJL.

# From James W. Wallace

DEAR SIR                                    Aquia\* Sept 13<sup>th</sup> 14

A stage passenger this (11 oclock AM) moment from Baltimore, says the Enemy has landed 12 miles below Baltimore; and that our army (17,000 strong) has gone to meet him.

If Winder has the command of the Militia Baltimore will share the fate Washington.

Respects to the Monticello[1] family & M<sup>rs</sup> & M<sup>r</sup> Bankhead

God bless you Sir                          JAMES W. WALLACE

NB. I shall See you in a few days                 J W W

\*8 miles below Dumfries

RC (DLC); endorsed by TJ as received 21 Sept. 1814 and so recorded in SJL.

Brigadier General William Henry WINDER commanded the American forces at the disastrous battle of Bladensburg. Despite questions about his leadership, James Monroe, as acting secretary of war, placed Winder under Major General Samuel Smith of the Maryland militia during the American defense of Baltimore (Malcomson, *Historical Dictionary*, 41–3, 611–2).

[1] Manuscript: "Monticllo."


# From Donald Fraser

SIR—                                    New York Sept<sup>r</sup> 14<sup>th</sup> 1814.

Permit me to present for the Honour of Your acceptance, a copy of a small work which I recently published—The Benevolence of your Disposition, will induce you to pardon the freedom of the following communication—I have two Sons in the U. States army[1]—The eldest, <u>Donald</u>, is now aid to Genl Porter, at Fort Erie, he was also, aide camp to Gen<sup>l</sup> <u>Pike</u> & carries his <u>Sword</u> & pistols, presented to him by Mrs Pike—He's been twice wounded, at the Capture of "Little York" & "Fort George" My youngest Son, Upton, Sheridan, Fraser is a Subaltern in the 15<sup>th</sup> Regt.—

Having lost by misplaced confidence & villainy—the fruits of nearly a whole life of arduous industry I'm now, comparatively, poor.—At Sixty years of age—my means of support being the small emolluments derived from a circulating Library, which is very unproductive at present; as[2] <u>fighting</u> is more necessary than <u>reading</u> at the present Crisis—I am Desirous to obtain the appointment of a <u>Chaplain</u> to some Brigade in the army—When I arrived in this country forty years ago, I preached in New England—received a liberal Education—& humbly conceive that I'm competent to Discharge the Duties of a Chaplain—Tho, I may not be able to Deliver a Theological Discource, I trust that I can impress upon the minds of the Soldiery patriotic Sentiments & moral injunctions—Will you have the Goodness to solicit the worthy <u>President</u> of the U. States or Secretary of war, to Grant me the Desired appointment?—

I have the Honour to be, with great regard for your talents and character, Sir, your humble Servant          DONALD FRASER SENR

RC (DLC); dateline at foot of text; endorsed by TJ as received 21 Sept. 1814 and so recorded in SJL. Enclosure: Fraser, *An Interesting Companion for a Leisure Hour: or, an Historical, Geographical, and Chronological Compendium: containing a brief but comprehensive history of England, Ireland, Scotland, and Holland: together with a variety of curious articles, both miscellaneous and Masonic, not generally known* (New York, 1814; Poor, *Jefferson's Library*, 4 [no. 124]).

The battles of YORK (later Toronto) and FORT GEORGE took place on 27 Apr. and 27 May 1813, respectively (Malcomson, *Historical Dictionary*, 206–8, 620–2).

¹ Manuscript: "arny."
² Manuscript: "as, as."

# From Thomas Cooper

DR SIR                                                    [ca. 15 Sept. 1814]

Some time ago I promised the Editor of the Port folio a paper on education, but I neglected it till your letter came. If the inclosed shd be worth publication, I will send it for that work. Pray oblige me by any remarks that occur to you, so that I may make it as useful as I can; and return it to me. I presume your purpose will be answered by that mode of communication.          THOMAS COOPER

RC (MHi); undated; endorsed by TJ as a letter of 15 Sept. 1814 received 30 Sept. 1814 and so recorded in SJL; additional notations by TJ on verso: "probably Carlisle" and "returned the letter it covd of Sep. 15." Enclosure: Cooper to TJ, 15 Sept. 1814.

# From Thomas Cooper

DEAR SIR,                                          *Carlisle, 15th Sept.* 1814.

I reply to your queries, as to the branches of science expedient to be taught in a university.

The great difficulties in the outset, are, at what age and with what qualifications should a young man enter a university? How long should he continue in such an institution before he be permitted to take a degree?

As to the first question—I would state it as a position which to my mind is supported by proofs so numerous and decisive as to admit of no controversy, that a young man turned out into the world with an intimate knowledge of the Latin, Greek and French languages, a readiness at Latin composition, and with a competent knowledge also of mathematics, algebra and fluxions, is better qualified both for active life, and literary pursuits, and will have attained more facility in acquiring other branches of knowledge, than by any other possible mode of education in use at the present day.

For proof of this, I can safely refer to the men of eminence whom I have personally known, and that without an exception. Among the persons of this description known to yourself, I am aware, that there may be half a dozen partial exceptions: can you count more? But review the prominent characters of the last two centuries, and the proof from induction is complete.

In England, the question has been agitated within a few years: my friend Dr. Barrow, in his treatise on education, has ably defended the old system: Dr. Rennell, dean of Winchester, took the side that Dr. Rush took here; he was opposed by Dr. Vincent of Westminster and by Dr. Ireland. I believe the opinion of the literary world there is settled on the subject. In this country, from the general want of a good classical education among us, the question can hardly be appreciated; and there is a general want also of literary stimulus, owing to the very superficial acquirements with which a young man leaves college, under the idea of having received a finished education: yet the innovaters upon the old plan of school instruction do not seem to gain ground even here. I am glad of this: among many bad omens, it appears to me to augur well.

In England the dissenters have for these twenty years taken the opposite side of the question; and, in their seminaries, deprived the learned languages of much of the time usually devoted to them, which they have given to the sciences. Doubtless there were many of these sectarists who were an ornament to their county; but they have been persons educated *in the old school*. Our friend Priestley was of middle age, before he turned his attention to scientific pursuits.

Within these half dozen years, the literary young men of England, as I hear, affect a kind of encyclopedic knowledge, just as the Martinets in the new fashion of school tactics, would have a boy run the gauntlet of the sciences, and stop for a moment at each member of the circle. To me, this seems the way to turn out sciolists, and to blunt the edge of curiosity, by forcing upon youth a mere *smattering* of knowledge, which they will be apt hereafter to consider as sufficient for all the purposes of life, because it will enable them to chatter upon a variety of subjects, of which they know but little, save the names. Indeed, the chances are, that a man who knows a little of every thing, knows nothing profoundly.

Our boys and girls here are educated much upon the same general plan: the boys are turned into the world as accomplished men, before they have acquired enough of language, or of science, to make it pleasant from its having become easy: the harshness of compulsion has not passed away; the acerbity of school discipline yet remains; and what has been thus half learned is never again applied to. So, we teach our girls music and drawing and French: we make them quit their studies while the acquiring of such accomplishments is still painful; and the instant they become wives, these tasks, as they are considered, are most gladly laid aside, never to be resumed.

With these notions, I would never confer a degree on a young man leaving the university, until he could (inter alia) read with perfect facility, Horace Juvenal and Tacitus; Demosthenes and Sophocles: unless he could on the spot convert a page of English into Latin, and then into French; faultless as to the grammar: and unless he could give evidence of competent knowledge in Euclid; in conic sections; in algebra as far as cubic, quadratic and biquadratic equations, and the equations of curves; in spherical trigonometry; and at least some progress in fluxionary calculus. Let any one read Cumberland's life, and he will find that this is not so much as is exacted for the degree of Bachelor of Arts at Cambridge: and since some late discussions, the exercises both at Oxford and Cambridge, are more strict than they used to be in my time. They are not now satisfied, as in my day at Oxford, with doing *generals*, doing *juraments* and reading *Wall Lectures:* a portion of classical learning that in this country would be considered as profound, is now exacted from the candidate for a mere bachelor's degree. Five and thirty years ago I passed well enough by construing a page in Horace, another in Demosthenes, and another in the easy Greek of Euripides, together with a few answers in Euclid, in logic, and some other trifling branch of education. This will not do there now. Why ought it to do here? But here, we turn out boys as accomplished men, before they are half out of their boyhood; and they go into the world knowing nothing well, with an unconquerable conviction that they know all that is to be known upon every subject of useful or polite knowledge. In most of our seminaries they are taught elocution too! that is, the art of talking without understanding; as if all accomplishment depended upon well-turned periods alone. This is a national evil. Is it not sickening to hear men get up in our legislatures and talk for hours, not to say days, upon a new question, with as much self complacency as if they had studied and comprehended it, *ab imo?*—I am well aware of all the common place objections to Latin and Greek—to the uselessness of wasting so many years on words, to the exclusion of things—on *dead* languages, thrown aside in common life—to the neglect of scientific knowledge—to the immorality of the classic pages, as well as the absurdities of ancient mythology. I know too, on the other hand, the common places about these authors' being models of style and of taste, which they are not in any thing like the degree pretended—about the knowledge of ancient history and ancient manners they furnish; which I acknowledge may be well attained in the present day from compilations—about the facilities they afford to the accurate knowledge of modern languages, which is well founded—about the propriety of employing early youth in the learning of words before they can be made to comprehend things; which is true also, and which Madame de Stael has well urged[1]—about the key the dead languages afford to much knowledge locked up in modern as well as ancient authors; which is also undeniable—about the necessity of a tolerable knowledge of Latin and Greek to understand the allusions and quotations in works of taste, in every known modern language; which also cannot be gainsaid—about the necessity of Greek and Latin to understand the very terms used in chemistry, in natural history, in medicine, anatomy and other sciences; which also no man of science will deny—about the necessity of Greek and Latin to understand not merely the proofs, but many of the doctrines of christianity at first hand; which I presume the clergy will for the most part admit. All this and much more I have read and considered on the subject: but I am not ultimately governed by these considerations. I am decided by what I have known and seen. All the great men in my time, who have contributed to sway the destinies of nations—all the eminent men of literature and of science, whom I have known, personally or by character, have been educated as I have suggested. North, Fox, Burke, Pitt, Wyndham, Sheridan, Tooke, &c. &c.

I insist upon French as necessary to be made a familiar acquisition, because French science, and French literature, is at the head of European science and literature. I know the English and the anglo-Americans do not like to acknowledge this: but they cannot deny it.

In astronomy, in mathematics, and in natural history, the French authors undoubtedly take the lead. What Englishman competes with La Place, La Lande, Carnot, La Grange, Cuvier, La Marck, &c. In chemistry and in general literature, they are on a par with the English, at least in their publications: and though chemical and mechanical knowledge are not so universally diffused among the manufacturers of France as in England, yet the prejudices of the old regime do not now stand in the way of this diffusion among the French. To a man of literature and to a scientific man, therefore, and to a well educated man generally, a familiar acquaintance with the French language is indispensible. German would be very useful, and Italian very pleasant, but they do not bear so immediately on our literary wants as the French.

In such a university, then, as you propose, I would rigidly prohibit the entrance of every youth, who had not entered his sixteenth year—who could not translate, parse, and scan Virgil and Ovid, Homer and Zenophon—who was not a proficient in all the rules of arithmetic, and in the mensuration of superficies and solids of every description. If the university is to be converted into a grammar school, there is an end of its utility as a university: if necessary, connect a grammar school with it. Exclusively confined to the higher branches of knowledge, its trustees ought *rigidly* to exact from those who enter, a proficiency in common school education, as a previous and *indispensable* requisite. In conformity with common opinion and with modern notions of utility in education, I would consent that the professors of the university should teach, 1st, The classics not usually recited in schools. Before a youth enters the university, I take for granted he has read Justin, Eutropius, Cornelius Nepos, Sallust, Cæsar's Commentaries, Cicero de Officiis, Cicero's Orations, as prose writers among the Latin prose authors: Ovid's Metamorphoses, Virgil's Eneid, and Horace among the Latin poets: the Greek Testament, the Tabula Cebetis, the Encheiridion of Epictetus, some dialogues of Lucian, Zenophon's Cyropedia, and Homer among the Greek poets. I take for granted also that he has attended very little to Latin prose or verse composition, without frequent exercise in which, I aver no man can read with ease and pleasure, or accurately comprehend the authors in the Latin language.—Hence at the university, the classical tutor will have to teach Livy, Tacitus, Suetonius—Horace again, parts of Catullus, Tibullus, Propertius, Juvenal and Persius; and I think Lucan and Lucretius; and if time allow, Statius: the opinions of Lucretius may be remarked upon in reading him; or he might be read with the

Anti-Lucretius of Cardinal Polignac. In Greek, Zenophon's Anaba-
sis, Herodotus, Demosthenes, Pindar, Euripides, Sophocles, with the
poetæ minores, or some of them.

This course should be attended with lectures and frequent exami-
nations on ancient laws, manners and customs: and on the principles
of taste in verse and prose composition; including examples and illustrations, both of faults and beauties, from classic authors. Blair's
Lectures, and Irving's[2] Elements of Composition, should be made
use of at this stage, with the antiquities of Potter and Du Bos, Adams
and the travels of Anacharsis.

During this course, the student should read ancient history at his
leisure hours, and be examined thereon. Plutarch's Lives, Rollin
(though an old woman who retails gravely the *fabulas aniles, et quic-
quid Græcia mendax audet in historiâ:*) Gillie's and Mitford's Greece,
Hooke's Roman History, and Gibbon's decline and fall of the Roman
empire. I know the objections which some rigid characters would be
inclined to make to this author: but he is indispensible for a knowledge of the transactions of the periods he describes. Nor can I believe
that it is enough to operate the downfall of christianity, to pen a few
sneers on the conduct of the more violent among the early proselytes:
or that we need start at every ill-founded and trifling objection, as the
objections of Gibbon are generally considered. Nor do I deem it the
aspen character of christianity, to tremble at every breath of opposition? Is it not easy, moreover, in conversing upon this author, to
show, where the case really is so, that the statements are made on
prejudiced and inimical authority, and that they do not bear upon the
proofs internal or external, on which the truth and excellency of
christianity rest? The evidence of christianity by Hartley, Priestley,
Watson and Paley, will furnish the best counterpoise to the sarcasms
of Gibbon, which our language affords.—This classical course,
should be accompanied with two Latin prose, and two Latin verse
compositions every week, for the first year: during which period, assiduous attention should also be given to the French language. Beside this, nothing more ought to enter into the first year's studies, but
logic, metaphysics, Euclid's elements, and trigonometry. The course
of logic and metaphysics, the classical tutor should be competent to—
Duncombe, Watts, or Condillac for logic: but in metaphysics, the
Ontology in Latin of Hutcheson, and Belsham, and Stewart on the
human mind: not either the one or the other, but in point of fairness
both Stewart and Belsham are indispensible. By attending recitations
four hours a day all this may be well accomplished: except the classical course which should occupy three days a week for the first year,

and at least two during each succeeding year: as to the classics indeed, my rule should be *nulla dies sine pagina.* 2. During the second year, classics, with Latin and French composition; conic sections, spherical trigonometry, algebra, fluxions, geography. 3 During the third year, classics, with Latin and French composition twice a week. Mathematics twice a week. The rest to be occupied by those branches of natural or mechanical philosophy, whose demonstrations chiefly depend on mathematical science, rather than ocular demonstration. Such as the principles of the composition and resolution of forces: the general laws of mechanical power on the plan of Carnot's papers. The exhibition and demonstration of the usual mechanical powers, the wedge, the lever, the screw, &c. and their applications in common life. Hydraulics, hydrostatics, pneumatics, optics and the elements of astronomy. 4th year. Chemistry, electricity, galvanism, magnetism, mineralogy (never omitting two lectures weekly, in classics and composition.) Lectures on the theory of general politics, political economy and statistics.

Such is the course I would adopt. The general practice of every European university, so far as I know, is, to exact a four years' course of study preparatory to a degree. I am sure less will not suffice, if you wish for a good course. If parents will not let their sons *sacrifice*, as they may call it, so much time, they must give up, what in Europe would be called a good education. If the circumstances of the country[3] will not bear a good course of study, the plan must be renounced. What I propose is not quite so much as is required in France, Germany, and England: for if I have added a branch or two, I have struck off others taught there.

Such an institution as I recommend, will turn out men of the world, and ought to be exclusively under the control of men of the world as trustees.

For the above purposes, you would want a classical, a mathematical, and a chemical tutor, or professor, with assistants if necessary. There should also be teachers of French, of drawing, of dancing, of the manual exercise, of the broad sword exercise, and of fencing with the small sword. Perhaps the classical tutor might undertake the lectures on history, politics, political economy, and statistics: but it would not be easy to find a gentleman so qualified. The mathematical professor ought to teach also, natural philosophy and geography.

I have said nothing about the evidences of christianity as a branch of study: nor of a course of lectures on the law of nature and nations: nor any thing on anatomy or general physiology. I think it best to let the several professions adopt their own course of study. When the general plan has been pursued to its end, the student will be qualified for any future plan of literary life.

Nor have I mentioned a course of modern history and belles lettres reading. But to young men who will seek for books of this description, it would be worth while to recommend that they should not be perused in an accidental and desultory manner, by which half the pleasure as well as half the profit of such a course will be lost. Even reading for amusement should be entered on with a plan; for by system it may be converted into a course of instruction as well as pleasure.

Such a course should comprehend, as history, the elements of modern history by Millot: then the authors on English history, Hume, Henry, Smollet, and Bisset's continuation of Hume; Memoirs of James II. and of the period of the revolution of 1688 by Dalrymple; and Bellsham's house of Brunswick; Robertson's Scotland.

As to other nations; for France read the memoirs of Philip de Comines, a book extremely interesting from its naiveté: Sully's memoirs, memoirs of De Retz; Voltaire's age of Louis XIV. and XV. Justamond's life of Louis XV. The impartial history of the French revolution from the new Annual Register in two volumes, octavo, and Stephens's memoirs of the French war. For Spanish history, Robertson's America, his Charles V. Watson's Philip II. Clavigero's history of Mexico. For the history of literature, Roscoe's Leo X. House of Medicis, Godwin's life of Chaucer, Mrs. Dobson's life of Petrarch, and Berington's Abelard. Voltaire's Charles XII. Anquetil has published an excellent series of French historical books, Esprit de la Ligue,[4] Esprit de la Fronde, Histoire des Croisades, Louis XIV.[5] Sa Cour et le Régent,[6] Intrigues du Cabinet. The history of our own country may be read in Ramsay, Gordon, and Marshall. A commencement of oriental history may be made by Richardson's very curious dissertation prefixed to his Persian dictionary, but published separately: and Dow's Hindostan. Raynal's history of the Indies can hardly be depended on. Voluminous as this course seems, with industry, a youth[7] may get through it by the time he is two and twenty, without any thing that can be called labour. The British poets should be read in the order wherein they are commented on, in that very pretty book, Dr. Aikin's Letters to a young lady on a course of English poetry; which, with Dr. Johnson's Lives of the Poets, will give some just ideas of criticism upon the works of the British Poets. Shakspeare, Beaumont, and Fletcher, and Massinger must be read as the classic dramatists of the old school. The other plays may be perused in any of the collections, such as Bell's British Theatre, or Mrs. Inchbald's collection. The next class of indispensable reading which should succeed the poets, is the miscellaneous periodical papers of the British writers, which for the gradual changes in dress, amusements, manners, customs, and fashionable literature, as well as of style, should be read in the order of their dates of publication. First the Tatler, Spectator, Guardian, and Freeholder; then the Adventurer, the Rambler, the Idler, the World, the Connoisseur, the Babler, the Citizen of the World, the Mirror, the Lounger, the Observer, and Winter's Evenings; about fifty volumes in all. The novel writers may be perused in Mrs. Barbauld's collection, and include also, all the works of Mrs. D'Arblay, (Miss Burney) Mrs. West, Mrs. Inchbald, Mrs. Opie, and Miss Edgeworth. Rabelais, Cervantes, and Le Sage's Gil Blas and Diable Boiteaux may be added; nor should Sterne be omitted, but with Dr. Feriar's commentary.

Thus have I delineated what I believe is the usual course of reading of a man of good education in England, excepting the French poets, dramatists, and novelists.

To a young man who reads French, Racine, Corneille, and Voltaire, as tragic writers, and Moliere as the first of French comic authors will occur of course. J. B. Rousseau, Boileau, Voltaire, Fontaine, De Lisle, among the men, with Madame and Mademoiselle Deshouillers, and the exquisitely tender pieces of that extraordinary woman Margauerette Elionore Clotilde among the female writers will not be forgotten: some plays of Dident, Destouches, D'Avaure, La Fare, and Gui Joli are worth reading.

Among the French novelists I know of few to recommend; I should not say much in favour of Diderot, Crebillon, Louvet, or P. Le Brun; but Rousseau's Eloisa and Emilius, and his Letters from the Mountains are the finest specimens of ardent language extant, ancient or modern; nor should the pretty tales of Voltaire which are not *Roman*, nor the tales of Florian which are, be omitted, if they fall in the way of perusal.

If a young man's days are well employed at school and at the university till the age of twenty or twenty-one; and his leisure hours employed on such a course as this afterwards, he may have read with sufficient attention every book I have mentioned by the time he is five-and-twenty: a period quite early enough in my opinion for a young man to begin the world for himself. Indeed what is there in the preceding course, that a young man of literary education is not *expected* to be acquainted with in England? and why not here? You and

I will not see the day when it is so, but I shall be glad to contribute my efforts to hasten it.

With my best respects, and good wishes, adieu,     T. C.

Printed in *Port Folio*, 3d ser., 5 [Apr. 1815]: 349–59; at head of text: "Copy of a Letter to a Friend on University Education." Recorded in SJL as received 30 Sept. 1814. Enclosed in Cooper to TJ, [ca. 15 Sept. 1814], and TJ to Cooper, 7 Oct. 1814.

William BARROW, a 1778 graduate of Queen's College, Oxford University, was generally supportive of the traditional classical curriculum in *An Essay on Education; in which are particularly considered the Merits and the Defects of the Discipline and Instruction in our Academies*, 2 vols. (London, 1802). The author Richard CUMBERLAND graduated in 1751 from Trinity College, Cambridge University (*ODNB*). GENERALS, or JURAMENTS were a part of the "succession of exercises for the Bachelor's degree" at Oxford University, at which Cooper had matriculated in 1779 (Dumas Malone, *The Public Life of Thomas Cooper, 1783–1839* [1926; repr. 1961], 4–5). The WALL LECTURES, also called "sex solennes lectiones" were often "delivered *pro forma* to the bare walls of an empty room" (Alfred Denis Godley, *Oxford In The Eighteenth Century* [1908], 173, 178). AB IMO: "from top to bottom."

ANACHARSIS: Jean Jacques Barthélemy, *Voyage du Jeune Anacharsis en Grèce* (Paris, 1788; for a later ed. see Sowerby, no. 41). FABULAS ANILES . . . IN HISTORIÂ: "old wives' tales, and all the other lies that Greece dares tell as history," derives from Juvenal, *Satires*, 10:174–5, in *Juvenal and Persius*, ed. and trans. Susanna Morton Braund, Loeb Classical Library (2004), 380–1. NULLA DIES SINE PAGINA: "not a day without a page." A work on LA FRONDE, *L'Esprit de la Fronde* (Paris, 1772–73), was sometimes attributed to Louis Pierre Anquetil but actually written by Jean Baptiste Mailly. Mailly also wrote on DES CROISADES (*L'Esprit des Croisades* [Amsterdam, 1780]), but Cooper may have had in mind Joseph François Michaud's *Histoire des Croisades* (Paris, 1812). D'AVAURE: possibly François Antoine Devaux.

[1] *Port Folio*: "ugred."
[2] *Port Folio*: "Irvine's."
[3] *Port Folio*: "couutry."
[4] *Port Folio*: "Ligne."
[5] *Port Folio*: "XII."
[6] *Port Folio*: "Requet."
[7] *Port Folio*: "young."

# Thomas Cooper's Notes on University Curricula

[ca. 15–22 Sept. 1814]

It appears to me desireable, that in an University, should be taught

| 1 | Languages | { | antient. Latin. Greek |
| | | | modern. French. |
| 2 | Mathematics. | | Plane and Spherical[1] Trigonometry. Algebra. Fluxions. |
| | Nat. Philosophy | | Mechanics. Hydraulics. Hydrostatics. Pneumatics. Optics. Magnetism. Winds. Clouds. Meteors. Dew. Vapours. |

3 Chemistry
{ Chemistry as applied to Agriculture, Arts, & Manufacture.
Electricity and Galvanism, & their connection with Chemistry.
Mineralogy and Geology.

4 {

Ethics
{ Natural Theology. Foundation of moral obligation.
Duties of a man, and of a citizen.

Metaphysics
{ Ontology. Cause & effect. Nominalists & realists. Abstract Ideas. Species intelligibiles &c history of these questions to the time of Locke.
Liberty & Necessity. Hobbes. Leibnitz &c

Ideology
{ Scotch School. Reid. Dugald Stewart.
English School. Hartley. Priestley. Belsham.
French School. De Mairan. Condillac. Cabanis. Destut Tracey.
Connection of Ideology with Physiology.

Logic
{ Account of the Logic of Aristotle.
Logic as applied by the schoolmen, its uses & abuses. Aquinas. Bradwardine. scotus.
Modern abridgements of Watts, Duncan &c
Exercises in Syllogisms, their properties & laws.

5 History
{ Spirit of antient & modern history. Progress of civilization in laws, language & manners. History of forms of Government. Theory of Politics. Political Economy & Statistics. Political Arithmetic or arithmetical questions dependant on these Subjects

6 Natural history
{ Elements of Anatomy & Physiology natural history of Animals.
Botany on the systems both of Linnæus & Jussieu, which is now necessary.
History of Man, his races, varieties, migrations, manners and habits in various ages, climates & geographical situations

7.   Law.

⎱ Law of nature and of nations. Civil law.
⎰ Characters & varieties of the State Codes as to
⎰ their general features.
⎰ Municipal Law as applicable to the United
⎰ states, wherein of common, statute, &
⎰ chancery Law.

Drawing. Fencing & the Manual exercise.

I think it should be scrupulously exacted, that no young person should be admitted a member of the university, who cannot pass an examination in some of the easier classics, and in the common rules of Arithmetic; including vulgar & decimal fractions, & the mensuration of superficies & solids. For this purpose, would not a grammar school connected with, but at some distance from the university be of use? The boys at a grammar school, are such nuisances in the bounds of an university, that the two Institutions ought not to be near each other. I speak from experience here, and elsewhere. I take the present as I take every opportunity of urging (whether in Season or out of Season) the great value of incessant translations in & out of the languages that are to be taught.

The preceding plan appears to me to require 7 or 8 professors.— It might be filled up, not at once, but gradually.

MS (DLC: TJ Papers, 201:35725); entirely in Cooper's hand; undated.

Evidently a partial response to TJ's 25 Aug. 1814 letter to Cooper, this document is filed by DLC with the RC of Cooper to TJ, 22 Sept. 1814, but it could also have accompanied his letter of 15 Sept. 1814.

[1] Manuscript: "Sperical."

# From Horatio G. Spafford

ESTEEMED FRIEND—                              Albany, 9 Mo. 15, 1814.

Events that have occurred since I last had the pleasure to write thee, have made it probable that I must defer my journey to Washington to a later period than October.

Grateful for thy past favors, I regret to give thee any further trouble. But, it appears to me that the removal of Doct. Thornton from the Patent Office, must follow now, as a thing of course. And in this view, my wishes bound, at once, to Washington, as his Successor. May I use the freedom to request of thee to Name my wishes to the President. The place would suit me exactly, & Administration would find me not ungrateful. A few days since I wrote the President, but did not then know of the conduct attributed to the Doctor, in the late disasters at the Capital. A man should have friends about himself. Had I known more about it, I would have suggested my wishes to the President.

The P.O. in this City, is yet in the hands to which Pickering gave it! I pray thee to accept renewed assurances of my most respectful regards. May I expect to hear from thee, on the above subject?

H. G. SPAFFORD.

RC (MHi); endorsed by TJ as received 24 Sept. 1814 and so recorded in SJL.

William THORNTON asserted in the *National Intelligencer* that he had saved the federal PATENT OFFICE during the invasion and burning of Washington by convincing the British that it contained only private property. In response, Washington mayor James H. Blake defended his own actions and disputed Thornton's heroic narrative (Washington *National Intelligencer*, 7, 9, 12 Sept. 1814). Spafford WROTE to President James Madison on 13 Sept. 1814 expressing his unwillingness to join the military because of his Quaker beliefs (DLC: Madison Papers). George W. Mancius was in charge of the post office IN THIS CITY.

# From Joseph C. Cabell

DEAR SIR,                                    Warminster. 17th Sepr 1814.

The dangers of our country will be my apology for troubling you with this letter. I wish to draw your attention to the important subject of our financial difficulties, & particularly those which will present themselves to the Genl Assembly at its next session: and to sollicit the favor of you to put me in possession of any hints, or plans which you may think adapted to the crisis. I went to Richmond when the Governor issued his proclamation. When I called on him, he informed me that the enemy was expected every day; that a large militia army was assembling which would in a few days be competent to repel any assault that would probably be made: but that this army must be disbanded for want of support, unless money could be procured: that there was no money in the Treasury & none at Washington: that our only resource for the emergency was a Loan from the Banks, to the amt of 50, or 100,000$ in anticipation of the Revenue; but that the Banks had declined lending, on the ground that they were already in advance to the state to the amt of $160,000—& that it was utterly out of their power to lend[1] a further sum, without imminent danger of inability to pay their notes: that he had exhorted them to hazard every consequence, sooner than suffer the country to be laid open to the incursions of the British army, but had found them deaf to his remonstrances: that[2] it was yet possible that those institutions might be prevailed on to lend the state, provided the application should be seconded by members of the Gen[l] Assembly: and that he wished me to undertake to renew the application on his behalf, supported by such arguments as it might be in my power to urge. I waited on some of the officers of the two Banks, in compliance with the Governor's Request. Among the arguments[3] used, I stated that tho' a stoppage of paym[t] of specie, was in itself a great evil, yet I considered it less than that the enemy should march to Richmond & blow up our capitol, & I had no hesitation in believing that the Gen[l] Assembly would not be unmindful of the favor of cooperation by the Banks at so critical a period. After some deliberation, the two Banks agreed to advance the sum of $140,000, for the use of the state—which added to their previous advances, would make an aggregate of $300,000. The day after this loan, the Farmer's Bank stopped payment in specie: & the next day the Virginia Bank also stopped: but under a promise to reopen their issue of specie, as soon as it could be got down from Lynchburg. Upon enquiry I learned they expected $20,000—which w[d] last but a few days: owing to the Great drain of specie to supply change for the use of the army. The Virginia Bank perhaps will go on—but I think it will not. The Farmer's Bank certainly will not. The alledged cause, of this suspension, is the late suspension in the northern Towns.[4] The want of change was sensibly felt in consequence of this measure. It was believed by some that individuals had hoarded and were hoarding specie. It was feared that the supplies for the army, so much wanted, would be affected by fears of the solidity of the paper: and a meeting of the merchants was talked of, to support the character of the notes.—Almost our whole revenue has been, or will have been anticipated by the[5] 10th Oct[r]. So many of the people are called out or have left home, that the sheriffs will probably in many instances find it difficult to collect the taxes. The Gen[l] Gov[t] owed Virginia last winter, upwards of $400,000, & passed a law to provide for paying the debt—but from some cause or other the acc[t] has not been settled & paid in conformity to the act—and now they have no money. An army of 10, or 12,000 men is now guarding Richmond, not to mention the force at Petersburg & in the northern neck. For the present, we are compelled to support this force, the expence of which is & will be vast indeed; & one of the first duties of the Assembly will be to adopt measures for this purpose. We have a right to expect that Congress will take from our shoulders this heavy burthen, but that Gov[t] is without money, & we must defend ourselves, at every cost & hazard, trusting in ultimate remuneration. I came up on 13th ins[t] to prepare my affairs for a long absence on the Assembly—I w^d wish [to] carry some[6] useful ideas with me, when I join the Senate—& I take the liberty once [more to] ask the kindness of you to furnish me with such suggestions as you may deem useful for the occasion. I will use them under such restrictions as you may think proper to impose. I should be happy to call on you; but I[7] shall be so engaged in settling my necessary affairs, I am not certain it will be in my power to pass thro' Albemarle. By the 5^th Oct^r I count on leaving home. I wish to obtain Col. nicholas's consent that he may be put in nomination as our next Governor.

I am, d^r Sir, with the most sincere respect & esteem, y^r friend & Humb: Serv^t
JOSEPH C. CABELL

RC (ViU: TJP-PC); mutilated at seal; addressed: "Thomas Jefferson esq. Monticello Albemarle"; stamped; postmarked Warminster, 17 Sept. 1814; endorsed by TJ as received 19 Sept. 1814 and so recorded in SJL.

By a PROCLAMATION issued 1 Sept. 1814, Governor James Barbour called the Virginia General Assembly back into session beginning on the second Monday in October 1814 (Richmond *Enquirer*, 3 Sept. 1814).

[1] Cabell here canceled "any."
[2] Cabell here canceled "he saw no."
[3] Cabell here canceled "I urged."
[4] Cabell here canceled "Such was the state."
[5] Cabell here canceled "time."
[6] Preceding two words interlined above seal tear in an unidentified hand.
[7] Cabell here canceled "must try to make at least some."

# From José Corrêa da Serra

SIR                              Chambersburgh 20 Sept^r 1814
After having visited your western states, and attempted in vain to pass through the mountains directly from Lexington (Ky) to Monticello, i have been obliged to come back to Pittsburgh and to this place, from whence as soon as i receive an answer from Philadelphia, that is to say in two or three days i will proceed to pay my respects to you. In the mean time i address to you these few Lines, because the moments are precious in these circumstances, and i entreat your forgiveness for the impatience of my American feelings.

Last year i passed three months in the eastern states from whence i did not return to Philadelphia but in winter, i lived with all parties but chiefly with the Leaders of the opposition. I am convinced that though many of them are so by party feelings, or by private interests, still there is among them more treason than from what i remember of our conversations, you seemed aware of. Among their followers the greater number by far is composed of dupes whom the Leaders keep together by manyfold artifices, but who are at the bottom very good americans. Treason is more to be feared in the present moment than in any epoch of your history, the only talent ever known in Lord Castlereagh was that of an artful and succesful intriguer. This Last French catastrophe is a striking proof in all its details, and what is more surprizing though Less important, he has in the same time outwitted the Pope and his Cardinals, and by his artifice has rendered them irrevocably his tools to sow discord among the Irish R. Catholics. Would it not be this[1] a fit moment to give rise in the eastern states to committees of public safety? They are an american institution. It seems that if they were prudently instituted and directed they could do much good and prevent the execution of much treasonable plans and practices. You may expect that the Leaders and their trumpets will cry aloud but even that might be made to recoil on them. Party name ought not to exclude any one from being members, all are to be invited as in common danger, but noted party men are to be excluded. I am persuaded that this thing wisely executed will separate from their ranks a vast number of followers. Moments of danger, and invasion are the proper time for such institutions, because all the sincere of whatever party agree in them by the presence of danger; the guilty alone are against them, and they Loose the dupes who followed them. You and the actual government know better the properer steps to be taken, but i expect your pardon for thus meddling in your public affairs. In every case i entreat you to destroy this note because a Portuguese is in circumstances worse than if he had sworn allegiance to the crown of Great Britain.

My best compliments to M^r and M^rs Randolph, and may all sort of happiness fix itself in Monticello.

I am with the greatest veneration
Sir Your most obedient serv^t         JOSEPH CORRÈA DE SERRA

RC (DLC); endorsed by TJ as received          [1] Thus in manuscript.
30 Sept. 1814 and so recorded in SJL.

# Deposition of Craven Peyton in
## *Jefferson v. Michie*

The deposition of Craven Peyton taken at the house of John Watson in the town of Milton on the 20^th day of Sep^t 1814 in a suit depending in the County Court of Albemarle in Chancery between Thomas

Jefferson Complainant and David Michie Def[t] under a commission to us directed—the deponent being sworn saith[1] that in 1801 the deponent having purchased from T M Woodson Certain portions[2] of the Estate of the late Bennett Henderson which had fallen to his son James L Henderson which was adjoining the town of Milton, and he sold the same to the Comp[t] Thomas Jefferson who thereupon engaged this deponent to purchase for him such[3] other of the portions of the estate of the said Bennett Henderson as were offered for sale, that this Dep[t] being in Kentucky in the succeeding year 1802 at the house of Elizabeth Henderson widow of said Bennett Henderson then purchased from her, the life estate in all the lands[4] which she held in right of dower of the Estate of her deceased Husband Bennett Henderson except in the mill then standing & in the ware house[5] and with an allowance to John Henderson her son to remain in the mansion house for the terms & on the Conditions specified in the deed which she then made to the said Peyton for all which he agreed to give and did make good to her as per her receipt[6] the sum of two hundred & fifty pounds, that in this purchase he acted on behalf and in trust[7] for the Comp[t] Thomas Jefferson altho he was never named to the said Elizabeth as[8] Concerned therein, that at the time of the said purchase neither the widow nor[9] any other person mentioned a syllable[10] of her[11] ever having given to her son John or to any other person a right to make a Canal through her dower lands, nor had he the least notice[12] or suspicion that she had ever given to him or any other such a right—That in 1804 he purchased further from the s[d] Elizabeth her remaining rights in the mill & warehouse which had been excepted out of her former deed,[13] that in 1806 the said John Henderson the son being greatly indebted made a deed to James Lewis and a Certain Matthew Henderson for Certain property therein described among which were all the rights which he held in any of the lands of his father adjoining Milton, whether by descent[14] or purchase in trust for the payment of his debts and other purposes as in the deed specified, and soon after being in Jail took the benefit of the insolvent law by giving in a schedule[15] of his estate in which were specified his rights in the lands mentioned in the deed to his trustees and was thereon discharged from Jail. That the trustees having advertized the land for sale and proceeded to make sale, the same was struck out to James Lewis one of the Trustees as the highest bidder, whether in his own right or as trustee or by bidder[16] this dep[t] does not recollect,[17] that about 2 years afterwards this deponent purchased from the said James Lewis all the rights of the said Jno Henderson in the said lands of his father adjoining Milton for the sum of $750 which he made good to him said James, that a bill of Injunction was at that time depending in the Court of Appeals wherein this dep[t] was nominal Plt and the said J Henderson was Def[t] Concerning the title to the dower lands aforesaid, and that this dep[t] after purchasing all the rights of the s[d] John, the Def[t] in that bill gave himself no[18] trouble after about the suit because holding now the rights of both Plt & Def[t] a decree for either would Confirm his right[19] and that his Counsel accordingly in 1812 suffered his bill to be dismissed in favour of the Def[t]—that in all these transactions he acted in trust for the Comp[t] Tho Jefferson without fee or reward or Committing himself in any way which Could lay him under the least responsibility to the s[d] Comp[t] his services having been rendered merely as a friend and that he stand at this moment wholly disinterested[20] in the issue or Consequences of the present suit[21]—that[22] after he had purchased from James Lewis the rights of the said John Henderson in the said lands and never before he heard that David Michie the Def[t] set up some claim in them, but that he never had any reason to believe they had any foundation in law or equity, nor did he ever expect they would be seriously brought forward until after the dismissal of his bill in the Court of Appeals as aforesaid, he learned that the said David Michie Considered that Circumstance as favourable to him and thereon[23] made a forcible entry and detainor of some[24] of the said lands from which he was afterwards removed on process of forcible entry & detainor, that he has heard that there were[25] articles of agreement and Covenant for Conveyance[26] said to have been entered into between the said J Henderson & D Michie in 1804 in which it is stated that the said David[27] was to give to the said John the sum of $500[28] for one half of the s[d] mill & lots 8 & 9 and of the Canal grounds attested by a single witness but never offered for record until July 1812 and has heard[29] of a[30] Copy of a deed from the said John to the said David acknowledging the payment of one additional sum of $500 for further interests in the premises dated in 1812 which Considerations[31] the deponent had ever believed to have been nominal only and not to have been realy paid and that accordingly the said John Henderson in a conversation with this deponent[32] easter sunday last—declared that $200 was all that was actually paid or to be paid by the said David[33] and that after the desolution of the injunction before the Court of Appeals, and that it was from great persuasion he said John was induced to take it,—and this deponent further saith not—

CRAVEN PEYTON

Albemarle County to wit

The before going deposition taken and sworn to in due form this 20th Sept 1814.

JNO WATSON

JS OLD

Tr (ViU: TJP-LBJM); at head of text: "Depositions"; entirely in George Carr's hand. Dft (Mrs. Charles W. Biggs, Lewisburg, W. Va., 1950); in TJ's hand, with two emendations by Peyton as noted below; undated; on reused address cover to TJ; enclosed in TJ to Peyton, 6 Sept. 1814.

A missing letter of this date from Peyton to TJ is recorded in SJL as received 24 Sept. 1814 from Monteagle. For an overview of Peyton's role in *Jefferson v. Michie*, see Haggard, "Henderson Heirs."

[1] Dft begins here.

[2] Preceding two words, thus in Tr, reworked in Dft to "a certain portion."

[3] Word interlined in Dft in place of "some."

[4] Preceding four words interlined in Dft.

[5] In Dft TJ here canceled "for which he paid her the sum of £250."

[6] Preceding four words not in Dft.

[7] Thus in Dft. Tr: "acted in behalf on part."

[8] Tr: "or." Dft: "as."

[9] Tr: "or." Dft: "nor."

[10] Tr: "sylable." Dft: "syllable."

[11] Tr: "his." Dft: "her."

[12] Word interlined in Dft in place of "knolege."

[13] Sentence to this point interlined in Dft in place of "that in 1804. this dep. also purchased from the sd J. H. all his rights."

[14] Tr: "decent." Dft: "descent."

[15] Tr: "shedule." Dft: "schedule."

[16] Preceding three words interlined in Dft, with "&" instead of "or."

[17] Dft: "knows not."

[18] Dft here includes "further."

[19] Text from "because" to this point interlined in Dft.

[20] Tr: "discharged." Dft: "disinterested."

[21] Dft here adds "and moreover that he possesses a written discharge from the complt of all responsibility to him for his transactions aforesaid respecting any of the lands which were the property of the sd B. H."

[22] In Dft TJ here canceled "during these transactions."

[23] In Dft TJ here canceled "took forcible possession."

[24] Tr: "use." Dft: "some."

[25] In Dft Peyton reworked preceding four words from "seen the supposed <*deed*>."

[26] Preceding four words interlined in Dft.

[27] Tr: "the said Davie." Dft: "the said D."

[28] Dft: "£500."

[29] Tr: "herd."

[30] In Dft Peyton reworked "seen also the" to "herd also of a."

[31] Tr: "Conditions." Dft: "considerations."

[32] Remainder of Dft reads: "on the       day of       of this present year declared that they had not been paid, and that he never recieved but the sum of       Dollars, and that but very lately as a consideration for the said conveyances."

[33] Tr: "Davie."

# Deposition of Richard Price in
## *Jefferson v. Michie*

The deposition of Richard Price taken at the house of John Watson in the town of Milton on the 20ʰ day of September 1814 in a suit depending in the County Court of Albemarle in Chancery between Thomas Jefferson Complainant and David Michie Defᵗ under a Commission to us directed.

The deponent being first sworn on the holy evangelist deposeth and saith that some time in the spring of 1804 he saw John Henderson son of Bennett Henderson in the town of milton in possession of an instrument of writing under which he claimed the right of Conducting a mill race through the dower land of his mother Elizabeth Henderson adjoining the town of milton That the deponent mentioned to the said John that he should be ashamed to produce such an instrument in Court the same being interlined in the most obligatory part, particularly that part under which he claimed the right of Conducting a mill race through said Mʳˢ Hendersons dower land: the said John replied that the Conveyance was interlined before signed, and the deponent observed that a note of the interlineation was made at the bottom of said writing.

The Deponent having been asked whether he believed that the instrument he saw in possession of John Henderson was realy and bona fide executed by Mʳˢ Henderson in the manner & form in which he saw it?

Answers that he doth not actually know whether the interlineation was made before or after the instrument was executed by Mʳˢ Henderson but believes it was afterwards and therefore he made the aforesaid observation—Having been asked whether from his acquaintance with the actions character & principles of the said John Henderson, he believed him Capable of an act like the one imputed to him by the former question? Answers that he hath been acquainted with the said John Henderson twelve years and doth think him Capable of Committing such an act.

Having been asked what is the general opinion so far as it has reached him of the Correctness and fair dealing of the said John between man & man Saith that so far as the acts of the said John have Come to his knowledge they have not been fair, and it is a general opinion that they have not been fair.

Having been asked whether he was positive as to the time when he saw the said John in the possession of the instrument relating to the mill race? Sayeth that it was in the spring of the year 1804 to the best of his recollection and of this he is pretty Certain but not positive.

Having been asked whether it was before or since he heard of the Controversy which had taken place between Craven Peyton & the s$^d$ John relative to the mill site & race that he saw the said paper in possession of the said John? Says that it was since, for the Conversation was brought up by talking of which had the better right.

Having been asked whether he had given an opinion at that time or at any time before his first deposition was taken on this subject as to which had the better right? says he never had.

Having been asked whether he had not had many disputes both in & out of Court with the said John? and whether he did not entertain a strong enmity against him? Saith that he hath had many disputes with the said John in and out of Court but at this time hath no animosity against him whatsoever.

Having been asked whether Kemp Catlett was a subscribing witness to the paper before mentioned relating to the mill race? Answers that he was. Having been asked about his disputes with the said John and whether he believed that he has had disputes of the Same nature with his own, with most men$^1$ who have had much dealing with him? Answered that he had with a good many as he believed.

Having been asked whether he had any Conversation with Kemp Catlett who is said to be a witness to the afores$^d$ instrument$^2$ about the same, and what was that Conversation? Answered that he had at the time the said Jno showed the instrument; and the s$^d$ Catlett said he did not know whether it was interlined or not, at the time he signed as a witness.

Having been asked whether he was Certain that the instrument of writing before alluded to was signed by Elizabeth Henderson, and from his view of it at the time, if it might not have been signed by James Henderson, or some other member of the family? Answered that he believed that M$^{rs}$ Hendersons name was to it but who signed it he Could not tell.

Having been asked whether he believed that the writing before alluded to was a Copy or the original paper, or whether the said John told him it was a Copy? Says that he believes the instrument produced by the said John was the original as the name of Kemp Catlett who was a witness thereto appeared to be in his own hand writing, and the said John did not say it was a Copy.

Having been asked whether he knew the date of the instrument aforesaid and whether he knew it was the same which is said to be lost? Answers that he does not—And further this deponent saith not.                                            RICH^D PRICE

Albemarle County to wit

The before going deposition taken and sworn to in due form before us this 20^h of Sep^t 1814                              JNO WATSON
JA^S OLD

Tr (ViU: TJP-LBJM); entirely in George Carr's hand.

Richard Price (d. 1827) operated an ordinary in the town of Milton. Price carried goods from Milton to Monticello for TJ, who stopped occasionally at Price's establishment for meals and supplies. TJ praised Price's honesty and his gardening skills when he recommended him to Louis H. Girardin as a source for plant seeds (PTJ, 28:471–4; Woods,

*Albemarle*, 57, 298; Albemarle Co. Order Book [1800–01], 406; *MB*; TJ to Girardin, 31 Mar. 1813; Albemarle Co. Will Book, 9:42).

For Price's FIRST DEPOSITION on this subject, given on 17 May 1805 in the case of *Peyton v. Henderson*, see note to Bill of Complaint in *Jefferson v. Michie*, 16 June 1813.

[1] Thus in manuscript.
[2] Manuscript: "intrument."

# From Thomas Cooper

DEAR SIR                                     Carlisle Sep. 21. 1814

I send you remarks on your letter to Mr Carr: not much differing from the spirit and substance of my former letter.

I do not disagree with you in the least as to the measure of national happiness in the two countries, but the worst government in other respects is certainly the most powerful. Your plan of a Militia, I and Gen^l John Steele took pains to recommend about the year 1802–3 but he was then in the Senate, & the suggestion cost him his popularity. The Romans and Greeks were an agriculture and a military people, by inclination, by necessity, by profession. They were not Nations bouticaires. You cannot make a set of Shopkeepers public Spirited, or brave, or energetic for the community. They exert no talent, they live to get money, and to eat and drink.

A military, or even a manufacturing nation is far superior both in energy and knowledge. But either your plan of Militia must be adopted, which there is not virtue and self denial among us suffic^t to accomplish, or we must have a standing Army; which I think may be so managed as to be less formidable than in times past.

As to Banks, I have laboured for years on y^r Side of the question, to no avail. I am not sorry to observe the approaching Crisis.

My Emporium stops with the number now printing. My publishers are afraid of risking their capital these war times. Adieu. May God bless you.

THOMAS COOPER

RC (MHi); endorsed by TJ as received 30 Sept. 1814 and so recorded in SJL. Enclosure: Cooper to TJ, 22 Sept. 1814.

Cooper's FORMER LETTER on university education was dated 15 Sept. 1814. NA-TIONS BOUTICAIRES: "nations of shop-keepers."

# The Sale of Thomas Jefferson's Library to Congress

I. THOMAS JEFFERSON TO SAMUEL H. SMITH, 21 SEPT. 1814
II. THOMAS JEFFERSON TO SAMUEL H. SMITH, 21 SEPT. 1814

## EDITORIAL NOTE

Having learned through the newspapers of the British destruction on 24 Aug. 1814 of the 3,000-volume Library of Congress, Jefferson quickly decided to offer his large personal library as a replacement. On 21 Sept. he sent his proposal and a manuscript catalogue to his old friend Samuel H. Smith, federal commissioner of the revenue and former publisher of the Washington *National Intelligencer*, requesting that both be submitted to Congress for its consideration. While agreeing to accept any legislative valuation and payment plan, Jefferson specified that his library must be purchased in its entirety or not at all. Smith forwarded Jefferson's letter to Senator Robert H. Goldsborough, chair of the congressional Joint Library Committee, on 3 Oct. Four days later Goldsborough introduced a joint resolution authorizing the committee to negotiate with Jefferson for the purchase of his library. The Senate passed the resolution on 10 Oct. The House of Representatives added its approval nine days later with an amendment, to which the Senate consented on 20 Oct. 1814, that Congress retain the right to approve or reject the final contract. At Smith's prompting, on 29 Oct. Jefferson asked the Georgetown bookseller Joseph Milligan "to take the trouble of actually counting the numbers of every page of the Catalogue, distinguishing separately the folios, 4.$^{tos}$ 8$^{vos}$ and 12$^{mos}$ so as to inform him [Smith] how many there are of each format, which would enable him to set a value on the whole." The formula ultimately settled on was $10 per folio, $6 per quarto, $3 per octavo, and $1 per duodecimo volume. The Library Committee having accordingly received from Smith the "precise terms of sale" for Jefferson's library—6,487 volumes for $23,950, with deductions to be made if the actual count fell below the number of books recorded in the catalogue—Goldsborough presented the Library Bill to the Senate on 28 Nov. It passed in the upper chamber on 3

Dec. 1814 and won approval on 26 Jan. 1815 in the House. On 30 Jan. 1815 President James Madison signed into law "An Act to authorize the purchase of the library of Thomas Jefferson, late President of the United States."

Congressional support for the bill was, however, far from unanimous. In the House of Representatives, in particular, Federalists strongly opposed the sale. Their "objections to the purchase were generally its extent, the cost of the purchase, the nature of the selection, embracing too many works in foreign languages, some of too philosophical a character, and some otherwise objectionable." Federalist legislators Cyrus King and Timothy Pickering each offered amendments under which Congress would buy only the most suitable portions of Jefferson's library. Motions to postpone the vote in the House failed on 26 Jan. 1815 by only six and seven votes. King's proposition that the Library Committee be "authorized and directed to select therefrom, all such books, as, in their opinion, are not useful or necessary for Congress, and to cause the same to be sold, and the proceeds thereof invested in other books for the use of Congress" fell short on the same day. Although the bill did pass, it was no landslide. Seventy-one members, some 47 percent of those voting in the House, opposed the purchase.

While preparing his library for shipment to Washington the following spring, Jefferson counted 6,707 volumes in his possession, 220 more than had been reported to Congress. Although this presumably entitled him to an additional $1,172.50, he neither retained the surplus books nor demanded extra funds from Congress. Jefferson did successfully lobby to have Milligan come to Monticello to assist him in filling the spaces between the books and shelves with scrap paper, wrapping the best bindings, inserting slips between the books, and "with the catalogue in his hand, [checking to] see that every book is on the shelves." Ten wagons filled with Jefferson's nailed-up book presses left Monticello beginning in the middle of April, with the last one departing on 8 May 1815. They all arrived safely in Washington after a weeklong journey and were set up in Blodget's Hotel, the nation's temporary capitol.

Jefferson used the funds from the sale to reduce his sizable debts, paying what he owed to Tadeusz Kosciuszko, William Short, and others. However, he found himself unable to restrain what he called in 1818 his "canine appetite for reading" and almost immediately began buying replacements. During the eleven years left to him he acquired—and presumably read or perused—about 1,600 volumes.

On the day the last of his books left Monticello, Jefferson wistfully remarked that "an interesting treasure is added to [Washington, D.C.], now become the depository of unquestionably the choicest collection of books in the US. and I hope it will not be without some general effect on the literature of our country." In both regards Jefferson proved to be correct. Although approximately two-thirds of his library was consumed by fire in 1851, the surviving 2,465 volumes are now among the Library of Congress's most prized possessions. Moreover, beginning in 1998 a diligent effort to reconstruct the original library has replaced most of the editions lost in that conflagration or in other ways. Even more important, the acquisition of Jefferson's wide-ranging collection made clear that the Library of Congress would not long remain solely a reference tool for a handful of legislators, but would grow over time into a great national institution seeking to encompass all of human knowledge (*ASP, Misc.*, 2:246, 253; *JS*, 5:533–4, 538, 539, 561–2, 565 [7, 10, 20, 21 Oct., 28 Nov., 3 Dec. 1814]; *JHR*, 9:479, 482–3, 486, 689–91 [17, 18, 19, 21 Oct. 1814, 26 Jan. 1815]; *Annals*, 13th Cong., 3d sess., 398, 1105 [17 Oct. 1814, 26 Jan. 1815]; *U.S. Statutes at Large*, 3:195; Smith to TJ, 21 Oct. 1814, 30 Jan. 1815; TJ to Milligan, 29 Oct. 1814, 27 Feb. 1815; TJ to Smith, 29 Oct. 1814, 27 Feb., 8 May 1815; Milligan to TJ, 16 Nov. 1814, 31 July 1815; TJ to Madison, 23 Mar. 1815; TJ to Alexander J. Dallas, 18 Apr. 1815; TJ to John Adams, 17 May 1818; Douglas L. Wilson, *Jefferson's Books* [1996], 12–5, 47, 51; Malone, *Jefferson*, 6:172–8, 181).

# I. Thomas Jefferson to Samuel H. Smith

DEAR SIR                                                    Monticello Sep. 21. 14.

I am imposing a task on your friendship which needs much apology, and will be explained in the letter accompanying this. it is to offer my library to the library committee of Congress. I would not have trespassed on your time so much, but that I hope it will give you little trouble. the delivery of the accompanying letter (which is written separately with that view) and the Catalogue will enable them to give you their yea, or nay. as the subject however cannot but be interesting, and I shall feel anxiety until I know their inclinations, you would greatly oblige me by informing me of them as soon as you can form a probable conjecture what they are likely to decide. present me respectfully and affectionately to mrs Smith and accept assurances of my great attachment and respect.                    TH: JEFFERSON

RC (DLC: J. Henley Smith Papers); at foot of text: "Samuel Harrison Smith esq." PoC (DLC); endorsed by TJ. Enclosure: TJ to Smith, 21 Sept. 1814, second letter, printed immediately below.

# II. Thomas Jefferson to Samuel H. Smith

DEAR SIR                                                    Monticello Sep. 21. 14.

I learn from the Newspapers that the Vandalism of our enemy has triumphed at Washington over science as well as the Arts, by the destruction of the public library with the noble edifice in which it was deposited. of this transaction, as of that of Copenhagen, the world will entertain but one sentiment. they will see a nation suddenly withdrawn from a great war, full armed and full handed, taking advantage of another whom they had recently forced into it, unarmed, and unprepared,[1] to indulge themselves in acts of barbarism which do not belong to a civilised age. when Van Ghent destroyed their shipping at Chatham, and De Ruyter rode triumphantly up the Thames, he might in like manner, by the acknolegement of their own historians, have forced all their ships up to London bridge, and there have burnt them, the tower, & city, had these examples been then set. London, when thus menaced, was near a thousand years old, Washington is but in it's teens.           I presume it will be among the early objects of Congress to recommence their collection. this will be difficult while the war continues, and intercourse with Europe is attended with so much risk. you know my collection, it's condition and extent. I have been 50. years making it, & have spared no pains, opportunity or expence to make it what it[2] is. while residing in Paris I devoted every afternoon I was disengaged, for a summer or two, in examining all the principal bookstores, turning over every book with my own hands, and putting by every thing which related to America, and indeed whatever was rare & valuable in every science. besides this, I had standing orders, during the whole time I was in Europe, in it's principal book-marts, particularly Amsterdam, Frankfort, Madrid and London, for such works relating to America as could not be found in Paris. so that, in that department, particularly, such a collection was made as probably can never again be effected; because it is hardly probable that the same opportunities, the same time, industry, perseverance, and expence, with some knolege of the bibliography of the subject would again happen to be in concurrence.           during the same period, and after my return to America, I was led to procure also whatever related to the duties of those in the high concerns of the nation. so that the collection, which I suppose is of between 9. and 10,000. volumes, while it includes what is chiefly valuable in science and literature generally, extends more particularly to whatever belongs to the American statesman. in the diplomatic and Parliamentary branches, it is particularly full. it is long since I have been sensible it ought not to continue private property, and had provided that, at my death, Congress should have the refusal of it, at their own price. but the loss they have now incurred makes the present, the proper moment for their accomodation, without regard to the small remnant of time, and the barren use of my enjoying it.           I ask of your friendship therefore to make for me the tender of it to the library committee of Congress, not knowing myself of whom the committee consists. I inclose you the catalogue, which will enable them to judge of it's contents. nearly the whole are well bound, abundance of them elegantly, and of the choicest editions existing.[3] they may be valued by persons named by themselves, and the payment made convenient to the public. it may be, for instance in such annual instalments as the law of Congress has left at their disposal, or in stock of any[4] of their late loans, or of any loan they may institute at this session, so as to spare the present calls of our country, and await it's days of peace and prosperity. they may enter nevertheless into immediate use of it, as 18. or 20. waggons would place it in Washington in a single trip of a fortnight.—I should be willing indeed to retain a few of the books to amuse the time I have yet to pass, which might be valued with the rest, but not included in the sum of valuation until they should be restored at my death, which I would carefully provide for, so that the whole library, as it stands in the catalogue at this moment should be theirs, without any[5] garbling. those I should like to retain would be chiefly classical and Mathematical, some few in other branches, & particularly one of the five encyclopedias in the catalogue. but this, if not acceptable, would not be urged. I must add that I have not revised the library since I came home to live, so that it is probable some of the books may be missing, except in the chapters of Law and divinity, which have been revised, and stand exactly as in the catalogue. the return of the Catalogue[6] will of course be needed, whether the tender be accepted or not. I do not know that it contains any branch of science which Congress would wish to exclude from their collection. there is in fact no subject to which a member of Congress may not have occasion to refer. but such a wish would not correspond with my views of preventing it's dismemberment. my desire is either to place it in their hands entire, or to preserve it so here. I am engaged in making an Alphabetical Index of the authors' names, to be annexed to the catalogue in order to facilitate the finding their works in the catalogue, which I will forward to you as soon as compleated. any agreement you shall be so good as to take the trouble of entering into with the committee, I hereby confirm. Accept the assurance of my great esteem and respect.

Th: Jefferson

RC (ICU: Butler-Gunsaulus Collection); penciled notation at foot of text in an unidentified hand: "Nov 28. Congress agreed to purchase the library for 23,950 Dollars." PoC (DLC); at foot of first page: "Samuel H. Smith esq." Enclosed in preceding document. Printed in Georgetown *Federal Republican*, 18 Oct., and Washington *Daily National Intelligencer*, 27 Oct. 1814.

In 1807 the British navy bombarded COPENHAGEN and captured the Danish fleet in order to insure that Napoleon would gain no naval strength if the Danes abandoned their neutrality in his favor. During the 1667 Battle of CHATHAM, or Medway, Dutch commanders Willem Joseph van Ghent and Michiel Adriaanszoon de Ruyter executed a successful raid on British naval vessels that helped the Netherlands to negotiate a victorious end to the second Anglo-Dutch war (Gijs Rommelse, *The Second Anglo-Dutch War (1665–1667): Raison d'état, mercantilism and maritime strife* [2006], 180–2).

The CATALOGUE of TJ's library here enclosed was most likely the fair copy of 1812 with which he replaced an extant manuscript catalogue that he had probably begun early in the 1780s (MS in MHi). The new catalogue also evolved as TJ's library continued to grow, and it was later passed on to the librarian of Congress, George Watterston, for use in creating a print edition. Watterston retained the catalogue after publication, and its subsequent history is unknown (*PTJ*, 6:216; Sowerby, 1:ix–x; TJ to Thomas Cooper, 10 July 1812). A reconstruction of this catalogue completed by Nicholas P. Trist in 1823 at TJ's request is now at DLC: Rare Book and Special Collections (Trist to TJ, 18 Oct. 1823; TJ to Trist, 13 Apr. 1824; James Gilreath and Douglas L. Wilson, eds., *Thomas Jefferson's Library: A Catalog with the Entries in His Own Order* [1989]).

¹ *Federal Republican* here adds, in brackets, "after two years offensive war."
² *Daily National Intelligencer* here adds "now."
³ Word not in *Federal Republican* or *Daily National Intelligencer*.
⁴ TJ here canceled "kind."
⁵ *Federal Republican*: "my."
⁶ *Daily National Intelligencer* substitutes "which" for preceding five words.

# From John Vaughan

D SIR                                    [received 21 Sept. 1814]

Hoping M Correa will be with You I inclose a line from myself with a European Packet—from which I trust much Satisfaction will be derived—Excuse this hasty line—Our minds are much Engaged but now somewhat relieved¹

Yˢ sincerely                                    JN VAUGHAN

RC (MHi); undated, endorsed by TJ as received 21 Sept. 1814 and so recorded in SJL. Enclosure not found.

¹ Manuscript: "relived."

# From Thomas Cooper

DEAR SIR                                    Carlisle 22 Septʳ 1814

I have carefully considered the plan of University education you [se]nt¹ me. In addition to my former letter on the same subject, written before I [ha]d² seen yours to Mʳ Carr, I send you the following remarks.

I agree, that in a school of the first grade (usually called in this section of the Union a Grammar School) every thing should be taught, that every citizen of whatever class, ought to know: the grammar of his own language—arithmetic and mensuration—geography. I think it is just that the Institution in its character of a <u>College</u>, should[3] furnish the means of instruction in every branch of knowledge that a well-educated gentleman is expected to know; and in its character of an <u>University</u> it should furnish Professors in those particular branches of science which are usually pursued with a view to subsistence, and wherein degrees or other honorary marks of approbation are or ought to be conferred: thus marking the three grades which your plan embraces.

I consider it as indispensible to a good system of education, that education should not be[4] terminated till the close of the nineteenth year <u>at the soonest</u>: I should greatly prefer the close of the twentieth.

It is a question of great importance, and of great difficulty too, not to throw into the course of education of the second grade, more branches of knowledge than can be well taught and well learnt between the commencement of the fifteenth and the commencement of the twentieth year. On the best reflection I can give to this part of the subject, it ought not to comprehend more than the following branches.

1st Latin and Greek, pursued unremittingly untill translation out of, and translation into these languages, both in prose and verse become easy and familiar: then and never till then, will antient authors be perused with a proper Relish of their beauties, & become as they may be to the end of life, sources of instruction and elegant amusement. Without this acquirement, so common on the European Continent, no branch of natural philosophy, of natural history, of chemistry, medicine, surgery, can be satisfactorily pursued. The Stores of knowledge from 1600 to 1800 are in a grea[t] measure wrapt up in the dead languages: they are the languages of men of science or rather of science itself in Germany in the present day. There is not in Europe a book of belles lettres reading, that can be perused with pleasure without a knowledge of its classical allusions.

To the attainment of these languages <u>frequent composition in verse</u> is indispensible. A dozen latin verses, will require more thought, and impress more knowledge, than twice the number of pages of translation. I dwell upon this, from the great, and growing, and culpable neglect of this exercise in all our places of education. Hence, when Horace & Virgil and Ovid have been partially read at school, they are thrown aside for life, with us. The languages like music will never be

resorted to as a source of pleasure, untill their use and application
have become so familiar, as to be like our own language not an effort
of memory & voluntary association, but mechanical. Then indeed, the
attainment is truly worth having.

Hence, no intermission of classical reading & composition sh$^d$ be permitted, till the studies of the second grade, and the education of the
Gentleman are over.

2$^{ly}$ To this grade, the knowledge of the french language is in my
opinion essential. Essential to be spoken and written with ease & accuracy. At least as much of profitable and of pleasurable knowledge is
locked up in that language as in our own: it has long been, it is, and
I think it will continue to be the pass-port language of Europe.

3$^{ly}$ A knowledge of mathematics including not a slight knowledge of
Algebra & fluxions. These are so applicable to future scientific pursuits, that I sho[uld] be apt to entertain a Cambridge-predilection for
them.

4.$^{ly}$ A course of Chemistry, Mineralogy, and the chemical principles of
Agriculture Modern requirements have rendered these necessary:
and they afford the key to so much practical knowledge, that we cannot dispense with them. They will occupy three lectures a week for a
Year, or thereabout.

Chemistry ought to include, Heat, Light, Electricity, Galvanism,
Magnetism, [so] far as the teaching these branches of knowledge depends on experimental demonstration.

4$^{ly}$ The Mathematical part of Natural philosophy, Physico-
Mathematics, Including, Optics, Hydrostatics, Hydraulics, Pneumat-
ics, Acoustics; and Dynamics with models. This would occupy (with
Astronomy) one lecture a week during a Year.

5$^{ly}$ Lectures on Logic, Ideology or if you please Metaphysics; the theory of Language.

6$^{ly}$ Lectures on the Theory of Composition, and what is usually called
Taste, in writing, whether in prose or verse.

These 2 last w$^d$ not occupy more than one lecture a week each per
half year.

7$^{ly}$ Lectures on the Theory of Politics or Government, & its history,
beginning with the Politics of Aristotle, an excellent book. On statistics, & Political Economy. On the Spirit of general History. These w$^d$
occupy about 40 or 50 lectures. Perhaps a few Lectures on Ethics
and the general Principles of natural Law, might be added to these,
but I should not insist on it.

I believe, with historical reading by way of amusement, introducing also the french writers on History, as books to be read for the attainment of the french Language: and devoting some time to fencing with the small sword and back sword, the manual exercise and dancing—a young man's time will be very sufficiently filled up for five years, if these branches of knowledge be attended to not slightly and superficially, but duly.

I reject Anatomy, the Theory of Medicine, Zoology, Botany, and the Law of nature and nations, first because they are too technical to be considered as branches of general education: secondly because I do not think there is room or time to admit them in such a course: thirdly because I do not believe you can procure a Chemist competent to Chemistry, Mineralogy, Electric[ity] common & voltaic, Zoology and Botany: nor could he find the time [to] teach all these. Neither can you find a mathematician competent to Anatomy and the Theory of Medicine beside pure mathematics and natural philosopy. I think you require too many attainments a[nd] too many hours to be occupied.

As to the third or professional grade of Education. I agree to

1$^{st}$ A Department for teaching the duties of a Civil architect, and of a Civil Engineer, which for some years might be united. The art of laying out grounds might naturally be joined to this. But you have not, & cannot have at least for a Century in the United states, the means of founding a school of Painting, Sculpture or Music. Your drawing school, which is the first branch of this Department, should be well furnished with Casts and Prints.

2$^{ly}$ Department of military and naval Architecture, is indispensible: and including the mathematical part of this[5] department with models & a laboratory is enough of itself, without embracing rural economy, technical philosophy medecine and Surgery. These or some of them I should include in

3$^{ly}$ The Department of medecine. Including Anatomy, Physiology, Materia Medica, a renewal of the chemical course; Nosology, Therapeutics &c to which sh$^d$ be added Botany, Zoology, comparative Anatomy—

I w$^d$ reject the Department of technical philosophy; because no man can have the necessary knowledge—because men meaning to be tradesmen will not be able to attend it—because defects in the minute parts of the Knowledge of trades, will bring the Lectures into contempt among the people who are meant to be benefitted by them—because natural philosophy & Chemistry, will afford a sufficiency of principles, to guide the manipulations of most Arts and Trades.

I reject the Department of Theology: for reasons numerous and I think very weighty, but which need not be repeated. Where there exists a national system of religion, there ought to be a church establishment to support it, and regular seminaries in which should be taught the dogmata and their defences which the nation has thought fit politically to adopt. If religion be politically necessary, then teach it without regard to the truth of the adopted system: but if you are to teach theology in your university on the ground of its truth, who is to judge which System is true?

Suppose you teach Ecclesiastical History: any body can read it at home. Who can read it at all, with prejudices in favour of any System?

Will you teach the Evidences of Christianity, internal and external? Is it not fraud unless you teach the objections also? What seminary will venture upon this? Avoid this: it is a Noli me tangere.

4$^{ly}$ I would have a department of Law. To begin with the Law of nature and nations: then to proceed to the History and Elements of the Civil Law. Then to the history of the feudal Law. Then to the history of maritime Law, through the Laws of Rhodes, Oleron, Wisbeach &c to the Commentators on the french Code Valin, Emerigon. Then Brown, Azuni most grossly abused by the abettors of Aristocracy or rather of British Polity, Galliani, Lampredi.

Then the history of English Law Bracton, Fleta, with Reeves.

Further than this I w$^d$ not go. I think your State ought to annex some privileges to degrees taken after three years study in the last or Professional Grade.

Pray accept these hints and remarks, using or rejecting as you see good. Accept too of my best wishes for the success of the establishment, and your health and comfort.                    THOMAS COOPER

RC (DLC); edges chipped; endorsed by TJ as received 30 Sept. 1814 and so recorded in SJL. Enclosed in Cooper to TJ, 21 Sept. 1814.

For the PLAN OF UNIVERSITY EDUCATION YOU SENT ME, see TJ to Peter Carr, 7 Sept. 1814, which TJ sent to Cooper on 10 Sept. 1814. Cooper's FORMER LETTER ON THE SAME SUBJECT was dated 15 Sept. 1814. CAMBRIDGE-PREDILECTION: by the middle of the eighteenth century the tripos, or Senate House examination, with a heavy emphasis on mathematics, had become the only road to a degree at Cambridge University in England (W. W. Rouse Ball, *A History of the Study of Mathematics at Cambridge* [1889], 99, 187–210). Rhodian law is the earliest known system or code of MARITIME LAW, dating from about 900 B.C. (*Black's Law Dictionary*). The medieval maritime laws of OLERON, an island in the Bay of Biscay, and Visby or Wisby (WISBEACH), a port on the Baltic sea, appeared in Estienne Cleirac, *The Ancient Sea-Laws of Oleron, Wisby, and the Hanse-Towns, Still in Force*, trans. Guy Miege (London, 1686; Sowerby, no. 2099).

[1] Word stained.
[2] Word stained.
[3] Cooper here canceled "teach."

[4] Cooper here canceled "considered."
[5] Preceding three words interlined.

# To Joseph C. Cabell

DEAR SIR                                    Monticello. Sep. 23. 14.

Your favor of the 17th is just recieved. I shall answer it, as usual, frankly, adding my suggestions to those you may recieve from others, or concieve yourself, that your own good judgment may examine all things and hold fast that which is good. having before imposed on you the Corvée of reading my general sentiments on the subject of our finances, I may be the shorter now. I then thought it so important for the nation to enter into it's rights in the circulating medium, that I proposed the legislative resumption of them, and the gradual abolition of the banks of paper-discount[1] and of their paper. it would have been a difficult task; but to get along with the war otherwise I thought more difficult. Providence has now done the work for us. the banks from North to South, are all bankrupt, and have so declared themselves; covered indeed under the thin[2] pretext of preventing our enemies from drawing off all our specie, and their assurance that they will reassume business at a proper time. but I presume they will not invite the public authorities to inspect their books and vaults to see if the latter contain one third of what the former will prove they have in circulation. their notes, already rejected by some, recieved with hesitation by others, may drag on a few weeks longer, for want of all other circulation. but they are essentially defunct; and it is incumbent on the public authorities to act on that ground. to Congress it certainly should belong exclusively; and I presume they will immediately commence supplying the circulation with treasury notes. if bottomed on taxes, they will be recieved as willingly as gold and silver. if not so bottomed, they will soon, if not at the first, be on a footing with the bank notes & old Continental. they should, in the first place, issue as much as would repay all they have borrowed from the banks, requiring the banks to throw them[3] into circulation, in exchange for their own notes:[4] & they should issue as much more as will carry us thro' the ensuing year. if they were to buy up with treasury notes, the certificates of all their former loans, they would scarcely furnish as much medium as is necessary to let us down easily from the present excess. taxes then redeeming annually one tenth of their issues, would gradually reduce them to a competent circulation; and whenever they should fall below that, the metals would come in & keep it up to it's wholsome level.

But these measures may not perhaps be adopted by Congress, and would besides be too dilatory for the wants of our state, which you represent as urgent. the question then is whether we ought not to do ourselves what I have said it is the more peculiar duty of Congress to do? I acknolege a difficulty arising from the words of the constitution of the US. and the construction which some may put on them, and that construction too which is safest for the general interest. the states are prohibited from 'emitting bills of credit.' it is impossible however but that these words must have some limitation to their meaning. they cannot mean, for instance, that a state may not give to those to whom it owes a debt which it cannot yet[5] pay, an acknolegement of what it owes. our state, for example, has been in the constant practice of issuing by it's Auditor, certificates of what it owes to the bearer, whether the treasurer can pay them immediately or not; and this has never been deemed a breach of the constitution. continue this practice then. you owe the banks 300,000.D. give them Auditors' certificates of from 50. down to 5.D. declaring that 'the state owes them so many dollars, which shall be paid to them or bearer out of the proceeds of such a tax, within such a term, or as much sooner as may be from other resources.' and let the banks give out these certificates in exchange for so much of their own notes. you owe present sums also to your militia, contractors & furnishers, and will be incurring new debts thro' the ensuing year. authorise the giving them due-bills countersigned by the Auditor, to a corresponding effect. suppose these, with the debt to the banks, amount to 400,000.D. lay taxes of 40,000.D. annual amount for 10. years, appropriate them sacredly to the sole object of paying off that amount of these bills annually, and let them be recievable moreover in taxes. were bank bills in credit, it might be necessary to make the Auditors notes bear interest. but they will be taken now of necessity, and greedily,[6] without interest, as the bank notes were. their bearing an interest would produce two great evils. 1. they would be hoarded and the circulation starved. 2. you would be 20. instead of 10. years redeeming the debt, by the same tax, were you to allow the same interest which the United States give.

But the United States owe you 400,000.D. as soon then as this is paid, call in our own notes in exchange for those of the US. let the tax cease from that moment, and with it the example of being in contact with the constitution. that example continued might lead to new deluges of paper circulation, and to new revolutions and convulsions in private fortunes. we shall now experience these in a higher degree than on the death of the old Continental money: but this evil is incurred and cannot be cured; and it was long ago visible to experience & observation that the bank mania had siesed our citizens so universally as to admit no other remedy than ruin. that is now upon them, and will I hope convince the legislatures that it is the interest of all that all should relinquish the right of establishing banks of paper-discount, and that neither should that power be given to Congress; because it is an expedient which runs so certainly to abuse & the ruin of private fortunes, that no such power ought to be granted by the people to any of their public functionaries. the proceedings I propose, in order to secure us permanently against the recurrence of this catastrophe, should declare that no bank note should be ever again transferable, or ever again be evidence of a debt, or effect the discharge of a debt. but for this the legislature will not be ripe until they are overwhelmed by the abyss of ruin, now only beginning.

Accept these suggestions, which have been invited by your own request; use them for your own consideration only, or that of confidential friends, and be assured of my great friendship and respect.

Tʜ: Jᴇꜰꜰᴇʀꜱᴏɴ

RC (ViU: TJP); at foot of first page: "Joseph C. Cabell esq."; endorsed by Cabell, with his additional notation: "on the Finances of Virginia." PoC (NN: James Monroe Papers). Enclosed in TJ to James Monroe, 24 Sept. 1814.

Article 1, section 10 of the United States Constitution prohibits states from EMITTING BILLS OF CREDIT.

[1] Reworked from "of discount for paper."
[2] TJ here canceled "veil."
[3] Word reworked to "these notes" in PoC.
[4] Word canceled in PoC.
[5] Word interlined.
[6] Comma supplied from PoC.

# To James Madison

Dᴇᴀʀ Sɪʀ                                        Monticello Sep. 24. 14.

It is very long since I troubled you with a letter, which has proceeded from discretion, & not want of inclination, because I have really had nothing to write which ought to have occupied your time. but in the late events at Washington I have felt so much for you that

I cannot withold the expression of my sympathies. for altho' every reasonable man must be sensible that all you can do is to order, that execution must depend on others, & failures be imputable to them alone, yet I know that when such failures happen they afflict even those who have done everything they could to prevent them. had G$^l$ Washington himself been now at the head of our affairs, the same event would probably have happened. we all remember the disgraces which befel us in his time in a trifling war with one or two petty tribes of Indians, in which two armies were cut off by not half their numbers. every one knew, and I personally knew, because I was then of his council, that no blame was imputable to him, and that his officers alone were the cause of the disasters.

they must now do the same justice.—I am happy to turn to a countervailing event, & to congratulate you on the destruction of a second hostile fleet on the lakes by M$^c$Donough; of which however we have not the details. while our enemies cannot but feel shame for their barbarous atchievements at Washington, they will be stung to the soul by these repeated victories over them on that element on which they wish the world to think them invincible. we have dissipated that error. they must now feel a conviction themselves that we can beat them gun to gun, ship to ship, and fleet to fleet: and that their early successes on the land have been either purchased from traitors, or obtained from raw men entrusted of necessity with commands for which no experience had qualified them, and that every day is adding that experience to unquestioned bravery.

I am afraid the failure of our banks will occasion embarrasment for a while, altho it restores to us a fund which ought never to have been surrendered by the nation, and which now, prudently used, will carry us thro' all the fiscal difficulties of the war. at the request of mr Eppes, who was chairman of the committee of finance at the preceding session, I had written him some long letters on this subject. Col$^o$ Monroe asked the reading of them some time ago, and I now send him another, written to a member of our legislature, who requested my ideas on the recent bank-events. they are too long for your reading, but Col$^o$ Monroe can, in a few sentences, state to you their outline.

Learning by the papers the loss of the library of Congress, I have sent my catalogue to S. H. Smith, to make to their library committee the offer of my collection, now of about 9. or 10,000. vols. which may be delivered to them instantly, on a valuation by persons of their own naming, and be paid for in any way, and at any term they please; in stock, for example, of any loan they have, unissued, or of any one they may institute at this session; or in such annual instalments as are at the disposal of the committee. I believe you are acquainted with the condition of the books, should they wish to be ascertained of this. I have long been sensible that my library would be an interesting possession for the public, and the loss Congress has recently sustained, and the difficulty of replacing it, while our intercourse with Europe is so obstructed, renders this the proper moment for placing it at their service. Accept assurances of my constant & affectionate friendship and respect.

TH: JEFFERSON

RC (DLC: Madison Papers, Rives Collection); addressed: "James Madison President of the US. Washington"; franked; postmarked Milton, 28 Sept. PoC (DLC).

Arthur St. Clair and Josiah Harmer were the military OFFICERS who engaged in disastrous battles against Indians in the Northwest Territory during the

1790s (Washington, *Papers, Pres. Ser.*, 5:371–8, 6:361–5, 668–70, 11:291–316). Commander Thomas Macdonough won a major naval victory ON THE LAKES near Plattsburgh, New York, 11 Sept. 1814 (Malcomson, *Historical Dictionary*, 302–4). The letter to a MEMBER OF OUR LEGISLATURE was TJ to Joseph C. Cabell, 23 Sept. 1814.

# From Philip Mazzei

STIMATISSIMO, E CARISSIMO AMICO,                Pisa, 24 7bre, 1814.

Per mezzo del Sig.<sup>r</sup> David Bailei Wandeny, Console degli Stati Uniti a Parigi, mi pervenne la carissima e amorevolissima sua del 29 xbre, 1813, alla quale feci subito una breve risposta, e la mandai al Sig.<sup>r</sup> Guglielmo Enrigo Crawford, nostro ministro Plenipotenziario in Francia, per mezzo del nostro Console all'Isole Boreali, il quale (venendo da Livorno per andar'a Parigi, e di là ritornare al suo Posto) ebbe la bontà di trattenersi un giorno e una notte in casa mia colla sua numerosa e angelica famiglia. Questa la mando al Sig.<sup>r</sup> David Bailei Wandeny, come la precedente.[1]

Ò tradotto la sua lettera per comunicarla agli Amici qui, a Livorno, a Lucca, e a Firenze. Il tutto è stato letto con sommo piacere, a riserva del tradimento del nostro primo Generale, e il massacro alle frontiere, che ànno eccitato lo sdegno, e l'ira universale.

Il Sig.<sup>r</sup> Bernardo Lessi, Legale sommo, stato Auditore qui e a Livorno, poi Avvocato Regio in Firenze, Auditore al Supremo Tribunal di Giustizia, ed è ora Membro del Real consulta (che rappresenta il Sovrano) mi ci rispose come segue

"Ò letto l'interessante lettera di Jefferson con sommo piacere, ed ò ammirato l'uomo di Stato, l'amico dei suoi simili, l'amico vostro.[2]

Non lasciai trascorrere un momento per comunicarla al Fabbroni, ed eccovi la sua risposta."

(Sono veramente grato all'Amico Filippo, e a voi, per la comunicazione dell'interezzante lettera. Il candore che vi regna, e il carattere di chi la scrive, danno la più alta autenticita ai fatti, che Stanno in contrasto con i fatti riferiti dai novisti venali. Avrei curiosità di sapere quel che è seguito dal Gennaio a questa parte.)[3]

Continovazione della lettera di Lessi.

"Intanto ritorno nelle vostre mani l'interessantissima lettera di Jefferson, ed unisco al plico i recapiti riguardanti l'eredità del Bellini. Le sorelle morirono, e l'erede è un certo Prete Fancelli, in correspettività dei soccorsi caritatevoli dati alle medesime quando erano in vita. La Luisa, che fa testamento, stava[4] in casa sua, ed era trattata ed assistita come se fosse stata sua sorella. I recapiti che vi mando non ànno firma di mercanti, per quanto abbiano tutte le altre legalizzazioni. Non vorrei che restassero infruttuosi, giacchè ànno costato mille impazzamenti."

Ella si ricorderà, che mandai al Sig[r] Bracken la procura delle sorelle del Bellini per[5] vendere il moro, la mora, e i mobili, che lasciò il fratello. Le sopraddette carte di procura sono voluminose, e costerebbe molto il mandarle a Parigi per la posta; onde aspetterò che vengano a Livorno i nostri bastimenti mercantili, dei quali si spera che ne venranno molti, e presto; ma intanto La prego d'informarsi di quel che à fatto Bracken, onde poter'agire subito che riceverà le sopraddette carte.

Ella mi dice: "Il messaggio del Presidente all'apertura del Congresso vi darà un dettaglio esatto della nostra condotta. Conoscendo il vostro affetto per questo Paese, e il vostro desiderio per la sua prosperità, ò creduto che la relazione dei suoi eventi vi avrebbe fatto piacere." Desidero di vederlo; ma se non me lo manda presto, non lo vedrò. Si ricordi, che ò 11 anni più di Lei, come ne à Ella più di Madison. E, oltre il peso di 84 anni che terminerò il 25 del prossimo xbre, ò le gambe gonfie, e soffro molto, dovendo tenere una fasciatura con un piombo, che pigia fortemente sul pube, per impedire all'intestino Colon l'introito nello scroto, dove inevitabilmente produrrebbe un'ernia incarcerata.

Le son molto grato della vendita della mia casa e lot in Richmond, il cui prodotto à superato la mia aspettativa; ma gradirei che mi fosse rimesso immediatamente per più motivi. Ella probabilmente saprà, che l'insaziabile tirannia di[6] Napoleone à rovinato tutti i Paesi dove à potuto dominare,[7] e che gl'individui più strapazzati e angariati sono stati i conosciuti, o supposti nemici del potere arbitrario. Conseguentemente io sono stato uno dei piu perseguitati, onde le mie finanze ànno molto sofferto, e mi sarebbe di gran sollievo il poter ritirare il prodotto del mio stabile immediatamente,[8] poichè la grande scarsezza del denaro, causata dal Tiranno, fa sì che il denaro può impiegarsi adesso con mallevadoria territoriale a uno per 100 il mese. Io dunque preferirei volentieri il rilasciare al Compratore una somma discreta, piuttosto che aspettare uno, o 2 anni a riceverne il capitale. La prego di farmi ottener l'intento, riflettendo ancora, che[9] difficilmente si può ottenere dagli Esecutori Testamentari la circospezione e l'attenzione d'un marito e d'un padre.[10]

Mi confermo ex corde qual sempre fui dal momento che La conobbi, e sarò usque ad mortem,

Suo cordiale amico,

FILIPPO MAZZEI.

P.S. Di questa ne manderò altre copie con i bastimenti Americani, che venranno a Livorno.

ESTEEMED, AND DEAREST FRIEND,      Pisa, 24 September, 1814.
I received your most kind and precious letter dated 29 December 1813 through Mr. David Bailie Warden, United States consul at Paris. I immediately wrote a brief reply and sent it to Mr. William Henry Crawford, our minister plenipotentiary in France, by way of our consul in the Balearic Islands (who was traveling from Leghorn to Paris and from there returning to his post). He along with his numerous and angelic family were good enough to stay a day and a night at my home. As with the preceding letter, I am sending this through Mr. David Bailie Warden.

I translated your letter so as to communicate it to friends here, in Leghorn, Lucca, and Florence. The contents were read with great pleasure, except for the sections on the betrayal of our foremost general and the massacre at the border, both of which have roused universal disdain and anger.

Mr. Bernardo Lessi, an excellent lawyer, formerly auditor here and in Leghorn, later royal advocate in Florence and auditor of the supreme court of justice, and now a member of the royal council (which represents the sovereign), answered me as follows
"I read Jefferson's interesting letter with great pleasure and admire him as a statesman, a friend to his fellow man, and to you. I did not let a moment pass before communicating it to Fabbroni, and here is his response."

(I am truly grateful to our friend Philip and to you for communicating this interesting letter. Its pervasive candor and its author's character lend the utmost authenticity to the facts it contains, which contrast with those reported by writers for hire. I would be curious to know what has happened since January.)

Lessi's letter continues.
"In the meantime I am returning Jefferson's most interesting letter to you, and I am including in the package the documents regarding Bellini's estate.

His sisters have died, and the heir is a certain Father Fancelli, who is being compensated for the charitable care he gave the sisters during their lifetime. Luisa, who wrote the will, lived in his home and was treated and cared for as if she were his sister. The papers I am sending you do not have the merchants' signature, although they have all the other legal authentications. I hope these papers will not prove useless, especially as they have already caused a thousand headaches."

You will recall that I sent the Bellini sisters' power-of-attorney to Mr. Bracken to allow him to sell the negro, the negress, and the furniture left by their brother. The abovementioned proxy papers are voluminous, and it would cost a great deal to send them to Paris by mail; therefore I will wait for our cargo ships to come to Leghorn. We hope many will soon come; but in the meantime I would ask you to please find out what Bracken did, so as to be able to act quickly as soon as you receive the above papers.

You say to me: "The President's message at the opening of Congress will give you an exact account of our actions. Knowing your affection for this country and your wishes for its prosperity, I thought that a report on its events would please you." I wish to see it; but if you do not send it to me soon, I will not. Remember, I am eleven years your senior, exactly as much older as you are than Madison. And, in addition to the weight of my eighty-four years, which I will reach next 25 December, my legs are swollen and I am in great pain, as I have to wear a support belt with a lead seal that presses heavily against my groin in order to prevent my colon from entering my scrotum, where it would inevitably produce a strangulated hernia.

I am very grateful to you for the sale of my house and lot in Richmond, the proceeds of which surpassed my expectation. But I would prefer, for a number of reasons, for it to be remitted to me immediately. You probably know that Napoleon's insatiable tyranny has ruined all the countries he has managed to dominate, and that the known, or alleged, enemies of arbitrary power have been the most battered and oppressed. Consequently I have been one of the most persecuted, and as a result my finances have suffered greatly. I would be greatly relieved if I could collect the income from my estate immediately, especially as the scarcity of money, on account of the tyrant, is such that one can now invest in landed securities at a rate of one percent per month. Therefore I would gladly prefer to discount substantially the sale price to the buyer, rather than have to wait one or two years to receive the principal. Please help me to accomplish this, recalling again how difficult it is to get the same kind of care and attention from estate executors that one gets from a husband or a father.

I pledge myself from my heart, as I have been since the moment I met you and will always be until death,

Your cordial friend, PHILIP MAZZEI.

P.S. I will send other copies of this by the American ships that come to Leghorn.

RC (DLC); addressed: "Thomas Jefferson Esq^re, at Monticello, in the county of Albemarle, in Virginia"; notation by TJ on address cover: "forwarded to me in a letter of D. B. Warden of Oct. 20. 14."; endorsed by TJ as received 15 July 1815 and so recorded in SJL. Dupl (DLC); dated 18 Sept. 1814; in Elisabetta Mazzei's hand, with the signature and postscripts in Philip Mazzei's hand; differs somewhat from RC, with only the most significant variations noted below; endorsed by TJ as a "dupl." dated 18 Sept. 1815 and received 25 Oct. 1815. Translation by Dr. Adrienne Ward. Enclosed in David Bailie Warden to TJ, 20 Oct. 1814, and Thomas Appleton to TJ, 26 Aug. 1815.

SJL records the receipt on 6 Oct. 1815 of an additional text of this letter, with TJ's notation that it was a "duplicate" of the 18 and 24 Sept. 1814 letters (the latter referred to by its 15 July 1815 date of receipt). This additional text evidently enclosed the Bellini estate documents described below at TJ to Robert Saunders, 25 Dec. 1815.

Mazzei's BREVE RISPOSTA of 21 Aug. 1814, not found, was enclosed to TJ on 18 Oct. 1815 by John Martin Baker, the CONSOLE ALL'ISOLE BOREALI, and is recorded in SJL as received from Pisa on 13 Jan. 1816. Mazzei states that he, TJ, and James Madison were separated in age by intervals of 11 ANNI, but they were actually born in 1730, 1743, and 1751, respectively.

[1] Sentence not in Dupl.
[2] Dupl: "il vero Amico vostro" ("your true friend").
[3] Omitted closing parenthesis editorially supplied.
[4] Dupl here adds "e morì" ("and died").
[5] Dupl here adds "autorizzarlo a" ("to authorize him to").

[6] Dupl: "dell'Iniquo" ("of the iniquitous").
[7] Dupl: "invadere" ("to invade").
[8] Dupl: "in Ritchmond" ("in Richmond").
[9] For preceding three words Dupl substitutes "poichè (ottre il maggior fratto che produrrebbe quì)" ("since [aside from the greater profit it would produce here]").
[10] Remainder of Dupl reads as follows: "E quanto alla somma da rilasciarsi al Compratore, mi rimetto interamente alla sua discretezza. N:B: Questa l'indirizzo al Sig.re David Bailei Wandeny, e ne manderò delle copie subito che verranno a Livorno i nostri Bastimenti Americani. Intanto mi confermo ex corde (qual sempre fui dal momento che ebbi la fortuna, e la consolazione di conoscerla). Suo vero, e cordiale Amico, [in Mazzei's hand hereafter] Filippo Mazzei. La mano non mi serve bene, onde ò fatto fare questa copia alla mia Figlia, e Le ne farò fare dell'altre. N.B. Questa è la seconda copia della risposta al Signnor Tommaso Jefferson, e parte nel Bastimento          , Capitano          , il dì          " ("As far as the price to charge the buyer, I leave that entirely to your discretion. N:B: I am addressing this to Mr. David Bailie Warden and will send copies as soon as American ships come to Leghorn. In the meantime, I pledge myself from my heart (as I have been since the moment I had the good fortune and consolation of meeting you) your true and cordial friend, Philip Mazzei. As my hand does not serve me well, I had my daughter make this copy, and I will have her make others. N.B. This is the second copy of my reply to Mr. Thomas Jefferson, and it leaves on the ship          , Captain          , on the          day").

# From Joseph Milligan

DEAR SIR                                George Town Sep.t 24 1814

I returned here on Monday-night at 10 o'clock, after having visited Richmond, Petersburg and Norfolk. In each of those places I found great military Preperations, and a Spirit of Unanimity amongst the citizens, that Surpassed my most Sanguin expectations. In Norfolk I was particularly attracted by the great, and (I trust) Successful, efforts that have been made to render that place Secure. If they be not attacked before Christmas I think 30,0000 of the enemy would make no impression on the place if defended by 10,000—even Militia—unless they lay regular siege, and in that case they[1] would Soon be compelled to raise the Siege, by reinforcements that would immediately be Sent from Petersburg and Richmond. But to come more immediately to the object of this letter.

On Tuesday-morning I called on the Secretary of State; he informs me that the Library of Congress "with all that thereunto appertained," was consumed on the memorable 24th of August;—therefore, your truly magnanamous offer of the Monticello Library to Congress, will be very acceptable. If Congress should purchase it, to literary men it would be a great privelege to be permitted at all times of the year to have free access, not to take away the Books, but, to read in the Library and make extracts: therefore the place of Librarian would be well to be a distinct office from the clerk of the House of Representatives. If they do take it every thing that I can do in arranging it Shall be done, and I will keep the Library for this session free of cost. By this I would have it clearly understood that it is not my wish to fish for it; as a permanent thing, for I would not accept a place of profit under any Government.

You will please communicate with the Secretary of State on the Subject—and enclose the catalogue to him.

I will immediately on receipt of it arrange to have it printed.

I Shall, in a few days, Send you a few Books by the way of Fredericksburg, to the care of my friend Cap[t] W[m] F. Gray; to whom I have written to undertake the little agency that you spoke of. I could not see him on my return as he was in Camp with his men.

The Great Hotel makes a very convenient house for both houses of Congress with a sufficient number of committee Rooms, and a large room for the Washington Post-Office.

The news from england, of this day by an arrival at charleston I have enclosed to you.

In two or three days I will write to you the State of the Public Ruins.

My Sincere Respects to Mrs. Randolph, Mrs. Bankhead, Mrs. Carey and their respective families.

with great respect
yours.

JOSEPH MILLIGAN

RC (DLC); addressed: "Thomas Jefferson. Esquire, Monticello. Virginia"; franked and postmarked; endorsed by TJ as received 30 Sept. 1814 and so recorded in SJL. Enclosure not found.

Blodget's was the GREAT HOTEL.

[1] Manuscript: "the."

# To James Monroe

DEAR SIR                                          Monticello Sep. 24. 14.

The events which have lately taken place at Washington, & which truly disgrace our enemies much more than us, have occupied you too much to admit intrusions by private & useless letters. you seem indeed to have had your hands full with the duties of the field and the double duties of the Cabinet. the success of M<sup>c</sup>Donough has been happily timed to dispel the gloom of your present meeting, and to open the present session of Congress with hope and good humor. to add however to our embarrasments, it happens to be the moment when the general bankruptcy comes upon us, which has been so long and so certainly impending. the banks declare they will not pay their bills, which is sufficiently understood to mean that they cannot. altho' this truth has been long expected, yet their own declaration was wanting to fix the moment of insolvency. their paper is now offered doubtingly, recieved by some merely from the total absence of all other medium of payment, and absolutely rejected by others; and in no case will a half-disme of cash be given in change. the annihilation of these institutions has come on us suddenly therefore, which I had thought should be suppressed, but gradatim only, in order to prevent, as much as possible, the crush of private fortunes. this catastrophe happening just as our legislature was about to meet, a member of it requested my thoughts on the occasion. these I have expressed in the inclosed letter, and as it forms a sequel to those I had lent you before, I send it for your perusal. altho' I am not willing they should be handed about promiscuously to friend and foe, yet if the communication of them to particular and confidential characters can do any good, I should leave that to your discretion, and only ask their return as soon as that shall have been done.          Having learnt by the public papers the loss of the library of Congress, I have sent my catalogue to S. H. Smith with an offer of the whole collection, as it stands, to the library committee, to be valued by persons named by themselves, delivered immediately, and paid for in such stock, or otherwise, & at such epoch as they may chuse after the days of peace &

prosperity shall have returned. you know the general condition of the books, & can give them information should they ask any. I salute you always with sincere affection & respect    TH: JEFFERSON

RC (NN: Monroe Papers); at foot of text: "Col⁰ Monroe." PoC (DLC); endorsed by TJ. Enclosure: TJ to Joseph C. Cabell, 23 Sept. 1814.

GRADATIM: "step by step; gradually" (*OED*).

# To John L. E. W. Shecut

DEAR SIR                                Monticello Sep. 25. 14.

Your favor of Aug. 17. has been recieved but lately, and I learn from it with satisfaction that you are occupied in digesting a Theory of Medecine which you think will be free from the inconsistences which have hitherto been found in all others. for myself, I must candidly own I have little faith in the theories hitherto offered; and the less, because they change as often as the fashions of caps and gowns. whether all the fluids & solids which compose the animal machine, their action on one another, & that of the surrounding bodies on them, and the natural substances which are found to reestablish order when it has been disturbed, will ever be known to man, is yet to be seen. but to be a candidate for the discovery of a theory which, answering these views, shall be permanent as the Elements of Euclid, is certainly a laudable object of ambition: and if I do not look forward with entire confidence in the accomplishment of your hopes, I do it with sincere good wishes for success, as well for the advancement of your reputation & benefit, as for the good it will produce to the human race. for myself, the remaining term of life is too short to feel a personal interest in it: and satisfied with that which has been indulged to me and always till lately with the blessing of health,[1] I do not know that I should be thankful to him who should lengthen it.        With respect to your wishes to obtain a secretaryship in some of our foreign legations, in order to get your work printed, I must observe that the appointment of secretaries of legation was tried by the government for a while, but soon abandoned from the inconveniences it produced, & the former practice was reverted to of permitting every minister to select his own private secretary; an office not equal to the other either in emolument or respectability. but the application for this must be to the principal appointed. whether any office can be obtained from the government which placing you near them might afford an opportunity of printing, I am not able to say, having long-withdrawn myself from that kind of interference from a necessity imposed on me by the multitude of applications, & the supplicating attitude in which it kept me constantly before the government. the most effectual enquiry & sollicitation you could employ would be by your members of Congress, who would be on the spot when a foreign mission is named, or an office vacated, & whose recommendations, more than any others, have weight with the government. I should with pleasure give aid to your views in any way which should be consistent with the laws I have been obliged to lay down for my own conduct: and with every wish for the accomplishment of your views, I tender you the assurance of my great esteem & respect.                                   Th: Jefferson

PoC (DLC); at foot of first page: "Doct' L. E. W. Sheecut"; endorsed by TJ.

INCONSISTENCES: "inconsistencies" (*OED*).

[1] Preceding nine words interlined.

# To Thomas B. Wait

Sir                                   Monticello Sep. 25. 14.

Your favor of the 8th has been duly recieved. not being certain that I form a correct idea of the character of the state papers you propose to publish and to what extent your views may go, I will notice & observe on them specifically.

1. Diplomatic correspondence. the whole of this in MS. is doubtless in the office of State. the parts not heretofore permitted to be made public, would not, I presume be now permitted. the residue has been printed from session to session of Congress, on loose sheets for the use of the members, and published in the newspapers & especially in the National Intelligencer from 1801. & Fenno's paper preceding that epoch.

2. Reports of the heads of departments; printed always for the use of the members, and in Fenno and the National Intelligencer.

3. Reports of Committees, & Motions of particular members, printed always for the use of the members. such of these as have been approved, are entered of course on the Journals of the House, where they may be found. those rejected remain only in the loose sheets printed for the members. I hardly suppose however that you would think these abortive reports & motions worth reprinting.

Some of the members of Congress have been in the habit of preserving these loose sheets, and stitching them together in annual volumes: and I have no doubt this has been done by some members of your state, but a file of Fenno's papers till 1800. & of the National Intelligencer afterwards, will compleatly supply all the Diplomatic correspondence which has ever been made public, and the reports of the heads of departments; and they will be found within the periods of the sessions of Congress.

The loose sheets having been printed for the use of members only, I did not recieve them fully. whether those preserved for the use of the two houses of Congress were saved or not, I am not informed. the MS. papers of the department of State I understand were all preserved.

In thus indicating to you sources from which these several descriptions of papers may certainly be obtained, I have the less regret in being myself unable to furnish them. I have little doubt they may be procured from individual members of Congress, and none at all that a file of Fenno's papers to 1800. & of the National Intelligencer afterwards will furnish the whole from the commencement of the government. with wishes of success to your undertaking, I tender you the assurance of my respect.                    TH: JEFFERSON

PoC (DLC); at foot of first page: "Mr Thos B. Wait"; endorsed by TJ.

FENNO'S PAPER: the *Gazette of the United States* was published with varying subtitles at New York by John Fenno, 1789–90, and at Philadelphia successively by John Fenno, 1790–98, John W. Fenno, 1798–1800, and Caleb P. Wayne, 1800–01 (Brigham, *American Newspapers*, 1:645, 2:912–3).

# From Edward Coles

Washington Sep: 26th '14

I must be permitted again to trouble you, my dear Sir, to return my grateful thanks for the respectful and friendly attention shown to my letter in your answer of the 25th ulto. Your favorable reception of sentiments not generally avowed if felt by our Countrymen, but which have ever been so inseparably interwoven with my opinions and feelings as to become as it were the rudder that shapes my course even against a strong tide of interest and of local partialities, could not but be in the highest degree gratifying to me. And your interesting and highly prized letter, conveying them to me in such flattering terms, would have called forth my acknowledgements before this but for its having been forwarded to me to the Springs, and from thence it was again returned here before I received it, which was only a few days since.

Your indulgent treatment encourages me to add—that I feel very sensibly the force of your remarks on the impropriety of yielding to my repugnancies in abandoning my property in Slaves and my native State. I certainly should never have been inclined to yield to them if I had supposed myself capable of being instrumental in bringing about a liberation, or that I could by my example meliorate the condition of these oppressed people. If I could be convinced of being in the slightest degree useful in doing either, it would afford me very great happiness, and the more so as it would enable me to gratify many partialities by remaining in Virginia. But never having flattered myself with the hope of being able to contribute to either, I have long since determined, and should, but for my bad health ere this, have removed, carrying along with me those who had been my Slaves, to the Country North West of the river Ohio.

Your prayers I trust will not only be heard with indulgence in Heaven, but with influence on earth. But I cannot agree with you that they are the only weapons of one at your age, nor that the difficult work of cleansing the escutcheon of Virginia of the foul stain of slavery can best be done by the young. To effect so great and difficult an object great and extensive powers both of mind and influence are required, which can never be possessed in so great a degree by the young as by the old. And among the few of the former who might unite the disposition with the requisite capacity, they are too often led by ambitious views to go with the current of popular feeling, rather than to mark out a course for themselves, where they might be buffetted by the waves of opposition; and indeed it is feared these waves would in this case be too strong to be effectually resisted, by any but those who had gained by a previous course of useful employment the firmest footing in the confidence and attachment of their Country. It is with them, therefore, I am persuaded, that the subject of emancipation must originate; for they are the only persons who have it in their power effectually to arouse and enlighten the public sentiment, which in matters of this kind ought not to be expected to lead but to be led; nor ought it to be wondered at that there should prevail a degree of apathy with the general mass of mankind, where a mere passive principle of right has to contend against the weighty influence of habit and interest. On such a question there will always exist in society a kind of vis inertia, to arouse and overcome which require a strong impulse, which can only be given by those who have acquired a great weight of character, and on whom there devolves in this case a most solemn obligation. It was under these impressions that I looked to you, my dear sir, as the first of our aged worthies, to awaken our fellow Citizens from their infatuation to a proper sense of Justice and to the true interest of their country, and by proposing a system for the gradual emancipation of our Slaves, at once to form a rallying point for its friends, who enlightened by your wisdom and experience, and supported and encouraged by your sanction and patronage, might look forward to a propitious and happy result. Your time of life I had not considered as an obstacle to the undertaking. Doctor Franklin, to whom, by the way, Pennsylvania owes her early riddance of the evils of Slavery, was as actively and as usefully employed on as arduous duties after he had past your age as he had ever been at any period of his life.

With apologizing for having given you so much trouble on this subject, and again repeating my thanks for the respectful and flattering attention you have been pleased to pay to it, I renew the assurances of the great respect and regard which makes me most sincerely
Yours　　　　　　　　　　　　　　　EDWARD COLES

RC (DLC); endorsed by TJ as received 30 Sept. 1814 and so recorded in SJL. RC (NHi: Thomas Jefferson Papers); address cover only; with Dft of TJ to Patrick Gibson, 21 Nov. 1814, on verso; addressed: "Th: Jefferson Monticello Milton Virginia"; franked; postmarked Washington, 28 Sept. FC (NjP: Coles Papers); entirely in Coles's hand.

Benjamin FRANKLIN, writing in his capacity as president of the PENNSYLVANIA Society for Promoting the Abolition of Slavery, submitted a petition in the last year of his life asking the United States Congress to abolish slavery and end the slave trade. Both houses considered the petition in February and March 1790 along with two similar documents by groups of Quakers, but after intense debate Congress concluded that, with the exception of the foreign slave trade, slavery was an internal affair of the states that it had no authority to regulate (Linda Grant De Pauw and others, eds., *Documentary History of the First Federal Congress* [1972–　], 8:314–38).

# To Miles King

SIR　　　　　　　　　　　　　　　Monticello Sep. 26. 14
I duly recieved your letter of Aug. 20. and I thank you for it, because I believe it was written with kind intentions, and a personal concern for my future happiness. whether the particular revelation

which you suppose to have been made to yourself were real or imaginary, your reason alone is the competent judge. for, dispute as long as we will on religious tenets, our reason at last must ultimately decide, as it is the only oracle which god has given us to determine between what really comes from him, & the phantasms of a disordered or deluded imagination. when he means to make a personal revelation he carries conviction of it's authenticity to the reason he has bestowed as the umpire of truth. you believe you have been favored with such a special communication. your reason, not mine, is to judge of this: and if it shall be his pleasure to favor me with a like admonition, I shall obey it with the same fidelity with which I would obey his known will in all cases. hitherto I have been under the guidance of that portion of reason which he has thought proper to deal out to me. I have followed it faithfully in all important cases, to such a degree at least as leaves me without uneasiness; and if on minor occasions I have erred from it's dictates, I have trust in him who made us what we are, and knows it was not his plan to make us always unerring. he has formed us moral agents, not that, in the perfection of his state, he can feel pain or pleasure from any thing we may do: he is far above our power: but that we may promote the happiness of those with whom he has placed us in society, by acting honestly towards all, benevolently to those who fall within our way, respecting sacredly their rights bodily and mental, and cherishing especially their freedom of conscience, as we value our own. I must ever believe that religion substantially good which produces an honest life, and we have been authorised by one, whom you and I equally respect, to judge of the tree by it's fruit. our particular principles of religion are a subject of accountability to our god alone. I enquire after no man's, and trouble none with mine: nor is it given to us in this life to know whether your's or mine, our friend's or our foe's are exactly the right. nay, we have heard it said that there is not a quaker or a baptist, a presbyterian or an episcopalian, a catholic or a protestant in heaven: that, on entering that gate, we leave those badges of schism behind, and find ourselves united in those principles only in which god has united us all. let us not be uneasy then about the different roads we may pursue, as believing them the shortest, to that our last abode: but, following the guidance of a good conscience, let us be happy in the hope that, by these different paths, we shall all meet in the end. and that you and I may there meet and embrace is my earnest prayer: and with this assurance I salute you with brotherly esteem and respect.                                                            TH: JEFFERSON

PoC (DLC); at foot of first page: "M^r Miles King."

In the Bible, Jesus taught his followers to JUDGE OF THE TREE BY IT'S FRUIT (Matthew 7.15–20, 12.33; Luke 6.43–5).

John Adams had recently cited George Whitefield's assertion that THERE IS NOT A QUAKER OR A BAPTIST, A PRESBYTERI-AN OR AN EPISCOPALIAN, A CATHOLIC OR A PROTESTANT IN HEAVEN (Adams to TJ, 3 Dec. 1813).

# From Samuel E. Mifflin

Philadel^a N^o 179 Chesnut St at Ann Em opposite the State House
[ca. 26 Sept. 1814]

I wish to know of you Sir, whether you recollect to have observed during the American War, by the then general Thomas Mifflin any opposition to have been made to the sanctity and <u>spirit</u> of General Washington Whether that opposition and the eternal spring of patriotism given to the American breast by the genius the <u>valour</u> the intelligence and the virtue of <u>Mifflin</u> did not rescue this Country from impending destruction and from impending devastation in all it's borders: Whether the valour of Thomas Mifflin did not shine conspicuous before the eternal spirit and whether his fame has not been injured by the indigence of the quaker Society, whether the little want of principle of virtue of intelligence of liberality in the State of which he was a member has not or whether[1] the envy and enmity of private families have not infringed upon his rights and glory and whether the vanity of others, Virginians as well as Pennsylvanians, You as well as General Washington whose passions whose sentiments may have been actuated upon by others, has not served to form a thick volumino[us] dark threatning impenetrable cloud, which has served to obscure the most resplendent rays of one of the brightest suns that ever was created in the Hemisphere[2] of[3] patriotism You must know Sir, for I will inform you, by this letter which, I hope you will read for the sake of your manners as a man of Your genius as a Philosopher of your virtue as an american citizen & that one of the most conspicuous of any that Pennsylvania is changing in habits in manners & in religion that the Mifflin family are determined to bring about a revolution in their sentiments or perish in the attempt for their name (that of the Mifflins) shall no longer be held at the whims the caprices and the frowns of others for Pennsylvania shall rise some parts of her in virtue in honour in intelligence and in renown and this by the virtue of the Mifflin family alone if General Mifflin whose virtues rise conspicuous in the canopy of heaven has not had justice done Justice shall yet be done him; for I <u>will</u> rescue this country of the United States of America including the boundless regions of Louisiana which you were inquisitive in purchasing together with the indigent John Randolph who supported you in that measure during Your illustrious and ever memorable administration from the eternal disgrace of the contempt of the inspired the glorious the illustrious Mifflin, Sir, I declare before the canopy of heaven that he was a greater a more illustrious a more virtuous a more truly benevolent patriotick charater than has been any American that ever existed (and[4] equal) not even excepting You the illustrious Jefferson or General Washington.[5]

S. E. MIFFLIN

RC (DLC: TJ Papers, 202:35993–4); undated; edge trimmed; addressed: "His Excellency Thomas Jefferson late President of the United S. Monticello Virginia"; postmarked Philadelphia, 26 Sept.; endorsed by TJ as received 30 Sept. 1814 and so recorded in SJL.

Samuel Emlen Mifflin (b. 1790) was the son of Quaker reformer Warner Mifflin and Anne Emlen Mifflin, a Quaker preacher and abolitionist. In an 1813 letter to another family member, a cousin described Samuel as "in a state of derangement—the symptoms occasionally varying—sometimes violent—and sometimes more moderate—but never even apparently removed (as far as I can learn) since his first attack" (Hilda Justice, *Life and Ancestry of Warner Mifflin* [1905], 19; John Lynch to TJ, 25 Dec. 1810; Lloyd Mifflin Sr. to Joseph Mifflin Jr., 6 Nov. 1813 [PLF: Mifflin Papers]).

THOMAS MIFFLIN (1744–1800), merchant and public official, was a native of Philadelphia. He served in both Continental Congresses before accepting a position as George Washington's aide-de-camp in 1775, for which warlike activity the Quakers disowned him. Mifflin was appointed the Continental army's first quartermaster general later that year and rose to major general in 1777. After controversy regarding his tenure as quartermaster drew the attention of Congress, he resigned from the military in 1779. His reputation was further marred by rumored involvement in an organized plot to replace Washington during the winter of 1777–78. Mifflin returned to the Continental Congress, 1782–84 (with service as president, 1783–84), signed the United States Constitution in 1787, presided over the convention that drafted the 1790 Pennsylvania constitution, and was elected to three consecutive terms as a moderately Republican governor of Pennsylvania, 1790–99 (*ANB*; *DAB*; Heitman, *U.S. Army*, 1:708; Washington, *Papers, Rev. War Ser.*, 1:56–7; *PTJ*, 7:275).

[1] Manuscript: "whethe."
[2] Preceding seven words interlined.
[3] Mifflin here canceled "true of unequalled unparallelled unconquerable."
[4] Mifflin here canceled "if we except them shurly none others are nearly."
[5] Mifflin here canceled "your frien."

# Statement of Albemarle County Taxes and Court Fees

Thomas Jefferson Esq:

| | | | | |
|---|---|---|---|---|
| 1814 | To the commonwealth of Virginia | | | Dr. |
| Sep$^{tr}$ | Rev: on | 5374$\frac{3}{4}$ acres land | | $59.73 |

| | | |
|---|---|---|
| 72 Negroes above 16 | | |
| 14 ditto under | | |
| 26 Horses | | |
| 1 Phæton value | 150$ | |
| 1 ditto | 100 | 111.52 |
| 1 Gig | 50 | |
| 1 M-Mill | | |
| 1 Toll Mill | | |
| 1 Saw ditto | | |

| | |
|---|---|
| County & Parish levy on 5 white and 72 black tytheables @ 31 cts | 23.87 |
| Thomas Jefferson & C° for tax on 266$\frac{2}{3}$ acres land | 1.11 |
| | $196.23 |
| Mrs M Lewis' dft | 8.24 |
| Tickets—vs Hasting Marks and his Ex$^{tr}$ | 7.39 |
| ditto—  vs W$^m$ Short | 5.29 |
| C Peyton for transfer ticket Henderson to him for Your benefit  }0.75 | 15.70 |
| Same, for Your proportion of Clerk's ticket Hendersons deed to him for }2.27  } 3.02 your benefit | |
| Tickets vs Yourself | 10.15 |
| | 10.15 |
| | $230.32 |

| | |
|---|---|
| 1814 | |
| Sep$^{tr}$ 27 | By draft on Gibson and Jefferson for the amount of above account payable the 25$^{th}$ October next |

CLIF: HARRIS D SHFF
for
CH$^s$ B. HUNTON S, A, C

MS (MHi); in Harris's hand; composed in two sittings; endorsed by TJ: "Sheriff Albemarle taxes and tickets Sep. 1814"; with TJ's apparently unrelated calculations totaling $134.84 on verso.

Clifton Harris (b. ca. 1785) was still in Albemarle County in 1853. He served as deputy sheriff until at least 1817. Harris pledged $100 to Central College, and in 1836 he supported Martin Van Buren's presidential candidacy. The 1850 census described him as a teacher (Woods, *Albemarle*, 221; *MB*, 2:1303, 1338; Cabell, *University of Virginia*, 406; *Richmond Enquirer*, 13 Feb. 1836; DNA: RG 29, CS, Albemarle Co., 1850; *MACH* 19 [1960/61]: 57).

Charles B. Hunton (d. 1818) was sheriff of Albemarle County, 1813–15. He was appointed a county magistrate in 1791, took a leading role in the organization in 1808 of a volunteer unit, the Albemarle Military Association, and published a short newspaper essay on "Fly-Proof Wheat" in the year before his death (Woods, *Albemarle*, 299, 374, 376, 379, 400; Richmond *Enquirer*, 24 Dec. 1808; *Richmond Enquirer*, 24 June 1817; Albemarle Co. Will Book, 8:104).

M-MILL: "manufacturing mill."

# To Dabney Carr

DEAR SIR                                        Monticello Sep. 27. 14.

I thank you for setting me to rights as to my notices. I had trusted that an old experienced magistrate had[1] given his certificate[2] according to the existing laws, and therefore did not look into them. I now send you one in due form, and have corrected the others. I have set a long day in yours on consultation with judge Holmes. I return you also the paper you inclosed me.

I think you take the affair at Washington more to heart than it deserves. There is not a capital in Europe which has not been in the hands of Bonaparte except S$^t$ Petersburg and London. and London itself by the acknolegement of their own historians when de Ruyter destroyed their ships at Chatham & sailed triumphantly up the Thames might have been burnt by him, had the examples of Copenhagen and Washington been then set. be assured it disgraces England more than it does us. it will work well in two ways; it places them in Europe in the attitude of Barbarians, and has roused our citizens who were really sunk in apathy. ever affectionately yours.

TH: JEFFERSON

RC (Ancient and Honorable Artillery Company of Massachusetts, Faneuil Hall, Boston, 1954); addressed: "The honble Dabney Carr Winchester"; franked; postmarked Milton, 29 Sept.; endorsed by Carr. PoC (DLC); endorsed by TJ. Enclosures not found.

Carr probably sent the PAPER YOU INCLOSED ME in his letter to TJ of 5 Sept.

1814, not found, but recorded in SJL as received 15 Sept. 1814 from Winchester. SJL also records a missing letter from Carr of 1 Nov. 1814, received 15 Nov. 1814 from Winchester.

[1] TJ here canceled "done."
[2] In enhancing the faint PoC, TJ made this word plural.

# To Patrick Gibson

Dear Sir                                          Monticello. Sep. 27. 14.

I have not learned whether at the last renewal of my note to the bank, it was enlarged or not, and in the present doubtful state of our medium I do not know whether I ought to wish it, except so far as to cover my taxes in Bedford & here, for which I must draw on you in a few days, and 50.D. which I must request you to send me by return of mail. the credit of the bank paper has become of doubtful tender, since their declaration that they will not pay their notes; and resting now on public opinion only should that take alarm, we may be without a medium to make any payment. perhaps it might be secured by a declaration of support by our merchants such as has been made by those to the North. I have urged mr R. Randolph to send me on a supply of jugs, and desired Capt Oldham to chuse and forward to me 73. panes of glass of particular sizes, for which he will ask payment of you; and I must ask the favor of you to send me a dozen bottles of oil, & 10. or 12. gross of corks. I presume payment has been made for my flour. I have good crops of wheat and tobº on hand, which I shall endeavor to get down early in the hope of their meeting a peace. I expect to leave this for Bedford within about 10. days & to be there a month or 6. weeks.

Accept the assurance of my great esteem and respect.

Th: Jefferson

PoC (ViU: TJP); at foot of text: "Mr Gibson."

# From Samuel E. Mifflin

Dear Sir                                          [ca. 27 Sept. 1814]

I have written a letter addressed to you by the Post. I want to tell you now, Sir who I am in order that you may know how to act in this contest for victory between the different families of the united States of America including Virginia and Pennsylvania since General Thomas + Mifflin was resident in the latter State and his actions were so minute as to sanctify Virginia in wrath with Pennsylvania Delaware and Maryland. You know that the Virginians are a base

+ The contest always existed in fact among the Philadelphians who despised Thomas Mifflin without the authority of their God and between the Philadelphians & the Virginians as you yourself must know.

people when compared with the noblemen of England or the native born Sons of America of New England for their defiance of the Creator is the contempt of the Holy of Holies since they, meanly, having it in their power, usurp the different offices under the different governments of the United States of America with the extensive territory of Louisiana in north America bordering on the Spanish Dominions and on the Pacif Oce and which you have assisted in purchasing to the eternal renown to your (at present)[1] glorified name. But the fact is the intruding quaker families of Philadelphia in Pennsylvania and the families of Virginia even those not quakers many of them comeing up here to Philadelphia on a visit have in their way sanctified the Mifflin family in baseness[2] forever. But this "eternal blazon" must no longer be. The Mifflin family and the Mifflin name is the greatest in the world as by the authority of the word of God it is testified. The Mifflin family are inspired by the Holy Ghost to protect man from the vanity of the quakers, to protect America from the contempt of Devils. I am the son of Warner Mifflin of the Eastern Shore of Virginia by birth and whose eldest Son by another venter was and is the great nephew of Joseph Galloway who joined the British standard during the American War. That eldest son lives in the State of Delaware at present in Kent County where his father formerly lived and a delightful State it is thereabouts. You know Dover to be the Capital marked on the maps in the centre of the State in Kent County By referring to the maps of the State you will see the Capital Dover marked and a village called Camden about five miles from thence which belonged formerly to my uncle Daniel Mifflin my fathers brother and which during the American War had that name of Camden attached to it in consequence of his my uncle Daniel Mifflin's attachment to the British. You know that it's not equal to Maryland in point of magnitude nor to the State of Virginia in point of magnitude but that the rights of Property ought to be protected from the vanity of the rich is a question of magnitude but that they ought to be protected from the intrusions of the ignorant and the wicked is a matter of fact. Joseph Galloway was a good man and one who venerated his god. He was born on the Eastern Shore of Maryland and in Delaware he had great[3] nieces who got connected with my father as above stated. He was a good he was a great man having been a member of the first Congress having been a member of the Legislature of Pennsylvania[4] under the British government where his speeches were great & glorious.

yrs                                                   S. E: MIFFLIN

RC (DLC: TJ Papers, 202:35999–36000); undated; addressed: "Thomas Jefferson Esqʳ late President of the United States Monticello Virginia"; franked; postmarked Philadelphia, [27?] Sept.; endorsed by TJ as received 5 Oct. 1814 and so recorded in SJL.

ETERNAL BLAZON quotes from William Shakespeare, *Hamlet*, act 1, scene 5: "But this eternal blazon must not be To ears of flesh and blood." The eldest son of WARNER MIFFLIN and his first wife, Elizabeth Johns, was his namesake Warner Mifflin (Hilda Justice, *Life and Ancestry of Warner Mifflin* [1905], 16, 18).

¹ Omitted closing parenthesis editorially supplied.
² Mifflin here canceled "with the Emlens."
³ Word interlined.
⁴ Manuscript: "Legislature of Pennsylvania Legislature."

# To James Oldham

DEAR SIR                                          Monticello Sep. 27. 14.

Being in immediate want of some glass to keep the winter out of our broken windows, I must trespass on your friendship, as being a judge of the quality to look out for the following sizes, to wit.

50. panes  12  I. square
20. panes  12. by 18 I.
3. panes  24. by 18 I.

mr Gibson will be so good as to pay the bill, and if you will have the box lodged with him, I will direct a boatman to call for it in whose care I have particular confidence. accept the assurance of my esteem & best wishes.                                    TH: JEFFERSON

PoC (MHi); at foot of text: "Capᵗ James Oldham"; on verso of reused address cover to TJ; endorsed by TJ.

# To Richard Randolph

DEAR SIR                                          Monticello Sep. 27. 14

I am now engaged in brewing a year's supply of malt strong beer, which however I have no chance of saving but by a supply of quart jugs from you. I recieved (I think) 10½ dozen. and must ask the favor of 4. gross more for which mr Gibson will pay your bill. be so good as to inform me when they will be ready. if lodged at mr Gibson's I will direct a waterman on whom I can rely to call for them. Accept the assurance of my esteem and respect          TH: JEFFERSON

PoC (MHi); at foot of text: "Richard Randolph esq."; on verso of address cover to RC of John H. Cocke to TJ, 27 Aug. 1814; endorsed by TJ.

# To Thomas Ritchie

DEAR SIR                                    Monticello Sep. 27. 14.

In a letter of Aug. 19. I proposed to you to publish the tran[s]lation of an inedited work of Mʳ Tracy, to which I will ask the favor of an answer, as, if you cannot do it, I must engage some other. I wi[ll] also ask the return of two letters from Dʳ Maese of Philadelphia and mr Greer of Baltimore inclosed in mine of Aug. 14. Accept the assurance of my esteem and respect.

                                            TH: JEFFERSON

PoC (MHi); edge trimmed; at foot of text: "Thomas Ritchie esq."; on verso of address cover to RC of Thomas Jefferson Randolph to TJ, 31 Aug. 1814; endorsed by TJ.

TJ's LETTER OF AUG. 19, not found, is recorded in SJL. His letter to Ritchie of AUG. 14., which is actually dated 15 Aug., was recorded in SJL under the earlier date.

# To John Barnes

DEAR SIR                                    Monticello Sep. 30. 14.

The object of the present letter is merely to save 5. dollars. the inclosed Alexandria bill for that amount[1] can yet I presume be past with you, in which case you will place it to credit in our account. no bank-bill of another state is now recieved with us; those of our own state are refused by many, and recieved by others only from doubtful debtors, and for want of all other medium. they will rub along some weeks longer perhaps, but are effectually defunct; as the declaration of the banks against paying their own notes is considered as a declaration of bankruptcy. how fortunate is it, my dear Sir, that we have saved our friend Kosciuzko, by withdrawing his funds from the bank in the moment we did. for him to have lost his capital, the price of his blood spilt for us, & now his only resource for life, would have overwhelmed me with affliction while I should have lived. ever affectionately yours

                                            TH: JEFFERSON

RC (NN: photostat in John T. Finley Papers, 1946); at foot of text: "Mʳ Barnes." PoC (DLC); on verso of address cover to RC of James W. Wallace to TJ, 7 Sept. 1814; endorsed by TJ.

[1] Preceding three words interlined.

# To Joseph C. Cabell

DEAR SIR                                         Monticello Sep. 30. 14.

In my letter of the 23ᵈ an important fact escaped me which, lest it should not occur to you, I will mention. the monies arising from the sales of the glebe lands in the several counties, have generally I believe, and under the sanction of the legislature, been deposited in some of the banks. so also the funds of the literary society. these debts, altho' parcelled among the counties, yet the counties constitute the state, & their representatives the legislature, united into one whole. it is right then that owing 300,000 D. to the banks, they should stay so much of that sum in their own hands as will secure what the banks owe to their constituents as divided into counties. perhaps the loss of these funds would be the most lasting of the evils proceeding from the insolvency of the banks. ever your's with great esteem & respect.                                TH: JEFFERSON

RC (ViU: TJP); addressed: "Joseph C. Cabell esq. of the Senate of Virginia now at Richmond"; franked; postmarked Milton, 2 Oct.; endorsed by Cabell. PoC (DLC).

TJ's interest at this time in the security of the funds resulting from the SALES OF THE GLEBE LANDS, property appropriat-ed to public use after the disestablishment of the Anglican Church in Virginia, presumably grew out of his service on a committee of the trustees of the Albemarle Academy that hoped to obtain Albemarle County's share of this money for that institution (Minutes of the Albemarle Academy Board of Trustees, 3 May 1814).

# José Corrêa da Serra's Memorandum on Religious Education

[after 30 Sept. 1814]

I have read with attention and ruminated your plan of school, and as you are above compliments i will only tell you that i would have been proud of having planned it, so much i find it proportionate to the actual degree of improvement of human mind, and to the present state of your nation. I differ nevertheless in one point from you, which is the Theological branch, not for the reasons of Dʳ Cooper, because persuaded as i am that superstition and religion in the bulk of mankind must always exist, they being the natural result of the inequal proportion with which the different mental faculties are generally coupled in the human nature, it is much better to neutralize them, than to Leave them alone to work according their caustic nature. You have done much in America to neutralize them, by withdrawing any support from government, and breaking their old alliance, but that is not yet all; the best means of neutralizing them is by Learning infused in their ministers

The question is; if it is best to have the clergy of the most considerable sects, composed of gentlemen or vulgar people? of Learned or ignorant men. David Hume has in some manner resolved the first question, and there may be no doubt as to the second. If they are Learned they will in proportion be Liberal minded and neutralize the absurdities incidental to their creeds, if ignorant they will go on deeper and deeper into fanaticism and nonsense, which as you know are and will always be very epidemical and dangerous diseases.

I wish therefore that there may be an opening Left in the University in order to have Learned clergymen, but their studies there to be real things, in which all sects agree (to avoid the just objections of M$^r$ Cooper to Theology and ecclesiastical[1] history) and of such nature that not only neutralize fanaticism, but protect important branches of Learning which otherwise will have no support amongst you.

1. Natural Theology, which pretending to ground on reason the principles of general religion, makes them conversant with Metaphysics and the philosophy of human mind
2. Hebrew and its relation with oriental languages and oriental Litterature, in order to understand the Bible; the greek is already in the plan of the college
3. What is called Eruditio Biblica that is to say the knowledge of facts and things necessary or useful to understand the Bible. It is incr[e]dible what number of capital books exist on this object. Two works of the first eminence in natural history are the Hierozoicon of Bochart and the Hierobotanos of Celsius, on the animals and plants of the Bible. This branch of Learning carries a man to the deep recesses of the history of the Asiatic world, and to what remains of the first ages of mankind. The critical history of the books of the Bible, must make one of the chief articles of this branch.

All these studies have the natural effects of neutralizing fanaticism and enlarging the mind, to the contrary of what elements of Divinity and[2] ecclesiastical history, whatever they may be must naturally have.

These few words are sufficient for you who[3] will see in a moment the consequences. As for the other objections of D[r] Cooper, they have put me in mind of many a rich atlas full of precious maps some minutely topographical, others geographical in different scales, but wanting a Mappemond in which they are found in their relative proportions, and positions.

MS (DLC: TJ Papers, 202:36077); in Corrêa da Serra's hand; one word faint; undated, but apparently written during Corrêa da Serra's autumn 1814 visit to Monticello, and certainly composed after the receipt by TJ on 30 Sept. of Thomas Cooper's letter of 22 Sept. 1814; endorsed by TJ: "Correa."

For the PLAN OF SCHOOL, see TJ to Peter Carr, 7 Sept. 1814. Cooper gave his REASONS for omitting theology from a university curriculum in his letter to TJ of 22 Sept. 1814. ERUDITIO BIBLICA: "biblical education." On the ANIMALS AND

PLANTS OF THE BIBLE, Corrêa da Serra cited Samuel Bochart, *Hierozoicon Sive bipertitum opus de Animalibus Sacræ Scripturæ*, 2 vols. (London, 1663), and Olof Celsius, *Hierobotanicon, sive de Plantis Sacræ Scripturæ, dissertationes breves*, 2 vols. (Uppsala, 1745–47). Mappemonde (MAPPEMOND): "map of the world" (*OED*).

[1] Word interlined in place of "natural."
[2] Corrêa da Serra here canceled "natur."
[3] Word interlined in place of "that."

# From Patrick Gibson

SIR                                    Richmond 30th Septem[r] 1814
A short absence from town prevented me from informing you sooner of the fate of your note renewed on the 9th and which I enlarged to $3900—under the impression that the system of curtailing, which was then pursuing and which it was expected would be continued, must soon reduce it below the amount you required, this system however has been discontinued for the present, in consequence of the necessary absence of most of their customers, but will no doubt be again resumed so soon as it can be done without too much risk— their determination not to issue any more specie, became a matter of necessity growing out of a similar determination made by all the banks to the North, it subjects us to very great inconvenience for the want of change, but is felt in no other way, I know of no other support the Merchants could give but by taking the notes, which they do as heretofore—As requested in your letter of the 27th I inclose you $50 and shall send you by Johnson a Crate of Jugs, a dozen bottles of

oil (for which I had to pay $16) and the Corks and shall pay M<sup>r</sup> Old-ham for the Glass on application—I am

    With great respect         Your ob<sup>t</sup> Serv<sup>t</sup>    PATRICK GIBSON

Fine family flour      $6
   Ordinary S. fine     "4

I have sent only 8 Gross of Corks which is all I could procure—

RC (ViU: TJP-ER); endorsed by TJ as received 5 Oct. 1814 and so recorded in SJL. RC (DLC); address cover only; with PoC of TJ to John H. Cocke, 23 Oct. 1814, on verso; addressed: "Thomas Jefferson Esq<sup>re</sup> Monticello"; franked; postmarked Richmond, 1 Oct.

# Appendix

## Supplemental List of Documents Not Found

JEFFERSON'S epistolary record and other sources describe a number of documents for which no text is known to survive. The Editors generally account for such material at documents that mention them or at other relevant places. Exceptions are accounted for below.

From Edward Parker, 18 Dec. 1813. Recorded in SJL as received from Philadelphia on 24 Dec. 1813.

From Samuel McCaleb, 25 Apr. 1814. Recorded in SJL as received from Lovingston on 30 Apr. 1814.

From Samuel Overbury, 10 May 1814. Recorded in SJL as received from Franklin, Tennessee, on 26 June 1814.

To Mr. Wright, of Nelson County, 2 Aug. 1814. Recorded in SJL.

To Johnson & Warner, 17 Aug. 1814. Recorded in SJL.

From Johnson & Warner, 26 Aug. 1814. Recorded in SJL as received from Richmond on 29 Aug. 1814.

# INDEX

Aboville, François Marie, chevalier (later comte) d': and opossums, 210, 211n

Abraham (Old Testament patriarch), 220

*Abrégé du Système de la Nature, de Linné, Histoire des Mammaires* (J. E. Gilibert), 626

*Un Abridgment des plusieurs cases et resolutions del Common Ley* (H. Rolle), 126

*An Abridgment of Waldo's Rudiments of English Grammar* (J. Waldo), 320

*Acacia nilotica.* See gum arabic tree

*An Account of Expeditions to the Sources of the Mississippi* (Z. M. Pike), 31

*An Account of the American Antiquarian Society,* 47

*An Account of the life, writings, and inventions of John Napier, of Merchiston* (D. S. E. Buchan and W. Minto), 252, 253n, 255

*An Account of the People called Shakers* (T. Brown), 555, 633

Achilles, 477

acoustics: study of, 638, 639, 686

*Acta Sanctorum* (J. de Bolland and others), 220

An Act concerning the commercial intercourse between the United States and Great Britain and France (*1810*), 41, 44n

Act for regulating Conveyances (*1792*), 535

An Act for the assessment and collection of direct taxes and internal duties (*1813*), 45–6n

An Act for the relief of Oliver Evans (*1808*), 108, 109n, 171, 173n

An Act laying an embargo on all ships and vessels in the ports and harbours of the United States (*1813*), 70n

An Act to authorize the purchase of the library of Thomas Jefferson (*1815*), 679–80

An Act to establish Public Schools (*1796*), 637, 642n

An Act to promote the progress of useful Arts (*1793*), 171–3, 510n

Adam, Alexander, 662

Adams, Abigail Smith (John Adams's wife): health of, 26; identified, 6:298n; reading habits of, 217; TJ in-

troduces W. C. Rives to, 369; TJ sends greetings to, 455

Adams, John: on aristocracy, 64–7, 477, 479; on Condorcet, 23–4, 477, 481n; on education, 480–1; on French Revolution, 479; on Genghis Khan, 477; on Great Britain, 477; health of, 220, 451; on human progress, 23–6, 476–7; identified, 4:390–1n; letter returned to, 150; letters from, 23–7, 64–8, 73–8, 216–21, 476–82; letters to, 146–51, 368–9, 451–5; and memoir on D. Rittenhouse, 216–7; mentioned, 471; on Napoleon, 477–8; on Plato, 74–7, 478–80; presidency of, 530, 576; on J. Priestley, 25, 26; and J. Priestley's writings, 74–7, 218–20, 221; on religion, 23–6, 73–7, 217–20, 476–7; W. C. Rives proposes to visit, 451, 476; on J. Taylor of Caroline, 217, 221n, 478–9, 481n; TJ introduces W. C. Rives to, 368–9

Adams, John Quincy: mentioned, 480; minister to Russia, 434; as peace negotiator, 201, 202n, 433, 434, 473–4; presidential prospects of, 560

Adams, Samuel: mentioned, 476

Adams, Samuel G.: Richmond merchant, 189

Addison, Joseph: *Cato: A Tragedy,* 312n

*Adriano in Siria* (P. Metastasio), 452, 455n

*The Adventurer,* 665

*Aeneid* (Virgil), 661

Aeschines: A. Auger's translation of, 259; TJ recommends, 447

*Aesop's Fables:* quoted by W. Short, 224, 225n

Æthelberht I, king of Kent: laws of, 125, 147

Africa: peoples of, 533

African Americans: military service by proposed, 532–4. *See also* slavery; slaves

agate, 261

*The Age of Louis XIV* (Voltaire), 664

*The Age of Louis XV* (Voltaire), 664

Aggy (TJ's slave): medical care of, 387

Agricultural Society of Bavaria: diploma from received by TJ, 505; membership conferred on TJ, 505

agriculture: books on, 626; contour plowing, 79–80; corn-shelling

468; petitions for incorporation of, 145n; W. Short on, 223; TJ on, 128, 133–4, 149–50, 168, 169–70, 211–2, 314–6, 442–3, 653–5, 689–91, 692, 699, 710, 713, 714; in Virginia, 134, 144, 145n, 185, 203, 669–71, 689–91, 710, 713, 714, 716

Barbauld, Anna Letitia: *The Female Speaker*, 665

Barber, Mr. *See* Barbour, James

Barbour, James: and access to records, 256; as governor of Virginia, 33, 61, 62n, 190, 232, 669–70, 671n; identified, 4:415–6n; issues proclamation, 669, 671n; letter to, 256; and War of *1812*, 623, 632

Baring Brothers & Company: identified, 440n; letter to, 439–40; and remittances to T. Kosciuszko, 421, 431n, 432, 437, 441, 442, 456, 499

Barlow, Joel: death of, 428n, 490; identified, 1:589–90n; Obituary by P. S. Du Pont de Nemours and K. E. Oelsner, 525; U.S. minister to France, 428n

Barnes, John: account with T. Kosciuszko, 432, 456–7, 499; on defense of Washington, D.C., 554, 617–8; handles financial transactions, 261, 261–2, 284, 294, 323, 456–7, 553–4, 572, 713; health of, 284, 294; identified, 1:32n; introduced to G. W. Campbell by TJ, 354; and T. Kosciuszko's American investments, 9–10, 46, 169–70, 189, 192–4, 211–2, 215–6, 233–4, 261, 283–4, 294, 314–6, 333–4, 353, 354, 355, 363, 369, 380–1, 421, 431–2, 432, 437, 440, 440–1, 442–3, 456–7, 475, 499, 553–4, 572, 617, 713; letters from, 46, 189, 192–4, 215–6, 233–4, 283–4, 294–5, 323, 333–4, 334–5, 363, 369, 380–1, 421–2, 431–2, 437–8, 456–7, 469–70, 470–2, 499–500, 553–4, 617–8; letters to, 169–70, 211–2, 261, 261–2, 314–7, 353–4, 440–1, 572, 713; on prospects for peace, 437, 499–500; reports on visit with W. Short, 469–70, 471–2; on stability of banks, 192–4; TJ pays, 441, 517, 552, 572, 602, 617; TJ's account with, 422, 441, 617, 713; as TJ's agent, 333, 353, 713; travels to Philadelphia, 363, 381, 456, 457, 469–70, 470–2

Barnet, Isaac Cox: identified, 5:463–4n; letter to, 50; sends books to TJ, 50;

and D. B. Warden's removal as consul, 428n, 429n

Barney, Joshua: and contested congressional election, 177n

Baronio (Baronius), Cesare: quoted, 24

Barraud, John Taylor: forwards books for D. B. Warden, 90; identified, 5:500n

Barrow, William: *An Essay on Education*, 658, 666n

Barthélemy, Jean Jacques: *Voyage du Jeune Anacharsis en Grèce*, 662, 666n

Barton, Benjamin Smith: and American Philosophical Society, 281n; and classification of animals, 152; and J. Delaplaine's *Repository*, 295, 302, 562; *Elements of Botany*, 626; identified, 1:521n; on Indians, 289; introduces A. B. Woodward, 288; letter from, 288–9; letter to, 281; mentioned, 399; sends packages to TJ, 308

Barton, William: identified, 5:371–2n; letters from, 398–400, 511–2; letters to, 446–7, 555–6; *Memoirs of the Life of David Rittenhouse*, 150, 151n, 216–7, 398, 512, 554; *Select American Biography*, 398–400, 446–7, 511; TJ pays, 555–6; on war and U.S. society, 511–2

Barziza, Antonio, Count: and L. L. Paradise's estate, 372; TJ as agent for, 372

Bassano, Hugues Bernard Maret, duc de, 490, 491n

bath: portable, 187–8, 325, 326n, 345

Batteux, Charles: *Histoire des Causes Premières*, 75, 148

Baudoin, Francis, 66

Baudoin, Jean, 66

Baudouin de Toulouse, 66

Baxter, John: *A New and Impartial History of England*, 629

Bayard, James Ashton: as peace negotiator, 198, 201, 202n, 429n, 433

Bayly, Mr. (of Germantown, Pa.): and hydrostatic engine, 232, 233n

beans: chickpea, 326; and Pythagoras, 218, 221n

Bear Creek plantation (part of TJ's Poplar Forest estate): roads through, 71, 430

Bear Meat (Cherokee Indian): militia service of, 161

Béarn family: and Albigensian heresy, 65

Beasley, Reuben Gaunt: as agent in London, 198

birch trees: F. A. Michaux on, 52

bird pepper, 326, 567, 568n

Birdwood (Gilmer family's Henry Co. estate): E. Trist at, 501–2

Bishop, Joseph: paid by TJ, 459, 460n, 460

bison, American (buffalo), 302

Bisset, Robert, 664

black-eyed peas (cowpea), 288

Blackstone, William: *Commentaries on the Laws of England*, 125–7, 148, 249, 628; and Magna Carta, 67; mentioned, 129, 223

*Blackstone's Commentaries* (S. G. Tucker), 616, 617n, 628

Bladensburg, Battle of, 621–4, 656n

Blair, Hugh: *Lectures on Rhetoric and Belles Lettres*, 629, 662; TJ references, 630

Blake, James Heighe: mayor of Washington, D.C., 669n

Bland, Richard: and protection of slaves, 603, 605n; TJ on, 411, 548, 603; and Two-Penny Act (*1758*), 546

Blanque, Jean: Louisiana legislator, 227

Blodget's Hotel (Washington, D.C.), 680, 698, 699n

Blumenbach, Johann Friedrich: and classification of animals, 152, 208–9, 210; *Manuel D'Histoire Naturelle*, 626

boats: impressment of, 123, 135, 156; transfer goods to and from Richmond, 94–5

Bochart, Samuel: *Hierozoicon*, 715, 716n

Boerstler, Charles, 525

Boileau, Nicolas, 665

Bolingbroke, Henry St. John, Viscount: J. Adams on, 74, 78n, 480

Bolland, Jean de: *Acta Sanctorum*, 220

Bollman, Justus Erich, 128

Bonaparte, Joseph, king of Spain: and Napoleon's abdication, 537

Bonaparte, Napoleon. *See* Napoleon I, emperor of France

Bonne, Rigobert: *Atlas Portatif à l'usage des Colleges*, 116–7

*"The Book!" or, The Proceedings and Correspondence upon the subject of the Inquiry into the Conduct of Her Royal Highness The Princess of Wales*, 34, 36n, 270, 410, 500

books: on agriculture, 626; on astronomy, 626; on belles lettres, 629; biographical, 50, 295–6, 302–3, 330; on botany, 245n, 626; on brewing, 259, 285, 292; on chemistry, 626; classi-

cal, 259; on criticism (literary), 629; dictionaries, 286, 458, 633, 646; on economics, 5–6, 598, 628; encyclopedias, 683; on ethics, 627; on geography, 389, 626; on government, 628; on grammar, 320, 458; on history, 139, 155, 190, 286, 389, 629; on hydraulics, 302, 386; on law, 125–7, 146–8, 228, 249, 249–50, 257–8, 292, 627–8, 683; on mathematics, 250–3, 286, 458, 626, 683; on morals, 286, 458; on natural history, 389; on natural law, 627; on natural philosophy, 626; on New York, 169, 248, 264; on oratory, 629–30; on physics, 282, 292; on plants, 458; on politics, 628, 682; on religion, 74–7, 148, 218–21, 286, 595, 627, 633, 646, 683; on rhetoric, 629; satires, 60, 62n; sent by Bradford & Inskeep, 289; sent by N. G. Dufief, 286, 292, 633, 646; of speeches, 331–2, 373–4; on spelling, 320; TJ recommends to J. Minor, 625–31; TJ recommends to B. Moore, 625–31; on zoology, 626. *See also* Jefferson, Thomas: Books & Library

Boothroyd, Benjamin: *The History of the Ancient Borough of Pontefract*, 389

Boscovich, Ruggiero Giuseppe: on law of forces, 557, 560n

Bossut, Charles: *Essai sur l'Histoire Génerale des Mathématiques*, 626

Boston, Mass.: British evacuation of during Revolutionary War, 101, 103n

botany: books on, 244–5, 626; study of, 638–41, 667, 687

Botta, Carlo Giuseppe Guglielmo: identified, 2:529–30n; *Storia della guerra dell'Independenza degli Stati Uniti d'America*, 616, 617n

Bourdaloue, Louis: *Sermons*, 627

Bowditch, Nathaniel: praised, 217

Bowdoin, James (*1726–1790*): governor of Massachusetts, 65, 67n

Bowdoin, James (*1752–1811*): identified, 3:96n; mentioned, 65; nephews of adopt surname, 66–8

Bowdoin, James Temple: adopts uncle's surname, 67n

Bowdoin (Winthrop), James: adopts uncle's surname, 67–8n

Bowdoin, Sarah. *See* Dearborn, Sarah Bowdoin (James Bowdoin's widow; Henry Dearborn's second wife)

Bowdoin College, 65

*et Particulière*, 626; mentioned, 34, 480

building materials: plank, 461; window glass, 710, 712, 717

Bullock, James: witnesses a deed, 353

Bunyan, John: *The Pilgrim's Progress*, 26

Burgh, James: *Political Disquisitions*, 628

Burk, John Daly: *The History of Virginia*, 547, 550n, 629

Burke, Edmund: criticized, 74; education of, 660; *Reflections on the Revolution in France*, 74, 78n

Burnet, William: family of, 520, 595–6; royal governor, 520, 521n, 596

Burney, Fanny, Madame d'Arblay: *Cecilia*, 65; in collegiate curriculum, 665

Burnside, Samuel McGregore: identified, 47–8n; letter from accounted for, 521n; letters from, 47–8, 595–6; letters to, 115–6, 520–1; as recording secretary of American Antiquarian Society, 47, 115, 520, 521n, 595–6

Burr, Aaron (*1756–1836*): alleged conspiracy of, 206, 207n, 235–6, 238–9; TJ on, 648; treason trial of, 148, 151n; western expeditions of, 206, 236, 239

Burrall, Charles: as Baltimore postmaster, 229, 230n, 231–2; criticized, 231; Federalist sympathies of, 244; identified, 230n; letters from, 229–30, 231–2, 262; letter to, 243; lives with TJ in Philadelphia, 230n, 244; thanks TJ, 262; TJ recommends to J. Madison, 243, 244, 262

Bushnell, David: submarine inventor, 513n, 621; torpedoes of, 512, 620–1

butter: churning, 82

Cabanis, Pierre Jean Georges: in collegiate curriculum, 667; *Rapports du Physique et du Moral de l'Homme*, 385–6

Cabell, Joseph Carrington: and Albemarle Academy, 714; on banks, 144, 669–71; and Central College, 266; identified, 2:489–90n; letters from, 5–6, 33, 144–6, 184–5, 230, 669–71; letters to, 133–5, 176–7, 689–91, 714; and Rivanna Company, 5, 33, 145, 184–5; and TJ's ideas on finance, 5–6, 133–4, 144, 149–51, 185, 230, 510, 669, 671, 689–91, 692, 693n, 714; as

Virginia state senator, 5, 33, 133–5, 144–5, 168, 169n, 176–7, 184–5, 669–71, 689–91, 714

Cade, John (Jack) (rebel leader): compared to Napoleon, 477

Cadore, duc de, Jean Baptiste Nompère de Champagny: French foreign minister, 463

Caesar (TJ's slave; b. *1774*): hat for, 124

Caesar, Julius: *Commentaries on the Gallic and Civil Wars*, 661; mentioned, 24, 373, 447, 477, 495, 551n

Caffarena, Edward: identified, 634n; letter from, 634; sends seeds to TJ, 634; vice-consul at Genoa, 634

Caldwell, Charles: identified, 318–9n; letters from, 317–9, 328–9; letter to, 410–2; and *Port Folio*, 317–9, 328–9, 410–2; visits Monticello, 319n

calendar: Julian, 436, 437n; reform of Gregorian proposed, 436–7

Calendi, Giuseppe: copies paintings for TJ, 340–2

calico, 558

Callaway, Abner Early: Bedford Co. land of, 430; identified, 5:468n

Callender, James Thomson: and sedition law, 206, 207n

Callis, William Overton: and H. Marks's estate, 518

Calvin, John: mentioned, 74

Cambacérès, Jean Jacques Régis de, 490

Cambridge University, 659, 686, 688n

Camden, William: biographies by, 629, 631n

Camm, John: and Two-Penny Act (*1758*), 546

Campbell, George Washington: J. Barnes introduced to by TJ, 354; identified, 354–5n; letter to, 354–5; and remittances to T. Kosciuszko, 334, 353, 354, 380; as secretary of the treasury, 316, 317n, 334, 354; and TJ's letters on finance, 510

Camp Fairfield (Henrico Co.): Virginia militia at, 600–1, 609n, 632

Canada: British troops in, 91, 97–8, 350, 360; W. Short on U.S. acquisition of, 138; support for American conquest of, 501; TJ anticipates American conquest of, 7–8, 10, 11, 14, 35, 88, 90–1; TJ on, 56; Upper, 14, 35, 88, 138, 530, 531; and U.S. fishing rights, 451, 452–3, 455n, 478, 501; U.S. invasion of, 10, 12, 14, 35, 42–3, 51, 56, 61, 88, 90–1, 194–5, 525n, 530–1

Chisholm, Hugh (*cont.*)
from, 380; letter to, 357–8; plastering at Poplar Forest, 297, 380, 400; stonework at Poplar Forest, 380; and wing of offices at Poplar Forest, xlvi, 380

Chisholm, Isham: identified, 5:5n; TJ pays, 45

Chittenden, Martin: proclamation of, 61–3

Chouteau, Augustus: recommends R. Easton, 365, 366n

Christianity: doxology, 385, 386n; M. King on, 586–9; and law, 146–8, 190–1, 217, 257; relics, 220

*The Christian's Victory Over Death and the Grave. A Sermon … on the decease of Elizabeth Lady Temple* (J. S. J. Gardiner), 67

Christmas: and mince pies, 78

chub, Roanoke, 260

Cicero, Marcus Tullius: *Cato Maior de senectute*, 627; *De Officiis*, 627, 661; T. Law quotes, 467, 468n; orations of, 661; quoted, 74, 78n; *Somnium Scipionis*, 627; TJ on, 453; TJ recommends, 447, 630; *Tusculan Disputations*, 627; writings on government, 479

cider: apple, 381, 382n, 444–5

*The Citizen of the World*, 665

Claiborne, William Charles Coles: governor of Louisiana, 226, 227n; identified, 1:179–80n; plants requested from, 287, 321

Clark, Christopher Henderson: identified, 2:323–4n; letter to, 430; TJ seeks legal assistance from, 430

Clark, Daniel (of Knaresborough, England): and E. Aram's murder trial, 375, 377, 378n

Clark, Daniel (of Louisiana): death of, 61

Clark, Thomas: identified, 6:166n; letters from, 139–41, 232; letters to, 190, 256–7; *Naval History of the United States*, 139, 140n, 141n, 155, 190, 256; proposed history of the United States, 139–40, 190, 232, 256, 256–7; TJ introduces to J. Barbour, 256

Clark (Clarke), William: identified, 1:511n; and journals of Lewis and Clark Expedition, 31, 63

Clarke, John (ca. *1687–1734*, British author): *A New Grammar of the Latin Tongue*, 458

Clarke, John (*1766–1844*): identified, 5:680n; letter from, 16–23; letter to, 158; plan for increasing enlistment of regular troops, 16–20, 158, 159; on U.S. position internationally, 20–1; on wartime political wrangling, 21–2

Clarke, Mary Anne: *Evidence and Proceedings upon the Charges preferred against the Duke of York, in 1809*, 34, 36n

classics: collegiate education in, 480, 661–2, 663, 668, 685–6

Clavigero, Francesco Saverio: *Storia Antica del Messico*, 664

Clay, Charles: carding machine for, 79, 114, 116; identified, 2:78n; letter from, 116; letters to, 79, 114; makes payment for TJ, 387

Clay, Henry: carries TJ's letters to Europe, 222; as peace negotiator, 138, 139n, 197, 201–2, 223–4

Clayton, Maj. (of Culpeper Courthouse): letter to, 551; and package for TJ, 460, 551

clergy: British sympathies of, 57–8, 248; TJ on, 248

Clinton, DeWitt: and A. Burr conspiracy, 206, 235, 239

Clinton family: as aristocrats, 67

Clopper, Francis C.: patent agent, 438, 486, 507, 523, 552–3, 568

cloth. *See* textiles

clothing: coats, 72, 73n; hats, 71, 124; homespun, 187; shoes, 332; for slaves, 71, 191

Clotilde, Marguerite Éléonore. *See* Surville, Clotilde de (Marguerite Éléonore Clotilde de Vallon-Chalys)

clover: as crop, 71, 83, 179; threshing of, 81–2

Cochrane, Sir Alexander: invites U.S. slaves to join British military, 534n

Cocke, James: militia service of, 161

Cocke, John Hartwell: identified, 3:136n; letters from, 301, 608–9; letters to, 300, 513–4; militia service of, 608, 632; TJ purchases horse from, 300, 301, 513–4, 608; and TJ's letters on finance, 230

Cocke, William: identified, 5:652n; letter from, 160–2; on campaign against Creek Indians, 160–2

*Code de Commerce* (D. Raynal), 90

*Code d'Instruction criminelle*, 90

*A Code of Gentoo Laws, or, Ordinations*

shad, 321, 332, 333n, 448; TJ purchases, 321, 332, 333n, 552n
fisheries, Canadian: U.S. rights to, 451, 452–3, 455n, 478, 501
Fiske, John (ca. *1601–77*), 199
Fiske, John (*1744–97*): family of, 199; as Revolutionary War naval officer, 198–9; TJ on, 242
Fiske, Moses, 199
Fiske, Samuel, 199
Fitch, John: and steamboats, 113n
Fitzherbert, Sir Anthony: *La Graunde Abridgement*, 126
Fitzwhylsonn & Potter (Richmond firm): and *Edinburgh Review*, 367, 388, 389–90; identified, 3:599n
flax: spinning of, 570, 593
*Fleta seu commentarius Juris Anglicani sic nuncupatus*, 257, 688
Fletcher, John (dramatist), 664
*Flora Carolinæensis* (Shecut), 566
Florian, Jean Pierre Claris de, 665
Florida: acquisition of by U.S., 42–3; TJ on U.S. acquisition of, 7, 8, 11, 51; and War of *1812*, 7–8, 20
flour: British seize, 623, 624, 642, 644n; distilled into whiskey, 240; machinery for manufacture of, 107, 111–2, 131–3; milling of, 32; from Poplar Forest, 72, 94–5, 402; price of, 72, 114–5, 123, 141, 155, 166, 188, 212, 215, 222, 240, 241, 290, 307, 346, 401–2, 412, 433, 441, 457, 513, 514–5, 515, 516–7, 518, 717; at Richmond, 69, 86, 114–5, 412, 441, 513, 515, 516–7, 572, 717; sale of, 69, 141, 166, 179, 263, 430–1, 433, 441, 448, 457, 459, 513–4, 514–5, 515, 516–7, 518, 572, 710; transported to Richmond, 94–5, 123. *See also* Monticello (TJ's estate): flour from
Flournoy, Thomas C.: Fourth of July Speech of, 462–7; identified, 5:331n; letter from, 462; letter to, 522; sends speech to TJ, 462, 522; on War of *1812*, 462–6
fly. *See* Hessian fly
Foix family: and Albigensian heresy, 65
Fonblanque, John de Grenier: *A Treatise of Equity*, 628
Fontenelle, Bernard Le Bovier de: on Plato, 454, 455n
food: apples, 78, 381–2, 444–5, 492; asparagus, 288; bacon, 45; beef, 649; beets, 54, 55; black-eyed peas (cow-

pea), 288; bread, 649; butter, 82; chickpeas, 326; herring, 448; hominy, 82; lemon acid, 594, 602; peas, 71, 288, 356; pies, 78; salt, 124, 180, 649; shad, 321, 332, 333n, 448; veal, 442n. *See also* alcohol; coffee; corn; flour; oil; rice; spices; sugar; tea
Forber (Faber), Mr.: and carding machines, 79, 114, 116
Foronda, Valentín de: identified, 1:471n; letter to, 50–2; letter to mentioned, 107, 222; sends writings to TJ, 50–1; on Spanish colonial policy, 50–1, 393–4
Fort Erie (Upper Canada), 501, 502n, 656
Fort George (Upper Canada), 656, 657n
Fosgate, Bela: D. Holt recommends, 49; identified, 49n; letter from, 48–9; and torpedo, 48–9
Fossombroni, Vittorio: *Memorie Idraulico-Storiche sopra la Val-di-Chiana*, 302
Foster, Augustus John: British minister to U.S., 41, 44n
Fourth of July: orations, 462, 462–6, 522
*Fourth Annual Exhibition of the Columbian Society of Artists and the Pennsylvania Academy. May 1814*, 401, 443–4
Fox, Charles James: education of, 660; *A History of the Early Part of the Reign of James the Second*, 629
France: allies invade, 259; Berlin and Milan decrees, 87, 462–4; Bourbon dynasty, 350, 351n, 385, 592; freedom of the press in, 422, 539, 607; and Great Britain, 21, 23n, 298–9, 462–4; and Lafayette, 536–41; G. Logan's unofficial peace mission to, 38; Louis XVIII's constitutional charter, 537, 542n; Napoleon's constitution, 350, 425, 476; oppression in, 598–9; revolutionary calendar, 455n; W. Short on, 224–5; TJ on, 409–10, 450; and U.S., 187, 424. *See also* Barlow, Joel: U.S. minister to France; Crawford, William Harris: U.S. minister to France; Institut de France; Napoleon I, emperor of France
Francis I, emperor of Austria: daughter of marries Napoleon, 426n; makes peace with France, 423–4; and Napoleon, 410n, 423–4, 537

Gelston, David: identified, 1:282n; letters from, 263, 307–8; letter to, 282; sends seeds to TJ, 263, 282, 307–8

*Genealogical, chronological, historical, and geographical atlas* (Las Cases), 90

*A general system of nature, through the three grand kingdoms of animals, vegetables, and minerals* (C. Linnaeus; trans. W. Turton), 626

Genet, Edmond Charles: mentioned, 217

Genghis Khan: mentioned, 477

*The Gentleman Farmer* (Kames), 626

geography: books on, 389, 626; collegiate education in, 480, 638, 639, 663, 667; elementary education in, 637, 640, 685. *See also* Lambert, William; maps

geology: study of, 667; of Vermont, 357. *See also* mineralogy

George III, king of Great Britain: P. Henry on, 495, 548; and impressment, 465–7; and partitions of Poland, 298; TJ on, 34, 36n, 410

George, Prince Regent (later George IV, king of Great Britain): criticized, 60–1; on impressment, 464; as Prince of Wales, 34, 36n, 87, 96; TJ on, 410

Georgetown, D.C.: *Federal Republican*, xlv–xlvi, 434 (*illus.*)

Gérard de Rayneval, Joseph Mathias: *Institutions du Droit de la Nature et des Gens*, 627

German language: study of, 480, 661

Gerry, Elbridge (*1744–1814*): identified, 1:573n; as vice president, 313, 314n

Gessner, Conrad: works of, 389

Ghent: peace negotiations at, 156n, 424–5, 499–500, 516, 541; Treaty of (*1814*), 455n

Gibbon, Edward: *The History of the Decline and Fall of the Roman Empire*, 629, 662; mentioned, 74, 480

Gibson, Patrick: account with TJ, 472, 516–8, 716; and currency for TJ, 212, 222, 241, 263, 268, 346; and embargo, 300; and goods for TJ, 188–9, 488, 710, 712, 716–7; and gunpowder for TJ, 155, 291, 307; identified, 4:523n; letter from accounted for, 552n; letters from, 69–70, 86–7, 114–5, 141, 188–9, 215, 222, 241, 268, 307, 346, 412, 457–8, 472, 491–2, 602, 716–7; letters to, 72, 123, 155–6, 212, 263, 290–1, 401–2, 433, 459–60, 516–8, 551–2, 555, 572–3, 710; letters

to accounted for, 87n, 180n, 241n, 346n; and nailrod for TJ, 155, 188, 472, 602; payments made for TJ, 45n, 72, 154, 155, 347, 349, 367, 402, 433, 434, 457, 488, 522, 552, 554–5, 555, 572, 594, 602, 617, 618n, 633, 646, 649, 710, 717; and payments to TJ, 72, 86, 123, 141, 155, 457, 491; and plows for TJ, 246; and TJ's bank note, 69, 215, 222, 241, 263, 268, 491, 551–2, 555, 572, 710, 716; and TJ's corn contracts, 263, 459–60; and TJ's flour, 69, 72, 86, 114–5, 123, 141, 155, 188, 212, 215, 222, 241, 263, 290, 307, 346, 401–2, 412, 430, 433, 457, 459, 491, 513–4, 514–5, 515, 516–7, 572; and TJ's tobacco, 263, 307; and window glass for TJ, 712. *See also* Gibson & Jefferson (Richmond firm)

Gibson & Jefferson (Richmond firm): and books acquired by TJ, 289; flour sold for TJ, 300, 441, 513–4, 514–5; identified, 1:44n; letters to accounted for, 458n, 472n; payments made for TJ, 72n, 178, 182, 231, 290, 291n, 552n, 556, 564–5, 568–9, 708; and TJ's corn contracts, 460n. *See also* Gibson, Patrick

gigs: taxes on, xlv

Gilbert, Sir Geoffrey: TJ recommends works by, 628

Giles, William Branch: identified, 3:205n; as U.S. senator, 22, 23n

Gilibert, Jean Emmanuel: *Abrégé du Système de la Nature, de Linné, Histoire des Mammaires*, 626

Gill (TJ's slave; b. *1792*). *See* Gillette, Gill (TJ's slave; b. *1792*)

Gillespie, Robert: identified, 509–10n; invents still, 509; letter from accounted for, 510n; letter to, 509–10

Gillette, Dick (TJ's slave; b. *1790*): travels to Poplar Forest, 71

Gillette, Gill (TJ's slave; b. *1792*): health of, 71; as wagoner, 71, 124, 179–80

Gillette, Ned (TJ's slave; b. *1786*): and earthworks at Monticello, 400

*Gilliam v. Fleming*: chancery case, 99; and settlement of accounts, 174

Gillies, John: *The History of the World, from the reign of Alexander to that of Augustus*, 662

Gilmer, Francis Walker: and improvements at Monticello, 501

*La Graunde Abridgement* (R. Brooke), 126

*La Graunde Abridgement* (A. Fitzherbert), 126

Gray, William F.: forwards packages to TJ, 698; identified, 2:482–3n

Great Britain: and African Americans in military service, 532–4; allegedly mentioned in Bible, 36–7; American supporters of, 57–8, 248–9; attacks Copenhagen, 653, 681, 709; and colonization, 39; constitution of, 558; educational system in, 658–9, 666n; financial situation of, 39, 468; and France, 21, 298–9, 424, 462–4; House of Commons, 373, 545, 547–8; House of Lords, 545, 547–8; laws of, 125–7, 190–1, 217, 257; G. Logan's unofficial peace mission to, 38–44; manufacturing in, 39, 559; and Massachusetts, 92, 452–3, 455n, 478; navy of, 10–1, 350; Orders in Council (*1807*), 39–40, 41–2, 44, 51, 87, 96, 167, 452, 462–4, 542; peace with, 359–60; W. Short on, 224; society in compared with U.S., 650–3, 678; and Stamp Act (*1765*), 495, 496–7; TJ compares U.S. slaves to British underclass, 651–2; TJ on history of, 367–8; TJ on war with, 10–2, 13–4, 33, 87–8, 96–8, 158, 159–60, 213, 409–10, 451, 452–3, 519, 524, 601, 691–2; TJ proposes arson in, 11; treatment of prisoners of war by, 11–3; and U.S., 187, 298–9, 424. *See also* Embargo Act (*1807*); George III; George IV; Jefferson, Thomas: Opinions on; Pinkney, William; Wellesley, Richard Colley Wellesley, Marquess

Greek language: study of, 658, 660–1, 666, 685–6, 715; TJ on, 447; translations from owned by TJ, 259

Greene, Mr. (publisher), 494

Greene, Nathanael: portrait of, 498; seeks reimbursement of small sum, 64

Greenhow, Samuel: and Bible Society of Virginia, 178, 182–3; identified, 1:244n; letter from, 182–3; letter to, 178

Greenup, Christopher: and depositions in *Jefferson v. Michie*, 596–7; and Henderson case, 117; letters from accounted for, 597n; letter to accounted for, 597n

Greer, George: identified, 508–9n; letter from, 523–4; letter from mentioned, 713; letter to from W. Thornton, 508–9; as patent agent, 506, 507, 568

Gregory XIII, pope: reforms Julian calendar, 436

Grenet, Abbé: *Atlas Portatif à l'usage des Colleges*, 116–7

Griffin, Burgess: identified, 2:97n; Poplar Forest overseer, 44; and TJ's bond, 515–6

groceries: purchased by TJ, 180, 212. *See also* food

*The Grounds of Christianity Examined, by Comparing the New Testament with the Old* (G. B. English), 435n

*The Guardian*, 665

*Guerriere*, HMS (frigate), 465, 467n

gum arabic (medicinal), 387

gum arabic tree, 16

Gummere, John: American Philosophical Society member, 437n

gunpowder: sent to TJ, 188, 189, 307; TJ orders, 155, 291

gypsum (plaster of paris): used as fertilizer, 83

Habington, William: *The Historie of Edvvard the Fourth, King of England*, 629, 631n

Hackley, Harriet Randolph (Richard Hackley's wife): greetings to, 394; M. J. Randolph's correspondence with, 328

Hairston, George: military service of, 226–7

Hal (laborer): paid for work, 45

Hale, Sir Mathew: and *King v. Taylor*, 147–8; and witch trial at Bury Saint Edmunds, 147, 151n

Hale, Thomas: *A Compleat Body of Husbandry*, 626

Halhed, Nathaniel Brassey, trans.: *A Code of Gentoo Laws, or, Ordinations of the Pundits*, 221n

Hall (Hal) (TJ's slave; b. *1767*): hat for, 124

Hall, John Elihu: address cover to, xliv, 434 (*illus.*); *American Law Journal*, 95–6, 241–2; identified, 5:176n; letter from, 241–2; letter to, 95–6

Hamilton, Alexander (*1757–1804*): admires British government, 102–4; *The Federalist*, 628; and portrait for J. Delaplaine's *Repository*, 498

son estate, 117–8, 352; identified,
6:316n; letter from, 117–8; letter to,
596–7; and Milton lands, 117–8,
596–7

*Horse-Hoeing Husbandry: or, An Essay
on the Principles of Vegetation and
Tillage* (J. Tull), 626

horses: S. Carr loans, 625, 632; medical
conditions of, 301; at Poplar Forest,
124; and plows, 80; and threshing
machines, 83; taxes on, 708; TJ loans,
625; TJ purchases, 300, 301, 513–4,
608; wartime treatment of, 649

Hoüard, David: *Traités sur les Coutumes
Anglo-Normandes*, 125

Houbraken, Jacobus: as engraver, 399,
400n

Houdetot, Elisabeth Françoise Sophie de
La Live de Bellegarde, comtesse d':
TJ's acquaintance with, 404

household articles: beer jugs, 154, 155,
204, 710, 712, 716; carpet, 73; carriage handles, 360; corks, 155, 188,
189, 710, 717; counterpanes, 348;
earthenware, 154, 602; napkins, 348;
razor strops, 260, 270; tablecloths,
348. *See also* building materials;
clothing; tools

House of Representatives, U.S.: debates
in, 560n; journals of, 701; and office of
postmaster general, 196; and purchase
of TJ's library, 679–80; qualifications
for membership in, 144–5, 176–7, 184.
*See also* Congress, U.S.

Howard family: as aristocrats, 67

Howel, Dr.: and E. Aram's murder trial,
378

Hubbard, Jame (TJ's slave; father of
James Hubbard): hat for, 124

Hubbard, James (Jame) (TJ's slave):
identified, 3:412–3n; sold by TJ, 45

Hubbard, Phill (TJ's slave): hat for, 124

Hughes, Wormley (TJ's slave; b. *1781*):
and earthworks at Monticello, 400

Hughes Crab apple. *See* Hewes Crab
apple

Hull, Isaac: American naval commander,
465

Hull, William: and surrender of Northwest Army, 8, 9n, 10, 11, 12n, 14, 87,
89n, 91–3, 525

Humboldt, Friedrich Wilhelm Heinrich
Alexander, Baron von: *Essai politique
sur le royaume de la Nouvelle-Espagne*,
29; family of, 541; identified, 1:24–5n;
letter to, 29–32; observations in natu-

ral history, 210; *Recueil d'observations
astronomiques*, 29; and D. B. Warden,
506

Humboldt, Karl Wilhelm von: Prussian
ambassador, 541

Hume, David: in collegiate curriculum,
664; criticized, 74; *The History of
England, from the Invasion of Julius
Caesar to the Revolution in 1688*, 249,
527–8, 532n; mentioned, 480, 629,
715

Hunt, Samuel: dispute with G. Granger,
206, 207n; and D. Madison, 207n

Hunton, Charles B.: identified, 709n;
sheriff, 708; and TJ's taxes, 708–9

*The Husbandry of the Ancients* (A. Dickson), 626

Hutcheson, Francis: in collegiate curriculum, 662; *A Short Introduction To
Moral Philosophy*, 458, 627

Hutchinson, James, 217

Hutton, Charles: *A Course of Mathematics*, 250–1, 253n; *A Mathematical and
Philosophical Dictionary*, 251, 253n

Hyde de Neuville, Jean Guillaume:
identified, 4:374–5n; and Louis
XVIII, 404

hydraulics: and manufacturing, 558;
study of, 638, 639, 663, 666, 686

hydrodynamics: study of, 638, 639

hydrostatic engine, 232–3, 268–9

hydrostatics: and manufacturing, 558;
study of, 638, 639, 663, 666, 686

hysteria, 388

ideology: study of, 638, 640, 667, 686

*The Idler*, 665

Ignatius of Loyola, Saint, 26

Illinois Territory: immigration to, 93–4

*Illustrations of Prophecy* (J. L. Towers),
36, 38n, 98, 99n

*Illustrations of Sterne* (J. Ferriar), 665

impressment: of American seamen,
464–6, 542–3; of boats, 123, 135,
156; laws regarding, 374n; and
Northern Europe, 350; TJ on, 51–2,
87, 96, 167

*An Inaugural Oration delivered at
Burlington, August 1, 1811* (J. Chamberlain), 357, 447

Inchbald, Elizabeth: *The British Theatre*,
665; in collegiate curriculum, 665

India (Hindustan; Indostan): and
British military, 68n, 533–4; and
sepoy system, 534

# INDEX

# INDEX

Lomax, Judith: identified, 6:464n; letter from, 16; *The Notes of an American Lyre*, 260, 270; sends seeds to TJ, 16

Lomax, Thomas: identified, 1:631n; as P. Mazzei's friend, 89

London: compared to Washington, D.C., 682; and second Anglo-Dutch war, 682, 684n; TJ suggests burning of, 11. *See also* Russell, Jonathan

Long, Mr.: militia service of, 161

Long, Stephen Harriman: and hydrostatic engine, 232–3

looms, 402, 405–7, 438, 486, 492, 506–7, 507, 508, 523–4, 552–3, 568, 570, 572

Loony (Looney), Joseph: militia service of, 161

Loony (Looney), Peter: militia service of, 161

lotteries: for Albemarle Academy, 265, 337–8, 339, 426–7

*Louis XIV, Sa Cour, et le Régent* (L. P. Anquetil), 664

Louis XVIII, king of France, 404, 450, 451n; restoration of, 423–4, 425, 537–8, 540, 542n

Louisiana (state): economy of, 384; and French-language Bibles, 183; resistance to draft in, 226, 227; and War of *1812*, 227, 384; works on, 242, 383–4

Louisiana Territory: TJ's role in purchasing, 706–7, 711. *See also* Lewis, Meriwether

*The Lounger*, 665

Louvet de Couvray, Jean Baptiste, 665

Loveday, Septimus: and E. Aram's murder trial, 378

Lovett, John: and O. Evans's petition to Congress, 113n

Lucan: in collegiate curriculum, 661

Lucian: dialogues of, 661

Luciani, Sebastiano: portrait of Columbus, xliii–xliv

Lucretius (Titus Lucretius Carus), 661–2

Ludlow, Edmund: *Memoirs*, 629

Ludwell, Frances: and P. Ludwell's estate, 371

Ludwell, Philip: estate of, 329, 371–2

Lundy's Lane, Battle of, 525n

Luther, Martin: J. Adams on, 23, 74, 480

*Lycée ou Cours De Littérature Ancienne Et Moderne* (J. F. La Harpe), 26

Lynchburg, Va.: fish shipped to, 448; price of tobacco at, 124; specie sent from, 670; TJ on, 482–3

Lyons, James: identified, 175n; letter from accounted for, 175n; letter to, 174–5; and J. Wayles's estate, 174, 175

Lyons, Peter: and J. Wayles's estate, 174, 175n, 175

Lysias: A. Auger's translation of, 259, 285

Macaulay, Catharine: *The History of England from the Accession of James I. to that of the Brunswick Line*, 629

McCaleb, Samuel: letter from accounted for, 719

M'Calla, Daniel: *The Works of the Rev. Daniel M'Calla*, 518–9

McClure, David: sells books, 282

McClure, George: Niagara campaign of, 159–60

McClure (McLure), William: identified, 4:143n; recommended by TJ and T. M. Randolph, 240–1

McCreery, William: and contested Congressional election, 176, 177n

McCulloch, James H. (father of James H. McCulloh): collector at Baltimore, 343, 351

McCulloh, James H. (son of James H. McCulloch): identified, 343–4n; introduced by J. Monroe, 351; introduced by J. H. Nicholson, 343; proposed western exploration by, 343, 351, 379; *Researches on America; being an attempt to settle some points relative to the Aborigines of America, &c.*, 344n; scientific interests of, 343, 351; visits Monticello, 379; visits Natural Bridge, 379

Macdonough, Thomas: U.S. naval commander, 692, 699

McGavock, Jacob: militia service of, 161

machines: carding, 79, 114, 116; cornshelling, 83–4; drill plow, 246–7, 306; O. Evans's patent machinery, 106, 107–9, 131–3, 154, 170–3, 386; hydrostatic engine, 232–3, 268–9; loom, 438, 486, 506–7, 507, 508, 523–4, 552–3, 568, 570, 572; and patent rights, 606–7; portable bath, 187–8, 325, 326n, 345; sawing, 84–5; spinning, 558; spinning jenny, 240, 325, 570, 593; steam engine, 558; straw-

identified, 4:86n; TJ's transactions with, 94–5, 402
Mitchill, Samuel Latham: and mineralogy, 363
Mitford, William: *The History of Greece*, 662
*Modern Geography* (J. Pinkerton): TJ recommends, 626
Mohican Indians, 521n
Molière, Jean Baptiste Poquelin, 665
Moll, Karl Marie Ehrenbert von, baron: and Agricultural Society of Bavaria, 505; identified, 5:272n; letter to, 505
Monroe, Elizabeth Kortright (James Monroe's wife): and British destruction in Washington, D.C., 616; visits Highland estate, 272
Monroe, James: and conveyances to Europe, 437; and Highland–Indian Camp boundary dispute, 70–1, 136, 157, 159, 168, 169n, 197–8, 271, 405, 487, 510, 591–2; identified, 1:349n; introduces J. H. McCulloh, 351; letters from, 197–8, 351, 487–8; letters to, 159–60, 355, 510–1, 699–700; letter to, from J. J. Monroe, 310–3; Loudon Co. land of, 487, 488n; and remittances to T. Kosciuszko, 334, 353, 355, 380, 456; as secretary of state, 41, 44n, 156n, 158n, 197, 198, 224, 225n, 429n, 499, 541, 656n, 698, 699–700; and W. Short's land, 70–1, 157–8, 487, 510, 591–2, 594–5, 655; and TJ's letters on finance, 488, 510, 692, 699; visits Highland estate, 272, 308, 351
Monroe, Joseph Jones: accuses TJ of opposing J. Madison, 310–2; dispute with P. Carr, 310–1; identified, 5:158–9n; letter from, to James Monroe, 310–3
Montalto, 400n
Montbeillard, Philibert Guéneau: and Buffon's *Histoire Naturelle*, 626
Monteagle (C. Peyton's Albemarle Co. estate), 535
Montebello, Duchesse de. *See* Lannes, Louise Antoinette, Duchesse de Montebello
Montesquieu, Charles Louis de Secondat. *See* Destutt de Tracy, Antoine Louis Claude: *Commentary and Review of Montesquieu's Spirit of Laws*
Montfort, Simon de, 66

MONTICELLO (TJ's estate): barn at, 44; brewery at, 712; builders at, 448–9; carpentry supervisors at, 619–20; climate at, 302; corn crop at, 431; deer at, 260; domestic manufacturing at, 240–1, 507, 508; earthworks at, 400; Entrance Hall described, 593, 621; flour from, 72, 115, 123, 166–7, 433, 457, 513–4, 514–5, 515, 572; gardens, 116; oat crop at, 461; roads at, 400; schooling at, 647; stonework at, 297, 331, 448–9; tobacco crop at, 710; weaving at, 240–1; wheat crop at, 166–7, 461, 710. *See also* naileries

*Visitors to*

Caldwell, Charles, 319n; Carr, Peter, 536; Corrêa da Serra, José, 7, 29, 55, 716n; Darnall, Joseph R., 121, 122; Dehon, Theodore, 368n; McCulloh, James H., 379; Woodward, Augustus E. B., 309n, 353

Montpellier (Montpelier; Madison's Orange Co. estate): J. Madison at, 323, 359, 365; G. Stuart portrait of TJ at, 303, 341
Montreal, 8, 9, 10, 12, 14, 16n, 30–1, 90–1, 531
Montucla, Jean Étienne: *Histoire des Mathématiques*, 250, 626
Moore, Andrew: identified, 6:537n; letter to, 485–6; as marshal for district of Va., 484–5, 485–6; and package for TJ, 33, 145; as Va. legislator, 549
Moore, Bernard (d. ca. *1775*): identified, 631n; TJ recommends books for son of, 625–31
Moore, Bernard, Jr.: TJ recommends books for, 625–31; TJ retranscribes letter to, 625–30
Moore, John, trans.: *Lettres D'Un Voyageur Anglois Sur La France, La Suisse Et L'Allemagne*, 389
Moore, Thomas (*1779–1852*): *Intercepted Letters; or, the Twopenny Post Bag*, 34, 60, 62n
More, Hannah: *Practical Piety*, 586, 590n
More, Thomas: *The workes of Sir Thomas More Knyght*, 629, 631n
Moreau, Jean: death of, 61, 63n, 228; W. Short on, 224, 403–4
Morgan, George: and A. Burr conspiracy, 236, 238n

with Great Britain, 20; religion in, 327, 390–1; resists Napoleonic rule, 23n, 327; TJ on, 50–1, 326–8, 390–1, 392, 450; and U.S., 50–1; and U.S. land claims, 42–3. *See also* Bonaparte, Joseph, king of Spain; Charles IV, king of Spain; Ferdinand VII, king of Spain; Onís y González Vara López y Gómez, Luis de

*The Spectator*, 665

Spelman, Sir Henry: *Glossarium Archaiologicum*, 127

spices: bird pepper, 326, 567, 568n

spinning jennies, 570, 593

spinning machines: described, 558; TJ on, 13–4, 54, 88, 92, 406

spirits (alcohol), 180

Staël Holstein, Anne Louise Germaine Necker, baronne de: on acquisition of language, 660; identified, 5:452–3n; and Lafayette, 541

Stamp Act (*1765*): resolutions opposing, 493–5, 496–7, 544–5, 546–7, 549–51

Stanard, B. (militia officer), 600

Staples, John: as patent agent, 154, 155; identified, 5:93–4n; letters to, 154, 346–7; makes castings for TJ, 346–7, 517; and plow moldboards for TJ, 552n

Stark, John: Revolutionary War officer, 87

State Department, U.S.: forwards letters, 222; papers of, 701, 702. *See also* Graham, John

*State Papers and Publick Documents*: prospectus for, 644–6, 701–2; published by T. B. Wait & Sons, 646n

statics: study of, 638, 639

*Statistique élémentaire de la France* (J. Peuchet), 90

*The Statutes at Large* (W. W. Hening): publication of, 190, 292; sources for, 228

steamboats: report on, 68; for U.S. river navigation, 56–7, 113n

steam engine, 113n, 558

steel: engraving on, 559; purchased by TJ, 180

Steele, John: identified, 2:506–7n; and TJ's plan for militia, 678

Stephen (TJ's slave; b. *1794*): hat for, 124

Stephens, Alexander: *The History of the Wars which arose out of the French Revolution*, 664

Steptoe, William: account with TJ,

387–8; as doctor, 387; identified, 388n

Sterne, Laurence: in collegiate curriculum, 665; TJ recommends sermons of, 627

Stevens, Alexander Hodgdon: forwards works to TJ, 90; identified, 6:373n

Stevens, Edward: as Va. legislator, 549

Stevens, William: TJ pays, 459, 460n

Stewart, Dugald: in collegiate curriculum, 662, 667; *Elements of the Philosophy of the Human Mind*, 627

Sthreshly, Robert B.: and Albemarle Academy, 267, 282, 293, 335, 570; identified, 6:554n; sells corn to TJ, 290, 291n

stills: R. Gillespie invents, 509

*Storia Antica del Messico* (F. S. Clavigero), 664

*Storia della guerra dell' Independenza degli Stati Uniti d'America* (C. G. G. Botta), 616, 617n

stoves: stone, 361–3

Stovin, George: and E. Aram's murder trial, 376

Strange, John: *Reports of Adjudged Cases in the Courts of Chancery, King's Bench, Common Pleas, and Exchequer*, 147–8

Strong, Caleb: Massachusetts governor, 129

Stuart, Archibald: identified, 2:93–4n; TJ's cloth forwarded to, 460

Stuart, Gilbert: identified, 526–7n; letter to, 525–7; "Medallion" profile of TJ, 525–7; portrait of J. Madison by, 295; portraits of TJ by, 296, 303, 341, 342n, 429, 497–8, 522, 525–7, 562; TJ on, 526

Stukeley, William: and E. Aram's murder trial, 376

subscriptions, for publications: journals, 344, 388–90. *See also* books

subscriptions, non-publication: for Albemarle Academy, 265, 337–8, 339

Suetonius (Gaius Suetonius Tranquillus): in collegiate curriculum, 661; reliability of, 24

sugar: from beets, 54, 55; brown, 180; refined, 180; TJ orders, 434

Sullivan, Mr.: and W. Janes's looms, 523

Sully, Maximilien de Béthune, duc de: *Memoires de Maximillien de Bethune, Duc de Sully*, 664

Sully, Thomas: identified, 4:356–7n; portrait of B. Rush, 296n

THE PAPERS OF THOMAS JEFFERSON are composed in Monticello, a font based on the "Pica No. 1" created in the early 1800s by Binny & Ronaldson, the first successful typefounding company in America. The face is considered historically appropriate for The Papers of Thomas Jefferson because it was used extensively in American printing during the last quarter-century of Jefferson's life, and because Jefferson himself expressed cordial approval of Binny & Ronaldson types. It was revived and rechristened Monticello in the late 1940s by the Mergenthaler Linotype Company, under the direction of C. H. Griffith and in close consultation with P. J. Conkwright, specifically for the publication of the Jefferson Papers. The font suffered some losses in its first translation to digital format in the 1980s to accommodate computerized typesetting. Matthew Carter's reinterpretation in 2002 restores the spirit and style of Binny & Ronaldson's original design of two centuries earlier.

✧